THE
NEW BOOK
OF
KNOWLEDGE

THE NEW BOOK OF KNOWLEDGE

Scholastic Library Publishing, Inc.
Danbury, Connecticut

VOLUME 17

S

S, the 19th letter in the English alphabet, was the 21st letter in ancient Hebrew and Phoenician alphabets and the 18th letter in the classical Greek alphabet. The Hebrews and Phoenicians called it *shin*. The Greeks called it *sigma*.

Phoenician letter names were also used as words. The letter name *shin*, for example, was also the Phoenician word for "tooth." Some language scholars believe that the form of the letter *shin* was a simplified picture of a tooth. It looked like this:

In adapting the Phoenician alphabet to their own language in the 700's B.C., the Greeks turned the letter on its side. The Etruscans, an ancient people of northern Italy who conquered Rome, based their alphabet on a Greek model. The Romans learned the alphabet from the Etruscans. The S used in English today is the same as the S of the Romans.

In the English language, S has two main sounds: an S sound, as in the word *soup*; and a Z sound, as in the word *has*. The letter usually has the S sound at the beginning of a word, as in *salt*, or when two S's come together, as in *assassin*. The Z sound usually comes when the S is between two vowels, as in the words *reason* and *chosen*. Among the exceptions to these rules are the words *dessert* and *evasive*. The letter S also has a SH sound, as in the words *sugar*, *sure*, and *mission*. In some words, such as *isle* and *aisle*, the S is silent.

The letter S is found in many abbreviations. In chemistry S is the abbreviation for sulfur. In geography S stands for south or southern. The letters S.S. before the name of a ship, as in S.S. *United States*, mean steamship. The letters SS when referring to an airplane mean supersonic, as in SST—supersonic transport. In school an S may indicate either a satisfactory or superior grade. In the names of many organizations S stands for society, as in PSA for Photographic Society of America.

Reviewed by MARIO PEI
Author, *The Story of Language*

See also ALPHABET.

SOME WAYS TO REPRESENT S:

The **manuscript** or printed forms of the letter (left) are highly readable. The **cursive** letters (right) are formed from slanted flowing strokes joining one letter to the next.

The **Manual Alphabet** (left) enables a deaf person to communicate by forming letters with the fingers of one hand. **Braille** (right) is a system by which a blind person can use fingertips to "read" raised dots that stand for letters.

The **International Code of Signals** is a special group of flags, used to send and receive messages at sea. Each letter is represented by a different flag.

International Morse Code is used to send messages by radio signals. Each letter is expressed as a combination of dots (.) and dashes (——).

SACAGAWEA
(1787?–1812?)

Sacagawea was a Lemhi Shoshoni Indian woman who served as an interpreter for U.S. Army captains Meriwether Lewis and William Clark and their Corps of Discovery on their famous expedition (1804–06) to explore the Louisiana Territory and find a route to the Pacific Ocean.

Sacagawea (pronounced sah-kah-gah-WEE-ah, meaning "Bird Woman") was born in east central Idaho about 1787. In 1800 she was captured by the Hidatsa tribe, who took her to their village along the Knife River in present-day North Dakota. There she became the wife of Toussaint Charbonneau, a French-Canadian fur trader.

In late October 1804, Lewis and Clark and the Corps of Discovery arrived at the junction of the Knife and Missouri rivers, where they built Fort Mandan at which to spend the winter. Charbonneau and Sacagawea, who was then about 17, joined the expedition as interpreters. Before the party left on their journey the following April, Sacagawea gave birth to a son named Jean-Baptiste, whom Clark nicknamed Pompey.

In August 1805, the expedition encountered a band of Shoshoni, now led by Sacagawea's brother, Cameahwait. Sacagawea was overjoyed to see him and easily persuaded him to give the explorers horses, which they needed to reach the Pacific.

Several years after the expedition ended, Sacagawea and her husband took Pompey to St. Louis, where Clark became his legal guardian and helped him obtain a formal education. Sacagawea probably died in 1812, although some sources say she resettled among the Shoshoni in Wyoming and died there in 1884. In 2000, the Sacagawea Golden Dollar was minted in honor of her accomplishments.

BARBARA KUBIK
Lewis and Clark Trail Heritage Foundation, Inc.

SACRAMENTO. See CALIFORNIA (Cities).

SADAT, ANWAR EL- (1918–1981)

Anwar el-Sadat, a leading political figure in the Arab world, served as president of Egypt from 1970 until he was assassinated in 1981.

Sadat was born on December 25, 1918, in a small village in the Nile River delta. He graduated from the Egyptian Military Academy in Cairo in 1938. In 1942, during World War II, Sadat was dismissed from the army and sent to prison for cooperating with Nazi German agents against Egypt's British-backed government. He was reinstated in 1950 and became a member of the officers' committee that later overthrew Farouk, the king of Egypt. Egypt was declared a republic in 1953, and Sadat held several posts in the new government, including that of vice president (1964–67; 1969–70).

Sadat succeeded Gamal Abdel Nasser as president in 1970. His goals included Arab unity and the recovery of lands lost in wars with Israel. In 1971 he proposed a federation of Arab republics, with Syria and Libya. But this union never became truly effective. In 1973 he launched an attack against Israeli forces and regained complete control of the Suez Canal and later signed agreements reducing Israel's presence in the Sinai.

Sadat once said that working for peace in the Middle East was his "sacred mission." In 1977 he took the extraordinary step of traveling to Jerusalem to discuss the possibilities of peace. He was the first Arab leader to visit Israel. Then in 1978, Sadat met with Israeli prime minister Menachem Begin and U.S. president Jimmy Carter in the United States to develop a framework for a peace treaty. For this, Sadat and Begin shared the 1978 Nobel Peace Prize.

Sadat's bold actions were sharply criticized by other Arab leaders. After the treaty was signed, most other Arab countries broke off diplomatic relations with Egypt. He was assassinated by Muslim extremists in Cairo on October 6, 1981.

Reviewed by DON PERETZ
State University of New York at Binghamton

SAFETY

Every year people are injured or killed in accidents or other kinds of harmful situations. A knowledge of safety rules combined with common sense and good judgment can often help people avoid the risk of injuries and prevent many types of serious accidents.

An important source of information on safety in the United States is the National Safety Council. Founded in 1913, this organization is dedicated to the reduction of accidental deaths and injuries and to the prevention of diseases. The council works with groups representing industry, government, and local communities to ensure the health and safety of Americans. It provides information on safety and sponsors and organizes health and safety programs throughout the country. The safety tips that follow, just a few of the many people should be familiar with, are based on recommendations of the National Safety Council.

Whether you are walking or driving, it is important to look left and right before crossing a street or going through an intersection. Always move with the green light, never the red.

▶ **CUTS, BROKEN BONES, AND BITES**

Cuts and broken bones are common injuries that can result from a variety of situations. Many cuts and broken bones are caused by falls, one of the most common accidents. People can fall at home, at work, at school, or at play. They can fall while walking, running, riding a bicycle, skating, or performing other activities. Or they can fall because they trip over something, slip on a wet or oily surface, or lose their balance. The chances of falling are increased by illness or by being tired or in a hurry. Safety precautions such as keeping floors clean and uncluttered and paying attention to where you are going can help reduce the risk of falls and the injuries that result from them.

Cuts and scratches can also result from carelessness with tools, with everyday utensils such as knives and forks and pens and pencils, as well as from contact with broken glass or sharp objects. These injuries can lead to serious infections if not treated properly. Always use the right tool or utensil for a job and do not improvise by using something else. Cutting tools should also be stored out of the reach of small children, and broken glass or broken objects with sharp edges should always be picked up and thrown away.

Cuts and broken bones suffered in traffic accidents can be especially serious. Most of these accidents are the result of carelessness or recklessness, such as driving while sleepy, driving too fast, crossing a street against the light, or running into the street between parked cars. Traffic accidents can also be caused by unsafe vehicles. Safety devices such as seat belts, air bags, and improved braking systems can help reduce injuries from traffic accidents. Other safety tips include looking left, right, and left again when crossing a street; obeying all traffic rules; walking on sidewalks or on the far side of the street or road; wearing seat belts; and keeping vehicles in good working order.

Insect bites and stings can be dangerous, especially if a person is allergic. Some people, for example, are very allergic to bee venom, and a sting can lead to unconsciousness, difficulty in breathing, and even death if not treated promptly. Insect repellents can provide some protection from insect bites, and the use of insect sprays around the house can help reduce the insect population. If a stinging insect lands on your body, swiftly brush it away; slapping the insect may cause it to sting. Animal bites or scratches can be dangerous if the wound becomes infected. Therefore, it is important to avoid contact with strange animals, especially wild animals, and to treat your own animals with respect. Playing too roughly with a pet can sometimes result in a bite or scratch.

▶ POISONING, CHOKING, AND SUFFOCATING

Each year, thousands of people are harmed by poisoning, choking, or suffocating. Every household contains substances such as detergents, disinfectants, insect sprays, weed killers, and medications. All of these products have important uses, but they can cause illness, injury, and even death if not used properly. Because they like to put things into their mouths, young children are at risk of being poisoned by these substances. Poisoning at home can be prevented by storing products properly and by keeping dangerous substances clearly marked and out of the reach of children. To prevent the misuse of medications, it is important to read labels carefully and then to follow their directions. Poisoning among older adults is often the result of their taking the wrong medication or the wrong dose of a medication. By handling and storing foods properly, especially items that can spoil easily, the risk of food poisoning can be reduced.

Because small children often do put things in their mouths, they are at risk of choking on small objects that can become lodged in their throats. To prevent children from choking, keep small objects out of their reach and make sure their food is cut into small pieces. Adults can choke if they have eaten their food too quickly or have not chewed it adequately. They, too, should avoid eating large pieces of food. To keep yourself from choking it is also a good idea not to talk with food in your mouth.

Suffocation is another hazard for small children. Infants can suffocate or strangle if they become trapped between broken crib parts or if they get tangled in blankets or other bedding. To avoid such dangers, be sure cribs are secure and that bedding is placed over sleeping infants properly. Children of all ages can suffocate if they place plastic bags over their heads or strangle if they become tangled in loose cords on clothing or household furnishings. Therefore, it is important to store plastic bags out of the reach of children and to examine their clothing carefully. Loose cords should be removed or tied properly.

▶ BURNS, ELECTRIC SHOCKS, AND FIRE

Burns and electric shocks are not as common as other types of injuries, but they can be extremely dangerous. Burns can range from small blisters to wounds that can be life-threatening. Many burns occur in the kitchen around or near the stove and microwave oven. A pot of boiling liquid, a hot pan, or hot grease from a skillet can cause serious burns. People can also burn themselves on hot irons or other appliances. Fire, of course, is a leading cause of burns.

Burns can be prevented by following certain safety precautions. Keep hot pots and pans out of the reach of children, and use potholders or padded gloves when handling

If you are going skating, always wear a helmet and protective pads. Do not leave objects on stairways where someone, including yourself, could trip over them, and never leave a wet spill on the floor. Anyone could slip on it and get hurt seriously in a fall.

them. Stand back from skillets that contain hot grease. Open hot ovens and covered pots or pans with caution. Handle electrical appliances such as irons with care. Learn and follow fire safety rules. (For more information about fire prevention and safety, see FIRE FIGHTING AND PREVENTION in Volume F.)

Many home fires are the result of faulty or inadequate electrical wiring. Electricity is also responsible for electric shock injuries. When the human body comes into contact with a strong electric charge, the muscles contract violently. A serious electric shock may paralyze the muscles or nerves, and death can result if the heart muscles or nerves that control breathing become paralyzed. Remember to replace old electrical cords with new ones that have the Underwriters Laboratories (UL) label. Do not overload electric outlets with numerous plugs or unplug an appliance by pulling on its cord. Never touch an electrical appliance with wet hands or use one near a sink or bathtub or while any part of your body is touching or in water.

▶ **INJURIES FROM SPORTS**

Sports activities can result in all types of injuries. Accidents while bicycling, skiing, skating, playing basketball or baseball, hiking, and other activities can cause cuts and broken bones. Boating, scuba diving, and swimming accidents can result in drowning. Accidents with rifles, pistols, shotguns, and bows and arrows can cause serious wounds, and even death. Not wearing suitable clothing for outdoor activities in cold weather can lead to serious problems. One is **hypothermia**, a condition in which the body temperature becomes dangerously low; another is **frostbite**, a condition in which the body tissues are injured or destroyed by exposure to extreme cold. Activities in hot weather can lead to sunburn and to **dehydration**, a dangerous loss of moisture from the body.

There are many different safety precautions that should be taken while participating in sports activities. While bicycling or skating, for example, it is important to wear a helmet to protect the head and padding to protect the knees, elbows, and other parts of the body. In water sports, a knowledge of boating and water safety rules is essential. These rules include using life jackets, carefully supervising children, being cautious when in or

---

SAFETY TIPS*

- Keep stairways and halls well lighted.
- Wipe up spills on floors as quickly as possible.
- Use containers with child-resistant lids to store medications and other substances that could be harmful to young people.
- Dispose of medications that have passed their expiration dates.
- Keep harmful household products in their original, labeled containers, and store them in locked cabinets.
- Do not unplug electrical appliances while they are in use.
- Avoid placing electrical cords under carpeting and rugs.
- Wear safety glasses or goggles when working with power tools.
- Keep power tools and portable appliances unplugged and store them in a safe place when they are not in use.
- Read and follow instructions and warnings on all equipment, appliances, chemical substances, cleaning products, and medications.
- Avoid participating in strenuous or possibly dangerous activities when you are ill or tired.
- Keep emergency phone numbers (police, fire, medical, poison control center, and others) next to each phone in your home.

*Based on publications of the National Safety Council

---

around water, and not being alone if at all possible. Activities involving firearms, knives, or bows and arrows require a thorough knowledge of those weapons, and specific safety rules for the care and use of the weapons should be strictly followed. When not in use, all weapons should be placed in locked storage areas. Before participating in any sport, it is important to know its possible dangers and to take the right safety precautions to prevent injuries.

Reviewed by CAROLE HUYBRECHT
Program Coordinator, National Safety Council

See also BICYCLING; BOATS AND BOATING; DRIVER EDUCATION; ELECTRICITY; FIRE FIGHTING AND PREVENTION; FIRST AID; GUNS AND AMMUNITION; HUNTING; OCCUPATIONAL HEALTH AND SAFETY; POISONS; SWIMMING.

SAGAN, CARL. See NEW YORK CITY (Famous People).

SAGINAW. See MICHIGAN (Cities).

SAHARA

The world's largest desert, the Sahara extends across a vast expanse of northern Africa, from the Atlantic Ocean in the west to the Red Sea in the east. It covers about 3.5 million square miles (9 million square kilometers), an area nearly equal to that of the United States, and makes up about 30 percent of Africa's total land area. From north to south, the Sahara stretches from the Atlas Mountains and the Mediterranean Sea to the Niger River and Lake Chad. In the south the desert merges into a region of sparse grassland called the Sahel. Various parts of the Sahara are known by different names, such as the Libyan, Arabian, and Nubian deserts. The name "Sahara" itself comes from an Arabic word meaning either "desert" or "steppe."

The Land and Climate. The Sahara consists of high, shifting sand dunes called **ergs**, rocky desert uplands called **hammadas**, and flat gravel plains called **regs**. Rocks and gravel cover most of the surface. Sand covers only about 10 percent of the land. Much of the desert consists of a plateau that lies about 2,000 feet (600 meters) above sea level. The highest points are in the Ahaggar and Tibesti uplands.

The Sahara is both very dry and very hot. Average rainfall is less than 10 inches (250 millimeters) a year. Summer temperatures

High, shifting sand dunes called ergs (*top*) cover only a part of the Sahara. Most of the rest consists of rocky uplands and gravel plains. A large but sparsely inhabited region, the Sahara historically has been the home of nomadic people (*left*). Occasional oases, or fertile, watered areas (*above*), dot the otherwise barren landscape.

often reach 120°F (49°C), and the world's highest temperature—138°F (58°C)—was recorded at Azizia, in Libya. Yet rock carvings and paintings that have been found show that the region was once fertile. The dry beds of rivers and lakes can still be seen.

The People. The Sahara is vast but sparsely populated. The only densely settled part is in Egypt, in the valley of the Nile River. Elsewhere, Arab and Berber tribes live on oases, watered by underground springs or wells, or travel as nomads from one oasis to the next with their camels and goats. The best known of the nomads are the Tuareg, a Berber people. In religion, most of the people are Muslims.

Although large areas of the desert are empty, a well-watered oasis can support several thousand people. Dates are the chief crop. Cereal grains, fruits, and vegetables are also grown where there is enough water. Nomadic herders frequently stop at the oases for food and drink. Camel

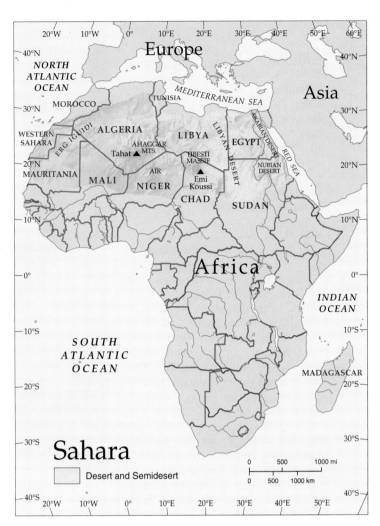

The Sahara is rich in a variety of mineral resources, including oil and natural gas. This refinery is in Libya, one of the region's major oil producers.

caravans deliver news, exchange goods, and carry date crops to the cities for export.

History and Economy. British explorers Dixon Denham, Hugh Clapperton, and Walter Oudney were the first Europeans to cross the Sahara from north to south. They started from Tripoli, Libya, in 1822 and reached Kano, Nigeria, in 1823.

The mineral resources of the Sahara are rapidly being developed. Huge oil, gas, and coal reserves were first discovered in 1956. There are also deposits of copper, lead, zinc, salt, and phosphates. Trucks now cross the Sahara on four major roads equipped with refueling stations, and paved highways extend from Algeria into Mali and Niger.

Reviewed by HOWARD CRITCHFIELD
Western Washington University

See also DESERTS; OASES.

SAIGON. See HO CHI MINH CITY.

SAILING

Sailing, a popular pastime and sport, combines adventure with the freedom of the high seas. Sailboats range in size from one-person crafts to racing yachts that may have a crew of twenty or more. All sailors need to master many skills, from the hoisting of sails to the reading of navigation charts.

▶ HISTORY OF SAILING

Sailing dates back thousands of years. The ancient Egyptians and Greeks used sails on their boats, as did the Romans. Beginning in the 1400's, Europeans explored the world on sailing ships. In early times, these ships were used mainly for fishing, in battles, and to transport people and cargo. The first boats that were designed specifically for pleasure sailing probably were made by the Dutch in the early 1600's. The sport of yachting became popular among wealthy Europeans and Americans during the 1700's and 1800's. The word "yacht" comes from the Dutch word *jaghtschip*, which means "hunting ship."

Today, sailing is enjoyed by many people. Materials such as fiberglass and aluminum have lowered the production costs of sailboats, making them more affordable. In addition, some sailboats are relatively small, so it is easy to transport them on trailers or car roofs. Sailing programs offered by local communities and organizations such as the Red Cross, Boy Scouts, and Girl Scouts have made sailing accessible to thousands of people. Competitive events, such as the America's Cup race and the Olympics, have focused attention on sailing as well and increased its popularity.

▶ PARTS OF A SAILBOAT

There are many different types and sizes of sailboats. A catboat, the simplest, has one sail supported by a **mast**, a single vertical pole. Adding a smaller sail, a **jib**, in front of the mast turns the boat into a sloop. A cutter has two jibs in front of the mast. Other sailboats have additional masts, which add sail area for

It is an exciting moment for a crew when the wind fills the sailboat's large, colorful spinnakers, giving it the power to cut through the water with the wind.

more power. A smaller mast behind the main mast is a **mizzenmast**, and a mast in front of the main mast is a **foremast**. Depending on the size of the additional masts and their locations, sailboats are called yawls, ketches, or schooners. Sailboats with twin **hulls**, or bodies, are catamarans, and three-hulled boats are trimarans.

The most distinctive features of a sailboat are the vertical mast and the **boom**, a horizontal pole attached to the lower portion of the mast. The mast and the boom are also known as **spars**. The main mast and its boom support the **mainsail**, the principal sail that catches the power of the wind and propels the sailboat forward. Other sails include the triangular-shaped jibs, which help a boat sail close to the direction of the wind, and the balloon-shaped **spinnaker**, which is used for sailing before the wind, or sailing with the wind coming from behind the boat.

The Parts of a Single-Masted Sailboat

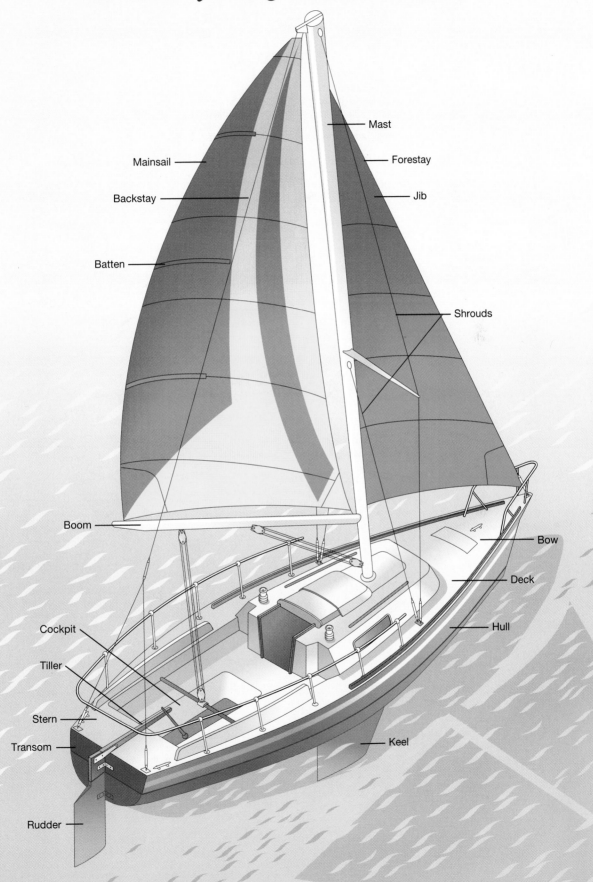

Mast

Mainsail

Forestay

Backstay

Jib

Batten

Shrouds

Boom

Bow

Deck

Cockpit

Hull

Tiller

Stern

Transom

Keel

Rudder

The Positions of a Sailboat

WIND

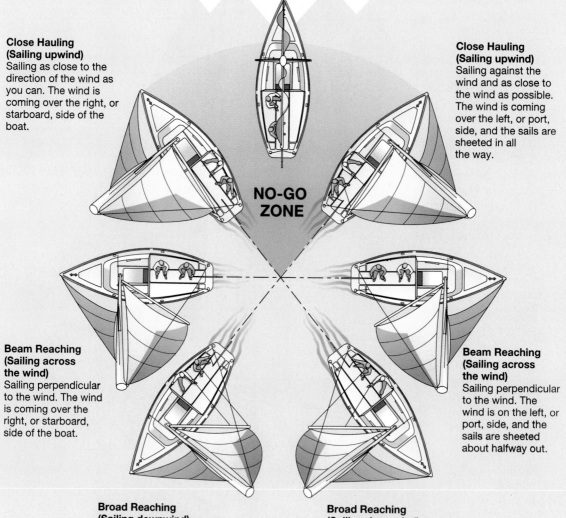

**Luffing
(No-go zone)**
The center of this zone is the direction of the wind. When a boat enters this zone, the sail will flap, or luff, so it cannot develop the power to move the boat forward.

**Close Hauling
(Sailing upwind)**
Sailing as close to the direction of the wind as you can. The wind is coming over the right, or starboard, side of the boat.

**Close Hauling
(Sailing upwind)**
Sailing against the wind and as close to the wind as possible. The wind is coming over the left, or port, side, and the sails are sheeted in all the way.

**NO-GO
ZONE**

**Beam Reaching
(Sailing across the wind)**
Sailing perpendicular to the wind. The wind is coming over the right, or starboard, side of the boat.

**Beam Reaching
(Sailing across the wind)**
Sailing perpendicular to the wind. The wind is on the left, or port, side, and the sails are sheeted about halfway out.

**Broad Reaching
(Sailing downwind)**
Sailing away from the wind but at an angle to it. The wind is coming over the right, or starboard, side.

**Broad Reaching
(Sailing downwind)**
Sailing away from the wind. The wind is coming over the left, or port, side, and the sails are sheeted perpendicular to the wind.

Masts are supported and kept upright by the **standing rigging**, the steel wires or ropes attached to the upper part of a mast. The rigging includes **stays**, which are attached to the bow (front) and stern (rear) of the boat, and **shrouds**, which are attached to the starboard (right) and port (left) sides of the boat.

The ropes, or lines, that manipulate the sails are the **running rigging**. This rigging includes the **halyards**, the lines that raise and lower the sails, and the **sheets**, the lines that pull the sails in or let them out depending on the boat's direction in relation to the wind. Pulling the sails in or letting them out is called trimming the sails.

Other key parts of a sailboat are the **rudder**, which is used to steer the boat, and the moveable **centerboard** or the fixed **keel** under the hull that provides stability and keeps the boat from sliding sideways when going toward the wind. Large boats usually have a keel instead of a centerboard.

▶ PRINCIPLES OF SAILING

A sailboat cannot sail directly into the wind. If a boat is pointed into the wind, its sails flap, or **luff**, and the boat goes nowhere. For a boat to sail, it must point at an angle to the wind, or it must have the wind come from behind it.

A sailboat facing into the wind at about a 45 degree angle is **beating**; its curved sails catch the wind and propel the boat forward. Steering a boat away from the wind and letting out the sails is known as **easing the sheets**. Sailing as close to the direction of the wind as possible with the sails pulled in tightly is **close-hauling**. Sailing with the wind coming over the side of the boat is known as **reaching**. There are two types of reaching. In beam reaching, the boat is sailing perpendicular to the wind, or sailing across the wind. In broad reaching, the boat is sailing away from the wind at right angles. **Running** is sailing before the wind when the wind is coming from directly behind the boat.

Two basic maneuvers, tacking and jibing, are used to position the boat properly in relation to the wind. In **tacking**, the boat moves in a zigzag motion facing into the wind. During a series of tacks, the sails are shifted from one side to the other in order to catch the wind. In a starboard tack, the wind is blowing from the right side of the boat. In a port tack, it is blowing from the left side. Changing tack is known as coming about. In **jibing**, the boat moves in a zigzag motion with the wind coming from behind the boat.

▶ SEAMANSHIP

Sailing involves much more than knowing how to trim the sails. It also involves good seamanship—the knowledge and skill needed to operate and navigate a sailboat safely.

Sailing is governed by rules that determine which boat has the right of way in various situations. For example, a boat on a starboard tack has the right of way over a boat on a port tack. When two boats are on the same tack, the one closest to the direction of the wind must give way to the other. Faster boats must stay away from slower boats. In general, sailboats have the right of way over motor-powered boats, except for large commercial vessels that are unable to maneuver easily. All sailors must know and follow the rules in order to prevent collisions.

Sailors also must have a knowledge of navigational signals, such as buoys, in order to know where it is safe to sail. They must have navigational skills such as how to read a sailing chart and how to plot and follow a course. It is important to understand and anticipate changes in weather and to know what to do during bad weather. Sailors should also know how to swim and survive in water, and they must always wear lifejackets whenever the boat leaves the dock.

During a race, a crew needs to be at its best to maneuver its sailboat quickly around a marker according to the rules.

Glossary of Sailing Terms

There are many technical terms for the parts of a boat and the maneuvers of sailing. Some important sailing terms and their definitions are given here.

ABEAM: Off to the side; 90 degrees from the bow.

AFT: At or toward the stern.

ASTERN: Behind a boat; backward.

ATHWARTSHIPS: At right angles to the fore-and-aft line of the boat.

BALLAST: A weight in the centerboard or keel that helps provide stability.

BATTENS: Long, thin pieces of wood inserted in pockets along the leech of a sail, used to help the sail keep its proper shape.

BEAM: The width of a boat at its widest point.

BILGE: The curved part of the hull below the waterline. Also, the inside of the hull at the very bottom of the boat.

BLOCK: A frame with grooved rollers or pulleys for hauling lines.

BOOM: The pole attached at right angles to the lower part of the mast. The foot of a sail is fastened to it.

BOW: The front of the boat.

BUOY: A floating marker used for navigation.

CAPSIZE: To overturn.

CENTERBOARD: A flat wooden or fiberglass fin let down into the water under the boat from inside a box in the center of the boat. It gives the boat stability and keeps the boat from slipping sideways when going windward.

CLEAT: A metal or wood fitting with two projecting horns or arms, around which lines are secured.

CLEW: The lower outside, or after, corner of a sail.

COCKPIT: The area where the crew sits and the tiller is located.

DINGHY: A small boat, often carried or towed by a larger boat, which is used to get to and from shore.

FOOT: The lower edge of a sail.

FORE-AND-AFT: From front to back; lengthwise.

HALYARD: A line for hoisting a sail.

HEEL: To tilt sideways.

HULL: The body of the boat.

KEEL: A fixed and weighted lead or metal projection, usually V-shaped, from the center of the bottom of the boat down into the water. The keel provides stability.

LEECH: The outside, or after, edge of a sail.

LEEWARD: Away from the wind; the sheltered side.

LUFF: The front edge of a sail; the flapping of sails.

OUTHAUL: A line used to haul the foot of a sail taut along a boom.

PAINTER: A line fastened to the bow of a small boat, used for tying it up to a pier or a mooring.

PORT: The left side of the boat, as you face forward.

QUARTER: The part of the boat between the beam and the stern.

RAIL: The outer side of the boat's deck.

RUDDER: The device that swings in the water at the stern of a boat. It is attached to the tiller and controls the steering of the boat.

SHEAVE: A roller set in a block, often at the top of a mast or the end of a boom, over which a line such as a halyard or an outhaul runs.

SHEET: A line used to trim a sail. A sheet takes the name of the sail it controls, for example, mainsheet, jibsheet, and so on.

SHROUDS: Wires or lines that support the mast athwartships.

SPARS: The booms, gaffs, and masts of the boat.

STARBOARD: The right side of the boat, as you face forward.

STAYS: Wires or lines that support the mast from bow to stern.

STERN: The rear part of the boat.

TILLER: The wooden arm attached to, and used to control, the rudder of the boat. Some boats have a wheel for steering.

TOPSIDE: The part of the boat between the waterline and the rail.

TRANSOM: The flat or slightly curved surface across the stern of the boat.

WINCH: A mechanical drum, often with a handle, used to pull in sheets and halyards.

WINDWARD: On the side toward the wind; in the direction from which the wind is blowing.

▶ **RACING**

Many sailors enjoy the thrill of competition. Each year, there are hundreds of organized races at the local, national, and international levels. Contestants may compete either in boats with identical hulls and sails or in different types of boats. Races featuring different types of boats have rules that make the contest equal for all entries. A fleet race series, or regatta, involves many entries. Match races, such as the America's Cup race, feature only two boats that compete head-to-head. This famous race and its trophy got their names from the U.S. schooner *America*, which won the silver cup in 1851. In 1857, it was given to the New York Yacht Club to be used as an international challenge trophy, and the first race was held in 1870. Today the race is usually held every four years.

Shimon Van Collie
West Coast Editor, *Sailing Magazine*
See also Boats and Boating.

SAINT-GAUDENS, AUGUSTUS. See New Hampshire (Famous People).

SAINT KITTS AND NEVIS

St. Kitts and Nevis is a small nation located in the Caribbean Sea. It is composed of the two islands of St. Kitts (formerly St. Christopher) and Nevis, which are a part of the Leeward Islands chain of the West Indies. St. Kitts was the first British settlement in the West Indies. Nevis is of historical interest as the birthplace of Alexander Hamilton, one of the founders of the United States. The islands gained complete independence from Britain in 1983. Basseterre on St. Kitts is the capital and largest city.

People. Most of the people are descendants of African slaves first brought to the islands in the 1600's to work on the sugarcane plantations. More than three quarters of the population lives on St. Kitts, the larger of the two islands. English is the official language. The majority of the people are Protestants.

Land. Both islands are of volcanic origin and are mountainous. The highest point, Mount Misery, on St. Kitts, rises to 3,792 feet (1,156 meters). The southern part of St. Kitts is a narrow peninsula, with beautiful sandy beaches. The climate is tropical but moderate. Rainfall is abundant.

ST. KITTS AND NEVIS

Economy. The economy is based on agriculture. Sugarcane, grown on St. Kitts, is the main crop. Other important commercial crops are coconuts, peanuts, and cotton. Vegetables and fruits are grown for local use and some livestock is raised, but food must still be imported. Tourism and products manufactured for export are being rapidly developed.

History and Government. Christopher Columbus was the first European to visit the islands, in 1493. The British established a settlement on St. Kitts in 1623 and one on Nevis in 1628. In 1816 the nearby island of Anguilla was joined to the territory.

In 1967, St. Kitts, Nevis, and Anguilla were granted internal self-government as part of the West Indies Associated States. Anguilla, at its own request, was later separated from the two larger islands. It remains a British dependency. St. Kitts and Nevis won independence in 1983. In 1998 a referendum for independence was held on Nevis. It was not approved, but only by a narrow margin.

The British monarch, represented by a governor-general, is the country's ceremonial head of state. The head of government is the prime minister, who leads the majority party in the legislature, the National Assembly.

HOWARD A. FERGUS
University of the West Indies (Montserrat)

SAINT LAURENT, LOUIS STEPHEN. See CANADA, GOVERNMENT OF (Profiles).

FACTS and figures

THE FEDERATION OF SAINT KITTS AND NEVIS is the official name of the country.

LOCATION: Caribbean Sea.

AREA: 101 sq mi (261 km²).

POPULATION: 45,000 (estimate).

CAPITAL AND LARGEST CITY: Basseterre.

MAJOR LANGUAGE: English (official).

MAJOR RELIGIOUS GROUP: Protestant.

GOVERNMENT: Constitutional monarchy. **Head of state**—British monarch, represented by a governor-general. **Head of government**—prime minister. **Legislature**—National Assembly.

CHIEF PRODUCTS: Sugarcane, cotton, processed sugarcane, clothing, shoes, beverages.

MONETARY UNIT: East Caribbean dollar (1 EC dollar = 100 cents).

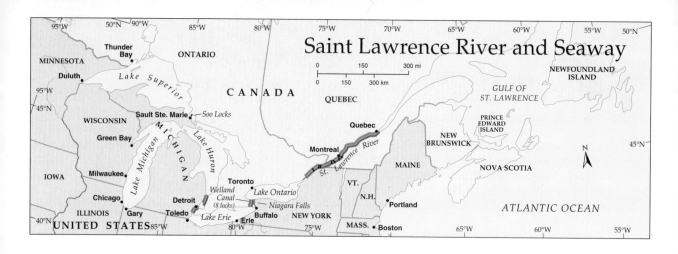

Saint Lawrence River and Seaway

SAINT LAWRENCE RIVER AND SEAWAY

The St. Lawrence River in southeastern Canada is one of the great rivers of the world. It is an international waterway with a unique place in the history and development of North America.

The St. Lawrence River begins at the eastern end of Lake Ontario. It follows a northeasterly course for about 760 miles (1,225 kilometers), flowing into the Gulf of St. Lawrence and the Atlantic Ocean. About one-fourth of the river's length forms the international boundary between the province of Ontario and the state of New York.

The drainage basin of the St. Lawrence River system is the third largest in North America. The five Great Lakes—Ontario, Erie, Huron, Michigan, and Superior—are part of the system. The main tributary rivers of the St. Lawrence River are the Ottawa, St. Maurice, Saguenay, Richelieu, St. Francis, and Chaudière, which all flow out of the province of Quebec. Major cities on the river include Montreal and Quebec City.

History of the St. Lawrence

Before the arrival of European explorers, the St. Lawrence River region was inhabited by several Native American tribes, including the Huron and the Iroquois. The French explorer Jacques Cartier (1491–1557) discovered the St. Lawrence River on his second voyage to the New World in 1535. Before entering the river, Cartier sheltered in a small bay leading off the gulf. He named the bay the St. Laurent because it was August 10, the feast day of that saint. Later, the English name "St. Lawrence" was given to both the gulf and river.

In 1608 another French explorer, Samuel de Champlain (1567?–1635), founded a settlement at the foot of a high cliff that loomed over a narrow section of the river. The Indians called this place Kebec, an Algonkian word meaning "narrowing of the waters." The French settlers called it Québec.

Beginning with Champlain's settlement, the St. Lawrence River played a leading part in the history of New France. Throughout the 1600's the tributaries of the river were the routes by which explorers, such as Pierre Radisson (1636–1710?), Médart Chouart, Sieur des Groseilliers (1625–98), and Robert Cavelier, Sieur de La Salle (1643–87), made their way into the continent. Following these same routes were traders in search of furs and missionaries seeking to spread Christianity to Native Americans.

The St. Lawrence area quickly became the scene of fierce warfare between the Iroquois and the French over the valuable trade in fur. The English on the Atlantic coast, who wanted to control the western fur trade, contributed to the conflict by encouraging the Iroquois to make surprise attacks on the French at Montreal.

The French later came into direct conflict with the British, and in September 1759 they were defeated by the British on the Plains of Abraham outside Quebec. Under the terms of the 1763 Treaty of Paris, all French territory in Canada was ceded to Great Britain.

The British built a great commercial empire based on fur and, later, timber. The St. Lawrence River was the route by which the furs were brought east to Montreal for shipment overseas to Great Britain and France. In the second quarter of the 1800's, timber replaced fur as the most valuable export. Later, grain became another important export shipped on the St. Lawrence.

The St. Lawrence Seaway

Because of its rapids, the St. Lawrence River was for many years unsuitable for large-scale shipping. In the late 1700's and early 1800's some efforts were made to overcome these natural barriers. Canals were dug and locks were built to bypass the rapids and connect the river with the Great Lakes.

By the 1900's there were 22 locks in the system. Freighters up to 250 feet (76 meters) in length could then move up and down the 224-foot (68-meter) difference in water levels between Montreal and Lake Ontario. But the canals were too narrow and shallow for larger freighters. Eastbound lake freighters had to unload and transfer their cargoes at Ogdensburg, New York, or Prescott, Ontario. Westbound ocean freighters had to unload and transfer their cargoes at Montreal. The canals and locks had to be widened and deepened.

In 1954 work began on two international projects: building the St. Lawrence Seaway and harnessing the river for hydroelectric power. New canals were dug and old ones enlarged. Bridges were built and old ones raised to accommodate taller ships. Some sections of the river were drained in order to build concrete dams and locks on bedrock. In several places the river was dredged to provide a deeper channel. Entire towns were relocated and the land they had occupied was flooded to create the Lake St. Lawrence power pool. This artificial lake, located about 75 miles (120 kilometers) southwest of Montreal, today helps generate 1.6 million kilowatts of hydroelectricity.

By April 1959, the new waterway was completed. In June 1959, the seaway was opened officially by Canada's Queen Elizabeth II and U.S. president Dwight D. Eisenhower. Soon the Montreal–Lake Ontario section alone was handling annually about four times as many tons of cargo as before.

The seaway can now accommodate ships more than 700 feet (213 meters) long carrying over 25,000 tons of cargo. Iron ore mined in Labrador is shipped westward through the Seaway to steel mills in the industrial heart-

The St. Lawrence River, connecting Lake Ontario and the Atlantic Ocean, is the second longest river in Canada. In 1959, the completion of a vast network of dams, locks, and canals known as the St. Lawrence Seaway extended the reach of the river system all the way to Lake Superior.

lands of Canada and the United States, and grain from the midwestern states and Prairie Provinces is shipped eastward through the Great Lakes, down the St. Lawrence River and then overseas. Because of the winter freeze-up, the St. Lawrence Seaway operates only about ten months of the year—from early March to the end of December on both the Montreal–Lake Ontario section and the Welland Canal.

Reviewed by MAURICE SMITH
Executive Director
The Marine Museum of the Great Lakes

SAINT LOUIS

St. Louis, Missouri's second most populous city, is a major industrial and transportation center located on the west bank of the Mississippi River.

In 1764, a French fur trader named Pierre Laclède sent his 14-year-old stepson, René Auguste Chouteau, and a group of workers to build a trading post on the Mississippi. They named their settlement Saint Louis, after the French king Louis IX, who was canonized by the Catholic Church in 1297. St. Louis thrived as a trading center. Then in 1803, the United States bought the Louisiana Territory from France, and St. Louis became an American frontier outpost.

Due to its location on the Mississippi River, the nation's foremost north-south transportation highway, St. Louis prospered and became a manufacturing center. In the 1870's it also became one of the nation's main railroad junctions. In 1904, to celebrate the 100th anniversary of the Louisiana Purchase, St. Louisans sponsored an impressive World's Fair that drew millions of visitors from around the world.

After the United States acquired the territory west of the Mississippi River in 1803, St. Louis became a major trading and industrial center, linking the established cities in the East to the developing western frontier.

Today St. Louis has a population of more than 348,000 and covers an area of 61 square miles (158 square kilometers). More than 2.5 million people live in its larger metropolitan area, which spreads out into nine counties, including several in Illinois.

St. Louis is a commercial and financial center. Nationally known firms turn out such varied products as cars and trucks, chemicals, processed foods, beer, clothing, aircraft, and spaceships. The city is also home to one of the nation's twelve Federal Reserve banks.

Forest Park, one of the largest municipal parks in the country, contains the world-famous St. Louis Zoological Park and the St. Louis Art Museum. Not far away is the world-renowned Missouri Botanical Garden. The St. Louis Symphony is one of the country's oldest symphony orchestras. The city's many colleges and universities include Washington University, St. Louis University, and the St. Louis campus of the University of Missouri. Professional sports are well represented. The St. Louis Rams play football in the Trans World Dome; the St. Louis Cardinals play baseball in the Busch Memorial Stadium; and the St. Louis Blues play hockey in the Kiel Center.

St. Louis has undergone several phases of civic improvement. While renewing the downtown area, city planners have preserved several historic sites, notably part of Laclède's original village and the Jefferson National Expansion Memorial, which includes the Gateway Arch. Designed by the architect Eero Saarinen, this towering stainless steel arch, a symbol of St. Louis as the Gateway to the West, stands as a monument to the pioneers and America's territorial expansion west of the Mississippi River.

Reviewed by LAWRENCE O. CHRISTENSEN
University of Missouri, Rolla

SAINT LUCIA

ST. LUCIA

St. Lucia is an island nation in the Caribbean Sea. It is the second largest of the Windward Islands, which form a part of the Lesser Antilles chain of islands of the West Indies. Once inhabited by Carib Indians, St. Lucia was colonized by the French and then by the British, who gained possession of the island in the early 1800's. St. Lucia won complete independence from Britain in 1979.

▶ THE PEOPLE

The Carib Indians died out after the European settlement of the island. Most of St. Lucia's people today are of black African ancestry, the descendants of slaves who were brought to the island in the 1600's and 1700's. Several thousand Asians, some whites, and people of mixed race make up the rest of the population.

English is the official language, but many St. Lucians also speak a dialect based on French. The great majority of the people are Roman Catholics.

▶ THE LAND

St. Lucia is a mountainous island of rugged beauty. Its highest peak, Morne Gimie (or

FACTS and figures

SAINT LUCIA is the official name of the country.

LOCATION: Caribbean Sea.

AREA: 238 sq mi (616 km²).

POPULATION: 140,000 (estimate).

CAPITAL AND LARGEST CITY: Castries.

MAJOR LANGUAGE: English (official).

MAJOR RELIGIOUS GROUP: Roman Catholic.

GOVERNMENT: Constitutional monarchy. **Head of state**—British monarch, represented by a governor-general. **Head of government**—prime minister. **Legislature**—parliament, consisting of the House of Assembly and Senate.

CHIEF PRODUCTS: Agricultural—bananas, coconuts, cocoa, vegetables and fruits. **Manufactured**—copra (dried coconut meat), coconut oil, plastics, textiles.

MONETARY UNIT: East Caribbean dollar (1 EC dollar = 100 cents).

Mount Gimie), rises to 3,145 feet (959 meters). On the southwestern coast, the cones of two volcanoes—Gros Piton and Petit Piton—rise majestically from the sea. Much of the landscape is covered with lush, green foliage.

St. Lucia has a tropical climate, with an average yearly temperature of 79°F (26°C). Rainfall is abundant and falls heavily on the high mountain slopes. Like other Caribbean islands, St. Lucia is subject to hurricanes, which have frequently been destructive.

Castries is St. Lucia's capital, largest city, and chief port. It is situated in a natural harbor on the northwestern coast. It has a population of about 50,000.

THE ECONOMY

The island's economy is dependent on agriculture, which employs more than one-third of the workforce. Bananas are the most important commercial crop and the chief export. Coconuts and cocoa are also major commercial crops. Various vegetables and tropical fruits are grown for food and for export.

St. Lucia's industry for a long time was limited to the processing of agricultural products. Factories now produce plastics, textiles, and other goods as well. The island's striking mountain scenery, pleasant climate, and unspoiled sandy beaches have made tourism a growing industry.

The mountains of Saint Lucia rise abruptly from the sea. Like most islands in the Caribbean, it is a popular tourist beach resort.

▶ HISTORY AND GOVERNMENT

St. Lucia was first settled by Carib Indians. It is thought that Christopher Columbus visited the island in 1502. But its inhabitants resisted early European attempts at colonization. The island came under British control in 1803. St. Lucia was part of the British Windward Islands colony until that colony was dissolved in 1959. The islanders were granted increasing control over local affairs. Full internal self-government came in 1967, but the British government remained responsible for St. Lucia's defense and foreign affairs.

Independence. St. Lucia gained complete independence from Britain in 1979 and is now a constitutional monarchy within the Commonwealth of Nations.

The British monarch, represented by a governor-general, is the head of state. The parliament, or legislative body, consists of the 17-member House of Assembly, which is elected by the people, and the 11-member Senate, which is appointed by the governor-general. The head of government is the prime minister. The prime minister and his cabinet must have majority support in the House of Assembly.

Recent Events. John G. M. Compton, head of the United Workers' Party (UWP) and a leader of the independence movement, was prime minister at the time of independence in 1979. In elections held later that year, the St. Lucia Labour Party (SLP) won a majority of seats in the House of Assembly, and its leader, Allan Louisy, became prime minister. Compton returned as prime minister from 1982 to 1996. His successor, Vaughn Lewis, was succeeded by SLP leader Kenny Anthony in 1997.

St. Lucia belongs to the Organization of Eastern Caribbean States (OECS), whose members also include Antigua and Barbuda, Dominica, Grenada, Montserrat, St. Kitts and Nevis, and St. Vincent and the Grenadines. OECS headquarters are in Castries.

Reviewed by THOMAS G. MATHEWS
Secretary-General, Association of Caribbean
Universities and Research Institutes

SAINT PAUL. See MINNEAPOLIS–SAINT PAUL.

SAINT PETERSBURG (FLORIDA). See FLORIDA (Cities).

SAINT PETERSBURG (RUSSIA)

St. Petersburg, often called the Venice of the North because of its many canals and magnificent beauty, is the second largest city in Russia. It lies in northwestern Russia on marshy land at the mouth of the Neva River, which flows into the Gulf of Finland, and includes many islands. At one time the capital of Russia, St. Petersburg today is regarded as the country's cultural center and has a population of about 4 million.

Because St. Petersburg lies close to the Arctic Circle, daylight hours during the winter are short. During the summer, there are days when sunlight is visible throughout the evening hours (called white nights). Seasonal temperatures are moderated by winds off the ocean, which also make the city particularly humid. Flooding is common.

The City. St. Petersburg has a distinctly Western flavor. Architects from France and Italy were commissioned by Russia's rulers to join with Russian architects in designing the city's fine squares, broad streets, parks, and stately buildings.

The main avenue, the Nevsky Prospekt, is lined with shops, apartment houses, and churches. The Nevsky Prospekt leads to the great square in front of the Admiralty, a naval college originally built as a

dockyard during the city's early years. The cathedral of St. Isaac, with its high golden dome, is nearby. Next to the cathedral is the Blue Bridge, one of the widest bridges in the world. A bronze statue of Peter the Great stands in the middle of the square and looks toward the Peter and Paul Fortress, the oldest building in St. Petersburg, which occupies an island in the Neva River.

The city is home to the State Hermitage Museum, one of the largest and most elegant museums in the world. Contained at first within the Winter Palace, once a royal residence, the museum has grown over the years and now includes many other historic buildings filled with works of art from all over the world.

Left: A statue of Peter the Great stands in St. Petersburg's great square. *Below:* The city is famous for its canals and Western architecture.

Among the many other places of interest are the State Russian Museum, dedicated strictly to Russian art; the Fëdor Dostoevski Museum, located in the last apartment the famed author lived in; and the Peterhof estate, once a summer residence for the czars and today famous for its lush parks and spectacular fountains.

One of the city's old palaces has been turned into the Palace of Pioneers and Schoolchildren. It has workshops, studios, sports areas, and dance rooms, and its brass band is quite famous. The city also has several puppet theaters for children, as well as two circuses. The Leningradsky Zoo, near the Peter and Paul Fortress, opened in 1865.

The Nevsky Prospekt, St. Petersburg's busy main avenue, is lined with many shops and apartment buildings.

St. Petersburg has many colleges and universities. Besides the St. Petersburg State University, there are schools for religion and philosophy, engineering and economics, and veterinary medicine.

Economic Activity. Because of the city's great works of architecture and collections of art, tourism is a major part of the economy. Its coastal location has also made the city ideal for shipbuilding and trade. Its leading manufactures are machinery, chemicals, and electrical equipment.

History. Named for Saint Peter, St. Petersburg was founded by Peter the Great in 1703.

When Peter became czar in 1682, Russia was far behind the rest of Europe in its development of science and industry. Peter was determined to make his country equal to the other European nations. By waging war on Sweden, he won some marshy land on the Gulf of Finland in 1703. In the same year he began to build his city, which he wanted to be a "window to the West." In 1712, Peter made St. Petersburg the nation's capital, replacing the old capital of Moscow. His successors developed the city into an important seaport and industrial center.

In 1914, at the beginning of World War I (in which Germany and Russia were opponents), the German form of the city's name was changed to the Russian form—Petrograd. In 1917, revolution broke out in the city. The czar was overthrown, and a provisional (temporary) representative government was established. Later that year, the provisional government was itself overthrown by V. I. Lenin and his Communist Party, who relocated the nation's capital to Moscow in 1918. Four years later, the Soviet Union was established. When Lenin died in 1924, Petrograd was renamed Leningrad in his honor.

In 1941, during World War II, Nazi Germany invaded the Soviet Union. In September 1941, Leningrad was encircled by German armies and underwent a 2½-year siege. While soldiers defended the city, women, children, and the elderly dug trenches and helped build fortifications. Although the people suffered greatly, hundreds of thousands dying from cold and hunger, the city held out until it was relieved in January 1944.

The city's last renaming followed a period of great political change in the Soviet Union. Following a vote by the city's residents to restore its original name, Leningrad became St. Petersburg in September 1991. Just months later, the Soviet Union collapsed, and the city became part of the new Russian Federation.

ELIZABETH SEEGER
Author, *The Pageant of Russian History*

See also HERMITAGE MUSEUM; PETER THE GREAT.

SAINTS

As it appears in the New Testament, the term "saint" refers to someone who is a faithful member of the Christian community. However, very early in Christian history, during the time of the Roman Empire (753 B.C.?–1453), the word began to be used to describe those persons who were persecuted and who died for their beliefs. These persons, called martyrs, were believed to be in heaven. Once in heaven, they were considered allies of God who could pray for those on Earth, and they were recognized in prayers during official church services. In the early 300's, after the period of the Roman persecutions, the term "saint" was also applied to Christian figures such as monks, missionaries, and church leaders who led heroic lives.

Until the 1200's, there was no official system to establish who was a saint. A community might begin to honor someone they considered a holy person in a certain place, such as at his or her tomb, or at a certain time, such as on the anniversary of the date of the person's death, which is called the person's **feast day**. Churches might also honor the same person by keeping and displaying **relics**, which were parts of the person's body or objects connected with them. On the person's feast day, the **legend**, or the life of the saint, would be read in church. It was not until A.D. 973 that the pope in Rome proclaimed a person a saint to be honored by the entire Catholic Church. In 1234, Pope Gregory IX decreed that saints could only be named by a pope, which is the practice in the Roman Catholic Church today.

The process by which a person is named a saint is called **canonization**. In canonization, a person is put on an official church list, or **canon**, and then may be honored in the church's public prayer, or **liturgy**. In the Roman Catholic Church, the canonization process starts with an investigation into the life of the person. After research is completed, the results are sent to Rome for further study by the Congregation for the Cause of the Saints. This group may then declare that the person can be called **Blessed**, or worthy of honor at the local level. This process is called **beatification**. After additional study, especially into miracles that are believed to have occurred through the aid of this person, he or she is canonized and called a saint. The saint is then honored in the entire church, and his or her name is inscribed in the calendar of saints' feast days. Other Christian churches, such as the Eastern Orthodox and the Anglican, have similar procedures for honoring saints. But Protestant churches do not formally name saints.

Many Christians pray to saints for divine favors. Throughout the history of Christianity, there have been many places, known as shrines, where people have gone to pray to saints, who are seen as models of how to live a life of faith, service to others, and self-sacrifice. Some saints have left written works, and some have been written about by others. These writings are used by people seeking inspiration and help in their lives.

The Christian churches that **venerate**, or honor, saints with special services do so on a specific day during the year. In the Roman Catholic and Anglican churches, the calendar of these feast days is called the **sanctoral cycle**. In the Orthodox church, it is known as the Menaion. Protestant churches do not venerate the saints formally.

Although many people identify saints only with Christianity, all the major religions of the world honor holy persons in similar ways. Judaism venerates very righteous and learned persons who are known as *zaddikim* or *Hasidim*. In Islam, living holy persons are honored with the title *pir* or *sheikh*, and these "friends of God" are venerated after their deaths with prayers at their tombs. In certain traditions of Buddhism, those who have reached *prajna*, or Enlightenment, and choose to remain on Earth to aid others to seek Enlightenment are called *bodhisattvas*, or "buddhas to be." In Hinduism, holy people called *saddhus* or *gurus* are honored both during their lives and after their deaths. Another common term for saint in certain Eastern traditions, such as Chinese Confucianism, is "sage," meaning a person who exemplifies and teaches wisdom.

LAWRENCE S. CUNNINGHAM
The University of Notre Dame

See also APOSTLES, THE; AQUINAS, SAINT THOMAS; AUGUSTINE, SAINT; BIBLE; BUDDHA; BUDDHISM; CHRISTIANITY, HISTORY OF; FRANCIS OF ASSISI, SAINT; HINDUISM; ISLAM; JEROME, SAINT; JOHN THE BAPTIST; JUDAISM; LOYOLA, SAINT IGNATIUS; PATRICK, SAINT; PAUL, SAINT; PETER, SAINT; RELIGIOUS HOLIDAYS; and profiles of saints on the following page.

The following are brief descriptions of some of the many saints whose feast days are celebrated.

Albertus Magnus, the patron saint of students of the natural sciences, was a German theologian, philosopher, and scientist noted for his work in the natural sciences and for his writings about the ancient Greek philosopher Aristotle. Feast day: November 15.

Ambrose, the patron saint of bishops and the French army, was important in the rise of Christianity during the decline of the Roman Empire. He is also the patron saint of beekeepers because, as a child, it was said that bees settled on his face but did not harm him. Feast day: January 27.

Anne, the patron saint of Quebec, was the mother of the Virgin Mary and the wife of Joachim. Because she was unable to have a child for many years, she is also the patron saint of childless women. Feast day: July 26.

Anthony of Padua, the patron saint of Portugal, was a Franciscan friar known for his eloquent preaching and his devotion to the poor. He was called a wonder-worker because of the many miracles attributed to him. Feast day: June 13.

Antony, the founder of monasticism, was a hermit in the desert for many years. Known as a healer, he is the patron saint of people with skin diseases. Feast day: January 17.

Benedict of Nursia, "the Patriarch of Western Monasticism," was known for his wisdom and holiness. The patron saint of monks, he wrote the most important rules for monks in the Western church. Feast day: July 11.

Bernadette of Lourdes, a French nun who as a young shepherdess was said to have had visions of the Virgin Mary at Lourdes, was known for her truthfulness and courage. She is the patron saint of shepherdesses. Feast day: April 16.

Boniface, an English monk, was a missionary to German tribes in the 700's. He is the patron saint of Germany. Feast day: June 5.

Bridget of Sweden, the patron saint of Sweden, founded an order for both monks and nuns. Although she was said to have had many visions, she was canonized for her virtue. Feast day: July 23.

Frances Xavier Cabrini (Mother Cabrini), a nun sent to the United States to work with Italian immigrants, became a U.S. citizen and founded convents, schools, and hospitals all over the world. The first foreign-born U.S. citizen to be canonized, she is the patron saint of immigrants. Feast day: December 22.

Catherine of Siena, the patron saint of Italy and of nurses, was a Dominican nun who nursed patients with leprosy and advanced cancer. She was also an influential spiritual leader during the Middle Ages. Feast day: April 29.

Cecilia has been known as the patron saint of music and musicians since the 1500's. She was martyred during the Roman persecutions. Feast day: November 22.

Christopher, the patron saint of travelers, was said to have carried travelers across a stream on his shoulders. His name means "Christ-bearer" because he was said to have once carried the Christ child in this way. Feast day: July 25.

Clare of Assisi, recently named the patron saint of television, was so moved by St. Francis of Assisi's preaching that she became a nun who founded an order of nuns dedicated to poverty. Feast day: August 11.

Elizabeth, the patron saint of pregnant women, was the mother of St. John the Baptist. Feast day: November 5.

Francis de Sales, a French churchman, converted the Protestants of Chablais from Calvinism to Catholicism. Known for his writing style, he is the patron saint of writers. Feast day: January 24.

George, the patron saint of England, is best known for the legend that told of his slaying a dragon and rescuing a king's daughter. Feast day: April 23.

Helena, the patron saint of archaeologists, was the mother of Constantine the Great, the first Christian emperor. According to tradition, Helena discovered the true cross in the Holy Land. Feast day: August 18.

John of the Cross, a Spanish Carmelite priest, was the author of the famous poem "Noche obscura del alma" ("Dark Night of the Soul"). He is the patron saint of poets. Feast day: December 14.

Joseph, a carpenter in Nazareth, was the husband of Mary and the foster father of Jesus. He is the patron saint of fathers and of manual laborers, especially carpenters. Feast day: March 19.

Lucy, the patron saint of those with eye diseases, according to legend had her eyes torn out and then miraculously restored. Her name means "light," and in Sweden her feast day is celebrated as a festival of light. Feast day: December 13.

Luke, the patron saint of artists as well as doctors, was a Greek physician, evangelist, and writer. He wrote the Acts of the Apostles and the Third Gospel. Feast day: October 18.

Mark, the patron saint of Venice, is the author of Mark's Gospel, one of the four gospels in the New Testament. He is often represented as a lion, his symbol as an evangelist. Feast day: April 25.

Martin de Porres, the patron saint of race relations, was known for his devotion to the poor, regardless of their race or color. Feast day: November 5.

Martin of Tours, the patron saint of beggars, was the first saint not to be martyred. According to legend, he gave half of his cloak to a freezing beggar, and then Christ appeared to him wearing the same cloak. Feast day: November 11.

Maurice and the Theban Legion were soldiers and the first African martyrs because they refused to take part in the killing of innocent Christians. Maurice, the legion's leader, is the patron saint of soldiers. Feast day: September 22.

Nicholas, the patron saint of Russia, according to legend provided the dowry for a poverty-stricken nobleman's three daughters. He is popularly known as Santa Claus. Feast day: December 6.

Pius X, the last pope to be canonized, is the patron saint of sick pilgrims because he established a society dedicated to taking sick people to the Italian shrine of Lapurdo. Feast day: August 21.

Rose of Lima, the "flower of Lima," was a Dominican nun who lived as a hermit in her order's garden, which became the spiritual center of Lima. She is the patron saint of South America, gardeners, and florists. Feast day: August 23.

Seton, Elizabeth Ann Bayley, the first native-born U.S. citizen to be canonized, founded the American Sisters of Charity, devoted to helping the poor and to teaching in parish schools. Feast day: January 4.

Teresa of Avila, the patron saint of Spain, founded the reformed Carmelites, who lived in poverty, hardship, and solitude. Feast day: October 15.

Therese of Lisieux, the "little flower," prayed for foreign missionaries. A Carmelite nun, she is the patron saint of foreign missions. Feast day: October 1.

Vincent de Paul, the patron saint of charitable societies, was a French priest who established the French Sisters of Charity and devoted his life to charitable deeds. Feast day: September 27.

SAINT VINCENT AND THE GRENADINES

St. Vincent and the Grenadines is an island nation in the Caribbean Sea, part of the Windward Islands of the West Indies. It is composed of the main island of St. Vincent and the northern half of the Grenadines, a chain of more than 100 small islands and islets. The southern half of the Grenadines belongs to the nation of Grenada. Formerly governed by Britain, St. Vincent and the Grenadines gained complete independence in 1979.

The People. The great majority of the people are descended from black African slaves who were brought to the islands in past centuries to work on plantations. Some islanders are of mixed black and Indian ancestry. There are smaller numbers of whites and Asians. The population is concentrated largely on the island of St. Vincent. The capital and largest city is Kingstown, on St. Vincent.

English is the official language. Most of the people are Protestants, while Roman Catholics make up a considerable minority. The Asians are mainly Hindus or Muslims.

The Land. St. Vincent is a rugged, mountainous island, formed by the action of volcanoes. Mount Soufrière, at its northern end, is the highest point, rising to 4,048 feet (1,234 meters). Only about one third of the island, mainly along the coast, is suitable for farming. The principal islands of the Grenadines

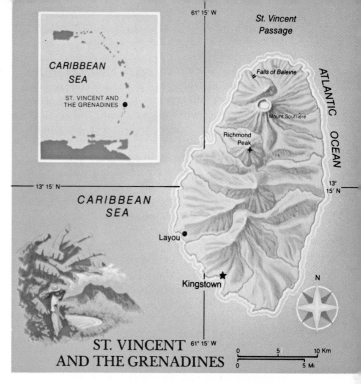

SAINT VINCENT AND THE GRENADINES is the official name of the country.

LOCATION: Caribbean Sea.

AREA: 150 sq mi (388 km²).

POPULATION: 116,000 (estimate).

CAPITAL AND LARGEST CITY: Kingstown.

MAJOR LANGUAGE: English (official).

MAJOR RELIGIOUS GROUPS: Protestant, Roman Catholic.

GOVERNMENT: Constitutional monarchy. **Head of state**—British monarch, represented by a governor-general. **Head of government**—prime minister. **Legislature**—House of Assembly.

CHIEF PRODUCTS: Bananas, arrowroot, coconuts, peanuts, carrots, ginger, nutmeg, mace.

MONETARY UNIT: East Caribbean dollar (1 EC dollar = 100 cents).

The rugged mountains of St. Vincent loom over the port of Kingstown, capital and largest city of the Caribbean island nation of St. Vincent and the Grenadines.

belonging to St. Vincent include Bequia, Canouan, Mayreau, Mustique, and Union Island. The climate is tropical, with pleasantly warm temperatures and abundant rainfall.

Economy. Agriculture is the main economic activity. Bananas are the most important commercial crop and the country's chief export. St. Vincent and the Grenadines is also the world's largest producer of arrowroot, a plant whose roots yield a starch used in making puddings and cookies. Other leading commercial crops include coconuts, peanuts, carrots, and such spices as ginger, nutmeg, and mace.

Industry is limited largely to the processing of agricultural products, although some manufacturing is developing. Tourism is growing in importance, especially in the Grenadines, where some of the uninhabited islets have been turned into resorts.

History and Government. The island of St. Vincent was originally settled by Arawak Indians. They were killed off by the more warlike Carib Indians, who came to the island from the mainland of South America.

It is believed that Christopher Columbus sighted the main island on Saint Vincent's Day in 1498. The Carib Indians resisted colonization by the French and British until the 18th century. Britain won possession of St. Vincent in 1783. Later it was administered as part of the British Windward Islands colony, until 1960. It gained internal self-government in 1967 and full independence as St. Vincent and the Grenadines in 1979.

St. Vincent and the Grenadines is a constitutional monarchy. The British monarch, represented by a governor-general, is the head of state. The head of government is the prime minister, who is the leader of the majority political party in the legislature, the House of Assembly. The House of Assembly has 13 elected members and 6 appointed senators.

Reviewed by THOMAS G. MATHEWS
Author, *Politics and Economics
of the Caribbean*

SAKHAROV, ANDREI.   See UNION OF SOVIET SOCIALIST REPUBLICS (Profiles).

SALADIN.   See MIDDLE AGES (Profiles).

SALAMANDERS.   See AMPHIBIANS.

SALEM.   See OREGON (Cities).

SALES AND MARKETING

It was once said that if you build a better mousetrap, the world will beat a path to your door. Business people today know that this is not true. To sell even the highest quality product, it must be marketed successfully. That is, the consumer must be told about the product, be persuaded to buy it, and be satisfied enough to buy it again.

Marketing includes all the activities necessary to develop a product and to move it from the producer to the consumer. These activities are called the four p's—product development, product placement, product pricing, and product promotion.

Product Development

The question "Can we make this product?" is often not as important as "Can we make a profit on this product?" Automakers could produce a car with only three wheels. But consumers prefer cars with four wheels. A three-wheeled model would not be profitable because not enough people would buy it.

Product development begins with **market research.** Firms that specialize in market research help manufacturers determine whether a market (a large enough group of potential consumers) exists for a product. They conduct surveys, asking people what kind of products they want, and they forecast probable sales of the product. How the product should be packaged is also very important and is analyzed carefully.

Through consumer education, people have become more aware of what they are buying and more careful about their purchases. This has had a great influence on how products are marketed.

Product Placement

Consumers buy two kinds of products—tangible, or physical, products such as clothing or cars; and intangible, or service, products such as theater tickets and insurance policies. Advice marketed by accountants, lawyers, and other consultants is another example of a service product. Consumers spend about half their buying dollars for tangible products and the other half for services.

Some products and services are sold directly to the consumer through commercials or through the manufacturer's salespeople. However, most products go through one or more intermediaries (dealers or agents) before they reach the consumer. The leading intermediates are **wholesalers** and **retailers.**

Wholesalers buy in large quantities and then resell the products in smaller quantities to retailers. Retailers then sell in even smaller quantities to consumers. Wholesalers perform several important services for retailers. They maintain warehouses, make deliveries, sell to the retailer on credit, and can also give advice on marketing.

The path taken by a product as it moves from producer to wholesaler to retailer to consumer is called the **channel of distribution.**

Product Pricing

Imagine that you have purchased a sweater from a retailer for $20. The retailer probably paid a wholesaler or the manufacturer around $10 for the same sweater. The difference between what a business charges you for a product and what it costs the business to make or buy the same item is called **markup.**

Consumers often feel that markups are too high. But they may be overlooking the costs a retailer must pay to make products easily available. Some of these costs are rent, advertising, utilities, salaries, interest expenses, and store fixtures.

Businesses follow one of three pricing policies. They price their merchandise higher than that of their competitor; they meet the competitor's price; or they sell below the competitor's price. How successful the pricing policy is depends greatly on the kind of competition a business faces. Because competition in the sale of most products is strong, the consumer has some assurance of paying a fair price.

Customer convenience is also a factor in pricing. Products sold in quick-service (convenience) food stores, for example, are almost always priced higher than identical items sold in a supermarket.

Product Promotion

The goal of promotion is to convince people to buy a product. The two main promotional tools are personal selling and advertising. Personal selling is the face-to-face, or personal, explanation of a product by a salesperson to a prospective consumer. Because personal selling is expensive, many retailers of food, drugs, and hardware operate on a self-service basis. Many departments in large chain stores are self-service.

Personal selling is still widely used to market products to industrial consumers. Many industrial products are highly technical, and the seller has to be able to explain in detail how the product works and how it will meet the buyer's needs. For example, in order to sell complex computer systems, the salesperson must be knowledgeable not only about the product but also about the competitor's product and about computer science in general.

Advertising is the impersonal presentation of information about a product. Television, radio, newspapers, magazines, billboards, and direct mail are the most widely used means of presenting advertisements to consumers. Manufacturers may hire an advertising agency to prepare ads and place them in the media.

Advertising seems very costly. A one-minute commercial during a televised event, for example, may cost $500,000. But that sum is small when you consider the number of people who may see the commercial. If 50,000,000 people watch the event, the cost of presenting the product to one customer is only one cent.

Packaging is another type of promotion. Some consumers will stop and look at a product simply because the packaging catches their eye, and may then buy the product.

Marketing by Nonprofit Organizations

Many enterprises that do not seek a profit also use marketing techniques to influence people. Some colleges advertise to attract students. Hospitals use marketing techniques to urge doctors to recommend their hospital to patients. Politicians do not simply run for office; they market themselves and their programs. Public-service announcements and commercials encourage people to do such things as vote, contribute to charities, and volunteer to help their communities.

The Future

Both businesses and consumers can profit by improved marketing techniques. Producers can make a profit only on a product that consumers really want. The result for consumers will be fewer but better products.

DAVID J. SCHWARTZ
Author, *Marketing Today*

See also ADVERTISING; MAIL ORDER; RETAIL STORES.

SALK, JONAS. See CALIFORNIA (Famous People).

SALT

Salt is a mineral that is vital to life. It is made up of sodium and chlorine, both of which play very important roles in good health. (Without salt, the fluids in the human body could not be kept in their proper balance.) Salt is also very important as an industrial chemical.

The value of salt has been known for thousands of years. The *Pen Ts'ao,* an early Chinese book on medicine, records more than 40 uses of salt to cure ailments.

The phrase "not worth his salt" probably became a saying in ancient Greece during the time when slaves were bought with salt. The word "salary" comes from the Roman practice of giving troops money to buy salt rations. The money for salt was called *salarium argentum* in Latin.

Salt was so important in the Middle Ages that governments often took over the salt trade. In many countries, no one was allowed to mine or sell salt without permission from the government, and all salt was taxed. In the years before the French Revolution, the French government passed a law forcing each peasant to buy a fixed amount of salt at very high prices. This unfair tax on salt was one of the causes that drove the people to revolt. Some countries today still have a government salt monopoly or put a tax on salt.

At the Great Salt Flats in Colombia, South America, seawater evaporates from shallow pools leaving salt behind. Workers mound it into piles to dry in the sun.

▶HOW DO WE GET SALT?

Common salt, a chemical combination of sodium and chlorine, is found in rocks throughout the world. Water is continually dissolving tiny amounts of salt from rocks and soil. Streams carry the dissolved salt to the sea, and every day the heat of the sun evaporates some of the water, leaving the salt behind. In this way the sea has slowly been growing saltier for millions of years. At present there is about ¼ pound of salt in each gallon (30 grams in each liter) of seawater.

If all the water evaporated from the sea, large deposits of salt would be left. This is exactly what happened millions of years ago when ancient seas dried up. Today these deposits, called **salt beds** or **rock salt**, lie beneath layers of rocks all over the world. The salt beds can be found at depths ranging from about ½ mile to more than 4 miles (1 kilometer to 6 kilometers) below the surface.

In some places, pressure of the earth's crust on deep-lying salt beds forced the salt into weak spots in the rock layers that lay above the beds. The salt was forced into the shape of gigantic columns. These formations are called **salt domes**.

▶PRODUCTION OF SALT

An increasing amount of salt is collected from nature each year. The present worldwide collection rate has reached nearly 150 million metric tons. Leading countries in the production of salt include the United States, China, Ukraine, Turkmenistan, Germany, and India. Salt is obtained from salt mines, brine wells, and the sea.

Mining. In mining salt a shaft is sunk through the earth until the salt bed is reached. Miners then dig into the wall of salt and use explosives to blast loose the salt. The chunks of salt are loaded on small freight cars, trucks, or conveyor belts and carried to the surface. There the rock salt is put through crushers and reduced to small particles.

Brine Wells. Getting salt from wells is much like getting oil from wells. In the simplest type of brine well, two pipes are driven into the salt deposit. Water is sent into the salt bed through one pipe and pumped back out through the second pipe. As the water passes through the salt bed, it dissolves the salt. The water and salt mixture is known as **brine**.

The water is removed from the brine by heat. The cube-shaped crystals used for table salt, food processing, and industrial operations are produced by evaporating the brine in a vacuum pan. Flake salt, which is dried for use in some foods and used undried for curing leather, is made by evaporating the brine in large, open, heated tanks.

Solar Salt. Solar salt is obtained from the sea or salt lakes by simply letting the sun dry out the water. The salty water, or brine, is pumped into a system of ponds or evaporating beds and left to evaporate. As the brine is pumped from pond to pond, minerals and chemicals other than salt settle on the bottom. When the last drop of water has evaporated in the final pond, the salt is harvested with special machines. Because this process needs a large amount of sunshine, little rainfall, and a good breeze, solar salt is usually produced around seacoasts.

▶ USES OF SALT

Salt companies produce more than 300 types of specialized salt for food processors, chemical companies, and other salt users.

Salt in Food

Salt is probably the oldest preservative and seasoning. It is so necessary to the functioning of animal and human bodies that life cannot go on without it.

Salt for Animals. Many kinds of animals search for salt deposits that lie at the earth's surface. These deposits are called **licks** because the animals lick the rock salt with their tongues. Many of the trails made by the animals on their way to the licks came to be traveled by people. Some roads now in use were once animal salt trails.

Today animals on farms are given feed with salt mixed into it. Blocks of pressed salt are also sometimes put out in the pasture.

Salt for Humans. The recommended intake of salt for healthy adults is ½ to 1½ teaspoons a day. Most of this is found naturally in foods. (Fresh foods usually contain less salt than processed foods, which are often prepared with salt.) Salt sold for table use often has iodine added to it to prevent a disease called goiter.

Many medical researchers believe that too much salt in the diet can lead to hypertension, or high blood pressure. This is a condition in which blood vessels constrict, or tighten. As a result, blood is pumped through the vessels with a dangerous amount of force. Not everyone develops hypertension from eating too much salt. But people who already have high blood pressure can usually improve their condition with a low-salt diet.

▶ SALT AND THE CHEMICAL INDUSTRY

Only a small amount of the world's total salt production goes into foods. Most of it is used by the chemical industry. In industrial nations, as much as 70 percent of the salt is put to some chemical use.

Salt is called a basic chemical. That means it is used in the production of many other chemicals, such as caustic soda (sodium hydroxide), used to make soap and paper. Chemicals made from salt are important in the manufacture of glass, synthetic fabric, leather, and fertilizer. Liquid sodium, made from salt, plays an important part in nuclear power plants as a cooling agent. Salt also goes into the manufacture of textile dyes and explosives.

▶ OTHER USES OF SALT

Salt on Roads and Highways. Sprinkling salt on icy roads has proved to be an inexpensive and effective method of keeping roads clear in winter. Millions of tons of salt are used every winter for this purpose.

Salt is also used in dirt and gravel roads. Mixing salt into the soil and gravel of roads gives the roads added firmness and strength to help them withstand weather. This addition of salt is called **stabilization** because the salt makes the roads more reliable.

Salt for Water Softening. Another interesting use of salt is in softening water. "Hard water" is water that contains fairly large amounts of calcium and magnesium solids. These chemicals cause scale (mineral deposits) on plumbing pipes and cooking utensils. Hard water is also responsible for the bathtub ring that is so well known to everyone.

Hard water is more than a cleaning nuisance. Scale left on equipment by the water can ruin many industrial processes. Water is softened by running it through a chemical filter that absorbs the calcium and magnesium from the water. The filter gives off sodium in exchange and can be used again and again if it is recharged with brine.

HERBERT PERKINS
Salt Institute

SALT LAKE CITY

Salt Lake City is the capital and largest city of Utah. Named for the famous Great Salt Lake located nearby, the city lies at the base of the Wasatch and Oquirrh mountain ranges on land that is partly desert. Nearly 182,000 people live in the city proper, which covers an area of 75 square miles (194 square kilometers). More than 1 million people live in the metropolitan area.

Salt Lake City is sometimes called the Crossroads of the West because of its importance as a distribution and transportation center. Other leading industries include salt processing, oil and mineral refining, biomedical products, and copper mining in the nearby Bingham Canyon Copper Mine, the largest open-pit copper mine in North America. Tourism is also an important industry.

Salt Lake City is the religious and cultural center for the Mormon Church—which is officially known as the Church of Jesus Christ of Latter-day Saints. Mormons make up about half the city's population. The first group of 148 Mormons, fleeing persecution in the Midwest, entered the valley of the Great Salt Lake on July 24, 1847. The sight that greeted them was that of a desert wilderness. But as their leader, Brigham Young, surveyed the valley, he said, "This is the right place." The spot where they first entered the valley is now marked at the mouth of Emigration

Canyon. And each year on July 24 the city commemorates their arrival with Pioneer Day, an official Utah state holiday.

Many of the places of interest in Salt Lake City reflect the influence of the Mormons. Temple Square, at the heart of the city, is the site of the Salt Lake Temple, the Assembly Hall, and the Tabernacle, home of the world-famous Mormon Tabernacle Choir.

Near Temple Square is the Family History Library, the world's largest library for genealogical research. The Utah State Historical Society Museum contains diaries of pioneers and other materials concerning Utah's history. The downtown area also includes Hansen Planetarium; the Salt Palace Convention Center; Abravanel Hall; the Salt Lake Art Center; and the restored Capitol Theatre, the home of the Utah Opera Company and Ballet West. The Delta Center is home to the Utah Jazz of the National Basketball Association and the Utah Starzz of the Women's National Basketball Association. In 2002 the city hosted the Winter Olympic Games.

Local schools of higher education include the University of Utah, Westminster College, the Latter-day Saints Business College, and Salt Lake Community College. The University of Utah also contains museums of fine arts, earth sciences, and natural history.

There is also much to see and do outside the city. Skiers enjoy famous mountain resorts, such as Alta and Snowbird. Other visitors can enjoy camping, fishing, hunting, and swimming—particularly in the Great Salt Lake, where the high salt content makes bathers float like corks.

MARIE RASMUSSEN
Salt Lake City Public Library

See also MORMONS; YOUNG, BRIGHAM.

Salt Lake City, the capital of Utah, is the state's largest city and headquarters of the Mormon Church (the Church of Jesus Christ of Latter-day Saints).

SALVATION ARMY

The Salvation Army is a Christian organization dedicated to "the advancement of the Christian religion …and of education, the relief of poverty, and other charitable objects beneficial to society or the community of mankind as a whole." Known primarily for its thrift stores and "red kettle" Christmas campaigns, the Salvation Army assists more than 5 million people in more than 100 countries every year.

Founded in London in 1865 by the Methodist evangelist William Booth (1829–1912), the organization's original goal was to help the spiritually and financially impoverished slum dwellers of London's Whitechapel district. Known as the Christian Mission, it was renamed the Salvation Army in 1878. Its first American branch opened in 1880.

The Salvation Army is organized according to military structure. Officers and volunteer workers, called Salvationists, provide shelter for the homeless, distribute meals to the hungry, supply emergency relief to victims of natural disasters, and offer alcohol-

and drug-rehabilitation programs as well as spiritual counseling. International headquarters are located at 101 Queen Victoria Street, London, England. United States headquarters are located at 615 Slaters Lane, Alexandria, Virginia 22313.

Reviewed by The Salvation Army

SAMOA. See WESTERN SAMOA.

SAMOSET (1590?–1653?)

Samoset was an Abnaki Indian sachem, or chief, of Pemaquid, a district at the mouth of the Kennebec River in southeastern Maine. As early as 1607, the English had sailed into Pemaquid's excellent harbor to fish and trade for furs. Samoset learned a little English from these visitors.

In the summer of 1620, Samoset traveled south to Cape Cod peninsula, the territory of the Wampanoag nation. The following December, a group of English founded Plimouth Colony at the base of Cape Cod. In March 1621, after observing the Plimouth colonists for several months, the Wampanoag sachem, Massasoit, sent Samoset to inform the colonists that their settlement lay in Wampanoag territory. Samoset strode confidently toward the strangers, greeting them with the words, "Welcome, Englishmen!"

The astonished colonists described Samoset as "a tall, straight man; the hair of his head black." Dressed only in a fringed breechcloth in spite of the cold March wind,

Samoset was pleased when the colonists put a coat around his shoulders. The entire afternoon, he sat with the English and described the Indian nations of the region to them.

Samoset returned to Massasoit with a message that the colonists wanted to trade for beaver and other furs. On another visit, he was accompanied by Squanto (Tisquantum), a Pawtuxet Indian. The two men announced that sachem Massasoit was now waiting to formally meet the settlers.

The climax of Samoset's diplomacy was the March 1621 treaty between Plimouth Colony and Massasoit of the Wampanoag Confederacy. Massasoit agreed to be "King James' man" in alliance with Plimouth. Samoset returned to Maine and in 1625 deeded about 12,000 acres (4,800 hectares) of Pemaquid territory to John Brown, an English settler. This is said to have been the first legal transfer of Indian land to an Englishman. Samoset died about 1653 and was buried in his family plot on Monhegan Island.

ALICE B. KEHOE
Professor of Anthropology, Marquette University

SAN ANTONIO

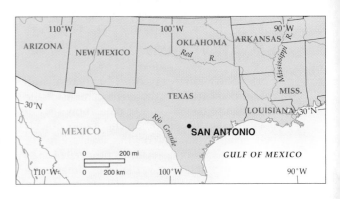

San Antonio, the third most populous city in Texas, is located on the San Antonio River in the south central part of the state. Approximately 1 million people live in the city, which covers an area of 328 square miles (850 square kilometers). More than half the population is of Hispanic origin, and Spanish is widely spoken.

A major manufacturing, banking, medical, and transportation center, San Antonio also serves as a wholesale, retail, and distribution center for the surrounding agricultural area. Other local industries include food processing, tourism, and the manufacture of clothing, leather goods, petroleum products, electronic equipment, and aircraft parts.

Institutions of higher learning in and around San Antonio include St. Mary's and Trinity universities, the University of Texas at San Antonio, and the University of Texas Health Science Center. Community colleges include San Antonio, Palo Alto, and St. Philips colleges.

San Antonio, Texas, is a center of commerce and a popular tourist destination. Its many attractions include four Spanish missions and the historic Alamo.

Named for Saint Anthony of Padua, San Antonio is often called Alamo City because the historic Battle of the Alamo was fought there in 1836 during Texas' war for independence. The Alamo is San Antonio's most visited attraction. Other historic sites include La Villita (the little town), a restoration of the original Spanish settlement; San Fernando Cathedral; the Spanish Governor's Palace; and four Spanish missions, including San Jose, now a national historic site. Other attractions include the Paseo del Rio (Riverwalk), a dining and shopping area along the San Antonio River; El Mercado, the largest Mexican market in the United States; Six Flags Fiesta Texas and Sea World amusement parks; the McNay Art Institute; and the San Antonio Art Museum. The Alamo Dome is home to the San Antonio Spurs of the National Basketball Association.

The mission of San Antonio de Valero (later known as the Alamo) and the presidio, or military post, of San Antonio de Bexar (or Bejar) were established in 1718. A group of Spanish immigrants established the nearby town of San Fernando de Bexar in 1731. By 1791 the settlements were collectively called San Antonio de Bexar. San Antonio remained under Spanish rule until 1821, then briefly belonged to Mexico before it became part of the United States in 1845. By the end of the 1800's, San Antonio had become a major shipping point for cattle.

Construction of Fort Sam Houston began in 1876. San Antonio and eventually its surrounding area became home to other U.S. military installations, among them Brooks, Kelly, Lackland, and Randolph air force bases. Today San Antonio is a popular retirement center for military personnel.

Reviewed by HENRY G. CISNEROS
Former Mayor, San Antonio

Carl Sandburg, American poet and historian, celebrated his country and the people who made its history in works that twice won the Pulitzer prize.

SANDBURG, CARL (1878–1967)

The American poet Carl August Sandburg was born in Galesburg, Illinois, on January 6, 1878. His parents came from Sweden. His father worked in a blacksmith shop.

Carl did odd jobs after school to help support his family. After finishing the eighth grade, he left school to work full-time. First he delivered milk; then he was a porter and a shoe shiner. He was always reading, however. He read encyclopedias, histories, biographies, and his sister's high-school textbooks.

When Carl was 19 he traveled to Kansas as a hobo, picking up odd jobs along the way. He saw small towns, prairie towns, and big cities and learned about all kinds of work. After a year he returned to Galesburg and worked as a house painter. In 1898 he enlisted to fight in the Spanish-American War and served in Puerto Rico. When he returned he entered Lombard College in Galesburg and worked on the switchboard at the fire department to support himself. He was captain of Lombard's basketball team, sang in the glee club, and edited college publications. He left in the spring of his senior year.

Sandburg's first volumes of poetry, *In Reckless Ecstasy* (1904) and *The Plaint of a Rose* (1905), and a book of essays, *Incidentals* (1905), were published privately by a former professor of his at Lombard. Sandburg went to Milwaukee in 1907 as district organizer for the Social Democratic Party of Wisconsin. In 1908 he married Lillian Steichen, sister of the photographer Edward Steichen. They had three daughters.

Sandburg wrote for various newspapers in Milwaukee and Chicago, where he moved in 1912. His first wide recognition as a poet came when some of his poems were printed in *Poetry* magazine. His poem "Chicago," which *Poetry* published in 1914, won a prize. *Chicago Poems* followed in 1916. Many books of his poems have been published since. His *Complete Poems* (1950) was awarded the Pulitzer prize for poetry in 1951.

Sandburg published many other works besides poetry. His coverage of the Chicago race riots of 1919 for the Chicago *Daily News* was published as a book, *Chicago Race Riots* (1919). Fairy tales he wrote for his daughters were published as *Rootabaga Stories* (1922) and *Rootabaga Pigeons* (1923).

Abraham Lincoln: The Prairie Years (1926) was followed by *Abraham Lincoln: The War Years* (1939), which won the Pulitzer prize in history in 1940. A shortened version of *The Prairie Years* for children was published as *Abe Lincoln Grows Up* (1928). *The American Songbag* (1927) contained songs Sandburg had collected over the years. He told his own story in *Always the Young Strangers* (1952). He wrote the prologue for Steichen's Family of Man exhibit, which was shown around the world and was later put into book form. Sandburg's only novel is *Remembrance Rock* (1948).

One of Sandburg's greatest works is *The People, Yes* (1936), a long historical poem about the American people—about the way they talk and the things they say and why.

In 1945, Sandburg settled at Connemara Farm in Flat Rock, North Carolina. There on July 22, 1967, the snowy-haired poet, folksinger, and biographer died at the age of 89.

Reviewed by REGINALD L. COOK
Middlebury College

One of Carl Sandburg's best-known poems and one of his Rootabaga stories follow. "Fog" was written after Sandburg had been studying Japanese haiku.

FOG

The fog comes
on little cat feet.
It sits looking
over harbor and city
on silent haunches
and then moves on.

▶ **THE SKYSCRAPER TO THE MOON AND HOW THE GREEN RAT WITH THE RHEUMATISM RAN A THOUSAND MILES TWICE**

Blixie Bimber's mother was chopping hash. And the hatchet broke. So Blixie started downtown with fifteen cents to buy a new hash hatchet for chopping hash.

Downtown she peeped around the corner next nearest the postoffice where the Potato Face Blind Man sat with his accordion. And the old man had his legs crossed, one foot on the sidewalk, the other foot up in the air.

The foot up in the air had a green rat sitting on it, tying the old man's shoestrings in knots and double knots. Whenever the old man's foot wiggled and wriggled the green rat wiggled and wriggled.

The tail of the rat wrapped five wraps around the shoe and then fastened and tied like a package.

On the back of the green rat was a long white swipe from the end of the nose to the end of the tail. Two little white swipes stuck up over the eyelashes. And five short thick swipes of white played pussy-wants-a-corner back of the ears and along the ribs of the green rat.

They were talking, the old man and the green rat, talking about alligators and why the alligators keep their baby shoes locked up in trunks over the winter time—and why the rats in the moon lock their mittens in ice boxes.

"I had the rheumatism last summer a year ago," said the rat. "I had the rheumatism so bad I ran a thousand miles south and west till I came to the Egg Towns and stopped in the Village of Eggs Up."

"So?" quizzed the Potato Face.

"There in the Village of Eggs Up, they asked me, 'Do you know how to stop the moon mov-ing?' I answered them, 'Yes, I know how—a baby alligator told me—but I told the baby alligator I wouldn't tell.'

"Many years ago there in that Village of Eggs Up they started making a skyscraper to go up till it reached the moon. They said, 'We will step in the elevator and go up to the roof and sit on the roof and eat supper on the moon.'

"The bricklayers and the mortar men and the iron riveters and the wheelbarrowers and the plasterers went higher and higher making that skyscraper, till at last they were half way up to the moon, saying to each other while they worked, 'We will step in the elevator and go up to the roof and sit on the roof and eat supper on the moon.'

"Yes, they were halfway up to the moon. And that night looking at the moon they saw it move and they said to each other, 'We must stop the moon moving,' and they said later, 'We don't know how to stop the moon moving.'

"And the bricklayers and the mortar men and the iron riveters and the wheelbarrowers and the plasterers said to each other, 'If we go on now and make this skyscraper it will miss the moon and we will never go up in the elevator and sit on the roof and eat supper on the moon.'

"So they took the skyscraper down and started making it over again, aiming it straight at the moon again. And one night standing looking at the moon they saw it move and they said to each other, 'We must stop the moon moving,' saying later to each other, 'We don't know how to stop the moon moving.'

"And now they stand in the streets at night there in the Village of Eggs Up, stretching their necks looking at the moon, and asking each other, 'Why does the moon move and how can we stop the moon moving?'

"Whenever I saw them standing there stretching their necks looking at the moon, I had a zig-zag ache in my left hind foot and I wanted to tell them what the baby alligator told me, the secret of how to stop the moon moving. One night that ache zig-zagged me so—way inside my left hind foot—it zig-zagged so I ran home here a thousand miles."

The Potato Face Blind Man wriggled his shoe—and the green rat wriggled—and the long white swipe from the end of the nose to the end of the tail of the green rat wriggled.

"Is your rheumatism better?" the old man asked.

The rat answered, "Any rheumatism is better if you run a thousand miles twice."

And Blixie Bimber going home with the fifteen cent hash hatchet for her mother to chop hash, Blixie said to herself, "It is a large morning to be thoughtful about."

SAN DIEGO

San Diego, the second largest city in California after Los Angeles, lies on the Pacific Coast near the Mexican border. Its hills and valleys, canyons, beaches, two large bays (San Diego and Mission), and the Pacific Ocean provide a splendid setting. The local climate is nearly ideal. Days are mild and sunny, even in winter.

Important industries include aerospace and electronics equipment, shipbuilding, and biotechnology. Local farms grow fruits, vegetables, flowers, and trees and raise dairy cattle. Tourism also makes a major contribution to the local economy. San Diego welcomes millions of visitors each year.

More than 1 million people, representing a variety of ethnic groups, live in the city proper. Nearly 3 million live in the greater metropolitan area, which covers San Diego County.

Places of Interest

Located on San Diego Bay are Point Loma, a high peninsula that protects the bay from the ocean; downtown San Diego, on the eastern shore; and Harbor and Shelter islands, with their hotels, restaurants, parks, and yacht harbors. The modern Convention Center is adjacent to Embarcadero Marina Park, also located on the bayside.

San Diego Bay provides some of the city's most interesting sights. The Maritime Museum is housed in three historic ships—the *Star of India*, a merchant vessel, built in 1863; the *Berkeley*, a ferry built in 1898; and the *Medea*, a steam-yacht built in 1904. A tour of the harbor on an excursion boat takes visitors past the country's largest naval fleet and huge shipyards. On Point Loma can be seen Cabrillo National Monument, which commemorates the landing in 1542 of Juan Rodríguez Cabrillo, and Point Lighthouse. Some excursion boats go out into the ocean. From December through February, watching the great gray whales on their annual migration from Alaska to Baja (Lower) California is a favorite pastime.

The Community Concourse, in the heart of San Diego's downtown area, contains city administration buildings and a convention and performing arts center. Northeast of the concourse is the 1,400-acre (567-hectare) Balboa Park, which contains a wide variety of interesting sites, including a planetarium, the Reuben H. Fleet Space Theater; the historic Spreckels Organ Pavilion, with its huge outdoor pipe organ; and several museums with collections ranging from fine art to aerospace history. The park's most famous attraction, the world-famous San Diego Zoo, has more than 3,000 animals contained in lush natural settings. At Wild Animal Park, 30 miles (48 kilometers) northeast of downtown, rare and

San Diego has one of the world's finest deepwater harbors, making the city a busy commercial port and a hub of naval and other military activities.

Balboa Park's most visited attraction is the San Diego Zoo. Covering 125 acres (50 hectares), it has one of the world's largest collections of animals and plants.

endangered species roam in large enclosures resembling their native habitats.

Old Town, north of the downtown section, is the site of San Diego's first settlement. North of Old Town is Mission Bay and its shoreline, which form the city's largest park. Mission Bay Aquatic Park is the home of Sea World, where seals, otters, penguins, and killer whales and other dolphins perform for visitors. The park also provides facilities for all kinds of water sports. The area's major-league sports fans root for the San Diego Chargers (football) and the San Diego Padres (baseball).

The San Diego area supports many cultural, educational, and research institutions. The city itself has its own symphony orchestra and ballet and opera companies. A summer Shakespeare festival is held in Balboa Park's Old Globe Theatre, and musical shows are performed outdoors at the Starlight Opera. La Jolla, a suburb of San Diego, has the world-renowned La Jolla Playhouse. It is also the site of the University of California at San Diego and the home of the Scripps Institution of Oceanography. The Salk Institute for Biological Studies, a nonprofit research organization, is located nearby. Other local colleges include San Diego State University and the University of San Diego.

History

In 1542, the mariner Juan Rodríguez Cabrillo explored the Pacific Coast of America for Spain and discovered San Diego Bay. Cabrillo claimed the area for Spain and named it San Miguel. Sixty years later, Sebastián Vizcaíno entered the harbor and renamed it San Diego (Saint James). Spain did not send any more ships until 1769, when Spanish soldiers arrived and set up a fort, and Father Junípero Serra, a Franciscan missionary, established the mission San Diego de Alcalá on Presidio Hill. Today the restored buildings of Old Town Historic park re-create the San Diego of the 1700's. The Junípero Serra Museum is nearby. The original mission, which was moved farther up the valley in 1774, is now restored and is surrounded by shopping centers, apartment complexes, and freeways.

The pueblo (village) of San Diego came under the control of Mexico in 1822, after that country declared its independence from Spain. The American flag was first raised over the pueblo in 1846, during the Mexican War, won by the United States in 1848. San Diego was incorporated as a city in 1850.

Naval activities and aviation have been important in the history of San Diego. U.S. Navy ships were anchored in the harbor as early as 1846, and the first naval base, a fuel depot, was built in the early 1900's. The first seaplane flight in the United States took place in 1911, when Glenn Curtiss flew his aircraft over the bay. The Panama-California Exposition of 1915-16, celebrating the completion of the Panama Canal, drew world attention to San Diego. The *Spirit of St. Louis*—the airplane in which Charles Lindbergh made the first nonstop flight across the Atlantic Ocean, in 1927—was built for him in San Diego. In the 1940's, during World War II, the airplane industry and military training camps brought thousands of people to San Diego, and many of them stayed on after the war.

Today, San Diego's population and industries are growing rapidly. To meet the need for mass transportation, a trolley-car line began operating in 1981. The bright red streetcars travel from the downtown area to the eastern and southern suburbs and go all the way to the Mexican border. Despite its growth, however, San Diego has retained a pleasant, small-town atmosphere.

ANNE GRAY
Author, *The Wonderful World of San Diego*
Reviewed by ABRAHAM J. SHRAGGE
University of California, San Diego

SANDSTONE.   See ROCKS (Sedimentary Rock).

SAN FRANCISCO

The British author Rudyard Kipling once said, "San Francisco has only one drawback...'tis hard to leave." Located on a peninsula between the Pacific Ocean and the fine natural harbor of San Francisco Bay, San Francisco is considered one of the world's most beautiful cities. Occupying an area of only 46 square miles (119 square kilometers), the city is built almost entirely on 42 hills. The quaint cable cars for which San Francisco is famous were introduced in 1873 to solve the problem of transportation on the steepest inclines.

San Francisco is one of the world's loveliest cities. The skyline, featuring the pyramid-shaped Trans-America Building, rises among quaint residential neighborhoods, known for their pretty Victorian-style houses.

San Francisco is California's fourth most populous city and home to nearly 777,000 people. The greater metropolitan area, including Oakland across the bay and San Jose to the south, has more than 7 million people. San Francisco has large communities of Japanese, Russians, Germans, English, Irish, Italians, Mexicans, Central Americans, Southeast Asians, and Filipinos. It is also home to one of the largest Chinese communities in the United States.

Together with Oakland, San Francisco provides port facilities and air terminal connections for much of the trade and commerce between the western United States and Asia, Hawaii, and Alaska. San Francisco is a leader on the West Coast in international banking, financial services, and insurance. Tourism, business and personal services, food processing, and clothing manufacturing also play a role in the city's economic life.

San Francisco has a mild climate. Even during September, the warmest month, the temperature seldom rises above 70°F (21°C). In winter it rarely drops below freezing. San Francisco's morning fogs are well known, but the afternoon hours bring mostly sunshine.

Places of Interest

From the Twin Peaks that dominate the center of the city, one can look straight down Market Street and across the Bay Bridge to Oakland. Another magnificent view is from Coit Memorial Tower on Telegraph Hill. From there it is possible to see the famous Golden Gate Bridge that spans the entrance to San Francisco Bay, a strait known as the Golden Gate.

Just east of the Golden Gate is Fisherman's Wharf and other reminders of San Francisco's long association with seafaring, such as the Hyde Street Pier and Maritime Museum. The Cannery and Ghirardelli Square, two former factories, have been transformed into attractive shopping centers.

The famed San Francisco Opera and the San Francisco Ballet occupy the War Memorial Opera House in the Civic Center, where the San Francisco Public Library is also located. Across the street, the Louise M. Davies Symphony Hall, a modern glass and concrete building, is home to the San Francisco Symphony Orchestra. Notable museums include the California Palace of the Legion of Honor, located in a spectacular setting overlooking the Pacific Ocean, and the Museum of Modern Art, in the recently redeveloped South of Market area near the downtown financial

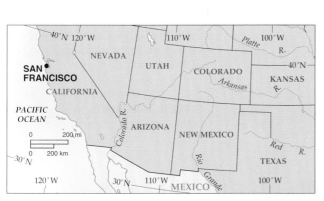

district. Golden Gate Park contains the M. H. de Young Museum, the Japanese Tea Garden, and the California Academy of Sciences, which operates the Morrison Planetarium and the Steinhart Aquarium. San Francisco State University and the medical, dental, and nursing facilities of the University of California are also located in the city.

Professional sports teams include major league baseball's San Francisco Giants and the National Football League's San Francisco Forty-Niners.

History

European voyagers explored San Francisco Bay in the 1600's. The first settlement was founded by the Spanish in 1776. At that time a site was chosen for a mission dedicated to Saint Francis of Assisi. The village that grew up around the Franciscan mission was called Yerba Buena. It remained under Spanish, and then Mexican, rule until 1846, when the United States flag was first raised over it. The next year it took the name San Francisco.

In 1848, gold was discovered at Sutter's Mill near Sacramento. Gold seekers poured into San Francisco and turned it into a rough-and-tumble boomtown. Many people realized that there was more profit in supplying the

San Francisco is famous for its steep streets and clanging cable cars. This form of public transportation is a favorite tourist attraction.

needs of the gold miners than there was in mining. Bankers and entrepreneurs financed much of northern California's expanding agricultural businesses, while others ventured into the import-export business with Asia.

On April 18, 1906, a terrible earthquake, measuring 8.3 on the Richter scale, shook the city. Fires raged for three days, destroying almost 500 city blocks. Approximately 2,500 people were killed. Rebuilding began at once, and the city celebrated its recovery in 1915.

During World War II, San Francisco became the nation's leading shipbuilding center. When the war ended in 1945, international delegates gathered there to draw up the charter creating the United Nations.

During the 1950's and 1960's, San Francisco attracted cultural innovators, literary and artistic dissenters, and a large gay and lesbian community. In the 1970's, the city became the first in the nation to elect an admittedly gay political official, Supervisor Harvey Milk, who was assassinated, along with San Francisco's mayor, George Moscone, by a political rival in 1978.

On October 17, 1989, San Francisco experienced another devastating earthquake, measuring 7.1 on the Richter scale. It claimed 67 lives, caused fires in the city's Marina District, and toppled parts of the Bay Bridge and the Embarcadero Freeway. The city quickly recovered, and today it continues to lure visitors and new residents from all over the world.

Reviewed by WILLIAM ISSEL
San Francisco State University

SANGER, MARGARET. See BIRTH CONTROL; WOMEN'S RIGHTS MOVEMENT (Profiles).

The Golden Gate Bridge is one of California's most familiar landmarks. Spanning the strait between the Pacific Ocean and San Francisco Bay, the bridge connects the city with Marin County to the north.

SANITATION

The word "sanitation" comes from the Latin word *sanitas*, which means "health." It refers to measures developed to protect people from infection and disease by safeguarding the quality of their air, water, land, and food. Modern sanitation measures include the purification of water and the removal, treatment, and disposal of liquid and solid wastes. Sanitation problems may vary from one part of the world to another, but most countries establish national and local sanitation standards and the measures and laws needed to uphold them.

▶ WATER AND WASTEWATER TREATMENT

Drinking water is purified in several ways. In the most common method, water is first filtered through fine sand to strain out impurities. Then a chemical, usually chlorine, is added to kill **pathogens**—disease-producing organisms such as bacteria and viruses.

Wastewater, or **sewage**, is a menace to health because it often contains substances that may contaminate food and drinking water. **Domestic sewage** is produced by normal home activities and includes such things as toilet drainage and wastewater from sinks, bathtubs, and washing machines. **Industrial sewage** includes liquid wastes from factories. Sewage is often discharged into a body of water or onto land. Before disposal, however, it is usually treated in some way so that the water or land will not become polluted.

In cities, sewage treatment often involves two processes. In the first, sewage flows into holding tanks where heavier substances settle to the bottom and lighter substances, such as oil and grease, float to the surface. The material that settles to the bottom, called **sludge**, is withdrawn and the material on the surface is skimmed off. The second process is a biological one in which bacteria are used to destroy most of the remaining organic wastes (wastes derived from living things). The wastewater is then treated with a disinfecting agent, usually chlorine, before being discharged.

In rural areas, sewage treatment often involves the use of septic tanks and leaching fields. Sewage flows to a septic tank—an underground tank of metal or concrete—where solid wastes settle to the bottom and are destroyed by bacteria. Liquid wastes then flow through a leaching field, made up of a system of drains laid just below the surface of the ground, and seep into the earth.

▶ SOLID-WASTE DISPOSAL

There are several types of solid wastes. **Garbage** consists chiefly of waste food that will decay. **Rubbish** includes plastics, paper, rags, bottles, and metal cans that will not decay. **Construction and demolition waste** includes wood, bricks, and stone from buildings. Other solid waste includes such things as old furniture and abandoned automobiles.

Solid wastes are becoming increasingly dangerous to public health in the United States. Most solid wastes in the United States are buried in **sanitary landfills**—special sites where wastes are buried according to certain sanitary guidelines. At landfills, solid wastes are dumped into specially prepared trenches or directly on the ground. The solid waste is then compacted as much as possible. By the end of each day it is covered with clean sand. A potential danger of landfills is that contaminants may seep through the earth and pollute water supplies.

Because space for new landfills is becoming scarce, other ways to reduce the volume of solid waste are being considered. One way is through incineration, or burning. However, burning contributes to air pollution unless incinerators are equipped with air-cleaning devices. Because these devices are costly, few solid-waste incinerators are used.

There are other ways to help reduce the amount of solid wastes disposed of each year. Among these are composting and recycling. In **composting**, garbage is exposed to controlled amounts of heat, oxygen, and moisture, which make it decay faster. The resulting decayed material, called compost, is used as a fertilizer. In **recycling**, items such as metal cans and newspapers are reprocessed so that the materials they are made of can be reused. Newspapers, for example, are turned into pulp from which new paper is made. Most disposable things could be recycled. Today, more and more communities are trying to solve their waste-disposal problems by recycling.

ERIC W. MOOD
School of Medicine, Yale University

See also AIR POLLUTION; DISEASES; FOOD PRESERVATION; PUBLIC HEALTH; VECTORS OF DISEASE; WATER POLLUTION.

SAN JOSE

San Jose, the third most populous city in California, is situated in the Santa Clara Valley, between the Santa Cruz Mountains and the Diablo Range, approximately 50 miles (80 kilometers) south of San Francisco. It is the seat of Santa Clara county.

A leading center of the computer and electronics industries, the San Jose area has been nicknamed Silicon Valley after the silicon chips that are used in the manufacture of computers. Other important regional industries include electronics manufacturing; the research and development of aerospace and medical technologies; and food processing, including winemaking.

Nearly 895,000 people live within San Jose's 170 square miles (440 square kilometers). The greater metropolitan area, which includes San Francisco and Oakland, contains more than 7 million people. One of the nation's fastest-growing cities, San Jose has a population that has more than doubled since

1970 and at the same time has become more diverse. A large percentage claims Hispanic or Asian heritage.

Founded in 1777 by a group of Spanish colonists, San Jose was named Pueblo de San Jose de Guadalupe, in honor of St. Joseph and the Guadalupe River, on which the city is situated. It later served as the first capital (1849–51) of California and was the first city to be chartered (1850) in the new state. San Jose developed commercially as a supply base for gold prospectors, and after the completion of a rail line to San Francisco in 1864, it became the distribution point for the surrounding agricultural area. Regional farms produce significant amounts of plums, apricots, and grapes.

San Jose's revitalized downtown district features a convention center and the San Jose Arena, home to the San Jose Sharks hockey team. The city is also home to San Jose State University, the oldest public educational institution in California, founded in 1857. San Jose City College is nearby.

Museums include the Rosicrucian Egyptian Museum and Art Gallery; the Rosicrucian Science Museum and Planetarium; the San Jose Museum of Art; the Children's Discovery Museum; and the Winchester Mystery House. The city is also famous for its many gardens. The Municipal Rose Garden contains more than 7,500 plants, including 158 varieties of roses. Alum Rock Park, just east of the city, contains mineral springs. Kelly Park features a zoo, Japanese tea garden, and the San Jose Historical Museum.

VINSON BROWN
Author, *It All Happened in Santa Clara County*

Reviewed by WILLIAM ISSEL
San Francisco State University

An aerial view shows some of the many computer-related firms in the San Jose area, nicknamed Silicon Valley after the silicon chip used in computers.

SAN MARINO

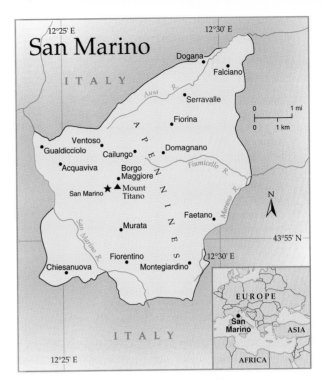

San Marino is the oldest republic in the world. It is also one of the world's smallest countries. It is located on the eastern slopes of the Apennines, a rugged mountain chain that runs the length of Italy.

People. The people of San Marino are surrounded by Italian territory and use Italian currency as their money. They speak Italian, and their culture has much in common with that of Italy. But the Sammarinese, as the people are called, have a proud tradition of independence that dates back about 1,700 years. Most Sammarinese are Roman Catholics. Nearly all can read and write. Education is compulsory from age 6 to 14.

Land. Most of San Marino is situated on Mount Titano in the Apennines. The mountain has three peaks and reaches a height of about 2,457 feet (749 meters). The capital, the city of San Marino, clings to the main peak. Streets wind up the slopes between turreted buildings and ancient fortifications.

One of the world's smallest countries, San Marino is located on the eastern slopes of the Apennines mountains and is surrounded by Italian territory.

Among the city's major tourist attractions are the Government Palace, the Church of St. Francis, and the Valloni Palace. The bones of St. Marinus (San Marino), the legendary founder and patron saint of San Marino, are said to be buried in the San Marino basilica.

Economy. Some 60 percent of the labor force is employed in services. Of these, tourism is especially vital to San Marino's economy. Key industries include the manufacture of clothing, electronics, and ceramics. Agriculture plays a smaller role in the economy; vineyards line the mountain slopes, and cattle and sheep graze in the meadows below. The country's main exports are building stone, lime, wood, chestnuts, wheat, wine, baked goods, hides, and ceramics. San Marino's postage stamps are sought by collectors throughout the world and are a chief source of income. The Italian government also provides an annual cash subsidy to San Marino.

History and Government. According to tradition, San Marino was founded in A.D. 301 by a stonecutter named Marinus. A Christian, he fled to Mount Titano to escape religious persecution at the hands of the Romans. On the mountain he built a tiny chapel. During the Middle Ages, a small community developed as others sought refuge there. The rugged terrain made invasion difficult.

REPUBLIC OF SAN MARINO (Repubblica di San Marino) is the official name of the country.

LOCATION: East central Italy.

AREA: 24 sq mi (62 km²).

POPULATION: 27,000 (estimate).

CAPITAL AND LARGEST CITY: San Marino.

MAJOR LANGUAGE: Italian.

MAJOR RELIGIOUS GROUP: Roman Catholic.

GOVERNMENT: Republic. **Head of state and government**—Secretary of State for Foreign and Political Affairs. **Legislature**—Great and General Council.

CHIEF PRODUCTS: Agricultural—wheat, grapes, corn, olives, livestock, cheese. **Manufactured**—postage stamps, textiles, electronics, ceramics, cement, wine.

MONETARY UNIT: Italian lira (1 lira = 100 centesimi).

It is said that in 1797 the French emperor Napoleon I offered San Marino additional territory. The people refused, explaining that their smallness and poverty were their greatest protection. In the 1800's, during the struggle for the liberation and unification of Italy, Italian patriots found temporary refuge in San Marino. Since 1862, San Marino has had a treaty of friendship with Italy.

Although San Marino was officially neutral in World War II, it suffered heavy damage from bombing. During the war, the republic provided sanctuary for many refugees.

The government of San Marino includes a 60-member elected legislature called the Great and General Council. The council elects ten of its members to the Congress of State, or cabinet. Two additional council members are elected to serve for six-month periods as Captains Regent. The Captains Regent preside over meetings of the Great and General Council and the Congress of State and act as the nation's co-chiefs of state; the Secretary of State for Foreign and Political Affairs acts as head of government. A variety of political parties are represented in the Great and General Council. In recent years the Christian Democrats have held the most seats. San Marino became a member of the United Nations in 1992.

Reviewed by DR. PAOLA SERGI
Italian Cultural Institute

SAN MARTÍN, JOSÉ DE (1778–1850)

José de San Martín was a hero of South America's struggle for freedom from Spanish colonial rule. He was born on February 25, 1778, in Yapeyú, in what is now Argentina. His father was a Spanish officer, and when San Martín was 9 years old, his family returned to Spain. He received a military education and served in the Spanish army.

In 1810, rebels took control of the Spanish colony of Río de la Plata (now Argentina, Uruguay, Paraguay, and part of Bolivia). San Martín resolved to help them. In 1812 he returned to Argentina and became a general in the rebel army. Argentina's independence was formally declared in 1816. But San Martín knew that to ensure it, he would have to drive the Spanish out of Chile and Peru.

In 1817, with an army of about 5,000, he began a march to Chile. This Army of the Andes, also led by the Chilean patriot Bernardo O'Higgins, defeated the Spanish at Chacabuco and at the Maipo River. Chile's independence was declared in 1818. San Martín named O'Higgins as the Chilean leader. For the next two years he assembled a fleet, then sailed north to attack the Spanish in Peru. In 1821, San Martín declared Peru independent and was named governor of the new nation.

By now patriot Simón Bolívar's forces were advancing from the north. In 1822, San Martín met Bolívar at Guayaquil, Ecuador. But they disagreed on how to organize the newly independent countries, and San Martín returned to Argentina. In 1824 he retired to Europe, where he died on August 17, 1850. Years later, Argentina came to regard him as its greatest national hero.

DAVID BUSHNELL
University of Florida

See also BOLÍVAR, SIMÓN; O'HIGGINS, BERNARDO.

SANTA CLAUS. See CHRISTMAS.

SANTA FE. See NEW MEXICO (Cities).

SANTA FE TRAIL. See OVERLAND TRAILS.

SANTIAGO

Santiago, the capital city of Chile, is the political, cultural, commercial, and industrial center of the nation. It stretches along both sides of the Mapocho River, on a wide plain with views of the majestic, snowcapped Andes mountains. The climate throughout the year is generally mild.

Santiago is one of the largest cities in South America. The population of the city exceeds 4.6 million. More than 5.6 million live in the greater metropolitan area. Most residents are of mixed Indian and European backgrounds. Many are descended from the Spanish immigrants who settled in the area in the 1700's and 1800's. But there are large groups of English, Scots, Germans, Swiss, and Italians as well.

The City. Although Santiago is a modern city with tall skyscrapers and broad, spacious avenues, it has managed to preserve much of its Spanish colonial past. At the heart of the city lies the Plaza de Armas, a square featuring the Cathedral of Santiago, built in the late 1700's. Another fine example of colonial architecture is the Palacio de la Moneda, the home of Chile's presidents, which dates from the early 1800's.

Santiago's cultural life is concentrated at the Municipal Center, where orchestras, dance groups, and opera companies regularly perform. The city is also graced with lovely hillside parks.

Santiago is an important educational center. The state-supported University of Chile is the largest institution of higher learning in the country. The Catholic University of Chile is noted for its programs in political science and journalism. The Biblioteca Nacional is one of the largest libraries in all of South America.

Economic Activity. As the political and financial capital of Chile, Santiago has an economy largely based on government, banking, and commercial services.

About half of all the manufacturing in Chile takes place in the city and in the surrounding province of Santiago. Many of the people work in factories on the edge of the city. They produce such goods as processed foods, textiles, chemicals, glassware, paper, machinery, and furniture. Street vendors in Santiago sell produce from local farms. Santi-

ago is also a famous wine center, as some of Chile's best vineyards are located nearby. However, agriculture as a whole is becoming less important as new factories are built on agricultural lands.

History. Santiago was founded in 1541 by the Spanish conquistador Pedro de Valdivia, who marched south along the Pacific coast from Peru to conquer and settle what is now known as Chile. In the 1500's the area was held by the Araucanian Indians. But most of them were killed during a long struggle with the Spanish for the land.

In 1817, José de San Martín occupied the city, after crossing the Andes from Argentina. The following year, Chile gained its independence, and Santiago became the capital. At the time, Santiago was the largest city in the country, although it had a population of just 20,000 people and only covered a 15-block area. In the mid-1800's, the city began to spread out along the Mapocho River. Santiago continued to grow throughout the 1900's as it became a major industrial center.

The people of Santiago are accustomed to dealing with environmental issues. Each year the city experiences several dozen earthquakes of varying strengths. It was almost completely destroyed by an earthquake in 1617, and some settlers thought the site should be abandoned. But the people returned to rebuild their city. Today many of the buildings are specially built to minimize the amount of damage caused. Flood-control projects have also been implemented to regulate the snow and ice melt from the mountains that floods the Mapocho River every spring. In addition, measures have been taken to control the growing amount of smog produced by traffic and industry.

JAMES NELSON GOODSELL
The Christian Science Monitor

Smaller residential areas lie on the outskirts of São Paulo, the largest city in Brazil and one of the largest cities in the world.

SÃO PAULO

São Paulo is the largest city in Brazil, the largest country in South America. The city is home to more than 9.5 million people. With a metropolitan population of more than 16 million, São Paulo is one of the world's largest cities. It is South America's leading commercial, industrial, and economic center—a city of shining skyscrapers, crowded streets, and busy factories.

The city produces most of Brazil's textiles, chemicals, medicines, cars, trucks, electrical equipment, rubber goods, and machinery. In fact, São Paulo accounts for 30 percent of all Brazilian industrial production. Some Brazilians say that the city of São Paulo is like a locomotive that pulls the rest of the country along economically.

To most Brazilians, São Paulo is a city of opportunity. Many of its people have come from the less developed areas of Brazil. People from all over the world have also flocked to São Paulo to seek their fortunes. Along with that of Portugal, the cultures of Italy, Lebanon, Germany, Spain, Japan, and other countries contribute to the city's ethnic variety. Many people consider São Paulo, together with the state of São Paulo in which it is located, almost a country within the country of Brazil.

The people of São Paulo, called *paulistanos*, are known for working hard. They are also fond of sports—particularly *futebol* (soccer), volleyball, basketball, and swimming.

Places of Interest

São Paulo sprawls out over gently rolling slopes on a plateau 2,493 feet (760 meters) above sea level. The city is centered on a square, the Praça da Sé, where Portuguese Je-

suits founded the city in 1554. Visitors can see replicas of São Paulo's first buildings in this area of old avenues, overpasses, and skyscrapers. Near the intersection of Avenida São João and Avenida Ipiranga is Edifício Itália, the tallest building in São Paulo, and a park called the Praça da República. The commercial center of the city is along Avenida Paulista. Coffee barons once lived in huge mansions on this avenue, which today is lined with skyscrapers. Beyond this area, the suburbs of São Paulo spread outward for many miles. Along the railroads, both inside and outside the city limits, are compact industrial districts. In the greater area, the urban and suburban sprawl engulfs the small farms that feed the city's millions of people.

São Paulo has a number of notable museums. These include the Museum of Art of São Paulo, the Museum of Contemporary Art, the Pinacoteca of the State of São Paulo, and the Ipiranga Museum, which houses a collection of historical artifacts. The Museum of Modern Art is found in Ibirapuera Park, along with the Planetarium. The Bienal, an important international art exposition held every two years, showcases modern art from around the world.

The city also boasts many fine universities, medical facilities, and scientific laboratories, including the Butantã Institute, a research center that gained fame for its development of snakebite serums. Hundreds of snakes and spiders are on display there. The Zoological Garden, one of the world's largest, has thousands of different species of animals from all over the world.

History

Jesuit missionaries founded São Paulo in 1554 as a base for exploring the interior of Brazil in search of Indian slaves and precious minerals such as gold and diamonds. In 1822, in São Paulo, Emperor Dom Pedro I declared Brazil's independence from Portugal. The settlement remained the small center of a modest agricultural region until the late 1800's, when it was discovered that the rich soil near São Paulo was ideal for growing coffee. São Paulo became the chief commercial center for the expanding coffee region.

As new railroads and factories were built, more and more people moved to São Paulo. In the 1900's, coffee wealth was used to build textile plants, shoe factories, and other industries. The availability of hydroelectric power also aided industrial growth. Gradually, the city became a center of industry, banking, and commerce for all of South America.

São Paulo's economic growth has been like a magnet attracting people and industry to the city. More and more cars crowd the streets. The multiplying industries have polluted the air. The influx of poor workers seeking jobs has led to the growth of *favelas*, or urban slums. Though it struggles with the problems of modern industrial growth, São Paulo is one of the most bustling and dynamic urban centers in the world.

IRENE FLUM GALVIN
President
The Communications Connection
Author, *Brazil: Many Voices, Many Faces*

Many important banks have offices in São Paulo. The city is South America's leading financial, commercial, and industrial center.

SÃO TOMÉ AND PRÍNCIPE

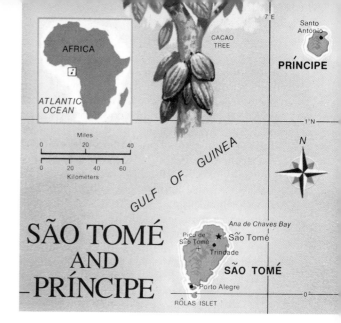

São Tomé and Príncipe is one of the smallest nations of Africa. The country consists of two islands located off the west coast of Africa in the Gulf of Guinea. Long a colony of Portugal, it gained independence in 1975.

▶ THE PEOPLE

The people are descended mainly from the original Portuguese colonists and the black slaves they brought from other parts of Africa. The land is rugged and much of the country is thinly settled. Most of the people live on São Tomé, the larger island. Many live on small farms on its northeast coast, but villages are scattered throughout the two islands. The capital and largest city, also called São Tomé, is situated on São Tomé island.

Most of the people are Roman Catholics, although some practice traditional African religions. The official language is Portuguese, but African languages are also spoken.

FACTS and figures

DEMOCRATIC REPUBLIC OF SÃO TOMÉ AND PRÍNCIPE (República Democrática de São Tomé e Príncipe) is the official name of the country.

LOCATION: Off the west coast of Africa.

AREA: 371 sq mi (960 km²).

POPULATION: 144,000 (estimate).

CAPITAL AND LARGEST CITY: São Tomé.

MAJOR LANGUAGE: Portuguese (official).

MAJOR RELIGIOUS GROUP: Christian (mostly Roman Catholic).

GOVERNMENT: Republic. **Head of state**—president. **Head of government**—prime minister. **Legislature**—National People's Assembly.

CHIEF PRODUCTS: Agricultural—cacao, coffee, copra, palm kernels, bananas, yams, cassava. **Manufactured**—palm oil, bread, clothing, processed fish and shrimp, beverages.

MONETARY UNIT: Dobra (1 dobra = 100 cêntimos).

▶ THE LAND

The islands are of volcanic origin. The scenery on São Tomé is impressive. There are rugged mountains covered with dense tropical vegetation, many waterfalls, and rushing rivers and streams spanned by natural bridges. The highest mountain, Pico de São Tomé, rises to 6,640 feet (2,024 meters).

The island of Príncipe lies about 90 miles (145 kilometers) northeast of São Tomé. It is less rugged than São Tomé and only about one-eighth as large. Several tiny, rocky islets also make up part of the country's territory.

▶ THE ECONOMY

The islands have long depended on the export of such crops as cacao (used in making cocoa and chocolate), coffee, and copra (dried coconut meat). But this source of income has been hurt by declining world prices and poor methods of cultivation. Farmers have been encouraged to plant a variety of crops, and fishing and tourism are being promoted. But much of the country's food must still be imported, and there is little industry.

▶ HISTORY AND GOVERNMENT

The islands were uninhabited when they were first sighted by Portuguese navigators in 1470 and 1471. Portuguese colonizers brought in African slaves to clear the land for sugarcane plantations. The islands became a busy center of slave trading and shipping. As production of sugar declined, the islands served chiefly as slave stations on the Portuguese slave route from Africa to the Americas.

Independence was achieved in 1975, and Manuel Pinto da Costa served as the country's first president. A new constitution in 1990 provided for a president, elected for five years directly by the people. The president appoints and shares power with a prime minister. The legislative body is the National Assembly, whose members are also elected to 5-year terms. Príncipe was granted self-government in 1995.

Miguel Trovoada won the country's first multiparty presidential elections in 1990 and was re-elected in 1996. He was succeeded by Fradique de Menezes in 2001. But the democracy was overthrown in 2003 in a military coup that was condemned by other nations. An agreement ending the coup called for the establishment of a new coalition government, increased power for the military, and laws concerning the distribution of oil revenues.

RICHARD J. HOUK
De Paul University

SARAZEN, GENE. See GOLF (Great Players).

SARGENT, JOHN SINGER (1856–1925)

John Singer Sargent, who worked mainly in Europe, became the most famous American portrait painter of his time. Later, he was recognized also for his landscapes.

Sargent was born to American parents in Florence, Italy, on January 12, 1856. He grew up in Europe and did not make his first visit to the United States until the age of 20. As a boy, he often went on sketching trips with his mother, who was an amateur artist. By the time he was 12, his parents recognized his talent, and he was given painting lessons.

In 1874, the family moved to Paris. There Sargent studied with a painter famous for his portraits of fashionable people of the day. From this teacher, Sargent also received training that prepared him to work in an impressionist manner. In 1877, one of Sargent's paintings was accepted at the Salon in Paris—the official exhibition of the French Academy of Art. His paintings were mainly society portraits—often flattering portraits of women in beautiful and stylish gowns.

In 1884, Sargent's *Portrait of Madame X* was criticized in Paris because the low neckline of the dress was thought to be immodest. A scandal followed, and Sargent moved to London, where he received many commissions for portraits. After 1887, he made regular trips to the United States to paint portraits. But during summers in England, he enjoyed painting landscapes in an impressionist style.

Toward the end of his career, Sargent became bored with portrait painting and began to refuse commissions. He painted a series of murals for public buildings in Boston. During the early 1900's, he spent most of his time painting brilliant landscapes in watercolors. He died in London on April 15, 1925.

WILLIAM H. GERDTS
City University of New York
Graduate School and University Center

Portrait of Madame X (1884), by John Singer Sargent. Metropolitan Museum of Art, New York.

SASKATCHEWAN

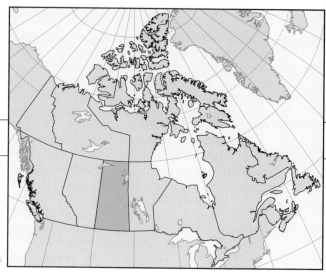

The green stripe in Saskatchewan's flag (above) represents the province's forests; the gold, its wheat fields. The provincial coat of arms (opposite page) shows sheaves of wheat and a lion symbolizing the British crown. The provincial flower is the prairie lily. The provincial bird (right) is the sharp-tailed grouse.

Great herds of bison once roamed the vast grasslands of the Canadian prairies. They were hunted only by the native Indian peoples for food and clothing. Then the fur traders came to the northern forests. They needed quantities of pemmican, made from bison meat, for food. By the time European settlers entered Saskatchewan, the bison had disappeared. Under treaties made between 1871 and 1877, most of the Indian peoples were resettled on reserves (reservations). During the next 50 years, productive farms and ranches took root in much of the native prairie grassland and part of the northern forest fringe.

▶THE LAND

Saskatchewan is one of Canada's three "Prairie Provinces" and is located between the other two, Manitoba and Alberta. It is a land of vast plains. There are no mountain ranges. The highest point—1,392 meters (4,567 feet)—is in the Cypress Hills in the southwest. The lowest elevations—less than 275 meters (900 feet) above sea level—are found in the northwest near Lake Athabasca and on the east where the Saskatchewan River enters Manitoba.

The Canadian Shield. The Canadian Shield occupies most of the northern third of the province. The Shield is a vast expanse of rock, forests, rivers, lakes, and swamps that extends over much of northern Canada. Some of the rocks that form the Shield are nearly 3,000,000,000 (billion) years old. Most of the soil that once covered the Shield was scraped away by glaciers as they moved southward during the Ice Age. The rocky landscape was grooved and roughened during their slow progress. Today many of the hollows carved by the moving glaciers are filled by lakes. These are joined to one another by rivers that often have waterfalls and rapids. Much of the area is covered by muskeg (peat bog). Pine and spruce forests grow in the better-drained areas. The rocks of the Canadian Shield contain valuable deposits of uranium, copper, zinc, gold, lead, and other minerals. Only a few settlements are found in this part of the province.

The Interior Plains. South of the Canadian Shield are the plains, lying mainly between 450 and 900 meters (1,500 and 3,000 feet) above sea level. They rise gradually toward the west and southwest. The sedimentary rock below their surface has been covered by glacial deposits, and rock outcrops are rarely seen. These sedimentary rocks were deposited millions of years ago, when seas covered the region. Some of these rock layers now contain fossil fuels—coal, petroleum, natural gas, potash, and other minerals.

Except for the Cypress Hills, the southwestern part of the plains is almost treeless. A central zone, where many groves of aspen interrupt the landscape, is known as the park belt. The park belt, in turn, merges with the commercial forests of mixed woods that occupy the northern section of the plains.

Soils. Differences in temperature and precipitation account for differences in soil, in plant life, and in the way the land is used. In the south, the natural vegetation is grassland.

FACTS AND FIGURES

Location: Central Canada. **Latitude**—49° N to 60° N. **Longitude**—101° 22′ W to 110° W.

Joined Canadian Confederation: September 1, 1905 (with Alberta, as the 8th and 9th provinces).

Population: 978,933 (2001 census). **Rank among provinces**—6th.

Capital: Regina, pop. 178,225 (2001 census).

Largest City: Saskatoon, pop. 196,811 (2001 census).

Physical Features: Area—251,365 sq mi (651,036 km²). **Rank among provinces**—5th. **Rivers**—Fond du Lac, Churchill, Saskatchewan and its North and South branches, Qu'Appelle. **Lakes**—Athabasca, Reindeer, Wollaston, La Ronge, Peter Pond, Cree, Diefenbaker. **Highest point**—

4,567 ft (1,392 m), in Cypress Hills.

Industries and Products: Agriculture; mining; manufacturing; forestry; fish; furs.

Government: Self-governing province. **Titular head of government**—lieutenant governor, appointed by the governor-general in council. **Actual head of government**—premier, leader of the majority in the legislature. **Provincial representation in federal parliament**—6 appointed senators; 14 elected member(s) of the House of Commons. **Voting age for provincial elections**—18.

Provincial Bird: Sharp-tailed grouse.

Provincial Flower: Prairie lily.

Provincial Motto: *Multis e gentibus vires* (From many peoples strength).

Here the soils are most suitable for growing wheat. In the drier, rougher southwest, the land is more suitable for ranching. North of the grassland in the zone of grasses and trees (the park belt) there is more moisture, and mixed farming is widespread. This zone gives way farther north to the mixed woods region, with poplar and spruce the most common trees of the commercial forests. In this northern section of poor soil and short growing season, there is little agriculture.

Rivers and Lakes. There are few permanent lakes and rivers in the south. The two main streams are the North and South Saskatchewan rivers. They begin in the western mountains of Canada and enter from Alberta, winding eastward across Saskatchewan to join as the Saskatchewan River before entering Manitoba. The need for water led to the damming of the South Saskatchewan near Outlook to form a large reservoir, Lake Diefenbaker. Intended primarily for irrigation, this reservoir also supplies water for the needs of cities, for power generation, and for recreational use.

Lakes, rivers, and other bodies of water cover about 12 percent of the province. But most of this water is in the northern forested region, outside the settled area. The Churchill River flows east and, together with rivers that flow into Lake Athabasca, drains northern Saskatchewan.

Two major dams are located on the Saskatchewan River—one at Squaw Rapids and the other upstream at Nipawin. Both dams were designed for electrical power production but also provide recreational facilities. Propos-

als for power development on the Churchill River were rejected in the 1970's for environmental reasons. However, the hydroelectric plant at Island Falls has supplied electricity to the copper and zinc mines and smelter at Flin Flon since 1928.

Wildlife. Woodland and Barren Ground caribou are found in the north. Moose and elk also live in the forest region. The white-tailed deer is the most abundant big game animal. Its range includes most of the interior plains, but it is most numerous in the wooded sections. Pronghorn antelope and mule deer are found in the rolling grasslands of southwestern Saskatchewan. Bears and wolves live in the northern forests, while the coyote is more typical of the southern grassland area. Beaver, muskrat, mink, and squirrel are among the Shield's fur-bearing animals.

The province is famous for its waterfowl. Ducks and geese nest in great numbers along the ponds, marshes, and lakes. Game birds—partridges, pheasant, and grouse—provide good hunting. White pelicans, blue herons, Canada geese, and other less plentiful species are protected in wildlife refuges.

Most of the commercial fishing is carried on in the lakes of the forest region. Whitefish, pickerel, lake trout, pike, and tullibee are the main species taken. Sport fishing is very popular in the province.

Climate. Saskatchewan has a difficult climate. Winters are cold and long, with frigid temperatures and blizzards. Summers are warm but short, with a frost-free period ranging from more than 100 days in the south to

less than 80 days in the northeast. The climate is dry, particularly in parts of the south. The wooded belt in the central part of the province is the wettest section. It receives about 400 millimeters (16 inches) of precipitation annually. Some of this precipitation comes in the form of snow. But most of it falls as showers between April and October.

Environment. Saskatchewan's most serious environmental concerns stem from soil erosion. On the farmlands there has been a general and long-term loss of topsoil. This has been blamed on crop practices, particularly summer fallow (the practice of preparing the land during the summer for sowing later in the year or the next year). Summer fallow is also blamed for an increase in the amount of farmlands affected by salt accumulation in the soil. Yet, summer fallow has been the farmers' traditional defense against the main enemy of agriculture—insufficient rainfall. Both private and governmental agencies have helped to introduce conservation measures.

The province has experienced both accidental and purposeful discharges of unwanted wastes from factories, mines, farms, and towns.

But although severe pollution has occurred in some areas, the problem is not of the scale common to more highly industrialized places. New factories and mining activities are subject to increasingly strict regulation.

▶ **THE PEOPLE**

The population of Saskatchewan is very small compared to the land area. Most of the people live in the southern part of the province, where there are grain farms, ranches, oil and gas wells, and potash mines. Northern Saskatchewan is forested and is almost unoccupied because of its severe climate, poor soils, and limited resources. There are Indian and métis communities, which depend on fishing, hunting, trapping, and forest work. Other settlements are based on mining and tourism. The lakes and rivers of the north provide good places for recreation.

The area that is now Saskatchewan was opened for settlement in 1870. Before that, Indian hunters were the only inhabitants. By 1901, Saskatchewan's population was still only 91,279. But in the next 35 years it increased rapidly, to more than 930,000. Most

Opposite page: A Ukrainian Orthodox church stands out in the flat landscape characteristic of Saskatchewan. *Left:* A combine is dwarfed by vast farmlands. Modern machinery has helped increase the size of the typical provincial farm. *Below:* The world-famous Royal Canadian Mounted Police display their fine horsemanship. The "Mounties" have their headquarters in Regina, Saskatchewan.

of the early settlers farmed the park belt and in the grasslands. Despite difficulties of climate, insect pests, and plant diseases, the region quickly became one of the great wheat-growing areas of the world.

Today less than 20 percent of the people in Saskatchewan live on farms, compared with about 4 percent for Canada as a whole. More than half of Saskatchewan's people live in urban areas, and half of these live in the largest cities, Regina and Saskatoon. Although the number living on farms is decreasing rapidly as more people move to urban centers, at the same time farms are becoming larger, partly as a result of improved farm machinery, which requires fewer farm workers.

The first white settlers came to Saskatchewan from many European countries, but most of the present population is Canadian-born. Ethnic groups, in order of their size, are British, German, Ukrainian, and Scandinavian. A recent emphasis on "multi-culturalism" (appreciation of the many cultures that have contributed to Canada's national character) has encouraged a new interest in traditional folkways, in language, and in other traditions.

In many primary schools, Canada's second language, French, is the language of instruction. Other languages are also taught.

Approximately 131,000 native peoples make their homes in Saskatchewan, including about 86,000 American Indians and some 45,000 métis. Inuit number close to 300. Many of the early European fur traders married Indian women. The children of these marriages became known as métis (from a French word meaning "mixed" or "half-caste"). The métis developed a well-organized society and a history of their own. They consider themselves a "nation," although today the word "métis" is also applied to many people who have Indian ancestry but who are not Treaty Indians (covered by treaties).

Many religions are represented. But the main church groups, in order of size, are Roman Catholic, United Church of Canada, Lutheran, Anglican Church of Canada, and Eastern Orthodox.

Health. In 1962, Saskatchewan became the first province to introduce a form of "medicare." The province provides a tax-supported program of medical aid for all.

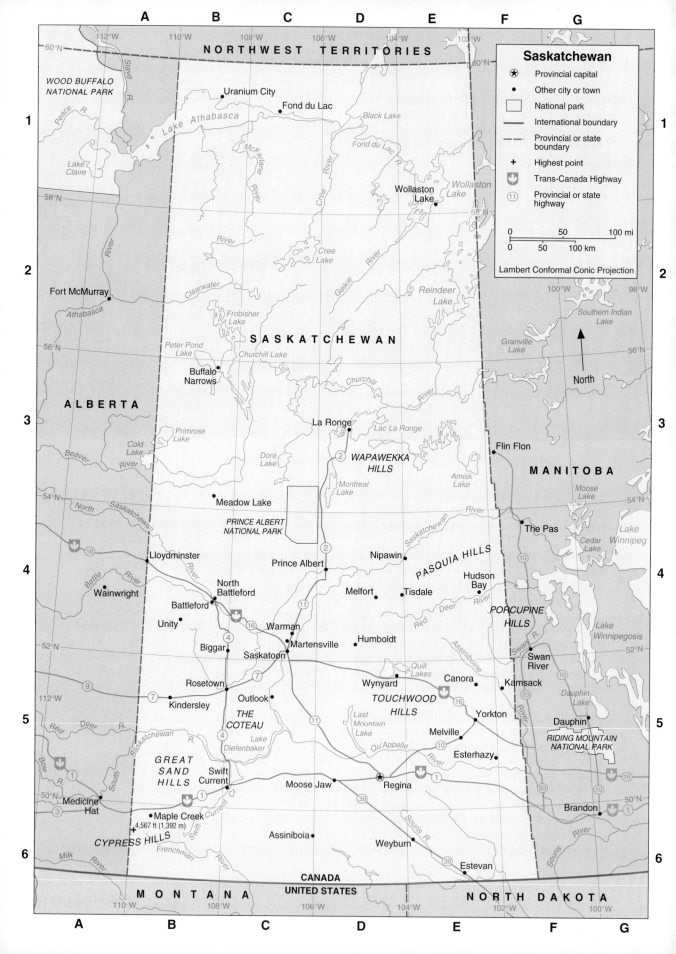

INDEX TO SASKATCHEWAN MAP

▶**EDUCATION**

The province has developed an excellent educational system that provides for both public and "separate" schools. Separate schools are operated by Roman Catholic school boards. Both are tax-supported and are controlled by the provincial department of education. School attendance is compulsory for children from 7 to 16 years of age.

Vocational courses and training in trades are offered both in high schools and in post-secondary institutes of applied arts and sciences. There is also a system of community colleges, providing instruction in a variety of fields. The province supports two universities —the University of Saskatchewan, in Saskatoon, and the University of Regina, in Regina.

Libraries and Museums. The first public library was established at Regina in 1908. Since then an extensive library system has been developed. It includes libraries in 18 of the larger urban centers and 7 regional library systems that serve approximately 300 other places across the province. The university libraries at Regina and Saskatoon are the largest. Major art galleries are the Mendel in Saskatoon and the Norman Mackenzie in Regina. The chief museums are described in the section on Places of Interest.

▶**PLACES OF INTEREST**

Saskatchewan has 17 provincial parks and almost 100 regional parks—all with recreational facilities. Places of special interest include museums and national parks.

Batoche National Historic Site is at Batoche, a village south of Prince Albert. It was the scene of the final battle of the last armed conflict in Canadian history—the Northwest Rebellion of 1885. On the field is Batoche Rectory, the only building that survived the battle.

Fort Battleford National Historic Park, at Battleford, contains a museum and a restored 1876 Northwest Mounted Police fort.

Prince Albert National Park, in central Saskatchewan, is one of the province's major recreational areas, with vast stretches of forestland and many lakes, streams, and beaches. It was established in 1927.

The Royal Canadian Mounted Police Museum and Barracks, in Regina, houses interesting exhibits depicting the history of the famous red-coated "Mounties," who have their national headquarters in Regina.

Wanuskewin Heritage Park, another national historic site, is located just outside Saskatoon. The area has been associated with the Northern Plains Indians for centuries, and this rich past is explored in numerous archaeological excavations.

Wascana Centre, surrounding Wascana Lake in Regina includes parks, the Legislative Building, the University of Regina, the Saskatchewan Centre of the Arts, and the Saskatchewan Museum of Natural History.

The Western Development Museum stresses the history of the settlement of western Canada. It has branches in North Battleford, Saskatoon, and Yorkton.

▶**INDUSTRIES AND PRODUCTS**

Because Saskatchewan has more than one third of Canada's total farmland, it is not surprising that farming is the main occupation. But mining and manufacturing have a part in the economy of the province.

Agriculture. Despite a decrease in the number of farms because of increased size and mechanization, there are still some 67,000 farms. Land is not farmed intensively. A considerable part is left fallow (unplanted) in summer to conserve moisture for the following year. Most of the best farmland is located in a zone that includes the moister edge of the grasslands and the fertile black soils of the park belt. In this zone the farm population is distributed thinly but fairly evenly. There are numerous hamlets and villages strung out along rail lines. Typically they are about 13 kilometers (8 miles) apart, and each has its own group of grain elevators. Most of the large towns and cities are also located in this

Grain elevators stand beside the railroad track near Viscount, Saskatchewan. These unique structures hold wheat in storage until it can be shipped by rail to its destination.

zone, for they also serve the needs of the agriculture industry.

In the drier southwest, ranching and some irrigated farming is important, while north of the populated area the forests take over. Spring wheat is the most important crop, both in dollar value and in amount of land planted. In an effort to get fair prices for their wheat, farmers have built their own co-operative grain elevators and have developed their own marketing service, known as the Saskatchewan Wheat Pool. The Canadian Wheat Board is the sole marketing agency for exporting wheat, barley, and oats. Feed grains for domestic use, together with oilseed and other crops, are marketed by the private grain trade. Other field crops include rapeseed, rye, and flax. Most farms concentrate on grain crops, but mixed farming—including cattle, hogs, and grain—is more common in the moister areas. Most cattle come not from the ranches, but from small herds kept on thousands of farms throughout the southwestern part of the province.

Mining. Petroleum, natural gas, helium, lignite coal, potash, and salt are mined in the southern Saskatchewan. Most of these products are shipped out in raw form. But most of the coal produced is burned in the thermalelectric plants at Estevan and Coronach. Metallic minerals are mined in the Canadian Shield.

Oil accounts for more than half the total value of Saskatchewan's mineral production. Most of the oil and natural gas are exported by pipeline, mainly to Ontario and the United States. Usually the amount of oil produced in Saskatchewan is about 10 percent of the total Canadian production. Lignite coal is mined near Estevan and Coronach.

Potash reserves in south central Saskatchewan are possibly the world's largest. Potash to be used as fertilizer and in manufacturing is exported chiefly to the United States and Japan and in smaller amounts to other countries. The value of potash produced is almost 30 percent of the total value of all minerals produced in the province. Other minerals mined in southern Saskatchewan include salt and sodium sulfate, which is recovered from the beds of shallow lakes.

Metallic minerals from the Shield include uranium, copper, and zinc. Together with minor amounts of gold and silver, these account for more than 10 percent of the total value of mineral production in the province. Uranium is the most important metallic mineral.

Forest Industries. Forest operations are confined to the commercial forest area north of settled Saskatchewan. Forest products include board timber, posts, poles, pulpwood, plywood, and fiberboard. The pulp mill at

Prince Albert, established in 1968, can produce large amounts of bleached sulfate pulp. It has created many jobs in the forest industry.

Manufacturing. Although manufacturing is not a strong part of the economy, Saskatchewan turns out a variety of products. Meatpacking plants, dairies, and flour mills process farm products both for local sale and for other markets in Canada and abroad. A second group of industries draws on natural resources to supply local demands. These include oil refining, cement making, brick manufacture, and the manufacture of wood products. Many industries, such as the food and beverage and metal-fabricating industries, are entirely local, while some others, such as agricultural machinery manufacture, have achieved international markets. Other manufactured products include clothing, electronics, and industrial chemicals.

Electric Power. In a plains region, natural sites for waterpower development are not common. Most of Saskatchewan's electricity is produced from lignite coal and natural gas. But several sites have been developed for the production of hydroelectric power. These include Island Falls on the Churchill River, Squaw Rapids on the North Saskatchewan River, and Gardiner Dam on the South Saskatchewan River. Others are planned.

▶ **CITIES**

Of the cities in Saskatchewan, only Regina and Saskatoon have populations of more than 100,000. The others vary in size from about 5,000 to 34,000. Regina and Saskatoon, centrally located in the settled region, are the chief trade and transportation centers.

Regina gained prominence when the Canadian Pacific Railway reached the townsite in 1872. It was proclaimed the capital of the Northwest Territories the same year and became the provincial capital in 1905. Its industries include the processing of agricultural products, oil refining, and the manufacture of steel pipe, cement, and fertilizer. Its educational and cultural institutions, many within the 920-hectare (2,300-acre) Regina Centre, include the University of Regina, museums, the Regina Symphony Orchestra, and the Globe Theatre. The city has a population of about 180,000.

Saskatoon was founded in 1883 on the banks of the South Saskatchewan River. A rail line from Regina reached it in 1890. After 1900, Saskatoon's growth was rapid as it became the center of a railroad network, and it has continued to be a major service and transportation center. Today's population is about 197,000. Its industries include meat packing, flour milling, and the manufacture of chemicals, agricultural equipment, and cement. Saskatoon is a commuting center for workers for the nearby potash mines. Its educational and cultural institutions include the University of Saskatchewan, founded in 1907; a number of museums; and a symphony orchestra.

Prince Albert, the third largest city in Saskatchewan, is a distributing center for a rich agricultural region and for the huge forest area to the north. Saskatchewan's only pulp mill is located in Prince Albert. Among the first settlers were the métis. In 1866 a Christian mission for the Indians was established at the site and named for Prince Albert, Queen Victoria's husband. The city's population is about 34,000.

Moose Jaw, with about 32,000 people, was formerly an important rail center. The city now serves a large agricultural area. Among its industries are meat packing and grain storage. Moose Jaw's recreational attractions include a Wild Animal Park and Crescent Park, which houses an art museum and other facilities.

Yorkton, with about 15,000 people, is the center of a rich farming area in the eastern park belt. Its major industries are food processing and the manufacture of farm equipment. Yorkton was founded in 1882 by colonizers from Ontario and was incorporated as a city in 1928. There are many lake resorts nearby, and the city is host to the biennial Yorkton International Film Festival.

Swift Current, with a population of nearly 15,000, is the largest urban center in southwestern Saskatchewan. It serves a large farming area devoted mainly to wheat and cattle, as well as nearby oil fields.

North Battleford, on the North Saskatchewan River northwest of Saskatoon, is a railroad terminal and distribution center for a mixed-farming area. It displaced historic Battleford as a major center in 1905, when the railroad was built on the north side of the North Saskatchewan River. North Battleford is attractively situated at the gateway to the lakes and recreation areas of northwestern Saskatchewan. It has nearly 14,000 people.

Regina, Saskatchewan's capital and largest city, was founded in 1882 on Pile of Bones Creek. Its residents have made the flat prairie town into a modern city.

Other cities with populations of 5,000 or more are **Estevan, Weyburn, Lloydminster,** and **Melfort.**

▶ TRANSPORTATION AND COMMUNICATION

Railroads serve the settled southern area of Saskatchewan, and most of the towns and villages are located along the railway. But no railways and few roads penetrate the northern half of the province. Paved highways connect all the cities and larger towns, but about 90 percent of Saskatchewan's roads are built of gravel or earth.

Saskatoon and Regina have major commercial airports. Smaller airports are located in other cities. Much of the north can be reached only by small ski- or float-equipped aircraft.

Saskatchewan's three daily newspapers are published in Regina, Saskatoon, and Prince Albert. Eight television stations originate in the province. In the north, satellite stations provide television broadcasts. Radio coverage is extensive, with more than 50 AM and FM stations serving the province.

▶ GOVERNMENT

Saskatchewan is a self-governing province. Like other provinces, it is led by a premier who heads the controlling party in the provincial legislature. A lieutenant governor, appointed by Canada's governor-general, is the titular head of the province. Saskatchewan is represented in the federal Parliament by 14 elected members of the House of Commons and 6 senators appointed by the governor-general. The voting age in provincial elections is 18.

▶ HISTORY

At the beginning of the 1700's, there were three well-defined Indian territories in Saskatchewan. Occupying the Shield were Chipewyan, with the Slave and Beaver on the west. Southward, on the forested plains, were the Cree. The grasslands were Assiniboine territory, although Gros Ventres and Blackfoot claimed the southwest.

The forest Indians traveled in small bands, on foot or by canoe, in search of food. In contrast, Indians of the grasslands had learned to organize in large groups to hunt the bison. The introduction of the horse and new weapons added to their mobility and successful organization to the point that they were able to resist the advance of European settlers on their land until the treaties of 1870. By the mid-1800's, however, many Indians had become dependent on European fur traders for a major part of their livelihood, and their own tribal loyalties and culture gradually weakened.

Fur Trade and Exploration. The Hudson's Bay Company had been engaged in the western fur trade since the 1670's. In 1690 the company sent Henry Kelsey to investigate the fur-producing potential of the interior. He returned with the first account of the area written in English. From New France (Quebec), explorer-traders pushed westward, and in 1737 the first report in French was provided by Sieur de la Vérendrye. French competition forced the Hudson's Bay Company to establish the first permanent settlement in Saskatchewan, at Cumberland House, in 1774. This location was chosen because it was a focus of water routes leading to Hudson Bay.

Early Settlement. During the 1850's and 1860's, métis bison hunters began to spend the winter in river valleys and along lake shores in southern and central Saskatchewan. In these settlements there developed a rough system of farming alongside hunting. The opening of the territory to homesteading in 1872 caused the métis to feel that their way of life was being threatened. On March 19, 1885, under the leadership of Louis Riel, the métis proclaimed the Provincial Government of the Saskatchewan and Batoche. Their protests soon led to armed rebellion, but the métis and their Indian allies were quickly defeated by soldiers from eastern Canada. Riel remains a controversial figure in Canadian history. A leader of two rebellions (in Manitoba in 1870 and Saskatchewan in 1885), he created dissension between French- and English-speaking Canadians that persists today.

The 20th Century. In the decade from 1901 to 1911, a rail network was constructed to accommodate the needs of immigrants who had been attracted to Saskatchewan—then a part of the Northwest Territories—by the government's offer of free or cheap land. They came from eastern Canada, the British Isles, the United States, and Europe. Saskatchewan's population grew by 400,000 during the decade, and by 1909, it was the chief wheat-producing province in Canada. But northern Saskatchewan was little affected. For a long time its tiny population consisted mainly of those in search of game, fish, and fur.

In 1905, Saskatchewan became a separate province. Despite World War I, recessions, and droughts, the population grew steadily. But in the 1930's severe drought and economic depression forced thousands of people to abandon their farms. Many left the province, and there was a large population loss over a period of several years.

Major economic changes began to occur in the 1950's. Valuable oil and natural gas discoveries brought new investment in exploration, recovery, and refinery construction. At the same time, the province's large potash resources were being developed. Both mining ventures created new demands for steel and other products and for labor and other locally supplied services. A long-faltering farm economy became strong again.

Agriculture remains the leading goods-producing industry, but the economy has become more diversified. Discoveries of oil, natural gas, and other minerals have made mining the second most important goods-producing industry. Services, however, account for the largest percentage of the province's gross domestic product (the total value of goods and services produced in a year).

Saskatchewan retains a strong sense of the future, in new breakthroughs in crops and crop yields and in the development of new markets for its raw materials and finished products.

J. HOWARD RICHARDS
University of Saskatchewan

SASSANIANS. See PERSIA, ANCIENT.

IMPORTANT DATES

1670	King Charles II of England granted ownership, trading rights, and governing powers of Rupert's Land (including present-day Saskatchewan) to the Hudson's Bay Company.
1690	Henry Kelsey, of Hudson's Bay Company, explored Saskatchewan.
1774	Samuel Hearne established the first permanent inland trading post—Cumberland House.
1821	Hudson's Bay Company merged with the North West Company.
1870	Canada bought Rupert's Land and made it part of the Canadian Northwest Territories.
1872	Canadian Government offered free land to settlers in Saskatchewan.
1882	Regina became territorial capital.
1885	Rebellion of Indians and Métis led by Louis Riel ended with the Battle of Batoche.
1905	Saskatchewan admitted to the Confederation as a province, with Regina the capital city.
1907	University of Saskatchewan founded in Saskatoon.
1924	Saskatchewan Wheat Pool organized.
1947	Saskatchewan became the first province to enact a tax-financed, free hospitalization plan.
1951–1953	Major oil and gas deposits discovered; significant uranium ore production started.
1963	Squaw Rapids plant on North Saskatchewan River provided hydroelectric power; first large production of potash.
1982	Legislation passed to establish a National Grasslands Park in the northern forest area.
1991	The New Democratic Party returned to power for the first time since its 1982 defeat by the Progressive Conservatives.
1993	Janice MacKinnon became the first woman appointed finance minister in Saskatchewan.
1996	Saskatchewan Wheat Pool became a public company.

SATELLITES

Imagine looking up into the night sky and seeing several objects that looked like our moon. That is what you would see if you lived on Jupiter or Saturn, because those planets have many moons, or satellites, instead of just one. Any natural object that orbits a planet is called a satellite.

Spacecraft and other objects launched from Earth to orbit a planet or the sun are called artificial satellites. These are discussed in the article SATELLITES, ARTIFICIAL, in this volume.

Of the nine planets in the solar system, only Mercury and Venus have no known satellites. The Earth and Pluto each have one satellite. Moon is the name of the Earth's satellite, and Charon is Pluto's satellite. Mars has two satellites, Phobos and Deimos. Each of the four remaining planets have many satellites. Saturn has 1 large satellite, Titan, and more than 40 small ones. Jupiter has more than 50 small satellites and 4 large ones: Io, Europa, Callisto, and Ganymede. Many of the known satellites were discovered by space probes, such as *Voyager 1* and *Voyager 2*. Others have been discovered with Earth-based telescopes.

How Planets Got Their Satellites

Astronomers think that the satellites were formed billions of years ago, at the same time as the sun and planets were formed. At that time, the solar system was a vast rotating disk of dust particles, ice, and gases. Over time, these materials condensed and accumulated into larger and larger bodies of matter, eventually becoming the planets. The gravitational force of each planet attracted smaller bodies of matter, which crashed into the planet and added to its size. However, some of the small bodies of matter did not crash, but began to circle the planet instead. These smaller objects became the planet's satellites.

Some satellites may have been formed as a result of collisions between a planet and other huge objects. The Earth's moon, for example, was probably formed when an object about the size of Mars collided with Earth, blasting an enormous amount of debris into space. As this debris circled the planet, it may have eventually fused to form the moon.

Other satellites were "captured" long after the planets were formed. The gravitational pull of the largest planets is so great that sometimes passing asteroids are captured and kept in orbits around them. Astronomers think that some of Jupiter's and Saturn's smaller satellites, as well as Neptune's large satellite, Triton, were originally asteroids because they travel in backward orbits.

A Host of Different Worlds

The Earth's moon is an unusual satellite because it is made up of very dry rocks. Most of the other satellites contain large amounts of water or other liquids in their interiors, and some are made up almost entirely of frozen water. For example, a thick layer of ice covers Europa, one of Jupiter's satellites. Beneath this layer may be an ocean of liquid water, which some scientists say could support life. Triton is covered with a snowlike layer of frozen nitrogen and appears very white. But other satellites are very dark. Deimos and Phobos, the satellites of Mars, are as dark as coal because they contain much black carbonlike material.

There is still much to learn about the satellites in the solar system. A major step was taken in 2005 when the *Huygens* space probe touched down on the surface of Titan, Saturn's largest satellite. The probe provided valuable information about Titan's dense atmosphere and mysterious surface.

RICHARD BERRY
Author, *Discover the Stars*
Reviewed by WILLIAM A. GUTSCH, JR.
President, The Challenger Center for
Space Science Education

See also ASTRONOMY; MOON; PLANETS; SOLAR SYSTEM; SPACE PROBES; articles on individual planets.

Photographs taken by the *Galileo* space probe in 1990 show the composition of surface areas of the Earth's moon. Deep blues indicate the metal titanium. Greens, yellows, and oranges indicate iron and magnesium.

SATELLITES, ARTIFICIAL

A natural object that revolves around a planet is called a **satellite**. Earth's moon is a natural satellite, as are the moons circling other planets in the solar system.

In addition to these natural satellites, there are thousands of artificial satellites, which have been designed and built on Earth and launched into space since the late 1950's. These artificial satellites are expanding our knowledge of space and our own planet.

Movements of Satellites

A satellite's movement in space is affected by the gravity of the object that it is orbiting. Earth's gravity pulls a moving satellite downward and makes it curve around the planet. To stay in this curved orbit, the satellite must maintain a certain speed. If it slows down too much, Earth's gravity will pull it back down toward the planet. If it travels fast enough, it can break free from Earth's gravity and travel out into space. The speed needed to do this is called **escape velocity**.

Once in orbit, a satellite moves at a certain speed unless acted on by some force. This tendency to continue moving or remain at rest is called **inertia**. When a satellite moves through Earth's atmosphere, friction forces it to slow down. The thinner the atmosphere, the less friction there is and the less a satellite's speed is affected.

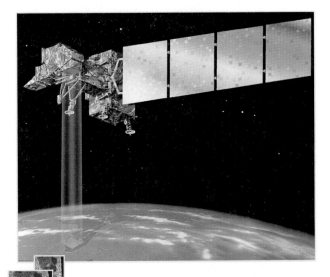

The speed that a satellite must maintain in order to stay in orbit is called its **orbital velocity**. This speed depends on the satellite's distance from Earth. The farther a satellite is from Earth, the slower it needs to move to remain in orbit.

The orbits of satellites are not perfectly circular. They follow an oval, or elliptical, path. In an elliptical orbit, the distance of a satellite from Earth varies. The closest point is called the **perigee**, and the farthest point is called the **apogee**. If the perigee is too low, atmospheric friction slows down the satellite and causes its orbit to decay, or decrease. If a satellite drops through the atmosphere, it usually burns up from the heat caused by friction.

Many satellites are launched from Earth in an easterly direction. This gives the satellite a boost of speed from Earth's rotation, since the satellite takes off in the same direction as Earth's rotational spin. This push enables the satellite to use less fuel for its launch. One common type of east-west orbit

Satellites, such as the *Landsat 7* shown above, can take detailed pictures of Earth's surface from space. In the picture below, Florida's Everglades show up darker than the built-up urban and farm areas around them.

is a **geosynchronous orbit** (also called a geo-stationary orbit). Satellites in this orbit circle Earth in 24 hours—the same period of time it takes Earth to rotate. As a result, the satellite always stays over the same spot on Earth. In a **polar orbit**, a satellite travels in a north-south direction over both poles. Satellites in a polar orbit are able to pass over all parts of Earth and observe a greater area of Earth's surface.

A space satellite is launched into orbit by a rocket called a **launch vehicle**. A satellite is usually placed at the top of the launch vehicle and protected by a metal shroud that is ejected after the satellite reaches orbit.

The first launch vehicles were military missiles that were also designed to carry warheads. Ground-based rockets are still used to launch most satellites. Some rockets are released from the air by large airplanes that can reach high altitudes. Other satellites are carried into space aboard the space shuttle, a reusable spacecraft piloted by astronauts. Once in orbit, astronauts remove the satellite from the shuttle's cargo bay. Rockets on the satellite then carry it to its proper orbit.

Uses of Artificial Satellites

In 1957, the Soviet Union launched the first artificial satellite, *Sputnik 1*. It was little more than a radio beacon, but it ushered in a new era of space exploration and communications. Today, many different kinds of satellites orbit Earth for a variety of uses.

Astronomy. Many satellites are used for astronomical research, since satellites can detect radiation from space that never reaches Earth's surface. On the ground, we can see visible light coming from stars, galaxies, and other objects in space. However, we cannot detect many other types of radiation—X rays, gamma rays, ultraviolet radiation, infrared radiation, certain radio waves, and microwaves—because they are absorbed by Earth's atmosphere. Satellites can detect these types of radiation, which reveal important information about the universe.

Earth Sciences. Satellites are also used to study Earth itself. Some, such as the *Landsat* satellites, take pictures of Earth's surface and collect data about the oceans, natural resources, and changes in our environment. Other satellites gather information about Earth's weather. This helps meteorologists make forecasts and warn people about hurricanes and other severe storms.

Communications. Satellites are also used for many types of communication. Radio broadcasts, television programs, and telephone calls are transmitted around the world by satellites. The first communications satellite, *Echo 1*, was launched in 1960. Today many communications satellites orbit Earth. Some transmit television signals to receiving "dishes" at millions of homes, enabling people to watch events from all over the world.

In the 1990's, several companies began launching dozens of low Earth-orbit satellites to form networks that cover the entire globe. These networks provide people with access to telephone services and computers from virtually anywhere.

Military Spying. The military uses special satellites that help with spying. One of the most famous United States spy satellites is the *KH-11*, known as Big Bird. Some military satellites can detect nuclear weapon tests or missile launchings. Others can help guide missiles and planes to their targets.

Navigation. One type of military satellite technology—the global positioning system, or GPS—has recently found many civilian applications. This system is a network of some 24 satellites that continually transmit signals at precise intervals. From nearly any point on Earth's surface, a person with a GPS receiver (a device that picks up the signals) can determine his or her location. GPS receivers are now installed in many automobiles, ships, and airplanes as navigation aids.

Space Stations. A special type of satellite is the orbiting space station, where people live for months conducting research. The first one, *Salyut 1*, was launched in 1971 by the Soviet Union. The United States launched its first space station, *Skylab*, in 1973. On the Soviet *Mir* space station, launched in 1986, some crew members set records by remaining in space for more than a year. In 1998, the United States (in partnership with Russia, eleven European nations, Canada, Japan, and Brazil) began assembling the new *International Space Station*, the largest satellite ever.

JOSEPH KELCH
Davis Planetarium, Maryland Science Center

See also GRAVITY AND GRAVITATION; ROCKETS; SPACE EXPLORATION AND TRAVEL; SPACE SHUTTLES; SPACE STATIONS; SPACE TELESCOPES.

SATURN

Of the nine planets in the solar system, Saturn is one of the most beautiful. Other planets have colorful clouds, huge volcanoes, enormous craters, and great deserts of colored sand, but Saturn has a magnificent ring system. Through a telescope, the planet appears against the dark sky as a light yellowish ball with a gleaming white ring around it—truly a wondrous sight. Even without its ring system, Saturn is an impressive planet. The second largest planet in the solar system, it is an enormous ball with a diameter nine times greater than the Earth's. Along with Jupiter, Uranus, and Neptune, it is one of the gas giants of the solar system.

Saturn's Revolution and Rotation

Until Uranus was discovered in 1781, Saturn was the most distant planet known. The planet is more than nine times farther from the sun than the Earth is, so it takes much longer than the Earth to revolve around the sun. In fact, the planet takes 29.5 Earth years to make one orbit. Saturn rotates quickly on its axis, making one rotation in about 10 hours and 40 minutes. The planet's rapid period of rotation distorts its shape slightly, causing it to flatten at the poles and bulge at the equator.

Saturn's axis of rotation is tilted 26.7 degrees from the plane of its orbit. This causes the planet to be seen from different angles on Earth during its revolution around the sun. For half of each revolution, astronomers can see Saturn's northern hemisphere and the northern side of its ring system. For the other half of its revolution, astronomers can see Saturn's southern hemisphere and the southern side of its rings. Twice during each revolution the rings appear edge-on, but they are so thin that they cannot be seen without a very large telescope.

A World of Hydrogen and Helium

Like the other gas giants, Saturn consists mostly of gases. Most of its mass consists of hydrogen and helium gas—the two lightest and most abundant elements in the universe.

These two gases are clear, but when viewed through a powerful telescope, Saturn has colored belts of clouds enveloped in a dense, smoggy haze. These clouds and haze are caused by small amounts of methane, ammonia, and hydrocarbon molecules in the atmosphere. In the upper atmosphere, the hydrocarbon molecules condense into droplets, which cause the haze. Deeper down in the atmosphere, the ammonia and methane also condense, forming the thick clouds.

If it were not for the dense haze in its upper atmosphere, Saturn's cloud belts might be as colorful as those of Jupiter. While clouds of pure ammonia are white, colored clouds result when compounds containing carbon,

The *Voyager* space probes uncovered much information about Saturn's ring system, which for years had been a mystery to astronomers.

phosphorus, germanium, and other elements are present, as they are in Saturn's clouds. These compounds form shades of red, orange, yellow, and brown. In contrast to Jupiter, however, Saturn looks more pastel because layers of haze soften its cloud colors.

Saturn does not have a solid surface, only an enormously deep atmosphere that becomes denser and hotter toward the interior of the planet. Roughly halfway to the planet's core—about 20,000 miles (32,000 kilometers) deep—the atmosphere changes to a highly compressed mixture of molten metallic hydrogen and helium. The very center of Saturn may consist of a core of molten rock at a temperature of 22,000°F (12,000°C).

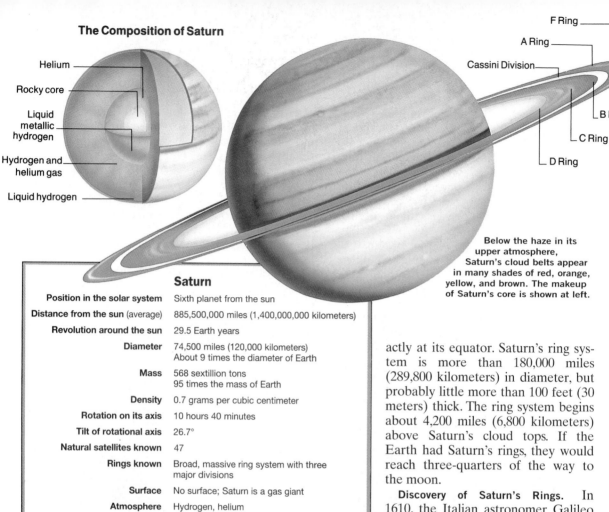

The Composition of Saturn

- Helium
- Rocky core
- Liquid metallic hydrogen
- Hydrogen and helium gas
- Liquid hydrogen

- F Ring
- A Ring
- Cassini Division
- B Ring
- C Ring
- D Ring

Below the haze in its upper atmosphere, Saturn's cloud belts appear in many shades of red, orange, yellow, and brown. The makeup of Saturn's core is shown at left.

Saturn

Position in the solar system	Sixth planet from the sun
Distance from the sun (average)	885,500,000 miles (1,400,000,000 kilometers)
Revolution around the sun	29.5 Earth years
Diameter	74,500 miles (120,000 kilometers) About 9 times the diameter of Earth
Mass	568 sextillion tons 95 times the mass of Earth
Density	0.7 grams per cubic centimeter
Rotation on its axis	10 hours 40 minutes
Tilt of rotational axis	26.7°
Natural satellites known	47
Rings known	Broad, massive ring system with three major divisions
Surface	No surface; Saturn is a gas giant
Atmosphere	Hydrogen, helium
Temperature (at cloudtop level)	−243°F (−153°C)
Symbol	♄
In mythology	Saturn, Roman god of agriculture

Saturn's Ring System

Saturn's most impressive feature is its system of rings, which is composed of trillions of chunks of ice ranging in size from particles as small as a grain of sand to boulders larger than a house. Although each chunk of ice orbits Saturn separately, together they appear as enormous rings encircling the planet ex-

actly at its equator. Saturn's ring system is more than 180,000 miles (289,800 kilometers) in diameter, but probably little more than 100 feet (30 meters) thick. The ring system begins about 4,200 miles (6,800 kilometers) above Saturn's cloud tops. If the Earth had Saturn's rings, they would reach three-quarters of the way to the moon.

Discovery of Saturn's Rings. In 1610, the Italian astronomer Galileo Galilei (1564–1642) looked at Saturn through a telescope. Unfortunately, Galileo's telescope was not powerful enough to allow him to see the ring system clearly. He could see that there was something unusual about the planet, but he concluded that Saturn was accompanied by two "attendants." Several years later, Galileo observed Saturn again, but the planet had revolved in its orbit so that the rings were nearly edge-on, making them very difficult to see. As a result, Galileo only saw the planet itself and not the rings. He wondered whether his eyes or his tele-

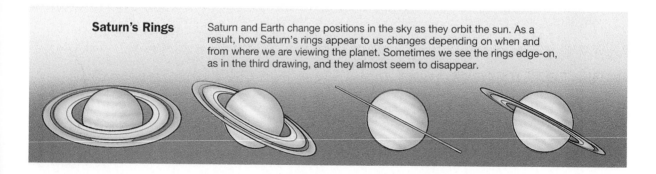

Saturn's Rings

Saturn and Earth change positions in the sky as they orbit the sun. As a result, how Saturn's rings appear to us changes depending on when and from where we are viewing the planet. Sometimes we see the rings edge-on, as in the third drawing, and they almost seem to disappear.

scope had deceived him in his earlier observations. Galileo died before he solved this mystery. In 1659, the Dutch astronomer Christiaan Huygens (1629–95) used a better telescope and saw that Saturn was encircled by a flat ring.

A System of Many Rings. A closer look, however, reveals that Saturn is surrounded by a system of three main rings. The outermost ring is called the A Ring. Closer to the planet, a dark, 2,900-mile (4,670-kilometer)-wide gap called the Cassini Division separates the A Ring from the B Ring, which is the brightest and whitest ring. The main ring closest to the planet is the faint C Ring, which is also called the Crepe Ring because it resembles crepe, a thin fabric that is almost transparent. More recently discovered rings include the very faint D Ring inside the C Ring, and the F Ring beyond the A Ring.

When the two *Voyager* space probes flew past Saturn in 1980 and 1981, the images they took provided amazing details about the structure of the rings. Each of the planet's main rings was found to consist of hundreds or even thousands of narrow "ringlets." These ringlets are too narrow and close together to be seen from Earth, and their number and structure are probably continuously changing over time.

It was also revealed that the ice particles forming the ringlets, and thus the rings themselves, vary in size. In the A Ring, for exam-

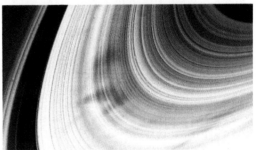

False-color images of the ringlets in Saturn's C Ring (blues and grays) and B Ring (orangy yellows) are used to indicate the variations in their composition (*top*). The mysterious "spokes" in Saturn's B Ring can be seen in the bottom photograph.

ple, many particles are the size of marbles. The B Ring is composed of larger chunks, some as big as a house, but with a mix of smaller chunks too. About three-fourths of the total mass of Saturn's ring system is in the B Ring.

The *Voyagers'* images also revealed dark spoke-like patches in the B Ring. These patches rotate around Saturn and continually break up and form again. Astronomers think these patches are due to fine electrically charged particles of dust or other dark material that is suspended just above the rings by Saturn's magnetic field.

This complex ring system is a result of gravitational resonances that push its particles into a particular path. These resonances occur because Saturn's ring particles and Saturn's satellites have different periods of revolution. For example, the Cassini Division is at a place where particles would take one half the time to orbit Saturn as its satellite Mimas. Because of this difference, the gravitational force of Mimas would pull on particles in that region and move them slightly. After millions of tiny gravitational pulls, the particles would move to a new orbit either closer to or farther from Saturn than the Cassini Division. This resonance with Mimas has thus created the gap that is the Cassini Division.

WONDER QUESTION

Where did Saturn's rings come from?

If all the chunks of ice in all of Saturn's rings were put together, they would form a satellite about 250 miles (400 kilometers) in diameter. In fact, astronomers suspect that the ring system may be the remains of a satellite that broke up long ago, or perhaps material that might have formed a satellite but for some reason never did.

Saturn's ring system cannot last forever. As chunks of material in the rings collide, they break apart into smaller and smaller pieces. Over long periods of time, such collisions will grind all the material into very fine particles. Magnetic and electrical forces that have little effect on large chunks of material will act to remove these fine particles from the rings. Astronomers disagree about how long Saturn's ring system will last—perhaps billions of years—but all agree that someday it will be gone.

Saturn's Satellites

Saturn has many satellites, or moons. Of the more than 40 known satellites, nine measure more than 62 miles (100 kilometers) across, while most of the remaining ones measure less than 12 miles (20 kilometers) across. Several are notable.

Titan. With a diameter of 3,200 miles (5,150 kilometers), Titan is Saturn's largest moon and the second largest in the solar system. It is the only moon with a dense atmosphere, which consists mostly of nitrogen and also methane and hydrocarbon molecules. The hydrocarbon molecules create a natural "smog," making Titan's surface invisible to the naked eye. Titan may be in a kind of pre-life state similar to the Earth's environment billions of years ago. However, since it is so cold, the possibility of life evolving on Titan is very remote.

Pandora and Prometheus. These two small potato-shaped satellites, about 71 and 90 miles (114 and 145 kilometers) in their longest dimension and about 52 miles (84 kilometers) wide, orbit Saturn on either side of the planet's F Ring. They are known as shepherd satellites because the force of their gravitational pulls keeps the material within Saturn's F Ring together, just as a shepherd keeps a flock of sheep together.

Mimas. This satellite, 244 miles (392 kilometers) in diameter, is the first large satellite beyond Saturn's ring system. It offers an important clue about how Saturn's ring system was formed. On the surface of Mimas is a very large crater, one-third the size of the satellite itself, which must have been formed by an impact with a large asteroid or other object. Astronomers think that if this impact were any larger, Mimas would have been shattered and its pieces might have formed yet another ring around Saturn.

Iapetus. Iapetus, 907 miles (1,460 kilometers) in diameter, is Saturn's outermost large satellite. It has a strange surface: One side is darker than coal, while the other side is very bright. Scientists do not know why this is so—perhaps something dark erupted from its interior or something dark from space hit Iapetus and covered part of its surface.

Titan

Mimas

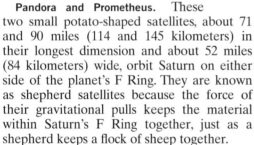

Iapetus

Phoebe. Phoebe, about 132 miles (212 kilometers) in diameter, travels in a **retrograde** orbit—meaning it moves in the opposite direction to the spin of Saturn. Its surface is dark, in contrast to most of Saturn's other moons, which are bright. Astronomers speculate that Phoebe may have come from the outer solar system and been captured by Saturn's gravity in the distant past.

Future Saturn Exploration

The future of Saturn exploration is happening right now. After a seven-year trip from Earth, the *Cassini* space probe reached Saturn in July 2004 and became the first artificial satellite to orbit the planet. During its four-year mission, *Cassini* will use a wide variety of instruments to provide detailed analyses of Saturn, its system of rings, and its moons.

The *Cassini* space probe has already made many new discoveries at Saturn, including a radiation belt between the innermost ring and the top of the planet's clouds; a large amount of dark material, or "dirt," within the rings' Cassini Division; a day- and nighttime glow to Titan created by emissions of methane and carbon dioxide in its atmosphere; an atmosphere surrounding the large moon Enceladus; and several new moons and rings.

Cassini carried with it another space probe, *Huygens*, which it released in December 2004 to study Titan. *Huygens* entered the moon's atmosphere in January 2005, and as it descended, it analyzed the atmosphere's chemistry, wind speeds, and temperature. When the probe landed safely on the surface, it revealed a rugged world of ridges, plains, and gullies, where liquid methane rains down and etches the surface with channels, deltas, and riverbeds. These geological processes are strikingly similar to those found on Earth.

RICHARD BERRY
Author, *Discover the Stars*

Reviewed by WILLIAM A. GUTSCH, JR.
President, The Challenger Center for Space Science Education

See also PLANETS; SATELLITES; SOLAR SYSTEM; SPACE PROBES.

SAUDI ARABIA

Saudi Arabia is a vast kingdom in the Middle East that is about one-third the size of the continental United States. Its population, however, is relatively small, for much of Saudi Arabia is desert, poorly suited to human habitation.

Saudi Arabia occupies most of the boot-shaped Arabian Peninsula in southwestern Asia. For much of its history, Arabia was isolated from the rest of the world. It was largely the home of nomadic Bedouin, who crossed the deserts searching for grazing land and water for their herds of camels, goats, and sheep. But two events, many centuries apart, greatly changed the character and fortunes of the region.

In A.D. 610 the prophet Mohammed began to preach the new faith of Islam. Soon an Islamic civilization spread across much of Asia, Africa, and into Europe, where it was halted by Christian armies. The second major event occurred in the 1930's, when enormous deposits of oil were discovered beneath Arabia's barren soil. Today the wealth from its vast oil reserves has helped transform Saudi Arabia from a desert kingdom into a modern state.

▶ PEOPLE

Saudi Arabia has a population of about 22 million, but about 25 percent of its residents are workers from foreign countries, known as expatriates. Of the total native population, 90 percent is Arab and 10 percent is Afro-Asian.

Language. Arabic, a member of the Semitic family of languages, is the official language of Saudi Arabia. Its significance comes from the belief that the Koran (Quran) was revealed to the Prophet Mohammed in the Arabic language.

Religion. All native Saudi Arabians are Muslims, and 90 percent of them belong to the Sunni branch of Islam. A significant number of Sunni Muslims conform to Wahhabism, a reform sect that follows strict interpretation of all the laws of Islam. Ten percent of Saudi

Saudi Arabians are an Arab people. Barren desert covers much of their land, which is situated on the Arabian Peninsula in the Middle East.

All Muslim women in Saudi Arabia must cloak their bodies and keep their faces covered while in public.

Arabians belong to the Shi'ite branch of Islam.

Islam's two major holy sites—Mecca and Medina—are situated in Saudi Arabia. Mecca draws about 3 million Muslim pilgrims from all over the world for the hajj (pilgrimage) to the Kaaba (cube-shaped holy site in Mecca) each year during the twelfth month in the Islamic calendar. Muslims are required to make this pilgrimage once during the course of their lives given that they are adult, able-bodied, and have the financial means to do so. The second holiest Islamic city is Medina. It is the city where the first Islamic state was established. The Prophet Mohammed's mosque and tomb are located there. For more information, see the articles ARABS, ISLAM, and MOHAMMED in the appropriate volumes.

Education. The government of Saudi Arabia provides free schooling from the primary through the university level. Girls and boys attend separate schools. Universities for men and colleges for women are located in Riyadh, the capital, and in other major cities such as Jidda, Medina, and Dhahran. An Islamic university in Medina trains religious leaders. The College of Petroleum and Minerals in Dhahran trains technicians and managers for industry. Many students attend colleges and universities abroad.

Way of Life. Until fairly recently, most of Saudi Arabia's people were nomadic or semi-nomadic. But the impact of modern economic, social, and political changes has led to the rapid growth of urban areas. By the year 2000, approximately 80 percent of the population lived in cities. Many former nomads, who once rode animals for transportation and lived in tents, now drive cars and live in modern apartments or houses subsidized by the government.

Those who still follow nomadic traditions travel through the desert during the autumn, winter, and spring months. In the summer, when grass and water are scarce, they may camp near an oasis, well-spring, or other permanent water source. They visit the towns and villages to sell their livestock, buy supplies, and visit friends. In late autumn, they resume the cycle.

Traditional village life in Saudi Arabia centers around a marketplace, a mosque (the Muslim house of worship), and a coffee-house, where men gather to talk. Houses are usually one or two stories high and are constructed of sun-dried bricks, stone, or concrete blocks. They are often built around an open courtyard.

Customs. Religion and family relationships have always played important roles in Saudi Arabian life, and the people are proud of their ancestral traditions and codes of honor. A household is typically made up of a husband and wife, their unmarried sons and daughters, and in some cases married sons with their wives and children. In the past, parents arranged their children's marriages, and men often had more than one wife. These practices, however, are now in decline.

In Saudi Arabia, the most socially conservative of the Arab countries, women are not allowed to drive cars or travel alone. But educated Saudi Arabian women are gradually moving into public life.

Dress. Traditional clothing for men consists of an ankle-length gown called a *thobe* or *jellaba*, over which may be worn an *aba*, or dark-colored cloak. The head covering is a large square cotton cloth called a *ghutra*. It is held in place by a black ropelike hoop called an *agal*.

In public, Saudi Arabian women cover their faces and wear long dark-colored garments that cloak their bodies from head to foot. However, at home they often wear western-style clothing.

▶ LAND

Land Regions. Saudi Arabia has several distinct geographical regions: the Western Highlands, the Central Plateau, the Northern Deserts, the Rub' al-Khali, and the Eastern Lowlands.

The Western Highlands lie along the Red Sea. The northern portion is called the Hejaz, and the southern portion is called the Asir. A narrow coastal plain called the Tihama separates parts of both regions from mountains that rise to the east. Jabal Sawda, the country's highest peak, rises 10,279 feet (3,133 meters) in the Asir.

The Central Plateau, called the Nejd, extends eastward from the mountains. This is a relatively level area, occasionally interrupted by low ranges and cut by wadis, or desert valleys. A chain of fertile oases extends down the plateau.

About one-third of Saudi Arabia is desert. The Northern Deserts are also known as the An Nafūd. Southern Saudi Arabia encompasses the Rub' al-Khali— or Empty Quarter. Because of the sweltering heat and lack of water, this vast area of continuous sand is one of the most inhospitable

and least known deserts in the world. The An Nafūd and Rub' al-Khali deserts are connected by the Ad Dahnā, a long, narrow belt of sand ridges.

The Eastern Lowlands, along the Persian Gulf, make up the lowest part of the country.

Rivers, Lakes, and Coastal Waters. Saudi Arabia is bordered by the Red Sea to the west and the Persian Gulf to the east. It has no permanent rivers or lakes. The many wadis are formed by temporary streams that carry water only after the infrequent rains.

Climate. Most of Saudi Arabia has a harsh desert climate, with frequent dust and sand storms and little rainfall. From May to September, the weather is very hot and dry. Temperatures drop rapidly after sunset, and the nights are relatively cool. Temperatures are lower along the coasts, but the humidity is higher. Temperatures are less extreme from October to May.

Natural Resources. Saudi Arabia has about one-quarter of the world's known reserves of oil and natural gas. It also has deposits of iron ore, gold, and copper.

FACTS and figures

KINGDOM OF SAUDI ARABIA is the official name of the country.

LOCATION: Arabian Peninsula in Southwest Asia.

AREA: 830,000 sq mi (2,149,700 km²).

POPULATION: 22,000,000 (estimate).

CAPITAL AND LARGEST CITY: Riyadh.

MAJOR LANGUAGE: Arabic (official).

MAJOR RELIGIOUS GROUP: Muslim (official).

GOVERNMENT: Monarchy. **Head of state and government**—king.

CHIEF PRODUCTS: Agricultural—Wheat, barley, tomatoes, melons, dates, citrus, livestock. **Manufactured**—petroleum refining, petrochemicals, cement, fertilizer, plastics. **Mineral**—petroleum.

MONETARY UNIT: Saudi riyal (1 riyal = 100 halalah).

Saudi Arabia's economy is dependent on its vast reserves of oil and natural gas. The country is the world's leading exporter of petroleum and natural gas.

▶ ECONOMY

Saudi Arabia is the world's leading producer and exporter of petroleum and natural gas. Because petroleum provides almost all of the country's income, the economy fluctuates with the rise and fall of world oil prices. In recent years, to diversify their investments, Saudi Arabians have put much of their wealth into foreign products and financial markets.

Services. The development of the oil industry and rapid economic growth has drawn many foreigners to Saudi Arabia. Many of these expatriates are employed by banks, restaurants, hotels, airlines, hospitals, shops, schools, and other service providers.

While praying, all Muslims must face in the direction of Islam's holiest site, the Kaaba in Mecca.

Manufacturing. Most Saudi industries are related to oil, such as the refining of crude petroleum and the manufacture of petrochemicals, fertilizer, and plastics. The expanding construction industry employs large numbers of workers. Steel mills and aluminum refineries are also being built. Other notable products include leather goods, clothing, and processed foods.

Agriculture. Only a fraction of Saudi Arabia's land is suitable for the cultivation of crops. Because there is a shortage of fresh water for drinking and irrigation, one of the most important industries is desalinization—the process by which seawater is transformed into drinking water and table salt.

Wheat, barley, tomatoes, melons, dates, and citrus are the most important crops. As domestic production cannot meet the needs of the growing population, most foods must be imported.

▶ MAJOR CITIES

Riyadh, the capital and largest city, has a population of about 3 million. In the older part of the city, the streets are narrow. The newer portion of Riyadh is a city of wide avenues lined with modern government buildings and royal palaces.

Jidda, Saudi Arabia's second largest city, has a population of approximately 2 million people. Located on the Red Sea, Jidda is the country's center of commerce, cultural activity, and a port of entry for millions of Muslim pilgrims and other visitors.

Mecca, the holiest site in all of Islam, is the country's third largest city, with a population approaching 1 million. For more information, see the article MECCA in Volume M.

▶ **CULTURAL HERITAGE**

Poetry and storytelling are common Arabian folk traditions. The Koran limits public performances of music and dance and prohibits artists from the making of graven images (objects of worship). However, hand-lettered Korans are produced, usually with illustrations based on complex geometric and floral designs. See the articles ARABIC LITERATURE and ISLAMIC ART AND ARCHITECTURE in the appropriate volumes.

▶ **GOVERNMENT**

Saudi Arabia is an absolute monarchy, ruled by a king according to the rules of *Sharia* (the laws of Islam). *Ulema* (Muslim religious leaders) advise the king, and ministers run the various departments, but major decisions are made by the king and his Council of Ministers. In 1992, King Fahd created a new governmental body, *Shura* (the Consultative Council), which advises the ministers and reviews laws.

▶ **HISTORY**

By the time the prophet Mohammed died in 632, most of the tribes of the Arabian Peninsula had embraced Islam. Within the next 100 years, Islam and Arab political control extended from India to Spain. But Arabia lost its place as the center of Islam. Its capital shifted first to Damascus, located in present-day Syria, and later to Baghdad, in present-day Iraq. Arabia became a subordinate province, although it remained important as the site of the holy cities.

After Mohammed's death, no ruler was able to control the entire peninsula. In the 1500's, the coastal regions acknowledged the authority of the Ottoman Turks, who had established an empire. The interior of the peninsula remained isolated and under the rule of several tribal leaders.

King Fahd ruled Saudi Arabia from 1982 until his death in 2005. His father, Ibn Saud, founded the kingdom in 1932.

The Saudis. In the 1700's, the Wahhabi movement, which sought to restore the original teachings of Islam, gained many followers. In the 1800's this movement came under the leadership of the Saudis, one of the ruling tribes of the region. As Wahhabism grew, the Saudis gained control of central and eastern Arabia. But their power diminished when the family split into rival factions. The Turks, seeing an opportunity, took over large areas of Arabia, and the Saudi leaders were forced to flee.

In 1902, Ibn Saud, one of the exiled Saudi leaders, recaptured Riyadh, the tribal seat. By 1926, Ibn Saud's power extended over almost all of the Arabian Peninsula. In 1932 the Kingdom of Saudi Arabia was proclaimed, with Ibn Saud as king.

Ibn Saud was succeeded on the throne by five of his sons: Saud (in 1953), Faisal (in 1964), Khalid (in 1975), Fahd (in 1982), and Abdullah (in 2005).

Recent History. When Iraq invaded Kuwait in 1990, neighboring Saudi Arabia became the springboard for the allied campaign in the Persian Gulf War (1991). Afterward, U.S. troops stayed in Saudi Arabia as part of Operation Desert Shield, using Saudi bases to police a "no-fly" zone in Iraq. They pulled out in April 2003 soon after Iraqi dictator Saddam Hussein was overthrown in a second war against Iraq.

In 2005, for the first time, Saudi men aged 21 or older were allowed to vote in nationwide elections to choose half the total number of municipal councilmen.

Reviewed by ALAM PAYIND
JENNIFER NICHOLS
Middle East Studies Center
The Ohio State University

SCANDINAVIA

Scandinavia is a name given to the region of northern Europe that includes the countries of Denmark, Sweden, and Norway. The name was first used by Roman geographers to describe the area between the Baltic and North seas, and it probably is related to the name of Sweden's southernmost province, which is called Skane. Originally it seems to have meant ''islands of mist or darkness.''

The Scandinavian countries are closely related in terms of their languages and culture. Because peoples from Scandinavia also settled in Finland and Iceland, these countries are often included in a larger region called *Norden,* which means simply ''the North.'' The modern languages of Denmark, Sweden, Norway, and Iceland all trace their origins to a Germanic tongue called Old Norse. The Finnish language is unrelated to the others.

▶THE LAND

Scandinavia is a region of peninsulas and islands. Sweden and Norway occupy the Scandinavian Peninsula and nearby islands.

SCANDINAVIA

The islands and peninsula of Jutland now occupied by Denmark were formed thousands of years ago by rock and soil pushed southward from the Scandinavian Peninsula by great sheets of ice.

The Nordic landscape ranges from the treeless mountains, fiords (steep-walled inlets of the sea), and plunging waterfalls of Norway to the low, rolling plains of Denmark, where tidy farms stretch as far as the eye can see. Sweden and Finland are characterized by vast forests of spruce and pine, sparkling lakes, and rushing rivers. Iceland is a land of active volcanoes, hot springs, and great glaciers.

Although Scandinavia lies as far north as Alaska, it has a much milder climate. Winters are often warmer and summers cooler than they are in the northeastern United States. This is because the warm waters of the Gulf Stream flow along the coast of Norway and steady southwesterly winds carry mild air across all of Scandinavia. Only in the highest mountains and in the northern interior—a region known as Lapland—are winters cold and snowy. North of the Arctic Circle, there is continual daylight in midsummer. In midwinter the sun never rises above the horizon. This region is sometimes called the land of the midnight sun.

▶PEOPLE AND CULTURE

Norden has about as many people as the state of California in the United States, although it covers an area about three times as large. The people generally live in cities and work in commerce, manufacturing, or service industries. Traditional activities—farming, fishing, and mining—employ fewer and fewer people. But they remain important to the economy of the region.

Small though they are, the Nordic countries have produced many great artists and scientists. In the music world we find composers such as Edvard Grieg and Jean Sibelius, as well as many famous opera stars. In literature, Hans Christian Andersen, Henrik Ibsen, and August Strindberg are some of the writers widely known beyond their national borders. Well-known scientists include botanist Carolus Linnaeus and atomic physicist Niels Bohr. Alfred Nobel was the founder of the Nobel prizes. Trygve Lie and Dag Hammarskjöld, the first two secretaries-general of the United Nations, are among the figures who have contributed to the cause of world peace. (Biographies of Grieg, Sibelius, Andersen, Ibsen, Linnaeus, Bohr, and Nobel can be found in the appropriate volumes. Biographies of Lie and Hammarskjöld can be found by consulting the Index.)

▶HISTORY

The Scandinavian peoples first appear in the pages of history shortly before the year A.D. 800, when fierce bands of Vikings swept out of their Scandinavian homeland across the North Sea to raid the coasts of Britain, Ireland, and France. Other Northmen pushed across the Baltic all the way to the Black and Caspian seas. During the Viking era, which lasted until about A.D. 1100, Scandinavian seafarers also probed into the Arctic to Spitsbergen and westward across the Atlantic to Iceland, Greenland, and even North America.

When the Viking era came to an end, the three Scandinavian kingdoms turned their attention in different directions. Denmark expanded southward into the borderlands of Germany, Norway to the west across the Atlantic, and Sweden eastward into Finland. But none of them was strong enough to keep the Hanseatic League, an organization of German commercial cities, from gaining control of the trade of northern Europe during the early Middle Ages.

In the 1300's the royal family of Norway died out. Both Norway and Iceland (which had been ruled by Norway since 1262) then came under the control of Denmark. Danish Queen Margrethe established the Kalmar Union in 1397, joining Denmark, Norway, and Sweden under a single crown. The Swedes broke out of the union in 1523 and finally pushed the Danes off the southern Swedish mainland in 1660, establishing the present boundary between the two countries. Sweden continued to expand in the Baltic region until Russia, under Peter the Great, checked the Swedish advance and then slowly began to push Sweden westward again.

Sweden lost Finland to Russia during the Napoleonic Wars. With the collapse of Napoleon's army in 1814, Sweden won control of Norway from Denmark, which had been allied with France. The Swedish king agreed to respect Norway's constitution and parliament. It seemed that war might break out between Sweden and Norway when the Norwegian parliament voted in 1905 to make Norway inde-

Norwegian fiords are a distinctive part of the landscape of Scandinavia. Fiords were carved out of the mountains by glaciers long ago.

pendent. But the two countries finally parted in peace. Finland declared its independence from Russia in 1917. Iceland was recognized as a sovereign country in 1918, but it remained linked to Denmark until 1944.

Although all of the Scandinavian countries managed to remain neutral in World War I, both Denmark and Norway were invaded and occupied by Germany during World War II. After the war, all of the Nordic countries joined the United Nations. Denmark, Iceland, and Norway also chose to become part of the North Atlantic Treaty Organization (NATO), while Sweden and Finland pursued a policy of neutrality. The Nordic countries co-operate on economic, social, and cultural matters through the Nordic Council, which was inaugurated in 1953.

Today the people of the Nordic countries enjoy some of the highest living standards in the world. Not only do they earn high incomes, but they also have excellent housing, schools, and health care facilities and generous social welfare benefits. They are proud of their long tradition of political and social democracy and rich cultural heritage.

VINCENT MALMSTROM
Dartmouth College

See also LAPLAND; SCANDINAVIAN LITERATURE; VIKINGS; and articles on individual countries.

SCANDINAVIAN LITERATURE

The earliest known literature in Scandinavia came into being during the period from A.D. 750 to 1100. This early literature was oral (handed down by word of mouth), and it was poetry. This poetry was given lasting written form in the 12th and 13th centuries.

Early Poetry, Sagas, and Ballads

The early poetry was of two kinds, skaldic and Eddic. Skaldic poetry was recited by the *skalds,* poets who wrote in a certain intricate style. Most of the poems were spoken in praise of some great warrior who was present. Other poems told of a great dead warrior's arrival in Valhalla, the hall of the slain, to feast with the warrior deities.

The other kind of early poetry is called Eddic. The term ''Edda'' was used by the historian Snorri Sturluson (1178?–1241), who wrote a book we now call the *Prose Edda.* The so-called *Poetic Edda* is a collection of ancient poems. Many of these poems are based on myths dealing with the gods, the creation of the world, and the relations between gods and mortals.

The heroic tradition is also found in a Scandinavian prose account known as the *Völsunga Saga.* The central theme is that of Sigurd the Dragonslayer and the half-divine Brynhild. Sigurd killed the dragon and set Brynhild free from her imprisonment in a circle of flame.

The word ''saga'' means ''tale'' or ''short historical account.'' The sagas are both religious and secular (worldly). They are both local and concerned with an entire kingdom.

The most famous are the family sagas that deal with Norwegian immigrants and settlers in Iceland. Based on oral traditions, they present unusually lifelike pictures in a plain, forceful style. The most famous family sagas are *The Saga of Burnt Njal, The Laxdale Saga,* and *Egil's Saga.* But more famous still is *Heimskringla: Sagas of the Norwegian Kings,* by Snorri Sturluson. It tells the story of the Norwegian dynasty from the legendary early days to the year 1177.

No complete Swedish saga, Eddic or skaldic poem, or history of kings has come down to us. In the late Middle Ages, Sweden and Finland were under one rule. The Finns produced in the *Kalevala* a great national epic, but it was not put into writing until 1835. The greatest Danish historian of the Middle Ages, Saxo Grammaticus (1150?–1220?) wrote in Latin, not Danish.

During the period from the 13th to the 16th century, the ballad and the folk dance swept over southern Scandinavia. Denmark became one of the richest sources of these ballads. In 1591, Anders Vedel published *One Hundred Ballads,* the first printed collection. Together with native religious hymns by Thomas Hansen Kingo (1634–1703) and others, they are among the finest achievements of the age.

Drama

In the 17th century the drama of France patterned itself after the classical drama of Greece and Rome. Scandinavian nobles and their courts imitated France. They spoke the French language, and they brought troupes of players from the French capital.

Denmark. Ludvig Holberg (1684–1754), a Danish historian and Latin scholar, wrote with amazing speed more than 20 comedies, doing for the western Scandinavian stage what the great dramatist Molière had done for the French stage. Many aspects of Copenhagen life were satirized in *Jeppe of the Hill* (1722) and *Erasmus Montanus* (1723).

During the first half of the 19th century, Copenhagen enjoyed a period made rich by the romantic tragedies of Adam Oehlenschläger (1779–1850). His subjects came mostly from ancient Scandinavian history and mythology. Some of the best of Oehlenschläger's plays are *Aladdin* (1805), *Aksel and Valborg* (1810), and *Kjartan and Gudrun* (1848).

Norway. When the golden age of the Danish drama passed, the younger theater of Norway came into the foreground and produced two first-rate writers, Bjørnstjerne Bjørnson (1832-1910) and Henrik Ibsen (1828–1906). Bjørnson's best dramas are his early attempts to throw a light on his country's history: *Sigurd Slembe* (1862) and *Sigurd the Crusader* (1872). They were followed by social dramas about the new business society.

Ibsen began by writing dramas on themes from folklore and history, later turning to mighty dramatic poems, such as *Brand* (1866) and *Peer Gynt* (1867). He became a master of the realistic play dealing largely with the problems of middle-class marriage, such as *A Doll's House* (1879), *Ghosts* (1881), *The Wild Duck* (1884), and *Hedda Gabler* (1890).

Sweden. The theater of Sweden came into the foreground with the brilliant works of August Strindberg (1849–1912). Following in the paths of Ibsen and Bjørnson, Strindberg began by writing historical plays but turned to dark, forceful drama in *The Father* (1887) and *Miss Julie* (1888). In the 1890's he created an original type of highly tense, personal play. Characteristic of his work are *The Dream Play* (1902) and *The Ghost Sonata* (1907).

Sweden's second great dramatist, Pär Lagerkvist (1891–1974), both followed Strindberg and broke away to new ground in plays designed to express the violence of world wars and the atomic age. Among his best-known dramas are *The Hangman* (1934) and *The Man Without a Soul* (1936).

Poetry

In the latter half of the 18th century, the Stockholm singer Carl Michael Bellman (1740–95) produced his famous tavern songs, notably those collected in *Fredman's Epistles* (1790) and *Fredman's Songs* (1791). Sweden also had three important poets in the first half of the 19th century: Esaias Tegnér (1782–1846), Erik Gustaf Geijer (1783–1847), and Per Daniel Amadeus Atterbom (1790–1855). Tegnér wrote his patriotic poem *Svea* in 1811 and the more famous *Frithiof's Saga* in 1825. Geijer composed fine patriotic poems. Atterbom wrote his best poems about nature, as did the Norwegian Henrik Wergeland (1808–45).

In Denmark, Adam Oehlenschläger was the most sensitive lyric poet during the first quarter of the 19th century. Nikolai F. S. Grundtvig (1783–1872) wrote hymns of great power. In Norway, Bjørnson was the greatest of the national songwriters of the 19th century. During the latter half of the century, Abraham Viktor Rydberg (1828–95) and Carl Snoilsky (1841–1903) in Sweden were poets of the first rank.

In the 20th century, lyric poetry has had a period of impressive blossoming. In Norway, Olaf Bull (1883–1933) and Arnulf Øverland (1889–1968) were leading poets, and Eino Leino (1878–1926) was Finland's finest lyric poet. In Sweden the names of Verner von Heidenstam (1859–1940), Erik Axel Karlfeldt (1864–1931), Gunnar Ekelöf (1907–68), and Erik Lindegren (1910–68) stand out. But the great poet Gustaf Fröding (1860–1911) looms as the genius of the time.

Prose

The Scandinavian novel first stirred a large reading public with the historical tales of the Danish writer Bernhard Severin Ingemann (1789–1862). He concentrated on the golden age of the Waldemars in Danish history. Hans Christian Andersen (1805–75) and Søren Kierkegaard (1813–55) are Denmark's world-renowned prose writers of the 19th century, Andersen with his fairy tales, Kierkegaard with his philosophical works.

In Norway the novel thrived after 1850, as did the drama of Ibsen and Bjørnson. The versatile Bjørnson wrote his peasant novels during the years 1857–72. In 1870 the popular storyteller Jonas Lie (1833–1908) published his first longer story, *The Visionary*. Lie was followed in the 1880's by novelist-playwright Alexander Kielland (1849–1906). The art of the novel continued to thrive in the 20th century. Knut Hamsun (1859–1952) published *Hunger* in 1890 and *Growth of the Soil* in 1917. Sigrid Undset (1882–1949), in the field of the historical novel, published a massive trilogy, *Kristin Lavransdatter* (1920–22). Olav Duun (1876–1939) wrote a still vaster series, about four generations of a Norwegian family, *The People of Juvik* (1918–23).

In Denmark, outstanding 20th-century poets and novelists included Henrik Pontoppidan (1857–1943), Johannes V. Jensen (1873–1950), Isak Dinesen (1885–1962), and Tom Kristensen (1893–1974).

The career of Sweden's novelist-poet Selma Lagerlöf (1858–1940) was long and distinguished, beginning with the novel *Gösta Berling* in 1891. Pär Lagerkvist has been mentioned as a dramatist and poet. He was also one of Sweden's leading novelists. A major theme of his works is the evil in the world. Among his best-known books are *The Dwarf* (1944), *Barabbas* (1950), and *Pilgrim at Sea* (1962).

THEODORE JORGENSON
Former Chairman of Scandinavian Studies
St. Olaf College (Minnesota)
Reviewed by EDWIN BONSACK
Library of Congress

See also ANDERSEN, HANS CHRISTIAN; IBSEN, HENRIK; NORSE MYTHOLOGY.

SCARLET FEVER. See DISEASES (Descriptions of Some Diseases).

SCARRY, RICHARD. See CHILDREN'S LITERATURE (Profiles).

SCHILLER, FRIEDRICH VON (1759–1805)

The dramatist, poet, and philosopher Friedrich von Schiller was a giant of German literature. His works promote the ideals of liberty and human dignity. His early writings, along with those of his contemporary Johann Goethe, were part of a key German literary movement called *Sturm und Drang* ("Storm and Stress").

Johann Christoph Friedrich von Schiller was born in Marbach, Württemberg, Germany, on November 10, 1759. His father was an officer in the army of the Duke of Württemberg, and young Schiller grew up in the service of the duke. But he disliked the strict discipline of life as a military physician and began to express his rebellious thoughts in writing.

His first play, *The Robbers* (1781), features a Robin Hood-like hero who seeks to right the wrongs of his father's court. It was an immediate success and established Schiller's reputation as a dramatist. His other plays from this period include *Intrigue and Love* (1784) and *Don Carlos* (1787).

From 1787 to 1792, Schiller devoted himself to writing historical works. He next turned to the study of philosophy. His philosophical views were expressed in essays such as *On Grace and Dignity* (1793) and in a number of poems.

Schiller's friendship with Goethe began in 1794, and the two collaborated on several works for literary journals published by Schiller. Returning to drama, Schiller wrote the three-part verse drama *Wallenstein* (1799), about the Thirty Years' War. In the last five years of his life he wrote some of his finest dramas: *Maria Stuart* (1800), about Mary, Queen of Scots; *The Maid of Orleans* (1801), about Joan of Arc; *The Bride of Messina* (1803); and *Wilhelm Tell* (1804). He died in Weimar on May 9, 1805.

Reviewed by PETER BRIGG
University of Guelph

See also GERMANY, LITERATURE OF (Goethe and Schiller); ROMANTICISM.

SCHINDLER, OSKAR (1908–1974)

During the Holocaust of World War II (1939–45), 6 million European Jews and other minorities were murdered by the leaders of Nazi Germany. Oskar Schindler, a German Catholic and industrialist, became known as one of the few who risked his life to help the persecuted. Owing to his courage, more than 1,100 Jews were spared from the Nazi death camps. They later came to be known as *Schindlerjuden* (Schindler Jews).

Oskar Schindler was born on April 28, 1908, in Zwittau, Austria-Hungary (now Svitavy, Czech Republic). In 1939, Schindler moved to Kraków, Poland, where he bought an enamelware factory from the Nazis. By this time, German-owned businesses, including his, were using Jews as slave laborers.

In Kraków, Schindler befriended high-ranking Nazi officers, and at the same time he secretly helped the Jews who worked for him. For example, his work rolls indicated that his Jewish employees were skilled blue-collar workers—but in fact they were lawyers, doctors, engineers, and even children. In 1943, when the Nazis began moving Kraków's Jews to a brutal labor camp, Schindler was allowed to set up a branch of the camp at his factory, where he saw to it that the Jews received proper food and medical care.

In October 1944, the Nazis began sending Jews to death camps. Once again Schindler acted. He compiled a list of about 1,100 names—all that he could afford in bribes—and tranported his workers to a work camp in Brünnlitz (now Brnenec, Czech Republic). In the spring of 1945, the Russian Army freed the Jews in the Brünnlitz camp. Many of the *Schindlerjuden* later went to Israel.

In 1963, Schindler was honored by the nation of Israel, where he was later buried. He died in Frankfurt, Germany, on October 9, 1974. His story became known around the world with the 1982 publication of the book *Schindler's List* by Thomas Keneally, which was made into a film by director Steven Spielberg in 1993.

THOMAS FENSCH
Editor, *Oskar Schindler and His List*

SCHLIEFFEN PLAN. See WORLD WAR I.

SCHLIEMANN, HEINRICH (1822–1890)

Heinrich Schliemann, the German archaeologist who discovered the site of the ancient city of Troy, was born in the northern German town of Neubukow on January 8, 1822. The son of a poor clergyman, he became a grocer's apprentice at 14. As a boy he was fascinated by the stories of ancient Greece, particularly Homer's epic poem the *Iliad*.

When he was 19, Schliemann was shipwrecked on his way to South America and landed in the Netherlands, where he found an office job in Amsterdam. On his own, he began to study Dutch, French, English, Spanish, Portuguese, Italian, Russian, and Greek. In 1846 he went to St. Petersburg, Russia, where he started a successful import business. He retired at age 41 to devote himself to archaeology (the study of past human life).

In 1870, Schliemann went to northeast Asia Minor (modern-day Turkey) to begin the search for the site of ancient Troy. He based his search almost entirely on clues in Homer's *Iliad* and on his own hunches. Believing the ruins of Troy lay somewhere in a mound on a plain near the Dardanelles, he began digging there with the help of some 100 workers. Schliemann discovered ancient walls and signs of a great fire. In the mound were nine cities, each one built on top of another. Schliemann was convinced that the Troy Homer described lay near the bottom; he dug through ruins of city after city. Soon he proclaimed that he had located Homer's city next to the bottom. Later excavations showed that Homer's city was actually the sixth Troy from the bottom.

Schliemann continued his excavations at Troy until the year he died, but he also did much work in Greece. Among other things, he unearthed many royal tombs at Mycenae, including what he believed was the tomb of Agamemnon. Archaeologists now know that these were the graves of people who had lived hundreds of years earlier.

When Schliemann died in Naples, Italy, on December 25, 1890, many came to honor him. Although his excavation methods were crude by today's standards, his work inspired many modern studies of ancient Greece.

DAVID C. KNIGHT
Author, science books for children

See also ARCHAEOLOGY; ILIAD; TROJAN WAR.

SCHMIDT, HELMUT (1918–)

Helmut Schmidt was chancellor (chief minister) of West Germany from 1974 to 1982. During the eight years of his chancellorship, he was one of Western Europe's most influential leaders.

Schmidt was born on December 23, 1918, in Hamburg. During World War II (1939–45), while serving as a lieutenant in the German army, he was taken prisoner at the Battle of the Bulge (1944–45). After the war, he completed his studies at the University of Hamburg.

In 1953, Schmidt, a supporter of the Social Democratic Party (SDP), was first elected to the Bundestag, West Germany's lower house of parliament. In 1969, Willy Brandt, the leader of the SDP, came to power and Schmidt was named defense minister. He was appointed finance minister in 1972. When Brandt resigned in 1974, Schmidt succeeded him as chancellor.

In the 1970's, a worldwide recession decreased the SDP's popularity. The party narrowly won the 1976 elections by forming a coalition government with members of the Free Democratic Party. In 1980, the coalition was re-elected by a larger majority.

Schmidt was widely credited with raising West Germany's influence in the world and keeping the economy reasonably strong. By the end of 1981, however, unemployment in West Germany reached its highest level in 25 years; and international tensions forced Schmidt to increase military spending while cutting the budget for social programs, which angered liberals in his own party. In October 1982, the Free Democrats withdrew from Schmidt's coalition, and he resigned following a vote of no confidence. Schmidt was succeeded as chancellor by Helmut Kohl, the leader of the Christian Democratic Union (CDU) Party. He remained a member of the Bundestag until he retired from politics in 1987.

ROBERT HALASZ
Contributor, *Current Biography*

SCHOENBERG, ARNOLD (1874–1951)

Arnold Schoenberg, a pioneer of 20th-century music, was born in Vienna, Austria, on September 13, 1874. As a boy, he learned to play the violin and the cello. When he was 18, he left school and worked as a clerk in a bank, studying music in his spare time. Deciding to make music his career, he began to compose. He admired the operas of Richard Wagner and wanted to write music like his.

In 1900 he began working on *Songs of Gurra*, a vast composition for four large choruses, solo singers, and a large orchestra. This work, based on medieval Danish history, was not finished until 1911. By that time Schoenberg wanted to write a different kind of music. He began composing strange new works, in which the notes seemed to wander wherever they pleased. Pieces written in this new style, sometimes called atonal music, are often very brief. Schoenberg's *Six Little Piano Pieces* (1911) last only about five minutes.

Next, Schoenberg began to work out rules for writing his new kind of music. He developed the "twelve-tone method" of composition. In this method every melody and harmony in a piece is drawn from a particular arrangement of twelve different notes. Schoenberg and his followers wrote many works using this technique.

In 1925, Schoenberg won a prestigious post at the Prussian Academy of Arts in Berlin, Germany. But he was dismissed by the Nazi government in 1933 because he was a Jew. He went to the United States, where he continued to teach and compose.

Among Schoenberg's works are four string quartets, a piano concerto, a violin concerto, and many orchestral pieces. He planned to finish his great opera *Moses and Aaron*, which had been left incomplete in 1932, but he did not live to compose the last act. Schoenberg died in Los Angeles on July 13, 1951.

DIKA NEWLIN
Author, *Bruckner, Mahler, Schoenberg*

SCHOOLS

Schools are places of learning, where teachers meet with students who have come for instruction in reading, writing, mathematics, science, and much more. Many schools also provide day care and health care services to the community. Elderly people learn new technology at night school. Job training is offered to adults. Cities and schools are becoming partners and sharing libraries, parks, pools, and athletic facilities.

In ancient times, when people lived by hunting and gathering, children had no need of formal schooling. But when populations increased and settlements grew, it made sense to gather all the children in one place, called a schoolhouse, and to employ experts called teachers. The first schools in the United States were set up in the 1600's by the colonists. In these private schools, the subjects were reading, writing, and religion. Children of all ages were taught together in one room.

In 1847, the Quincy Grammar School, the first graded elementary school in the United States, was built in Quincy, Massachussetts. It was a large building that was

The Country School by Winslow Homer shows a one-room schoolhouse of the 1800's. All grades were taught in the same room.

Charter school: an independent public school, often run by parents, teachers, or a community group, that operates under a special contract, or charter.

College: a school that offers education beyond secondary school. Usually colleges offer four-year programs leading to a bachelor's degree.

Community college: a junior college that serves a particular community.

Elementary school: a school that provides the first level of education, usually kindergarten through grade six.

Graduate school: a school that offers education after college, usually leading to a master's or doctor's degree.

High school: a secondary school for grades nine or ten through twelve.

Junior college: a school that offers two years of education after high school.

Junior high school: a secondary school usually for grades seven and eight.

Magnet school: a school that focuses on a specific subject, such as the performing arts, mathematics, or science.

Middle school: an intermediate school, usually for grades five through seven or eight.

Military school: a private school that teaches military organization and discipline.

Night school: classes offered at night by a college or university.

Nongraded school: a school that does away with formal grade structure, so that children proceed at their own pace.

Parochial school: a school supported by a church or religious body.

Preparatory school: a private school that prepares students for college.

Preschool or nursery school: a school that provides informal education for children below elementary school age.

Private school: a school that is not financed by the government.

Public school: in the United States and many other countries, a school operated by the local government, supported by tax money, and open to all children. In Britain, a privately funded secondary school that prepares students for university education.

Secondary school: a school that provides the second level of education, through grade twelve.

Summer school: classes held in summer so that students can make up work or speed up their education.

University: a school of higher education that offers graduate as well as bachelor's degrees. Most universities are made up of a number of colleges and professional schools.

Vocational school: a school that prepares people for skilled trades.

---

divided into twelve classrooms. One room was used for teaching each grade. For more than 100 years, most North American schools were designed in the manner of the Quincy school.

In the mid-1900's, schools began to change. Each year more and more young children go to nursery school (sometimes called preschool) before entering kindergarten or first grade. In many schools, teachers work together as a team to help students understand how many subjects play a part in solving a single problem. Most classes are made up of 20 to 30 students. Sometimes students work in small groups within their class.

Most students attend classes from September until June, but year-round schools are becoming popular. In a year-round school, students take several shorter vacations throughout the year instead of a long one during the summer.

In the United States, schools are classified as elementary and secondary. Most elementary schools have six or eight grades. Secondary schools usually consist of junior and senior high schools, each having three or four grades. Many communities now have middle schools, serving the middle years—grades five, six, seven, and eight.

Schools in Canada, Australia, New Zealand, and Scotland are organized similarly to those in the United States. In most other countries, students between the ages of 11 and 13 must decide whether they will go on to universities or into jobs requiring specific skills. They then enter either a vocational school or a school offering an intensive academic program. But comprehensive high schools offering both kinds of courses are increasingly common in Europe.

HAROLD B. GORES
President, Educational Facilities Laboratories, Inc.
Reviewed by DEBORAH MOORE
Director of Operations
Council of Educational
Facility Planners, International

See also EDUCATION; KINDERGARTEN AND NURSERY SCHOOLS; PREPARATORY SCHOOLS; UNIVERSITIES AND COLLEGES.

SCHRÖDER, GERHARD (1944–)

Gerhard Schröder was elected chancellor of Germany in 1998. He replaced Helmut Kohl, who had been chancellor of West Germany—and then a reunited Germany—for 16 years. Schröder took office as the head of a governing coalition that consisted of his own Social Democratic Party (SDP) and the smaller Green Party, Germany's environmentalist party. Political analysts described Schröder as a clever and ambitious campaigner who rose to power by moving his left-leaning party to the center.

Schröder was born on April 7, 1944, in Mossenberg, a small town in the state of Lower Saxony. His father was killed while fighting on the Russian front during World War II (1939–45). His mother worked as a cleaning woman to support her five children. Schröder left school at age 14, but later completed his university preparatory studies at night. In 1976 he earned a law degree from the University of Göttingen, where he had become president of a group of young SDP members known for their radical views.

In 1980, Schröder was elected to the Bundestag, the lower house of West Germany's parliament. In 1990, the year that West Germany and East Germany reunited, he became premier of Lower Saxony, one of Germany's largest states. He was re-elected in 1994 and 1998.

During the 1998 national campaign, Schröder promised to reduce unemployment, consider reducing taxes, and reform the welfare system. He also pledged to maintain strong relations with both the United States and the European Union (EU).

Schröder was re-elected chancellor in 2002. A key issue in this campaign was his opposition to U.S. military policy in Iraq. But in 2005, after a close election, he lost the chancellorship to Angela Merkel, leader of the conservative Christian Democratic Union Party.

ROBERT HALASZ
Contributor, *Current Biography*

SCHRÖDINGER, ERWIN. See PHYSICS, HISTORY OF (Profiles).

SCHUBERT, FRANZ (1797–1828)

Franz Schubert is one of music's most celebrated songwriters. Although he lived only 31 years, he wrote over 600 songs, nine symphonies (two are unfinished), 22 piano sonatas, and much choral and chamber music.

Franz was born in Vienna, Austria, on January 31, 1797. His father, a schoolmaster, was an amateur cellist. As a boy, Franz learned to play the piano, violin, and organ and sang in the church choir. When he was 11 he was admitted to the choir of the Court Chapel and to the training school for court singers.

Musical studies were easy for Franz. He had an uncommon talent for melody and soon began to compose. By age 17 he had written his first symphony. The great Beethoven admired his music.

In 1814, Schubert took a post as a teacher in his father's school. He continued to compose, writing his first song masterpieces, "Gretchen at the Spinning Wheel" and "The Erl King." He composed as many as 144 songs in 1815.

Schubert disliked teaching, and in 1818 he gave up his post at the school. He tried to find a post as a conductor or choirmaster but never again found a permanent position. He composed constantly, sometimes writing as many as eight songs in a day. Although Schubert sold many of his songs and piano pieces, he was usually short of money and often had to depend on the generosity of his friends. Few of his greatest compositions were publicly performed during his lifetime.

Among Schubert's most important works are the song cycles *Fair Maid of the Mill* and *The Winter Journey*. His finest symphonies are the Eighth, known as the "Unfinished" (although the Seventh Symphony is also incomplete), and his Ninth—and final—symphony, referred to as the "Great" C Major Symphony. Other outstanding works of his last years include several string quartets and piano sonatas, two piano trios, and a string quintet.

Schubert's health began to fail after he was infected with syphilis in 1822. He died on November 19, 1828.

ROBERT C. MARSH
Music Critic, *Chicago Sun-Times*

SCHULZ, CHARLES M. See MINNESOTA (Famous People).

SCHUMANN, ROBERT (1810–1856)

Robert Schumann, a great German composer, was born on June 8, 1810, at Zwickau. Although he showed great musical talent as a child, his widowed mother wanted him to study law. Robert tried this but did poorly because his mind was always on music. At age 20 he began at last to make music his career.

Schumann's first ambition was to be a concert pianist. In 1832 he developed a special device to strengthen his fingers, but it caused permanent injury to his right hand. This ruled out a concert career, and Schumann decided to turn his efforts to composing.

In Leipzig, Schumann fell in love with his music instructor's daughter, Clara Wieck (1819–96), a brilliant pianist. They wanted to marry, but Clara's father was against the match. The lovers applied to the courts, and in 1840 they were permitted to marry. Schumann expressed his joy in his compositions. In the first months after marrying Clara, he wrote over 100 songs, and shortly afterward, two of his four symphonies.

Schumann was particularly successful as a composer of short piano pieces. He gave each piece a title, and he liked to group several pieces into a suite, or set. *Carnaval*, one of Schumann's most popular works, is a suite of 21 pieces. Each paints a musical picture of characters and scenes at a masked ball.

During the later part of his life, Schumann worked as an orchestral conductor in Dresden and in Düsseldorf. Early in 1854 his health began to decline, and he suffered from imagined noises and depression. Fearful for his sanity, Schumann threw himself into the Rhine River. He was rescued and taken to a nursing home, where he died on July 29, 1856, at the age of 46.

KARL GEIRINGER
University of California (Santa Barbara)

SCHURZ FAMILY. See WISCONSIN (Famous People).

SCHWEITZER, ALBERT (1875–1965)

Dr. Albert Schweitzer had a distinguished career in several fields. He was a musician, philosopher, theologian, and medical missionary. The world remembers him best for his work among the sick in what is now Gabon, in western Africa.

Schweitzer was born in Kaysersberg, Alsace (then part of Germany), on January 14, 1875. Though not an outstanding student, he showed signs of a gentle, sensitive nature. At the age of 5 he began to study the piano, and at 9 he played the organ at church services.

As a young man, Schweitzer continued his studies in Paris, Strasbourg, and Berlin. He became an accomplished organist, an authority on the music of Johann Sebastian Bach, and a distinguished scholar in the fields of philosophy and religion. Two of his best-known books are a biography entitled *J. S. Bach* (1905) and a theological work, *The Quest of the Historical Jesus* (1906).

When Schweitzer was 30, the course of his life changed. To fit himself for what he called "the direct service of humanity," he began to study medicine. The year after he received his degree, he married Hélène Bresslau, and in 1913 the couple sailed to Africa. At Lambaréné, Schweitzer erected the first crude hospital. Within a year he and his wife had treated over 2,000 patients, many suffering from malaria, yellow fever, or leprosy.

After World War I, Schweitzer traveled throughout Europe trying to interest people in his hospital. He lectured, wrote, and gave organ recitals to raise money. In 1924 he returned to Lambaréné. He found that his hospital had suffered such neglect that he was forced to move it elsewhere.

For the rest of his life, Schweitzer remained in Africa, occasionally traveling abroad to meet with the publishers of his books and supporters of his hospital. In 1952 he was named winner of the Nobel Peace Prize. He used the prize money to improve the facilities of the hospital and set up a leper colony.

Schweitzer wrote that his philosophy was based on a deep and lasting "reverence for life." This idea influenced his entire career. He died at Lambaréné on September 4, 1965.

Reviewed by NORMAN COUSINS
Author, *Dr. Schweitzer of Lambaréné*

SCIENCE

Science is knowledge. Our word "science" comes from an old Latin word, *scientia*, which means "to know."

Everyone knows thousands of facts about the world. We know the names of plants, animals, cities, and states. It takes just a glance for some people to name the makes of cars or to recognize the faces of famous actors, musicians, and sports stars. But simply knowing facts is not science.

Knowledge becomes scientific when facts are collected and organized in a way that shows how they are related. Scientists use knowledge about these relationships to discover rules explaining how and why things happen. That knowledge is very powerful. Once we know how and why something happens, we can try to change it.

We may want to stop some things—diseases or earthquakes, for instance—from happening. In other cases, we may want things—such as airplanes and computers—to work faster. Using scientific rules, we can make predictions about diseases, computers, and other things. The predictions must be tested to see if they are right.

▶ THE SCIENTIFIC METHOD

Scientists test ideas and make new discoveries by following a set of procedures called the scientific method. The great English thinker Francis Bacon (1561–1626) gave us this important way of thinking about and solving problems. Bacon's ideas were part of a scientific revolution that occurred during the 1500's and 1600's. It led to our modern system of science. Over the centuries, other scientists added to Bacon's ideas.

Today there really is no one scientific method. Scientists in different fields use their own approaches and instruments to investigate problems. In general, however, the scientific method involves: 1) recognizing and stating the problem that needs to be studied; 2) gathering and organizing facts about the problem; 3) using logic to form an idea about the problem; 4) conducting experiments to test the idea; 5) using information, or data, from the experiments to draw conclusions.

In following the scientific method, researchers use facts to make **predictions**. A fact is something we know to be true from experience or observation. It is a fact that a rubber ball dropped from a window will bounce. A prediction is based on many observations of facts. Observe many times how a ball bounces, and you can predict how it will bounce when dropped again.

This article provides an overview of why science is different from other types of knowledge, how scientists make discoveries, what kinds of research scientists conduct, and how scientists communicate the results of their research. It also outlines the major milestones in science over the past 4,500 years. And it discusses the scientific challenges that lie ahead. A Wonder Question on pseudoscience explores some common mistakes in scientific reasoning.

Histories of specific fields are covered in the articles ASTRONOMY; BIOLOGY; CHEMISTRY, HISTORY OF; GEOLOGY; MATHEMATICS, HISTORY OF; MEDICINE; and PHYSICS, HISTORY OF. Advances in the applications of science are covered in such articles as ENGINEERING; INVENTIONS; and TECHNOLOGY.

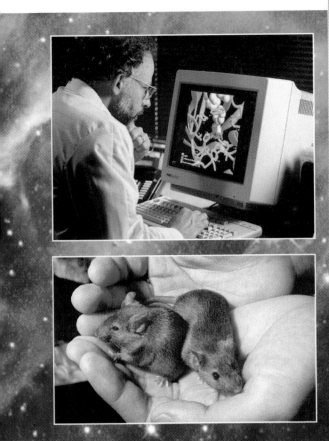

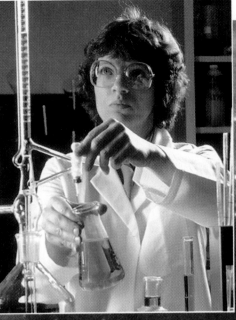

Scientists use many approaches to discover how and why things happen. *Background:* Astronomers use telescopes to study distant objects, such as the Tarantula Nebula. *Opposite page:* Physicists often use huge instruments, such as the underground Sudbury Neutrino Observatory in Canada, to study matter and energy. *This page:* Researchers in biology, chemistry, and medicine test theories by studying animals such as these cloned mice, using computers to simulate the behavior of molecules, and performing chemical reactions in the lab.

Eventually, scientists may develop a **hypothesis**, a guess or possible explanation for something. Suppose you observe 100 times that a ball dropped from 10 feet bounces 3 feet. Then you may decide that dropping it from 20 feet will result in a 6-foot-high bounce. At this point, you must carry out an experiment to test the hypothesis.

After a hypothesis is tested under many different conditions, researchers may develop a **theory**, or general rule. Dropping different balls from various heights may lead to a rule that explains how different balls bounce. The theory could also predict how balls made from new materials would bounce.

Some familiar theories include Isaac Newton's theory of gravity, Charles Darwin's theory of natural selection, and Albert Einstein's theory of relativity. Theories take a great deal of time and effort to develop and become accepted. Toppling an accepted theory, and replacing it with a new theory, can be difficult. Scientists demand a lot of evidence to accept that a new theory explains the world better than an existing theory does.

Scientific research also involves creativity, inspiration, and sometimes lucky accidents. For example, the non-stick material known as Teflon was discovered when scientists found a strange lump of material inside a gas cylinder. Researchers made the discovery, and worked backward to find out how it occurred. They then found many uses for Teflon as a coating for pots and other products.

During the entire process, scientists must remain objective, interested in facts obtained only through experimentation. Scientists must avoid letting personal beliefs, wishes, and opinions influence their research.

▶ WHAT SCIENTISTS DO

Scientists work in different subject areas, or branches. Two main branches of science are the physical sciences and the life sciences.

The **physical sciences** involve research on the structure and properties of nonliving things. These may range from the invisible particles that make up atoms to huge masses of stars called galaxies.

Astronomy, chemistry, geology, meteorology, and physics are among the physical sciences. Astronomy is the study of planets, stars, comets, and other objects in the universe. Chemistry deals with the composition, structure, and properties of substances, and changes that occur in substances. Geology is the study of rocks, minerals, fossils, and Earth's composition and history. Meteorology is the study of how changes in Earth's atmosphere produce weather. Physics focuses on matter and energy. Matter is the material that makes up everything in the universe, while energy is what makes matter change and move.

The **life sciences**, or biological sciences, involve the study of living things. Two main branches of the life sciences are botany and zoology. Botany is the study of plants. Zoology is the study of animals.

Several of the life sciences are called biomedical sciences because they are used in medicine. These include anatomy, cell biology, physiology, genetics, molecular biology, and biochemistry. Anatomy is the study of the structure of living things. Cell biology concerns the structure and function of cells.

Physiology deals with how living things function. Genetics focuses on how biological instructions called genes determine the traits of living things. Molecular biology is the study of proteins and other big molecules that are important in health and disease. Biochemistry is the study of chemical processes that occur inside living things.

Distinct boundaries once separated scientific branches, or disciplines. In modern science, however, research in one field often overlaps another. This has created new **interdisciplinary fields**, which use tools and ideas from two or more sciences. Biochemistry combines biology and chemistry. Biophysics combines biology and physics. Molecular biology involves genetics, cell biology, and biochemistry. Many important discoveries now occur in interdisciplinary fields.

Modern science is changing in other ways, as well. Most research today is done by teams, not individual scientists working alone in a laboratory. Teams are often **multidisciplinary**, with experts from several fields combining their knowledge and skills. Each works on different parts of a problem. Then they share their findings. Science is also more international now. Men and women from different countries work together, or collaborate, on research.

Kinds of Research

Experimental science involves discovering new knowledge by doing tests to see if a hypothesis is true. In an experiment, scientists carry out a series of steps, almost like a recipe. Scientists design and conduct experiments very carefully, making sure that observations and measurements are as accurate as possible.

Many medical experiments are called **clinical trials**. For example, in deciding whether a new drug is better than an old drug, physicians might compare the results of each medicine on separate groups of patients in a clinic or hospital. In a clinical trial, both groups must be as similar as possible. They must be of the same age and health, for instance. If one group were older or sicker, they might respond to a drug differently. That difference could lead to false results.

In order to avoid false results, experimental scientists reduce the chances for errors in several ways. They may repeat an experiment several times. Scientists also encourage other researchers to repeat the experiment. To be meaningful, or valid, an experiment must be repeatable. Any scientist who does the experiment in the same way should get the same results. Scientists use statistics to decide whether findings are valid.

Scientists also make discoveries with theoretical and observational research. **Theoretical research** involves thinking about a problem. Einstein developed the theory of relativity in this way. He worked it out in his mind, without doing experiments. Modern theoretical scientists usually add to their brainpower by using computers. Computers can model, or portray, a problem and show how it changes under different conditions.

Observational research is probably the oldest kind of science. It involves observing events in the natural world and drawing conclusions. Darwin developed his theory of natural selection, which describes how species evolve, by observing similarities among plants and animals in different parts of the world.

Many modern scientists still work this way, by collecting and analyzing data. Astronomers, for instance, discover the nature of planets, stars, and other celestial objects by observing light and other forms of radiation that the objects emit. Geologists gather data about the composition of ancient rocks. Many new discoveries in genetics come from observations about the location, structure, and function of genes.

Research can also be basic or applied. Basic research tries to uncover new knowledge that has no immediate practical use. Applied research seeks knowledge that can be used to create new products or in other practical ways.

Communicating Science

New discoveries join the body of scientific knowledge when they are published in scientific journals. Scientists make other researchers aware of their discoveries by writing reports, or manuscripts, for journals.

A manuscript tells why a scientist's research is important, outlines the methods used to make the discovery, and describes the findings. It also explains what the findings mean and how they add to what scientists already know. Scientists send manuscripts to the editors of a journal. The editors then send the manuscripts out for **peer review**: Several peers, or experts in the same field, are asked for opinions on whether the research is good enough to be published.

There are thousands of journals. Most are highly specialized. Scientists working in one

WONDER QUESTION

What is pseudoscience?

All too often, people reach false conclusions about the world because of mistakes, or fallacies, in scientific reasoning. Then real science becomes pseudoscience. "Pseudo" means false, deceptive, or fake. One common fallacy involves seeing links between things that actually are not related. Suppose your friend observes that more people get heat stroke on hot summer days. He also observes that more people eat ice cream on these days. So he concludes that ice cream causes heat stroke. Pseudoscience also creeps in when we mistake anecdotal evidence for objective evidence. Anecdotal evidence is "they say" evidence: "They say wearing a copper bracelet cures arthritis." "They say that reading in dim light ruins the eyes." Just because people say or believe something does not mean it is scientific fact. It takes objective experimentation to reach valid conclusions about the world.

field may not understand a journal published in another. A few are general journals, which print very important discoveries from all fields of science. Two of the most popular are *Science* and *Nature*.

In the late 20th century, scientists began publishing their findings in so-called online journals on the Internet computer network. Online journals can be published much faster than paper journals can. Rapid publication of research findings is important. Without publication, nobody would know about a discovery. The faster that news of a discovery spreads, the faster other scientists can use the knowledge in their own research.

Communicating scientific discoveries to the public also is important. It makes people aware of findings that can affect their own lives. Such knowledge helps citizens make more informed decisions when they vote on issues that involve science. Specialized writers and broadcasters called science journalists translate complex discoveries into language that everybody can understand. Many have college degrees in both science and journalism.

▶ **MODERN SCIENCE**

The roots of science can be traced back some 4,500 years ago, to ancient Egypt and Babylonia. These civilizations gave us our first systems of measuring quantities such as time and distance, as well as our first understandings of both

MILESTONES IN SCIENCE FROM ANCIENT TO MODERN TIMES

Science in Ancient Babylonia and Egypt (2500 to 500 B.C.)

Scientifically, the most advanced of the earliest civilizations were those of the Babylonians (who lived in what is now Iraq) and the Egyptians.

As early as 2500 B.C., the Babylonians had established standards for length, weight, and volume. The Babylonians also closely observed the change of seasons, as well as the movements of the sun, the moon, the stars, and the planets. These observations, which led to a method of measuring months and years, were the beginning of astronomy.

In addition to being great builders of pyramids, the ancient Egyptians were also advanced in medicine. Egyptian texts dating back to 2000 B.C. mention many medicines and describe basic **anatomy** (the structure of the human body) and **physiology** (the functions of the body).

Science in Ancient Greece and Alexandria (500 B.C. to A.D. 500)

Thales of Miletus (640?–546? B.C.) was one of the earliest Greek philosophers who tried to explain the world around him. His thinking led him to conclude that natural causes, not mythical forces, explained natural phenomena.

Although most Greek philosophers believed that all matter was made of four elements (earth, air, fire, and water), a different theory was suggested by Democritus (460?–370? B.C.). He believed that everything was composed of **atoms**— tiny particles that could not be divided into anything smaller.

Aristotle and Plato

The physician Hippocrates (460?–377? B.C.) and his followers were concerned with curing disease and understanding how it is caused. They speculated that the body contains four **humors**, or fluids. When a patient was ill, they believed, the humors needed to be brought back into balance.

For the philosopher Plato (427?–347? B.C.), the universe was fundamentally mathematical. He formed his ideas about nature by using logic, not observation, to make deductions. For example, the Greeks considered the sphere and circle to be perfect forms. Therefore, Plato said, the universe must be a sphere, and all natural motion must be circular.

An early Egyptian physician

celestial bodies and the human body. (You can read more about major scientific achievements throughout history in the accompanying feature, Milestones in Science from Ancient to Modern Times.)

However, most of what we know about the natural world and how it works has been learned in only the last hundred years or so. In fact, many of the greatest advances in modern science have occurred in just the latter half of the 20th century.

Physics

In recent decades, researchers in physics have moved toward their greatest goal—a **Grand Unification Theory** (GUT) to explain how everything in the universe works. Physi-cists recognize four forces, or kinds of interaction, between objects. These are gravity, the electromagnetic force, the strong nuclear force (which holds the centers, or nuclei, of atoms together), and the weak nuclear force (which causes subatomic particles to break down, or decay). Many physicists believe that these are parts of a single yet-to-be-discovered force.

By the 1970's, GUT researchers had shown that the electromagnetic force and the weak nuclear force were part of an underlying electroweak force. In the 1980's and 1990's, researchers developed new mathematical models that would also include the strong nuclear force. The final step would be to make gravity a part of this unified force.

One of Plato's students was the great philospher Aristotle (384–322 B.C.). Like Plato, Aristotle believed that the heavenly bodies move in perfect circles. But unlike Plato, Aristotle eventually used direct observation to find the causes of natural phenomena. For example, he carefully observed hundreds of plants and animals, and he developed a system of classifying them that was used for more than 2,000 years.

In the 300's B.C., the Greek city of Alexandria in Egypt was a center of learning. Here, Archimedes (287?–212 B.C.) combined proof by deduction and an experimental approach to nature. And Aristarchus (310?–230? B.C.) first proposed that Earth moved around the sun.

Greek science faded with the decline of ancient Greek civilization. It was not picked up anew until many centuries later.

Science in the Muslim World and Middle Ages (500 to 1500)

In the early centuries after the birth of Christ, Greek scientific thought was kept alive by Christians and later by Muslims in the Middle and Near East. Greek texts were translated into Arabic, the common language of Muslims. Knowledge of science spread through the Muslim world, which reached from Spain to central Asia in the 700's. Muslims also introduced the Hindu-Arabic numeral system and the technique of dealing with unknown quantities, called **algebra**.

The Crusades—wars waged by the Christians against the Muslims—brought Europeans into close contact with Muslim learning. Also during the Middle Ages, Chinese inventions such as gunpowder and papermaking were introduced into Europe.

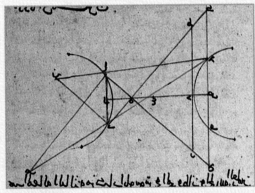

An ancient Muslim manuscript on optics

As trade between countries grew, so did the spread of ideas. Universities sprang up in England, France, and Italy.

Some medieval scientists, such as Roger Bacon in England (1214?–92?), stressed the importance of conducting experiments to prove scientific facts. However, it was difficult for scientists to disagree openly

Among many other advances were the development of "atom smashers." These machines allow scientists to break atoms apart and study subatomic particles. This knowledge has contributed to exciting new theories about how the universe formed 10 to 15 billion years ago, in an event known as the **Big Bang**.

Astronomy

In astronomy, a revolution occurred with the launching of robotic **space probes**—spacecraft having no human crews but equipped with cameras and other imaging devices. These probes have helped astronomers gain new knowledge about the composition of other planets in the solar system. A new generation of telescopes has allowed astronomers to look deeper into the universe and learn about events such as the birth of stars. Some of this new knowledge has come from more powerful land-based telescopes. More knowledge has come from Earth-orbiting instruments, such as the Hubble Space Telescope, which have much clearer views of space above Earth's atmosphere.

One of the most surprising discoveries made using telescopes in recent years has been the first evidence that planets orbit other stars. Future space telescopes may even allow astronomers to tell whether conditions on such extrasolar planets (those beyond our own solar system) are suitable for life.

An illustration from *Fabrica*

with the established views of Aristotle, which were shared by the Catholic Church.

The Renaissance and the Scientific Revolution (1500 to 1700)

By the middle of the 1500's, navigators had sailed around the world. The invention of the printing press increased the spread of knowledge. Ancient manuscripts were brought back to light. During this period, called the Renaissance (a French word meaning "rebirth"), new approaches to science were introduced.

The Belgian anatomist Andreas Vesalius (1514–64) challenged ancient Greek theories of the body. Vesalius believed in conducting his own studies of the body directly. His book, *Fabrica*, or *The Fabric of the Human Body* (1543), included detailed anatomical drawings.

During the 1600's, the movement to study science by observation and experimentation became a complete scientific revolution. The writings of English statesman and philosopher Francis Bacon (1561–1626) outlined the new scientific method.

The Italian Galileo Galilei (1564–1642) applied a mathematical and experimental approach to the study of motion. He showed how to calculate the path of an object shot from a cannon and how both light and heavy objects fall through the same distance at the same rate.

Galileo Galilei

Using the recently invented telescope, Galileo first observed the planet Jupiter's moons. This and other observations led him to support the theory (put forward earlier by Polish astronomer Nicolaus Copernicus) that Earth and the other planets move around the sun.

Also during this time, German astronomer Johannes Kepler (1571–1630) proved that all planets orbit the sun in elliptical (oblong) paths instead of circles.

In England, William Harvey (1578–1657) introduced the experimental method to biology. Harvey showed that the heart acts

Francis Bacon

Earth Science

Another revolution occurred in the Earth sciences with the emergence of the theory of **plate tectonics**. Plates are huge slabs of rocks. The word "tectonics" means "to build." According to this theory, Earth's surface is built from about a dozen huge plates that constantly move relative to each other, floating on molten material below. Plate tectonics has explained how today's continents formed from a single supercontinent that broke up 225 million years ago. It has also offered better explanations for why earthquakes occur.

Earth scientists have also discovered that certain chemicals, including those once used in aerosol sprays, can destroy the atmosphere's **ozone layer**. This blanket of gas protects living things from the sun's harmful ultraviolet rays. As a result of the discovery, the world's nations agreed to ban most uses of the harmful chemicals.

Research on Earth's climate has recently raised concern about **global warming**. Carbon dioxide and certain other gases in the atmosphere trap heat near Earth, just as glass traps the sun's heat in a greenhouse. This so-called greenhouse effect keeps Earth warm enough to support life. However, too much carbon dioxide, released from the burning of fuels, has increased this effect in the past century or so. Scientists predict that global

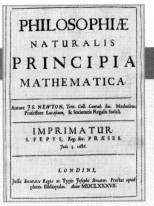

Isaac Newton's *Principia* laid the foundations of physics.

as a pump to keep the blood circulating through a system of arteries and veins.

In Holland, Anton van Leeuwenhoek (1632–1723) invented a single-lens microscope that let him observe tiny forms of life in drops of water. Using an improved compound microscope (with more than one lens), the Englishman Robert Hooke (1635–1703) later discovered that plants are made up of tiny structures, which he called **cells**.

Perhaps the greatest scientist during this time was Isaac Newton of England (1642–1727). In optics, Newton used a prism to show that white light is made up of rays of many colors. In his great work—called the *Principia*, or *Mathematical Principles of Natural Philosophy*—Newton used mathematics to show that the same laws of physics govern the motion of bodies both in the heavens and on Earth. Newton's work helped lay the foundations of physics.

To help spread the new knowledge of the scientific revolution, scientific societies were organized. These included the Academy of the Lynx in Rome, the Royal Academy of Sciences in Paris, and the Royal Society of London. Members of these groups shared ideas by publishing papers and holding meetings to discuss their experiments.

Rise of Experimental Science (1700 to 1800)

The 1700's were mainly a period of experimentation. New scientific instruments were developed and older ones improved. The balance (for weighing objects), the air pump, and many new electrical machines found much use during this time.

Joseph Black of Scotland (1728–99) conducted experiments to measure the flow of heat. He found that different materials absorbed different amounts of heat. He also discovered that heat can be "hidden," or absorbed within a substance, as it changes from a liquid to a gas.

Great advances were also made in understanding electricity. Experimenters discovered that electricity could be conducted, or carried, by certain substances, which they called **conductors**. In his famous kite experiment, the American statesman and scientist Benjamin Franklin (1706–90) showed that lightning was a form of electricity.

In Italy, Luigi Galvani (1737–98) noticed that when he touched a frog's leg muscle with pieces of brass and iron, the muscle

warming could disrupt agriculture, raise ocean levels, and have other harmful effects.

Chemistry

One breakthrough in chemistry was a better method of making, or synthesizing, new compounds. This method is called **combinatorial chemistry**. In the past, chemists trying to find new drugs might synthesize a few compounds in a week. With combinatorial chemistry, a single chemist can make thousands of compounds in the same time. Chemists have also developed automated ways of checking, or screening, big batches of compounds to tell which ones have promise as drugs.

In recent years, chemists have developed **nanotechnology**, which involves making ultra-small devices and other structures. They are about a nanometer, one billionth of a meter, in length—roughly the size of ten atoms placed end to end. Researchers hope to use nanotechnology to make miniature pumps that could be implanted in patients to deliver medicines, for example, and to make tiny electronic devices for faster computers.

Biology

Begun in 1990, the **Human Genome Project** (HGP) has revolutionized biology. A genome is the complete set of genes in any organism. The Human Genome Project's goal is to identify all 20,000 to 25,000 genes that

Antoine Lavoisier

Louis Pasteur

twitched. Another Italian scientist, Alessandro Volta (1745–1827), explained that a flow of electricity, or **electric current**, caused the twitch. Volta later constructed the first electric battery.

Also during the 1700's, the English chemist Joseph Priestley (1733–1804) discovered oxygen. The French chemist Antoine Lavoisier (1743–94) later proved that when substances burn, they combine with oxygen. Lavoisier outlined a whole new system of chemistry, in which elements are the basis of all chemical combinations.

Advances in Biology, Chemistry, and Physics (1800 to 1900)

Better microscopes enabled biologists to learn more about the structure and function of cells. For example, they found that most plant and animal cells contain a smaller body called a nucleus, and that all new cells are formed by the division of existing cells.

In the 1850's, French scientist Louis Pasteur (1822–95) disproved the theory that living things spring from nonliving things, such as air and soil. Pasteur showed that many diseases are caused by **microorganisms**, or germs. His discovery brought about antiseptic (germ-free) practices, which sharply cut down infections in hospitals.

Scientists also began thinking about **evolution**—how living things arise, or evolve, from simpler forms of life. In his studies of plants and animals, the English naturalist Charles Darwin (1809–82) observed that slight differences exist among organisms of any one kind, or species. According to Darwin's theory of **natural selection**, organisms with traits that help them survive will produce more offspring than those with unfavorable traits. The favorable traits will be passed on to more offspring, becoming more common in the general population. Over many generations, the organisms may become different enough to be considered a new species.

In the mid-1800's, the Austrian monk Gregor Mendel (1822–84) discovered the laws of **heredity**. Mendel's laws explained how physical features were handed down, or inherited, from parents to offspring. His work was forgotten for many years, but it paved the way for genetics.

In chemistry, experimenters learned more about how chemical elements combine. The

make up every human being. In addition to finding the chemical structures of these genes, HGP researchers have developed new computerized ways of using this information in medicine.

This project was made possible because of key advances in genetics. These include the development of new tools for detecting, decoding, and copying genes, as well as transferring them from one organism to another.

Scientists in industry have used such tools in **biotechnology**, which involves making biological products that are of practical use to humans. Biotechnology has led to genetically engineered medicines, food crops, and farm animals. These include livestock that are **clones**, or genetic copies, of one animal.

Cloning has allowed scientists to quickly produce large numbers of animals with desirable traits, such as the ability to produce more meat and milk.

Advances in genetics have also led to the discovery of human genes involved in birth defects, hereditary diseases, and more common conditions such as cancer, obesity, and heart disease. In the 1990's, a whole new field of medicine, called **gene therapy**, was born. Using gene therapy, doctors can treat disease by replacing abnormal genes with normal copies.

Medicine

Other medical advances include the invention of new diagnostic tools such as

English chemist John Dalton (1766–1844) revived Democritus' theory that all matter is made of atoms. Dalton believed that atoms from the same element are alike, but they differ from atoms of other elements in size, weight, and how they combine.

In the mid-1800's, the Russian chemist Dmitri Mendeleev (1834–1907) arranged all the known elements in a chart by the weights of their atoms. Elements having similar characteristics were placed in the same column. Soon, gaps in his chart were filled with the discovery of new elements. Mendeleev's chart served as the basis of our modern periodic table of the elements.

In physics, the English scientist Michael Faraday (1791–1867) discovered a way of producing an electric current in a coil of wire using a magnet. Faraday also proposed the theory of **fields of force**, which accounted for action that took place at a distance, such as magnetic attraction and repulsion.

Charles Darwin

Later, fellow English scientist James Clerk Maxwell (1831–79) developed Faraday's ideas into the theory of **electromagnetic waves**, such as light. The differences between electromagnetic waves are in their wavelengths.

In 1898, the French scientist Marie Curie (1867–1934) and her husband Pierre Curie (1859–1906) discovered two new elements, radium and polonium. Like uranium, these elements were found to give off radiant energy, or **radiation**. They called this phenomenon **radioactivity**.

Marie Curie

Science in the Early and Mid-20th Century

In 1900, the German physicist Max Planck (1858–1947) proposed the **quantum theory** of energy. This theory states that energy is radiated and absorbed in tiny bundles called quanta. The German-Swiss physicist Albert Einstein (1879–1955) later verified Planck's theory when he proved that light travels as quanta, or photons.

In his **theory of relativity**, Einstein showed how space, time, matter, and energy are all related, and how masses distort space and time to produce gravity. His theory helped astronomers learn much about stars and the energy they emit. And it predicted that matter could be converted into energy. Scientists used this knowledge to make the first atomic bombs and nuclear reactors.

computed tomography (CT), magnetic resonance imaging (MRI), and positron emission tomography (PET) scanners. These devices let doctors diagnose diseases with much greater accuracy.

Medical scientists have also developed powerful new drugs to treat cancer and heart disease. They have shown that people can reduce their risks of these conditions with better diets and lifestyles. Drugs to control the body's rejection of transplanted organs have greatly improved the success of kidney, heart, liver, and other organ transplants.

Computer Science

Computers and the Internet have given science a big boost. Powerful, inexpensive computers allow scientists to complete research faster and tackle complex problems that would have been impossible to solve before. The Internet has helped make research findings available sooner, and it has given scientists access to vast collections, or databases, of information. Much genetics research has been done by analyzing database information about genes.

▶ CHALLENGES FOR THE 21ST CENTURY

The rapid pace of scientific progress promises more benefits for humanity. Tomorrow's science has the potential to help people live longer, healthier, happier lives. People will have a deeper understanding of nature and greater control over it.

In astronomy, the American Edwin Hubble (1889–1953) showed that other galaxies existed beyond our own. He later observed that distant objects are moving away rapidly, suggesting that the universe is expanding. This finding supported the **Big Bang theory**, which states that the universe began billions of years ago with a giant explosion.

Chemistry also made great strides, especially in the development of new materials that do not exist in nature. The most important of these artificial, or synthetic, materials were **plastics**. These could be molded easily into various products, from bottles to automobile parts, or spun into new fabrics such as nylon.

A new science, called solid state physics, gave rise to two important technologies: the **transistor** and the **laser**. Invented in 1947, the transistor was made with materials called semiconductors. Since they could easily amplify and switch electronic signals, transistors found many uses in devices ranging from portable radios to computers. In 1960, the first optical laser was invented, using a ruby crystal that produced an intense beam of light. Lasers would later find many applications in electronics, medicine, and other fields.

In biology, one of the most important breakthroughs came in 1953, when James Watson of the United States (1928–) and Francis Crick of England (1916–2004) discovered the structure of the "molecule of life": **deoxyribonucleic acid**, or **DNA**. They showed that DNA is shaped like a double helix, or twisting ladder. The rungs of this ladder are pairs of compounds that spell out **genes**, the instructions in cells that determine how organisms look and function.

Much progress was also made in the study of humanity's origins. In the 1930's, in Tanzania, Kenyan-born Louis Leakey (1903–72) and his English wife Mary Leakey (1913–96) began unearthing the bones of extinct humanlike creatures. The findings suggested that humans descended from a common ancestor in Africa several million years ago.

New insights were also made about humanity's closest living relatives, the great apes. In the 1960's, English researcher Jane

Albert Einstein

A mushroom cloud rises from an atomic bomb test.

At the same time, serious concerns remain about modern science. Some experts worry that scientific advances can be used for evil as well as good. For example, knowledge of genetic engineering could be used to create terrible biological weapons, just as 20th-century advances in physics led to nuclear weapons. Or it could lead to the release of undesirable forms of genetically engineered organisms into the environment.

Experts also worry about scientific and mathematical literacy—the public's ability to understand scientific progress. Many elementary school and high school students have never learned basic scientific concepts. Likewise, many adults lack the knowledge necessary to be effective citizens in a society where science is so important. These realities point to the need for improved science education for everyone in the 21st century.

Big challenges lie ahead for tomorrow's scientists. These include conquering disease, finding new sources of energy, coping with environmental problems such as global warming, feeding the world's growing population in poor countries, and developing computers with the ability to think and reason as humans do.

MICHAEL WOODS
Science Editor, Washington Bureau
Pittsburgh Post Gazette and *Toledo Blade*

SCIENCE ACTIVITIES. See EXPERIMENTS AND OTHER SCIENCE ACTIVITIES; SCIENCE FAIRS.

Mary Leakey

Goodall (1934–) began her study of wild chimpanzees in Tanzania, while American researcher Dian Fossey (1932–85) focused on the mountain gorillas of Rwanda. Their observations uncovered the many humanlike aspects of apes.

Studies such as these also raised awareness about the threats faced by many species as a result of human activities, such as the destruction of forests. In 1962, the American naturalist Rachel Carson (1907–64) brought attention to another threat—pollution. In her book *Silent Spring*, Carson detailed the dangerous effects of pesticides on wildlife. Such work helped launch the modern environmental movement.

Jane Goodall and chimp

In medicine, perhaps the greatest achievements of the 20th century were **antibiotics** and **vaccines** to combat diseases caused by germs. The antibiotic penicillin, discovered in 1928 by Scottish scientist Alexander Fleming (1881–1955), saved people from infections that had once killed millions. In 1953, Jonas Salk (1914–95) developed a vaccine to protect people against the crippling disease polio.

In the early 1900's, important advances were made in understanding the human mind. Sigmund Freud of Austria (1856–1939) suggested that physical illnesses can sometimes have mental causes. He introduced a technique called **psychoanalysis** to help people deal with troubling memories. In Switzerland, Carl Jung (1875–1961) described different personality types that are common to many people. And he proposed that thoughts and feelings shared by all people influence the unconscious mind.

Scientists also began understanding the body's natural defenses, or **immune system**. Such knowledge enabled doctors to perform blood transfusions (in which blood is given to those undergoing surgery, for example) and later made organ transplants possible.

(You can learn about more recent scientific advances in this article's section on modern science, which begins on page 68.)

SCIENCE FAIRS

Have you ever wondered what type of soap is best for killing bacteria, which materials are the best insulators, or how different pesticides affect tomato plants? If you wonder about interesting questions such as these, you may be well on your way to designing an excellent project for a science fair.

Science fairs are events that allow students to present their own scientific research to teachers, scientists, and the general public, as

At science fairs, students can share their discoveries and make new friends. Participants create exhibits that explain the results of their research.

well as to make new friends who share similar science interests. These activities give students a chance to improve their research and communication skills while having fun.

Planning a Project. The key to preparing a good science project is selecting an interesting topic. Be curious—pose questions about the world around you. Ask yourself, "Do I care about the answers to these questions?" If you say yes, that means other people will probably be interested in what you discover.

To help find ideas for an interesting topic, visit a library, where you can browse science magazines and books and search for information using computer networks such as the Internet. Find out what scientists already know about the topic, and what they have yet to discover. Talk to other young people, teach-

ers, and scientists. If possible, join science clubs at your school or local museum. You may want to work on your project individually or with a team of other students.

After choosing a topic, think of some specific questions that you would like to try to answer. Keep in mind that your project should be unique—that is, it should not repeat what someone else has already done. Try to build upon the research that you read about by asking your own questions.

Before starting your project, it may be helpful to find a **mentor**—a teacher, scientist, or experienced student who can give you useful advice. This person can help you out when you are stuck and need some guidance. Your mentor should carefully go over the rules of the science fair with you before you begin.

Conducting an Experiment. A good science fair project follows the **scientific method**, a process that scientists use to gain knowledge through the results of experiments. The first step in this process is forming a **hypothesis**, an educated prediction about what you think will be the answer to a question. To figure out what kind of experiment you could carry out to test your hypothesis, you will probably have to do some more research. Find out how others have performed similar experiments and why they were successful or unsuccessful. This will give you valuable clues about designing your own experiment.

Next, write a list of the materials and apparatus (equipment) that you will need to carry out the experiment. Also, describe how to conduct the experiment by writing a **procedure**, a clear set of instructions. Before beginning, go over the materials and procedure with your mentor. Also, check with your mentor to make sure that the materials you need are not dangerous and that the experiment you plan to carry out will be done safely.

When you perform your experiment, keep careful records of your **observations**—what you see and measure—in a lab notebook. Take precise measurements using reliable rulers, stopwatches, and other instruments you may need. Document both expected and unexpected results. Usually, you will need to repeat your experiment a number of times in order to be sure of your results, which may be somewhat different each time. These differences can tell you how accurate your results are. They can also reveal possible sources of error in your experimental set-up.

Once you have enough results, you may begin your **analysis**—organizing your observations and measurements in ways that will let you see trends or patterns. You may wish to make graphs of your measurements, so

CHECKLIST AND TIPS FOR A SUCCESSFUL EXHIBIT

Before you begin to work on your exhibit, you should have certain information about the science fair and the types of exhibits it will include. The following checklist will be helpful:

✓ Where and when will the science fair be held? In what size and type of room will the exhibits be shown? At what times and on what days are you permitted in the room?

✓ How much space will you be allowed for your exhibit? Will you have a table on which you can place things? Where can you set up posters and signs?

✓ How will you get your exhibit to the science fair? Will you have anyone to help you carry and set up your exhibit? Will you have someone to help you watch your exhibit to prevent damage?

✓ What safety regulations must you follow? Are you permitted to use 110-volt electricity? What kinds of chemicals may you use? Are living things allowed to be part of your exhibit? If so, what kinds may you have, and how must you care for them?

Your exhibit should be eye-catching, and it should explain itself. Here are some tips to help you accomplish these goals:

✓ If you will have a table, you might make a large poster by fastening three sheets of poster board together with strong plastic tape, forming hinges. Such a poster can stand upright on the table, in front of which other parts of your display can be set. If you will not have a table, you can mount your poster and any light objects that can be fastened to it on a wall or standing bulletin board.

✓ Choose easy-to-read colors and sizes of type for your display. You might have the title in one color and large letters, the headings in a different color and medium-sized letters, and text under the headings in a third color and smaller letters. All text should be printed neatly and large enough so that visitors can read it from a distance of up to a yard (roughly a meter).

✓ Make the title, headings, and other text as brief as you can. Remember that visitors might not stay at your exhibit very long, so they should be able to understand the story of your project quickly. Do not try to cram too much into the exhibit—it will look cluttered, and the most important aspect of your project might not be clear.

✓ Models, photographs, drawings, and graphs attract attention. They may also give visitors a clearer understanding of your activity. If possible, display some of the actual equipment and materials you used in your project. You might want to show the activity actually taking place. Visitors always enjoy taking part in the activity themselves.

✓ What you yourself do during the science fair can be very important in attracting attention to your exhibit. You should be obviously interested in your project and in the entire science fair. You should offer to answer any questions that visitors might want to ask.

that you can see mathematical relationships between variables such as distance, volume, and time. Again, your mentor can serve as a helpful guide, offering suggestions that might clarify your results.

From the results and analysis of your experiment, you will be able to make appropriate **conclusions**. Your conclusions should state whether your experiment supported or disproved your hypothesis. You should also point out any errors that may have affected your results. This information is important for others who may try to improve upon your experiment in the future.

Communicating Your Findings. When professional scientists discover something new, they share their findings by publishing them in journals and discussing them at conferences. Science fairs give young people a similar chance to share their discoveries. In order to communicate your results, it is important to put together an effective written report and exhibit of your project. Keep your audience in mind. Your exhibit may be visited by people who know little about your area of research, so make sure that what you present is easy for the general public to understand.

Your report should begin with an **abstract**, a brief overview of your project stating your hypothesis and summarizing your findings. The report should also describe the materials and procedure you used, explaining how and why your experiment was conducted. And the report should contain an analysis of your results and the conclusions you reached.

Your exhibit should consist of a poster display that is organized so that others can quickly understand the important steps of your project. Make your poster as creative as you can to catch people's attention, but do not make it so flashy that it distracts people from your research. In addition to written text, use graphs, charts, and other images to explain your work. Remember, a picture is worth a thousand words.

Participating in Competitions. Now that you have finished the hard work of putting together your exhibit, you are ready for the fun part: competing in a science fair. There are many science fair competitions that take place every year on various levels across North America. If you are an elementary or middle school student, ask your teachers about local and city-wide competitions that you can enter. High school students can take part in regional and state or provincial competitions. If your exhibit is successful, you may be selected to participate in the International Science and Engineering Fair (ISEF), which brings together students from around the world.

Top high school students compete in the International Science and Engineering Fair (ISEF). Author Karen Mendelson is a two-time ISEF winner.

At these competitions, you will set up your exhibit, including your written report, lab notebook, poster, and other parts of your display, such as your apparatus. You will be asked to explain your project to judges, who typically include teachers and often scientists, as well as to students and other members of the general public. Explain your project in a logical manner and leave plenty of time for people to ask you questions. Teachers and other professionals can offer you suggestions on how to improve your work.

Entering science fair competitions will give you a lot of self-confidence. And by talking to fellow participants, you can get an idea of the type of work that other students your age are doing. Have fun sharing your science interest with others. You may also have the chance to interact with adult scientists and learn about their interesting careers. You may even be inspired to become a successful scientist in the future. So what are you waiting for? Let the science begin. Good luck!

KAREN MENDELSON
1997 Recipient, Intel Young Scientist Scholarship
1998 Recipient, Glenn Seaborg Nobel Visit Award
International Science and Engineering Fair

See also EXPERIMENTS AND OTHER SCIENCE ACTIVITES.

Science fiction often speculates about advances in science and technology. In *20,000 Leagues Under the Sea*, Jules Verne imagined an atomic submarine, the *Nautilus* (*pictured*), some eighty years before such a vessel became a reality.

SCIENCE FICTION

There is no definition of science fiction that pleases everyone. But it is possible to say that most science fiction deals in some way with change and the impact that science and technology have on people. It is a tool for understanding our lives now and imagining what our future might be.

The writer Ursula K. LeGuin compared science fiction to the thought experiments scientists conduct when they ask, "What if x happens? What if y is true?" Science fiction writers ask the same kind of theoretical questions and, like scientists, they use those questions to examine possibilities. The ideas of scientists are tested through experiment or observation. The ideas of science fiction writers are tested in readers' minds. Is the story convincing? Does the world it describes seem real?

▶ BEGINNINGS

Some people trace science fiction back to the ancient Greeks and Romans, who told stories about marvelous journeys, monsters, inventors, and magicians. Other people believe science fiction began in Europe in the 1500's and 1600's, when Thomas More wrote *Utopia* (about an imaginary, perfect land) and

Cyrano de Bergerac wrote *The Comical History of the States and Empires of the Moon and Sun*.

If science fiction is about technology and change, however, then we should look for its true beginning in a place and time when technological and social changes occurred more rapidly than ever before: England in the early 1800's.

At this time, the Industrial Revolution was changing how people lived and worked. Political revolutions at the end of the 1700's in the American colonies and France challenged old governments as well as traditional ideas about society. And it was this atmosphere of intellectual and social change that helped produce what has been called the first science fiction novel, *Frankenstein* (1818).

Written in 1816 by Mary Wollstonecraft Shelley, *Frankenstein* tells the story of a young scientist (Victor Frankenstein) who, having discovered the secret of creating life, produces a hideous monster that later destroys him. The novel introduces several themes that were continued in later science fiction, such as the creation of intelligent life and the problems caused by such creations.

Later in the 1800's, French author Jules Verne became the first master of modern science fiction. Verne found technology interest-

Biographies of the following authors who made important contributions to science fiction can be found in *The New Book of Knowledge*: Aldous Huxley, George Orwell, Jules Verne, and H. G. Wells.

Ray Bradbury

Octavia Butler

Brian Aldiss (1925–), born in Norfolk, England, served in the British Army in World War II. After the war, he worked in an Oxford bookstore and began writing fiction. In the 1960's he was associated with the experimental English science fiction magazine *New Worlds*. Among the work Aldiss produced during this period was a group of stories about Europe after a war in which mind-altering drugs were used as weapons. The stories were collected in the book *Barefoot in the Head* (1969). Between 1982 and 1985 Aldiss wrote the Helliconia trilogy.

Isaac Asimov (1920–92) was born in Petrovichim, Russia, and immigrated with his family to the United States in 1923. Asimov wrote with equal authority and skill about astronomy, biology, chemistry, physics, and history, producing over 500 books during his lifetime. He was best known, however, for his science fiction. In his short-story collection *I, Robot* (1950), Asimov invented the Three Laws of Robotics, a set of rules governing robots' behavior toward people. Other science fiction work by Asimov includes his famous Foundation series (1951–93), the novels *The Caves of Steel* (1954) and *The Gods Themselves* (1972), and the novella *The Bicentennial Man* (1976).

Ray Bradbury (1920–), was born in Waukegan, Illinois. He published his first story in 1938, and much of his early work appeared in pulp magazines. Bradbury's stories, however fanciful the location or situation they featured, were usually about people and the trials they must face in life. His classics include such novels as *The Martian Chronicles* (1950), *Fahrenheit 451* (1953), *Something Wicked This Way Comes* (1962), and the short-story collection *The Illustrated Man* (1951). Bradbury also wrote poetry, drama, and scripts for film and television.

Octavia Butler (1947–), born in Pasadena, California, was the first African American woman to earn a reputation as a science fiction writer. She sold her first stories at age 23 and her first novel, *Patternmaster* (1976), at age 28. She wrote mainly novels in series: the Patternmaster series (1976–84), the Xenogenesis trilogy (1987–89), and the Parable of the Sower series (1993–). One of her stand-alone novels is *Kindred* (1979). In 1995, Butler

Mary Shelley's *Frankenstein* is considered the first true science fiction novel. This engraving from an early edition of the book shows a less horrifying "monster" than later depictions.

ing and exciting, and his tales were full of marvelous inventions and daring adventures. He wrote over 60 novels, including *From the Earth to the Moon* (1865), *20,000 Leagues Under the Sea* (1870), and *Around the World in Eighty Days* (1873).

At the end of the 1800's, English writer H. G. Wells made his mark as the next great name in science fiction. Wells's interest in science (including Charles Darwin's theory of evolution) and social issues influenced his writing. His most famous science fiction is a series of short novels written in the late 1890's. These include *The Time Machine* (1895), in which an inventor travels to a future society; *The Island of Doctor Moreau* (1896), in which a scientist attempts to turn animals into humans; and *The War of the Worlds* (1898), about an invasion of Earth by Martians.

▶ **THE EARLY 1900'S**

Science fiction became popular in the United States during the early 1900's. Much of it was published in "pulp" magazines (named for the poor quality pulp paper on which many were printed) such as *Amazing*

received the prestigious MacArthur Foundation "genius" grant awarded to American artists and scholars.

Arthur C. Clarke (1917–) was born in Somerset, England. Clarke had been writing science fiction for about 20 years when he rose to world fame in 1968 with the release of the acclaimed motion picture *2001: A Space Odyssey*. It was based on Clarke's short story "The Sentinel" (1951), and Clarke collaborated on the script with the film's director, Stanley Kubrick. Some of his best work, such as *The City and the Stars* (1956) and *Childhood's End* (1953), combine his interest in technology and his fascination with the evolution of the human race.

Robert A. Heinlein (1907–88) was born in Butler, Missouri. He graduated from the U.S. Naval Academy in 1929 and served in the navy during World War II. Most of his adult life, however, was devoted to writing science fiction. Early in his career, from 1939 to 1942, he wrote for the pulp

Robert A. Heinlein

Ursula K. LeGuin

magazine *Astounding Science Fiction*. His first novel, *Rocket Ship Galileo* (1947), was followed by many novels and short stories. Some of them were written for young readers, including *Starman Jones* (1953), *Time for the Stars* (1956), and *Citizen of the Galaxy* (1957).

Ursula K. LeGuin (1929–), born in Berkeley, California, began publishing science fiction short stories in the early 1960's. *A Wizard of Earthsea*, the first of her fantasy Earthsea series, was published in 1968. The rest of the series included *The Tombs of Atuan* (1971), *The*

Farthest Shore (1972), and *Tehanu* (1990). *The Left Hand of Darkness* (1969) is perhaps LeGuin's most acclaimed book. Other important works include *The Dispossessed: An Ambiguous Utopia* (1974) and *Always Coming Home* (1985). LeGuin's work is concerned with social, political, and moral questions.

Gene Roddenberry (1921–91), born in El Paso, Texas, spent several years as a Los Angeles police officer before becoming a writer for television in 1954. He is most famous for *Star Trek*, which first aired in 1966. The show envisioned a future that is humane and hopeful, where men and women of different races and cultures work together as they explore the universe. The original show lasted only three years, but it eventually led to the first *Star Trek* motion picture in 1979. A new television series, *Star Trek: The Next Generation*, premiered in 1987 and lasted until 1994. This was followed by other television series that maintained Roddenberry's vision and legacy.

"Pulp" magazines introduced readers to classic science fiction tales, such as H. G. Wells's *The War of the Worlds* (*pictured*). They also showcased tales by new writers who later became masters in the field.

Stories. Founded in 1926 by Hugo Gernsback, *Amazing Stories* was the first major American science fiction magazine. The stories in these magazines were primarily action tales intended for boys and young men, full of technological marvels and thrilling adventures. *Astounding Stories* (later, *Astounding Science Fiction*) appeared in 1930, and when John Campbell became its editor in 1937, it began featuring stories with more serious themes. Many prominent science fiction writers, including Robert Heinlein, Ray Bradbury, Fritz Leiber, Isaac Asimov, Frederik Pohl, and Philip K. Dick, began their careers in magazines such as these and the many others that followed.

The most interesting science fiction in the 1930's and 1940's was not American, however. It was produced by three English writers: Aldous Huxley, George Orwell, and Olaf Stapledon. Huxley was not primarily a science fiction writer, but he produced several novels that fit the genre. The most famous is *Brave New World* (1932), which describes a future society in which modern biology and psychology are used to give people lives of shallow happiness at the expense of their individuality. George Orwell also ventured into science fiction on rare occasions. He wrote *1984* (1949), another disturbing vision of the future, in which England has become a bleak police state ruled by a harsh dictator called Big Brother. The science fiction novels of the English philosopher Olaf Stapledon are surveys of intelligent life, both human and non-human, over long expanses of time and wide reaches of space. His masterpiece is *Star Maker* (1937).

▶ THE LATE 1900'S

The late 1900's was a time of change for science fiction. Two influential American magazines, *Fantasy and Science Fiction*, founded in 1949 and edited by Anthony Boucher, and *Galaxy*, founded in 1950 and edited by H. L. Gold, helped bring greater respect to the field. Boucher and Gold had higher literary standards than the earlier pulp editors. A clever idea and thrilling action were no longer enough; Boucher especially wanted writing that was as good as writing outside the field of science fiction. Both editors were interested in stories about human behavior, emotions, and society.

Science fiction was largely an English-language field from the 1890's through the 1940's. This began to change in the 1950's with the emergence of writers such as Poland's Stanislaw Lem and the brothers Boris and Arkady Strugatsky in the former Soviet Union. However, English-language science fiction continues to dominate the field worldwide; much of today's foreign-language science fiction publishing consists of translations of English-language work.

The 1960's and early 1970's are often called the era of "New Wave" science fiction. For the first time, a large number of science fiction writers experimented with new writing styles and a wider range of subjects. In England, author Michael Moorcock took over as editor of the magazine *New Worlds*, turning it into the premier English-language science fiction magazine of the 1960's as well as a showcase for New Wave authors such as England's J. G. Ballard and Brian Aldiss and the American John Sladek. Especially noteworthy among New Wave authors is Samuel R. Delany, Jr., one of a handful of African American science fiction writers.

In the late 1960's, women began to enter science fiction in noticeable numbers. There had always been some women in the field, including C. L. Moore, Leigh Brackett, and Katherine MacLean. But women had been a minority among science fiction writers and fans as well. The writer Theodore Sturgeon commented in the 1970's that all the good new writers in the field, except James Tiptree, Jr., were women. Sturgeon did not know that Tiptree was, in reality, the pen name of the writer Alice Sheldon! One of the most prominent science fiction writers to emerge around this time was Ursula K. LeGuin, author of *The Left Hand of Darkness* (1969). Other women who began to publish in the 1960's and 1970's were C. J. Cherryh, Vonda McIntyre, and Octavia Butler.

The 1960's also saw the publication of the classic science fiction novel *Dune*. Written in 1965 by the American Frank Herbert, *Dune* was the first in a sprawling and complex six-book epic.

A new kind of science fiction called cyberpunk emerged in the 1980's. It was produced by authors who combined computer technology, skillful writing, and an attitude that seemed to come from tough-guy detective movies of the 1940's. The cyberpunk world, best seen in William Gibson's Neuromancer trilogy (1984–88), is a vast, dark place of poverty and crime. Most of the characters live on the margins of society, struggling to

---

Did you know that...

for a brief, terrifying time on October 30, 1938, thousands of people across the United States were convinced that science fiction had become science fact? On that night, radio news bulletins reported that an invasion force from Mars had landed in New Jersey and begun a destructive assault on Earth. Listeners who had tuned in at the start of the broadcast knew that the reports were actually part of a radio dramatization of the H. G. Wells novel *The War of the Worlds*. But the performance, by a young actor named Orson Welles and his Mercury Theatre company, was so convincing that it caused many others to panic in the belief that a Martian invasion was taking place. Welles, who gained instant celebrity, went on to become a noted motion picture actor and director. And his famous broadcast is considered a classic of radio's Golden Age.

The special effects of the motion picture *Star Wars* and its sequels gave imaginary worlds and characters a level of realism never before seen.

survive. The rich and powerful people who rule Earth are almost unreachable and no longer entirely human.

In the late 1980's, a number of other science fiction writers began to produce novels about complicated societies spanning vast regions of space and long periods of time. These authors include Joan Slonczewski (*A Door into Ocean*, 1986), Vernor Vinge (*A Fire upon the Deep*, 1992), and Paul McAuley (*Four Hundred Billion Stars*, 1988). Other authors wrote complex stories that encompassed many volumes. Examples include David Brin's Uplift saga, Gregory Benford's Galactic Center series, the Mars trilogy by Kim Stanley Robinson, and Lois McMaster Bujold's many novels featuring the popular character Miles Vorkosigan.

▶ **SCIENCE FICTION IN FILM AND TELEVISION**

After motion pictures were invented in the late 1800's, science fiction quickly entered the new medium. One of the very first films was a humorous science fiction tale, *A Trip to the Moon* (1902), by French filmmaker Georges Méliès. Another early film, *Metropolis* (1926), by German filmmaker Fritz Lang, provided a grim vision of society in the year 2000.

In the 1930's and 1940's, science fiction "serials" became popular. These were series of films that focused on a particular hero, such as Flash Gordon or Buck Rogers, and followed him on exciting adventures. The 1950's saw a more serious approach to science fiction films with such classics as *The Day the Earth Stood Still* (1951), *The Invasion of the Body Snatchers* (1956), and *The Incredible Shrinking Man* (1957).

Science fiction in film leaped to a higher level of artistry in 1968 with *2001: A Space Odyssey*, which set new standards for special effects and concept. Perhaps the peak of popular success, however, came with *Star Wars* (1977) and its sequels, against which all later science fiction films were measured.

On television, science fiction found its first success in the late 1950's and early 1960's with Rod Serling's *The Twilight Zone*, which had a literate and thought-provoking approach. Another series, *Star Trek*, developed a devoted following and went on to spawn a series of films and new television series that have become mainstays of science fiction. Science fiction became more popular on television in the 1990's with such acclaimed shows as *The X-Files* (which dealt with the paranormal as well as science fiction) and *Babylon 5*.

ELEANOR ARNASON
Author, *A Woman of the Iron People*
Reviewed by PETER BRIGG
Associate Professor
School of Literatures and
Performance Studies in English
University of Guelph

SCIENCE PROJECTS. See EXPERIMENTS AND OTHER SCIENCE ACTIVITIES.

SCOPES TRIAL

In 1925, John Thomas Scopes, a 24-year-old high-school science teacher, was arrested in Dayton, Tennessee. He was charged with teaching Charles Darwin's theory of evolution, which suggests that humans developed from simpler life-forms. Tennessee's Butler Act, which was passed earlier that year, had made it unlawful for any public school to teach a theory that challenged creationism—the story of God's creation of man as taught in the Bible.

The Scopes trial took place from July 10 to 21. It became popularly known as the monkey trial because most people thought, incorrectly, that evolutionists believed humans had descended from monkeys. Arguing for the prosecution was the famous orator and former presidential candidate William Jennings Bryan, who resolved to "protect the religious faith of our children." Leading the defense team, with the support of the American Civil Liberties Union (ACLU), was Clarence Darrow, the most famous defense lawyer of the era. Darrow promised to "smother Mr. Bryan's arguments under a mountain of scientific testimony." But to Darrow's dismay, Judge John Raulston did not allow a discussion of the validity of the theory of evolution. The only relevant question, he declared, was whether or not Scopes had broken a state law, which the defense openly admitted.

But on July 20, Darrow cleverly maneuvered Bryan into taking the stand as an expert witness on the Bible. During the long, grueling, and theatrical exchange between the two men, Darrow managed to embarrass Bryan, who grew increasingly confused and angry. (Bryan's supporters later claimed that the experience hastened his death, of a stroke, just five days after the trial ended.) Nevertheless, the jury found Scopes guilty, and Judge Raulston fined him $100.

In 1927, the Tennessee Supreme Court upheld the Butler Act but overruled Scopes's conviction on a technicality and revoked his fine. Evolution continued to be taught in Tennessee schools, even though the law against it was not repealed until 1967.

DON NARDO
Author, *The Scopes Trial*

SCORPIONS

From under a desert rock, a scorpion emerges at night to hunt. As it nears its prey, it arches its tail. With a quick strike, the scorpion stuns its victim.

Scorpions are among the oldest arachnids, which also include spiders, mites, and ticks. Scientists believe scorpions evolved from similar creatures that lived some 400 million years ago. Over 1,200 different species now inhabit various places throughout the world, including dry, tropical, and temperate climates.

Most scorpions are 1½ to 3 inches (about 4 to 7 centimeters) in length, although some are nearly twice that size. At the front of a scorpion's flat body are two appendages that end in pincers, used to capture prey. On either side of the body are four walking legs. The scorpion uses the curved stinger at the end of its tail to inject poison into its enemies and prey.

Scorpions feed on both arachnids and insects. After capturing and stinging its prey, a scorpion crushes it with jawlike parts. The scorpion then spits a digestive fluid over its prey, which turns into a liquid that the scorpion sucks up through its mouth.

Unlike egg-laying arachnids, scorpions give birth to live young. The young scorpions ride on their mother's back until they are old enough to manage on their own.

Scorpions seldom attack unless disturbed. The sting from most is painful but not fatal. The only species in the United States with a potentially fatal sting, *Centruroides sculpturatus*, is yellow to yellow brown with two black stripes on the back. It lives mostly in Mexico but also in Arizona.

Reviewed by JOHN A. JACKMAN
Department of Entomology, Texas A & M University

See also ARACHNIDS.

SCORSESE, MARTIN. See MOTION PICTURES (Profiles: Directors).

SCOTLAND

Scotland is one of the four political units that make up the United Kingdom of Great Britain and Northern Ireland. After nearly three centuries of political unity, however, the Scots remain a distinct people. Scotland's magnificent scenery, together with its colorful festivals and fascinating history, make the place a favorite destination for tourists.

Above: Eilean Donan in Loch Duich is one of the many interesting castles found on Scotland's west coast. *Right:* Scottish Highland bagpipes are among the country's most familiar symbols.

▶ PEOPLE

Scotland is smaller than England and has far fewer people. Because much of the land is rugged and isolated, the Scots, historically, have tended to be very independent.

The Scots are descended from the Celts and other tribes that migrated to the area from other parts of Britain and the European mainland before the 600's B.C. The name "Scotland" comes from the Scotti, one of the Celtic tribes that settled there.

Language and Religion. All Scots speak English—but with a distinctive "burr." Nearly 2 percent speak Gaelic, a language that originated with the Celts. Many Scots belong to the Church of Scotland, a Presbyterian sect of Protestantism.

Education and Libraries. Education is free and compulsory for children between the ages of 5 and 16. Higher education is provided at 13 universities. The largest are the universities of Edinburgh and Glasgow. The others include Aberdeen, St. Andrews, and Dundee. The National Library of Scotland, in Edinburgh, has about 5 million items.

Way of Life. The Scottish way of life is similar to that of the English, but the Scots have maintained many distinct customs. These include folk dancing, playing bagpipes, and wearing kilts and colorful tartans—the plaid patterns of the various Scottish clans.

Sports and Recreation. Scotland is best known for golf, as the game was developed there in the mid-1700's. Today, the Royal and Ancient Golf Club of St. Andrews is perhaps the most famous golf club in the world. Soccer and rugby games are widely attended.

Also popular are the Highland Games, which include track meets as well as folk dancing and bagpipe competitions.

▶ LAND

Scotland occupies the northernmost third of the island of Great Britain. With an area of 30,418 square miles (78,783 square kilometers), it is about the same size as the state of South Carolina. Included are some 800 offshore islands, fewer than one-fourth of which are inhabited. The most notable island groups are the Shetlands, the Orkneys, and the Outer and Inner Hebrides.

Land Regions. Scotland is divided geographically into Highlands, Lowlands, and Uplands. The fabled Scottish Highlands cover about two-thirds of the country. The Highlands are divided by Glen More (the Great Glen), a huge valley. The desolate and windswept moors and mountains of the northwestern Highlands include some of the most unspoiled country in Europe.

East and south of Glen More are the Grampian Mountains, rushing streams, lochs (lakes), and heather-covered moors. Here Ben Nevis, the highest mountain in the

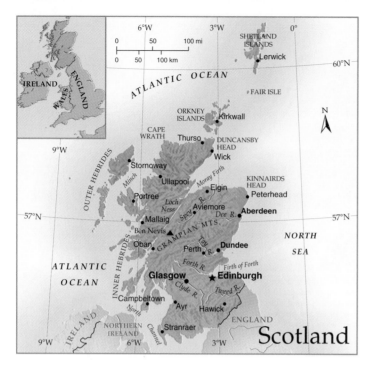

Scotland

varies from 120 inches (3,050 millimeters) in the west to about 25 inches (635 millimeters) in the east.

Natural Resources. Scotland is poor in natural resources. There are, however, deposits of coal, iron, granite, slate, and other minerals, located mainly in the Central Lowlands. Only about 15 percent of the land is forested.

▶ ECONOMY

Coal mining and steelmaking were once Scotland's major industries, but these have declined in recent decades. On the rise are industries related to the services, high technology, and offshore oil drilling.

Services. The service industries, especially those related to finance and tourism, are among the fastest-growing segments of Scotland's economy. Financial and business services alone employ more than 270,000 people.

Manufacturing. High-technology electronics industries now account for almost a third of Scotland's manufacturing output and half of its manufactured exports. Firms producing computers, software, automated-banking machines, and other high-technology equipment employ the most workers.

Dozens of other industries are associated with specific regions. World-famous Scotch whisky, Scotland's second largest export, is made chiefly in the northeast. The east central region is known for malting and brewing beverages. Jute is processed along the Tay River. Woolen textiles are produced in the southern regions. Tweeds are made in the Outer Hebrides. Aluminum is smelted in the

United Kingdom, rises to 4,406 feet (1,343 meters).

Some of the best farmland in the United Kingdom is found in the Central Lowlands, in the river valleys. This area is the center of Scottish commerce and industry.

The southernmost region of Scotland, the Southern Uplands, is similar to the Highlands but is less rugged. Grazing sheep dot the grass-covered hills and valleys.

Rivers, Lakes, and Coastal Waters. Although Scotland is surrounded on three sides by breathtaking views of the Atlantic Ocean and the North Sea, it is particularly known for its many beautiful lakes. Loch Lomond is the largest. Loch Ness, perhaps the most famous, is the source of a legend of a sea monster that has persisted for hundreds of years. Scotland's major rivers are the Dee, Tay, Forth, Clyde, and Tweed.

Climate. The Gulf Stream passes near the rugged northwestern coast, making Scotland's climate warmer than might be expected. Cool summers are followed by comparatively mild winters. Rainfall in Scotland

The raising of sheep is important to the economy of the Southern Uplands. Sheep provide mutton as well as high-quality wool for Scotland's tweed manufacturers.

Highlands, using the region's abundant hydroelectric power.

The offshore oil and gas industry is another major employer. Aberdeen, Scotland's northernmost major city, is the onshore base for much of the North Sea petroleum industry. The principal refinery is located at Grangemouth, where foreign supplies of heavier crude petroleum are imported. The Shetland Islands are a terminus for oil pipelines from the northernmost fields.

Agriculture. Livestock production dominates Scottish agriculture. Sheep and cattle are particularly important in the Uplands, where poor soils, rain, and low temperatures prevent crops from thriving. Cattle provide beef and milk. Sheep yield mutton and the high-quality wool used by Scotland's tweed manufacturers.

Scottish agriculture is highly mechanized. Fruits and vegetables—many of which are canned, frozen, or made into preserves—are grown in abundance, particularly north of the Forth River.

Aberdeen, Peterhead, and Mallaig are important fishing centers. Lobster and other shellfish have brought prosperity to several additional coastal settlements, as has fish farming, particularly of salmon. But many little towns have suffered from the sharp decline in herring stock off southwest Scotland and in the North Sea.

MAJOR CITIES

Edinburgh, Scotland's capital, is one of Europe's most beautiful cities. The central city is divided into two parts—the Old Town and the New Town. The Old Town, which dates from the 1000's, is rich in historic buildings, including Edinburgh Castle and the University of Edinburgh. Every summer, thousands of visitors attend the Edinburgh International Festival of Music and Drama. The city is also the seat of the Scottish Parliament.

Glasgow is Scotland's largest city. Situated on the banks of the River Clyde, which opens into the Atlantic Ocean, it is a major port and was once the center of Scotland's shipbuilding industry. Today it is a center of science, industry,

Above: The City Chambers and a monument to Sir Walter Scott grace Glasgow's George Square. *Left:* Sir William Wallace, a Scottish patriot and hero, was executed by the English in 1305.

and engineering. The city is home to the University of Glasgow, founded in 1451, and the University of Strathclyde. The city's beautiful St. Mungo's Cathedral dates back to the 1200's.

CULTURAL HERITAGE

Scotland's artistic heritage can be traced back to the bards—singers of poetic verses who flourished in the 1100's and passed down their art through the generations. Modern performing arts groups include the Royal Scottish National Orchestra, the Scottish Opera, and the Scottish Chamber Orchestra, all world renowned. Celtic music is highlighted each January at the Glasgow Royal Concert Hall. And every August and September, the annual Edinburgh International Festival of Music and Drama attracts tourists from all over the world.

In literature, Scotland was the birthplace of such renowned poets and writers as Robert Burns, Sir Walter Scott, Robert Louis Stevenson, and Sir Arthur Conan Doyle. Native Scotsmen who contributed in other fields of endeavor include the philosopher David Hume; business tycoon Andrew Carnegie; and many scientists and inventors, such as Sir Alexander Fleming, discoverer of penicillin, and Alexander Graham Bell, inventor of the telephone. Biographies of each of these figures can be found in the appropriate volumes.

On July 1, 1999, Queen Elizabeth II of the United Kingdom traveled along Edinburgh's Royal Mile to attend the opening of the new Scottish Parliament.

▶ HISTORY AND GOVERNMENT

Scotland's earliest settlement dates from about 4000 B.C. Thousands of years later, the Romans attempted to subdue the warring northern tribes. But eventually they withdrew south of Hadrian's Wall, which they built (A.D. 122–128) across northern England. The Picts and Scots, along with Britons, Angles, and eventually the Vikings, all contributed to the establishment of a Scottish kingdom by the 900's.

Most of Scotland's monarchs faced tragedy and rebellion. For example, King Duncan I (?–1040) was killed by his general, Macbeth (?–1057), who in turn was killed by Duncan's son Malcolm III (?–1093). Centuries later, the story of these events was told by the English playwright William Shakespeare in his celebrated play *Macbeth*.

After the death of Alexander III (1241–86), Scottish lords began fighting over the succession to the throne. England's King Edward I (1239–1307) invaded Scotland, declaring himself its overlord in 1292. But the Scots,

under the leadership of their first great hero, Sir William Wallace (1272?–1305), rose against Edward and defeated him at the Battle of Stirling (1297). The English later captured Wallace and executed him for treason. The Scottish revolt then continued under the leadership of Robert the Bruce (1274–1329), who was crowned King Robert I in 1306. He later defeated the English at Bannockburn (1314), and in 1328, the English signed a treaty recognizing Scotland's independence.

In 1371, the first Scottish king from the House of Stuart was crowned Robert II (1316–90). His descendants James I (1394–1437) and James II (1430–60) strengthened the central government. During this time, trade prospered and education flourished.

In 1502, James IV (1473–1513) tried to strengthen Scotland's ties with England by marrying Margaret Tudor (1489–1541), a daughter of Henry VII (1457–1509). But conflicts between James and Margaret's brother, Henry VIII, led to a border war. James was killed at the Battle of Flodden Field in 1513 and was succeeded by his son James V (1512–42). He, in turn, was succeeded by his infant daughter, Mary, Queen of Scots (1542–87). During Mary's reign, Scotland went through a religious reformation, banished its Catholic queen, and became a Protestant country.

In 1603, Mary's son, James VI (1566–1625), succeeded to the throne of England as James I. With the Act of Union in 1707, England (including Wales), Ireland, and Scotland were officially united under one parliament and one ruler. Ever since, Scottish nationalists have called for independence. Most people, however, support devolution—a return to power of an elected Scottish legislature.

A vote on devolution failed in 1979, but another succeeded overwhelmingly in 1997. The resulting Scotland Act of 1998 provided for the establishment of a 129-member Scottish Parliament and an Executive, seated in Edinburgh. The first elections to the new Parliament were held in 1999. Scotland continues to be represented in foreign affairs by 72 members in the British House of Commons.

Reviewed by British Information Services
New York City

See also JAMES; MARY, QUEEN OF SCOTS; ROBERT I (THE BRUCE).

SCOTT, DRED. See DRED SCOTT DECISION.

SCOTT, SIR WALTER (1771–1832)

Sir Walter Scott, poet and novelist, was born on August 15, 1771, in Edinburgh, Scotland. He spent much of his childhood on his grandfather's farm, where he learned local legends and loved to listen to songs and tales of Scottish heroes.

Scott went to Edinburgh University and became a lawyer like his father. But he was most interested in literature. He began to collect ballads, and then to write his own. His three-volume collection, *Minstrelsy of the Scottish Border*, was published in 1802–03. Then he published his own long poem, *The Lay of the Last Minstrel* (1805), a romantic story set in the border country of his childhood.

The book-length poems of the following years, such as *Marmion* (1808), brought him great success. With his earnings, he invested in a publishing business, and in 1812 he bought a beautiful estate called Abbotsford. There, with his wife, Charlotte, and their four children, he entertained visitors and lived like the noble Scottish lairds he wrote about.

But the sales of his poetry began to drop, and the publishing firm was almost bankrupt. Because he needed money, he began to write novels. His first novel, *Waverley* (1814), was even more successful than his poems.

Scott continued to produce historical novels, many of them set in Scotland. Two of his best works are *Rob Roy* (1817) and *Ivanhoe* (1819). Scott became the most famous novelist of his day, and in 1820 he was made a baronet.

Scott's publishing business finally collapsed in 1826, and he took over his partners' debts. He continued to work until his death on September 21, 1832.

JULIET MCMASTER
University of Alberta (Canada)

SCOTT, WINFIELD (1786–1866)

Winfield Scott served as commanding general of the United States Army from 1841 to 1861. Known as Old Fuss and Feathers for his attention to dress and discipline, he is best remembered for his brilliant campaigns that brought a successful conclusion to the Mexican War (1846–48).

Scott was born on June 13, 1786, near Petersburg, Virginia. In 1805 he attended William and Mary College but left to pursue law and, eventually, a military career.

When the War of 1812 broke out between the United States and Great Britain, Scott was made a lieutenant colonel. He was badly wounded at the Battle at Lundy's Lane (1814), but his extraordinary bravery made him an overnight hero and earned him a promotion to major general. In the 1830's he served in a series of Indian wars and in 1841 was appointed commanding general of the U.S. Army.

By the time the Mexican War began in May 1846, Scott was nearly 60, but his most significant military achievements were yet to come. In March 1847, his troops quickly captured the coastal Mexican city of Veracruz.

For the next six months, they fought their way toward Mexico City, winning battles at Cerro Gordo, Contreras, Churubusco, Molino del Rey, and Chapultepec. In September, Scott's forces captured Mexico City, bringing the war to an end. In 1852, the popular war hero ran for president against Franklin Pierce. However, his popularity was not strong enough to carry his crumbling Whig Party, and he was soundly defeated.

At the outset of the Civil War in 1861, Scott briefly served as one of President Abraham Lincoln's military advisers before retiring from the army in November at the age of 75. He died at West Point, New York, on May 29, 1866.

Reviewed by LEONARD L. RICHARDS
University of Massachusetts

SCOTTSDALE. See ARIZONA (Cities).

SCOUTING. See BOY SCOUTS; CAMP FIRE BOYS AND GIRLS; GIRL SCOUTS.

SCRANTON. See PENNSYLVANIA (Cities).

SCREWS. See NAILS, SCREWS, AND RIVETS.

SCUBA DIVING. See SKIN DIVING.

SCULPTURE

For thousands of years sculpture has filled many roles in human life. The earliest sculpture was probably made to supply magical help to hunters. After the dawn of civilization, statues were used to represent gods. Ancient kings, possibly in the hope of making themselves immortal, had likenesses carved, and portrait sculpture was born. The Greeks made statues that depicted perfectly formed men and women. Early Christians decorated churches with demons and devils, reminders of the presence of evil for the many churchgoers who could neither read nor write.

From its beginnings until the present, sculpture has been largely monumental. In the 15th century, monuments to biblical heroes were built on the streets of Italian cities, and in the 20th century a monument to a songwriter was built in the heart of New York City. Great fountains with sculpture in the center are as commonplace beside modern skyscrapers as they were in the courts of old palaces. The ancient Sumerians celebrated military victory with sculpture. The participants of World War II also used sculpture to honor their soldiers.

▶THE TYPES OF SCULPTURE

Sculpture can be divided into two classes: relief sculpture and sculpture in the round. There are three methods for making sculpture: modeling, carving, and joining.

Relief sculpture is sculpture in which images are set against a flat background. A coin is a good example of relief sculpture: the inscription, the date, and the figure—sometimes a portrait of a statesman—are slightly raised above a flat surface. When the image is only slightly raised, as with the coin, the sculpture is called low relief or **bas-relief**. The ancient Egyptians sometimes carved figures into a flat surface. This type of carving is known as sunken relief. Statues that are almost three-dimensional but still are attached to backgrounds are regarded as **high relief**.

Sculpture in the round is freestanding, attached to no background. Most statues and portrait busts are carved in the round.

Modeling is done with clay, wax, or some other soft, pliable material. The sculptor adds pieces of material and molds it to the desired shape.

Carving can be thought of as the opposite of modeling because it involves removing rather than adding material. With knife or chisel, the sculptor carves from a block of wood or stone until the form is made.

Joining, or **constructing**, was not widely practiced until the 20th century. In this method the artist uses pieces of wood, metal, or plastic and joins them together into a construction. The airy, abstract kind of forms that are popular in modern times lend themselves to the joining system.

Almost everyone has actually practiced all three methods of making sculpture. When you make a snake or clown of clay, you are modeling. Whittling a stick is carving, and playing with an erector set or building a model airplane is joining.

▶HOW THE SCULPTOR WORKS

We think of the sculptor as a creative, sensitive, and original thinker. Seldom, however, do we think of the physical demands that the

This article describes some of the materials, tools, and techniques used in sculpting. It also discusses the development of sculpture throughout history. Articles on the arts of individual countries, such as ITALY, ART AND ARCHITECTURE OF, include discussions of the sculpture produced in those countries. See also the names of periods and styles of art, such as GOTHIC ART AND ARCHITECTURE. Biographies of Giovanni Bernini, Constantin Brancusi, Donatello, Michelangelo, Louise Nevelson, Pablo Picasso, and Auguste Rodin—all of whom are mentioned in this article—can be found in the appropriate volumes of this encyclopedia.

art of sculpture makes on the artist. A sculptor's work can be backbreaking. Marble must be moved and cut. Wood must be carved and sandpapered. Clay must be pounded and kept in condition with day-to-day care.

The sculptor must have a great deal of technical knowledge. He or she must know a good piece of stone from a bad one and just how much force that stone can take before it cracks. The sculptor must judge the quality of woods and learn how much water different kinds of clays need to stay workable. For casting models, the sculptor must know the chemistry of metals and their melting points. And the modern sculptor is frequently a competent welder, riveter, and machinist as well as an artist.

Materials

Before beginning to work, the sculptor must decide what material to use. Materials range from something as rare and costly as ivory, which comes from elephants' tusks, to common clay. Good clay is highly prized, but almost anyone can afford it, since it is found in many places all over the world.

The sculptor must decide between a material that is permanent and one that must be made permanent. Each kind has its advantages and disadvantages. A stone like marble is, of course, very hard. Carving must be done with great strength and at the same time with great delicacy. Mistakes are difficult to repair, and too much force can cause breakage. But when a marble statue is carved and polished, the sculptor's work is done. Clay, in contrast, is very soft. The artist can experiment a great deal, adding pieces and remodeling sections. If a mistake is made, the error can be removed quickly. However, clay must be kept workable. Every day the unfinished work must be covered with damp rags, and from time to time the unused clay in the bin must be moistened with water and pounded. Moreover, when the modeling is finished, the statue is by no means ready for exhibition, for clay does not last long. Therefore, the statue must be converted to another kind of material. A number of systems may be used, each requiring additional work. These systems—pointing, firing, and casting—will be described later.

Perhaps because they are permanent, stone and metal have always been important materials for the sculptor. Other materials that have been used include wood, ivory, jade, bone, glass, and plaster. For sculpture that is to be converted to another material, clay is by far the most frequently used substance, but various kinds of wax have also been employed.

In modern times the sculptor has turned to new materials such as one of the plastics, fiberglass, stainless steel, and aluminum.

Sculpture has filled many roles in human life. Over the ages, much sculpture has been made for public display: to honor a religious deity (*opposite page*), to pay tribute to an important leader (*left*), or simply to make a public place more interesting (*right*).

A woodcarver uses a chisel to create a sculpture. Sculptors use chisels and other tools to remove pieces from a block of wood, stone, or other material.

Tools

Sculpting tools are an extension of the artist's hands. Some tools let a sculptor work a soft substance easily and precisely. Other tools allow the use of materials otherwise too hard to handle.

Loops of wire held in wooden handles can drag off large sections from a mass of clay more quickly and neatly than can a person's hands. Sticks or blades of wood, ivory, or light, flexible metals can give clean edges and draw fine lines across the surface of wax, clay, or soft metal. Hardwood and all forms of stone demand different kinds of tools. Hammers, mallets, chisels, and drills are needed for the process of carving. Today sculptors often use welding torches and soldering irons to join metal together for sculpture. Special machines that join or separate plastics with heat and pressure may also be used.

Pointing, Firing, and Casting

Many sculptors begin working from their sketches, while others work directly with their materials. Whatever the approach, the sculptor's aim is to produce a lasting work of art.

Pointing is not used very much today, but to sculptors in the past it was a dependable system for converting clay or wax sculpture into stone. First, the sculptor made a clay model of a statue. The sculptor then placed points, or marks, on the model, measuring the distances between the points. Using hundreds and sometimes thousands of points as guides, the exact proportions of the model could be transferred to the stone.

Firing is the only system that converts clay sculpture itself into a durable object. Not all clay sculpture is suitable for firing, for the system requires the object to be hollow and free from impurities and air bubbles. Therefore, as a rule, only small statues are fired. After the sculpture is completed, it must be left uncovered while the moisture in the clay evaporates. Then it is placed in a kiln, a high-temperature oven, and fired (baked) until very hard.

Casting is the most common system of converting a clay or wax sculpture into another material. There are many systems of casting, most of which are used in foundries. Basically, casting involves making a mold of the clay or wax model. This mold may be made of plaster, rubber, clay, or any of several other substances that are both workable and tough. If the sculpture is clay, the mold must be made in several parts, so that it can be removed from the model and then reassembled. If the figure is made of wax, the mold may be of one piece; for the mold can be heated, causing the wax to melt and run out. Hot liquid metal—usually bronze—is poured into the mold. When the metal has hardened, the mold is broken away and the sculpture is cleaned and finished.

▶PREHISTORIC SCULPTURE

Sculpture may be the oldest of the arts. People carved before they painted or designed dwellings. The earliest drawings were probably carved on rock or incised (scratched) in earth. Therefore, these drawings were as much forerunners of relief sculpture as of painting.

Only a few objects survive to show what sculpture was like thousands of years ago. There are, however, hundreds of recent examples of sculpture made by people living in primitive cultures. These examples may be similar to prehistoric sculpture.

From recent primitive sculpture and from the few surviving prehistoric pieces, we can judge that prehistoric sculpture was never made to be beautiful. It was always made to be used in rituals. In their constant fight for survival, early people made sculpture to provide spiritual support.

Figures of men, women, and animals and combinations of all these served to honor the strange and sometimes frightening forces of nature, which were worshiped as evil or good spirits. Oddly shaped figures must have represented prayers for strong sons, good crops, and abundant game and fish. Sculpture in the form of masks was worn by priests or medicine men in dances designed to drive away evil spirits or beg favors from good ones.

▶ SCULPTURE IN THE ANCIENT WORLD

The earliest civilizations of Egypt, Mesopotamia, the Indus Valley, and China gradually developed forms of writing about 3000 B.C. The people of these civilizations, like their prehistoric ancestors, also expressed deeply felt beliefs in sculpture.

Egypt

Egyptian sculpture and all Egyptian art was based on the belief in a life after death. The body of the Egyptian ruler, or pharaoh, was carefully preserved, and goods were buried with him to provide for his needs forever. The pyramids, great monumental tombs of Giza, were built for the most powerful early rulers. The pharaoh and his wife were buried in chambers cut deep inside the huge blocks of stone.

Life-size and even larger statues, carved in slate, alabaster, and limestone, were as regular and simple in shape as the tombs themselves. Placed in the temples and inside the burial chambers, these statues were images of the rulers, the nobles, and the gods worshiped by the Egyptians. The Egyptians believed that the spirit of the dead person could always return to these images. Hundreds of smaller statuettes in clay or wood showed people engaged in all the normal actions of life: kneading bread, sailing, counting cattle. These statuettes were astonishingly lifelike. Scenes carved in relief and painted in the tomb chambers or on temple walls described Egyptian life in all its variety.

Egyptian sculptors always presented ideas clearly. The pharaoh or noble is made larger than less important people. In relief sculpture every part of a figure is clearly shown. An eye looking straight forward is placed against the profile of a face, the upper part of the body faces front, and the legs are again in profile.

The Egyptians often combined features from various creatures to symbolize ideas. For example, the human head of the pharaoh Khafre is added to the crouching figure of a lion to form the Great Sphinx. This composition suggests the combination of human intelligence and animal strength.

Egyptian sculptors made standing and seated figures in the round and in relief. Changes in style reveal changed circumstances. The portraits of rulers of the Middle Kingdom (2134?–1778? B.C.) lose the strength and vigor of those of their ancestors at Giza. The faces are drawn, sad, and weary. A greater energy and force returns in the period of Egypt's greatest power, the New Kingdom (1567–1080 B.C.). Colossal figures like those of Ramses II at the entrance to his tomb at Abu-Simbel are broad, powerful, and commanding. A smaller portrait of Ramses II shows the smooth finish, precise craftsmanship, and elegance of late New Kingdom art.

Mesopotamia

The "land between the rivers," Mesopotamia, had a much less stable society than Egypt and lacked Egypt's vast amounts of stone for monumental sculpture. Its cities were often destroyed by floods and invading armies.

The earliest examples of sculpture in this region were formed of light materials: baked and unbaked clay, wood or combinations of wood, shells, and gold leaf. A group of stone figures from Tell Asmar depicts gods, priests, and worshipers in a way very different from Egyptian sculpture. These figures are cone-shaped, with flaring skirts, small heads, huge, beaklike noses, and large, staring eyes.

Stone sculpture from such heavily fortified city palaces as Nineveh, Nimrud, and Khor-

In ancient Egypt, useful objects such as furniture and musical instruments were often decorated with sculpture. This carved wooden head formed part of a harp.

sabad reveal the aggressive, warlike character of later (10th-century B.C.) conquerors of this region, the Assyrians. At the entrances of their palaces the Assyrians placed huge symbols of the king's might and majesty in the form of colossal guardian monsters—five-legged, winged bulls with human heads. Slabs of stone carved in relief with scenes of hunts, battles, victory banquets, and ceremonial rituals were placed along the lower walls inside the palaces.

A greater lightness and brilliance can be seen in a still later center of this region, Babylon. The Babylonians used brightly colored tiles in their reliefs.

Persian conquerors who occupied Babylon in the 6th century B.C. brought with them a tradition of fine craftsmanship. This skill persisted as they continued creating superb designs in bronze and gold. Sometimes the designs are purely abstract ornamental patterns; sometimes they are animal forms freely shaped into graceful figures. Relief sculpture

from the great palace of Darius at Persepolis (begun about 520 B.C.) retains some Assyrian features. The figures have heads with tightly curled hair and beards. Flat areas bounded by sharply cut lines contrast with richly patterned ones. The figures in this sculpture are softly curved and rounded; draperies are fine and light.

The easy, natural movements of these figures marching in stately procession along the walls of the palace at Persepolis may well reflect qualities of the most original sculptors of the era (6th century B.C.), the Greeks.

Aegean Civilization

Just a few examples of sculpture remain from the colorful Minoan civilization on the island of Crete. Ivory and terra-cotta; small statuettes of snake goddesses, priestesses, and acrobats; and cups with such scenes in relief as a bull being caught in a net or harvesters returning from the fields give lively suggestions of Minoans in action.

Opposite page: At the Persian palace of Persepolis, a stairway is decorated with relief sculptures of animals and the king's guards. *Far left:* The Lion Gate at Mycenae features sculptures of two massive lions, symbolic guardians of the city. *Near left:* For the ancient Greeks, a winged female figure, called a Nike, stood for victory.

Power passed from Crete to the mainland, but little sculpture from such sites as Tiryns or Mycenae has been found. The Lion Gate at Mycenae (about 1250 B.C.), with its two massive beasts guarding the entrance to the fortified city, is an exceptional monumental sculpture from this time. The beaten-gold mask of Agamemnon is memorable for its suggestion of the great heroes of Homeric legends. The mask was found buried with golden cups, daggers, breastplates, and other objects in the tombs and shaft graves of Mycenae.

▶ GREEK SCULPTURE

Around 600 B.C., Greece developed one of the great civilizations in the history of the world. Sculpture became one of the most important forms of expression for the Greeks.

The Greek belief that ''man is the measure of all things'' is nowhere more clearly shown than in Greek sculpture. The human figure was the principal subject of all Greek art. Beginning in the late 7th century B.C., sculptors in Greece constantly sought better ways to represent the human figure.

The Greeks developed a standing figure of a nude male, called the Kouros or Apollo. The Kouros served to depict gods and heroes. The Kore, or standing figure of a draped female, was more graceful and was used to portray maidens and goddesses. The winged female figure, or Nike, became the personification of victory.

The fact that Greek sculptors concentrated their energies on a limited number of problems may have helped bring about the rapid changes that occurred in Greek sculpture between the 7th century and the late 4th century B.C. The change from abstraction to naturalism, from simple figures to realistic ones, took place during this period. Later figures have normal proportions and stand or sit easily in perfectly balanced poses.

Historians have adopted a special set of terms to suggest the main changes in the development of Greek sculpture and of Greek art in general. The early, or Archaic, phase lasted about 150 years, from 625 to 480 B.C. A short interval called Early Classical or Severe, from 480 to 450 B.C., was followed by a half century of Classical sculpture. Late Classical indicates Greek art produced between 400 and 323 B.C., and Hellenistic art was made from 323 to 146 B.C.

The most important function of Greek sculpture was to honor gods and goddesses. Statues were placed in temples or were carved as part of a temple. Greek temples were shrines created to preserve the images of the gods. The people worshiped outdoors.

Greek sculpture changed with Greek civilization. Praxiteles' *Hermes* is slimmer and more elegant than the strong, vigorous *Spear-Bearer,* by Polykleitos. Figures by Skopas from the Mausoleum at Halicarnassus are harsher and more dramatic than the quiet, controlled figures by Phidias.

Hellenistic sculptors emphasized the human figure. They reflected the great changes in their world when they treated in new ways subjects traditionally favored by earlier Greek sculptors. A new interest developed in the phases of life, from childhood to extreme old age. Sculptors described their figures in as natural and exact a way as possible. An ill old woman hobbles painfully back from the market; a little boy almost squeezes a poor goose to death.

The Greeks were defeated by the Romans, but the Hellenistic style lasted for centuries. Greek sculpture survived because the Romans were greatly impressed by Greek art. From the early days of the republic, Romans imported examples of Greek art, ordered copies of famous Greek works, and commissioned Greek sculptors to do Roman subjects.

▶ETRUSCAN AND ROMAN SCULPTURE

Greek sculpture and Greek art had been exported to Italy long before Romans ruled the land. By the 7th and 6th centuries B.C. the Etruscans were firmly settled in Italy. Hundreds of objects have been and are still being found in vast Etruscan cemeteries. Some of the sculpture and many vases are Greek, while others are lively Etruscan translations of Greek forms. Many small bronze figures of farmers, warriors, or gods show the great talents of the Etruscans as metalworkers and sculptors.

Rome profited from the double artistic inheritance of Greek and Etruscan sculpture. The inventiveness of Roman sculptors added to this heritage. The most important contributions of the Roman sculptors were portraits.

The development of Roman sculpture was the reverse of that of Greek sculpture. Instead of progressing from fairly simple, abstract forms to more natural and realistic statues, Roman sculpture, once realistic, became far more simple and abstract.

▶EARLY CHRISTIAN SCULPTURE

Early Christian sculpture resembled the art of Rome. Sarcophagi (burial chests) found in Italy are all Roman in type, although they are given a special meaning by subjects, signs, or symbols important for Christians.

Sculpture, however, was not a natural form of expression for the early Christians. This was because one of the Ten Commandments forbids the making of graven (carved) images. Many early Christians interpreted this commandment, just as the Hebrews had, to mean that it was wrong to make any images of the human figure. Eventually church authorities decided that art could serve Christianity. It

was only the making of idols (false gods) that was regarded as a breach of the commandment.

In the 5th century A.D. the western half of the Roman Empire fell to invading Germanic tribes from northern and central Europe. These peoples soon became Christians and spread the religion throughout Europe. Unlike the Romans, the Germanic peoples had no tradition of human representation in art. Their art consisted mainly of complex patterns and shapes used for decoration. It influenced Christian art as much as Greco-Roman art did.

There are relatively few examples of sculpture made in the first 1,000 years of Christianity. Among these rare examples are portable altars, reliquaries (containers for the remains of Christian saints and martyrs), chalices, and other objects used in the services of Christian worship. These were shaped with great care and were often made of precious materials. Sculptors used the fragile and lovely medium of ivory in many ways. They carved it in relief for small altars or as covers for the Gospels, the Bible, or prayerbooks. Small, freestanding figures represented the Madonna and the Christ Child, angels, or Christian saints.

▶ROMANESQUE SCULPTURE

A new and brilliant chapter in Christian art began after the year 1000. For the next three centuries sculptors, architects, masons, carpenters, and hundreds of other craftsmen created some of the most impressive Christian churches ever built.

These artists worked on a bolder and larger scale than had been possible for hundreds of years. For their ideas they looked to the best examples of great structures they knew— Roman buildings. The term "Romanesque" suggests the Roman qualities of the art of the 11th and 12th centuries. Important changes were made by these later artists. German Romanesque churches differ from Italian ones, and Spanish from French ones. Ideas of carving, building, and painting circulated freely, for people often went on pilgrimages to worship at sacred sites in different countries.

An early 11th century example of Romanesque sculpture shows the way Roman ideas were translated. The bronze doors of the Cathedral of Hildesheim have ten panels with scenes from the Bible. The placing, purpose, and arrangement of these large doors clearly recall the 5th-century doors of Santa Sabina in

Opposite page: The Romans honored important leaders such as the Emperor Augustus by making statues of them for public display. *Left:* This small ivory relief carving from the early Christian period represents the archangel Michael. *Above:* Romanesque churches were heavily decorated with sculptures. This one, carved over the doorway of the Church of Ste.-Madeleine in Vézelay, France, features Christ and the apostles.

Madonna and Angels, by Luca della Robbia, is made of glazed and painted terra-cotta, a medium used by some Renaissance sculptors because it was less expensive than marble.

Rome. But the details are different. Small figures twist and turn freely. Their heads and hands are enlarged and stand out from the surface of the relief.

▶ GOTHIC SCULPTURE

Sculpture after the 12th century gradually changed from the clear, concentrated abstractions of Romanesque art to a more natural and lifelike appearance. Human figures shown in natural proportions were carved in high relief on church columns and portals.

As Gothic sculptors became more skilled, they also gained greater freedom and independence. Later Gothic figures are depicted much more realistically than those made during the Romanesque and earlier Gothic periods. The faces of the statues have expression, and their garments are draped in a natural way. Hundreds of carvings in the great Gothic cathedrals all over Western Europe presented aspects of the Christian faith in terms that every Christian could understand.

The great era of building drew to a close by the early 14th century. A series of wars and crises prevented the building of anything more than small chapels and a few additions to earlier structures. One finds only small statuettes and objects, used for private devotions, instead of the great programs of monumental sculpture that in the 13th century had enriched such cathedrals as those at Amiens, Paris, Rheims, Wells, Burgos, and Strasbourg.

▶ RENAISSANCE SCULPTURE

Jutting into the Mediterranean Sea, the Italian peninsula, at the crossroads of several worlds, had been the heart of the Roman Empire. Rome was the center of the western Christian world. Later, northeastern Italy—especially Venice—became the gateway to the Near East and the Orient. Italian artists never completely accepted the Gothic styles that dominated art in Western Europe. The reason is that Italian artists were surrounded by the remains of the Classical Age and exposed to the Eastern influence of Byzantine art. (The article BYZANTINE ART AND ARCHITECTURE appears in Volume B.)

As early as the 13th century the Italians planted the seeds of a new age: the Renaissance. Although the elements of medieval and Byzantine art contributed a great deal to the formation of Renaissance sculpture, Italian artists were interested in reviving the classical approach to art. (''Renaissance'' means ''rebirth.'')

The most significant change in art that occurred in the Renaissance was the new emphasis on glorifying the human figure. No longer was sculpture to deal only with idealized saints and angels; sculpted figures began to look more lifelike.

The relief sculpture of Nicola Pisano (1220–84) forecast the new age. In the late 13th century Pisano carved nude male figures on a church pulpit. (The nude figure had not

Top left: The figures carved on the doorways of Chartres Cathedral are outstanding examples of Gothic sculpture. *Top right:* A panel of the bronze doors created by the early Renaissance sculptor Ghiberti for the Florence Baptistery. *Bottom right:* Ghiberti's contemporary Donatello sculpted this bronze *David,* the first freestanding nude statue since ancient times. *Bottom left:* Some 60 years later, the great Michelangelo created his own version of David.

been used in sculpture since the fall of Rome.) Although Pisano obviously tried to copy the heroic figures of classical art, he knew little about human anatomy, and his work was still proportioned like Byzantine and medieval sculpture.

By the early 15th century the Renaissance was well under way. The sculptor Donatello created the first freestanding nude since classical times, a bronze figure of David. Donatello clearly understood the whole anatomy of the figure so well that he could present the young biblical hero with an ease and assurance. By the early 16th century the sculptural heritage of another Florentine, the great painter and sculptor Michelangelo Buonarroti, was such that his version of David is almost superhuman in its force and strength.

Donatello and his contemporaries Lorenzo Ghiberti (1378–1455) and Jacopo della Quercia (1378?–1438) made themselves the masters of both the freestanding human figure and sculpture in relief. Jacopo's stone panels at San Petronio, Bologna, are powerful and emotional. Ghiberti's famous bronze doors of the Baptistery in Florence show his control of the science of perspective and his masterful handling of the human figure.

A host of sculptors worked with these men and, in turn, trained younger sculptors. Their individual talents varied, and these were applied to a number of different sculptural problems. Christian themes continued to be important, but in addition, fountains, portraits, tombs, equestrian statues, and subjects from classical mythology were all created to meet a lively demand. Luca della Robbia (1400?–82) and others developed a new medium—glazed terra-cotta. It was a popular and attractive substitute for the more expensive marble.

Michelangelo unquestionably became the dominant figure in 16th-century sculpture, and he is thought by many people to be the greatest single figure in the history of art. All his sculpture, from the early, beautifully finished *Pietà* to the tragic fragment the *Rondanini Pietà,* left unfinished at his death, was made with skill and power. Michelangelo's contemporaries and the sculptors who lived in later years in Italy and elsewhere developed a more elegant, decorative style, relying on a smooth, precise finish and complex, elaborate designs. This style was called **mannerism.**

▶BAROQUE SCULPTURE

Sculptors in the 17th century continued to deal with the same wide variety of sculptural problems as their Renaissance predecessors, using the human figure as a form of expression. They reacted, however, against the mannerism of late 16th century sculptors. They worked instead for a return to the greater strength of Michelangelo and the energy and agility of 15th-century sculpture.

Giovanni Lorenzo Bernini (1598–1680) was, like Michelangelo, a gifted artist. In a long and productive career, he easily became the dominating figure in his own country and one of the major artists in Europe during a brilliant, creative period. Bernini's *David* reveals his admiration for Michelangelo and his own originality. It has the largeness and strength of Michelangelo's *David* but is a much more active and less tragic figure. Bernini's figures stand in dramatic poses—as though they were actors on a stage, reaching

out to the observer. As a result, we feel drawn toward them and their grace.

ROCOCO SCULPTURE

The basic qualities of 17th-century art were carried forward into the 18th century but were transformed for the taste of a different generation. The term "rococo" suggests the preference for gayer, lighter, and more decorative effects in sculpture and in all the arts.

Jean Baptiste Pigalle (1714–85) and Étienne Maurice Falconet (1716–91) show the same technical dexterity as Bernini, but their figures are slight and cheerful. The skill revealed in their delicate work, with its tiny, sweetly shaped figures and graceful movement, represents a marked change from the strong, religious intensity of Bernini's work.

Statuettes and statues of small groups were designed as pleasant and often witty additions to lovely rooms. The individual talents of the sculptors and their joint efforts created an or-

namental effect. The same brilliance and skill also created a group of superbly beautiful churches in southern Germany.

NEOCLASSIC AND ROMANTIC SCULPTURE

The pendulum of taste swung in a new direction in the late 18th century while Clodion (1738–1814) and other rococo sculptors were still active. This direction, called neoclassic to describe the deliberate return to classical subject matter and style, lasted in strength for nearly a century. The change can be seen in the work of the distinguished sculptor Jean Antoine Houdon (1741–1828). His statue of George Washington could be compared to a portrait of a Roman emperor.

The most commanding figure of neoclassical sculpture was the Italian Antonio Canova (1757–1822). Canova was a favorite of the kings and noblemen of Europe. His specialty was the monument in which a statesman or other important figure was dressed in the robes

Opposite page: Bernini's *David* is rendered in the dramatic style of the Baroque period. *Above:* Michelangelo's powerful *Moses* is a late Renaissance work. *Right:* Houdon's *George Washington* portrays the American president in the manner of Greek and Roman sculpture.

and garlands of classical figures. Canova frankly imitated antique sculptors. His *Perseus* and *The Pugilists* are exhibited in the Vatican with ancient classical sculpture.

During the 19th century many sculptors rebelled against the neoclassical tradition. They wanted their works of art to say something, to express an idea or a feeling. They wanted to copy nature, not the works of other sculptors. François Rude (1784–1855) was one of the first to react against the coldness of the neoclassical style.

An intensity of emotion brings to life the work of Antoine Louis Barye (1795–1875). *Jaguar Devouring a Hare* is an exciting scene of conflict and violent struggle.

▶RODIN

Although the Romantic movement was growing, many artists still preferred to work in the classical tradition followed in the academies. In the 1860's a young sculptor named Auguste Rodin was turned away three times from the École des Beaux-Arts, the academy in Paris. By the end of the century he was the most famous sculptor in France and throughout most of Europe.

Although Rodin sought to copy nature, he used many new techniques. Both the hollows and raised portions of a surface were important to Rodin. He experimented with the effects of light on the surface of forms, just as the impressionists were doing in painting. He carved figures in shadow or emerging from an unfinished block. Whether he praised the homely courage of the subjects in *Burghers of*

Above: The Romantic sculptor Antoine Barye made dramatic studies of animals, such as this scene of a boa and a stag. *Left:* The rugged surfaces of Rodin's *Burghers of Calais* (1884–86) create an interplay of light and shadow.

Calais or the lovers in *The Kiss*—their heads enshadowed—Rodin suggested the natural, unposed moments in life.

20TH-CENTURY SCULPTURE

The 20th century was an age of experimentation with new ideas, new styles, and new materials. Studies of the human figure gave way to new subjects: dreams, ideas, emotions, and studies of form and space. Plastic, chromium, and welded steel were used, as well as boxes, broken automobile parts, and pieces of old furniture.

Twentieth-century sculptors owed a great debt to Rodin. His tremendous output and variety inspired a new generation of sculptors to express new thoughts in an art form that had been repeating old ideas for 200 years. Although Rodin's successors tended to move away from both his realism and his literary subjects, his innovations had an important influence. Aristide Maillol (1861–1944) rejected Rodin's rough surfaces. The smooth figures of Maillol's stone and bronze works seem to rest in calm repose.

As artists of the Renaissance had used the rediscovered works of classical Greece and Rome for inspiration, artists of the 20th century looked to the simple and powerful forms of the primitive African and Oceanic art. Wilhelm Lehmbruck (1881–1919), the German sculptor, began under the influence of Maillol. Later Lehmbruck distorted his figures by making them unnaturally long in the manner of primitive art. The faces of *Women*, by Gaston Lachaise (1882–1935), suggest the sculpture of ancient India. The round, solid, and massive bodies seem to symbolize the vitality of womanhood.

Constantin Brancusi (1876–1957), a Romanian who worked mostly in Paris, combined Romanian folk traditions with the simplicity of African wood carving and Oriental sculpture. Brancusi sought absolute simplicity of form and purity of meaning. This simplicity and purity is found in such works as *New-Born* and *Bird in Space*.

Pablo Picasso, one of the greatest sculptors as well as perhaps the greatest painter of the 20th century, saw another quality in primitive

Modern sculptors often experiment with abstract forms. *Above:* A stabile by Alexander Calder. *Below:* Cubi IX (1961), a grouping of shapes by David Smith.

Some modern sculptors portray traditional subjects, such as human form, in nontraditional ways. *Above:* Pablo Picasso's *Head of a Woman (Fernande)* (1909). *Below: Family Group* (1949) by Henry Moore.

Bronze, 16¹/₄" high. Collection, The Museum of Modern Art, New York. Purchase.

art. In the simplicity of forms he saw that objects of nature are not necessarily solid masses but are made up of circles, squares, triangles, and cubes. This led to a style called **cubism,** which was developed by Picasso and Georges Braque. Picasso's *Head of a Woman* (1909) is one of the first cubist sculptures. In it Picasso divided the surface of a head into many different planes.

With Picasso and Brancusi, Jacques Lipchitz (1891–1973) was one of the most influential sculptors of the 20th century. His powerful bronze forms show his understanding of cubism and the simple strength of African art, as well as all the other movements in 20th-century art.

As World War I began, the atmosphere in Europe was anxious. Some artists reflected the tensions of the uneasy times in a new form of art called dada—meaningless, representing nothing, and opposed to all other art. ''Found objects'' and household items, such as the sinks and hangers of Marcel Duchamp (1887–1968), were exhibited as sculpture. At the same time, a group of Italian artists called **futurists** were excited by the pace of the machine age. Their sculpture showed objects in motion. Umberto Boccioni (1882–1916) was a leading futurist.

After World War I, the movement called **surrealism** developed. Many artists who had been cubists or dadaists became surrealists. The work of Jean Arp (1887–1966), with its fanciful forms that seem to float in space, belongs to this movement.

During the 1920's and 1930's, the constructivists built rather than carved or modeled their sculptures. The beauty of pure form and space excited them. The Russian brothers Naum Gabo (1890–1977) and Antoine Pevsner (1886–1962) used blades of metal and plastic to achieve an effect of lightness and transparency. Julio Gonzalez (1876–1942) introduced the use of forged iron. The tremendous influence of his technique is seen particularly in the work of Picasso, a student of Gonzalez in the technique of welding.

As modern sculpture developed, it became more and more individualistic, although it still showed its debt to the past. The long, thin figures of Alberto Giacometti (1901–66) seem to wander alone in a world without boundaries. Alexander Calder (1898–1976) created moving sculptures called mobiles and station-

Left: In sleek, streamlined works like *Bird in Space* (1940), Constantin Brancusi sought absolute simplicity of form. *Above:* In *Mirror-Shadow VII* (1985), Louise Nelson brought an assembly of complex parts into a unified whole.

ary ones called stabiles. The wire and metal-strip constructions made by Richard Lippold (1915–) evoke a feeling of delicate lightness. The steel geometric sculptures of David Smith (1906–65) have a sense of balance and order that pleases the eye.

In the 1960's and 1970's, still more new styles developed. Some artists chose to portray subjects from the everyday world around them—the Brillo boxes and soup cans of Andy Warhol (1930?–87), the surrealist boxes of Joseph Cornell (1903–72), the plaster hamburgers and "soft typewriters" of Claes Oldenburg (1929–). Others combined painting, sculpture, and "found objects," as in the work of Marisol Escobar (1930–). George Segal (1924–) used plaster casts of human figures in everyday poses. Louise Nelson (1900–88) combined small units of metal and wood (often table and chair legs, bed posts) into huge structures that she called "environments." Sculptors like Barnett Newman (1905–70) and Tony Smith (1912–80) created

massive pieces that are often shown outdoors. Some sculpture not only moves but is run by computer.

One dominant figure in the world of sculpture, Henry Moore (1898–1986), used traditional materials (wood, bronze, and stone) in exploring traditional problems of sculpture such as the seated figure and the reclining figure. He believed that the space shapes created by a sculpture are as important to its design as the solid forms, and he often put holes or openings in his sculptures. Moore also contrasted light and dark by curving his bronze figures inward and outward.

Form and space, reality, emotion, and perfect beauty are the interests of artists in all centuries. The 20th century only gave them new shape.

ELEANOR DODGE BARTON
Formerly, University of Hartford

See also BAROQUE ART AND ARCHITECTURE; DESIGN; MODERN ART; RENAISSANCE ART AND ARCHITECTURE; articles on individual artists and the art of specific countries.

The California sea lion, a marine mammal belonging to the eared seal family, has a long, tapering body and limbs that are modified into flippers.

SEA LIONS

Young sea lions always seem to be at play. Some will spend hours body surfing. Others may make a toy of a slow-moving lizard or a lost pair of eyeglasses, tossing it about in the water. In fact, the trained "seals" you see performing in zoos and theme parks are actually California sea lions.

Sea lions belong to a group of sea mammals, called pinnipeds, that also includes fur seals, seals, and walruses. The California sea lion is the most well known of the five kinds, or species, of sea lions. It makes its home in coastal waters from California to South America. Other sea lions live off the coasts of Alaska, Canada, Australia, and New Zealand.

Unlike true seals, sea lions have small outer ears. They also are able to walk by turning their hind flippers to face forward or backward. This allows sea lions extra mobility on land. To move about, they raise up their sleek, torpedo-shaped bodies and alternately move their front and rear flippers. In the water, sea lions use just the strong front flippers in a rowing motion.

▶SEA LIONS AND THEIR YOUNG

Each year, female sea lions, or cows, gather on beaches to give birth. Their single pups are born in late spring. Males, or bulls, establish breeding areas on these beaches. They gather the females that settle on their territory into harems. If one bull enters another bull's territory, a vicious fight may break out. Mating takes place after the pups are born.

Mothers tend their newborns carefully, learning to recognize them by smell and sound. Nourished by their mother's milk for five to six months, the pups grow quickly. By 1 month old, pups are swimming on their own. Fathers take no part in the care of young.

After the breeding season, which lasts about three months, California sea lions swim north for the winter. However, some females may stay on the breeding grounds year-round.

When fully grown, a California sea lion bull weighs about 836 pounds (380 kilograms) and reaches more than 6 feet (1.8 meters) in length. Cows are much smaller, weighing about 220 pounds (100 kilograms) and reaching a length of about 5½ feet (1.7 meters). The largest sea lions are the northern, or Steller, sea lions. These bulls may weigh up to 2,400 pounds (1,089 kilograms) and be more than 10 feet (3 meters) long!

▶THE LIFE AND ENVIRONMENT OF THE SEA LION

Sea lions eat mainly fish and squid. To catch their prey, they dive 85 to 243 feet (26 to 74 meters) underwater, usually staying there for a few minutes. Steller sea lions also eat small seals and fur seals, while New Zealand sea lions also eat penguins.

Sea lions are prey for such animals as large sharks and killer whales. Humans have hunted sea lions for their meat, blubber, and skins. Commercial fishers have killed the animals because they compete for fish and damage fishing gear.

Although hunting sea lions is now illegal, the numbers of northern sea lions have dropped severely. No one knows exactly why. Many sea lions drown when they become tangled in fishing nets. Another reason may be that heavy fishing has deprived sea lions of their food supply. Disease, which spreads very quickly through groups of sea lions, could also be a threat to their population.

CARRIE DIERKS
Denver Museum of Natural History
Reviewed by LOUIS GARIBALDI
Aquarium for Wildlife Conservation

See also FUR SEALS; MAMMALS; SEALS.

SEALS

On land, seals are slow and clumsy, moving their large torpedo-shaped bodies with great effort. But the water is their natural home and in it they are speedy and graceful swimmers. Plunging beneath the water's surface, some can dive up to 2,000 feet (610 meters) deep and stay underwater for more than an hour!

Seals are related to sea lions, fur seals, and walruses. All are sea mammals belonging to the order Pinnipedia, which is Latin for "wing-footed." Called pinnipeds, they evolved from land mammals 15 to 25 million years ago. Their land-dwelling ancestors were probably also the ancestors of today's weasels and bears.

The 18 living species, or kinds, of seals range over a wide area. Most seals live near the coasts of the Arctic and Antarctic oceans and in adjoining areas of the Atlantic and Pacific oceans. However, two species live in inland bodies of water, and one species lives in a freshwater lake.

►CHARACTERISTICS OF SEALS

At first glance, seals look much like sea lions and fur seals. These animals are all well adapted to life in water. They have sleek, rounded bodies, and instead of legs they have flippers, which look somewhat like fins. However, unlike their relatives, seals have no external ears. Also, while sea lions and fur seals can turn their hind flippers to face forward or backward, a seal's hind flippers always face backward.

The seal is like an elegant acrobat in the water. As the seal swims, its hind flippers make powerful, side-to-side slashing movements to propel the animal along. Its front flippers are used for slow rowing and steering. On land the hind flippers are nearly useless. The seal moves along the ground like a giant caterpillar, shifting its weight from front to back and bending its entire body.

A seal's fur is short and stiff and may range in color from light to dark. Some kinds of seals have spotted or ringed coats. The fur of the seal is too thin to offer much protection

Seals, such as the crabeater seal (*above*) and the Hawaiian monk seal (*left*), are water-loving creatures that crawl ashore only when it is time to rest or give birth.

from its cold environment. Rather, seals are protected from heat loss by a well-developed layer of fatty tissue, called blubber, that lies under the skin.

Even the smallest of seals are large animals. Male harbor seals, which are among the smaller seals, weigh up to 300 pounds (136 kilograms), while females weigh about 175 pounds (79 kilograms). The largest seals are the southern elephant seals— these males may weigh up to 8,000 pounds (3,629 kilograms)!

Seals have a keen sense of hearing. It is probably their most important sense, helping them to find their way and to detect danger. Their large eyes see well underwater, but not so well on land. Once they leave the water, seals depend more on their sense of smell to recognize each other and their enemies.

►THE LIFE OF THE SEAL

Most seals, including harbor seals and elephant seals, are very sociable. Thousands will crowd together on beaches. Other kinds of seals, such as bearded seals, stay by themselves except during the mating season.

Seals have different mating seasons depending on where they live. Some seals gather

Southern elephant seals, who are shedding their coats, crowd together on a beach. The seals will not eat during the process, which can take as long as 40 days.

"hauling out," on land or ice. Like all pinnipeds, seals are meat eaters, or carnivores. They catch fish, squid, shrimp, and other prey and tear the meat with their peglike teeth. Larger seals are also known to hunt penguins or small sharks.

▶ SEALS AND THEIR ENVIRONMENT

Seals may be prey for large sharks, killer whales, polar bears, and walruses. However, the main predators of seals are people. Northern peoples still make oil from seal blubber and leather from seal hides. Historically, some seals were also hunted for their pelts; with their thick white fur, newborn harp seals had been a popular target.

While there are some seals that are hunted for use as food, many more are killed because they are considered a nuisance. Commercial fishers have killed thousands of seals because the seals compete for fish and damage equipment. Many others die accidentally when they become trapped in fishing nets and drown.

Hunting is no longer a threat to most seals. Other human activities, such as oil spills and pollution, have resulted in the destruction of

every year on the same breeding areas. Females, or cows, arrive at the breeding grounds after the males. A week or so later, they give birth to a single pup. The pups, who are sometimes born in shallow water, can move about and swim almost immediately.

Mothers nurse their young for about a month. Nourished by extra-rich milk, the pups double their weight by the time they are weaned. Most seals are fully grown by 4 or 5 years of age.

Mating takes place soon after the pups are weaned. Among elephant seals, males guard their mates closely. They herd the females together and chase away other males who come too close.

After mating season, seals spend most of their time hunting out at sea. They may spend only a few minutes at a time resting, or

Right: Rearing their heads, male elephant seals challenge each other. The most successful fighters in a group will get to mate with the most females. *Below:* A harbor seal pup stays close to its mother.

the seal's habitat and contamination of its food supplies. Control of ocean pollution and efforts to protect the animal's environment are measures that will help make sure that seals will continue to thrive.

CARRIE DIERKS
Denver Museum of Natural History
Reviewed by LOUIS GARIBALDI
Aquarium for Wildlife Conservation

See also FUR SEALS; MAMMALS.

SEAS.   See OCEAN; OCEANS AND SEAS OF THE WORLD.

Summer ▶

Winter ▼

▲ Fall

◀ Spring

SEASONS

The Earth is constantly moving. Once each year it completes one revolution in its orbit around the sun, and once every 24 hours it completes one rotation on its own axis. The Earth's rotation on its axis is what causes day and night. The different periods of the year that are known as **seasons**—spring, summer, fall, and winter—are caused by the tilt of the Earth's axis and the revolution of the Earth around the sun. In most places, the different seasons bring changes in the length of daylight, in temperature, and in weather.

Seasonal changes occur because the Earth's axis is tilted at an angle of 23.5 degrees to the plane of its orbit around the sun. Because of this tilt, the Earth's North and South Poles are each turned toward the sun for part of the year and away from the sun for the rest of the year. When the North Pole is tilted toward the sun, it is spring and summer in the Northern Hemi-

sphere. The sun shines longer each day than it does in fall and winter, and it takes its highest and longest path across the sky on the first day of summer. For this reason, this is also the longest day of the year.

The seasons north and south of the equator are always the opposite of each other. During the time one pole is tilted toward the sun, the other pole is tilted away from it. Thus, while it is spring and summer in the Northern Hemisphere, it is fall and winter in the Southern Hemisphere. In winter, the days are shorter, the sun is low in the sky, and the sun's radiation is spread over a larger area. During fall and winter at either the North or South Pole, there is almost continuous night.

Some regions of the Earth experience fewer seasonal changes than others. This is especially true in areas near the equator, which receive about the same amount of sunlight all

Imagining the Celestial Sphere

Astronomers work out the dates of the astronomical seasons by imagining that the sun moves around the Earth and that the Earth stands still. They describe how the sun appears to move to someone on Earth, even though we know that in fact the Earth does move and that it revolves around the sun. They put the Earth at the center of a huge globe called a **celestial sphere**, which represents the sky. The sun's path around the Earth, which is called the **ecliptic**, is represented by a circle around the inner surface of this sphere. It takes the sun one year to make a trip around its ecliptic.

The Earth's axis intersects the celestial sphere at two points, which are called the **celestial poles**. The **celestial equator** lies midway between these poles,

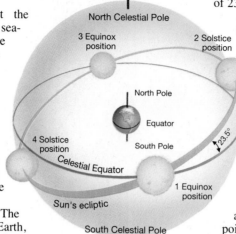

North Celestial Pole
3 Equinox position
2 Solstice position
North Pole
Equator
4 Solstice position
South Pole
Celestial Equator
23.5°
1 Equinox position
Sun's ecliptic
South Celestial Pole

and the sun's ecliptic lies at an angle of 23.5 degrees to it.

At the point where the sun's ecliptic crosses the celestial equator, its light "slices" the Earth exactly in half from pole to pole. This means that as the Earth spins, nearly every part of the planet experiences a day in which the length of daylight hours equals the length of darkness.

Astronomers say that the sun is at an **equinox**, or "equal night," position.

As the sun continues moving along its ecliptic, it reaches points above or below the celestial equator where it seems to stand still momentarily before descending or ascending back toward the celestial equator. Each of these stand-still points is called a **solstice**, from Latin words meaning "sun stands still." The solstice and the equinox points mark the beginning and end of the four astronomical seasons on Earth.

Why is it hotter in summer than it is in winter?

The sun is higher in the sky in the summer, and it shines down more directly on the Earth. As a result, the sun's rays are more concentrated. The days are also longer, which gives the sun more time to heat the Earth's surface.

In winter the sun is lower in the sky, and its light reaches the ground at a greater slant. Therefore, the rays of the sun are spread out over a larger area than they are in summer. The days are also shorter in winter, which means that the sun has less time to warm the Earth's surface.

In the illustration below, the flashlight represents the sun and the square represents a portion of the Earth's surface. The flashlight is giving out the same amount of light in both examples, A and B. But the light is spread out over a larger total area in B. Thus the square in A is getting more energy per second than the square in B.

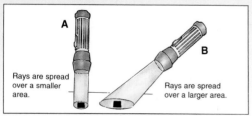

A
B
Rays are spread over a smaller area.
Rays are spread over a larger area.

year long and have little or no change in temperature throughout the year. These regions generally have only a rainy season and a dry season.

The Astronomical Seasons

Seasonal changes in temperature and weather characterize what are known as the climatic seasons. The beginnings and ends of these climatic seasons vary depending upon the place and the year. Scientists, however, have worked out specific dates for when what are known as the astronomical seasons begin and end each year.

The **summer solstice**, which occurs on June 20 or 21, is the date that summer begins in the Northern Hemisphere. This is the day of the year when the Northern Hemisphere experiences the most hours of daylight. December 21 or 22 marks the **winter solstice**, the beginning of winter in the Northern Hemisphere and the day with the fewest daylight hours. The beginning of spring, the **vernal equinox**, occurs on March 20 or 21. On this day, the sun appears directly above the equator, and the hours of daylight and darkness are equal. The

When the Seasons Begin in the Northern Hemisphere

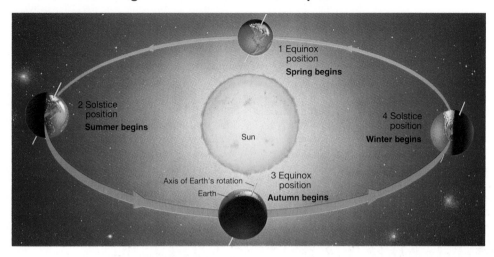

Points 1, 2, 3, and 4 in this drawing relate to the same points in the illustration of the celestial sphere on page 110. In the Northern Hemisphere, the spring, or vernal equinox, occurs at point 1. Then, as the Earth moves on, the sun seems to climb higher in the sky, and the hours of daylight become longer every day until the Earth reaches point 2, the summer solstice.

As the Earth moves away from point 2, the days gradually become shorter until the planet reaches point 3, the autumnal equinox. At this point the nights are as long as the days. Then, as the Earth travels toward point 4, the North Pole tilts away from the sun. The sun seems low in the sky at midday, and the days are short and the nights are long. Winter arrives with the winter solstice at point 4.

In the Southern Hemisphere the seasons are exactly opposite those in the Northern Hemisphere. When it is winter or spring in the Northern Hemisphere, it is summer or fall in the Southern Hemisphere. In this illustration, the vernal equinox in the Southern Hemisphere is at point 3, the summer solstice at point 4, the autumnal equinox at point 1, and the winter solstice at point 2.

A simple experiment will allow you to see how the seasons change as the Earth travels around the sun. You will need a globe and a lamp. Set the lamp in the middle of a darkened room and remove the shade so that the bulb is exposed. Place the globe on a table or a stand about 2 feet (60 centimeters) away from the lamp and at about the same height.

Tilt the globe so that the North Pole is pointed toward the light at about a 25-degree angle. This represents summer in the Northern Hemisphere. Now rotate the globe slowly on its axis. You will notice that more light falls directly on places in the Northern Hemisphere than on those in the Southern Hemisphere. The light falls on the North Pole continuously, but it does not reach the South Pole at all.

Now carry the globe slowly around the lamp, facing the light and keeping the base of the globe turned exactly as it was when you started. Observe where and how the light falls. You will notice that when you reach a point opposite from where you started, the Southern Hemisphere receives more direct light from the lamp. At that point it is summer in the Southern Hemisphere and winter in the Northern Hemisphere.

same is true for the beginning of autumn, the **autumnal equinox**, which occurs on September 22 or 23.

The path of the Earth's orbit around the sun is not a perfect circle. As a result, the planet's distance from the sun changes. The Earth is nearest the sun about January 1 and farthest away about July 1. The difference in distance is not enough to affect the seasons. But the dates marking the start of the astronomical seasons may differ from year to year because our calendar requires the addition of a full day every four years. The year with the extra day is known as leap year.

COLIN A. RONAN
Fellow of the Royal Astronomical Society

See also EARTH; SUN.

SEA STARS. See STARFISH.

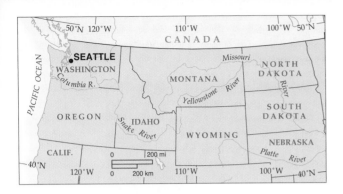

SEATTLE

Seattle, Washington, is the largest city in the Pacific Northwest and Washington's main center for trade, finance, marketing, and manufacturing. Its population is more than 560,000, and together with the cities of Everett and Tacoma, it is the center of a metropolitan area of more than 3.5 million people.

Situated in lowland amid mountains and forests, Seattle is one of the world's most scenic cities and is considered one of the most desirable places in which to live. It occupies a slender isthmus that is flanked by two bodies of water—saltwater Puget Sound to the west and freshwater Lake Washington to the east. The city itself covers an area of 92 square miles (238 square kilometers).

Seattle is graced with spectacular mountain views. The Olympic Mountains rise to the west and the Cascade Range, featuring Mount Rainier, rise to the east. These two ranges shelter Seattle from extreme temperatures and from most severe storms. Its climate is mild and moist. Temperatures average only 39°F (4°C) in January and 65°F (18°C) in July. Annual precipitation averages 39 inches (990 millimeters), with the heaviest rains falling from October through March.

Business and Industry

Seattle is famous for the manufacture of aircraft, especially jet-powered transports and military planes. Other important industries are based on forest products and fisheries. The port is a major shipping terminal for international trade between the United States and Asia. The area's main airport is Seattle-Tacoma International. Its two major daily newspapers are the *Seattle Post-Intelligencer* and the *Seattle Times*.

Education, Culture, and Recreation

The University of Washington, with an enrollment of about 30,000, is the largest university in the Pacific Northwest. Other regional institutions of higher learning include Seattle University and Seattle Pacific University. A number of community colleges also offer a variety of educational opportunities.

The creative arts are well represented. The Seattle Symphony and the Seattle Opera Association perform at Seattle Center, which was built for the Century 21 Exposition of 1962. The Space Needle, the symbol of the fair, towers above the center. Its observation deck offers a panoramic view of the city.

Local museums include the Seattle Art Museum, the Museum of History and Industry, and the Pacific Science Center, which features a planetarium and laser shows.

The mountains and water around Seattle offer year-round opportunities for recreation, and the city's vast park system provides ample open areas and playgrounds. The best known is Woodland Park, with its gardens, amusement park, and natural-habitat zoo. Other attractions include the Seattle Aquarium and the Seattle Funplex, an indoor recre-

The picturesque city of Seattle, Washington, is surrounded by mountains and water. Seattle's most familiar landmark, the Space Needle, is a towering structure that was built when the city hosted the World's Fair in 1962. Mount Rainier, in the Cascade Range, rises in the background.

ation and sports complex. SAFECO Field is home to the Seattle Mariners baseball team and the Seattle Seahawks football team. The SuperSonics and the Seattle Storm basketball teams play at KeyArena in the Seattle Center Coliseum.

History

The Seattle area was originally home to several Indian tribes, including the Duwamish and the Suquamish. In 1851 five pioneer families from Illinois settled on Alki Point, west of Elliott Bay, an arm of Puget Sound. They cut logs for shipment to San Francisco. The following year they moved to the eastern shore of Elliott Bay, which was a better port site, and named their settlement Seattle, after a Suquamish Indian chief.

Lumbering throughout western Washington expanded, and salmon fisheries developed in Seattle. The transcontinental Great Northern Railroad reached the city in 1884. It later brought miners and supplies destined for Alaska during the gold rush of 1897. By 1910, Seattle had become a major Pacific port.

Both world wars stimulated manufacturing, especially shipbuilding and airplane construction. Other Puget Sound cities grew along with Seattle. In the 1960's and early 1970's, employment in the airplane-manufacturing industry declined, and many people moved to the suburbs. More recently, increased trade with Asian countries has stimulated port activities. In 2001, Seattle experienced a 6.8 magnitude earthquake, the worst to hit the area in more than 50 years. Property damage was significant, but no deaths were reported.

OTTO F. JAKUBEK
Central Washington University

SEAWEEDS.   See ALGAE.

SECRET WRITING.   See CODES AND CIPHERS.

SEEDS.   See FLOWERS; PLANTS.

SEGREGATION

Segregation refers to the separateness of two or more groups living within the same society. The source of segregation is prejudice felt by a dominant group that feels superior to the other. Segregation usually refers to the separation of races within a common community, but segregated societies may also be based on prejudice against different religious beliefs or ancestry.

Although segregation is the product of prejudice and discrimination, these terms have different meanings. Prejudice is a dislike for certain people because of their race, religion, or ancestry. Discrimination is prejudice in action. It is evident wherever the dominant group deprives a minority of the same rights and opportunities that they themselves enjoy.

Whether brought about by custom or by law, segregation affects every aspect of daily life—where people can or cannot live, work, and go to school, what public facilities they can use, and even where they can sit when using public transportation.

▶ *DE JURE* AND *DE FACTO* SEGREGATION

Legal segregation is called *de jure* (Latin for "according to law"). Until the passage of the Civil Rights Act of 1964, segregation was still legal in several parts of the United States. But after this act and other civil rights legislation passed, it became illegal nationwide to practice segregation in public places.

De facto (Latin for "in fact") segregation exists in many places, even where fair housing and employment laws already have been passed. But people find ways to get around these laws. Employers might be complying with the law by hiring minorities, but no law prevents them from hiring minorities only for the most menial jobs. Homeowners may discriminate by refusing to sell or rent to certain people. Tactics might include pricing the property far beyond the potential buyers' reach or telling unwanted buyers that the property has already been sold. It is hard to prove in court that such actions by employers or homeowners are based on prejudice.

▶ SEGREGATION IN HISTORY

Segregation of one kind or another has been a part of most societies since the beginning of civilized life. Many peoples of the ancient world practiced segregation according to social classes. Slaves, often taken as prisoners

Before segregation was outlawed in the United States, it was common practice for African-Americans to use separate public facilities, especially in the southern states.

of war, had no rights of citizenship, and from birth their children faced lives of servitude.

Segregation by religion prevailed in Europe for centuries. People of some religions feared and hated those of other faiths, believing them to hold false doctrines and ungodly views. In almost every country, those who did not practice the religion of the majority were forced to live apart from the rest of the community in places that came to be known as ghettos. These people, especially Jews, lived in terror of persecution and death.

Colonial Slavery

As Europeans began to colonize the African, Asian, and American continents, segregation by color began. Often it was easy for the powerful Europeans to force their rule upon the native societies that they encountered. Once they had established rule, the Europeans imposed strict laws of segregation, usually in order to hold power over the native populations that outnumbered them.

The African slave trade began in the late 1400's. Blacks, chiefly from the west coast of Africa, were sold into slavery—sometimes by Europeans and often by African chiefs or Arab traders. As soon as slaves were introduced into the American colonies in the early 1600's, they were separated from mainstream society. The harsh conditions of slavery and the imposed isolation kept blacks in a powerless position for hundreds of years.

▶THE MOVEMENT TOWARD DESEGREGATION IN AMERICA

Many generations of Americans worked for the cause of racial equality. First they fought for the abolition of slavery, which was accomplished in 1865. But this achievement was compromised with the Supreme Court ruling *Plessy* v. *Ferguson* (1896), which declared that although blacks were considered equal under the law, there was nothing unconstitutional about separating them in society.

It was not until the mid-1950's, however, that the civil rights movement caught fire. Unlike previous movements, it was not limited to small groups. Eventually, Native Americans, Hispanic Americans, and other minorities also took part.

Many of the seeds of the movement were planted while the nation was engaged (1941–45) in World War II. Blacks and others fought as equals beside white soldiers in foreign countries. When the war ended and these soldiers returned to civilian life, they expected equal treatment.

The war also influenced the thinking of many whites in the United States who had fought Nazi racism. They began to recognize the kind of racism that they knew existed at home. Many rallied to the black cause. They believed that as long as freedom was denied any citizen, the rights of all were in danger.

The Supreme Court Ruling of 1954

In 1954 civil rights lawyer Thurgood Marshall headed the legal team that brought the issue of school desegregation before the U.S. Supreme Court. In the landmark case *Brown* v. *Board of Education of Topeka*, (Kansas), the high court overruled *Plessy* v. *Ferguson* and declared segregation in public schools unconstitutional. A few southern cities, such as Atlanta and Louisville, carried out the desegregation process with minimal disturbance. However, the schools in several other cities simply ignored the decision and continued to exclude blacks.

In 1957, Little Rock, Arkansas, drew national attention when the governor openly defied the government ruling and barred nine black students from enrolling at Little Rock's all-white Central High School. Federal troops were dispatched by President Dwight D. Eisenhower to protect the students and suppress the rioting and violence.

Montgomery, Alabama

In 1955, Rosa Parks, a black woman in Montgomery, Alabama, ignited the civil rights movement with a single act of courage. She refused a white bus driver's order to move to the back of the bus in which she was riding. When Parks was arrested and fined for her actions, Montgomery's African American community began a boycott of the city bus lines. Segregation on the buses ended after the case was taken to court. This was a major turning point in the history of the civil rights movement in the United States. It was the first time a segregation law had been nullified (made invalid) through the efforts of African Americans.

Civil Rights Leaders

During the Montgomery crisis, Martin Luther King, Jr., a Baptist minister, emerged as the chief leader of the civil rights movement. He and many others worked to end segregation and discrimination. Among them were Roy Wilkins (1901–81), a longtime director (1955–77) of the National Association for the Advancement of Colored People (NAACP); A. Philip Randolph (1889–1979), who led a labor union of black railroad car porters; Whitney M. Young, Jr. (1921–71), executive director (1961–71) of the National Urban League; Ralph Abernathy (1926–90), president (1968–77) of the Southern Christian Leadership Conference (SCLC); and Bayard Rustin (1910–87), who pioneered "freedom ride" protest marches into the South in 1947. Today the Reverend Jesse Jackson (1941–   ) is a chief spokesperson for minority rights.

School integration on a national scale proceeded slowly until passage of the Civil Rights Act of 1964, which empowered the federal government to withhold funds from segregated school districts. At first, efforts to desegregate were focused on the South, and by 1974 southern schools were far more integrated than northern schools. Efforts to achieve racial balance in northern states increased in the mid-1970's. Officials attempted to desegregate the public schools by busing less fortunate children into more affluent school districts. This practice often met with violent opposition.

▶ SEGREGATION TODAY

De facto segregation continues to be practiced in all parts of the world. For example, in Latin America the descendants of the native Indians have faced repression ever since the Spanish conquistadors took over their land beginning in the 1500's. India did not abolish its rigid caste system until 1949. For hundreds of years India had segregated fully 20 percent of its population, branding them "untouchables." Many segregation laws and practices were removed in several Asian and African colonies when they became independent nations after 1945, following World War II.

The best defense against *de facto* segregation is the growth of understanding and goodwill among people of all races, cultures, and religions. There are signs of such growth. For example, in the United States today, sincere efforts are made by many people to promote fair practices in housing and employment.

The battle against segregation is a very special kind of war. It is not a war against people but a war against certain ideas. In this war, victory does not mean conquering people. It means getting them to change their ideas. The ultimate goal of the civil rights movement is to establish a truly open society, in which each person is judged on his or her merit alone.

Reviewed by ELLIOTT RUDWICK
Kent State University

See also CIVIL RIGHTS MOVEMENT.

SEISMOLOGY. See EARTHQUAKES.

SELECTIVE SERVICE. See DRAFT, OR CONSCRIPTION.

Civil rights attorney Thurgood Marshall (center) celebrated a landmark victory with the Supreme Court ruling (1954) that declared segregation unconstitutional in the public schools.

SEMANTICS

Semantics is the study of meanings. In most cases it is impossible to learn a word's meaning from the word alone. We must know what the word represents—its **referent**. A key principle of semantics is that the connection between a word and its referent is something that people have agreed on.

Many English words have more than one meaning. Words that are spelled alike but have different meanings are called **homonyms**. Sometimes the different meanings of a homonym are unrelated—for example, a round object ("ball") and a formal dance ("ball"). But sometimes the meanings are related—for example, "fall" means both a downward movement and the season when leaves fall to the ground.

Even words that seem to have one meaning represent separate objects. Take the word "apple." Every apple is different from every other. We may use the name of the particular variety of apple, but even these names do not distinguish between individual apples.

Words that represent feelings—such as *love* and *fun*—are even harder to describe. A main problem in semantics is to discover how such words (called **abstract words**) come by their meanings.

Words that make us feel a certain emotion often do so not by what they represent but by what they suggest. The direct meaning of a word is its **denotation**; its suggested meaning is its **connotation**. When we call someone "Honey," we do not mean the substance made by bees. That is the word's denotation. What the word means as a nickname is its connotation. Words with different connotations can suggest very different things. Here is an example: I am *cautious*; you are *timid*; he is a *coward*. All three words have the same denotation—they describe a person who does not take chances. But what do these words tell us about the speaker's feelings?

The study of semantics reveals that all words have not only official meanings, but deeper meanings that shape our lives.

ANATOL RAPOPORT
University of Michigan

SEMICONDUCTORS. See MATERIALS SCIENCE; TRANSISTORS, DIODES, AND INTEGRATED CIRCUITS.

SENDAK, MAURICE (1928–)

Illustrator and writer Maurice Sendak was born in Brooklyn, New York, on June 10, 1928. As a boy, Sendak and his older brother used to write stories, illustrate them, and bind them into little books.

Though Sendak went to art school for a short time, he mainly learned about his profession on his own. As a teen he spent many hours sketching neighborhood children as they played. These children were represented in *A Hole Is to Dig* (1952), a book by Ruth Kraus that brought Sendak his first fame.

Sendak's ability to remember the sounds and feelings of particular childhood

Maurice Sendak's book *Where the Wild Things Are* has delighted children the world over. Sendak is famous for capturing the feelings of childhood through his illustrations and words.

moments were demonstrated in his best-known book, *Where the Wild Things Are* (1963), for which he won the 1964 Caldecott Medal. He later wrote and illustrated two companion books: *In the Night Kitchen* (1970) and *Outside Over There* (1981); the latter received a 1982 American Book Award. Sendak has said the three works are about "how children manage to get through childhood … how they defeat boredom, worries and fear, and find joy."

Sendak has illustrated some ninety children's books. In 1970, he won the international Hans Christian Andersen Medal for the body of his illustrated work, becoming the first American to receive this highest honor in children's book publishing. In 1996, U.S. president Bill Clinton presented Sendak with the National Medal of Arts. In recent years, the artist has designed sets and costumes for the ballet and for a number of grand operas in the United States and England.

SELMA G. LANES
Author, *The Art of Maurice Sendak*

★ SENEGAL

Senegal is an African nation of nearly 10 million people. It is located on the westernmost tip of Africa's great western bulge, on the coast of the Atlantic Ocean. Once a French colonial territory, Senegal gained its independence in 1960. Formerly dominated by a single political party, it has gradually moved toward a more democratic system of government.

▶ **PEOPLE**

Senegal's people belong to varied ethnic groups. The Wolof is the largest and makes up more than one-third of the population. Other ethnic groups include the Serer, the Fulani, the Tukulor, the Diola, and the Mandingo. More than half the population lives in the countryside, mainly as farmers in small villages. The others live in cities and towns. Most Senegalese are Muslims, and their religious leaders, the Marabou, have much economic and political influence. Some peo-

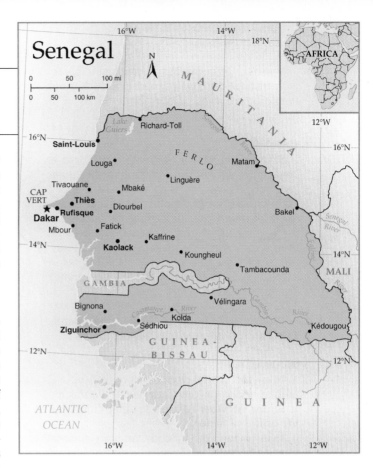

ple practice traditional African religions, and about 5 percent are Christians.

Most of the people speak Wolof, an African language. French, the official language, is used in government and in schools. Six years of primary education is compulsory.

▶ **LAND**

Most of Senegal consists of low plains, except in the southeast, where plateaus and hills reach a height of about 1,640 feet (500 meters). Much of the northern interior is semi-desert. The southern region, called the Casamance, is partly separated from the rest of the country by the nation of Gambia. The Casamance has a swampy coastal area and dense rain forests inland.

Senegal is drained by five rivers: the Senegal on the northern border; the Siné and the Saloum in the central part of the country; and the Gambia and the Casamance in the south.

The presidential palace in Dakar, Senegal's capital, is one of the city's most prominent and attractive landmarks.

Climate. Senegal has a tropical climate, with distinct dry and wet seasons. Maximum temperatures range from about 63 to 82°F (17 to 27°C).

▶ ECONOMY

Seventy percent of Senegal's workforce is engaged in agriculture. Peanuts are the main commercial crop.

Processed foods (mainly products made from peanuts) are the country's most important manufactured products, and canned tuna is its leading export. Chemicals and cotton textiles are also manufactured. Imported petroleum is refined at Dakar. Phosphates are mined for use in fertilizers.

Senegal's transportation system includes well-developed ports in Dakar and Saint-Louis and an international airport in Dakar.

▶ MAJOR CITIES

Dakar, the capital city, has a population of 2 million and is on the Cape Verde Peninsula. It is one of West Africa's leading cities and the center of Senegal's public life.

Thiès, a railroad junction and an agricultural and commercial center, is east of Dakar. **Kaolack** is an important inland port on the Saloum River. **Saint-Louis**, a northern port city, is believed to have been West Africa's first French settlement.

FACTS and figures

REPUBLIC OF SENEGAL (République du Sénégal) is the official name of the country.

LOCATION: West Africa.

AREA: 75,749 sq mi (196,190 km²).

POPULATION: 11,100,000 (estimate).

CAPITAL AND LARGEST CITY: Dakar.

MAJOR LANGUAGES: French (official), Wolof, other African languages.

MAJOR RELIGIOUS GROUPS: Muslim, traditional African religions, Christian (mainly Roman Catholic).

GOVERNMENT: Republic. **Head of state**—president. **Head of government**—prime minister. **Legislature**—National Assembly.

CHIEF PRODUCTS: Agricultural—peanuts, cotton, rice, cassava, millet, beans, sorghum, livestock. **Manufactured**—canned fish, peanut oil and other peanut products, cotton textiles, chemicals. **Mineral**—phosphates.

MONETARY UNIT: African Financial Community (CFA) franc (1 CFA franc = 100 centimes).

▶ GOVERNMENT

Senegal adopted a new constitution in 2001. A president, elected to serve a 5-year term, serves as head of state. A prime minister, appointed by the president, serves as head of government. Members of Senegal's 120-seat legislature, the National Assembly, are elected to serve 5-year terms.

▶ HISTORY

Flourishing kingdoms existed in the region before the first Europeans arrived in the 1400's. The French arrived in the 1600's, and in the late 1800's, Senegal became part of the colony called French West Africa, a federation of eight African territories.

Independence. In 1958, Senegal gained self-government as a member of the French community. The following year, Senegal joined with what is now the Republic of Mali to form the Mali Federation. Senegal withdrew from the federation in 1960, becoming a separate, independent republic.

Léopold Sédar Senghor, a well-known poet, became the country's first president in 1960 and held that position through successive elections until his retirement in 1980. Beginning in 1976, he introduced reforms that made Senegal one of the first multiparty states in Africa. In 1981, Senghor was succeeded as president by Abdou Diouf.

In 1982, Senegal and Gambia were united in a confederation called Senegambia. The union was dissolved in 1989.

Recent History. In 1982, a civil war erupted among separatists in the southern Casamance region. The crisis also created conflict with Senegal's southern neighbor, Guinea-Bissau.

In 2000, in his fourth presidential race, President Diouf was defeated by opposition leader Abdoulaye Wade, marking the first loss for Senegal's Socialist Party in forty years. Two years later, Senegal experienced one of the worst maritime disasters in history when a ferry carrying nearly 1,900 people was lost at sea.

In 2004, the Senegalese government signed a peace accord with the Casamance rebels, ending 22 years of civil war.

JON KRAUS
Political Science Department
State University of New York, Fredonia

SENSES. See BODY, HUMAN (The Nervous System).

SEOUL

Seoul, the capital of the Republic of Korea (South Korea), is one of the world's largest urban centers. Along with its suburbs, the city contains a population of more than 12 million, making it home to almost one out of every four South Koreans.

Seoul became the capital of the Republic of Korea in 1948. It was heavily damaged during the Korean War (1950–53) but was soon reconstructed into a vibrant modern city that became the center of South Korea's industrial "economic miracle." It is also South Korea's primary educational and cultural center.

The City. The original part of the city, north of the Han River, is congested, with tiny alleyways honeycombing vast blocks. It retains many relics of Seoul's past, among them restored royal palaces, ancestral shrines, and museums. In contrast, the area known as Kangnam (meaning "south of the river") has become a showcase of modern urban planning, with broad boulevards, apartment complexes, parks, arts centers, and industrial areas. The island of Yoido is home to the national legislature and many of the city's newest and tallest office buildings.

An ambitious river development project has transformed the Han from a muddy stream into a beautiful recreation area, with miles of public parkland along its banks. Along the Han are several sports facilities, including those built for the 1988 Summer Olympic Games as well as the Seoul World Cup Stadium, where Korea hosted the 2002 world soccer championships.

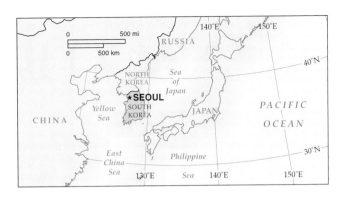

Economic Activity. After the Korean War, large numbers of rural Koreans migrated to the city in search of factory jobs. In the 1960's, with borrowed money and foreign aid, the workers began making and exporting textiles. Later they produced electronics, plastics, steel, chemicals, automobiles, ships, and high-quality computer components. Today Seoul provides more than half the country's industrial jobs.

Modern transportation has much to do with the city's economic success. Traffic flows on expressways, and underneath the city people move quickly and efficiently through the subway system. Some twenty bridges cross the Han River. Gimpo Airport, just outside the city, handles all domestic flights. An international airport operates at Inchon, Seoul's port on the Yellow Sea.

History. Seoul has been the focus of national life for more than 600 years. In 1396 it was chosen as the capital of the Chosŏn kingdom because of its location amid majestic mountains and streams. The heart of the government was the Kyongbok Palace, one of several historic sites in the old city that has been reconstructed.

After the fall of the monarchy in 1910, Seoul continued to serve as the colonial capital under Japanese rule. In 1945, Korea was liberated and divided into North and South Korea. Three years later, Seoul was established as the capital of South Korea.

DONALD N. CLARK
Trinity University

The Great South Gate, completed in 1398, stands in marked contrast to Seoul's modern skyscrapers. It was one of four original entryways into the old walled city.

September

The ancient Romans named September after the Latin word for "seven." In the old Roman calendar it was the seventh month of the year. In the Northern Hemisphere, September is the month when apples ripen, crops are harvested, birds migrate, and children return to school.

Place in year: 9th month.
Number of days: 30.
Flowers: Morning glory and aster.
Birthstone: Sapphire.
Zodiac signs: Virgo, the Virgin (August 23–September 22), and Libra, the Scales (September 23–October 22).

1
- Alberta and Saskatchewan became provinces in the Canadian Confederation, 1905
- German troops invaded Poland, starting World War II, 1939
- National holiday in Libya

2
- **Eugene Field** born 1850
- Great fire of London began, 1666
- Japan formally surrendered to Allies on V-J Day, 1945
- National holiday in Vietnam

3
- **Louis Sullivan** born 1856
- Great Britain signed Treaty of Paris, marking the end of the American Revolution, 1783
- First official Labor Day celebrated in U.S., 1894
- Liberation of Monaco Day in Monaco
- Independence Day in Qatar
- St. Marinus Day in San Marino

4
- U.S. swimmer Mark Spitz became first person to win seven gold medals in single Olympics, 1972

5
- **Jesse James** born 1847
- First Continental Congress met in Philadelphia, 1774

6
- **Marquis de Lafayette** born 1757
- **John Dalton** born 1766
- **Jane Addams** born 1860
- Massachusetts Bay Colony established, 1628
- President McKinley shot by an assassin, 1901
- Somhlolo Day in Swaziland

7
- **Elizabeth I** born 1533
- **Grandma Moses** born 1860
- Treaty signed with U.S., giving Panama control of the Panama Canal, 1977
- Independence Day in Brazil

8
- **Antonin Dvořák** born 1841
- First permanent white settlement founded in what is now America, Saint Augustine, Florida, 1565

9
- **Cardinal Richelieu** born 1585
- California became the 31st state, 1850

- National Liberation Day in Bulgaria
- National holiday in North Korea

10
- Oliver Perry won the Battle of Lake Erie, 1813
- Elias Howe patented the sewing machine, 1846

11
- **O. Henry** born 1862

12
- **Jesse Owens** born 1913
- First rocket to the moon launched by U.S.S.R., 1959
- Nationality Day in Cape Verde
- Popular Revolution Commemoration Day in Ethiopia

13
- **Walter Reed** born 1851
- **General John J. Pershing** born 1860
- **Arnold Schoenberg** born 1874

14
- **Ivan Pavlov** born 1849
- Great Britain and its American colonies adopted the Gregorian calendar, 1752
- Francis Scott Key wrote "The Star-Spangled Banner" during the British attack on Fort McHenry, 1814
- Mother Elizabeth Seton became first U.S.-born saint, 1975

15
- **James Fenimore Cooper** born 1789
- **William Howard Taft** born 1857
- Independence Day in Costa Rica; El Salvador; Guatemala; Honduras; Nicaragua

16
- *Mayflower* sailed from Plymouth, England, 1620
- *Cherokee Strip Day* in Oklahoma
- Independence Day in Mexico; Papua New Guinea

17
- Constitution of the U.S. signed at Constitutional Convention, 1787
- *Citizenship Day*
- *Constitution Day*

18
- **Samuel Johnson** born 1709
- **John George Diefenbaker** born 1895

- George Washington laid the cornerstone for the U.S. Capitol, 1793
- Independence Day in Chile

19
- President James Garfield died from an assassin's shot, 1881
- The cartoon character to be known as Mickey Mouse introduced in a Walt Disney film, *Steamboat Willie,* 1928

20
- Compromise of 1850 became law as resolution abolishing slave trade was passed by U.S. Congress, 1850

21
- **H. G. Wells** born 1866
- Independence Day in Belize

22
- **Michael Faraday** born 1791
- Nathan Hale executed as a spy by the British in New York City, 1776
- President Lincoln issued the preliminary Emancipation Proclamation, 1862
- Peace Corps became permanent agency of U.S. Government, 1961
- Independence Day in Mali

23
- John Paul Jones defeated the British in a naval battle during American Revolution, 1779
- National holiday in Saudi Arabia

24
- **John Marshall** born 1755
- **Konstantin Chernenko** born 1911
- U.S. President Dwight Eisenhower sent National Guard to enforce racial integration of schools in Little Rock, Arkansas, 1957
- Establishment of the Republic Day in Guinea-Bissau

25
- **William Michael Rossetti** born 1829
- **William Faulkner** born 1897
- Vasco Núñez de Balboa discovered the Pacific Ocean, 1513
- Twelfth Amendment added to U.S. Constitution providing for change in method of electing the president and the vice president, 1804
- First transatlantic telephone cable put into service, 1956

26
- **T. S. Eliot** born 1888
- **Pope Paul VI** born 1897
- **George Gershwin** born 1898
- National Day in Yemen

27
- **Samuel Adams** born 1722

28
- **Georges Clemenceau** born 1841
- William the Conqueror landed in England, 1066
- Birthday of Confucius in Republic of China

29
- **Lord Horatio Nelson** born 1758
- **Enrico Fermi** born 1901

30
- James Meredith escorted to classes at formerly all-white University of Mississippi by U.S. deputy marshalls, 1962
- Botswana Day in Botswana

First Monday in September: *Labor Day.* **First Sunday after Labor Day:** *National Grandparents' Day.* **Holidays that may occur in either September or October:** *Rosh Hashanah* (Jewish New Year) and *Yom Kippur* (Day of Atonement).

The calendar listing identifies people who were born on the indicated day in boldface type, **like this.** You will find a biography of each of these birthday people in *The New Book of Knowledge.* In addition to citing some historical events and historical firsts, the calendar also lists the holidays and some of the festivals celebrated in the United States. These holidays are printed in italic type, *like this.* See the article HOLIDAYS for more information.

Many holidays and festivals of nations around the world are included in the calendar as well. When the term "national holiday" is used, it means that the nation celebrates an important patriotic event on that day—in most cases the winning of independence. Consult *The New Book of Knowledge* article on the individual nation for further information on its national holiday.

SEQUOYA (1770?–1843)

Sequoya (also known as Sequoyah) was a Cherokee Indian who developed the first written Native American language. In his later years, he was also a Cherokee leader.

He was born in Loudon County, Tennessee, about 1770. His mother was the daughter of a chief, and his father may have been a trader or peddler named Gist. Sometimes Sequoya is called George Gist or George Guess.

Sequoya had no formal schooling, although historians think he probably visited various mission schools in the Southeast. It is also believed he learned to speak French, Spanish, and English. As a young man, he became a silversmith. He was lame, possibly because of a disease or inherited condition, or perhaps due to an injury received during the Creek War (1813–14). Like many other Cherokee, Sequoya fought alongside General Andrew Jackson's forces against the Creek Indians of the Southeast.

Through his contact with American missionaries and educators, Sequoya realized the value of reading and writing. He began to think his people could advance further if they had their own written language. Sequoya may have also believed this would help preserve Cherokee culture, which had been greatly undermined in the face of U.S. expansion into Cherokee lands.

In 1809, Sequoya began experimenting with a writing system, carving symbols on birch bark. At first he developed a system of pictographs (miniature pictures representing objects) but found it was too complicated to memorize. Although he was ridiculed by others, he continued trying different ideas. When he finally completed his system and tested it on his 6-year-old daughter, he saw that children could learn the language easily.

Sequoya presented his work to a tribal council in 1821. His system of writing, called a syllabary, consisted of 85 symbols, each representing a syllable in the Cherokee language. The chiefs approved the writing system, and within a few months thousands of Cherokee learned to read and write. Sequoya became an honored member of his tribe, and his writing system was praised by linguists around the world. The Cherokee National Council provided Sequoya with a yearly allowance as a reward.

In 1822 Sequoya traveled west to teach the Cherokee of Arkansas and Oklahoma to write. Soon parts of the Bible were printed in Cherokee. In 1827 the Cherokee used the new alphabet to write a constitution. In 1828 a newspaper called the *Cherokee Phoenix* was published. Printed in both English and Cherokee, its main goal was to help the Cherokee resist U.S. government efforts to drive them from their eastern homeland to a part of Indian Territory (in present-day Oklahoma).

Although the newspaper and writing system helped further resistance efforts, the Cherokee were eventually forced off their land. In 1838 they began their difficult journey west (known as the Trail of Tears), crossing the Appalachians on foot in the winter. Many died along the way.

Sequoya, a Cherokee Indian, developed the first Native American writing system. It consisted of 85 symbols, each representing a single syllable in the Cherokee language.

Sequoya, who had traveled west earlier, became a leader of the Western Cherokee and signed the Act of Union joining all Cherokee in 1839. He spent the last years of his life traveling among the Indian tribes, seeking a rumored long-lost band of Cherokee. His unsuccessful search took him into the mountains of Mexico, where he died in 1843.

A statue of Sequoya presented by the state of Oklahoma stands in Statuary Hall in Washington, D.C. The giant redwood trees known as sequoias (the Latin spelling of his name) are named after him.

Reviewed by DANIEL JACOBSON
Montclair State College

SERBIA AND MONTENEGRO

In 2003, the Federal Republic of Yugoslavia ceased to exist when its two republics approved a new constitution and formally renamed the country Serbia and Montenegro. Four of Yugoslavia's former republics—Slovenia, Croatia, Macedonia, and Bosnia and Herzegovina—had declared their independence between 1991 and 1992, leaving Serbia and its small neighbor Montenegro as the remnant of the Eastern European nation that had been created at the end of World War I (1914–18).

▶ PEOPLE

Serbia and Montenegro is home to nearly 11 million people, most of whom are of South Slavic origin. Serbs make up nearly two-thirds of

the total population. The rest is made up of Albanians, Montenegrins, Muslim Slavs, Croats, and Macedonians as well as smaller numbers of Magyars (Hungarians), Slovaks, Romanians, and Roma (formerly known as Gypsies).

Language. The official language of Serbia and Montenegro is Serbo-Croatian, which belongs to the South Slavic language group. It is written in two different alphabets: Serbs, like the Russians, use the Cyrillic alphabet, based on the original South Slavic script. Croats use the Latin alphabet.

Religion. Most Serbs and Montenegrins belong to the Eastern Orthodox Church. Croats are mostly Roman Catholics. Muslim Slavs exist in Serbia and Montenegro due to the rule of the Ottoman (Turkish) Empire. Many of the country's ethnic Albanians also are Muslims.

Education. Education in Serbia and Montenegro is free, and school attendance is required for children aged 7 to 14. Universities are located in Belgrade, Kragujevac, Niš, Novi Sad, Podgorica, and Priština.

Food and Drink. National dishes are served on special occasions. *Čulbastija*, grilled pork or beef, served with slivovitz (a brandy made from plums) is popular. Shashlik—meat (usually lamb) cut into small cubes and broiled on a skewer over an open fire—is a

The peoples of Serbia and Montenegro practice different religions. Most Serbs and Montenegrins (*above right*) are Eastern Orthodox Christians, while the majority of Kosovars (*above*) are Muslims. Golubac Castle on the Danube River (*right*) dates from the Middle Ages.

Serbia and Montenegro

Rivers. The lowlands are watered by the Danube River and its tributaries, the Sava and Tisza rivers. South of the Danube are the Drina, Morava, Vardar, Ibar, and Morača rivers. Scutari, the country's largest lake, is located near the Adriatic coast on the border between Montenegro and Albania.

Climate. In the lowlands, winters are cold and summers are hot and dry. In the interior highlands, winters are very cold. There are heavy rains in early summer, and summers are generally cool. Along the Adriatic coast, summers are warm and dry. Winter temperatures rarely reach freezing.

Natural Resources. Montenegro's mountains and about one-quarter of Serbia are covered with coniferous and deciduous forests, primarily oak and beech trees. The mountains of eastern Serbia contain most of the country's deposits of lignite (brown coal), smaller amounts of bituminous (soft) coal, and copper ore. Other important resources include lead and zinc in Kosovo, oil and natural gas in Vojvodina, and bauxite (aluminum ore) in Montenegro. Rivers and hot springs provide thermal and hydroelectric power.

favorite in Muslim areas. In villages and large towns, workers meet at the *kafana* (coffeehouse) to sip strong "Turkish" coffee and talk politics.

▶ LAND

Situated on the Balkan Peninsula of southeastern Europe, Serbia and Montenegro encompasses an area of 39,517 square miles (102,350 square kilometers). The country includes two autonomous provinces—Kosovo in the south (largely Albanian in population) and Vojvodina in the north.

Land Regions. Serbia is larger than Montenegro in both area and population. The lowlands of Vojvodina have the richest agricultural land. Valleys in the northwest have forests and patches of densely cultivated lands, but irrigation is needed to grow the area's main crops. Central and southern Serbia are mountainous.

Most of Montenegro (meaning "Black Mountain") is situated in the Dinaric Alps along the coast of the Adriatic Sea. It contains the Durmitor Massif. These mountains include Mount Daravica, which at 8,714 feet (2,656 meters) is the country's highest peak.

FACTS and figures

STATE UNION OF SERBIA AND MONTENEGRO is the official name of the country.

LOCATION: Southeastern Europe.

AREA: 39,517 sq mi (102,350 km²).

POPULATION: 10,700,000 (estimate).

CAPITAL AND LARGEST CITY: Belgrade.

MAJOR LANGUAGE: Serbo-Croatian (official).

MAJOR RELIGIOUS GROUPS: Eastern Orthodox Christian, Muslim.

GOVERNMENT: Republic. **Head of state**—president. **Head of government**—prime minister. **Legislature**—National Assembly (transitional).

CHIEF PRODUCTS: Agricultural—wheat and other cereal grains, fruits, vegetables, tobacco, livestock. **Manufactured**—transportation vehicles, military weapons and vehicles, electrical equipment, agricultural machinery, textiles, electronics, petroleum products, chemicals, pharmaceuticals, furniture. **Mineral**—lignite (brown coal), bauxite (aluminum ore), nonferrous ores (copper, lead, and zinc), iron ore, limestone.

MONETARY UNIT: Dinar (1 dinar = 100 paras) in Serbia; Euro (1 euro = 100 cents) in Montenegro.

ECONOMY

Services. Service industries, including retail trade and tourism, employ a significant number of workers. Tourism is an important source of foreign currency, as are moneys sent home by relatives working abroad.

Agriculture. About half the land is used for farming. The leading food crops are wheat, rice, and corn. Potatoes and other vegetables, tobacco, and a variety of fruits are grown, including olives, cherries, grapes, figs, peaches, pears, and plums. Forestry and livestock raising are also important to the economy.

Manufacturing. Serbia and Montenegro produce a variety of goods. The chief products are automobiles, trucks, military tanks and weapons, electrical equipment, agricultural machinery, textiles, electronics, and furniture. Chemicals, aluminum, and pharmaceuticals are also produced.

MAJOR CITIES

Belgrade is Serbia's as well as the nation's capital. Strategically located at the joining of the Sava and Danube rivers, it has been called the Key to the Balkans. For more information, see the article on Belgrade in Volume B.

Podgorica is the capital and largest city of Montenegro. It was founded by the Romans at the junction on the Zeta and Morava rivers in the A.D. 500's. From 1946 to 1992 the city was known as Titograd.

Other important cities include **Novi Sad**, the capital of Vojvodina; **Priština**, the capital of Kosovo; and **Subotica**, a largely Magyar city near the Hungarian border. **Kotor** and **Bar**, on the

A goatherd tends to her animals. Livestock raising, particularly in the mountainous regions, is important to the economy of Serbia and Montenegro.

Adriatic coast, are the country's chief ports.

GOVERNMENT

The government of Serbia and Montenegro is based on a constitutional charter ratified in 2003. The charter provides for a president of the union, a prime minister, and a five-member Council of Ministers in the areas of foreign affairs, defense, international economic relations, internal economic relations, and human and minority rights. It also provides for a one-house legislature, the Assembly, made up of 126 members—91 from Serbia and 35 from Montenegro. In addition, each constituent state has its own president and parliament.

HISTORY

Originally known as Illyria, the region containing Serbia and Montenegro was long a part of the Roman Empire. The South Slavs, who settled there in the A.D. 600's, came under the political and cultural influence of the Byzantine Empire. In the late 1100's, Stephen Nemanja founded the first independent Serbian state and became its first king.

Belgrade is the nation's capital and largest city. The bustling downtown area includes an outdoor mall that is closed to motor vehicles.

Serbia reached the height of its power during the 1300's, under King Stephen Dushan. But in 1389 the Ottoman Turks defeated Serbia and its allies at the historic Battle of Kosovo Polje. Thus began a period of Ottoman rule that lasted nearly 500 years. Due partly to its rugged landscape, Montenegro was able to repulse the Ottoman invasions. After 1516, Montenegro was ruled by Orthodox bishops, until it became an independent principality in 1878.

The Formation of Yugoslavia. When Serbia also won its independence in 1878, it began to gather all inhabited Serbian lands into a single state. Thus bitter hostility was provoked when Austria-Hungary annexed Bosnia and Herzegovina, with its large numbers of Serbs, in 1908. Then in 1914, a Serbian nationalist assassinated the Austrian archduke Francis Ferdinand, heir to the throne. This single event triggered the outbreak of World War I. When the war ended in 1918, Serbia led the movement to form the Kingdom of Serbs, Croats, and Slovenes under the Serbian royal dynasty. The new country, which now included Montenegro, was renamed the Kingdom of Yugoslavia in 1929.

World War I began soon after the Austrian archduke Francis Ferdinand and his wife were assassinated on June 28, 1914, by a Serbian nationalist opposed to Austria's domination.

Although Yugoslavia had been created by consent, not conquest, it was beset by internal disagreements, rivalries, and ambitions. Serbia was the most powerful of the states, and many non-Serbs saw Yugoslavia only as an enlarged Serbia. Belgrade, the Serbian capital, became the nation's capital, and the Serbian monarch, Peter I, became king.

The Croatians and Slovenes—mostly Roman Catholics with long-standing cultural ties to Austria—particularly resented the predominance of the Eastern Orthodox Serbs. Peter's son Alexander, who succeeded as king in 1921, was assassinated by a Macedonian nationalist in 1934.

After Yugoslavia was occupied by Nazi Germany in 1941 during World War II, it became a battleground between two rival guerrilla groups, the Serbian Chetniks and the Partisans, who were led by the Communist leader Tito (Josip Broz). At the war's end in 1945, Serbia became one of the republics of the new Socialist Federal Republic of Yugoslavia and came under Tito's command.

Yugoslavia Under Tito. Yugoslavia maintained close relations with the Soviet Union until 1948, when a dispute between Tito and the Soviet leader Joseph Stalin caused Stalin to expel Yugoslavia from the Soviet bloc. Tito had two great defensive advantages over Stalin. One was Yugoslavia's unusually rugged terrain. The other was that Tito, unlike other Communist rulers in postwar Eastern Europe, had not been brought to power by the Soviet military and so did not require its support. Yugoslavia gradually abandoned the highly centralized economic model of the Soviet Union in favor of a decentralized system of production with a mixture of state-owned and private enterprise. Tito's tight control over the country kept the old ethnic rivalries and hatreds in check. But after his death in 1980, the complex government structure began to break down. For more information, see the biography of Tito in Volume T.

The Breakup of Yugoslavia. By the late 1980's, Yugoslavia's economic system was on the verge of total collapse. Caught up in the revolutionary political and economic changes that shattered the Soviet Union and transformed Communist Eastern Europe, Yugoslavia began to break apart. Croatia and Slovenia demanded that Yugoslavia be made a loose confederation of states. This Serbia opposed. There was also disagreement over the replacement of the nation's Communist system with a democratic government and free-market economy. Serbia also claimed that the boundaries between the republics established by Tito were unfair to Serbs and tried to redraw them.

The crisis rapidly escalated in 1991. On May 15, assumption of the presidency by a Croat, dictated by the constitution, was blocked by Serbia. On June 25, Croatia and Slovenia proclaimed their independence, followed later in the year by Macedonia.

The first fighting in the civil war that followed took place in Slovenia, but it soon subsided. In Croatia, which had a much larger Serbian minority, war raged during the latter half of 1991. The greatest bloodletting, however, was in Bosnia and Herzegovina, with its diverse population of Serbs, Croats, and Muslims, following a declaration of independence in March 1992. In April, Serbia proclaimed itself and Montenegro the Federal Republic of Yugoslavia, the successor to the former Yugoslav state.

The Federal Republic. Slobodan Milošević, who had been president of Serbia since 1989, assumed control over the new republic. A Communist nationalist who had opposed the breakup, Milošević backed Serb attacks on Croatia and Bosnia and Herzegovina after they declared their independence. In 1992, in an effort to end Serbian aggression against the Croats and Bosnians, the United Nations imposed economic sanctions on Yugoslavia. A peace accord signed in Dayton, Ohio, ended the conflict in 1995.

Milošević became president of Yugoslavia in 1997. The following year, civil war broke out between the Serbs and the ethnic Albanians in Kosovo. News of Serbian atrocities prompted the North Atlantic Treaty Organization (NATO), led by the United States, to threaten force against the Serbs. When peace talks held in early 1999 failed to settle the dispute, NATO began air strikes against Serbian military targets. After the Yugoslav army withdrew from Kosovo, NATO ceased its offensive and installed peacekeeping forces to ensure the safe resettlement of refugees.

In 2000, a revolt swept through Yugoslavia when Milošević refused to acknowledge losing the presidential election to opposition candidate Vojislav Koštunica. Milošević finally stepped down when it became clear he had lost the support of the military. Koštunica assumed the presidency on October 5. In 2001,

In 1998, the Serbs began an aggressive civil war against ethnic Albanians in Kosovo. Hundreds of thousands of refugees fled across the border to Albania and Macedonia.

Milošević became the first former national leader brought to trial for war crimes by the International Court in The Hague.

A New Nation. In 2002, in response to a growing independence movement in Montenegro, the two republics agreed to a new federation pact so that each might assume semi-independence. When a new constitution was approved in 2003, Yugoslavia was officially renamed Serbia and Montenegro. Svetozar Marovic was elected its first president. As part of the agreement, the charter offered each state the right to hold a referendum in 2006 to decide if the union should continue or be split into two independent states.

In March 2003, the Serbian state's prime minister, Zoran Djindjic, was assassinated. The government declared a state of emergency. Zoran Zivkovic assumed the role of prime minister and promised to carry on Djindjic's policies.

Reviewed by JANUSZ BUGAJSKI
Director, Eastern European Project
Center for Strategic and International Studies

See also BALKANS; YUGOSLAVIA.

SERRA, FATHER JUNÍPERO. See CALIFORNIA (Profiles).

SERVICE INDUSTRIES. See INDUSTRY.

SETI. See LIFE (Life on Other Planets); RADIO ASTRONOMY (Feature).

SETON, SAINT ELIZABETH ANN BAYLEY. See SAINTS (Profiles).

SETS

A set is a collection. It may be a collection of objects—the coins in your pocket, the members of your family, or the fingers of one hand. A set may also be a collection of numbers or ideas. For instance, the counting numbers from 1 to 10 make up a set whose members are 1, 2, 3, 4, 5, 6, 7, 8, 9, and 10.

Sets can be compared with one another and can be handled mathematically in many ways.

▶ SYMBOLS AND TERMS

Mathematicians use symbols to stand for objects or to show relationships in sets.

The Set. A set can be described by listing its members, or elements, in braces **{ }** and by choosing a capital letter to represent, or stand for, the set. Thus a set of pets that includes a dog, cat, and rabbit may be shown this way:

$$X = \{dog, cat, rabbit\}$$

The elements of the set are listed inside the braces, and the X stands for the set of pets.

The symbol $\in$ means "is a member, or element, of." Imagine this set:

$$X = \{Leonard, Jose, Susan, Keisha\}$$

To write "Susan is a member of set X," you would use these symbols:

$$Susan \in X$$

The symbol $\notin$ means "is not a member, or element, of." "Harry is not a member of set X" is written with these symbols:

$$Harry \notin X$$

▶ TYPES OF SETS

There are many different types of sets. Sets are often classified by comparing them with each other.

Empty Sets. The empty, or null, set is a set that has no elements. Suppose you want to make a set of all the Siamese cats on your block. After searching out all the cats, you find that they are all tabby or Persian cats. Because there are no Siamese cats on your block, your set will have no elements. It is an empty set, and it can be written in two ways:

$$X = \varnothing \text{ or } X = \{ \}$$

Equal and Equivalent Sets. When two sets have exactly the same elements, they are said to be equal. Look at the example below. Set A and set B have the same elements, so they are equal sets.

$$A = \{ \blacktriangle , \bullet , \blacksquare \}$$
$$B = \{ \bullet , \blacksquare , \blacktriangle \}$$

When two sets have the same number of elements, even though the elements are different, the sets are said to be equivalent. Look at this example below. For each element in set A, there is one element in set B, and for each element in set B, there is one element in set A. There are three elements in each set. Thus sets A and B are equivalent sets.

$$A = \{ \blacktriangle , \bullet , \blacksquare \}$$
$$B = \{ \blacktriangle , \blacklozenge , \blacksquare \}$$

Disjoint Sets. Sets that have no elements in common are called disjoint sets. Look at the sets in the example below. One set consists entirely of fruits, and the other set contains only nuts. The two sets have no elements in common, so they are disjoint sets.

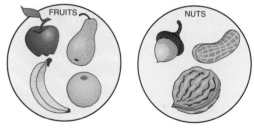

Included Sets. A set that is completely contained within a larger set is called an included set, or a subset. As shown in the example below, set A is a set of animals in a zoo, and set B consists of the animals in the

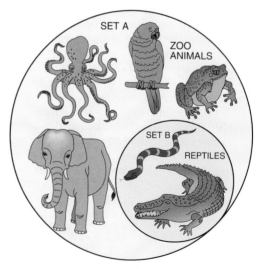

zoo that are reptiles. Thus set B is a subset of set A. To indicate a subset, the symbol ⊂ is used. For this example you would write B ⊂ A, meaning set B is a subset of set A.

▶ INFINITE SETS

Set theory was originally developed by the German mathematician Georg Cantor (1845–1918) to help in counting infinities, numbers so large that we sometimes call them uncountable. (See the Wonder Question What is infinity? in the article NUMBERS AND NUMBER SYSTEMS.)

Whole numbers, which are all of the counting numbers plus zero, make up a set. The set of whole numbers is an infinite set. It starts with 0, 1, 2, 3 and keeps going. No matter how many whole numbers you name, there is at least one more number you have not reached. For example, if you name six quintillion (6 followed by 18 zeros), then there is six quintillion one.

The set of even numbers—0, 2, 4, 6, 8, and so on—is also an infinite set. Are there more whole numbers than there are even numbers? You might think there are, since some whole numbers are even and some are not. But you will notice that you can match every whole number with an even number if you multiply the whole number by 2.

$$0\ 1\ 2\ 3\ 4\ 5\ 6\ 7\ 8$$
$$\updownarrow\ \updownarrow\ \updownarrow\ \updownarrow\ \updownarrow\ \updownarrow\ \updownarrow\ \updownarrow\ \updownarrow$$
$$0\ 2\ 4\ 6\ 8\ 10\ 12\ 14\ 16$$

This process continues through the entire set. For example, the number 637 from the set of whole numbers can be matched with the number 1,274 from the set of even numbers (2 x 637 = 1,274). Thus you can also say that for every even number there is a whole number. Because the two sets can be matched in this way, they have the same number of elements. However, not all infinite sets have the same number of elements.

▶ SET OPERATIONS

Sets can be compared and combined in many ways. The different ways of working with sets are called set operations. The two main kinds of set operations are **union** and **intersection**.

Union of Sets. The union, or joining, of two sets results in another set that contains all the elements of the two sets. Suppose set A contains all the people in John's family:

A = {Mother, Father, John, Margaret}

Suppose set B contains all the red-haired people John knows:

B = {Margaret, Tonio, Kevin, Sheila}

The union of set A and set B is the set that includes all of the elements of both sets. The symbol for union is ∪. So the union of sets A and B can be shown this way:

A ∪ B = {Mother, Father, John, Margaret, Tonio, Kevin, Sheila}

The new set can be described as the set of people that are either family members or that have red hair. Notice that Margaret is listed only once even though she is an element in both sets.

Intersection of Sets. Sometimes it is useful to know what elements are shared by two sets. Using the union of sets A and B above, you can see that Margaret is the only element common to both sets.

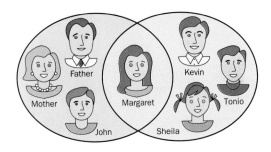

So the intersection of sets A and B is Margaret. The symbol for intersection is ∩. The intersection of sets A and B would be shown like this:

A ∩ B = {Margaret}

Knowing about sets and set operations is important to the understanding of basic mathematical ideas. Sets and set theory are used in algebra, geometry, probability, as well as in other areas of mathematics.

Reviewed by BRYAN H. BUNCH
Instructor of Mathematics, Pace University
See also MATHEMATICS; MATHEMATICS, HISTORY OF.

Then he fell on his head!
He came down with a bump . .
—*The Cat in the Hat*

And he puzzled three hours,
  till his puzzler was sore.
Then the Grinch thought of something
  he hadn't before!
"Maybe Christmas," he thought,
  "doesn't come from a store."
—*How the Grinch
Stole Christmas*

If you wish
you may go
by lion's tail.
—*Marvin K. Mooney
Will You
Please
Go
Now!*

SEUSS, DR. (1904–1991)

Have you met the Drum-Tummied Snumm, the wink-hooded Hoodwinks, and the Juggling Jot? Or the Lorax, the Sneetches, and the Yuzz-a-ma-Tuzz? Then you know Dr. Seuss, the author-illustrator who created a fantastic menagerie of more than 40 children's books. Millions of copies of the Dr. Seuss books have been sold, in 17 languages.

Dr. Seuss's real name was Theodor Seuss Geisel. He was born on March 2, 1904, in Springfield, Massachusetts, where his father was superintendent of the city parks and zoo. After graduating from Dartmouth College in 1925, Geisel studied at Oxford University in England. He had no formal art training, but after returning to the United States, he became an advertising illustrator.

His first children's book, *And to Think That I Saw It on Mulberry Street*, was published in 1937 with the author-illustrator listed as "Dr. Seuss." In this and later picture books—among them *The 500 Hats of Bartholomew Cubbins* (1938), *Horton Hears a Who* (1954), *The Lorax* (1971), *The Butter Battle Book* (1984), and *Oh, the Places You'll Go!* (1990) —nonsense, exaggeration, and rhyme are combined with a gentle moral.

According to Dr. Seuss, all of his books began with doodles that turned into zany characters. *The Cat in the Hat* (1957) uses only 175 different words to tell a story easy enough for first graders to read on their own. The Beginner Books that followed use simple words to tell of hilarious situations. Two favorites are *Green Eggs and Ham* (1960) and *Hop on Pop* (1963).

Dr. Seuss was also a designer and producer of animated cartoons. In 1950 he won an Academy Award for his animated short film *Gerald McBoing-Boing*. The television cartoon of his book *How the Grinch Stole Christmas* has become a Christmastime favorite. For his contributions to children's literature, Dr. Seuss received the Laura Ingalls Wilder Medal in 1980. He died on September 24, 1991.

NANCY LARRICK
Author, *A Parent's Guide to Children's Reading*

SEVEN WONDERS OF THE ANCIENT WORLD. See WONDERS OF THE WORLD.

SEWAGE DISPOSAL. See SANITATION.

SEWARD, WILLIAM H. See ALASKA (Famous People).

SEWING

Sewing—using a threaded needle to stitch together fabric or other material—is one of the oldest crafts. It dates to prehistoric times, when primitive people used bone or straw needles and grass or sinew thread to create fitted garments from animal skins.

Over time, sewing became more sophisticated, as did the materials used. People learned to soften animal skins and make textiles. They discovered how to make dyes from soil, plants, and insects. Fabrics became finer, designs became more elaborate, and needles became sharper.

Beginning in the late 1700's, mechanical stitching devices appeared. In 1846, Elias Howe received a patent for a sewing machine, based in part on others' inventions. In 1850, Isaac M. Singer was the first to mass-produce a sewing machine. Within a few years, thousands had been sold to homemakers across America.

Until modern times, all sewing was done either at home or by a professional seamstress or tailor. Ready-made clothes, curtains, quilts, and other home furnishings were not widely available. Although most people now buy these things in stores, others prefer making some of them at home. For many, sewing is a way to save money, as well as a means of personal expression. With a machine, one can create many things, from simple dresses and curtains to elaborate garments and slipcovers.

▶ **SEWING TOOLS**

Sewing requires three basic tools—a needle, thread, and scissors. Needles for hand sewing come in many sizes and lengths; the fabric, thread, and type of sewing determine which to use.

Thread comes in many different colors and types, even metallic. Cotton thread is suitable

Sewing is a popular and practical hobby. With today's sophisticated machines, and a wide range of fabrics to choose from, home sewers can produce many decorative and useful items.

for stitching cotton fabric, as well as linen, wool, dull rayon, and cotton and synthetic blends. Silk thread is appropriate for stitching silk, wool, shiny rayon, and fine linen. Synthetic thread, finer than most other kinds, is suitable for synthetic and knit fabrics. Buttonhole twist is a strong silk thread for handmade button holes, for attaching buttons, and for decorative stitching.

Thread also comes in different thicknesses and is numbered accordingly. The lower the number, the thicker the thread. When selecting thread, choose a shade that is a bit darker than the fabric because thread on the spool appears darker than a single strand.

Good, sharp scissors are also important when sewing. Scissors most commonly used for cutting fabric—dressmaker's shears—have a slightly bent handle and 6- or 8-inch blades. Smaller sewing scissors, sometimes called embroidery scissors, are used to cut thread and smaller bits of fabric.

Other items needed for sewing include straight pins and a holder (a pin cushion or magnetic dish), a seam ripper (to remove stitches or make buttonholes), a thimble (to protect the finger from pin pricks and to help push a needle through thick material), a tape measure, and tailor's chalk or a disappearing-ink pen (to temporarily mark fabric). For

TYPES OF STITCHES

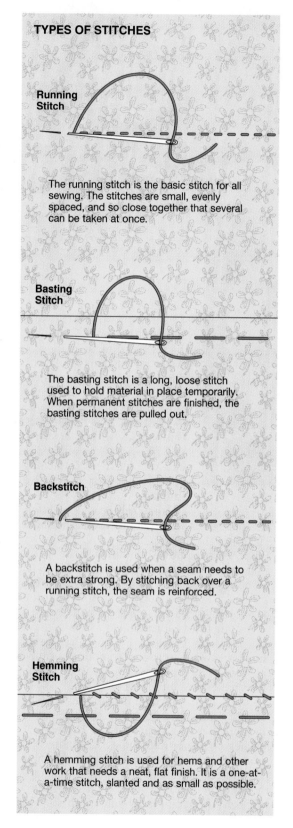

Running Stitch

The running stitch is the basic stitch for all sewing. The stitches are small, evenly spaced, and so close together that several can be taken at once.

Basting Stitch

The basting stitch is a long, loose stitch used to hold material in place temporarily. When permanent stitches are finished, the basting stitches are pulled out.

Backstitch

A backstitch is used when a seam needs to be extra strong. By stitching back over a running stitch, the seam is reinforced.

Hemming Stitch

A hemming stitch is used for hems and other work that needs a neat, flat finish. It is a one-at-a-time stitch, slanted and as small as possible.

machine sewing, one should also have extra machine needles and spare bobbins (thread holders) on hand.

Sewing Machines. Today's sewing machines are motorized devices operated by a foot or knee pedal. A good machine includes such features as a seam guide, bobbin winder, a reverse stitching function, and adjustable stitch lengths and widths. The newest machines are computerized, with hundreds of preprogrammed stitches, both functional and decorative. These machines can also run software to create thousands of designs for embroidery and other decorative stitching.

If you are just learning to use a sewing machine, it is a good idea to have someone with experience help you get started. This could be a friend or family member, or a sewing instructor. Many sewing machine retailers offer classes on how to use their machines. Sewing classes may also be available through community education programs, fabric and craft stores, and home economics programs in some schools.

▶ PATTERNS

Once you learn to operate a sewing machine, you should also know how to use a pattern. A pattern consists of tissue-thin pieces of paper that show how the fabric for a specific item is to be cut and sewn together.

Before opening the pattern, look at the envelope. This will include a drawing and written description of the finished item, suggested fabrics, a chart showing how much fabric to buy, and any notions that are needed (such as buttons, shoulder pads, and zippers). Next, read the pattern instruction sheet inside the envelope; this will guide you through each step. It is important to read all instructions before starting and note the pattern pieces to be used, cutting layout, and markings to be transferred from the pattern to the fabric.

Each pattern piece will have notches for matching with other pieces, a number or a letter to identify which piece it is, lines showing where to position pockets and buttonholes, arrows showing how to position the fabric, cutting lines, and the seam allowance. Hemlines, pleats, and tucks will also be indicated on the pattern pieces.

JOAN CAMPBELL
Home Sewing Association

See also NEEDLECRAFT; TEXTILES.

SEYCHELLES

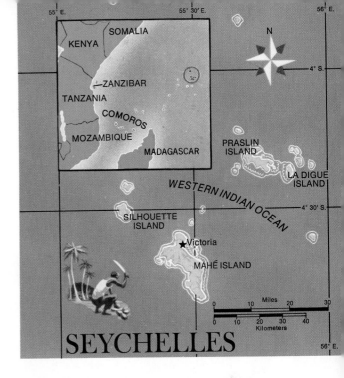

SEYCHELLES

Seychelles is a small nation made up of a chain of islands located in the Indian Ocean, about 1,000 miles (1,600 kilometers) off the east coast of Africa. Settled by the French in the 1700's, the islands later came under British rule. Britain governed Seychelles until 1976, when it gained independence.

People. The Seychellois, as the people are called, are mainly descendants of the early French settlers and black African slaves. Although both English and French are the country's official languages, the most commonly spoken language is Creole, a mixture of French and African languages. Most of the people are Roman Catholics.

The Seychellois live mainly on Mahé, the largest island. Victoria, the capital and largest city, is situated on Mahé Island.

Land. The Seychelles chain consists of 92 widely scattered islands, most of which are small and uninhabited. There are two island groups. The main group—centered around Mahé Island and including Praslin, La Digue, and Silhouette islands—is formed of volcanic rock. The smaller group is composed of coral.

FACTS and figures

REPUBLIC OF SEYCHELLES is the official name of the country.

LOCATION: Indian Ocean, off the east coast of Africa.

AREA: 176 sq mi (455 km²).

POPULATION: 80,000 (estimate).

CAPITAL AND LARGEST CITY: Victoria.

MAJOR LANGUAGES: English, French (both official), Creole.

MAJOR RELIGIOUS GROUP: Christian (mainly Roman Catholic).

GOVERNMENT: Republic. **Head of state and government**—president. **Legislature**—National Assembly.

CHIEF PRODUCTS: Canned tuna, cinnamon bark, copra (dried coconut meat).

MONETARY UNIT: Seychelles rupee (1 S rupee = 100 cents).

Economy. Seychelles' economy is based on tourism and agriculture. Coconuts are the main commercial crop. Important exports include canned tuna, cinnamon bark, and copra (dried coconut meat). The islands' pleasant climate, sandy beaches, and striking scenery, including many varieties of rare plants and birds, have made tourism the chief industry.

History and Government. Seychelles was uninhabited when French colonists established a settlement in 1768, bringing with them slaves from the African mainland. The islands were named for Marie-Jean Hérault des Séchelles, an attorney to King Louis XVI. Britain acquired control of the islands under the Treaty of Paris in 1814 and made them a British crown colony in 1903. Seychelles gained increasing self-government and won full independence in 1976.

The government is headed by a president. The legislature is the National Assembly. Both the president and the members of the Assembly are elected to 5-year terms. President France Albert René has been continuously reelected since he seized power in 1977. Under a constitution adopted in 1979, Seychelles was governed by a single political party. But a new constitution, approved in 1993, made the country a multiparty democracy.

HUGH C. BROOKS
Director, Center for African Studies
St. John's University (New York)

Far left: The great poet and playwright William Shakespeare was probably born in this house in Stratford-upon-Avon, England. *Near left:* A portrait of Shakespeare appears in the First Folio, the first collected edition of his plays. *Below:* Shakespeare's plays are well loved and widely performed. Here, *The Merchant of Venice* is performed in Stratford by England's famous Royal Shakespeare Company.

SHAKESPEARE, WILLIAM (1564–1616)

William Shakespeare, who is perhaps the greatest writer in the history of the world, was looked upon in his own day as little more than a maker of popular plays. Yet in this lies the key to his greatness. The theater of his day gave him freedom, and he in turn gave it the best that was in him.

Early Years in Stratford

Shakespeare was born in 1564, far from the world of the stage, in the little English town of Stratford on the river Avon. He is usually believed to have been born on April 23, but all that is known for certain is that he was baptized on Sunday, April 26. Stratford was a busy little town, and Shakespeare's father, a prosperous businessman, served for a time as its mayor. Shakespeare was brought up in a comfortable house on Henley Street along with several brothers and sisters.

Shakespeare, like other boys in Stratford, probably went to grammar school as soon as he could read and write. All of the students studied Latin. Shakespeare did not go on to a university. At 18 he married Anne Hathaway, who was eight years older than he was and the daughter of a neighboring farmer. During the next two years, they had three children, a girl named Susanna and then twins named Judith and Hamnet (a version of Hamlet).

London Actor, Playwright, and Poet

After the birth of the twins in 1585, there is no record of what Shakespeare was doing until he is mentioned, in 1592, as a London actor. It is possible he had spent those seven years training to be an actor—it was a difficult profession in those days, and only the best actors in England found work in London.

It was in London, not Stratford, that Shakespeare got his education, learning the ways of the theater and nearly everything else. There he found the books he read and the people he met—the foreigners, the old soldiers, the courtiers, the whole lively civilization of the late Renaissance. London was a port city of 250,000 people, and Shakespeare could not have come to it at a better time.

Many actors of the period were playwrights also, and by 1592 Shakespeare had written several plays. They are clearly the work of a young man, but they already show his great variety and his gift for pleasing an audience. His greatest popular success was a series of three plays called *Henry VI*, which gave a patriotic and very one-sided view of the English wars against the French. Almost as well liked was a bloody melodrama called *Titus Andronicus*. In a complete change of pace he also wrote a wild and funny farce called *The Comedy of Errors* and a graceful lyric comedy called *Love's Labour's Lost*.

The London theaters were closed in 1592 because of a plague, and Shakespeare turned to another kind of writing. He wrote two narrative poems, *Venus and Adonis* and *The Rape of Lucrece*, which he dedicated to the earl of Southampton. They were handsomely printed and greatly admired by the critics, and if Shakespeare had wanted to be a famous poet in his own day, he would have continued with this kind of writing.

Instead, he turned back to the life of the stage as soon as the theaters reopened in 1594. He joined a newly formed acting company called the Chamberlain's Men and never left them until he retired from the theater itself. He wrote all the rest of his plays for the Chamberlain's men and published no more poetry. The sonnets he wrote privately were published in 1609 without his consent.

The Chamberlain's Men and the Globe

The Chamberlain's Men were a remarkable group of people—excellent actors who were also business partners and close personal friends. The most famous actor in the company was Richard Burbage. Shakespeare was still an actor as late as 1608, appearing in other men's plays as well as his own.

Like all the other London companies, Shakespeare and his fellow actors were responsible for every detail of the plays they presented. They shared the ownership of the scripts, the costumes, and the properties, and they also shared equally in the money that was made. Shakespeare and his fellow actors worked together so successfully that after four years they decided to build a theater of their own.

The Chamberlain's Men called their theater the Globe and opened it in 1599. It was shaped like all the other theaters in London, a huge, unroofed amphitheater with the seats curving around a jutting stage. The stage was covered and built on several levels, so that anything could be shown, from underground caverns to city battlements. Plays always started at two in the afternoon to take advantage of daylight, as no artificial lighting was used. Anyone who could not afford the price of a seat could stand in front of the stage for a penny. Everyone in London came to see the shows—housewives, noblemen, visitors from abroad, and children. It was for this audience that Shakespeare wrote, and he obviously loved them just as much as they loved him.

Many of the plays he wrote for the Chamberlain's Men were on English history. With the exception of an early play called *King John*, all Shakespeare's history plays form a single linked story. He had already written the last part of this story in *Henry VI*, except for the melodramatic climax that he records in *Richard III*. Then he went back to the beginning with the sad and subtle play of *Richard II* and followed it with the two parts of *Henry IV* and with *Henry V*. He filled these four plays with all sorts of lively Englishmen, but the one the audience took to its heart was Falstaff, the fat soldier who did not like to fight. The Londoners found Falstaff so funny that Shakespeare finally gave him a comedy of his own in *The Merry Wives of Windsor*.

Shakespeare's great gift for laughter found expression in many ways. He wrote a lively farce, *The Taming of the Shrew*, and four graceful and poetic comedies, *Two Gentlemen of Verona*, *Twelfth Night*, *As You Like It*, and *Much Ado About Nothing*. He wrote *The Merchant of Venice*, with its famous trial scene between Portia and Shylock, and he filled the stage with fairies and music in *A Midsummer Night's Dream*.

Shakespeare also wrote three great tragedies for the Chamberlain's Men. The first was the lovely, heartbreaking story of *Romeo and Juliet*, the second was the great political drama of *Julius Caesar*, and the third was the dark and enthralling tragedy of *Hamlet*. All these stories were already known to London audiences, since Shakespeare almost never invented his own plots. It was what he did with them that made them immortal.

The King's Men

Queen Elizabeth died in 1603, and her cousin King James came to the throne of England. Fortunately, he enjoyed the plays of Shakespeare's company just as much as the great queen had, and from then on the company had a new name—the King's Men.

The King's Men opened the Christmas season at court by presenting Shakespeare's *Othello*, the tragedy of the Moor who killed his wife because he believed she was unfaithful to him. A few weeks later they presented Shakespeare's *Measure for Measure*, which must have been successful on the London stage or it would not have been shown before King James. *Measure for Measure* belongs to a group of plays—*All's Well That Ends Well*, *Troilus and Cressida*, and *Timon of Athens*—that some people have found unpleasant. But each has its own kind of effectiveness.

It was during the reign of King James that Shakespeare wrote three of his greatest tragedies: *Macbeth*, the dark and bloody tale of a husband and wife who commit murder to win the throne of Scotland; *Antony and Cleopatra*, the glittering love story of two people who could govern half the world but not themselves; and that vast, storm-ridden masterpiece *King Lear*. No subject was too difficult for Shakespeare to try.

Some say that Shakespeare's plays mirror his life. But he wrote these great tragedies at a time of personal peace, and he was writing light comedies in 1596, when his only son died. Shakespeare's private life had nothing to do with what he gave his audiences.

Last Years

He was mainly retired from the stage by about 1610, after giving his company a final series of comedies—*Cymbeline*, *The Winter's Tale*, and the magic loveliness of *The Tempest*. He did one more play for the company three years later, a history play called *Henry VIII*, which dealt with Queen Elizabeth's father, and collaborated with John Fletcher on *The Two Noble Kinsmen*.

Shakespeare lived mostly at his home in Stratford during these last years of his life. In 1597 he had bought a handsome brick house called New Place. In the following years he made several real estate investments in Stratford and London, and in 1609 he and his fellow actors bought a second theater, an indoor one called the Blackfriars.

Shakespeare died in Stratford on April 23, 1616, and was buried in the local church where he had been baptized 52 years earlier. The people of England did not know that their greatest poet had died. They thought of him only as a popular playwright and as an actor with an unusual reputation for gentleness. His two narrative poems were still in print, and so were his sonnets, but his great plays were merely acting scripts, stored for use at the Globe. Half of them had been published, but only in the cheap and often inaccurate little pamphlets that seemed good enough for anything as unimportant as plays.

Few people could believe that a theater script could also be a work of art. But two of the actors in Shakespeare's company, John Heminges and Henry Condell, were convinced that Shakespeare's plays were worth saving. They gathered all 36 plays together and published them in a large volume that is called the First Folio. They said they did it not for "self-profit or fame; only to keep the memory of so worthy a friend and fellow alive as was our Shakespeare."

Admiration for Shakespeare's works increased over the years. In fact, some people believed that a person born in a small town and educated only at the local grammar school could not have been clever enough to write such masterful plays. They proposed that Shakespeare was not the author of the plays that bear his name. Sir Francis Bacon and the Earl of Oxford are among those who have been suggested as the true playwright. These claims have very little evidence to support them, however, and they are not accepted by most scholars.

MARCHETTE CHUTE
Author, *Shakespeare of London*
Reviewed by JAY L. HALIO
University of Delaware

rief plot summaries of Shakespeare's plays are given on these pages. Famous quotes from some of the plays also appear.

All's Well That Ends Well (comedy, 1602?). Helena, a famed physician's daughter, cures the king of France of a severe illness. As a reward, she is promised a husband of her choice. She chooses young Count Bertram, whom she has always loved. Bertram, unhappy after the marriage, flees to Italy. Disguising herself, Helena follows and finally wins his love by proving her sincere devotion.

> Praising what is lost
> Makes the remembrance dear.
>
> Act V, scene 3

Antony and Cleopatra (tragedy, 1607). Mark Antony goes to Egypt and falls in love with Queen Cleopatra, betraying his wife, Octavia, who is in Rome. Octavius, Antony's ally and brother to Octavia, uses this insult to his family as an excuse to attack Antony with an army. Antony is defeated and kills himself. Cleopatra, hearing that Octavius wants to take her in triumphant procession through Rome, kills herself.

> My salad days,
> When I was green in judgment.
>
> Act I, scene 5

> Age cannot wither her, nor custom stale
> Her infinite variety.
>
> Act II, scene 2

As You Like It (comedy, 1599). Frederick banishes his brother, the rightful Duke, to the Forest of Arden, where the Duke lives with his followers. When the Duke's daughter, Rosalind, also is banished, she comes to the Forest of Arden disguised as a boy and calling herself Ganymede. Celia, Frederick's daughter, accompanies Rosalind and is disguised as a rural maiden. Orlando, a young man whom Rosalind met and loved in Frederick's court, finds the two girls. Orlando, fooled by her disguise, tells ''Ganymede'' of his love for Rosalind. After a series of episodes, the Duke regains his kingdom. Then a double wedding unites Rosalind and Orlando as well as Celia and Oliver, Orlando's brother.

> Well said: that was laid on with a trowel.
>
> Act I, scene 2

The Comedy of Errors (comedy, 1594?). Two sets of identical male twins, separated as children, meet each other as adults. Many problems arise because each brother has the same name.

Two are called Antipholus, and two are called Dromio. Mistaken identity causes great confusion until all are reunited happily. The modern play *The Boys from Syracuse* is an adaptation.

Coriolanus (tragedy, 1608). Coriolanus, a Roman aristocrat, defeats Rome's enemies, the Volscians, and their leader, Tullus Aufidius. Despite this service to Rome, the common people resent Coriolanus' haughtiness and drive him out of the city. The enraged Coriolanus joins the enemy and plots an attack on Rome, from which his friends cannot sway him. He gives in only to his mother, Volumnia, and his wife, Virgilia, who plead with him to spare the city. Aufidius accuses Coriolanus of being a traitor and has him killed.

Cymbeline (comedy, 1610). The legendary British king Cymbeline has two sons, Guiderius and Arviragus, who are brought up in the wilds of Wales by Belarius as if they were his own. Their sister, Imogen, marries Posthumus, a ''poor but noble gentleman,'' who is banished by the king. On a bet with an Italian named Giacomo, Posthumus tests his wife's virtue. Meanwhile, Cymbeline's second wife tries to have her son Cloten succeed to the throne. The intricate plot is unraveled when the faithful Imogen discovers her brothers, who defeat a Roman army with Belarius's help, Cloten is killed, and Imogen is reunited with her husband.

> Golden lads and girls all must,
> As chimney-sweepers, come to dust.
>
> Act IV, scene 2

Hamlet (tragedy, 1602). Hamlet, Prince of Denmark, returns home to learn that his father has died and his mother, Gertrude, has married Claudius, her late husband's brother. Hamlet hears from his father's ghost that he was murdered by Claudius. Hamlet resolves to avenge his father's death. In order to mislead Claudius, Hamlet pretends to be insane. He rejects Ophelia, whom he loves, and kills her father, Polonius, mistaking him for Claudius. Ophelia goes mad and drowns herself. Claudius, to save himself, plots to have Hamlet killed, but fails. In the end, Gertrude drinks from poisoned wine meant for her son; Hamlet kills Claudius; and in a duel Ophelia's brother, Laertes, is killed

Hamlet

by Hamlet. Hamlet himself dies of a wound from Laertes' poisoned sword.

Neither a borrower, nor a lender be . . . .

Act I, scene 3

Something is rotten in the state of Denmark.

Act I, scene 4

Though this be madness, yet there is method in it.

Act II, scene 2

The lady doth protest too much, methinks.

Act III, scene 2

Sweets to the sweet . . . .

Act V, scene 1

Henry IV, Parts I and II (history, 1597–98). During the early years of Henry's reign, revolts in Scotland are put down successfully by Henry Percy (also called Hotspur). But the king angers Hotspur by refusing to ransom Percy's kinsman, a captive of Welsh rebels. The angry Percy family joins the rebels. Meanwhile, Henry's son, Prince Hal, has been wasting his time in the company of Sir John Falstaff, a man of questionable reputation. But when Prince Hal hears of the rebellion, he rushes to his father's rescue and kills Hotspur.

In Part II, Hotspur is dead, but the uprisings continue. King Henry's second son, John of Lancaster, pretending to make peace with the rebel leaders, has them all killed in cold blood. When the king dies, Prince Hal succeeds as Henry V. His first act is to banish Falstaff, for Henry is becoming a responsible ruler.

Uneasy lies the head that wears a crown.

Act III, scene 1

Henry V (history, 1599). Henry believes he has a rightful claim to the French throne and invades France with his army. He not only wins a decisive military battle, but also wins the love of the French Princess Katherine of Valois and becomes the heir to the French throne. Marrying Katherine, Henry unites the two crowns in peace.

Henry V

Once more unto the breach, dear friends . . . .

Act III, scene 1

Henry VI, Parts I, II, and III (history, 1590–92). This cycle of three plays covers most of the period in English history known as "The Wars of the Roses." The name derives from a story, probably legendary, about members of the House of York, who plucked a white rose to represent them, and members of the House of Lancaster, who plucked a red one. These opposing aristocratic families engaged in civil war throughout the 1400's for supremacy in Britain. Shakespeare dramatized the rose garden scene in Part I, act 2, scene 4. Part I also dramatizes the rise and fall of Joan of Arc, whom the British fought in France.

Henry VIII (history, 1613). This is the last of Shakespeare's history plays, written many years after the others. In it, Katherine of Aragon, Henry VIII's first wife, is put on trial for divorce, and Henry marries Anne Boleyn. Anne gives birth at the end of the play to a daughter, Elizabeth (later recognized as England's most famous queen). The decline and fall of Cardinal Wolsey, once the most powerful man in England after the king, is also dramatized, along with the fall and execution of Wolsey's enemy, the Duke of Buckingham.

Julius Caesar

Julius Caesar (tragedy, 1599). Many Romans fear that Caesar's growing power is a threat to Roman freedom. A group of conspirators, among them Cassius and Caesar's friend Brutus, assassinate Caesar in the senate. In a fiery speech at Caesar's funeral, Marcus Antonius (Antony) stirs the Romans to such anger that the conspirators have to flee. A triumvirate is formed, and Brutus and Cassius die in the battle of Philippi.

Beware the ides of March.

Act I, scene 2

Yond' Cassius has a lean and hungry look . . . .

Act I, scene 2

For mine own part, it was Greek to me.

Act I, scene 2

Friends, Romans, countrymen, lend me your
ears . . . .

Act III, scene 2

King John (history, 1595–96). The reign of
King John of England (1167–1216) is the only
one that does not fit into Shakespeare's cycle of
English history plays beginning with *Richard II*.
John's weak claim to the throne is supported by
Philip Faulconbridge and disputed by Prince Ar-
thur, who is aided by the King of France. When
war between the countries ends in stalemate, the
Pope's agent, Cardinal Pandolph, arrives and pre-
vents peace. John later is poisoned by monks, and
Faulconbridge emerges as a voice for England.

King Lear (tragedy, 1606). The aging King
Lear of Britain decides to give each of his three
daughters a part of his kingdom. Two daughters
flatter him and receive their portions. The third,
Cordelia, refuses to give him empty praise and is
left without her share. She marries the King of
France, but later returns to protect her father
when the two false daughters oust him from his
kingdom. Lear recognizes Cordelia's genuine
love too late. Cordelia is hanged, and Lear dies
of grief.

I am a man
More sinned against than sinning.

Act III, scene 2

Love's Labour's Lost (comedy, 1594?). King
Ferdinand of Navarre and three friends—Lords
Biron, Dumain, and Longaville—swear to deny
love and devote three years to study. But when
the Princess of France arrives with three charming ladies, the four young men fall in love despite
their oaths. Each one secretly woos the lady of
his choice. In the end they have to admit openly
that love's power has triumphed.

Macbeth (tragedy, 1606). Macbeth, a general,
meets three witches who hail him as the future
king of Scotland. They also prophesy that the
children of his friend Banquo will sit on the
throne. Goaded on by his wife, Macbeth
murders King Duncan. Caught between fear and his growing greed for
power, Macbeth murders Banquo
and then others. Lady Macbeth
loses her mind under the strain
of her horrid memories and
kills herself. Macbeth is finally defeated by the army
of Malcolm (who is Dun-
can's son) and is slain by
the nobleman Macduff.

Life's but a walking
shadow, a poor player,
That struts and frets his
hour upon the stage,

Lady Macbeth

And then is heard no more; it is
a tale
Told by an idiot, full of sound
and fury,
Signifying nothing.

Act V, scene 5

Measure for Measure
(comedy, 1604). Duke Vin-
centio of Vienna assigns
Angelo to rid that city of
its evil. The stern Angelo
begins by sentencing young
Claudio to death for having
seduced Juliet. When Claudio's sister, Isabella, pleads
for his life, Angelo falls
passionately in love with Isabella and himself tries to
seduce her. Vincentio, who
has watched it all in the disguise of a monk,
scolds Angelo, unites Claudio and Juliet, and
helps everyone regain his senses.

Falstaff

The Merchant of Venice (comedy, 1595?). The
merchant Antonio borrows money from Shylock,
a moneylender, so that his penniless friend Bas-
sanio can woo the noble Portia. Instead of interest
on the loan, Shylock asks a pound of flesh from
Antonio's body, should he not repay in time. Antonio loses his best ships and cannot return the
money. Shylock, an embittered man, demands
his price, the pound of flesh. Portia attends Antonio's trial disguised as a lawyer. With a wise
argument, she makes Shylock see the impossibil-
ity of his demand and thus saves Antonio's life.

The quality of mercy is not strain'd,
It droppeth as the gentle rain
from heaven
Upon the place
beneath . . . .

Act V, scene 1

The Merry Wives of Windsor
(comedy, 1600–01). As
usual, Sir John Falstaff needs
money. He thinks he can get it
from Mistress Page and
Mistress Ford by making
love to them. But the
ladies compare notes
and decide to teach
Falstaff a lesson.
They invite him
to secret meet-
ings and then
play all sorts
of tricks on
Falstaff. He is
finally par-
doned by all.

Puck

A Midsummer Night's Dream (comedy, 1595). In a forest near Athens, elves and fairies flit about with their king and queen, Oberon and Titania. A group of rustic players rehearse a play. And four young people—Helena, Demetrius, Hermia, and Lysander—chase each other because each loves one who loves another. Oberon sends his servant Puck for a love potion. This potion causes Titania to fall in love with a donkey—actually one of the players, Bottom, whose head was changed into a donkey's by Puck. The four young people again fall in love with wrong partners, but Puck finally sets things straight.

Lord, what fools these mortals be!

Act III, scene 2

Much Ado About Nothing (comedy, 1599?). Benedick and Beatrice, both quick-witted and intelligent, are made to fall in love with each other by a clever scheme of their friends. Meanwhile another couple, Claudio and Hero, have to put up with the plots of jealous people before they can be happily united. Bumbling Constable Dogberry helps the lovers, oddly enough, through his own clumsiness.

Othello (tragedy, 1604). Othello, a Moorish general in Venice, marries Desdemona, daughter of the senator Brabantio. Othello has made his friend Cassio his chief lieutenant, a position wanted by Iago. Jealous, Iago plots vengeance and falsely accuses Desdemona of betraying her husband with Cassio. Othello, believing Iago, smothers Desdemona. When Iago's falsehood is discovered, Othello stabs himself and dies at his wife's side.

Bottom

Who steals my purse
  steals trash; 'tis something, nothing;
'Twas mine, 'tis his, and has been slave to thousands;
But he that filches from me my good name
Robs me of that which not enriches him,
And makes me poor indeed.

Act III, scene 3

O! beware, my lord, of jealousy;
It is the green-ey'd monster . . . .

Act III, scene 3

Pericles (comedy, 1608?). Pericles, Prince of Tyre, successfully solves the riddle that King Antiochus sets for all of his daughter's suitors but escapes in time to avoid death at the tyrant's hands. He later marries the daughter of King Simonides of Pentapolis, Thaisa, who gives birth to Marina. Returning to Tyre by ship, mother and daughter are lost at sea, and Pericles becomes terribly depressed. Marina is saved, however, and years later when she and her father are miraculously reunited, Pericles discovers that Thaisa is also alive and is reunited with her as well.

Richard II (history, 1595). King Richard exiles two nobleman—his cousin Henry Bolingbroke and the Duke of Norfolk—from England. When Bolingbroke's father, John of Gaunt, dies, Richard seizes his uncle's property to finance his wars. While Richard is fighting in Ireland, Bolingbroke comes back to England and takes the throne. Richard is imprisoned and murdered upon the secret order of Bolingbroke, now King Henry IV.

Richard III (history, 1592–93). Richard, younger brother of King Edward IV of England, seeks the throne for himself and gets rid of everyone who stands in his way. Richard has his elder brother George, Duke of Clarence, murdered. When King Edward dies, Richard seizes the crown, executes the defenders of Edward's widow, and has her two young sons murdered. The noblemen revolt, and the Duke of Buckingham is executed by Richard. But Richard is finally slain on the battlefield by Henry Tudor, who will become King Henry VII.

A horse! a horse! my kingdom for a horse!

Act V, scene 4

Romeo and Juliet (tragedy, 1595). Romeo Montague and Juliet Capulet, children of two feuding families of Verona, fall in love and are married by Friar Laurence. In a street fight Romeo kills Juliet's cousin Tybalt and is banished from Verona. Juliet, rather than marry Count Paris, takes a drug that makes her appear dead. Romeo, believing her dead, poisons himself at her side. When Juliet awakens and sees Romeo, she stabs herself. The two families, shocked by the tragedy, end their feud.

Good-night, good-night! Parting is such sweet sorrow

That I shall say good-night
till it be morrow.

Act II, scene 2

The Taming of the Shrew
(comedy, 1594?). Baptista
has two daughters. Bianca,
the younger, has many suitors, while her older sister,
Katharina, is a shrew whose
temper frightens men away.
Baptista will not allow
Bianca to marry until Ka-
tharina is off his hands. The
gentleman Petruchio comes
along and marries Katharina
and after the wedding sets
out to "tame" his new wife.
In very clever ways he
shows he that he can be

Romeo and Juliet

even more ill-tempered than she. Meanwhile,
Bianca manages to marry the man of her choice,
Lucentio.

And thereby hangs a tale.

Act IV, scene 1

The Tempest (comedy, 1611). Prospero, ma-
gician and former Duke of Milan, lives on a
lonely island with his daughter Miranda and two
servants, Ariel and Caliban. With his magic,
Prospero one day causes a violent tempest in
order to shipwreck a boat and wash its passengers
ashore. The passengers are Prospero's brother,
Antonio; Alonso, King of Naples; and Prince Ferdinand, son of Alonso. Antonio and Alonso had
ousted Prospero from Milan, and Prospero makes
them see their guilt. The two restore Prospero to
his dukedom, and he renounces his magic powers. Ferdinand and Miranda, who have fallen in
love, are united, and all return to Italy.

Misery acquaints a man with strange bedfellows.

Act II, scene 2

We are such stuff
As dreams are made on, and our little life
Is rounded with a sleep.

Act IV, scene 1

Timon of Athens (tragedy, 1605?). Timon, a
rich nobleman of Athens, squanders his fortune
against the best advice of his loyal steward, Fla-
vius. When his money is all gone, he discovers
that most of his friends are false. Filled with bit-
terness, he becomes a hermit, living in a cave
even after discovering a treasure of gold. One of
his true friends, Alcibiades, who had been banished from Athens, then returns to revenge himself and Timon on the Athenian aristocracy.

Titus Andronicus (revenge tragedy, 1591?). In
the 300's B.C., Titus returns to Rome leading the
queen of the Goths, Tamora, in triumph. He
swears allegiance to Saturninus,
eldest son of the previous emperor
of Rome, who then takes Tamora
for his wife. Tamora's revenge
against Titus for executing her
sons is bloody and terrible, surpassed only by Titus' against her,
when he kills her other sons, Chiron and Demetrius, and serves
them to her and Saturninus at a
banquet. Titus then kills his
daughter, Lavinia, whom Chiron
and Demetrius had raped and mu-
tilated, and stabs Tamora. Saturninus kills him, and Lucius, Titus'
son, kills Saturninus.

Troilus and Cressida (tragedy,
1601?). Troilus, a Trojan prince
fighting in the Trojan War, is
heartbroken because his beloved Cressida is
taken to the Greek camp in exchange for a Trojan
prisoner. During a time of truce, Troilus arrives
in the Greeks' camp, only to discover that Cressida has betrayed him with a Greek soldier. When
the Greek hero Achilles hears of the slaying of
his best friend, he kills Hector, Troilus' brother,
and the war is resumed.

Twelfth Night, or What You Will (comedy,
1600). Orsino, duke of Illyria, loves Olivia, who
in turn loves Orsino's page and messenger. Unfortunately, this page is a girl, Viola, in disguise,
and Viola loves Orsino. The confused triangle is
finally disentangled when Olivia unites with Sebastian, Viola's twin brother, and Viola, shedding her disguise, marries Orsino.

If music be the food of love, play on . . . .

Act I, scene 1

The Two Gentlemen of Verona (comedy,
1592?). Valentine and Proteus, two friends who
live in Verona, travel to Milan to seek their fortune. Proteus forgets his own beloved, Julia, and
falls in love with Silvia, the sweetheart of Valentine. Proteus also arranges that Valentine be
banished from the court of Silvia's father, the
Duke of Milan. Silvia flees, Proteus follows, and
Julia, disguised as his page, goes with him, hoping to win him back. Finally Proteus is brought
to his senses and the couples are reunited.

The Winter's Tale (comedy, 1611). Leontes,
king of Sicilia, accuses his wife, Hermione, of
betraying him with his friend Polixenes. Polixenes escapes to Bohemia, and Leontes throws
Hermione into prison. When he realizes his mistake, it is too late; Hermione is reported dead.
Sixteen years later, when Leontes' daughter is
about to marry Polixenes' son, Leontes is overjoyed to learn that his wife is alive.

SHALE.   See ROCKS (Sedimentary Rock).

SHANGHAI

Shanghai is the largest city in China. Located on the country's east coast, the city (whose name means "on the sea") sits on both banks of the Huangpu River near where the Yangtze (Chang) River empties into the East China Sea. It is a major international port and is China's commercial, financial, and manufacturing center.

Shanghai is a municipality, meaning it is directly administered by China's central government in Beijing. The municipality consists of the city proper plus several surrounding counties and has a population of about 17 million. The area is one of the wealthiest in the country, and the average annual income per person is the highest in China. The climate is mild, with winter temperatures rarely reaching freezing and summer temperatures averaging around 80°F (27°C).

▶ THE CITY

Shanghai is divided into two sections—Puxi on the west bank of the Huangpu River and Pudong on the east. The city's most famous site is the Bund, a scenic boulevard running along the river's west bank and lined with hotels and office buildings built by Western nations in the 1920's. The Bund is a favorite place for morning and evening strolls. Mainland China's tallest building, the Jin Mao Building (1,381 feet/421 meters) is located in Pudong, as are the Oriental Pearl Television Tower and the Shanghai stock exchange. In 1999, a new international airport was also opened in Pudong.

Nanjing Road, connected to the Bund, is the city's busiest street. Clothing stores and restaurants attract crowds of shoppers. In the old international settlements further inland, restaurants, cafés, coffee shops, and bars are busy well into the evening.

The oldest part of Shanghai has recently been restored. The beautiful Yu Yuan Garden, built during the Ming dynasty (A.D. 1368–1644), provides visitors a glimpse of how wealthy imperial merchants once lived.

Shanghai's Pudong section, on the east bank of the Huangpu River, is the city's financial center and site of some of its most modern architecture.

The garden is surrounded by small lanes lined with specialty shops. Nearby, the Jade Buddha Temple displays two magnificent statues of the Buddha carved in white jade.

The Shanghai Museum is one of the finest in China, with a vast collection of bronze items from the Shang (1523–1000's B.C.) and Zhou (1000's–221 B.C.) dynasties as well as many examples of traditional Chinese art.

Several universities are also located in Shanghai. These include Fudan, East China Normal, and Tongji universities.

In the late 1990's Shanghai completed a new subway system, a series of highways, and several bridges across the Huangpu River. These have eased the city's traffic problem.

▶ ECONOMIC ACTIVITY

Shanghai's major industries include the manufacture of automobiles, electronics, telecommunications equipment, machinery, textiles, iron, steel, pharmaceuticals, and petrochemicals. The city aims to be an international center of finance, trade, and services.

▶ HISTORY

Prior to 1842, Shanghai was a small, unremarkable fishing town. After China's defeat by the British in the Opium War (1839–42), however, it prospered. The Treaty of Nanjing, which settled the war, identified the city as one of five Chinese ports to be opened to Western trade. The treaty required the introduction of extraterritoriality, which meant that foreigners living in those ports were not subject to Chinese law.

Western traders eventually established two major settlements in Shanghai: the French Concession and the International Settlement, each with its own foreign laws and officials. The city became a major industrial center. Shipbuilding and repairs, textile production, and food processing were major industries. Westerners also built China's first skyscrapers in the city. Because of its many movie theaters, universities, and luxurious hotels—as well as for its early use of electricity, telephones, and streetcars—Shanghai became known as the Pearl of the Orient.

However, Shanghai's great wealth coexisted with staggering poverty. Rural peasants in the new textile factories often worked long hours in unsafe conditions. Crime and political unrest were also problems.

The Bund runs along the west bank of the Huangpu River. The boulevard, lined with Western-style buildings, is a popular place for morning and evening strolls.

Shanghai after 1945. Shanghai was returned to Chinese control at the end of World War II (1939–45), after which the country was engulfed by civil war. When the Communists defeated the Nationalist Party in 1949, ending the civil war and establishing the People's Republic of China, Shanghai declined. Foreigners left, small shops and the big textile and ship-building factories were taken over by the state, international trade declined, and traffic in the port dwindled.

Nonetheless, Shanghai remained China's major industrial center. But Beijing taxed much of what Shanghai earned and redistributed it to poorer parts of the country. One-sixth of the central government's revenues came from Shanghai.

Since 1989, Shanghai's economy has improved dramatically. In 2002, the Chinese unveiled the world's first commercial maglev, or magnetic levitation train, linking Shanghai with the international airport in Pudong.

ANNE F. THURSTON
Johns Hopkins University
School of Advanced International Studies

SHARKS, RAYS, AND CHIMAERAS

No other group of fish has caused so much curiosity, confusion, and fear throughout human history as the **Chondrichthyes**—the sharks, rays, and chimaeras. These fish are diverse in their appearance and habits and include forms ranging from giant plankton feeders and colorful reef-scavengers to some of the ocean's fiercest predators.

Most sharks and rays live in marine waters. They can be found from the tropics to the poles and from the shallows to the deepest ocean basins. Several species of rays live fully in fresh water, and some species of sharks enter fresh water occasionally.

All Chondrichthyes have a skeleton that is made of cartilage. Unlike bone, which is hard and inflexible, cartilage is strong and flexible. The only true bone that is found in sharks is in the roots of their teeth. Sharks and rays have bodies that are covered with small, dense, toothlike scales, which give the skin a rough feel.

Sharks, rays, and chimaeras are carnivores (meat eaters). They may be scavengers or predators, and the types of prey vary greatly among these groups. They eat no plants of any kind.

▶ SHARKS

Most sharks have an elongated body shaped like a torpedo, a strong tail, and fins

Sharks inhabit most parts of the ocean. The Caribbean reef shark (*top*) dwells in shallow waters near coral reefs in the Caribbean sea. The more ferocious great white shark (*above*) prefers cooler waters.

for steering and lift. Sharks' fins are relatively rigid and are formed by the cartilage skeleton and covered by a layer of dense skin.

Sharks lack the air-filled swim bladder that allows most other fish to stay afloat. Instead, sharks have large oil-filled livers. Since oil is less dense than water, the liver gives sharks some buoyancy. However, they must also rely on the lift provided by their fins to keep them afloat. Sharks will sink when not swimming because they do not have this added lift.

Like other fish, sharks do not breathe air but get oxygen from the water through their gills. Most species of sharks and rays have five pairs of gill openings, but a few species have six or seven. Each gill opening contains a system of many tiny blood vessels called **capillaries**. As the shark pumps water into its mouth and out through its gills, oxygen from the water is absorbed and carbon dioxide is eliminated by the capillaries. This process is called **respiration**.

A commonly held but mistaken idea is that all sharks must swim constantly to remain alive. Some sharks do rely on the water pressure generated by swimming to force water into their mouths and through their gills for respiration. However, many species of sharks have strong muscles that can pump water over their gills even when the shark is not moving.

Sharks' teeth are specialized for effective capture and eating of prey. Sharks have at least one row of fully functional teeth at any time. Three to seven rows of replacement teeth are located behind every functional tooth.

Senses

Sharks have specialized senses that allow them to easily detect and locate prey. One of the most important shark senses is touch. Sharks have many nerve endings located throughout their skin that detect even the faintest vibrations and movements in the water. They also have sensors called the **ampullae of Lorenzini**, which are very small pores found throughout the body but especially on the head. These sensors are **electroreceptors**, which give sharks, rays, and chimaeras the unique ability to detect the weak electrical impulses given off by living organisms. The sense of smell in sharks and their relatives is also sensitive, and many predatory sharks can locate the odor of their prey from miles away. Vision in most sharks is comparable to that of humans, but some deepwater sharks have good vision even in dark waters.

Feeding

Methods of feeding vary widely among shark species. Some sharks are predators. They may chase down their prey or catch it in swift surprise attacks. Or they may simply cruise an area looking for less active prey lying on the ocean bottom.

The three largest species of sharks are plankton feeders. They feed passively by swimming and taking in large volumes of water, which is filtered as it passes over the gills. Structures called gill rakers act like sieves to strain out small fish and plankton that the sharks swallow without chewing.

Mating and Reproduction

All sharks, rays, and chimaeras reproduce by internal fertilization, a characteristic uncommon in other groups of fish. After courting a female shark, the male shark grasps the female's body or fins with his teeth to help hold her in place. He then inserts a structure called a **clasper**, a modified extension of the pelvic fin, which passes sperm into the female's **cloaca** where the eggs are fertilized.

Some species of sharks lay the fertilized eggs among vegetation or rocks, and the offspring hatch several months later. Other species retain the fertilized eggs within the body. The young are born after they emerge from the egg. Some species produce live young that have a direct circulatory and nutritional connection with the mother while in the womb. The connection is similar in function to the placenta in mammals.

Young sharks are miniature but fully functioning versions of adults. Since there is no parental care, baby sharks must immediately begin life on their own.

Specific Sharks

More than 400 species of sharks are known. Several of the most studied are described below.

Angel Shark. With its flattened body and wide fins, the angel shark resembles a ray, but it is a shark. It often lies half-buried in the sediment of the ocean floor and, with a lightning fast lunge, ambushes unsuspecting prey that wanders by.

Basking Shark. The basking shark is the second largest species of shark, and it is a plankton feeder. It was once hunted for its large oil-filled liver, but populations have been severely reduced in many areas of the world by overfishing.

Bull Shark. The bull shark is a large, bold predatory shark. It is able to travel into shallow coastal waters and even into fresh waters. This species has been caught hundreds of miles upstream in large rivers, such as the Amazon, Mississippi, and Tigris rivers.

Dogfish. Often called the spiny dogfish because of the sharp spines that are found in front of their dorsal fins, this species is commonly used for dissections in anatomy courses and is used as food in many countries. Dogfish sometimes form large schools and often compete with fishermen by preying on other species of commercial fish.

Great White. The great white is perhaps the largest and most active predatory shark. These fish can reach 20 feet (6 meters) in length, and they prey on other sharks, seals, sea lions, and dolphins. Although they have a worldwide distribution, great whites are found most often in cooler waters where their marine mammal prey is most abundant.

Hammerhead. The hammerhead group is made up of several different shark species. Each has a distinctive flattened and widened head that resembles the head of a hammer. Scientists guess that the widened head helps the ampullae of Lorenzini detect prey buried in bottom sediments.

Nurse Shark. Often seen sleeping motionless on the ocean bottom, the nurse shark is a common predator of tropical reefs. It uses suction to extract small fish and crustaceans from coral reefs and rocky cracks and crushes them with its powerful jaws and blunt teeth.

Thresher Shark. There are three different species of thresher shark. All have a distinctive elongated tail that is used as a lasso to corral small schooling fish or as a whip to stun and kill larger fish.

Tiger Shark. The tiger shark gets its name from the distinctive spots on young sharks that fade away as the sharks reach adulthood. Tiger sharks are large and potentially dangerous predators of the tropics. Their diet is one of the most diverse of any species of shark. Their usual prey consists of fish and sharks, but they also eat squid, crustaceans, sea turtles, marine mammals, seabirds, and occasionally humans. Tiger sharks are also scavengers and will eat nearly any type of waste.

Whale Shark. Reaching lengths of up to 60 feet (18 meters), the whale shark is the largest fish alive, but it is a harmless plankton feeder. It is found mainly in the tropics, where its gentle nature, large size, and attractive spotted pattern make it a favorite attraction for scuba divers.

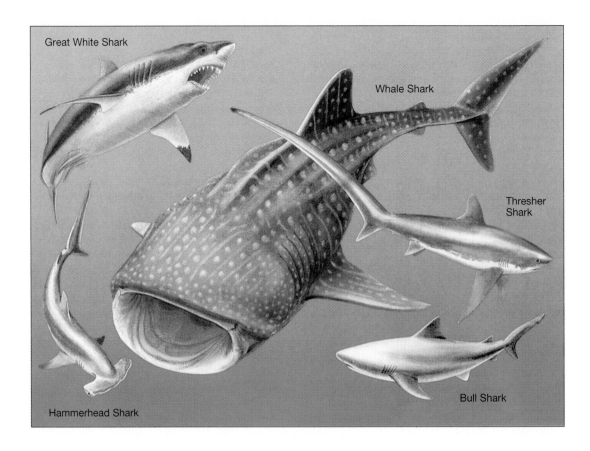

Great White Shark

Whale Shark

Thresher Shark

Bull Shark

Hammerhead Shark

The bluespotted stingray often lies camouflaged on the ocean floor, waiting for a meal of mollusk or crab.

Sharks and People

Human activities, such as fishing, swimming, and snorkeling, often take place in the waters where sharks live. But sharks and humans do not always coexist peacefully.

Shark Attacks. To most people, few experiences seem more frightening than a shark attack. But of the nearly 400 species of sharks known, only a dozen species are potentially dangerous to humans. Worldwide, fewer than 100 shark attacks are reported each year. Fewer than a third of these are fatal. Given the fact that tens of thousands of bathers, divers, swimmers, and surfers use beaches that are well within the ranges of many predatory sharks every day, it is surprising that shark attacks do not happen more often.

Because attacks on humans are uncommon, it appears that humans are not a normal part of the diet of most sharks. In some cases of shark attacks, human-related activities, such as divers harassing a shark, may provoke the attack. In unprovoked attacks, it is often a single shark that attacks a lone bather. In these cases, it is thought that sharks mistakenly attack humans, believing them to be their normal prey of seals and dolphins.

Ecological Consequences of Overfishing. As the top predators in marine environments, sharks and rays help maintain the balance in the food chain of their ecosystems. But human activities such as fishing are placing increasing pressure on these species. Recent evidence shows a worldwide decrease in the populations of many sharks.

Sharks replace their populations very slowly. Thus overfishing can happen quickly, and populations of some shark species are so low that they are considered commercially extinct. Some species of sharks and rays are legally protected. Monitoring these populations is essential for assuring the long-term viability of commercial fishing and maintaining the role of sharks and rays in the careful balance of nature.

▶ RAYS

Rays, which include the stingrays, electric rays, sawfish, guitarfish, mantas, and skates, are similar to sharks in most ways. But unlike sharks, rays have a flattened body, a long snout, and side fins that are expanded to look like wings. These features allow rays to lie securely on the ocean bottom to wait for prey, but several species are free-swimming plankton feeders.

The mouth of most rays is on the underside of the snout, which allows them to feed on bottom-dwelling organisms more easily. Rays breathe by pumping water in through two holes located behind their eyes and pumping it out through their gills.

Stingrays have a sharp, jagged barb (stinger) that they use as defense against potential predators. The barb may inject a mildly toxic (poisonous) mucus. Many species of rays are fished for the meat in their large winglike pectoral fins.

▶ CHIMAERAS

The chimaeras are an ancient and odd group of fish that are normally found in cool, deep waters. Like sharks and rays, they have a skeleton made of cartilage and a large liver, but they also have several unique features. For example, they have only a single pair of gill openings; thin, flexible fins; a flattened scaleless body; and a jaw that contains a sharp, beaklike tooth plate rather than teeth. Male chimaeras also have several hooked clublike organs on the head and pelvic fins that they probably use in mating. Very little is known about the chimaeras.

Douglas J. Long
California Academy of Sciences

See also Fish.

SHAW, GEORGE BERNARD (1856–1950)

George Bernard Shaw, one of the most influential playwrights of the 20th century, was born in Dublin on July 26, 1856. His early life was not happy. His father was an irresponsible man who drank too much and could not support his family properly. His mother was a disappointed, unhappy woman who found more pleasure in studying music than in raising her children. Bernard and his two sisters received little love and attention from their mother when they were young, and his memories of these days were often bitter.

Although he did not like school, Bernard was a good, bright, curious student. His lifelong interest in everything from music and art to machines and medicine began in school. When he was 15, he went to work in an office. He did well as a clerk, but after five years he decided that he wanted to be a writer. In 1876 he left Ireland and went to London, where he began to write seriously. His early works, mostly novels, were not at all successful, but he eventually gained a reputation as a good, if not always kind, critic of music, drama, and the other arts.

Shaw was friendly with Beatrice and Sidney Webb, who were interested in making many social reforms in England. Together they were the most powerful members of the Fabian Society, a Socialist organization to which Shaw gave much time and effort for many, many years. Many of the controversial ideas endorsed by the society are expressed in Shaw's plays.

In 1898 Shaw married a wealthy, intellectual, independent woman named Charlotte Payne-Townshend. There was little romance in their courtship and marriage, but they lived happily together until her death in 1943. She encouraged him in many ways, helping him in his work and bringing to his home life some of the peace and order that he had missed in his earlier years.

At the time of his marriage Shaw had already written some of the plays on which his fame rests—*Arms and the Man* (1894), *Candida* (1894), and *The Devil's Disciple* (1897). In 1904 Harley Granville-Barker (1877–1946) became the producer of the Royal Court Theatre and began presenting Shaw's plays. Shaw introduced new subjects and theater techniques in his plays, and at first his public following was small. His comedy about relations between England and Ireland, *John Bull's Other Island* (1904), drew favorable attention, however, and *Major Barbara* (1905) increased his fame.

Shaw's greatest popularity as a playwright is perhaps based on two plays, *Pygmalion* (1912) and *Saint Joan* (1923). He wrote the part of Eliza Doolittle, the poor Cockney girl in *Pygmalion,* for the noted actress Mrs. Patrick Campbell. Shaw said that he fell in love with her "30 seconds after meeting her." Their romance did not last long, but it has become famous through the publication of their love letters. *Pygmalion* is the play on which the celebrated musical *My Fair Lady* is based.

Saint Joan was a great success. The story of the courageous, independent, misunderstood Maid of Orleans appealed to Shaw, and he treated his subject with humor and compassion. Shaw was awarded the Nobel prize for literature in 1925 but refused to accept the prize money. Instead he asked that the funds be used "to encourage understanding in literature and art between Sweden and the British Isles."

Shaw wrote some 50 plays, as well as many essays. These essays were often published as prefaces to his plays. In addition, he wrote many books and pamphlets on politics, economics, religion, social customs, art, music, and the theater. His correspondence was enormous. He continued to take a lively interest in everything and to express his opinions freely on any subject until the end of his long life. His thin frame and full white beard were familiar to newspaper readers throughout the world, and his witty and direct statements were constantly quoted. He was a firm vegetarian and a shrewd businessman who drove a hard bargain. To the public he often seemed strange but always interesting. To his friends he was known as a basically shy man, honest in word and thought.

Shaw died at his home in Ayot St. Lawrence, England, on November 2, 1950. For many years he had been interested in simplified spelling, and in his will he left money for the creation of a new alphabet.

PHILIP DRISCOLL
Formerly, Brandeis University

SHEEP

Most sheep are raised on rangelands and farms. A few live wild in mountain country. But wherever they live, sheep are alike in many ways. Their teeth are developed for grazing on grasses, weeds, and the leaves of shrubs. They have eight incisor teeth in the front of the lower jaw for biting plants. Larger cheek teeth in both jaws are used for grinding. Their feet are hoofed.

The females of many domestic breeds of sheep are hornless. But both males and females of many wild sheep grow horns. The male's horns are large and may be very wide at the base. The female's are smaller.

It is usually easy to tell sheep from goats. In general, male goats, unlike male sheep, have beards, and they give off a strong odor. A goat's horns usually grow upward and backward. A sheep's horns usually grow out to the sides, then curve in a spiral. The tails of domestic goats usually turn up. The tails of domestic sheep turn down. Almost all sheep have a gland between their toes that gives off a scented substance. Goats do not.

There are many different kinds of wild and domestic sheep. But all of them are considered varieties of one main kind.

Male sheep are called **rams**. Females are called **ewes**. Ewes give birth to one or two young, called **lambs**, usually in the spring.

▶ DOMESTIC SHEEP

Sheep raising began thousands of years ago, probably in Asia. Certain kinds of wild sheep were raised for their skins, milk, and meat. Later they were also raised for wool.

Domestic sheep differ from wild sheep in some ways. They usually have longer tails and somewhat smaller horns than wild sheep have. Domestic sheep have coats of wool. Wild sheep have shorter, stiffer hair.

Domestic sheep provide people with food and clothing. They are also a source of leather, soap, and glue. The fatty substance, or grease, taken from sheep's wool is widely used as a softening agent in ointments and creams. It is commonly called **lanolin**.

▶ WILD SHEEP

The Rocky Mountain bighorn is much like other kinds of wild sheep in habits and appearance. Its coat is grayish brown above and white below. It has a short, black tail.

The Rocky Mountain bighorn lives in western mountains, from Canada to Mexico. It is a graceful, quick-moving animal. Its padded feet help it grip slippery surfaces. Bighorns move about in small bands. Except during the mating season, many bands consist of mothers with their young. Males form separate bands.

Another North American sheep is the Dall sheep. It looks much like the Rocky Mountain bighorn but is pure white in color. Its relative the Stone's sheep is brownish black. Both live in Alaska and northwest Canada.

Other kinds of wild sheep include the mouflon; the urial; and the argali. The mouflon, the only kind of wild sheep still found in southern Europe, lives in Corsica and Sardinia. It is a small reddish brown sheep with a dark line running along its back. The urial has long, slender horns. It lives in Asia Minor, the southern part of the former Soviet Union, and Iran. The argali of Asia is the largest of all wild sheep.

The aoudad and the bharal are like sheep in some ways and like goats in other ways. The aoudad lives in northern Africa. It is brownish yellow in color. A mane of long hair grows along its body from its chin to between its front legs. The bharal looks somewhat like a goat but lacks the goat's strong odor. It lives in Tibet and western China. Bands of wild mouflon and aoudads have been introduced to some rough range areas of the United States.

CARL S. MENZIES
Texas A & M University

See also HOOFED MAMMALS.

SHELLEY, PERCY BYSSHE (1792–1822)

One of the greatest English lyric poets, Percy Bysshe Shelley, was born on August 4, 1792, near Horsham, Sussex. He was the eldest son of a family of seven children. He used to entertain his brother and sisters by making up stories about fantastic creatures living in their house and grounds. When Shelley was 10, he went to boarding school. In 1804 he entered Eton.

Because he had his own interests and did not mix with the other boys at school, Shelley was treated cruelly. The boys called him "Mad Shelley" for his original ideas and eccentricities. Shelley was interested in science and conducted his own experiments. He wrote horror stories and began *Queen Mab,* a philosophical poem that was published in 1813.

Shelley went on to Oxford in 1810, but he had been there less than a year when he published a pamphlet called *The Necessity of Atheism.* When he refused to admit his authorship of the pamphlet, the university officials expelled him.

Shelley's life from then on was generally unsettled and often clouded with debts and disappointments. At 19, he married 16-year-old Harriet Westbrook. They were separated in 1814. Shelley then eloped to Europe with Mary Godwin, whom he married in 1816 after Harriet had drowned herself. Shelley and Mary had three children, only one of whom lived beyond childhood. Mary, also a writer, is remembered most for her novel *Frankenstein* (1818). After settling in Italy in 1818, the Shelleys often saw Lord Byron, although the two poets were very different in character.

Shelley's first poem to reach many readers was *Alastor, or the Spirit of Solitude* (1816). In 1820 his *Prometheus Unbound,* a lyrical drama based on classical models, was published. Around this time, he also wrote his best-known odes, including "To a Skylark" and "Ode to Heaven." Some, such as "Ode to the West Wind," are partly autobiographical. The death of the English poet John Keats inspired Shelley to write *Adonais* (1821). He was working on a long poem, "The Triumph of Life," when he met his own death. On July 8, 1822, his boat was capsized in a storm off the coast of Italy, and he was drowned.

Reviewed by RANDEL HELMS
Arizona State University

To Night

I

SWIFTLY walk o'er the western wave,
Spirit of Night!
Out of the misty eastern cave
Where, all the long and lone daylight,
Thou wovest dreams of joy and fear
Which make thee terrible and dear,
Swift be thy flight!

II

Wrap thy form in a mantle gray,
Star-inwrought,
Blind with thine hair the eyes of Day;
Kiss her until she be wearied out.
Then wander o'er city and sea and land,
Touching all with thine opiate wand—
Come, long-sought!

III

When I arose and saw the dawn,
I sighed for thee;
When light rode high, and the dew was gone,
And noon lay heavy on flower and tree,
And the weary Day turned to her rest,
Lingering like an unloved guest,
I sighed for thee.

IV

Thy brother Death came, and cried,
Wouldst thou me?
Thy sweet child Sleep, the filmy-eyed,
Murmured like a noontide bee,
Shall I nestle near thy side?
Wouldst thou me?—And I replied,
No, not thee.

V

Death will come when thou art dead,
Soon, too soon—
Sleep will come when thou art fled.
Of neither would I ask the boon
I ask of thee, beloved Night—
Swift be thine approaching flight,
Come soon, soon!

Ozymandias

I met a traveller from an antique land
Who said: "Two vast and trunkless legs of stone
Stand in the desert. Near them, on the sand,
Half sunk, a shattered visage lies, whose frown,
And wrinkled lip, and sneer of cold command,
Tell that its sculptor well those passions read
Which yet survive, stamped on these lifeless things,
The hand that mocked them, and the heart that fed:
And on the pedestal these words appear:
'My name is Ozymandias, king of kings:
Look on my works, ye Mighty, and despair!'
Nothing beside remains. Round the decay
Of that colossal wreck, boundless and bare
The lone and level sands stretch far away."

SHELLS

Many kinds of animals grow hard external covers, or shells, to protect their bodies from predators and the environment. Turtles, crustaceans (such as crabs, lobsters, and shrimps), and even some microscopic organisms all have very distinct kinds of shells. However, when most people think of shells, they think of the shells of mollusks. Mollusks are a group of invertebrates (animals without a backbone) that includes snails, clams, oysters, mussels, and nautiluses. This article discusses the shells of mollusks.

▶ MOLLUSK SHELLS

There are five primary kinds, or classes, of mollusks: gastropods, bivalves, cephalopods, chitons, and scaphopods. Most of these animals have shells. The main exceptions are land and sea slugs, octopuses, and squids. While crustaceans and some kinds of insects continually shed and replace their shells as they grow, in a process called molting, a mollusk has only one shell during its lifetime.

Shelled mollusks are born with shells, and as they grow, their shells grow with them. Specialized tissue along the mantle, the skin-like envelope covering the animal's soft body, continuously adds thin layers to the edge of the shell's opening. This gradual buildup of new shell material is called **accretion**.

The shell material consists of several layers of calcium carbonate crystals and protein, which makes the shell strong as well as slightly flexible. The outer layer of a shell, called the **periostracum**, protects the rest of the shell. In the **prismatic layer**, the crystals of calcium carbonate are shaped like prisms. Some shells have an inner **nacreous layer**, in which the calcium carbonate and protein form a lustrous material called nacre, or mother-of-pearl. Mother-of-pearl is the substance that builds up inside oysters to form pearls.

Mollusk shells are found in a variety of colors, including white, gray, pink, silver, or brown. Some shells have vivid spots, bands, or stripes of black, red, yellow, and sometimes green. A shell's coloration often serves as camouflage, helping the animal blend into its surroundings. Coloration may also serve to attract mates or as a warning to predators.

The largest mollusk shells belong to giant white clams, whose shells can grow more than

The shells of snails are formed by a series of coils or whorls that typically produce a tapered, spiral shape. *Clockwise from top left:* Cone shells are popular with collectors, but the snails living in them often inflict venomous stings. Limpet shells stop coiling early in the snail's life and form into a flat disc. Lister's conch is found in the Indian Ocean. Trumpet triton shells have been used as horns by native peoples living on islands in the Pacific Ocean. The spikes on the shells of the arthritic spider conch and the thorny whelk may help protect the animals from predators. Cowry shells are usually smooth and oval.

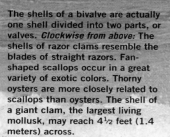

The shells of a bivalve are actually one shell divided into two parts, or valves. *Clockwise from above:* The shells of razor clams resemble the blades of straight razors. Fan-shaped scallops occur in a great variety of exotic colors. Thorny oysters are more closely related to scallops than oysters. The shell of a giant clam, the largest living mollusk, may reach 4½ feet (1.4 meters) across.

4½ feet (1.4 meters) wide. The smallest shell is that of the snail *Ammonicera japonica*, whose shell has a diameter of only about 0.014 inch (0.35 millimeter).

Gastropods. Gastropods (from the Greek words meaning "stomach-foot") are the largest group of mollusks. They include snails and slugs (which have no shells) that live on land and in fresh and salt water. Snail shells grow in a process called **coiling**, in which a spiral is formed by a succession of coils or **whorls**. The whorls of the shell become larger and wider as the animal grows, and the animal lives in the last or last few whorls. Limpets are a kind of snail in which coiling stops at an early stage of growth, resulting in a flat, saucer-shaped shell.

The surface of snail shells may be smooth or have ribs, knobs, spines, or a combination of these. These features may strengthen the shell and may also protect it from predators that would try to swallow or bore into it.

Bivalves. Bivalves are mollusks with shells divided into two parts, or valves, and they include ani-mals such as clams, oysters, mussels, and scallops. The two parts of a bivalve shell are connected by a flexible ligament, which acts like a hinge. When a set of muscles is contracted, the two valves close against each other. When these muscles relax, the valves separate.

Some bivalves are wedge-shaped, which helps them burrow into the sand or mud. The shells of mussels and some oysters are streamlined to help protect the animal from pounding waves. The fan-shaped shell of a scallop helps the animal travel short distances when it squirts water out of its shell.

Cephalopods. Most cephalopods (from the Greek words meaning "head-foot"), such as squids and octopuses, do not have shells. However, fossil records indicate that many different kinds of shelled cephalopods lived in the oceans millions of years ago. Fossils

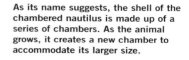

As its name suggests, the shell of the chambered nautilus is made up of a series of chambers. As the animal grows, it creates a new chamber to accommodate its larger size.

How to Start a Shell Collection

Shell collecting is a hobby enjoyed by many people. If you would like to collect shells, look through various books on shells or explore a museum's invertebrate collection to help you decide what kind of shell interests you the most. Some people collect only one kind of shell—scallops or cone-shells, for example—while others collect shells from a particular habitat or geographic location. Some people even specialize in collecting shells of just one color.

Among the best places to look for shells are beaches, mudflats, and breakwaters. As you gather each shell, make sure it is not still inhabited; if it is, carefully put it back where you found it. After you bring your shells home, wash them thoroughly to remove any sand or remains of the mollusks that lived in them. To make the shells shine, gently polish them with a

soft cloth or apply a thin coat of mineral oil. Record the common and scientific names of your shells, as well as when and where you found them, and then store them in a dry place out of direct sunlight.

of one such group of animals, called ammonites, have been found that measure up to 6 feet (2 meters) in diameter.

The best-known shelled cephalopod living today is the chambered, or pearly, nautilus. It resembles the extinct ammonites and lives in the Indian and Pacific oceans. This animal grows a shell with internal chambers that can be filled with or emptied of water, allowing the animal to move up or down in the ocean. The animal lives in the last and largest chamber of the shell.

Chitons. Chitons are flat, oval-shaped mollusks found in most oceans of the world, usually in shallow coastal areas. Their shells are composed of eight (or sometimes seven)

Chitons have flat, oval shells formed by a series of overlapping plates. Some species can grow to 1 foot (0.3 meter) in length.

overlapping plates that are hinged together, which makes it easy for the animals' bodies to conform to the rocky surfaces on which they live.

Scaphopods. Scaphopods (from the Greek words meaning "shovel-foot") are often called tusk shells because their long, narrow shells resemble teeth or tusks. The shapes of these shells help the animals burrow into the sand.

▶ **CAREERS IN SHELL STUDIES**

The scientific study of mollusk shells is called conchology, and it is always linked with the study of mollusks, which is called malacology. Although there are no academic programs in the United States devoted solely to conchology or malacology, there are many institutions (such as universities, research centers, and natural history museums) that emphasize the study of mollusks through programs in zoology, marine biology, ecology, genetics, and other related subjects.

JOSÉ H. LEAL
Director, The Bailey-Matthews Shell Museum

See also MOLLUSKS; OCTOPUSES, SQUIDS, AND OTHER CEPHALOPODS; OYSTERS, CLAMS, AND OTHER BIVALVES; PEARLS; SNAILS AND SLUGS.

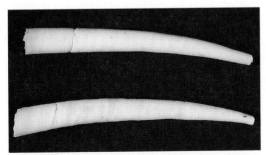

Scaphopods are also called tusk shells because their long and narrow shape resembles a tusk, or tooth. This shape helps the animal burrow into the sand.

SHENYANG

Shenyang (formerly called Mukden) is one of China's leading industrial cities. It is the capital of Liaoning province and the chief city of China's Northeastern region, commonly known as Manchuria. The city is located on the Hun River on the southern Manchurian plain. It has a population of about 4 million.

Shenyang is a transportation center and the most important manufacturing city in the northeast. It produces heavy machinery, electrical equipment, automobiles, trucks, locomotives, machine tools, and chemicals. The city also processes agricultural products.

History. Shenyang was an early center of Chinese settlement in southern Manchuria. The city was captured by the Manchus, a nomadic people of the region, who made it their capital in 1625. The Manchus later conquered all of China, establishing the Ch'ing (or Manchu) dynasty, which ruled until 1912.

In the early years of the 1900's, Shenyang was dominated first by Russia and then Japan. In 1931, Japanese troops began the conquest of Manchuria. The Japanese used as an excuse for their action the so-called Mukden Incident. They falsely claimed that Chinese had blown up part of a Japanese-owned railroad near Mukden, as the city was then called. The city was restored to China in 1945, along with the rest of Manchuria, when Japan was defeated in World War II.

HYMAN KUBLIN
City University of New York, Brooklyn College
Author, *The Rim of Asia*

SHEPARD, ALAN B. See NEW HAMPSHIRE (Famous People); SPACE EXPLORATION AND TRAVEL (Profiles).
SHERIDAN, PHILIP HENRY. See CIVIL WAR, UNITED STATES (Profiles: Union).
SHERMAN, JAMES S. See VICE PRESIDENCY OF THE UNITED STATES.
SHERMAN, ROGER. See CONNECTICUT (Famous People).

SHERMAN, WILLIAM TECUMSEH (1820–1891)

William Tecumseh Sherman was one of the Union Army's leading generals during the U.S. Civil War (1861–65). He was born in Lancaster, Ohio, on February 8, 1820. His father, a judge, named him after the Shawnee Indian chief Tecumseh. When Sherman was 9, his father died, and he was brought up by a family friend. He later attended the U.S. Military Academy at West Point, New York, graduating in 1840.

Civil War. When the Civil War broke out, Sherman was appointed a colonel in the Union Army. He rose to become General Ulysses S. Grant's most trusted officer. When Grant became general in chief in 1864, Sherman took command of all Union forces in the southwest. In September of that year, he captured Atlanta, Georgia. He evacuated the people from the city and then, on November 15, burned everything in it of military value. That day, with an army of 62,000, he began his famous March to the Sea. His intent was to "make Georgia howl" by destroying crops in a wide path to Savannah. Sherman did not attack an army—he was almost unopposed. Instead, he attacked the South's ability and will to fight.

After capturing Savannah, Sherman marched north and continued his destructive course into South Carolina. On April 26, 1865, the Confederate general Joseph E. Johnston surrendered to Sherman. Seventeen days earlier, General Robert E. Lee had surrendered to Grant. The Civil War was over.

When Grant became president in 1869, Sherman succeeded him as commanding general (1869–84) of the Army. Because of his broad strategies, Sherman has been called the first modern general. When urged to run for the presidency in 1884, Sherman refused, saying, "I will not accept if nominated and will not serve if elected." He died on February 14, 1891, in New York City.

ARI HOOGENBOOM
City University of New York, Brooklyn College
See also CIVIL WAR, UNITED STATES.

SHIPS AND SHIPPING

Ships have played a vital role in human history. They have enabled people to cross oceans, lakes, and rivers that were once impassable; to transport large loads of goods over long distances; and to discover and explore the farthest reaches of the world. And some of the most important inventions, including the magnetic compass and the chronometer, were developed for use on ships.

▶ KINDS OF SHIPS

The term "ship" is typically applied to any vessel measuring at least 40 feet (12 meters) long and weighing more than 40 tons. Any vessel smaller is called a boat, although fishing vessels and submarines are always known as boats whatever their size. Modern ships are made in many different designs to accommodate their many different uses. Ships are used for recreational activities, for military purposes, and to transport raw materials and finished products to and from ports all over the world.

Sailing Ships

Today's large sailing ships, also called **tall ships** or **windjammers**, are not used to transport people or goods as they were before the invention of steam power. These ships are used to train people, particularly naval and coast guard cadets, in the craft of sailing; for exhibitions and educational purposes; for racing; and for nostalgic cruises and tours that provide opportunities to experience the excitement and adventure of the age of sail. For more information on sailboats and similar craft, see the article SAILING in Volume S.

Passenger Ships

There are two basic kinds of ships that carry passengers. **Ocean liners** provide vacationers with leisurely and comfortable cruises, often to exotic locations such as the Caribbean. These ships typically include shops, theaters, swimming pools, spas, casinos, and restaurants. For more information, see the article OCEAN LINERS in Volume O.

Ferries carry people and vehicles across rivers or small bodies of water. They are commonly used by commuters to get to and from work. The oldest continuously operated ferry, which crosses the Connecticut River between the towns of Rocky Hill and Glastonbury, has been in ser-

Supertankers carry large amounts of crude oil across the oceans. They are among the largest merchant ships.

vice since 1655. Two kinds of ships occasionally used as ferries are **catamarans**, which have two separate hulls of equal size, set parallel to one another and held together by a framework; and **hydrofoils**, which skim over the water on winglike fins.

Military Ships

A wide variety of ships serve in navies throughout the world. The United States Navy includes **destroyers**, originally built to

Frigates are among the many different kinds of ships used by navies throughout the world for combat, deploying troops, or delivering supplies to other ships.

attack and destroy torpedo boats; **cruisers**, which are capable of attacking targets in the air, under water, and on the surface of the water; the immense **aircraft carriers**; **amphibious assault ships**, which deploy aircraft and troops at beach landings; **fast combat support ships**, designed to provide rapid delivery of supplies to other Navy ships; and **submarines**. Aircraft carriers and submarines are often powered by nuclear reactors. For more information on military ships, see the articles SUBMARINES in Volume S and UNITED STATES, ARMED FORCES OF THE (The United States Navy) in Volume UV.

Merchant Ships

Merchant ships, also called **cargo ships**, **commercial ships**, or **freighters**, are specially designed to efficiently and safely transport a wide variety of goods, as well as perform a wide variety of services, across the world's waterways. They are typically powered by diesel engines, which are more fuel-efficient and less costly to install than steam turbine engines. Sails are rarely used on modern merchant ships.

Merchant ships are manned by civilians known as merchant mariners. In the United States, the Coast Guard oversees the certification of mariners for service on merchant vessels. Six state Merchant Marine academies and the U.S. Merchant Marine Academy, located at Kings Point, New York, train men and women to be licensed deck and engineering officers in the Merchant Marine. The International Maritime Organization, formed in 1948, establishes safety standards for international shipping.

Merchant ships are classified according to the kinds of goods they carry: dry or wet. Dry goods include minerals, grains and other foods, and numerous kinds of manufactured products. **Container ships** are one of the most widely used dry-cargo ships. Before container ships, most dry cargo was unpacked from trucks and loaded piece by piece into the vast holds of ships by dockworkers using forklifts, cranes, and other equipment. Once the ship reached its destination, the cargo was unloaded and repacked onto trucks in the same slow process. Container ships were developed in the 1950's to accommodate a different method of loading and carrying cargo: At their place of manufacture, many pieces of cargo are packed in a large metal container that is then carried to the dock on a flatbed truck. The entire container is then loaded onto the vessel and stacked in special holds. This method of shipping saves time and reduces transportation costs.

Another kind of dry-cargo ship is the **roll on-roll off**, or RO-RO. The cargo carried on a RO-RO ship is rolled aboard in wheeled containers instead of lifted by a crane. The **pure**

WONDER QUESTION

Why are the left and right sides of a ship called port and starboard?

Ancient ships had their rudders, or steering boards, on the right side of the stern of the ship. This gave rise to the Anglo-Saxon word *steorbord*, which means "steer side." When ships came into port to load and unload, they were tied up with their left sides closest to the dock to prevent damage to the rudder. Thus, the left side became known as the port side. Port used to be called larboard, from Middle English *ladeborde*, which referred to the loading side of a ship.

that they could sit on a floating piece of wood and paddle with their hands to move along. But such a craft could be easily tipped over and had little room to carry cargo. Eventually, people learned that a more useful boat could be made by tying several pieces of floating wood together.

The first primitive ships were rafts constructed of bundles of reeds tied together.

Above: A tugboat guides a large ferry into port. *Right:* Container ships are specially designed to carry cargo that has been packed into large metal containers before being loaded on board.

car truck carrier, or PCTC, is built specifically to carry cars and light trucks. **Dry bulk carriers**, or **bulkers**, carry dry, loose goods such as grain and coal.

Wet cargo consists primarily of crude oil and refined oil products. Small tankers called **product tankers** transport refined products such as gasoline, lubricating oil, and chemicals. Larger **tank vessels**, or **supertankers**, transport great quantities of crude oil across the oceans. The largest tanker ever built is the *Jahre Viking*, launched in 1975. It measures more than 1,500 feet (457 meters) long and can carry more than 4 million barrels of crude oil (one barrel equals 42 gallons, or 159 liters). Some tank vessels that operate in United States waters are built with double hulls—an outer hull and an inner hull—separated by an empty space. The theory behind this kind of construction is that if the ship runs aground, only the exterior hull will be ruptured, leaving the interior hull undamaged and preventing millions of gallons of oil from spilling into the sea.

Oil is also transported on **barges**, which have no engines or crew, towed by **tugboats**. Tugboats are also used in harbors to assist ships in docking and undocking.

▶ HISTORY OF SHIPS AND SHIPPING

The ancestor of the ship was probably a simple tree branch or log. People discovered

Drawings and models found in ancient Egyptian tombs show that reed ships were used on the Nile River several thousand years ago.

Animal skins were another material used by early shipbuilders. In Mesopotamia (an ancient region in the Middle East), floats made of animal skins were attached to wooden platforms. These rafts, called *keleks*, could be floated downstream with a load of goods and then dismantled. The skins could be carried back upstream on horseback to be used to make another raft.

Animal hides were also used to make skin boats. The hides were stretched over a circular wooden framework. These round boats were called *gufas* in Mesopotamia.

In countries with abundant forest, wood was the natural material for shipbuilding. Bark canoes and dugout canoes (hollowed-out logs) were the earliest types of wooden ships.

Mediterranean and European Ships

The people around the Mediterranean Sea were among the earliest to use ships in large numbers. The Egyptians, who did not venture far from the Nile River, built ships made of

Why are ships christened with champagne?

Ships are christened with champagne as a way of bestowing good luck. This ritual is very old. The Vikings christened their ships with blood, human sacrifices, and religious rituals. The Romans and Greeks used water as a sign of purification in blessing a new ship. During the Middle Ages, blood was replaced with red wine, which was drunk in a religious ceremony on board the ship as it was launched. At some point, champagne replaced red wine because it was more expensive and was thought more fitting to the occasion. At first the champagne was poured onto the ship's deck. Today a champagne bottle, which is enclosed in a metal mesh covering to protect against flying glass, is smashed on the bow.

wooden planks as early as 2500 B.C. Large trees were scarce in Egypt, so the Egyptians built their ships from short lengths of timber joined together and held in place with wooden pins. Some of these early ships were more than 100 feet (30 meters) long. They were powered by oars as well as a square sail supported by a single mast.

The Phoenicians (from present-day Lebanon) sailed all over the Mediterranean Sea, into the Atlantic Ocean and as far north as the Baltic Sea. For centuries the Phoenicians were the world's leading sea traders.

The ancient Greeks were also notable seafarers. The design of their warships, called **galleys**, is known from sculptures and from paintings on vases. Rows of oars were used to propel the ship, but it also had one or more square sails, each on its own mast. Steering was done with a **rudder**, which consisted of a very large oar on the side of the ship near the back, or **stern**. Often two oars were used, one on each side. On their fronts, or **bows**, the galleys had heavy rams that were used for smashing into enemy vessels. The ram was a sharp, strong beak of metal that stuck out from the ship's bow beneath the waterline. Galleys were swift, but they had little room for cargo, and they were not very seaworthy.

During the 100's B.C., the Romans replaced the Phoenicians as the dominant sea power in the Mediterranean. Roman shipbuilders copied their basic designs from Phoenician vessels but introduced some new features, such as decking to provide shelter for those on board. Roman warships were built as boarding vessels. The Romans would get alongside an enemy ship and extend a wooden platform from their deck to the enemy's deck. The soldiers then crossed the platform and captured the enemy ship.

The large population of Rome depended for much of its food on grain imported from Egypt and North Africa. The cargo ships that transported the grain were large, broad, solidly built vessels that were slow but seaworthy. A Roman cargo ship could carry 248 tons of grain at a time. The ship's high stern curved up into a carved swan's head. There was a large sail on the mast. A smaller sail was mounted on a long pole called a **spar** that extended forward from the bow. The addition of the smaller sail, a Roman invention, made the ships easier to maneuver in the wind than those of the Phoenicians and

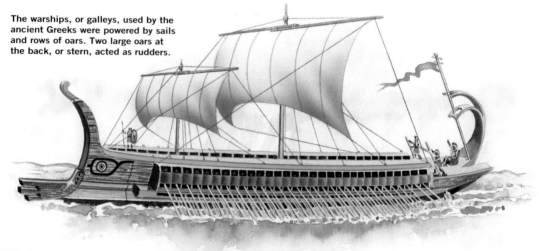

The warships, or galleys, used by the ancient Greeks were powered by sails and rows of oars. Two large oars at the back, or stern, acted as rudders.

Greeks. Cargo ships had no rowers, so they relied on sails.

In northern Europe the most skilled and daring sailors were the Vikings of Scandinavia (Denmark, Sweden, and Norway). Their ships were open (there were no decks), double-ended (the stern and bow had the same shape), and about 75 feet (23 meters) long. On the bow was a carving of a sea serpent's head. A large and often brightly colored sail was attached to the tall mast. There were 15 or 16 rowers on each side of the vessel. The Vikings raided the coasts of Europe and sailed to Iceland, Greenland, and North America from about A.D. 800 to about 1050.

Viking leaders were often buried in their ships together with their treasures. Earth was piled up over the ship to form a mound. The remains of Viking ships found in these mounds show that they were built differently from the ships that Mediterranean peoples built. The bodies, or **hulls**, of Mediterranean ships were **carvel-built**—made of planks joined edge to edge. Viking ships were **clinker-built**, with the planks overlapping one another like roof shingles. Eventually all deep-sea ships were carvel-built.

The Age of Sail

In the Middle Ages (A.D. 500–1450), sea trade and exploration increased. Larger ships were built to carry more cargo and to travel across the open sea. Sails replaced oars as the chief means of propelling ships. Instead of only one mast with one huge sail, two or three masts with several smaller sails on each were used. Dividing the sails in this way made them easier to handle, especially in rough weather. The largest mast (usually in the center) was called the **mainmast**, the one in front was the **foremast**, and the one in the rear was the **mizzenmast**. The **spritsail** was the small sail projecting from the bow on a spar (called a **bowsprit**). Open ships were mostly replaced by decked ships, and the steering rudder was moved from the side of the ship to directly behind the stern.

Until late in the 1500's, warships carried both sails and oars. The sails were rarely used

Beginning in the late 1500's, Spanish galleons and other warships abandoned oars and fought their battles entirely under the power of sail.

in battle, however, because it was easier to use oars to maneuver the ships at close range. Naval battles consisted mostly of trying to board and capture enemy ships. The battle of Lepanto in 1571, in which the Spanish and Italians defeated the Ottoman Turks, was the last naval battle fought in this way. In 1588 the first great naval battle fought entirely under sail took place between the Spanish Armada and the English fleet. The opponents kept at a distance from each other and blasted away with cannons, which were just coming into widespread use on ships.

Ships and Shipping in the New World. Settlers in North America, or the New World, needed ships to keep in touch with the homeland and to travel along the coasts of the continent. Since the interior of the land was still a trackless forest inhabited by often hostile Native Americans, most transportation had to be by ship.

The need for ships and the abundant supply of raw materials to build them helped shipbuilding grow rapidly in the American colonies. During the 1700's, the Americans developed the **schooner**, a ship with two or more masts and sails on each that stretched toward the bow and stern (a style called **fore-**

The last great ships of the age of sail were the Yankee clippers. These large streamlined ships were very fast and carried more sails than any ships before them.

and-aft rigging). These ships were used mostly for trading. By the time the American Revolution began in 1775, many British merchant ships were built in the colonies.

Whaling also helped the growth of the merchant fleet in the colonies. Whale oil for fuel was in great demand, and whales abounded in the waters off the Atlantic coast. By 1775 the American whaling fleet consisted of about 300 ships.

After gaining its independence in 1783, the young American nation had to compete for

WONDER QUESTION

What are flotsam, jetsam, and lagan?

Under maritime law, goods lost or deliberately thrown overboard from a ship at sea are distinguished by their condition when found. If an item is found floating on the surface, it is called **flotsam**. If an item is cast overboard to lighten a ship and sinks or is washed ashore, it is called **jetsam**. And if an item is found with a floating buoy attached to it indicating the owner, it is called **lagan**. If the owner of flotsam or jetsam does not make a proper claim to the item, it belongs to whoever recovered it. If found, lagan must be returned to its owner.

trade with the merchant fleets of England, Spain, the Netherlands, and France. The ships of these nations were well protected by their navies, but unprotected American merchant ships were the prey of pirates. In 1794 the United States Congress authorized the building of armed warships called **frigates** to protect American merchant ships. The frigate *United States*, launched on May 10, 1797, was the first ship of the United States Navy.

Transatlantic Ships and Shipping. Scheduled sailing-ship service across the Atlantic began in 1818 when the Black Ball Line began a regular New York to Liverpool run. The ships were called **packet ships** because they carried packets of mail as well as passengers and cargo. The packet ships were larger than regular merchant vessels. They took an average of 23 days to cross the Atlantic from west to east and 40 days the other way. (The difference in sailing time was due to winds and currents.)

Although steamships were being developed, the era of sailing ships was not quite over. During the 1840's, the greatest of all sailing ships—the **clippers**—took to the seas. These giant sailing craft, designed and built in American and Canadian shipyards, were often called **Yankee clippers**. Later, Britain began building clippers too.

Sturdily constructed of the finest wood, the clippers carried more sails than any sailing ships before them. The sails stretched from one side of the ship to the other in a style called **square-rigging**. Clippers were large, streamlined, beautiful, and incredibly fast for sailing ships. In 1852 the clipper *Challenge* sailed from near the coast of Japan to California in 18 days. The *Andrew Jackson*, another clipper, made the voyage from Liverpool to New York in 15 days in 1860. This was as fast as the best steamships of the time.

Steam Power and Metal Ships

The first steam-powered vessel crossed the Atlantic in 1819. This was the *Savannah*, an American sailing ship that had been fitted with a steam engine and had paddle wheels on each side. However, most of the voyage was made under sail; the engine, which frequently broke down, was used only when the wind subsided. It took the *Savannah* 29 days to cross the ocean—longer than the packet ships.

As steam engine design improved, steam power became more reliable than sail. If the wind dies down, a steamship goes ahead at full speed, while a sailing ship lies helpless. Winds blowing the wrong way can slow a steamboat but not stop it. But they can keep a sailing ship from reaching its destination.

Another important development was the metal hull. Metal hulls are more durable than wooden ones. They are not attacked by the shipworm—which eats away wooden hulls unless the wood is specially protected—and they do not rot. Metal hulls are also stronger than wooden ones of the same weight. And it is easier to build large hulls out of metal than out of wood.

Oceangoing British ships of iron were in service by the late 1830's and were making transatlantic voyages by the 1850's. The United States, which concentrated for a few years on clipper ships, lagged behind in the building of iron ships. Only after the Civil War ended in 1865 was iron used on a wide scale for shipbuilding in the United States. The first United States iron ships for transatlantic service were built in 1872–73.

In the 1870's, steel, which was lighter and stronger than plain iron, replaced iron for shipbuilding. During the next 30 years almost all European ships were built of steel.

The means of powering ships also improved during the late 1800's. Screw propellers replaced paddle wheels, and new high-speed turbines for ships were developed. The diesel engine began to be used in ships around the time of World War I (1914–18).

The use of steel and more powerful engines made it possible to build larger ships than ever before. Passenger liners became more luxurious, freight ships had huge capacities, and massive warships were built. New types of ships also appeared. The oil tanker, with special tanks built in for carrying oil, was designed in the 1870's. Before that time oil had to be transported in barrels placed aboard ship.

Beginning in the 1940's, passenger liners began losing customers to airplanes, which were a faster and less expensive way of traveling between the United States and Europe.

By the time jet planes began offering regular transatlantic service in 1958, passenger ships had ceased to be the primary method of carrying people between the continents.

The world's first nuclear-powered submarine, the *Nautilus*, was launched by the United States in 1954. The first merchant ship to use nuclear power, the *Savannah*, began service for the United States in 1962. But because some international ports were concerned about safety and refused to allow the nuclear-powered ship to dock, the *Savannah* was retired in 1971.

Before the mid-1900's, the primary means of crossing the oceans was on steel passenger liners with powerful engines and often luxurious accommodations.

Ships will continue to play an important role in the global economy. In 2001, about 80 percent of the United States' merchandise sent overseas was transported by ships. The number of U.S.-operated merchant ships has declined, but the average vessel size has increased. These larger ships, which can carry three times as much cargo as older vessels, are more economical to operate. At the same time, improvements in marine electronics, navigational systems, and engines have produced safer and more efficient ships of all kinds.

EDWIN M. HOOD
President, Shipbuilders Council of America
Reviewed by STEVEN P. ANDERSON
Director, Vessel Operations
E-Ships, Inc.

See also BOATS AND BOATING; HYDROFOIL BOATS; NAVIGATION; OCEAN LINERS; SUBMARINES; TRANSPORTATION; UNITED STATES, ARMED FORCES OF THE.

SHOES

Shoes protect our feet against cold and wet, dirt, and cuts and bruises. But the appearance of shoes seems to matter almost as much as the protection they offer. Shoe styles change from year to year and from season to season. There are shoes for everyday, shoes for special occasions, and shoes for sports. Shoes come in many colors and materials.

The first shoes were probably simple sandals woven out of vegetable fibers, such as papyrus, or pieces of animal hide that early people wrapped around their feet to protect them from the natural environment. As time went on, shoes of many kinds were made.

People began to wear certain types of footwear to show their occupation or their rank in society. Some shoe styles became so fanciful that the wearer had difficulty walking. During the Middle Ages, members of the European upper classes wore shoes with pointed toes that sometimes extended so far beyond the foot that the points had to be stuffed with moss or wool to retain their shape. Knights' metal shoes also had long pointed toes, which secured them in their horses' stirrups and showed their rank as warriors (longer toes meant a higher rank). By the 1500's, first platform shoes (chopines) and later high heels were invented—impractical forms of footwear that are still in style today. However, not all shoe styles were impractical. Wooden clogs served as a humble yet durable form of footwear worn by the working classes for hundreds of years.

Knight's shoe, 1400's

Early shoemakers, or **cordwainers**, used a crescent-shaped knife to cut out the leather parts of shoes. Holes were punched in the leather with a pointed instrument called an awl, and the pieces were stitched together to make the **upper**. The upper was then stretched over a wooden foot-shaped form called a **last**. Finally the sole was attached using wooden pegs and, later, nails. With the invention of the

Papyrus sandals, ancient Egypt

sewing machine, shoemaking began to be mechanized. But mass production of shoes did not begin until the 1850's, when a machine was designed that could stitch together the sole and the upper parts of a shoe.

Today shoes are made using computers and other high-tech equipment. Some designers and manufacturers use computer-aided design and computer-aided manufacturing (CAD/CAM) to create the look and the construction details of the shoe. After a design is accepted for mass production, devices called cutters—similar to cookie cutters—are made out of metal in the shape of a shoe pattern and are pressed into the material chosen for the shoes. After cutting, the pieces are stitched together by machine and stretched over a plastic last. The

Platform sandal, 1580's

shoes are completed with the addition of soles and heels glued in place using extremely strong adhesives.

Although shoes may be made out of many different types of materials, they have traditionally been made of leather (such as goatskin or calfskin) or fabric (such as silks and twills) in the western world. Innovative synthetic materials such as polyvinyl chloride (PVC), a durable plastic, and Lycra are increasingly used in contemporary footwear. Shoemakers are always trying out new materials to increase the performance, comfort, and durability of the shoes we wear.

Embroidered shoe, 1700's

Reviewed by ELIZABETH SEMMELHACK
Curator
The Bata Shoe Museum

SHORT STORIES

The term "short story" explains itself. It is fiction—that is, it is an imaginary story—and it is short. But because there are so many different kinds of short stories, the term is almost impossible to define.

For one thing, how short is "short"? Some stories are only 1,000 words long. Others are 20 times as long. Edgar Allan Poe said that a short story should be short enough to be read at a single sitting. Reading time will differ, of course, with different readers. In general, however, any story shorter than 20,000 words is called a short story. A longer story is called a novelette (up to 40,000 words) or a novel (over 40,000 words). Most short stories are from 3,000 to 6,000 words long (equal to about 3½ to 7 pages with no pictures in *The New Book of Knowledge*).

The short story differs in important ways from longer fiction. Many things happen in a novel. In most short stories only one thing happens. Most novels take place over a long period of time. The time span in the short story is usually short—often no longer than a day or even an hour. Novels change scenes frequently. Most short stories occur in only one place. Most novels have many characters. Short stories seldom have more than three or four. Most novels tell us a great deal about the people in them—what they look like, how they talk and act, what they think, and what they are like and why. In contrast, short stories have only enough space to tell us a few things about a character and to develop a single character trait, such as selfishness or kindness. Devices that help make stories seem real, such as description, are more fully developed in the novel than in the short story. In fact, short-story writers try to make their stories come alive by suggestion or implication. They try to make one detail suggest many others, the way a dusty blackboard can suggest an entire schoolroom. So the "short" of "short story" involves much more than just the number of words.

Early History

The short story as we know it today is not yet 200 years old. It first appeared in the 19th century, when the magazine had just been invented and magazine editors wanted short fiction and articles. But the origins of the short story are much older. Probably the first people told stories almost as soon as they learned to talk—stories about brave deeds in battle or exciting hunts. Eventually some of these were written down and collected. Some of the earliest known tales come from ancient Egypt. The stories now called *The Arabian Nights* were first told in India and the Middle East hundreds of years ago. Except for the fact that they use rhyme, rhythm, and a regular stanzaic form, folk ballads are very much like short stories. Parts of the Old Testament, such as the story of Ruth, are really short stories.

About 1350 the Italian writer Giovanni Boccaccio published a collection of prose tales called *The Decameron*. Some 40 years later Geoffrey Chaucer, an English poet, wrote a book of 24 stories called *The Canterbury Tales*. Both these works are forerunners of the modern short story.

But, generally, before 1700, writers who had stories to tell preferred to use other literary forms, such as drama and poetry. During the 18th century the novel, or long prose story, became popular. In the early 19th century, short stories began to appear at the same time in four countries: Germany, the United States, France, and Russia.

The 19th Century

Short stories appeared first in Germany. In 1812, Jacob and Wilhelm Grimm published their first collection of fairy tales. Seven years later E. T. A. Hoffmann's first tales appeared. Hoffmann's tales are called gothic. This means that they deal with the supernatural and are intended to frighten a reader. Hoffmann could be called the father of the ghost story. Hoffmann and the brothers Grimm greatly influenced two early American short-story writers, Washington Irving and Edgar Allan Poe.

During the 19th century the short story became very popular in the United States. In 1819, Washington Irving published his *Sketch Book*. One story in it, "Rip Van Winkle," is usually considered to be the first American short story. Within 15 years Poe's stories were appearing. And in 1842, Poe wrote a review of Nathaniel Hawthorne's *Twice Told Tales* in which he tried to define a short story and list the rules a writer should follow in writing one. It was the first time a writer had done this. Poe said that a short story should be short enough to be read at a single sitting; should create in the reader a single emotional effect (terror, for example, or sadness); and should be so economical that every word in it would be absolutely necessary. Modern short-story writers think that stories can have other purposes than just to make a reader feel something. But Poe's principles of unity and economy (a story should stick to one purpose and not waste words) are still basic principles of storywriting.

While Poe was writing Gothic horror stories (such as ''The Pit and the Pendulum''), detective stories (such as ''The Purloined Letter''), and psychological studies of insane people (such as ''The Fall of the House of Usher''), another American writer, Nathaniel Hawthorne, was writing a different kind of story. Hawthorne was interested in theme—in what a story meant. He liked to use symbols—concrete objects that stand for abstract ideas (the way a cross is the symbol for Christianity). Thus, in ''The Birthmark'' the birthmark on the wife's otherwise beautiful face stands for human imperfection (moral as well as physical). The young doctor's desire to remove the birthmark stands for humans' constant attempts to be perfect. The wife's death, when the birthmark is removed, means that human beings can never be perfect and live.

Bret Harte was the first American to write local-color stories. The United States was a country of many sections. In each section people talked differently, dressed differently, and followed different customs. The local-color story shows these differences. Harte is the inventor of the Western.

Meanwhile, in France, the short story was taking a different direction with the work of Guy de Maupassant. Maupassant's teacher was the novelist Gustave Flaubert, whose main characteristics were objectivity and realism. Maupassant was one of the two most influential writers in the history of the short story.

The other was Anton Chekhov, a Russian. In Russia the short story was taking still another form. Character was, of course, important in French stories. But what happened was as important as the person to whom it happened. Russian writers, however, were telling stories in which there was little or no plot but much characterization. Probably the first story of this type was Nikolai Gogol's ''The Overcoat''—a story so important that another Rus-

sian writer, Fëdor Dostoevski, said later, ''We all spring from Gogol's 'Overcoat.' '' Ten years later, in 1852, Ivan Turgenev published his *Sportsman's Sketches*. Late in the 19th century Chekhov learned from these two writers to write stories in which nothing ever seems to happen. In them ordinary people (shoemakers, cabdrivers, peasants, teachers) are put in commonplace, undramatic, real-life situations. The stories are not exciting or dramatic. In fact, there often seems to be no story at all. Yet, if we read them carefully, we get to know the people in them—what they are like, how they feel—much more intimately than we ever get to know the people in more exciting stories or even in realistic stories like those of Maupassant.

The Modern Short Story

Since the end of the 19th century, the short story has flourished in most countries of the Western Hemisphere. It has been most popular in the United States and England. In these countries the rise of popular magazines read by millions of people created a demand for short stories. The readers of these magazines wanted entertaining stories that were exciting or humorous. They liked sentimental themes and happy endings, and they liked stories that could be read quickly and easily. Beginning in the late 1800's, many writers produced these popular short stories.

From the stories of Guy de Maupassant, popular-story writers learned the art of plotting. After Maupassant many writers relied on well-constructed plots to organize their stories. O. Henry (William Sydney Porter) was a popular-story writer who often used the surprise ending as a plot technique. His type of story is still imitated today. Other skilled and successful writers of popular short stories were Rudyard Kipling, Richard Harding Davis, Robert Louis Stevenson, W. Somerset Maugham, and F. Scott Fitzgerald.

Another group of writers did not want to build their stories around plot. Some of these writers, such as Katherine Mansfield and Eudora Welty, followed the example of Anton Chekhov and wrote plotless stories. Others, such as Henry James, James Joyce, John Dos Passos, Virginia Woolf, Ernest Hemingway, Katherine Anne Porter, and D. H. Lawrence, experimented with new methods of telling a story.

Some writers felt that what happened in a story was not nearly so important as the people to whom it happened. One writer whose stories are written to explain people to us is Sherwood Anderson.

Other writers felt that the life shown in some popular stories was false. They wanted their stories to tell the truth about life. Ernest Hemingway said that he spent ten years trying to learn how to put down not "what you were supposed to feel, and had been taught to feel" but "what you really felt . . . what really happened."

Some writers felt that neither plot nor character in a story was as important as theme or meaning. Important writers of thematic short stories are Joseph Conrad, Stephen Crane, Ernest Hemingway, William Faulkner, and Thomas Mann.

Other writers wrote social-protest stories. Such writers as Theodore Dreiser, Ring Lardner, John Dos Passos, and John Steinbeck did not think life in the United States was perfect. Their stories criticize American society and the American way of life. Less direct criticism of society occurs in more recent stories by such writers as Irwin Shaw, J.D. Salinger, John Updike, and Bernard Malamud.

Another type of serious short story is the fantasy. Most stories show us a world that is very like the world we live in. The fantasy writer gives us a world totally unlike the world we know. The modern science-fiction story is usually a fantasy. Though most fantasies are written solely to entertain us, many tell a truth about life that the author could not tell if he wrote a realistic story. The stories of Franz Kafka, William Sansom, and Flannery O'Connor are often fantasy stories that are thematic and serious.

VIRGIL SCOTT
Michigan State University

Short stories can be written in many different styles, and they can be about almost any subject imaginable. The following excerpts, by three American masters of the short story, illustrate some of this variety.

A further sampling of short stories may be found by consulting the biographies of Arthur Conan Doyle, Nathaniel Hawthorne, and Washington Irving in *The New Book of Knowledge.* Excerpts from stories by these authors are included with their biographies.

▶**THE TELL-TALE HEART** by Edgar Allan Poe

True!—nervous—very, very dreadfully nervous I had been and am; but why *will* you say that I am mad? The disease had sharpened my senses —not destroyed—not dulled them. Above all was the sense of hearing acute. I heard all things in the heaven and in the earth. I heard many things in hell. How, then, am I mad? Harken! and observe how healthily—how calmly I can tell you the whole story.

It is impossible to say how first the idea entered my brain; but once conceived, it haunted me day and night. Object there was none. Passion there was none. I loved the old man. He had never wronged me. He had never given me insult. For his gold I had no desire. I think it was his eye! Yes, it was this! One of his eyes resembled that of a vulture—a pale blue eye, with a film over it. Whenever it fell upon me, my blood ran cold; and so by degrees—very gradually—I made up my mind to take the life of the old man, and thus rid myself of the eye forever.

Now this is the point. You fancy me mad. Madmen know nothing. But you should have seen *me.* You should have seen how wisely I proceeded—with what caution—with what foresight —with what dissimulation I went to work! I was never kinder to the old man than during the whole week before I killed him. And every night, about midnight, I turned the latch of his door and opened it—oh, so gently! And then, when I had made an opening sufficient for my head, I put in a dark lantern, all closed, closed, so that no light shone out, and then I thrust in my head. Oh, you would have laughed to see how cunningly I thrust it in! I moved it slowly—very, very slowly, so that I might not disturb the old man's sleep. It took me an hour to place my whole head within the opening so far that I could see him as he lay upon his bed. Ha!—would a madman have been so wise as this? And then, when my head was well within the room, I undid the lantern cautiously—oh, so cautiously—cautiously (for the hinges creaked)—I undid it just so much that a single thin ray fell upon the vulture eye. And this I did for seven long nights—every night just at midnight—but I found the eye always closed; and so it was impossible to do the work; for it was not the old man who vexed me, but his Evil Eye.

▶**THE GIFT OF THE MAGI** by O. Henry

[Della] stood by the window and looked out dully at a great cat walking a gray fence in a gray backyard. Tomorrow would be Christmas Day, and she had only $1.87 with which to buy Jim a present. She had been saving every penny she could for months with this result. Twenty dollars a week doesn't go far. Expenses had been greater than she had calculated. They always are. Only $1.87 to buy a present for Jim. Her Jim. Many a happy hour she had spent planning for something nice for him. Something fine and rare and sterling —something just a little bit near to being worthy of the honor of being owned by Jim.

There was a pier-glass between the windows of the room. Perhaps you have seen a pier-glass in an $8 flat. A very thin and very agile person may, by observing his reflection in a rapid sequence of longitudinal strips, obtain a fairly accurate conception of his looks. Della, being slender, had mastered the art. Suddenly she whirled from the window and stood before the glass. Her eyes were shining brilliantly, but her face had lost its color within twenty seconds. Rapidly she pulled down her hair and let it fall to its full length.

Now, there are two possessions of the James Dillingham Youngs in which they both took a mighty pride. One was Jim's gold watch that had been his father's and his grandfather's. The other was Della's hair. Had the Queen of Sheba lived in the flat across the airshaft, Della would have let her hair hang out the window some day to dry just to depreciate Her Majesty's jewels and gifts. Had King Solomon been the janitor, with all his treasures piled up in the basement, Jim would have pulled out his watch every time he passed, just to see him pluck at his beard from envy.

So now Della's beautiful hair fell about her rippling and shining like a cascade of brown water. It reached below her knee and made itself almost a garment for her. And then she did it up again nervously and quickly. Once she faltered for a minute and stood still while a tear or two splashed on the worn red carpet.

On went her old brown jacket; on went her old brown hat. With a whirl of skirts and with the brilliant sparkle still in her eyes, she fluttered out the door and down the stairs to the street. Where she stopped the sign read: "Mme. Sofronie. Hair Goods of All Kinds." One flight up Della ran, and collected herself, panting. Madame, large, too white, chilly, hardly looked the "Sofronie."

"Will you buy my hair?" asked Della.

"I buy hair," said Madame. "Take yer hat off and let's have a sight at the looks of it."

Down rippled the brown cascade. "Twenty dollars," said Madame, lifting the mass with a practised hand.

"Give it to me quick," said Della.

▶ **TWO SOLDIERS** by William Faulkner

Me and Pete would go down to Old Man Killegrew's and listen to his radio. We would wait
until after supper, after dark, and we would stand
outside Old Man Killegrew's parlor window, and
we could hear it because Old Man Killegrew's
wife was deaf, and so he run the radio as loud as
it would run, and so me an Pete could hear it plain
as Old Man Killegrew's wife could, I reckon,
even standing outside with the window closed.

And that night I said, "What? Japanese?
What's a pearl harbor?" and Pete said, "Hush."

And so we stood there, it was cold, listening to
the fellow in the radio talking, only I couldn't
make no heads nor tails neither out of it. Then the
fellow said that would be all for a while, and me
and Pete walked back up the road to home, and
Pete told me what it was. Because he was nigh
twenty and he had done finished the Consolidated
last June and he knowed a heap: about them Japanese dropping bombs on Pearl Harbor and that
Pearl Harbor was across the water.

"Across what water?" I said. "Across that
Government reservoy up at Oxford?"

"Naw," Pete said. "Across the big water. The
Pacific Ocean."

We went home. Maw and pap was already
asleep, and me and Pete laid in the bed, and I still
couldn't understand where it was, and Pete told
me again—the Pacific Ocean.

"What's the matter with you?" Pete said.
"You're going on nine years old. You been in
school now ever since September. Ain't you
learned nothing yet?"

"I reckon we ain't got as fer as the Pacific
Ocean yet," I said.

We was still sowing the vetch then that ought
to been all finished by the fifteenth of November,
because pap was still behind, just like he had
been ever since me and Pete had knowed him.
And we had firewood to git in, too, but every
night me and Pete would go down to Old Man
Killegrew's and stand outside his parlor window
in the cold and listen to his radio; then we would
come back home and lay in the bed and Pete
would tell me what it was. That is, he would tell
me for a while. Then he wouldn't tell me. It was
like he didn't want to talk about it no more. He
would tell me to shut up because he wanted to go
to sleep, but he never wanted to go to sleep.

He would lay there, a heap stiller than if he
was asleep, and it would be something, I could
feel it coming out of him, like he was mad at me
even, only I knowed he wasn't thinking about
me, or like he was worried about something, and
it wasn't that neither, because he never had nothing to worry about. He never got behind like pap,
let alone stayed behind. Pap gave him ten acres
when he graduated from the Consolidated and me
and Pete both reckoned pap was durn glad to get
shut of at least ten acres, less to have to worry
with himself; and Pete had them ten acres all
sowed to vetch and busted out and bedded for the
winter, and so it wasn't that. But it was something. And still we would go down to Old Man
Killegrew's every night and listen to his radio,
and they was at it in the Philippines now, but
General MacArthur was holding um. Then we
would come back home and lay in the bed, and
Pete wouldn't tell me nothing or talk at all. He
would just lay there still as a ambush and when I
would touch him, his side or his leg would feel
hard and still as iron, until after a while I would
go to sleep.

SHREVEPORT. See LOUISIANA (Cities).

SHREWS

It may not often be seen in meadows and fields, but hidden in the long grass or in burrows just under the surface of the ground lurks a ferocious creature. It feeds almost all the time, day and night, with only short rest periods between hunting trips. Each day it devours more than its own weight in food. This creature is the shrew —the smallest mammal on land!

All shrews are very small, usually about 5 inches (10 centimeters) long and about 1.2 ounces (34 grams) in weight. The smallest of all—Savi's pygmy shrew—is only 2.5 to 3 inches (6 to 8 centimeters) long, including its tail. It weighs less than a penny, only $\frac{1}{14}$ ounce (2 grams). Shrews are found throughout the world except the polar regions, Australia, New Zealand, and most of South America.

Shrews and Their Young. Most shrews in northern lands court and breed from spring to autumn. In warmer regions, shrews mate all year round. Sometimes males fight each other for mates. The winner courts the female, calling to her with low twittering sounds. A female shrew may have three or four litters of babies during just one mating season.

About three weeks after breeding, the female prepares a nest of grass or dry leaves under a log or in an abandoned burrow. Here she gives birth to a litter of four to seven babies. The babies are born blind and hairless. They weigh only $\frac{1}{28}$ ounce (1 gram) and are about the size of a jelly bean.

In a few days, hair begins to grow. Even before their eyes open, the babies begin to crawl out of the nest. The tiny shrews follow their mother in a train, each using its teeth to hold onto the tail of the one in front. By 2 weeks of age their eyes are open. They are fully grown by the time they are 5 or 6 weeks old. If the young shrews are not killed by other animals or by disease, they usually live for about a year.

The Life of a Shrew. The shrew is a nervous creature with a body that functions at an incredibly fast rate—its heart may beat 1,000 times a minute. Highly active, the shrew works continually to satisfy its enormous appetite. If left without food, a shrew would starve to death within hours.

Generally, shrews are found near streams or other moist places. Some, called water

The short-tailed shrew is just one of the more than 200 different kinds of shrews. Most shrews have dark fur, tiny eyes and ears, and long, pointed snouts.

shrews, spend much of their life in water. They build dens along the banks of ponds, lakes, and streams. Water shrews are excellent swimmers, and catch fish, insects, and frogs while swimming underwater.

Homes for land shrews may be under stones or bushes, in networks of tunnels it has dug, or even in vacant burrows made by mice or other animals. When winter comes, shrews may move into barns and other buildings. They use their long snouts and excellent sense of smell to hunt insects, spiders, and other invertebrates. Some shrews have a poisonous substance in their saliva that allows them to kill animals much larger than themselves.

The Shrew and Its Environment. Although two or more kinds of shrews may be found living in the same area, most shrews are solitary animals. They come together only during the breeding season. At other times, shrews are fierce fighters, quick to defend their territory against one another. They rise up on their back legs as they attack one another.

The most dangerous time of year for the shrew is the winter. Shrews do not hibernate, and their constant search for food often drives them into the open, where they are easy prey for birds such as owls and hawks. Weasels and other small meat-eating animals also attack shrews. However, the skin glands of the shrew produce a very strong, bad-tasting substance that stops most predators from eating the tiny creatures.

JENNY TESAR
Author, *Introduction to Animals*
Reviewed by DOUGLAS FALK
Assistant Curator
New York Zoological Society

SHRIMPS

Shrimps are sometimes called the insects of the sea. In fact, people who fish for shrimps often call them "bugs." As seafood they are called shellfish, but shrimps—along with their relatives the lobsters, crabs, and crayfishes—are properly called **crustaceans.** Crustaceans are aquatic (water) animals with a usually-stiff outer covering, called an **exoskeleton,** and many limbs (legs and feelers).

▶PHYSICAL DESCRIPTION

About 2,500 species, or kinds, of shrimps are known. Each species has special features that set it apart from other species, but the body plan of all shrimps is the same. A shrimp's body includes a head, thorax (trunk), and jointed abdomen (tail). The head and thorax are covered by a shieldlike part of the exoskeleton, called the **carapace.** On the head are feelers (antennules and antennae) and mouthparts.

The thorax bears five pairs of legs, gills with which the shrimp breathes, and includes various internal organs. The jointed abdomen is almost completely filled with muscles. It bears tiny flattened limbs, called **swimmerets,** and a finlike tail fan at the end. Within the abdomen is the threadlike intestine, sometimes incorrectly called the "vein" in seafood recipes.

Adult shrimps range in body length from less than ½ inch (1 centimeter) long to more than 8 inches (20 centimeters) long, not including the long, whiplike antennae. Females are usually larger than males. The tiniest shrimps weigh much less than an ounce, but the tails alone of food shrimps may weigh 1½ ounces (43 grams).

Shrimps are often colored to match the surroundings in which they live. They may be sand colored if they live on the sandy bottom of a pond, stream, or ocean, green or brown if they live among seaweeds, or even striped red or orange if they live near corals or sponges with such patterns. Some species are even able to change color to match different backgrounds.

In the deep sea, where sunlight cannot penetrate, shrimps are colored red, probably because red appears black in the dark. Some deep-sea shrimps (like many other deep-sea animals) have **photophores,** organs that pro-

Shrimps are found in all the world's oceans as well as in some freshwater lakes and streams. They serve as an important food source for a variety of aquatic animals.

duce light like that of fireflies. All of these colorations help to conceal the shrimps in their environment.

▶HABITAT

Shrimps live in almost all the world's aquatic environments. Most species live in the sea, from shallow coastal bays to great ocean depths. Freshwater shrimps live in ponds, lakes, and streams on all the continents except Antarctica.

Shrimps are most commonly found along ocean shorelines and on shallow offshore banks where food and safe shelter are plentiful. Shrimps may conceal themselves in plant growth, coral reefs, or in soft muddy or sandy bottoms. Some shrimps, such as the snapping shrimps, burrow into live sponges. Others burrow into solid coral.

Mud shrimps and ghost shrimps live in tubelike burrows 3 feet (1 meter) deep. Cleaner shrimps are visited at their homes in tropical reefs, called cleaning stations, by fishes that patiently allow the shrimps to crawl over their bodies picking off parasites, foreign matter, and dead skin.

Some shrimps that have somewhat permanent homes live in male-female pairs. Others swarm by the thousands in deep ocean waters. These mid-water species seldom come to rest on any solid surface. Their bodies contain oil that helps them float, so they waste little energy swimming.

▶ DIET AND LIFE CYCLE

Shrimps obtain food in a number of ways. They filter water through tiny hairs that catch food particles. They scrape surfaces with their mouthparts. Or they dig, cut, or grasp food with pincers. Depending on the species and the particular environment, shrimps eat tiny plants (such as algae), bacteria, decaying particles of larger plants or animals, or small animals (such as worms).

Shrimps produce many offspring—up to thousands at one time. Females of some species simply release their eggs into the water. Other females show some parental care by attaching the eggs to hairs on their swimmerets and then cleaning and fanning the eggs until they hatch.

Newly hatched shrimps may look much like the adults, but the young of most species are **larvae,** which are quite different in appearance. Like other crustaceans, shrimps grow by shedding their exoskeletons in a process called **molting.** (Exoskeletons cannot grow and expand like the skin on our bodies.) A new, larger exoskeleton hardens on the shrimp each time an old one has been shed.

Most shrimps live from a few months to about two years, if they are not first eaten by the many kinds of fish and sea mammals that consume them as food. In polar waters, where life processes of cold-blooded animals move slower than in warm tropical waters, shrimp may reach ages of up to 8 years.

▶ COMMERCIAL USES

Some of the largest and most valuable fisheries, or fishing areas, in the world are shrimp fisheries. Along with lobsters, shrimps earn more per pound for the fisher than almost any other seafood. In 1985 the commercial catch in the United States alone was more than 300,000,000 pounds (136,000,000 kilograms) of tails, worth almost $500,000,000. Fisheries in the Indian and Pacific oceans produce even more.

In the United States, Louisiana and Texas are the leading shrimp-producing states. In addition to the United States, Mexico and Ecuador are leading shrimp-producing nations.

Most shrimps are caught in funnel-shaped nets, called trawls, which are towed along the ocean bottom by boats known as shrimp trawlers. Catches are made in relatively shallow coastal waters—up to 150 feet (45 meters) deep—where vast swarms of shrimps live.

Shrimps are also cultured, or raised, by rearing the larvae to adult size in saltwater ponds. This "shrimp farming" is practiced mainly in Southeast Asia and South America.

AUSTIN B. WILLIAMS
National Marine Fisheries Service
Author, *Shrimps, Lobsters, and Crabs*
of the Atlantic Coast of the Eastern
United States, Maine to Florida

Shrimp fishing is an important industry in many parts of the world. Most shrimps, such as these off the coast of Maine, are caught in nets, but in some regions shrimps are raised in saltwater ponds.

SHUFFLEBOARD

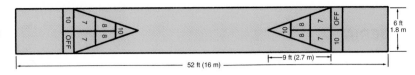

Shuffleboard is a popular game that may be played on any smooth, level surface, usually concrete or wood. It is played with disks and cues that have heads curved to fit the disks. The object is to push, or "shoot," the disks so that they land in scoring areas.

The scoring areas are in two triangles that point toward each other on the court. The area nearest the tip of the triangle is worth 10 points. The middle is worth 8, and the base is worth 7. Behind the base is an area marked "10 off."

Each player, or team of two players, has four disks, red or black. The players stand behind the "10 off" area. In singles, both begin at the same end of the court. They take turns in shooting their disks at the scoring areas at the opposite end. Besides trying to score with their own disks, they may try to knock the opponent's disks from a scoring area into the "10 off" area or out of bounds. When all disks have been played, the players go to the other end of the court.

In doubles, one member of each team plays at each end of the court. The players at one end shoot the disks; then the others play.

Points are counted after all eight disks have been played. To score, a disk must be completely within a scoring area. It may not be on a line. If a disk lands in the "10 off" space, 10 points are deducted from the player's score. The games may consist of 50, 75, or 100 points.

The regulation court is 52 feet (16 meters) long and 6 feet (1.8 meters) wide. A shuffleboard cue may not be more than 6 feet 3 inches (1.9 meters) long. A disk is 6 inches (15 centimeters) in diameter.

Reviewed by PARKE CUMMINGS
Author, *The Dictionary of Sports*

SIAM. See THAILAND.

SIBELIUS, JEAN (1865–1957)

Jean Sibelius, Finland's greatest composer, was born in Hämeenlinna on December 8, 1865. As a boy, he learned to play the piano and violin. When Sibelius was 20, he went to Helsinki to study law. But he soon quit the university to study music at the Helsinki Conservatory. There he wrote compositions for strings that were highly praised when first performed in 1889.

After further study in Berlin and Vienna, Sibelius returned to his native land. He studied the history and legends of Finland. Deeply patriotic, he expressed the love he felt for his country in his music. He composed the first of several works based on the *Kalevala*, the Finnish national epic, in 1892. In the same year he married Aino Järnefelt. They had six children.

In 1893, Sibelius became a professor at the conservatory. But four years later the Finnish Government began to give him money that allowed him to devote his time to composing.

Although Sibelius never used Finnish folk music in his orchestral works, he captured the spirit of such music perfectly. His symphonic poems (long compositions for symphony orchestra) *En Saga* (1892) and, above all, *Finlandia* are the most popular of Sibelius' works that express his patriotic feelings. *Finlandia*, which was first performed in 1900, became an anthem of freedom for the Finnish people in their struggle to win independence from Russia.

In 1904, Sibelius moved to a home near Helsinki, where he lived for the rest of his life. He completed the Violin Concerto in 1905. The Fourth Symphony appeared in 1911, the Fifth Symphony in 1915. In 1914 he went to the United States to conduct the first performance of his symphonic poem *The Oceanides*.

In 1924, Sibelius finished the last of his seven symphonies. Music to accompany performances of Shakespeare's *Tempest* (1925) and the symphonic poem *Tapiola* (1926) were his last important works. He died in Jarvenpaa on September 20, 1957, and was honored as a hero by the Finnish people.

Reviewed by SIXTEN EHRLING
The Juilliard School

SIBERIA

Siberia is a vast region of a vast country. It makes up the eastern and northern part of the Russian Federation (formerly the Russian republic of the Soviet Union) and extends from the Ural Mountains to the Pacific Ocean. Siberia has an area of about 5,000,000 square miles (12,950,000 square kilometers) and a population of some 40 million.

▶THE LAND

Siberia has three main regions.

West Siberia, the smallest and most populous region, lies between the Ural Mountains and the Yenisei River. Most of West Siberia is a flat, marshy plain. Agriculture and dairy farming are important in the south. The main cities of West Siberia are Novosibirsk, Omsk, Tomsk, Tyumen, and Barnaul. The Kuznetsk Basin is Russia's richest source of coal. It also has large deposits of oil.

East Siberia, which is largely mountainous, stretches from the Yenisei River to beyond the Lena River. East Siberia is one of the Russian Federation's leading sources of gold. Diamonds, mica, iron ore, coal, graphite, nonferrous metals, and waterpower resources (especially on the Angara River) are among the region's other assets. East Siberia's leading cities are Krasnoyarsk, Irkutsk, Chita, Ulan-Ude, Cheremkhovo, and Yakutsk. The climate can be extremely harsh in winter. Near the Arctic Circle, temperatures of $-90°F$ ($-68°C$) have been recorded, the lowest in the world outside of Antarctica.

The Far East extends along the entire Pacific coastline of the Russian Federation. It is mainly a mountainous region. But rich farms in the Amur and Ussuri river valleys produce wheat, oats, soybeans, and sugar beets. The region's industries include the manufacture of iron and steel, oil-refining, lumbering, and machine building. Coal is mined on Sakhalin island and in the Bureya River basin. Gold is mined in the great Kolyma Gold Fields. Iron ore, lignite, lead, zinc, and silver are also mined. There are rich oil fields in western Siberia. Fishing and lumbering are important in the south, and fur trapping and reindeer herding in the north. The region's best-known and most important city is Vladivostok. It is an important port, a naval base, and the terminus of the Trans-Siberian Railroad. The Baikal-Amur Mainline Railroad, completed in 1984, provides additional access to Siberia's wealth of natural resources.

▶HISTORY

The first Russian explorers penetrated Siberia in the 1200's to establish fur-trading posts. Russia's conquest of the region began in the 1500's. All of West Siberia belonged to Russia by the 1600's. The Amur and Ussuri basins did not become a part of Russia until 1860.

From the 1600's on, Siberia was a Russian penal colony. It was a dreaded place of exile for political prisoners and criminals. The region's vast size and its extremes of climate made settlement difficult. With the completion of the Trans-Siberian Railroad in 1905, Siberia became an important industrial and agricultural region. During World War II, Siberia provided much-needed iron and grain to the Soviet war effort.

Reviewed by ALOYS A. MICHEL
Dean of the Graduate School
University of Rhode Island

SICKLE-CELL ANEMIA. See DISEASES (Descriptions of Some Diseases).

SICKNESS. See DISEASES.

In some parts of Siberia, roads still are made of logs.

SIERRA LEONE

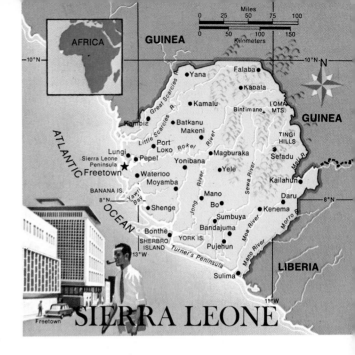

SIERRA LEONE

Sierra Leone is a small nation in West Africa. It is situated on the coast of the Atlantic Ocean on the western bulge of the continent. Sierra Leone means "lion mountains." The name originated with 15th-century Portuguese explorers, who thought the sound of thunder in the coastal mountains resembled a lion's roar. Formerly governed by Britain, Sierra Leone gained independence in 1961.

▶THE PEOPLE

Of Sierra Leone's many ethnic groups, the largest are the Mende and Temne, most of whom live in the interior. Freetown, the capital, largest city, and chief port, was founded in the 18th century as a home for freed slaves. Their descendants, known as Creoles, make up most of the population in and around Freetown today.

Language and Religion. English is the official language of the country. Mende is widely spoken by people in the south, and Temne is used in the north. Krio, derived from English with added words from African languages, serves as a form of communication among the different groups. About half the people practice traditional African religions. Some are Muslims and smaller numbers are Christians.

▶THE LAND

Sierra Leone is a land of great variety. The low, swampy coastline is broken by the mouths of rivers, such as the Scarcies in the north and the Sewa and Moa in the south. Near Freetown a marked change in the landscape occurs. There the mountains of the Sierra Leone Peninsula rise 2,000 to 3,000 feet (600 to 900 meters) in height. Their green, forested slopes frame the Freetown harbor on the Rokel River estuary.

Farther inland the land becomes a broad plateau. In the far eastern part of this region,

In the Sierra Leone Peninsula, the mountains rise abruptly from a flat coastal plain. They were first sighted by 15th-century Portuguese explorers who gave them their name, which means "lion mountains."

171

peaks in the Loma Mountains and the Tingi Hills rise to over 6,000 feet (1,800 meters).

Relatively few people live in the northern region, which has a long dry season that makes farming difficult. Cattle are raised on the plateau. Rainfall is heavier in the south.

▶ **THE ECONOMY**

Sierra Leone's economy is based mainly on agriculture and mining. Rice is the most important food crop. The chief commercial crops include coffee, cacao, and palm kernels. Diamonds are Sierra Leone's most valuable export.

▶ **HISTORY AND GOVERNMENT**

Early History. European contact with what is now Sierra Leone began with the explorations of the Portuguese Pedro da Cintra about 1460. The region became a source of slaves as early as the 1500's. In 1787 a leader in the British movement to abolish slavery, Granville Sharp, founded a colony of freed slaves at what is now Freetown. After Britain outlawed the slave trade in 1807, any slaves captured by the British were freed in the colony. In 1896, Britain established a protectorate over the interior of the region. Sierra Leone won increasing self-government, and in 1961 it gained complete independence.

Recent History. Between 1968 and 1985, Siaka Stevens was the nation's dominant political figure. He served first as prime minister

Freetown is the capital, largest city, and chief port of Sierra Leone. It was originally founded in the 1700's as a home for freed slaves.

and then as president. He was succeeded by General Joseph Saidu Momoh.

In 1992, Momoh was overthrown. The leaders of a second coup, in 1996, stepped down shortly after. A new elected civilian government signed a peace accord in November 1996 to end a civil war that had begun in 1991. But the fighting soon resumed.

In 1997, President Ahmad Tejan Kabbah was overthrown by Major Johnny Paul Koroma, who named himself head of the Armed Forces Revolutionary Council and joined forces with the rebels. In 1998 a West African peacekeeping force captured Freetown and ousted Koroma. Kabbah was reinstalled as president on March 10, 1998. But the fighting, which included widespread rebel atrocities against civilians, continued. The war was declared officially over in 2001, when United Nations peacekeeping forces were stationed throughout the country. Kabbah was reelected by a landslide in 2002.

H. R. JARRETT
University of Newcastle (Australia)

FACTS and figures

REPUBLIC OF SIERRA LEONE is the official name of the country.

LOCATION: West Africa.

AREA: 27,700 sq mi (71,740 km²).

POPULATION: 5,450,000 (estimate).

CAPITAL AND LARGEST CITY: Freetown.

MAJOR LANGUAGES: English (official), Mende, Temne, Krio.

MAJOR RELIGIOUS GROUPS: Muslim, traditional African, Christian.

GOVERNMENT: Constitutional democracy. **Head of state and government**—president. **Legislature**—House of Representatives.

CHIEF PRODUCTS: Agricultural—Rice, coffee, cacao, palm products. **Manufactured**—diamonds, bauxite, rutile, iron ore.

MONETARY UNIT: Leone (1 leone = 100 cents).

SILICONES

Silicones are chemical compounds that are used in the manufacture of paints, plastics, agricultural products, paper, and many other important substances. They are an unusual and useful group of compounds that contain the elements silicon, oxygen, and carbon.

In making silicones, the chemist uses coal or oil as the source of the organic (carbon-containing) part of the silicone. The inorganic part is obtained from sand, which is made up of silicon and oxygen. The atoms of carbon, silicon, and oxygen are made to combine to form the silicone polymers, which are long, chainlike molecules.

It is the special properties of the silicones that have made them different from other natural or synthetic polymers. These properties include stability at high temperatures, water repellency, formation of thin films with unusual surface properties, and inertness toward most other chemicals. (An inert substance is one that will not react very easily with any other substance.) Chemists have learned to make many kinds of silicones that take advantage of these special properties.

Because of these properties, silicones have hundreds of uses. Scientists have made various types of silicone rubber and coatings that do not lose their properties in extreme heat or cold. Heat-resistant silicone coatings are used to seal the heat-shield tiles on the U.S. space shuttle. Cold-resistant silicone rubber is made into gaskets (seals) for airplane doors. The rubber keeps its elasticity at altitudes where temperatures are far below freezing.

Some silicones are key ingredients in adhesives. Adhesives are materials that are used to bond two surfaces together. Other silicones are used as release agents. These silicones work just the opposite from adhesives. They prevent two surfaces from sticking together.

Silicone finishes on clothing and furniture fabrics provide properties that cannot be achieved with ordinary organic finishes. Silicones give the fabrics a soft feel and can make them repellent to water, wrinkles, and some stains. Polishes that contain silicone are easily rubbed on automobiles and wood furniture. They leave a shiny, water-resistant film on the surface.

Other silicones can be used safely in intimate contact with the human body. Because of this property, silicones have found increased and widespread use in cosmetics and medical applications. In medicine, silicones are used in the manufacture of drugs, contact lenses, and the fabrication of body implants, such as joint replacements.

Certain silicones are used to reduce or eliminate foaming in food processing. They are also added to antacid tablets or liquids. On the other hand, some silicones cause foaming. They are essential in the manufacture of foams used as insulation in houses and refrigerators or as cushions in furniture or automobile seats.

Ordinary oils and greases break down and lose their lubricating ability in machines or engines that must operate at very high or very low temperatures. But lubricants made with silicones withstand extreme temperatures without breaking down.

Scientists were studying the chemistry of the element silicon during the 1800's and early 1900's, but it was not until about 1930 that the usefulness of silicone polymers was discovered. The wide variety of properties that are available in silicones helped them become part of many manufacturing processes. Today the silicones are a group of more than than 5,000 different compounds and form the basis of a worldwide industry.

Reviewed by J. R. BARBER
Silicones and Urethane Intermediates Division
Union Carbide Corp.

Silicones are known for their many unusual properties and hundreds of uses. When added to car wax, they produce a water-resistant finish and a brilliant shine.

SILK

Silk is a natural fiber than can be woven or knitted into fabric for a variety of uses. Clothing, upholstery, draperies, lampshades, and strings for musical instruments are a few of the products in which silk may be used.

The delicate silk fiber is actually spun by the fat white larvae of a white moth. The larvae are called silkworms because they look like little worms. Silkworms feed on the leaves of the mulberry tree.

Silk has a fascinating history. It was discovered in China more than 4,000 years ago. Around 2640 B.C., it is said, the legendary emperor Huang-ti asked his bride, Hsi-Ling-Shih (Lei-Tus) to study the little worms that were destroying the mulberry trees in the imperial gardens. The young empress gathered some of the cocoons and took them into the palace to see what they were made of. She dropped a cocoon into a bowl of steaming water. To her amazement, a cobweblike tangle separated itself from the cocoon. She picked up the gauzy mass and found that one slender thread was unwinding itself almost without end from the cocoon. Hsi-Ling-Shih had discovered silk.

She was so pleased with the soft, fine thread that she wove a ceremonial robe for the emperor out of the cocoon threads. Soon robes of brightly dyed silk were worn by all the court for important ceremonies. But the common people of China were not permitted to use silk until about 1150 B.C.

To people living in other lands, silk was a rare curiosity. Occasionally, a piece of the gauzy material changed hands in the markets of the Western world, but no one could discover how it was made. A few curious traders ventured to China, but the Chinese jealously guarded the secret of their spinning silkworm. Many baffled traders thought that silk was a fleece that grew on trees. But to make sure their secret was truly safe, the Chinese searched all travelers leaving China. If any silkworms or mulberry cuttings were found, the carrier was instantly put to death. Still, knowledge of the silk moth eventually spread, and silkworms were raised in nearby countries.

Silk was still a mystery in the Western world, however. A king would pay a fortune for a scrap of the delicate material. Silk remained a rarity in the West until Alexander the Great conquered the Persian Empire in the 4th century B.C.

Alexander's conquest brought about an increase of goods exchanged between the East and the West. With the founding of the powerful Han dynasty about 200 B.C., the Chinese, too, became more eager to trade their precious silk. Caravans of silk-laden camels slowly plodded across China to Persian trading stations such as Samarkand. From Samarkand the Persians carried the silk to Damascus, the marketplace of the ancient world, where East and West met. At Damascus the Persians demanded high prices for their exotic cargo. Since all silk came to the Western world by this dangerous and difficult route, Greek or Roman nobles had to pay the price set by the Persians or do without their luxurious silk.

The 6th-century Byzantine emperor Justinian decided that control of such a prize as silk must be taken from the Chinese and the Persians. Justinian sent two monks to China. Risking their lives, they found the secret of the fabric of splendor. They brought back to Byzantium a supply of mulberry seeds and silkworm eggs. According to legend, they hid the seeds and the eggs in the hollow cores of their walking sticks. People at the court of Justinian watched the silkworms weaving their delicate threads, and the mystery of silk was solved.

▶SERICULTURE

Silk culture, or sericulture, is the care of the little insect that produces the silk thread. It is very delicate work that requires attention and patience throughout the entire cycle of the silk moth, from egg to cocoon.

The breeder moths for silkworms are selected very carefully. The eggs undergo many tests to make sure they are free of the least taint of disease, which might spoil the quality of the silk. The eggs are left to hibernate in the mountains and other cool areas during the winter. When the mulberry trees begin to show their leaves in the spring, the eggs are taken out of storage and incubated. In about a week they hatch into tiny silkworms. The silkworms are maintained under very clean conditions on trays, which must be constantly refilled with strips of mulberry leaves, the silkworm's food.

The baby silkworm is only a tiny creature, but it has a ravenous appetite. It eats voraciously for four to five weeks, and it outgrows its skin four times. The process of discarding a skin that has become too tight is known as **molting**. After the fourth molt, the silkworm grows to be about 3 to 4 inches (8 to 10 centimeters) long. During this period of its life, the appetite of the silkworm is extraordinary.

An idea of the amount of mulberry leaves that silkworms eat can be gained from the following facts: 2½ acres (1 hectare) of land planted with mulberry trees usually yields about 10 tons of leaves. On the average, this would feed 250,000 silkworms from egg to cocoon. Only 20 percent would be eaten before the fourth molt. Eighty percent would be eaten afterward. These silkworms would produce about 125 pounds (55 kilograms) of raw silk.

When the silkworm has completed the process of eating and growing, it begins to spin its cocoon. By moving its head in the pattern of a figure eight over and over again, it spins a continuous thread around its body. Soon it disappears from sight, but continues to make the cocoon snug and tight from the inside. The silkworm must be left undisturbed as it spins, or its artistry may be less than perfect. A disturbance might even cause the silkworm to die.

In about ten days the cocoon is heated to destroy the silkworm. If the worm were allowed to develop into a moth, the long silk thread would be broken as the moth burst from its cocoon.

The silk threads of the cocoon are covered with a natural gum that helps hold the cocoon together. The cocoons are put in basins of hot water to free the threads, just as in the days of the ancient Chinese. When the threads have begun to unwind from the cocoons, several of them are twisted together and guided onto reels. The threads from each cocoon may be as long as 1,300 yards (1,200 meters). About 2 pounds (1 kilogram) of raw silk gives about 3 million yards (2.8 million meters) of thread.

The silk from the reels can be treated in two different ways. Silk for many dress fabrics and for rough, nubbly materials such as shantung is woven with the natural gum still in it. Then the gum is usually boiled off. This is also the method used to make materials for transparent curtains. To make fine brocades and damasks, the silk is first boiled and then dyed. The dyed silk goes through a process known as **throwing**, or **twisting**. Several threads are twisted together to make a firm strand of raw silk.

China, India, Japan, Brazil, and South Korea are among the leading silk-producing countries in the world today.

Reviewed by Franco Scalamandre
Scalamandre Silks, Inc.

Silkworms, which spin the delicate silk fiber, are fed fresh mulberry leaves *(right)*. Raw silk is wound on giant reels *(below right)*. After the raw silk is dyed, weavers work at looms *(below)* to create beautiful designs.

Silk-screen printing was an ideal technique for the pop artists of the 1960's who playfully imitated the bold forms and bright colors of commercial art. (*Campbell's Soup Cans: 1965* by Andy Warhol)

SILK-SCREEN PRINTING

Silk-screening is a printing method used by artists and professional printers. The process is closely related to ordinary stenciling.

Artists' fine-art prints made by the silk-screen process are called **serigraphs.** Serigraphs are made by forcing ink through a tightly stretched silk screen. Parts of the screen—the areas that will not be printed—are coated with a sealer, such as shellac, to prevent ink from passing through. The screen therefore acts as a stencil. In making serigraphs of many colors, printers need a stencil for each color.

No one knows how old the stencil is. The idea is so simple that historians believe stencils may have been used thousands of years ago. The silk-screen stencil is believed to have been invented in Asia as long ago as A.D. 500. By the 1600's, silk-screen printing was a highly developed art in China and Japan. It spread gradually to Europe. Samuel Simon, of England, received the first patent for silk-screen stencil printing in 1907.

Preparation of the Silk Screen

To make a silk screen, the artist builds a wooden frame that is a little larger than the prints that will be made. A piece of fine silk is stretched tightly over the frame and nailed to the sides. For a long time silk was the only fabric with a weave small enough for the process. But today screens made of nylon, cotton, or steel wire are also used. The covered frame is hinged to a base or table, silk side down. The screen is then ready to be used over and over again.

There are several ways to make the silk screen into a stencil. In the simplest method, the artist makes a drawing on the screen. Then, using shellac or glue, the artist paints around the design. The area to be printed is left uncoated. Another way is to paint the design on the screen with lithographic tusche (a grease-based ink), then cover the entire screen with glue. After the glue coating dries, kerosene is wiped over the surface of the screen removing the tusche from the places where the artist has drawn. Many other techniques can be used. The only requirement is that the shapes to be printed must remain uncoated.

Printing the Serigraph

After the sealer dries, the silk screen is a stencil, ready to be used for printing. A piece of paper is placed under the screen. A creamy opaque or transparent ink is placed on the border along one side of the screen. With a **squeegee**—a square-edged strip of hard rubber attached to a handle—the ink is spread across the screen so that it penetrates the unsealed areas. This procedure may be repeated for as many prints as are needed. If prints of many colors are wanted, a different screen is usually prepared for each color.

The Uses of Silk-Screen Printing

Many artists make serigraphs, and the silk-screen process is as popular for making prints as are the more traditional techniques, such as woodblock printing, etching, and lithography. Silk-screen printing is a splendid technique for printing bold posters and signs. Commercial printers often use the technique for printing advertisements because silk-screening is much less expensive than most other printing methods.

In recent years, the silk screen has been used more and more by manufacturers, fashion designers, and commercial artists. Toys, bottles, glasses, and wallpaper can be decorated with serigraph designs. Silk-screened fabrics are a popular choice for draperies.

Reviewed by JOHN SPARKS
Maryland Institute, College of Art

SILVER

Silver is a precious metal with a wide variety of uses. It has been valuable for thousands of years not only for its decorative qualities but also as a metal for coins. In more recent times, people have found many more uses for this soft, white metal.

Silver has become important in making photographic film, welding alloys, and electrical contacts. It is used in purifiers that keep water safe to drink. It is part of a cream used to heal skin burns. It is used on huge curved mirrors that collect sunlight, which is then changed to electricity and heat energy. If a silver compound is added to the water in a vase of cut flowers, the growth of bacteria will be prevented, and the flowers will last longer.

The Metal and Its Properties

Silver conducts electricity and heat better than any other metal. Silver, the whitest of all metals, is the best backing material for mirrors because it reflects light better than other metals. Silver is also very easy to shape. Only gold can be worked with greater ease. The rarity of silver also adds to its value.

Pure silver is very soft. Therefore, to increase its usefulness, small amounts of other metals are added to it. Sterling silver is 92½ percent silver and 7½ percent copper. For 173 years, until 1965, United States coins contained 90 percent silver and 10 percent copper. In 1965 a law was passed that prohibited the future use of silver in making quarters and dimes. The law also reduced the amount of silver in half-dollars from 90 to 40 percent. Many countries produce special silver coins in honor of an important person or event. These coins are eagerly sought by collectors and investors.

How Silver Is Found in Nature

Silver is sometimes found in nature as native, or solid, metal. More often it is combined with other metals and nonmetals in mineral ores.

Most silver is found as traces in ores containing gold, copper, lead, or zinc. Many of the copper ores and gold ores from which silver is recovered contain only one part of silver to 30,000 parts of other materials. Since it

---

FACTS ABOUT SILVER

CHEMICAL SYMBOL: Ag (from Latin word *argentum*).

ATOMIC WEIGHT: 107.88

SPECIFIC GRAVITY: 10.49 (10½ times as heavy as water).

COLOR: White.

PROPERTIES: Soft and easily shaped; is the best conductor of electricity and heat, and has highest reflectivity, of any metal; forms compounds that are easily broken down; resists corrosion by the atmosphere.

OCCURRENCE: Sometimes found in nature as a metal; usually occurs in association with gold, copper, lead, or zinc in complex ores.

---

is necessary to separate several metals from the ore, the smelting and refining processes are quite complex.

Leading silver-producing nations include Canada, Mexico, Russia, Peru, the United States, and Australia.

The History of Silver

Gold and copper were probably the only metals that people used before silver. Some silver ornaments found in the Middle East date back to about 3500 B.C. The Book of Genesis in the Bible mentions silver as part of Abraham's wealth. In Europe, silver mining probably started no earlier than 500 or 600 B.C. Because ways to work silver were known in early times and because it was scarce, silver was used as money at an early date.

For many centuries India, China, and other countries of Asia used more silver than the rest of the world. In India, the women wore as many silver bracelets as they could afford. The working people hoarded silver coins. The wealthy people collected great quantities of silver in the form of large ornaments.

Despite the demand for silver, very little was produced during the Middle Ages because Europe's supplies of silver were limited and mining was not highly developed. Production increased greatly after silver mines were discovered in Mexico, Peru, and Bolivia in the 1500's. Much later, in the 1700's, silver mines were discovered in the United States and Canada.

Since 1492, two-thirds of the silver produced in the world has been mined in the Americas. Much of it has been exported to

Why is high-quality silver called "sterling"?

The word "sterling" possibly has been used for high-quality silver ever since the 1200's. At that time merchants in northern Germany were making coins containing a high percentage of silver. The coins made in England contained little silver. Since both types of coins were common in England, the English began to distinguish the better-quality German coins from their native coins by calling the German coins easterlings, because they came from the east. It is likely that common English speech gradually turned the word "easterling" to "sterling." The quality of silver known as sterling later became used for commercial silver, as well as for coins. The standard for English sterling was set in the 1500's and is now accepted worldwide.

Europe and Asia, and at times the supply of silver has been quite low in North America. During the United States Civil War, silver dollars and many other silver coins disappeared from circulation. This happened because the industrial demands for silver caused the metal itself to become more valuable than the silver coins. After the Civil War large silver-mine discoveries in the Rocky Mountains brought the price of silver down.

Again, in the early 1900's, the United States ran short of silver because so much was going to India to help avoid a collapse of its currency system. A silver-purchase act passed by the United States in 1934 directed the Treasury to purchase silver. The United States then began piling up large quantities. But with recent increases in the use of silver, the United States is again rapidly running out of its supply. This caused United States government officials to change the metallic content of dimes, quarters, and half-dollars in 1965.

Industrial Uses of Silver

Silver's ability to conduct electricity and its resistance to corrosion make it valuable in the electrical and electronic industries. Silver alloys are used for forming electrical contact points and to coat ceramic parts of electrical devices. A silver compound is used in corrosion-resistant batteries.

The silver-mercury alloys (called **amalgams**) used by dentists to fill cavities contain 33 percent silver, 52 percent mercury, 12 percent tin, and small amounts of copper and zinc. This mixture remains soft long enough for the dentist to fill a cavity and shape the filling before the metal hardens.

There are many other useful silver alloys. Bearings in aircraft engines use a silver alloy because it is moderately hard, conducts heat well, and does not combine readily with iron. Silver alloys also make good solders for fastening joints in such items as refrigerator tubing, where extra strength and corrosion resistance are needed.

Silver compounds in large quantities are used in photography. The silver compound used in photographic film is sensitive to light. Silver compounds are also used in medicines and in making some inks.

Decorative Silver

Sterling silver is used to make decorative pieces of considerable value. Silver makes beautiful and useful tableware, but it is so expensive that for years there were attempts to make cheaper substitutes for it.

The first substitute for solid sterling silver was silver-clad copper, known as **Sheffield plate** because it was made largely in Sheffield, England. Introduced in 1742, it is made by adding a thin sheet of silver to a sheet of copper and rolling them into one sheet. Sheffield plate was used for making coffeepots, candlesticks, and similar pieces.

Electroplated silver, which is produced by a process discovered in 1844, has replaced Sheffield plate. In electroplating, a bar of silver and an object made of cheaper metal are placed in a chemical solution. When an electric current is passed through the solution, silver gradually coats the metal object.

TAYLOR LYMAN
Formerly, American Society for Metals

See also JEWELRY; KNIVES, FORKS, AND SPOONS; MONEY.

SILVERSTEIN, SHEL. See CHILDREN'S LITERATURE (Profiles).

SIMENON, GEORGES. See MYSTERY AND DETECTIVE STORIES (Profiles).

SINATRA, FRANK. See NEW JERSEY (Famous People).

SINGAPORE

Singapore is a small island nation, about 3½ times the size of Washington, D.C., located off the southern tip of the Malay Peninsula in Southeast Asia. Its neighbors are Malaysia to the north and east and Indonesia to the south, west, and east. Although small in size, Singapore is a prosperous nation. The heart of the country is its capital city and port of Singapore. Located at a crossroads of international trade, Singapore's port is one of the busiest in the world.

Singapore came under British rule in the 1800's and was long a key outpost of the British Empire. It won full independence in 1963 as a member of the Federation of Malaysia. It left the federation in 1965, becoming the independent Republic of Singapore.

▸ **PEOPLE**

Singapore was only lightly populated at the time of its founding as a British trading settlement in the early 1800's. Today it is a multi-ethnic society—one composed of vari-

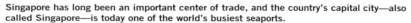

ous peoples—as well as one of the world's most densely populated countries. Much of Singapore's growth came from immigration. Slightly more than 75 percent of its people are Chinese. Malays, the original inhabitants of the region, are the second largest ethnic group, making up about 15 percent of the

Singapore has long been an important center of trade, and the country's capital city—also called Singapore—is today one of the world's busiest seaports.

SINGAPORE • 179

population. The other major ethnic groups are Indians and Pakistanis. A small number of Europeans, mainly of British background, also live on the island.

Each of Singapore's ethnic groups has maintained its traditional customs and pattern of living. At the same time, because of the diversity of the population, toleration for others has become a way of life (although the Malay minority has occasionally charged that it is discriminated against by the Chinese community). This toleration has been encouraged by the government, which seeks to create from its various peoples a distinct Singaporean national identity.

Language. Singapore has four official languages: Malay, Chinese (Mandarin dialect), English, and Tamil (a language of southern India). Malay is also the national language. English is widely used in government administration and commerce and is a principal language of instruction in schools.

Religion. The religions of the Singaporeans reflect their origins and include the world's major faiths. The Chinese are mostly Buddhists and Taoists. The Malays and Pakistanis are predominantly Muslims. Most Indians are Hindus. About 10 percent of the population is Christian. Freedom of worship is guaranteed under the constitution.

Education. Singaporeans have a high regard for education. The country's literacy rate (the percentage of its people able to read and write) is over 90 percent.

Primary schooling begins at age 6 and lasts for six years. It is followed by either four or five years of secondary education, depending on whether students choose short or extended study. Entrance to secondary school depends on the results of examinations taken after completion of the primary grades.

Students who do not continue in the secondary school academic system may attend vocational, craft, or technical schools. The National University of Singapore was formed in 1980 from the merger of the University of Singapore and Nanyang University.

▶ **LAND**

Singapore consists of a main island and a number of smaller islands and islets. A causeway across the narrow Johore Strait links Singapore island with the mainland of Malaysia. The causeway carries a road and a railway. South of Singapore's main island is the Singapore Strait, which separates Singapore from the islands of Indonesia. Its location between the South China Sea and the Indian Ocean has made Singapore an important transit point for Southeast Asian as well as worldwide shipping.

The island of Singapore has a generally flat terrain, broken only by a few rolling hills. In the center of the island is an area of rain forests. Mangrove swamps rim the coastal areas. The city and port of Singapore lies at the southern tip of the island.

Climate. Singapore has a tropical climate, marked by high temperatures and humidity and heavy rainfall. Maximum yearly temperatures average 88°F (31°C). Rainfall averages about 94 inches (2,400 millimeters) a year.

Food vendors and outdoor eating areas crowd a Singapore street. About 65 percent of the country's people live in the city and its surrounding areas.

ECONOMY

Singapore owes its prosperity to its strategic location for trade and its natural deepwater harbor. The constant flow of raw materials, industrial machinery, and manufactured products creates work for many thousands of people. While trade is the backbone of the economy, the government in recent years has been extremely successful in developing local manufacturing. At the Jurong Industrial Estate, for example, goods of a wide variety are manufactured in a complex of hundreds of factories. Although Singapore has no petroleum reserves, it is a center for the production of petroleum products.

Only a small part of the island of Singapore is farmed. The chief agricultural products are rubber, copra, fruits, vegetables, and poultry. Most of its food, however, must be imported. The country has no natural resources, but it has one of the world's largest oil-refining facilities. Electronics and ship repair are important industries. Singapore is also a center of international banking.

MAJOR CITIES

Singapore is also the name of Singapore's capital and largest city. About 65 percent of the country's people live in the city and its surrounding areas. It is the seat of government as well as the center of commerce and industry. Broad boulevards and towering skyscrapers contrast with narrow winding streets, along which are crowded rows of homes and shops. The city's heavy traffic is controlled by an advanced traffic management system, and the rapid transit system utilizes a network of underground tunnels.

HISTORY AND GOVERNMENT

In 1819, Sir Stamford Raffles, an agent for a British trading company, took the lead in establishing British rule over Singapore. Singapore became a colony in 1867, and the British developed it into a major commercial center and a strong naval base. During World War II (1939–45), Singapore was occupied by the Japanese.

Independence. Singapore was a British crown colony from 1946 until 1959, when it gained self-government. In 1963 it joined the newly formed Federation of Malaysia but withdrew in 1965 to become a nation in its own right.

FACTS and figures

REPUBLIC OF SINGAPORE is the official name of the country.

LOCATION: Southeast Asia.

AREA: 267$\frac{1}{2}$ sq mi (692.7 km^2).

POPULATION: 4,425,000 (estimate).

CAPITAL AND LARGEST CITY: Singapore.

MAJOR LANGUAGES: Chinese, Malay (national), Tamil, English (all official).

MAJOR RELIGIOUS GROUPS: Buddhist, Muslim, Christian, Hindu, Taoist.

GOVERNMENT: Republic. **Head of state**—president. **Head of government**—prime minister. **Legislature**—Parliament.

CHIEF PRODUCTS: Agricultural—rubber, copra, fruits, vegetables, poultry. **Manufactured**—electronics, oil drilling equipment, petroleum refining, rubber processing and rubber products, processed food and beverages.

MONETARY UNIT: Singapore dollar (1 S dollar = 100 cents).

Singapore's government is based on the British system. Members of Parliament, the legislative body, are elected by the people for a maximum of five years, although new elections may be called at any time within that period. The head of state is the president, elected to a 6-year term. The head of government is the prime minister, who is the leader of the majority party or a majority coalition in Parliament and is appointed by the president. The People's Action Party (PAP) has held a majority in Parliament since 1959.

Singapore's current president, Sellapan Rama Nathan, was elected in 1999 and re-elected in 2005. Lee Hsien Loong was named prime minister in 2004.

HYMAN KUBLIN
City University of New York, Brooklyn College
Author, *The Rim of Asia*
Reviewed by PATRICK M. MAYERCHAK
Department of International Studies
Virginia Military Institute

SINGING. See VOICE TRAINING AND SINGING.

SIOUX FALLS. See SOUTH DAKOTA (Cities).

SIOUX INDIANS. See INDIANS, AMERICAN (On the Prairies and Plains).

SISYPHUS. See GREEK MYTHOLOGY (Profiles).

SITTING BULL. See INDIANS, AMERICAN (Profiles: On the Prairies and Plains); SOUTH DAKOTA (Famous People).

SKATEBOARDING

Skateboarding began in the United States in the early 1960's, when California teenagers attached roller skates to wood boards so that they could practice "surfing" on the sidewalk. The ride was far from perfect. Bumpy roads and stones often stopped the small skate wheels and this sent the sidewalk surfers sprawling.

In the 1970's, manufacturers responded to this fad by using improved wheels and boards. Newer plastic wheels made out of polyurethane were larger and softer than skate wheels. These plastic wheels provided a smoother ride and excellent traction. The wheels were mounted on special shock absorbers called trucks that made boards easier to maneuver. Improved boards came in different models and were made of different woods as well as plastic, fiberglass, and aluminum. With the new equipment, the sport caught on quickly, and today more than 20 million people all over the world are skateboarding. Some of them even use custom-made skateboards.

▶COMPETITIVE SKATEBOARDING

While most people skateboard for fun, some do it competitively. Professional skateboarders can compete in a variety of events. In **downhill**, skateboarders race down a hill against each other or against the clock. In **sla**lom, they weave at breakneck speeds around plastic cones. Skateboarding teams compete in **cross-country**, with each member completing part of an obstacle course in the shortest possible time. In **bowl riding**, competitors perform tricks on the side walls of a circular cement bowl. In **freestyle**, competitors perform individual routines, which may include high jumps, handstands, and 360's (circles on one pair of wheels).

The popularity of both competitive and recreational skateboarding has led to the creation of special skateboard parks. These parks have concrete hills, bowls, flat areas, and sometimes cross-country courses where skateboarders can practice. Some of these parks have even been built indoors so that skateboarders can use them throughout the year.

▶SAFE SKATEBOARDING

Safety equipment is very important in skateboarding. Skateboarders out for fun or in competition should always wear it to help prevent serious injuries in case of falls. Skateboarders should also take care of their equipment and boards so that everything is in good working order.

MICHELE AND TOM GRIMM
Authors, *Hitchhiker's Handbook*
Reviewed by SALLY ANNE MILLER
International Skateboard Association

SKATING. See ICE-SKATING; ROLLER-SKATING.

SAFE SKATEBOARDING

Skateboarding requires balance and coordination. It can be dangerous. These rules can help you avoid injury:

- Always wear shoes when skateboarding. Athletic shoes are best because they give you a good grip on the board.
- Always wear a helmet, gloves, knee pads, and elbow pads. Wrist guards, hip pads, and padded pants give you further protection.
- Take good care of your equipment. Before you ride, check the board for cracks and splits. Be certain that nuts and bolts are tight, trucks are adjusted properly, and wheels can turn freely.
- Try to skate in areas reserved for skateboarding, such as skateboard parks.
- If you are allowed to skateboard on a sidewalk, watch out for pedestrians.
- If you must skateboard on a street, obey all traffic signs, signals, and regulations.
- Never skate on a busy street or on a street where it is hard for cars to see you.
- Never skateboard at night, when you cannot see potholes or obstacles in time to avoid them.
- Never allow a bicycle, car, or other vehicle to tow you on a skateboard.

SKELETAL SYSTEM

Just as a building has a sturdy inner framework to help support it and hold its shape, the human body also has an inner framework: the skeleton. The main function of the skeleton is to provide strength and support for other structures of the body. But that is not the only thing it does. Bones work together with muscles to allow body parts to move. Bones also help protect some of the soft and delicate organs of the body, such as the brain and spinal cord. The ribs help protect organs in the chest and also take part in the movements of breathing.

Although they seem hard and unchanging, bones are living tissues. Minerals such as calcium are constantly entering and leaving the bones. Hollow areas inside some bones are filled with bone marrow, in which billions of new blood cells are formed each day.

▶STRUCTURE

The skeleton of a human being is divided into two main parts. The bones of the skull and face, the vertebral column, the breastbone, and the ribs make up the **axial skeleton**. They form the long axis of the body, like a central supporting rod. The other bones make up the **appendicular skeleton**. The shoulder bones and arm and hand bones form the upper part, while the hip bones and leg and feet bones form the lower part.

Axial Skeleton

The eight bones of the skull are fitted tightly together to form the bowl-shaped **cranium** that covers and protects the brain. In a young baby, whose head is still growing, there are gaps between some of the cranial bones. As an individual develops, the bones grow together to form one solid structure.

If the spinal column were just as rigid as the skull, you would not be able to nod your head or bend over. The spine must be flexible yet must provide support and protection. Both of these needs are satisfied by a series of 26 separate bones, the **vertebrae**. Tough, cordlike **ligaments** tie the vertebrae firmly together.

The vertebrae get progressively larger from the top (joined to the skull) downward. The seven vertebrae in the neck region are called **cervical vertebrae**. Then come twelve **thoracic vertebrae** in the chest region, followed by five **lumbar vertebrae** in the lower body.

The Skull and Spinal Column

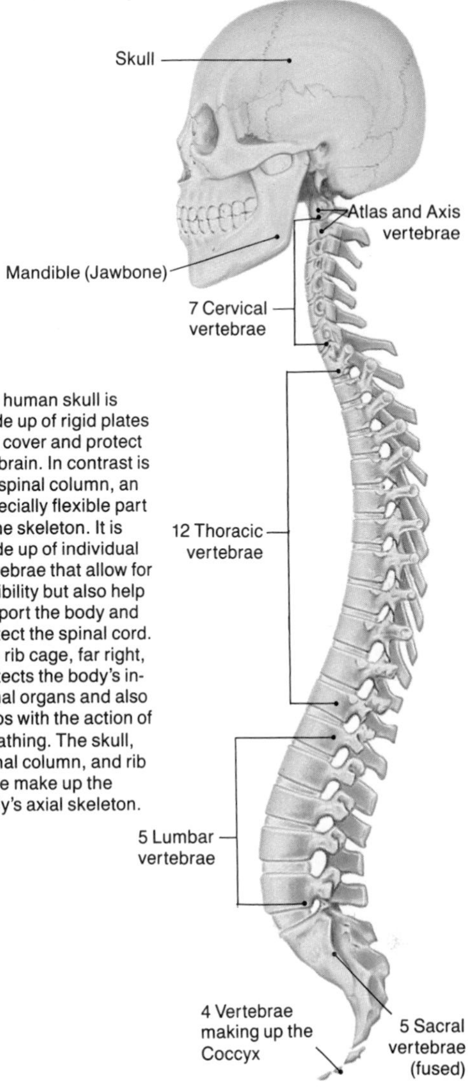

The human skull is made up of rigid plates that cover and protect the brain. In contrast is the spinal column, an especially flexible part of the skeleton. It is made up of individual vertebrae that allow for flexibility but also help support the body and protect the spinal cord. The rib cage, far right, protects the body's internal organs and also helps with the action of breathing. The skull, spinal column, and rib cage make up the body's axial skeleton.

Labels on figure:
- Skull
- Atlas and Axis vertebrae
- Mandible (Jawbone)
- 7 Cervical vertebrae
- 12 Thoracic vertebrae
- 5 Lumbar vertebrae
- 4 Vertebrae making up the Coccyx
- 5 Sacral vertebrae (fused)

The last bones in the spinal column, the **sacrum** and **coccyx**, are actually formed from separate vertebrae that have fused together.

Appendicular Skeleton

The appendicular skeleton is made up of a variety of bones. The shoulder girdle includes the **clavicles** (collar bones) and the **scapulae** (shoulder blades). Three long bones, the **humerus**, **radius**, and **ulna**, provide the framework for each arm. A group of pebblelike **carpals** (wrist bones) and a series of miniature long bones, the **metacarpals** and **phalanges**, form the wrist, hand, and fingers.

The hip girdle and legs follow a similar pattern, but the bones are larger and heavier. The **pelvis** (hipbone) is formed from three separate bones that have fused. The three long bones in the leg are the **femur**, **tibia**, and **fibula**. The **patella** (kneecap) protects the front of the knee joint. The bones of the ankle and foot are the **tarsals** (corresponding to the carpals in the wrist), the **metatarsals**, and the **phalanges**.

▶ BONES

Bones come in a variety of sizes and shapes, but they can all be grouped into four main types: long, short, flat, and irregular.

Long bones, found in the arms and legs, have a rodlike shaft and knoblike ends. The largest are the femurs, in the legs, but this group also includes some rather small bones, such as the phalanges in the toes. The shafts of the long bones are actually hollow cylinders, a design that is strong yet lightweight. The hollows are filled with bone marrow. The bone itself is composed of two layers. The outer part of a long bone is formed from a very hard and dense **compact bone**. The inner parts, especially in the knobby ends, look more like a lacy network or sponge. This kind of bone is called spongy or **cancellous bone**. Some bone marrow is also found here. The joint surfaces of the long bones are covered with

gristly **cartilage**, which cushions the contacts with other bones.

Short bones are cube-shaped and consist of cancellous bone inside a thin shell of compact bone. Examples are the carpals in the wrist and the tarsals in the ankle.

Flat bones are built like a sandwich, with flat plates of compact bone enclosing a layer of cancellous bone. The ribs, the shoulder blades, the breastbone, and most of the bones of the skull are flat bones.

Irregular bones are a catchall group that includes all the bones that do not fit into the other categories. The three tiny bones in the

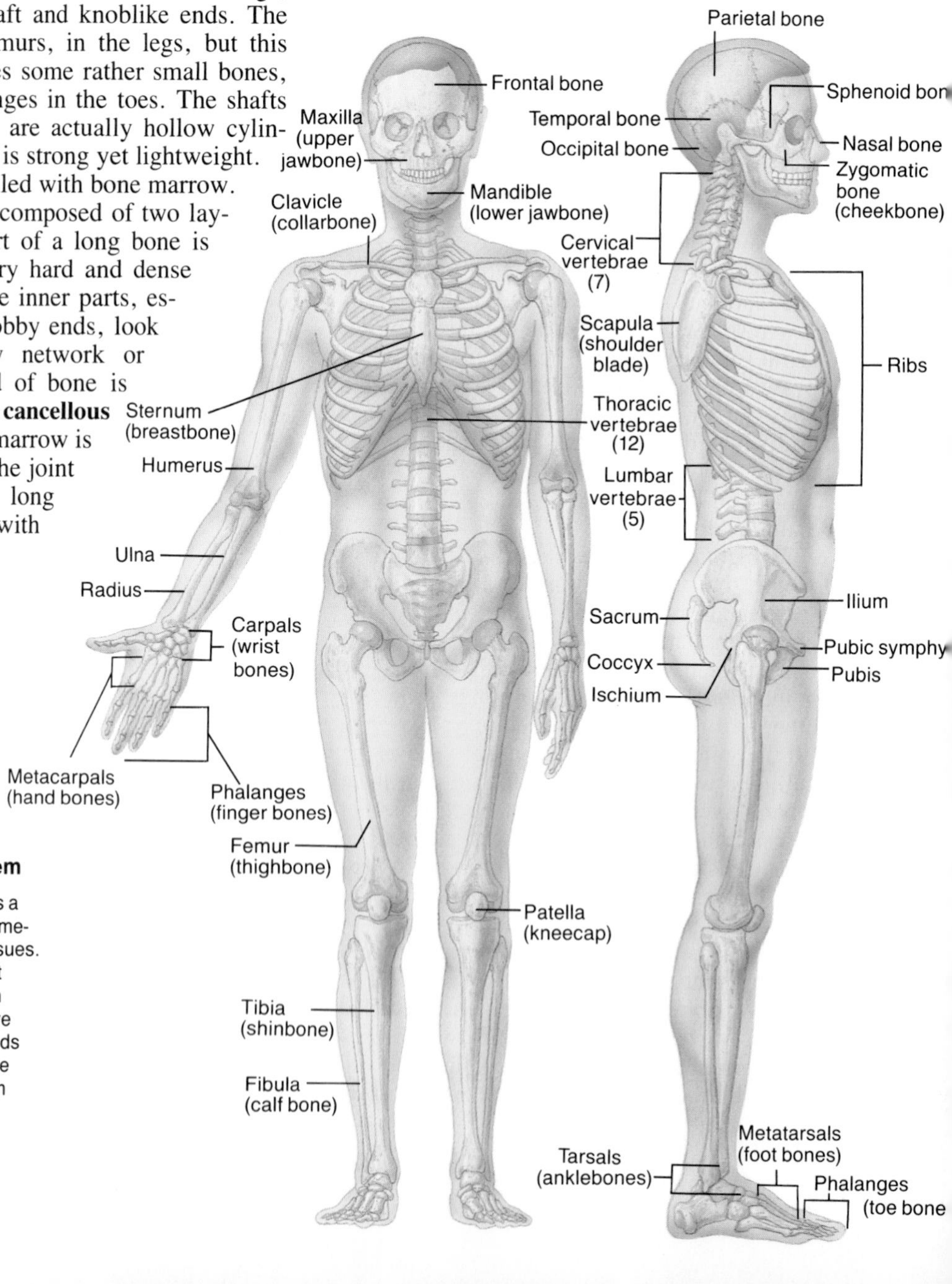

Parietal bone
Frontal bone
Maxilla (upper jawbone)
Temporal bone
Occipital bone
Sphenoid bone
Nasal bone
Zygomatic bone (cheekbone)
Mandible (lower jawbone)
Clavicle (collarbone)
Cervical vertebrae (7)
Scapula (shoulder blade)
Ribs
Thoracic vertebrae (12)
Sternum (breastbone)
Humerus
Lumbar vertebrae (5)
Ulna
Radius
Sacrum
Ilium
Carpals (wrist bones)
Coccyx
Ischium
Pubic symphysis
Pubis
Metacarpals (hand bones)
Phalanges (finger bones)
Femur (thighbone)
Patella (kneecap)
Tibia (shinbone)
Fibula (calf bone)
Metatarsals (foot bones)
Tarsals (anklebones)
Phalanges (toe bones)

The Skeletal System

The human skeleton is a hard, strong, living framework for the body's tissues. It provides the support needed so that we can stand upright and move about freely. It also holds internal organs in place and shelters them from injury.

ear are irregular bones; their shapes are described by their names: the hammer, anvil, and stirrup.

Bone Structure and Growth

You probably think of bone as something hard and dry, like a stone. Actually, bone is more like reinforced concrete. Mineral salts, chiefly calcium carbonate and calcium phosphate, provide hardness. They are deposited in a tough, rubbery network reinforced by fibers that give the bone strength. Your leg bones can stand up to a force of one ton without snapping or bending. Stainless steel cannot do as well!

The bony substance itself is arranged in long cylinders. The cylinders are nested one inside another. Living cells in small hollows between the bony cylinders build or reshape the bone when needed. Some of the bone cells, called **osteoblasts**, form new bone during periods of growth or when broken bones are healing.

In most people, growth of the bones is completed during the teen years. Boys typically grow for a few years longer than girls and usually grow larger. Even when bone growth is complete, however, the bones continue to change. Heavy exercise stimulates the bones to grow larger, heavier, and stronger. Inactivity may result in a loss of minerals from the bones, so that they become brittle and weak and may break easily. This condition, called osteoporosis, may develop gradually as a person ages.

Bone Marrow

The hollows inside bones are filled with spongy bone marrow. Some bone marrow is red, from the pigment hemoglobin that is pro-

duced there. Red blood cells are formed in the red bone marrow, going through a sequence of development that gradually transforms generalized **stem cells** into the hemoglobin-carrying mature red cells.

Some bone marrow stem cells develop into white blood cells, the body's roving disease fighters. However, not all of the body's white blood cells are produced in the red bone mar-

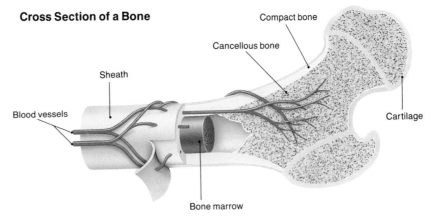

Bones are amazingly strong for their light weight. In this cutaway view of a femur you can see why. Beneath a sheath, or covering, and a layer of dense compact bone is a light, spongy mass called cancellous bone. Some bone marrow, which is where blood cells are produced, is found here as well as in the bone's hollow shaft. Blood vessels supply the bone with nourishment and oxygen. Cartilage at the end provides cushioning where the bone forms a joint.

Cross Section of a Bone

Compact bone

Cancellous bone

Sheath

Blood vessels

Cartilage

Bone marrow

Different Types of Joints

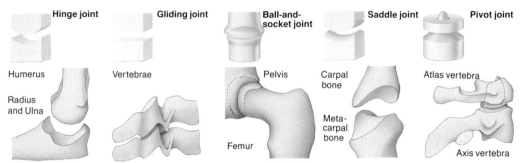

Hinge joint   Gliding joint   Ball-and-socket joint   Saddle joint   Pivot joint

Humerus

Radius and Ulna

Vertebrae

Pelvis

Femur

Carpal bone

Meta-carpal bone

Atlas vertebra

Axis vertebra

Joints permit movement between many of the bones in our skeleton. The shape of the bones in the joint (as well as the attached ligaments and muscles) determines what kind of movement takes place. For example, the hinge joint in the arm allows the arm to bend in only one direction. The pivot joint in the neck allows the head to move from side to side as well as up and down. Five of the body's joints are shown here.

row; some white cells are formed in the lymph nodes and spleen.

JOINTS

If the bones in our bodies were all joined rigidly together, we would be as immovable as statues. Instead, most of the bones are linked together in joints that permit a wide range of movement.

Some joints are actually **fixed** and rigid. The skull would not be a very effective protection for the delicate brain tissue inside if the bones that form it could flap up and down. Instead, the bones of the skull grow together at the edges to form a solid plate.

Most of the joints between bones permit movement of one kind or another. The movements at a joint are limited by the shape of the bones that are in contact with each other, the tightness of the ligaments holding them together, and the action of muscles.

In **gliding joints**, the bone surfaces slide over one another, permitting limited movement. Gliding joints are found between the vertebrae and in the carpals of the wrist and tarsals of the feet. **Hinge joints** work like the hinge on a door, permitting a back and forth movement. The knees and elbows have hinge joints; the knuckles of the fingers are also examples of this type.

Pivot joints are a special type of hinge joint, in which a ring rotates around a pivot. A pivot joint between the first two vertebrae permits you to turn your head, while a pivot joint between the two bones of the forearm (the radius and ulna) permits twisting motions such as

turning a doorknob. **Saddle joints**, named for their shape, permit more motion than hinge joints. The joint at the base of the thumb is a saddle joint. The freest movement, in almost any direction, is permitted by **ball-and-socket joints**. The shoulder and hip have ball-and-socket joints that permit the arms and legs to not only be raised and lowered, but also to be swung around in a circle.

When two surfaces move in contact with each other, friction can generate heat and wear them away. The bones in moving joints are protected from friction in several important ways. Their contact surfaces are coated with smooth, slippery cartilage. In addition, the joints are lubricated by the fluid called **synovial fluid**. Shock-absorbing cartilage **disks** or fluid sacs called **bursae** may also help to cut down the wear and tear on joints.

Aging can bring changes that stiffen the joints. Less synovial fluid is produced, cartilage is replaced by bone, and bony spurs may form. **Arthritis** is an inflammation of the joints that can deform them and limit movement. There are two main kinds: **Osteoarthritis** is an effect of aging, due to the damaging effects of friction on the joint cartilages; **rheumatoid arthritis** is a general inflammation of the synovial membranes, which thicken, damage the joint cartilage, and then are invaded by fibrous tissue that limits movement.

ALVIN SILVERSTEIN
College of Staten Island, CUNY
VIRGINIA SILVERSTEIN
Co-author, *The Skeletal System*

See also BODY, HUMAN; FEET AND HANDS.

SKIING

Skiing is one of the most popular winter sports in the world. The excitement of skiing down the slopes of a mountain or through a quiet, snow-filled forest attract millions of people to the sport.

▶TECHNIQUES AND EQUIPMENT

There are two types of skiing: mountain, or **Alpine**, skiing, and cross-country, or **Nordic**, skiing. Each type requires its own special equipment and special style of skiing.

Alpine

Alpine skiing includes pleasure skiing down mountain slopes as well as competitive events. Safety and control are very important. Alpine skiing is exhilarating and fun.

Ski techniques have changed through the years. For many years it was thought that perfect skiing form was vital to the skier's ability to get down the hill. In **parallel skiing**, skiers were required to keep their ankles together. Because of the emphasis on form, it took years to learn to ski properly. Skiers started by learning how to slide down the most gentle of slopes. They kept the front tips of their skis angled toward each other. This technique was called a **snowplow** but is now called a **wedge**. It allowed skiers to stay at slower speeds. Skiers would practice that technique until they were able to ski with their skis parallel.

During the late 1960's and early 1970's, this learning method changed. Skiers started learning on short skis. A method known as **GLM**, or graduated length method, became popular. Using shorter skis, beginners learn parallel skiing almost at once in addition to the wedge. As they progress they gradually use longer and longer skis.

This new teaching method allowed many people to enjoy the sport sooner, which was a major cause of the amazing growth of skiing during the 1970's.

Alpine ski equipment also changed as new materials were used for skis and boots. For many years, skis were made of wood and boots were made of leather. Then ski manufacturers began experimenting with plastics, metals, fiberglass, and other manufactured materials. Laced, leather boots gave way to boots with buckles, foam inner linings, and other materials that molded to the foot. The

Spraying snow in his wake, a young skier twists and turns over a slalom course. Whether competitive or recreational, skiing is an exciting winter sport.

newer boots give skiers more protection, extra strength in turning, and they are warmer.

Skis went through many different types of design. They became shorter, which made turning easier, and wider, which added stability. Injuries from falls were frequent. So **safety bindings** were developed that allow skiers to be released from their skis in falls but that keep the skis securely attached to their feet while they are skiing. A strap was attached to the binding and tied around the skier's legs. In this way, if a skier were to fall and the skis to be released, the straps would keep the skis from sliding off down the hill. A braking attachment was later developed to replace this strap method. It stops skis on the snow once they are released.

Before trying to ski, skiers should prepare their bodies with exercise. During the fall months, most skiers try to do conditioning exercises, especially those that stretch the muscles. Most ski coaches also recommend running or jogging.

Nordic

Nordic skiing includes ski jumping and cross-country skiing. Ski jumping is an event for highly trained competitors. It is not meant to be a leisure sport. Cross-country is meant for the casual skier as well as the competitive skier. It is skiing across country, uphill and down, over flatland, and often along forest trails. When not skiing downhill, the skier moves by striding and by thrusting the ski poles. Because of these activities, cross-country skiing is strenuous and good exercise.

In preparing for a season of cross-country, skiers must do exercises that strengthen their legs and their cardiovascular system (heart and blood vessels). It is important to stretch the leg muscles and to be able to cover distances

Cross-country skiing is an excellent form of exercise, and its popularity has greatly increased in the last several years.

over the snow without getting winded. Bicycle riding, jogging, and running are good ways for cross-country skiers to train for their sport.

Teaching techniques for cross-country skiing vary little from instructor to instructor. Skiers are taught how to glide over the snow, use their poles, make step turns, and brake on downhill runs.

The number of Nordic touring centers in North America grew in the 1970's. These centers offer rental equipment, waxing informa-tion, instruction, and touring trails. Many ski touring groups sponsor cross-country trips. There are prepared trails on national and state forestland.

It is much less expensive to purchase cross-country or Nordic ski equipment than Alpine gear. Skiers need cross-country or touring skis, a simple binding, cross-country shoes, poles, and a wax kit if waxless skis are not used.

Freestyle or Hot Dog Skiing

Freestyle skiing grew in popularity during the late 1960's and early 1970's. It began on the bumps, or moguls, of steep trails. These bumpy snow fields, called **mogul runs**, were created when snow was pushed up into small mounds by many skiers turning in the same place. It was found that by skiing off of these bumps instead of around them, a new sport, called **hot dog skiing**, could be practiced.

There had been a sport called **freestyle skiing** for many years, but this was not really "free" since skiers had to follow rules and ski required forms. Judges gave points on style, as do figure-skating judges.

As bump skiing grew in popularity, skiers looked to other, freer forms. **Aerials**, or aerial acrobatics, were developed as a part of free-style skiing.

Then a third form, called **ballet**, was devel-oped. It was done to music and was closer to what had started as freestyle. Skiers performed with music and they followed choreographed routines.

▶ COMPETITION

Ever since people started to ski, there have been contests to determine which skier could ski the fastest, jump the farthest, or run the fastest on skis.

Competition exists in all levels of skiing. Major competition is regulated by the Interna-tional Ski Federation (FIS, from its French name). The FIS holds World Ski Champion-ships every two years, and skiing events are an important part of the Winter Olympic Games that are held every four years.

While the World Ski Championships and the Olympics are the major events of skiing, Alpine skiing has a continuous competition known as the World Cup. It is a series of ski races held at sites throughout the Alpine world each season. Skiers gain points for finishes in

Alberto Tomba of Italy (*right*) and Marc Girardelli of Luxembourg (*below*) were among the top-rated men's Alpine skiers at the 1992 Winter Olympics in Albertville, France. Tomba took the gold medal in the Men's Giant Slalom and the silver medal in the Men's Slalom. Girardelli won the silver medal in both the Men's Super Giant Slalom and Men's Giant Slalom.

each race. A man and a woman are crowned World Cup champions each season. All forms of ski racing have shown increased popularity in the United States in recent years.

Alpine Events

There are four competitive events for Alpine skiers—slalom, giant slalom, downhill, and parallel.

Slalom. Slalom racing is done on an intermediate slope with courses of about 50 gates. A gate is an opening between two flags of the same color through which skiers must pass. If the racers miss a gate, they are disqualified unless they climb back and go through the missed gate. The skier must be able to turn well on this course, the shortest of the Alpine races. Racers make two runs down two courses. They either walk up along the side or ski down the outside of each course and memorize the gates so that when they race, they can anticipate each set of gates.

Giant Slalom. This race is also done through a series of gates. It is thought of as a dash, not a distance run. Skiers must attack the gates with smooth, well-carved turns, but not the fierceness of the slalom. Racers must have excellent acceleration. Each racer makes two runs down the course. The total time of both runs is combined to determine the final standings.

Downhill. This is the glamour event of Alpine racing. It is simply a race to determine which skier can get from the top of a mountain to the bottom fastest.

While downhill is always just one run, a downhill race actually takes three days. Skiers are required to put in at least one day of training on the downhill course. Then, on the day before the race, each skier must complete a nonstop training run just as if it were a race. On race day the skiers again start at the top and ski to the bottom. The best time wins. There are control gates on most downhill runs.

They are used to keep the skier from getting up to speeds that the skier cannot control. Downhill skiers often reach speeds of about 115 to 130 kilometers (70 to 80 miles) an hour.

Parallel. The fourth and newest form of Alpine racing is parallel racing. In this event two skiers begin at the top of two courses that have been made as similar as possible. They ski side by side. The first skier down breaks a timing beam. The second finisher stops the clock, and the interval between their finishes is computed. The skiers then switch courses and ski again. The time is again computed to determine the winner.

Nordic Events

There are two major forms of Nordic ski competition—cross-country skiing and ski jumping

Cross-Country. In international competition, such as the Olympics and the World Championships, there are races of 15, 30, and 50 kilometers (9.3, 18.6, and 31.1 miles) for men and 5, 10, and 20 kilometers (3.1, 6.2, and 12.4 miles) for women. The races pit each skier against every other skier. Places are awarded on the basis of the time taken to cover the distance. In addition there is a relay for men, in which each of four skiers from each national team skis 10 kilometers, and a women's relay, in which each woman skis 5 kilometers. The relays are scored on the combined time of the four members of each team.

Many other cross-country races are held, including marathons of up to 60 kilometers (37.3 miles).

Ski Jumping. While there are ski jumps of various sizes, the two sizes for international competition are 70 meters (230 feet) and 90 meters (295 feet). Ski jumpers slide down a snow-covered track, take off at the end, fly through the air, and land on a specially built landing hill far below. Winners are determined by a combination of the distance jumped and style points, which are awarded by the judges for how skiers looked in the air and how well they landed.

One form of Nordic competition brings together the talents of the ski jumper and the cross-country skier. In the **Nordic combined**, the athlete jumps off the 70-meter jump one day and then competes in a 15-kilometer race the next.

Another Nordic competition combines the skills of cross-country skiing and marksmanship. The **biathlon** is a carryover from the days of ski and shoot competition among soldiers, and it is still an Olympic and World Championship sport. The Olympic Games have three biathlon events—a 20-kilometer test, a 10-kilometer test, and a relay for four skiers, each of whom skis 7.5 kilometers (4.7 miles). While out on the course, the skier carries a rifle and shoots at specific targets. The score is a combination of the time on the course and the number of targets hit.

▶SAFETY

Whether a skier is a champion or just a beginner, safety is an important part of skiing. All beginning skiers, both Alpine and cross-country, should receive adequate instruction from a competent and qualified teacher. Proper physical conditioning is necessary for any sport and will certainly reduce the chance of injury. Skiers should do a few stretching exercises and spend some time in the cold before pushing off for a first run.

Before skiing, skiers should be aware of snow conditions—light, powdery snow, for example, requires different techniques from those used on hard, crusty snow.

Skiers should not ski alone, and they should stay on marked trails. Ski areas will have trails for skiers of different abilities, such as beginners, intermediates, and experts. Skiers should never attempt to ski on a trail that is too hard for them.

It is important to ski safely and courteously, watching out for other skiers. Never ski when you are overtired. If you are injured, stay where you are and wait for the Ski Patrol, highly trained rescue skiers who patrol the area for skiers in trouble. Ski clothing should be warm, lightweight, wind-resistant, and as moisture-proof as possible. Sunglasses and goggles will help prevent eyestrain and protect your eyes from the sun's ultraviolet rays.

▶SKI AREAS

There are thousands of ski areas located throughout the world. Snowmaking equipment allows ski areas to make snow by spraying water under pressure into the cold air. It is possible to rent skiing equipment at many ski areas. In addition, skiing lessons are usually available.

Students at a ski school learn to regulate their speed by keeping the front tips of their skis angled toward each other, a technique called a snowplow.

How do skiers get up the mountains and hills they wish to ski down? Various systems, called **ski lifts**, have been used to pull skiers up the slopes. In the **rope tow**, skiers hang on to a long rope that travels up the mountain over a system of pulleys. In **T-bar** and **J-bar** lifts, skiers lean against bars that are pulled uphill by a series of poles and a cable. In a **chair lift**, the skiers sit in a chairlike device that is attached to a cable running up the mountain.

▶ HISTORY

Skiing began as a means of transportation. Scenes of people wearing crude skis have been found scratched on the walls of ancient caves. In the United States, skiers delivered the mail in the snowy mountains of the West, and gold miners and ranchers used skis for transportation and sport. But early skis were long and cumbersome, and each skier had to carry a long pole to accomplish turns. In the late 1800's, an Austrian, Mathias Zdarsky, developed the idea of two poles for balance and shortened his skis. Zdarsky is known as the father of Alpine skiing.

The two forms of skiing, cross-country and Alpine, each developed independently. Cross-country skiing came first, but Alpine was the form of skiing that grew popular first. After World War I, enterprising business people de-veloped rope tows to pull skiers to the tops of hills. Later, wide development of the ski lift ushered in a boom for the sport of Alpine skiing.

Nordic skiing, including ski jumping as well as cross-country skiing, had been popular in the midwestern United States in the 1800's. The first skiing competitions were among the Nordic skiers. But the popularity of cross-country skiing did not keep pace with that of Alpine skiing. Cross-country was practiced by only a few who enjoyed hiking through the woods on skis. Then, in the 1970's, there was a rebirth of cross-country skiing. New skiing trails were cut everywhere, and Nordic equipment was improved.

Today skiing is popular in all its forms. It is an exciting and invigorating wintertime activity that people of all ages can enjoy.

DON A. METIVIER
Editor and Publisher, *Ski Racing* magazine

SKIN. See BODY, HUMAN.

Basic equipment for snorkeling includes a face mask, flippers, and a breathing tube called a snorkel.

SKIN DIVING

Skin diving gives the feeling of complete freedom in a world where you seem to have no weight. Underwater you have the sensation of flying. You glide by scenery as beautiful and spectacular as any on land. You can float over grassy plains and great sandy deserts. You can drift effortlessly over submerged mountains or cruise down the face of a sheer rock cliff. An underwater leap could take you all the way to the surface.

Little was known about skin diving before World War II, but during the war, lightweight equipment for swimming underwater was developed. Swimming with this equipment soon became a popular sport, and today there are millions of skin-diving enthusiasts.

The term "skin diving" was originally used to differentiate between the sport of diving and the work of deep-sea divers, who wore cum-

bersome diving suits and helmets and used air lines connected to the surface. A sport diver often wore only a bathing suit, with bare skin exposed to the water. As sport diving became popular and new equipment such as the wet suit was introduced, the original reference to diving in bare skin lost its meaning. Today, skin diving refers to any underwater diving in which there are no lines connecting a diver to the surface. Divers who use *s*elf-*c*ontained *u*nderwater *b*reathing *a*pparatus (scuba) are known as scuba divers. Divers who limit their activities to the length of time they can hold their breath are called snorkel divers.

▶SKIN-DIVING BASICS

While skin diving can be as safe as any other sport, it is foolish to try to dive without first learning something about the equipment and how to use it. An average swimmer in good health can easily learn to use the basic equipment of snorkel diving. Before trying to use scuba, however, a person should take a complete course in diving from a trained instructor.

Basic Equipment

The most basic piece of equipment in snorkeling and scuba diving is a face mask. It is the window through which a diver can see clearly the secrets of the underwater world. The face mask forms an airtight seal around the diver's eyes and nose and places an air space between the eyes and the water that eliminates blurred vision.

Having the nose inside the face mask is important because it lets the diver equalize pressure during dives and prevents a face squeeze. A face squeeze occurs when water pressure pushes the diver's face into the mask and makes it feel as if suction were pulling the mask tight. If a diver does not do something about this, it can cause black eyes. The solution is to blow a little air from the nose into the mask while descending. This will also help prevent ear pain caused by increased pressure.

Another important piece of diving equipment for both snorkeling and scuba diving is a pair of swim fins, or flippers. Without these, skin diving would be almost impossible. Flippers give divers great speed and power and the ability to move about without using their hands. Flippers take much of the work out of diving. They should fit snugly but not be too tight or too loose. If they are too tight, they cause cramps. If they are too loose, they chafe and create sores on the feet. Divers can choose either flexible flippers or rigid ones. Flexible flippers can be kicked at a fast rate without tiring the leg muscles. Rigid flippers require a slower kick but give more power when the speed of the kick is increased.

A basic piece of equipment for snorkeling is the snorkel, a breathing tube with a mouthpiece. The snorkel eliminates the need to raise the head above water to take a breath. Using a snorkel, a swimmer can float face down on the surface of the water and still breathe. A person can also dive beneath the surface, and air pressure from holding the breath keeps water out of the lungs. Back on the surface, the diver blows the water out of the tube and starts breathing again. Some snorkels have a J-shaped top with an enclosed float at the end. When diving below the surface, the float rises and prevents water from entering the tube.

Two other necessities for safe skin diving are a float and a friend. Never dive alone, and always take a float to use as a life raft in case of an emergency or just to rest.

Self-Contained Underwater Breathing Apparatus (Scuba)

Until fairly recently, it was extremely complicated to take an air supply underwater. Divers faced problems of changing pressures and moving about freely. Diving with an air supply was restricted to highly trained individuals using complicated, cumbersome deep-sea suits and helmets with high-pressure air lines that reached to the surface.

In 1943, Captain Jacques-Yves Cousteau and Emile Gagnan invented the Aqua-lung. (You can see a picture of Jacques-Yves Cousteau and the Aqua-lung in the article INVENTIONS in Volume I.) With this new piece of equipment, divers were no longer connected by an air line to the surface or weighted down with heavy equipment. Instead, they were able to carry their air supply with them in high-pressure cylinders strapped to their backs.

Breathing with a modern aqualung is as automatic and natural as breathing without one. A special in-mouth air regulator attached to a compressed air tank automatically adjusts the breathing air to exactly the same pressure as that of the surrounding water. There are no valves to adjust, and all the diver needs to do is breathe. The tank and regulator provide air at exactly the right pressure, no matter what the depth.

With the introduction of the aqualung, the popularity of skin diving increased dramatically. Along with it came various kinds of new equipment as well. Cold-water suits, or wet suits, were developed to keep divers warm in icy water. Powerful spear guns were designed that enabled skin divers to hunt sharks, barracuda, and other fish. Pressure-proof watches, depth gauges, and compasses were developed to help divers keep track of their time, depth, and direction, and special cameras were designed, which opened the new field of underwater photography.

Uses of Scuba Diving. Today, scuba diving is used for more than just recreational purposes. Police departments train squads in scuba diving in order to search underwater for weapons or other evidence. Fire departments train skin-diving rescue crews to recover accident victims from the water and firefighting squads to fight waterfront fires burning beneath piers, docks, and wharves.

Scuba diving is also used in such fields as underwater salvage, mining, construction, and archaeology. Scuba divers have recovered sunken logs in lakes and mined gold from the bottoms of streams and rivers. They have also laid pipelines over coral reefs, recovered cargo from sunken ships, and found ancient artifacts at the bottom of oceans and seas.

New uses for scuba diving are still being developed. Our knowledge of the seas is still in its infancy, and the possibilities for the future seem

At one time, an expert deep-sea diver needed to use a heavy diving suit and a helmet connected to an air supply on board a ship. This limited the diver's ability to move about freely and work underwater.

almost unlimited. Among these are the construction of underwater research facilities, farming on the ocean bottom along the continental shelves, and extracting minerals from the seafloor or from seawater itself.

▶TECHNIQUES AND SAFETY RULES

Despite the relative safety of skin diving, there are some risks as in any sport. However, divers who know the limitations of diving and follow safety rules are usually in little danger.

Among the most important things a skin diver must learn are the effects of air and water pressure and how to deal with pressure changes. While diving, it is very important that all air spaces inside the diver's body be maintained at exactly the same pressure as that of the surrounding water. The slightest differ-

This scuba diver uses a compressed air tank to breathe underwater. A face mask, wet suit, flippers, and a vest filled with air that helps the diver float (a buoyancy compensator) are also essential for deep-sea diving.

ence in pressure will cause pain and may damage vital tissues or organs.

Protecting the Ears. A difference in pressure is the reason why people sometimes feel ear pain when diving to the bottoms of swimming pools. The water pressure pressing against the eardrum is greater than the air pressure inside the ear. The pressure can usually be equalized and the ear pain stopped by holding the nose and blowing. This is called "popping" your ears. Skin divers do the same thing to equalize pressure as they descend. If they did not, the water pressure could rupture their eardrums. For this reason, experienced skin divers never dive while suffering from head colds or while wearing earplugs. In these cases, pressure would build up inside the ears, and the eardrums would rupture.

Protecting the Lungs and Vital Organs. It is important to realize that a person walking on the surface of the earth is actually walking underneath an ocean of air. At sea level, the pressure of this air on the body is 14.7 pounds per square inch (1.036 kilograms per square centimeter). At a depth of 33 feet (10 meters) underwater, the weight of the water doubles this pressure, and air is compressed to one half its normal volume. As a result, when a diver breathes with scuba at a depth of 33 feet, it takes twice as much air to fill the lungs. If a diver rose to the surface without exhaling, this excess air would expand inside the lungs and could rupture the lung tissue and permit air bubbles to enter the bloodstream. This is called air embolism. If the air bubbles lodge inside blood vessels of the heart or brain, serious injury and even death could result.

Other Safety Tips. There are a variety of other things divers must learn in order to dive safely. For example, they must know how long their air supply will last at different depths, what to do when the air runs out, and what to do if their mask is knocked off, a mouthpiece is lost, or a piece of equipment malfunctions. Divers should also avoid diving in water not known to be safe.

These techniques and safety tips, and many more, are taught by competent diving instructors in the safety of a swimming pool. With such training comes the confidence, knowledge, and experience that will make skin diving a safe and enjoyable experience.

BILL BARADA
Contributing editor, *Skin Diver Magazine*

With its back arched and its tail raised, the striped skunk warns enemies to stay away or risk being sprayed with a foul-smelling liquid.

SKUNKS

If you suddenly meet a skunk face to face —stand still. If you do not make any sudden movements, chances are good that the little black-and-white mammal will continue on its way and leave you alone. But if you jump about or shout, you may learn firsthand how the skunk defends itself.

▶THE SKUNK'S DEFENSE

When a skunk is disturbed, its first response is to stamp its feet, which is a signal for the intruder to keep away. If this does not work, it will arch its back, raising its plumed tail in a vivid display of warning. If the intruder continues to advance, the skunk will whirl quickly and fire round after round of evil-smelling liquid at the enemy.

Not only does the spray have a disgusting odor, but it causes firelike stinging when it hits sensitive tissues of its victim, such as those in the nose. It can cause temporary blindness if it gets in the victim's eyes and vomiting if it gets in the mouth.

Musk glands inside the skunk's body store this powerful fluid until it is needed. Then strong muscles force it out through two small openings, one on each side of the base of the tail. Aiming accurately, the skunk can shoot this clear amber fluid a distance of more than 10 feet (3 meters). The odor can be carried as far as a mile away by the wind.

▶SKUNKS AND THEIR HOMES

Skunks, which all have black-and-white striped or spotted fur, are found only in North and South America. The most common North American species, or kind, is the striped skunk. It can be found from southern Canada southward through most of the United States and into Mexico. The striped skunk is about the size of a house cat.

Besides the striped skunk, three other kinds of skunks live in North America. The smallest of these is the little spotted skunk, which ranges over much of the United States, Mexico, and Central America. It seldom weighs more than 3 pounds (1.4 kilograms). The hooded skunk looks very much like the striped skunk. It is found from southern Arizona and New Mexico to Central America. The hognosed skunk gets its name from its long piglike snout. It is found in many of the same areas as the hooded skunk. However, the hognosed skunk is the only kind of skunk that is found in South America.

▶HOW SKUNKS LIVE

Skunks are nocturnal—that is, they are active during the night and rest during the day. During cold winter months skunks remain in their sleeping dens most of the time. During mild spells, however, they may be up and about in the nighttime. In February and March the males hunt for mates. About nine weeks after mating, the female skunk bears four to seven blind and almost naked young in her underground den. The youngsters grow rapidly. When they are about 6 weeks old, they begin to follow their mother on her nightly rambles.

Despite its disagreeable scent, the skunk is usually a mild and inoffensive animal. It never uses its weapon except to defend itself. And the skunk helps farmers by eating great quantities of harmful insects and their grubs. It also eats rodents and other small animals as well as fruit, bulbs, and eggs.

ROBERT M. McCLUNG
Author, science books for children

Experienced skydivers sometimes link up in formations before opening their parachutes. Different body positions help steer the skydivers into place.

SKYDIVING

One of the world's most exciting sports is skydiving—parachuting from airplanes for fun. Although sport parachuting dates back to the 1930's, skydiving's popularity began in the late 1950's. Today there are training centers and clubs in many parts of the world. The United States Parachute Association has more than 23,000 members. Its rules allow people 16 years and older to jump.

After several hours of training, a beginner may make the first jump, from a minimum altitude of 3,000 feet (915 meters). Pre-jump training includes instruction on jumping, parachute control, and landing techniques. Some beginners make their first jump with an instructor. Others jump alone, using a safety line from the airplane, called a static line, that opens the parachute automatically.

Upon leaving the airplane, skydivers, or jumpers, assume the "arch position"—back arched with arms and legs spread apart. During free-fall (before opening the parachute), this position provides stability and reduces the speed of the fall to about 120 miles (190 kilometers) per hour. It also enables jumpers to control their movement through the air. Depending on altitude, a jumper can perform maneuvers for as long as 75 seconds by changing position during the free-fall.

The parachute opens when the jumper pulls a release line, called the rip cord. The para-chute slows the jumper's fall, allowing him or her to float safely to the ground. To land, the jumper faces into the wind, with legs together and knees bent to absorb shock. Because of modern parachute designs, many jumpers can make soft, stand-up landings.

Parachuting equipment weighs about 25 pounds (11 kilograms). All jumpers wear two parachutes—a main parachute and an emergency one. Both are usually attached to the parachutist's back with a body harness. A one-piece jumpsuit, soft footwear such as sneakers, and a protective helmet cover the parachutist's body. Beginners sometimes carry a small radio to receive guidance from an instructor on the ground.

Experienced skydivers compete in several different types of competition. The most popular is formation skydiving in which four or eight jumpers link up in formations during free-fall. Points are awarded for the number of formations completed during a specified time. In style contests, individual jumpers do a preset series of maneuvers during free-fall. In accuracy contests, the jumper must land on a ground target during a series of several jumps. Some jumpers are so skilled that they can land exactly on the target time and time again.

Canopy relative work, or CRW, is a competition in which jumpers make formations by standing on one another's open parachutes. In freestyle competition, jumpers do flips, loops, stands, and other unusual poses during the free-fall. They also may move through the air standing on skis or a skateboard. World championships in each type of competition are held every two years.

Record-making jumps sometimes bring attention to the sport of skydiving. Large formations during free-fall have been completed successfully with 150 jumpers!

Safety is an important component of skydiving. Even after careful training, jumpers still follow direction from an experienced jump master, who supervises jumpers as they exit the airplane. Equipment is checked and rechecked to make sure that it operates properly. Classes are offered by clubs and training centers to improve jumpers' skills, so that each and every jump is as safe and fun as possible.

Reviewed by JACK GREGORY
Safety and Training Director
United States Parachute Association

SLANG

Slang words are words that are widely used in informal speech and writing but are not accepted for formal use. They may be new words or old ones used with a new meaning. The desire to say old things in a new way leads to slang. When something becomes very common in our daily life, we are likely to make up new words for it. Slang is a part of every profession, trade, sport, school, and social group.

Sometimes slang is used in a way that seems to be cruel or unkind, as when a person is called an egghead, sourpuss, beanpole, or jerk. Most slang is limited to certain areas, but some words, such as "okay," are carried around the world by newspapers, radio, television, motion pictures, and tourists. Slang is popular because it is catchy and timely. Most slang has a very short life. It meets a momentary need or expresses a temporary opinion. Yet some words now considered standard began as slang—words such as *taxi, flapjack, booster, pep, hoax, bogus, carpetbagger, sky-scraper,* and *fan* (from *fanatic*).

Slang is invented the same way formal language is. Its basis is usually metaphor (a word or phrase that ordinarily means one thing is used for another thing in order to suggest a likeness between the two). Money, for example, is called bacon, scratch, loot, shekels, dough, bucks, and bread. One's home is referred to as a pad, shack, dump, diggings, or hole in the wall. Death may be described as croaking or kicking the bucket. To be drunk is to be three sheets to the wind, stewed, stoned, pickled, plastered, bombed, pie-eyed, or soused. Failure is referred to as not getting to first base, striking out, blowing it, hitting a foul ball, flunking, getting nailed, or running into a stone wall. To be discharged from a job is to be sacked, bounced, fired, or axed.

Some slang words imitate the sound made by something, as *bam, click, kerplunk, ker-smack, plunk, razz, wham,* and *whoopee.* Other words come from longer expressions or from words with similar sounds, as when the name of something is unknown or forgotten and it is called a whatsit, whozis, widget, or thingamajig.

Abbreviations often become slang terms, as d.t.'s (delirium tremens), D.A. (district attor-ney), and M.C. (master of ceremonies). Shortened or clipped words are slang, as *biz* (business), *natch* (naturally), *vet* (veteran or veterinary), *delish* (delicious), *gym* (gymnasium), *math* (mathematics), and *lab* (laboratory). A headline in *Variety* is a good example of the use of this and other types of slang: STIX NIX HICKS PIX. It means that people in the sticks, or rural areas, did not like a motion picture that made fun of them.

Learned words may be imitated in slang, as *discombobulate, rambunctious, scrumptious,* and *hocus-pocus.* Two words may be telescoped into one, as in *slanguage* (slang and language), *brunch* (breakfast and lunch), and *skyjack* (sky and hijack).

Foreign languages are a source of slang, as in *klutz* (from a Yiddish word meaning "blockhead"), *toot sweet* (from the French phrase *tout de suite,* "at once"), *padre* (Spanish for "parson" or "father"), *hombre* (Spanish for "man"), *hoosegow* (from the Spanish word *juzgado,* "court of justice"), and *cala-boose* (from the Spanish word *calabozo,* "prison").

People often object to slang because they believe it is impolite, is connected with low-class society, weakens vocabulary, and has a limited life span. Yet slang gives to speech and writing a liveliness that makes its use in light moments quite appropriate. A command over language involves the power to make up new expressions or use old expressions for new purposes.

HARRY R. WARFEL
Author, *Language: A Science of Human Behavior*

SLATE. See ROCKS (Metamorphic Rock).

RHYMING TERMS IN SLANG

chitchat	honky-tonk
chowhound	hot rod
claptrap	hotshot
crumb bum	hot spot
culture vulture	howdy doody
date bait	hustle-bustle
deadhead	nitwit
double-trouble	plug-ugly
eager beaver	rootin'-tootin'
even steven	sad sack
fuddy-duddy	silly Billy
greasy grind	slaphappy
gruesome twosome	sure cure
gyp joint	thriller-diller
hi-fi	walkie-talkie

SLAVERY

Slavery is a system in which one group of people is subjected to the power and force of another group. Slavery has existed in various societies throughout history with varying degrees of harshness. In most of these societies, slaves were considered the property of others. They were forced to work without payment other than of food, clothing, and shelter, could be freely sold or given away, and were deprived of all basic human rights.

The practice of slavery is very old. It probably first came about when a victorious warrior captured and enslaved his defeated enemies instead of killing them. Historical writings confirm that slavery flourished in the ancient civilizations of Egypt, Greece, Rome, and in the Middle East and Asia. Although it went into decline in Christian Europe during the Middle Ages (A.D. 500–1500), it was reintroduced at the beginning of the modern age, when the creation of colonial empires required unlimited numbers of laborers. This led to the establishment of the African slave trade, in which, over a period of about 300 years, approximately 10 million black Africans were subjected to forced labor.

The economic benefits of slave labor were the primary reason people of conscience had such difficulty getting slavery abolished. Slavery was the very issue that led to the American Civil War (1861–65), the bloodiest conflict the country has ever known. The victory of the antislavery Union forces led to **emancipation**, the abolition of slavery, in the United States in 1865.

Slavery has long since been illegal in most of the world's civilized societies and is condemned by members of the United Nations. However, even today the practice survives in some parts of Latin America, Africa, the Middle East, the Far East, and anywhere people are unprotected by law and persistently deprived of their fundamental rights as human beings.

Throughout the ages, defenseless people who lack government protection have been enslaved, stripped of all basic human rights. For more than three centuries, millions of Africans were captured and forced to labor in European colonies. This photograph was taken in the 1880's in the Belgian Congo, a colony in central Africa.

▶ ANCIENT TIMES

Historical writings tell us that slavery existed throughout the ancient world. In the Code of Hammurabi, a series of laws issued before 1750 B.C., King Hammurabi of Babylonia described how slaves should be treated and even outlined ways in which they might buy their own freedom. In the Bible, a book of the Old Testament called Exodus describes how the Israelites were enslaved by the Egyptians around 1200 B.C., until Moses came and led them to freedom. The writings of Homer also indicate that slavery existed in Greece as early as 1200 B.C.

Egypt

Ancient Egyptian society depended on slave labor, which was provided for the most part by prisoners of war, criminals, and people who could not pay their debts. The poor could sell themselves and their children. Egypt was the center of the ancient slave trade. The Egyptians bought slaves from the neighboring countries of Ethiopia, Nubia, and Assyria and shaved their heads so they might easily be identified.

Carvings from an early Egyptian tomb illustrate the flogging of slaves. Military conquests after 1570 B.C. dramatically increased the number of slaves in Egypt.

Greece

Although the actual condition of slavery in Greece was less harsh than that in Egypt, children were in constant danger of being kidnapped and sold, and anyone who came into debt could be enslaved at any time.

Certain classes of Greek slaves were treated better than others. Household slaves and certain artisans and public workers could actually save up money to buy their freedom, and the state would sometimes free slaves who had served the public, such as soldiers. Freed slaves could petition for full citizenship. However, state-owned slaves, who did farm and road work, were not treated well at all, and those assigned to work in the appalling conditions of the silver mines were often chained together and whipped.

The Roman Empire

After the Romans conquered Greece, Egypt, North Africa, and Gaul, they took thousands of prisoners as slaves. Roman slaves, like the Greeks', were divided into two classes—public and private. Until about A.D. 100, Roman masters held the power of life and death over their slaves. Some, for the thrill of gambling, trained their slaves to be gladiators, then placed them in mortal combat against other gladiators or wild beasts.

By A.D. 150, Christians began pressing for more humane treatment of slaves, and the laws began to change. Masters no longer had the power of life and death, and freed slaves no longer could sell themselves or their children. Under Constantine I (280?–377), the first Christian emperor, and Justinian I (483–565), new laws prepared the way for the change from slavery to serfdom.

▶THE MIDDLE AGES

Agricultural serfdom in medieval Europe was similar to slavery, except that masters did not own their serfs outright. Under the **manorial system**, which reached its height in the 1100's, serfs worked sections of land held by the lords of the local manor in exchange for protection. For their loyalty and faithful service, especially in times of war, some serfs were given the right to a bit of land, the first step toward emancipation. But slavery in Europe sprang to life again in the 1400's, when an interest in new trade routes led Europeans to unexplored lands.

▶THE AFRICAN SLAVE TRADE

In 1442, Antam Gonçalvez, a Portuguese sea captain in the service of Prince Henry the Navigator, brought ten black men from the west coast of Africa to the Portuguese city of Lisbon to be sold as slaves. By 1460, Portuguese ships were carrying 1,000 Africans a year, and by the end of the century, they also were supplying slaves to Spain.

To the Spanish Colonies

In 1492, Christopher Columbus founded the first colonial settlement on the island of Hispaniola. The Spanish attempted to enslave the native Carib Indians to raise food and mine gold, but the idea of working for someone else baffled the Caribs and they refused. Later attempts to enslave the native peoples of South and Central America failed for other reasons. Infectious European diseases proved deadly to the Native Americans.

In 1505 the Spanish governor of Hispaniola was given permission to import black African slaves to replace the Indians. The first were imported from Portugal, but to meet the great demand, slave traders soon turned to Africa, where the supply seemed unlimited.

Many Native Americans did not understand the concept of forced labor and died while attempting to escape the brutality of the Spanish and Portuguese conquistadors.

To the English Colonies

The slave trade to the English settlements in the New World began in 1619 when about 20 Africans were sold by a Dutch trader in Jamestown, Virginia. Slavery in the English colonies was, at first, a system of indentured servitude. After working for a master for not more than 21 years, the slave was freed. But by 1663, both Virginia and Maryland had laws stating that "all Negroes or other slaves, [and] all Negroes to be hereafter imported, shall serve *durante vita*"—for the rest of their lives. Under the new form of slavery, the children born to slaves also became the master's **chattel**, or personal property.

British abolitionist Thomas Clarkson was instrumental in securing passage of antislavery legislation in Great Britain. In 1840 he addressed delegates attending the World Anti-Slavery Convention in London.

In 1715 there were about 23,000 slaves in Virginia and similar numbers in Maryland and the Carolinas. There were fewer in the New England colonies, where the rocky soil was not suited to large-scale farming. But New Englanders were nevertheless deeply involved in the slave trade. Slave ships were built in New England shipyards, and New England rum was a factor in what became known as the **triangular trade** between New England, Africa, and the West Indies. New England rum was traded for slaves in Africa. The slaves, in turn, were sold in the West Indies for money, which was then used to buy the molasses New Englanders needed to make more rum. Because the transport of the slaves across the Atlantic Ocean was the second stage of this three-stage process, it became known as the **Middle Passage** (see inset).

▶ SLAVERY IN THE UNITED STATES

Thoughtful Americans were opposed to slavery even before the Revolutionary War. Although many of the founders of the United States, including George Washington and Thomas Jefferson, owned slaves, some were against instituting slavery into the laws of the new nation.

In the first draft of the Declaration of Independence, Jefferson called the slave trade "a cruel war against human nature itself, violating its most sacred rights of life and liberty," but he was forced to remove the antislavery language from the final draft.

George Washington said that one of his first wishes was to see slavery wiped out, and he freed some of the blacks who fought in the Revolutionary War. In 1777, Vermont be-

The Middle Passage

Slave traders, called slavers, purchased only the strongest Africans to transport across the Atlantic. Men, women, and children, sometimes chained hand and foot, were crammed tightly aboard ships for the voyage. The conditions on this Middle Passage, as the crossing was called, were so brutal that during the 400 years of slave trading, one out of every five died, some from the contagious diseases of the whites and many others from scurvy. By the time the transatlantic slave trade ended in the 1800's, about 10 million black African slaves had been imported to the Americas, and possibly 2 million more had died before they ever reached shore.

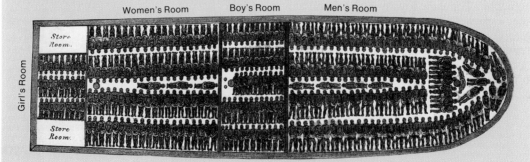

came the first state to abolish slavery altogether, followed by Massachusetts in 1783. Pennsylvania provided for the gradual abolition of slavery in 1780, as did Connecticut and Rhode Island in 1784.

At the Constitutional Convention of 1787, Jefferson, James Madison, and Alexander Hamilton argued to outlaw slavery. Although they did not get their way, the Constitution allowed that after 20 years, Congress could enact a law to end the slave trade. In 1807,

Slavery Flourishes in the Cotton Kingdom

The South's economy relied on cotton, tobacco, sugarcane, and other cash crops. The planting, harvesting, and processing of these crops required hard, intensive labor. Southern plantation owners made enormous profits using free slave labor.

Most slaves worked in the fields and were called field hands. Thousands more served as cooks, maids, valets, and coachmen, and a selected few did the skilled work of masons,

Testimony of Rosa Blackwell, from a Letter to the Editor published by William Lloyd Garrison in the *Liberator* (November 7, 1862).

"The person who claimed me as their slave owned two plantations. During the life of the old gentleman, the slaves were well treated. After his death, the plantations came into the possession of his son. Then came a change. The hands were obliged to go to work at 4 o'clock in the morning, and if they did not finish their task, had to stay till 11 at night. The overseer was a very cruel man, who applied the lash freely, and at all hours of the day.

"The slaves had for their weekly allowance a peck of corn and a half a peck of sweet potatoes, and were never allowed a piece of meat, unless they should take sometimes a hog on their own account, for which they were severely whipped. . . ."

Congress passed such a law, which went into effect on January 1, 1808. But even though slaves could no longer be imported, the institution of slavery and the domestic slave trade continued uninterrupted in the South.

The Colonization Movement

In 1816, the American Colonization Society was formed in the United States to re-locate freed black slaves to Liberia (meaning "free land") on the west coast of Africa. The movement found many supporters in both the North and the South. Many Northerners sincerely wished to help free blacks establish a democratic society of their own. But in some parts of the South, where freed slaves competed with unskilled white workers for jobs, many whites thought it useful simply to remove the competition. Of course, the United States was as much home to the free blacks born and raised there as to the white natives, and few African Americans, free or slave, wanted to be shipped off to a strange land.

carpenters, wheelwrights, and blacksmiths. The field hands lived the hardest lives and were the most cruelly treated, which made them the most likely to protest their slave condition. Slaves were far more likely to run away than to revolt, but rebellions, such as the Nat Turner uprising in 1831, only frightened slave owners into inflicting harsher disciplinary measures, ranging from branding and maim-

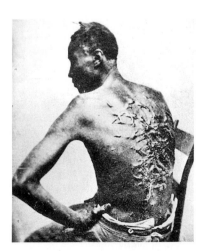

A slave named Peter sat for this picture in Baton Rouge, Louisiana, on April 2, 1863, during the Civil War. In his own words he explained, "Overseer Artayou Carrier whipped me. I was two months in bed sore from the whipping. My master come after I was whipped; he discharged the overseer."

Aesop (620?–560? B.C.), the gifted story-teller, was born in Phrygia, Thrace. He was a slave in the wealthy household of a Greek named Iadmon on the island of Samos. Aesop wove fantastic animal fables, such as "The Fox and the Grapes," that also illustrated shortcomings in human nature. Aesop became so famous he was ordered to serve the emperor Croesus.

Spartacus (?–71 B.C.), a shepherd from Thrace, was taken prisoner by the Romans and trained as a gladiator. In 73 B.C. he escaped and fled to the crater of Mt. Vesuvius, where he raised an army of more than 40,000 other runaway gladiators and slaves. His forces devastated Roman armies in the Servile War but were defeated by Crassus at the Silarus River, where Spartacus was killed.

Saint Patrick

Phillis Wheatley

Saint Patrick (389?–461?), born in Britain, became the patron saint of Ireland. Although the details of his life are unclear, it seems that at the age of 16, Patrick was captured by Irish raiders and sold as a slave in Ireland, where he labored as a shepherd. After six years, he escaped and eventually made his way to Gaul, where he studied for the priesthood. Ordained a bishop in 432, he returned to Ireland, determined to convert the Irish to Christianity. (For more information, see the article PATRICK, SAINT in Volume P.)

François Dominique Toussaint L'Ouverture (1743–1803) was born a slave in the French West Indies. He participated in the Haitian slave uprisings of the 1790's, and through his efforts and leadership, Haiti became the first independent nation in Latin America. (For more information, see the article TOUSSAINT L'OUVERTURE in Volume T.)

Phillis Wheatley (1753?–84) was the first black woman to gain recognition for her poetry in colonial America. Born in Senegal, West Africa, she was taken on a slave ship to Boston, Mass., at the age of 8. She astonished her owners, the Wheatleys, with her talents. She began writing poetry at 13. Several of her poems and her translation of Ovid were later published and received wide praise. In 1778 Phillis was freed and she married, but her husband was imprisoned for debt and she died in poverty. Her works include *Poems on Various Subjects: Religious and Moral* (1773).

Denmark Vesey (VEE-zee) (1767–1822), born in Africa, became a slave to a slave-ship's captain at a young age. For twenty years Vesey sailed between the Virgin

ing to hanging. For more information on slave life, see the article AFRICAN AMERICANS (Plantation Bondage Era) in Volume A.

Southern planters needed new and fertile land on which to grow cotton, so they used their political power to promote the spread of slavery westward. By 1848, the area under cotton cultivation, known as the Cotton Kingdom, stretched all the way from South Carolina to Texas.

The Great Debate

The question of extending slavery into new states and territories aroused bitter opposition between proslavery and antislavery groups. Most Northerners supported the **Wilmot Proviso** (1846), which called for the prohibition of slavery in western territories; most Southerners, however, opposed it. Attempts at compromise, such as admitting to the United States the same number of new "slave states" as "free states" only led to increased violence and stricter fugitive slave laws.

The 1852 publication of Harriet Beecher Stowe's novel *Uncle Tom's Cabin* helped pop-

ularize the antislavery movement. But the activities of such radical abolitionists as William L. Garrison (1805–79), Frederick Douglass (1817–95), and John Brown (1800–1859) only increased the hostilities of slaveholders. For example, John Brown's raid on Harpers Ferry, Virginia, on October 16, 1859, made Southerners so angry that they began what Garrison described as a "reign of terror," randomly arresting and abusing innocent travelers from the North. John Brown's raid brought the issue of slavery to a head.

War for Emancipation

Eventually most Southerners felt that the only way to maintain their independence and their self-proclaimed right to own slaves was to secede (withdraw) from the United States and form their own nation. One by one the Southern states seceded, and on April 12, 1861, Jefferson Davis, president of the new Confederate States of America, ordered an all-out assault on Fort Sumter, a U.S. Army post in South Carolina. Thus began the great Civil War (1861–65).

Islands and Haiti, and in 1800 he got an opportunity to buy his freedom when he won $600 in a lottery. As a freedman, Vesey settled in Charleston, S.C. He worked at carpentry and later became a Methodist church minister. Vesey planned a black insurrection that would take over the entire city of Charleston. He recruited hundreds of supporters through his church. The insurrection was planned for July 1822, but the plan was exposed to white authorities by a black informant. Vesey and 34 other blacks were hanged.

Nat Turner (1800–1831) was born a slave in Southampton County, Va. His master taught him to read. Turner was a preacher, known to slaves throughout the South as the Prophet. In 1831, believing himself an instrument of God's will, Turner led what many consider the deadliest slave revolt in American history. The uprising began when Turner and four followers killed five members of his master's family as they slept. During the next two days they roamed the countryside, killing dozens of slaveholders and recruiting slaves to join the rebellion. In the end Turner and 17 of his followers were hanged. The rebellion struck terror

Nat Turner

in the hearts of slaveholders and led to more repressive laws, forbidding masters to teach slaves to read and forbidding slaves to gather in groups of any kind.

Frederick Douglass (1817–95) was one of the most influential leaders and eloquent speakers of the antislavery movement. Born a slave on a large plantation in Tuckahoe, Md., he escaped to the North in 1838. Douglass eventually settled in Rochester, N.Y., where he became editor of the highly influential antislavery newspaper, the *North Star*. His home was a station on the Underground Railroad.

Profiles

(For more information, see the article DOUGLASS, FREDERICK in Volume D.)

Robert Smalls (1839–1915) engineered one of the most daring escapes in Civil War history. Born a slave in Beaufort, S.C., Smalls was forced to serve the Confederacy as a pilot for the transport steamer, the *Planter*. In 1862, boldly disguised as the ship's captain, Smalls secreted the warship past several Confederate forts and out of Charleston harbor. Along the way, he even managed to stop to rescue 15 other slaves, including his family. After serving out the war on the Union side, Smalls returned to South Carolina and became a delegate to the South Carolina Constitutional Convention. He then served in the state legislature (1868–75) and in the U.S. House of Representatives (1875–79).

On January 1, 1863, in an effort to strengthen the Northern cause, U.S. president Abraham Lincoln issued the Emancipation Proclamation. The document, which proclaimed that slaves in the Confederate states were free, was intended to rouse the blacks to join the U.S. Army and help the North fight their former masters. But it was not until 1865, when the 13th Amendment was passed, that slavery was formally abolished in the United States. (For more information, see EMANCIPATION PROCLAMATION in Volume E.)

▶ **SLAVERY IN RECENT TIMES**

In the 1900's, several other nations took steps to end slavery. In 1911 a revolt led by Emiliano Zapata freed the Indians of Mexico and Guatemala from 35 years of bondage they had experienced under the regime of Mexican dictator Porfirio Díaz; in the 1930's, the League of Nations found sufficient evidence of slavery in Saudi Arabia, Ethiopia, and Liberia to draw up a general agreement against it; and in 1945, in response to the evidence of forced labor of millions in German concentra-

tion camps and Soviet labor camps, the United Nations established the Permanent Commission on Human Rights. This commission prepared a declaration affirming the right of all people to life, liberty, and asylum (safe refuge); to security and privacy; and to all the freedoms implied by democracy.

Further U.N. conventions strengthened antislavery declarations. But tragically, even today many millions of unprotected peoples of all races and religions throughout the world are forced into labor and other forms of human bondage, deprived of all personal rights.

JAY SAUNDERS REDDING
Author, *Lonesome Road:
The Story of the Negro in America*
Reviewed by MEGAN MCCLARD
Metropolitan State College of Denver

See also ABOLITION MOVEMENT; AFRICAN AMERICANS (Plantation Bondage Era); BROWN, JOHN; CIVIL WAR, UNITED STATES; COMPROMISE OF 1850; DOUGLASS, FREDERICK; DRED SCOTT DECISION; EMANCIPATION PROCLAMATION; KANSAS-NEBRASKA ACT; LINCOLN, ABRAHAM; MISSOURI COMPROMISE; STOWE, HARRIET BEECHER; UNDERGROUND RAILROAD; UNITED STATES, HISTORY OF THE (Slavery and the Missouri Compromise; The States Divided).

SLEEP

All living creatures need to sleep or at least have periods of complete rest. Otherwise, the mind and body become too tired to work properly. Comparatively little is known about what causes a person to fall asleep. There are many theories, but no one theory is accepted by all scientists.

What Happens During Sleep? Sleeping people are unconscious—unaware of what is going on around them. But unlike the unconsciousness that comes from fainting or injury, the unconsciousness of sleep can be quickly ended. A strong shake or loud noise will awaken most sleepers at once.

Both the mind and body continue to work during sleep, but many body functions slow down. Breathing is slower and deeper. The heart beats slower, and blood pressure is lower. Arms and legs are limp. Since it is difficult to achieve this degree of relaxation during waking hours, sleep offers more opportunity to recover from fatigue than quiet rest.

Body temperature becomes lower during sleep, and this makes people feel chilly. That is why a sleeper must be covered. People who are used to being up during the day and sleeping at night will have a drop in body temperature at night, even if they stay up all night. People who work at night and sleep during the day will have a drop in body temperature during the day, whether they go to bed or not.

People do not remain in one position during sleep. They shift about and turn from side to side. It is possible to sleep while sitting up or, when very tired, while standing. Some animals, particularly birds, sleep regularly in a standing position. Dolphins sleep with half the brain asleep and the other half awake.

Even though the sleeper is unconscious, many reflexes are still active. A sleeper will pull a hand or foot away if tickled. He or she is not aware of doing this, because the parts of the brain that control voluntary movements are at rest.

The depth of sleep is not the same throughout the whole period of sleep. Depth is measured by the amount of sound needed to awaken the sleeper. The first cycle of sleep is the deepest, lasting about 1½ hours. This is followed by lighter sleep. These 1½-hour cycles continue throughout the night. Toward the end of the night there is less deep sleep and more of the lighter sleep.

Research has proven that these two types of sleep—the light sleep when dreams occur and deep, nondreaming sleep—are both important in learning and for remembering what is learned. Everyone dreams while asleep, although people may not remember their dreams when awake. The ability to dream appears to play a part in making people feel refreshed upon awakening.

Getting Enough Sleep. The amount of sleep a person requires varies with age. In general, people need less sleep as they grow older. On average, 2-year-olds need twelve hours of sleep at night and one to two hours of nap. Children between the ages of 6 and 9 need about eleven hours, while a 12-year-old may do well with ten hours. Most adults need from seven to nine hours daily.

People who get less sleep than they need for several nights in a row may find they become irritable and have difficulty thinking clearly. They may find it hard to learn and remember and may be more prone to make mistakes. They may also be more likely to get sick or to have accidents.

Getting Ready for Sleep. Sleep comes on more readily when a person is relaxed and quiet. Worry or excitement can cause insomnia, a state of sleeplessness. It is not always possible to avoid thoughts that keep one awake at night, but there are routines that help people fall asleep, such as taking a warm bath or listening to soothing music. Going to bed at the same time each night is very helpful in establishing a sleep pattern. A comfortable bed and a darkened, quiet room will aid sleep, as will avoiding eating big meals or watching television close to bedtime.

Some studies suggest that sleep is important for people's physical and emotional well-being. It could also have other functions that scientists may discover by using new techniques, such as brain imaging, for studying people while they sleep.

PHYLLIS RYBA
Downstate Medical Center (New York)
Reviewed by ROSALIND D. CARTWRIGHT
Author, *Crisis Dreaming:
Using Your Dreams to Solve Your Problems*

See also DREAMING.

SLEET. See RAIN, SNOW, SLEET, AND HAIL.

SLOVAKIA

Slovakia

Slovakia (officially, the Slovak Republic) is a nation situated in east central Europe. Formerly part of Czechoslovakia, it became an independent country in 1993, when Czechoslovakia was divided into the Czech Republic and the Slovak Republic. Slovakia is the smaller and less populous of the two countries. The Slovaks had joined with the Czechs to form Czechoslovakia in 1918. The division of Czechoslovakia came about only a few years after the collapse of the Communist regime that had long governed the country. It resulted from basic disagreements between Czech and Slovak leaders on the country's future.

See the separate article on the Czech Republic in Volume C.

▶THE PEOPLE

Ethnic Groups, Language, Religion. About 85 percent of Slovakia's people are Slovaks. Hungarians are the largest ethnic minority, with about 11 percent of the population. Gypsies and other groups make up the remainder. The Slovaks, like the Czechs, are a West Slavic people, and the Slovak and Czech languages are so similar that the two peoples can readily understand each other. Most of the country's inhabitants are traditionally Roman Catholics. There are also some Protestants and members of the Orthodox Church. Many Slovaks, particularly in urban areas, consider themselves to be nonbelievers. In rural areas, however, the people have retained a strong attachment to religion.

Slovakia After Communism. The quality of life was greatly impaired during the forty years of Communist rule of Czechoslovakia. Democratic freedoms and human rights were

Northern Slovakia is a rugged, mountainous region covered with forests at its lower elevations. The mountains are the High Tatra, part of the Carpathian system.

A farmer and his horses plow a field in southern Slovakia. The country's only lowland region, the south forms part of the Danubian plain that extends into neighboring Hungary. The major crops include grains such as rye, wheat, and corn, as well as potatoes and flax (from which linen is made). Once almost entirely agricultural, Slovakia now has an economy in which industry has become first in importance.

suppressed. The Communist practice of emphasizing heavy industry while neglecting the production of consumer goods led to the lowering of the standard of living. The downfall of the Communists in 1989 was thus expected to bring rapid improvement in the life of the people.

As far as human rights and political freedoms were concerned, most of these expectations were satisfied. But economic improvements have been more difficult to achieve. The changeover from the government-managed and state-controlled economy of the Communist era to a free-market system has resulted in the closing of factories that were unprofitable, the layoff of unneeded employees, and widespread price increases.

FACTS and figures

SLOVAK REPUBLIC is the official name of the country.

LOCATION: East central Europe.

AREA: 18,933 sq mi (49,035 km²).

POPULATION: 5,270,000 (estimate).

CAPITAL AND LARGEST CITY: Bratislava.

MAJOR LANGUAGE: Slovak.

MAJOR RELIGIOUS GROUP: Roman Catholic.

GOVERNMENT: Republic. **Head of state**—president. **Head of government**—prime minister (appointed by the president). **Legislature**—Slovak National Council.

CHIEF PRODUCTS: Agricultural—wheat, rye, corn, potatoes, flax, livestock. **Manufactured**—metals, engineering equipment, refined petroleum, petrochemicals. **Mineral**—coal, iron ore, small deposits of other minerals.

▶THE LAND

Slovakia is a landlocked country bordered by five other nations. Poland lies to the north, the Czech Republic to the west, Hungary to the south, Austria to the southwest, and Ukraine to the east.

Landforms. The country's northern boundary is formed by the Carpathian Mountains, which reach their highest point, 8,737 feet (2,663 meters), in the High Tatra. The entire northern part of Slovakia is rugged and mountainous and is covered with forests in the lower elevations. The southern portion is a lowland that is a natural extension of the Danubian plain of Hungary. Slovakia is drained by several rivers, including the Danube, which provides it with an important water route to the Black Sea.

Climate and Natural Resources. Slovakia has a continental climate, marked by moderately warm summers and cold winters. Temperatures and the amount of rainfall vary, however, depending on altitude. In the High Tatra winters are bitterly cold and rainfall reaches 50 inches (1,270 millimeters) or more a year.

Slovakia has deposits of numerous minerals, including coal, iron ore, petroleum, and natural gas, but most are not found in sufficient quantities for industrial use. Since much of the country is forested, timber is one of its most important natural resources.

Chief Cities. Bratislava is Slovakia's capital, commercial center, and largest city, with a population of about 450,000. Situated on the Danube, it was first settled by Slovaks in the A.D. 700's. During the 1600's and 1700's, it served as the Hungarian capital at a time when

Slovakia was ruled by Hungary. Formerly known as Pressburg, it became the center of a Slovak revival after the creation of Czechoslovakia in 1918.

Košice, in southeastern Slovakia, is the country's second largest city. An important site since the Middle Ages, it is now a leading industrial city and transportation center.

▶ THE ECONOMY

While under Hungarian rule, Slovakia's economy remained largely agricultural. But after becoming part of Czechoslovakia, a slow process of industrialization began. It gained momentum during the Communist era with the government's stress on heavy industry. Today's manufactures include metal products, processed foods and beverages, electricity and heating fuels, chemicals, machinery, and transport vehicles.

About one-third of Slovakia's land is suitable for cultivation. The main crops are wheat, rye, corn, potatoes, and flax (from which linen is made). Livestock is also raised.

▶ GOVERNMENT

Slovakia's government is based on a constitution adopted in September 1992. The legislature, or lawmaking body, is the Slovak National Council, whose 150 members are elected for 4-year terms. The president is elected for five years by a three-fifths majority of the National Council. The president appoints and shares executive authority with the prime minister. A Constitutional Court, made up of ten judges appointed by the president, ensures that no laws are passed that do not agree with the constitution.

▶ HISTORY

Early History. Slavs first settled in what is now Slovakia in the A.D. 400's. In the 800's they were united with the Czechs in the empire of Great Moravia and were converted to Christianity. But in 907, Great Moravia was attacked by the Magyars (or Hungarians), and the Slovaks fell under their rule.

Slovak culture declined under Hungarian domination. But in the late 1700's, a renewed interest in the Slovak language and ethnic heritage strengthened Slovak national consciousness. Meanwhile, their Czech cousins, now under the rule of the dual monarchy of Austria and Hungary, were also undergoing a cultural revival.

Creation of Czechoslovakia. When World War I broke out in 1914, two exiled Czech leaders, Tomáš Masaryk and Eduard Beneš, initiated a movement to gain independence from Austria-Hungary. Milan Štefánik, a Slovak, became a high-ranking member of the Czechoslovak National Council that was set up to head the independence movement. With Austria-Hungary's defeat in the war and the breakup of its empire, a new Czechoslovak nation came into existence on October 28, 1918. It united Slovakia with the Czech lands of Bohemia and Moravia, a portion of Silesia, and the province of Ruthenia.

Although this union benefited Slovakia economically and culturally, many Slovaks soon felt dominated by the central govern-

Czechoslovaks marched to protest the invasion of their country by the Soviet Union and four of its allies in 1968. The portrait is that of Alexander Dubček, a Slovak and moderate Communist leader, whose reforms had stirred the hearts of the people after years of harsh Communist rule. The sign reads "Go Home," referring to the invaders. The Dubček government was overthrown by the Soviet armies, and Czechoslovaks had to wait until 1989 for the restoration of democracy.

The fall of the Communist regime in 1989 was soon followed by disagreements between Czech and Slovak leaders over the country's future. Here a Slovak calls for his republic's independence, which was peacefully achieved in 1993 with the breakup of Czechoslovakia.

ment in Prague, the national capital, situated in Bohemia.

A Slovak State. In 1938, the Nazi German dictator Adolf Hitler annexed the Sudetenland, a border region of Czechoslovakia, and part of Ruthenia was transferred to Hungary. Meanwhile, Slovak leaders gained autonomy (self-rule), and Jozef Tiso, a Roman Catholic priest turned politician, became prime minister of the new Slovak state.

In 1939, Hitler took control of Bohemia and Moravia but allowed Slovakia to become an independent country under German protection. When World War II broke out in 1939, Slovakia was forced to become Germany's ally.

Restoration and Communist Rule. With Germany's defeat in 1945, the Slovaks and Czechs were reunited in a restored Czechoslovakia. But in 1948, Communists, backed by the Soviet Union, seized control of the government. They ruled for the next forty years.

In January 1968, in a bold attempt to liberalize the harsh system, high-level Communist functionaries replaced the die-hard Communist party leader, Antonín Novotný, with Alexander Dubček, a moderate Slovak Communist. During this period, known as the "Prague Spring," Dubček's reforms stirred the hearts of Czechoslovaks as well as many other peoples around the world. However, in August 1968, the reformist government was overthrown by the Soviet Union and four of its allies. In 1969, Gustáv Husák, a Slovak, replaced Dubček and reinstated strict Communist control.

Fall of Communism and Separation. In 1989, Communism collapsed throughout Central and Eastern Europe. Czechoslovakia's Communist government fell after massive demonstrations spearheaded by the Czech Civic Forum and the Slovak Public Against Violence. A democratic government was formed, headed by Václav Havel (a Czech) as president and Marian Čalfa (a Slovak) as prime minister.

But differences between the Czechs and Slovaks soon threatened the new democratic federation. Representatives of the largest Czech political party, the Civil Democratic Party (ODS), insisted on the preservation of a close federation and a speedy replacement of the socialist-style state-controlled economy with a capitalist free-market system. Vladimír Mečiar, the leader of the major Slovak party, the Movement for Democratic Slovakia (HZDS), favored a looser confederation, with more authority given to local governments, and a slower pace of economic change. When compromise proved impossible, the country was divided peacefully on January 1, 1993. Michal Kováč was elected president of the new Slovak Republic, and Mečiar, as head of the ruling party, became prime minister.

Recent History. In 1998, when the 5-year term of President Kováč expired, Mečiar prevented the election of a successor and assumed the powers of the presidency until August 1998. The following month, after a coalition of opposition parties won control in parliamentary elections, Mečiar resigned and a new government led by Mikulás Dzurinda of the Slovak Democratic Coalition (SDK) was sworn in. Important goals for Dzurinda's government included stronger ties with the West and membership in the North Atlantic Treaty Organization (NATO) and the European Union (EU). In 1999 Rudolf Schuster was elected president.

In the 2002 parliamentary elections, Dzurinda was returned to power as head of a new coalition of pro-Western parties. Ivan Gasparovic succeeded Schuster as president in 2004. That same year, Slovakia became a member of both NATO and the EU.

EDWARD TABORSKY
Author, *Communism in Czechoslovakia*

SLOVENIA

Slovenia was one of the six republics that made up the former nation of Yugoslavia. It gained its independence in 1991. The northernmost of the former republics, Slovenia is bounded by Austria on the north, Hungary on the east, Croatia on the south, and Italy and the Adriatic Sea on the west.

▶ PEOPLE

Nearly all of Slovenia's people are ethnic Slovenes. They speak Slovenian, which belongs to the South Slavic branch of languages, and most are Roman Catholic. Their religion, relatively high standard of living, and long association with Italian and Austrian cultures have made the Slovenes, like the neighboring Croats, much more Westernized than the people of the other former Yugoslav republics.

The picturesque city of Ljubljana (pronounced lee-oo-blee-AHN-a), the capital and largest city of Slovenia, is situated on the Ljubljanica River.

▶ LAND

Slovenia occupies the northwestern corner of the Balkan Peninsula. Thick forests cover nearly half the country, and much of the rest is hilly or mountainous. Triglav mountain, Slovenia's highest peak, rises 9,395 feet (2,864 meters) in the Julian Alps near the Italian border. The mountain regions are cold and snowy in the winter and mild and rainy in the summer. The weather is mild along the Adriatic coastline. Tourists are attracted to Slovenia's northern lakes and its beaches on the Adriatic.

▶ ECONOMY

Manufacturing and trade provide about 60 percent of Slovenia's income and give its people the highest income per capita (per person) of all the former Yugoslav republics. Leading manufactures include metal products, electronics, trucks, electric power equipment, wood products, textiles, chemicals, and machine tools. Slovenia also has significant deposits of coal, mercury, and oil.

Agriculture, another important sector of Slovenia's economy, employs about two-thirds of the workforce. Potatoes, hops, wheat, sugar beets, and corn are the major crops. Cattle, sheep, and pigs are raised as livestock.

▶ MAJOR CITIES

Ljubljana, with a population of about 300,000, is the nation's capital, largest city, and cultural center. It is located in central Slovenia on the Ljubljanica River, a tributary of the Sava River. The city was founded by the Romans in the first century B.C.

Maribor, the country's second-largest city, was founded in the 1100's on the Drava River.

▶ HISTORY AND GOVERNMENT

The ancestors of the Slovenes moved into the region as early as the A.D. 500's. But unlike the Serbs and Croats, they were never able to establish their own independent state, and they quickly fell under foreign, mainly German, control and influence.

Foreign Influences. In the early 800's, Slovenia came under the domination of Austria, a border region of Charlemagne's great Holy Roman Empire that later became part of a vast empire ruled by the Habsburg dynasty. At the same time, smaller numbers of Slovenes settled in northern Italy, where they were ruled by what was then the city-state of Venice. Thus, for a thousand years, the Slovenes were influenced by German, Austrian, and Italian culture. Only the peasant farmers kept the old Slavic language and customs alive.

In 1809, the conquering French general and emperor Napoleon Bonaparte combined the Habsburgs' territories in Serbia, Croatia, and Slovenia into the short-lived Illyrian Provinces. Under French rule, the Slovenes experienced a brief national revival of their language and culture.

Yugoslavia. After the Habsburgs' empire collapsed in 1918 at the end of World War I (1914–18), Slovenia became a part of the new Kingdom of Serbs, Croats, and Slovenes (renamed the Kingdom of Yugoslavia in 1929). But Yugoslavia was politically unstable, and it fell apart when it was occupied by Nazi Germany and its allies in 1941, during World War II (1939–45). Slovenia itself was divided up among Germany, Italy, and Hungary.

At the war's end, Slovenia became part of the Socialist Federal Republic of Yugoslavia, a Communist state established by Tito (Josip Broz). It was built around a federal system based on ethnic republics, but it was ruled firmly by Tito. After his death in 1980, however, the country's complex government structure and unstable economy rapidly approached collapse. Yugoslavia was also faced with rising ethnic hostilities.

Independence. In 1990, Slovenia, eager to adopt a democratic form of government and a free-market economy, first demanded that Yugoslavia be converted into a loose confederation of states. Then in June 1991, it formally proclaimed independence. Serbia, the largest of the republics, refused to accept this and dispatched federal military forces to Slovenia. After hostilities had taken some 200 lives, a truce was arranged and the federal forces withdrew. Slovenia's independence was recognized by the international community, and in 1992 it was admitted to the United Nations. In 2004, Slovenia joined both the North Atlantic Treaty Organization (NATO) and the European Union (EU).

Slovenia's government is headed by a prime minister, who is elected by the legislature, the Drzavni Zbor (National Assembly). Its 90 members are elected to 4-year terms. A president is popularly elected to serve a 5-year term as head of state. Milan Kucan, Slovenia's first president, was succeeded in 2002 by Janez Drnovšek.

Reviewed by JANUSZ BUGAJSKI
Center for Strategic and International Studies

FACTS
and figures

REPUBLIC OF SLOVENIA is the official name of the country.

LOCATION: Southeastern Europe.

AREA: 7,827 sq mi (20,273 km²).

POPULATION: 2,000,000 (estimate).

CAPITAL AND LARGEST CITY: Ljubljana.

MAJOR LANGUAGE: Slovenian.

MAJOR RELIGIOUS GROUP: Roman Catholic.

GOVERNMENT: Republic. **Head of state**—president. **Head of government**—prime minister. **Legislature**—Drzavni Zbor (National Assembly).

CHIEF PRODUCTS: Agricultural—potatoes, hops, wheat, sugar beets, corn, grapes, livestock. **Manufactured**—metal products, lead and zinc smelting, electronics, trucks, electric power equipment, wood products, textiles, chemicals, machine tools. **Mineral**—coal, mercury, oil.

MONETARY UNIT: Tolar (1 tolar = 100 stotin.)

SMITH, JOHN (1580–1631)

John Smith was an English soldier and explorer who helped found Jamestown, Virginia, the first permanent English colony in America. He was born in Willoughby, England, in 1580. While still in his teens he became a soldier and had many adventures. By his own account, he defeated three Turks in duels and killed yet another who had made him a slave.

In 1606, Smith joined a group of colonists bound for Virginia. On the voyage, Smith was accused of mutiny and arrested. When the ships reached America, the sealed orders of the Virginia Company of London were opened, revealing that Smith had been appointed to the colony's governing council. Because he was not allowed to serve at first, Smith went on an exploring expedition.

In his *General Historie of Virginia* (1624), Smith said that during this time away from the colony, he and some companions were captured by Indians. As he was about to be killed, he was saved by Pocahontas, the daughter of

Legend says Chief Powhatan spared John Smith's life at the insistence of his daughter, Pocahontas.

Chief Powhatan. Though no one knows if the tale is true, it is known that Pocahontas later befriended the colonists and brought them food.

On his return to Jamestown, Smith was arrested again but was soon freed. Eventually he became the colony's most successful leader. He set the colonists to work building houses and establishing farms, and during the severe winter of 1608–09 he saved them from starvation by persuading the Indians to give them corn.

In 1609, Smith was injured in an explosion and returned to England. Five years later he came back to America, explored New England, and made the first accurate map of the coast. His book *A Description of New England* (1616) gave the region its name. The Pilgrims later used his books and maps. Smith returned to England, where he died on June 21, 1631.

Reviewed by JOHN J. WATERS
University of Rochester

SMITH, JOSEPH (1805–1844)

Joseph Smith was the founding prophet and first president of the Church of Jesus Christ of Latter-day Saints. He was born in Sharon, Vermont, on December 23, 1805. His family later settled in Palmyra, New York.

From 1820 to 1827, Smith had a series of religious experiences. He claimed that God and Jesus had appeared to him in a vision. Later he said an angel had shown him where to find some ancient writings, which told of the ministry of Jesus Christ among the people of ancient America, after his resurrection. These writings were translated and published as *The Book of Mormon*.

In 1830, Smith organized a new church in Fayette, New York. Although the church drew many converts, Smith and his followers were driven out of New York, then Ohio, and then Missouri. In 1839 they finally settled in Illinois, where they built a new city called Nauvoo. Smith served as the president of the church and later became mayor.

Under Smith's leadership, the Mormons opposed slavery and, until 1890, allowed men more than one wife. These beliefs made the Mormons very unpopular and led to violent persecution. On June 27, 1844, after he had announced his candidacy for president of the United States, Joseph Smith was shot to death by a mob. Two years later, Brigham Young, Smith's successor as leader of the church, left Nauvoo and led his followers west to the valley of the Great Salt Lake. Today, Salt Lake City, Utah, is the church's world headquarters.

L. DON LeFEVRE
The Church of Jesus Christ of Latter-day Saints

See also MORMONS; YOUNG, BRIGHAM.

SMITH, MARGARET CHASE. See MAINE (Famous People); UNITED STATES, CONGRESS OF THE (Profiles: Senators).

SMITHSONIAN INSTITUTION

From its earliest days, the Smithsonian Institution in Washington, D.C., has promoted science and culture in the United States and throughout the world. Every year millions of people visit its museums, art galleries, and other exhibits.

The Smithsonian is an independent establishment supported by federal funds and by nonfederal gifts, grants, and endowments. It is governed by a board of regents composed of the chief justice of the U.S. Supreme Court, the vice president, three members of the House of Representatives, three senators, and nine private citizens. This board selects the secretary, who serves as the executive officer and director of all Smithsonian activities.

Museums. The Smithsonian museums contain nearly 150 million objects and specimens from almost every branch of science, art, and history. The original Star-Spangled Banner is on display, as well as the famous Hope Diamond. Gowns of all the first ladies can be seen. Also on exhibit are the plane flown by Charles Lindbergh in the first nonstop solo flight across the Atlantic Ocean in 1927 and the command module that carried the first astronauts to the moon in 1969.

Bordering the National Mall in Washington, D.C., are the Smithsonian Institution Building (known as the Castle), the Hirshhorn Museum and Sculpture Garden, the Arts and Industries Building, the Freer Gallery of Art and Arthur M. Sackler Gallery, the National Museum of American History Behring Center, the National Museum of Natural History, the National Museum of African Art, the National Museum of the American Indian, and the National Air and Space Museum. A second air and space museum, the Steven F. Udvar-Hazy Center, is located at Washington Dulles International Airport outside the city.

Many additional attractions are located near the Mall, including the Smithsonian American Art Museum and Renwick Gallery and the National Portrait Gallery. The Anacostia Museum and Center for African American History and Culture is located in a historic section of southeast Washington. The National Zoological Park (National Zoo) is in Rock Creek Park. And the National Postal Museum is located downtown, near Union Station. The Cooper-Hewitt National Design Museum, in New York City, contains the country's largest collection of decorative arts.

Scientific Research Centers. The Smithsonian is the oldest professional scientific research organization in the United States. It has several research centers. The Archives of American Art in Washington, D.C., provides documentation on American artists since colonial times. The Smithsonian Astrophysical Observatory (SAO) in Cambridge, Massachusetts, conducts research in astrophysics. The Smithsonian Tropical Research Institute (STRI) conducts research in biology in Panama. The Smithsonian Environmental Research Center (SERC) on Chesapeake Bay conducts environmental studies.

The staff of each individual Smithsonian museum also carries out research in its own specialty areas. Large collections of specimens, artifacts, and documents are made available for use by the staff members and visiting scientists.

Outreach Programs and Publications. Smithsonian outreach programs include the Asian Pacific American Program, the Center for Education and Museum Studies, the Center for Folklife and Cultural Heritage, Latino Initiatives, the National Science Resources Center, Smithsonian TV, and the Smithsonian Associates. Smithsonian materials are also displayed at approximately 150 affiliated museums across the country.

The Smithsonian publishes many books, magazines, and catalogs related to the collections. The monthly *Smithsonian* magazine publishes articles on science, the arts, and history and on the results of special research studies the institution has conducted.

History. The Smithsonian was established with a gift from an English scientist, James Smithson (1765–1829). Smithson, as far as is known, never visited the United States. In his will, he left more than $500,000 "to found, at Washington under the name of the Smithsonian Institution, an Establishment for the increase and diffusion of knowledge among men." Congress accepted the gift in trust, and in 1846, President James K. Polk signed the legislation that founded the Smithsonian.

ALVIN ROSENFELD
Director, Office of Public Affairs
Smithsonian Institution

SMOG. See FOG AND SMOG.

Anti-smoking campaigns stress that smoking causes disease and poses a danger to nonsmokers. Campaigns aimed at young people try to lower the percentage of teenagers who smoke.

SMOKING

Smoking is the practice of inhaling tobacco from a pipe, cigar, or cigarette. The custom of smoking tobacco is thought to have started in the Americas. In the late 1400's, English and Spanish explorers returning from the New World brought back to Europe the custom of pipe smoking, which they had learned from the Indians. Cigarette smoking may have started among the Aztecs of Mexico, who smoked shredded tobacco rolled inside corn husks.

Until the 1900's tobacco was used mainly in cigars, chewing tobacco, and snuff. Later cigarette smoking became popular and increased sharply after World War I (1918) and again after World War II (1945).

In 1964 the United States Public Health Service released a landmark document, *Smoking and Health: Report of the Advisory Committee to the Surgeon General*, which concluded that smoking is a major cause of cancer of the lung, mouth, and throat. Since then, researchers have shown that each year cigarette smoking causes more than 300,000 premature deaths in the United States alone. These deaths are principally from heart disease, cancer, and chronic (long-lasting) obstructive lung disease, such as emphysema.

In 1965, Congress adopted legislation requiring that all cigarette packages carry a warning about the health hazards of smoking. Today, four different warning labels are placed on cigarette packages and advertisements: (1) Smoking by Pregnant Women May Result in Fetal Injury, Premature Birth, and Low Birth Weight; (2) Cigarette Smoke Contains Carbon Monoxide; (3) Smoking Causes Lung Cancer, Heart Disease, Emphysema, and May Complicate Pregnancy; and (4) Quitting Smoking Now Greatly Reduces Serious Risks to Your Health. Cigarette advertisements on radio and television have been banned since 1970.

Tobacco smoke also affects nonsmokers ("passive" or "involuntary" smoking). The 1986 Surgeon General's Report, *The Health Consequences of Involuntary Smoking*, came to three major conclusions: (1) Involuntary smoking is a cause of disease, including lung cancer, in healthy nonsmokers; (2) The children of parents who smoke have more respiratory infections, such as pneumonia and bronchitis, than the children of nonsmokers; (3) The separation of smokers and nonsmokers may reduce, but does not eliminate, the exposure of nonsmokers to environmental tobacco smoke. These findings support the recent trend toward restricting or banning smoking in public places and in the workplace. In addition, individuals and various organizations, including state governments, have taken legal action against tobacco companies to recover some of the staggering health-care costs related to smoking.

Campaigns aimed at educating the public about the health hazards of smoking have been very successful. Studies show that 90 percent of the U.S. adult population now recognizes that cigarette smoking causes lung cancer, heart disease, and emphysema. Unfortunately, statistics show that teenagers are still attracted to smoking. Each day, almost 3,000 teens become regular smokers.

It is critical that people recognize the dangers of smoking before they consider taking up the habit. Smoking causes smoker's cough, a lower capacity for exercise, addiction to nicotine, and, in the long run, severe disability and death.

C. EVERETT KOOP, M.D.
Former Surgeon General
United States Public Health Service

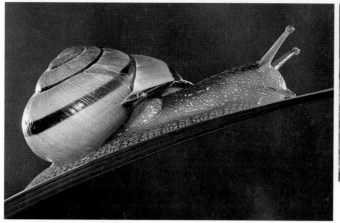

Snails and slugs live on land and in water. *Left:* Land snails are found in many parts of the world. *Above:* Saltwater slugs often have exotic coloration.

SNAILS AND SLUGS

Snails and slugs are gastropods (from Greek words meaning "stomach-feet"). They belong to a group of invertebrates (animals with no backbone) called mollusks, which also includes clams, mussels, squids, and other animals. There are about 100,000 species of gastropods, making them the largest group of mollusks.

Characteristics of Snails and Slugs. The body of a typical snail consists of a head, a foot, and a visceral hump. The mouth, eyes, and tentacles are located on the head. Behind the head is the foot, on which the snail glides along by muscular contractions. Above the foot is the visceral hump, which contains most of the inner organs. The visceral hump is covered by a skin-like tissue called the mantle, and the mantle is covered by the shell. The shell is usually shaped in a spiral coil, but it can also be shaped like a deep dish or a flat plate.

Slugs are snails that lack a shell. A slug's internal organs are in its foot, which is covered by a shield-shaped mantle.

Snails and slugs have a varied diet. Some species feed on live and decaying plants. Other species feed on living animals.

Gastropods can be male or female, or one individual can possess both male and female reproductive organs. Most gastropods lay eggs from which larvae or fully formed young hatch. Others give birth to live young.

The smallest gastropod, *Ammonicera japonica*, has a shell diameter of only about 0.014 inch (0.35 millimeter). The largest, the Australian trumpet snail, can reach about 30 inches (76 centimeters) in length.

Terrestrial and Aquatic Snails and Slugs. Terrestrial gastropods live on land. The garden snail, which lives in Europe, North America, and many other parts of the world, has a round shell mottled with a variable pattern in brown, gray, and yellow. Several snail species live in the trees of tropical and subtropical areas around the world. Their shells are often brightly colored or striped. There are many species of terrestrial slugs.

Other snails and slugs are aquatic, meaning they live in fresh or salt water. Freshwater gastropods are most abundant in stagnant and slow-moving bodies of water that are rich in vegetation. Their shells occur in many different shapes and colors. Some species use gills to obtain oxygen from the water, while other species have lungs and breathe air at the water's surface.

Saltwater gastropods come in many shapes and sizes. Conchs have small to very large and heavy shells with a large opening. Cowries have egg-shaped, glossy shells with beautiful color patterns and a narrow, slit-like opening. Whelks have oval or tower-like shells, often with knobs, folds, or spiral ridges. Numerous kinds of slugs live in marine habitats, and many are very colorful.

Snails and Slugs and Their Environment. Some gastropods damage gardens and crops, while others are intermediate hosts for parasites that cause serious diseases in humans and cattle. But gastropods also play a vital role in their habitats. They are an important food for other animals, such as fish and birds, and many species are eaten by people.

JOCHEN GERBER
Division of Invertebrates
Field Museum of Natural History

SNAKES

Snakes are reptiles. Like other reptiles, they have scales and cannot regulate their body temperatures from within. But the most distinctive feature of snakes is their shape. Their bodies are long tubes and they have no legs.

More than 2,900 species of snakes have been identified. Snakes inhabit nearly all parts of the planet and are found both in the water and on land. The greatest numbers are found in the tropics, but many snakes are native to temperate zone regions. Some have even been found living above the Arctic Circle. No snakes are native to Ireland or the Hawaiian Islands.

▶ CHARACTERISTICS OF SNAKES

Snakes are **ectotherms**, which means their body temperatures vary depending on the environment. A snake spends much of its time seeking conditions that help it maintain a comfortable body temperature. Many terrestrial snakes raise their body temperatures by basking in the sun; they lower their body temperatures by moving into shade or going underground. Desert snakes are generally nocturnal (active at night). They stay cool during the day by remaining underground, and they elevate their body temperatures at night by making contact with warm sand or rocks. Aquatic snakes bask on tree limbs or shoreline to raise their body temperatures above that of the water.

Snakes' closest relatives are lizards. Although the two groups share many traits, snakes have some distinguishing characteristics. Snakes do not have functional limbs, but this trait alone is not enough to distinguish them because some lizards have no legs or have legs that are too small to be detected easily. Snakes are carnivores (meat eaters). They eat only other animals and their eggs, while some lizards eat plants. Snakes also have fixed, clear eyelids rather than moveable eyelids. Most snakes have only one lung, and their other body organs, including the liver, heart, and kidneys, are quite elongated. Also, snakes shed their scaly skin all at once, leaving a hollow skin that is an exact inverted copy of the body surface. Some lizards have one or more of these traits, but none have all of them.

To ward off its enemies, a cobra tries to appear bigger than it is. It displays a threatening posture by rising up and flaring its hood.

Most **herpetologists** (scientists who study reptiles) believe that snakes evolved from lizardlike ancestors that gradually lost their limbs after developing burrowing habits. The oldest known fossils of snakes are 100 to 125 million years old.

Snakes have more vertebrae than other animals. This greatly increases their flexibility and allows them to move in ways that other animals cannot. Although no snakes have any sign of the forelimbs, some species, including tiny blind snakes and giant pythons, have an undeveloped pelvic girdle (the bony arch of the skeleton that supports the hind limbs), and a few have external rear appendages that are too small to function as legs. The appendages may be used by males in courtship.

Locomotion

Snakes must use special techniques for movement because they have no limbs. At least six methods of snake locomotion have been described. The most common form of movement is **lateral undulation**. The snake

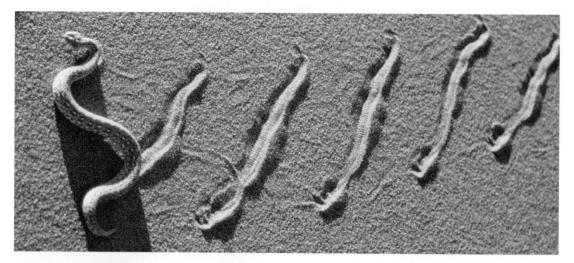

Snakes use different methods of locomotion depending on the surface over which they are moving. An adder uses sidewinding to move across the loose desert sands (*above*). A black rat snake climbs straight up a tall tree using rectilinear locomotion *(left)*.

presses different points of its body against fixed points in the environment, such as rocks on the ground or the branches of a tree, and its longitudinal muscles (those running lengthwise along the body) contract alternately. This causes the snake to move forward in an S-shaped motion.

Slide-pushing also involves alternate contraction of the body muscles. Snakes use slide-pushing on low-friction surfaces, such as those that are smooth or slippery. They may appear to be thrashing helplessly but, in fact, are moving forward at a slow pace.

Snakes use **concertina locomotion** to move vertically or horizontally on surfaces where lateral undulation would not be effective. Vipers and boas use concertina locomotion to move up trees or other straight objects such as bamboo. The snake curls its tail and lower body around the trunk of a tree and then stretches the front of its body upward, hooking its neck around the tree at a higher point. After getting a firm grip with its neck and forebody, the snake releases its tail and pulls its lower body up. The process is repeated and the snake slowly ascends.

Sidewinding is used as the main method of locomotion by a few species. The snake presses its rear end against the ground and lifts its front portion to one side so that its head lands several inches away from its tail. In doing so, its midbody lifts from the ground and is moved forward. Sidewinding is highly effective for the Saharan Desert horned viper and the sidewinder of the American Southwest. These snakes must move across loose, fine-grained desert sands, where lateral undulation is difficult.

Boas, pythons, and some vipers use **rectilinear locomotion** as their primary form of movement. To move forward in a straight line, the snake contracts muscles on both sides of its body and uses its belly scales as anchor points. Rat snakes can climb straight up a brick wall using rectilinear locomotion.

One type of African viper moves with a jumping movement called **saltatorial locomo-**

tion. The snake straightens its body rapidly from front to rear. This causes its entire body to lift from the ground and move forward.

Snakes show great agility in a variety of situations and are sometimes perceived to move rapidly over the ground. However, the maximum speed of even the fastest snakes, such as coachwhips and mambas, is less than 10 miles (16 kilometers) per hour.

Snake Teeth and Jaws

Some snakes have highly specialized teeth. For example, the slug-eating snakes of tropical America have elongated front teeth that are used to extract live snails from their shells. Vipers and pit vipers have movable, hollow, open-ended fangs located on the front of the upper jaw. When a pit viper closes its mouth, the fangs fold neatly inside, as if on a hinge. Cobras and sea snakes have grooved fangs that are fixed on the front of the upper jaw. When these snakes close their mouths, the fangs slip into a slot in the lower jaw. Snakes such as the African vine snake have grooved teeth in the rear of the upper jaw. The grooves allow the passage of venom or saliva. But because their teeth do not

transfer venom rapidly into the bloodstream of another organism, rear-fanged snakes must hold their victims in their mouths for long periods to introduce the venom. Nonvenomous snakes without specialized teeth are said to be **aglyphous**.

Snakes swallow their prey whole, without chewing, and have powerful digestive systems that can dissolve bones and other body parts. Some snakes eat animals that are very large relative to their own size. A snake's jaws are designed to fit prey larger than its head. The snake's lower jaw is divided in two. The two halves are connected by flexible ligaments that allow each side to operate independently. The connection between the upper and lower jaws is made of pressure-resistant bones that allow the jaw to stretch when a large food item passes through. After a big meal, many snakes can go for weeks or months without consuming any food, although they require water more frequently.

Snake Diets

Snakes feed on almost every type of land and freshwater animal and some marine species as well. Some snakes have very special-

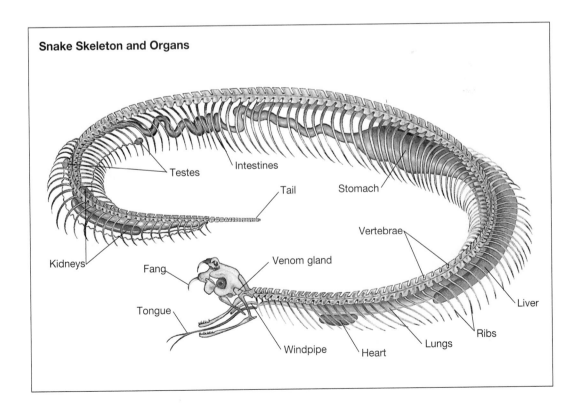

Snake Skeleton and Organs

Testes · Intestines · Tail · Stomach · Vertebrae · Kidneys · Fang · Venom gland · Liver · Tongue · Windpipe · Heart · Lungs · Ribs

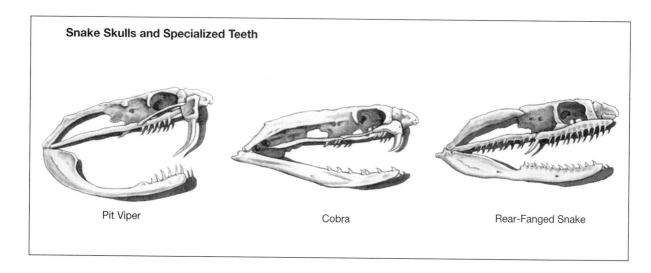

Snake Skulls and Specialized Teeth

Pit Viper

Cobra

Rear-Fanged Snake

ized diets and eat only a single type of prey. Sea snakes, for example, eat mainly moray eels. Adult mud snakes of North America eat only giant southeastern salamanders. Blind snakes eat only termites, some North American black-headed snakes eat primarily centipedes, and pine snakes, bull snakes, and large rattlesnakes eat mostly small mammals and some birds.

Other snakes, such as racers and copperheads, eat diverse diets made up of insects, amphibians, reptiles, birds, and mammals. Some snakes even eat other snakes. The king snake will attack and eat venomous species such as rattlesnakes. It is immune to their venom. Cottonmouths and racers are cannibalistic and will eat smaller individuals of their own species.

Snakes' diets often change as they develop from juveniles to adults. For example, some rat snakes eat primarily lizards as juveniles, but they eat mammals and birds as adults.

Hunting and Capturing Prey

Snakes use many different techniques to find and overpower their prey. Rattlesnakes and other large species sit and wait in a concealed position for a meal to come along. A rattler may coil beside a path used by small mammals. If necessary, it will wait for days for an opportunity to strike and kill a passing rabbit or rat.

Some snakes actively seek their prey. This is known as wide-ranging foraging. A gopher snake may enter a small mammal burrow looking for a meal, and a red-bellied water snake may search for frogs along a river bank.

Other snakes lure prey to them. Young copperheads and Australian death adders wiggle their yellow-tipped tails in imitation of a worm. A small lizard or frog, thinking a meal is available, will come close enough to be captured by the snake.

Snakes use two main approaches for killing their prey—constriction and poisoning with venom. Constrictors squeeze their prey very tightly by coiling their body around it. This kills the animal by suffocation, not by crushing bones or body parts. The tightly wrapped coils exert constant pressure so that each time the victim exhales,

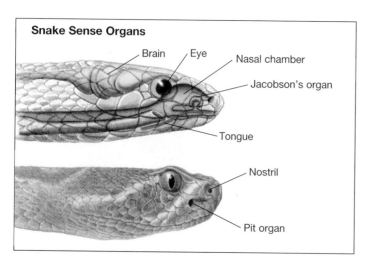

Snake Sense Organs

Brain

Eye

Nasal chamber

Jacobson's organ

Tongue

Nostril

Pit organ

the coils squeeze tighter. The squeezing prevents the animal from inhaling and restricts the flow of blood. Constrictors are found worldwide. They range in size from 30-foot (9-meter) pythons and anacondas to 1-foot (30-centimeter) scarlet king snakes.

Other snakes use venom to obtain their prey. Some venomous snakes grab their victims and hold on to them while injecting them with venom. Others, such as rattlesnakes, may bite a rat or rabbit that then runs for many feet before collapsing. To eat its prey, the snake must track the animal's trail through the forest.

Some venoms are extremely powerful. Large pit vipers and members of the cobra family can deliver a bite that will kill a rat or mouse in a few seconds. The qualities of venom are specific to particular species or groups of snakes. Different venoms affect prey in different ways.

Snake Senses

Snakes use several well-developed senses to gather information about their environment. Although they have no external ears or ear openings and cannot hear airborne sounds, some snakes seem to be highly sensitive to vibrations transmitted on the ground or through water. The details of this sense are not well understood for most species.

Snakes' eyes never close. Each eye is covered by a fixed, transparent scale instead of a moveable eyelid. This gives even a sleeping snake the appearance of being alert. Snakes that live in the trees or on the ground have good vision. Snakes, such as blind snakes, that spend most of their lives underground have undeveloped eyes and no functional vision.

Snakes use their forked tongues to detect airborne smells and to pick up chemical molecules from surfaces. The tongue tips are touched to a sense organ known as the **Jacobson's organ** in the roof of the mouth. Using its forked tongue and Jacobson's organ, the snake can identify pheromones and other chemical cues and use them to determine another animal's direction of travel. This is how rattlesnakes find prey that have run long distances after being bitten. Male snakes of many species use this sense to follow a female's trail in the correct direction.

Some snakes, including pit vipers and some boas and pythons, have developed a sense

Snakes swallow their prey whole, and some snakes eat meals that are very large relative to their own size. Their jaws are specially designed for this task. Here, an egg-eater snake's jaws expand over an egg that is larger than its head (*top*). The snake slowly moves the egg farther into its mouth (*middle*). When the egg is completely swallowed (*bottom*), muscles in the snake's neck will contract, and spines on its vertebrae will pierce the egg. The contents of the egg will be swallowed and the shell spit out.

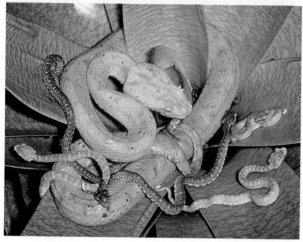

Most snakes, such as gopher snakes (*left*), hatch from eggs. But some snakes, such as vipers (*below left*), garter snakes, and others, give birth to live young.

as **shivering**. Similarly, some pit vipers remain with their newborn young for several days after birth. This may be a form of protection for the babies.

Snakes that live in temperate zones are usually hatched or born in the late summer or early autumn. The young snakes attempt to feed before cold weather sets in. During winter, snakes remain dormant throughout most of North America. In the colder mountainous or high-latitude regions, snakes will often migrate to underground communal dens for the winter.

Snakes grow steadily during the warm periods of their first year, as long as food is available. Some species take two or more years to reach maturity. Most species of snakes mate in the spring, although a few species are known to mate in the fall.

In many snake species, one sex is significantly larger than the other. Among species in which males are larger, male combat takes place during the mating season. Combat varies among species but usually consists of the two snakes raising the front halves of their bodies and trying to push each other over. The battle resembles an arm wrestling match. The loser typically crawls away, leaving the winner to mate with the female.

Snakes are one of the most poorly studied of the major groups of animals. The life histories, basic reproductive cycles, and environmental interactions of a few snake species have been investigated, but such information is minimal for most species.

▶ SPECIFIC TYPES OF SNAKES

Herpetologists recognize 15 to 18 different families of snakes. Snakes are grouped into families based mostly on the structures of their skulls and teeth. Modern genetic techniques have clarified some relationships among snakes.

Most snakes belong to the largest family, Colubridae, which is made up of more than 1,700 species. This family contains many common harmless snakes, such as garter snakes, which are aglyphous. But it also contains a number of venomous rear-fanged species. The boomslang and African vine snake are

unknown in other animals. These snakes can detect very small differences or changes in infrared radiation (heat). To do this they use facial pits located either between the eye and nostril (pit vipers) or on the lips (boas and pythons). This sense is both sensitive and directional. It allows a snake to locate potential prey in total darkness by detecting its body heat.

Mating and Life Cycle

Snakes differ in the way they produce offspring. Most snakes lay eggs, but some give birth to live young. Snakes that lay eggs are said to be **oviparous**. Those that produce live young are called **viviparous**.

A few species of snakes exhibit parental care. For example, large female pythons coil around their eggs and incubate them by generating body heat through a process known

SNAKE SAFETY

What should you do if you find a snake? What should you do if you are bitten?

Bites from venomous snakes can be serious, but lethal bites from snakes are rare in North America. About 8,000 people are bitten by venomous snakes in the United States each year and less than 20 die. In comparison, more than 200,000 venomous snakebites occur annually in India. About 20,000 of these are fatal.

In the United States there are four main types of venomous snakes—rattlesnakes, copperheads, cottonmouths (also called water moccasins), and coral snakes. Rattlesnakes, copperheads, and cottonmouths are pit vipers. They are widely distributed throughout the United States. Coral snakes belong to the cobra family and are found mainly in the southern states. Except for Maine, Alaska, and Hawaii, all states have at least one venomous snake species. But venomous snakes make up fewer than 20 percent of the snake species found in the United States. Therefore, it is relatively unlikely that a snake you encounter in the wild is venomous.

If you spend time hiking, camping, or picnicking in wilderness or snake-inhabited areas, it is a good idea to be cautious. Wear heavy boots in tall grass and keep to well traveled, clearly marked paths as much as possible. Do not put your hands into any hidden opening where snakes could be present. Although most snakes that you encounter will not be venomous, it may be difficult to identify some snakes. Therefore, if you find a snake, the safest approach is to move away. Many snakebites result from someone trying to pick up or kill a snake.

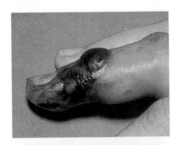

Venomous snakebites can cause swelling and infection of the tissue surrounding the bite (*top*). Serious bites must be treated with antivenin. Venom collected from snakes by the process of milking (*above*) is injected into horses or other animals to produce antibodies for use in antivenin.

A person's first priority if bitten by a snake should be to get to an emergency treatment facility quickly. The bite victim should avoid excessive activity, however, as increasing the heart rate could cause the venom to spread more rapidly. Some authorities suggest applying suction immediately to the puncture holes made by the fangs to remove some of the venom. A device called a venom extractor is sold for this purpose. If possible, the bitten extremity should be immobilized in a position lower than the heart.

First aid treatments such as incisions, tourniquets, and chilling the limb for long periods are not recommended. Although special first aid treatments are effective in some situations and regions of the world, in the United States the best option is to seek professional treatment immediately. If you are traveling to a region of the world in which venomous snakes are common, learn more about the special precautions you should take.

If a snakebite is serious, a doctor may administer **antivenin** (also called antivenom), which acts to neutralize the venom. Most antivenin is produced by injecting horses with small amounts of venom that has been collected from snakes through the process of "milking." The natural antibodies produced by the horses in response to the venom are collected. Not everyone can be given antivenin made in this way. People who are allergic to horses can have severe allergic reactions. In 2000, the Food and Drug Administration approved a new kind of antivenin derived from sheep. This antivenin is not yet in wide use but is believed to be less allergenic.

The red, black, and gold coloring of the nonvenomous scarlet king snake (*above left*) mimics the bright coloring of the more dangerous coral snake (*above right*).

capable of delivering a lethal bite to a human.

Colubrids are found throughout the world, except Antarctica, New Zealand, and some Pacific Islands. They live in a variety of habitats—in the trees, on land, in the water, and underground. Colubrids have belly scales as wide as their bodies. Some snakes in this family lay eggs, while others give birth to live young.

Most colubrids are not classified any further, but several subfamilies are recognized. One subfamily includes almost 200 species of water snakes, garter snakes, and their close relatives. Another subfamily includes the colorful mud and rainbow snakes, hognose snakes, and the extraordinarily slender vine snakes of tropical America.

The viper family (Viperidae) contains more than 200 species of snakes. It is made up of vipers and pit vipers. Vipers include adders, Russell's viper—a major cause of snakebite in India and Myanmar—and the African Gaboon viper, which has fangs over 2 inches (5 centimeters) long. Pit vipers are named for the deep pit found between the

eye and the nostril on each side of the head. They include the rattlesnakes, cottonmouths, and copperheads of North America; the fer-de-lance and related species of Central and South America; and the lance-headed vipers of Southeast Asia.

Members of the viper family are found worldwide except for Australia and the eastern Pacific Islands. These snakes have heavy bodies and hollow fangs that fold inside when the mouth is closed. Many of these snakes produce powerful venom, and the snakes in this family are often considered quite dangerous. However, some deliver relatively mild bites, and many bites to humans are provoked by unnecessary harassment of the snake.

More than 280 species of snakes belong to the cobra family (Elapidae), including mambas, coral snakes, and sea snakes. The venom of cobras and other snakes in this family is **neurotoxic** (poisonous to the nervous system). It can paralyze the nerves of the respiratory system, causing the bite victim to stop breathing.

Many species in the cobra family are native to Africa, Asia, and Australia. The king cobra, which can reach lengths of 18 feet (5.5 meters), is the largest venomous snake in the world. The hiss of a king cobra sounds like a

The Western diamondback rattlesnake gives a warning signal that it is going to strike by shaking the rattle on its tail.

Some sea snakes live permanently in the sea. Although they can hold their breath for long periods of time, sea snakes must eventually come to the surface to breathe.

The giant constrictors—boas and pythons—belong to the family Boiidae, which includes more than 60 species. Most are found in the tropics; however, the rosy boa and rubber boa live in temperate climates. Boa constrictors, anacondas, and some pythons are among the largest snakes in the world. But other members of the family, such as the African sand boas, are very small. Members of this family kill their prey by constriction. Some boas and pythons look very similar, but an important difference is that boas give birth to live young, and pythons lay eggs.

Most of the remaining snake families contain only a few species. The blind snakes are an exception. More than 300 species of blind snakes are contained within three families. These snakes are small burrowers with primitive characteristics.

▶ PREDATORS OF SNAKES

Snakes can become prey to a variety of predators. Carnivorous mammals, raptors and other birds, alligators and crocodiles, large fish, bullfrogs, and spiders will eat snakes. Juvenile snakes are especially susceptible to enemies. Some snakes use venom to defend against predators. Pit vipers, true vipers, and cobras are well known for using venom to defend against humans. Nonvenomous species use other means of defense against enemies. They escape into the water or into holes in the ground. Some snakes may try to scare off a predator by hissing or expanding the neck and head region. Many species of snakes

growling dog. Black mambas are among the most dangerous snakes in the world because of their large size, fast movement, and potent venom. The taipan of northern Australia has one of the most poisonous venoms known.

The 60 species of sea snakes reach lengths of 3 to 6 feet (1 to 2 meters). They have highly toxic venom, but humans are seldom bitten. Some sea snakes have paddle-shaped tails. Their nostrils are located on top of the snout and can be closed with a valve. Some live permanently in the sea. The largest group of snakes ever reported was a solidly packed line of millions of sea snakes in the Pacific Ocean. The line was 10 feet (3 meters) wide and 50 miles (80.5 kilometers) long.

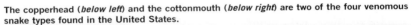

The copperhead (*below left*) and the cottonmouth (*below right*) are two of the four venomous snake types found in the United States.

defecate and release foul-smelling glandular secretions when captured. Often snakes simply try to hide from their enemies.

▶ SNAKE CONSERVATION

Snakes in many regions of the world are in danger. Habitat loss, environmental pollution, and overhunting all contribute to decreased numbers of snakes. In the United States the eastern indigo snake, the San Francisco garter snake, and the copperbelly water snake of the Midwest are protected under the U.S. Endangered Species Act. One of the most dramatic and unexplained declines of a snake population in the United States is that of the southern hognose snake, which has not been observed in most of its former range in the Southeast for more than a decade. In other parts of the world, populations of several boa and python species have declined due to the harvesting of wild snakes for their skins. And some species of snakes may have been over-collected for the pet trade. Changes in public attitudes toward snakes and stricter environmental laws to protect them will be necessary to ensure the continued existence of the many species making up this fascinating group of animals.

J. WHITFIELD GIBBONS
Professor of Ecology, University of Georgia and
Savannah River Ecology Laboratory

See also LIZARDS; REPTILES.

SNEAD, SAM. See GOLF (Great Players).
SNOW. See RAIN, SNOW, SLEET, AND HAIL.

SNOWBOARDING

Snowboarding is a winter sport that resembles skateboarding or surfing done on snow. The rider stands on a single wide board and slides down a snow-covered slope. Snowboarding is enjoyed worldwide as a recreational pastime and a competitive sport.

Snowboards come in many shapes and sizes. The length and width depend on how the snowboard will be used, as well as on the rider's height, weight, and foot size. Snowboards are usually made of wood coated with a tough, durable plastic. They have metal edges to help the rider turn. The rider wears special boots that are secured to the board with plastic or metal bindings.

Recreational snowboarding is usually done on the same slopes used for skiing or at special parks. These parks usually include a halfpipe—a U-shaped trench dug in the snow; snowboarders slide up and down the sides and perform flips and other tricks while in the air.

The two basic forms of competitive snowboarding are Alpine and freestyle. In Alpine snowboarding, snowboarders race downhill around gates marked by flags in the snow. Freestyle snowboarding includes the halfpipe and other courses that challenge the snowboarders' skill.

Many international snowboarding competitions are held each year, including the U.S. Open, the Grand Prix, and the World Cham-

Snowboarding is a very popular winter sport. Skilled snowboarders often perform acrobatic maneuvers high in the air.

pionships. Snowboarding became an official Olympic sport at the 1998 Winter Games.

Snowboarding has its origins in a toy invented in 1965 by Sherman Poppen of Michigan. He bound two skis together and attached a rope to the front for the rider to hold while sliding down a hill. By the 1970's the toy had evolved into a single board with no handle, and it had become widely popular. Very few ski areas permitted snowboarding during the 1980's, but that changed as snowboarding became the fastest-growing sport in the late 1990's and early 2000's.

SCOTT FLANDERS
Consultant, U.S. Ski and Snowboard Association

SNOWMOBILES

Snowmobiles, or motorized sleds, were an important development in winter travel and recreation. Before these vehicles became available, snow made it impossible to reach some places except by dogsled or snowshoes. Now snowmobiles can reach areas where other vehicles cannot go.

Snowmobiles are used to deliver mail, rescue people, and provide emergency medical help. Ranchers, hunters, and trappers sometimes use snowmobiles. Snowmobiles are also used for recreation and for racing.

Some people say that snowmobiles are noisy and that they do damage to the environment. For this reason, snowmobile clubs have set rules for the correct and safe use of snowmobiles. In some areas laws cover their use.

Snowmobiles can speed over the top of deep snow because they have two steel runners, like skis, mounted in the front. The vehicle is propelled by a wide tread, or track, that pushes against the snow. Drivers steer snowmobiles with handlebars and by leaning their bodies to the left or right. Snowmobiles

Snowmobilers wear heavy, warm clothing. Protective helmets and seat belts are required by law in many areas.

can go about 50 miles (80 kilometers) an hour. Racing models may go more than 90 miles (145 kilometers) an hour.

In 1930, Joseph-Armand Bombardier, a Canadian, patented the first snowmobile operated by traction. But his vehicles were big and heavy and were difficult to maneuver. A light snowmobile that could be driven easily was first developed in 1958. Snowmobiles then grew rapidly in popularity.

Reviewed by EDWARD RADLAUER
Author, *Snowmobiles*

SOAP. See DETERGENTS AND SOAP.

SOAP BOX DERBY

Each year thousands of competitors between the ages of 10 and 15 enter a race for motorless coaster cars known as the Soap Box Derby. The competitors come from the United States, Canada, and other countries.

The competition begins with local races, which are held in many cities. Boys and girls 10 to 12 years old race in the junior class. Those 12 to 15 race in the senior class. Winners of the local races represent their cities in the All-American Soap Box Derby, as the world championship race is called.

About 200 local winners go to Akron, Ohio, in early August for the world championship. On race day three competitors at a time speed their cars down the track, which is 953.75 feet (290.7 meters) long. Cars must start from a standstill on a special inclined ramp. Pushing the car to start it is not allowed. Senior champions win college scholarships, while junior champions win other prizes. There are also awards for car construction and design.

The official rule book has instructions and designs to help car builders. Derby rules set limits on car size and weight. Each car must have an official set of wheels, and—for safe stopping—a single drag brake. Car bodies are mostly made of wood. The young person who races the car must do most of the building, but some adult help with power tools and paint is permitted.

The All-American Soap Box Derby was first run in 1934. It is sponsored by clubs and businesses in Akron. Many companies also sponsor cars for the races.

Reviewed by EDWARD RADLAUER
Author, *Soap Box Winners*

Competitors in the Soap Box Derby must build their own cars following the official rules for size and weight.

SOCCER

Soccer may be the world's most popular sport. It is played by more than 150 million people in more than 178 countries, and it is estimated that more than 2 billion people now follow the World Cup competition.

Even though no one really knows when the game of soccer was first played, some sort of recreation that involved the kicking and chasing of a round object has existed throughout history. Historians think that soccerlike games were played in ancient Greece, Rome, Egypt, and China.

Modern soccer began in England, where the first set of rules was published in 1863 by the London Football Association. This gave the sport a clearly defined set of standards and a name: association football. Somehow, the word soccer was derived from "assoc.," a short form of "association."

Soccer developed very quickly in England, and by 1888 the first professional league had been created. English travelers and settlers spread the game throughout the world. The English spread soccer worldwide, but people in different countries adopted new and different ways to play the game. Today, there are various styles of play depending upon the nation or culture in which the game is played.

There are also different names for soccer in other languages—*fútbol* in Spanish, *calcio* in Italian, *fussball* in German, and so on. Even though there are many names for soccer, it is played with the same rules around the world, often before huge crowds.

Soccer is both a recreational and a competitive sport. Competitive soccer is played on every level—from a junior team of 6-year-olds through high school and college and up to club, professional, and national teams.

Often a player will need to head the ball to keep it from a defender or to pass it to a teammate moving toward the opposing team's goal.

▶ SOCCER IN THE UNITED STATES

There are professional soccer leagues in most countries, including the United States. Soccer has been played in the United States in one form or another for more than 100 years. It is rapidly increasing in popularity, but it is only just becoming one of the major sports.

In 1913 the United States Soccer Federation (USSF) joined the International Federation of Association Football, or FIFA, from its French name, headquartered in Zurich, Switzerland. FIFA now has more members than the United Nations, indicating the worldwide following of the sport. The United States Soccer Federation, which is headquartered in Chicago, Illinois, is responsible for regulating all soccer programs in the United States.

In the United States, soccer's popularity began to grow tremendously in the late 1960's, as many more schools and colleges started to play the game. Soon after the North American Soccer League (NASL) was founded in 1967, soccer became a popular spectator sport. It became even more popular in 1975 when the New York Cosmos hired the Brazilian who was considered the game's best player, Edson Arantes do Nascimento, better known as Pelé. (For more information about him, see the article PELÉ in Volume P.)

The North American Soccer League ceased operations in 1985. However, professional soccer continues in the United States. For men, the top outdoor league is Major League Soccer. There are also indoor leagues, such as the Major Indoor Soccer League

(MISL) and the World Indoor Soccer League (WISL). Women's professional soccer is represented in the United States by the W-League and the Women's United Soccer Association (WUSA). For information about soccer for children, see the feature Youth Soccer accompanying this article.

Growth in Participation

Soccer is one of the fastest-growing participation sports in the United States. The number of people playing soccer grew from about 500,000 in 1973 to more than 17 million in 2002. Twelve million of those players were under the age of 18.

Soccer is expected to continue its rapid growth in the United States. Where money is scarce for school athletic programs, the low cost of fielding a soccer team also makes it a good choice—only shorts, shirts, shoes, shin guards, and a ball and a playing field need to be provided.

▶ THE PLAYERS AND THE FIELD

A soccer team consists of eleven players. There is one goalkeeper and ten other players used as forwards, midfielders, and defenders. The forwards are usually the goal scorers. The defenders try to stop the opposing team from scoring. The midfielders coordinate play between the forwards and defenders. For example, when the defenders get the ball from the opposing team, they often pass the ball to the midfielders, who start the offensive attack.

Other terms besides defender, midfielder, and forward are used to denote players' positions. Defenders are also called fullbacks or backs. Defenders may also be called sweepers or stoppers. Sweepers are the last line of defense before the goalkeeper. Stoppers play just in front of the sweepers. Goalkeepers try to prevent goals from being scored by stopping shots or taking the ball away from opposing players. They can sometimes start an attack by kicking or throwing the ball to a teammate. Midfielders are also called halfbacks or, sometimes, linkmen because they link the defense with the offense. Forwards are also called strikers because they strike for the goal. The central striker is also called the targetman, and the other forwards may be called wingers, since they form the outside wings of the attack.

In the past, certain players who played between the midfielders and the forwards were

8 FT.

24 FT.

SOCCER BALL   SOCCER GOAL

PLAYER'S POSITIONS	
RF Right forward	ORD Outside (right) defender
LF Left forward	ST Stopper (central defender)
ORM Outside (right) midfielder	SW Sweeper (central defender)
OM Offensive midfielder	OLD Outside (left) defender
DM Defensive midfielder	G Goalkeeper
OLM Outside (left) midfielder	

Soccer Field and Players' Positions

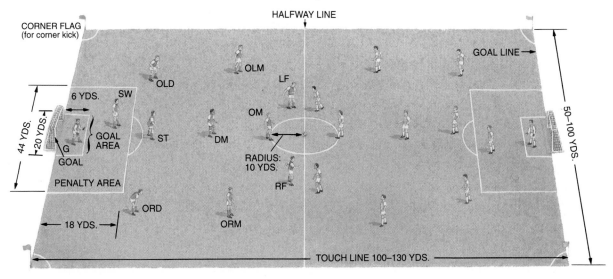

HALFWAY LINE

CORNER FLAG
(for corner kick)

GOAL LINE →

OLM

OLD

LF

6 YDS.   SW

OM

44 YDS.   20 YDS.

ST   DM

GOAL AREA

G

GOAL

RADIUS: 10 YDS.

50–100 YDS.

PENALTY AREA

RF

18 YDS.   ORD

ORM

TOUCH LINE 100–130 YDS.

Deep concentration is needed by players trying to dribble the ball downfield or keep it from being kicked away by a defender.

called inside players. In recent years, as formations have changed, the inside players have moved either forward or backward to become strikers or midfielders.

Players wear cleated, not spiked, shoes with knee-length socks, shorts, and either long- or short-sleeved shirts. All players should also wear shin guards.

Soccer is played with a round ball covered with leather. It must be from 27 to 28 inches (69 to 71 centimeters) in circumference and must weigh from 14 to 16 ounces (397 to 454 grams). The circumference of the ball used in youth soccer is 25 inches (64 centimeters).

The Field

The soccer field is typically from 100 to 130 yards (90 to 120 meters) long and from 50 to 100 yards (46 to 90 meters) wide. Fields used in international matches have slightly different dimensions.

The boundary lines on the long side of the field are called touch lines. Those on the short sides are called goal lines.

The goals stand in the center of the goal lines. Each goal consists of two wooden or metal posts 24 feet (7.3 meters) apart, joined at the top by a crossbar that is 8 feet (2.4 meters) above the ground. A net is usually attached to the back of the goal. The net is helpful because it stops the ball when it goes in the goal. In this way everyone can be sure that the ball has passed between the two posts and under the crossbar to score a goal.

The goal area is a rectangle in front of each goal. It is 20 yards (18 meters) wide and extends 6 yards (5.5 meters) in front of the goal. The goalkeeper cannot be charged in the goal area by an opponent.

The penalty area is 44 yards (40 meters) wide and extends 18 yards (16.5 meters) in front of the goal. The penalty area is important because defenders are seriously penalized if they break certain rules in that area. In such cases, a member of the offensive team gets a kick from the penalty spot 12 yards (11 meters) in front of the goal. Only the goalkeeper can attempt to block the kick.

▶ **HOW THE GAME IS PLAYED**

Before a game starts, the team captains flip a coin to decide which team will kick off. They also choose the goals their teams will defend. The teams change goals at the beginning of the second half. The team that did not kick off to start the game kicks off for the second half.

Teams kick off from the center spot, a point in the middle of the halfway line. Players line up on their own half of the field with three players on the kicking team usually standing close to the ball. Opponents must be at least 10 yards (9 meters) away from the ball. One of the attackers kicks the ball forward to a teammate to start. After each goal, play resumes with a kickoff. The team that is scored against kicks off.

As in basketball or hockey, the object is to score points by putting the ball into the opposing team's goal while preventing the opposing team from scoring. When a player gets the ball into the opposing team's goal, either by kicking it or hitting it with another legal part of the body, the player scores a goal that counts one point. In international, professional, and collegiate play, the game consists of two 45- minute halves with an intermission no more than 15 minutes long. Youth soccer games are shorter, usually two 30- to 40-minute halves. The game is won by the team that scores the most points.

Offensive play tries to advance the ball into opposition territory through team play. This is done by passing the ball from player to player while keeping it from defenders. When in a position to do so, a player kicks or **heads** the ball (hits the ball with the head) in the direction of the opponent's goal. Defensive players try to clear the ball from their area by intercepting passes and by using other legal methods to stop the team trying to score.

The offensive team's aim is simply to put a player with time and room to spare in a shooting position near the opposing goal. It does not matter whether that player is supposed to be a forward or a defender.

Soccer is an exciting, fast-paced game that requires great physical endurance. On average, a midfielder will run up to 7 miles (11 kilometers) in a 90-minute match. Play rarely stops. Players move up and down the field almost constantly. Play is stopped only when a goal is scored, when a foul occurs, or when a player is seriously injured. Since most rules prohibit players from returning to a game once

they have been removed, soccer players often continue to play with injuries.

Ball Control

Ball control is one of the most important elements of soccer. Players may **trap** the ball (bring it under control) with any part of their body except their hands. Only goalkeepers are allowed to use their hands. After gaining control of the ball, the player may pass it to another player or dribble it downfield. The ball is **dribbled** (pushed along the ground by the feet of a player) by using the instep, the inside, or the outside of the foot. For a long pass the instep is usually used to kick the ball. The player's head is also used in ball control. Players hit the ball with their foreheads to pass, intercept, and shoot the ball at the goal.

While a player has control of the ball, the player's teammates try to find an open area to receive a pass. The opposing team tries to intercept the ball. In soccer a defensive player is allowed to **tackle** the ball. This is done by kicking the ball away from the ballhandler.

▶ RULES OF THE GAME

The most basic rule of soccer is that no player except the goalkeeper is allowed to touch the ball with the arms or hands, and goalkeepers may use their arms and hands only within the penalty area.

International rules allow a maximum of two substitutions, and no one who has left the game is allowed to return. In the United States, the National Collegiate Athletic Association (NCAA) permits five substitutes who are allowed to leave and re-enter the game.

Under international and collegiate soccer rules, one referee and two linesmen officiate

Soccer players must have physical strength and agility to perform well during a game, whether they are trying to stop the ball (*above*) or prevent a goal from being scored (*right*).

at a game. In high school, two referees often are used. The referee acts as the timekeeper and enforces the rules. The main job of the referee is to control the game with the help of the linesmen. The linesmen notify the referee when a team should be awarded a throw-in, a corner kick, or a goal kick and when a player is offside or has committed a foul. It is the referee who makes the final decision in all disputes.

Offsides and Free Kicks

A difficult rule to understand in soccer is the **offside** rule. A player is offside if the player is nearer or equal to the opponent's goal than the ball is at the time the ball is being played by a teammate. But there are exceptions to this rule. A player is not offside if she or he is in the defending half of the field or is farther from the goal line than two opponents. A player is not offside if the ball was last touched by an opponent or if the player received the ball directly from a goal kick, corner kick, or throw-in.

For violations such as offside, obstruction, and dangerous play, an **indirect free kick** is given to the opposing team. The player taking the indirect free kick is not allowed to kick the ball directly into the goal. The ball must first be touched by another player before entering the goal.

The opposing team gets a **direct free kick** if a player kicks, trips, jumps at, violently charges, charges from behind, strikes, holds, or pushes an opponent or intentionally touches the ball with the hands or arms. A goal may be scored on a direct free kick without the ball being touched by another player.

If any direct-free-kick offense is committed by a defending team in its own penalty area, the opposing team is given a **penalty kick** from the penalty spot, which is 12 yards (11 meters)

YOUTH SOCCER

From a beach in Rio de Janeiro in Brazil, to an empty lot in Europe, to a playground in the United States, soccer is one of the most popular sports played by young people throughout the world. On some occasions, thousands of people watch youth competitions.

The two largest youth tournaments in the United States are the USA Cup (Blaine, Minnesota) and the Dallas Cup (Dallas, Texas). Six hundred youth teams from 16 countries and 40 states participate in the USA cup tournament, as thousands of spectators view the week-long competition.

▶ GROWTH AND POPULARITY

In the United States there has been a rapid growth in the participation of young people in soccer from the late 1970's to well into the 1990's. The United States Soccer Federation (USSF) reported that some 1.8 million young players were registered in 1992. This was more than double the number of players in 1980, and three times the number that was registered in 1977. The United States Youth Soccer Association (USYSA), the American Youth Soccer Organization, and smaller youth organizations such as Soccer for America's Youth also experienced rapid increases in membership during this period.

Youth soccer is a sport that is popular with both boys and girls. It is also one of the few sports where a town, a city, or a school-league team may be composed of both girls and boys.

in front of the goal. Only the player taking the shot and the goalkeeper are allowed inside the penalty area during this shot.

Throw-Ins and Corner Kicks

The ball is out of play when it has completely crossed a goal line or touch line and when the game has been stopped by the referee. When the ball has crossed the touch line, the team that last touched it loses possession. An opposing player puts the ball back into play with a **throw-in**. The throw must be an overhead, two-handed delivery. As the player releases the ball, both feet must be touching the ground on or outside the touch line. When the ball has crossed the goal line, it is put back into play by either a goal kick or a corner kick, depending on which team last touched the ball. If the defensive team last touched it, a **corner kick** is taken by

WORLD CUP CHAMPIONS

MEN'S

1930	Uruguay	1974	West Germany
1934	Italy	1978	Argentina
1938	Italy	1982	Italy
1950	Uruguay	1986	Argentina
1954	West Germany	1990	West Germany
1958	Brazil	1994	Brazil
1962	Brazil	1998	France
1966	England	2002	Brazil
1970	Brazil		

WOMEN'S

1991	United States
1995	Norway
1999	United States
2003	Germany

In addition to programs of national soccer organizations, there are other soccer programs in many towns and cities. A town or city may have its own leagues organized by age levels and perhaps administered by the recreation department. A team will play other teams from the same town. At times boys and girls play on the same teams.

Youth soccer organizations were founded to develop the game of soccer among players under the age of 19. State youth soccer associations develop and administer soccer in each state with the regional and national organizations overseeing their activities.

Youth soccer groups administer the game from the under-8 to the under-19 age groups, with varying approaches depending on the division. Participation is recognized as the key factor at the lower age levels. This means that every youngster in attendance will play during at least part of the game. Participation, rather than winning, is the main objective. There is a shift in emphasis to competitiveness as players reach the divisions for older players.

Youth soccer groups often host teams from Europe and South America in exchange programs. Some U.S. teams travel abroad to play in foreign competitions.

the offensive team from the corner on the side on which the ball went out. If the ball was last touched by the offensive team, the defensive team takes a **goal kick**. The ball is placed on a corner of the goal area within the field and it is kicked from there.

A goal cannot be scored if the ball was thrown or carried in by the hand or arm of a player. A shot scores a goal only if the entire ball crosses the goal line between the goal posts and below the crossbar.

▶ THE WORLD CUP

Soccer's highest competitive prize is the World Cup championship. Every four years, the top soccer-playing nations compete for the honor of being called the outstanding soccer-playing country in the world. All nations belonging to the International Federation of Association Football are eligible to compete in qualifying competitions, which determine the teams that will join the host nation and the previous champion to play for the World Cup.

The first World Cup (for men only) was played in 1930 at Montevideo, Uruguay. It has been held every four years since then at a different site, except during World War II (1939–45), when competition was suspended. The women's World Cup made its debut in 1991, and is also held every four years.

Soccer is also included in the Olympic Games. The men's competition was first held in 1900, and women's soccer became an official Olympic sport in 1996.

JIM FROSLID
United States Soccer Federation

SOCIALISM

Socialism is an economic theory that favors public or government ownership of some or all of the means of production. This is in contrast with the belief in the ownership of production by private individuals.

There are many types of socialism. They vary in the amount of public ownership desired and in their methods of operation. In some countries, the government controls all forms of production. In others, state control over the economy is less complete, usually involving ownership of banks, transportation, and public utilities. Socialism thus takes many forms, economically. Politically, it may also vary, from totalitarian to democratic forms of government.

History of Socialism

The Industrial Revolution started in England in the middle of the 1700's and spread to Western Europe in the 1800's. The Industrial Revolution introduced the factory system, with its cruel working conditions—the 14-hour day, child labor, and low pay. Many owners of the factories (capitalists) became very rich. There were no laws to keep them from forcing these bad conditions upon the workers. There were some men, however, who felt that the system was unjust. They believed that the workers should be given better working and living conditions. They also thought that the workers should share the ownership of the factories with the capitalist owners. These men, who stressed co-operative economic living, included Robert Owen (1771–1858), François Marie Charles Fourier (1772–1837), and Claude Henri de Rouvroy, Comte de Saint-Simon (1760–1825). They were called Utopian Socialists because they wished to create a new society that would solve the economic problems of the day.

A German economist and writer, Karl Marx, disagreed with the Utopian Socialists. He believed that the capitalist system would destroy itself and that eventually all countries of the world would adopt a socialist system. Marx said that the workers should own and operate the means of production and that they should control the government.

Influenced by Marx's thinking, socialist groups and parties began to organize in Europe. To hasten the arrival of socialism, Marx said, the workers should band together and overthrow, by force of revolution if necessary, the existing governments. This troubled many socialists, who felt that if socialism was going to occur anyway, violence should not be used. Thus began the struggle between those who felt that revolution was necessary and those who wanted to revise Marx's theories. The revisionists became known as social democrats. They wanted to achieve socialism legally, through popular elections.

By the end of the 1800's, social democratic parties in Europe were large and well respected. They did not want a radical change but rather a gradual one aimed at improving the conditions of all working men.

There were others, however, who still felt that socialism could only be achieved through violence and revolution. In the first years of the 1900's they broke away from the socialist parties and formed their own groups. They called themselves Communists. They differed from the social democrats, or socialists, because they called for the complete and immediate establishment of socialism. The Communists were willing to use violent revolution to obtain their goals. Their aims were partially achieved in the Russian Revolution of 1917.

Social democrats, too, have found success. The victory of the British Labour Party in the United Kingdom's national elections in 1945 enabled the government to assume the operation of some British industries. Other countries in Europe, following the United Kingdom's lead, control some industries, while allowing private ownership in others. Today socialist parties advocate social and economic reforms as their main goals.

Thus, socialism has traveled many different paths. While promising a better world, socialists argue among themselves as to how this better world should be realized. The major impact of socialism today has shifted from the industrialized nations to the underdeveloped countries, which are struggling to emerge from their dependence upon agriculture.

Reviewed by ALBERT ALEXANDER
New York City Council on Economic Education

See also CAPITALISM; COMMUNISM; INDUSTRIAL REVOLUTION; MARX, KARL.

SOCIAL SECURITY

Many people worry about how they will pay for food, housing, and medical care if they are too old or too ill to work. Today, most developed countries have programs to help them obtain such necessities throughout their lives. These systems are generally known as social security.

One part of social security called public welfare, or public assistance, helps poor people who are aged, blind, or disabled or who have children to support. Governments provide public-assistance payments to those who need them most, and the cost is usually covered by general taxes.

Another part of social security—social insurance—consists of payments that are made to people regardless of need. One type of social insurance pays benefits to those who cannot work because of age or disability. Another provides money for medical care. In some countries, payments are made to all families with children under a certain age. Two other kinds of social insurance programs are covered in separate articles: UNEMPLOYMENT AND UNEMPLOYMENT INSURANCE and WORKERS' COMPENSATION.

▶ **HISTORY**

The need for social security developed in the late 1700's with the growth of industry. Instead of making their living off the land, many people in England and North America began working for wages in factories and mills. But wages could stop suddenly when a worker grew old or sick or when business activity fell off.

In response to this, workers in some industries formed benefit societies. Working members of a benefit society would contribute to a fund. This fund would be used to help members who could not work because of old age or sickness.

Gradually European countries adopted social security laws that provided these societies with government funds for social services. Germany became the first country to introduce sickness insurance (1883) and old-age insurance (1889). By the late 1930's, most of Europe had such programs.

By this time, too, many U.S. states had passed laws providing special relief for dependent children, the blind, and needy older

A social security card contains the number assigned by the government to keep track of a person's earnings and benefits throughout his or her lifetime.

people. Reformers had campaigned for years for a national social insurance system. The need for such a system became sharper in the 1930's, during the Great Depression. Millions of people lost their jobs and many faced starvation. This experience helped bring about a national social security system under the Social Security Act, which was passed in 1935. This act created several public-assistance programs, including unemployment insurance and old-age insurance. Over the years, eligibility requirements for social insurance payments have been broadened, and benefits have been increased.

▶ **UNITED STATES PROGRAMS**

In the United States, the term "social security" is used to refer to a program that provides benefits for retired older people, widows and orphans, and the severely disabled. The basic idea of this insurance is simple. During their working years, employees, their employers, and self-employed people pay taxes on their earnings. These taxes are called contributions. This money is used to pay benefits to workers (and their dependents) whose earnings have stopped due to retirement, disability, or death. Excess contributions that are not needed to pay current benefits go into special funds to pay benefits in the future. This program is administered by the Social Security Administration, an independent agency of the United States government since 1995.

Social security taxes consist of a specific percentage of a worker's wages, with an equal amount paid by the worker's employer. All workers participating in the program have a separate record of earnings. This record is identified by a unique social security number that is kept throughout a person's lifetime and keeps track of his or her record.

Anyone who has paid social security taxes on wages for at least ten years (though this need not be ten consecutive years) is eligible to receive social security benefits, regardless of other income. Fewer years of work are required for young workers seeking disability or survivor benefits.

The amount of the benefit payment depends on the amount of earnings in a person's account and the age at which the benefit payments begin. The earlier a person retires, the lower the payment will be. Full retirement benefits are paid at full retirement age. This was originally 65, but is gradually increasing each year until it reaches age 67 in the year 2027.

Medicare

Another type of social insurance benefit within the social security system is called Medicare. This pays hospital bills for people age 65 and over who are eligible for benefits under social security and the railroad retirement system. People who are eligible for hospital benefits may also get coverage of other medical bills by paying a monthly premium. Medicare was authorized by Congress in 1965.

▶ CANADIAN AND OTHER NATIONAL PROGRAMS

Canada has a number of social insurance programs. In the Canada Pension Plan, workers and employers contribute to a fund. Retired workers can begin to receive benefits at age 65, but they can get larger benefits if they continue to work until age 70. The amount of the benefit is based on the person's earnings. The plan also makes payments to disabled workers and to the surviving members of a worker's family after death. It covers all the provinces except Quebec, which has its own pension plan.

The Old Age Security program is designed to provide a pension for all Canadians 65 and older. People who have little or no income except this pension can receive additional payments under the Guaranteed Income Supplement program. Canada also pays monthly allowances to all families with children under 18. The Medical Care Act, in effect since 1968, provides medical insurance for all Canadian residents.

Social insurance programs in many countries are more extensive than the programs in the United States. In Britain, for example, medical care is provided through the National Health Service and the cost is covered by insurance and taxes. Britain and France are among the countries that, like Canada, pay allowances to families with children. Some Scandinavian countries make similar payments to all older people.

▶ THE FUTURE OF SOCIAL SECURITY

Today the social security systems in many countries are facing serious financial problems. Unemployment and inflation (the rising cost of goods and services) have helped to create these problems. When many people are out of work, less money goes into the social security program and more goes out. And as the cost of living goes up, so do the amounts of social insurance payments. In the United States, social security payments are based on the rate of inflation. This means they increase with each rise in the cost of living.

A decline in the number of workers has also created problems within the social security system. In recent years there have been fewer workers due to decreasing birthrates in previous years, but more money is needed for benefits because people are now living longer.

In 1983 the U.S. Congress passed legislation aimed at reducing social security costs. The legislation called for an increase in employee contributions, which were to rise in stages until 1990. In addition to gradually raising the retirement age to 67, benefits for people who retired early would be reduced. However, beginning in the year 2000, workers who reached full retirement age could collect retirement benefits even if they continued to work. In addition, the new legislation delayed some cost of living increases and reserved the right to freeze such increases if social security funds were low. It was hoped that these measures, together with other reforms, would keep social security costs under control.

ROBERT GREEN
University of Connecticut
Reviewed by STANLEY A. TOMKIEL III
Attorney at Law

See also OLD AGE; UNEMPLOYMENT AND UNEMPLOYMENT INSURANCE; WELFARE, PUBLIC; WORKERS' COMPENSATION.

SOCIAL STUDIES

"Social studies" is a name given to a particular part of a school's program of instruction. In the social studies, pupils learn how people use the earth to satisfy their needs for food, clothing, and shelter. They learn how people form governments and protect themselves from danger. They learn about humankind from the earliest beginnings to the present time. The word "social" in "social studies" means that these studies look at how people live together in neighborhoods, communities, states, and in the world of nations.

The subject matter of the social studies comes mainly from history and geography. But certain aspects of sociology, economics, political science, anthropology, and psychology are also included. These subjects are called the social sciences. Subject matter for social studies also comes from current happenings, such as a national election or a world problem. Sometimes the topics selected for social studies are those that are important to the pupils themselves, such as a school election or learning to live safely.

What the Social Studies Are Supposed to Do

The whole school program helps to make pupils better citizens. But social studies include learnings of a special type that have to do with education for citizenship.

The learnings that make up the social studies are of three types. The first is the development of understandings. These learnings consist of knowledge and facts about how people live and work. They include history, which is the story of humanity's past. They include geography, which helps pupils learn about the earth as their home. By studying economics, pupils learn how people use the earth to make a living and how they produce, consume, and trade goods. To be a good citizen in today's world, one needs to know many things about the world and its people. Social studies help pupils do this.

A second group of learnings has to do with ideals, appreciations, and values. Pupils not only need to know about their country but are expected to have feelings of pride and loyalty toward it. They need to value the freedoms they enjoy and appreciate the work of those who contributed to the making of their

In social studies classes, students learn to be good citizens of their own countries and to understand how and where citizens of other countries live.

nation. In the United States, citizens believe in rules and laws. People must not only know what these laws are but must learn to respect and obey them. The great American document of freedom, the Declaration of Independence, states the belief that all people are created equal. These learnings mean much more than simply knowing something. They mean that citizens are expected to behave in ways that represent the values and ideals of their nation. Through the social studies, people are helped to understand these beliefs.

The third group of social studies learnings is called skills. A social studies textbook contains maps, charts, graphs, and special words. These have little meaning to a pupil who does not have the skills to use them. Map reading, using references, making outlines, preparing reports, and reading charts are all important skills in the social studies. Other skills include thinking critically about topics, taking charge of a meeting, contributing to a discussion, and presenting a report to a group.

Programs of Instruction

For many years most schools taught the social studies as separate subjects. The subjects most commonly taught were history, geography, and civics. Civics is the study of government and laws. Some schools still teach these separate subjects. But they call the entire program social studies.

Many schools select topics for study, such as "Our Community," "Latin-American Neighbors," or "Life in Ancient Rome." These topics become units of study that may take a class several weeks to complete. In the process the teacher combines learnings from history, geography, economics, and other social sciences that will help the pupils gain a better understanding of the topic. Study units are sometimes planned around problems such as "How Do Workers in the Neighborhood Help Us?" "How Have Inventions Changed Our Lives?" or "How Do Citizens Work for Good Government?"

Social studies programs are sometimes planned around things that people do when they live together in groups. For example, all groups of people have ways of protecting and governing themselves. They educate their young. They produce, distribute, and consume goods. They have ways of communicating with each other, and they have some system of religious beliefs. A pupil might develop a good understanding of a community, a culture, or a country by studying the ways in which people perform these important activities.

In recent years many schools have been experimenting with a plan of organizing social studies around key ideas called concepts. Such concepts are selected from the social sciences, and the pupils learn more about them each year as they go through school. For example, the idea "When people live together in communities, they need some system of government" is one that is often selected. Young children learn how this applies to their own community, while older students can learn more complex ideas about how governments are organized and what they can and cannot do.

Schools in the United States, therefore, organize their social studies programs in a number of ways, but any of these different plans may properly be called social studies. All of them include a study of the history, government, and geography of the United States.

Materials of Instruction

Social studies programs use a great variety of instructional materials to help pupils learn. The most important of these are books, encyclopedias, maps, globes, reference books, films, filmstrips, and pictures. Many of the social studies topics and subjects are such that the pupils cannot learn about them directly. They cannot visit all of the countries studied, nor can they see firsthand the things that happened a long time ago. But with good instructional materials pupils can learn about distant places, relive exciting adventures in history, and appreciate the people of the past who helped to shape the world's history.

Besides the usual materials of instruction, many teachers use television, field trips, museums, and real objects that children can handle. Radio and television programs and recordings are also used. In addition, some teachers make use of guest speakers, free materials, newspapers, and other current-events publications. Materials for today's social studies are interesting and colorful. The textbook, while still important, is no longer the only tool used for learning in a modern program of social studies education.

Instructional Practices

Teachers use a variety of activities to help pupils learn and to give them practice in using skills. Reading is important as a way of gaining information. Pupils also discuss topics, work together in small groups, conduct interviews, present ideas through dramatics, take field trips, hold elections and political conventions, engage in creative writing, and plan and work together. These activities are used to achieve important goals in social studies. As a member of a study committee the pupil learns to work in a responsible way with others, to plan a job, and to carry it through to completion. To present a play, make a model, or paint a mural, a pupil must do much reading and research to get correct knowledge and facts. Many activities are used to build skills such as critical thinking, doing research, using references, learning to use maps and globes, exercising leadership, and working with others. These are important not only in social studies but in life outside school.

JOHN JAROLIMEK
University of Washington

SOCIAL WORK

The chief aim of social work is to help people with the problems that come up in their everyday lives as individuals, members of groups, or citizens of a community. The social worker is prepared to work with people facing difficulties they cannot handle alone. Social workers are employed by public and voluntary agencies, hospitals, youth organizations, settlement houses, schools, courts, and community-planning agencies.

Human problems are varied and complicated. They may be due to poverty and poor housing, physical or mental illness, unemployment, family misunderstandings, or discrimination. One of the tasks of the social worker is to help the person or group to gain understanding of the difficulty and to plan ways in which it can be met.

Throughout history people have shown a willingness to help their neighbors in trouble. Social work had its beginnings in this concern for the well-being of neighbors. In earlier days the poor were helped through simple acts of charity, but as the numbers of the needy increased, this was not enough. Institutions were provided to care for dependent children, the aged, the handicapped, and the sick. Too often in the past it was thought that being in trouble was a person's own fault. Little attention was paid to the real causes of distress.

At the turn of the 20th century, however, there came new knowledge from psychiatry and the social sciences. It brought a greater understanding of the forces that keep people from being useful and happy. Social work changed from a program of "doing for" people to a program of "working with" people to help them achieve fuller and more satisfying lives. Helping them to help themselves became a central purpose. It was recognized too that goodwill was not enough to help people solve their problems. Trained minds were needed as well. Gradually principles and methods were developed that grew into today's skilled profession of social work.

▶ THE PRACTICE OF SOCIAL WORK

Social problems in today's society demand expanded social services. These services should be available to all parts of the population. The services should represent new ideas and methods and be geared to today's special needs. However, these needs are not always met by government or private agencies. Social-work groups are now interested in providing for the establishment and maintenance of services of high quality.

Social workers use a variety of methods. Some work directly with families and individuals through family-service agencies, public-assistance bureaus, schools, prisons, and other institutions. In person-to-person talks with the individual or family, the social worker tries to learn the facts, as well as how people feel about their difficulties. If necessary, specialists in fields such as legal aid, medicine, and housing may be called in to help.

Social workers in general or mental hospitals are part of a team that includes doctors and nurses. They help patients understand what is wrong and how to co-operate with treatment. They help families deal with the problems that come up when a person needs hospital care.

Social agencies are greatly concerned with the well-being of children. While plans are made for foster-home care for children who have been made homeless by the death or desertion of parents, social workers work with the children so they will not feel alone. The social worker, under legal authority, plays an important part in arranging adoptive homes for children.

Social workers also work with groups of people in community centers, settlement houses, youth organizations, and centers for old people. They help plan programs aimed at giving group members opportunities for recreation and new interests and for experiences in democratic living.

Social workers are active in neighborhoods where young people sometimes get into trouble with the law. Many of these young people come from homes that offer little encouragement or hope for the future. Some young people, on the other hand, are rebelling against wealth and affluence.

The gangs that young people may join often engage in unlawful activities. To meet this problem, social workers are employed to work in the places where the gangs meet. The worker is always on hand to help individuals work out family or personal problems. The worker gets members interested in projects of value, and may gradually win their trust by standing by when they get into trouble.

Some social workers use their skills in urban planning, rural-development programs, and community projects that will meet the health and welfare needs of the area.

There are also experienced social workers who qualify for private practice. They work as self-employed counselors or consultants. Some seek further education and move into administrative, teaching, or research positions.

Jobs in social work include working with people in many different settings, both at home and abroad. Highly skilled social workers are employed in the Peace Corps, the various units of the United Nations, and special projects overseas.

▶ PREPARATION FOR SOCIAL WORK

Social workers in the United States are recruited from all groups. There is need for active recruitment of people of varying religious, cultural, and racial backgrounds, with special emphasis on blacks, Mexican-Americans, Puerto Ricans, and Indians. Social work is changing, developing, and adapting to new demands and new situations. As part of the new approach, beginning jobs for workers with limited academic preparation are opening up.

Many American colleges and universities offer social-work educational programs in the junior and senior years. Two-year junior or community colleges in many places are offering technical training that prepares students for some beginning jobs.

Education at the graduate level is essential for highly skilled clinical practice and for supervisory, teaching, and administrative jobs. Graduate study provides both classroom and field instruction. Undergraduate programs also offer field experience in which the student can have the opportunity to put classroom work into practice.

In other parts of the world, social-work education may be organized within universities, usually at the undergraduate level. In continental Europe, in some parts of Africa, and in a number of Latin-American countries, independent institutions provide education for social work, although in many of these places university training is favored.

▶ SOCIAL WORK AS A CAREER

What influences young people to become social workers? Those who choose this career usually do so because they genuinely care about people and wish to help them lead productive, satisfying lives. Social workers believe that most people can be helped to help themselves. The opportunity to help people secure their rights, protect their freedoms, and reach their highest level of development makes social work appealing and gratifying.

Salary levels are improving, and the many different situations in which social work is practiced give it great appeal for ambitious young people. In fact, social work is one of the fastest-growing careers in the United States. The profession is expected to grow by 30 percent by 2010. Nearly 600,000 people in the United States now hold degrees in social work.

For information about accredited schools of social work, contact the Council on Social Work Education at 1600 Duke Street, Alexandria, Virginia 22314.

MARGARET WILLIAMSON
Formerly, School of Social Work
Columbia University
Reviewed by National Association
of Social Workers

See also ADDAMS, JANE; WELFARE, PUBLIC.

SOCIOLOGY

Sociology is the study of people's behavior as it is influenced by interaction with other people. Sociologists are the experts who try to find out about human relationships and how those relationships are affected by people living and working together.

What happens, for example, when people go to school, join organizations, take jobs, or move to a new community? Sociologists have a scientific interest in understanding how and why people act the way they do. Some human behavior causes problems—such as crime and unemployment—for the individual or others. Sociologists alone cannot solve these and other social problems. By finding possible causes and explanations, they can help people lessen them.

In addition to doing research studies, most sociologists teach, either in colleges or in high schools. Soon sociology will also be taught in the elementary schools. Students who study sociology find out what is known about human behavior. Sometimes this helps them to understand themselves and others better.

▶ HOW SOCIOLOGY DEVELOPED

Probably people have always tried to understand and explain their own behavior. But Auguste Comte (1798–1857), a French philosopher, was the first to put into words the need for studying the problem. He suggested that "We need a special science to explain man to himself, just as we already have a science of stars, plants, and rocks." Comte gave sociology its name by combining the Latin word *socius* with the Greek word *logos,* thus forming a word that can be thought of as meaning "science of relationships."

Frédéric Le Play (1806–82) got people to write down exactly how they spent their time every day of the week. In this way he could tell how different behavior was connected with different surroundings. In England, Herbert Spencer (1820–1903) read reports by travelers and missionaries in all lands. He tried to explain that all human societies developed and grew in the same way, even though their cultures might be very different. In the United States, William G. Sumner (1840–1910) became famous for his explanation of how social customs started and their influence on people's actions.

The best of the early studies were done by Émile Durkheim (1858–1917) in France, Georg Simmel (1858–1918) and Max Weber (1864–1920) in Germany, and Charles H. Cooley (1864–1929) and William I. Thomas (1863–1947) in the United States. Durkheim suggested several theories about the causes of suicide and the origins of religion. He then collected all the information available to test each of these theories. He found that suicide victims were mostly lonely people who did not understand the customs of their society very well. Religion began when people developed a strong sense of membership in a new group.

Weber also studied religion, but he was interested in how different religions created different attitudes toward work and business. Simmel was the first great student of conflict—such as wars, labor strikes, race prejudice. Cooley studied children and the way in which they grew up in the family and play group. Thomas studied the problems of immigrants to the United States.

By the 1940's sociology had become an accepted department at most universities and colleges in Europe and the United States. Sociology also spread to Japan, India, and some countries of South America. In most of the nations of Africa and Asia very little or no sociology is studied.

▶ WHAT SOCIOLOGISTS STUDY TODAY

Sociologists who are called **demographers** study the number of people who are born and who die, the number of people who live in different places, and where and why people move. An important problem the demographers are trying to solve is "overpopulation"—why there are too many people in certain parts of the world. Some study the **community**—in city, town, and open country. They show how people's behavior is influenced by the kind of place in which they live. A number of sociologists specialize in **social psychology**. They seek to find out the basic reasons people act the way they do, regardless of the society or community they happen to live in. Still others study **social organization**. This may be in the form of institutions, like the family, the factory, the farm, the school, the church. Or it may be in the form of great classes of people, such as the members of minority or economic groups.

A great number of sociologists study the behavior that causes special **problems** in society. Crime, poverty, race prejudice, and overpopulation have already been mentioned. In addition there are also studies of drug addiction, alcoholism, mental illness, poor housing, slum living, continuing ill health, divorce, and all the other difficulties people have made or have to face for one reason or another. One specialty that has received much attention in recent years deals with the problems of older people. These problems include their lower income, the lack of things for them to do, their need for a special kind of housing, and how they face illness and death.

Most sociologists are interested in **social change**—that is, how society and human behavior change. They study the causes of change in inventions, laws, revolutions, fashions, disasters, and social movements.

▶ **HOW SOCIOLOGISTS DO THEIR STUDIES**

It is not easy to study people. Sociologists have had to develop special methods of gathering information and putting it together so that it makes sense. These are called **methods of research**, and some sociologists spend all their time developing such methods. Seldom can sociologists use laboratories, but sometimes nature makes experiments that sociologists can observe carefully.

They can observe human behavior simply by watching how people act, or they can get people to answer questions. They can even read—with permission—the letters and diaries of the individuals under observation. Sometimes sociologists actually join organizations or gangs, work in factories or offices, or get placed in prisons or schools just to study human behavior in these surroundings. Sometimes sociologists observe only a few selected things about a large number of persons or groups. At other times sociologists want to learn as much about one person or group as possible. When this is the case, the sociologist has a complete case study.

Once sociologists have their information, they must organize it and seek to find out what it means. To do this, they may compare several groups or persons. They may show how the groups have changed over a period of time. They may point out what characteristics the people usually have. When they write up their studies, sociologists may use case reports and statistics. Or they may just tell in an exact way what they have seen and heard.

There are thousands of such studies published every year in books and special magazines. Although sociology is still a young field of study, it already has much to teach about how people behave in society.

ARNOLD M. ROSE
University of Minnesota

SOCRATES (470?–399 B.C.)

Socrates was a Greek thinker and teacher. He was born in Athens about 470 B.C. and was put to death there in 399. He was married to Xanthippē, who was such a scold that her name is now used to mean "shrew." For some time Socrates worked as a stonemason and sculptor. Then he grew interested in philosophy. He spent the rest of his life thinking about philosophy and discussing it with practically everyone he met.

Socrates did not teach in the regular way. He held no classes and gave no lectures and wrote no books. He simply asked questions. "What is courage?" "Why do people do wrong actions?" When he got an answer, he asked more questions, like a cross-examination, until very often the other man admitted he could not give any more answers.

Socrates asked his questions in order to make people think about ideas they took for granted. Some men admired this very much. They became fast friends of Socrates and joined in his philosophical discussions for many years. Others thought he was simply trying to destroy good old ideas about religion and morality without putting anything in their place. Some of the young men whom he knew well became traitors to their country and led a revolution that overthrew the democratic government. The Athenians rose against them and killed them. After democracy had been restored, Socrates was brought to trial. He was accused of introducing new gods to Athens and of corrupting young men's minds.

Socrates did not take these charges seriously and would not ask for mercy. So he was condemned to die by drinking a cup of hemlock. Many people, then and later, thought the sentence was unjust because it denied freedom of speech. Others believe that he deserved to die because his pupils nearly destroyed the Athenian state. In any case his courage and independence have always been admired. His most famous pupil, Plato, became a great philosopher and made Socrates the chief character in most of his books.

GILBERT HIGHET
Formerly, Columbia University

SOFTBALL

Softball, a game similar to baseball, originated in the United States as an indoor substitute for baseball. In 1895, Lewis Rober, a member of the Minneapolis Fire Department, invented softball as an indoor game for firefighters to play in their spare time. Today softball is played by more than 37 million people in 80 countries.

The name "softball" is misleading because the modern softball is as hard as a baseball. But the large size of the ball makes it easier to handle than a baseball.

Softball and baseball are similar in many ways. Both games are played on a diamond with a bat and ball by two teams of nine players. However, softball is played on a smaller diamond, the ball is larger and heavier, the bat is lighter, and the game is played for seven innings rather than the nine of baseball. Another important difference between the games is the way the ball is pitched. In baseball, the ball is usually pitched overhand; in softball, the ball must always be pitched underhand.

Though softball started as an indoor sport, it soon became a popular outdoor game. In 1908, the National Amateur Playground Ball Association was organized to promote the outdoor play of the game and to draw up rules. Although the rules for softball have changed over the years, they are now standardized.

Softball is easy for people of all ages to play, and the equipment is inexpensive. Softball became popular soon after it was invented. But for several years it remained an

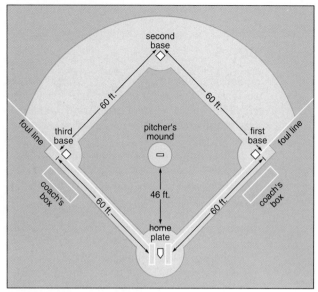

A softball field

unorganized sport without an official name. It was known by such names as kitten ball, diamond ball, mushball, indoor-outdoor, recreation ball, and playground ball. In 1926, it was named "softball" by Walter Hakanson of the Denver, Colorado, YMCA. But the name was not official until 1933.

Softball is the most popular amateur team sport in the United States and an important part of the physical education and recreation programs of more than 90 percent of the junior and senior high schools in the United States.

In many countries softball is a part of the intramural school athletic programs for both boys and girls and is one of the activities in their national physical fitness programs. In the military forces of many countries, softball ranks as the most popular of all sports. In most cases, the United States military forces have introduced softball overseas, but Peace Corps volunteers can be given the credit for taking the game to remote regions of the world.

Television has been instrumental in the growing popularity of the game. Telecasts of world softball championships have been very popular with TV sports fans. In 1996, softball became an Olympic sport at the Summer Olympic Games in Atlanta, Georgia.

No other major sport has remained so completely an amateur game. Softball started as a game to be played for fun, and it is still played that way.

DON E. PORTER
Executive Director, Amateur Softball Association

In softball, the ball must be pitched underhand.

SOILS

Soil is a thin layer of loose material on the surface of the earth. Above the soil is the air. Beneath it is solid rock. Soil can be a few inches deep, or it can go down several feet.

Soil is a mixture of organic and inorganic materials. The organic part consists of living things and the remains of once-living things. The inorganic part is made up of particles of rocks and minerals—that is, of substances that were not formed by living things.

Our word "soil" comes from the Latin word *solum,* which means "floor" or "ground." The Latin root tells you something about the importance of soil. Soil is the ground, or foundation, of all life on land. It supports the plants on which men and all other living beings depend.

▶ WHERE SOIL COMES FROM

When the earth was very young, there was no soil. There was only water, air, and rock. But over millions of years weather worked on the surface of the solid rock. Rain and wind and water wore it down. Freezing and thawing cracked and broke off pieces of rock.

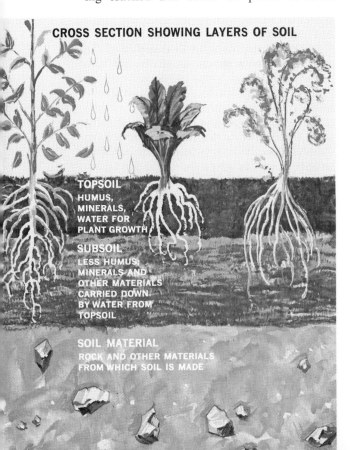

CROSS SECTION SHOWING LAYERS OF SOIL

TOPSOIL
HUMUS, MINERALS, WATER FOR PLANT GROWTH

SUBSOIL
LESS HUMUS; MINERALS AND OTHER MATERIALS CARRIED DOWN BY WATER FROM TOPSOIL

SOIL MATERIAL
ROCK AND OTHER MATERIALS FROM WHICH SOIL IS MADE

CAN CHANGES IN TEMPERATURE BREAK UP ROCKS?

To find out, try this demonstration at a cook-out. After the food has been cooked but while the coals are still glowing, place several kinds of rocks in the coals. You may see some of the rocks crack almost immediately.

In about 10 minutes, when the rocks have become very hot, rake them out of the coals, using a metal rake or other long-handled tool. Examine the rocks for cracks. Some rocks will be broken.

Heat makes a solid, such as a rock, expand. The outside of the rock may expand so much that it breaks away from the cooler inside.

Very slowly a layer of loose rock particles formed. Such wearing away is called **erosion**.

In time the remains of plants and animals were added to the particles of rocks and minerals. The result was what is now called soil.

▶ WHAT CAUSES DIFFERENCES IN SOILS

The soil in one place is never exactly the same as the soil in another place. You have probably noticed this if you have traveled in different parts of the country or moved from one town to another. Some soils look dark. Others are gray. Still other soils are yellow or reddish.

You have probably noticed also that pine forests flourish in some places and tall grasses in others. Soils contain different amounts of the basic minerals needed for plant growth. Since each kind of plant has its own special needs, each kind grows best in a particular type of soil. Plants in turn change the soil in which they grow. Plants use up minerals as they grow. When they die, their remains become part of the soil, and in time minerals are put back into the soil.

Many other living and nonliving things affect the soil. Taken together, they determine the type of soil that is found in a particular place.

Among the things that determine soil type are the size of the rock particles, the climate of the region, the location of the particular place, and the way man uses the soil.

▶ WHAT SOIL CONSISTS OF

Soil is made of rock and mineral particles and of living and once-living things. Its texture—or feel—depends on the size of the

Clay: Very fine particles with diameters less than .00008 inch.

Silt: Particles coarser than clay with diameters ranging from .00008 to .002 inch.

SIZE OF ROCK PARTICLES IN SOILS

Sand: Particles coarser than silt with diameters ranging from .002 to .08 inch.

Loam: A mixture of clay, sand, and silt. When mixed with humus, loam makes a fertile garden soil.

inorganic particles and on the amount of organic matter present. Soil texture is one of the first things that a farmer, rancher, or other person wishing to use soil must examine. It determines the way a particular soil should be worked.

The Size of the Rock Particles

Most soils are a mixture of fine, medium, and coarse particles. A soil mixture made up of very fine particles is called **clay**. A soil made up of somewhat coarser particles is called **silt**. A soil of still coarser particles is called **sand**. Sand may range from very fine—though not so fine as silt—to very coarse. Finally, soil may contain a high percentage of pebbles and gravel. A soil mixture of sand, clay, and silt is called **loam**. When

---

DO GROWING PLANTS BREAK UP ROCKS?

To answer this question, try planting bean or pea seeds in a "rock." You will need an empty coffee can (1-pound size is best), plaster of paris, water, and about nine seeds.

Soak the seeds for 8 to 12 hours before you start. (This hastens the sprouting.)

Put a cup of dry plaster in the coffee can. Stir in water slowly until the plaster is like thick mud. If the plaster seems too runny, add a little more dry plaster.

Plant the seeds quickly, before the plaster hardens. Each seed should be about ¼ inch below the surface of the plaster. Put the can in a warm place but not in direct sunlight.

In about a week look at the plaster "rock." What happens to the plaster on top of the seeds as the plants grow?

---

loam is well mixed with organic matter, it makes a fertile, or productive, garden soil.

Soil is made up of water and air, as well as organic and inorganic matter. The size of the rock particles determines how much water and air enter soil and remain there. Clay, for example, packs tightly. It soaks up and holds water easily. (This makes clay a heavy soil.) But a soil packed very tightly may act like concrete, slowing down the growth of plant roots. In a light, sandy soil there are more air spaces between particles. Water runs through easily. However, when water runs off too easily, soil dries out. Important minerals may be leached, or drained, out of the soil.

In a soil that produces good crops, particles are usually coated with a film of water. Substances needed for plant growth have to be dissolved in water in order to be absorbed by plants.

Humus

The decaying organic matter in soil is called humus. Humus separates otherwise tightly packed rock particles, thus allowing more air and water to enter the soil. Humus also provides food for bacteria and other micro-organisms (very tiny living things) in soil. These micro-organisms decay, or break down, dead organic matter, forming substances that plants can use.

Humus is important to soil fertility, or productivity. Farmers add humus to soil in the form of manures (animal wastes), composts (decaying plant materials), cover crops, and the remains of crops, such as roots and stems. A cover crop is one that is planted between the harvesting of one crop and the planting of the next. The crop is plowed under while still green. (That is why the farmer calls such crops green manure or green fertilizer.) After the crop decays, it becomes humus.

The Living Part of the Soil

The soil contains many living things. All help the soil in some way. For example, the roots of plants grow down into the soil. Thus, plants hold the soil and prevent it from being blown or washed away.

Many kinds of animals live in the soil. Rodents, such as ground squirrels and moles, make their burrows there. Their tunnels and holes let more air and water into the soil. Still smaller animals, such as beetles and ants, millipedes and centipedes, slugs and snails, and spiders and mites feed on organic matter, thus starting the process of decay. The body wastes of these animals enrich the soil. The most important of all these animals are the earthworms. Like tiny plows, they turn over the soil and improve it in many ways.

In addition, countless numbers of microorganisms are present in soil, feeding on particles of organic matter. As they feed they break the organic material into minerals, gases, and liquids. These decay products are broken down still further by other microorganisms. There result new combinations of the basic elements. Plants can then use the substances for growth.

There are 10 elements that all plants need, though in varying amounts. Three of these are present in either air or water or in both. They are oxygen, hydrogen, and carbon. The others are a result of decay. These elements are nitrogen, phosphorus, potassium, calcium, magnesium, iron, and sulfur. (Nitrogen is plentiful as a gas in the air, but plants cannot use nitrogen in this form.)

▶THE EFFECTS OF CLIMATE AND LOCATION ON SOILS

The activities of living things in the soil, as well as soil texture, determine how fertile a particular soil may be. However, climate and location are also important.

Map shows distribution of various soils throughout the world. Climate and location are important in determining the kind of soil a particular area has.

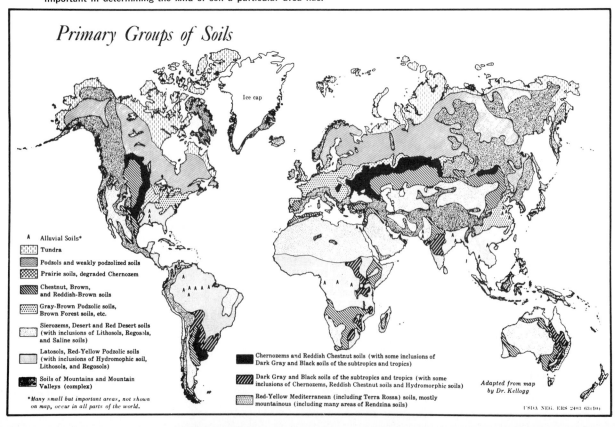

Primary Groups of Soils

Ice cap

▲ Alluvial Soils*

Tundra

Podzols and weakly podzolized soils

Prairie soils, degraded Chernozem

Chestnut, Brown, and Reddish-Brown soils

Gray-Brown Podzolic soils, Brown Forest soils, etc.

Sierozems, Desert and Red Desert soils (with inclusions of Lithosols, Regosols, and Saline soils)

Latosols, Red-Yellow Podzolic soils (with inclusions of Hydromophic soil, Lithosols, and Regosols)

Soils of Mountains and Mountain Valleys (complex)

*Many small but important areas, not shown on map, occur in all parts of the world.

Chernozems and Reddish Chestnut soils (with some inclusions of Dark Gray and Black soils of the subtropics and tropics)

Dark Gray and Black soils of the subtropics and tropics (with some inclusions of Chernozems, Reddish Chestnut soils and Hydromorphic soils)

Red-Yellow Mediterranean (including Terra Rossa) soils, mostly mountainous (including many areas of Rendzina soils)

Adapted from map by Dr. Kellogg

USDA NEG. ERS 2493-63(10)

Climate

The climate of a particular region determines the way soil develops and weathers. Temperature and rainfall, for example, affect the rate at which rocks are broken down. They affect the rate of decay and also the speed with which elements are lost from the soil.

Soil builds up rapidly in moist, warm climates, for example. High temperatures and moisture favor plant life. They also speed up the process of decay. Soil forms more slowly in colder, northern regions, where fewer plants can grow and the decay process is slow. Little soil develops in dry desert basins. There surface water evaporates, leaving salts that harm plants.

Soils are often classified according to the climate, or climatic zone, in which they form. The five most common groups are tundra, podzolic, latosolic, chernozemic, and desert.

In very cold climates **tundra** soil develops. This is usually a black muck, rich with humus.

Why Should Topsoil Be Conserved?

To observe the importance of topsoil for plant life, try growing peas or some other fast-sprouting seeds in topsoil and in subsoil. The results may give you an idea of the importance of soil conservation.

Materials Needed

Two flower pots, pea seeds, water, topsoil, and subsoil.

Procedure

Fill one pot with topsoil from a flower garden or from a bag of potting soil. Label the pot "topsoil."

Fill the other pot with subsoil. Label the pot "subsoil." You can get subsoil from a badly eroded hillside or from a place where the foundations for a building are being dug. You can also get subsoil by digging down through the topsoil in a garden to a depth of at least 1 foot.

Plant five seeds in each pot, following the planting instructions on the seed package. (Most seeds will sprout more quickly if you have soaked them overnight.) Add the same amount of water to the soil in each pot. Set the two pots side by side in a warm place. Be sure both pots receive the same amount of light. Water the pots every 2 days, always giving both pots the same amount of water.

Record the progress of the plants each day. Compare the plants in the two pots.

Observing the Differences in Soil Particles

For this demonstration you will need several types of soil, some quart-size jars, water, a teaspoon, and a magnifying glass.

Place a cup of one type of soil in a jar. Fill the jar with water. Cover the top of the jar with your hand or with a lid. Gently shake up the contents of the jar.

Let the jar stand for 4 to 5 hours. The heaviest soil particles settle out first, and the lightest ones last. Humus will float on top for some time. Humus is the part of the soil that contains most of the nutrients plants need for growth.

When the water has completely cleared, carefully remove spoonfuls of the particles from each layer and examine the particles with the magnifying glass. Can you see why some particles are heavier than others?

Repeat this with the other soil samples. Can you see differences in the textures of the various soils?

The topsoil—that is, the top layer of soil, which contains living things—thaws for only a short time each year. Lichens, mosses, and many small, low plants grow in it, but trees cannot. The subsoil—the soil below the topsoil, which contains no life—is permanently frozen.

In cool moist climates—such as those of the northern parts of Asia and North America—**podzolic** soil forms. "Podzol" comes from a Russian word for "ashes," and podzolic soil is usually gray or white with patches of brown humus. Such soils are often acid because certain minerals have been leached (washed) out.

In hot moist climates, **latosolic** soil is found. The term comes from the Latin for "brick," and latosolic soil is often brick-red or yellow. Plants grow well in such soils, and the soil is usually rich with decaying matter.

In mild dry climates, **chernozemic** soil develops. The term comes from the Russian words for "black earth," and chernozemic soils are usually black. Such soils are usually covered with prairie grasses.

In hot dry climates, **desert** soil forms. This soil is light-colored or reddish. It supports a few grasses and small shrubs, but little humus builds up.

Location

Soils, like the parent rocks, are worn away by erosion (the process of weathering). Soil is washed off mountainsides by melting snow, for example. Soil collects in valleys. When rivers overflow their banks, they deposit soil on the flooded plains. Soil builds up at the mouths of great rivers such as the Mississippi. Often, therefore, the depth and quality of soil depend on its location.

Accordingly, soil scientists sometimes classify soil by the way soil is deposited. For example, soil may be carried by rivers and streams and then deposited on flooded plains and at river deltas. Such soil is called **alluvium**, or **alluvial soil**. **Till** is soil that has been deposited by glaciers. Till, which is sometimes called **boulder clay**, is a coarse clay mixed with gravel and boulders. **Loess** is a fine sandy loam that has been deposited by strong winds. If treated correctly, loess can be made to produce excellent crops.

▶ **THE EFFECT OF HUMAN ACTIVITY ON SOIL**

People's actions may speed up or slow down the slow natural process of soil erosion. Unless we are careful, we can destroy in a short time fertile topsoil that took thousands of years to develop.

TESTING TO SEE IF SOIL IS ACID

You have probably heard a gardener or a farmer talking about how acid or alkaline a certain soil is. Acid soils are good for some plants, such as beans, clover, and peaches. Alkaline soils are better for others, such as beets and tomatoes. There is no one soil condition that is ideal for all crops.

You can test soils yourself by using litmus paper. Litmus paper is a paper treated with colored vegetable dye. Acids turn blue litmus to red. Alkalis turn red litmus blue. You can get litmus paper in most drugstores and hobby shops.

Dig up samples of various soils. You may start, for example, by testing a sandy soil, loam, and clay. Put a handful of the first sample into a clean paper cup. Wet the sample thoroughly with water. Then press the blue litmus paper into the soil.

If the paper turns pink, the soil is acid. If the paper does not change color, try the red litmus paper. If the paper turns blue, the soil is alkaline. Use a fresh piece of litmus paper for each soil sample.

If one or more of your samples test acid, you can make the soil less acid. You can do this by adding gardener's lime. Stir lime into your sample, a teaspoonful at a time. Test the soil with the blue litmus paper after each addition, until it ceases to react.

For example, good soil is constantly covered over when houses, factories, and roads are built. Once roofs have replaced roots, the soil is lost.

When forests are cut down and replaced with crops, the soil is changed. With continual planting of the same crops, cleared forest land stops producing in 5 years. Crops exhaust (use up) the elements that took many years to build up. If the elements are not replaced, the soil loses its fertility. If the land is left bare between crops, winds and rains may carry off the topsoil.

Through such careless uses of soil, the continental United States has lost almost 3 billion acres of productive farmland. Fortunately, however, the Department of Agriculture now helps people plan the wise use of the remaining soil. Geologists (scientists who study the earth) and other soil experts study soils and prepare surveys and maps. These soil surveys and maps tell about such things as soil textures and types.

A person wishing to use land for a certain crop or for grazing or for an airport consults these surveys and maps. Land whose soil is too poor for agriculture might be good enough for grazing. Land too poor to provide food for cattle might instead be fine for an airport, and so on.

Fertile land that is planted to food crops can be **conserved**, or protected, in various ways. Erosion can be slowed by such things as contour plowing and crop rotation. Contour plowing follows the curve of the land, thus slowing down the flow of water—and soil—from the top of a slope to the bottom. Crops are rotated —that is, first one kind of crop is grown in a field, then another—so that the repeated planting of the same crop will not exhaust minerals. Organic and chemical fertilizers are added to replace the minerals that are used up. Cover crops are grown to prevent soil erosion between crops. Various other measures are taken to control the floods and the droughts that are the result of the washing and blowing away of soil.

With good management, people can save and even improve the fertile topsoil on which our life depends.

WALTER SINGER
The New York Botanical Garden

See also BACTERIA; CONSERVATION; GEOLOGY; MINERALS; ORES; ROCKS; WORMS.

SOLAR ENERGY

The sun radiates vast amounts of energy, which nourishes all life on Earth and is the driving force behind the planet's weather patterns and other natural cycles. People have been using solar energy for many thousands of years, and scientists continue to discover new and better ways of harnessing and using it.

The Earth receives several thousand times more energy from the sun than is used by all the people in the world at any moment. In order to take advantage of this vast and continuous energy supply, we have learned to convert solar energy into forms of energy that we can use for heating, power, and transportation.

▶ USING SOLAR ENERGY IN BUILDINGS

Solar energy systems developed for buildings can help meet the energy needs of the people who live or work in them in many ways. Such systems are often described as either **passive** or **active**. Passive systems rely on the design and materials of the building to distribute light and heat from the sun without mechanical help. Active systems use pumps or fans.

Daylighting. Daylighting, a passive use of solar energy, makes the most efficient use of sunlight because it does not have to be converted to another form of energy. A daylit building uses specially designed windows to let sunlight into interior spaces, which reduces the need for electrical lighting. This can save a significant amount of electricity, especially in office buildings, schools, and other large buildings that are used mostly in the daytime. Well-designed daylighting also makes work spaces more attractive and pleasant to be in.

Solar Heating and Cooling. In climates with cold winters, solar energy can provide between 35 and 75 percent of the heating needs of a passive solar home. A good passive solar design includes **glass**, **mass**, and **insulation**. The building should have south-facing windows to let in sunlight, which provides heat when it strikes the interior of the home. Objects such as furniture, walls, and floors store the heat in their mass during the daytime and slowly release it at night. Tile floors and masonry walls designed into the building increase the mass and, therefore, the heat-storage capacity of the building. Insulating walls and ceilings also help to hold heat in.

In warm climates, the goal of passive solar design is to keep the sun's heat out of a building. This is done by carefully positioning the building and its window placements to reduce the amount of heat it absorbs during daylight hours, and by using roofing overhangs that block the sun and encourage natural air movement within the building. Passive cooling design also includes the planting of trees to provide shade.

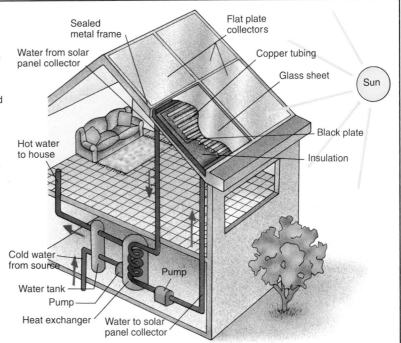

A Solar-Heated House

Solar water heaters used in homes are active solar heating systems used to heat water for showers, washing, and other household tasks. Typically, a solar collector is placed on the roof and connected by copper pipe to a heat exchanger and a storage tank inside the house. Inside the collector, a black metal plate absorbs heat from the sun and transfers it to a liquid antifreeze mixture running through copper tubing. The plate and tubing are sandwiched in between insulation on the back and glass on the front of the collector, which is held together by a sealed metal frame. The heated liquid is pumped through the heat exchanger, where it gives up its heat to the water in the storage tank. The heated water can then be used in the home. A backup gas or electric water heater ensures that hot water is available on cloudy days.

Sealed metal frame
Flat plate collectors
Water from solar panel collector
Copper tubing
Glass sheet
Sun
Hot water to house
Black plate
Insulation
Cold water from source
Pump
Water tank
Pump
Heat exchanger
Water to solar panel collector

A 2-megawatt photovoltaic plant in Sacramento, California

▶ SOLAR THERMAL POWER PLANTS

In a solar thermal power plant, sunlight is converted to heat energy and used to generate electricity. Special collectors concentrate sunlight in order to achieve the high temperatures needed for this type of system. Advanced systems use rows of trough collectors or a central receiver surrounded by mirrors.

Trough Collector Systems. Trough systems contain curved metal reflectors arranged in long rows. With the help of small computers, they track the sun during the day and reflect sunlight precisely onto heat-collecting, glass-covered steel pipes held several feet away. Oil is pumped through the pipes to absorb the heat, and it is then used to produce the steam needed to drive a large electric generator.

Central Receiver Systems. These systems consist of a tall tower surrounded by thousands of mirrors called **heliostats**. The heliostats track the sun and continuously reflect beams of sunlight to the top of the tower. There the sunlight is converted to heat and absorbed by a heat-transfer fluid. The heat is then used to power a steam-driven electric generator or it is stored for later use.

Photovoltaic Systems. Photovoltaic (PV) systems use solar cells to convert sunlight directly to electricity. A solar cell is a thin, waferlike device usually made of a semiconductor material such as silicon. This material produces an electric current when sunlight strikes its surface. This current is then used to provide power where it is needed. Solar cells are generally interconnected in a sealed panel called a **module**, and modules can be connected to form an **array**. Electrical current from a PV array is either used directly or it is stored in low-voltage **batteries** for use when the sun is not shining.

Stand-alone PV systems are most commonly used to provide electricity in locations not reached by the electrical distribution system of a centralized power company. In countries with large rural areas not served by a central utility, PV is a cost-effective and reliable source of electricity. PV has brought electricity to homes, schools, and hospitals in thousands of villages around the world.

In countries with extensive power supply networks, small PV systems are cost-effective ways to provide electricity to remote homes near a power pole and for small electrical needs, such as water pumping and highway signs.

Large-scale PV systems use large fields of PV arrays to generate electricity for private or government-owned power companies around the world. These systems usually do not include battery storage but are connected directly to a power grid. Some utilities in the United States have installed grid-connected PV systems on the rooftops of residential and commercial buildings to provide extra power during periods of high electrical demand.

PV arrays are also being used in several places throughout the world to charge the batteries of electric vehicles. Solar energy has also been used to provide the electricity needed to create hydrogen, which can then be used as a transportation fuel.

Benefits of Solar Energy

Much of the interest in solar energy is related to our environmental concerns about using fossil fuels as well as our safety concerns over the use of nuclear power. Solar energy can be a reliable alternative to energy sources that cause pollution or other environmental or safety hazards. Solar energy can also have significant benefits for local and national economies from the development of energy-producing industries that create jobs within a country.

BURKE MILLER THAYER
American Solar Energy Society

SOLAR SYSTEM

Our solar system consists of the sun and all of the other objects—planets and their satellites, asteroids, comets, and interplanetary gas and dust—that orbit it. The solar system is shaped like a disk with the sun at its center.

The largest objects orbiting the sun are the planets: Mercury, Venus, Earth, Mars, Jupiter, Saturn, Uranus, Neptune, and Pluto. Mercury is the closest planet to the sun. Pluto is often the most distant, but at times the elliptical, or oval, shape of Pluto's orbit brings it inside the orbit of Neptune. When this happens, Neptune is farther from the sun than Pluto.

Several planet-like objects have been found in the outer solar system. One such object, called Sedna, is about three-fourths the size of Pluto. These objects may be part of belts or clouds of distant (and mostly small) objects. Some scientists think Pluto is one of these objects and should not be called a planet.

Thousands of tiny objects called asteroids also orbit the sun, most of them located within the large gap that exists between the orbits of Mars and Jupiter.

Comets—chunks of ice, rocks, and dust— also travel around the sun. The orbits of most comets keep them far beyond the orbit of Pluto. When they do enter the inner solar system, heat and other radiation from the sun cause them to develop long, beautiful tails.

Dust and gases scattered throughout the solar system are what remain of the materials used in its formation.

▶ SOLAR SYSTEM THEORIES

A few Greek philosophers and astronomers who lived about 300 B.C. suggested that the sun was the center of the solar system. However, until the middle of the 1500's, most astronomers thought that the Earth was the center of the entire universe and that everything, including the sun, moon, planets, and stars, revolved around it. This is how things can appear to be from our viewpoint on Earth.

Then, in 1543, the Polish astronomer Nicolaus Copernicus (1473–1543) published a theory stating that Earth and the other planets revolve around the sun in circular orbits. Copernicus did not provide evidence to support his theory, but he noted that the mathematics needed to describe a sun-centered system was simpler than the mathematics needed to describe an Earth-centered system.

In the early 1600's the Italian astronomer Galileo Galilei (1564–1642) became the first scientist to look at the sky with a telescope. He discovered that the planet Venus goes through phases like the Earth's satellite, the moon. He reasoned that this could happen only if Venus orbited the sun rather than the Earth, which supported Copernicus' theory.

By 1618, the German astronomer Johannes Kepler (1571–1630) was also studying the planets' motions. He, too, concluded that the planets orbit the sun, but he also realized that instead of traveling in perfect circles, each planet travels in an elliptical path.

▶ ORBITS OF THE PLANETS

Kepler's discoveries of the orbits and motions of the planets became known as Kepler's three laws of planetary motion.

The sun is the star at the center of our solar system. It is only a medium-sized star, but compared to the planets, the sun is enormous. More than 1 million globes the size of the Earth could fit inside it. Like other stars, the sun is a ball of very hot gases that shines with its own light and gives off its own heat. That light and heat make life possible on Earth.

Kepler's first law states that each of the planets travels in an orbit around the sun and that the shape of its orbit is an ellipse, or oval, with the sun positioned near one end of the oval (see Figure 1). This means that the distance between a planet and the sun varies as the planet travels along its orbit. When a planet is at the closest point to the sun in its orbit, it is at **perihelion** (from the Greek words for "near" and "sun"). When a planet is at its farthest point from the sun in its orbit, it is at **aphelion** (from the Greek words for "away"

elliptical path, the line (which will increase and decrease in length) moves across an imaginary surface. Look at Figure 2, which shows the same planet at four different points in its orbit, marked 1, 2, 3, and 4. According to Kepler's second law, the total area marked A equals the total area marked B. A planet will take the same amount of time to sweep out area A, from point 1 to point 2, as it will take to sweep out area B, from point 3 to point 4. In order to do this the planet will move faster while going from point 1 to point 2, when it is

Kepler's First Law

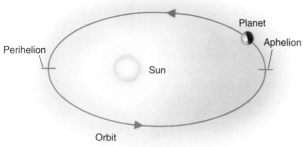

Figure 1. The distance between the sun and a planet varies when the planet is in an elliptical, or oval, orbit around the sun. The planet is closest to the sun at perihelion and farthest away from the sun at aphelion.

Kepler's Second Law

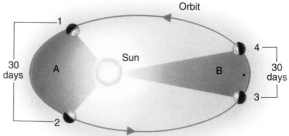

Figure 2. A planet in an elliptical orbit around the sun will sweep out equal areas in its orbit in equal amounts of time. It will move across area A, from points 1 to 2, in the same amount of time that it takes it to move across area B, from points 3 to 4.

and "sun"). Our Earth, for example, is at perihelion in early January of each year, when it is about 91.4 million miles (147 million kilometers) from the sun. During early July the Earth is at aphelion, when it is about 94.5 million miles (152.1 million kilometers) from the sun.

Kepler's second law describes how a planet's speed changes as it travels around the sun. A planet traveling in an elliptical orbit travels fastest when it is closest to the sun, at perihelion, and it travels slowest when it is farthest from the sun, at aphelion. For example, the Earth travels at a speed of 18.8 miles (30.3 kilometers) per second at perihelion, whereas at aphelion it is traveling slightly slower, at 18.2 miles (29.3 kilometers) per second.

In addition to describing how planets travel at different speeds, Kepler's second law also states that a planet moves across, or "sweeps out," equal areas in its orbit in equal amounts of time. This is sometimes called the "law of equal areas." Imagine a line drawn from the sun to a planet. As the planet travels in its

closer to the sun, than while moving from point 3 to point 4, when it is farther away from the sun.

Kepler's third law relates a planet's distance from the sun to the time it takes the planet to make one revolution around the sun. The closer a planet is to the sun, the faster it goes and the less distance it has to travel to complete one orbit around the sun. The farther a planet is from the sun, the slower it travels and the distance it has to travel increases. As a result, its period of revolution and its year are longer.

Kepler's observations led him to describe some of the motions of the planets, but he was unable to explain why the planets move as they do.

Gravitation and Planetary Orbits

In the late 1600's the English scientist and mathematician Sir Isaac Newton (1642–1727) added to our understanding of what causes the planets to orbit the sun as they do. Using a form of mathematics called calculus, Newton was able to show that the force that holds objects to the Earth, which became known as the force of gravity, also holds the planets in their orbits around the sun.

The story about Newton being hit on the head with an apple and thereby discovering the "law of gravity" may not be true. But it is possible that seeing an apple fall from a tree helped Newton come up with the idea that the same invisible force that can pull an apple from a tree to the Earth also holds the moon in its orbit around the Earth and keeps the planets moving in their orbits around the sun. This force, the force of gravity, he went on to suggest, is universal. It controls the motions of all objects in the solar system.

Newton went an important step beyond this, however, by calculating what the force of gravity depends on. By carefully observing the motions of various planets, the Earth's moon, and objects on Earth, Newton determined that the strength of the gravitational force between any two objects depends on the masses of the two objects and the distance between them. (The mass of an object depends on the amount of matter it is made of.) Newton found that the more massive two objects are, the greater the force of gravity between them. If you double the mass of either object, the gravitational force doubles. If you double the mass of both objects, the force is four times greater. However, if you double the *distance* between the two objects, the gravitational force lessens and becomes one-fourth as great

as it was originally. Newton also stated that two objects such as the Earth and the moon exert a gravitational force on each other, that it is not correct to think only of one object, the Earth, as having a gravitational force on the other, the moon.

Newton further determined that without gravity or some other outside force, an object such as our moon or a planet once in motion would travel through space in a straight line forever. The moon follows an orbit around the Earth because the tendency of the moon to travel straight off into space is countered by the force of gravity between the Earth and the moon. If the moon were not moving, it would fall into the Earth. Its motion combined with the force of gravity causes the moon to fall toward the Earth each second by the same amount at which the Earth is curving out of the way. In the same way, gravity and the motions of the planets keep them orbiting the sun.

The speed at which an object travels is also significant. If an object travels too slowly, gravity from the object it is orbiting may pull it out of its orbit. An artificial satellite that orbits only 150 miles (242 kilometers) above the Earth must travel at about 17,500 miles (28,175 kilometers) per hour to keep from falling to the Earth. It will take the satellite about 1½ hours to complete each revolution or orbit around the Earth. The moon is about 240,000 miles (386,000 kilometers) away from Earth. The force of gravity on the moon

BODE'S LAW

The numbers 0, 3, 6, 12, 24, 48, 96, and 192 are first written out in a line. Notice that each number, except 3, is twice as big as the number before it.

| 0 | 3 | 6 | 12 | 24 | 48 | 96 | 192 |

The number 4 is then added to each number:

| 4 | 7 | 10 | 16 | 28 | 52 | 100 | 196 |

In this row, number 4 represents Mercury, 7 represents Venus, 10 represents the Earth, and so on. The planets are placed under the numbers in the order of their distances from the sun. Each planet (except Neptune and Pluto) is given a number. The space under number 28 is left blank because there is no known planet whose distance from the sun

fits here. However, Ceres, a large asteroid, is located at about this position.

4	7	10	16	28	52	100	196
Mercury	Venus	Earth	Mars		Jupiter	Saturn	Uranus

To find the distances of the planets from the sun, the number of each planet is first divided by 10, which is the Earth's number. The result is then multiplied by 93,000,000 miles (150,000,000 kilometers), the Earth's average distance from the sun.

For example, Venus is number 7; the Earth is number 10. $7 \div 10 = \frac{7}{10}$. $\frac{7}{10} \times 93,000,000 = 65,100,000$ miles, (or, in kilometers, $\frac{7}{10} \times 150,000,000 = 105,000,000$). This is close to the correct distance between Venus and the sun.

is therefore much less than it is on the artificial satellite, so the moon only needs to travel at about 2,186 miles (3,519 kilometers) per hour to maintain its orbit. However, it takes the moon nearly a month to make one complete orbit around the Earth. In the same way, the sun's gravitational force is greater on Mercury, the closest planet to the sun, than it is on Pluto, which is usually the farthest planet from the sun. Mercury orbits the sun at an average speed of 29.8 miles (47.9 kilometers) per second while Pluto has to move along at an average speed of only 2.9 miles (4.7 kilometers) per second to maintain its orbit.

▶DISCOVERY OF THE ASTEROIDS

In 1772, Johannes Bode (1747–1826), a German astronomer, pointed out that there was a curious mathematical relationship in the distances of the planets from the sun. See the table on page 243. The table shows how Bode's law works and how to find the distances of the first seven planets from the sun. (The distances of Neptune and Pluto cannot be calculated using Bode's law. Kepler's third law, which states that the orbital motions of planets are faster or slower depending on their distance from the sun, results in more accurate figures for the distances, and it is used to make exact calculations for all the planets.)

At first, Bode's law included only the planets known in 1772. When Uranus was discovered in 1781, it also fitted the pattern. The only puzzling thing about the pattern was the gap at number 28 between Mars and Jupiter.

After the discovery of Uranus, astronomers began to search for a planet they thought might be at a distance corresponding to number 28 in the Bode pattern, but they were unsuccessful. Then, early in 1801, the Italian astronomer Giuseppe Piazzi (1746–1826) was observing the night sky through a telescope and noticed a starlike object that did not behave like a star, which keeps its position in relation to other stars night after night. This object changed its position slightly each night.

By observing its motions, he was able to plot its orbit around the sun. He concluded that the object was a tiny planetlike object, or asteroid, about 500 miles (800 kilometers) in diameter. He named it Ceres. When its distance from the sun was calculated, it corresponded to number 28 in Bode's table of the planets. A year later another asteroid was dis-

covered, and many more have since been found orbiting the sun in the gap called the main belt, which is between the orbits of Mars and Jupiter. More than 1,700 asteroids have been named and their orbits worked out. Many more have been discovered, but their orbits have not yet been plotted. Asteroids, many of which are quite irregular in shape, are thought to be made up of small pieces of rock and metal that never formed a planet.

▶THE PLANETS AS SEEN FROM EARTH

When people looked at the night sky in ancient times, they noticed that the planets known at that time—Mercury, Venus, Mars, Earth, Jupiter, and Saturn—and the Earth's moon, as well, moved through an area like a narrow band that went all the way around the sky. This band also appeared to be divided into twelve **constellations**. Constellations are groups of stars that form unchanging patterns in the sky. Throughout the year, the sun also moved through the same region of the sky.

This region became known as the **zodiac**, from the Greek word for "circle." When Uranus and Neptune were discovered, they, too, were found to move through the zodiac. As a result, people discovered that it was not necessary to look all over the sky for a planet, you only needed to look along the zodiac.

For many hundreds of years, astronomers did not know why the planets were seen in this region until they discovered that the orbits of most of the planets are almost in the same plane as the orbit the Earth follows around the sun. Observers on Earth looking at the planets see them all along this plane or band in the sky. The constellations are the background of stars that observers see as they look along the band in which the planets are moving.

Different planets also appear to go through different motions in the sky. To understand this, we can divide them into two groups—those closer to the sun than the Earth are

Within an area of space 100,000 light-years across is a spiral galaxy known as the Milky Way galaxy. There are about 300 billion stars in the Milky Way galaxy, among them a medium-sized yellow star we call the sun. Orbiting the sun are the nine planets and their satellites, the asteroids and comets, and the interplanetary gas and dust that make up the solar system. Although it is shown magnified here, our entire solar system takes up only a tiny dot of space in the Milky Way galaxy, which itself is only one of the millions of galaxies in the universe.

Milky Way galaxy

Saturn

Mars

Mercury

Venus

Jupiter

Sun

Earth

Neptune

Uranus

Inner asteroid belt

Comet

Pluto

The path of the Earth's orbit around the sun is called the ecliptic plane. Most of the planets orbit the sun in about the same plane. The exception is Pluto, whose orbit is tilted 17° to the ecliptic plane of the solar system.

Sun

Earth

Ecliptic plane

To a viewer on Earth, planets such as Mars, Jupiter, and Saturn sometimes seem to stop and reverse direction before moving forward again in their orbits. Examples of such retrograde motion are shown in this display at the Munich Planetarium.

known as the **inferior** planets and those farther from the sun than the Earth are known as the **superior** planets.

The inferior planets are Mercury and Venus. To an observer on Earth, it seems that their motion in our sky is a gradual swinging back and forth relative to the sun. At times they may be found to the left of the sun; at other times they are found to the right of the sun. This effect happens because compared to the distance and speed of the Earth's orbit around the sun, the inferior planets have shorter distances to travel and they travel at a faster rate. They overtake the Earth more than once before it completes one orbit, so we see them at these different points in their orbits.

When Mercury and Venus lie to the left of the sun in our sky, they set after sunset and are seen in the western sky during twilight. When they lie to the right of the sun in our sky, they rise before the sun and are seen in the eastern predawn sky. When Mercury and Venus round the far side of the sun, they are said to be in **superior conjunction**. When they pass between the Earth and the sun, they are said to be in **inferior conjunction**.

The superior planets—Mars, Jupiter, Saturn, Uranus, Neptune, and Pluto—appear to have very different motions in the sky. They can be seen anywhere along the zodiac from very near the sun's position in the sky to opposite the sun in the sky. Because the Earth travels faster in its orbit and has a shorter distance to travel around the sun than the superior planets do, our planet orbits the sun more than once before they complete one orbit. As a result, we see them at many different points in their orbits.

When a superior planet lies on the far side of the sun, it cannot be seen because of the sun's glare. Gradually, however, because the Earth is moving around the sun more quickly, the superior planet will emerge from the sun's glare and it will rise in the eastern sky a short time before sunrise. Each morning, as the Earth gradually rounds the sun and approaches the planet, the planet will rise earlier and earlier, getting higher and higher in the eastern sky before the rising sun floods the sky with light.

Eventually, the Earth in its speedier course will be in a position to swing past the superior planet. When the planet lies directly opposite the sun in our sky, the planet will rise in the east as the sun sets in the west. At this point, astronomers say the planet is in **opposition**.

During this time, the planet also appears to make a curious change in its motion in our sky. Around the time of opposition, the planet seems to stop its eastward motion against the background stars, reverse its direction for several nights or weeks, stop again, and then resume its normal eastward motion. Astronomers refer to this phenomenon as a **retrograde**, or backward, motion.

To understand what is happening, we must remember that the Earth is going around the sun faster than the superior planet. As the Earth speeds past the slower-moving planet, it appears to us that the planet is traveling backward. This can be compared to passing a car on the highway. If you were in a car going fast enough to pass another car, the car you passed would appear to be going backward as you sped by it. We have visual clues to watch that let us know we are actually passing a slower car. But the planets are merely dots moving silently through the sky, where there are no real visual clues to help us.

▶ **SATELLITES OF THE PLANETS**

Among the nine known planets in the solar system, Mercury and Venus have no satellites, or moons. Pluto and Earth each have 1 satellite. Mars has 2, Neptune has 13, Jupiter has 61, Saturn has 31, and Uranus has 25. The diameters of the moons range from about 2.5 miles (4 kilometers) to more than 3,200 miles (5,200 kilometers).

Some of the satellites orbiting the planets travel at great speeds. For example, Phobos, one of Mars's satellites, completes one orbit in about 7½ hours, which is one-third the length of a day on Mars. Therefore, Phobos goes around Mars three times in one day and appears to travel backward in the Martian sky. Two of Jupiter's satellites and two of Neptune's satellites also complete a single orbit in about 7 hours. Other satellites have longer orbital periods depending on how far away they are from the planets they orbit. Just like the planets orbiting the sun, the farther a satellite is from a planet, the longer it takes to revolve around the planet.

▶ **COMETS AND METEOROIDS**

Besides the planets and their satellites, interplanetary gas and dust, and the asteroids,

---

See For Yourself

How to Make a Solar System Model

Our solar system is so enormous that it is difficult to get a good idea of its size, but you can make a model that will help you get a better idea of the comparative sizes of the planets.

Materials needed:

a ruler	scissors
a compass	nine large pieces of
a pencil	paper or cardboard
string	tape

You will make your solar system model by drawing and cutting out circles of different sizes to represent the planets. In the model, each inch (2.54 centimeters) is equal to 2,642 miles (4,254 kilometers). For example, the diameter of the Earth is 7,926 miles (12,760 kilometers), so the Earth's diameter in the model will be 3 inches (7.6 centimeters).

Use the table on the right as a guide to create planets in circles of the correct size. One way to draw circles is by using a compass. The compass should be opened to a width equal to the radius of the planet model you are drawing. (The radius of a circle is one-half its diameter). For example, for Earth you will open your compass to a distance of 1½ inches (3.8 centimeters) between the pencil tip and the compass point. You can measure this distance using a ruler.

The radius for the model of Jupiter is 16³/₄ inches (42.5 centimeters). Most compasses are not large enough to open this far. A good way to make a large circle is by using a piece of string and a pencil. Cut a piece of string that is about 20 inches (51 centimeters) long. Make small loops in the string that are 16³/₄ inches (42.5 centimeters) apart. Tighten one loop around a pencil. Hold the other loop with your finger. Draw a circle by keeping your finger still, like the point of the compass, and moving the pencil around in a circle.

Planet Sizes for Solar System Model

Planet	Diameter	Radius
Mercury	1 inch (2.5 centimeters)	½ inch (1.3 centimeters)
Venus	3 inches (7.6 centimeters)	1½ inches (3.8 centimeters)
Earth	3 inches (7.6 centimeters)	1½ inches (3.8 centimeters)
Mars	1½ inches (3.8 centimeters)	¾ inch (1.9 centimeters)
Jupiter	33½ inches (85.1 centimeters)	16¾ inches (42.5 centimeters)
Saturn	28½ inches (72.4 centimeters)	14¼ inches (36.2 centimeters)
Uranus	12 inches (30.5 centimeters)	6 inches (15.2 centimeters)
Neptune	11½ inches (29.2 centimeters)	5¾ inches (14.6 centimeters)
Pluto	½ inch (1.3 centimeters)	¼ inch (0.64 centimeter)

Cut out each circle. If you like, you can color each one to look like the planet it represents, using an astronomy book as a guide. Tape a piece of string to each planet and hang them in the correct order from a bulletin board or from the ceiling. In this model the sun would be about 27 feet (8.3 meters) in diameter.

Although the sizes of your planets are correctly to scale, their distance from one another is not. To place them at the correct distance from one another, you would need a very large model. Using planets of the size you have drawn, the distances between the sun and Mercury and between each of the planets would be as follows:

Sun to Mercury 1,137 feet (347 meters)
Mercury to Venus 984 feet (300 meters)
Venus to Earth 813¹/₂ feet (248 meters)
Earth to Mars 1,536 feet (468 meters)
Mars to Jupiter 10,797 feet (3,291 meters)
Jupiter to Saturn 12,731 feet (3,880 meters)
Saturn to Uranus 28,318 feet (8,631.5 meters)
Uranus to Neptune 31,974 feet (9,746 meters)
Neptune to Pluto 27,726 feet (8,451 meters)

Pluto would be 22 miles (35 kilometers) from the sun using this scale model!

there are two other kinds of natural objects orbiting the sun. These are comets and meteoroids.

Comets. A comet is a mass of ice, rocks, and dust. After several spacecraft flew past Halley's comet in 1986, scientists determined that it was rich in compounds of carbon, hydrogen, oxygen, and nitrogen. The nucleus of a comet may be several miles across but may not be very round. While some of it is made up of frozen water, like snowballs on Earth, other ices including frozen carbon dioxide, ammonia, and methane are also usually present, as well as carbon, silicates, and other materials. There are probably thousands of comets in our solar system, but most have very large orbits that always keep them far from the sun in the frozen depths of space. Many comets may have remained unchanged since the beginning of the solar system and may contain clues to what conditions existed then.

Sometimes, however, the gravitational pull of Jupiter and the other giant planets can gradually change a distant comet's orbit and start the comet on a journey to the inner solar system. As the comet nucleus draws closer to the sun, the sun's heat gradually begins to vaporize the outermost layer of ice, releasing dust particles and gases. Geyser-like jets form on the comet's surface, shooting gas and dust into space. This material forms a cloud called the **coma**, which envelopes the icy nucleus and gives the comet a round, fuzzy appearance as it nears the orbit of Mars.

Two long tails—one of gas and one of dust—flowed out of the nucleus of Comet West in 1976 during its journey through our solar system.

As the comet draws still closer to the sun, the pressure of the sun's light pushes the released dust particles away from the coma and out into space. In addition, the solar wind—particles streaming off the sun—collides with and pushes the dirt particles and gas outward and away from the comet. This causes the comet to grow a tail (or sometimes two tails, one of gas and the other of dust) that always points away from the sun. Most comets rarely enter the inner solar system; others visit frequently. Halley's comet appears every 76 years; a few comets appear more frequently.

Meteoroids. Meteoroids are pieces of rock and metal that orbit the sun. Most meteoroids are small, ranging in size from microscopic dust grains to pebbles the size of driveway gravel. A few, however, can be the size of a house or larger. Some are debris left behind from older, disintegrating comets whose ices continue to evaporate during their approaches to the sun. The debris released by the vaporized ices spreads out around the comet's orbit, forming a stream of meteoroids.

The Earth encounters meteoroids every day as dust-size particles slowly filter down through the atmosphere. Larger pieces, even those the size of grains of sand, can travel through the upper atmosphere at speeds of up to about 40 miles (64 kilometers) per second. Friction with the atmosphere causes them to heat up and glow brilliantly. These glowing meteoroids are known as **meteors**, and from the ground they can sometimes be seen at night. Although they are not stars, they are often also referred to as shooting stars.

Debris from disintegrating comets usually travels in swarms. When the Earth crosses through one, a **meteor shower** takes place. Some meteor showers occur at the same time each year. Others can produce 60 or more meteors an hour that are visible to the naked eye.

If a meteoroid is sufficiently large, it may not completely vaporize on its journey through the atmosphere. The remaining fragment can strike the Earth; then it is known as a **meteorite**. More than 100 meteorite craters have been found on our planet. The largest is more than 110 miles (180 kilometers) in diameter and is located in the Yucatan Peninsula in Mexico.

▶THE FORMATION OF THE SOLAR SYSTEM

One of the most basic questions we can ask about our solar system is, How did it form?

Scientists get clues by looking far out into space. Throughout our galaxy, the Milky Way galaxy, and beyond it, they see huge clouds of gas and dust lit up by the light of young stars. These stars were formed from dust and gases present in the clouds.

The force of gravity is also involved in the process of star formation. Dust and gases are not distributed evenly within the clouds in space. The more matter there is in a particular region of a cloud, the stronger the force of gravity is in that region. If a region is particularly dense, the gravitational force in that region will become strong enough to cause that part of the cloud to begin to collapse. As the collapse continues, nearby gas and dust will be drawn toward the collapsing region and add to its gravitational pull. The energy of the matter falling toward the center of the region is transformed into heat. If enough matter collapses, internal temperatures in the region will reach about 9 million°F (5 million°C). Hydrogen atoms will collide with such force that they bond to create helium and give off energy. Where once there was only a collapsing region inside a cloud, there is now a star.

Scientists think that this same set of circumstances may have formed our own star, the sun, about 4.55 billion years ago. In the case of the sun, however, not all of the collapsing gas and dust went into its formation as a star. Instead, it is thought that small amounts continued to orbit the sun at various distances as the whole region of the cloud began to flatten out. Clumps began to form within this revolving disk of materials as dust particles collided and stuck together. The gravitational force within these clumps grew, and they attracted and adhered to other clumps creating still larger bodies called **planetesimals**. The more massive of these planetesimals attracted still more of the material in the disk and grew to become the planets. Other planetesimals evolved into the satellites of the planets or cooled to become the objects we know today as asteroids, meteoroids, and the nuclei of comets.

Data from the *Voyager* space probes and other spacecraft suggest that the cores of the planets formed first and that the atmospheres of some planets may have resulted from the release of internal gases by volcanic activity. In the case of the giant planets, gases in their atmospheres may have been pulled in from

Images of the star Beta Pictoris display a gaseous disk orbiting the star, which has characteristics similar to the disk that probably orbited the sun prior to the formation of the planets in our solar system.

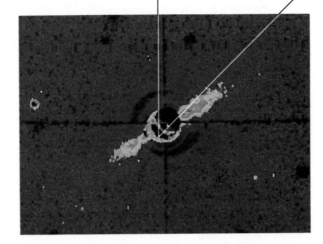

space by the gravitational pull of the cores of the planets as they formed.

Scientists have found many stars surrounded by large disks of dusty material. They have also seen planets along with dust around the same star. These observations suggest that planets form out of thick disks of dust, gradually clearing them out.

About 150 planets are known to orbit stars other than the sun. These extrasolar planets are usually detected indirectly. "Wobbles" in the motion of some stars suggest that large planets are orbiting them. In some cases, the planet passes between the star and Earth, causing the star's light to dim. In 2005, the first extrasolar planets were observed directly. Scientists hope that the study of extrasolar planets will help us understand our own solar system.

WILLIAM A. GUTSCH, JR.
Chairman, American Museum-
Hayden Planetarium

See also ASTRONOMY; COMETS, METEORITES, AND ASTEROIDS; CONSTELLATIONS; GRAVITY AND GRAVITATION; MOON; PLANETS; SATELLITES; SATELLITES, ARTIFICIAL; SPACE PROBES; SUN; UNIVERSE; articles on individual planets.

SOLDERING. See WELDING AND SOLDERING.

SOLIDS

Any piece of matter that has a definite shape is a solid. Wood is a solid. So are salt, sugar, rubber, diamonds, iron, and wax.

Sometimes it is extremely difficult to squeeze a solid out of shape. Such a solid is **hard**; iron and diamond are hard. A solid that can easily be squeezed out of shape is **soft**. Rubber and wax are examples of soft solids. Rubber will spring back into its original shape after it is squeezed. Wax will not. Because of these properties, rubber is **elastic** and wax is **plastic**.

Liquids (such as water) and gases (such as air) are kinds of matter that do not have definite shapes. Yet liquids, gases, and solids are all made up of tiny particles, or **molecules**. The particles behave differently in each type of matter.

The particles in solids are very strongly attracted to one another. Because of this they take up positions close to one another and are firmly held in place. That is why a solid has a definite shape.

The particles in a liquid are also close together, but they are not firmly held in position. For that reason, a liquid has no definite shape. It can flow and will take the shape of the container it is in. It will spread out on a flat surface such as a tabletop.

The particles in gases are not close to one another. They spread apart as far as possible. They will also take the shape of a container, but only if it is tightly sealed. Otherwise the particles will escape out of the opening into the surrounding air.

Actually, the particles in a solid are not entirely motionless. They vibrate about the place in which they are located, like a person standing in one place but shifting from foot to foot. The amount of vibration depends on the temperature. The higher the temperature is, the stronger the vibration.

If the temperature rises high enough, the vibration becomes so strong that the individual particles break away from each other. They begin to slide about freely. The solid **melts** and becomes a liquid.

The temperature at which this happens is called the **melting point**. Each solid has its own melting point. Ice melts at 32°F (0°C), lead at about 621°F (327°C), and tungsten at about 6100°F (3400°C).

The reverse is also true. Substances that are ordinarily liquid can become solid if cooled to a low enough temperature. As the temperature drops, the particles of the liquid move less and less rapidly until they come to be fixed in place. Mercury becomes solid at about −40°F (−40°C). Grain alcohol becomes solid at about −179°F (−117°C). Even a gas, if cooled sufficiently, can become a liquid first and then a solid. For example, oxygen becomes a liquid at −297°F (−183°C) and freezes to become a solid at −360°F (−218°C).

Very often, when a solid is formed, the particles take up orderly positions in a geometric pattern. When this happens, **crystals** are formed. Crystals are pieces of solid matter that have fixed geometric shapes. These shapes are brought about by the arrangement of the particles that make them up.

Each solid substance always crystallizes into its own particular shape. Ordinary salt, for instance, always crystallizes into little cubes. The salt crystals may differ in size, but they are all the same shape. The study of crystal shapes is called **crystallography**.

In recent years chemists have learned to make pure crystals. These are crystals made up of a single type of particle with hardly any impurities (particles of other types). Such crystals have very useful properties. This is also true when crystals contain certain impurities that are added in just the proper amounts.

Crystals of silicon are good examples of this. When small quantities of certain impurities are added to them, they can carry an electric current in one direction but not in the other. It is sometimes very useful to let a current go through such a "one-way gate."

Such crystals can be combined to form transistors. These are tiny devices that can control electric currents and make them stronger. Transistors can do all the work of radio tubes, which are much larger. Transistors have made possible today's electronic wristwatches, pocket calculators, computers, and many other electronic devices. The study of the electrical and other properties of crystals is called **solid-state physics**.

ISAAC ASIMOV
Author, *Asimov's New Guide to Science*
Reviewed and updated by ROBERT GARDNER
Author, *Science Projects About Chemistry*

See also CRYSTALS; ELECTRONICS; GASES; LIQUIDS; MATTER; TRANSISTORS, DIODES, AND INTEGRATED CIRCUITS.

The story of Solomon's offer to split a baby in two in order to determine who was its real mother is often used as an example of his wisdom. (*The Judgment of Solomon*, Poussin)

SOLOMON

Solomon, son of King David, ruled Israel from about 961 to 922 B.C. His name comes from the Hebrew *shelomoh*, which is related to the word meaning "peaceful." His rule was a time of peace for Israel.

The Bible says that God appeared to Solomon one night in a dream. God said, "Ask what I shall give thee." Solomon answered, "Give thy servant an understanding heart to judge thy people, that I may discern between good and bad." God was pleased that Solomon had asked for this. He answered, "I have given thee a wise and an understanding heart. . . . And I have also given thee that which thou hast not asked, both riches, and honor: so that there shall not be any among the kings like unto thee all thy days."

Solomon's glory was great. He built a magnificent temple in Jerusalem. He enlarged the wealth of his country. He raised knowledge and wisdom to a high place in his kingdom.

The temple was built with the aid of King Hiram of Tyre, who supplied skilled artisans and wood from the cedars of Lebanon. Solomon also built a royal palace, strong fortifications, and a fleet of ships. He sent his ships to trade in far-off lands. His fame spread to the Queen of Sheba. She came to Jerusalem to test his wisdom with difficult questions. His answers pleased her so much that she gave him great treasures of gold and spices and precious stones.

A well-known story demonstrating the wisdom of Solomon concerns two women who both claimed the same baby. Solomon called for a sword, and he said, "Divide the child in two, and give half to the one, and half to the other." The child's real mother immediately offered to give the child to the other woman, and in this way the wise Solomon determined who the real mother was. He knew that the real mother would never let her child be killed.

Solomon's people were not always happy under his rule. He forced those who were not Israelites to build his buildings. He sold 20 cities to Hiram when he needed money. He married foreign wives, which was against the Israelites' religion, and built shrines to their gods. After his death some of his people revolted and set up independent kingdoms.

Nevertheless, Solomon received what God had promised him—wisdom and riches and honor. His story is told in I Kings. The Song of Songs is sometimes called the Song of Solomon, but most scholars think that Solomon was not really the author. Some of his words of wisdom are thought to be a part of the collection of Proverbs.

LLOYD R. BAILEY
Duke University

SOLOMON ISLANDS

The Solomon Islands is a nation in the Pacific Ocean, located about 1,200 miles (1,900 kilometers) northeast of Australia. It is composed of a number of large islands and many smaller ones, stretching across the southwestern Pacific. The nation of the Solomon Islands includes the southern part of the larger Solomon Islands chain. The northern Solomons are part of the nation of Papua New Guinea. A former British protectorate, the Solomon Islands gained its independence in 1978.

The People. Most Solomon Islanders are Melanesians, a dark-skinned people of the Western Pacific. English is the country's official language, but at least 80 different languages and dialects are spoken throughout the islands. The most commonly used form of communication is Melanesian Pidgin, a simplified form of English with words from other languages. Most islanders are Christians.

The people live mainly in small, widely scattered villages along the coasts of the larger islands. Most are subsistence farmers, growing food for their own needs.

The Land. The major islands include Guadalcanal (the largest), Malaita (the most pop-ulous), Santa Isabela, Choiseul, New Georgia, San Christobel (or Makira), and the Santa Cruz group. The large islands are mountainous, with dense rain forests covering most of their interiors. The smaller ones are mainly low-lying atolls, or rings of coral surrounding a lagoon. The capital and largest city, Honiara, is situated on the island of Guadalcanal.

The climate is generally hot and humid. Rainfall is heavy, especially in inland areas.

FACTS AND FIGURES

SOLOMON ISLANDS is the official name of the country.

THE PEOPLE are known as Solomon Islanders.

LOCATION: Southwestern Pacific Ocean.

AREA: 10,983 sq mi (28,446 km^2).

POPULATION: 280,000 (estimate).

CAPITAL AND LARGEST CITY: Honiara.

MAJOR LANGUAGES: English (official), Melanesian Pidgin, many other local languages and dialects.

MAJOR RELIGION: Christian (mainly Protestant).

GOVERNMENT: Constitutional monarchy. **Head of state—** British monarch, represented by a governor-general. **Head of government**—prime minister. **Legislature—** National Parliament.

CHIEF PRODUCTS: Coconuts, copra (dried coconut meat), palm kernels, palm oil, rice, cocoa, frozen and canned tuna, timber, yams, sweet potatoes, cassava.

MONETARY UNIT: Solomon Islands dollar (1 SI dollar = 100 cents).

NATIONAL ANTHEM: "God Save Our Solomon Islands."

Most Solomon Islanders live in villages situated along the coastal areas of the larger islands. Inland areas, which are covered by dense rain forests, are thinly populated.

Economy. Agriculture, fishing, and forestry are the mainstays of the islands' economy. Coconuts are the most important commercial crop, and copra (dried coconut meat) is a leading export. Palm kernels and palm oil, rice, and cocoa also are exported. Frozen and canned fish (mainly tuna) are one of the islands' chief sources of export income. The forests provide timber for export.

History and Government. Little is known of the early history of the Solomons, although its people originally may have come from Southeast Asia. The first Europeans to see the islands were the Spanish in the 1500's, who named them after the biblical King Solomon. Traders and missionaries later visited the islands. In the late 1800's, Britain established a protectorate over the southern Solomons.

The Solomons gained worldwide attention during World War II. Occupied by Japan in 1942, the islands, particularly Guadalcanal and New Georgia, were the scene of major battles between Japanese and U.S. military and naval forces. After the war, the islands gained increasing self-government and won complete independence in 1978.

THE SOLOMON ISLANDS

The Solomon Islands is a constitutional monarchy. The British monarch, represented by a governor-general, is the head of state. The head of government is the prime minister, who leads the majority party in the one-house legislature, the National Parliament.

HAROLD M. ROSS
St. Norbert College (Wisconsin)

SOLON (638?–559? B.C.)

Solon was a statesman who laid the foundation for democracy in the ancient Greek city-state of Athens. He was born in Athens about 638 B.C. It was ruled at the time by a few rich, powerful families. They took over land from poor farmers and drove them out of Athens or made them slaves. The people were about to revolt, when, in 594 B.C., Solon, who was known to be fair and wise, was called in to reform the Athenian constitution.

Solon drew up a clear, simple plan that balanced the rights of the citizens. It had built-in safeguards to keep any one group from oppressing the others. Solon began by passing a law that canceled all debts owed by the poor to rich landowners and forbade that anyone be enslaved for debt in the future. Then he divided the citizens into four classes according to the property they owned, each with a different share in the government. Finally, Solon wrote a code of laws, simpler and less brutal than the existing laws.

Solon then left Athens for ten years, hoping the Athenians would make the constitution work without him. He traveled to foreign countries, studying how they were governed. On his return, he found that the Athenians had accepted some of his proposals but were still fighting over others. To advise them, he wrote wise political poems to explain his ideas. These are the earliest known poems in Athenian literature.

Civil strife went on until a strong leader called Pisistratus seized power and made himself dictator. Soon after that, in about 559 B.C., Solon died. But his reforms were not forgotten. Fifty years later Athens became a democracy based on his plan.

GILBERT HIGHET
Columbia University

SOLTI, SIR GEORG. See ORCHESTRA CONDUCTING (Profiles).

SOLZHENITSYN, ALEKSANDR. See UNION OF SOVIET SOCIALIST REPUBLICS (Profiles).

SOMALIA

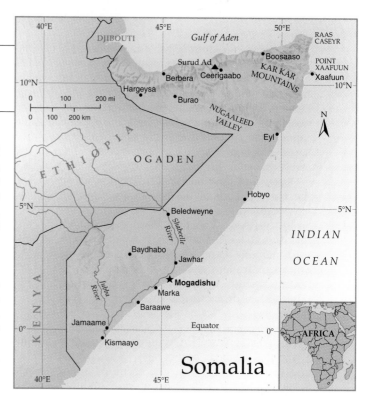

Somalia

Somalia, in eastern Africa, is one of the world's poorest nations. It has a population of 7.2 million. Somalia is bordered by the Indian Ocean to the east and the Gulf of Aden to the north, along the projection of land known as the Horn of Africa.

▶ **PEOPLE**

Many Somalis are nomadic or semi-nomadic herders of livestock; others are settled farmers. Most are gathered into clans—large groups of people who consider themselves related—and almost all are Sunni Muslims. Recent warfare has created many challenges for Somalis, including widespread malnutrition, famine, the collapse of the national government and all public services, and rule by warlord armies.

Most people speak Somali, the official language, which did not become a written language until 1972. Some also speak English, Arabic, and Italian. Education is free but not mandatory. Due to recent civil strife, most children do not attend school.

▶ **LAND**

The far northern part of Somalia consists of hills and low mountains, which reach to about 8,000 feet (2,440 meters). To the south and west is a region of low plateaus. The largest rivers are the Shabeelle and the Jubba. The southwestern part of Somalia is

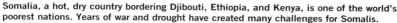

Somalia, a hot, dry country bordering Djibouti, Ethiopia, and Kenya, is one of the world's poorest nations. Years of war and drought have created many challenges for Somalis.

largely savanna, or grassland. Only about 13 percent of the country is suitable for farming.

Climate. The climate is generally hot and dry with little rain and recurring drought. Average temperatures range from 75 to 88°F (24 to 31°C).

▶ ECONOMY

Somalia's economy is based chiefly on farming and livestock. Bananas are the biggest commercial crop. Income from Somalis who work in foreign countries has become essential to the economy, as has financial assistance from other nations.

▶ MAJOR CITIES

Mogadishu, Somalia's capital and largest city, is located on the coast of the Indian Ocean. It has a population of about 500,000. Other important cities are **Kismaayo** in the south and **Berbera** on the coast of the Gulf of Aden in the north.

▶ HISTORY AND GOVERNMENT

Somalia was an ancient center of trade. Arabs arrived in the 900's. Large-scale European colonization began in the late 1800's, with Britain controlling the north and Italy the south. Britain gained control of Italian Somaliland in 1941, during World War II (1939–45).

Independence. British Somaliland won independence on June 26, 1960. On July 1, 1960, it joined with the former Italian Somaliland to create independent Somalia. The country was governed as a parliamentary democracy until 1969, when the army, led by General Mohammed Siad Barré, took over the government. A new constitution was adopted in 1979. But real power remained with Siad Barré, who was head of the military, president, and head of Somalia's only legal political party.

Recent History. Clashes with Ethiopia in the 1970's and 1980's strained the Somali economy. This resulted in civil war and opposition to Siad Barré, who was overthrown in 1991. In 1992 the Somali National Movement (SNM) proclaimed an independent Somaliland Republic in the north. Although civil war ended there, it continued in the south.

Years of war and drought created widespread famine. Because Somalia lacked a functioning central government, American

troops were sent there in 1992 to monitor the distribution of emergency food supplies. In 1993 this responsibility was taken over by the United Nations. But what had begun as a humanitarian gesture soon turned into a military operation after a number of U.N. peacekeeping troops and Americans were killed by followers of clan warlord Mohammed Farah Aidid. The last U.S. troops left Somalia in 1994 (although other United Nations troops remained), and the violence continued.

In 2004, Somalia's major warlords finally called a truce and agreed to form a new parliament based on equal representation of the four major clans. The new government elected a president, former army colonel and warlord Abdullahi Yusuf. He announced plans to hold elections under a new constitution within five years' time.

Somalia was one of several East African nations affected by a massive underwater earthquake that occurred off the coast of Indonesia on December 26, 2004. Enormous waves, traveling more than 4,000 miles (6,400 kilometers), killed at least 100 Somalis.

JON KRAUS
State University of New York, Fredonia

SONAR. See RADAR AND SONAR.

SONATA. See MUSIC (History of Western Musical Forms).

SONNETS. See POETRY

SOUND AND ULTRASONICS

The everyday world is filled with all kinds of sounds—the murmur of voices, the blaring horn of an automobile, the distant putt-putt of a lawn mower, the buzzing of a mosquito. Each of these common sounds is different from the others. And it is easy to tell all of them from hundreds of other sounds.

There are still other sounds, however, that are too high-pitched to be heard by the human ear. These sounds are called **ultrasonic** sounds, or **ultrasound.** Some animals, such as dolphins and bats, make and hear these sounds. Scientists have built special instruments to produce and detect ultrasonic sound.

In this article you will read how sounds are produced and why they are different from one another. You will also read how ultrasound has been put to use.

▶**HOW SOUNDS ARE PRODUCED**

All sounds are produced by a certain kind of motion. Suppose you stretch a rubber band and then pluck it. The band moves back and forth so rapidly that its motion appears blurred. The sound you hear comes from its motion. Such very fast, back-and-forth motions are called **vibrations.** Vibrations are the source of all sounds.

Pluck a guitar string. You will hear a musical sound. If you place your finger lightly on the string, you can feel the vibrations. They produce the sound. When you stop the vibrations, you stop the sound.

Sound Travels Through a Medium

Sound travels from a vibrating object to your ear by means of a medium, or sound carrier. The medium may be a solid, a liquid, or a gas. Air, a mixture of several gases, is the most common carrier of sound as far as people are concerned. If there is no medium to carry the sound to our ears, we cannot hear the sound. For example, the moon has no air. Astronauts on the moon cannot speak directly to each other but must communicate by radio.

▶**THE SPEED OF SOUND**

A person seated beyond the outfield of a ballpark sees a batter swing at the ball. An instant later the person hears the crack of a bat as it hits the ball. You usually hear a clap of thunder a short time after you see the bolt of

You can demonstrate that sounds are caused by vibrations. Strike a tuning fork to produce a tone and then dip the fork into water. Watch out for splashing!

lightning that caused the sound. Such common experiences demonstrate that the speed of sound is slower than the speed of light.

Careful measurements show that the speed of sound depends on the medium. For example, sound travels through the air at a speed of about 1,100 feet (335 meters) a second. Sound travels about 4 times as fast in water as it does in air. Sound travels even faster in solids. In steel and in aluminum, the speed of sound is about 15 times faster than it is in air.

Changes in temperature can change the medium enough so that sounds travel through it at a different speed. For example, sound travels slightly faster in warm air than in cold air. However, at a given temperature all sounds in the same medium have the same speed.

▶**SOUND WAVES**

Sounds travel from a vibrating object to your ear by means of compression waves in the air. To understand what a compression wave is, you can try an experiment with a coil spring toy made up of many flat metal coils. (One such toy of this type is called a Slinky.) The spring stretches open easily and then returns to its original shape. This flexibility makes it useful for the experiment.

First, find a yardstick or other stick about 3 feet (1 meter) long. Slide it through the center of the spring. Ask a helper to hold one end of the stick firmly. With your right hand hold your end of the stick and one end of the spring at the same time. With your left hand hold the free end of the spring. Now you can stretch the spring back and forth along the stick.

If you slide your left hand back and forth along the stick in a regular motion, a wave will move down the outstretched spring from one end to the other. The individual turns of the spring move only slightly out of position, yet the wave motion travels all along the coils.

To understand how this happens, think about the movement of the spring in slow motion. When you first move the end of the spring toward yourself, the coils nearest your hand are compressed. When you let go, the coils immediately spring apart, or expand, which compresses the next section of coils along the spring.

One such compression and expansion is called a **cycle.** Scientists call a wave made of many compressions and expansions a **compression wave.** Many compression waves pass along the spring as your hand continues to jiggle the end of the spring.

Molecules of air behave in much the same flexible way. When pushed by a vibrating object, air molecules bunch up, or compress, and then expand. The effect is passed along to neighboring molecules as compression waves of sound. The invisible compression waves travel through the air, gradually becoming weaker and weaker until the sound waves die out altogether. Diagrams of compression waves in a coil spring and in air molecules are shown below.

▶**CHARACTERISTICS OF SOUND WAVES**

A vibrating object sends out sound waves through the air in all directions. The waves travel outward in ever widening "shells," one inside the other. If you could see sound waves, they would look somewhat like round balloons of different sizes, one inside the other. The balloons would represent the compressions of air molecules, and the space between the balloons would represent the expansions. The vibrating body, the source of the sound, would be in the center of the smallest balloon.

Wavelength and Frequency

The distance between one compression and the next is called the **wavelength** of a sound wave. The human ear can hear sounds whose wavelengths in air are from a little less than ¾ inch (2 centimeters) to about 69 feet (21 meters) long.

An object that vibrates 500 times per second causes a sound wave that vibrates at the rate of 500 cycles per second. This rate is called the **frequency** of the sound wave. Instead of cycles per second, the term **hertz** (abbreviated Hz) is often used. This unit was named for Heinrich Hertz, a German scientist. For example, a bell or a piano string that vibrates 250 times per second produces a sound wave with a frequency of 250 hertz.

Depending on the rate of vibration, sound waves are described as being of low, medium, or high frequency. Thus, a 22-hertz wave is considered a low-frequency wave, while a wave of 7,000 hertz is a high-frequency wave.

There is a relationship between the wavelength and the frequency. Short wavelengths have a high frequency. Long wavelengths have a low frequency. There is also a connection between the frequency and the **pitch.**

The compressions and expansions of a moving coil spring are similar to the movement of air molecules when pushed by a vibrating object. An arrow indicates the distance one air molecule moves from its normal, or undisturbed, position. This distance is called the amplitude of the sound wave.

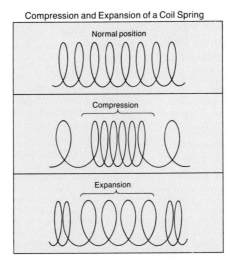

Compression and Expansion of a Coil Spring

Normal position

Compression

Expansion

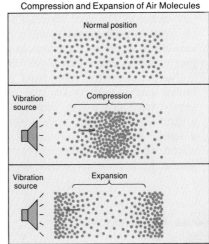

Compression and Expansion of Air Molecules

Normal position

Vibration source — Compression

Vibration source — Expansion

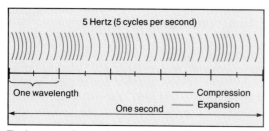

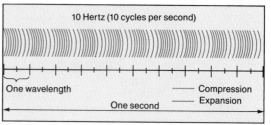

The frequency of a sound wave is determined by the number of cycles (compressions and expansions) that occur in 1 second. Sound waves of two different frequencies, measured in hertz, are shown here.

Pitch

A whistling or screeching sound has a high pitch. A deep or rumbling sound, such as you get from the low notes on a piano, has a low pitch. The pitch of a sound depends on its frequency. A high frequency (many cycles per second) produces a high pitch. A lower frequency (fewer cycles per second) produces a lower pitch.

You can show that the pitch of a sound depends on the frequency by plucking a stretched rubber band. If you pluck a loosely stretched rubber band, the frequency of the sound waves produced may be so low that you can see the vibrations of the rubber band. The sound you hear has a low pitch. Stretch the rubber band tightly and pluck it again. Its vibrations are so fast that you see only a blur, and the sound has a higher pitch.

Think of how an electric fan sounds when you turn on the switch. At first the fan turns slowly, and the air particles around it vibrate slowly. A low-frequency sound wave is produced, and you hear a low-pitched hum. As the fan whirls faster, the air particles vibrate faster. A higher-frequency sound wave results, and you hear a higher-pitched hum.

Amplitude, Loudness, and Intensity

A sound wave is a disturbance of the particles in the medium, or sound carrier. As each particle is disturbed, it moves back and forth a tiny distance. The distance each particle travels from its undisturbed position is called the **amplitude** of the sound wave. In general, the greater the amplitude, the louder the sound.

Pluck a stretched rubber band gently. It vibrates gently and strikes the air particles gently. Each air particle is made to move only a short distance—that is, the sound wave has a small amplitude. You hear a soft, gentle sound. If you pluck the rubber band with a greater force, each air particle moves a greater

How We Hear

The human ear can hear sounds of many different frequencies and intensities. It can tell the difference between an explosion and a pistol shot. It can hear a lion roar and a mouse squeal. What happens when sound waves reach your ears? How do you detect and identify the sounds?

The ear receives sound waves and changes them into electrical signals that are passed on to the brain. When the brain receives the signals, it translates them into the sensation of sound. You can read more about how the ear works in the article BODY, HUMAN (The Sense Organs).

Audible sounds are those that the human ear and brain can detect and identify. If such sounds are made weaker and weaker, they may still strike the ear but may not produce the sensation of hearing. This is because their intensity is too low to be detected by the human ear. These sounds belong to a group called inaudible sounds. They are said to be below the **threshold of hearing,** or the point at which hearing begins.

A person's ability to hear a sound depends on the frequency of the sound wave as well as its intensity. Most people are able to hear sounds in the frequency range between about 16 hertz and 20,000 hertz. Some people are able to hear sounds whose frequencies are a little higher or a little lower than this average range of audible frequencies.

Your state of health may also determine what range of frequencies you can hear. For example, if you have a cold in the head, you may not be able to hear some low or some high frequencies that you can hear normally. And as people grow older, they are often unable to hear the high-frequency sounds that were audible to them when they were young.

Today the sound of music that is amplified through loudspeakers or headphones has introduced a new health hazard. When sound levels are too high, the hearing of a young person can be so badly damaged as to resemble that of an elderly person with impaired hearing. You can read more about hearing-related problems in the article DEAFNESS in Volume D.

distance. The sound wave has a greater amplitude, and you hear a louder sound.

Loudness depends on each person's sense of hearing. Loudness may not be the same for two people sitting next to each other and listening to the same sound. One person may have a keener sense of hearing than the other. Therefore scientists cannot measure the loudness of a sound because it may be different for each person who hears it.

Scientists can, however, measure the **intensity** of a sound. Intensity refers to the amount of energy in the sound, no matter who hears it.

Think back to how you made a rubber band produce sounds of different loudness. When you plucked the rubber band gently, it produced a soft sound. When the rubber band was plucked with greater force, you put more energy into the sound. That produced a sound wave of greater amplitude. The sound had a greater intensity and was louder to your ears. It would sound louder to most people with normal hearing.

Measuring Intensity of Sound

Scientists can measure the intensity of a sound by measuring the amplitude of the sound wave. This intensity is called the **sound level.** It is measured in units called **decibels.** One decibel is the smallest change in intensity that can be detected by most people.

Here are the decibel units of some sample sounds:

Faintest whisper most people can hear: 0 decibels.
Whisper loud enough to be heard 5 feet (1.5 meters) away: 20 decibels.
Ordinary conversation at a distance of 3 feet (1 meter): 65 decibels.
Traffic on a busy street: 80 decibels.
Noisiest spot at Niagara Falls: 95 decibels.
A loud, amplified rock band: 100 decibels.

A sound level of 120 or more decibels is painful to the ears of most people. If you stood near an 11-inch (280-millimeter) heavy military gun that was being fired, the sound would be very painful to your ears. The sound level is about 230 decibels. For this reason, soldiers usually use ear protectors when they are near a big gun or cannon that is about to be fired.

Both the intensity and the loudness of a sound decrease rapidly as you move away from the sound source. Sound waves have energy. As the waves move away from their source, the energy spreads out over an ever increasing space. At a great distance from the source of the sound, the energy is so spread out that any one spot receives only a tiny bit of energy. If you are standing a great distance from the source of the sound, only a very small amount of the energy reaches your ears, and you hear only a tiny sound.

▶BEHAVIOR OF SOUND

Sound waves can behave in ways that produce a number of different special effects. Some of these effects may cause the sound to be repeated or to be louder or blurred. If you have ever heard an echo, you have heard one of these effects.

Echoes

Suppose you shout across a canyon. Part of the sound wave you have produced with your voice strikes the opposite wall of the canyon and bounces back. The sound is reflected from the canyon wall. You hear the sound of your voice returning. This returned sound is what is known as an echo.

In order for you to detect a definite echo, the reflecting surface must be at least 55 feet (16.75 meters) away from you. The reason for this has to do with the speed of sound and the way we hear.

When you shout, at first you hear your own voice. This sensation of sound lasts in your mind for about $\frac{1}{10}$ second. Thus, if you are to hear a separate echo, the sound must take at least $\frac{1}{10}$ second to cross the canyon and return. This is the minimum time that must pass before the sensation of the original shout has died out in your mind.

In this minimum time of $\frac{1}{10}$ second, sound travels about 110 feet (33.5 meters). If the canyon wall is 55 feet away, the sound will make a round trip of about 110 feet. You will be able to tell the difference between the shout and its echo, but you cannot do this if the wall is any closer. If the wall is more than 55 feet away, you may hear a clear, distinct echo of your shout as the sound wave bounces back.

Reverberation

The reflection of sound sometimes causes an effect called reverberation. In some large auditoriums and gymnasiums, for example,

Experiments with sound and accurate tests of sound equipment are often carried out in an anechoic chamber. Boxlike compartments on the walls, ceiling, and floor trap sound waves and prevent any sound from being reflected.

sounds are reflected many times from the floor, walls, and ceiling. When the sound waves bounce around between these surfaces, the original sound is repeated many times. But no distinct, separate echoes are heard. Each echo has mixed with the others that are reflected from various parts of the room. This overall effect is called reverberation.

Reverberation is measured by making a sharp sound, like the crack of a pistol, and measuring the time it takes for all the echoes and re-echoes to die out. This time is called the **time of reverberation.** If the time of reverberation in an auditorium is too long, speech sounds run together and it is hard to understand the speaker. If it is too short, the room sounds "dead" and not enough sound reaches the listeners. A certain amount of reverberation is necessary in auditoriums, especially for the enjoyment of music.

Acoustics

Acoustics is the science that is concerned with the behavior of sound. It also means the way sounds echo or reverberate in an auditorium or concert hall. People say, "The acoustics of this concert hall are very good," or "This auditorium has poor acoustics."

Engineers and architects must take into account the problems of echoes and reverberation when they plan auditoriums, concert halls, and other public places. They must design the room so that there are no echoes. But

they do want some reverberation, which is necessary for good acoustics.

The amount of reverberation can be controlled by placing special materials on the floor, walls, and ceiling of a room. Porous materials, such as wool, felt, and cork, are good sound absorbers. When sound waves enter the pores of these materials, the vibrations of the particles of the air are stopped. Sound-reflecting materials can be positioned in a room, especially auditoriums and concert halls, to help create desirable reverberations.

Sound-absorbing tiles, called acoustical tiles, line the ceilings of many restaurants, reducing the clatter of dishes and the noise made by the voices of many people. Soft draperies, carpets, and wall hangings help to reduce reverberation in auditoriums and concert halls.

The presence of people in an auditorium also affects the acoustics. The clothing and bodies of people absorb some of the sound waves. In an empty auditorium, listen to the way your voice sounds. It sounds different than when most of the seats are filled.

For special experiments, scientists often use a room called an anechoic chamber. Anechoic means without echoes. The walls, ceiling, and floor of such a room are constructed of sound-absorbing materials built into compartments of various sizes. Different size compartments trap sounds of different wavelengths. The result is a room in which almost no sound is reflected. Such a chamber reveals the true sound quality of instruments and voices. The anechoic chamber is useful for making very accurate measurements of sound and for testing microphones and other devices.

Natural Frequency

When you strike an object and make it vibrate, the force of your blow determines the intensity of the sound wave. But the frequency of the sound wave does not depend on the force of your blow. The frequency depends on the size, shape, and material of the object. Every vibrating object has its own frequency of vibration. This is called its natural frequency.

For example, the metal of a bell vibrates at its own natural frequency no matter how hard the clapper inside the bell strikes the metal. A tuning fork—a two-pronged "fork" used by musicians and singers to get a pure tone—is constructed to vibrate at a certain frequency. If it is constructed to vibrate at 440 cycles per second, this is its natural frequency.

Sympathetic Vibrations

Suppose two neighboring objects have the same natural frequency. One of the objects is made to vibrate. Its sound waves reach the second object and strike against it. Because the frequency of the sound waves is the same as the natural frequency of the second object, the waves start the second object vibrating. Both produce the same note. The second object is in **sympathetic vibration** with the first.

Suppose a tree crashes to the ground in a forest where there is no one to hear it. Does the sound exist?

There would be no *sensation* of sound, because a sensation can exist only if there is a brain to receive the sensation "signal." But there would be a sound, because a sound is a disturbance in the air. The crashing tree sends out sound waves even if they are not received by an ear and changed into the sensation of sound.

Why do you hear a roaring sound, like the sound of the sea, when you hold a large snail or conch shell over your ear?

Some very soft sounds in the air around you match the natural vibrating frequencies of parts of the shell or air spaces within the shell. The shell and its air chambers vibrate in sympathy, resonating and amplifying the sounds outside. You do not really hear the "sound of the sea" as many people think. You hear amplified sounds from the air around you.

If you have two tuning forks of the same frequency, you can hear sympathetic vibrations. Hold each tuning fork at its stem and make one vibrate by striking it against the edge of a table. After the tuning fork has sounded for a few seconds, stop its vibration by moving your hand up to the prongs. You can then hear the same sound coming from the second fork, because it is in sympathetic vibration with the first.

Sympathetic vibrations can cause an avalanche. In a mountainous region, a large mass of rocks and snow may be piled loosely on a steep slope. The sound waves from a human voice or from some other source may cause some rock and snow particles to vibrate sympathetically. This small motion is sometimes enough to start the large mass of loosely piled material tumbling down the mountainside.

Resonance

An effect called resonance occurs when a number of small repeated pushes cause a large vibration. Resonance increases the amplitude, and thus the intensity, of a sound.

For an example of how resonance occurs, think of a child sitting on a swing. You give the swing a push, and it starts moving in an arc. If you continue giving a small push each time the swing is at its highest point, the swing soon moves through a wide arc. Although each push is small, you have timed the pushes so that their effect adds up, producing the large back-and-forth motion.

The swing has a natural frequency at which it moves back and forth. Your pushes, if timed to this natural frequency, add up to make the wider arc. If you push at a faster or a slower rate, the swing comes almost to a stop. Resonance takes place only when you push at the natural frequency of the swing.

The sounds made by wind instruments in music are reinforced (strengthened) by resonance. The resonance comes from a column of air inside the instrument. Thus, the sound of a trumpet or a bugle is reinforced by resonance of the air inside the instrument.

Forced Vibration

Sometimes an object can be made to vibrate at a frequency other than its natural frequency. Its back-and-forth motion is then called forced vibration. A common example of forced vibration is in the eardrum. When sound waves

When two sound waves reach your ears at the same time, the compressions and expansions of one wave interfere with the compressions and expansions of the other wave. The result is a series of loud and soft pulses, called beats. This effect is usually only noticeable when the sound waves are very pure, such as in musical notes, and when the two sounds have very nearly the same frequency.

strike the eardrum, they cause it to vibrate at the frequency of the received sound wave.

You can use a tuning fork to produce forced vibrations. Strike the tuning fork to make the prongs vibrate, and listen to the sound for a moment. The sound is quite soft. Now place the stem of the fork against the top of a table. The sound at once becomes much louder. The vibrations of the fork force the tabletop to vibrate at the same frequency as the tuning fork. The table's larger size sets more air in motion than the tuning fork alone does, and you hear a louder sound.

Many musical instruments are designed so that forced vibrations amplify their sounds. In a violin, for example, vibrating strings force the wood to vibrate—thereby increasing the sound made by the strings. The forced vibration of the sounding board of a piano amplifies the sound made when a note is struck.

Interference and Beats

If two musicians play a tone of the same frequency, the two sounds combine. The result is a louder sound. But if two tones of only slightly different frequencies are played together, a series of loud and soft sounds is heard. This effect—of loud and soft sounds occurring one after the other—is called beats.

Beats are caused by the interference of two sound waves. When the compressions and expansions of two different sound waves reach your ear at the same time, they reinforce each other. The sound becomes louder. But when the compressions of one wave reach your ear at the same time as the expansions of the

other, they interfere with each other. For a moment, almost no sound is heard.

You can hear beats by using two tuning forks that have the same frequency. Change the frequency of one fork slightly by putting a thin rubber band around one of its prongs. Then strike the forks. You will hear the repeated loudness and softness as regular pulses. These are beats.

It is annoying to hear more than four or five beats per second, and beats can spoil music. Musicians in an orchestra tune their instruments in unison so that all will produce the same pitch, or frequency. This eliminates the possibility of beats on identical pitches, and the instruments are said to be "in tune."

However, this applies only to notes of the same name, such as all "A" notes. In modern, or "tempered," tuning, all other intervals are very slightly out of tune and actually generate beats. This system is used to equalize the various intervals between the half-steps of the musical scale. These beats, described as "shimmers," give the characteristic richness to groups of notes played together as chords.

Doppler Effect

Have you ever noticed the change in pitch of a train whistle or automobile horn as the vehicle approaches and then passes you? As the sound source comes toward you, the pitch sounds higher. When the source is nearest you, you hear the sound at its normal pitch. Then as the source of sound moves away from you the pitch drops. This change in pitch is called the Doppler effect, after Christian Doppler, a 19th-century Austrian scientist.

An automobile horn, like a train whistle, always vibrates at the same frequency. The apparent change in frequency in the sound wave is caused by the motion of the automobile. When the vehicle approaches you, it is moving in the same direction as the sound waves coming from the horn. The sound waves are pushed closer together. Your ear receives more vibrations each second than the horn actually sends out. This gives the effect of a higher frequency, and you hear a higher-pitched sound.

After the car passes you, the opposite effect takes place. The horn still sends out the same sound waves but is moving away from the waves. The sound waves are spaced farther apart, and your ear receives fewer vibrations a

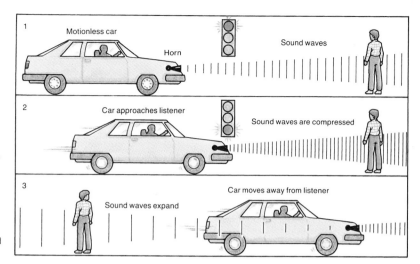

The Doppler Effect

The sound of an automobile horn is heard at a normal pitch when the car is motionless (1). As the car approaches a listener, the sound waves are compressed, and the horn sounds higher pitched (2). After the car passes, the sound waves are spaced farther apart, and a lower-pitched sound is heard (3).

second than the horn sends out. This gives the effect of a lower frequency, and you hear a lower-pitched sound.

The Doppler effect occurs whenever distance is changing between the source of sound and the listener. For example, you will hear a change in pitch if you are driving past a parked car whose horn is blowing. The amount of change depends on how fast the sound source or the listener is moving. If the speed of the sound source or the listener is great, the change in pitch is great. If the speed is slow, the change in pitch is less.

▶**MUSICAL SOUNDS**

What determines whether a vibrating object will produce a noise, a pleasant sound, or a musical tone?

When compressions and expansions of a sound wave follow each other in an even, regular order, the sound is pleasant. People usually call it music. When the compressions and expansions follow each other in an uneven, irregular pattern, the sound we hear is a noise.

Hammering on a steel tank produces a loud noise. The metal of the tank vibrates unevenly. It sends out compressions and expansions that do not follow each other in a regular pattern. A note played on the piano is a musical tone because the strings that produce the tone send out a regular pattern of compressions and expansions. A skilled pianist plays enjoyable music by producing a series of regular vibrations that blend well together. A child banging on the piano keyboard produces unpleasant noises.

An exception to this rule is the sound of percussion instruments. Cymbals and most drums produce random combinations of frequencies, usually considered noises. However, when the bursts of noise are skillfully played in organized combinations, noise is converted into music.

Fundamentals and Overtones

A tuning fork is a specially constructed device that vibrates at only one particular frequency. However, most vibrating objects vibrate at several frequencies at the same time.

To understand how an object can vibrate at several frequencies at once, look at the figure below. A string is stretched between the two posts. When plucked in the middle, the string vibrates as a whole, as in (A). When plucked halfway between the middle and either end, the string again vibrates as a whole. But each half of the string vibrates separately as well (B). Depending on where it is plucked, the string can be made to vibrate as a whole and also in three or more separate parts, as in (C) and (D). The parts vibrate at a different frequency from the vibration of the whole string.

Depending on where it is plucked (indicated by arrow), a string will vibrate at several different frequencies. Harmonics, or overtones, are produced when parts of the string vibrate differently than the string as a whole.

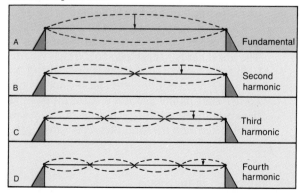

DEMONSTRATIONS YOU CAN DO WITH SOUND

MAKE A SET OF MUSICAL GLASSES

You need:

    8 drinking glasses (4 large and 4 small)
    water
    a pencil

Set the glasses in a row. Pour different amounts of water into the glasses.

    Use the pencil to strike each glass near the top. Listen to the tones produced by the different lengths of the water columns in each glass.

    Experiment with the amounts of water and the order of the glasses until they begin to resemble the sounds of a musical scale. One such arrangement is shown in the diagram below. However, all glasses are different, so your result may look a little different than the diagram. If you have a test-tube rack and eight test tubes, the eight tubes also can be made to produce the tones of a musical scale.

SHOW HOW THE VIBRATIONS OF A TUNING FORK ARE PASSED ON AS THE FORK PRODUCES A SOUND

You need:

    4 table-tennis balls
    4 strings, each 8 inches (20 centimeters)
    transparent tape
    a tuning fork

With the tape, attach a string to each ball. The balls should swing freely from the strings.

    Tie the free ends of the strings to a support, such as a towel rack. The balls should be about ¼ inch (0.5 centimeter) apart, and the string must not touch the wall or any other solid object.

    Strike the tuning fork and hold it to your ear for a moment to be sure it is producing a sound. Then hold it close to the first ball. Watch how the ball swings as the vibrations from the tuning fork strike it. Notice how the vibration is transmitted to the other balls.

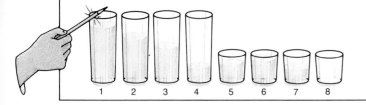

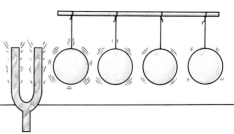

The tone produced by the vibration of the string as a whole is called the fundamental tone of the string. The tones produced by the vibrations of the parts are called overtones or harmonics.

Musical instruments are designed to produce both a fundamental tone and overtones. In stringed instruments the strings vibrate as a whole and in sections, producing fundamentals and overtones. When a wind or woodwind instrument is played, the column of air in the instrument vibrates as a whole and in sections, producing both fundamentals and overtones. The metal or skin of percussion instruments produces overtones as well as fundamentals.

The different combinations of fundamentals and overtones give the sound of each musical instrument its special quality. Two instruments playing the same note sound different because each instrument produces different overtones. You might say that each has its own "recipe" of fundamentals and overtones.

Like different musical instruments, each human voice has its own sound-wave recipe. The vocal cords in each person's throat vibrate with frequencies and overtones that depend on the size, thickness, length, and tension of the cords. The amount and force of the air passing between the cords as a person speaks also helps determine the kind of sound waves produced. This makes it possible for you to identify many different voices, just as you can tell the difference between the sound of a piano and a flute.

►ULTRASONICS

The human ear generally cannot hear sound waves whose frequency is higher than about 20,000 hertz. Such high-frequency waves are called ultrasound or ultrasonic waves. ("Ultra" means "beyond," and "sonic" means "sound.") Ultrasonic waves may have frequencies as high as millions of hertz. They can never be heard by a person.

Ultrasonic waves can be produced in several ways. One method requires a thin slice of a quartz crystal. (Quartz is a common mineral. It has the unusual property of responding to a changing, or alternating, electric current by vibrating in step with the current.) High-frequency alternating current is fed into the quartz. The crystal vibrates in step with the current and produces an ultrasonic wave. Another method makes use of an electromagnet with a special core usually made of the metal nickel. When a high-frequency alternating current is passed through the electromagnet, the nickel core expands and contracts slightly. This sets up ultrasonic vibrations in the surrounding medium.

Uses of Ultrasound

Ultrasonic waves have a very short wavelength. (Short wavelengths have a high frequency.) Because of this, many waves—and their energy—are packed into a small space. Scientists have found ways of putting this concentrated energy to use in scientific research, in industry, and in medicine.

Ordinary sound waves move outward in all directions. But the very short wavelengths of ultrasonic waves make it possible to beam ultrasound in a straight line. Scientists have used straight ultrasonic beams in systems called **sonar** to locate submarines, schools of fish, and other solid objects underwater.

In sonar systems, sound reflections, or echoes, are used to detect the solid objects. A pulse, or burst, of ultrasonic waves is sent out from an instrument on a ship. The ultrasonic waves travel underwater in a straight line until they strike a solid object. The waves are then reflected and received at an instrument on board the ship.

To measure the depth of the ocean a type of sonar system called a **fathometer** is used. An operator aboard a ship beams an ultrasonic wave down into the water. The time it takes for the echo of the sound wave to return to the instrument on the ship gives the operator the depth of the water.

Ultrasound is used in industry to detect flaws hidden deep inside metals or other solid materials. An ultrasonic wave is beamed into the part to be tested. The way in which the beam is echoed back into a receiving device tells whether there is a defect in the material and where the defect is.

An ultrasonic wave passed through a liquid makes the liquid vibrate very fast. The vibration can shake up paint to mix it thoroughly, homogenize milk by breaking up the fat particles, and clean tools, machine parts, dishes, and other solid objects.

Ultrasound is used experimentally to break down the cell walls of bacteria. In medicine it is used to help detect brain injuries, to trace blood flow through various parts of the body, and for certain kinds of surgery. In dentistry, a dental drill controlled by ultrasonic vibrations can neatly penetrate or cut into tooth enamel, creating very little friction or heat in the gum tissue. Certain ultrasound frequencies can be used to penetrate muscles and create heat, thereby stimulating circulation.

A mother and her family watch monitor screens during an ultrasound test. Ultrasounds safely pass through the mother's body to produce an image of her unborn baby.

An interesting application of ultrasound is in ultrasonic holography, a method of producing three-dimensional pictures with ultrasound. This is possible because ultrasound waves can easily travel through soft body tissues. When they reach denser layers of bone and cartilage, the waves are reflected back. Computers store and compare the images to generate three-dimensional pictures. With this technique it is even possible to safely detect the form of an unborn baby inside its mother's womb.

Ultrasonics and Animals

Some animals can hear ultrasonic sounds. For example, dogs can hear the high-pitched sound of a dog whistle that most people cannot hear. There are some animals that have built-in sonar systems. Dolphins have a sort of sonar system that they use to locate fish and obstacles in the water. Bats, too, have a sonar system. They find their way about in darkness by uttering ultrasonic squeaks that are echoed back to them from solid objects like walls. Because animal sonar is so efficient, scientists are studying these animals to learn their "ultrasonic secrets."

WILLIAM C. VERGARA
Director of Advanced Research
The Bendix Corporation

Reviewed by LARRY KETTLEKAMP
Author, *The Magic of Sound*

See also NOISE.

In a sound recording studio, music is saved in a permanent form for later playback.

SOUND RECORDING

Sound recording is a means of preserving sound in a permanent, physical form so that it can be reproduced at a later time. Almost any kind of sound can be saved with sound recording equipment. Music on a cassette tape and speech on a motion picture sound track are two familiar examples of recorded sound.

▶ WHAT IS SOUND?

Sounds are made up of **pressure waves** that travel through gases, liquids, and even solids. These pressure waves are typically caused by the vibration of objects, such as a guitar string or the larynx (voice box) in our throats.

Any moving object causes the molecules in the air around it to bunch up and then spread apart. When the molecules bunch up, a region of high pressure is created in the air. When the molecules spread apart, a low pressure region is formed. A series of high and low pressures creates the pressure waves that make up sound. When the pressure waves reach our ears, we hear the sound.

We cannot see sound, but we can see a good representation of it by using an instrument called an **oscilloscope**. What appears on the screen of an oscilloscope is a representation of the shape of the pressure wave, or **sound wave**. This shape is called the **waveform**. From this waveform scientists can study the various physical properties of the sound wave. For more information, see the article SOUND AND ULTRASONICS in this volume.

▶ HOW SOUND IS RECORDED

There are four kinds of materials used to record sound: phonograph records (the least-used material today), magnetic tapes, motion picture film, and optical discs. All recording is done only on the surface of these materials.

To record sounds on a recording material, the sound waves in the air are first converted by a microphone into waveforms of electricity. These electrical waveforms have nearly the same shape as the original sound waves.

The electricity is then used to "write" the waveforms onto the recording material. This can be done **mechanically**, as in the case of the phonograph record; it can be done **magnetically**, as in the case of a magnetic tape (which includes tape used in videocassette recorders); or it can be done **optically**, as in the case of a motion picture sound track or an optical disc such as an audio compact disc (CD).

Reproduction, or playback, of sound is essentially the reverse of recording. The recorded patterns are converted back to electrical waveforms nearly identical to the originals. These waveforms are amplified (made larger) and sent to a loudspeaker or headphones, where they produce sounds that are close imitations of the originals.

The term **fidelity** is used to describe how closely the reproduced sound matches the original. The term **high fidelity**, or **hi-fi**, refers to high quality sound reproduction.

Recording on Tracks. Because many minutes or even hours of sound are usually preserved during a recording session, a recorded waveform must be stretched out in one long, continuous track. The groove of a phonograph record, for example, is a continuous spiral that starts at the outside of the disc and ends near the inside. Spacing of the grooves on successive turns is less than $\frac{1}{1,000}$ of an inch (25 micrometers). (A human hair is about 100 micrometers in diameter.) If we were to change a record's spiral groove to a straight line, the line would be greater than a mile in length.

A similar spiral track is employed in the optical disc. There are 15 times the number of tracks on optical discs in the same-sized area as there are on phonograph records. The tracks are so close to each other that they have a spacing similar to that of the wavelength of light. When white light reflects from the closely spaced tracks, it is broken up into its color components. That is why we see rainbow colors on the surface of an optical disc.

The magnetic tape in a cassette (a small, enclosed plastic case) is a few hundred feet long. The open reels of a large tape recorder can hold several thousand feet of tape. The recording track is as long as the magnetic tape, but a tape can have several recording tracks along its width. A person can record to the end of one track and then continue to record on the next track going in the opposite direction. This can be done as many times as there are tracks.

Stereophonic Sound. When we listen to live music or other sounds, slightly different vibrations reach our left and right ears. Reproduced sound seems more realistic if it re-creates those slight differences. This can be done by using two microphones and individually recording the sounds reaching each microphone. The recorded sounds are then played back through two separate loudspeakers or headphones.

Each separate sound path is called a **channel**. Reproducing sound this way is called stereophonic sound, or simply **stereo**. (Recorded sound made up of a single channel is called **monophonic sound**.) Stereo phonograph records have each channel recorded on opposite sides of the groove. Stereo tapes have two parallel tracks.

▶PHONOGRAPH RECORDS

The phonograph record stores sound waveforms in the form of a shallow groove cut by a sharp stylus (needle) into the surface of a master disc. The sound waveform is "written" onto the disc by moving the stylus from side to side. This forms a graph, or diagram, of the waveform—hence the name "phonograph," meaning "sound-writing." A mold of the master disc is made, and that mold is used to press out copies.

To play back a phonograph record, a pointed stylus is placed in the shallow groove.

The record turns at a steady speed—33⅓ revolutions per minute (abbreviated 33⅓ rpm) for long-playing records. The standard speed for "singles" is 45 rpm. As the record turns, the stylus wiggles slightly from side to side as it follows the groove on the disc. The motion of the stylus is turned into an electrical waveform by the phonograph pickup cartridge. The waveform is then amplified and turned into sound by the loudspeakers or headphones.

▶MAGNETIC TAPE

The sound pattern on the surface of a magnetic tape is invisible, because we cannot see magnetism. If we could see the recorded waveforms on a tape, they would appear as a line of tiny permanent magnets placed end to end along the length of a track.

A magnetic tape is made of a thin ribbon of clear plastic that is usually less than ¹/₁,₀₀₀ inch (25 micrometers) thick. This ribbon is coated on one side with billions of microscopic magnetic particles.

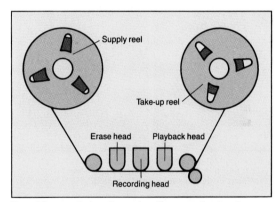

Sound is recorded on tape when the recording head arranges magnetic particles on the tape in a pattern that corresponds to the original sound waves.

Magnetic waveforms are created by pulling the tape over the surface of a small electromagnet called a **recording head**. The electrical signal from the microphone changes the strength and direction of the current in the coils of the electromagnet. The changing magnetic field from the electromagnet produces the magnetic pattern on the track.

The original sound can be reproduced by pulling the tape across another electromagnet called a **playback head**. This time the electromagnet is not driven by an electrical signal. It uses the principle of magnetic induction in which moving magnetic lines of force produce an electrical signal. This signal is amplified and fed to a loudspeaker or headphones.

▶ MOTION PICTURE SOUND TRACK

A motion picture sound track runs along one edge of the same film that contains the motion picture images. It provides sound for the picture being projected onto a theater screen.

Sound for a motion picture is recorded on special magnetic tape at the same time that the pictures are exposed on photographic film. The sound track is transferred to the film as a series of light and dark regions along the film's edge. These regions may be thick and thin horizontal lines or a single black vertical line that varies in width.

To reproduce the sound, a beam of light is projected on the sound track in the motion picture projector. The amount of light that passes through the film varies as the light and dark

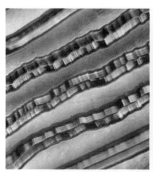

Magnified images of grooves on a phonograph record (*left*) and pits on a compact disc (*right*) show two of the surfaces on which sound can be stored.

regions pass by. A device called a **photodetector** converts the varying brightness into an electrical waveform that closely matches the originally recorded sound waveform.

▶ DIGITAL RECORDING OF SOUND

Sound recording machines fall into two categories—analog recorders and digital recorders. Thus far we have been describing analog recording, in which sound waveforms are written directly onto the surfaces of recording materials.

Another very different way to record sound is called digital audio recording. Digital recording uses electronic devices that are similar

to computers. In this method sound waveforms are first measured and converted to numbers. Because computers are involved, these numbers are represented in binary form as a series of zeros and ones. They are then "stored" on a tape as a series of magnetic reversals (reversal = 1, no reversal = 0) or on a compact disc as a series of pits in the track (pit edge = 1, no pit edge = 0).

To reproduce the sound, a compact disc player uses a tiny laser to send light onto the pits in the track. The light reflects onto a photodetector, which transforms the pattern of pits into an electrical signal. A tiny computer-like electronic device receives that signal, recognizes the series of digits, and reproduces the original waveform as an electrical signal.

A digital audio tape player reproduces sound in much the same way except that it uses a playback head instead of a laser and photodetector.

Digital audio recording is considered a technical advance over analog recording, in part because the reproduced sound has less distortion. That is, the played-back waveforms more closely resemble the original waveforms.

Compact Discs (CD's). The audio compact disc, like the phonograph record, is made of plastic pressed by a master disc. Recording is done by a tiny spot of laser light, which is focused onto the surface of the spinning master disc. This spot is turned on and off by the bits of a digital audio signal. As this happens, small oval spots are exposed onto the surface of the master disc. The spots are arranged in a spiral track.

The master disc is then chemically developed, much like photographic film. The exposed spots are washed away, leaving tiny pits in the disc's surface. From this a metal master disc is made for pressing out plastic copies.

To play back sound from a compact disc, the disc is placed into a CD player, where it spins at approximately four revolutions per second. As it spins, a tiny spot of laser light follows the spiral track of pits. The pits change the amount of light reflected from the disc as they pass under the spot. This changing light is directed into a photodetector. The photodetector changes the light to a series of on-off electrical pulses that represent the binary digits of the original recording. Finally, the pulses are changed to a sound waveform by a special computer-like converter.

MODERN STEREO SYSTEMS

Today's music listener has a wide variety of equipment choices for making and enjoying recorded sound. The following audio components, in combination, make up a complete stereo system:

The **record player** consists of a rotating turntable, a stylus (needle) contained in a cartridge, and a tonearm that holds the stylus in position in the record groove. The **compact disc player** has now become a primary stereo component, in many cases replacing the record player. A **cassette tape recorder** also is often included in a modern stereo system.

The compact disc player was introduced in the early 1980's and quickly became popular. It has replaced the record player in most stereo systems.

The **tuner** receives radio broadcasts, usually both AM and FM stations. The **preamplifier** strengthens the electrical signal coming from the record player or other components. It also contains volume and tone controls for the stereo system.

The **power amplifier** provides power to the loudspeakers. It may be combined with the preamplifier in a component called an **integrated amplifier**. The integrated amplifier and the tuner are often combined in one housing called a **receiver**.

Loudspeakers are made up of **drivers**, which convert electrical energy into mechanical motion, thereby creating sound waves in the surrounding air. The driver that handles low-frequency sounds is relatively large and is called a **woofer**. High-frequency sounds are handled by a small driver, called a **tweeter**. Many loudspeakers also include a third driver that operates only at middle frequencies. Headphones are simply miniature loudspeakers that are held in place on the ears.

HISTORY OF SOUND RECORDING

The phonograph was the first practical means of sound recording. Invented by Thomas Edison in 1877, the early phonograph recorded sound on a groove cut into the surface of a hollow cylinder. The cylinder was later replaced by the flat phonograph disc we use today.

Early motion pictures contained no sound, and moviegoers had to read printed dialogue projected on the screen between scenes. But in the 1920's, phonograph records were synchronized with the film projectors (which

made the sound and the action occur at precisely the same time). Soon the optical sound track was invented, and sound recording was combined with the images on the film.

The ancestor of the magnetic tape recorder was the wire recorder, developed in the late 1890's. The first machine to use magnetic tape was called a **magnetophone**, developed in Germany in the late 1930's.

Reel-to-reel tape recording machines came into general use in the 1950's. Tape recording was adapted to the eight-track cartridge and was very popular in the 1960's. Today the smaller cassette tape is the most familiar form of tape recording for consumer use. Digital audio magnetic tapes are also available. One kind is called the digital audio tape (DAT) cassette and is used widely by professional recordists. Another is called the digital compact cassette (DCC).

Compact discs were developed in the mid-1970's and became widely available in the early 1980's. Recordable compact discs became available in the early 1990's. One type of CD can be recorded on only one time. Another type is called the MiniDisc (MD). Because the MD recorder uses a combination magnetic and optical system, MD's can be recorded on many times.

PETER VOGELGESANG
Staff Scientist, 3M
Reviewed by DELOS EILERS
Senior Specialist, 3M

See also HIGH-FIDELITY SYSTEMS; PHONOGRAPH; SOUND AND ULTRASONICS; VIDEO RECORDING.

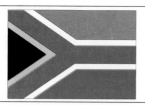

SOUTH AFRICA

The Republic of South Africa is situated at the southern tip of Africa, where the Atlantic and Indian oceans meet. Its neighboring countries are Namibia on the northwest; Botswana and Zimbabwe on the north; and Mozambique and Swaziland on the northeast. The small nation of Lesotho is an enclave of (lies within) South Africa. In area, South Africa is nearly as large as the European nations of Britain, France, and Sweden combined. Although it is not the largest country on the African continent, South Africa is the most highly industrialized and the most prosperous.

▶ THE PEOPLE

South Africa has a varied population. About 72 percent of the people are black Africans. Whites (sometimes called Europeans) make up about 16 percent of the population. Other groups are the Coloureds (mixed black African and other races) and the Asians (mostly East Indians). The whites have long controlled the country and most of its wealth.

Blacks. Most black South Africans are Bantu, which refers to a large language family spoken across much of central and southern Africa. The word "Bantu" itself means "the people." There are a number of Bantu tribes in South Africa, including the Xhosa, the Zulu, the Sotho, and the Tswana. The tribes differ in language, dress, and customs. Although the various Bantu languages are related, there are differences among them, and members of different tribes may have trouble understanding one another. To be able to communicate, many blacks learn to speak a simple common language called Fanagalo. Others speak Afrikaans and English, which are two

One of the world's most scenic cities, Cape Town lies at the southwestern tip of the African continent, on the blue waters of Table Bay. Behind the city is the massive outcropping of Table Mountain. Cape Town is South Africa's oldest city, the second largest in population, and the site of the Parliament, or national legislature.

of the country's eleven official languages. The others are the major Bantu languages. In religion, some black South Africans follow traditional African faiths, but the majority belong to the Protestant or Roman Catholic churches or to independent churches that combine traditional and Christian beliefs.

South Africa also has small numbers of Khoikhoi and San who were among its earliest inhabitants. The San, a shy people, retreated before the newcomers into the Kalahari Desert, where most now live.

Traditional Black Life. Traditionally, most blacks lived off the land, growing crops and raising cattle. The land now available to blacks is not sufficient to support them all, however. Many have had to leave their villages to find work in the cities, in the mines, or on the large white-owned farms.

Traditional African dress is usually now worn only on special occasions and varies from tribe to tribe. Xhosa men, for example, wear colorful woven wrappers and carry goatskin bags that can hold small tools or other necessities. The women wear dyed oxhide skirts, hooded shawls, and colorful beaded bracelets and armbands. The Sotho, who live in a cool climate, wear woolen garments. Black South African villages are called kraals. A typical Zulu kraal consists of a number of beehive-shaped, one-room thatched houses built around a large animal pen.

Whites. There are two main groups of whites, the Afrikaners and the English. The Afrikaners are descended from the Dutch who first went to South Africa with the Dutch East India Company in the 1600's. They were joined by French and German Protestants who left their countries to escape religious persecution. Today these people form a very close-knit group. The majority of Afrikaners belong to the Dutch Reformed Church. Their language is Afrikaans, which resembles Dutch.

British settlers began to arrive in South Africa in the early 1800's. Many of the English-speaking whites live and work in the larger cities. Most are members of the Anglican (Episcopal), Methodist, Presbyterian, or Roman Catholic churches. South Africa also has a small Jewish community.

Coloureds and Asians. The Coloureds are descendants of intermarriages between the early Dutch settlers, Malayan slaves, Khoikhoi, and other Africans. Most Coloureds

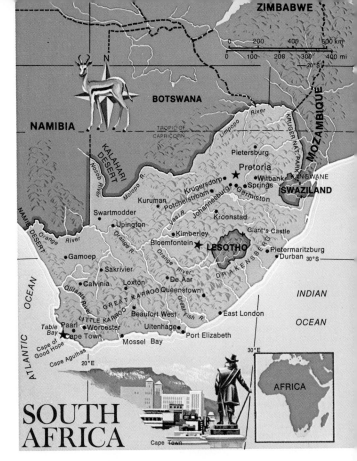

have light-brown skin and speak Afrikaans. Their way of life is more like that of whites than black Africans.

Asians were first brought to South Africa from India in the late 1800's to work on the sugar plantations. Almost all follow the Hindu or Muslim religions.

Race Relations. Until 1993, relations between South Africa's various peoples were based on a strict system of racial separation called apartheid. Established by the white minority government, apartheid dominated every aspect of South African life. Racial classification determined who could vote and where people could live, work, and go to school. Most of the country was reserved for whites. Areas known as tribal homelands, or Bantustans, were set aside for the blacks.

Several of the homelands were declared independent by the South African government. They included Transkei, Bophuthatswana, Venda, and Ciskei. But they remained economically dependent on South Africa, and no government, aside from South Africa itself, ever recognized their independence.

However, since black workers were needed in South African industry, agriculture, and as domestic servants, most lived outside the homelands in special townships near the places where they worked. Because blacks were not allowed to own land outside the homelands, those who lived in the townships had no political rights there, although they had some control over local affairs.

Some of the racial laws were relaxed or abolished in the late 1980's and early 1990's, and both the system of apartheid and the homelands themselves were done away with entirely following the approval of a new constitution in 1993. See the Government and History sections of this article.

Education. The political changes that South Africa is undergoing also will affect its educational system. The apartheid laws provided for separate education for the various racial groups. Educational requirements differed. White, Coloured, and Asian children were required by law to attend school between the ages of 7 and 16. Education for black children was only required between the ages of 7 and 11, and only about half actually completed their last year. Black schools also received considerably less funding.

South Africa has a number of fine universities. Formerly segregated, they began to admit students of all races in the 1980's.

▶**THE LAND**

A Country of Great Variety. South Africa is a land of great beauty and variety. In the far south, the city of Cape Town lies on curved, picturesque Table Bay. Around the city are vineyards, fruit orchards, farms, factories, and gardens. Table Mountain rises steeply behind the city. A mountain ridge divides the fertile farmland from the plateaus a little farther north. The Great Karroo, a plateau area, is used as pasture for sheep. The land then rises in giant rocky steps to the High Veld (high grassland country) of the north. This is an area of good farmland, which is also rich in gold and other minerals. Corn grows well on the flat, open veld.

Farther north the land changes to wooded savanna. Then it drops down to the steamy forest through which the Limpopo (Crocodile) River flows to the Indian Ocean.

The Drakensberg mountain range forms a sharp spine parallel to the Indian Ocean in the east. At the edge of the Drakensberg is the Great Escarpment, which falls sharply to the coastal plain below. On the plain are citrus fruit orchards and sugarcane plantations. South Africa's chief river, the Orange, rises in the Drakensberg and flows toward the Atlantic Ocean.

Above: Strollers in Johannesburg, South Africa's largest city, reflect the country's varied population, which includes whites, blacks, people of mixed race, and Asians. *Right:* The striking South African landscape is as varied as the people. The eastern part of the country, seen here, consists of a high, grassy plateau and rolling hills that lead up to the Drakensberg mountain range.

Climate. South Africa has a generally mild climate, with few extremes of hot or cold. This is due largely to the influence of the surrounding waters. Average annual temperatures range from 73°F (23°C) in the north to about 54°F (12°C) in the south.

Rainfall is heaviest in the Drakensberg mountain range and along the eastern coast, where an average of 40 inches (1,000 millimeters) falls each year. Other areas, especially in the west, are dry, with a desert or semi-desert climate.

▶ **THE ECONOMY**

Manufacturing and Mining. Manufacturing is the most important part of South Africa's economy. Steel products are the chief manufactures. Other important industrial products are building materials, chemicals, processed foods, shoes, and clothing.

South Africa is one of the richest countries in the world in terms of mineral wealth. It produces more than half of the world's supply of gold, which is its single most important export. Its gold-mining center is in the Witwatersrand ("white water ridge") in the north. South Africa is also a major ex-

Gold is mined at the Witwatersrand. South Africa produces more than half of the world's gold, which is the country's most valuable single export.

porter of quality diamonds. It is one of the world's leading producers of uranium, manganese, and vanadium. There are, in addition, large deposits of coal, iron ore, platinum, and other minerals. South Africa obtains much of its energy from coal.

Agriculture. About 14 percent of South Africans make their living from the soil. Corn is the chief food crop. Known as "mealies," it is a staple food of the blacks. Wheat, oats, and barley are also grown. Sugarcane, citrus fruits, and wine grapes flourish in South Africa's mild climate. Cattle, sheep, and pigs provide meat, dairy products, and wool.

▶ **MAJOR CITIES**

South Africa has three national capitals—Cape Town (legislative), where Parliament is housed; Pretoria (administrative), where the prime minister and cabinet maintain their offices; and Bloemfontein (judicial), where the Supreme Court sits.

Johannesburg, South Africa's largest city, was founded in 1886 as a gold-mining town. Today it is the heart of South Africa's industry and trade. Its industries include breweries, flour mills, and plants that produce chemicals and clothing. Never far from view are the yellow mounds of the dumps from the gold mines that brought great wealth to South Africa.

Cape Town is South Africa's second city in population, manufacturing, and trade. Founded in 1652, it is South Africa's oldest city. Besides the Parliament, its famous buildings include Government House, the Dutch

---

FACTS and figures

REPUBLIC OF SOUTH AFRICA is the official name of the country.

LOCATION: Southern Africa.

AREA: 441,444 sq mi (1,221,037 km²).

POPULATION: 40,400,000 (estimate).

CAPITAL: Cape Town (legislative), Pretoria (administrative), Bloemfontein (judicial).

LARGEST CITY: Johannesburg.

MAJOR LANGUAGES: Afrikaans, English, various Bantu languages.

MAJOR RELIGIOUS GROUPS: Christian, traditional African religions, Hindu, Muslim, Jewish.

GOVERNMENT: Republic. **Head of state and government**—president. **Legislature**—Parliament, consisting of the National Assembly and National Council of Provinces. (Fully effective in 1999.)

CHIEF PRODUCTS: Agricultural—corn, wheat, and other grains, sugarcane, citrus fruits, wine grapes, livestock and livestock products. **Manufactured**—steel products, building materials, chemicals, processed foods, shoes, clothing. **Mineral**—gold, coal, diamonds, uranium, manganese, iron ore, vanadium, platinum.

MONETARY UNIT: Rand (1 rand = 100 cents).

Reformed Church Synodical Hall, and Groote Schuur, once the home of Cecil Rhodes.

Durban, on the Indian Ocean, is the third largest city. It is South Africa's chief port and a major industrial center. Most of the country's Asians live in or near Durban.

▶ GOVERNMENT

The 1993 interim constitution under which the country's first all-race elections were held in 1994 created a government of national unity. All parties receiving at least 5 percent of the vote were included in the cabinet. The former ruling National Party withdrew from this government in 1996 to become the official opposition.

South Africa adopted a new constitution in 1996, under which new elections were held in 1999. The new constitution provides for a parliament consisting of two houses: the National Assembly, elected directly by the people, and the National Council of Provinces, whose members are appointed by the country's provincial legislatures. The president is elected by the National Assembly and is limited to two 5-year terms.

South Africa was formerly divided into four provinces—Cape Province, Natal, Orange Free State, and Transvaal. These have been subdivided into nine new provinces: Northern Cape, Western Cape, Eastern Cape, Mpumalanga, Northern Province, North-West, Gauteng, Free State, and KwaZulu/Natal.

▶ HISTORY

Early History. Little is known of the early inhabitants of the southern tip of Africa, but people have lived there for some 9,000 years.

The Portuguese navigator Bartholomeu Dias was the first European to see the Cape of Good Hope, in 1488. The first European colony was founded there in 1652. It was used by ships of the Dutch East India Company as a stopover point on the way to the East Indies. The early Dutch settlers found San and Khoikhoi when they arrived. Bantu-speaking people soon began to move into the area.

Dutch-Bantu Rivalry. Little by little the Dutch began to move into new areas in search of more land for their cattle. In 1779, Xhosa tribes crossed the Great Fish River and were driven back by the Dutch. This was the first of many clashes over grazing lands between the Dutch and the Bantus.

Among the various Bantu groups moving south from central Africa were the Zulus. They developed into a powerful nation under the leadership of Chief Chaka. The African tribes on the plateau were caught between the Dutch moving northward along the coast with their cattle and the Zulus pushing southward with their herds. One tribe, the Ndebele, burned everything to the ground as they fled from Chaka's warriors. They eventually settled north of the Limpopo River in Zimbabwe. Tribes now known as the Basuto moved into the Drakensberg for security.

The Great Trek. At the end of the Napoleonic Wars in 1815, the British took over Cape Province from the Dutch. After the 1820's, more and more British settlers went to the Cape. The Dutch people, called Boers (from the Dutch word for "farmer"), opposed the British settlement. By this time the Boers had few ties to Europe. They were, in a sense, a white tribe in a continent of black tribes, with a distinctive way of life they wanted to keep. Rather than adjust to the British, the Boers left the Cape. Beginning in 1835–36, they set out on the Great Trek, a long journey northward. They established new settlements in what became the Transvaal and the Orange Free State.

The Boer War (1899–1902) pitted the Dutch Boers, such as these artillerymen, against British troops. The Boers were eventually defeated.

Diamonds, Gold, and War. Two discoveries changed South Africa's history. In 1867 diamonds were discovered near Kimberley in the Orange Free State, and in 1886 rich gold deposits were found on the Witwatersrand in the Transvaal. These discoveries brought a flood of immigrants, mainly from Britain. Among them was a young Englishman, Cecil Rhodes, who eventually gained control of the diamond mines and became prime minister of the Cape Colony. His dream was to place the two Boer republics under British rule. In 1899 the Boer leader Paul Kruger, president of the Transvaal, declared war on the British to prevent their taking over his republic.

Union. After the defeat of the Boers in 1902, leaders on both sides decided to form a union. Thus the country became independent in 1910 as the Union of South Africa. It was composed of the two British colonies (Cape Colony and Natal) and the two Boer republics. (See the article on the Boer War in Volume B and the biography of Rhodes in Volume QR.)

The Nationalists and Apartheid. In 1948 the Nationalist Party, dominated by Afrikaners, came to power. Under the Nationalists, apartheid became the official policy of the government. Only whites were permitted to vote. Separate residence areas were established for whites and nonwhites. Blacks who sought work outside their homelands were required to obtain and carry passes. In 1960 a number of blacks demonstrating against the pass laws were shot and killed by police in Sharpeville. In 1961, South Africa left the Commonwealth of Nations rather than change its racial policies. It took its present name, Republic of South Africa, that same year.

Apartheid became the subject of international protests. Attempts were made to force South Africa out of the United Nations. South African athletes were barred from international sports events, and many nations instituted economic sanctions against the country.

The adoption of a new constitution in 1984 gave some representation to the country's Coloureds and Asians. But blacks were still denied political rights in South Africa, and violent anti-government demonstrations swept through many black communities.

Recent History. Under P. W. Botha, who served as prime minister and then president from 1978 to 1989, the government made

In 1994, F. W. de Klerk (center) was succeeded as president of South Africa by Nelson Mandela (right), the country's first black leader. The two men shared the 1993 Nobel Peace Prize for ending apartheid.

some reforms of the apartheid system. F. W. de Klerk, who succeeded Botha as president in 1989, abolished most apartheid restrictions. He ordered the release, in 1990, of the black South African leader Nelson Mandela, after nearly 26 years of imprisonment. De Klerk also lifted the ban on the African National Congress (ANC), the anti-apartheid organization that Mandela helped found.

In 1993 an interim post-apartheid constitution was adopted, and in 1994 the first elections were held in which blacks were allowed to vote. The result was a victory for the ANC, and Mandela became the country's first black president. A new, permanent constitution was proclaimed in 1996. The ANC won an even larger share of the vote in the 1999 elections. ANC leader Thabo Mbeki succeeded Mandela as president on June 16, 1999.

In general elections in April 2004, the ANC won a landslide victory, assuring a second 5-year term for Mbeki. When Mandela retired from public life in May, he praised Mbeki but advised him to address the crisis of the country's rising AIDS epidemic.

KATHERINE SAVAGE
Author, *The Story of Africa*

Reviewed by HUGH C. BROOKS
Director, Center for African Studies
St. John's University (New York)

See also MANDELA, NELSON.

SOUTH AMERICA

South America ranks fourth in area and fifth in population among the world's continents. One of the two continents of the Western Hemisphere, it is linked to North America by the Isthmus of Panama. South America is bounded by various bodies of water: the Caribbean Sea on the north, the Atlantic Ocean on the northeast and east, the Pacific Ocean on the west, and on the south, the Drake Passage, a strait connecting the two oceans.

On the map, South America looks roughly like an inverted triangle, with its broadest landmass in the north and tapering almost to a point in the south. At its widest, it measures about 3,200 miles (5,150 kilometers) from east to west. It extends some 4,600 miles (7,400 kilometers) from north to south.

South America has some of the most impressive geographical features of any continent. The Andes, which run its entire length, are the world's longest mountain chain; Aconcagua, in the Argentinean Andes, is the highest mountain in the Western Hemisphere. The Amazon, which empties into the Atlantic Ocean, is the world's largest river in volume of water flow, and its enormous drainage basin is covered by the world's most extensive area of rain forests. Angel Falls on the Churun River in Venezuela is the highest waterfall in the world, while Chile's Atacama Desert, where it has not rained for centuries, is considered the driest region on earth.

South America is home to twelve independent countries, of which Brazil is by far the largest and most populous. Suriname is the smallest, both in area and population. South America also includes two nonindependent territories: French Guiana, an overseas department of France; and the Falkland Islands, a British crown colony.

The people are chiefly of Indian, Spanish, and Portuguese descent. But there are also significant numbers of South Americans of other European, African, and Asian origin as well as many of mixed ancestry. The Indians, the original inhabitants, were supplanted by the Spanish and Portuguese, who, beginning in the early 1500's, explored, conquered, and then colonized the region. Together with later settlers and immigrants, the three groups constitute the present-day population of the continent.

South America makes up most of the larger cultural region known as Latin America, which also includes Mexico, Central

America, and many of the islands of the Caribbean Sea. These three regions, although geographically part of North America, share a common heritage and historical experience with South America. For more information, see the articles LATIN AMERICA; LATIN AMERICA, ART AND ARCHITECTURE OF; LATIN AMERICA, LITERATURE OF; and LATIN AMERICA, MUSIC OF in Volume L.

Some of the many aspects of South America: *Opposite page:* A Peruvian funerary mask; a gaucho herding sheep on the Pampas, Argentina's most fertile region. *Above:* A Brazilian worker sifting coffee beans. *Left:* A vineyard in the Elqui River valley in north central Chile, which produces grapes for the nation's popular wines. *Below left:* The snow-covered Andes Mountains, one of the world's longest and highest mountain systems, tower above a crystal-clear lake in southern Argentina. *Below:* A trail made by the Inca Indians high in the Peruvian Andes.

▶ THE LAND

South America can be divided into three main geographical regions: the Andes in the west, the Eastern Highlands in the east, which include the Brazilian and Guiana highlands, and a vast lowland in the interior that also contains a distinctive upland area, Patagonia, in the southeastern part of the continent.

Geographical Regions

The Andes occupy the entire western strip of South America. This mountain system stretches from Venezuela in the north to Tierra del Fuego at the continent's southern tip. The Andes are not one continuous mountain chain of geologically related rocks but, rather, a series of ranges with varied landforms. They reach their highest point at Argentina's Aconcagua, the highest mountain peak in the Western Hemisphere, which rises to 22,834 feet (6,960 meters).

The Andes drop abruptly toward the Pacific Ocean, leaving a very narrow coastal plain. Scattered throughout the mountains are valleys of various sizes, where most of the population is concentrated. Except for southern Chile, where numerous inlets make the coastline a maze of channels and islands, the Pacific coast is largely unindented. Historically, the Andes have tended to hinder transportation and communication between east and west, making the economic development and unity of the continent more difficult. See the article on the Andes in Volume A.

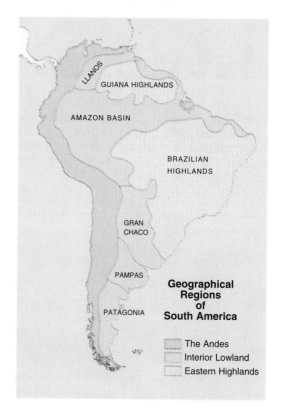

Geographical Regions of South America

- The Andes
- Interior Lowland
- Eastern Highlands

The Eastern Highlands have two distinct sections—the Brazilian Highlands and the Guiana Highlands.

The eroded, or worn-down, mountains of the Brazilian Highlands are the oldest part of the South American continent. Consisting mainly of gently rolling hills, with a few imposing plateaus, they extend southward from the Amazon River basin through a large area of Brazil, Uruguay, and parts of Paraguay and Bolivia. The highest elevation is in the Pico da Bandeira in eastern Brazil. At the Brazilian coastline (except in the northeast), the highlands break off abruptly into a series of steep cliffs called the Great Escarpment. The region has excellent farming and grazing land as well as a wealth of mineral resources.

The Guiana Highlands are a mixture of rounded hills, low mountains, plateaus, and narrow valleys. They stretch across the southeastern half of Venezuela into southern Guyana, Suriname, French Guiana, and

Venezuela. The region is known to have a variety of mineral deposits, but its natural resources are still largely undeveloped.

The Interior Lowland lies between the Andes and the Eastern Highlands. Within this great north-south expanse are the Llanos, the Amazon Basin, the Gran Chaco, the Pampas, and Patagonia.

The Llanos is an area of rolling, grassy plains ("llanos" means "plains") situated in Colombia and Venezuela and watered by the Orinoco River.

Most of the Amazon Basin, the vast area drained by the Amazon River, is covered by dense rain forests. A narrow strip of this region extends eastward to the Atlantic, separating the Guiana and Brazilian highlands.

The Gran Chaco is a wild, sparsely settled plain consisting of scrub vegetation and grasses occupying parts of Bolivia, Paraguay, and northern Argentina. South of the Gran Chaco is the Pampas, or grasslands, of Uruguay and Argentina. This is one of the

Above: Glaciers abound in the Andes in Southern Argentina, a cold and remote region near the Chilean border.

Opposite page: A plateau between the peaks of the Andes of north central Ecuador provides rich agricultural land.

Right: The Atacama Desert in Chile is one of the driest places on earth, but it is rich in sodium nitrate and other minerals.

northeastern Brazil. Mount Roraima, on the border between Venezuela and Guyana, is the highest point. The land is covered by dense forests, with occasional small areas of savanna, or tropical grassland. Magnificent waterfalls tumble from the plateaus, among them Angel Falls, situated on the headwaters of the Caroní River in southeastern

most productive of the continent's agricultural regions.

Patagonia is situated south of the Pampas. Stretching from the Colorado River to the southern tip of the continent, it faces the eastern edge of the Andes.. It consists mainly of high plateaus rising steeply from the Atlantic Ocean and cut by deep

COUNTRIES OF SOUTH AMERICA

COUNTRY	CAPITAL
Argentina	Buenos Aires
Bolivia	La Paz (administrative)
	Sucre (legal)
Brazil	Brasília
Chile	Santiago
Colombia	Bogotá
Ecuador	Quito
Guyana	Georgetown
Paraguay	Asunción
Peru	Lima
Suriname	Paramaribo
Uruguay	Montevideo
Venezuela	Caracas

NONINDEPENDENT TERRITORIES OF SOUTH AMERICA

TERRITORY	STATUS
Falkland Islands (Islas Malvinas)	British dependency; claimed by Argentina
French Guiana	Overseas department of France

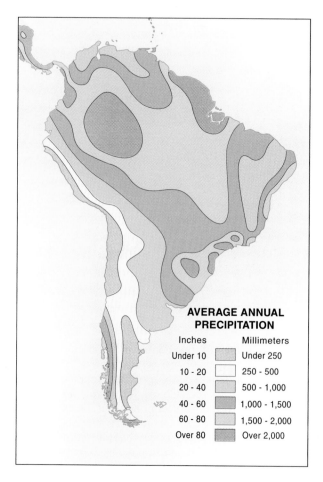

AVERAGE ANNUAL PRECIPITATION

Inches		Millimeters
Under 10		Under 250
10 - 20		250 - 500
20 - 40		500 - 1,000
40 - 60		1,000 - 1,500
60 - 80		1,500 - 2,000
Over 80		Over 2,000

INDEX TO SOUTH AMERICA PHYSICAL MAP

South America

North America

CARIBBEAN SEA

NORTH ATLANTIC OCEAN

90°W 80°W 70°W 60°W 50°W 40°W 20°N
20°N

VENEZUELA
Pico Bolívar ▲
10°N 10°N

MALPELO ISLAND
(Col.)

Angel Falls
Mt. Roraima ▲ **GUYANA**
SURINAME **FRENCH GUIANA** *(Fr.)*

COLOMBIA
GUIANA HIGHLANDS
LLANOS
Orinoco R.

ANDES
Magdalena

Rio Negro
Japurá R.
ECUADOR ▲
Chimborazo ▲
0° *Amazon* R. **MARAJÓ ISLAND** 0°

GALÁPAGOS ISLANDS *(Ecu.)*

A M A Z O N
B A S I N

CAPE SÃO ROQUE

AGUJA POINT
Marañón R.
Juruá *Purus* *Madeira* *Tapajós R.* *Xingu R.*

PACIFIC OCEAN

Huascarán ▲
Ucayali R.
PERU

A N D E S

BRAZIL

Paulo Afonso Falls
10°S

Lake Titicaca
Illampu ▲
BOLIVIA
Lake Poopó

MATO GROSSO

BRAZILIAN HIGHLANDS
Tocantins R.
Parnaíba
São Francisco

Três Marias Res.
Pico da Bandeira ▲
20°S

ATACAMA DESERT
Paraguay R.
PARAGUAY
GRAN CHACO
Pilcomayo R.
Furnas Res.

Tropic of Capricorn Tropic of Capricorn

SAN FÉLIX ISLAND *(Chile)* SAN AMBROSIO ISLAND *(Chile)*

Río Salado
Paraná R.
Iguazú Falls

CHILE

SOUTH ATLANTIC OCEAN

JUAN FERNÁNDEZ ISLANDS *(Chile)*

Aconcagua ▲
Río Salado
ARGENTINA
30°S
Uruguay R.
URUGUAY

PAMPAS
Río de la Plata

Río Colorado

CHILOÉ ISLAND
Chubut R.
VALDÉS PENINSULA

40°S

TAITAO PENINSULA
Cerro San Valentín ▲

P A T A G O N I A

FALKLAND ISLANDS *(U.K.)*

Strait of Magellan

SOUTH GEORGIA *(U.K.)*

TIERRA DEL FUEGO

CAPE HORN

50°S

North ↑

Legend

■	Tropical Rain Forest
■	Coniferous/Evergreen Forest
■	Deciduous Forest
■	Chaparral
■	Grassland
■	Desert and Semidesert
■	Alpine Tundra
□	Ice Sheet

0 500 1,000 mi
0 500 1,000 km

Azimuthal Equal-area Projection

110°W 100°W 90°W 80°W 70°W 60°W 50°W 40°W 30°W 20°W

canyons. An arid, cool, and windswept region, with only limited vegetation, it is subject to frequent storms the year round. It makes up approximately one-quarter of Argentina's total land area.

Rivers and Lakes

The interior lowland is drained by three great river systems, the largest of which is the Amazon. Second in importance is the Río de la Plata. The third main river system is the Orinoco.

The Amazon. The Amazon is exceeded in length only by the Nile in Africa. It carries more water than any other river in the world, draining an area nearly as large as Australia. Originating high in the Peruvian Andes and fed by hundreds of tributary rivers in six countries, it crosses the widest part of South America before emptying into the Atlantic off northeastern Brazil. See the article on the Amazon River in Volume A.

Río de la Plata. The Río de la Plata is formed by the Paraná and its principal tributaries, the Paraguay and Uruguay rivers. It is South America's most important inland waterway. The Paraná rises in the highlands of

With a total drop of 3,212 feet (979 meters), Angel Falls in Venezuela is the world's highest waterfall.

southeastern Brazil and flows in a generally southerly direction along the eastern border of Paraguay. It then crosses into Argentina, where the Uruguay joins it to form the Río de la Plata estuary on the Atlantic between Uruguay and Argentina.

The Orinoco. From its headwaters in the Guiana Highlands, the Orinoco River flows northeastward through Venezuela to the Atlantic Ocean. More than half of the Orinoco is navigable by fairly large ships. A small stream called the Casiquiare links the Orinoco to the Amazon by way of the Río Negro.

Other Major Waterways. The Magdalena is the principal river of Colombia and its chief artery of trade. Together with its main tributary, the Cauca, it flows northward through Colombia's Andean ranges to the Caribbean Sea.

The São Francisco is the main waterway leading to the interior of eastern Brazil. It rises in the Brazilian Highlands and flows in a northeasterly direction, parallel to the coast, before turning abruptly on its journey east to the Atlantic Ocean. Navigation along its route is interrupted by the Paulo Afonso Falls.

A village floating on reeds on Lake Titicaca. Situated in the Andes on the Bolivia-Peru border, Titicaca is South America's largest lake and the world's highest navigable body of water.

Lakes. South America has relatively few lakes. The largest, Lake Maracaibo, is situated on the continent's northern coast, in western Venezuela. The Maracaibo basin is one of the major oil-producing regions. Lake Titicaca, which forms part of the border between Peru and Bolivia, in the Andean region, is the world's highest navigable body of water. Nearby is the much smaller Lake Poopó, about half Titicaca's size. Lagoa dos Patos, in southern Brazil, is actually an arm of the Atlantic Ocean. A low peninsula separates it from the open sea.

Islands

Aside from Tierra del Fuego in the far south and along the heavily indented southern coast of Chile, South America has few significant islands. Some of the more important ones are described below.

The Juan Fernández Islands, lying off the central Chilean coast, are of interest chiefly because of their association with the story of Robinson Crusoe. A Scottish seaman,

Alexander Selkirk, shipwrecked there in the early 1700's, became the model for the fictional Crusoe. The main island is now called Robinson Crusoe. (Chile also governs Easter Island, far out in the South Pacific, but it is not considered a part of the continent.)

The Galápagos Islands, situated about 600 miles (965 kilometers) off the coast of Ecuador, are famous for their distinctive animal life, which includes the giant Galápagos tortoise. The Caribbean island of Margarita is an integral part of Venezuela. The Falkland Islands in the South Atlantic, although under British rule, were long claimed by Argentina, which calls them Islas Malvinas. The Falklands were the site of a brief war between Britain and Argentina in 1982.

Climate

South America has varied types of climate. These are influenced by such factors as elevation, distance from the equator, winds and currents, and nearness to the surrounding oceans and seas.

South America does not have the extremes of temperature found in North America. Its great northern bulge lies on or near the equator, giving this large area of the continent a tropical climate, except in the higher elevations of the Andes. The Amazon Basin, Guiana Highlands, much of the Brazilian Highlands, and some coastal areas are hot and humid the year round, with heavy rainfall and temperatures averaging about 80°F (27°C).

Much of the narrower, southern half of the continent has more distinct winter and summer seasons, although winters are generally mild. Since the region is south of the equator, the seasons are reversed, with winter falling between June and August and summer between December and February. A Mediterranean type of climate is found in central Chile and parts of Argentina, which benefit from the moderating influences of the surrounding oceans.

An aerial view of the lower Amazon River floodplain. The Amazon, the second longest river in the world after the Nile, is South America's most important river.

Because of their great height, the Andes act as a climatic barrier, blocking the passage of moisture-laden winds from the east and contributing to the semi-arid and desert conditions of the Peruvian coast and northern Chile. The coldest regions of South America are in Tierra del Fuego and the Andes, where temperatures can fall below 32°F (0°C). Some of the highest temperatures occur in the Gran Chaco, with readings well above 100°F (38°C) common in summer.

Except for the arid regions, rainfall is generally plentiful or adequate throughout most of the continent. Some tropical areas have separate wet and dry seasons. Snow falls mainly in the higher Andes, where many of the peaks are permanently snow covered.

Natural Resources

South America's considerable natural resources include areas of good soil, abundant deposits of many minerals, and a great diversity of plant and animal life.

Soils. The continent has two main types of fertile soils. One is alluvial, or soil deposited by rivers, found in the floodplains of the rivers. The other is the grassland soil found in the Pampas of Argentina and similar areas of Uruguay. Soils of the desert areas can also be made to produce crops if irrigated. The least fertile are mountain soils, which are too thin and stony, and soils of the tropical forests, whose nutrients have been washed away by the heavy rainfall.

Vegetation. More than 40 percent of South America is forested. Most of this consists of tropical rain forest, or selva, occupying the Amazon Basin, parts of the Guiana and Brazilian highlands, and the Pacific coast of Colombia. Among the numerous varieties of trees found here are mahogany, rosewood, Brazil nut, wild rubber, palm, and cacao. Plants and tropical flowers, including many kinds of orchids and giant water lilies, grow in profusion. Tropical thorn trees and other scrub vegetation cover much of the Gran Chaco. Small areas of evergreen forest are found in southern Brazil and central Chile.

The extraordinary diversity of the Amazonian selva is now threatened by deforesta-

The llama (*top*) and the vicuña (*right*), both relatives of the camel, are used as beasts of burden in many areas of South America, especially in the Andean region. The red howler monkey (*above*) inhabits the Orinoco River basin of Venezuela. Orchids (*above right*) grow in profusion in the rain forests of northern South America.

tion. This is due to a number of factors, including increased road building, logging, and the growth of new settlements.

About 30 percent of the continent consists of grasslands. The tropical grassy plains, or savanna, that cover parts of Venezuela and Colombia and much of the Brazilian Highlands are most suitable for grazing cattle. The temperate grasslands of the Pampas of Uruguay and eastern Argentina are utilized

The jaguar (*above*), a threatened species, inhabits the forests and grasslands of South America. The anaconda (*right*) is a water snake that can grow to a length of 25 feet (7.6 meters). This one has just made a meal of a caiman, a small alligator-like reptile.

for farming as well as cattle raising.

Animal Life. South America's wild animal life is as varied as the continent itself. The larger mammals include great cats such as the jaguar and mountain lion and the smaller ocelot. The sure-footed llama, alpaca, guanaco, and vicuña—all relatives of the camel—have traditionally been used as pack animals in the high Andes and are also prized for their fine wool.

Other distinctive forms of wildlife are the capybara, the world's largest rodent, which may exceed 100 pounds (45 kilograms) in weight; the piglike peccary; the vampire bat; the howler monkey; the giant armadillo; and the anaconda, a water snake that can reach a length of 25 feet (7.6 meters).

South America is also home to many unusual species of fish. These include the voracious piranha, which feeds in schools that can devour large prey in minutes; the electric eel; and the air-breathing lungfish.

South America is thought to have more species of birds than any other continent. The rain forests are home to tiny, jewel-like hummingbirds and various kinds of vividly colored parrots, macaws, and large-beaked toucans. Larger birds include the rhea, a kind of ostrich, which inhabits the savannas; the harpy eagle, which is large enough to prey on monkeys; and the Andean condor, the largest of its kind, with a wingspan of some 10 feet (3 meters).

Minerals. South America has abundant deposits of many kinds of minerals, although these resources are not distributed evenly across the continent. The regions richest in mineral production are in the Eastern Highlands, parts of the Andes, and northwestern Venezuela.

The faces of South America reflect its people's Indian, African, and European ancestry. *Clockwise from top left:* A young gaucho, or cowboy, on Argentina's Pampas; schoolgirls on a park bench; girls in costume for the pre-Lent Carnival in Rio de Janeiro, Brazil; young people in the traditional dress of their ancestors, the Incas, who had a powerful empire long before the arrival of Europeans; an Amazonian Indian from north central Brazil.

suitable for extensive human settlement because they are very densely forested, extremely mountainous, or too barren for cultivation. Like its mineral resources, the continent's population tends to be very unevenly distributed.

Distribution and Growth

The great majority of the people live along the fringes of the continent, often on the

Brazil is the world's second largest producer of iron ore, after China, and Chile ranks as one of the world's two leading copper-mining countries (the United States is the other). Bolivia is among the world leaders in tin production. Venezuela has South America's largest petroleum deposits and is a major oil exporter. Colombia has the continent's only sizable coal deposits. It produces much of its gold and is one of the world's chief sources of emeralds. Brazil is also a major producer of bauxite (aluminum ore) and manganese. Peru exports significant amounts of lead, zinc, and silver, while Chile has, in addition to copper, large deposits of sulfur and nitrates.

▶ THE PEOPLE

South America covers about 12 percent of the world's land surface but contains less than 6 percent of its people. Many areas of the continent are not

Left: Young Colombian girls enjoy a rainy day. *Above:* Brazilians turn out by the thousands to cheer on their favorite soccer team at Rio de Janeiro's Marracana Stadium. Soccer is South America's favorite sport.

coastal areas or within a relatively short distance from them. Much of the interior is sparsely inhabited. The most heavily populated region stretches along the Atlantic coast from Belém, near the mouth of the Amazon in Brazil, to Buenos Aires, on the Río de la Plata in Argentina. A second, smaller area of high population density extends from Bogotá, in Colombia, to the Pacific coast between Ecuador and central Peru. Population distribution has been strongly affected by growing urbanization, or the movement of people from the countryside to the cities.

Blacks were originally brought to the continent as slaves during the early colonial period; their descendants now live chiefly in parts of Brazil and in northern coastal areas. South Americans of Asian origin include East Indians, who make up more than half the population of Guyana; Chinese, found mainly on the Pacific coast; and Japanese, who have settled largely in Brazil and Peru. There are also scattered communities of Syrians and Lebanese.

People of mixed race make up more than half of South America's population. The largest single ethnic group consists of mestizos (a Spanish term), who are of Indian and European ancestry. They are found in many parts of the continent but primarily in Venezuela, the Andean countries, and Paraguay.

Above: In Venezuela, a carnival spirit accompanies the celebration of the annual Feast of Corpus Christi, a Roman Catholic holiday. **Right: Christ the Redeemer**, a huge statue, overlooks Rio de Janeiro, Brazil.

South America's population is increasing rapidly, due to improved living conditions and a traditionally high birthrate. Its average population growth, about 1.8 percent a year, is second only to that of Africa. Growth rates for individual countries can vary widely, however, ranging from about 2.8 percent in Paraguay to less than 1 percent in Uruguay. More than one-third of the population is under 15 years of age.

Ethnicity

Most of South America's Indian population is concentrated in two distinct regions, the high Andes (particularly in such countries as Bolivia, Peru, and Ecuador) and the tropical rain forests. Argentina, central Chile, Uruguay, and southern Brazil have populations of predominantly European ancestry.

Language and Religion

Spanish and Portuguese are the continent's dominant languages. Portuguese is the official language of Brazil, and Spanish that of most of the other countries. Numerous Indian languages are also spoken, and many Andean Indians know no Spanish, speaking only Quechua or Aymara. Bolivia, more than half of whose people are Indians, has made

Like other South American capitals, Buenos Aires has many beautiful public squares. Overlooking this square is the Palace of the National Congress, the seat of Argentina's two-chamber legislature.

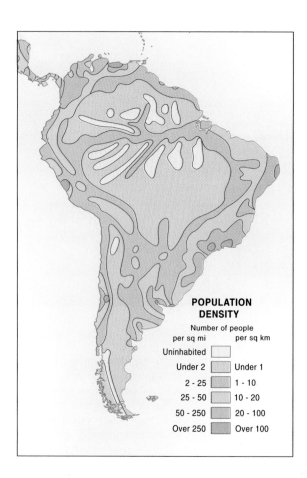

POPULATION DENSITY

Number of people

per sq mi		per sq km
Uninhabited		
Under 2		Under 1
2 - 25		1 - 10
25 - 50		10 - 20
50 - 250		20 - 100
Over 250		Over 100

INDEX TO
SOUTH AMERICA POLITICAL MAP

★ Capital City

Shopping malls like this one in São Paulo, Brazil, offer consumers a wide variety of goods, while markets in towns such as Otavalo, Ecuador, offer local products.

Quechua and Aymara official languages, along with Spanish. Aymara is one of the two official languages of Peru. In Paraguay the Guaraní Indian language is used by so many people that it is considered an official language.

Guyana, Suriname, and French Guiana differ from the rest of South America in that their official languages are English, Dutch, and French, respectively. Other languages spoken—including German, Italian, Polish, Hindi and other East Indian languages, Chinese, and Japanese—reflect the varied national origins of many South Americans.

Roman Catholicism was brought to South America by the Spanish and Portuguese and remains the religion of the great majority of the people. In some areas, particularly the central Andean highlands, the Indians combine Roman Catholicism with elements of their earlier, traditional religions. Some African religious practices and beliefs are followed in parts of Brazil, including the *macumba* ceremonies and other voodoo rites.

Protestantism came to South America with small groups of European Protestant immigrants and missionaries from the United States, but its influence is relatively slight. Argentina has the continent's largest Jewish community. Most South Americans of Chinese ancestry are Buddhists, and those of East Indian descent are either Hindus or Muslims.

Education

All South American countries provide free public education. In addition, there are numerous private schools, many of them church sponsored. Education levels vary widely, however, from country to country and between rural areas and the cities. The literacy rate, or percentage of people able to read and write, ranges from a high of more than 96 percent in Guyana to about 78 percent in Bolivia.

There are numerous universities, in addition to colleges and techni-

More than three-fourths of South America's population is concentrated in and around the metropolitan areas of such major cities as Bogotá, the capital of Colombia.

The increasing movement of rural people to such South American cities as São Paulo, Brazil (*above*), has been accompanied by the growth of slums, such as these (*left*) in Rio de Janeiro, Brazil.

cal schools. Some universities date from the first century of the colonial era. The oldest, the National University of San Marcos in Lima, Peru, was founded in 1551.

▶ CITIES

The rapid growth of South America's cities began in the second half of the 1900's, as increasing numbers of people arrived from the rural areas attracted by the possibility of a better life. Today, about 75 percent of the population is concentrated in and around the metropolitan areas of the major cities. Uruguay, Argentina, and Chile have the largest urban populations, while Guyana, Suriname, and Bolivia have the smallest. The inability of the cities to absorb all the new-comers, however, has resulted in severe overcrowding, the growth of slums and shanty-towns, and problems of unemployment or underemployment.

South America's largest urban centers are São Paulo, Rio de Janeiro, Buenos Aires, Lima, Bogotá, and Santiago.

São Paulo, Brazil's most populous city and the center of its industry, is the largest city in South America and its fastest growing metropolitan area. Rio de Janeiro, Brazil's second largest city and chief port, is famed for its magnificent site on one of the world's most scenic harbors. Buenos Aires, Argentina's capital and chief port, is a cosmopolitan city reflecting its varied European heritage. Lima, Peru's capital and leading city, was founded in 1535 by Francisco Pizarro, conqueror of the Inca Indian empire. Bogotá, capital and chief city of Colombia, lies high in the Andes, more than 8,600 feet (2,600 meters) above sea level. Santiago, Chile's capital and commercial center, is situated in the heart of the country's wine-producing region.

Articles on each of these cities can be found in the appropriate volumes.

▶ THE ECONOMY

Agriculture has long been the mainstay of South America's economy. Industrialization

toes, which can be grown in the harsh environment of the Andes. Major commercial crops include coffee, bananas, sugarcane, wheat, and cacao (or cocoa beans). Brazil is the world's leading exporter of coffee, followed by Colombia. Brazil and Ecuador are the continent's major exporters of bananas, and Brazil is also a world leader in the production of sugarcane and cacao. Argentina's Pampas and other regions produce enormous

The rain forests of the Amazon Basin are a source of valuable hardwoods. But the destruction of these forests through logging and other human activities poses a serious threat to the environment.

quantities of wheat, sorghum, and other grains, as well as flax, citrus fruits, potatoes, tea, and grapes.

Brazil and Argentina are the continent's major cattle-raising countries, particularly beef cattle. Argentina leads in sheep raising and wool production, with Uruguay second in importance.

Manufacturing

Manufacturing is concentrated mainly in and around the major cities. Brazil, Ar-

was relatively slow in developing, since, historically, the continent was viewed chiefly as a source of agricultural commodities and raw materials, particularly its minerals. Manufacturing has been steadily increasing in importance, however. Fishing and the processing of forest products are also significant economic activities in certain areas.

Agriculture

Only about one-third of South America's farmable land is currently under cultivation. Small areas of intensively farmed land are often separated by vast expanses of unused land. While commercial crops are usually grown on large estates or plantations, the bulk of the continent's agriculture consists of subsistence farming, that is, the cultivation of basic food crops, most frequently on small plots of land.

Corn, a staple of the diet for much of South America, is the most widely grown food crop. Rice is also cultivated, as are pota-

Corn, shown here being dried at a Bolivian farming settlement, is South America's most widely grown food crop and a staple of the diet for most South Americans.

gentina, and Chile are the most highly industrialized of the South American nations. Brazil, the continent's industrial giant, produces a variety of manufactured goods, including textiles, steel, processed foods, motor vehicles, aircraft, chemicals, and electronic equipment. Argentina's major industries are based chiefly on meatpacking and the manufacture of wool textiles and leather goods. Chile produces wood and wood products (including paper), transportation equipment and machinery, processed fish, and wines. Venezuela's economic development has centered around its large petroleum industry.

Mining, Fishing, and Forestry

Gold, silver, and gems were first mined by the Indians, and it was this evidence of the continent's great mineral wealth that attracted early European explorers and colonizers. For information on mineral production, see the preceding section Natural Resources (Minerals).

Manufacturing, including food and beverage processing, is increasingly important to the economies of South America. Chilean wines (*left*), Colombian steel (*right*), and Brazilian automobiles (*below*) are among the continent's products.

Fish are important both as a source of food and as an export. Peru and Chile have the continent's largest commercial fishing industries. Peru ranks as one of the world's leading fishing nations, its most valuable catches being anchovies and pilchards (sardines). Much of the catch is processed as fish meal, used in animal feed.

South America has few of the softwood forests necessary for the production of lumber. But the tropical rain forests are a source of valuable hardwoods, chiefly mahogany and rosewood, which are used to make fine furniture. Other important forest products include rubber, nuts, tannin (used in tanning leather), palm oil, waxes, and chicle (the base for chewing gum). Brazil is the leading exporter of forest products.

Trade

Although South America now exports increasing quantities of manufactured goods to foreign countries—particularly clothing and shoes—agricultural products and minerals are still its chief exports. The most important are petroleum, coffee, iron ore, soybeans, copper, beef, corn, bananas, and cacao. Manufactured goods, including machinery and transportation equipment, are among the major imports.

The United States and Western Europe are the continent's major trading partners. Efforts to increase trade among the South American countries led to the formation of the Latin American Free Trade Association (LAFTA) in 1960 and its successor, the Latin American Integration Association (LAIA), in 1980. Composed of ten South American nations (Suriname and Guyana have not joined) and Mexico, the association sought to gradually reduce tariffs, or import taxes, among the member countries and, eventually, to eliminate all trade barriers among them.

Transportation

Historically, transportation across the continent has been hampered by natural land barriers. Population centers developed chiefly along the coastal areas because of the difficulty in penetrating much of the interior. In the past, only the navigable waterways made it at all possible to reach many inland areas. Today, there are networks of roads and railways, with the most extensive transportation systems found in Brazil, Argentina, and Chile. Most South American countries have national airlines, and air service often provides the only access to some sites, particularly in the rugged Andes.

The Spaniard Francisco Pizarro meets with Atahualpa, leader of the Incas of Peru, in 1532. Pizarro, who later lured Atahualpa into an ambush and had him executed, completed the conquest of the Inca Empire in 1533.

▶ **HISTORY**

The first people in South America, the ancestors of the Indians, probably came from the continent of North America by way of Central America, whose narrow shape made it a natural land bridge. The early peoples engaged in hunting, food gathering, and primitive forms of agriculture.

Indian Civilization

A number of Indian civilizations existed in the region before the arrival of the Europeans. At the time of the Spanish conquest, the most highly developed was that of the Incas, who lived in the Andean highlands of what are now Peru and Bolivia. They had an elaborate system of roads and farmed their hilly land by terracing it and using a system of irrigation. The Incas ruled a vast empire stretching from southern Colombia to northern Chile and Argentina and unified it under one government and one language, Quechua, still spoken by their descendants. For more information, see the article INCAS in Volume I. For extensive information on South America's entire native population, see INDIANS, AMERICAN, also in Volume I.

Discovery and Conquest

The first-known European to reach South America was Christopher Columbus, who landed at the mouth of the Orinoco River on his third voyage of discovery, in 1498. Columbus' explorations established Spain's claims in the Western Hemisphere. Portuguese claims to Brazil were bolstered by Pedro Álvares Cabral's expedition to its coast in 1500. A year later the navigator and mapmaker Amerigo Vespucci (for whom the Americas were named) confirmed that South America was a distinct continent, not a part of Asia as was previously thought.

Exploration was followed by rapid conquest and colonization. The first permanent Spanish settlement on the continent, San Sebastián, was established in present-day Colombia by Alonzo de Ojeda in 1510. Spanish adventurers known as conquistadores, drawn to the region by the lure of gold and

The rich cultural heritage of early Indian civilizations can be seen in artifacts such as this stone figure from the San Agustín National Archaeological Park in Colombia.

silver, quickly overcame the native peoples. Although relatively few in number, the Europeans were better armed and equipped, and the Indian rulers were often weakened by civil war.

In the 1530's, Peru, the heart of the Inca Empire, fell to a force of less than 200 men led by the conquistador Francisco Pizarro. Pizarro established a new capital, Lima, which became the center of Spain's South American empire. For more information on this period of European exploration, see the articles PIZARRO, FRANCISCO in Volume P and EXPLORATION AND DISCOVERY (Spain and Portugal Divide the World Between Them) in Volume E.

Spanish colonial rule saw the introduction of Spanish culture. This palace in Lima, Peru, reflects Spain's Moorish architectural style.

Colonial Rule

The chief colonial official was the viceroy, who served as the monarch's personal representative. Eventually, Spanish South America was divided into three viceroyalties: Peru in the west (first established in 1544), New Granada in the north (founded in 1717), and La Plata in the south (founded 1776). Portugal's colony of Brazil was divided into northern and southern states in 1750 but was then reunited in 1775, with Rio de Janeiro as its capital.

Roman Catholic priests had arrived with the first colonists, to convert the Indians to Christianity. In addition to its religious activities, the church operated schools and hospitals, and it remained a powerful force both during and after the colonial era.

The production of minerals, chiefly gold and silver, was the main economic activity in the Spanish colonies. One-fifth of the wealth produced went to the monarch as the "royal fifth." Agriculture was based on Indian practices and improved upon by the Europeans, who introduced new crops and the large-scale cultivation of livestock. Indians worked in the mines and as farm laborers, often under harsh conditions.

Brazil's economy was at first based largely on agriculture. Sugarcane was the main commercial crop, produced by Indians and then by black slaves. Gold and diamonds were later discovered in the interior.

Revolution

Stirrings of discontent with colonial rule began in the late 1700's and increased in the early 1800's. The movements for independence in South America (similar movements arose in Mexico and Central America) were led chiefly by *criollos*, persons of pure Spanish ancestry who had been born in the colonies. Well educated and often quite wealthy, the *criollos* resented the monopoly on high political office held by officials sent from Spain. Some were also influenced by the ideals of liberty represented by the recent American and French revolutions. The invasion of Spain by Napoleon I in 1807 and the

IMPORTANT DATES

A.D. 300?–1000? The Tiahuanaco, Mochica (early Chimu), and Nazca cultures flourished in Peru and Bolivia.

1100?–1525? Inca Empire expanded to embrace lands and peoples extending from southern Colombia to northern Chile and Argentina.

1498 Christopher Columbus landed at the mouth of the Orinoco River on his third voyage of discovery.

1500 The Portuguese navigator Pedro Álvares Cabral reached the coast of Brazil.

1510 Alonzo de Ojeda founded the first permanent Spanish settlement at San Sebastián (in present-day Colombia).

1532–33 A Spanish force under Francisco Pizarro conquered Peru, center of the Inca Empire.

1544 Viceroyalty of Peru established.

1551 National University of San Marcos, first university in South America, founded in Lima, Peru.

1810 Independence movements against Spanish rule began in what are now Argentina, Colombia, and Venezuela.

1824 Final defeat of the Spanish armies in South America.

1830 Ten of the twelve present-day South American nations came into existence.

1865–70 War of the Triple Alliance pitted Paraguay against Argentina, Brazil, and Uruguay.

1879–84 Chile fought Bolivia and Peru in the War of the Pacific.

1890 The first meeting of the International Conference of American States was held, marking the beginning of the Pan American Union.

1932–35 Paraguay fought Bolivia in the Chaco War.

1933 The United States adopted the Good Neighbor Policy in its dealings with Latin America.

1948 Organization of American States (OAS) was chartered.

1960 Latin American Free Trade Association (LAFTA) was founded.

1966 Guyana (formerly British Guiana) became an independent nation.

1975 Suriname (formerly Dutch Guiana) became an independent nation.

1980 LAFTA was succeeded by the Latin American Integration Association (LAIA).

1982 Falkland Islands were invaded by Argentina but were recaptured by Britain after a brief war.

2001 The countries of the Western Hemisphere agreed to create a free trade zone in the Americas by 2003.

---

overthrow of the monarchy gave them their opportunity to revolt.

The leaders in the struggle for independence—including such figures as Simón Bolívar, José de San Martín, and Bernardo O'Higgins—suffered early defeats against Spanish troops before victory was finally achieved, in 1824. Only Brazil had no major war of liberation, winning independence from Portugal peacefully in 1822. By 1830, ten of the twelve present-day South American nations had come into being. Guyana (formerly British Guiana) gained independence in 1966, and Suriname (the former Dutch Guiana) did so in 1975. Biographies of Simón Bolívar, Bernardo O'Higgins, and José de San Martín can be found in the appropriate volumes.

Problems of Independence

The years following independence were difficult ones. Unlike Brazil, which was a monarchy until 1889 and relatively stable, the new Spanish-speaking republics were frequently torn by political conflict. Typically, this pitted conservatives against liberals. The conservatives, who consisted mainly of the large landowners, favored a strong central government. The liberals, who were mainly from the cities, sought a more decentralized form of government and a reduction in the power and influence of the church. Unstable governments led to the rise of military rulers.

Simón Bolívar, "the Liberator," freed Venezuela, Colombia, Ecuador, Peru, and Bolivia from Spanish rule in the 1820's.

Argentina's President Juan Perón (1946–55 and 1973–74) was one of the many South American leaders brought to power by military coups in the 1900's.

Relations among the South American countries themselves were often strained by territorial and other disputes, which led to several long and bloody wars. Paraguay lost more than half its population in the War of the Triple Alliance (1865–70) against Argentina, Brazil, and Uruguay. Chile fought Bolivia and Peru in the War of the Pacific (1879–84). Paraguay again went to war, against Bolivia, in the Chaco War (1932–35).

The Modern Era

South America's economic development was spurred during the second half of the 1800's by the growth of overseas markets for its minerals and agricultural products. Immigration, chiefly from southern Europe, also increased. The outbreak of World War I in 1914 made the continent's raw materials even more important. Although the worldwide Great Depression of the 1930's brought on an economic crisis, conditions improved during the years of World War II (1939–45).

The postwar period was marked by the beginnings of industrialization, rapid urbanization, and increasing demands for economic and political reforms. With most South American countries dependent on exports of one or two basic commodities, a drop in world prices often caused the economy to falter. The resulting discontent led to the growth of revolutionary political movements. During the 1950's and 1960's, ineffective governments were often overthrown by the military. A pattern of military regimes alternating with civilian rule lasted until the early 1990's, when democratically elected governments were restored throughout the continent.

The Future

South America has a promising future but also a number of problems. In contrast to the early years of independence, the nations of the continent realize that cooperation is vital to all their interests, and many have banded together in regional pacts. In addition to the Latin American Integration Association, these include the Organization of American States (OAS), the Andean Common Market, Mercosur, and the proposed Free Trade Association of the Americas. For more information, see the article ORGANIZATION OF AMERICAN STATES (OAS) in Volume O.

The continent's continuing problems include the rapidly growing population; poverty within the Indian, rural, and unemployed urban populations; and a shortage of educational fa-

Peru's President Alberto Fujimori was popular for his fight against terrorism in the 1990's but was dismissed from office in disgrace in 2000.

cilities in many areas. Furthermore, there is a staggering burden of foreign debt owed by many countries of the region, which has forced their governments to adopt austerity measures that limit development efforts.

KEMPTON E. WEBB
Columbia University
Author, *Latin America*

See also articles on individual South American countries.

SOUTH CAROLINA

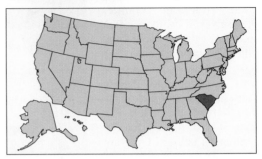

In 1629, King Charles I of England granted a charter for all lands in North America between 31 and 36 degrees north latitude. This entire region—which today would make up most of the southern United States—was called Carolana or Carolina, in the king's honor. More than 40 years later, English settlers arrived in the southern part of the grant. The settlement they founded at Charles Town (now Charleston) was the first in what became South Carolina.

South Carolina's nickname, the Palmetto State, dates from Revolutionary War times. Early in the war, South Carolina patriots built a fort on Sullivans Island at the entrance to Charleston Harbor. The 16-foot (5-meter) walls were built of sand reinforced by logs from the palmetto trees that grow along the Carolina coast. On June 28, 1776, well-armed British warships attacked the fort. Inside were 400 men under the command of Colonel (later General) William Moultrie. At nightfall, after ten hours of bombardment, the British retreated, with all their ships damaged and losses of about 200 men. In the fort the casualties were low. The palmetto fortress walls had stopped the British cannonballs from reaching their target.

South Carolina is located on the Atlantic Coast in the southeastern United States. From its beautiful ocean beaches in the east to the Blue Ridge Mountains in the west, the state's scenic attractions, mild climate, and colonial charm have made it a popular tourist destination.

With one of the most prosperous economies of all the southern states, South Carolina has a reputation as a good place to do business. In addition to tourism and other services, the manufacture of fabrics and other textiles is a leading source of income, particularly in the mountains. Farms yield a wide variety of produce, and each year festivals around the state celebrate everything from catfish and collards to peaches and poultry.

South Carolina, one of the original 13 colonies, has played a crucial role in the history of the nation. In the 1700's it experienced more Revolutionary War battles and skirmishes than any other state. In the 1800's it led the fight for states' rights and was the first state to secede (withdraw) from the Union, a direct cause of the Civil War. And the Civil War began in South Carolina in 1861, when Confederate forces fired on Fort Sumter, in Charleston Harbor.

▶ LAND

South Carolina is shaped like a triangle. The Atlantic Ocean, the Savannah River, and the North Carolina border form its three sides. The land gradually rises in elevation from the sea-level beaches of the Atlantic shore in the east to the crests of the Blue Ridge in the west.

Land Regions

South Carolina includes parts of two large natural land regions—the Coastal Plain and the Appalachian Highlands, containing the Piedmont and the Blue Ridge.

The Coastal Plain, an area known in South Carolina as the Low Country, covers about two-thirds of the state. Near the ocean the land is flat and often swampy, with many saltwater marshes containing interesting and valuable plant and animal life. The northern part of the coast has a continuous sandy beach, which attracts many vacationers. The rest of the coast is fringed by a chain of islands known as the Sea Islands. Inland the plain becomes gently rolling and is covered

Opposite page, clockwise from left: **Golfers finish a round at Hilton Head Island, a leading coastal resort. Historic buildings line the streets of Charleston, the state's oldest city. Cypress trees rise from the water at Cypress Gardens, north of Charleston.**

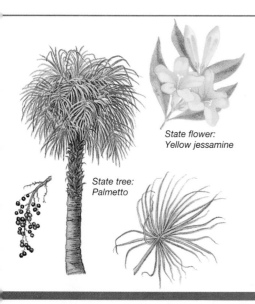

State flower:
Yellow jessamine

State tree:
Palmetto

FACTS AND FIGURES

Location: Southeastern United States; bordered on the north by North Carolina, on the east by the Atlantic Ocean, on the south by the Atlantic Ocean and Georgia, and on the west by Georgia.

Area: 31,189 sq mi (80,779 km^2); rank, 40th.

Population: 4,012,012 (2000 census); rank, 26th.

Elevation: *Highest*—3,560 ft (1,085 m), at Sassafras Mountain in Pickens County; *lowest*—sea level, along the Atlantic Ocean.

Capital: Columbia.

Statehood: May 23, 1788; 8th state.

State Mottoes: *Animis opibusque parati* ("Prepared in minds and resources"); *Dum spiro, spero* ("While I breathe, I hope").

State Songs: "Carolina"; "South Carolina on My Mind."

Nickname: Palmetto State.

Abbreviations: SC; S.C.

State bird:
Carolina wren

with forests. In the west, the plain rises to a belt of low hills, called the Sand Hills.

The Appalachian Highlands, a vast upland region of the eastern United States, covers the northwestern part of the state. South Carolinians call this area the Upstate or the Up Country. It consists of two sections—the Piedmont and the Blue Ridge.

The Piedmont is separated from the Coastal Plain by the fall line—the point where rivers tumble over rapids down to the Coastal Plain. This dividing line is actually a strip of land as much as 10 miles (16 kilometers) wide. The countryside of the Piedmont is rolling and dotted with hills called monadnocks. These hills are made up of very hard rock, which has resisted the forces of erosion. Some of the better-known monadnocks are Little Mountain, northwest of Columbia, and Kings Mountain, near the North Carolina border.

The Blue Ridge is a rugged, mountainous area that occupies only a small part of South Carolina, in the northwest corner of the state. Sassafras Mountain, the highest point in the state, is a crest of the Blue Ridge. Other notable peaks are Caesars Head and Pinnacle Mountain.

Rivers, Lakes, and Coastal Waters

South Carolina is drained by an extensive system of rivers and streams. The major rivers flow southeast, from the western highlands to the Atlantic Ocean. The Santee and its tributaries make up the most important system. The Santee is formed by the joining of the Wateree and the Congaree rivers, southeast of Columbia. The Congaree is formed at Columbia by the joining of the Saluda and the Broad rivers. The Pee Dee River, in the eastern part of the state, has two main tributaries—the Little Pee Dee and the Lynches. The Savannah River forms most of the state's boundary with Georgia.

Many dams have been built on South Carolina's rivers to generate electricity, improve navigation, and provide flood control. These dams have formed large reservoirs. Some of the largest are the J. Strom Thurmond, the Richard B. Russell, and Hartwell reservoirs on the Savannah River and Lake Marion and Lake Moultrie on the Santee and Cooper rivers. The state has no large natural lakes.

Measured in a straight line, South Carolina has 187 miles (300 kilometers) of coastline on the Atlantic Ocean. Including the shores of all the islands, sounds, and inlets, the shoreline measures 2,876 miles (4,630 kilometers).

Climate

South Carolina's climate is generally mild and pleasant. Summers are hot and humid in most of the state, but the mountains are considerably cooler. Temperatures in July average 80°F (27°C). Winters are generally mild. Temperatures in January average 45°F (7°C).

Annual precipitation averages 50 inches (1,270 millimeters) and is well distributed throughout the year. Rain and snow are heaviest in the mountains.

Plant and Animal Life

More than 60 percent of South Carolina is forested. Loblolly and longleaf pines dominate the Coastal Plain. Oaks, sweet gum, and cypress also grow in swampy areas. A mixture of oak, hickory, and pine trees is characteristic of the Piedmont and the Blue Ridge country. Commercial hardwoods include oak, sweet gum, black gum, and yellow poplar.

Decorative flowering trees and shrubs, particularly dogwoods and azaleas, thrive in South Carolina's mild, moist climate.

South Carolina has two national forests—Francis Marion National Forest, in the eastern part of the state, and Sumter National Forest, in the Up Country. South Carolina's climate is ideal for many flowering shrubs and trees, including azaleas and dogwoods.

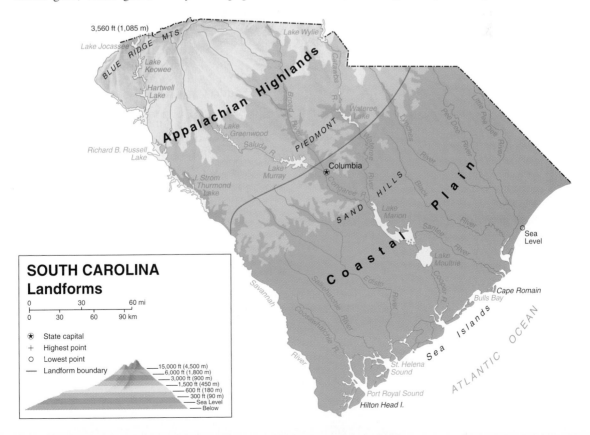

3,560 ft (1,085 m)

Lake Jocassee

Lake Wylie

BLUE RIDGE MTS.

Lake Keowee

Hartwell Lake

Richard B. Russell Lake

J. Strom Thurmond Lake

Catawba R.

Appalachian Highlands

Broad River

Lake Greenwood

Saluda R.

PIEDMONT

Wateree Lake

Wateree River

Little Pee Dee River

Big Pee Dee River

Lynches River

Columbia

Congaree R.

SAND HILLS

Lake Murray

Black River

Coastal Plain

Lake Marion

Santee River

Sea Level

Lake Moultrie

Cooper R.

Cape Romain

Bulls Bay

Savannah River

Salkehatchie River

Edisto River

Sea Islands

Coosawhatchie R.

St. Helena Sound

ATLANTIC OCEAN

Port Royal Sound

Hilton Head I.

SOUTH CAROLINA
Landforms

0   30   60 mi
0   30   60   90 km

⊛ State capital
+ Highest point
○ Lowest point
— Landform boundary

15,000 ft (4,500 m)
6,000 ft (1,800 m)
3,000 ft (900 m)
1,500 ft (450 m)
600 ft (180 m)
300 ft (90 m)
Sea Level
Below

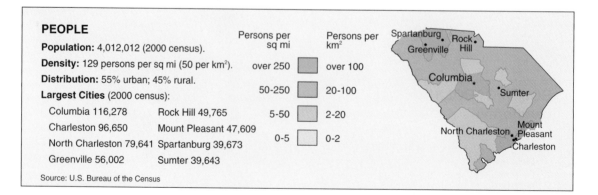

South Carolinians include people from many backgrounds. *Left:* Strollers take in an outdoor exhibit in Charleston. *Below:* A man pauses near a barber shop.

White-tailed deer are numerous in South Carolina. Smaller animals include opossums, raccoons, and foxes. Game birds include pheasants, doves, quail, wild turkeys, ducks, and geese.

Many species of saltwater fish and shellfish are found in the coastal waters. Shrimp, blue crabs, and oysters are the most important commercially. The rivers and lakes contain catfish, crappie, bass, bream, perch, and many other kinds of fish.

Natural Resources

South Carolina is committed to conserving natural resources such as soils, forests, and water supplies. Conservation programs seek ways to protect coastal areas, marshlands, and plant and animal life. Areas such as the Con-garee and the Santee swamps have been set aside as permanent wilderness areas. Beach erosion, land use, and hazardous waste disposal are other environmental issues important in the state.

The soils of the Coastal Plain are mostly sandy loams and are yellow in color. Soils in the Piedmont vary in texture from sandy loams to clay loams. Generally they are red in color. Soil conservation efforts have helped halt erosion in many areas.

South Carolina has an abundance of nonmetallic minerals. Among these are limestone, granite, sand and gravel, and various kinds of clay. Gold is also mined.

▶ PEOPLE

Many South Carolinians are descended from Europeans and Africans who arrived in the 1700's. The first white settlers were English and Scottish. They were followed by groups of Swiss, French, Irish, and German immigrants. African slaves were brought to South Carolina by the colonists about 1670.

Today African Americans make up close to 30 percent of the population. Asian Americans are the next largest minority. Native

PEOPLE

Population: 4,012,012 (2000 census).

Density: 129 persons per sq mi (50 per km²).

Distribution: 55% urban; 45% rural.

Largest Cities (2000 census):

Columbia 116,278	Rock Hill 49,765
Charleston 96,650	Mount Pleasant 47,609
North Charleston 79,641	Spartanburg 39,673
Greenville 56,002	Sumter 39,643

Persons per sq mi	Persons per km²
over 250	over 100
50-250	20-100
5-50	2-20
0-5	0-2

Source: U.S. Bureau of the Census

Americans, the original people of South Carolina, are represented by a small group of Catawba Indians. Some of them live on a reservation south of Rock Hill.

South Carolina's population has grown dramatically in recent years. Many businesses have moved to the state for its mild climate and low taxes, and that has attracted workers from other regions.

The 1980 census showed that for the first time in its history, South Carolina had more urban residents than rural residents. That trend has continued. More than 55 percent of the state's residents now live in urban areas.

Education

Public elementary and secondary schools in South Carolina have a combined enrollment of more than 655,000 students. In all, there are 1,097 public schools in the state in 92 school districts.

South Carolina is home to 33 colleges and universities, as well as 16 technical colleges offering specialized training. The University of South Carolina, founded in 1801, is the state's largest institution of higher education. The main campus is in Columbia. Regional campuses are located throughout the state. The College of Charleston in Charleston, chartered in 1785, is South Carolina's oldest college. Other state-supported four-year institutions include the Citadel (Military College of South Carolina) and the Medical University of South Carolina, both in Charleston, and Clemson University, in Clemson.

Among South Carolina's private colleges and universities are Bob Jones University and Furman University in Greenville and Wofford College and Converse College in Spartanburg.

Libraries, Museums, and the Arts

South Carolina's first library was founded in Charleston in 1698. Thomas Bray, a noted clergyman, sent the collection from England. The modern system of free public libraries was established about 1912.

The best-known museums in South Carolina are the Gibbes Art Gallery and the Charleston Museum in Charleston; the Columbia Museum of Art and the State Museum in Columbia; Brookgreen Gardens, an outdoor sculpture museum near Georgetown; and the Greenville County Museum of Art in Greenville. The Charleston Museum, founded in 1773, is said to be the country's oldest public museum.

Since 1977, Charleston has been the site of the Spoleto Festival, U.S.A., a celebration of the arts organized by composer Gian Carlo Menotti. The Peace Center in Greenville and the Koger Center in Columbia both host touring theatrical productions, concerts, and other cultural events. Columbia's Town Theatre (founded in 1919) is one of the oldest community theaters in the country.

▶ ECONOMY

For its first 200 years, South Carolina was primarily an agricultural state. Rice, indigo (a plant used to make dye), wheat, tobacco, and

PRODUCTS AND INDUSTRIES

Manufacturing: Textile products, especially synthetic fabrics; chemicals and related products; nonelectrical machinery; clothing; paper and paper products; electric and electronic equipment; rubber and plastic products; fabricated metal products.

Agriculture: Tobacco, soybeans, cattle and calves, hogs, eggs, milk, peaches, corn, broilers, turkeys, forest products, cotton, tomatoes, watermelons, peanuts.

Minerals: Stone, clays, sand and gravel.

Services: Wholesale and retail trade; finance, insurance, and real estate; business, social, and personal services; transportation, communication, and utilities; government.

*Gross state product is the total value of goods and services produced in a year.

Percentage of Gross State Product* by Industry

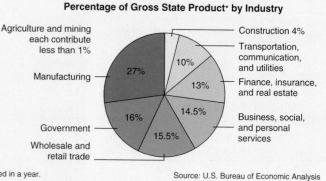

Agriculture and mining each contribute less than 1%

Manufacturing — 27%

Government — 16%

Wholesale and retail trade — 15.5%

14.5% — Business, social, and personal services

13% — Finance, insurance, and real estate

Transportation, communication, and utilities

10%

Construction 4%

Source: U.S. Bureau of Economic Analysis

Above: Vacationers wade into the Atlantic Ocean at Myrtle Beach. Miles of sandy beaches have helped make tourism a major industry in South Carolina.
Below: A textile worker inspects cotton thread at a textile mill. Textiles rank first among South Carolina's manufacturing industries.

Services

Service industries lead the state's economy. South Carolina's scenic, historic, and recreational attractions have made tourism a major industry. Coastal beaches, lakes, golf courses, tennis facilities, and excellent hunting, fishing, and boating areas offer nearly year-round recreation. Many people work in hotels, restaurants, and other businesses that cater to vacationers. Tourist, retirement, and health-care services are especially important along the coast.

In central South Carolina, especially around Columbia, state government is the major source of employment. Military installations at Charleston, Columbia, and Parris Island also provide many jobs. Retail trade and financial and computer services are growing in importance.

Manufacturing

Manufacturing has traditionally been a major source of employment in South Car-

cotton were its most important crops. Early industries included the manufacture of textiles, pottery, bricks, and iron utensils. However, manufacturing was slow to develop in the state until after the Civil War.

In the late 1800's, the textile industry began to develop rapidly. South Carolina's mild climate, abundant waterpower, and plentiful supplies of labor made it a center of textile manufacturing. Today, with a thriving tourism industry and significant foreign business investments, South Carolina's economy has become increasingly diverse.

olina. Textile manufacturing, which is concentrated in the Piedmont, still ranks first among the manufacturing industries. Textile mills spin and weave cotton, woolen, and synthetic yarns and fabrics. Other factories finish the cloth and turn it into clothing and other articles.

South Carolina has been successful in attracting foreign investment, and this has helped manufacturing grow. South Carolina's chemical industry has grown rapidly. Forest products, especially pulp and paper, are a major source of manufacturing income. Other important industries produce automobiles and other machinery, paper, electric and electronic equipment, rubber and plastic products, and products made of metal.

With a final polish, a new car rolls off the line at a BMW automobile plant in Spartanburg. The plant, built in the 1980's, has helped the economic growth of the region.

Agriculture

South Carolina's leading crop is tobacco, followed by soybeans, corn, cotton, and peaches. More peaches are grown in South Carolina than in any other state except California. Other crops include wheat, oats, peanuts, sweet potatoes, cucumbers, watermelons, and tomatoes.

Livestock, poultry, and egg production are important agricultural activities, as is dairying. One of South Carolina's specialties is squab (young pigeon).

Mining and Construction

South Carolina's most valuable minerals are stone, clays, and sand and gravel. Quarries producing crushed granite and blocks of granite for use in building are located in the middle and upper Piedmont. South Carolina is a leading producer of kaolin, a fine white clay used in making ceramics and as a filler in paper products. Most of the kaolin comes from Aiken County. Sand and gravel deposits are widespread in the Coastal Plain. Glass and glass products, such as fiberglass, are made from the finer sands. South Carolina is a leading producer of vermiculite, a mineral that is related to mica. Mined in the northwestern part of the state, vermiculite is used primarily as an ingredient in making plaster, insulation, and mulch.

A warm climate and a ready supply of lumber and other materials help make South Carolina a prime area for construction year-round. Construction accounts for only a small part of the state's economy, but it has become more important as the state's need for new homes and new and expanded business facilities has grown.

Harvested tobacco leaves are taken from the field to be dried. One of South Carolina's first cash crops, tobacco remains important to the state's economy.

Places of Interest

Middleton Place, near Charleston

Robert Mills Historic House and Park, in Columbia

Brookgreen Gardens, near Murrells Inlet, is a showplace of art and nature. It was developed in the 1930's by Archer and Anna Hyatt Huntington on the site of four colonial rice plantations. More than 500 sculptures from the 1800's and 1900's are exhibited among 2,000 species of plants.

Congaree Swamp National Monument, near Columbia, is a floodplain of the Congaree River. This protected area contains a fine example of a southern hardwood forest.

Cypress Gardens, near Charleston, was created from a reservoir once used for irrigating rice fields. Giant cypress trees draped in lavender and gray moss rise from the dark waters of the lake. Masses of daffodils, azaleas, and camellias bloom along the shore.

Fort Moultrie, on Sullivans Island, was built during the War of 1812. It is named in honor of Charleston-born William Moultrie, a Revolutionary War general, legislator, and governor of South Carolina (1785–87 and 1792–94). The site of the original fort on the island, which Moultrie and his men defended against the British in 1776, is now under the waters of Charleston Harbor. In front of the existing fort is the grave of Osceola, a famous Seminole leader. Osceola was captured during the Seminole Wars in Florida and imprisoned at Fort Moultrie, where he died in 1838.

Fort Sumter National Monument is on a tiny artificial island in Charleston Harbor. On April 12, 1861, Confederate troops opened fire on Fort Sumter, a federal (Union) fortification. These were the first shots fired in the U.S. Civil War. The monument includes a museum and the ruins of the brick and stone fort. The fort was named for Thomas Sumter (1734–1832), a Revolutionary War hero.

Fort Sumter National Monument, in Charleston Harbor

Kings Mountain National Military Park, near York, is one of the largest military parks in the United States. On this site on October 7, 1780, American troops won an important battle of the Revolutionary War. Most of the patriots were Up Country mountain folk who fought Indian-style, firing from behind trees and rocks.

Middleton Place, near Charleston, is said to have the oldest landscaped gardens in the United States. The original owner of the plantation was Henry Middleton, who served as president of the First Continental Congress. On the grounds are a rice mill, a springhouse (where foods were kept cool), and one wing of the Middleton mansion, built about 1755.

Ninety Six National Historic Site is located in a town called Ninety Six near Greenwood. The site was an important trading village during colonial days.

Penn Center Historic District, on St. Helena's Island near Beaufort, includes the site of the first school for freed slaves in the South, established during the Civil War.

Riverbanks Zoo and Botanical Gardens, in Columbia, is one of the top zoos in the United States. Animals live in replicas of their natural habitats, separated from people by space and water rather than cages.

Robert Mills Historic House and Park is located in the heart of Columbia. Mills, one of America's most celebrated architects, designed this mansion, built in 1823. Mills also designed the Washington Monument in Washington, D.C.

Woodrow Wilson's Boyhood Home, in Columbia, was the home of the 28th president of the United States from 1871 to 1875. The two-story white frame house is maintained as a museum.

State Recreational Areas. South Carolina's many state parks include a variety of scenic and historical attractions. For information, contact the South Carolina Department of Parks, Recreation, and Tourism, P.O. Box 71, Columbia, South Carolina 29202.

Transportation

South Carolina has a well-developed system of local roads and highways. All together, there are about 64,000 miles (103,040 kilometers) of roadway. Interstate highways 20, 26, and 85 are important routes.

Fifteen commercial airlines serve South Carolina. The state's major airports are in Charleston, Columbia, and Greenville. South Carolina's railroads are used mainly for freight. The state has about 2,500 miles (4,025 kilometers) of railway track.

Charleston is South Carolina's chief seaport. It is the leading U.S. Atlantic port in the South and boasts modern shipping container facilities. The Intracoastal Waterway provides storm-free passage for pleasure boats and for barges loaded with commercial goods.

Communication

South Carolina's first newspapers started in Charleston in 1732. Today 15 daily and about 80 weekly newspapers are published in the state. The largest daily is *The State*, published in Columbia. Other leading dailies include the *Greenville News* and the *News and Courier*, in Charleston.

South Carolina's first radio station, WSPA, started broadcasting in Spartanburg in 1929. There are about 165 radio stations broadcasting in the state today. The first television station, WCOS-TV, was started in 1953 in Columbia. The state is currently served by about 30 television stations.

▶ CITIES

Columbia, the capital and largest city, is located at the headwaters of the Congaree River, in the middle of the state. The original settlement, called Granby, was established in the early 1700's. A site across the river was chosen for the state capital in 1786, after heated debate between Up Country farmers, who wanted a central location, and Low Country plantation owners, who did not want the capital moved from Charleston. The state legislature first met there in 1790.

State government is the largest employer in Columbia. The city is also an educational and cultural center, with theaters, concert halls, and museums. Riverbanks Zoological Park is known for its innovative exhibits. Columbia is also the home of Fort Jackson, the largest training center of the U.S. Army.

Gracious homes and a band of green parkland line Charleston's historic waterfront. The city has retained much of its colonial charm, even while serving as a major port and manufacturing center.

Charleston, founded by the English in 1670, was the early capital of South Carolina. At first the settlement was called Charles Town, in honor of King Charles II, but the name was changed to Charleston at the end of the Revolutionary War.

Today, as a major seaport, Charleston receives ships from all over the world. It is also a manufacturing city, and it is home to air force and navy bases. But the city retains much of its colonial charm. Buildings and streets have been reconstructed and preserved, making Charleston a popular tourist destination. Charleston is also a famous cultural center. Dock Street Theater, opened in 1736, was the first playhouse in the United States used solely for giving dramatic productions. The Charleston Museum, the oldest museum in North America, has a collection of artifacts depicting Low Country life from the time of the first settlers to the present day. Cabbage Row, a courtyard off Church Street, was the model for Catfish Row in DuBose Heyward's novel *Porgy*. The novel was the basis for George Gershwin's opera *Porgy and Bess*.

Greenville is the manufacturing and commercial heart of the Piedmont. This area's leading industry has long been textile manufacturing. In recent years, it has become the U.S. headquarters for many international corporations. Greenville is the home of the Peace Center for the Performing Arts and the Shriners' Hospital for Crippled Children, one of the most modern facilities of its kind.

Rock Hill is in the north central part of the state, in the heart of the Piedmont. It has evolved from an agricultural city to a center of industry. Factories produce cotton and synthetic yarns and textiles, paper products, and other goods. Glencairn Gardens, a botanical park, graces the heart of the city.

Spartanburg is located next to Greenville. Along with that city, it has seen major growth. From the mid-1980's to the mid-1990's, Spartanburg County led the state in job creation and capital investments. Among the companies that helped the area grow is the German automobile maker BMW, which operates an assembly plant there. The Spartanburg Art Center, Twitchell Auditorium at Converse College, and several museums make Spartanburg a growing arts and educational community.

INDEX TO SOUTH CAROLINA MAP

● County Seat   Counties in parentheses   ★ State Capital

▶ **GOVERNMENT**

South Carolina has had a number of constitutions since independence was declared in 1776. The present government is based on a constitution that was adopted in 1895.

The chief executive of the state is the governor. Other elected state officers include the lieutenant governor, secretary of state, attorney general, and treasurer.

The legislative branch of the government, known as the General Assembly, is made up of a senate and a house of representatives. The General Assembly meets every year on the second Tuesday in January.

The judicial branch consists of the state supreme court, the court of appeals, the family court, and a number of circuit courts. Most counties have county courts, which handle primarily minor cases.

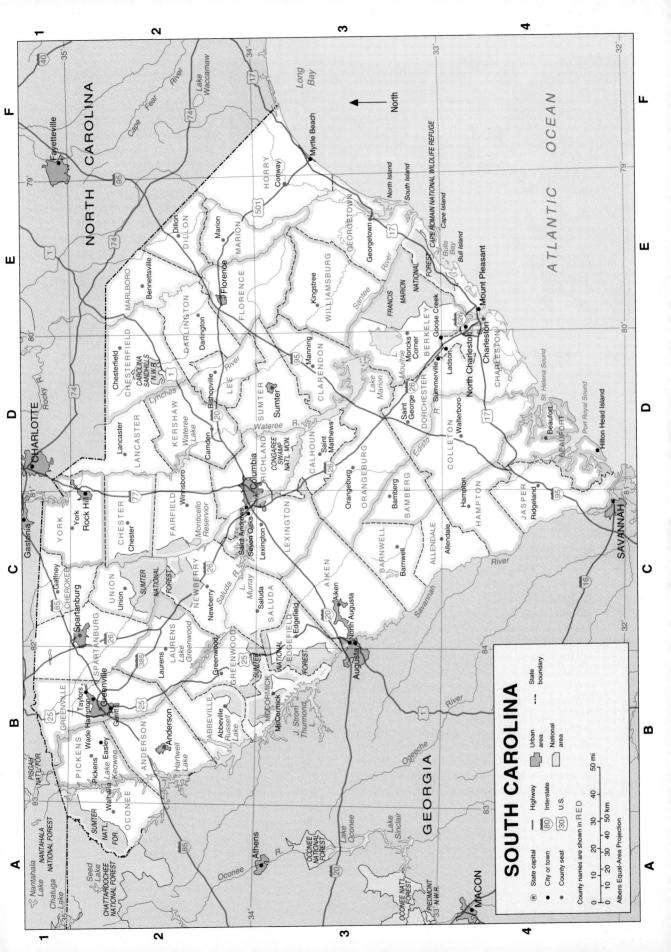

SOUTH CAROLINA

✪	State capital
⊛	City of town
•	County seat

County names are shown in RED

—	Highway
⑧⓪	Interstate
③⓪	U.S.

◼	Urban area
◻	National area
---	State boundary

0 10 20 30 40 50 mi
0 10 20 30 40 50 km

Albers Equal-Area Projection

NORTH CAROLINA

GEORGIA

ATLANTIC OCEAN

North

Columbia

Charleston

Greenville

Spartanburg

Florence

Sumter

Myrtle Beach

CHARLOTTE

FAYETTEVILLE

SAVANNAH

AUGUSTA

ATHENS

MACON

GASTONIA

South Carolina's legislature, known as the General Assembly, meets in the State House in Columbia, the state's capital and largest city.

GOVERNMENT

State Government
Governor: 4-year term
State senators: 46;
  4-year terms
State representatives: 124;
  2-year terms
Number of counties: 46

Federal Government
U.S. senators: 2
U.S. representatives: 6
Number of electoral votes: 8

For the name of the current governor, see STATE GOVERNMENTS in Volume S. For the names of current U.S. senators and representatives, see UNITED STATES, CONGRESS OF THE in Volume U-V.

▶ **HISTORY**

People lived in South Carolina as long as 11,000 years ago, but little is known about them. When Europeans first came to the area in the early 1500's, several dozen Native American tribes lived there. The largest groups were the Cherokee in the northwest and the Catawba in the Coastal Plain and Piedmont regions.

Over the years of European exploration and settlement, the Native Americans were forced from their lands. Only a small group of descendants of South Carolina's earliest people still live in the state.

Discovery and Exploration

The first Europeans to set foot in South Carolina were the Spanish. In 1521, Lucas Vázquez de Ayllón, a judge from the Caribbean island of Hispaniola, sent a ship to explore the Atlantic coast of North America. On the return trip, the ship's cargo included a number of Indians captured from the Carolina coast.

The first attempt to establish a colony was made in 1526. In that year Ayllón himself arrived with about 600 settlers, some African slaves, and dozens of horses. He founded San Miguel de Gualdape somewhere along the coast. The exact site of the colony is not known, but some historians have suggested it was at Winyah Bay, near present-day Georgetown. The colony failed after only a few months because of fever and starvation.

In 1562, Jean Ribaut (or Jan Ribault), a French naval officer, led a group of Huguenots (French Protestants) into Port Royal Sound. They constructed a fort, which they named Charlesfort, on Parris Island. Supplies grew short, and eventually the fort was abandoned. The Spanish established a fort and mission in 1566 in the same area, which they called Santa Elena. At one time it was the largest and most successful Spanish colony on the South Atlantic coast. But in 1587 it, too, was abandoned.

English Settlement

In 1629, King Charles I of England granted Carolina to his attorney general, Sir Robert Heath. But Heath failed to bring settlers to the province, and in 1663, King Charles II re-granted Carolina to eight government officials known as lords proprietors.

The first permanent settlement in South Carolina was made at Albemarle Point on the western bank of the Ashley River in April 1670. In 1680 the colony, known as Charles Town, was moved to the peninsula between the Ashley and Cooper rivers (Oyster Point). The colony prospered, but from the beginning the settlers were dissatisfied with the way the lords proprietors governed them. In 1719 they called a special assembly and declared themselves free of proprietary rule. They chose James Moore as their governor and requested royal rule.

During the royal period, South Carolina's economy was based on fur trading and the cultivation of rice and indigo. Charles Town became a major seaport. Several hundred vessels carrying goods to the northern colonies, the West Indies, and Europe passed through the harbor each year. The city also became a leading cultural center in North America.

The Revolutionary War

As time passed, many colonists became dissatisfied with the methods of royal control. In 1765, South Carolina sent delegates to the Stamp Act Congress to protest taxes imposed on the colonists by the king and his ministers.

In July 1774, a provincial congress elected delegates to the Continental Congress in Philadelphia and virtually took over the government of South Carolina. The royal governor fled in September 1775, five months after the Revolutionary War broke out. On March 26, 1776, South Carolina established an independent government.

During the Revolutionary War, the British attempted to take Charleston but were defeated at Sullivans Island on June 28, 1776. A second attempt in 1779 also failed, but the British finally succeeded in taking Charleston in 1780. Other important battles were fought at Kings Mountain (October 7, 1780) and at Cowpens battlefield (January 17, 1781). In all, South Carolina experienced about 200 Revolutionary War battles and skirmishes.

In 1787, four years after the United States won its independence from England, South Carolina sent four delegates to the Constitutional Convention in Philadelphia. Among them was Charles Pinckney, who contributed many valuable suggestions to the U.S. Constitution. South Carolina ratified (approved) the Constitution on May 23, 1788. It was the eighth state to do so.

Statehood

During the War of 1812, South Carolina contributed men and materials to the American forces. But during the years that followed, South Carolinians began to oppose the strong powers of the federal government. The state especially opposed high tariffs (taxes on exported goods). They were

Revolutionary War general Francis Marion is shown here crossing the Pee Dee River. Known as the Swamp Fox, he harrassed the British Army with his daring guerrilla-style raids.

thought to be harmful to cotton farmers, who grew crops chiefly for export. Under the guidance of John C. Calhoun, the state legislature passed the Ordinance of Nullification (1832), which declared the tariff acts of 1828 and 1832 null and void (invalid) in South Carolina. Armed conflict between the federal government and South Carolina was narrowly avoided, partly because a compromise tariff was passed in 1833.

By this time, cotton had become the state's leading crop. Planters relied on slave labor to tend and harvest cotton. Thus slavery became linked to South Carolina's economy. As opposition to slavery grew in the North, South

Famous People

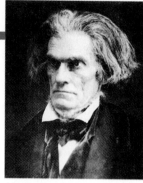

John C. Calhoun

Consult the Index to find more information in *The New Book of Knowledge* about the following people who were born in or are otherwise associated with South Carolina: Revolutionary War general Francis Marion (1732–95); slave revolt leader Denmark Vesey (1767–1822); President Andrew Jackson (1767–1845); Vice President John C. Calhoun (1782–1850); abolitionists and women's rights advocates Sarah Grimké (1792–1873) and Angelina Grimké (1805–79); U.S. representatives Joseph Hayne Rainey (1832–87) and Robert Smalls (1839–1915); educator Mary McLeod Bethune (1875–1955); labor leader Joseph Lane Kirkland (1922–99); tennis champion Althea Gibson (1927–2003); and civil rights leader Jesse Jackson (1941–).

James Francis Byrnes (1879–1972), born in Charleston, was an accomplished legislator, jurist, and statesman. He served his state and his country in many ways—as a U.S. representative (1911–25); U.S. senator (1931–41); U.S. Supreme Court justice (1941–42); secretary of state (1945–47) under President Harry S. Truman; and governor of South Carolina (1951–55).

Larry Doby (1923–2003), born in Camden, was the first African American to play on an American League baseball team, the Cleveland Indians. Doby played Negro League baseball while studying at Long Island University on scholarship. After serving in the navy during World War II, he rejoined the Newark Eagles. On July 5, 1947, he signed with the Indians. When the Indians won the World Series the next year, he became the first black player on a world championship team. Doby was inducted into the National Baseball Hall of Fame in 1998.

Julia Mood Peterkin (1880–1961), born in Laurens, was an author who drew on her experiences as the wife of a rich cotton planter. She wrote several novels depicting the lives of blacks in South Carolina. Her novel *Scarlet Sister Mary* won the Pulitzer Prize for fiction in 1929.

Elizabeth Lucas Pinckney (1722?–93), born in the West Indies, introduced the cultivation of indigo, used to make blue dye, to colonial South Carolina in the 1740's. Her sons **Charles Cotesworth Pinckney** (1746–1825) and

---

Carolinians began to fear that slavery would be restricted. Between 1850 and 1852, a strong movement for secession (withdrawal from the Union) developed in South Carolina. It failed due to the lack of cooperation from other Southern states.

Parts of Charleston, including Secession Hall (*shown*), were destroyed by Union soldiers toward the end of the Civil War.

The Civil War and Later Times

On December 20, 1860, South Carolina became the first state to secede from the Union. The war began when Confederate troops fired on Fort Sumter, in Charleston Harbor, in April 1861. More than 60,000 South Carolinians fought for the Confederacy. Union general William T. Sherman's march through South Carolina in early 1865 resulted in great destruction to the state, including the burning of Columbia, the capital. The State House was one of the few buildings in that city to survive.

The Reconstruction Period after the war was especially difficult in South Carolina. Little progress was made in economic development. Reconstruction ended in 1876, when Wade Hampton, a conservative, became governor.

In the years that followed, segregation—the separation of blacks and whites in society—

Julia Mood Peterkin

Larry Doby

Thomas Pinckney (1750–1828), both born in Charleston, were brilliant statesmen. Charles was a delegate to the Constitutional Convention of 1787 and was appointed minister to France in 1796. Thomas served as governor of South Carolina (1787–89) and as U.S. minister to Great Britain (1792–94). As special envoy to Spain (1795) he concluded the favorable treaty of San Lorenzo, which recognized U.S. boundary claims and allowed free navigation on the Mississippi River by Americans. **Charles Pinckney** (1757–1824), a Charleston-born cousin of the Pinckney brothers, was a governor of South Carolina (1789–92, 1796–98, and 1806–08) as well as a U.S. senator (1798–1801), U.S. minister to Spain (1801–05), and U.S. representative (1819–21). At the Constitutional Convention of 1787, he submitted the Pinckney Draught, which greatly influenced the final wording of the U.S. Constitution.

John Rutledge (1739–1800), born in Charleston, was a delegate to the Stamp Act Congress in 1765 and to the Continental Congress in 1774 and 1776. He later served as governor of South Carolina (1779–82) and as chief justice of the United States (1795), although his appointment was never confirmed by the U.S. Senate. **Edward Rutledge** (1749–1800) served with his brother John as a South Carolina delegate to the Continental Congress in 1774. In 1776 he signed the Declaration of Independence. He also served as governor (1798–1800).

James Strom Thurmond (1902–2003), born in Edgefield, was governor of South Carolina from 1947 to 1951. In 1948 he ran for president as the candidate of the States' Rights Democratic (Dixiecrat) Party. He was the longest-serving U.S. senator (1955–2003) in history, retiring at age 100.

---

became increasingly commonplace. Opportunities for black South Carolinians were severely limited, and their civil rights were all but ignored.

Modern Times

During World War I (1914–18), industry, especially textile manufacturing, developed rapidly in South Carolina. In the 1920's, however, the state's cotton industry was severely damaged by the invasion of the boll weevil. Many farmers turned to other crops, such as corn and tobacco.

After World War II (1939–45), the state continued to develop industrially. However, many African Americans moved north to avoid racial discrimination and limited economic opportunities. This trend continued until the 1960's, when the civil rights movement brought an end to segregation and legal discrimination in the state. Although the change was mostly peaceful, there was some violence. The most serious incident took place in 1968 at Orangeburg, where state police shot three black protesters. Two years later, three African Americans were elected to the state legislature. Many others have since served in state and local offices.

Meanwhile, improving economic conditions brought more employment opportunities. Thousands of people (including many African Americans originally from South Carolina) moved to the state from other parts of the country. In the 1970's, the state's population grew nearly twice as fast as the national average. Growth continued through the 1990's.

In September 1989, South Carolina experienced the most serious natural disaster in its history. Hurricane Hugo smashed into the Carolina coast near Charleston and traveled inland through Columbia. The storm destroyed thousands of homes and businesses. Assistance from the federal government and private agencies poured in, but rebuilding was slow and difficult.

Recent Trends

In the years since the hurricane, South Carolina's economy and its people have grown increasingly diversified, as international corporations have brought jobs to the state. At the same time, South Carolina has tackled important issues, such as improving education by strengthening public schools and colleges to create a stronger economic base and more job opportunities for its people.

ANN ADDY
South Carolina State Library

See also THIRTEEN AMERICAN COLONIES.

SOUTH DAKOTA

When the U.S. Congress divided the Dakota Territory in 1889, the southern half became the state of South Dakota. The name Dakota came from the region's Native American Sioux tribes, who called themselves Dakota, Nakota, *or* Lakota, *words in their language that mean "friends" or "allies."*

South Dakota's official nickname, the Mount Rushmore State, refers to the national memorial featuring the faces of four U.S. presidents—George Washington, Thomas Jefferson, Theodore Roosevelt, and Abraham Lincoln. This famous landmark, the state's most popular tourist attraction, also inspired the state slogan, "Great Faces, Great Places." Other South Dakota nicknames include the Sunshine State, for the state's many days of sunny weather, and the Coyote State, for the state animal. Ring-necked pheasants, the state bird, are so plentiful that South Dakota has also been called the Pheasant Capital of the World.

State flag

South Dakota is located in the midwestern United States, in the geographical center of the North American continent. The Missouri River, the region's major waterway, flows through the state, cutting it into two roughly equal sections. To the east lie gentle hills and fertile soils. To the west lie the Black Hills, the highest mountains east of the Rockies; the Badlands, a wasteland of weirdly eroded spires, ridges, and cliffs; and the endless horizons of the vast Great Plains.

The majority of South Dakotans live either in the eastern third of the state or in the Black Hills in the west. Sioux Falls, the state's largest city, is located in the southeast, near the borders of Iowa and Minnesota. Rapid City, the state's second largest city, is popularly known as the Gateway to the Black Hills. Pierre, the state capital, lies on the east bank of the Missouri River near the center of the state.

South Dakota's economy is based more heavily on agriculture than that of most other states. Wheat, oats, rye, corn, soybeans, and sorghum, the most valuable crops, are grown in the east. Cattle, sheep, and other livestock are raised in the west. Notable services and industries include food processing, health care, banking, and lumbering. Tourism, one of

the state's fastest-growing industries, has been fueled by an ever-growing interest in the region's fascinating history.

Pioneering farmers first settled in eastern South Dakota in the mid-1800's. Good wheat crops later brought more homesteaders, leading to what was known as the Great Dakota Boom. The Sioux Indians were pushed westward across the Missouri River to the plains. When gold was discovered in the Black Hills in 1874, prospectors skipped over the Indian-held lands to settle the western part of the territory. The gold rush of 1876, the struggle of the Sioux to hold on to their lands, and the stories of such pioneers as Laura Ingalls Wilder, known for her autobiographical tales in the *Little House* series, breathe color and life into the past and the present.

▶ **LAND**

South Dakota lies within a broad belt of plains country that extends through the center of North America from the Arctic Ocean to the Gulf of Mexico. Much of South Dakota is covered by rolling plains, interrupted by hills, valleys, or stretches of flat land. Mountains rise in the far western part of the state.

Opposite page, clockwise from top left: Pioneer life can be experienced at the Laura Ingalls Wilder Festival in De Smet. Cowboys prepare to ride bulls in Newall. Mount Rushmore National Memorial is known as the Shrine of Democracy.

State flower:
Pasqueflower

State tree:
Black Hills spruce

FACTS AND FIGURES

Location: North central United States; bordered on the north by North Dakota, on the east by Minnesota and Iowa, on the south by Nebraska, and on the west by Wyoming and Montana.

Area: 77,121 sq mi (199,744 km^2); rank, 17th.

Population: 754,844 (2000 census); rank, 46th.

Elevation: *Highest*—7,242 ft (2,207 m), at Harney Peak in Pennington County; *lowest*—962 ft (293 m) above sea level, at Big Stone Lake in Roberts County.

Capital: Pierre.

Statehood: November 2, 1889; 40th state.

State Motto: *Under God the people rule.*

State Song: "Hail, South Dakota."

Nickname: Mount Rushmore State.

Abbreviations: SD; S.D.; S. Dak.

State bird:
Ring-necked pheasant

Banded buttes, beautifully colored with varying layers of sandstone, are one of the most striking features of Badlands National Park on the Missouri Plateau.

Land Regions

South Dakota lies within two major land regions. They are the Central Lowland and the Great Plains.

The Central Lowland covers the eastern third of South Dakota. During the Ice Age, glaciers smoothed rough features, filled in valleys, and changed drainage patterns. When the ice sheets melted, they left behind loose soil, gravel, and boulders called drift.

In the northeastern part of the state, a low trench called the **Minnesota Valley** became an outlet for an ancient glacial lake. Today

the lowest parts of the trench form two lakes—Lake Traverse and Big Stone Lake.

West of the Minnesota Valley lies a rough highland country known as the **Prairie Hills**. Dozens of small lakes and ponds were formed in the Prairie Hills when chunks of ice broke away from the glaciers and melted, leaving holes in the glacial drift.

West of the hill country is the **James River Valley**, created by the flow of melting glacial waters. Occasional low ridges and knobby hills add variety to the generally flat landscape.

The Great Plains, the largest land region in South Dakota, can be divided into three sections—the Missouri Plateau, the High Plains, and the Black Hills.

The **Missouri Plateau** begins at the Missouri Escarpment, a gentle slope that crosses the state from north to south. To the west of the slope is a belt of rough country called the Missouri Hills, which marks the end of the

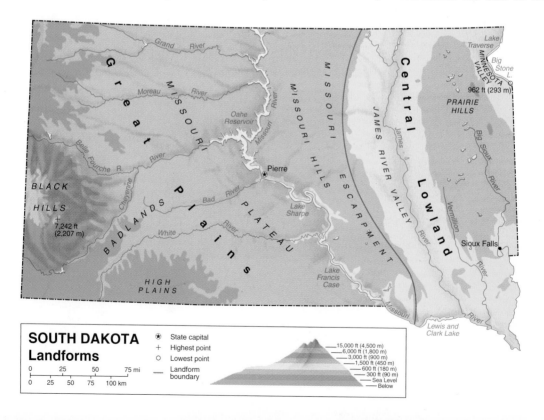

SOUTH DAKOTA Landforms

0   25   50   75 mi
0   25   50   75   100 km

⊛ State capital
+ Highest point
○ Lowest point
— Landform boundary

15,000 ft (4,500 m)
6,000 ft (1,800 m)
3,000 ft (900 m)
1,500 ft (450 m)
600 ft (180 m)
300 ft (90 m)
Sea Level
Below

glaciated part of South Dakota. West of the Missouri Hills lies a vast, rolling upland and the Missouri River valley. The northwest contains many low, steep-sided, flat-topped hills called buttes, with names such as Castle Rock, Thunder, and Deers Ears.

In some places on the Missouri Plateau, wind and water have eroded the sand and gravel, creating an area of unusual rock formations known as the Badlands. The Big Badlands, between the Cheyenne and the White rivers, form the largest single area of badlands in the state.

A small part of the **High Plains**, a region that extends into South Dakota from Nebraska, is made up largely of sand dunes. A steep, eroded cliff called the Pine Ridge marks the northern boundary of this region.

The **Black Hills**, which are actually very old mountains, are made mostly of granite. Several peaks rise above 7,000 feet (2,134 meters),

including Harney Peak, the state's highest point. This region is also known for its limestone and sandstone ridges called hogbacks, which were carved by swift-flowing streams. In some areas, underground water has also carved remarkable caves, such as those found in Wind Cave National Park.

Rivers and Lakes

Almost all of South Dakota is drained by the Missouri River. The Missouri's principal tributaries in the west—the Grand, Moreau, Cheyenne, Bad, and White rivers—flow eastward. The Missouri's tributaries in the east—the James, Vermillion, and Big Sioux rivers—flow southward.

South Dakota's largest lakes are reservoirs, created by damming the rivers. Oahe, the state's largest reservoir, lies north of Pierre on the Missouri River. Other reservoirs of notable size include Lake Sharpe, Lake Francis Case, and Lewis and Clark Lake. Lake Traverse and Big Stone Lake, both located on the boundary with Minnesota, are the largest natural lakes in the state.

Climate

South Dakota is exposed to warm, moist air masses from the Gulf of Mexico and cold, dry air masses from Canada. As a result, South Dakota experiences hot summers and cold winters. Average January temperatures range from 10°F (−12°C) in the northeast to 25°F (−4°C) in the southwest. Average July temperatures range from 68°F (20°C) to 75°F (24°C). However, changes in temperature are frequent and sometimes extreme.

Left: Granite spikes called the Needles challenge rock climbers in Custer State Park in the Black Hills. *Below:* Big Sioux Falls is located on the Big Sioux River in the Central Lowland, a well-watered region where agriculture flourishes.

South Dakota's precipitation comes largely from air masses that form over the Gulf of Mexico. The southeast receives the heaviest amount, about 25 inches (635 millimeters) a year, while the northwest receives an average of 14 inches (356 millimeters) a year. Most of the precipitation occurs as rain from April through September. Snowfall generally is not very heavy, although it usually remains on the ground until spring. Like other plains states,

Bison are native to the plains of South Dakota. State and national parks systems maintain some of the world's largest bison preserves.

South Dakota has occasional blizzards—a snowstorm accompanied by high winds and bitterly cold temperatures. The coldest areas are the north central and northeastern parts of the state.

Plant and Animal Life

South Dakota has about 2 million acres (800,000 hectares) of forestland. The most plentiful tree, the ponderosa pine, is harvested for commercial products. Smaller stands of softwood trees include spruce and juniper. About half the forestland is located in the Black Hills National Forest in the southwest and Custer National Forest in the northwest. Scattered areas of hardwood timber are found along the Missouri River and in the northeast.

Prairie grasses covered most of South Dakota before the sod was broken by non-Indian farmers. Still, more than 28 million acres (11.2 million hectares) of grasslands remain, mostly west of the Missouri River. Much of this is used for grazing livestock. South Dakota has three areas of national grasslands—the Grand River National Grassland in the northwest, the Buffalo Gap National Grassland in the southwest, and the Fort Pierre National Grassland, south of the capital.

Numerous animals make their home in South Dakota. The brightly colored ring-necked pheasant, the state bird, was imported from China in the 1890's. Other game birds include prairie chickens, grouse, and wild turkeys. During migration season, thousands of ducks and geese stop to rest and feed in the Missouri Valley.

Mule deer, white-tailed deer, and antelopes are among the state's most plentiful large game animals. South Dakota also has many American bison (often called buffalo). They live in scattered herds, chiefly in national parks in the Black Hills, where they are protected, and in central South Dakota, where they are raised for commercial purposes.

Brook trout, rainbow trout, and brown trout are found in the cold mountain streams of the Black Hills. Walleyed pike, northern pike, black bass, and other warm-water fish are common in the lake district of the north-

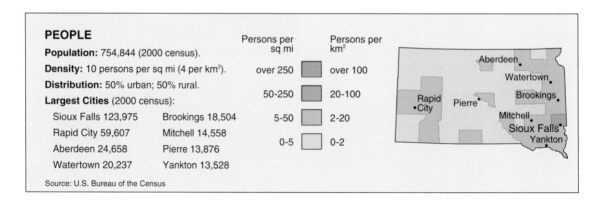

PEOPLE

Population: 754,844 (2000 census).

Density: 10 persons per sq mi (4 per km²).

Distribution: 50% urban; 50% rural.

Largest Cities (2000 census):

Sioux Falls 123,975	Brookings 18,504
Rapid City 59,607	Mitchell 14,558
Aberdeen 24,658	Pierre 13,876
Watertown 20,237	Yankton 13,528

Source: U.S. Bureau of the Census

Persons per sq mi	Persons per km²
over 250	over 100
50-250	20-100
5-50	2-20
0-5	0-2

east. Many varieties are also found in the reservoirs on the Missouri River.

Natural Resources

South Dakota's greatest natural resources are its soils and rich mineral deposits.

Most of the land east of the Missouri River is covered by a fertile soil called chernozem, from the Russian words for "black earth." Made up of partially decomposed plant and animal material, these dark soils are considered among the most productive in the world. Thinner, less productive chestnut soils—that are grayish brown in color—are found west of the Missouri River. Sandy soils are found in the High Plains. Gray soils are found in the wooded Black Hills.

The state has taken a number of steps to conserve its natural resources. Dams have been built to check soil erosion and provide a measure of flood control. Forests have been replanted. Shelterbelts (barriers of trees and shrubs) have also been planted to prevent soil erosion. Grasslands have been set aside and wildlife is protected in refuges.

The Black Hills contain most of South Dakota's mineral resources. The vein of gold discovered there in the 1870's is still being mined. Other minerals found in the Black Hills include silver, mica, feldspar, lithium, beryl, and uranium. Deposits of lignite—a low-grade soft coal—are located in the northwest. Petroleum is also found in western South Dakota. Manganese can be found along the Missouri River north of Chamberlain. The state also has plentiful supplies of sand and gravel and high-grade granite.

▶ PEOPLE

Soon after the Civil War ended in 1865, numerous people in search of good farmland decided to try their luck in the Dakota Territory. Many came from neighboring states, such as Minnesota and Iowa, and were quickly joined by immigrants of various European nationalities, especially Germans and Norwegians. Today many of the names in South Dakota are German or Scandinavian in origin. Smaller groups came from the British Isles and from eastern Europe.

About 8 percent of all South Dakotans are of Native American ancestry, a higher percentage than in most other states. The majority belong to nine different Sioux tribes and live on reservations, chiefly west of the Missouri River. Less than 1 percent of the population is African American.

Education

The first school in South Dakota was a log cabin built in Bon Homme County in 1860 that was torn down when the logs were needed to build a stockade. A second school was built at Vermillion in 1862. It also served as the town's first church, community hall, and voting place.

The University of South Dakota, founded in Vermillion in 1882, is South Dakota's oldest state-supported institution of higher learning.

A public school system was established by the first Dakota territorial legislature in 1862. School districts, first organized in 1865, increased in number as new settlers arrived. Most of the rural schools were built during the 1920's, the period of greatest expansion of the school system. Now consolidated schools have replaced many of the rural schools.

The first territorial legislature also passed a measure that created the University of South Dakota at Vermillion. This institution began to offer instruction at the college level in 1882. South Dakota State University, in Brookings, was chartered as a territorial agricultural college in 1881. It became a university

in 1964. The South Dakota School of Mines and Technology is located in Rapid City. Other state universities are located in Aberdeen, Madison, and Spearfish.

South Dakota also has one tribal university, Sinte Gleska University on the Rosebud Indian Reservation, as well as tribally sponsored community colleges on the Pine Ridge, Sisseton-Wahpeton, and Cheyenne River reservations. Private colleges and universities include Augustana College and the University of Sioux Falls in Sioux Falls, Dakota Wesleyan University in Mitchell, Huron University in Huron, and Mount Marty College in Yankton.

Libraries, Museums, and the Arts

The Dakota territorial legislature passed a law in 1887 that allowed towns to establish public libraries and collect taxes to support them. Among the first to establish libraries were Sioux Falls and Aberdeen. The Sioux Falls Public Library and Aberdeen's Alexander Mitchell Library are now the largest circulating libraries in the state. Specialized law and medical collections are found at the University of South Dakota in Vermillion.

The South Dakota State Historical Society, located at the Cultural Heritage Center in Pierre, has collected and preserved state records since 1902. The society's library of books and newspapers and its museum showcase the state's

Murals made of corn kernels and other grains adorn the interior and exterior walls of the Corn Palace in Mitchell.

PRODUCTS AND INDUSTRIES

Manufacturing: Industrial machinery and equipment; processed foods, including packed meats, flour, animal feed, and dairy products; scientific instruments; electronic and electric equipment; lumber and wood products.

Agriculture: Cattle and calves, corn, soybeans, wheat, hogs, dairy products, sunflowers, hay.

Minerals: Gold, stone, petroleum, sand and gravel.

Services: Wholesale and retail trade; finance, insurance, and real estate; business, social, and personal services; transportation, communication, and utilities; government.

*Gross state product is the total value of goods and services produced in a year.

Percentage of Gross State Product* by Industry

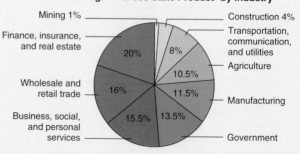

Mining 1%
Construction 4%
Transportation, communication, and utilities 8%
Finance, insurance, and real estate 20%
Agriculture 10.5%
Wholesale and retail trade 16%
Manufacturing 11.5%
Business, social, and personal services 15.5%
Government 13.5%

Source: U.S. Bureau of Economic Analysis

heritage from the time of the earliest inhabitants to the present. A museum in Rapid City called the Journey focuses on the natural and cultural history of the Black Hills. Exhibits at the Adams Museum in Deadwood feature the region's early mining history. The Soukup and Thomas International Balloon and Airship Museum in Mitchell traces the history of lighter-than-air flight.

Left: Wheat is one of South Dakota's most important field crops. *Below:* Casino gambling has become an important source of income in Deadwood, a major tourist destination. *Bottom:* More gold is mined in South Dakota than in any other state.

The Agricultural Heritage Museum at South Dakota State University in Brookings traces the state's agricultural history. The South Dakota Memorial Art Center, also in Brookings, houses a collection of regional artwork. The Oscar Howe Center in Mitchell displays paintings by the Dakota Sioux artist for whom it was named. The Dahl Fine Arts Center in Rapid City displays the works of many fine regional artists. The Shrine to Music Museum at South Dakota State University in Vermillion contains more than 5,000 musical instruments from all time periods.

The South Dakota Symphony, headquartered in Sioux Falls, performs classical and popular music throughout the state. One of the most popular outdoor theatrical productions in the Great Plains—the Passion Play—occurs each summer in Spearfish. Based on accounts of the last seven days in the life of Jesus Christ, the production continues a tradition begun in Europe during the Middle Ages.

▶ ECONOMY

South Dakota, a major farming and ranching state, ranks high in the production of both grain and livestock. But most South Dakotans are employed in occupations other than agriculture, particularly wholesale and retail trade, government, tourism, health care, manufacturing, and mining.

Services

About 39 percent of all the service people employed in South Dakota work in the growing health care industry. Sioux Falls has become a regional medical center for eastern South Dakota and parts of Minnesota and Iowa. Profits from hotels, restaurants, and other businesses dependent on tourism and recreation are also increasing.

Manufacturing

The processing of food products is South Dakota's leading manufacturing activity. The state's largest meat-packing plant is in Sioux Falls. Construction materials, such as cement, bricks, and tiles, are manufactured in Rapid City and Belle Fourche. Sawmills throughout the Black Hills produce lumber and other wood products. The state's fastest-growing manufacturing industries include the production of computers and metal products, such as tools and industrial machinery, and printing and publishing.

Agriculture

A large portion of South Dakota's agricultural income comes from the raising and feeding of beef cattle, hogs, and sheep. The

Deadwood

The Corn Palace, in Mitchell

Badlands National Park lies between the White and Cheyenne rivers in the southwestern part of the state. The park contains a fantastic array of eroded land-forms, including ravines, ridges, low hills, and cliffs. Some formations look like tow-ers, cathedral spires, or castles. Fossil remains of prehistoric animals are also found there.

The Corn Palace, an unusual exhibition center in Mitchell, takes its name from the multicolored corn kernels used each year to decorate both the outside and the inside of the building. The kernels are combined with other grains and tree branches to create murals.

Crazy Horse Memorial, located in the southern Black Hills, honors the region's Native American heritage. The massive granite carving depicts the famous Lakota warrior Crazy Horse seated on his horse. The project, begun in the 1940's by sculptor Korczak Ziolkowski, is still in progress.

Custer State Park, covering a vast tract of countryside in the Black Hills, is one of the largest state parks in the nation. Known for its great abundance of wildlife, it contains one of the world's largest herds of bison. Sylvan Lake, in a northern portion of the park, is a beautiful artificial lake famous for the huge, steep rocks that rise abruptly from the water's edge. A scenic highway passes through spikes of granite formations called the Needles.

Deadwood, located in the Black Hills, was known as one of the most lawless towns in the Wild West. Several well-known personalities, including Wild Bill Hickok, Calamity Jane, and Preacher

Crazy Horse Memorial

Smith, are buried nearby in Mount Moriah Cemetery. Profits from casino gambling are now used to preserve and restore the historic downtown district.

Fort Sisseton State Park, west of Sisseton, is the site of a fort built during a Sioux uprising in the 1860's. Its many restored buildings show what a typical fort in the Indian country looked like.

Hill City has one of the few narrow-gauge railroads still operating in the United States. The 1880 steam railroad offers scenic views of the Black Hills.

Indian Reservations, located throughout the state, are popular tourist sites. The six largest are the Lower Brule and Crow Creek reservations in the central part of the state; the Cheyenne River and Standing Rock reservations in the north central part of the state; and the Pine Ridge and

Rosebud reservations in the south and west.

Jewel Cave National Monument, west of Custer, is a limestone cavern in the Black Hills that is more than 104 miles (167 kilometers) long, making it the third longest cave in the world. The cavern received its name from the colorful crystal formations that line its many chambers and passageways.

Mount Rushmore National Memorial, South Dakota's most popular tourist attraction, is a giant carving on a granite cliff in the Black Hills. Designed by the sculptor Gutzon Borglum, the memorial features the faces of four great presidents, symbolizing four great American achievements: the founding of the nation (George Washington); territorial expansion (Thomas Jefferson); unification (Abraham Lincoln); and conservation (Theodore Roosevelt). The Mount Rushmore memorial has become known as the Shrine of Democracy.

Wind Cave National Park, north of Hot Springs, is famous for its limestone cavern, which contains a seemingly endless maze of passageways and chambers lined with delicately colored crystal formations in a honeycomb pattern known as boxwork. The cave gets its name from the sound the air makes as it blows through a small natural opening. The park also serves as a refuge for bison and other protected animals.

Wounded Knee Battlefield, located in the South Dakota Badlands, was the site of the last major battle between the Lakota Sioux and U.S. troops in 1890. The historic village of Wounded Knee is located nearby on the Pine Ridge Reservation.

State Recreation Areas. For more information on South Dakota's state parks and other places of interest, write to the South Dakota Division of Parks and Recreation, 523 E. Capitol Avenue, Pierre, South Dakota, 57501.

most profitable field crops are corn, soybeans, and wheat. Hay, sunflowers, oats, sorghum, potatoes, rye, and flax are also grown. Some of the corn, wheat, and other grains are processed into food for livestock.

Beef cattle and other livestock bring about as much revenue to South Dakota as all of the state's field crops combined.

Mining and Construction

South Dakota is the nation's leading producer of gold. Most of the gold, as well as some silver, comes from the Homestake Mine in Lead (pronounced LEED). Mica and feldspar are also mined in the Black Hills. Feldspar is used to make glass and chinaware. Mica has many uses in the electrical industry. Clays from Butte County are used to make brick. Oil is produced in the western and west central parts of the state. Several counties produce cement and sand and gravel, used in the construction of buildings, roads, and dams. Granite from the Milbank area has been used to build monuments.

Transportation

South Dakota's first "highway" was the Missouri River. It was the major transport route for the Native Americans and early explorers, missionaries, and fur traders. The first steamboat to travel on the upper Missouri, the *Yellowstone*, made its way to Fort Pierre in 1831.

Covered wagons brought the first pioneers to eastern South Dakota until the railroads reached Sioux Falls and Yankton in the 1870's. The discovery of gold in the Black Hills led to a rapid increase in railroad building in the 1880's. Today, fewer miles of track are maintained and are used mainly to carry freight.

South Dakota's highway system includes two interstate highways. One (I-90) runs east and west across the south central part of the state. The other (I-29) runs north and south, close to the eastern boundary. Numerous other federal and state highways crisscross South Dakota. The highways in the Black Hills provide especially scenic views.

South Dakota has dozens of small airports, many of them privately owned. The two largest public airports, served by major airlines, are located in Sioux Falls and Rapid City.

Communication

South Dakota's oldest newspaper is the *Yankton Press and Dakotan*, first published in 1861. The state now publishes more than 120 weekly newspapers and a dozen dailies. The *Sioux Falls Argus-Leader* and the *Rapid City Journal* have the widest circulations. South Dakota's broadcasting industry is represented by more than 40 radio and 12 television stations.

▶ CITIES

South Dakota is primarily a rural state. About half the people live on farms or ranches or in communities of fewer than 2,500 persons. The rest live in the larger towns and cities, especially in the east. South Dakota's cities are relatively small. Only one, Sioux Falls, has a population exceeding 100,000.

Sioux Falls, South Dakota's largest city, was named for the nearby falls of the Big Sioux River. The city is a regional center for commerce, industry, and health care.

Rapid City is the largest urban area in western South Dakota. Many of its service industries are geared to tourists visiting the Black Hills.

Pierre (pronounced PEER) is the capital of South Dakota. Located on the eastern bank of the Missouri River in the center of the state, it was founded as a ferry landing for the bustling town of Fort Pierre across the river. The town began to grow rapidly after 1880, when the railroads began stopping there. Pierre was selected as the temporary state capital in 1889 and became the permanent capital in 1904.

Today Pierre is an important regional trading and distribution center for the large surrounding farming area. Points of interest in and around the city include the state capitol building, the South Dakota State Historical Society, and Lake Oahe.

Sioux Falls, South Dakota's largest city, is located on the Big Sioux River in the eastern part of the state. First settled in 1857, the site was quickly abandoned due to a series of Indian raids. But settlers soon returned after a military fort was established there in 1865. Sioux Falls was chartered as a city in 1883.

Today the city is the commercial, industrial, and health care center for southeastern South Dakota and nearby areas in Minnesota and Iowa. It is also an important center for the marketing and distribution of livestock. Food processing is the leading industry, while credit-card banking enterprises and the computer industry are becoming increasingly profitable. The Earth Resources Observation Systems Data Center (EROS), a federal agency that processes and archives millions of pictures of the Earth taken by aircraft and

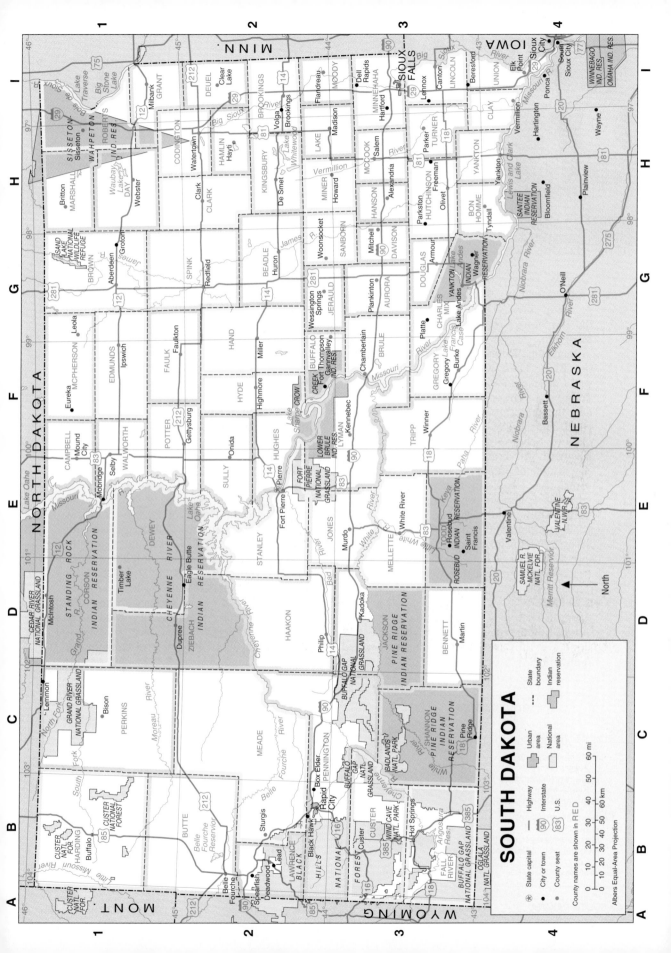

SOUTH DAKOTA

* State capital
● City or town
● County seat
County names are shown in RED

Highway
State boundary
Interstate
Indian reservation
U.S.

Urban area
National area

0 10 20 30 40 50 60 mi
0 10 20 30 40 50 60 km

Albers Equal-Area Projection

Pierre has been the capital of South Dakota since statehood in 1889. The capitol building was completed in 1910.

space satellites, is located nearby. Other points of interest include the scenic falls of the Big Sioux River and the Old Courthouse Museum.

Rapid City, located on the eastern edge of the Black Hills, was founded in 1876, two years after gold was discovered in the area. Today it is a shopping and distribution center and the major tourist headquarters for the Black Hills. Rapid City is home to the South Dakota School of Mines and Technology. Ellsworth Air Force Base, just north of the city, is a major employer.

Aberdeen, located in the fertile James River valley, is a shipping and railroad center for northeastern South Dakota. First settled in 1880, it became the regional headquarters for several federal government agencies, including the Bureau of Indian Affairs. Local industries specialize in machinery and tools.

▶ GOVERNMENT

South Dakota is governed under the constitution adopted in 1889, the year of statehood. But the constitution has been amended many times.

The governor heads the executive branch, assisted by a lieutenant governor, secretary of state, attorney general, treasurer, auditor, and commissioner of schools and public lands. These elected officials serve 4-year terms.

The legislative branch is made up of two houses—a senate and a house of representatives. Members of the legislature meet annually and serve 2-year terms. The people of South Dakota may call for referendums to reject laws passed by the legislature if enough people sign a petition to put a law to a general vote.

The supreme court is the highest court in the state. Supreme court justices serve 8-year terms. The lower courts include circuit courts, located in eight districts, as well as county and municipal courts.

▶ HISTORY

During the 1600's, South Dakota was inhabited by the Arikara Indians, who lived in villages along the Missouri River. Chiefly a farming people, they grew corn, beans, squash, and other crops and traded with the region's nomadic tribes. Around 1800, the Arikara—weakened by smallpox epidemics—were displaced by the Dakota, Lakota, and Nakota Sioux, who themselves had been forced out of Minnesota and Wisconsin. The Sioux gradually absorbed all of South Dakota as their hunting ground, pushing the Cheyenne and other nomadic tribes farther west.

Exploration and Early Settlement

The first non-Indians to see South Dakota were probably Louis and François Gaultier de Varennes, sons of Pierre Gaultier de Varennes, Sieur de la Vérendrye, a French explorer and fur trader from Canada. In 1743, they took possession of the land for France. As proof of their visit, they inscribed and buried a lead plate that was discovered near Pierre in 1913. After 1743, other French fur traders established small trading posts along the James and Missouri rivers.

GOVERNMENT

State Government
  Governor: 4-year term
  State senators: 35;
    2-year terms
  State representatives: 70;
    2-year terms
  Number of counties: 66

Federal Government
  U.S. senators: 2
  U.S. representatives: 1
  Number of electoral votes: 3

For the name of the current governor, see STATE GOVERNMENTS in Volume S. For the names of current U.S. senators and representatives, see UNITED STATES, CONGRESS OF THE in Volume U-V.

After the United States bought the Louisiana Territory in 1803, President Thomas Jefferson appointed Meriwether Lewis to head an expedition to explore the region, which included present-day South Dakota. In 1804, Lewis, his co-leader William Clark, and other members of the expedition passed through South Dakota, traveling northwest along the Missouri River.

After Lewis and Clark published accounts of their travels, several American fur companies established trading posts along the Missouri River. The main post in South Dakota was founded in 1817 near the junction of the Bad and the Missouri rivers. It was later rebuilt and renamed Fort Pierre Chouteau after a leading trader from St. Louis. Eventually the name was shortened to Fort Pierre. It became the first permanent settlement in South Dakota.

The fur trade became increasingly profitable after 1831, when steamboat travel eased the transport of goods. However, the fur trade ended in the 1860's due to a diminishing supply of furs, the outbreak of the Civil War, and battles with the Indians in the Dakota Territory.

Territorial Days

In 1857, small non-Indian agricultural settlements were established around Sioux Falls. Two years later, after the Indians vacated the area, the towns of Vermillion and Yankton were established. Although there were fewer than 3,000 people in all the southeastern settlements, the Dakota Territory was organized in 1861. It stretched northward to the Canadian border and westward to the foothills of the Rocky Mountains. Yankton served as the territorial capital until 1883, when the capital was moved to Bismarck, the present-day capital of North Dakota.

Active settlement of the Dakota Territory increased in the 1870's and early 1880's due to generally heavy rainfall that produced abundant crops. Thousands of farmers from neighboring states and from Europe moved into the region. The period of settlement between 1878 and 1885 became known as the Great Dakota Boom. Dakota's population continued to grow after the railroads reached the eastern settlements in the 1870's and were extended to the Missouri River in the 1880's.

Another important spur to the settlement of Dakota was the discovery of gold in the Black Hills. Rumors of gold there were confirmed in 1874 by a military expedition led by Lieutenant Colonel George A. Custer. Even though the Black Hills were reserved for the Indians by treaty, a full-scale gold rush was under way by 1876. In that year the towns of Deadwood and Lead were settled.

The occupation of the Black Hills caused an Indian uprising that led to the Battle of the Little Bighorn in Montana, where Custer and his troops were massacred by an allied force of various plains Indian tribes. The loss of Custer and his men caused a public outcry that increased the U.S. government's determination to contain the Indians. The Sioux were finally compelled to give up the Black Hills in 1877.

Statehood

In February 1889, Congress passed an act dividing the Dakota Territory into two parts—North Dakota and South Dakota—enabling each one to prepare for statehood.

Many of the Lakota Sioux Indians shown in this August 1890 photograph were killed four months later in the Wounded Knee massacre.

Famous People

Consult the Index to find more information in *The New Book of Knowledge* about the following people who were either born in or are otherwise associated with South Dakota: fur traders Pierre Chouteau (1789–1865) and Manuel Lisa (1772–1820); Sioux leaders Red Cloud (1822–1909), Spotted Tail (1826?–81), Gall (1840?–94), and Crazy Horse (1849?–77); Wild West legends Calamity Jane (1852–1903) and James Butler ("Wild Bill") Hickok (1837–76); children's author Laura Ingalls Wilder (1867–1957); Mount Rushmore sculptor Gutzon Borglum (1867–1941); and Vice President Hubert H. Humphrey (1911–78).

L. (Lyman) Frank Baum (1856–1919), author of the children's classic *The Wonderful Wizard of Oz* (1900), was born in New York but spent three years in Aberdeen (1888–91), where he published a newspaper called the *Aberdeen Saturday Pioneer*. Many of the characters and situations Baum depicted in his 14 *Oz* novels (1900–20) were based on the people he met and the events that took place while he was living in South Dakota. He left the state in 1891.

Laura Ingalls Wilder

Oscar Micheaux

Gertrude Simmons Bonnin (1875–1938), a civil rights activist and author, was born in the southern half of the Dakota Territory. A Yankton Dakota Sioux whose Indian name was *Zitkala-Sa* ("Red Bird"), Bonnin wrote about the legends and traditions of her people and published them in *Old Indian Legends* (1901) and other books. She later became a social activist, speaking out against the poor living conditions endured by those on Indian reservations. In 1926, she formed the National Council of American Indians to bring urgent issues to the attention of the U.S. Congress. Bonnin served as an adviser for the 1928 Meriam Commission that brought improvements to reservations.

Tom Brokaw (1940–), a leading television journalist and news anchor, was born in Webster. After he graduated from college in 1962, he worked in radio before joining NBC News in 1966. He was NBC's White House correspondent from 1973 to 1976, and from 1976 to 1992 he hosted NBC's popular *Today* show. He became the sole anchor of *NBC Nightly News* in 1993 and is the program's managing editor. For his coverage of major news events, he has won many journalism awards as well as seven Emmy Awards. Brokaw also wrote the highly acclaimed book *The Greatest Generation* (1998), about Americans who came of age during the Great Depression and World War II.

Amanda E. (Mandy) Clement (1888–1971), born in Hudson, was baseball's first professional female umpire. She umpired as many as sixty games a season in the Dakotas, Minnesota, Iowa, and Nebraska. She used her earnings to pay her own way through college. For her role as the first woman umpire, she was inducted into the South Dakota Baseball Hall of Fame in 1982 and is recognized by

---

On November 2, 1889, President Benjamin Harrison signed documents admitting both states into the Union. During the official ceremony, the names of the states were covered so that no one would ever know which state was signed into law first. Pierre, South Dakota's temporary state capital, was established as the permanent capital by elections in 1890 and again in 1904.

The Massacre at Wounded Knee

In 1890, South Dakota experienced its last armed conflict between U.S. troops and the Sioux. Having failed to discourage the Indians from practicing the Ghost Dance religion—which the Indians believed would drive the whites from their lands—the government decided to take action. On December 15, federal troops tried to arrest Chief Sitting Bull, who they believed was encouraging the Ghost Dance. A fight broke out, and Sitting Bull and his son Crow Foot were killed. Two weeks later, more than 350 Lakota Sioux, led by Chief Big Foot, were overtaken by federal forces near Wounded Knee Creek and forced to surrender. On December 29, as the troops attempted to disarm the Indians, a battle erupted. More than 140 Indians, many of them women and children, were killed as the troops began to fire. For more information, see the article INDIANS, AMERICAN (On the Prairies and Plains) in Volume I. This final defeat of the Sioux opened up much of western South Dakota to pioneer settlement.

The Early 1900's

During the years of World War I (1914–18), high wheat prices and a series of rainy years brought agricultural prosperity to South Dakota. But in the early 1930's, just as the national economy was crippled by the Great Depression, a drought struck the plains states, ruining crops and leaving families in poverty. Thousands of people began to leave the state.

the Baseball Hall of Fame in Cooperstown, New York.

Oscar Howe (1915–83), an artist, was born on the Crow Creek Indian Reservation. Overcoming poor eyesight, bad health, and poverty as a child, he attended the Studio of Indian Art in Santa Fe, New Mexico, and the Indian Arts Center in Lawton, Oklahoma. During the 1940's, he painted murals for the South Dakota Artists Project and began to design the murals for the Corn Palace in Mitchell. His internationally acclaimed paintings depict the traditions and symbols of his Yanktonais Sioux heritage. Howe served as Artist Laureate of South Dakota from 1960 until his death.

George Stanley McGovern (1922–), born in Avon, served two terms as a U.S. representative (1957–61) and three terms as a U.S. senator (1963–81). A scholar of foreign policy and a champion of the American farmer, McGovern was the Democratic Party's choice for president of the United States in 1972. Although his humanitarian platform included a

George S. McGovern

pledge to end the Vietnam War, he was soundly defeated by his Republican opponent, Richard M. Nixon. In 1984 he made another bid for the presidency but was not nominated.

Oscar Deveraux Micheaux (1884–1951), a novelist and filmmaker, was born in Metropolis, Illinois. The son of former slaves, Micheaux went to South Dakota in 1904 to homestead on the Rosebud Indian Reservation, where he wrote his first novel, *The Conquest: The Story of a Negro Pioneer* (1913). After organizing a film company in New York City, Micheaux returned to South Dakota to film *The Homesteader* (1919), the first feature-length film directed by an African American and starring African Americans. Micheaux directed more than thirty popular "race movies," including *Body and Soul* (1924), which introduced the future star Paul Robeson; *Exile* (1931); and *The Betrayal* (1948).

Sitting Bull (1831?–90), a chief of the Hunkpapa Sioux, was born on the Grand River. In the 1870's he was involved in a number of conflicts with U.S. troops, in-

Sitting Bull

cluding the famous Battle of the Little Bighorn in Montana (1876). In 1877 he was forced to retreat into Canada. Four years later he returned to surrender. He was imprisoned for two years and then confined to the Standing Rock Indian Reservation in South Dakota. In 1890 he was killed by federal troops who had been sent to arrest him for allegedly encouraging the Ghost Dance religion.

When the United States became involved in World War II in 1941, South Dakota's economy began to recover, with the establishment of air bases and other defense installations in the state. The war also caused increased demand for South Dakota's minerals and agricultural products.

In 1944, the U.S. Congress authorized the construction of dams and reservoirs in the Missouri River basin. Completed in the mid-1960's, they provided South Dakotans with new sources of electricity and recreation.

Modern Times

In the latter half of the 1900's, a series of civil rights movements swept the nation. In 1973, members of the American Indian Movement (AIM), a civil rights organization, seized the village of Wounded Knee on the Pine Ridge Reservation to protest the U.S. government's treatment of Native Americans. Among their demands were increased funding for schools, health care, and job training.

In the 1980's, casino gambling became a major source of income in the town of Deadwood and on the Indian reservations nearest to the Minnesota and Iowa borders. State lotteries were also launched to raise money for the state government.

Meanwhile, South Dakota's population slowly increased. Most new residents settled in the larger eastern cities or in the Black Hills. At the same time, many of South Dakota's smaller, rural towns lost population.

Many of the state's economic difficulties have resulted from supporting a small population scattered over a large area. For example, it has proved very expensive to maintain good schools and road systems. And although South Dakota's industry continues to grow, it has failed to attract large numbers of new permanent residents. Wisely, residents have concentrated on developing their state's tourism industry.

NANCY TYSTAD KOUPAL
South Dakota State Historical Society

SOUTHEAST ASIA

Southeast Asia is a geographical region located south of China and east of India. Because of its location, it has been called the crossroads of the East. With the rapid modernization of its societies, the importance of the region has grown economically, politically, and strategically.

Five of the eleven countries of Southeast Asia—Vietnam, Laos, Cambodia, Thailand (formerly known as Siam), and Myanmar (formerly known as Burma)—are situated on the Asian mainland. Four are island countries—the Philippines, Indonesia, East Timor, and Singapore. Malaysia belongs to both the mainland and the islands of Southeast Asia. It includes most of the Malay Peninsula, plus Sarawak and Sabah on the island of Borneo, much of which is part of Indonesia. Brunei, situated on the north coast of Borneo, has the smallest population of the Southeast Asian countries. Indonesia has the fourth largest population in the world, after China, India, and the United States.

▶ PEOPLE

Southeast Asia is home to many different peoples and cultures. The peoples represent various races, speak different languages, and follow their individual customs and ways of life. All together, Southeast Asia has a population of more than 510 million and is growing at about 1.6 percent each year.

Some of the earliest peoples to dwell in the region were Negritos and Malays. Over time they were joined by migrants from what is today South China. These later peoples became the ancestors of the Laotians, the Thais (Siamese), the Burmese, and the Vietnamese. The long-time inhabitants of the region are often divided into two categories: mainland and island peoples.

Communities of ethnic Chinese have long lived throughout Southeast Asia. In Singapore, more than 75 percent of the population is of Chinese origin. About one-third of Malaysia's people are of Chinese ancestry. Ethnic Chinese make up less than 5 percent of the population in Vietnam and Indonesia. People from India and Europe are also found in many countries throughout the region.

Languages. The descendants of the island peoples who came to Southeast Asia thou-

Left: In Buddhist countries, including Myanmar, it is customary for boys entering adulthood to spend time as monks. *Below left:* Dance is a major art form in Thailand and other Southeast Asian countries. *Below:* Rice, shown being harvested in Indonesia, is the basic food in most of the region.

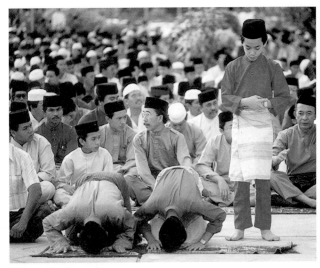

Left: Most of Southeast Asia is made up of islands, such as Palawan, in the western Philippines. *Right:* Islam is the major religion of the Southeast Asian island nations. Muslims, such as these worshipers in Brunei, are taught to pray five times each day.

sands of years ago speak languages similar to the Malayo-Polynesian family of languages. One of these, Malay, has been used by the island peoples as a trading language for centuries. Malay is the national language of Malaysia, where it is called Bahasa Malaysia, and of Indonesia, where it is called Bahasa Indonesia. The national language of the Philippines is called Pilipino.

Because geography isolates the people of the mainland, many different languages are spoken there. Some mainland languages are related to Chinese. The Lao language of Laos is similar to the Thai language of Thailand. The Mon-Khmer language of Cambodia belongs to a different language family. Mountain peoples speak more than 100 different languages or dialects.

During the colonial era, educated people in Southeast Asia spoke at least one European language—English, French, or Spanish. Today English is the most common foreign language and is used in international commerce. English is the official language of Singapore. It is also the most widely taught second language in Southeast Asia. In Chinese and Indian communities, the languages of the old homelands are still very much alive.

Religion. Religion has shaped the life and culture of people all over Southeast Asia. Some of the finest monuments are buildings and statues erected by devout worshipers. The most important religious holidays—Tet in Vietnam; Ramadan in Brunei, Malaysia,

and Indonesia; Songkran in Thailand; Christian holidays in most of the Philippines—are occasions for family members, neighbors, and friends to gather for prayers and feasts.

Hinduism came to Southeast Asia from India, but today it is practiced only on the island of Bali, in Indonesia. Buddhism also came from India and from China. Buddhism struck deep roots in Myanmar and Thailand. It remains important in Laos, Cambodia, and Vietnam, although the Communist governments that came to power there after 1975 tried to lessen its influence.

On the islands, there was greater contact with Muslim sea traders from the Middle East. Islam gradually became the major religion of Indonesia, Malaysia, and the Philippines. The Spanish introduced Christianity to the Philippines, where it soon displaced Islam except on parts of Mindanao Island and in the Sulu archipelago to the south. Other European nations brought Christianity to the areas they controlled. But today the Philippines is the only country in all of Asia where most of the people are Christians.

People throughout Southeast Asia have deep respect for their ancestors. Many also believe in animal and natural spirits and set up elaborate spirit houses with flowers and offerings of food. It is quite common for people in Southeast Asia to combine a belief in spirits with other religions.

Rural Life. The majority of Southeast Asians still spend their lives in and around

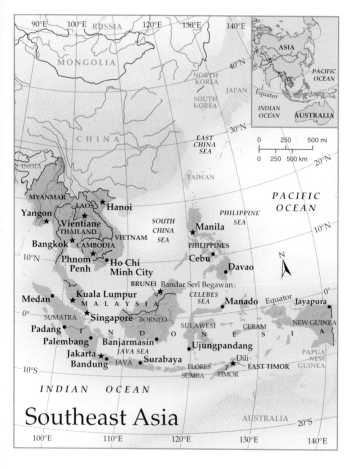

Southeast Asia

rural, agricultural villages. Historically, villagers have worked together to plant and bring in their crops. In many rural areas, modernization and urbanization are breaking down this cooperation.

Village people come to larger towns to mill their rice and sell some of it to rice traders. They also sell their vegetables, animals, fish, or other products, which are then resold in the cities.

Hill tribes in Myanmar, Laos, and Vietnam practice "slash-and-burn" cultivation techniques. They cut down and burn patches of tropical forest and plant their crops among the stumps. When the soil becomes less fertile, they move to another spot in the forest to make new clearings. This age-old practice has done much harm to the environment, but it has been very difficult to get the people to change their ways.

City Life. City life in Southeast Asia has changed markedly in recent decades. In most countries, an increasing number of villagers have moved to the cities to find jobs in construction or modern industries, although many return to their villages to help their families at harvest time.

A middle class of relatively wealthy people has grown up in the more developed countries of Southeast Asia. It includes business people, doctors, lawyers, and government officials. Middle-class people generally live in modern houses or apartments and can afford household help and their own automobiles.

Left: Many rural houses in Southeast Asia are built on stilts to keep them dry during seasonal floods. *Right:* Motor scooters and motorcycles have largely replaced bicycles as the common means of transportation in most Southeast Asian cities, such as Vietnam's Ho Chi Minh City.

Left: The Mekong, one of the world's great rivers, rises in the mountains of Tibet, China, and flows 2,600 miles (4,200 kilometers) to the South China Sea. *Below:* Tropical rain forests, such as this one on Borneo, are threatened by overlogging and land clearance.

Food. Dishes vary greatly in style from one area to another, but rice, fish, and coconuts are some of the main foods of Southeast Asia. Rice is the main course at almost every meal. It is often seasoned with fish sauce, greens, or hot red peppers. Many kinds of vegetables and fruits are eaten.

Customs and Traditions. Southeast Asia is known for its wide variety of cultures and traditions. Each country has its own heritage of storytelling, music and song, folk tales, and theater, although there are similarities in the music and dance forms of Thailand, Cambodia, and Indonesia.

In the countryside, the tradition of parents choosing marriage partners persists. In the cities, this practice is less common. Young couples often move into the homes of their parents. The roles of women in Southeast Asia vary greatly. In much of the region, women run the small businesses and control the family's finances. But society, for the most part, is dominated by men.

▶ **LAND**

Southeast Asia has a total land area of about 1.8 million square miles (4.7 million square kilometers). Two of its countries, Indonesia and the Philippines, are archipelagoes made up of thousands of islands. For centuries, mountains have separated the peoples of the mainland, while water has linked the people of the islands.

Land Regions. Few other regions in Asia are as rich in geographical features. Vast sec-

tions of the mainland and the islands are blanketed with tropical forests. There are many mountain ranges, plateaus, plains, and broad stretches of grassland. Large bodies of water include the Andaman Sea, the Gulf of Thailand, the South China Sea, the Philippine Sea, the Sulu Sea, the Celebes Sea, and the Java Sea.

Rivers. Southeast Asia is cut by many great rivers. Of these, the Mekong is the longest. Others include the Red River in Vietnam, the Chao Phraya in Thailand, and the Irrawaddy and Salween in Myanmar. These rivers are navigable for great distances and are important transportation systems.

Climate. Rainfall is heavy throughout Southeast Asia. Near the equator there are no distinct seasons, and there are brief downpours almost every afternoon. In much of the area the seasons are controlled by the monsoon winds, which blow from one direction for months at a time. The northeast monsoons, which are generally dry, begin in October. In the late spring, strong winds begin to blow across the ocean from south of the equator. For the next few months, during the main growing season, there is rain almost every day—sometimes drizzling, sometimes pouring and then clearing.

Natural Resources. Among Southeast Asia's most valuable resources are oil and natural gas, with the richest fields located mainly in the territorial waters of Indonesia, Malaysia, and Brunei. There are large tin deposits in Malaysia and Indonesia. Gemstones and potash are Thailand's most valuable minerals, and Myanmar is noted for its emeralds. Most of the region's coal is found in northern Vietnam.

Fertile soils and vast forests are other important natural resources. The most productive soils are found in the river valleys and in areas where volcanic eruptions have enriched the soil. Southeast Asia used to be densely covered with valuable hardwoods, but the forests are vanishing due to overlogging and the burning of vast areas to clear land.

▶ ECONOMY

Southeast Asia was once one of the poorest regions of the world. Until the 1970's, most of the people earned their living from farming. A majority of the people still engage in agriculture, but several countries are rapidly industrializing. Some have made dramatic economic progress. The standard of living for most people in several countries is now above the poverty line.

The individual countries of Southeast Asia are at very different levels of economic development. Myanmar, Laos, and Cambodia are still extremely poor. Singapore, Malaysia, and Thailand are the most developed, while Indonesia and the Philippines are still in relatively early stages of development. Brunei has only one source of income—its huge oil and natural gas reserves in the South China Sea—and is extremely wealthy. Vietnam is slowly moving from a Communist to more of a free market economic system.

Countries such as Singapore have often been called the economic "tigers" of Asia and have been held up as examples for other developing countries in Africa and South America to follow. In 1997, however, Thailand experienced a severe recession. Its effects soon spread to Indonesia and Malaysia. The economic crisis in Southeast Asia was compounded by weakness in the economies of its neighbors to the north, Japan, South Korea, and China.

Manufacturing. The electronics industry, which produces television and radio sets and computer parts, is well established in Thailand, Malaysia, the Philippines, and Singapore, and it is spreading to

Left: The electronics industry is one of the fastest-growing segments of Southeast Asia's economy. *Below:* Farmers in Vientiane, Laos, sell a wide variety of produce at outdoor markets. *Far left:* Southeast Asia is the source of most of the world's natural rubber. All of the trees on Southeast Asian rubber plantations were grown from seeds harvested in Brazil in the 1800's.

Vietnam. Thailand is the regional center for automobile production. Textiles and clothing, shoes, and other apparel are made throughout Southeast Asia. Many international companies have opened factories there because costs are lower and workers are plentiful.

Tourism. Southeast Asia's beautiful mountain and beach resorts, historical monuments, exotic foods, and friendly peoples make it the destination of millions of tourists each year. Tourism is one of the region's largest sources of income.

Agriculture and Forestry. The rainy climate is well suited to the cultivation of rice, which remains the chief crop throughout the region. Thailand and Vietnam are among the world's leading producers of rice. The islands of Indonesia were once known as the Spice Islands, and spices have long been valued exports from there as well as from Vietnam. Malaysia is one of the world's leading exporters of rubber, which is also an important product of Indonesia, Cambodia, Vietnam, and Thailand. Tobacco, sugar, copra (dried coconut meat), jute, palm oil, groundnuts (peanuts), coffee, tea, bananas, pineapples, and soybeans are the other major agricultural products. Water buffalo are still used for plowing and all kinds of heavy work in rural areas, although tractors and mechanical plows are gradually replacing them.

Frozen shrimp exports have become a major source of income for several countries. Teak, sandalwood, camphor, and rosewood are among the woods exported from the tropical forests. Cheap softwoods suitable for making plywood are also exported.

Mining. Vietnam has large reserves of coal and exports much of it to Japan. Tin is mined extensively in Malaysia and Indonesia. Cobalt, nickel, and other metals are found beneath the waters of the South China Sea.

Energy. Indonesia, Malaysia, and Brunei are major exporters of oil and natural gas. Thailand, Vietnam, and the Philippines are also producers but cannot fully satisfy their own energy needs. Hydroelectric plants along the Mekong River supply electricity to Laos and northern Thailand.

Trade. Southeast Asian countries rely heavily on exports of natural resources and light manufactured goods for income. They export mainly to Japan, the United States, and European countries.

Southeast Asia is an important producer of oil and natural gas, much of it from offshore fields. This oil rig is located off the coast of Vietnam.

Transportation. Roads in many parts of rural Southeast Asia are made of dirt or gravel. Roads connecting major towns and cities are more likely to be paved. Bangkok, Manila, and Singapore are the main hubs for international air travel.

Communication. Private radio and television sets are common in Southeast Asian cities, and telephone service is widely available. Most country people also have access to radios and television sets, which are often located in village public areas.

▶ **MAJOR CITIES**

Bandar Seri Begawan, the capital of Brunei, is home to almost all of Brunei's population. Its landmarks include the sultan's gold-domed, 1,788-room palace, the largest in the world.

Bangkok, the capital of Thailand, used to be known as the Venice of the East, for its klongs (canals), which are now paved over with bustling highways. Its colorful temples and vibrant nightlife attract many tourists. See the article on Bangkok in Volume B.

Dili became the capital of East Timor when the country achieved independence in 2002. Founded as a Portuguese colonial settlement in 1637, Dili is East Timor's chief port and center of commerce.

Hanoi, the capital of Vietnam, has graceful lakes and tree-lined boulevards. Since the

Above: Singapore is the most urbanized country in Southeast Asia. *Right:* The twin Petronas Towers in Kuala Lumpur, the capital of Malaysia, are among the tallest buildings in the world. Completed in 1996, they rise to 1,483 feet (452 meters).

1980's, the city has increasingly attracted foreign companies eager to do business in Vietnam. See the article on Hanoi in Volume H.

Ho Chi Minh City, the former capital of South Vietnam, is the commercial center of Vietnam. See the article on Ho Chi Minh City in Volume H.

Jakarta, also known as Djakarta, is the capital of Indonesia. It is the country's leading banking and business center and the foremost city on the island of Java. See the article on Jakarta in Volume JK.

Kuala Lumpur, the capital of Malaysia, is a cosmopolitan city with a mixed ethnic population of Chinese, Malays, Indians, and Europeans. It is the primary center for banking, business, and communication. The city's landmarks include the twin Petronas Towers, among the tallest buildings in the world. Like other cities in the region, Kuala Lumpur suffers from the environmental problems and overcrowding that often accompany rapid modernization.

Manila is the capital and largest city of the Philippines. The Makati section of Metro Manila is one of the leading financial services and business centers in Asia. See the article on Manila in Volume M.

Phnom Penh, situated on the banks of a tributary of the Mekong River, became the capital of Cambodia in the mid-1400's, after the fall of the Khmer Empire. The city was virtually emptied in 1975, when the Khmer Rouge drove its residents out into the countryside. Since repopulated, it has retained little of its former elegance.

Singapore, a city-state (both a country and a city), is one of Asia's most important financial and business centers. See the article on Singapore in this volume.

Vientiane, the capital of Laos, is a sleepy town on the banks of the Mekong River. It is less well known than Luang Prabang, the capital of the former Kingdom of Laos that is the country's main tourist attraction.

Yangon (formerly Rangoon) is Myanmar's capital, largest city, main port, and center of industry. Its most famous landmark is the Shwe Dagon Pagoda.

▶ **HISTORY**

Human settlement began early in Southeast Asia. The remains of Java man, estimated to be 500,000 years old, were found in Indonesia in 1891. Northeastern Thailand may have been the site of the earliest rice cultivation in Asia.

The Chinese conquered the Vietnamese in 111 B.C. and ruled northern Vietnam until A.D. 939. Many kingdoms in Southeast Asia have paid taxes to China and recognized its power. But only the Vietnamese were ruled by the Chinese for a long time and adopted some aspects of Chinese civilization.

In Myanmar, Thailand, Cambodia, and Laos, local kings practiced many Indian customs and accepted Buddhism or Hinduism. By 1300 many of the region's island rulers, influenced by traders from the Middle East, began to be converted to Islam.

The great kingdoms of Southeast Asia began to flourish in the A.D. 900's and often waged war against each other. The Burmese and the Thais were enemies for centuries. The Cambodians (Khmers) were bitter enemies of the Thais, the Vietnamese, and the Chams (who lived in what is now Vietnam). Wars destroyed the great ancient cities and temples that now exist only as ruins.

The Colonial Period. When Europeans first visited Southeast Asia in the early 1500's, powerful states existed in what are now Myanmar, Thailand, Vietnam, and Indonesia. The Portuguese and Spanish were the first to arrive. Portugal dominated the spice trade through its control of the Straits of Malacca. Spain occupied key parts of the Philippines and began a rule that lasted 300 years. The Dutch captured Malacca in 1611, then extended their control over the Indonesian islands. In 1819 the British built a new city, Singapore, on the Straits of Malacca and eventually gained control of the Malay Peninsula.

In a series of wars during the 1800's, the British made Burma (present-day Myanmar) a colony, and the French made colonies of Vietnam, Laos, and Cambodia. The United States took the Philippines from Spain in 1898. Only Thailand, through clever diplomacy, managed to remain independent.

The colonial powers drew handsome profits from their empires. Economic development centered on products that could be exported. Education of the native population was carefully restricted. Only the United States made a serious effort to prepare its colonial subjects, the Filipinos, for independence. Elsewhere, the domination of the Europeans was intensely resented.

Independence. World War II (1939–45) hastened the movement of the Southeast Asian countries toward independence. During the war (1941–42), the Japanese briefly conquered all of Southeast Asia. After the war, in 1946, the United States granted independence to the Philippines. The European powers tried to regain control of their colonies but found national leaders everywhere prepared to fight them. The British granted independence to Burma in 1948; to Malaya in 1957; and to Singapore, Sabah, and Sarawak in 1963, when they joined with Malaya to form Malaysia. In 1965 Singapore left Malaysia to become an independent nation. In 1949, after a prolonged struggle, the Dutch were persuaded to grant independence to Indonesia (known then as the Dutch East Indies).

Indochina. In 1945, following the Allied victory in World War II, France tried to regain control of its Vietnamese colonies by force of arms. The First Indochina War ended in 1954 with the defeat of the French at Dien Bien Phu. The Geneva Accords divided Vietnam into Communist North Vietnam and non-Communist South Vietnam and also gave Cambodia and Laos their independence. (For more information, see the article GENEVA ACCORDS in Volume G.)

The division of Vietnam led to the Second Indochina War, which lasted twenty years and became known as the Vietnam War. During

The ruins of Angkor Thom, an 800-year-old walled city in northern Cambodia, are among the world's most splendid architectural wonders.

this war, the United States backed South Vietnam, while North Vietnam received massive aid from the Communist governments of the Soviet Union and China. The war eventually expanded into Laos and Cambodia. (For more information, see the article on the Vietnam War in Volume UV.)

The withdrawal of U.S. forces from South Vietnam in the early 1970's led to the defeat of South Vietnam by the North. American-supported governments in Cambodia and Laos collapsed at the same time. North and South Vietnam were unified under a Communist government in 1976. The war left all three countries devastated, their economies disrupted, and millions of people homeless.

After the war, as many as 2 million Cambodians died under the harsh regime of the Communist Khmer Rouge. From 1979 to 1991 the country was ruled by a government installed by an invading Vietnamese army. The United Nations administered Cambodia from 1991 to 1993. Despite multiparty elections in 1993 and 1998, Cambodia remains politically unstable and impoverished.

Vietnam began to move toward a free-market economic system in 1986 and is gradually lifting itself out of poverty. In 1995 it was the first Communist nation admitted to the Association of Southeast Asian Nations (ASEAN). Laos also remains Communist.

Elsewhere, the governments of the region have succeeded in holding their countries together in the difficult years since independence. The region has contrasting political systems. Some countries remain undemocratic (Brunei, Cambodia, Laos, Myanmar, Singapore, and Vietnam). Some are democratic or moving steadily in that direction (Thailand, the Philippines, and Malaysia). Indonesia has a tradition of strong, authoritative leaders, but it is changing dramatically. In 1998, its president, General Suharto, was forced to resign after more than 30 years in power.

Southeast Asia Today. Southeast Asia is vastly different from what it was at the end of World War II. Some of Southeast Asia's

The Association of Southeast Asian Nations (ASEAN) was founded during the Vietnam War by the region's non-Communist countries. Today it includes all of Southeast Asia except Cambodia. Its concerns are primarily economic.

urban areas are as modern as those of Europe or the United States, although the rapid growth of cities has led to many social problems. In the mountains, jungles, and other remote rural areas, life remains much as it was hundreds of years ago. The rural standard of living has improved, but there is still a large gap between rich and poor in most countries.

Southeast Asia's new industries and strong exports are indicators of continued economic development, and its nations have become part of the global trading community. With the expansion of the ASEAN into a regional free-trade group and the joint development efforts along the Mekong River, these diverse nations have made peace with each other and share a new sense of regional community.

On December 26, 2004, a massive earthquake occurred in the Indian Ocean. It unleashed a sea surge (tsunami) that devastated Indonesia, Malaysia, Myanmar, and Thailand, and killed tens of thousands of people.

HYMAN KUBLIN
City University of New York, Brooklyn College
FREDERICK Z. BROWN
School of Advanced International Studies

See also BANGKOK; BORNEO; HANOI; HO CHI MINH CITY (SAIGON); JAKARTA; MANILA; VIETNAM WAR; articles on individual countries.

SOUTH KOREA. See KOREA, SOUTH.

SOUTH POLE. See ANTARCTICA.

SOUTH-WEST AFRICA. See NAMIBIA.

SOUTH YEMEN. See YEMEN.

SOVIET UNION. See UNION OF SOVIET SOCIALIST REPUBLICS.

SOYBEANS

The soybean is a plant grown widely throughout the world. It is important as a source of oil and protein for people and animals. It is also used in the manufacture of many products, such as paint, floor coverings, and soap.

The soybean plant is upright, leafy, and bushy. It grows to about 3 feet (1 meter) in height. Soybean plants can stand a great deal of dry weather. The variety of the plant grown in moderate temperatures takes about 120 days to grow from seed to full size. The varieties that are grown in tropical areas may take 170 days. The plant usually produces two or three beans in each pod. The beans, or seeds, may be of many different colors—yellow, green, black, brown, or shades of these colors. Almost all the soybeans grown commercially in the United States are of the yellow variety. In 2001, genetically modified seeds that were resistant to certain broad-spectrum herbicides were used to plant 68 percent of the U.S. soybean crop.

Soybeans are highly nutritious. In Asia they are called the meat of the field because they are used the way eggs and meat are used in Western countries. A cup of soybean concentrate will supply an average adult's daily need for protein, vitamins, and minerals.

Traditional soybean foods that are common in Asia are soy sauce, soybean paste (a mushy food used to flavor rice and vegetables), soy milk (a preparation made from ground-up soybeans that have been boiled, filtered, sugared, and salted), soy cheese (a fermented product that is similar to dairy cheese), soybean sprouts, and tofu.

In the United States, foods made from soybeans are becoming more common, in part because of increased awareness of the health benefits associated with soybeans. For example, a diet high in soy protein has been linked to decreased risk of heart disease. Popular soybean foods include meatless patties and nuggets; roasted soybeans; and soy milk, cheese, and yogurt. Soy protein is

The United States produces about 2 billion bushels of soybeans each year—they are the third largest cultivated crop, after corn and wheat. The beans form inside pods that are covered with fine hairs (*left*). Each pod contains two to three beans.

also added to some cereals, energy bars, breads, and other foods.

However, in the United States most of the soybean crop is still used to produce oils for food and industrial use and as protein meal for livestock feeds. Soybean oil is used in greater quantity than any other vegetable oil in producing hydrogenated shortening. It is also widely used in salad dressings.

Soybeans have been grown in China and Japan for thousands of years. The beans were first sent to the United States in 1804 in a ship traveling from China. At first, Americans grew the plant as a curiosity. Later, traders brought information from Asia about the plant's value. Soybeans were then grown for livestock forage and as a soil-building crop. Today soybeans are a very valuable crop. The United States is the world's largest producer, led by the midwestern states. Soybeans are also an important crop in Brazil, Argentina, China, India, Paraguay, and Canada.

Reviewed by GLENN H. POGELER
Formerly, National Soybean
Processors Association

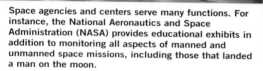

Space agencies and centers serve many functions. For instance, the National Aeronautics and Space Administration (NASA) provides educational exhibits in addition to monitoring all aspects of manned and unmanned space missions, including those that landed a man on the moon.

SPACE AGENCIES AND CENTERS

Space agencies and centers are organizations dedicated to developing and maintaining national space programs. They train astronauts as well as conduct research and development of various kinds of science and technology that can be applied to space exploration and travel.

Although the United States' National Aeronautics and Space Administration is perhaps the best-known space agency in the world, it is not the only one. There are similar agencies in other countries, including Russia, Canada, Japan, and China.

▶ NATIONAL AERONAUTICS AND SPACE ADMINISTRATION

The National Aeronautics and Space Administration (NASA) was founded on October 1, 1958. It was designed to develop space exploration systems and to demonstrate those systems in flight. By 1962, Project Mercury, the first of NASA's programs, had achieved its main objectives: Alan Shepard became the first American in space, and John Glenn became the first American to orbit the Earth. Thereafter, the focus of the space pro-

gram shifted to landing an astronaut on the moon. The Apollo program was developed to achieve this goal, and in 1969, Neil Armstrong became the first person to set foot on the moon. After the Apollo program ended in 1972, NASA developed the space shuttle, which has been instrumental in the development and construction of the *International Space Station*.

In addition to its manned spaceflight missions, NASA also develops programs to study the Earth and explore the solar system and deep space with unmanned vehicles. Among NASA's many successful unmanned missions have been the *Pioneer* and *Voyager* probes to the outer planets, the *Spirit* and *Opportunity* Mars rovers, the *Galileo* probe to Jupiter, the *Cassini* probe to Saturn, and the four Great Observatories: The Hubble Space Telescope, the Compton Gamma-Ray Observatory, the Chandra X-Ray Observatory, and the Spitzer Space Telescope. For more information about these projects, see OBSERVATORIES, SPACE EXPLORATION AND TRAVEL, SPACE PROBES, and SPACE TELESCOPES in the appropriate volumes.

To maintain its various space programs, NASA relies on a number of special facilities across the country and throughout the world. These include the Johnson Space Center, the Kennedy Space Center, the Jet Propulsion Laboratory, the Marshall Space Flight Center, and the Ames Research Center.

Johnson Space Center. The Johnson Space Center (JSC), founded in 1961, is located about 20 miles (32 kilometers) southeast of Houston, Texas. It is NASA's primary center for the design, development, and testing of spacecraft; the selection and training of astronauts; and the development of the *International Space Station*. It is responsible for managing the space shuttle program as well.

Kennedy Space Center. The Kennedy Space Center (KSC), located on Florida's central Atlantic coast, was founded in the early 1960's as the launch site for the Apollo lunar landing missions. It is now NASA's primary center for assembling, testing, checking, and launching space vehicles and their payloads, including the space shuttle.

Jet Propulsion Laboratory. The Jet Propulsion Laboratory (JPL), founded in 1936, is administered for NASA by the California Institute of Technology as NASA's center of operations for unmanned missions in the solar system. The JPL has been responsible for designing, building, and testing most of the very successful space probes that have explored the planets, asteroids, and comets. The JPL also receives images and other data from these spacecraft for enhancement and analysis.

Marshall Space Flight Center. NASA's Marshall Space Flight Center, located in Huntsville, Alabama, was founded in 1960. It manages key propulsion hardware and technology for the space shuttle program and oversees science and hardware for the *International Space Station*. The center will also help develop the space transportation and propulsion systems that will succeed the space shuttles.

In 2005, the ESA space probe *Huygens* (bottom) landed on the surface of Saturn's moon Titan.

NASA Ames Research Center. The NASA Ames Research Center at Moffett Field, California, was founded in 1939 and conducts research and technology development in support of various NASA missions. This research and development includes studying comets, searching for planets around distant stars, robotics, airborne infrared astronomy, and astrobiology.

▶ **EUROPEAN SPACE AGENCY**

The European Space Agency (ESA) was established in 1975. Based in Paris, France, the ESA is concerned with space activities that take place throughout Europe. It ensures cooperation among European countries in space research and technology. Much of ESA's work is centered on contracting European companies to build launch vehicles and satellites. Three of its main projects have been Eutelsat, a telecommunications satellite network; Eumetsat, a weather satellite system; and Arianespace, a French company responsible for building launchers. Two of ESA's greatest accomplishments were the design and construction of the *Mars Express* and *Huygens* space probes. The *Mars Express* probe has sent back thousands of high-resolution color images of Mars' canyons, craters, mountains, plains, deserts, and polar caps. The *Huygens* probe, carried to Saturn aboard NASA's *Cassini* probe, became the first probe to land on a moon other than the Earth's when it touched down on the surface of Titan in 2005. The probe sent back images and other important data about the moon's surface and atmosphere.

▶ **CANADIAN SPACE AGENCY**

The Canadian Space Agency was founded in 1989 and is maintained by Canada's Ministry of State for Science and Technology. The program monitors space-related activities from various departments throughout the Canadian federal government. Its main objectives are to develop space technology to

Space agencies in many countries, including the United States, Russia, Japan, and Canada, have contributed to the design and construction of the *International Space Station*.

recent years, the Russian Federal Space Agency has cooperated with NASA in building and manning the *International Space Station*.

▶ CHINA NATIONAL SPACE ADMINISTRATION

The China National Space Administration is China's central space agency. Its responsibilities include enforcing the country's space policies and managing national interests in space science, technology, and industry. Most missions have been related to communications and scientific studies, but in 2003 China became the third nation to launch a person into space.

▶ JAPAN AEROSPACE EXPLORATION AGENCY

The Japan Aerospace Exploration Agency (known as JAXA) was founded in 2003. It conducts space-related research; develops satellites, space probes, and their launch vehicles; trains researchers in space science; helps choose and train astronauts; and supports public education about space.

meet practical needs, to develop competitive space industries, and to maintain a position of excellence worldwide in the exploration of space. Its activities include crop monitoring, sea-ice surveillance, air-traffic control, the Canadian astronaut program, and the promotion of foreign sales for Canadian space technology and products.

The Canadian space program maintains close ties with programs in other countries. Canada has also cooperated with the United States on a satellite communications project and with the former Soviet Union on search-and-rescue technology. Canada is a cooperative member of the European Space Agency.

In 2003, China became the third nation to put a person in space. Astronaut Yang Liwei orbited the Earth 14 times and landed safely 21 hours after liftoff.

▶ RUSSIAN FEDERAL SPACE AGENCY

The Soviet Union developed many space agencies and programs before its breakup in 1991. Space projects are now headed by the Russian Federal Space Agency.

Early space achievements by Russia included the launching of the first artificial satellite, *Sputnik*, in 1957; unmanned landings on the moon, Venus, and Mars; and launching the first manned orbital mission in 1961. In

▶ SPACE EDUCATION

Some space agencies and centers also provide exciting learning programs, exhibits, and other educational materials that encourage young people to study space science, mathematics, and related fields. Other organizations have been established solely for this purpose.

The Challenger Center for Space Science Education. Founded in 1986 by the seven families of the crew that died in the U.S. space shuttle *Challenger*, the Challenger Center for Space Science Education provides positive educational experiences for students in science, math, and technology. It also provides in-depth training in these areas for teachers.

It supports more than 50 Challenger Learning Centers throughout the world, where students and teachers are given the opportunity to work on science and engineering teams to solve problems and reach goals on simulated spaceflight missions. The first Challenger Learning Center was opened at the Houston Museum of Natural Science in 1988.

The United States Space and Rocket Center. The U.S. Space and Rocket Center opened in Huntsville, Alabama, in 1970. The center has a space science museum with exhibits that include the *Saturn V* rocket that launched the Apollo astronauts on their flights to the moon, a full-scale space shuttle orbiter mock-up, and the original capsule trainers for the Mercury and Gemini programs. The space shuttle orbiter mock-up was used to test equipment and launch procedures for space shuttle flights. The *Skylab* prototype, which was used to test procedures during the missions to the U.S. space station in the 1970's, is also on display.

There are more than 1,500 objects at the center, all connected with the history of the U.S. space program. It also has the Space-dome IMAX theater that shows space- and science-related films on a towering screen. Visitors can also tour the Marshall Space Flight Center.

The United States Space Camp. The U.S. Space Camp is located next to the U.S. Space and Rocket Center in Alabama. Founded in 1982, it consists of various programs that allow students of all ages to explore many aspects of spaceflight and astronaut training. In addition to learning the history of the space program, students also take part in simulated space missions, using orbiter and mission control mock-ups. In the orbiter, they fly the spacecraft or go on space walks. In mission control, they monitor the simulated flight from liftoff to touchdown. Students can also try some of the devices that are used to train astronauts, including a multi-axis training simulator, which spins on three axes at the same time; a space walk simulator, called a five degrees of freedom (FDF) training simulator; and a microgravity training chair, which was used during the Apollo program to teach astronauts what it would be like to walk on the moon. There are programs for children, adults, children with adults, and for people with visual or hearing impairments.

A young visitor to the U.S. Space and Rocket Center in Hunstville, Alabama, spins in a multi-axis trainer, which simulates being in an orbiting spacecraft.

Space camps have also been established in other countries, including Turkey, Japan, and Belgium.

Young Astronaut Program. The Young Astronaut Program was developed by the Young Astronaut Council in 1984. The program consists of chapters located in every U.S. state and in many foreign countries. Young astronauts learn about science, mathematics, and space technology through experiments and activities, and they share their ideas with other young astronauts at conferences.

Other Organizations. Many science museums and technology centers also feature exhibits and programs about space, such as planetariums, instructional classes, and special activities. For instance, the Smithsonian's Air and Space Museum in Washington, D.C., contains many spacecraft, rockets, and other exhibits related to space science and exploration.

LOIS M. CAMPBELL
The Pennsylvania State University

Reviewed by WILLIAM A. GUTSCH
President, The Challenger Center for Space
Science Education

See also ASTRONAUTS; SPACE EXPLORATION AND TRAVEL; SPACE RESEARCH AND TECHNOLOGY.

SPACE EXPLORATION AND TRAVEL

For centuries, people have dreamed of leaving the Earth and traveling through space to visit the moon and explore other planets and stars. During the past thirty years, some of these dreams have become realities. Spacecraft have orbited the Earth and sent back data to ground-based scientists. They have traveled to other planets and transmitted images and information that have helped to expand our knowledge of the solar system. People have gone into space to orbit the Earth and even to visit the moon.

In 1992, a United States satellite, the Cosmic Background Explorer (COBE), detected slight variations or ripples in the background microwave radiation coming from far out in space. This information may be helpful in determining how the universe evolved.

Despite such achievements, space exploration is still in its infancy considering the vast scope of the universe and the many unanswered questions about it. For example, scientists estimate that there are 10 billion stars like our sun in the Milky Way galaxy, perhaps a million of which may have planets orbiting around them. Scientists want to know if these planets exist, and if they do, are any of them like those in our solar system, or do any harbor intelligent beings or other forms of life.

Someday, as a result of space exploration and travel, scientists may be able to solve the mysteries of the universe. Their discoveries may also change our view of life on Earth and of our planet's role in the universe.

The Andromeda galaxy (*opposite*), the closest major galaxy to our Milky Way, is 2.2 million light-years (13.2 trillion miles) away. To reach it seems an impossible dream—but reaching the moon seemed impossible until the first of the *Saturn* rockets (*right*) was developed. The new *International Space Station* may pave the way for future voyages to other planets lasting several years. Astronauts like Jerry Ross, atop a robot arm on an *Atlantis* space shuttle mission (*opposite*), have already practiced how to build in outer space.

▶ WHAT IS SPACE?

Our home, the Earth, is a small planet that orbits a medium-sized star known as the sun. Surrounding the Earth is its atmosphere, which extends for hundreds of miles above the planet's surface. Near the surface the atmosphere is dense, but its density decreases as the distance above the surface increases. High above the Earth's surface, the atmosphere finally ends and space begins.

While no one knows for certain where space ends, scientists do know that it extends in all directions for unimaginably long distances. For a better understanding of the vast distances of space, consider these facts: The star closest to our sun is about 25 trillion miles (40 trillion kilometers) away, and this distance is considered small compared to the size of the known universe. There are billions of stars in our galaxy, the Milky Way, and there are billions of galaxies, each containing billions of stars all traveling through space.

Reaching Into Space

Compared to the vastness of space, spacecraft from Earth have traveled only very small distances. For example, in 1983, the space probe *Pioneer 10* became the first artificial object to pass beyond the outer planets of our solar system—about 3.7 billion miles (5.9 billion kilometers) from the sun. It took the space probe more than eleven years to make that journey. *Pioneer 10* continues to travel out into space, making it the most distant artificial object. Human beings themselves have trav-

eled no farther away from Earth than the moon—only about 250,000 miles (400,000 kilometers). The longest human spaceflight planned for the near future is one to Mars, which when it is nearest to the Earth is about 34.6 million miles (55.7 million kilometers) away.

Even though spacecraft have not traveled into the far reaches of outer space, a great deal of information has been obtained about the moon and the Earth's atmosphere and climate. In addition, space probes and satellites have sent back data about the other planets and their satellites, the stars, and other objects in space. In the future, scientists hope to learn much more about space, including whether or not intelligent life exists anywhere else in the universe. A program called SETI, for *s*earch for *e*xtra*t*errestrial *i*ntelligence, is also attempting to find the answer to this question by listening for radio signals in space that may be from intelligent beings.

▶ LEAVING THE EARTH

Before reaching space, scientists had to solve the problem of escaping from the Earth's gravity—the force that pulls objects toward Earth and prevents them from floating off into space. A spacecraft leaving Earth must travel fast enough to overcome this strong gravitational pull. The speed needed to overcome the Earth's gravity, called **escape velocity**, is

---

A number of articles cover topics relating to astronomy and space. To locate these topics, see ASTRONAUTS; ASTRONOMY; BLACK HOLES; COMETS, METEORITES, AND ASTEROIDS; CONSTELLATIONS; COSMIC RAYS; ECLIPSES; GRAVITY AND GRAVITATION; MILKY WAY; MOON; NEBULAS; OBSERVATORIES; PLANETARIUMS AND SPACE MUSEUMS; PLANETS; PULSARS; QUASARS; RADIATION; RADIATION BELTS; RADIO AND RADAR ASTRONOMY; ROCKETS; SATELLITES; SATELLITES, ARTIFICIAL; SOLAR SYSTEM; SPACE AGENCIES AND CENTERS; SPACE PROBES; SPACE RESEARCH AND TECHNOLOGY; SPACE SHUTTLES; SPACE STATIONS; SPACE TELESCOPES; STARS; SUN; TELESCOPES; UNIVERSE; and articles on the individual planets— MERCURY, VENUS, EARTH, MARS, JUPITER, SATURN, URANUS, NEPTUNE, and PLUTO.

SOME SPACE TERMS

Abort—To halt a spaceflight.

Aerobraking—Use of large atmospheric brakes to slow a spacecraft. Aerobraking saves propellant.

Apogee—Point in the orbit of a heavenly body or an artificial satellite at which it is the farthest from Earth.

Astronaut—A word meaning "sailor of the stars," which the U.S. space program adopted for a person trained to pilot, navigate, or participate in a spaceflight.

Attitude—Position of a spacecraft compared to a reference point, such as the horizon of the Earth.

Biosatellite—Satellite that carries living matter into space to gain information on the effects of weightlessness and radiation.

Blockhouse—Reinforced concrete building that protects against heat or an explosion during spacecraft launchings. It contains the electronic instruments that control the launchings.

Booster—Rocket engine used to set a vehicle in motion.

Burnout—Time at which rocket fuel stops burning.

Capsule—Self-contained unit, or module, on a rocket where astronauts, animals, or instruments are housed. It is usually recovered after flight.

Cosmonaut—A word meaning "sailor of the universe," which the former Soviet Union's space program adopted for a person trained to pilot, navigate, or participate in a spaceflight.

Countdown—Process of checking out all the necessary equipment and systems before launch. The counting proceeds in reverse, so that it tells the amount of time remaining until lift-off.

Cutoff—To shut off fuel flow in a rocket engine.

Destruct—Order to destroy a rocket that is not working correctly after it leaves the launchpad.

Docking—Maneuver in spaceflight in which two vehicles approach one another and join together.

Drogue—Parachute used to stabilize a spacecraft while it is descending to Earth after re-entering the atmosphere.

Eccentricity—Amount by which the orbit of a spacecraft deviates from being a true circle.

Escape velocity—Speed at which an object must move so that it can escape the gravitational pull of the body from which it is launched. Escape velocity from the Earth is about 7 miles (11 kilometers) per second. From the moon it is 1.5 miles (2.4 kilometers) per second.

Free flight—Unpowered flight while in orbit.

Gantry—Structure with platforms on different levels used to assemble and service a rocket on its launchpad.

Gimbal—Rocket mounting that allows a rocket to be swung around so that it may be fired in a desired direction.

Heat shield—Spacecraft covering that absorbs heat and protects the astronauts during re-entry.

Hold—Pause in a countdown to clear up a problem.

Launch complex—Installations used to launch a rocket.

Launchpad—Platform from which a rocket is launched.

Launch vehicle—Rocket or combination of rockets used to launch a spacecraft.

LOX—Abbreviation for liquid oxygen, used as a propellant in many rockets.

Module—Self-contained unit of a spacecraft.

NASA—National Aeronautics and Space Administration, the government agency that directs the U.S. space program.

Oort Cloud—An area more than 100 billion miles (161 billion kilometers) from the sun believed to be the source of many comets. The comets and other debris in this cloud are thought to be left over from the formation of the solar system.

Orbit—Curved path that a planet, satellite, or spacecraft takes around a celestial body. Most orbits are elliptical, or oval shaped.

Orbital period—Time it takes a planet, satellite, or spacecraft to make one revolution in its orbit.

Orbital velocity—Speed that a spacecraft must reach in order to orbit the Earth.

Perigee—Point in the orbit of a heavenly body or an artificial satellite at which it is closest to Earth.

Propellant—Material burned in a rocket to provide thrust. There are liquid propellants and solid propellants.

Re-entry—A spacecraft's descent into the Earth's atmosphere.

Rendezvous—Close approach of one spacecraft to another while in flight.

Retro-rocket—Rocket that fires in the direction in which a space vehicle is moving. It is used to slow down the vehicle.

Satellite—Natural or artificial body that revolves around a larger body, such as a planet.

Soft landing—Landing that does not damage the instruments aboard a spacecraft.

Solar cell—Device used to convert the energy of sunlight into electricity. Solar cells are one of the main sources of power for artificial satellites.

Stage—A propulsion unit of a rocket. After each stage uses up its fuel, it is released from the rocket.

Sustainer—Rocket engine that keeps a space vehicle moving after reaching a speed given to it by its booster engine.

Telemetry—Method of obtaining a measurement from one place (an orbiting satellite, for example) and transmitting it to another place, such as a tracking station, back on Earth.

Tenth planet—Some experts believe that a tenth planet may exist in the solar system 8 to 10 billion miles (13 to 16 billion kilometers) from the sun.

Thrust—Propelling force provided by rocket engines.

Tracking station—Earth-based station containing instruments used to follow the path of a space vehicle.

Weightlessness—Condition of zero gravity in a spacecraft when the pull of gravity is balanced by other forces resulting from the motion of the spacecraft.

about 7 miles (11 kilometers) per second, or 25,000 miles (40,000 kilometers) per hour. Reaching escape velocity does not mean that a spacecraft has freed itself completely from the Earth's gravitational pull, which extends far out into space. But it does mean that the spacecraft will not fall back to Earth even if no additional power is used. As the spacecraft continues to move away from the Earth, the gravitational force weakens until it no longer has a significant effect on the spacecraft.

For a spacecraft to enter orbit around the Earth, it must reach a speed called **orbital velocity**. The orbital velocity will depend upon how far above the Earth the craft is supposed to orbit. For example, a spacecraft must attain an orbital velocity of about 17,500 miles (28,000 kilometers) per hour to orbit the Earth at a distance of 100 miles (160 kilometers). A slower orbital velocity is needed to keep a spacecraft in orbit farther from Earth.

A spacecraft is sometimes put into a temporary, or parking, orbit before it is sent farther out into space. There are two reasons for doing this. A spacecraft launched directly into space would need more powerful, more expensive rockets. Scientists have also found that it is easier to aim a spacecraft toward its destination if it is put into a parking orbit first.

Rockets and the Space Age

It was the development of rockets that enabled spacecraft to escape Earth's gravity and travel into space. The first rockets were invented by the Chinese who, as early as A.D. 1000, put gunpowder into sections of bamboo and used them as weapons. Later, in the 1600's, the English scientist Sir Isaac Newton formulated the laws of motion that explain the principle of how rockets work. But it was not until the 1900's, with the development of liquid propellant rockets, that spaceflight became a possibility. The first long-range rockets were built in the 1940's during World War II. After the war, rocket research led to even more powerful rockets, such as the *Saturn V*, that were capable of launching a spacecraft from the Earth's surface and putting it into orbit around the planet.

The space age truly began on October 4, 1957, when what was then the Soviet Union sent the first artificial satellite, *Sputnik 1*, into orbit. On April 12, 1961, the Soviet cosmonaut Yuri Gagarin became the first person to

travel in space. His spacecraft, *Vostok 1*, made one orbit around the Earth and then returned home. But perhaps it was the first landing of human beings on the moon that has been the most exciting event in space travel so far. On July 20, 1969, U.S. astronaut Neil Armstrong climbed down from the lunar landing module of his spacecraft, *Apollo 11*, and placed his foot on the surface of the moon. For the first time, a human being was standing on ground other than that of the Earth.

▶TO THE MOON AND BACK

The Apollo space program, which was developed to fly astronauts around the moon and land them there, was the most ambitious spaceflight effort undertaken by the United States. This program was built on the successes of earlier Mercury and Gemini programs, which first put Americans in space and in orbit around the Earth and developed techniques that would be needed for more advanced space missions. The first Apollo spacecraft to fly to the moon was *Apollo 8*, which entered lunar orbit and then returned to Earth in December 1968. The success of the *Apollo 8* mission gave a tremendous boost to the Apollo program because it showed that human beings could navigate to and from the moon successfully. After two additional Apollo missions, American astronauts were ready to fly to the moon and to try a lunar landing.

On July 16, 1969, Eastern Standard Time, the *Apollo 11* spacecraft lifted off its launchpad. Neil Armstrong, Michael Collins, and Edwin Aldrin began their historic mission to the surface of the moon.

1

The *Apollo 11* Mission

On July 16, 1969, the *Apollo 11* spacecraft was launched from Cape Kennedy (later renamed Cape Canaveral), Florida. The launch vehicle was the *Saturn V*, a three-stage rocket as high as a 28-story building. Aboard the spacecraft were three American astronauts—Neil A. Armstrong, Edwin E. Aldrin, Jr., and Michael Collins.

At launch, the first stage of *Saturn V* was fired. After two and one-half minutes, the rocket and the spacecraft located at its nose had risen to an altitude of 38 miles (61 kilometers) and had reached a speed of 6,000 miles (9,700 kilometers) per hour. Its work done, the first stage of the rocket dropped away and fell into the ocean far below. The spacecraft was now freed of the enormous weight of the first stage and its fuel. At this point, the second stage of the rocket fired, pushing the spacecraft to an altitude of 115 miles (185 kilometers) and a speed of more than 15,000 miles (24,000 kilometers) per hour. When the second stage of the rocket had used all its fuel, it also separated and tumbled earthward. The third stage of the rocket then ignited and put the spacecraft into a parking orbit. After reaching parking orbit, the third stage rocket shut down. It remained attached to the rest of the spacecraft, however, because it would be needed again later in the voyage to push the spaceship out of orbit and toward the moon.

When a spacecraft is being launched, it cannot simply be pointed toward an object like the moon because the object is moving through space. Instead, it must be aimed at a point in space where the object will be when the trip ends. For the *Apollo 11*, this meant aiming for a point in space where the moon would be in three days, the length of time it would take the spacecraft to get there. Setting the course of *Apollo 11* required great accuracy. While the spacecraft was in its parking orbit, computers constantly checked and compared the positions of the Earth, the moon, and the spacecraft, which were all moving at different speeds in different directions. The computers did millions of calculations to determine the exact course to the moon, the

About three minutes after lift-off, the first stage of the *Saturn V* rocket is cast off *Apollo 11* and falls into the Atlantic Ocean far below.

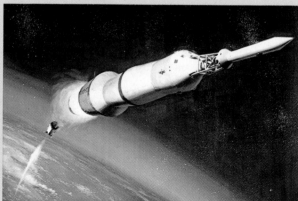

2

exact extra speed that the rocket's engines would have to provide, and the exact second when the rocket's third stage would have to fire again.

The moment for firing the third stage came during *Apollo 11*'s second orbit around the Earth. At that moment, the rocket's third-stage engine was ignited and allowed to burn for about five minutes, the amount of time needed to increase *Apollo 11*'s speed to escape velocity. The push of the rocket forced *Apollo 11* out of orbit and on a course toward the moon. After the third stage engine-burn stopped, the rocket separated from the spacecraft and fell away.

At this point, there was no need to push the *Apollo 11* spacecraft any more. Although the Earth's gravity acted to slow down the spacecraft, *Apollo 11*'s enormous speed kept it from falling back to Earth. As *Apollo 11* approached the moon, it sped up again as the moon's gravity began to pull it forward. At just the right moment, *Apollo 11*'s rocket engine was fired forward, slowing the spacecraft and placing it into orbit. *Apollo 11*'s engine was then fired again to adjust the orbit so that the spacecraft circled about 69 miles (111 kilometers) above the moon's surface. As *Apollo 11* sped over the sunlit side of the moon, the three astronauts could see mountains and craters on the lunar surface. They also saw dark, dry areas that appeared to be smooth and flat. The goal of the astronauts was to land on one of these areas called the Sea of Tranquility.

The *Apollo 11* Spacecraft. The *Apollo 11* spacecraft was made up of three sections, or modules—the **command module**, the **service module**, and the **lunar module**. The command module (CM), also called the **capsule**, housed the astronauts and contained the instruments and controls for operating the spacecraft and communicating with the Earth. It was the only part of the spacecraft that returned to Earth after the mission was completed.

The service module (SM) was located below the command module. Its rocket engine provided the push, or **thrust**, that slowed the spacecraft as it approached the moon. A rocket used for slowing a spacecraft is called a **retro-rocket**. As *Apollo 11* neared the moon, the astronauts turned the spacecraft so that the service module's retro-rocket faced the direction of flight, and then fired the rocket to slow the spacecraft and place it in orbit. This rocket provided the thrust that started *Apollo 11* on its return trip to Earth. The service module also held the electrical system for the spacecraft and fuel for the rocket engine.

The third section of *Apollo 11* was the lunar module (LM), sometimes called the "bug" because it had four spidery legs. These legs, which were folded during flight and then extended before landing, supported the lunar module while it was on the moon's surface. The lunar module was really two spacecraft. The lower part, with the legs, was the **descent stage**. The thrust of its rocket engine was downward, which allowed the LM to settle gently onto the moon's surface. The upper part was the **ascent stage**, which also had its own rocket engine. When the astronauts were ready to leave the moon they stood in the ascent stage and its engine was fired. The en-

The second stage of the *Saturn V* rocket lifts the spacecraft to about 115 miles above the Earth. When its fuel is used, it too is cast off.

The third stage of the *Saturn V* rocket is fired and puts *Apollo 11* into its proper parking orbit. On its second revolution, the rocket is ignited again to push *Apollo 11* on its way to the moon.

gine's thrust pushed the ascent stage upward, leaving the descent stage behind.

Landing on the Moon

High above the lunar surface, *Apollo 11* orbited the moon while two of the astronauts prepared for the lunar landing. Armstrong and Aldrin, wearing space suits, left the command module and crawled through a narrow tunnel into the lunar module. For several hours they checked the instruments and controls of the LM because their lives would depend on how well it functioned. When all was ready, the LM **undocked**, or separated, from the rest of the spacecraft. A burst of its rocket engine slowed the LM, and it started its descent toward the moon's surface. The combined command and service module (CSM) continued orbiting with Collins as pilot.

During its descent, the lunar module was tracked by radar on the CSM and by powerful radar equipment on Earth. A computer aboard the LM depended on this radar to control its movements. When the LM was 300 feet (90 meters) above the moon's surface, the astronauts took control and flew a short distance to a smooth landing place and then eased the spacecraft down. When the lunar module's spidery legs touched the surface, the first human beings had landed on the moon.

After landing, the astronauts' first task was to prepare the lunar module for quick lift-off in case of emergency. Instruments were rechecked and the computer and controls were reset. The astronauts then strapped portable life-support systems on their backs. Like large backpacks, these life-support systems supplied oxygen for breathing and contained an air conditioning system to protect the astronauts from the extreme temperatures of the moon. The packs also contained the radio equipment that allowed the astronauts to communicate with each other and with the control center on Earth. These radios were also able to report automatically to doctors at the control center. They supplied information about the breathing rate, heartbeat, and blood pressure of each astronaut.

After several hours of preparation, the astronauts opened the hatch of the lunar module. Neil Armstrong slowly made his way down a ladder to the moon's surface. A television camera and microphone on the lunar module allowed millions of people on Earth to see the first human being step on the moon and hear Armstrong say, "That's one small step for a man, one giant leap for mankind."

On the moon, the astronauts began their scientific work. They collected rocks and soil samples to be studied by scientists on Earth. They set up sensors to record vibrations caused by moonquakes or volcanic eruptions. They also set up a device to measure the **solar wind**—the flow of electrified particles from the sun—and a laser mirror to help determine the accurate distance of the moon from Earth.

Armstrong and Aldrin spent two and one-half hours on the moon before climbing into the ascent stage of the lunar module. Before liftoff, they tracked the combined command and service module (CSM) with radar to determine exactly where it was and the course it was following. When the CSM's position and course were established, the astronauts fired

After Armstrong and Aldrin settle in the lunar module (LM):
5 Panels around the LM are blown free.
6 The combined command and service module (CSM) with Collins on board is released. It turns and docks with the LM.
7 The docked craft separate from the third stage of the *Saturn V* rocket and cast it off.
8 The service module rocket fires and pushes the craft into lunar orbit.

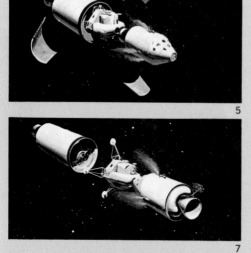

5

6

7

8

While Michael Collins orbits the moon in the command and service module (CSM) (*left*), Armstrong and Aldrin plant the United States flag on the surface of the moon (*below*).

the rocket engine of the ascent stage of the lunar module. Three hours later they caught up with the CSM and the two sections of the spacecraft moved slowly toward each other and **docked**, or joined together. The astronauts then climbed back into the CSM.

Returning to Earth

Now it was time to start back to Earth. The lunar module was released from the CSM and the rocket engine of the CSM was fired. The engine's thrust pushed the CSM out of lunar orbit and on a course toward Earth. Only one or two small corrections in course were needed during the long ride home.

As *Apollo 11* neared Earth, the pull of the Earth's gravity grew stronger and the spacecraft fell faster and faster toward the planet. As it approached the end of its journey, the spacecraft was traveling at the same speed at which it left Earth. At a point outside the Earth's atmosphere, the rocket engine of the service module was fired for the last time, and the service module separated from the command module. The thrust of this firing set the command module on a path called the **re-entry corridor**, which would bring it into the atmosphere at exactly the right slant. Too steep a slant would cause it to burn up as it plunged through the atmosphere. Too flat a slant would

The lunar module, called the *Eagle*, separates from the CSM and descends toward the moon's surface. It approaches the surface (rear) and lands in an area known as the Sea of Tranquility. Neil Armstrong tells mission control, "The *Eagle* has landed."

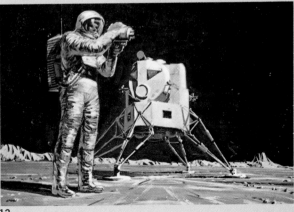

The astronauts conduct scientific observations and experiments on the surface of the moon. They work for more than two hours before returning to the *Eagle* and lifting off. They dock with the CSM three hours later.

make it bounce off the atmosphere and fly out into space. As the command module entered the atmosphere, friction produced an enormous amount of heat that caused parts of it to glow white-hot. However, the blunt end was covered with a heat shield made of special plastic to protect the spacecraft and its crew. Before reaching the atmosphere, the astronauts turned the module so that this blunt end faced forward. As the heat increased, the plastic slowly melted and boiled away, but it kept the heat away from the astronauts.

The resistance of the atmosphere slowed the spacecraft down. When the command module was about 20,000 feet (6,000 meters) above the Earth's surface, small parachutes called **drogues** opened to steady it and slow its descent some more. Then, at 10,000 feet (3,000 meters), larger parachutes opened to lower the module slowly to the Pacific Ocean. After touchdown, it floated on the ocean's surface while Armstrong, Aldrin, and Collins waited for helicopters to pick them up. The astronauts and the command module were then flown to nearby ships for their return home. There were eleven successful Apollo missions: *Apollo 7– Apollo 17,* which spanned the years 1967–72 and included six lunar landings.

After Apollo, a program was developed during the 1970's to provide a fleet of reusable vehicles to take astronauts and satellites into space. It was called the Space Transportation

Parachutes steady the command module's approach to the Earth's surface. After splashdown, helicopters pick up and fly it and the astronauts to nearby ships.

System (STS). Five space shuttles were put into use over several years: *Columbia* (1981—destroyed during re-entry in 2003), *Challenger* (1983—destroyed during launch in 1986), *Discovery* (1984), *Atlantis* (1985), and *Endeavour* (1992).

These reusable spacecraft were also developed because of the high cost of putting astronauts in space. Before the space shuttle was developed, each spacecraft launching required the use of new rockets and capsules. The shuttle, however, can return to Earth and land like an airplane. Since the first shuttle mission in April 1981, numerous flights have carried astronauts into space to conduct research and gather data and to launch satellites into space.

The astronauts cast off the LM and ignite the rocket that pushes them onto a course toward Earth. Before it enters Earth's atmosphere, the service module separates from the command module (*above*). The command module reverses its position so that it can enter the Earth's atmosphere at the proper slant (*right*).

Mission control monitors every aspect of a spaceflight on an array of screens. Special devices track the spacecraft's speed, distance, and direction. The activities and physical condition of the crew are also monitored.

▶ NAVIGATION, TRACKING, AND MONITORING

In space there are no fixed landmarks to indicate position. Yet a spacecraft is expected to travel immense distances to its destination and perhaps land within a few hundred yards of a specific target. Navigating a spacecraft to achieve this goal requires the help of many engineers and technicians and the use of complex equipment and systems.

Navigating in Space

During every spaceflight, computers are at work on Earth and on board the spacecraft making millions of calculations needed during flight. Any small error, such as an error in speed or direction, must be corrected quickly so that the spacecraft is not carried off course. Aboard the spacecraft, a navigation apparatus called the **inertial guidance unit** indicates to the computers whether the spacecraft is pointed toward its target or toward Earth. A part of the unit called the **accelerometer** measures changes in the spacecraft's speed. This information is stored in a computer so that it can be used later in setting up maneuvers to correct the course of the spacecraft.

There are several forces in space that must be considered when planning spaceflights be-cause they can upset the position, or **attitude**, of a spacecraft. Sunlight and the gravitational pull of other planets are two such forces. Sunlight presses gently on all objects. On Earth this tiny pressure is not significant, but in space it can nudge a spacecraft out of its proper path. Although the gravitational pull from distant planets is very weak during most of a spacecraft's flight, it is still strong enough to turn the spacecraft slightly, causing small course errors. Another upsetting force comes from within the spacecraft itself. This is a **torque**, or twisting force, that occurs whenever any motor in the spacecraft is running. The spacecraft is twisted in the direction opposite to the way the motor turns. To compensate for these upsetting forces, an **attitude control system** is built into the spacecraft to help it maintain its position and orientation. This system operates a group of small rocket engines called **thrusters** that keep the craft pointed in a particular direction and prevent it from turning or tumbling.

Tracking the Spacecraft

When *Apollo 11* flew to the moon, its location, speed, and direction were tracked by radar transmitters in a special Apollo tracking network. Three dish-shaped antennas, each 85 feet (26 meters) in diameter, made up the main part of the network. Other tracking networks are used to follow space satellites and probes.

For flights to the planets, additional factors must be considered in tracking a spacecraft. Scientists must determine the orbits of the planets and their positions relative to the Earth, and the effects another planet's gravity will have on a spacecraft's path, or **trajectory**. They then track the spacecraft's speed, distance, and direction to make sure the spacecraft remains on course.

The Doppler Effect. Scientists use the principle behind the Doppler effect to help track the movement of a spacecraft. Sound travels in waves. If the object transmitting or receiving the sound is moving, the wavelength and frequency of the sound wave change. This is called the Doppler effect. If the transmitter and receiver are approaching each other, the frequency increases and the wavelength gets shorter. If they are moving apart, the frequency decreases and the wavelength gets longer.

Using the Doppler effect, space navigators determine a spacecraft's velocity and acceleration. The time it takes a radio signal to travel from the spacecraft to Earth can then be used to determine the spacecraft's distance from Earth. The direction of the spacecraft is determined by analyzing the Doppler effect and other information, as well as factors such as the Earth's rotation and its revolution around the sun. The combined measurements of velocity, acceleration, distance, and direction,

together with data on the gravitational effects of the sun and planet, enable navigators to calculate the spacecraft's exact trajectory through space.

Monitoring Systems and Crew

Even during the quietest moments of a spaceflight, many things are happening on board the spacecraft. Doctors working with flight controllers must know such things as the breathing rate, pulse rate, blood pressure, and body temperature of each crew member. Ground-based engineers need information about temperatures and pressures within the spacecraft, the condition of its machinery and instruments, and whether any dangerous situations may be arising. Scientists need information about the characteristics of planets and their satellites (such as data on their gravitational and magnetic fields) and information on atoms and molecules in space.

Much of this data is gathered by devices called sensors, which can detect and measure pressures, temperatures, radiation, pulse rates, and so on. The measurements are changed into radio signals that are beamed back to scientists on Earth. The technology concerned with systems that gather and send this information is called **telemetry** (from Greek words meaning "measuring at a distance").

▶SURVIVAL IN SPACE

On Earth, people move about comfortably under the influence of Earth's gravity, and they extract oxygen from the air to breathe. The Earth's atmosphere protects them from deadly radiation and falling meteorites. Earth also has abundant supplies of water, which is necessary for survival. When people venture into space, however, they leave the only known place where they can live naturally.

G-Forces and the Human Body

During the first few minutes after a spacecraft is launched, an enormous force pushes astronauts down

Astronaut Brian Duffy uses an inflated globe to demonstrate how Earth is observed from space. Activities from the *Atlantis* STS-45 space shuttle mission were shown to American classrooms after the flight.

Atlantis STS-45
Commander Charles
Bolden (top right) grabs
a straw for his drink.
Crew members Brian
Duffy (bottom), Dirk
Frimout (left), and
Kathryn Sullivan
(middle) try to keep
their food from floating
away as they adjust to
microgravity conditions.

in their seats. You may have felt this force, although much more gently, in a rising elevator. As the elevator accelerates, you can feel the pressure of the floor against your feet. The force that holds you to the Earth and pulls you down is gravity.

The normal gravitational force that holds you to the Earth has a strength of 1 g. (The *g* stands for "gravity.") The pull of 1 g on your body is what is commonly called your weight. Suppose you stood on a scale inside an elevator as it accelerated upward. You would find that you had suddenly gained a few pounds. This is because gravity pulls you down and causes your body to resist being moved upward. This resistance has the effect of making you slightly heavier. The g-force on your body would be a little greater than the normal 1 g.

On early spaceflights, g-forces built up to 10 g as the spacecraft accelerated during launch, and also reached very high levels when the spacecraft slowed down. Care had to be taken to prevent these high g-forces from injuring the astronauts. Scientists learned that astronauts can withstand up to 10 g for about two minutes without harm if they are lying down and facing in the same direction as the spacecraft is moving. Their bodies must also be trained to withstand the strain.

Aboard the U.S. space shuttles, the g-forces are never greater than 3 g. Since this is well within the physical limitations of most people, it allows individuals who have not had special training to go into space. It also allows the space shuttle to carry equipment that would be damaged by high g-forces.

Weightlessness and Its Effects

By the time a spacecraft reaches escape velocity or orbital velocity, there are no more high g-forces. In fact, even Earth's 1 g-force is gone. As a result, people aboard the spacecraft experience **weightlessness**, or zero gravity (0 g), a state in which they feel absolutely no gravitational pull. In a state of weightlessness, people feel lighter than a feather and float because they weigh nothing at all.

Several things are usually done to help crew members deal with weightlessness. Lines are strung in the spacecraft cabin so that crew members can pull themselves along in the directions they want to go. The soles of shoes and the floor of the cabin are covered with a special burrlike fabric that will stick to another similar surface. It is very similar to the Velcro that is used today as a fastener for clothes. This fabric enables crew members to walk around inside the spacecraft cabin during weightlessness. Astronauts are also carefully trained to live in weightless conditions. They learn how to move, eat, drink, and handle tools. They also learn how to sleep in a floating position, held in place in a type of sleeping bag attached to the walls of the spacecraft.

During periods of weightlessness, it is very important for astronauts to do certain exercises or there may be damage to their hearts, blood vessels, bones, and muscles, which are all adapted to the gravity of Earth. Astronauts who spend a few months in weightless conditions do not seem harmed, but doctors are concerned about the possible effects of weightlessness during long voyages if muscles and other bodily systems are not utilized as they are on Earth.

Space Sickness

One problem that affects many astronauts is space sickness, a violent motion sickness characterized by nausea, headaches, sweating, and vomiting. Space sickness is apparently caused by the absence of gravity. In the weightless environment the brain does not seem to be able to cope with the conflicting

messages it receives from the eyes and the balance organs in the inner ear. As a result, a person's equilibrium, or sense of balance, is disrupted. After a few days, the body adapts to the weightless environment, but during the first few days of spaceflight, space sickness can make astronauts very uncomfortable. In many instances, certain drugs and mental training have been able to control the symptoms of space sickness.

Life-Support Systems

On Earth, every time you take a breath, fresh air is pushed into your lungs. That could not happen in space because there is no air and no air pressure to make air move. Instead, space is an almost perfect vacuum—an empty area with no air or atmosphere. Because of this vacuum, astronauts need special life-support systems to survive.

One type of life-support system is the pressurized space suit. This suit maintains proper air pressure and temperature and also supplies oxygen for breathing. It is made out of many layers of strong synthetic materials that can protect an astronaut from the vacuum of space and other dangers, such as radiation. A pressurized space suit is bulky, however, and it is uncomfortable and tiring to be inside one for very long. Therefore, scientists have created ways to provide a "shirtsleeve environment" for astronauts when they are inside the spacecraft. In this environment, the cabin is pressurized and its air is conditioned to protect astronauts from the extreme cold of space, the heat of the sun, and the heat of re-entry into the Earth's atmosphere. The cabin's air conditioning system also purifies the air, removes moisture and carbon dioxide from the air, and adds fresh oxygen to it. Within the cabin,

Did you know that . . .

astronaut and geologist Harrison H. Schmitt was the first scientist to explore the moon and also the last person to set foot on the moon? After *Apollo 17* (December 7–19, 1972) settled in the Taurus-Littrow valley, Schmitt and Eugene Cernan roamed the moon's surface for 21 miles (33.8 kilometers) in three moon walks. They discovered orange-colored soil and collected 242 pounds (108.9 kilograms) of rocks. Among the rocks collected was one that was 4.42 billion years old.

Lettuce is growing in this working model of a "salad machine," which contains nutrient-enriched water but no soil. It is being designed to function on long voyages in space to provide astronauts with a variety of fresh vegetables such as carrots, peppers, tomatoes, radishes, onions, and cucumbers.

Astronaut Kenneth D. Bowersox on board the *Columbia* STS-50 space shuttle mission that focused on scientific experiments in microgravity conditions. He holds an autoclave used here to grow zeolite crystals in a sterile environment. The zeolite crystal growth furnace is the circular container at left.

crew members wear light, comfortable space suits that allow great freedom of movement and that can be pressurized quickly in an emergency.

When astronauts leave the shirtsleeve environment of the cabin, they must wear pressurized space suits and carry portable life-support systems. The Apollo astronauts who walked on the moon, for example, wore backpacks with special equipment that could keep them alive for up to four hours. An astronaut's backpack contains a small air conditioning system and a small battery to supply power. Oxygen for breathing and for pressurizing the space suit is stored in a small tank within the backpack. A ventilating system forces oxygen through the space suit and the pack and removes carbon dioxide and other contaminants, as well as perspiration.

Several radio transmitters in the backpack make up a communications system. One transmitter permits crew members to talk to each other and to ground controllers on Earth. Other transmitters relay information about the physical condition of the person wearing the space suit and about the oxygen supply, the pressure and temperature within the suit, and the strength of the battery in the backpack.

Food, Water, and Wastes

The food that astronauts eat on board a spacecraft must be nutritious, easy to eat, and convenient to store. Most ordinary foods are too bulky and heavy to take on a spaceflight, and many spoil if they are not refrigerated. Some foods used in space are dehydrated and

freeze-dried, which is a process that removes water, leaving only a dry powdery or pastelike substance. Freeze-dried, dehydrated foods weigh as little as one tenth of their original weight. They take up very little space and can be kept in plastic bags at room temperature without spoiling. Before eating the freeze-dried food, an astronaut adds some water to the dry food while it is in the plastic bag and mixes the contents until the food is soft. The food can then be squeezed out of the bag or sometimes eaten with a spoon. Astronauts sometimes warm up frozen and chilled foods as well.

Astronauts must have water for drinking, washing themselves, and preparing freeze-dried foods. On long trips, devices called **fuel cells** are used to produce pure, fresh water. They also produce electricity for the spacecraft. When oxygen and hydrogen are piped into the fuel cells, the two gases combine, forming water. Electricity is produced during this reaction.

A special problem during spaceflight is how to deal with bodily wastes, such as perspiration, urine, and solid waste. Liquid wastes, such as perspiration and urine, are processed in a special purifying system that separates the water from the other materials in the wastes and purifies the water so it can be used again. Solid waste materials are stored in plastic bags that are discarded after returning to Earth.

Space Food in the Future. A trip to Mars will take about two and one-half years. Although this is a long time, space travelers will probably carry processed food and use chemi-

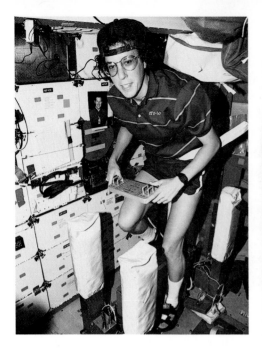

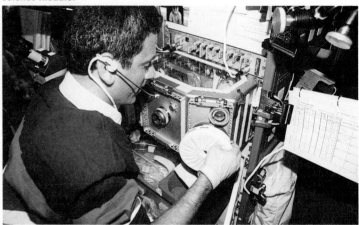

On board the *Columbia* STS-50 mission, Ellen Baker (*left*) uses the bicycle ergometer to maintain muscle tone in weightless conditions. Lawrence DeLucas (*below*) works with the Multipurpose Glovebox used for scientific experiments that cannot be done in an open science module.

cal purifying systems for atmosphere and water. For longer trips, on-board "space farms" will probably be developed to provide most of the food needed. The biological processes of growing plants could also be used to purify water and the spacecraft's atmosphere. A space station 40 feet (12 meters) long and 14 feet (4 meters) across could house a farm large enough to support a crew of four.

▶DANGERS OF SPACEFLIGHT

Astronauts in space face a number of dangers quite unlike the dangers on Earth. One of the most obvious dangers is the lack of atmosphere in space and the vacuum that exists there. Without life-support systems, astronauts would be quickly killed by the space environment. Space holds other dangers as well, including the physical and emotional stresses of spaceflight itself.

Physical and Emotional Stress

The environment aboard a spacecraft can be physically and emotionally stressful. Spacecraft are rather small, and there is little room for astronauts to move around or to have any real privacy. In a spacecraft environment, astronauts are also deprived of many of the emotional, physical, and sensory stimulations they experience in their lives on Earth. Astronauts must also cope with the constant worry of life-threatening dangers to themselves and the spacecraft. Such conditions can be very stress-

ful and can lead to conflicts among crew members, impaired judgment, and actions and behaviors that could endanger lives. While short missions do not pose a problem, long missions might cause tremendous stress.

Early spaceflights lasted only a few hours or a day, and stress was not a serious problem. Scientists were not sure, however, how astronauts would react to longer flights. To find out, they developed special test chambers to imitate the conditions in a spacecraft. Volunteers lived and worked in these test chambers for long periods of time, while scientists carefully observed them and kept records of their reactions. These tests helped scientists improve the methods of choosing and training astronauts.

Several other things can be done to reduce the stresses of spaceflight. Spacecraft cabins can be designed to allow privacy and provide room for recreation and exercise. Private spaces can be personalized. Astronauts can be given plenty of opportunities to rest, to engage in enjoyable activities, and to communicate with loved ones back on Earth. Such measures can be quite effective in reducing levels of stress.

Dangers from Micrometeoroids

Space is not completely empty. Floating around in it are countless tiny particles of solid matter called micrometeoroids. Although most of these particles are much smaller than grains of sand, they move through space at tremendous speeds—from 70,000 to 160,000 miles (112,000 to 258,000 kilometers) per hour.

Space is so vast that micrometeoroids are widely scattered throughout it, even though there are billions of them. Usually micrometeoroids pose no great danger to a spacecraft. Sometimes, however, they occur in great swarms. A spacecraft traveling through a swarm may be hit by some particles, which could puncture the skin of the spacecraft. While tiny puncture holes may not be dangerous, a larger hole could allow air to escape from the spacecraft cabin and cause the air pressure to decrease quickly. If too much air escaped and the air pressure decreased enough, breathing would become impossible. While such an accident is unlikely, astronauts are trained to respond almost automatically. Helmets are snapped into place, space suits are pressurized, and the oxygen supply is turned on. Safe within their space suits, the astronauts can devote their attention to repairing the damage to the spacecraft.

Danger from Radiation

In addition to micrometeoroids, space contains tiny, invisible particles of matter, known as radiation, that are emitted by the sun and other stars. These radiation particles travel at speeds ranging from 1 million miles (1.6 million kilometers) per hour to many times faster. There are many types of radiation, including X rays, ultraviolet rays, gamma rays, radio waves, and infrared rays.

Radiation can be very dangerous to life. Exposure to some radiation can cause physical illness and other serious health problems. Exposure to large amounts of radiation can cause death. On Earth, the atmosphere surrounding the planet acts as a filter to prevent most harmful radiation from reaching us. The radiation that gets through the atmosphere is weakened enough to make it relatively harmless. In space, however, there is no atmosphere to filter out harmful radiation particles.

Surrounding the Earth are two regions of strong radiation, discovered in 1958 by the American scientist James A. Van Allen. Known as the **Van Allen belts**, they are doughnut-shaped and one lies inside the other. They begin about 400 miles (640 kilometers) above the Earth and extend outward for about 12,000 miles (19,000 kilometers).

The early spaceflights did not go far enough into space to reach the Van Allen belts, but scientists planning the Apollo moon missions had to consider the danger from these belts. There was less danger than had been feared. *Apollo 8*, which carried the first astronauts to orbit the moon, was launched directly through the Van Allen belts. However, the thickness of the spacecraft's skin and the metals used in its construction helped shield the astronauts from radiation. The spacecraft also moved very fast, so it was in the heavy radiation zone for only a short time.

Another radiation danger results from solar "storms" on the surface of the sun. During these storms, great eruptions of energy called **solar flares** sometimes burst out from the sun, causing unusually intense radiation to spread outward in space. Astronauts who are exposed to this radiation, especially those working outside a spacecraft, are in serious danger. Protecting them against intense radiation requires the development of some type of heavy shielding. But even with the best shielding, some radiation might still harm them. Some scientists propose using intense electromagnetic fields that could shield astronauts by "pushing" radiation away. Fortunately, the most severe solar flares usually occur during the active parts of an eleven-year solar cycle, and the worst radiation occupies only a portion of the space around the sun.

Columbia **STS-50 mission commander Richard Richards talks with students from Georgia (on the monitor). This Amateur Radio Experiment was used on several shuttle flights, and it gave many students and radio "hams" a chance to talk to astronauts who are also licensed radio operators.**

The following profiles describe pioneering astronauts and cosmonauts whose missions have become "famous firsts" in the history of human spaceflight.

Yuri Gagarin

Yuri Gagarin (1934–68), born on a collective farm in the Smolensk region of Russia, became the first human to travel in space on April 12, 1961. The Soviet cosmonaut's *Vostok 1* capsule completed one orbit around the Earth before landing safely near the Volga River in Russia. Gagarin, the youngest person ever to fly in space, was to take part in the later Soyuz spaceflight program, but he was killed in the crash of a trainer jet.

Alan Shepard (1923–98), born in East Derry, New Hampshire, was the first American in space when his *Freedom 7* spacecraft, part of the U.S. Mercury spaceflight program, reached an altitude of 117 miles (187 kilometers) during a 15-minute flight, on May 5, 1961. In 1971, he commanded the *Apollo 14* mission and was the fifth person to walk on the moon. (You can read more about him in the article NEW HAMPSHIRE (Famous People) in Volume N.)

John Glenn (1921–   ), born in Cambridge, Ohio, became the first American to orbit the Earth, on February 20, 1962. After circling the planet three times in almost five hours, the Mercury astronaut splashed down in his capsule in the Atlantic Ocean. In 1998, at age 78, Glenn returned to space aboard the shuttle *Discovery*, becoming the oldest person in space to date. (A biography of Glenn appears in Volume G.)

Gordon Cooper (1927–2004), born in Shawnee, Oklahoma, was the first American to release a satellite from a spacecraft, on May 15, 1963, during the last Mercury flight. Cooper became the first person to make two orbital flights when he commanded the *Gemini 5* mission in 1965.

Valentina Tereshkova (1937–   ), born near Yaroslavl, Russia, became the first woman in space, on June 16, 1963. The Soviet cosmonaut's spacecraft, *Vostok 6*, remained aloft for more than 70 hours,

Valentina Tereshkova

completing 48 orbits. Before becoming a cosmonaut, Tereshkova had been a textile-factory worker and an amateur parachutist.

John Glenn

Aleksei Leonov (1934–   ), born in Listvyanka, Siberia, was the first person to walk in space, on March 18, 1965. The Soviet cosmonaut remained floating above Earth, protected inside his spacesuit and attached by a tether to the *Voskhod 2* spacecraft, for 10 minutes.

Virgil "Gus" Grissom (1926–67), born in Mitchell, Indiana, and **John Young** (1930–   ), born in San Francisco, California, were the first two-person crew to fly aboard a U.S. spacecraft, on March 23, 1965. Their vessel, *Gemini 3*, was also the first to make changes in orbit and the first to use an onboard computer. Grissom later died in the first fatal U.S. space program accident during an *Apollo 1* launch demonstration. (See the accompanying feature, Space Accidents and Disasters.) Young also joined the Apollo

Alan Shepard

James Irwin works on lunar rover.

"Buzz" Aldrin steps off lunar lander.

program, becoming the ninth person to walk on the moon. He later became one of the first space shuttle astronauts.

James Lovell (1928–), born in Cleveland, Ohio, **William Anders** (1933–), born in Hong Kong, and **Frank Borman** (1928–), born in Gary, Indiana, became the first astronauts to fly around the moon, on December 24, 1968. The astronauts orbited the moon ten times before returning safely to the Earth aboard their *Apollo 8* spacecraft. During their mission, the crew read from the Bible's Book of Genesis as part of a Christmas greeting to the Earth from the moon.

Neil Armstrong (1930–), born in Wapakoneta, Ohio, stepped out of *Apollo 11*'s lunar lander to become the first person to walk on the moon, on July 20, 1969. He was soon followed by his fellow crew member, astronaut **Edwin "Buzz"**

Aldrin (1930–), born in Montclair, New Jersey. Armstrong's first words after setting foot on the dusty lunar soil have become famous: "That's one small step for man, one giant leap for mankind." (A biography of Armstrong appears in Volume A.) Aldrin wrote about the pressures of the mission in his autobiography *Return to Earth* (1973), in which he described his later nervous breakdown and recovery.

James Irwin (1930–1991), born in Pittsburgh, Pennsylvania, and **David Scott** (1932–), born in San Antonio, Texas, became the first astronauts to ride a vehicle on the surface of the moon, on July 30, 1971. The crew of the *Apollo 15* brought with them the first lunar rover—a four-wheeled buggy, powered electrically, that could be driven on the moon's dusty surface at speeds of up to 8 miles per hour (13 kilometers per hour). The lunar rover, which also accompanied the next two Apollo missions, enabled astronauts to cover as much as 22 miles (35 kilometers) of terrain and collect various samples of moon rocks and soil to bring back to Earth.

Robert Crippen (1937–), born in Beaumont, Texas, and veteran astronaut John Young became the first astronauts

John Young and Robert Crippen

to fly in a space shuttle, on April 12, 1981. After nearly six years without a human presence in space, the United States launched the space shuttle *Columbia*. It was the first reusable spacecraft that could reach orbit, return through the atmosphere, and land like an airplane. This first mission of the shuttle, commanded by Young and piloted by Crippen, gave an important boost to the U.S. space program.

Sally Ride (1951–), born in Encino, California, became the first American woman in space, aboard the space shuttle *Challenger*, on June 18, 1983. At age 31, she was also the youngest U.S. astronaut to date. You can read more about her in the article CALIFORNIA (Famous People) in Volume C.

Sally Ride

Guion Bluford

Guion Bluford (1942–), born in Philadelphia, Pennsylvania, was the first African American in space, aboard the space shuttle *Challenger*, on August 30, 1983. The mission also marked the first time a shuttle was launched and landed during the night. The U.S. Air Force colonel flew aboard three other space shuttles, in 1985, 1991, and 1992.

Bruce McCandless (1937–), born in Boston, Massachusetts, was the first human satellite, walking in space freely without a tether, on February 7, 1984. The American astronaut wore a jet-propelled backpack, which enabled him to move around in space about 320 feet (97 meters) away from the space shuttle *Challenger*. Afterward, McCandless commented on his experience with a play on Neil Armstrong's words: "That may have been one small step for Neil, but this was a heck of a big leap for me."

Marc Garneau (1949–), born in Quebec City, Canada, became the first Canadian in space, aboard the space shuttle *Challenger*, on October 5, 1984. The flight was also the first to carry seven crew members. In his 1996 flight aboard the space shuttle *Endeavour*, Garneau was part of a team that released a satellite carrying the first large inflatable space structure—an antenna the size of a tennis court.

Mae Jemison (1956–), born in Decatur, Alabama, was the first African American woman to travel in space, aboard the shuttle *Endeavour*, on September 12, 1992. In addition to being a chemical engineer, medical doctor, and teacher, she also speaks fluent Russian, Japanese, and Swahili. She is a jazz dancer and choreographer. And she once appeared in an episode of the television series *Star Trek: The Next Generation*.

Eileen Collins (1956–), born in Elmira, New York, became the first woman to pilot a space shuttle, the *Discovery*, on February 3, 1995. During that mission, the shuttle made the first rendezvous with a Russian space station, flying as close as 37 feet (11 meters) from *Mir*. The shuttle crew also tested a new system designed

Bruce McCandless

Marc Garneau

to help ground-based radar stations better track small pieces of space debris, which could pose a danger to satellites and other orbiting spacecraft. In 1999, she became the first female commander of a shuttle, the *Columbia*, which carried the Chandra X-ray Observatory into space.

Norman Thagard (1943–), born in Marianna, Florida, was the first American to be launched into space aboard a Russian spacecraft, on March 14, 1995. Thagard traveled on a Soyuz flight to the space station *Mir*, where he lived and worked with two Russian cosmonauts for 115 days. He returned to Earth on July 7 aboard the space shuttle *Atlantis*, which had joined *Mir* on June 29, 1995.

Jerry Ross (1948–), born in Crown Point, Indiana, and **James Newman** (1956–), born in the Trust Territory of the Pacific Islands, were the first spacewalking construction workers to begin assembling the *International Space Station*, on December 5, 1998. The astronauts were part of the shuttle *Endeavour*'s crew, which used a robot arm to join the station's first two pieces—the U.S. module *Unity* (brought up by the *Endeavour*) and the Russian module *Zarya* (launched earlier). Ross and Newman ventured outside the shuttle to attach cables and other equipment for the station. A new spacewalk record was set as Ross finished his seventh in a series of walks totaling more than 44 hours.

SPACE SHUTTLES AND STATIONS

Many space missions in the future will depend on a permanent station orbiting high above the Earth. In 1998, the United States, in partnership with 15 other countries—Russia, Canada, Japan, eleven European nations, and Brazil—began assembling the *International Space Station*, or *ISS*. It was the largest science project ever undertaken, costing $60 billion and taking an expected five years to complete. Plans called for a station powered electrically by an array of solar panels as wide as a football field, with living and working quarters as large as the combined cabin size of two 747 jetliners—enough for a crew of up to seven scientists and astronauts. (You can read more about the *ISS* in the article SPACE STATIONS in this volume.)

The first two pieces, or modules, of the space station were carried into orbit, one by the U.S. shuttle *Endeavour* and the other by a Russian rocket. Shuttle astronauts started assembling the modules in space in what would be a series of missions to build the station piece by piece. They and future space construction workers will rely on various tools developed for the shuttles, such as the Remote Manipulator System (a robotic arm that

Did you know that...

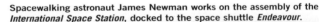

some humans have spent many months living in space? On March 22, 1995, Russian cosmonaut Valery Polyakov returned to Earth after orbiting in the *Mir* space station for a record-breaking 438 days. During his mission, he circled the Earth about 7,000 times. The next year, on September 26, 1996, American astronaut Shannon Lucid (*shown above*) returned home from the *Mir* after a 188-day stay—the longest time any woman had spent in space. You can read more about her in the article OKLAHOMA (Famous People) in Volume O. Polyakov's and Lucid's endurance records boosted hopes that humans could survive a journey to Mars one day.

moves objects in and out of the shuttle's cargo bay) and the MMU (*manned maneuvering unit*) that allows shuttle astronauts to "fly" and work in space without using a tether connected to a spacecraft.

The construction of an orbiting station will provide experience that can then be used in building lunar landing bases or research sta-

Spacewalking astronaut James Newman works on the assembly of the *International Space Station*, docked to the space shuttle *Endeavour*.

tions on the moon or on another planet. A space station also will provide an opportunity for astronauts and scientists to live and work in space for long periods of time, testing the long-term effects of weightlessness and exposure to the environment of outer space.

This ambitious project is not the first space station to orbit the Earth. The first experimental space station, *Salyut* ("Salute") *1*, was launched by the former Soviet Union in 1971. Several teams of cosmonauts visited the station

Various new kinds of spacecraft, such as the *X-38* (*above*), have been considered to supplement or replace the space shuttle fleet.

and conducted experiments. The Soviet Union put several other small space stations in orbit as well, including other *Salyut* stations and the *Mir* ("Peace") space station. Cosmonauts aboard the *Mir* set the record for the longest time human beings have re-

mained in space. The first U.S. space station to orbit the Earth was *Skylab*, launched in 1973. Several crews visited and worked in *Skylab* before it re-entered the Earth's atmosphere and disintegrated in 1979. *Skylab* provided information and experience that helped make many subsequent U.S. space shuttle flights successful.

Since the 1980's various new kinds of spacecraft have been proposed to supplement, if not eventually replace, the space shuttles. But these craft proved impractical. After the space shuttle *Columbia* was destroyed in 2003, the three other shuttles were grounded and work halted on the construction of the *International Space Station* as concern grew that the aging shuttles were obsolete and unsafe. The remaining space shuttles were upgraded to

WONDER QUESTION

What kinds of animals have traveled in space?

On November 3, 1957, a female dog named Laika became the first living creature to be sent into space. Launched by the Soviet Union aboard the *Sputnik 2* satellite, Laika traveled in a sealed cabin that contained equipment for recording her pulse, respiration (breathing), blood pressure, and heartbeat. On January 31, 1961, the United States sent a male chimpanzee named Ham (*shown here*) into space, aboard a *Mercury* capsule similar to the one that the first American astronaut, Alan Shepard, flew inside less than four months later. Human beings were sent into space only after dogs, chimpanzees, and other animals proved capable of surviving the stresses of rocket launches and spaceflight. In later years, astronauts brought many other kinds of animals—rats, mice, frogs, fish, fruitflies, even jellyfish—into space to study

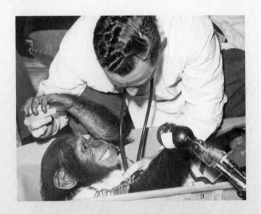

how their bodily systems reacted to weightlessness. Scientists hope the results of these studies and future biology experiments in space will help them better plan for longer missions, which will be needed if human beings are to visit other planets.

Skylab, the first U.S. space station, served as an orbiting laboratory for several crews of astronauts.

ensure they did not meet the same fate as the *Columbia*, but a new, different kind of manned spacecraft would be needed to continue servicing the space station, return astronauts to the moon, or even reach Mars. For more information, see the article SPACE SHUTTLES in this volume.

▶ **SPACE PROBES AND SATELLITES**

Since the launch of *Sputnik* in 1957, many spacecraft have been sent to explore space without people on board. These **space probes** and **space satellites** have observed and studied the Earth, aimed telescopes and other sensitive instruments at the planets, stars, and galaxies, and even landed on other planets to obtain soil and atmosphere samples. Since the earliest probes, which focused on the Earth and its moon, space probes have flown by all of the inner planets of the solar system and even landed on Venus and Mars. The information they have gathered has greatly expanded our knowledge of these neighboring planets. Among the most ambitious space probe missions have been voyages to explore the outer planets of the solar system. After voyages lasting many years, these probes—such as *Pioneer 10* and *11* and *Voyager 1* and *2*—relayed images and data of these distant worlds and some of their moons. Space probes have also been sent to study comets, asteroids, and the sun.

In the late 1990's, NASA introduced the next generation of space probes that would carry out the agency's "New Millennium" missions, aimed at developing technologies for faster, better, and cheaper spacecraft in the 21st century. The first of these probes,

In 1998, *Deep Space 1* became the first space probe powered by ion propulsion. This low-cost system uses electricity generated by the craft's solar panels to turn a gas into a stream of electrically charged atoms, providing thrust.

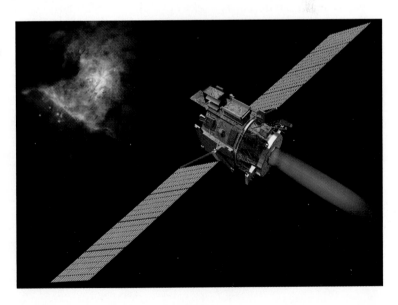

SPACE ACCIDENTS AND DISASTERS

Every manned spaceflight is carefully planned and executed to ensure the safety of its crew. However, spaceflight remains very dangerous, and several accidents have occurred over the years.

On January 27, 1967, astronauts Virgil Grissom, Edward White, and Roger Chaffee died inside their *Apollo 1* capsule when a fire broke out during a launch demonstration. The crew became the first U.S. casualties of the space age. Three months later, on April 24, Soviet cosmonaut Vladimir Komarov was killed when his *Soyuz 1* spacecraft became tangled in its parachute during its descent back to Earth.

Perhaps the most suspenseful spaceflight was that of the *Apollo 13* mission, which blasted off for the moon on April 11, 1970. The crew—James Lovell, Fred Haise, and John Swigert—never got the chance to set foot on the lunar landscape, however. Two days after launch, an oxygen tank in their spacecraft ruptured, crippling the power and life-support systems. The crew managed to use the engine of the craft's lunar module *Aquarius* to accelerate them around the moon and back to Earth, where they landed safely on April 17.

The next year, on June 29, 1971, after spending a record-breaking 23 days aboard the world's first space station, *Salyut 1*, three Soviet cosmonauts died from rapid decompression (loss of air pressure) inside their *Soyuz 11* spacecraft during its re-entry.

On January 28, 1986, just 73 seconds after liftoff, the U.S. space shuttle *Challenger* exploded after one of its solid-fuel booster rockets malfunctioned. The explosion killed all seven crew members—Francis Scobee, Michael Smith, Judith Resnik, Ellison Onizuka, Ronald McNair, Gregory Jarvis, and Christa McAuliffe (who would have been the first schoolteacher in space).

On February 23, 1997, the first in a series of mishaps threatened the lives of crew members aboard the space station *Mir*. An oxygen generator caught fire, burning for 14 minutes and filling the Russian station with smoke. Over the next few months, other equipment on the aging station began failing. On June 25, a cargo ship crashed into *Mir*, smashing an electricity-generating solar panel and puncturing part of the station's hull. No one was injured during those incidents, but new equipment had to be sent to the station, and crew members had to work for several months both inside and outside *Mir* to repair the damage.

A second U.S. space shuttle disaster occurred on February 1, 2003, when the *Columbia* was destroyed as it re-entered the Earth's atmosphere. All seven crew members—Americans Rick Husband, William McCool, Michael Anderson, David Brown, Kalpana Chawla, and Laurel Clark, and Israeli Ilan Ramon—were killed. An investigation revealed that insulation from the liquid fuel tank broke loose during liftoff and collided with the shuttle's left wing, damaging it. When the shuttle re-entered the Earth's atmosphere at the end of its mission, intensely hot air penetrated the wing, melted internal structures, and led to the destruction of the shuttle.

Debris from the space shuttle *Columbia* streaked across the sky after the craft broke apart on re-entry in February 2003. The accident was a grim reminder of the dangers of spaceflight.

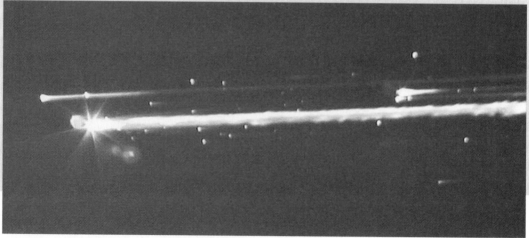

The *Galileo* probe has provided a great deal of scientific information about Jupiter (right) and its moons, such as Io (left).

Deep Space 1, was launched in 1998. It was also the first spacecraft powered by an ion propulsion system, instead of conventional solid or liquid rocket fuel. This type of system uses electricity generated by solar panels to turn a gas, such as xenon, into a stream of electrically charged atoms, called ions. These ions shoot out of the craft at about 60,000 miles (100,000 kilometers) per hour, providing a small but steady thrust.

Scientists will continue to explore the solar system using crewless space probes such as *Galileo*, sent in 1989 to study Jupiter and its moons. In 2004, the *Cassini* space probe arrived at Saturn to study the planet, its rings, and its moons. *Cassini* also deployed another probe, the *Huygens*, which landed on the surface of the moon Titan.

Space probes may also play an important role in preparing the way for astronauts to land on Mars and to visit the moon again. Some scientists even envision a probe mission to another star—a voyage to Alpha Centauri, the closest group of stars to the sun, would take 100 years if a spacecraft could travel 10,000 miles (16,000 kilometers) per second. In some ways, space probes have

been heroes of space exploration, providing a means to visit other worlds that people cannot yet reach.

In the coming years, scientists will learn a great deal more about space also as a result of the activities of space satellites and space-based astronomy. Orbiting satellites containing powerful telescopes and other equipment are able to "look" farther into space than Earth-bound telescopes can, and they are beginning to help astronomers solve some of the mysteries of our solar system and the universe. The orbiting Hubble Space Telescope has provided spectacularly detailed and colorful images showing the birth and death of stars and even the first visible signs of planets in neighboring solar systems. Instruments in satellites can also examine radiation in space that never reaches the Earth's surface and tell us more about distant stars and galaxies. (For more information, see the articles SATELLITES, ARTIFICIAL; SPACE PROBES; and SPACE TELESCOPES in this volume.)

▶ FUTURE SPACE EXPLORATIONS

One of the central quests of space exploration is to discover whether life exists anywhere else in the solar system. Life evolved on Earth because the planet lies at just the right distance from the sun to allow water to remain liquid and temperatures to be moderate. Without these two conditions, life as we know it could not exist.

Search for Life on Other Planets

Among the other planets in our solar system, Mars appears the most likely to have supported life at some time in its history. But Mars is farther from the sun than the Earth, and so it is much colder. It has some water,

After it reached Saturn in 2004, the *Cassini* space probe deployed the *Huygens* probe, which landed on the surface of the moon Titan.

frozen in polar ice caps and perhaps in its soil, much like the permafrost in Earth's arctic lands. Mars also has a thin atmosphere, composed mostly of carbon dioxide. Scientists think that long ago the planet may have had sufficient amounts of atmosphere and surface water to support life. Although studies of the planet's surface have not revealed any signs of life, future probes will no doubt look for remnants of life at the sites of Martian lakes that no longer exist.

Some scientists believe that remnants of Martian life may have already been found in several meteorites that came from Mars and crashed on Earth. In the late 1990's, NASA scientists discovered tiny wormlike features

resembling fossilized bacteria in meteorites found in Antarctica, Egypt, and India. The meteorites varied in age from 4 billion years to 165 million years, suggesting that life once existed—and perhaps still exists—on the red planet. Other researchers were skeptical, arguing that the microscopic features might not be signs of life at all. The debate will no doubt continue until more convincing evidence can be found in samples of Martian soil brought back to Earth by future space probes.

Another possible candidate for life in the solar system may be Europa, Jupiter's large ice-covered moon. Scientists think that some form of life could exist under Europa's ice, just as it does in frozen lakes of Antarctica. In the late 1990's, the *Galileo* space probe found signs of ice that had melted and shifted, indicating warm slush or even liquid water beneath Europa's cracked icy surface. Some scientists speculate that a gravitational "tug of war" exerted by Jupiter and its other moons could keep large parts of Europa's ocean liquid. If that is so, then Europa may harbor some form of marine life— perhaps similar to creatures found thriving around hot deep-sea vents on Earth. Future space probes, designed to peer below Europa's surface using ice-penetrating radar, may offer further clues.

Human Bases and Colonies in Space

Someday we may be able to establish permanent bases on the moon or perhaps Mars. The moon is the most likely site because it is close to Earth and its weaker gravity would allow spacecraft to use less fuel when taking off from its surface. The moon also contains various mineral resources that could be used in building a base. In 1998, the space probe *Lunar Prospector*, in orbit above the moon's poles, found signs of frozen water—the raw material from which hydrogen fuel and breathable oxygen could be extracted and used by future lunar colonists. (You can read more about this discovery in the Wonder Question, Is there water on the moon? in the article MOON in Volume M.)

FAMOUS MEETINGS IN SPACE

December 15, 1965

The crews of *Gemini 6* and *Gemini 7* were the first to carry out a successful rendezvous of two spacecraft. The vessels came within a foot of each other, preparing astronauts for later dockings of spacecraft. The Gemini program gave the United States valuable experience for the subsequent Apollo moon program.

June 6, 1971

Three cosmonauts flying in the *Soyuz 11* spacecraft met up with the world's first space station, *Salyut 1*, which had been launched by the Soviet Union on April 19, 1971. The crew lived on board the station for three weeks before their fatal return to Earth. (You can read more about them in the accompanying feature, Space Accidents and Disasters.) Over the next eleven years, the Soviets launched six more Salyut stations.

May 25, 1973

Three astronauts flying in an *Apollo* spacecraft met up with the first American space station, *Skylab*, which had been launched by the United States on May 14, 1973. They were the first of three crews to visit the station over a period of nine months. Numerous biology and chemistry experiments were carried out in *Skylab*'s weightless environment. Astronauts also made many observations of the Earth, the sun, and the stars. *Skylab* was to remain in orbit until it could be refueled by a space shuttle, but the station's orbit decayed more rapidly than expected. On July 11, 1979, *Skylab* became the largest spacecraft to fall back to Earth, disintegrating in the atmosphere and showering debris over the Indian Ocean and uninhabited regions of Australia.

July 17, 1975

The first docking of an American spacecraft and a Soviet spacecraft marked a period of cooperation between the two rival countries in space. The joint *Apollo-Soyuz* mission required a universal docking module, through which each crew was able to pass to visit the other's vessel.

April 6, 1984

The crew aboard the space shuttle *Columbia*, launched on this date, met up with the *Solar Maximum* satellite. Spacewalking astronauts carried out the first repair of a satellite in orbit, replacing its electronics box, which scientists used to study the sun.

June 29, 1995

The first docking of a U.S. space shuttle and the Russian space station *Mir* also created the largest spacecraft ever in orbit, with a combined weight of almost half a million pounds (about 225 tons).

The U.S. space shuttle *Atlantis* approaches the Russian space station *Mir*.

December 5, 1998

The crew aboard the space shuttle *Endeavour* met up with the Russian module *Zarya*, the first piece of the *International Space Station*, and connected it to the second piece, the U.S. module *Unity*. (See the accompanying profile of shuttle astronauts Jerry Ross and James Newman.)

If we establish bases on the moon, these bases will be excellent sites for astronomical research. The far side of the moon, for example, would be ideal for telescopes because there would be no glare from the sun and no atmospheric distortion. With near-perfect viewing conditions, astronomers could search for planets around other stars in the galaxy, conduct long-term studies of stars and other distant objects, and look much farther into space than with any Earth-based telescopes. The moon would also be an ideal site to listen for radio signals that might come from intelligent life elsewhere in the universe.

Much farther in the future lies the possibility of voyages to other stars. With current methods of rocket propulsion, however, a trip to the nearest star would take many more years than exist in a person's lifetime. Space travel within our Milky Way galaxy, therefore, will probably require spaceships to be "colonies," with generations of inhabitants whose entire lives will be spent on board the space colonies as they travel on their journeys.

Given enough time and advances in technology, it might even be possible to colonize other parts of the galaxy. In the 1990's, scientists began discovering planets orbiting other stars beyond our own. It may also be possible to build floating space colonies around nearby stars. These colonies would be located in regions of space near enough to a star so

Did you know that...

temperatures in space can be twice as high or twice as low as those in the hottest or coldest places on Earth? Near our planet and the moon, spacecraft in direct sunlight can heat up to a scorching 250°F (121°C). In shadows, temperatures can plummet to a frigid –250°F (–156°C). Such an extreme range is the reason why spacecraft—and spacesuits of astronauts who work outside their vessels—have to be specially designed to avoid absorbing or losing too much heat.

that there would be enough light, heat, and solar energy for human beings to survive.

More practical than colonies far out in space would be an orbiting space colony near the moon with room for 10,000 people. The colony could be built of lunar material, which would be easy to transport from the moon's surface because the weak gravitational force would allow rockets to take off easier than they can on Earth. Solar energy would supply an unlimited amount of power to the colony.

The Days Ahead

While exciting to contemplate, centuries-long space voyages, bases on the moon, and human colonies in space will not come about for many years. However, space tourism has become a reality. In 2001, American businessman Dennis Tito became the first civilian to pay for a trip into space. He joined a Russian crew on an eight-day mission to the *International Space Station*. And in 2004, the first manned commercial spaceflight was made by the rocket plane *SpaceShipOne*.

Achievements in space have been truly remarkable. Yet the future may hold even greater triumphs. The day may come when human beings explore and inhabit the distant reaches of space and unravel the mysteries of the universe and of life within it.

PETER W. WALLER
Ames Research Center, NASA

See also ASTRONAUTS; ASTRONOMY; GRAVITY AND GRAVITATION; MOON; OBSERVATORIES; PLANETS; RADIATION BELTS; RADIO ASTRONOMY; ROCKETS; SATELLITES, ARTIFICIAL; SOLAR SYSTEM; SPACE AGENCIES AND CENTERS; SPACE PROBES; SPACE RESEARCH AND TECHNOLOGY; SPACE TELESCOPES; articles on individual planets.

A future human base on Mars might include living and working quarters (powered by solar panels), a vehicle for exploring the planet, a greenhouse for growing food, and a launch vehicle for returning to Earth.

This painting of the flight of *Voyager 1* shows the space probe on its path across the solar system. *Voyager*s *1* and *2* sent revealing pictures and new information about the planets Jupiter, Saturn, Uranus, and Neptune and their satellites back to Earth.

SPACE PROBES

Most spacecraft are sent into space without astronauts or scientists on board. Many of them are space probes sent beyond the orbit of the Earth to explore and study distant objects in our solar system.

There are many possible destinations for space probes. Some have been placed into orbits around the sun to study the space between the planets. Some make flybys of planets or satellites of planets; some have even landed on the surface of planets. Others enter orbits around some of these distant worlds. On-board instruments such as cameras, radar, and other sensors send to astronomers on Earth valuable new information about the solar system.

Space probes are often sent on voyages lasting many years. Because people are not yet able to travel huge distances or remain in space for many years, space probes let us explore places we cannot reach in person.

The First Space Probes

Sputnik I, launched by the former Soviet Union on October 4, 1957, is usually considered a space probe even though it only orbited the Earth. Since no other object made by human beings had ever ventured into space, it was the first to "probe" the unknown environment around the Earth.

During the 1950's and 1960's, the Earth's moon was a frequent target of space probes.

Some, like the *Ranger* probes launched by the United States, carried cameras that sent back pictures to Earth before smashing into the moon's surface. Others orbited the moon and mapped its surface in great detail. By the mid-1960's, space probes had landed successfully on the moon's surface, leading the way for the first human exploration of the moon at the end of that decade.

Probes to Venus

As the moon was being studied, space probes began arriving at other planets to gather data and to search for signs of life. The earliest target was Venus, the planet closest to Earth. Observations of Venus from Earth showed a planet covered by clouds, and some astronomers thought Venus might be covered with thick rain forests. The thought that life might exist there made Venus an attractive choice for space probes.

The former Soviet Union was the first to attempt an interplanetary voyage to Venus with the launch of *Venera 1* on February 12, 1961. Radio contact was lost before the probe reached the planet, however, and nothing more was ever heard from it.

The launch of *Mariner 1* on July 22, 1962, was America's first attempt to reach Venus. It was also unsuccessful. Shortly after it was launched, the rocket carrying the probe veered off course and had to be destroyed. A little more than a month later, however, the United

States successfully launched *Mariner 2*, which became the first probe to reach another planet. It discovered that Venus had a surface temperature of more than 750°F (416°C) and an atmosphere dense with clouds.

In 1975, *Venera* probes launched by the former Soviet Union were the first to land on Venus and to send back pictures of its surface. Color photographs and radar maps of the surface of Venus from the *Venera* probes and the U.S. *Magellan* probe launched in 1989 revealed new details about Venus.

Probes to Mars

After the first visits to Venus, attention shifted to Mars, where it seemed more likely that life might be found. The first attempts also began with failures. *Mars 1*, launched by the former Soviet Union in 1962, stopped transmitting before it reached the planet. The U.S. *Mariner 3*, launched in 1964, suffered a power loss and could not function properly. However, the United States was ready to launch *Mariner 4* a few weeks later, and it reached Mars on July 15, 1965.

The equipment on these early space probes was primitive by today's standards. *Mariner 4* had a simple camera that could take only 22 black-and-white pictures, and it took 20 days to transmit them back to Earth. The images showed many craters and dry plains. Later *Mariners* were better equipped. They photographed more of the planet's surface and detected a thin atmosphere with little oxygen and temperatures far below zero.

The First Planetary Orbiter. *Mariner 9*, the first probe to orbit a planet, reached Mars in November 1971. The probe took thousands of pictures, some of which revealed giant volcanoes. The orbiter also found countless channels that seemed to have been formed by flowing water. These discoveries suggested that Mars may have had a more Earthlike past. If life had developed then, might some form of life still exist? To find out, a probe would have to land on Mars.

Landing on Mars. The former Soviet Union's *Mars 2* and *Mars 3* space probes both reached the planet within a few weeks of *Mariner 9*. *Mars 2* ejected a small capsule containing a Soviet flag and became the first human-built craft to reach the surface. *Mars 3* sent another lander to transmit pictures of the planet's surface. However, less than two minutes after touchdown, transmission stopped for unknown reasons.

In 1976, the U.S. *Viking 1* and *Viking 2* space probes entered orbit around Mars. *Viking 1* sent its lander to the surface, and within seconds its cameras were getting images. Within weeks, soil samples were being studied for signs of life. *Viking 2* began adding further data about six weeks later.

In 1997, two more American spacecraft visited the Red Planet. The *Mars Pathfinder* spacecraft and its robotic rover, *Sojourner*, landed on July 4 to investigate Martian surface and atmospheric features. On September 11, the *Mars Global Surveyor* eased into orbit around Mars to conduct a two-year mapping and data-collecting mission.

The United States' Mars Surveyor '98 program consisted of two probes: the *Mars Polar Lander* and the *Mars Climate Orbiter*. In September 1999, the *Orbiter* was lost just as it arrived because of an error in its navigation. The *Lander* was to touch down in December 1999. However, contact was lost with that craft after it was due to land.

Mars continues to be a popular target for space probes. In 2004, the twin Mars Exploration Rovers *Spirit* and *Opportunity* touched down on opposite sides of the planet and began to analyze Martian rock and soil for evidence of water. As the rovers discovered compelling—but not conclusive—evidence for the past presence of liquid water, they also provided vast amounts of information about the planet's geology.

Planet Hopper

The U.S. *Mariner 10* was the first probe to use the gravity of another planet to help propel it to another planet. This process, called gravity assist, was crucial to plans for exploring the outer planets of the solar system. It has been used by other probes to alter their direction and increase their speed.

Three months after its launch in November 1973, *Mariner 10* reached the planet Venus. The images of Venus transmitted from the cameras on *Mariner 10* were the first good pictures of the planet's clouds. Special cameras sensitive to ultraviolet light revealed details not easily seen in normal light. These images helped astronomers better understand the planet's winds and structure of its cloud layers.

IMPORTANT SPACE PROBES

COUNTRY	CRAFT	LAUNCHED	FLIGHT INFORMATION
U.S.S.R.*	*Sputnik 1*	Oct. 4, 1957	First artificial satellite.
U.S.S.R.*	*Luna 3*	Oct. 4, 1959	First photographs of far side of the moon.
U.S.A.	*Mariner 2*	Aug. 27, 1962	First planetary flyby (Venus).
U.S.A.	*Ranger 7*	July 28, 1964	First close-up images of the moon's surface.
U.S.A.	*Mariner 4*	Nov. 28, 1964	First photographs of the surface of Mars.
U.S.S.R.*	*Luna 9*	Jan. 31, 1966	First soft landing on the moon.
U.S.A.	*Surveyor 1*	June 2, 1966	Moon lander analyzed soil on moon; sent back 10,000 photographs of the moon's surface that were used to select landing sites for Apollo moon landings.
U.S.S.R.*	*Luna 17*	Nov. 10, 1970	Landed automated vehicle on the moon, which made studies of the moon's surface.
U.S.A.	*Mariner 9*	May 30, 1971	First probe to orbit a planet; orbited Mars; sent back first close-up photographs of Mars and analyzed its atmosphere.
U.S.A.	*Pioneer 10*	March 2, 1972	First close-up probe of Jupiter; sent back photographs of the planet; provided information about Jupiter's atmosphere and its structure.
U.S.A.	*Pioneer 11*	April 5, 1973	Flybys of Jupiter (Dec. 1974) and Saturn (Sept. 1979); detected a polar icecap on one of Jupiter's satellites; discovered one more ring around Saturn and possibly more satellites.
U.S.A.	*Mariner 10*	Nov. 3, 1973	First good pictures of Venus' clouds; first close-up photographs of Mercury.
U.S.S.R.*	*Venera 9/10*	June 8, 1975 June 14, 1975	Landed on Venus; analyzed surface and studied cloud cover.
U.S.A.	*Viking 1/2*	Aug. 20, 1975 Sept. 9, 1975	Landed on Mars; sent back first photographs taken from the surface of another planet; analyzed the planet's soil and atmosphere; measured temperature on Martian surface.
U.S.A.	*Voyager 2*	Aug. 20, 1977	Flybys of Jupiter (July 1979), Saturn (Aug. 1981), Uranus (Jan. 1986), and Neptune (Aug. 1989). Discovered volcanic activity on Jupiter's moon, Io; provided first close-up photographs of the rings and satellites of Jupiter, Saturn, Uranus, and Neptune.
U.S.A.	*Voyager 1*	Sept. 5, 1977	Flybys of Jupiter (March 1979) and Saturn (Nov. 1980).
ESA**	*Giotto*	July 2, 1985	Flew to within 400 miles of Halley's comet; took detailed images of comet's nucleus.
U.S.A.	*Magellan*	May 4, 1989	Mapped Venus' surface and collected data on the planet's gravity field.
U.S.A.	*Galileo*	Oct. 18, 1989	Orbited Jupiter; released separate probe into the planet's atmosphere; found evidence of liquid salt water on three of the large moons.
U.S.A./ESA**	*Ulysses*	Oct. 6, 1990	First to study polar regions of the sun.
U.S.A.	*NEAR Shoemaker*	Feb. 17, 1996	First spacecraft to land on an asteroid (Eros); analyzed asteroid's geology, mass, and other properties.
U.S.A.	*Mars Pathfinder*	Dec. 2, 1996	Landed on Mars; delivered first surface rover, *Sojourner*; analyzed atmosphere, weather, and geology.
U.S.A.	*Cassini*	Oct. 15, 1997	Studied Saturn, its rings, and moons; deployed *Huygens* probe, which landed on Titan.
U.S.A.	*Genesis*	Aug. 8, 2001	Collected samples from the sun's solar wind and returned them to Earth.
U.S.A.	*Spirit/ Opportunity*	June 10, 2003/ July 7, 2003	Twin surface rovers deployed on Mars; found evidence of liquid water in planet's past.
U.S.A.	*Deep Impact*	Jan.12, 2005	Deployed device that collided with comet Tempel 1; studied results of impact.

*The former Soviet Union
**European Space Agency

Magellan

Ulysses

With a gravity assist from Venus, *Mariner 10* flew to Mercury, where it took thousands of pictures of the heavily cratered planet. It also gathered information about the planet's core, atmosphere, and magnetic field.

Outward Bound

Only the United States has sent space probes to the outer planets. *Pioneer 10*, launched in 1972, became the first probe to reach Jupiter, and *Pioneer 11* followed about a year later. Relatively simple spacecraft, these probes helped pave the way for later, more advanced probes. Both are now outside the orbit of Pluto.

The real stars of outer planet exploration were *Voyager 1* and *Voyager 2*. Launched by the United States in 1977, these probes completed the most ambitious planet flyby missions ever attempted.

When the *Voyager* probes reached Jupiter, they took incredible pictures of the planet's clouds and its largest satellites. They also discovered a thin ring around Jupiter that was not visible from Earth. From Jupiter, *Voyager 1* sped on to Saturn, arriving in November 1980. The probe took pictures of the planet and of Titan, its largest satellite. The probe discovered that Titan had an atmosphere denser than the Earth's and composed mostly of nitrogen. But Titan was too cold, around −290°F (−145°C), to have liquid water that might support any forms of life.

Voyager 1 was unable to visit more planets due to the course it followed to get a close look at Titan. *Voyager 2*, however, took a path that allowed it to study Saturn's rings more closely and that placed it on course for encounters with the more distant planets. When *Voyager 2* reached Uranus in January 1986, it took pictures of the planet's rings, discovered ten new satellites, and detected a magnetic field on the planet. In August 1989, *Voyager 2* arrived at Neptune. As it flew past the planet, it discovered six satellites, several rings, and fascinating cloud features in the planet's stormy atmosphere.

Voyager 1 and *Voyager 2* have now joined *Pioneer 10* and *Pioneer 11* in exploring the region of space beyond the known planets. The *Voyager* probes have enough power to operate until about the year 2020.

One of the latest "voyagers" to the outer solar system was also a great success. The *Galileo* probe was launched in October 1989 to study Jupiter and its moons. Upon reaching Jupiter in 1995, *Galileo* deployed a probe of its own that penetrated the planet's thick clouds and analyzed the physical properties of the atmosphere.

Galileo discovered strong evidence of liquid water on some of Jupiter's large moons, as well as noticeable surface changes on Io because of the moon's active volcanoes. The probe also found less water than predicted in Jupiter's atmosphere, where wind speeds of over 400 miles (640 kilometers) per hour were recorded.

In 2004, the *Cassini* space probe arrived in orbit around Saturn and began a four-year mission to study the planet, its rings, and its moons. The probe soon found two new moons and a new radiation belt.

Also during its mission, *Cassini* deployed another probe, the *Huygens*. The *Huygens* penetrated the atmosphere of the moon Titan and landed on the surface.

Other Probes

The planets are not the only targets of space probes. When Halley's comet entered the inner solar system in 1986, the European Space Agency's *Giotto* approached to within 400 miles (640 kilometers) of the comet's nucleus and provided the most revealing pictures of a comet to date. On January 2, 2004, the United States' *Stardust* rendezvoused with the comet Wild-2 and collected samples of dust from its coma. The probe is expected to return the samples to Earth early in 2006. The American space probe *Deep Impact* rendezvoused with the comet Tempel 1 in July 2005. It deployed a device that collided with the comet's core and then analyzed the results of the impact.

In 2001, the American *NEAR* (*Near Earth Asteroid Rendezvous*) *Shoemaker* probe became the first spacecraft to land on an asteroid. In 2003, Japan and the United States launched *Hayabusa*, which will land on another asteroid, take samples, and return to Earth by 2007.

JOSEPH KELCH
Davis Planetarium
Maryland Science Center

See also OBSERVATORIES; SPACE EXPLORATION AND TRAVEL; SPACE RESEARCH AND TECHNOLOGY; SPACE TELESCOPES; articles on individual planets.

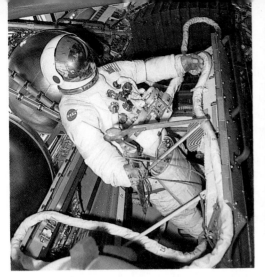

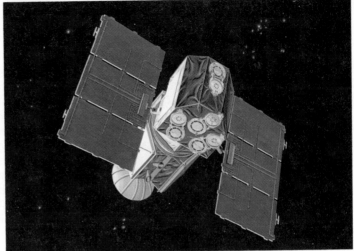

Space suits (*left*) allow astronauts to travel in space and walk on the moon. Artificial satellites, like the Extreme Ultraviolet Explorer (*above*), take scientific instruments beyond our atmosphere and give astronomers on Earth better images of distant star systems to study.

SPACE RESEARCH AND TECHNOLOGY

After a journey of more than 47 million miles (75 million kilometers), there—filling the viewing screen—is the planet Mars. As the spacecraft passes high above the planet, the crew and passengers can see huge volcanoes, ancient shorelines and riverbeds, rock-strewn plains, and a vast canyon stretching for more than 2,500 miles (4,000 kilometers) that would dwarf the Grand Canyon on Earth. As the spacecraft approaches the Martian base, they see the dome that protects its inhabitants from the hostile Martian atmosphere. The spacecraft fires its braking rockets and glides to the base's landing field.

This image of humans traveling in a spacecraft to Mars might seem fanciful. Yet by the middle of the 21st century, a spaceflight such as this may be quite common. Where has space exploration taken human beings so far and where might it take them in the future?

Traveling in Space

People have long dreamed of traveling in space. In 1865, for example, the French writer Jules Verne (1828–1905) wrote *From the Earth to the Moon*, a novel about space travel. Verne described a giant cannon so powerful that it could propel a spacecraft to the moon. However, with no method of propulsion of its own, Verne's craft could only orbit the moon; it could not descend to its surface or return to the Earth. To turn a dream such as Verne's into reality, it was necessary to develop ways to overcome Earth's gravity and propel a spacecraft into space.

Important steps toward achieving spaceflight were taken in the 1940's during World War II when efforts to build better weapons led to major advances in rocket technology. The most important was the V-2 rocket designed by German engineers. Although V-2 rockets could reach altitudes of about 100 miles (160 kilometers), they were not powerful enough to blast a satellite into orbit.

It was not until 1957 that the world's first artificial satellite, *Sputnik 1*, was sent into space. Launched by the former Soviet Union, *Sputnik 1* was essentially an aluminum sphere 23 inches (58 centimeters) in diameter with four antennas for transmitting radio signals to Earth. The most important component was the rocket used to launch the satellite. Approximately 124 feet (38 meters) tall, it used clusters of rocket engines and was much more powerful than the V-2 rocket. It was powerful

Five powerful F-1 engines and heat-resistant metal alloys were used on the *Saturn V* rocket that launched the U.S. Apollo astronaut missions to the moon.

enough to overcome the Earth's gravity and propel *Sputnik 1* into Earth orbit.

The rocket that launched *Sputnik 1* was dwarfed by the one built by the United States to carry its Apollo astronauts to the moon in 1969. This U.S. rocket, the *Saturn V*, was 364 feet (111 meters) tall. The first stage of *Saturn V* had five F-1 rocket engines, the largest and most powerful rocket engines ever built. When an F-1 engine was operating it created enormous force, consumed 6,000 pounds (2,700 kilograms) of propellants per second, and generated temperatures of up to 5072°F

"Robby" is the model of a rover being developed for missions to Mars and other planets. Its computers, cameras, and arms will allow it to move along planned routes on the surface of a planet, take pictures, grasp and examine soil and rock samples, and send data back to Earth.

(2800°C). Ordinary metals could not withstand conditions such as these, so special metal alloys were used, which was an important step in the development of spaceflight.

Robot Spacecraft and Artificial Satellites

Since the launch of *Sputnik 1* in 1957, the majority of spacecraft have been robot space satellites and space probes controlled by ground-based computers. These spacecraft have been used for a number of purposes, including scientific research, communications, weather monitoring, military spying, and the exploration of the solar system.

In 1976, *Viking 1* and *Viking 2* arrived at Mars. Each spacecraft consisted of an "orbiter" and a "lander." Upon reaching Mars, the landers separated from the orbiters and descended to the planet's surface, while the orbiters began to transmit images of the planet back to Earth. Attached to each *Viking* lander was a mechanical arm with a clawlike apparatus at the end. With this arm and claw, the lander was able to dig small holes in the Martian surface and gather samples of soil. The

landers also contained miniature scientific laboratories that performed biological and chemical tests on the Martian soil samples and the atmosphere. Among the equipment in these laboratories were X-ray spectrometers, which analyzed the soil and searched for iron, calcium, aluminum, and other elements. Other instruments tested for the presence of living substances such as micro-organisms, but no evidence of life on Mars was found. The search for life beyond planet Earth continues to be, nevertheless, one of the central quests of space exploration.

A common problem of all spacecraft, including *Viking 1* and *Viking 2*, is how to generate power and keep their electrical systems working. If the electrical systems fail, the spacecraft will "die." Therefore, each spacecraft needs to generate, store, and distribute electrical energy. This problem has been solved by using batteries and solar arrays— paddle-shaped structures that stick out from the body of the spacecraft. These solar arrays enable the spacecraft to utilize the large and free supply of solar energy from the sun. To capture this energy, special sensors called photovoltaic cells are mounted on the solar arrays, and the spacecraft is carefully positioned so that the arrays are pointed toward the sun. The photovoltaic cells gather sunlight and convert it into electrical energy.

Unfortunately, the intensity of the sun's solar energy decreases as the distance from the sun increases. As a result, spacecraft traveling far away from the sun must use other methods of generating power. This was the case with *Voyager 1*, which explored the outer planets of the solar system. Since *Voyager 1* was so far away from the sun, power was provided by a radioactive substance called plutonium dioxide. As this substance decays, it generates heat. The heat is then converted into an electrical current. This method of generating power is useful for long interplanetary space trips that take a spacecraft far from the sun.

Voyager 1 is now racing toward the stars. The distances to the stars are so vast that it would take the spacecraft, which is traveling 350 million miles (560 million kilometers) per year, nearly 80,000 years to reach even Alpha Centauri, the closest group of stars to the sun. The power supply of *Voyager 1* will be used up long before the spacecraft can travel to the farthest reaches of space.

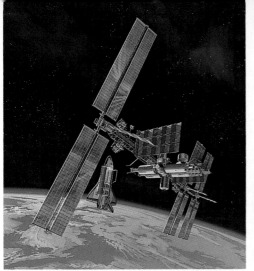
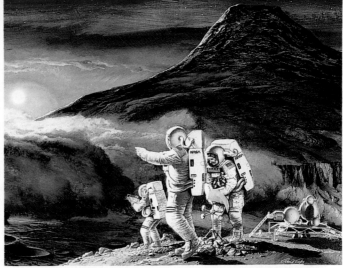

Once a space station similar to this early design (*left*) is in orbit, people will be able to live and conduct research in space. The activities of such space pioneers may lead to the human exploration of other planets, beginning with a landing on Mars (*right*).

Future Research and Technology

Until much faster spacecraft can be developed, human beings will be restricted to exploring the solar system. This is important too, however, because there are still many things to be learned about Earth from nearby space. The National Aeronautics and Space Administration (NASA) has started a program called "Earth Science Enterprise." As part of this program, a number of satellites examine the Earth's atmosphere, continents, and oceans from several hundred miles in space. The information gathered by these research satellites helps scientists determine such things as changes in the Earth's climate and in the ozone layer that shields human beings from the sun's harmful ultraviolet rays. While programs such as this rely on current space technology, many future programs will require new and increasingly complex technology.

Future human exploration of space will involve the construction of orbiting space stations where people can live for extended periods of time and conduct scientific research. These stations could also be used as bases for missions to repair damaged spacecraft and travel farther out in space.

In the 1980's, the United States and space agencies in Japan, Canada, and Europe began to work on a permanent space station called *Freedom*. The original design proved to be too expensive, so a scaled-down station, which could operate for 10 to 15 years after completion, was chosen. The first pieces of this *International Space Station*, as it is now called, were assembled by astronauts aboard the U.S. space shuttle *Endeavour* in 1998. Since one of the major goals of this new effort is to expand international participation in space, the design includes equipment developed by the United States, the European Space Agency, Russia, Canada, Japan, and Brazil.

The *International Space Station* will serve as an orbiting laboratory where astronauts can live and work for periods of up to 90 days. Plans call for carrying out studies on the long-term effects of weightlessness on living things and for developing manufacturing processes that could lead to new kinds of materials for industry and medicine.

An important role for future space stations may be to act as servicing and refueling depots for journeys to the moon and Mars. Although Venus is the closest planet to Earth, Mars is expected to be the first planet visited by astronauts. Data gathered by space probes have revealed surface temperatures on Venus of 860°F (460°C) and an extremely dense atmosphere composed mostly of carbon dioxide. Landing on Venus would pose extraordinary problems.

The astronauts' mission to Mars will be very challenging. For one thing, the round trip will take about three years and require a complex spacecraft. Difficult or not, astronauts are scheduled to walk on the surface of Mars sometime around the year 2020 or shortly after. Perhaps you will be among them.

ROBERT W. SMITH
National Air and Space Museum

See also SATELLITES, ARTIFICIAL; SPACE EXPLORATION AND TRAVEL; SPACE PROBES; SPACE STATIONS.

Space shuttle *Discovery* lights up the predawn sky as it is launched on an early mission by its fiery rocket boosters.

SPACE SHUTTLES

The first astronauts in space traveled in spacecraft that could be used only once. Because each mission required a new spacecraft and new rockets to propel it into orbit, space flight was very expensive. In 1981, astronauts from the United States traveled into space for the first time in a reusable spacecraft called a **space shuttle.** This airplane-like craft is launched into orbit like other spacecraft. But it can also return to Earth and land on a runway so that it can be used again. The use of a space shuttle has helped human exploration of space. With the shuttle, space missions can be flown more often and at less cost.

The United States Space Shuttle

The U.S. space shuttle program has a fleet of several shuttles in operation, including *Discovery*, *Atlantis*, and *Endeavour*. Each is capable of remaining in orbit for ten days or more. The shuttles can perform a variety of duties, such as placing satellites in orbit, repairing damaged satellites, studying the Earth and distant objects in space, and conducting experiments to study the effects of space travel on the human body.

Launching the Shuttle. The space shuttle is launched from a vertical position, with its nose pointing up into the sky. The shuttle vehicle itself, known as the orbiter, is attached to a large disposable fuel tank called the external tank. The fuel in this tank is pure liquid hydrogen and liquid oxygen. Attached to the external tank are two solid rocket boosters, or SRB's. These booster rockets use a solid fuel that is a mixture of chemicals, including aluminum and ammonia. Once the fuels in these SRB's are ignited, the power of the rockets cannot be adjusted or turned off.

The SRB's provide the main power needed during the first two minutes of launch to get the shuttle off the ground and moving quickly. They then separate from the rest of the shuttle at a point where they can fall into the ocean. There they can be retrieved and used again. After the SRB's fall away, the space shuttle main engines (SSME's) on the orbiter continue supplying power. These engines use the fuel from the external tank. The SSME's continue to burn for another six minutes until the shuttle has reached its orbiting altitude. These engines then shut down, and the external fuel tank is cast off. This tank is the only part of the shuttle that is not reused.

Changing Velocity, Orbit, and Position. After the shuttle reaches orbiting altitude and the SRB's and external tank are gone, the orbital maneuvering system (OMS) engines on the orbiter are used to change the velocity of the shuttle and to increase or decrease its altitude. They are also used to slow its re-entry into the Earth's atmosphere at the end of the mission. Forty-four tiny engines, all part of the reaction control system (RCS), are scattered around the nose and tail sections of the orbiter. These small engines control the position of the shuttle while in orbit. They help move the shuttle away from a satellite it has placed in orbit, or point the cargo bay away from or toward the Earth or sun. These engines use the same fuel (a mixture of liquid fuels) as the OMS engines, and they can use the OMS fuel tanks if necessary.

Carrying a Cargo. The large cargo bay of the shuttle is what makes it such an all-purpose spacecraft. The cargo bay is 60 feet (18 meters) long and 15 feet (4.6 meters) wide. Its doors are opened immediately after the shuttle reaches orbit, and they remain open until just before the craft re-enters the

On May 13, 1992, three *Endeavour* astronauts completed the first successful mission to capture an orbiting satellite—the *Intelsat VI*—and then relaunch it from space into its proper orbit.

Earth's atmosphere. This is done because the doors contain radiators that help cool the cabin in the front of the shuttle. Also, the solar panels on the doors convert sunlight into electricity.

Several small satellites, or one large one, can be carried in the shuttle's cargo bay. It can also hold telescopes and other instruments. In the mid-1990's, the shuttle was used to carry crews and cargo to the Russian space station *Mir*. And since the late 1990's, the shuttle has been very useful in building the *International Space Station*.

Re-entry. The shuttle fires its OMS engines to begin its descent to Earth. Upon entering the atmosphere, it is moving at about 17,000 miles (27,370 kilometers) per hour. Moving at such a great speed produces tremendous heat due to friction with the atmosphere. To resist this heat, the shuttle is covered with special tiles. Without these tiles the shuttle would burn up during re-entry.

The orbiter drops back to Earth like a glider, using its wings and tail section to maintain stable flight. Just before touchdown, landing gear emerges from the shuttle's underside, and it lands just like an airplane.

The *Challenger* and *Columbia* Accidents. In 1986, cold weather contributed to a malfunction in one of the space shuttle *Challenger*'s solid rocket boosters during launch. The spacecraft was destroyed and all seven astronauts on board were killed. Afterward, the boosters were redesigned and new rules were created to manage launch safety.

In 2003, the space shuttle *Columbia* failed, killing its seven-member crew. A piece of insulating foam broke off the external fuel tank during launch and damaged the shuttle's heat-resistant tiles. This allowed intensely hot air to penetrate the wing during re-entry, destroying the craft. Shuttle flights were stopped until the space shuttle *Discovery* flew a mission in 2005. By then, it seemed the foam problem had been solved. However, foam again fell off the fuel tank. This time it caused no harm, and the craft landed safely. NASA said it would ground the shuttles again until the foam problem was solved for certain.

Other Space Shuttles

The former Soviet Union developed a shuttle, the *Buran* ("blizzard"), in 1982. A test flight took place in 1988. However, the project ended with the breakup of the Soviet Union in 1991. And the European Space Agency developed the *Hermes* during the 1980's, but budget cuts canceled the project in the 1990's.

Discovery lands after a successful mission to deploy a tracking station that can communicate with low Earth-orbiting space satellites and shuttles.

The Future

Plans are under way to create a new kind of manned space vehicle to succeed—or at least supplement—the aging American space shuttles, which will probably be retired by about 2015. One possibility is the Crew Exploration Vehicle (CEV), which may abandon the winged design of the shuttle and use capsules like those in the Apollo program.

JOSEPH KELCH
Davis Planetarium, Maryland Science Center

See also ASTRONAUTS; SATELLITES, ARTIFICIAL; SPACE EXPLORATION AND TRAVEL; SPACE STATIONS.

SPACE STATIONS

Human beings have yet to walk on Mars or travel to worlds beyond our solar system, but we have already taken the first steps to getting there. Since the early 1970's, astronauts have been preparing for such voyages—aboard space stations orbiting high above Earth.

A space station is any structure that provides a place for people to live and work for long periods of time in space. Like any artificial satellite, a space station maintains its orbit by traveling at just the right velocity and altitude to overcome Earth's gravity. As a result, people and things inside the station experience almost perfect weightlessness, or a **microgravity environment**.

An artist's view of the *International Space Station* shows the crew's living and working quarters (center) and the large solar panels that will power the station.

Early Space Stations. The first true space station, *Salyut 1*, was launched by the former Soviet Union in 1971. It was followed by several other Salyut stations and by *Mir*, launched in 1986. Some Russian cosmonauts remained aboard *Mir* for more than a year. In 1973, the United States launched its first space station, *Skylab*. During a nine-month period, this orbiting workshop housed three different crews of astronauts, who performed various astronomical studies and other scientific experiments.

In 1981, the United States launched the space shuttle *Columbia*. It was the first in a series of reusable spacecraft designed to carry satellites into orbit and to serve as short-term orbiting platforms for conducting research. In the 1990's, shuttle crews also worked with cosmonauts aboard *Mir*, helping them prepare for the next major space station project.

The *International Space Station*. Originally planned as the U.S. space station *Freedom*, this project later became known as the *International Space Station*, or *ISS*. Led by the United States, the project is a joint effort with Russia, 11 western European countries, Canada, Japan, and Brazil. When the station is finished in 2006, it will house a crew of up to seven scientists and astronauts at any one time. Power will be supplied by an array of electricity-generating solar panels as wide as a football field.

In 1998, the first two pieces, or modules, of the space station were carried into orbit, one by a Russian rocket and the other by the U.S. shuttle *Endeavour*. The shuttle's crew then joined the modules in space. These space construction workers use specialized tools, such as a Canadian-made robotic arm, to build the station piece by piece.

Because of its microgravity environment, the *ISS* will provide scientists with a unique laboratory for conducting research and developing new technologies. Studies on the long-term effects of weightlessness on living things may help shed new light on human health and disease. These studies may also pave the way for future human missions to other planets. In addition, scientists will be able to develop manufacturing processes that take advantage of the near gravity-free conditions of space. These processes could lead to new kinds of materials for various types of electronic devices, medical products, and other uses.

Space Stations of Tomorrow. Some experts predict that future space stations will be entire "cities" orbiting Earth or even distant planets. Large numbers of people would live and work in these huge structures, which might rotate to simulate gravity inside. Until then, such dreams will continue to inspire space pioneers to carry on humanity's exploration of the universe.

Reviewed by KYLE HERRING
Public Affairs, NASA Johnson Space Center

See also SATELLITES, ARTIFICIAL; SPACE EXPLORATION AND TRAVEL; SPACE RESEARCH AND TECHNOLOGY; SPACE SHUTTLES.

SPACE TELESCOPES

How can scientists get a clear look at objects in outer space? How can they search for planets that might orbit nearby stars?

Telescopes have been used to study the heavens for over 300 years. But Earth-based telescopes have a serious handicap. The atmosphere surrounding Earth interferes with almost all radiation reaching us from space. For example, radiation in the form of light from distant objects is distorted by the atmosphere, making stars appear to twinkle. (See the Wonder Question, Why do stars twinkle? in the article STARS in this volume.)

Light is just one form of energy given off by stars. Stars also emit invisible energies, including radio waves, infrared, ultraviolet, gamma, and X rays. Except for light and radio waves, almost all of this energy is screened out by Earth's atmosphere.

The Hubble Space Telescope (*shown at left*, docked to the space shuttle *Endeavour*) has taken spectacular images of many celestial objects, including the star-forming towers of gas in the Eagle Nebula (*above*).

▶ **EARLY SPACE TELESCOPES**

The first space telescopes were designed to observe these screened-out invisible energies. As early as 1947, rockets carried instruments high into Earth's atmosphere to measure ultraviolet and X rays. By the 1970's, telescopes mounted on satellites were observing these and other invisible energies.

In addition to being unaffected by atmospheric distortions of visible light, space telescopes can observe other types of radiation that are blocked by the atmosphere. Instruments attached to the telescopes gather information and transmit it back to Earth.

Early space telescopes included the International Ultraviolet Explorer and the Einstein X-Ray Observatory (named after physicist Albert Einstein), both launched in 1978; and the Infrared Astronomical Satellite, launched in 1983.

▶ **TODAY'S SPACE TELESCOPES**

In the 1980's, the National Aeronautics and Space Administration (NASA) began planning four space telescopes, called the Great Observatories. The first of these, the Hubble Space Telescope, was launched in April 1990. It was followed by the Compton Gamma-Ray Observatory in April 1991, the Chandra X-Ray Observatory in July 1999, and the Spitzer Space Telescope in August 2003.

Hubble Space Telescope

The Hubble Space Telescope (HST) is designed to observe visible light and ultraviolet and infrared radiation. It is named after the American astronomer Edwin Hubble (1889–1953). Its orbit around Earth, at an average altitude of 370 miles (600 kilometers), lasts 95 minutes.

The Hubble is a reflecting telescope. Light enters the telescope and strikes a primary mirror. It is then reflected back to a secondary mirror, which redirects the light back through a small hole in the center of the primary mirror. The light is then analyzed by one of the Hubble's scientific instruments.

Some of the scientific instruments used on the Hubble over the course of its operation have been repaired, upgraded, or completely replaced during periodic service missions by astronauts aboard space shuttles. Among the instruments used on the Hubble have been a wide field/planetary camera, which photographed large sections of the sky as well as the planets in our solar system; and a Space Telescope Imaging Spectrograph (STIS), which analyzed the light from an object in space to determine what elements it was made of, how fast it was traveling, and if it was moving toward or away from the Earth.

The Hubble has photographed giant storms on Mars, collisions of distant galaxies, the birth of stars, strangely shaped regions of swirling dust and gases, and the evaporation of a gas planet closely orbiting a distant star. And in 1994, Hubble captured remarkable images of comet Shoemaker-Levy as fragments of its nucleus collided with Jupiter.

In 2005, plans to extend the Hubble's operations were canceled. The Hubble's successor, the James Webb Space Telescope, is scheduled for launch in 2011.

Compton Gamma-Ray Observatory

The Compton Gamma-Ray Observatory was designed to detect gamma rays—the most powerful, or energetic, form of electromagnetic radiation. This space telescope was named after the American physicist Arthur Compton (1892–1962). Because gamma rays do not penetrate Earth's atmosphere, except at extremely high energies, they cannot be detected by ground-based observatories.

Gamma rays are detected when they interact with matter, so the number of gamma-ray events recorded depends on the size of the detector. The Compton has instruments as large as a subcompact car.

The Compton made the first comprehensive map of the entire sky. It also discovered the nearby remains of a recent supernova and a new class of high-energy gamma-ray sources called gamma-ray quasars. The Compton's mission ended when it re-entered Earth's atmosphere in 2000 and burned up.

Chandra X-Ray Observatory

The Chandra X-Ray Observatory was named after the Indian astrophysicist Subrahmanyan Chandrasekhar (1910–95). The Chandra is designed to study sources of X rays, including stars, exploding stars called supernovae, and matter falling into black holes.

X rays from celestial objects are focused by mirrors inside the Chandra and directed at special instruments. A high-resolution camera records the number and strength of the incoming X rays. Various spectrometers analyze the spectrum of the X rays.

Among Chandra's discoveries were a massive black hole swallowing material at the center of the Milky Way Galaxy; pulses of X rays emanating from the polar regions of Jupiter; and an immense rotating disc of extremely hot gas moving through a distant galaxy. The Chandra also found signs of hidden dark matter, which may make up most of the mass of the universe.

The Spitzer Space Telescope

The Spitzer Space Telescope was originally called the Space Infrared Telescope Facility (SIRTF) but was renamed soon after launch in honor of the American astrophysicist Lyman Spitzer, Jr. (1914–97.) The Spitzer is designed to detect infrared radiation emitted by celestial objects, such as small, dim stars or forming planets hidden by thick clouds of dust and gas.

The Spitzer's scientific instruments include a reflecting telescope, an infrared camera, an infrared spectrograph, and a multiband imaging photometer.

The Spitzer has revealed newborn stars once hidden by dark clouds of gas; organic material within dusty discs orbiting young stars; and a clear, detailed image of one galaxy absorbing, or "eating," another.

▶ OTHER SPACE TELESCOPES

Other telescopes have been launched into space. Two are operated by the European Space Agency. The International Gamma-Ray Astrophysics Laboratory (INTEGRAL) will make various X-ray observations and create a gamma-ray map of the entire sky. The X-ray Multi-Mirror Mission (XMM-Newton) uses three X-ray telescopes to detect more X-ray sources than any other orbiting observatory. A third, the High Energy Transient Explorer (HETE-2), is jointly operated by the United States, Japan, France, and Italy. It is designed to detect bursts of gamma rays as well as survey X-ray sources. A fourth is NASA's Swift Gamma-Ray Burst Mission. Swift is a three-telescope platform that can detect and quickly aim itself at sources of intense gamma radiation. These sources are often stars that die spectacular, explosive deaths.

DAVID GHITELMAN
Author, *The Space Telescope*

See also ASTRONOMY; OBSERVATORIES; PULSARS; QUASARS; RADIATION; SPACE EXPLORATION AND TRAVEL; TELESCOPES.

SPAIN

Spain is the fourth largest European country in area, after Russia, Ukraine, and France. Situated in southwestern Europe, it occupies most of the Iberian Peninsula, which it shares with its smaller, western neighbor, Portugal. Spain is bounded by the Atlantic Ocean on the northwest and the Bay of Biscay (an arm of the Atlantic) on the north. In the northeast, the Pyrenees mountains divide it from France and the rest of the European continent. On the southeast and east, Spain borders the Mediterranean Sea, with the Strait of Gibraltar narrowly separating it from North Africa.

Spain's geographical position has greatly influenced its history. With its long Mediterranean coastline, it became a crossroads of early civilizations in the region. Its closeness to Africa brought a Moorish invasion and conquest, which added a new element to its development.

Beginning in the late 1400's, Spain took a leading role in the exploration and colonization of the Americas, where it built a vast empire. Although its empire is gone, the Spanish language and cultural heritage remain very much alive throughout most of Latin America, and its glory is still reflected in Spanish art, architecture, literature, and music.

Articles on Spanish art and architecture, language and literature, and music can be found following this article.

▶ PEOPLE

The Spanish are the descendants of varied peoples and the inheritors of many cultures. In prehistoric times, the native Iberians absorbed the culture of the Celts, a people then

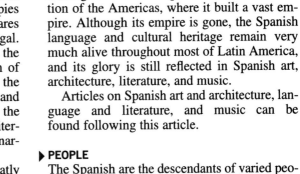

Galicians (*right*), Basques (*below right*) and Majorcans from the Balearic Islands (*below*) show cultural diversity in their various forms of traditional dress. The fortress of Alcázar in Old Castile (*far right*) was once the residence of kings.

widespread across much of Europe. Celtic customs, such as circle dances, wall and ball games, and the use of crude bagpipes, are still found in the Basque provinces of the Pyrenees. The language of the Basques is not Celtic, however, and although they are an ancient people of the region, related only to the French Basques across the Pyrenees, their origins are still a mystery.

The Phoenicians, a people of the eastern Mediterranean, and their successors, the Carthaginians, arrived later. They were followed by the Greeks and Romans, who added their classical cultures to the Spanish mix. The Romans, who called the region *Hispania* (giving it its present name) ruled it for nearly 600 years. Their cultural contributions included the Latin language, from which Spanish derived. The fall of the Roman Empire in the West in the A.D. 400's increased the movement of Germanic tribes, dominated by the Visigoths, into northern and central Spain. Their descendants can be seen today in the blond, blue-eyed Spaniards who are not uncommon in some areas of the country.

A greater cultural upheaval came in the early 700's, when Muslims from North Africa, including Arabs and Berbers, commonly known as Moors, conquered most of the peninsula. Andalusia in the south became the heartland of Muslim Spain. Two other peoples also made their appearance at this time. Jews from North Africa added to the small Jewish communities who had lived in Iberia since early Roman times. They eventually created a distinct group, the Sephardim, whose language, Ladino, is a mixture of Hebrew and early Spanish. Gypsies, or *Gitanos*, arrived in Spain from Asia Minor. Although never large in numbers, their striking flamenco music and dance has made them familiar figures, partic-

**Historical Regions
of Spain**

ularly to tourists. Many gypsies still live in the mountains of Andalusia.

In the early Middle Ages, the far north, which had resisted the Muslim conquest, attracted European settlers who had originally been drawn to its Christian holy places. At about the same time, northern Catalonia became, culturally, a part of Provence as a result of migrations from this area of France.

Language. Castilian Spanish is the country's official language, but Catalan, Galician, Basque, and other languages also have official status within their regions. All but Basque are Romance languages—that is, they are derived from Latin.

Catalan, the language of Catalonia in northeastern Spain, is similar to the Provençal of southern France. Galician, spoken in Galicia in the northwest, is distantly related to Portuguese. Basque, or Euskera, as the Basques call it, is spoken in the Basque provinces of northern Spain. It is unrelated to any other language in the world. Spanish ranks as the world's third most widely spoken language, after Mandarin Chinese and the Hindi of India.

Religion. Most Spaniards are Roman Catholics. There are small Protestant, Jewish, and Muslim communities. Although expelled from the country in past centuries, Spain's Jews and Muslims have had significant revivals in recent years.

Women in Andalusia wear a distinctive and classic style of traditional dress. Andalusia is Spain's largest and most populous historical province.

Spain

10°W **5°W** **0°** **5°E**

Bay of Biscay

FRANCE

Gulf of Lion

La Coruña • Castropol • Gijón • Santander • San Sebastián

Santiago • Lugo • Oviedo • Bilbao • Pamplona • ANDORRA • Port-Bou

Pontevedra • GALICIAN MTS. • CANTABRIAN MTS. • León • Vitoria • Pico de Aneto

Vigo • Ourense • Miño R. • Burgos • Logroño • Gerona

Zamora • Pisuerga R. • Valladolid • Saragossa • Lérida • Barcelona

Douro R. • Calatayud • Tarragona

Salamanca • Segovia • SIERRA DE GUADARRAMA • Tortosa

Tormes R. • Ávila • SIERRA DE GREDOS • Guadalajara • Teruel • Castellón de la Plana • Inca • Artá

SIERRA DE GATA • Madrid • Cuenca • Valencia • MINORCA

PORTUGAL • Tagus R. • Toledo • Aranjuez • Gulf of Valencia • Palma • MAJORCA

Cáceres • MONTES DE TOLEDO • Júcar R. • IBIZA • ISLA DE CABRERA

Valencia de Alcántara • Guadiana R. • Ciudad Real • ISLA DE FORMENTERA

Badajoz • Mérida • Segura R. • Alicante

SIERRA MORENA • Linares • Murcia

Córdoba • Guadalquivir River • Jaén • Cartagena

Ayamonte • Huelva • Seville • Granada • Almería

Gulf of Cádiz • Antequera • Mulhacén • SIERRA NEVADA • *Mediterranean Sea*

Cádiz • Jerez • Málaga

Algeciras • GIBRALTAR (U.K.) • CEUTA (Sp.) • ISLA DE ALBORÁN (Sp.)

Strait of Gibraltar • MELILLA (Sp.) • ALGERIA

MOROCCO

Canary Islands (SPAIN)

Lanzarote • Fuerteventura

La Palma • Tenerife • Pico de Teide

Isla de La Gomera • Gran Canaria • *ATLANTIC OCEAN*

Ferro

EUROPE

AFRICA

Education. A basic education is free and required by law for all Spanish children between the ages of 6 and 16. It consists of six years of primary school followed by two two-year courses of secondary school. Students may then either take one or two years of vo-cational training or the two-year *bachillerato* course for entrance to a university. Spain has numerous universities; the oldest, at Sala-manca, was founded in 1218.

Sports. Soccer is by far the favorite national sport. It draws enormous crowds, and televised matches are among the most popular programs shown. Basketball has become increasingly popular. Golf, tennis, and skiing also attract many Spaniards. Bullfighting, thought of as typically Spanish, is still popular, but not as widely attended as it once was. Jai alai, a game of dazzling speed resembling handball, originated in the Basque region. For more information, see the article BULL-FIGHTING in Volume B and the article JAI ALAI in Volume J-K.

Bullfighting is a contest between the courage and grace of the matador and the strength and stamina of the bull.

Festivals, Music, and Dance. Many Spanish festivals are associated with religious holidays. Two of the largest are the pre-Lenten Holy Week celebration in Seville and the San Isidro observance following Lent in Madrid, the capital. Every Spanish town and village also has a fiesta dedicated to its patron saint.

Music and dance have always been a part of Spanish life. Many Spanish dances, such as the bolero, fandango, and Gypsy flamenco, are well known. Also popular is the *zarzuela*, a type of musical comedy. In classical music, Spain has produced a number of excellent composers and performers. For more information, see SPAIN, MUSIC OF.

Food and Drink. Each part of Spain has its own particular cuisine, or way of preparing food. Regional specialties include the *cocido*, or boiled beef, of Madrid and the casseroles of Catalonia. In Valencia and Murcia the speciality is *paella*, a combination of rice, shellfish, and chicken. *Gazpacho*, a form of vegetable soup served cold, is a favorite in the south, while the Basque provinces are noted for their fish dishes. Wine accompanies most meals.

▶ **LAND**

Spain is a rugged land of mountains and high plateaus deeply indented by river valleys.

Land Regions. The coastal regions, particularly the Mediterranean shore, are fairly narrow but agriculturally fertile and have some of the densest concentrations of people. The plateau region of the central peninsula is the Meseta. It includes both Old and New Castile and forms the core of Spain. Mountain areas lie at the edge of the Meseta. The Cantabrian Mountains to the north and the Sierra Morena to the south define the region. The Sierra de Guadarrama near Madrid, the Sierra de Gredos, and the Montes de Toledo run diagonally through it, dividing it into a higher, northern meseta and a lower, southern meseta. The highest point on the mainland is Mulhacén, which rises to 11,407 feet (3,477 meters) in the Sierra Nevada in the southeast.

Rivers and Coastal Waters. The largest area of lowland is the valley of the Guadalquivir River in Andalusia. Other major rivers include the Tagus, Douro, Miño, and Guadiana, which flow into the Atlantic Ocean, and the Ebro (the largest river entirely within Spain), which empties into the Mediterranean Sea. Only short portions of the Guadalquivir and Tagus are navigable, or usable by ships. The rivers, particularly the Ebro, are an important source of irrigation in a land where rainfall is generally sparse.

Spain's varied landscape ranges from the high Pyrenees mountains in the northeast, which separate it from the rest of Europe, to the long, lush coastline along the Mediterranean Sea in the south. Its geographical position has greatly affected Spain's history.

Olive trees stretch as far as the eye can see in Andalusia, Spain's southernmost region and one of its chief agricultural areas. Spain is one of the world's leading producers of olives and olive oil.

Islands. The Balearic Islands in the Mediterranean and the Canary Islands in the Atlantic also form part of Spain's territory. The Balearic group consists of four main islands, of which Majorca is the largest and most populous. The Canary chain lies off the southwestern coast and consists of seven main islands. Tenerife, the largest Canary island, is the site of Spain's highest peak, Pico de Teide, which rises some 12,198 feet (3,718 meters).

Climate. Spain's climate varies according to region. The north and west have a maritime climate with moderate temperatures and generous rainfall. But rainfall decreases sharply as one moves south and a Mediterranean climate prevails, marked by mild winters and hot, dry summers.

Natural Resources. Except for the river valleys, Spain has only limited areas of fertile soil. Slightly more than one-third of the land is under cultivation. The country's once-extensive mineral resources still include deposits of coal, iron ore, potash, mercury, and copper, but mining has declined in importance. Spain obtains more than one-third of its electricity from nuclear power; the rest of its energy is derived from imported oil. The only remaining large areas of forest are in the north.

▶**ECONOMY**

For most of its history, Spain was primarily an agricultural country. However, services and manufacturing have now surpassed agriculture in terms of economic importance.

Services. Tourism has become one of the country's main sources of income. More than 30 million tourists visit Spain each year, attracted to the many coastal resorts and to its historic cities and cultural sites. Service industries, of which tourism is a large part, account for about half of Spain's gross domestic product, or GDP (the total value of goods and services produced in the country in one year).

Manufacturing. Manufacturing and related industries employ more than one-third of Spain's workforce and make up about one-third of its GDP. Most heavy industry is located in the north, particularly in the Basque provinces, Aragon, and Catalonia, although in recent years the areas around the cities of Madrid and Valencia have also become industrialized. The chief manufactured

FACTS and figures

KINGDOM OF SPAIN (Reino de España) is the official name of the country.

LOCATION: Iberian Peninsula in southwestern Europe.

AREA: 194,896 sq mi (504,782 km²).

POPULATION: 40,000,000 (estimate).

CAPITAL AND LARGEST CITY: Madrid.

MAJOR LANGUAGES: Castilian Spanish (official), Catalan, Galician, Basque, others official within their regions.

MAJOR RELIGIOUS GROUP: Roman Catholic.

GOVERNMENT: Constitutional monarchy. **Head of state**—king. **Head of government**—president of the government (prime minister). **Legislature**—National Assembly (composed of the Congress of Deputies and the Senate).

CHIEF PRODUCTS: Agricultural—wheat, rice, and other grains, olives, oranges, cork, grapes, livestock. **Manufactured**—automobiles, steel, chemicals, textiles, wines, shoes and other footwear, ships, processed foods. **Mineral**—coal, iron ore, potash, mercury, copper.

MONETARY UNIT: Euro (1 euro = 100 cents).

Twilight bathes the Avenida de José Antonio (*right*), one of the main thoroughfares in Madrid, Spain's capital and largest city. A statue of Christopher Columbus (*below*) towers over Barcelona, the historical capital of Catalonia and Spain's second largest city.

products include automobiles, steel, chemicals, textiles, processed foods, and shoes and other footwear. Shipbuilding and fishing are other major industries.

Agriculture. Historically, settled agriculture in Spain began in Andalusia. This region supplied grain to the Roman and Moorish empires. Agriculture spread to the rest of the country.

Most farms in the south are *latifundia*, or large estates worked by hired labor. In the north, farms are small, often just a few acres in size. The small farmers of the north, particularly of Galicia, and the landless farmworkers of Andalusia are among Spain's poorest.

Wheat, rice, and other grains are the chief crops. Oranges are an important export. Spain is one of the world's leading producers of olives and olive oil and a major producer of wine and cork. The most famous Spanish wine, sherry, took its name from the city of Jerez in the southwest, where it is made.

▶ **MAJOR CITIES**

The great majority of Spain's people live in urban areas. The largest cities are briefly described here.

Madrid, the capital and largest city, is situated on the Meseta plateau, in the heart of Spain. Originally an alcázar (fortress) founded by Muslims, the site fell to Christian forces in 1083. The Castilian court located permanently here in 1561.

Madrid endured a three-year siege by the Nationalists under General Francisco Franco during the Spanish Civil War (1936–39). See the article MADRID in Volume M.

Barcelona, the historical capital of Catalonia, is Spain's second largest city and chief port. Settled by the Phoenicians, it was, according to local tradition, named for the Carthaginian family of Barca. It grew to im-

portance in Roman times and became a political and economic power during the Middle Ages under the counts of Barcelona. The city's fortunes subsequently fell, a victim of its rivalry with Madrid and Castile. Industrialization transformed Barcelona during the late

The whitewashed buildings of Marbella on the Costa del Sol ("sun coast") on the Mediterranean Sea are typical of the cities of southern Spain.

1800's. During the Spanish Civil War, it was a center of resistance to the Nationalists, and the postwar Franco regime banned all aspects of Catalan culture. Its choice as the site of the 1992 Summer Olympic Games helped in its revival. See the article BARCELONA in Volume B.

Valencia, a Mediterranean port city, lies in a fertile agricultural region famed for its oranges. Founded by the Romans, it was one of the chief cities of Muslim Spain.

Seville (Sevilla), the largest city of southern Spain, is situated on the Guadalquivir River. An important city under the Romans and Visigoths, it became one of the centers of Muslim culture.

▶ CULTURAL HERITAGE

For information on the wealth of Spain's cultural achievements, both past and present, see the articles SPAIN, ART AND ARCHITECTURE OF; SPAIN, LANGUAGE AND LITERATURE OF; and SPAIN, MUSIC OF following this article.

▶ GOVERNMENT

Spain is a constitutional monarchy with a parliamentary form of government. Under the 1978 constitution, the king is the head of state. The parliament, or National Assembly, is known as the Cortes. It is made up of the Congress of Deputies and the Senate, both elected for 4-year terms. The king appoints the president of the government, or prime minister, who heads the Council of Ministers. The prime minister is chosen from the political party winning the largest number of seats in the Cortes.

Spain is divided into 50 provinces, each with an elected assembly and a governor appointed by the central government. There are also 17 autonomous communities, based on the country's historic regions. Each autonomous community has a regional parliament and cultural autonomy, including the right to use its own language.

Spain's overseas territories now consist of two tiny enclaves in North Africa—Ceuta and Melilla—both of which lie within Morocco.

▶ HISTORY

Early History. The Phoenicians, a seafaring and trading people who originated in what is now Lebanon, reached southern Spain in about 1000 B.C. They founded some of its earliest towns, including Málaga and Cádiz. Greeks established a string of colonies along the eastern coast between 600 and 400 B.C. The Carthaginians, descendants of the Phoenicians, established their power in Cartagena, the southern port city named for them. Rome's defeat of Carthage in the 200's B.C. brought Roman rule to the peninsula. Spain became a vital part of the Roman Empire, four of whose emperors were of Spanish origin. The Visigoths who succeeded the Romans held sway in Spain for some 200 years, when a new people invaded Spain from the south.

Muslim Spain. In A.D. 711, Muslims from North Africa (known as Moors), led by the Moroccan general Tariq, crossed to Gibraltar, where they defeated an army under Roderick, one of several Visigothic kings. The Muslim conquest spread rapidly northward, crossing the Pyrenees into what is today France. The defeat of the Muslims at the Battle of Tours in 732, however, forced them back into Spain, where for the next 700 years their culture dominated the peninsula.

Córdoba in Andalusia became the capital of the Umayyads, the dominant Muslim dynasty, and the region became the heartland of Muslim Spain. Under the Umayyad rulers, the system of irrigated agriculture was im-

Muslims from North Africa, known as the Moors, conquered Spain in the early 700's. Their northward advance was halted at the Battle of Tours in 732.

proved and the cultivation of rice, citrus fruits, and other crops was introduced. Crafts and technology brought from the Middle East exceeded what was then known in the rest of Europe. Córdoba and other Spanish cities became centers of intellectual life, as poetry, science, mathematics, medicine, and philosophy flourished.

The Umayyad dynasty collapsed in 1031, in part because of religious conflicts among the Muslims. A civil war led to the emergence of new Muslim dynasties, including the Almoravid (1086–1147) and the Almohad (1147–1212). Neither of these, however, reached the level of power and sophistication of the Umayyad.

The Christian Reconquest. Muslim decline also came about as a result of the renewal of Christian strength and culture in the north. The kingdom of León organized a resistance to the Muslims that became very much like a holy war. León became the center of the later kingdom of Castile, which took the lead in ending Muslim domination in Spain. During a long military campaign, Castile added the Basque provinces, Valencia, and Andalusia to its domain. The rival kingdoms of Aragón and Catalonia vied with Castile for Navarre (later lost to France), and together they conquered the Balearic Islands, Sicily, and Naples.

The fall of Toledo (1085), Córdoba (1236), and Seville (1248) left only the kingdom of Granada in Muslim hands. But in 1492, Granada surrendered, completing the Christian reconquest of Spain. Its fall also led to the expulsion of Spanish Jews and Muslims who refused to convert to Christianity.

The Spanish Empire. Spain's power and influence grew due to the marriage of Queen Isabella I of Castile (1451–1504) and Ferdinand II of Aragón (1452–1516), which led to the union of Spain's two largest kingdoms in 1479. Ferdinand and Isabella sponsored the voyages of Christopher Columbus, leading to the discovery of the Americas in 1492 and opening the way for Spain to colonize an empire in the West.

In 1496, the couple's eldest daughter, Joanna (Juana), married into Austria's Habsburg dynasty, rulers of the Holy Roman Empire. Thus the succession of Joanna's son, Charles I (1500–58), to the Spanish throne in 1516, began nearly 200 years of Habsburg rule in Spain. Charles was elected Holy Roman emperor in 1519 and thereafter was known as Holy Roman Emperor Charles V.

The marriage of Ferdinand II of Aragón and Isabella I of Castile united the two most powerful kingdoms in Spain. The monarchs sponsored the explorations of Christopher Columbus (pictured), who discovered the New World in 1492.

More German than Spanish, Charles V involved Catholic Spain militarily in the Protestant Reformation and brought it into conflict with France and the Ottoman Turks. In 1522, he divided his vast empire into Spanish and Austrian branches.

In the meantime, the Americas were becoming an outlet for those seeking fame and wealth abroad. The 1494 Treaty of Tordesillas had given Spain control of all American lands west of Brazil. Within a half century after Columbus' first voyage, Spanish conquistadors had colonized nearly two thirds of the Western Hemisphere, while Spanish priests had converted many native Indians to the Catholic faith. For more information, see the articles COLUMBUS, CHRISTOPHER; EXPLORATION AND DISCOVERY (North and South America); and FERDINAND AND ISABELLA in the appropriate volumes.

Spain reached the height of its power under Charles' son, Philip II (1527–98). Unlike his father, Philip was thoroughly Spanish. By the end of his reign, Spain ruled Portugal and the Low Countries (including what is now the Netherlands, Belgium, and Luxembourg) as well as much of Italy, the Canary Islands, and North Africa. In addition, Spain's vast colonies in the Americas included all of present-day Mexico, Central America, the American Southwest, and the Philippine Islands, named for Philip himself. For more information, see the article PHILIP in Volume P.

Philip II ruled the Spanish Empire (1556–98) at the height of its power. Many Spanish colonies were settled during this time, including the Philippines, which was named for him.

Decline of Spanish Power. Spain's decline in power was nearly as swift as its rise. In 1566, the Dutch began a long-drawn-out revolt against Spanish rule in the Low Countries, one of its richest lands. The Dutch Revolt proved costly to Spain and eventually led to the formation of the Dutch Republic in 1581. That same decade, while attempting to invade the British Isles in 1588, the great Spanish fleet known as the Armada was soundly defeated by British naval forces in the English Channel, marking the first successful challenge to Spanish sea power. Together these events ended Spain's hopes of extending Catholic rule in Protestant northern Europe. For more information, see the article SPANISH ARMADA in this volume.

Philip II's successors were mostly of limited ability. As wars drained its resources, Spain resorted to borrowing enormous sums of money. This policy depleted its treasure of gold and silver from the Americas, causing massive inflation and bankrupting the country. Under Philip IV (1605–65), Portugal regained its independence (1640), and Spanish troops were defeated by the French at the Battle of Rocroi (1643).

Despite these economic and military setbacks, Spanish art and literature flourished in the late 1500's and early 1600's. For more information on the most prominent artists and writer of the era, see the separate biographies GRECO, EL; VELÁZQUEZ, DIEGO; and CERVANTES, MIGUEL DE in the appropriate volumes.

War of the Spanish Succession. The last Spanish Habsburg king was Charles II (1661–1700). Before he died childless in 1700, he named as his heir the Bourbon prince Philip of Anjou (1683–1746), a grandson of the French King, Louis XIV. Other European powers, fearing the power of a combined France and Spain, supported a rival candidate— the Archduke Charles, the second son of Leopold I (1640–1705), Holy Roman emperor and ruler of Austria.

In 1701, Philip's accession as Philip V of Spain set off the War of the Spanish Succession between the French and Austrians. The following year, Britain, Prussia, and the Netherlands entered the war on the side of Austria. In Europe the Grand Alliance failed to conquer Spain, but the great English general, the Duke of Marlborough, succeeded in driving the French out of Germany and the Low Countries with his victories at the battles of Blenheim (1704), Ramillies (1706), Oudenaarde (1708), and Malplaquet (1709).

In the painting *The Third of May, 1808*, Spanish artist Francisco Goya portrayed French troops firing on the Spanish during the Peninsular War.

The succession of Ferdinand's infant daughter, Isabella II (1830–1904), in 1833 was opposed by the supporters of Ferdinand's brother Don Carlos, setting off the first Carlist War (1833–39). A military revolt in 1868 forced Isabella to give up the throne. A new constitutional monarchy was proclaimed in 1869, but it lasted only until 1873. A short-lived republic, from 1873 to 1874, was torn by the second Carlist War (1872–76). It was overthrown by the army, which placed Isabella's young son, Alfonso XII (1857–85), on the throne in 1875.

The 1900's.   Spain's imperial decline continued as the 1900's approached. Defeat in the Spanish-American War (1898) stripped it of Cuba, Puerto Rico, the Philippines, and its Pacific Island colonies. For more information, see the article SPANISH-AMERICAN WAR in this volume.

At home, political differences frustrated attempts to create a more liberal Spanish society. Opposition to the church had become widespread because of its support of large landowners and unpopular governments. The country was further divided by the gulf between rich and poor. Increasing social unrest eventually brought about a military dictatorship (1923–30) under General Miguel Primo de Rivera.

Second Republic.   In the 1931 local elections, a victory by opponents of the monarchy forced King Alfonso XIII (1886–1941) to leave the country, after which the Second Republic was proclaimed. The new republican govern-

General Francisco Franco led the Nationalist forces during the Spanish Civil War (1936–39). He then ruled Spain as dictator until his death in 1975.

In 1713 the British and Dutch quit the war by signing the Peace of Utrecht, which declared that France and Spain never be united. The Austrians fought on for another year. The 1714 Treaty of Rastatt left Philip V with control over Spain and Spanish America, but the Austrians gained most of Spanish Italy and the Spanish Netherlands (in present-day Belgium). Britain, now clearly the leading maritime power in Europe, gained Gibraltar, Minorca, Nova Scotia, and recognition of rights to Newfoundland and Hudson's Bay. Later Bourbon monarchs, though more capable than Philip, were nevertheless unable to restore Spanish power.

Peninsular War and Loss of Empire.   In 1808, Napoleon Bonaparte, the emperor of France, invaded Spain. He forced Ferdinand VII (1784–1833), Philip V's great grandson, to give up the throne and then made his own brother, Joseph Bonaparte, king of Spain. The move provoked a popular uprising. The conflict that resulted, known as the Peninsular War (and in Spain as the War of Independence) lasted until 1814, when British and Spanish forces drove out the French.

The war had caused nationalist feelings to soar, and a democratic constitution was proclaimed in 1812. But its failure to address colonial concerns led to the loss of most of Spain's empire in the Americas.

Period of Turmoil.   Ferdinand VII, restored to the throne after Napoleon's downfall in 1814, refused to accept the constitution, leading to an uprising (1820–23) that was put down only with the help of French troops.

The city of Barcelona hosted the Summer Olympic Games in 1992. The opening ceremonies (pictured) were among the most spectacular in the history of the Olympics.

ment adopted a number of economic and social reforms, but in so doing, it alienated the church, the army, and the large landowners. In 1933 those conservatives returned to power. But new elections held in 1936 resulted in a narrow victory by the Popular Front, now composed of liberals, Socialists, and some Communists. Fears of even greater radical change led to an army revolt that launched the Spanish Civil War (1936–39).

Civil War. The republic was supported by the Loyalists (or Republicans), who received aid from the Soviet Union and attracted volunteers from more than twenty nations. They were opposed by the Nationalists, who were aided by Nazi Germany and Fascist Italy. Superior military aid from Germany and Italy ultimately enabled the Nationalists under General Francisco Franco (1892–1975) to win the war with the fall of Madrid in April 1939. One million people were killed or wounded in the conflict, and another million Loyalists fled the country. For more information, see the article SPANISH CIVIL WAR.

The Franco Regime. Franco ruled Spain as a dictator for more than 35 years. As *caudillo* (leader), he was chief of state, commander of the armed forces, and head of the only legal political party, the Falange. He kept Spain out of World War II through artful diplomacy, began its postwar industrial development, and gave up most of its remaining African territories. In 1969 he named Prince Juan Carlos, grandson of Alfonso XIII, as his eventual successor. See the article FRANCO, FRANCISCO in Volume F.

Recent History. After Franco's death in 1975, the monarchy was restored, and the prince assumed the throne as Juan Carlos I (1938–   ). The next year, Spain gave up its last large African dependency, Spanish Sahara (now known as Western Sahara). Under its new king, Spain quickly re-established a democratic government, and in 1977 the first free elections since before the civil war were held.

Spain became a member of the North Atlantic Treaty Organization (NATO) in 1982 and of the European Community (now the European Union, or EU) in 1986. In 1999, the Spanish adopted the euro, the EU's common currency, as a further step toward European economic integration. In 2003, Spain was among the few western European nations to openly support an American-led war against Iraqi dictator Saddam Hussein.

On March 11, 2004, the worst terrorist attack in Spanish history took place when bombs exploded at several commuter train stations in Madrid, killing nearly 200 people and injuring at least 1,000 more. The prime minister, José María Aznar López, was quick to blame ETA, a Spanish terrorist group that has long sought independence for Spain's Basque population. But it was soon learned that Al Qaeda terrorists were likely responsible, possibly in retaliation for Spain's support of the war in Iraq. Three days after the attack, regularly scheduled national elections were held. The public, still reeling from the tragedy, abandoned Aznar's Popular Party and instead brought to power the Spanish Socialist Workers' Party, whose leader, José Luis Rodríguez Zapatero, had campaigned to withdraw Spanish troops from Iraq. Troops were recalled soon after.

ROBERT W. KERN
Editor, *Historical Dictionary of Modern Spain*

SPAIN, ART AND ARCHITECTURE OF

Spanish art reflects the variety of Spain itself. An ancient land, divided by mountain ranges, Spain has been home to many groups of people with extremely different origins, speaking different languages and following different religions.

▶BEGINNINGS

The earliest art found in the Iberian Peninsula, where Spain is located, dates from the Old Stone Age. About 13,000 B.C., ice-age hunters painted magnificent images of buffalo and other animals in vivid natural colors on the ceiling of a cave at Altamira on the northern coast.

From 1100 to 400 B.C., people from Greece, Phoenicia, and Carthage settled in Spain. It is common to see their art, as well as that of Syria and Egypt, mixed with central European forms in native Iberian art of this period. Objects of high quality in bronze, glass, gold, and stone have been

Right: The *Dama de Baza*, made about 400 B.C., is an early example of Spanish sculpture. *Below:* The immense roof of the Great Mosque at Córdoba is supported by rows of columns and horseshoe arches.

found, including the large figures, presumably goddesses, called *damas* ("ladies") in Spanish. Most famous are the *Dama de Baza* and the *Dama de Elche* (both about 400 B.C.).

The Romans came to Spain about 218 B.C. Over the course of the next one hundred years, Roman legions brought much of the Iberian peninsula into the empire. Remains of Roman walls, bridges, and aqueducts (structures for transporting water) can be found in every corner of Spain. Greek and Roman sculptures, mosaics, sarcophagi (coffins), jewelry, glass, and everyday objects have also been found in large numbers.

Christians became the most important group in Spain after Christianity became the official religion of the Roman Empire in A.D. 325, although there was also a Jewish population. Increasing political weakness in the western Roman Empire led to invasion by Germanic tribes such as the Visigoths, who entered Spain in the 400's. The Visigothic contribution to the arts in Spain was limited. Like other Germanic tribes, the Visigoths made wonderful jewelry. Their buildings were influenced by those of the Byzantine (Eastern Roman) Empire. Visigothic builders also introduced a new architectural form: the horseshoe arch, which would become a basic element in later Spanish architecture.

▶MOORISH ART

The Moors, originally from North Africa, invaded Spain in 711 and ruled much of southern Spain for several centuries. The Moors followed the Islamic faith, but their rulers allowed the existing Jewish and Christian communities to function. The rulers of the expanding Christian kingdoms in northern Spain also often allowed other religions to exist. The resulting *conviviencia* ("living together") produced a rich multi-ethnic culture. The cities of Córdoba, Seville, and Toledo became important world centers of art, literature, and scholarship.

Early Period. The best-known monument of early Spanish Islamic art is the Great Mosque at Córdoba. The mosque was begun in 786 by

Abd al-Rahman I, who had established a kingdom in Córdoba in 756. The architecture of the mosque—essentially a great covered area for group prayer with a courtyard outside—blends many ancient influences. The rows of arches that hold up the immense roof (covering almost 3 acres of floor) are derived from the Roman aqueduct at Mérida, including the use of alternating color in the stones of the arches. (The horseshoe arches themselves are Visigothic in origin.) The mosaics of the *mihrab*, a decorated niche indicating the direction to Mecca, are Byzantine in inspiration, as are many of the capitals (tops of columns). Other capitals show Greek and Roman influences. The building became the starting point for later Islamic architecture in Spain.

Middle Period. The kingdom of Córdoba came to an end about 1000. Islamic Spain broke up into a number of small kingdoms called Taifas, which increasingly lost territory to the Christian kingdoms of northern Spain. As the northern kingdoms expanded, Christians who had been living under Islamic rule moved north, bringing with them a style of art and architecture, known as **Mozarabic**, that combined European and Arabic influences.

The Taifas also suffered a series of invasions from Africa to the South, one of which brought the Almohads, who created a strong kingdom centered at Seville from the 1100's until 1248. Few examples survive of Almohad architecture, which featured brick buildings with elaborate carved stone decoration and glazed colored tiles. Of the great mosque erected in Seville by the Almohad emperor Yacoub al-Mansur in the 1190's, only the patio and minaret (now the bell tower of Seville's Christian cathedral) still stand. The importance of Almohad art is nevertheless very great, for it was this style that would be passed on to the Christian conquerors as **mudéjar** art. In fact, what one thinks of as the most typically "Moorish" building in Seville—the Alcázar, or royal palace—was largely built by Christian kings in the mudéjar style.

Late Period. The fall of Seville in 1248 left only the southeastern corner of Spain in Islamic hands. Nevertheless, a great kingdom

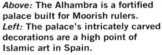

Above: The Alhambra is a fortified palace built for Moorish rulers.
Left: The palace's intricately carved decorations are a high point of Islamic art in Spain.

was built by the Nasrid dynasty at Granada from the 1300's until its final defeat by the Catholic monarchs Ferdinand and Isabella in 1492. The Nasrid princes erected the Alhambra, a fortified palace with beautiful gardens set into the mountain foothills overlooking Granada. With their intricately carved decorations and colorful tile work, the buildings of the Alhambra seem like a vision from the *Arabian Nights*. In addition to its beautiful architecture, the Alhambra is filled with pools and fountains, exotic plants, and fruit trees—a true oasis in the dry climate of southern Spain.

▶**ROMANESQUE**

In Asturias, the part of Spain not conquered by the Moors, a simple style of art and architecture, with Byzantine and Visigothic influences, arose in the 800's and 900's. In the Christian capital of León, Mozarabic architects built churches using the **basilican** plan, featuring a wide central aisle, called a nave, and side aisles with lower roofs. They also used Byzantine columns and horseshoe arches. León artists made beautiful hand-painted books, called illuminated manuscripts.

In Catalonia and Valencia, from about 1000, churches were built in the solid Romanesque style, with thick walls, massive columns, and round arches. Catalonian Romanesque painting is lively and almost modern in design. It includes **frescoes** (paint-

style in the 1700's). León was an important center of Romanesque painting, which spread throughout Castile.

▶ GOTHIC

The Romanesque period lasted into the mid-1200's, when the Gothic style, which had originated in France, appeared in Spain. Gothic churches were taller and less heavy than Romanesque churches, with pointed arches instead of rounded ones and thin columns that soared upward. Léon Cathedral, which was built from the late 1200's through the 1300's in an almost purely French manner, has glorious stained-glass windows that fill the interior with beautifully colored light.

An even richer and more varied effect was achieved in the cathedral at Burgos, begun by an international team in the 1200's but decorated in the 1400's. In its design, the cathedral follows the late French **flamboyant** (literally, "flame-like") style. It also incorporates the **arabesques** (curving designs) and lace-like carving of mudéjar art. This style of Spanish Gothic is often called Isabelline Gothic, after Queen Isabella. The Carthusian Monastery of Miraflores, near Burgos, decorated in the 1490's, has an Isabelline altarpiece designed

ings on plaster) on church walls and ceilings and **panel paintings** (paintings on wood) for the fronts of altars.

In the 1000's, millions of Christian pilgrims from all over Europe visited the tomb of St. James at Santiago de Compostela in Galicia. Hotels and hospitals were established along the pilgrimage routes, and many churches were built. The churches often had French influence but also were built in local Romanesque styles, with influences from Mozarabic and, eventually, mudéjar art. An outstanding example is the church of San Martín in Frómista near Palencia, which became the model for many later buildings. Another is the interior of the great cathedral at Santiago de Compostela (the exterior was rebuilt in the baroque

Adoration of the Shepherds, a painting by El Greco, has the elongated figures and crowded setting typical of the late Renaissance style known as mannerism.

(*plateros*). Classical forms were used as well. Painting and sculpture from the 1400's and early 1500's also show a mix of influences. The work of Castilian painters, such as the artist known as the Master of the Catholic Kings, shows heavy Flemish (Belgian) influence. In Aragón, Valencia, and Catalonia, Italian influence could also be found, although individual artists, such as Luis Dalmau of Valencia, were sent to study in Belgium.

After 1500, the Italian Renaissance became increasingly influential in Spain; many noble families built their palaces in the new style. Italian influence continued throughout the 1500's during the reigns of Charles V and his son Philip II. Philip invited many Italian artists to decorate the Escorial (begun 1562), the huge palace-monastery at the foot of the Guadarrama mountains near Madrid. The plain, severely classical style of this vast building complex came to be called **Herreran**, after the principal architect, Juan de Herrera.

The late Renaissance style called **mannerism** was represented in Spain by the sculptor Alonso de Berruguete and by one of the greatest painters of all time, the Italian-trained Greek, Domenikos Theotokopoulos, who was called El Greco in Spain. El Greco used the elongated figures and crowded settings typical of mannerism.

by the French artist Gil de Siloe. In contrast, Gothic churches in Catalonia, such as the church of Santa María del Mar, Barcelona, seem elegantly streamlined.

▶RENAISSANCE

The Renaissance began in Italy about 1400. *Renaissance* is a French word meaning "rebirth." The period was given this name because there was a rebirth of interest in the learning and the arts of the classical age of ancient Greece and Rome. Like the rest of Europe outside Italy, Spain was slow to adopt the new style in the 1400's.

During the reign (1474–1516) of Isabella and Ferdinand, the Isabelline Gothic mixed with a Renaissance style of architecture known as **plateresque**—so called because its fine decoration resembled the work of silversmiths

Las Meninas, a portrait of a young princess and her attendants, is among the greatest works of Diego Velázquez, one of the masters of Spain's Golden Age.

Elaborately carved and gilded structures called retables often decorated churches built in the Spanish late baroque, or Churrigueresque, style.

THE GOLDEN AGE

The period from about 1550 to 1700 in Spanish culture is called the Golden Age. At its outset, Spain was the most powerful country in Europe and the ruler of the New World. Although Spain's political power slowly crumbled, its artistic achievements reached a peak in the 1600's.

The Valencian painter Jusepe de Ribera spent his entire career in Italy, often working for the Spanish viceroys of Naples, who brought his paintings back to Spain. Ribera's works were painted in a style known as **tenebrism**, which is characterized by strong contrasts of light and dark, in the manner of the Italian painter Caravaggio.

Diego Velázquez created realistic paintings that often represented complicated ideas. For example, his famous painting *Las Meninas* ("The Maids of Honor"; 1656) shows the young princess Margarita and her attendants visiting the studio of the artist in the royal palace, but the work also appears to comment on the artist's own position at court.

Francisco de Zurbarán specialized in religious subjects, depicting them in an intensely reverent tenebrist manner. Bartolomé Murillo created religious paintings in the **baroque** style, filled with color and movement. His works include rich landscapes and breathtaking visions of heaven as well as quieter portraits and images of the Madonna.

Golden Age Spanish sculpture was often religious and made of painted wood. In many cases, the sculptures are still paraded through city streets during religious festivals. The sculptors—Juan Martinez Montañés, Alonso Cano, Pedro de Mena, Francisco Salzillo—are little known outside Spain.

1700'S AND 1800'S

In 1700, the Spanish throne passed to a Frenchman, Philip V, grandson of King Louis XIV of France. Spanish art entered several decades of uncertainty, with French and Italian influences once again becoming very powerful in painting, sculpture, and furniture design. In architecture, however, Spain developed its own version of the late baroque style, called **Churrigueresque** after the architect José Churriguera. The **retable**, a structure behind the church altar, was a characteristic feature of Churrigueresque architecture. Sometimes spanning the entire width and height of the church, the retables were elaborately carved and gilded (covered with gold).

This portrait of a young aristocrat was painted by Francisco Goya. One of Spain's most original artists, Goya painted a wide range of subjects.

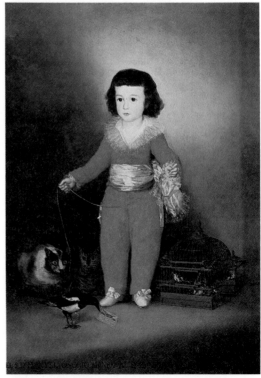

Guernica, by the great modern artist Pablo Picasso, portrays the suffering and destruction caused by the bombing of a Basque village in the Spanish Civil War.

Goya. Although many fine Spanish painters worked in the 1700's, they are often forgotten beside one of the greatest Spanish artists of all time, Francisco Goya. Goya was born near Zaragossa in Aragón and trained in Italy before returning to work in Madrid. In 1792, a mysterious illness almost killed him. Thereafter, his works took on a darker and more emotional quality. The Napoleonic wars (1808–14) affected Goya deeply. In 1810 he began his *Disasters of War* etchings, and he devoted one of his most important canvases, *The Third of May, 1808* (1814), to the heroes of the Spanish resistance. From 1819 to 1823, Goya produced a series of fantastic wall paintings, now called the "Black Paintings," that look forward to modern art.

After Goya, much Spanish art of the 1800's seems bland, although there were artists of great achievement, such as Vicente López, the Madrazo family, Aureliano de Beruete, Mariano Fortuny, Emilio Sánchez Perrier, and Joaquín Sorolla.

▶THE MODERN ERA

At the end of the 1800's, in Barcelona, a particularly active early modern group of artists and architects, including Antonio Gaudí, Ramón Casas, Isidro Nonell, and the young Pablo Picasso, began pushing Spanish art onto new ground. Picasso, along with fellow Spanish painters Joan Miró, Juan Gris, and Salvador Dalí, and the sculptor Julio González, went to Paris. There, Picasso and his French colleague Georges Braque created the abstract style called **cubism**, in which an object is often shown from several different angles at the same time. In the 1920's, Miró and Dalí became involved with the **surrealist** movement, which applied modern psychological theories to art. Dalí created unsettling dreamlike images in a sharply focused realistic manner. Miró is known for his brightly colored abstract paintings of fantastic imaginary worlds populated by make-believe creatures.

Many people feel that Picasso's greatest work is the large mural (wall painting) that he produced in 1937 to protest the bombing of the Basque village of Guernica during the Spanish Civil War (1936–39). *Guernica* combines nightmarish images of suffering and destruction in a highly expressive cubist arrangement. Like the newsreels and newspapers of the era, the scene is depicted in black and white, as if the color had drained out along with the lives of the victims.

Spain continued to produce great artists after the war, although their freedom of expression was often limited by the dictatorship of General Francisco Franco (ruled 1939–75). Among the best known of the artists active from 1950 to the present is Antoni Tàpies, from Barcelona, whose works are associated with the **abstract expressionist** movement in the United States. After Franco's death in 1975, Spanish modern art exploded into two decades of creativity, with older masters such as Miró, Tàpies, Antonio Saura, and Eduardo Chillida inspiring many younger artists.

MARCUS B. BURKE
Adjunct Professor of Religion and the Arts
Yale University

SPAIN, LANGUAGE AND LITERATURE OF

Spanish, one of the most important languages in the world, is the official language of Spain and its possessions and of most Latin American countries. It is one of the five working languages of the United Nations.

Some of the world's literary masterworks were written in Spanish. Many, including *Don Quixote*, are known to English-speaking people in translation.

▶SPANISH LANGUAGE

Like French, Italian, and Portuguese, Spanish is a romance language. The term comes from the Latin word *romanice*, meaning "in the Roman fashion."

The Romans first reached Spain in 218 B.C., and they gradually conquered the land. Roman customs and language were adopted by the peoples of the country. The only pre-Roman language to survive was Basque, which is still spoken in the Basque provinces of northern Spain and southern France. After two hundred years of conquest, Spain became an important part of the Roman Empire.

Then, in the A.D. 400's, Germanic tribes called the Visigoths gained control of most of the Iberian Peninsula. The Visigoths took the former Latin culture for their own and added little to the native language.

In 711, Arabic-speaking Moors from the Near East and North Africa conquered all of the peninsula except for a thin strip of mountain valleys in the north. These Muslim conquerors stayed until 1492 and helped develop the most outstanding culture of the time in western Europe. Christians were allowed to keep their religion and language. This language, called Mozarabic, stemmed from Visigothic Latin. Spanish was not altered by the presence of Arabic, but it did borrow from it some 4,000 words.

About 718, Christians began their long fight to reconquer Spain from the Muslims. The struggle lasted almost 800 years, and during that time Christian kingdoms were formed. A romance language developed in each separate kingdom: Galician-Portuguese in Galicia and what is now Portugal, Catalan in Catalonia, Castilian in Castile, and so on. The kingdom of Castile in central Spain gradually became the leading power, and its language had a wide influence. "Castilian language" and "Spanish language" came to mean the same thing.

As early as the 1200's, King Alfonso X of Castile made the spelling of Spanish words easier and more regular. He gave Castilian a phonetic spelling—that is, the words are spelled the way they are pronounced.

In the 1500's and 1600's, the Spanish language reached its maturity. It spread to the New World as Spaniards began to colonize present-day Latin America. Spanish varies in local accents, usages, and vocabulary, but it has a single grammar and written form.

▶SPANISH LITERATURE

Most of the great literature of Spain has been written in Castilian.

Early Middle Ages (1000–1400)

Jarchas, short lyric poems written in Mozarabic in the 1000's, are thought to be the earliest examples of Spanish literature. The first known Castilian texts date back to the 1100's. For the most part they are poems that were sung by wandering minstrels. The best-known example is *Poema de mio Cid (Poem*

An early woodcut shows the famous Spanish warrior Rodrigo Díaz de Vivar, known as *Cid* ("lord"). His deeds are the subject of the great Castilian epic *Poem of the Cid*, written about 1140. Like other poems of that era, it was sung by wandering minstrels.

of the Cid; about 1140), an epic poem about the hero Rodrigo Díaz de Vivar.

In the 1200's a new type of poetry began to take the place of the minstrel form. This was "clerical" or "learned" poetry, so called because the most learned people of the time—the clergy—wrote it. The greatest poet in the clerical form was the monk Gonzalo de Berceo, the first Castilian poet known to us by name.

The 1200's saw great intellectual growth. King Alfonso X of Castile, called "the Wise," gathered many scholars to write important works in history, science, and law. This marked the first time learned prose was written in Spanish rather than Latin.

The first prose fiction appeared in the 1300's. King Alfonso's nephew, the Infante Don Juan Manuel, wrote *Conde Lucanor* (*Count Lucanor*; 1335), a collection of 51 stories, each with a moral. The 1300's also saw the work of the most original Spanish poet of the time: Juan Ruiz. His masterwork is *El libro de buen amor* (*The Book of Good Love*), a mixture of fables, love stories, legends, satires (writing that ridicules human vices), and other forms.

King Alfonso X was a patron of literature and learning. During his reign (1252–84), Spanish was first used for scholarly writings.

Late Middle Ages (1400–1500)

The 1400's were both the high point and the end of the Middle Ages. Poetry had belonged to the minstrels and the priests. Now it belonged to troubadours, who sang of courtly love. Under Juan II of Castile, the *Cancionero de Baena* (*Songbook of Baena*) was compiled about 1445.

Romances, or ballads, are considered among the richest expressions of Spanish literature. The oldest romances are anonymous poems of the 1300's and 1400's, which were sung to the accompaniment of a musical instrument. These romances have inspired some of Spain's greatest poets.

An outstanding poet of the early 1400's was Íñigo López de Mendoza, Marquis of Santillana, who was known for his sonnets. Another was Jorge Manrique, known for his touching *Coplas por la muerte de su padre* (*Couplets on the Death of His Father*; 1476).

In prose there was Alfonso Martínez de Toledo, a moral and witty satirist. In *El Corbacho* (1438) he accuses women of trickery. Among the greatest Spanish works of all time is the novel *La Celestina* (1499) by Fernando de Rojas. It is the story of two young lovers whose lives are controlled by the greedy and evil woman called Celestina.

The first complete plays in Spanish literature date from the 1400's, such as the short religious dramas of Gómez Manrique. Two playwrights straddle the late 1400's and early 1500's: Juan del Encina and Gil Vicente. Encina, the father of Spanish drama, was also a composer and poet well schooled in the works of Latin and Italian writers. His most important plays are pastoral love dramas written in the early 1500's. A Spanish-Portuguese actor, director, and dramatist, Vicente borrowed from such popular literature as ballads and books of chivalry. His *Comedia del viudo* (*Play About the Widower*; 1514) is a humorous play about the marriage of two brothers to a widower's daughters. Bringing together poetry, music, and dance in drama, Encina and Vicente provided a solid base for later Spanish theater.

Renaissance (1500–1550)

The Renaissance was a cultural revival of the literature, art, and learning of classical Greece and Rome. It began in Italy in the 1300's and reached Spain in the late 1400's. The early Renaissance in Spain saw the publication of the first Castilian grammar book—the first written for a modern European language—by Antonio de Nebrija in 1492.

Don Quixote charges at a windmill—which he imagines to be a giant—with disastrous results in this scene from *Don Quixote*, the great novel by Cervantes.

In lyric poetry the first important figure of the 1500's was Garcilaso de la Vega. His first eclogue (a type of pastoral poem) describes the sad love affair of two shepherds and is regarded as his masterpiece.

Fray Luis de León, a professor of theology at the University of Salamanca, wrote moral and religious poems. A leading figure in Spain's mystic school, his greatest prose masterpiece is *De los nombres de Cristo* (*The Names of Christ*; 1583). Two of Spain's greatest saints, Teresa of Ávila and John of the Cross, are famed for their writings about the mystical union of the soul with God.

▶ THE GOLDEN AGE (1550–1680)

During the period known as the Golden Age, many of Spain's greatest literary figures wrote, and all the arts flourished.

The Novel. The books of chivalry were a kind of novel, with plots built on the marvelous adventures of pure and brave knights. The most famous of these novels is *Amadís de Gaula* (*Amadís of Gaul*; 1508), by Garcí Rodríguez de Montalvo.

Another popular type of fiction was the Moorish novel, which concerned the heroic adventures of Moors. A famous example is the anonymous *Historia del Abencerraje* (*Story of the Abencerraje*; 1565).

Pastoral novels are artificial in manner. They tell of the loves of shepherds and nymphs who often represent real-life people. The most famous pastoral novel is *La Diana* (1559) by Jorge de Montemayor.

The picaresque novel originated in Spain. It features *pícaros* (rogues), who usually tell about their adventurous lives as outlaws or petty criminals. The anonymous *Lazarillo de Tormes* (1554) is the first example of this kind of novel. Another rogue appears in *Guzmán de Alfarache* (1599–1604), by Mateo Alemán. This novel gives a bitter portrait of life in several Spanish and Italian cities.

It took the genius of Miguel de Cervantes to combine all these types of novels into one novel of great scope, *Don Quixote* (Part I, 1605; Part II, 1615). It is a masterpiece of world literature. As a parody of the already old-fashioned chivalric novels, *Don Quixote* outwardly tells of the adventures of an old gentleman, Don Quixote, and his peasant squire, Sancho Panza. But the story is far more. It is a criticism of life and human nature in Cervantes' day.

Cervantes is Spain's greatest literary figure. It has been said that his reputation could stand on his *Novelas ejemplares* (*Exemplary Tales*; 1613), which are short stories of wit and wisdom, or on his satirical short plays, *Entremeses* (*Interludes*; 1615).

Drama. The most important figure in Golden Age drama is Lope de Vega, at different times a soldier, priest, and doctor of theology. Lope wrote little prose, but he produced a huge number of poems and dramas. In *Arte nuevo de hacer comedias* (*New Art of Writing Plays*; 1609), he said that plays should be a mixture of comic and tragic elements and did not have to follow classical rules. Lope is credited with as many as 1,800 full-length plays. Among his best-known works is *Fuenteovejuna* (1619), the story of a town that rebels against a corrupt governor. Another important play is *Peribáñez* (1614).

Tirso de Molina, a monk, was the best of Lope's followers, excellent in both comedies and serious plays. In his *Burlador de Sevilla* (*Seducer of Seville*; 1630), he created the immortal figure of Don Juan.

Another great playwright of the Golden Age was the Mexican-born Juan Ruiz de Alarcón. His best play is *La verdad sospechosa* (*The Suspicious Truth*; 1630).

The last outstanding Golden Age playwright was Pedro Calderón de la Barca, a priest. He wrote some 180 plays, more formal and elaborate in style than those of his contemporaries. *La vida es sueño* (*Life is a Dream*; 1635), *El alcalde de Zalamea* (*The Mayor of Zalamea*; 1643), and some short religious dramas are the best of Calderón's output.

Poetry. The great poet Luis de Góngora wrote in a highly cultured and complicated style. His work can be understood only by someone knowledgeable in classical Greek and Latin languages and mythology. His most outstanding work is the ornate and beautiful *Soledades* (*Solitudes*; 1613).

Luis de Góngora was among the greatest poets of Spain's Golden Age. He used an extremely complex poetic style that became known as Gongorism. This portrait of Góngora was painted by one of the outstanding artists of the Golden Age, Diego Velázquez.

Francisco de Quevedo wrote some of the finest love poetry in Spanish literature. He is known for his witty and involved style in prose. His most famous work is the picaresque novel *El buscón* (*The Swindler*; about 1608). His *Sueños* (*Visions*; about 1610) is a masterful satire of the society of his time.

Contemporary with Quevedo was Baltasar Gracián, a keen critic of his times. Besides his philosophical treatises and moral maxims, Gracián wrote an allegorical novel, *El criticón* (*The Big Critic*; 1651–57).

Epic poetry was also popular in the Golden Age. The best example is Alonso de Ercilla's *La Araucana* (1569–89), about the Spanish conquest of the Araucanian Indians of Chile. The patriotic poetry of Fernando de Herrera is filled with rich imagery. Herrera was the founder of the Seville school of poetry, which perfected the sonnet form.

1700's

When the French king Philip V came to the Spanish throne in 1701, Spanish writers began to imitate French writers of that time, who were inspired by the writings of classical Greece and Rome. This neoclassicism, or new classicism, stifled the literary creativity of the traditionally free-spirited Spaniards. The 1700's produced no literary figures equal to those of the Renaissance or the Golden Age.

1800's

Romanticism. Literature called "romantic" has to do with the imagination and emotions rather than reason and intellect. A romantic movement arose in Spain about 1830.

The first truly romantic writer in Spain was the Duke of Rivas. His themes revolve around Spain's legends and heroic past. His most famous work is the drama *Don Álvaro o la fuerza del sino* (*Don Alvaro, or the Power of Fate*; 1835). Antonio García Gutiérrez is famous for his play *El trovador* (*The Troubadour*; 1836). José Zorilla wrote many plays, of which the best known is *Don Juan Tenorio* (1844).

Both Zorilla and the Duke of Rivas also wrote poetry. Another romantic poet was José de Espronceda. One of his best works is *El diablo mundo* (*The Devilish World*; 1841).

The outstanding figure of Spanish romanticism was Gustavo Adolfo Bécquer. His poems, collected in *Rimas* (*Rhymes*; 1860), reflect his dark and sentimental view of life.

The most important type of prose within Spanish romanticism was *costumbrismo*— short sketches of contemporary life that range from the quaint to the satirical. The journalist Mariano José de Larra, whose pen name was Fígaro, excelled at this kind of writing.

Realism. A literary movement known as realism began about the mid-1850's. Realist writers wanted to reproduce current reality in all its aspects. Many of their novels took place in their native regions of Spain.

Cecilia Böhl de Faber, a writer from Andalusia, in southern Spain, wrote the first realistic novels under the pen name Fernán Caballero. Another Andalusian, Pedro Antonio de Alarcón, is remembered for his short stories and his witty novel *El sombrero de tres picos* (*The Three-Cornered Hat*; 1874). Juan Valera, also an Andalusian, wrote *Pepita Jiménez* (1874), a novel about a young man who leaves the priesthood to marry a widow.

These novelists described the south of Spain. José María de Pereda wrote of the long-forgotten northern provinces, especially his native Santander. His *Peñas arriba* (1895) tells of a middle-class city man who finds himself in a different world—the mountain country, with its own traditions, language, and vivid landscape.

The greatest Spanish novelist of the 1800's was Benito Pérez Galdós. Free of regionalist tendencies, his novels deal with Spanish history and the contemporary life of Madrid. *Episodios nacionales* (*National Episodes*; 1873–1912), a series of 46 novels, show how history affects ordinary people. *Doña Perfecta* (1876) shows the tragedy that comes from religious bigotry. Several novels of Madrid portray the conflicts of a city. Of these, *Fortunata y Jacinta* (1886–87) is perhaps the best Spanish novel of the 1800's. In the four-volume series *Torquemada* (1889–95), Pérez Galdós deals with the internal conflicts of a miser. *Misericordia* (*Compassion*; 1897) concerns Christian idealism.

Naturalism. Several Spanish novelists were influenced by the French writer Émile Zola, who wrote in a style called naturalism. Like the realists, the naturalists wrote about ordinary Spaniards, but they emphasized the hard and unhappy lives of the lower social classes. They tried to describe their characters in a scientific manner. Some of Pérez Galdós' best novels contain elements of naturalism.

A leading naturalistic writer was Emilia Pardo Bazán, a native of Galicia, in northwestern Spain. Her best-known novels are *Los pazos de Ulloa* (*The Ulloa Estate*; 1886) and its sequel, *La madre naturaleza* (*Mother Nature*; 1887).

Leopoldo Alas, whose pen name was Clarín, was one of the best novelists and critics of his time. His best novel is probably *La Regenta* (1884–85), a psychological study of a tragic female character, Ana Ozores.

The most popular and internationally famous of the naturalists was Vicente Blasco Ibáñez. His novels *Sangre y arena* (*Blood and Sand*; 1908) and *Los cuatro jinetes del Apocalipsis* (*The Four Horsemen of the Apocalypse*; 1916) have been filmed several times. However, his real value rests on novels set in his native Valencia, notably *La barraca* (*The Cabin*; 1898).

Early 1900's

The Generation of 1898. In 1898, Spain lost the Spanish-American War and the last of its empire. A group of writers and critics, called the Generation of 1898, concerned themselves with the nature of Spain and its decline since the Golden Age. Although their examination of Spain's problems produced no political or social reforms, it left a rich literary legacy.

The most forceful and original spokesman for the Generation of 1898 was Miguel de Unamuno. He struggled not only with the question of Spain's problems but also with the

Benito Pérez Galdós was a leading Spanish novelist of the 1800's. He wrote historical novels and works about contemporary life.

problem of belief in God and what that belief does to one as an individual. Unamuno expressed himself in various literary forms: play, poem, novel, and especially essay. His best-known essay is *Del sentimiento trágico de la vida* (*The Tragic Sense of Life*; 1913).

Azorín, whose real name was José Martínez Ruiz, was the foremost literary critic of his generation. He traveled throughout Spain, seeking the eternal values of his country. Ramón del Valle-Inclán was a delicate stylist and bitter satirist. Several of his books give poetic interpretations of his native region, Galicia. His four *Sonatas* (1902–05) have a sad beauty. In other plays and novels he presents a grotesque vision of Spain.

While style was the main concern of Valle-Inclán, plot mattered most to the Basque novelist Pío Baroja. Baroja wrote in a simple, matter-of-fact style, revealing everything he thought wrong with Europe in general and with Spain in particular.

In poetry the most important figure was Antonio Machado. In his lyrics he tried to capture the history and spirit of Spain. He described his native province in *Campos de Castilla* (*Castilian Fields*; 1912).

In contrast to this deeply poetic writer is the dramatist Jacinto Benavente, winner of the Nobel Prize for literature in 1922. His quietly satirical plays, such as *Los intereses creados* (*The Bonds of Interest*; 1907), deal mostly with the middle-class citizens of Madrid.

Later Generations. Two outstanding writers, Juan Ramón Jiménez and José Ortega y Gasset, belong to what may be called the Gen-

Poet and dramatist Federico García Lorca was at the center of a group of writers known as the Generation of 1927. His collection of poems called *Gypsy Ballads* established his reputation throughout the Spanish-speaking world. García Lorca was killed at age 38 in the Spanish Civil War.

eration of 1914. Jiménez received the Nobel Prize for literature (1956) for his lifelong dedication to lyric poetry. He wrote in a personal style, carefully polished yet natural. Among his works is a children's classic about the life of a donkey, *Platero y yo* (*Platero and I*; 1917).

Ortega y Gasset's *La rebelión de las masas* (*The Revolt of the Masses*; 1930) deals with the modern "mass man," who has no individuality because society does not allow it. A philosopher, Ortega y Gasset also wrote brilliant essays on aspects of modern culture.

A later group of writers is sometimes called the Generation of 1927. These writers brought a new lyricism and poetic national feeling to their writing. The best known is Federico García Lorca. He is famous for *Romancero gitano* (*Gypsy Ballads*; 1928), poems that capture the

DAYS OF THE WEEK

Monday	*lunes*
Tuesday	*martes*
Wednesday	*miércoles*
Thursday	*jueves*
Friday	*viernes*
Saturday	*sábado*
Sunday	*domingo*

NUMBERS

one	*uno*	six	*seis*	eleven	*once*
two	*dos*	seven	*siete*	twelve	*doce*
three	*tres*	eight	*ocho*	twenty	*veinte*
four	*cuatro*	nine	*nueve*	twenty-one	*veinte y uno*
five	*cinco*	ten	*diez*	one hundred	*cien*

SOME WORDS IN EVERYDAY USE

book	*libro*	girl	*muchacha*
boy	*muchacho*	house	*casa*
cat	*gato*	mother	*madre*
church	*iglesia*	paper	*papel*
dog	*perro*	pencil	*lápiz*
family	*familia*	school	*escuela*
father	*padre*	time	*tiempo*

MONTHS OF THE YEAR

January	*enero*	July	*julio*
February	*febrero*	August	*agosto*
March	*marzo*	September	*septiembre*
April	*abril*	October	*octubre*
May	*mayo*	November	*noviembre*
June	*junio*	December	*diciembre*

color and magic of his native Granada. His *Poeta en Nueva York* (*Poet in New York*; 1940) is another collection of poems. García Lorca's plays, such as *Bodas de sangre* (*Blood Wedding*; 1933) and *La casa de Bernarda Alba* (*The House of Bernarda Alba*; 1936), have been produced all over the world.

Later 1900's

The Spanish Civil War of 1936–39 brought great loss of life and talent to Spain. Many Spanish writers have written about the war and its aftermath.

The modern Spanish writer Camilo José Cela is known for the grim realism and biting satire of his novels. One of his best-known works is his first novel, *Pascual Duarte's Family*. Cela was awarded the Nobel Prize for literature in 1989.

Poetry and Drama. The poets Pedro Salinas and Jorge Guillén tried to attain "pure poetry" in their early writings. Their later poems show their concern with life in the modern world. Vicente Aleixandre, a surrealist poet, received the Nobel Prize for literature in 1977. The poetry of Blas de Otero and José Hierro reveal their unhappiness with social conditions. Two of the better-known poets of the Generation of 1950 are Angel González and Claudio Rodríguez.

Antonio Buero Vallejo is considered the best contemporary dramatist. His play *Historia de una escalera* (*Story of a Staircase*; 1949) describes the unhappy lives of several families who live in an old apartment house in Madrid. His many social dramas generally end on a hopeful note. In contrast, Alfonso Sastre's plays of social protest are usually more pessimistic.

Prose Fiction. One of the best Spanish novelists of the 1900's was Ramón Sender. His masterpiece is *Requiem por un campesino español* (*Requiem for a Spanish Peasant*; 1960), in which a priest causes the death of a young man.

Camilo José Cela won the Nobel Prize for literature in 1989, mainly because of his famous novel *La familia de Pascual Duarte* (*Pascual Duarte's Family*; 1942). It concerns the tragic life of a criminal who does not know why he commits a series of crimes. Another important novel by Cela is *La colmena* (*The Hive*; 1951), a satire.

José María Gironella uses realistic descriptions in his long novels about the causes, events, and aftermath of the Civil War. An-other major novelist of the 1900's was Miguel Delibes. His novels reveal his unhappiness with the decline of rural Castile. They also deal with people's relationship to their environment. His best novel is probably *Cinco horas con Mario* (*Five Hours with Mario*; 1966), in which a woman talks to her husband's corpse.

Nada (*Nothing*; 1945) is Carmen Laforet's first and best novel. It tells the story of a young woman who comes to Barcelona to find her own identity. The novelist Ana María Matute has also written short stories and children's stories.

Juan Goytisolo criticizes the Civil War, the Catholic Church, Spanish society and politics, and Western civilization in such works as *Reivindicación del Conde don Julián* (*Vindication of Count Julian*; 1970) and *Makbara* (1980). The novels of Carlos Rojas concern the devilish and the supernatural, religious crises, and the search for social justice.

Nonfiction. The teacher and philosopher Xavier Zubiri influenced a generation of contemporary thinkers, notably Pedro Laín Entralgo. Laín's profound essays on philosophy, science, and literature were collected in *La espera y la esperanza* (*Waiting and Hope*; 1957) and other major works. Fernando Savater is among the most outstanding of more recent philosophers. He has also written fiction and drama. One of his best books is *La tarea del héroe* (*The Hero's Task*; 1982).

MARGARITA UCELAY DA CAL
Barnard College
REVIEWED BY DONALD W. BLEZNICK
University of Cincinnati

SPAIN, MUSIC OF

Music is a part of everyday life in Spain. The music of Spain is, above all, its folk music, which is made and enjoyed by the people themselves. But through the years Spanish musicians and composers have also created much art music (sometimes called classical music)—for church and court as well as for the opera house and concert hall.

▶FOLK MUSIC

Spanish folk music is as varied as the regions from which it comes. It can be joyous or sad, peaceful or intense. Folk music is heard at weddings and funerals, at *romerías* (festive pilgrimages to rural shrines), at *verbenas* (street festivals), and at solemn religious processions.

Andalusia, in southern Spain, is known for the music that accompanies the region's traditional flamenco, the best known of the gypsy dances. Flamenco dance forms include the dignified *alegrías*, the humorous *bulerías*, and the energetic *farruca*. Andalusians are known for the perfection of their guitar playing, their rich store of folk songs, and their skill with castanets and tambourines.

Asturias and Galicia, in northern Spain, produce music for the *pericote* and the *muñeira*, the regional dances. The *gaita*, or bagpipes, and drums of various sizes are instruments typical of these regions. In Aragon and Catalonia, to the east, the *jota* and the *sardana* are danced to the music of the *fluviol*, or Spanish flute, and drums.

Spanish performing artists have gained worldwide recognition. Through his concerts and recordings, guitarist Andrés Segovia did much to establish the popularity of the classical guitar.

A flamenco dancer embodies the drama of Spain's traditional folk music. Flamenco dance, which is usually accompanied by guitar, originated in the region of southern Spain called Andalusia.

▶ART MUSIC

Music in Spain at the beginning of the Christian era was created mainly for use in services of the Roman Catholic Church. After the invasion of Spain by the Moors, who brought with them their own music and many new instruments, a secular (nonreligious) music developed. This was the courtly music of the troubadours, heard in Spain's medieval castles, and the music of the *juglares*, minstrels who went from town to town composing for the common people.

The Renaissance. In the 1500's, Spanish church music reached great heights with the works of Tomás Luis de Victoria, who wrote a masterful *Requiem Mass* (1605), Cristóbal de Morales, and Francisco Guerrero. Antonio de Cabezón was the greatest organ composer of the period.

Secular music continued to develop in the courts of Castile and Catalonia. The most popular instrument of the period was the *vihuela*, an early version of the guitar. Many collections of music for *vihuela*, and later for guitar, were published. Among the best known were *The Master* (1536) by Luis de Milán, *Songs of the Sirens* (1547) by Enríquez de Valderrábano, and *Orpheus' Lyre* (1554) by Miguel de Fuenllana.

The major forms of secular music were the *romance* and the *villancico*. *Romances* were songs or ballads based on legends or folktales. The word *villancico* comes from *villano*, or "villager." These songs were generally part-songs with popular themes. Secular music also included music written for plays. For 200 years, playwrights used music in their drama. Foremost among these writers was Juan del Encina, who also composed the music for his plays.

The 1600's and 1700's. The marriage of music and drama continued in the 1600's with

Left: Isaac Albéniz, seen here at the piano with his wife, was a virtuoso pianist as well as a composer. His masterpiece *Iberia* is a suite of piano pieces that evoke Spanish places and scenes.

Below: Manuel de Falla, shown here in a drawing by Pablo Picasso, brought Spanish music to new heights. His compositions draw upon Spain's folk music traditions.

the works of Pedro Calderón de la Barca. Because Calderón alternated dialogue with music and dance, some of his works are acknowledged as forerunners of the *zarzuela*, a kind of musical play that became very popular with Spanish audiences.

Instrumental music also thrived during this period. Organist-composers Francisco Correa de Araujo and Juan José Cabanilles elaborated on the simpler organ styles of the 1500's. Chamber music (music performed by small ensembles) flourished at the Spanish court.

Opera came to maturity in the 1700's. *A Rare Thing* (1786), by Vicente Martin y Soler, is one of Spain's operatic masterpieces.

The 1800's and 1900's. The *zarzuela* increased in popularity during the 1800's. A master of the form was Francisco Asenjo Barbieri. His *zarzuelas*, such as *Bread and Bulls* (1864), often employed themes from Spanish folk music.

The use of Spanish themes to create a "national" music was encouraged by the composer and music scholar Felipe Pedrell. His writings and teachings influenced three of Spain's greatest composers—Isaac Albéniz, Enrique Granados, and Manuel de Falla. Albéniz' masterpiece *Iberia* (1909) is a suite of twelve piano pieces that capture in music the special characteristics of the regions and cities of Spain. Granados' opera *Goyescas* (1916), inspired by works of the Spanish painter Francisco Goya, evokes social life in Spain in the 1700's.

De Falla is considered the outstanding Spanish composer of his day. His music incorporates Spanish dances and folklore and reflects the spirit of his native Andalusia. Among his most widely known works are two ballets, *Love, the Sorcerer* (1915) and *The Three-Cornered Hat* (1919), and a composition for piano and orchestra, *Nights in the Gardens of Spain* (1909–15).

Other modern composers, notably Federico Mompou, Joaquim Homs, Xavier Montsalvatge, and Joaquín Rodrigo, continued to draw on Spanish themes. Rodrigo achieved worldwide fame for his brilliant *Concerto of Aranjuez* (1939), a concerto for guitar and orchestra. A later generation of composers, including Luis de Pablo and Cristóbal Halffter, embraced modern techniques such as serialism, producing music that was less identifiably Spanish.

In the realm of performance, Spain has given the world a number of outstanding musicians: the singers Plácido Domingo and Victoria de los Angeles; the pianists José Iturbi, Amparo Iturbi, and Alicia de Larrocha; the classical guitarist Andrés Segovia; and the cellists Gaspar Cassado and Pablo Casals.

RAMÓN MARTÍNEZ OCARANZA
Conservatory of Music, Mexico City

The mysterious explosion of the USS *Maine* in Cuban waters in 1898 led the United States to declare war on Spain. Although the war lasted less than four months, it made the United States a world power and cost Spain the last important colonies of its once vast empire—the Philippines, Guam, Puerto Rico, and Cuba.

SPANISH-AMERICAN WAR

A terrific explosion shattered the quiet harbor of Havana, Cuba, at 9:40 P.M. on February 15, 1898. The United States battleship *Maine* had blown up, costing the lives of 260 American crewmen. Experts now think that the blast was caused by a ship's fire that set off its ammunition supply. But at the time, the cause was unclear, and the explosion started what John M. Hay, the U.S. ambassador to Great Britain, called "a splendid little war."

▶ BACKGROUND OF THE WAR

In 1895 the Cuban War for Independence broke out against Spanish colonial rule. Spain put down this revolt with extreme brutality, killing thousands of innocent civilians as well as rebels. In the United States there was widespread sympathy for the Cuban people by 1897. Newspapers such as William Randolph Hearst's New York *Journal* and Joseph Pulitzer's New York *World* printed gruesome, and often highly exaggerated, accounts of Spanish atrocities. This "yellow journalism," or sensationalized reporting style, was intended to whip up war fever in the United States, and it worked.

To the many Americans who believed that it was the destiny of the United States to expand beyond its continental frontiers, the Cuban revolt presented the United States with an excuse for a war with Spain. Yet President William McKinley remained calm. Rather than demand war, he persuaded Spain to grant limited self-government to Cuba, which touched off further rioting in Havana by Spanish sympathizers.

In January 1898 the USS *Maine* was sent to Cuba to protect American lives there; it was exploded three weeks later. By April 19, the U.S. Congress had recognized Cuba's independence, and by April 25 Congress declared that a state of war had existed with Spain for four days. Americans rallied to the slogan, "Remember the *Maine*!"

▶ THE BATTLE OF MANILA BAY

The war to free Cuba actually began on the other side of the world—in the Philippine Islands, a Spanish possession in the Pacific. U.S. Assistant Secretary of the Navy Theodore Roosevelt, acting on his own initiative in the absence of his superior, ordered Commodore George Dewey and his fleet to proceed from Hong Kong to capture or destroy the Spanish fleet in the Philippines.

On May 1, 1898, Dewey's Asiatic Squadron bore down on the Spanish vessels in Manila Bay. "You may fire when you are ready, Gridley," Dewey calmly told Captain Charles V. Gridley, commander of the flagship *Olympia*. The Americans fired often and well, destroying all of the Spanish ships. No American ships or crewmen were lost, and Dewey became an overnight hero.

▶ CUBA BLOCKADED

In the meantime, the main American battle fleet, led by Rear Admiral William T. Sampson, went in search of the Spanish fleet in Cuban waters. The Spanish fleet managed to slip by the American vessels and into Santiago harbor on Cuba's southeastern side. However, Admiral Sampson then blocked the harbor to keep the Spanish from getting back out again.

THE CUBAN MELODRAMA.

"Yellow journalists" portrayed the Cuban situation as a theatrical melodrama—with the United States (the hero) protecting Cuba (the damsel in distress) from Spain (the evil villain).

The U.S. Navy was now ready to convoy Army troops to Cuba. Under the command of General William R. Shafter, the Fifth Army Corps, of about 25,000 troops, was assembled at Tampa, Florida. Among its most colorful regiments was the First Volunteer Cavalry, recruited by General Leonard Wood and the newly appointed Lieutenant Colonel Theodore Roosevelt, who had resigned his post at the Navy Department to join in the fighting. Because so many of this regiment's recruits were cowboys, they were called the Rough Riders.

As it happened, the War Department's organization was so poor that the troops were issued woolen winter uniforms for a campaign in the tropics. Furthermore, the transport ships did not have enough room for all of the troops and none for the cavalry's horses, which they had to leave behind.

▶ THE FIGHT FOR SANTIAGO

A force of about 18,000 troops landed unopposed near the city of Santiago, Cuba. In a hail of rifle bullets, action began at nearby Las Guásimas. The Americans pushed on through narrow jungle trails until they reached the village of El Caney and the ridges known as Kettle Hill and San Juan Hill. There the enemy waited in blockhouses and trenches.

Spanish resistance was stubborn as the Americans moved forward and took El Caney on July 1. Below San Juan Hill the Rough Riders were pinned down by heavy Spanish rifle fire. They waited for reinforcements and then stormed San Juan Hill, where they won a decisive victory.

On July 3, Spanish Admiral Pascual Cervera and his fleet tried to slip past the American blockade that had kept them in Santiago harbor since the end of May. But American warships, under the command of Rear Admiral Sampson and Commodore Winfield Scott Schley, moved quickly and sank the Spanish fleet in less than four hours. Spanish troops in Cuba, thus deprived of reinforcements, surrendered on July 17.

On July 25, the Americans invaded Puerto Rico and captured it with little resistance. Back in the Philippines, U.S. troops entered Manila on August 13 and occupied the city, unaware that an armistice signed with Spain the previous day had ended the war.

Of the more than 5,500 Americans who had died during the war, more than 90 percent perished not in battle but from diseases, such as dysentery, malaria, and yellow fever.

▶ RESULTS OF THE WAR

A peace treaty was signed in Paris on December 10, 1898, and was ratified by the U.S. Congress the following February. Although the war had ended quickly, it had far-reaching effects. Spain ceded the Philippines, Guam, and Puerto Rico to the United States, which almost overnight gained a vast colonial empire with a population of 8 million. Cuba was under the control of the U.S. military until 1902, when Cuba became independent. The following year, the United States built a naval base at Guantánamo Bay, and the U.S. Navy grew in strength. Furthermore, the war had made evident the need for a faster route between the Atlantic and Pacific oceans. In 1904, under the direction of Theodore Roosevelt, who by then had become president, the United States began building a canal across Panama.

FAIRFAX DOWNEY
Author, *Sound of the Guns*

Reviewed by ALBERT MARRIN
Author, *The Spanish-American War*

See also CUBA; PHILIPPINES; PUERTO RICO; REED, WALTER; ROOSEVELT, THEODORE; TERRITORIAL EXPANSION OF THE UNITED STATES.

SPANISH ARMADA

In 1588, King Philip II of Spain, a Roman Catholic and the mightiest ruler in the Christian world, set out to crush the opposition of Queen Elizabeth I of England, Europe's most powerful Protestant monarch. For many years Spain had sought to dominate England and restore Catholicism there.

In July 1588, determined to overpower England, Philip sent a fleet of 130 ships, known as the Armada, from Lisbon into the English Channel to assist an invasion of England from the Spanish Netherlands (centered in present-day Belgium). The Armada was soon attacked by a fleet of English warships, which, though smaller, were superior sailing vessels. During nine days of engagements, the Spaniards retained their formation. But when they anchored off the coast of France to board additional troops, they found that their invasion force was not yet ready to sail. The English then inflicted considerable damage on the Armada before a strong southwesterly wind drove it into the North Sea.

With no clear plan for recovery, the Spanish commanders then ordered a retreat to Spain via the hazardous northern route around the British Isles. This proved disastrous. A succession of violent and unseasonal storms lashed the fleet as it passed north of Scotland and down the west coast of Ireland. Ship after ship was smashed or driven ashore. Only a remnant of the once-powerful Armada returned to Spain.

The defeat of the Armada caused a significant loss of power for Spain, while England and its formidable navy—led by such brave captains as Sir Francis Drake and Martin Frobisher—grew in influence and prestige.

JEREMY BLACK
University of Exeter

SPANISH CIVIL WAR

On July 17, 1936, an uprising of troops in Spanish Morocco sparked a murderous civil war in Spain. After three years of fighting, revolutionary forces toppled Spain's elected republican government and installed a dictatorship under General Francisco Franco that endured for nearly forty years.

The Spanish Civil War resulted from an ideological clash between extreme left- and right-wing political groups. The liberal Republicans (also called Loyalists) included socialists, labor unionists, landless peasants, intellectuals, communists, and radical Marxists. The conservative Nationalists were mostly members of the military, the clergy, wealthy landowners, and fascists belonging to the Falange political party.

Hostilities between the two groups were long-standing. In 1931, after years of social upheaval, Spain's king, Alfonso XIII, was banished from the country, and a new liberal government proclaimed the Second Republic (an earlier attempt had failed in 1874). It then passed many social and economic reforms. But the conservatives regained power after the 1933 elections and immediately overturned many of the liberal reforms. This caused a popular uprising, which the government brutally suppressed. When power shifted back to the liberals in 1936, General Franco staged a revolt that quickly spread throughout Spain. The liberal government, known as the Popular Front, raised an army of its own and a brutal war began. By the end of 1936, the Nationalists had conquered the western half of Spain, and the country was split in two. The war ended when Nationalist forces occupied Madrid on March 28, 1939.

The Spanish Civil War attracted enormous interest worldwide. The Nationalists received foreign support from Fascist Italy and Nazi Germany, while the Republicans received aid from the Soviet Union. The United States and most other western powers did not intervene, but public sympathies generally supported the Republicans, and thousands of idealistic foreigners opposed to fascism died fighting for their cause.

JEREMY BLACK
University of Exeter

See also FRANCO, FRANCISCO.

SPANISH SUCCESSION, WAR OF THE. See SPAIN (History).

SPARTACUS. See SLAVERY (Profiles).

SPEARE, ELIZABETH GEORGE. See CHILDREN'S LITERATURE (Profiles).

SPECIAL OLYMPICS

Special Olympics is an international program of athletic training and competition for children and adults with mental retardation. Special Olympics is not a single athletic event or a once-every-four-years gathering. Rather, it is a continuous program that brings the joy of sports to millions of families, offering people with mental retardation the opportunity to participate in a rewarding community event.

History. Special Olympics was founded by Eunice Kennedy Shriver, sister of President John F. Kennedy. In the early 1960's, she noted the lack of opportunities for physical fitness training for people with mental retardation. She began a day camp in the backyard of her home in Rockville, Maryland, that offered sports and games to children with mental retardation. From that first camp—dubbed "Camp Shriver"—grew the idea of a more formal program of sports training and competition. The first Special Olympics Games were held on July 19–20, 1968, at Soldier Field in Chicago, Illinois. The Games drew 1,000 athletes of all ages from the United States, Canada, and France. The Special Olympics movement was born.

Through Special Olympics, people with mental retardation can experience the joy and sense of accomplishment that come with participating in many kinds of athletic events.

Special Olympics Today. Special Olympics now includes more than 1 million athletes in over 150 countries participating in 16,000 events each year. In the United States, each state has its own chapter, and many communities have local chapters as well. The Special Olympics World Games, a gathering of athletes from countries all over the world, are held every two years. Like the regular Olympics, the Special Olympics World Games alternate between Summer and Winter Games.

The athletes participate in more than just the games; they serve on the boards of directors at all levels of the organization, helping guide the movement in new and exciting directions. They also serve as spokespersons for the organization, appearing on television and speaking before students, business leaders, and civic groups. Many athletes receive training as coaches and are certified to hold team and individual practice sessions, preparing their teams for competition. Athletes may also be trained and certified as game officials. Volunteers have become a vital part of the Special Olympics movement; families, friends, celebrities, and other supporters donate their time and effort to help organize athletic events.

Special Olympics has developed the Unified Sports Program, which groups people with and without mental retardation in teams based on skill level. This approach has helped break down negative stereotypes about people with mental retardation.

From July 1998 to July 1999, Special Olympics celebrated its 30th anniversary. Activities included carrying a torch along the Great Wall of China and a concert at Egypt's pyramids.

Special Olympics athletes have accomplished far more than most people thought was possible in 1968. Through the years, the athletes have proved themselves capable of athletic performances equal to those of people without mental retardation. Their spirit and determination is given voice in the Special Olympics' motto: "Let me win. But if I cannot win, let me be brave in the attempt."

CHRIS PRIVETT
Media Relations Manager
Special Olympics, Inc.

SPEECH

Speech is a most valuable possession. People use it to make friends; and it helps them obtain the things they need. With speech people can persuade, inform, and amuse. Speech is a powerful weapon. Throughout history it has influenced the way people behave and has changed the course of nations.

A person's speech tells a great deal about the speaker. It shows personality and education. Speech can indicate the speaker's feelings about other people.

Good speech depends on what is said and how it is said. Speech is made up of sounds blended into syllables, of syllables blended into words, and of words blended into phrases and sentences. This final blending must be acceptable to listeners. The speaker should use a clear, pleasant voice and say words distinctly and loudly enough so that listeners can understand them.

Informal Speech. A person's speech changes according to the situation. When talking to family or close friends, for example, one would speak naturally and freely. Speech may include some slang expressions. On other occasions a more formal pattern of speech would be used.

Good speech cannot make up for a lack of ideas or for ideas of little value. In daily life the ideas expressed may be simply those that have to do with the business of living. Frequently, however, people carry on friendly conversations and discussions in which they share ideas on many subjects.

Good conversationalists are usually curious about the world and interested in people. They listen, observe, and read. They have their own opinions, but they respect the opinions of others. They support their opinions with facts.

Public Speaking. Occasionally it is necessary to speak before a group. The speaker must be well prepared. He or she must understand the topic clearly, selecting and organizing the ideas that will interest listeners most.

Some speakers write their speeches and then either say them from memory or read them. Others make notes that are sometimes just key words. Usually the best way is to give a speech without the use of notes. To do this, the speaker keeps a plan in mind and practices giving the speech before the presentation. People like to have a speaker look at them, and the speaker gets clues from the audience. Their expressions tell how well the talk is being received.

If note cards are used, key words, phrases, or short sentences can suggest the important areas of a speech. Quotations should be written out, to give the exact words of their authors. Charts, pictures, and other materials can help illustrate a talk.

When giving a speech, the speaker should stand quietly and appear confident. By beginning with some pleasant remarks, he or she can help to bring about a friendly feeling with the audience. The faces of the members of the audience indicate whether they can hear and understand. If they cannot, the speaker must speak more loudly, slowly, and clearly and present the topic in a different way—perhaps more simply.

The lips, teeth, tongue, jaw, and palate are used to make sounds that then make up syllables and words. The speaker must make sounds distinctly enough to be understood. The blending of sounds into syllables and words is called pronunciation. The best guide for acceptable pronunciation of everyday words is the speaker's ear—trained to listen to how teachers and other educated persons pronounce words. The dictionary is the best guide for unfamiliar words. In using the dictionary, the speaker must recognize syllables and markings for sounds and accent.

▶THE SPEAKING MECHANISM

The human voice is produced by the throat and mouth using the larynx, pharynx, tongue, teeth, and lips. The larynx is a muscular tube in the throat with several sections of stiff cartilage. (The largest section forms a ridge known as the Adam's apple.) The larynx contains the vocal cords that are the source of sound in the voice.

Sound begins when air passes over the muscular vocal cords and makes them vibrate. You can feel the vibrations if you hold your hand to your throat as you speak. When the vocal cords are pulled tight by muscles in the larynx, the vibrations produce a high-pitched sound. When the vocal cords are loosened, they produce a lower tone.

These vibrations are used to teach deaf people to speak. A deaf person cannot hear words, but he or she can "feel" words by touching the throat (and watching the mouth) of someone who is speaking. By imitating what they feel and see, many deaf people can learn to talk.

The cavities of the throat (pharynx) help reinforce the sound coming from the vocal cords. The tongue, teeth, and lips all help shape the sound into syllables and words that are recognized as speech.

Characteristics of the Voice. A voice has volume, pitch, and quality. Volume is related to the energy of the stream of air and to the type of resonance provided. Pitch is related to the tension, length, and thickness of the vocal cords. The vibration of the cords produces vocal tone. Quality depends on tone and on the resonance that reinforces this tone. For instance, if there is not enough nasal resonance, a person sounds like someone who has a cold. When there is too much, it sounds as though the person is talking through the nose.

Pronunciation. In order to speak, one must be able to make different sounds. The consonant sounds P, B, and M are all made with the lips. But they are made in different ways. The sounds P and B are called stops, because the sound is held and then suddenly released. M is called a nasal continuant, because it is resonated in the nose and goes on and on, or continues. P is made without voice. It is pronounced without any vibration of the vocal cords and with the breath stopped briefly by closed lips. M and B are made with voice. If you say P without adding a vowel and put your hand on your larynx, you will feel no vibration. But if you say B in the same way, you will feel vibration. Thus, each consonant has three characteristics: the place where it is made, the way it is made, and the presence or absence of voice.

Vowels are all voiced continuant sounds. They are made by changing the positions of the jaw, lips, and tongue. When you say EE, as in "me," the tongue is bunched in the front of the mouth. But when you say OO, as in "too," the tongue is bunched in the back of the mouth. When you say EE, as in "me," the tongue is high. But when you say the A in "cat," the jaw drops and the tongue is low. For some vowels the lips are more rounded than for others. For instance, to make the sound of UE in "blue," the lips are decidedly rounded, whereas for the sound of EA in "meat," they are spread. The place where the tongue is bunched and the tongue's height at

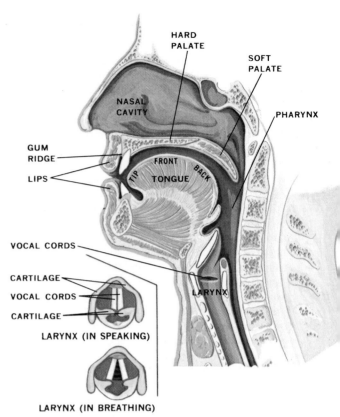

The speaking voice is produced by muscular structures in the throat and mouth. Vocal cords in the larynx are pulled tight and vibrate to produce sound.

that instant are mainly responsible for the differences in vowel sounds.

Consonants and vowels blend together into syllables and words. The pronunciation of words keeps changing because people do not make the effort to keep pronunciation constant. For example, the K in "knife" and "know," the T in "castle," and the B in "lamb" are no longer pronounced. "Nature" now has a CH sound in it. These changes have already taken place. Others are taking place all the time. Many educated Americans now omit (incorrectly) the first R in "surprise" and the N in "government."

The consonants and vowels that are blended into words are then blended into phrases and sentences for purposes of communication. The speaker's expression of ideas, their reception by listeners, and the listeners' reaction make up the cycle of communication.

MARDEL OGILVIE
City University of New York, Lehman College
Reviewed by JOHN H. CORCORAN
Glassboro State College (New Jersey)

A speech therapist can help this youngster overcome her nervousness about not being able to speak clearly by helping her understand what is causing the problem and showing her how to correct it.

SPEECH DISORDERS

People who have some problem with their speech that interferes with communication may be said to have a speech disorder. This type of speech makes it difficult for a listener to understand the speaker. The disorder may draw attention to itself rather than to what is said. It may also cause great concern to the speaker. Perhaps as many as twelve people out of one hundred have a speech disorder.

Problems of Articulation. Articulation is the production of speech sounds, made with the lips, tongue, and soft palate, together with the teeth and hard palate. The three major problems of articulation are substitution, omission, and distortion of sounds. In substitution of sounds, a person might say "balentine" for "valentine," substituting the B sound for the V sound. An example of an omission of a sound would be "tep" instead of "step," in which the S sound has been omitted, or left out. The sounds most often produced in a distorted manner are L ("yittle" for "little"), R ("wabbit" for "rabbit"), and S ("thun" for "sun"). Distortion of sounds is the most common articulation problem of young children.

The articulation problem known as **lisping** involves either substitution or distortion of the S sound. In a frontal lisp the S sound is usually substituted by a TH sound, as in "thun" or "bithicle." With a lateral lisp the S sound is distorted by being made with air rushing over the sides of the tongue and out the sides of the mouth.

When a person with an articulation problem begins speech correction, much time is spent in listening to the correct pronunciation of the sound. The student is taught to be able to tell the difference between the right sound and the wrong sound. He or she learns to produce the proper sound first by itself, then in syllables, words, phrases, and, finally, in conversation.

Some articulation problems may be temporary, such as those found in "baby talk." A child may come to school with one or several sound problems. But through kindergarten and first and second grades, the child simply outgrows the problems.

Stuttering. Stuttering is a speech disorder that is marked by involuntary repetition or interruption of sounds, as in "b-b-ball." There are two categories of stuttering. Primary stuttering is usually found in young children who repeat sounds easily and without effort. They do not know that this speech differs from that of others. If the problem is ignored, it will usually disappear or lessen as the child gets older. But secondary stuttering may develop if children are made aware that others are worried about their speech. As a result, youngsters may become anxious and develop fears of speaking situations as well as an overly critical attitude about how they sound. This in turn leads to greater hesitation and lack of fluent (smooth and effortless) speech.

Eventually secondary stutterers become tense and fearful of most speaking situations. They may develop physical reactions to forcing out words, such as tightening the muscles of the face and mouth. This creates a cycle of more fear and more stuttering.

Since there are many theories about the cause of stuttering, there are just as many or more therapies to help the stutterer. Relaxation, rhythmical patterns, breathing techniques, self-concept development, and many other procedures are used to help the stutterer become a more fluent speaker.

Voice Disorders. Voice disorders include such problems as pitch that is too high or too low to suit the age or sex of the speaker; a voice that is always loud or always soft; voice qualities such as harshness, breathiness, or a nasal sound; and a narrow range of expression or a completely expressionless voice (monotone).

Voice disorders may stem from emotional problems or personality factors. Or they may be the result of physical problems that require medical treatment. Sometimes the problem is due to imitation of poor voice standards. If there is no physical or emotional reason for the disorder, treatment usually consists of presenting the speaker with a good speech model to listen to and imitate.

Most speech and voice disorders do not have a physical cause. But some are the result of physical conditions such as cleft palate, cerebral palsy, or hearing loss.

Speech pathologists (also called speech therapists and speech correctionists) are professionals who help people become better speakers and develop self-confidence, both in school programs and in speech clinics. Speech pathologists are involved in research at universities and hospitals throughout the world.

Further information on speech disorders or on careers in speech correction can be obtained by writing to the American Speech/Language/Hearing Association, 10801 Rockville Pike, Rockville, Maryland 20852.

JOHN H. CORCORAN
Glassboro State College (New Jersey)

SPELLING

What do the letters *g-h-o-t-i* spell? To find out, decode the word like this:

Give *gh* the sound they have in "enouGH."

Give *o* the sound it has in "wOmen."

Give *ti* the sound they have in "naTIon." What do you get? You get the name for animals that live in water. The usual spelling is *f-i-s-h*. The playwright George Bernard Shaw (1856–1950) gets credit for first spelling "fish" the "ghoti" way. By doing so, he showed how hard it is to spell English correctly. It is one of the hardest languages in the world for spelling.

Why is correct spelling so important? Imagine how hard it would be to read if everyone spelled words differently. Readers would find it almost impossible to figure out what authors want to say.

How You Start to Spell

Your writing career begins when you are very young. At about 3 years old, you grab a pencil and draw squiggles on a piece of paper. When you are done, you proudly show off your "writing." You discover that you can represent "words" on a sheet of paper. Your squiggles are your first attempt at writing.

A year passes and during this time you develop new knowledge. You now know that special lines, called letters, are used to write words. You also learn that the letters represent sounds. You try to match letters with sounds, but the results are rarely accurate. "I want to play" might become "I wnt tu pla." You were not taught to spell "want" as "wnt." Instead, you invent spellings that look to you like the words you are hearing. The use of invented spelling is an important stage in your writing development.

At about 5 years old, however, you know that there is a standard way to spell words—the dictionary way. You also know that your invented spellings may not match the dictionary entries. Like most children, you have a natural desire to spell words right. Even while using invented spelling for most words, you begin to memorize the dictionary spelling for others. You probably learn to spell your own name first. Then you begin to learn a variety of two- and three-letter words such as *no*, *go*, *cat*, and *dog*. As time passes, you continue to learn the correct spelling for more and more words and use invented spelling less often.

▶ HOW TO MASTER SPELLING

By the time you are an adult, you will know thousands of words. How will you learn to spell all of them? During your first years in school, you learn that certain letters represent certain sounds. The more you know about the sounds the letters make, the better speller you will be. It can be hard, though, to remember all the spelling variations in English. Think of the letter *o*. It makes different sounds in all of these words: *pot, coat, cow, oil, book, boot,* and *women*. You must have a good memory to recall all of these different sounds. The kind of memory you need is **auditory memory**, or memory for things you hear.

Auditory memory alone, however, will not do. How will you remember that "cent" is the word that means money and "sent" is the word for sending things? You also need a good **visual memory**, or memory for the way words look when written. If you want to spell a word that begins with the S sound, you have two choices—the letter *s* or the letter *c*. How do you know which letter to use? "Sink" fits the picture you have for that word while "cink" does not. "City" fits a different picture while "sity" does not.

Spelling Rules

Even though English is tricky, there are some rules you can rely on most of the time. If you memorize the most important rules, your spelling will improve. It is easy to remember one of the rules because it is a poem:

"Write *i* before *e* except after *c*, or when sounded like A as in 'nEIghbor' and 'wEIgh.' "

This rule will help you spell "chief" and "receive" correctly. The rule has exceptions, though. *Weird, height,* and *neither,* for instance, do not follow the rule.

Here are three rules of adding endings to words. They are good rules to memorize.

1. When a final *y* comes after a consonant, change the *y* to *i* before adding *ed, er,* or *est* endings.
   Fry becomes *fried. Silly* becomes *sillier. Funny* becomes *funniest.*

2. Drop the final *e* before adding *ed, er,* or *ing* endings.
   Hope becomes *hoped. Dance* becomes *dancer. Write* becomes *writing.*

USE WHAT YOU READ

A Memory Game

Here is a game that can help strengthen your visual memory. Play it with a friend. You need a magazine that has lots of full-page pictures. Study a single picture for one minute. Then hand the picture to your friend. Your friend will ask you five questions about the picture. For instance, what color was the couch? How many flowers are in the vase? You get one point for every question you can answer correctly. Then switch roles. Have your friend study a new picture and you ask the questions. Play two or three rounds. See who has the most points at the end of the game.

---

3. When a word has a short vowel sound followed by a single consonant, double the final consonant before adding *ed, er,* or *ing* endings.
   Hop becomes *hopped. Spin* becomes *spinner. Nap* becomes *napping.*

Memory Tricks

Do you find it hard to remember the correct spelling of the word "separate"? You are not alone. "Separate" is among the 100 words most frequently misspelled by college students. The spelling of a word like "separate" is hard to remember even though you study rules and sounds and try to make a visual picture. When a word is so hard to memorize, you need a memory aid.

When you think of "separate," think of "Eee! A rat!" Why? *E* is the first vowel in "s-*e*-parate." *E* is followed by "a rat" (sep-*a-rat*-e).

If you try, you can invent similar tricks for any words you have trouble spelling.

▶ WRITING AND SPELLING

Should you worry about correct spelling while you write a story or a report? Yes and no. Certainly, you should make an effort to spell the words you know correctly, even in a first draft. Otherwise you may not be able to reread your own writing. Do not worry too much about spelling while getting your thoughts down on paper, however. If you want to include a word you do not know how to spell, invent a spelling for it. Then draw a line under the word to remind you to check it carefully when you proofread.

After you finish your first draft, edit your work. This means changing words so your thoughts are clear and easy to understand. Only after editing should you worry about proofreading, or carefully checking your spelling. It may seem strange, but the best way to proofread your paper for spelling is to read backward. Start with the last word in the paper and go word by word backward until you reach the first word. When you do this, it is easier to concentrate on spelling. That is because when you read forward you tend to get caught up in the meanings of the words. When you read backward, there are no distractions since the meanings are lost.

While proofreading, you will probably discover two kinds of spelling mistakes. First, you will find words that you misspelled by accident. You know the right spelling for "beach," but you accidentally wrote "baech." Now is the time to correct this error. Second, you will see words you are fairly sure you have misspelled. In these cases, however, you do not know how to spell them correctly. How can you find the correct spelling for these words? You could ask someone. This method is not reliable, however, since you cannot always find a good speller when you need one. The most reliable method is to use a dictionary. Many people resist using a dictionary because they find it difficult to look up words. The more you use a dictionary, however, the easier it gets.

Modern technology can also help writers perfect their spelling. A person who is lucky enough to have a computer can get a computer program that locates spelling mistakes and offers suggestions for correcting the errors. These "spelling checkers" are electronic proofreaders and automatic dictionaries.

Unfortunately, a computer cannot make English spelling more predictable. You have to live with hard-to-spell English for your entire life. With a little effort, however, correct spelling does not have to be too difficult to achieve.

PEGGY KAYE
Author, *Games for Learning*

See also LEARNING; READING; STUDY, HOW TO.

SPELUNKING

Spelunking, the sport of cave exploring, is like mountain climbing underground, in the dark. Like mountain climbing, spelunking can be an exciting, but potentially dangerous, hobby. Many of the same obstacles—high rock walls, narrow ledges, and rivers and lakes—are faced by both spelunkers (people who explore and map caves as a hobby) and mountaineers; and both need endurance, a desire for adventure, and plenty of experience.

Spelunkers, also known as cavers, often explore "wild" caves. These are caves that have not been opened to tourists. Sometimes, spelunkers find and explore caves that were previously unknown or unexplored.

In the United States most spelunkers belong to local caving clubs, usually chapters ("grottoes") of the National Speleological Society (N.S.S.). Some spelunkers who are also

A spelunker spends a quiet moment contemplating the fragile beauty of hanging rock formations within a chamber of the Old Guarena Cave in Spain.

skin divers belong to underwater caving groups. They often belong to both the N.S.S. and a diving club. They explore the large pools and deep springs found in many caves.

Spelunking offers plenty of adventure. But it can be dangerous unless safety rules are carefully observed. The following are the most important safety rules.

1. Never go into a cave alone. Spelunkers usually work in groups of four or more, including at least one experienced caver. An injured or trapped caver needs company while others go for help.

2. Always tell someone outside the cave where you will be and how long you plan to stay there, and keep to your schedule.

3. Mark your route into a cave with arrows pointing back to the entrance. Scratch these arrows in soft mud, chalk them on hard rock, or make them of small stones.

4. Gain your knowledge of caves and caving in the company of experienced spelunkers. Most of the necessary skills can be learned only by actual experience, although rope practice and rock climbing should be learned in a safe place before you go into a cave.

5. Always carry at least three reliable kinds of light. Wear a miner's helmet with a carbide lamp. Carry a flashlight with fresh batteries and candles with plenty of matches in a waterproof container. Be sure to have extra batteries, bulbs, carbide, and so on.

6. All equipment must be in perfect condition because your life depends on it. Before you take rope into a cave, inspect it carefully for obvious signs of wear and test its strength.

Another important rule is not so much for safety as for conservation: You should leave a cave exactly as you found it. Along with delicate rock formations, there are many living organisms that are found within caves. Do not remove or harm cave-dwelling plants and animals, stones, mineral samples, or anything else you find in a cave.

PETER VAN NOTE
Member, National Speleological Society

See also CAVES AND CAVERNS; MOUNTAIN CLIMBING.

SPENSER, EDMUND (1552?–1599)

One of Shakespeare's greatest contemporaries, the English poet Edmund Spenser was born in London, probably in 1552. Though his parents were poor, he attended the Merchant Taylors' School from its founding in 1561 until 1569, when he left for Pembroke Hall, Cambridge University. At Cambridge he received his B.A. in 1573 and his M.A. in 1576. His friend Gabriel Harvey introduced him to the earl of Leicester and the poet Sir Philip Sidney. It was to Sidney that Spenser dedicated his first major work, *The Shepheardes Calender* (1579), a series of short poems about country life. Sidney, like Leicester, was Spenser's patron.

In 1579 Spenser married Machabyas Childe, and they had two children. In 1580, as secretary to the new governor, Spenser moved with his family to Ireland (then under English rule), where he wrote most of his later poetry. He held a number of minor posts and eventually rose to High Sheriff of Cork in 1598. From 1586 on, his home was Kilcolman Castle, whose surrounding landscape is reflected in his poetry.

Spenser is perhaps best known for his great epic poem, *The Faerie Queene.* For it he invented a uniquely rhymed nine-line stanza that has since been called the Spenserian stanza. The poem was to include twelve books on twelve different virtues, but Spenser did not live to complete them all. Part one (Books I–III; 1590) was dedicated to Queen Elizabeth I, who granted him a special yearly pension. After his first wife died, he married Elizabeth Boyle, for whom his sonnet sequence *Amoretti* and a marriage poem, *Epithalamion,* were written (1595). Another marriage poem, *Prothalamion* (1596), was written for the wedding of the earl of Worcester's daughters. The second part of *The Faerie Queene* (Books IV–VI) also appeared in 1596.

In 1598, Kilcolman was burned by Irish rebels. The Spensers barely escaped. Broken in spirit, the poet died in London in 1599 and was buried in Westminster Abbey.

JAY L. HALIO
University of Delaware

SPICES. See HERBS AND SPICES.

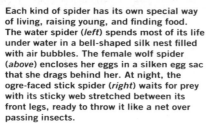

Each kind of spider has its own special way of living, raising young, and finding food. The water spider (*left*) spends most of its life under water in a bell-shaped silk nest filled with air bubbles. The female wolf spider (*above*) encloses her eggs in a silken egg sac that she drags behind her. At night, the ogre-faced stick spider (*right*) waits for prey with its sticky web stretched between its front legs, ready to throw it like a net over passing insects.

SPIDERS

Moving gracefully along the delicate woven threads of a web or hanging aloft from a silken line, the spider is a common sight. The small eight-legged creature can be found on every continent except Antarctica, in almost every kind of habitat on land and in water. Fields, woods, swamps, caves, mountains, and deserts are all home to the spider.

Spiders are **invertebrates**, or animals without backbones, that belong to a large class of animals (Arachnida) known as arachnids. There are more than 30,000 known kinds of spiders, although scientists believe there may actually be 50,000 to 100,000 different kinds. Most spiders are brown, black, or gray and range in size from about ⅕ inch (5 millimeters) to 3½ inches (89 millimeters).

▶THE CHARACTERISTICS OF SPIDERS

The appearance and size of each kind, or species, of spider varies greatly. However, there are two basic characteristics that all spiders share: All spiders have the same body plan and, with rare exceptions, they all have the ability to spin silk.

The Body of a Spider

If you look carefully at a spider, you will notice that its body is divided into two parts with a slender "waist" between the parts. The front part, which consists of the head and thorax joined together, is called the **cephalothorax**. The hind part is called the abdomen.

The eyes of the spider generally are located on the top of its head. Most spiders have eight eyes. As a rule, a spider has poor eyesight and apparently does not smell or hear in the way other animals do. But a spider's sense of touch is highly developed. Its entire body, including its mouthparts and legs, is covered with fine sensory hairs that can detect the slightest movement.

Below its eyes, the spider has a mouth. Its mouthparts consist of a pair of short appendages called **pedipalps** and another pair of appendages called **chelicerae**, which end in pointed, hollow claws, or fangs. Poison glands open at the tip of each fang. When a

The External Body Structures of a Spider

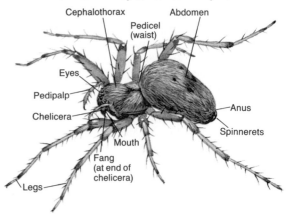

spider's chelicerae close on its prey, the fangs are inserted into the victim and poison is injected into the struggling creature. Once the poison has taken effect and the victim is dead or paralyzed, the spider uses its pedipalps to squeeze body juices out of its prey.

Glands located in the rear part of a spider's body produce silk. Scientists have found that there are seven different kinds of silk glands. Each kind of gland has its own shape and produces its own kind of silk. The glands open through tiny holes on the ends of small nipple-like organs called **spinnerets**. The spinnerets are at the hind end of the abdomen. In most spiders there are three pairs of spinnerets. In other kinds there may be one pair or two or up to six pairs.

Attached to the body of the spider are four pairs of jointed legs. The spider uses its first pair of legs, which typically are much longer than the other legs, to feel its way, in much the same manner that insects use their antennae, or feelers.

A Spider's Silk

All spiders spin silken fibers. These threads are finer than human hair and strong enough to hold 4,000 times the spider's own weight!

Silk Production. The spider's silk is formed in the spider's silk glands and comes out as a liquid thread that hardens on contact with air. Most spiders have at least three kinds of silk glands and can make at least three kinds of silk. The different kinds of silk have qualities that make them useful for special tasks.

All spiders make a silk used for binding up prey. Almost all female spiders produce another kind of silk for wrapping up their eggs. Some spiders have two or more kinds of silk for making webs.

Most spiders make a fine kind of silk known as a **dragline**. Wherever a spider goes, it spins this silk as a lifeline. If the spider falls, it can pull itself up again. A frightened spider can use the dragline to escape an enemy by dropping to the ground and then running off.

Weaving a Web. You have probably seen the tangled web of a house spider strung up in a corner or woven under a chair. There are many other types of webs. On a short walk through a meadow you can probably find three or four types. Grass spiders make a large funnel of silk in tall grass or on the ground near a hole or under a rock. The purseweb spider spins its tube-shaped web under stones or along the sides of trees.

The most handsome webs are those made by the orb-weaving spiders. The common garden spider is one of the orb-weavers. Its web is shaped like a wheel, with long sticky spirals covering the "spokes." The spider usually weaves its web at night, relying almost entirely on its sense of touch.

First the garden spider spins a line across an open space and anchors the line securely to a twig or other surface with a special kind of silk. This line then serves as a guideline. The spider adds other guidelines until it has made a large square or triangle secured at the points. Within this frame the spider weaves a wheel with many spokes. Next, starting at the center

The web of the orb-weaving spider (*right*) begins with a single guideline that is carried by the wind until it attaches to a twig or other object. Other guidelines are added (1) to make a frame. Silky threads run like spokes of a wheel (2) from the center to the frame. A temporary spiral (3) holds the spokes in place. A spiral of sticky threads (4) is spun and the temporary lines removed.

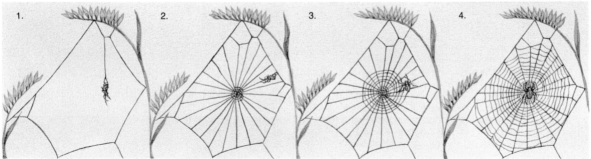

A jumping spider (*left*) can leap a distance of 8 inches (20 centimeters) to capture its prey. The grass spider (*right*) rushes out from its funnel-shaped web to grab its victim.

of the wheel, the spider circles round and round, laying down a silken scaffolding.

The spider is now ready to lay down the sticky silk that traps insects. Up to this point the spider has used a firm, dry silk. Now it uses sticky, elastic silk. The spider starts at the center. As it goes, it cuts away the scaffolding with its fangs. When the sticky spiral is finished, a garden spider spins a zigzag band of silk through the center.

Even though a spider's web is a sticky trap for unsuspecting prey, a spider does not get caught in its own web. There are two reasons for this. The chief one is that a spider runs along its web on the dry silk threads. It avoids the sticky, insect-catching ones. Also, a spider's feet are oily, and the oil helps to keep the spider from sticking.

▶THE LIFE OF A SPIDER

During its lifetime, every spider must perform certain tasks. A spider must find food, defend itself against enemies, and produce young. Each kind of spider goes about these tasks in its own way. Yet for each species, the behaviors all function to provide the same result: to improve the chances of survival.

Catching Prey

All spiders capture other animals for food. Spiders feed mainly on insects, although some spiders capture mice, small fish, frogs, and tadpoles to eat. Some spiders depend on the webs they spin to capture their prey. Usually web-spinning spiders, which include the grass spider and the garden spider, have poor vision. So rather than seek out prey, they wait for their victims to come to them. Other spiders are hunters, such as the wolf spider, the jumping spider, and the trap-door spider. Some stalk their prey on land, waiting for the chance to pounce; others lie in wait to ambush

The intricate web of communal spiders stretches across a fence. The web's lacy tangles hold several nests in addition to twigs, leaves, and the remains of prey.

Did you know that . . .

the class Arachnida takes its name from the mythological character Arachne? According to an ancient Greek legend, Arachne was a young girl who spun marvelously fine threads and wove beautiful cloth. She was so proud of her skills, the ancient Greeks said, that she challenged the goddess Athena to a spinning and weaving contest. Indeed, Arachne's cloth was perfect. The perfection of Arachne's work so enraged Athena that she destroyed her rival's work. Then she struck Arachne, turning her into a spider that would forever spin and weave.

What is the largest spider?

The largest spider is the hairy, long-legged tarantula found in the South American jungles. Some of these are so big that they can capture and eat mice and small birds. The largest tarantula found measured 10 inches (25 centimeters) long with its legs stretched out—about the size of a dinner plate!

an unsuspecting animal. Still others live near water and hunt water insects, small fish, and tadpoles.

Web Spinners. The grass spider makes its funnel-shaped web near a hiding place such as a hole in the ground or under a rock. When an insect gets inside the wide-spreading mouth of the funnel web, it is trapped. While the victim is trying to escape, the spider rushes out from its hiding place and grabs it.

The garden spider is another web spinner. It sits in the center of the web, waiting. When an insect is caught in its web, the spider rushes to its prey and sinks its fangs into the struggling victim to poison it.

Hunters. The fast speed of the wolf spider makes it an excellent hunter. It runs after its prey and springs on it. Wolf spiders are often large and hairy. You may have seen one of these active hunters scampering over dead leaves or roaming a sandy beach.

From its hiding place, the trap-door spider waits to ambush its victim. A trap-door spider can dig a burrow about 1 inch (2.5 centimeters) wide and 8 inches (20 centimeters) deep. It lines the burrow with silk and makes a tight-fitting lid hinged with silk at one side. Some trap-door spiders dig a side burrow off the main one. Sometimes the side burrow runs to the surface and has a second trapdoor. The spider conceals its hiding place with pieces of leaves and other vegetation. When a beetle or other insect strays nearby, the spider pops out and grabs it.

Defenses

Spiders have many enemies, including snakes, wasps, birds, frogs, and even other spiders. Camouflage, distraction, hiding, and fleeing are some of the methods that spiders use to defend themselves against enemies.

Some spiders use decoys to distract their enemies. Certain orb-web spiders wrap up the remains of insects or egg cocoons and place them in their webs. When an enemy, such as a wasp, comes in for the attack, it is distracted by the decoy. While the wasp is occupied, the spider can safely escape.

Fleeing is one means of defense that is used by all spiders. Many spiders use their drag-lines to help them flee from danger. When a spider becomes frightened, it drops to the ground from its dragline and runs off.

Producing Young

Some spiders are communal spiders. They live in a common web that contains several nests and may spread as wide as 4 square yards (3.3 square meters). Other spiders live alone. But, whether a spider is part of a large community or lives alone, it must go through the same steps to produce offspring.

Courtship and Mating. When an adult male reaches maturity, it immediately sets about

Hiding inside its burrow, a trap-door spider is safe from enemies such as birds and lizards. The California trap-door spider shown here can hold the lid of its burrow shut against a pull of almost forty times its own weight.

A bright yellow flower offers camouflage protection to the yellow crab spider. The flower also helps lure prey for the spider—the innocent honeybee that is attracted by the sight and scent of the blooms soon becomes a meal for the hidden crab spider.

When seeking a mate, male spiders perform a variety of courtship activities. The garden spider (*above*) spins a silken bridge to the female's web, then vibrates the thread to get her attention.

Most spiders abandon the young spiders, or spiderlings, once they hatch. But the wolf spider (*left*) protects her young by carrying them on her back. Soon the spiderlings will jump off and fend for themselves.

looking for a mate. Once it has found a female of the same species, the male spider sets about courting the female. In some species of spiders, such as the nursery web spiders, the male presents the female with a gift of food that it has captured. The male jumping spider moves his body in a dance to show off vividly colored parts of his body. Still other species attract the female by vibrating the threads of the female's web.

The male and female mate following courtship. During mating, the male uses his pedipalps to transfer sperm (the male sex cells) into special openings on the underside of the female's abdomen. The female stores these sperm in her body. Weeks or even months may pass before the female is ready to lay her eggs (the female sex cells).

The number of eggs laid by a female spider depends on the species size. An average-sized female lays about 100 eggs. But a large female spider may lay up to 3,000 eggs at one time. Before laying eggs, most female spiders prepare a silken egg sac to protect the eggs. Once the egg sac is complete, the female lays her eggs. As the eggs pass from the female into the egg sac, they are fertilized with the sperm she has stored in her body. Once the eggs are

fertilized, the egg sac may be attached to the web or some other object, such as a plant, or carried by the female until the eggs hatch.

Development of the Young. Inside the eggs, the young spiders grow. Soon the eggs hatch, but the young spiders, called **spiderlings**, stay inside the egg sac until warm weather arrives. Usually spiderlings **molt**, or shed their skin, for the first time within the egg sac. When the spiderlings emerge from the egg sac, they look just like their parents except that they are very much smaller.

While they are still young, spiderlings engage in a form of air travel called **ballooning**. The spiderling runs up and poises on grasses and tall plants. When a breeze comes along, the spiderling spins out long streamers of silk. The breeze lifts the streamers, and the spider floats away. Some spiders have been carried this way more than 200 miles (322 kilometers) out to sea. Others have been found floating 2,000 feet (610 meters) up in the air.

Spiderlings continue to grow and usually will undergo from 4 to 14 molts before becoming an adult. Once they reach adulthood, most spiders live alone. The life span of spiders varies; however, in areas with temperate climates, most live about a year. Tarantulas are one of the exceptions. They are a long-living species. The males live about 10 years, while the females have been known to live for more than 20 years.

▶ **SPIDERS AND THEIR ENVIRONMENT**

Many people fear spiders and kill them on sight. But very few of these animals are truly dangerous to people. In North America only the sac spider, the brown recluse spider, and a few kinds of widows and tarantulas are poisonous to people. Unless these spiders are provoked, they rarely bite human beings. They usually play dead or run away. Even when a person is bitten by a poisonous spider, there may only be a mild reaction. In general, spiders help rather than harm people. They eat many insects that destroy food crops and carry disease.

Ross E. Hutchins
Author, *Trails to Nature's Mysteries*

Reviewed by May R. Berenbaum
Department of Entomology
University of Illinois

SPIELBERG, STEVEN. See Motion Pictures (Profiles: Directors).

SPIES

For thousands of years, wherever information has been kept secret, there have been spies. Governments are particularly interested in learning about the political and military secrets of their enemies. One way to obtain this information, called **intelligence**, is through spying, which is also known as **espionage**.

In addition to discovering the secrets of their rivals, governments go to great lengths to keep their own activities undercover. So they also employ spies, called **agents**, to catch foreign spies or to feed them with false information. This is known as **counterespionage**.

Most spies work for their own country's foreign intelligence agency. In the United States it is the Central Intelligence Agency (CIA); in Great Britain it is called MI5 or MI6; in France, the *Deuxième Bureau*, and in Russia, the Russian Security Service (formerly the KGB). Some spies, however, spy against their own government on behalf of a foreign country. Most of these do so because they believe their own government is evil or corrupt. There are also a few spies who do not work for any specific government but will gather and sell secrets for personal profit.

The most important function of espionage is to gather information about another country's weapons and armed forces. Among the questions intelligence services want answered are, "What sort of new weapons does the enemy have?" "How many soldiers are in their army?" and "How well trained and equipped are they?" However, they are also interested in learning political and industrial secrets. They want to know whether a foreign government is popular or if it is likely to be overthrown. They also want to know about civilian matters such as the efficiency of their roads, railways, and factories. All in all, a spy wants to build up as complete a picture as possible of the country under investigation.

Much of what is described in spy novels and motion pictures gives a very inaccurate picture of the life of a typical agent. Spies, such as Ian Fleming's James Bond, are shown living a glamorous life full of fast cars, clever gadgets, casino gambling, and other amusements. In reality, most spies are highly trained and dedicated civil servants, who quietly and patiently gather scraps of information they think might prove useful to their employers.

Espionage is a very dangerous occupation. To prevent other people from suspecting that

WONDER QUESTION

What are some types of espionage agents?

Agents provocateurs encourage, lead, and often betray political movements or revolutions in a country in order to create conditions that will benefit their own country.

Assassins are trained to murder important leaders or members of opposition forces.

Combat spies are specially trained personnel employed behind enemy front lines to secure information.

Counterspies work specifically to discover and hinder the activities of other spies. An effective method of counterespionage is to permit the enemy network to function while one learns its operations and the identity of its agents. In this way it may be possible to destroy the network.

Double spies work for both sides and get information by pleasing both friend and foe.

Industrial spies gather plans and new developments and steal patents, to get information from strategically important industries.

Kidnappers are skilled in capturing military or political opponents for the purpose of extracting information from them.

Listening posts are spies and counterspies who record conversations or listen to airwaves for coded messages. For years the Russians listened in on the American embassy in Moscow through a secret microphone hidden behind the emblem of the American eagle.

Photographic spies are space satellites, launched by the more scientifically advanced nations. These small "spies in the skies" orbit the earth, taking pictures of the geography and the military installations of other countries. Their reports are relayed by television or other electronic devices to receiving stations on earth.

Scientific spies are trained scientists who steal or sell secret scientific information. Because modern warfare depends on scientific and technological advances, scientists are carefully screened for loyalty.

Sitters collect information, plan their moves, and wait patiently for the time when their knowledge will be useful.

Traitors are persons who willingly join an enemy of their country.

Profiles
(in historical sequence)

Scipio Africanus Major (Publius Cornelius Scipio) (236?–183 B.C.) was a great Roman general, whose spying techniques helped him defeat Hannibal at Zama (202 B.C.) during the Second Punic War. Scipio's spies in Africa sent up smoke signals to give him information about his enemy's troop movements. Without them, Scipio probably would not have won an important series of battles.

Alfred the Great (A.D. 849–99?), born in Wantage, Berkshire, ruled Wessex (871–899), an Anglo-Saxon kingdom in southeastern England. In 878, while at war with Guthrum, the Danish king of Mercia, Alfred disguised himself as a minstrel and sneaked into the Danish camp. By eavesdropping on Guthrum's plans, Alfred was able to defeat him the following day at the Battle of Edington. A biography of Alfred the Great appears in Volume A.

Sir Francis Walsingham (1530?–90), born in London or Chrislehurst, England, was principal secretary (1573–90) to Queen Elizabeth I of England and a master at gathering intelligence. As head of the secret service, he ran a huge network of spies throughout France, Spain, and Italy. His information helped convict Mary, Queen of Scots, of treason. He also informed Elizabeth about the planned attack of the Spanish Armada in 1587, a year before it was due to sail. Armed with Walsingham's information, Sir Francis Drake was able to surprise and destroy a large part of the enemy fleet.

Samuel Pepys (1633–1703), born in London, England, and best remembered for his remarkable diary depicting England in the 1600's, was an English public servant and a spy. While secretary of the admiralty under King Charles II, he stole a key from the pocket of a sleeping Dutch diplomat and unlocked his desk. From it Pepys removed important secret documents which he passed along to the English king.

Nathan Hale (1755–76), born in Coventry, Conn., was a spy for General George Washington during the American Revolutionary War. Hale went behind enemy lines, where he obtained maps and other strategic information. On his return to the American camp, Hale was caught by the British. Denied a trial, he was sentenced to death by hanging. Before his execution on September 22, 1776, the American patriot spoke his immortal last words, "I only regret that I have but one life to lose for my country." A biography of Nathan Hale appears in Volume H.

John André (1750–80), born in London, England, was a major in the British Army during the American Revolutionary War under the command of General Henry Clinton in New York. André was sent to meet with Benedict Arnold, an American traitor, who gave André the plans of the American fort at West Point on the Hudson River. While carrying the incriminating documents, André was captured by the Americans. Tried by George Washington's officers for espionage, he was hanged on October 2, 1780.

Belle Boyd (1843–1900), born in Martinsburg, Va., was a Confederate spy during the American Civil War. She used charm to obtain information from Northern officers, which she then passed along in secret code to officers in the South. Twice imprisoned but released for lack of evidence, she was captured a third time but escaped to England with her guard.

Mata Hari

Mata Hari (Margaretha Geertruida Zelle) (1876–1917), born in Leeuwarden, the Netherlands, was accused of spying for the Germans during World War I. An exotic dancer, she took the name Mata Hari (meaning Eye of the Dawn in Javanese) and performed on stage in Paris. She kept company with several French and other Allied officers, from whom she apparently obtained military secrets. Although it is now unclear whether she actually passed any information to the Germans, she was tried and convicted of espionage in 1917 and shot by a French firing squad.

Whittaker Jay David Chambers (1902–61), born in Philadelphia, Pa., was an American journalist and a self-confessed secret agent for the Soviet Union. Chambers was an editor with *Time* magazine when he appeared before the House Committee on Un-American Activities in 1948. He claimed he had renounced Communism and avoided imprisonment by naming other Soviet agents. Among those he named was **Alger Hiss**, (1904–96), born in Baltimore, Md., a former U.S. State Department official (1937–45), who had advised President Franklin D. Roosevelt during World War II. As evidence, Chambers took then U.S. congressman Richard M. Nixon to his farm in Maryland and showed him some microfilm he had hidden in a hollowed-out pumpkin. The film contained documents that Chambers said Hiss had typed up and given to him to deliver to the Soviets. Hiss, who denied knowing Chambers, was twice brought to trial on charges of perjury (lying under oath). Hiss was convicted on January 21, 1950, and sent to prison. He was released in 1954. The case sparked further charges of Communist infiltration in the U.S. government by Senator Joseph McCarthy. In 1992 former Soviet agents claimed they had no evidence that Hiss had spied for them.

Klaus Emil Julius Fuchs (1911–88), born in Rüsselsheim, Germany, was a physicist who fled Nazi Germany in 1933. Knowledgeable of both the British and American atomic bomb projects, in 1950 he was found guilty of having passed classified (secret) information to the Soviets. He was sentenced to 14 years in prison but was released in 1959.

Scipio Africanus Major

Nathan Hale

Ethel and Julius Rosenberg

they are spying, agents usually have to assume a false identity, or **cover**, and take great care not to attract attention to themselves, as the penalty for those who are caught is usually a long prison sentence and sometimes death.

Modern spying is highly technical and makes use of all forms of sophisticated equipment. Electronic eavesdropping, or bugging, devices are used to overhear conversations and telephone calls. Microfilm, microdots, and secret codes are used to record and distribute information discreetly. Specially designed aircraft and satellites are deployed to gather vital information about military installations and troop movements.

Industrial espionage has become commonplace in recent years. These days, a single trade secret can be worth millions of dollars, so some large companies have employed spies to keep them informed about their competitors' new products and technical developments. Also, to protect their own interests, many companies have had to employ security forces to make sure they themselves are not being spied on.

FRANK SMYTH
Author, *The Detective in Fact and Fiction*

See also CENTRAL INTELLIGENCE AGENCY; CODES AND CIPHERS.

SPINGARN MEDAL

The Spingarn Medal is an award presented annually by the National Association for the Advancement of Colored People (NAACP). The purpose of the award is to honor African-Americans of outstanding achievement who also inspire young people to achieve. The award was established in 1914 by Joel Elias Spingarn (1875–1939), one of the several white liberals who helped establish the NAACP, a civil rights organization.

Spingarn was born into a wealthy New York City family. After earning a doctorate of philosophy (Ph.D.) from Columbia University, he taught literature there from 1899 until 1911. Spingarn believed that one must act on one's convictions, not merely write and talk

about them. He once wrote, "Virtue is never solitary; it takes part in the conflicts of the world." He purchased and operated a club to provide destitute African-Americans with food and recreation. Through this venture, he met W.E.B. Du Bois, editor of *Crisis*, the official paper of the NAACP. In 1910, Du Bois supported Spingarn's request to join the year-old NAACP. Spingarn later served as the organization's chairman of the board and treasurer. When he died in 1939, his will provided for the continued annual funding of the award given in his name.

MEGAN MCCLARD
Metropolitan State College of Denver

A table of medal winners follows.

SPINGARN MEDAL WINNERS

Year	Name	Profession	Year	Name	Profession
1915	Ernest E. Just	Biologist		Carlotta Walls	
1916	Charles Young	Police organizer	1959	Duke Ellington	Musician
1917	Harry T. Burleigh	Musician	1960	Langston Hughes	Author
1918	W. S. Braithwaite	Poet, author	1961	Kenneth B. Clark	Psychologist
1919	Archibald H. Grimke	Politician, author	1962	Robert C. Weaver	Government administrator
1920	William E. B. Du Bois	Educator, editor	1963	Medgar W. Evers	Equal rights activist
1921	Charles S. Gilpin	Actor	1964	Roy Wilkins	Civil rights leader
1922	Mary B. Talbert	Douglass memorial organizer	1965	Leontyne Price	Singer
1923	George W. Carver	Botanist	1966	John H. Johnson	Publisher
1924	Roland Hayes	Concert singer	1967	Edward W. Brooke	Politician
1925	James Weldon Johnson	Author	1968	Sammy Davis, Jr.	Entertainer
1926	Carter G. Woodson	Educator	1969	Clarence M. Mitchell, Jr.	Lawyer
1927	Anthony Overton	Insurance underwriter	1970	Jacob Lawrence	Artist
1928	Charles W. Chesnutt	Author, lawyer	1971	Leon H. Sullivan	Equal rights activist
1929	Mordecai W. Johnson	University president	1972	Gordon Parks	Photographer
1930	Henry A. Hunt	Educator	1973	Wilson C. Riles	Educator
1931	Richard B. Harrison	Actor	1974	Damon J. Keith	Lawyer
1932	Robert R. Moton	Educator	1975	Henry Aaron	Baseball player
1933	Max Yergen	Interracial mediator	1976	Alvin Ailey	Dancer, choreographer
1934	William T. B. Williams	Educator	1977	Alex Haley	Author
1935	Mary McLeod Bethune	Educator	1978	Andrew J. Young, Jr.	Politician
1936	John Hope	Educator	1979	Rosa Lee Parks	Civil rights activist
1937	Walter F. White	Civil rights leader	1980	Rayford W. Logan	Educator
1938	No award given	-	1981	Coleman Young	Politician
1939	Marian Anderson	Concert singer	1982	Benjamin E. Mays	Educator, theologian
1940	Louis T. Wright	Surgeon	1983	Lena Horne	Entertainer
1941	Richard Wright	Author	1984	Thomas Bradley	Politician
1942	A. Philip Randolph	Labor leader	1985	Bill Cosby	Entertainer, educator
1943	William H. Hastie	Equal rights activist	1986	Benjamin L. Hooks	Civil rights leader
1944	Charles R. Drew	Surgeon, researcher	1987	Percy E. Sutton	Lawyer, politician
1945	Paul Robeson	Singer and actor	1988	Frederick Patterson	Educator
1946	Thurgood Marshall	Lawyer, judge	1989	Jesse Jackson	Politician, civil rights leader
1947	Percy L. Julian	Chemist	1990	L. Douglas Wilder	Politician
1948	Channing H. Tobias	Civil liberties activist	1991	Colin L. Powell	Army general
1949	Ralph J. Bunche	U.N. mediator	1992	Barbara Jordan	Educator
1950	Charles H. Houston	Lawyer, educator	1993	Dorothy I. Height	Humanitarian
1951	Mabel K. Staupers	Nurses' rights activist	1994	Maya Angelou	Author
1952	Harry T. Moore	Civil liberties activist	1995	John Hope Franklin	Historian
1953	Paul R. Williams	Architect	1996	A. Leon Higginbotham	Judge
1954	Theodore K. Lawless	Dermatologist	1997	Carl Rowan	Journalist
1955	Carl Murphy	Publisher	1998	Myrlie Evers Williams	Civil rights leader
1956	Jackie Robinson	Baseball player	1999	Earl G. Graves	Businessman
1957	Martin Luther King, Jr.	Civil rights leader	2000	Oprah Winfrey	Talk show host
1958	Mrs. Daisy Bates; Minnijean Brown; Elizabeth Eckford; Ernest Green; Thelma Mothershed; Melba Patillo; Gloria Ray; Terrence Roberts; Jefferson Thomas;	Civil rights activist; first black students to attend desegregated Central High School in Little Rock, Arkansas	2001	Vernon E. Jordan, Jr.	Civil rights leader, lawyer
			2002	John Lewis	Civil rights activist
			2003	Constance Baker Motley	Senior U.S. district judge
			2004	Robert L. Carter	Senior U.S. district judge
			2005	Oliver W. Hill	Civil rights leader, lawyer

SPINOZA, BARUCH (1632–1677)

The philosopher Baruch (or Benedict) Spinoza was born in Amsterdam on November 24, 1632. His parents, who were Jewish, had been driven from Portugal by religious persecution. As a young man, Spinoza studied under Frans van den Ende, a former Jesuit, and explored the philosophy of René Descartes. Spinoza began to question established religious doctrines and traditions. His criticism of the Bible, his rejection of personal immortality, and his radical notions about God attacked the foundations of both orthodox Judaism and Christianity.

Spinoza was expelled from the Jewish community for his beliefs. He moved several times, earning a living by grinding lenses and tutoring. Friends published some of his philosophical studies, but church authorities prohibited the circulation or reading of his works. Spinoza's greatest work, the *Ethica ordine geometrico demonstrata (Ethics Demonstrated in the Geometrical Manner)*, was not published until after his death. He died of tuberculosis on February 21, 1677.

For a century after his death, Spinoza was dismissed as an unimportant atheist philosopher. Gradually it was realized that this quiet, humble man had developed, through careful reasoning, a clear conception of God as the ultimate good. He taught that people should act not in relation to time or circumstance but in relation to the eternity of God.

Reviewed by HOWARD OZMON
Author, *Twelve Great Philosophers*

SPINY ANTEATERS. See PLATYPUS AND SPINY ANTEATERS.

SPIRITUALS. See HYMNS (Spirituals and Other Folk Hymns).

Sponges, such as the purple tube sponge (*above*), vase sponge (*above right*), and tennis ball sponge (*right*), are underwater animals that spend their adult lives attached to objects, such as rocks, on the seafloor.

SPONGES

A sponge is a many-celled animal that is found in all the seas of the world. Sponges live at all depths, from the shoreline out. At the water's edge at low tide, almost any rock you can turn over will have some kind of sponge growing on the underside.

Some sponges live alone. Others live in colonies. All told, there are some 5,000 different kinds of sponges. Most kinds live in the sea. A few kinds live in fresh water. None live on land.

Sponges are among the animal kingdom's strangest members, for they look much more like plants than animals. In its simplest form, it is little more than a hollow tube, open at the upper end and attached for support at the lower end. In color sponges may be green, brown, yellow, red, orange, or white. They may be shaped like fans, domes, vases, bowls, or trumpets. They may branch like trees. Or they may be flattened masses of spongy tissue spread out on the surface of underwater rocks, shells, or wood. Some sponges are less than 1 inch (2.5 centimeters) long. Others are almost 3 feet (.9 meter) in height or width.

Adult sponges never move about and seem to be rooted in place. If you touch one, it does not react. A sponge does not have a head or mouth. It has no eyes, ears, feelers, or other sense organs. If a living sponge is cut in two, all that can be seen is a slimy mass with holes or channels running through it. A sponge has no heart, stomach, muscles, blood vessels, or nervous system.

▶HOW A SPONGE FEEDS

The chief thing that makes a sponge an animal is the way it feeds. A sponge captures its food. It does not make its own food, as green plants do.

As the sponge feeds, water is taken in through tiny openings, called ostia, that are all over the outside of the sponge. When the water comes in, so do tiny animals and plants. The tube wall of the sponge acts like a sieve, or filter, to strain the tiny plants and animals out of the water. Then the water is forced out of the sponge through a hole, called an osculum, at the top of the animal. Water is forced in and out of the sponge by the beating action of microscopic, whiplike threads. These are called flagella (singular: flagellum). The flagella line the inner parts of the sponge.

The cells with flagella are also the cells that capture food. Around the bottom of each fla-

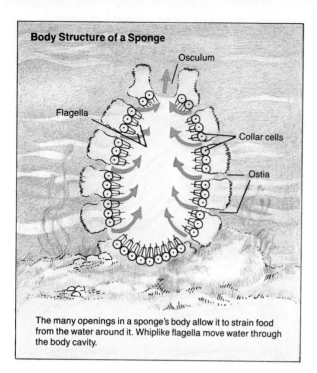

Body Structure of a Sponge

Osculum

Flagella

Collar cells

Ostia

The many openings in a sponge's body allow it to strain food from the water around it. Whiplike flagella move water through the body cavity.

gellum there is a growth that looks like a collar. It gives the cells their name, collar cells. Food is caught on the sticky surfaces of the collars. Some of the food is digested by the collar cells. Some is passed on to the rest of the sponge by a special kind of cell that wanders throughout the sponge.

▶THE SPONGE SKELETON

A sponge is a kind of living sieve. But even a sieve needs support. Part of the sponge tissue acts as a skeleton. It stiffens the whole sponge. As a result, the sponge can keep its shape in currents of water.

Sponges are classified by the kind of skeleton they have. One kind has a skeleton made of tough, horny fibers. (Cleaned and dried, this skeleton becomes the kind of sponge you can buy in shops.) Another kind has a skeleton made of needlelike crystals of lime or chalk. Still another kind has a glassy skeleton. Deep-sea glass sponges have skeletons of beautifully made glass structures something like the steel framework of a high building. Perhaps you have seen the skeleton of a sponge known as Venus's Flower Basket in a museum of natural history.

The shape of a sponge depends mostly on where the sponge lives. In still water, sponges usually have the shape of a vase—narrow at the bottom and wide at the top. In deep ocean

the floor is soft ooze. Here the vase-shaped glass sponges usually have an anchoring structure made of long glass fibers. These hold the main body of the sponge clear of the ooze. Along the shore there is always wave action of some sort. Here sponges spread out like thick carpets.

▶HOW SPONGES REPRODUCE

A sponge may reproduce by forming egg cells and sperm cells. The sperm cells are set free in the water. The egg cells stay in the sponge. They are fertilized by sperm cells from another sponge. A fertilized egg becomes a tiny larva. It has flagella. Swimming with its flagella, the larva leaves the sponge. Soon after, it attaches itself to a support and grows into a young sponge.

A sponge may also reproduce by budding. Cells grow out from the body, forming a small sponge. The small sponge may remain attached to the parent. Or it may drop off and attach itself to a support.

▶USES FOR SPONGES

People have long made use of sponges with horny skeletons. Natural sponges are still used today, although we often buy factory-made sponges of rubber, plastic, or glass. There are sponge fisheries in parts of the world where the horny sponge grows in warm, shallow seas, including the eastern section of the Mediterranean Sea and the waters off the shores of the Bahamas, Cuba, and Florida.

The horny sponges, brought up by divers, are usually placed in shallow, brackish ponds to rot, and put in the sun to dry. The tissue rots away, leaving the bleached skeleton, which is what most of us call a sponge.

Sponges can also be farmed. They are cut up, fastened to small rocks, and planted in warm, shallow water. In about four years each piece grows into a full-sized sponge, ready for harvesting.

N. J. BERRILL
McGill University

SPOTTED TAIL. See INDIANS, AMERICAN (Profiles).
SPRINGFIELD (Illinois). See ILLINOIS (Cities).
SPRINGFIELD (Massachusetts). See MASSACHUSETTS (Cities).
SPRINGFIELD (Missouri). See MISSOURI (Cities).
SQUANTO. See INDIANS, AMERICAN (Profiles).
SQUARE DANCING. See FOLK DANCE.

SRI LANKA

Sri Lanka (formerly called Ceylon) is an island nation of South Asia. Located in the Indian Ocean, just off the southeastern coast of India, it has been famed since ancient times for the lush beauty of its landscape. Early travelers to the island called it the Pearl of the Orient. Once governed by Britain, it gained its independence in 1948. It adopted its present name of Sri Lanka ("beautiful island") in 1972.

▶ THE PEOPLE

Ethnic Groups, Language, Religion. Sri Lanka's people belong to several ethnic groups. The largest group is the Sinhalese, who make up nearly 75 percent of the population, and live mainly in the southwestern part of the island. They speak Sinhala and are mostly Buddhists. Tamils make up about 18 percent of the population. One group of Tamils (often called Sri Lankan Tamils) have lived on the island for many centuries. A second group (usually called Indian Tamils) arrived from

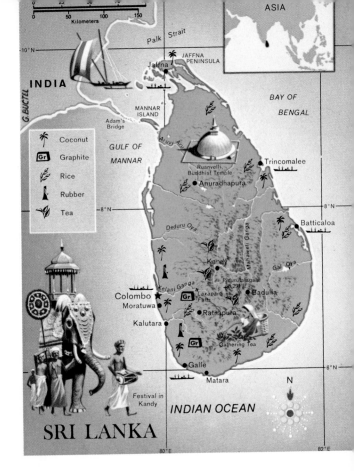

SRI LANKA

FACTS AND FIGURES

DEMOCRATIC SOCIALIST REPUBLIC OF SRI LANKA is the official name of the country.

THE PEOPLE are known as Sri Lankans.

LOCATION: Island in the Indian Ocean in South Asia.

AREA: 25,332 sq mi (65,610 km²).

POPULATION: 16,400,000 (estimate).

CAPITAL AND LARGEST CITY: Colombo.

MAJOR LANGUAGES: Sinhala (official), Tamil (national).

MAJOR RELIGIONS: Buddhist, Hindu, Muslim, Christian.

GOVERNMENT: Republic. **Head of state and government—** president. **Legislature**—Parliament.

CHIEF PRODUCTS: Agricultural—rice, tea, rubber, coconuts. **Manufactured**—textiles, copra (dried coconut meat), coconut oil, wood products, cement. **Mineral**— graphite, gemstones, kaolin.

MONETARY UNIT: Sri Lankan rupee (1 rupee = 100 cents).

NATIONAL ANTHEM: *Sri Lanka Matha* ("Mother Sri Lanka").

South India in the 19th century. Tamils live chiefly in the north and east. Their language is Tamil and most are Hindus.

Other Sri Lankans include Muslims of Arab origin, Europeans, and people of mixed race. There is also a small group of Veddas, descendants of the island's first inhabitants. A small minority of the people are Christians.

Way of Life. The great majority of Sri Lankans live in rural areas. Less than 25 percent live in cities or towns. Traditional dress for men consists of a long cloth tied at the waist and a shirt or jacket. The women often wear brightly colored saris. Sri Lankans educated in Western-type schools frequently wear Western-style clothes. Sri Lankan cooking is much like that of India. Rice is the basic food and is usually served with curried meat, fish, and vegetables.

Education. Sri Lanka has one of the highest literacy rates (87 percent) in Asia. All public and much of the private education is free, from kindergarten through the universities. Schools are found in all the towns and cities and in nearly every village. Girls and boys

A main avenue in Colombo, the capital, major port, and the most important commercial center of Sri Lanka.

Rice paddies in tea plantation. Tea is the major crop of Sri Lanka, and rice is the staple food of the people.

Many women work in the construction industries of Sri Lanka.

Workers in gem pits of southwest Sri Lanka looking for precious and semiprecious stones.

between the ages of 5 and 14 are required to go to school. The languages used in the schools are Sinhalese and Tamil. English is also taught in some schools and universities. It is widely spoken and read.

▶ THE LAND

Sri Lanka is separated from India by the shallow Palk Strait, which at its narrowest point is 35 kilometers (22 miles) wide. Other nearby neighbors are the Maldive Islands to the west and the Andaman and Nicobar Islands to the east.

The island of Sri Lanka is shaped like a teardrop. It is 435 kilometers (270 miles) long from north to south, and its greatest width is slightly more than half that distance. Sri Lanka is a little smaller than the country of Ireland and about half the size of the state of Florida in the United States.

Sri Lanka has a variety of landforms, and parts of the island contain some of the world's most beautiful scenery. The south central part is mountainous, with elevations of about 900 to 2,100 meters (3,000 to 7,000 feet). An upland zone of hills and plateaus surrounds the mountains and spreads out like a number of giant steps leading to the ocean. Elevations in the upland range up to 900 meters (3,000 feet). The rest of the island is a rolling lowland, which is broad in the north and narrow on the east, west, and south. In the extreme north is the Jaffna Peninsula, with its numerous offshore islands.

Sand dunes and lagoons are found along the coast in many areas. Some lagoons are open to the sea, and these form deep indentations along the coast. A coral reef lies close to the shore, although in most places it is submerged and cannot be seen.

Lakes and Rivers.   The rivers of Sri Lanka are short and flow outward from the highlands to the ocean. Although there are many rivers in Sri Lanka, only two of them are over 160 kilometers (100 miles) long. In the north and northeast, the rivers are dammed to form "tanks," or reservoirs, which are used for supplying water for drinking, washing, and irrigation. Many waterfalls are found in places where the rivers tumble over the edge of the highlands. The falls provide some of the most attractive spots on the island.

Climate.   Because of its nearness to the equator, Sri Lanka has high temperatures throughout the year. There is little difference between the temperatures of day and night. The average annual temperature in the lowlands is about 27°C (80°F). Cooler conditions are found in the highlands, where the average annual temperature ranges from 15 to 20°C (59 to 68°F), depending on elevation.

Rainfall varies greatly in Sri Lanka. Some parts of the island receive less than 1,000 millimeters (40 inches) annually, while other sections receive five times that amount. Most of Sri Lanka's rainfall comes from the southwest and northeast monsoons of South Asia. (The term "monsoon" is from the Arabic word *mausin,* which means "season.")

May to September is the season of the southwest monsoon. This season can bring a rainfall of more than 1,500 millimeters (60 inches) to the southwestern and south central parts of Sri Lanka, which are called the Wet Zone. The northeast monsoon season is from December to February. During this period northern and eastern Sri Lanka receive from 640 millimeters (25 inches) to more than twice that amount of rain. Additional rain from storms and thundershowers falls in all areas in the periods between the monsoons.

Natural Resources.   A variety of important minerals have been found in Sri Lanka, but much exploration remains to be done. Graphite, the leading mineral export, is found in large deposits in the southwest. The old crystalline rocks of the southwest contain many kinds of gemstones, such as sapphires, rubies, moonstones, and topazes. Other minerals include monazite (for nuclear power), kaolin (for ceramics), and mineral sands (for paint, aircraft parts, and glass).

In the past Sri Lanka had dense forests, but during hundreds of years most of them have been cleared for cropland. About two fifths of Sri Lanka is still covered with heavy forest, and many sections are set aside as forest preserves. The forests provide hardwood timber for construction, plywood, and paper products.

Soils in Sri Lanka vary greatly from place to place, but nearly all are related to the laterites, which are tropical, red-colored soils. These range from good to poor in quality, depending on local climate, conditions of terrain, and the use of the soils in the past.

Good locations for hydroelectric power plants are found along the rivers in the south central highlands, where rainfall is abundant.

Plants and Animals. Sri Lanka is the home of over 3,000 types of plants. A large number of them are not found anywhere else in the world. Among the most beautiful are the many orchids, hibiscus, and bougainvillea.

Wild elephants still live in the forests, but it is believed that only about 4,000 survive. One of the strangest creatures on the island is the loris, a slow-moving animal that has very large eyes and is about the size of a squirrel. More than 350 species of birds live in Sri Lanka. The island has two large reserves for the protection of wildlife.

▶ THE ECONOMY

Agriculture plays a vital part in Sri Lanka's economy, employing about one-third of the workforce. The most important food crop is rice, the staple of the Sri Lankan diet. The chief commercial export crops are tea, natural rubber, and coconuts, which are grown on nearly three-fifths of the cultivated land.

The most important products include textiles and clothing, wood products, cement, and a variety of consumer goods. Although Sri Lanka has no petroleum of its own, it refines and then exports imported petroleum.

▶ HISTORY AND GOVERNMENT

History records the arrival in Sri Lanka of an Indian prince named Vijaya about 543 B.C. His marriage to a local princess is said to have started the Sinhalese dynasty.

The first Europeans in Sri Lanka were the Portuguese, who came to the island in 1505. They were driven out by the Dutch in 1658. At the end of the 1700's, the British captured Sri Lanka from the Dutch and governed the island until 1948, when it gained complete independence as Ceylon.

Ceylon's first prime minister was D. S. Senanayake. In 1956, Solomon Bandaranaike became prime minister. He was assassinated in 1959 and was succeeded in 1960 by his widow, Sirimavo, who became the world's first woman prime minister. Her party was defeated in the 1965 elections but was returned to power in 1970. In 1972, Ceylon was renamed Sri Lanka. Bandaranaike was succeeded as prime minister by Junius Richard Jayewardene in 1977.

Under constitutional changes that went into effect in 1978, Sri Lanka adopted a presidential form of government. Jayewardene became the nation's first president and won re-election in 1982. Ranasinghe Premadasa, who succeeded him as president in 1988, was assassinated in 1993. He was succeeded by Dingiri Banda Wijetunga. In 1994 the presidency was won by the Bandaranaikes' daughter, Chandrika Bandaranaike Kumaratunga. She was re-elected in 1999 and again in 2000.

The president, elected for a 6-year term, appoints a cabinet, which is headed by a prime minister. Parliament, the legislative body, consists of only one house. Its 225 members are also elected for six years.

Sinhalese-Tamil Conflict. From 1983 until the signing of a permanent cease-fire agreement in 2002, Sri Lanka was torn by violent conflict between the Sinhalese and the Liberation Tigers of Tamil Eelam (LTTE), separatists seeking a politically independent Tamil homeland in northeastern Sri Lanka. As many as 65,000 people died in the civil war.

In 2004, Kumaratunga formed an alliance between her Sri Lanka Freedom Party (SLFP) and the leftist People's Liberation Front (JVP), to oppose self-government for the Tamil minority. Her party won the parliamentary elections, and Mahinda Rajapakse was named prime minister. The LTTE suspended peace talks with the government and rejected a peace offer they felt did not meet its demands for control of the Tamil region. The JVP abandoned the coalition in 2005.

On the morning of December 26, 2004, the world's most violent earthquake in forty years ruptured the seafloor under the Indian Ocean, triggering deadly tsunamis. Sri Lanka, after Indonesia, was the country most affected. More than 38,000 Sri Lankans were killed. About 1 million were left homeless.

In August 2005, Sri Lanka's foreign minister was assassinated. LTTE members were immediately suspected of committing the crime. That November, Rajapakse was elected president. He appointed another former prime minister, Ratnasiri Wickremanayaka, prime minister. Both men opposed Tamil self-government or power-sharing and favored reconsidering the 2002 cease-fire agreement.

DAVID FIRMAN
Towson State University (Maryland)

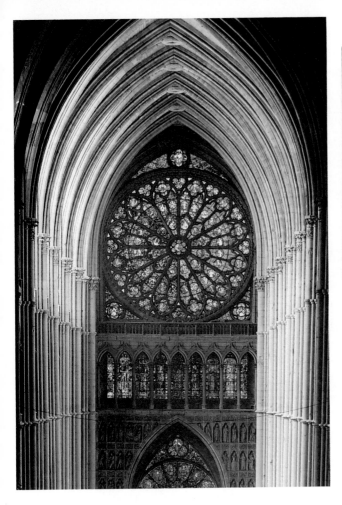

Left: Radiant stained-glass windows like this "rose" window in Reims Cathedral, France, enhance church interiors. The windows often depict scenes from the Bible. *Above:* An example from All Saints Cathedral, England, shows the return of the Prodigal Son.

STAINED-GLASS WINDOWS

Entering a Gothic cathedral on a sunny day is like stepping into a rainbow. Beams of sunlight passing through the stained-glass windows bathe the church in rich reds, blues, and greens.

"Stained glass" is the term used for pieces of colored glass joined together by strips of lead to form a picture or design. Stained glass is most often used for windows, because the beauty of the glass is best seen when light passes through it.

The process of coloring glass was probably invented in ancient Egypt. But it was during the Middle Ages that the making of stained-glass windows developed as a major art. Stained-glass windows were an important feature of churches built in the Gothic style, which first arose in the mid-1100's. The windows filled the church interiors with light and color, delighting worshipers with their beauty.

The windows were not only beautiful; they also served an educational purpose. During the Middle Ages, the church was the center of learning. There were few books, and only a handful of people could read. The designs in the first stained-glass windows usually depicted scenes from the Bible. Such scenes were important tools in teaching Christian beliefs to the people. In later years, workers' guilds and wealthy merchants paid for windows that glorified not only saints and kings but the donors themselves.

The artisans of the Middle Ages perfected techniques for making stained-glass windows, many of which are still used today. On a large white board, the artisan drew a picture the same size as the window. He numbered each section of the picture according to color. Over the drawing he placed pieces of glass that had already been colored—with metallic oxides—while the glass was being made. Then, following the outline of the drawing, he cut out the shapes with a hot iron. Finally the artisan cut strips of lead to fit between the pieces of glass. The lead did more than hold the pieces together; it became part of the design. The lead strips outlined sections of glass and kept the colors from appearing to overlap. Large windows were given a framework of iron bars for added strength.

Strangely, perfecting stained-glass techniques did not improve the windows. The bubbles in the first glasses and the unevenness of

Top: Windows designed by Louis C. Tiffany marked a revival of stained glass. *Above:* Space is the theme of a window in Washington (D.C.) National Cathedral. A piece of moon rock is embedded in the glass.

their surfaces made the sunlight seem to dance. The later glasses, with fewer imperfections, had less sparkle. Originally, paint was used only for small details, such as the features of a face. Beginning in the 1500's, more paint was used. Less light passed through the painted surfaces, and stained glass lost much of its power and majesty.

For about 200 years the use of stained glass declined, and it was not revived until the 1800's. Religious groups and wealthy people sought the excellent workmanship of the glassmakers Louis Comfort Tiffany (1848–1933), John La Farge (1835–1910), and others to decorate their churches and mansions.

When war loomed in Europe in the 1930's, windows were taken apart piece by piece and stored in safe places. After the war the windows were carefully put back.

New methods of production and ideas of design have changed the appearance of stained glass. But one thing has never changed: the magic effect of sunlight pouring through colored glass.

Reviewed by JANE HAYWARD
The Cloisters, New York City

See also DECORATIVE ARTS; GLASS; GOTHIC ART AND ARCHITECTURE.

Stalin (at right) met with U.S. president Harry S. Truman (center) and British prime minister Clement Attlee at the Potsdam Conference in Germany in 1945, near the end of World War II. At the conference, the Allied leaders called for the unconditional surrender of Japan and arranged for the division of Germany into four zones of occupation.

STALIN, JOSEPH (1879–1953)

For nearly 25 years, Joseph Stalin held absolute power in the Soviet Union and in the world Communist movement. He began his life, however, in humble surroundings. His original name was Iosif Vissarionovich Dzhugashvili, and he was born on December 21, 1879, in Gori, Georgia—then a part of Russia but now an independent country. His father was a poor shoemaker who barely earned enough to feed his family. When he was nearly 15, Iosif entered a seminary to study for the priesthood. But in 1899 he was expelled for revolutionary activities.

Early Career. During the early 1900's, he served as an organizer for the Bolsheviks, the forerunners of the Soviet Communist Party. He was arrested several times and exiled to Siberia, but he escaped. About 1913 he took the name Stalin, meaning "man of steel."

When revolution swept through Russia in 1917, Stalin had already attracted the attention of the Bolshevik leader, Lenin. By 1922, Stalin had become general secretary of the Communist Party. On his deathbed, Lenin warned of Stalin's inclination to tyranny and called for his removal as party secretary. But Lenin's warning was disregarded by his successors.

Rise to Power. After Lenin's death in 1924, Stalin gradually took power. By 1929 he was dictator of the country. Under his rule the Soviet Union was transformed into a totalitarian state in which the Communist Party exercised control over nearly all aspects of the country's economic, political, and intellectual life. In the 1930's he began a series of purges that led to the arrest and execution of his former opponents and even of his own lieutenants. Millions of ordinary citizens were also imprisoned or executed.

In 1939, Stalin signed a nonaggression pact with Adolf Hitler, the leader of Nazi Germany, which gave Hitler a free hand to invade Poland, setting off World War II. In June 1941, in spite of the pact, Germany invaded Russia. Eventually the German troops were repelled, and Stalin took control of countries in Eastern Europe that the Soviet Army had liberated from the Germans. This and other policies of Stalin led to a conflict with Western Europe and the United States that came to be called the Cold War.

Stalin was twice married and had three children. He died on March 5, 1953. Three years later his successors denounced his brutalities. A process of "de-Stalinization" was begun under Nikita Khrushchev, his eventual successor. Places named for Stalin were renamed, and in 1961, his body was removed from its place of honor in the Lenin Mausoleum.

BERTRAM D. WOLFE
Author, *Three Who Made a Revolution*

See also COMMUNISM; KHRUSHCHEV, NIKITA; LENIN, VLADIMIR ILICH.

STAMP ACT. See REVOLUTIONARY WAR.

A stamp collection can be built around a single subject or many. This collector's interests include butterflies, flowers, and space.

STAMPS AND STAMP COLLECTING

Stamp collecting is a hobby that appeals to many people. Some people enjoy gathering colorful stamps and organizing them. Others are interested in the history, geography, and culture of the countries whose stamps they collect. Still others like stamps because of the subjects pictured on them. Almost every stamp collector dreams of finding a "sleeper," a rare or valuable stamp that has been unnoticed among stamps worth little or nothing.

Modern postage stamps had their origin in the 1800's. In 1837 an Englishman, Sir Rowland Hill (1795–1879), devised a new system for paying postal fees. Before this time in most countries, the person who received a letter had to pay the postage. It was Hill's idea to have the sender attach a stamp to show that the postage had been paid. His idea was put into use in 1840, when Great Britain issued the first postage stamp. On this stamp, called the Penny Black, was a picture of Queen Victoria and the words "Postage" and "One Penny."

Stamp collecting began as soon as the Penny Black stamp went on sale. Since it was the first and only postage stamp in existence, it was a great curiosity. Many people collected Penny Blacks as souvenirs; some even tried to cover the walls of a room with them.

In 1847 the United States government issued two stamps—a ten-cent stamp bearing a portrait of George Washington and a five-cent stamp with a picture of Benjamin Franklin. While these were the first official government-issued stamps, U.S. postmasters had issued their own stamps before this. These earlier stamps are known as Postmaster's Provisionals and they are quite valuable today.

Soon other countries began to issue stamps and collectors kept as many as they could find. In those days it was fairly easy to collect all existing stamps. Since then, however, so many thousands of stamps have been issued around the world that it would be impossible for any individual to collect all of them.

▶**STARTING A STAMP COLLECTION**

To become a stamp collector a person must acquire stamps, and this can be done many ways. Some start by getting duplicate stamps from friends who are collectors. Once you become known as a collector, other friends will probably save stamps for you as well.

Most collectors also buy stamps from stamp dealers, some of whom advertise in magazines or newspapers. Some dealers sell stamps outright; others sell on approval. When buying on approval, you request an approval selection and pay only for the stamps you keep.

The cheapest way to buy stamps is by getting a mixture, which is simply a batch of unsorted stamps. Some dealers sell mixtures by weight, at so much per pound. A mixture contains canceled stamps, most of which have been issued recently. When a letter goes through the mail, the post office puts a cancellation mark on the stamp. This mark prevents people from using the stamp again. Most stamps in mixtures have been torn from envelopes and are attached to bits of paper. Mixtures often contain duplicates and are not likely to include valuable stamps. However, there is always the chance of finding a "sleeper."

Stamps are also available in packets or in sets. A packet of stamps contains no duplicates. It is therefore more expensive than a mixture, but a packet usually provides more stamps for the money. A set of stamps contains all the stamps issued by a government at one time. Sets may be complete or broken. A broken set has one or more stamps missing.

Established collectors also add to their collection by trading stamps with other collectors. You can almost always find some stamps you want among another collector's duplicates. At the same time, other collectors may want some of your duplicates.

▶ORGANIZING YOUR STAMPS

Once you have acquired stamps, the next step is to sort and prepare them for mounting. When sorting stamps, set aside those that are stuck to paper. These stamps must be separated from their backings. Do not try to rip the stamps loose or you may damage them. Instead, soak them in lukewarm water until they float free from the bits of paper to which they are attached. Then place the stamps between two clean white blotters to remove excess moisture. After that, they should be placed on clean paper to dry. To prevent stamps from wrinkling while they are drying, place them between two blotters and set a weight on them overnight. When handling stamps, you should use tongs or tweezers rather than your fingers to prevent them from becoming soiled.

Clean, dry stamps are ready to be sorted. The first step in sorting is to arrange the stamps by country of origin. Make a separate pile of stamps you cannot identify. After your stamps have been sorted, you may either mount them in albums or file them in envelopes to be mounted at another time. Ordinary correspondence envelopes may be used, or you may want to buy special glassine or transparent plastic envelopes from stamp dealers.

▶RATING THE CONDITION OF STAMPS

Before mounting stamps in an album, you must sort them again, this time according to their condition. If you have duplicates, you should select the best ones for your album. The value of a stamp depends upon two things: rarity and condition. Stamps are graded into the following five categories:

Superb: Stamps in this category are like new, with clean, fresh color. They have no creases or tears. The stamp design is centered perfectly, with even margins. Perforations are perfect and complete. If the stamp has not been canceled and the gum on the back is undamaged, it is in **mint** condition. If the stamp has been canceled, the cancellation mark should be light and legible.

Very fine: This is a physically perfect stamp. However, the color may be slightly off-shade, it may have a heavier cancellation mark, or the margins may be slightly uneven. It is not quite as good as a superb stamp.

Fine: This is a stamp without defects or blemishes but not up to very fine standards.

Good: This is a stamp with no tears or creases. The color may be faded, it may be heavily postmarked and canceled, or it may be printed off center.

Poor: These are stamps of the lowest quality. They may be torn or creased or have thin spots. Keep poor stamps only if they cannot be replaced.

▶MOUNTING YOUR STAMPS

You are now ready to mount your stamps in an album. You should try to buy the best album you can afford. A good album has room

CHILE. The 30-centavo stamp was issued in 1900 with a 5-centavo surcharge. This stamp was surcharged twice because one of the impressions was upside down. The error gives the stamp its value.

GUATEMALA. This "First Issue Fraud" fooled many collectors before it was exposed as a fake. It was circulated in 1867, 4 years before the Guatemalan government actually issued its first stamp.

CANADA. Imperfect plate production doubled some of the details (called a double transfer) on this 1851 three-penny stamp. Collectors prize such stamps.

UNITED STATES. An 1861 Wells Fargo "Pony Express" stamp. Payment of $1 assured delivery of mail from California to the east in about 8 days using stagecoaches and pony riders. Letters bearing a government 3-cent stamp were sent by covered wagon and took 8 weeks.

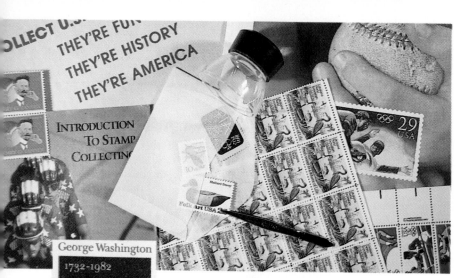

Important people and events in the history and culture of a country can be illustrated by stamps. A magnifier, clear envelopes, and tweezers will help you select and enjoy an interesting collection.

for many stamps, and the space where each stamp belongs is clearly marked. These spaces are arranged in chronological order—by the dates the stamps were issued. Many spaces have a picture of the stamp that belongs there, so all you have to do is mount a stamp over a matching picture.

Many collectors prefer to make their own albums instead of buying them. Any large loose-leaf notebook with a hard cover will do. The loose-leaf pages can be removed or added as you need them. Graph paper makes a good stamp album page; the ruled lines serve as guides for arranging stamps in even rows. When you make your own album, you can liven up the pages by making drawings or adding interesting notes. You can also arrange the pages in any way you like.

Stamps should be mounted on only one side of each page; otherwise they may tear as you turn the pages. Use stamp hinges to fasten the stamps. These hinges are made of thin, tough paper coated on one side with the same type of gum used on the backs of postage stamps. To use a hinge, fold down about one third of it, with the gummed side out. Lightly moisten this small gummed section and press it against the back of the stamp. The folded edge of the hinge should be near the top of the stamp. Now moisten the other gummed side of the hinge and press the stamp into its proper place in the album, holding it down for a few moments until it dries. A dry hinge can be easily removed from both the stamp and the album without tearing the stamp or leaving marks.

▶IDENTIFYING STAMPS

When you sorted your stamps, there were probably some you could not identify. You may be able to match some of these to the pictures in a commercial stamp album. To identify others, you will need to refer to special stamp catalogs.

When using catalogs, look for an illustration that matches the stamp you want to identify. You must look carefully, perhaps using a magnifying glass, because differences between stamps are often hardly noticeable. The illustrations in the catalog have numbers under them that refer to information about each stamp. You may find more than one reference to a particular stamp: What do you do?

In this case, you must do a bit of detective work and check four clues: the stamp's design, color, perforations, and watermark.

Matching your stamp's design to the ones shown in the catalog takes care of the first clue. Reading the descriptions of the stamps in the catalog may take care of the second clue—the stamp's color. If your stamp's color matches, your search may be over. Don't be fooled by slight color differences; a stamp's color may fade over the years. If there is more than one stamp of that color you will have to search further.

Early stamps were simply printed in rows on a large sheet, and the user had to cut them apart. These are called **imperforate** stamps. Later stamps were separated by rows of tiny slits, or **roulettes**, so they could be torn apart. Most modern stamps are separated by rows of tiny holes, called **perforations**. These perforations are made in different sizes, and catalogs show "perf" numbers for each stamp.

To check the third clue you must find the stamp's "perf" number. This can be done by using a perforation gauge, which looks like a ruler with rows of tiny dots on it. Place your stamp on the gauge so that its perforations match one of the rows of dots, then read the number on the scale. If it matches one of the stamps described, your search is at an end.

Several stamps, however, may have the same "perf" number, so you will have to check the fourth clue—the watermark. A watermark is a design placed in paper at the time it is manufactured. It cannot be seen with the naked eye. To bring out the watermark, place the stamp facedown in a small, shallow black dish and cover it with a few drops of refined benzine. If a watermark shows up, compare its design with those illustrated in the catalog.

If you fail to identify a stamp by design, color, perforations, or watermark, recheck your efforts. You will probably find that you have made an error somewhere.

▶ **CHOOSING A STAMP COLLECTION TOPIC**

Serious collectors do not attempt to collect every stamp in existence. There are far too many to collect and it would be too costly to collect them all. Most collectors, therefore, specialize in only certain types of stamps. Some collect stamps of only one country. Others may collect stamps of only one particular color or stamps with odd shapes. It is also possible to build a variety of **topical** collections, in which all the stamps relate to one topic. Ideas for such collections may include such things as airplanes, animals, athletes, birds, flowers, presidents, ships, writers, and so on. Every person can find some topic around which to build a collection.

HARRY ZARCHY
Author, *Stamp Collector's Guide*

STANFORD, LELAND. See CALIFORNIA (Famous People).

STANLEY, HENRY MORTON (1841–1904), AND DAVID LIVINGSTONE (1813–1873)

Henry M. Stanley   David Livingstone

Stanley and Livingstone are familiar names in the history of the exploration of Africa.

David Livingstone was born on March 19, 1813, at Blantyre, Scotland. A doctor and missionary, he went to Africa in 1840 to preach Christianity, tend the sick, and explore the "dark continent." In 1866 he set out to find the source of the Nile River, but when several years passed without word, many people thought he had died. So in 1869, James Gordon Bennett, the publisher of the New York *Herald*, sent reporter Henry Morton Stanley to look for him.

Henry Morton Stanley was born John Rowlands in Denbigh, Wales, on January 28, 1841. As a young man he sailed to New Orleans and took the name Stanley, the name of a cotton broker who had adopted him. After fighting in the American Civil War (1861–65), Stanley became a reporter. He was covering Britain's attack on Ethiopia when he was sent to find Livingstone.

On November 10, 1871, after a difficult two-year journey, Stanley found Livingstone, barely alive, at Ujiji, a village on Lake Tanganyika. His greeting "Dr. Livingstone, I presume?" became famous.

Livingstone remained in Africa and died on May 1, 1873. Stanley was hired by King Leopold II of Belgium to establish outposts in the Congo (now the Democratic Republic of Congo). Knighted in 1899, he died in England on May 10, 1904.

SANFORD H. BEDERMAN
Georgia State College

See also EXPLORATION AND DISCOVERY (Stanley and Livingstone).

STANLEY, WENDELL. See VIRUSES (The Discovery of Viruses).

STANTON, EDWIN McMASTERS. See CIVIL WAR, UNITED STATES (Profiles: Union).

STANTON, ELIZABETH CADY (1815–1902)

American reformer Elizabeth Cady Stanton organized the first women's rights convention in the United States (1848). One of the most radical thinkers of the early women's movement, she believed that women had an absolute "birthright to self-sovereignty."

Born Elizabeth Cady on November 12, 1815, in Johnstown, New York, she grew up in a time when women faced routine discrimination. At 24 she married Henry B. Stanton and began working on behalf of women. Then in 1848 she helped organize the first U.S. women's rights convention in Seneca Falls, New York (July 19–20).

At the convention, Cady Stanton unveiled her Declaration of Rights and Sentiments, which was based on the Declaration of Independence. It contained what were then revolutionary demands—that women be admitted into universities, trades, professions, and the ministry; that the equality of men and women be recognized; and, most shocking of all, that

women be given the right to vote. Thereafter, women's rights conventions became almost an annual event.

In 1854, while fighting for women's property rights with Susan B. Anthony, Cady Stanton became the first woman to address the New York State legislature. She was also the first woman to try to run for Congress: In 1866, after the Civil War had ended and the slaves were freed, she was so bitterly disappointed that Congress was considering extending the vote to African American men but not to women that she ran for office in protest.

In 1869, Cady Stanton and Anthony founded the National Woman Suffrage Association, which in 1890 became the National American Woman Suffrage Association. Cady Stanton died on October 26, 1902.

KATHRYN CULLEN-DUPONT
Author, *Elizabeth Cady Stanton and Women's Liberty*

See also ANTHONY, SUSAN B.

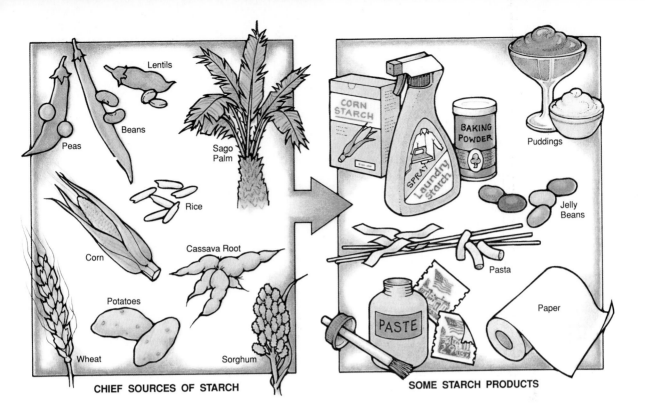

CHIEF SOURCES OF STARCH

Lentils

Beans

Peas

Sago Palm

Rice

Corn

Cassava Root

Potatoes

Wheat

Sorghum

SOME STARCH PRODUCTS

CORN STARCH

SPRAY Laundry Starch

BAKING POWDER

Puddings

Jelly Beans

Pasta

PASTE

Paper

STARCH

Starch is a food material that is stored in plants. It may be found in seeds (as in kernels of corn, rice, or wheat), in roots (tapioca), in tubers (potatoes), or in stems (the sago palm and other trees). The starch supplies food for growing seeds and for plants during their resting periods.

Starch is also an important food for people. It is a carbohydrate—a compound made up of carbon, hydrogen, and oxygen. In the process of digestion, starch is changed into sugars that the body uses for energy.

People eat starch in its natural form in potatoes, rice, and other starchy vegetables. Flour is a starch made from the seeds of rice, wheat, corn, or other plants. Starches are used to thicken puddings, gravies, and sauces. A large quantity of starch is used to brew beer and to make other alcoholic beverages. Prepared baking powders contain starch, as do candies such as jelly beans and gumdrops.

Starch also has many commercial uses. The paper industry uses large amounts of starch to strengthen paper and to give it a smooth surface. Glues made from starch are used to make cardboard boxes and paperboard. The textile industry uses starch to strengthen fibers and to stiffen fabrics such as organdy. Laundry starch is used to stiffen shirts and other clothes.

Starch is used in dusting powders and in ointments and pastes. It is used as a binder in tablets such as aspirin and in making sand cores for casting metals. It is even used to thicken the mud used in drilling oil wells.

The plants in which starch is found in large, easily available quantities are corn, wheat, rice, arrowroot, sorghum, potatoes, cassava (tapioca), and sago palms. Corn supplies most of the starch that is produced commercially in North and South America. Potatoes supply most of the commercial starch in Europe. In Asia rice is the chief commercial source of starch.

Pure starch is a tasteless, odorless white powder made up of tiny round or oval grains (granules) that can be viewed through a microscope. The granules vary in shape and appearance, depending on the plant from which they come.

Starch does not dissolve in cold water, alcohol, or ether. The test to identify starch is simple. If iodine solution is added to it, starch turns a dark color, usually blue.

ELBERT C. WEAVER
Co-author, *Chemistry for Our Times*

STARFISH

Starfish, or sea stars, are among the world's most beautiful and unusual animals. These creatures, which are not fish, are most often shaped like five-pointed stars. They are found throughout the world's oceans, from the icy waters of the Arctic and Antarctic to the warm waters of tropical coral reefs. While many different types live on rocky or sandy areas close to shore, other deep-sea starfish bury themselves in the mud on the ocean bottom. Some even are found at depths as great as 19,800 feet (6,035 meters).

The 1,800 living species, or kinds, of starfish are members of a larger group of sea invertebrates (animals without backbones) called echinoderms. Other echinoderms include brittle stars (also called serpent stars), sea urchins, basket stars, sand dollars, sea lilies, and sea cucumbers.

A dazzling array of spiny-skinned creatures called starfish dwell in the world's oceans. Each kind, no matter how different it might appear from another, has a similar form made up of arms regularly arranged around a central body.

▶ THE CHARACTERISTICS OF STARFISH

Starfish occur in an amazing variety of colors, textures, and shapes. They vary in color from bright yellow to deep purple. The starfish's thin covering of skin, which can be spiny, smooth, or knobby, is stretched over a tough internal skeleton made of thin plates of calcium. The skeleton protects the starfish's internal organs and gives the animal its special shape. Starfish range in size from 3/8 inch (1 centimeter) to almost 3 feet (1 meter) across.

The body of the starfish consists of a central disk with arms radiating outward. Most starfish have 5 arms, but some species have as many as 50 arms! At the tip of each arm is an eyespot that is sensitive to light. The starfish's mouth is located in the middle of the central disk, on the underside of its body.

A unique feature of the starfish is its water-vascular system—a network of tubes that run throughout its body. The starfish gets much of its oxygen and some nutrients directly from the seawater that is forced through the tube network.

The starfish also relies on its water-vascular system to help it move. If you turned over a starfish, you would see that the underside of each arm is covered with tiny suction cups, which are really the muscular ends of the tubes that make up the water-vascular system. Called tube feet, these suction cups are pushed out, to grip, or drawn back, to release, as the water pressure within the tubes is increased or decreased.

To move forward, the starfish extends one arm and grips the surface with its tube feet. Then it pulls its body forward. It continues moving forward by stretching its arm in front of it, grasping the surface, and pulling itself forward. This form of locomotion is sure, but slow. Most starfish amble along at about 3 yards (2.7 meters) per hour.

Some starfish also use their tube feet to help them feed.

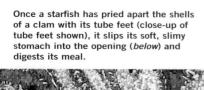

Once a starfish has pried apart the shells of a clam with its tube feet (close-up of tube feet shown), it slips its soft, slimy stomach into the opening (*below*) and digests its meal.

They wrap their arms around shelled animals, such as clams. With their tube feet, they pry the shell apart, applying steady pressure until the animal can no longer hold its shell closed. An opening of 1/25 inch (1 millimeter) or less is enough for the starfish. It feeds by pushing its stomach out through its mouth and down through the opening of the cracked clam. Digestive juices from the starfish's stomach go to work, breaking down the prey within its own shell.

Starfish have a remarkable ability. When attacked, the starfish will sacrifice its arms to escape a predator's grasp, and then regrow them (*left*)! A starfish stands on the tips of its arms (*below*) to release its eggs into the water.

▶ THE LIFE OF STARFISH

A few species of starfish are hermaphrodites. That is, they have both male and female parts and can fertilize their own eggs. Most, however, have two separate sexes. At spawning time, the female releases millions of eggs into the water at the same time as the male releases millions of sperm. Water currents bring these reproductive cells together, and many of the eggs are fertilized.

Some kinds of starfish that live in very cold water brood their fertilized eggs by holding them within the body cavity until the young hatch. For most starfish, however, the release of reproductive cells signals the end of their parental duty. The young starfish develop completely on their own. Within a few days of fertilization, the eggs become microscopic, free-swimming larvae. The tiny bean-shaped starfish larvae have hairlike projections called cilia extending from their sides like hundreds of slender oars. They drift along, feeding on single-celled creatures floating in the water.

Some larvae escape the fish, corals, jellyfish, and other animals that feed on them. Within a few weeks or months, those that survive anchor themselves to the ocean bottom and undergo a change into their adult form. A new mouth forms on one side and tiny arms grow from the central disk. At first the young starfish may be no bigger than the head of a pin. Day by day it grows, and within a couple of months, it reaches its adult size. By 1 year of age, the starfish produces its own eggs or sperm and contributes to a new generation of starfish.

New starfish are also produced by the process of regeneration. If a starfish is torn in half, both halves will grow new arms. The result is two identical starfish. Regeneration usually requires that the piece of starfish include at least one whole arm and part of the central disk. But in some starfish, a whole animal can regenerate from just a piece of an arm.

▶ STARFISH AND THEIR ENVIRONMENT

Because of their powers of regeneration, starfish became serious threats to commercial oyster and clam beds. Years ago, fishers that caught starfish in their nets used to try to kill them by chopping them up and throwing them back in the sea. Their catch of oysters and clams continued to dwindle until they learned that starfish regenerate when they are chopped up, producing more animals.

In recent years, starfish have continued to plague oyster and clam beds as well as coral reefs, especially those in the South Pacific. The coral-eating crown-of-thorns starfish has undergone a population explosion on many reefs and has killed off huge amounts of living coral. Human disturbance of the reefs, pollution, and overharvesting of shelled predators may create a more favorable environment for the starfish—permanently tipping the balance of nature in favor of the hardy starfish.

ELIZABETH KAPLAN
Series Coauthor, *Ask Isaac Asimov*

STARS

When you look at the sky on a clear dark night, you can see hundreds of points of light in the sky. These are stars. Although they look faint, stars are actually large, extremely bright balls of gas that emit enormous amounts of light, heat, and other forms of energy.

Our sun is a star, but unlike most stars, which are very far from Earth, the sun is relatively close—about 93 million miles (150 million kilometers) away. Other stars are so far away that their distance is measured in **light-years** rather than in miles. One light-year is the distance that light travels in one year—nearly 6 trillion miles (9.6 trillion kilometers).

It takes light from the sun about eight minutes to reach Earth. The nearest star to Earth after the sun is Alpha Centauri, which is about 4 light-years away. The brightest star in our sky is Sirius, which is about 8 light-years from Earth. Sirius is larger and hotter than the sun, but it appears much smaller and dimmer because it is so far away. Many of the stars you see in the sky are hundreds or thousands of light-years away.

▶ LEARNING ABOUT STARS

Special instruments attached to telescopes enable astronomers to measure the physical properties of stars. Brightness, for example, is measured by special electronic cameras. In measuring a star's brightness, or magnitude, astronomers must distinguish between its **apparent magnitude** (its brightness as it appears from Earth) and its **absolute magnitude** (the brightness it would have if all stars were the same distance from the Earth). Absolute magnitude allows astronomers to compare the actual brightness of the stars.

Temperature is determined by measuring the intensity of a star's light in different colors with an instrument called a **photometer**. And a star's composition can be determined by using a **spectrometer**, a device that measures wavelengths of light.

The most difficult property to measure is a star's distance. To calculate the distance to a star from Earth, astronomers must measure its **parallax** (how much the star appears to shift in the sky when viewed from different points

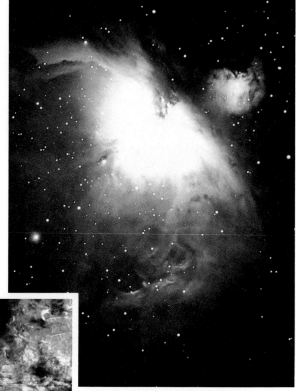

A spectacular cloud of gas surrounds intensely hot star clusters deep within the Orion Nebula (*above*). A Hubble Space Telescope image of the glowing gases at the edge of the nebula (*inset*) helps astronomers evaluate the possibility of new star formation within the cloud.

in space). Astronomers determine a star's parallax by measuring its position over six months, during which time the Earth has moved between different points in its orbit in space. From these observations, they can calculate the star's parallax and use mathematical formulas to calculate its distance from the Earth. The stars are so far away that all but a few of the nearest ones have a parallax shift of less than 1/10,000 degree. Measuring such shifts is difficult. (See parallax in ASTRONOMY in Volume A.)

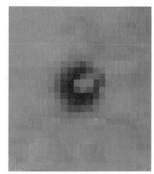

This image of a dark cloud of dust and gas shows a young, reddish star silhouetted against the background of the Orion Nebula. Astronomers think that within a few million years the cloud may develop into planets orbiting the star.

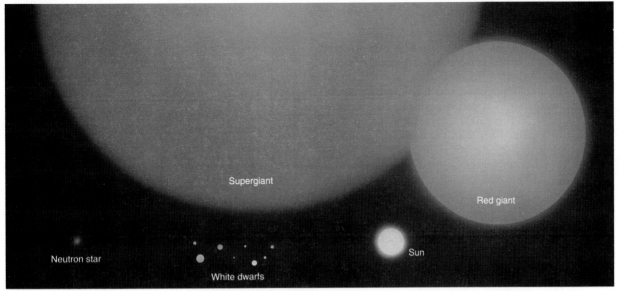

Supergiant

Red giant

Neutron star

White dwarfs

Sun

Stars vary greatly in size. Red supergiants are the largest stars and neutron stars are the smallest. Our sun is an average star. It is much larger than a white dwarf but much smaller than a red giant or a supergiant.

▶DIFFERENT TYPES OF STARS

Astronomers have surveyed thousands of stars in the sky. As a result, they have learned that stars differ in brightness, size, and color. A star's color depends on how hot it is. Very hot stars appear blue; slightly cooler stars may appear blue-white, white, or yellow; and the coolest stars appear orange or red.

The dimmest stars in the universe are **red dwarfs**. Our sun shines a million times brighter than most red dwarfs. Red dwarf stars are dim because they are relatively small and cool. A typical red dwarf has a temperature of about 5400°F (3000°C). That may seem very

Although it is a relatively small star, this ultraviolet image of the sun shows the force of its energy. An erupting solar prominence disrupts the sun's atmosphere as it ejects streams of hot gases far out into space.

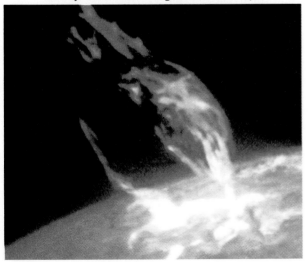

hot, but it is rather cool for a star. The best-known red dwarf is Proxima Centauri, a tiny companion star to Alpha Centauri. Proxima Centauri is about the same distance from Earth as Alpha Centauri is, but because it is so dim, it can only be seen through a telescope.

The brightest stars are known as **blue supergiants**. A typical blue supergiant shines a million times brighter than the sun, and its temperature may be as high as 108,000°F (60,000°C). In size, it may be as much as 100 times larger than the sun. We know of very few blue supergiants, but because they are so bright, they can be seen far away in space. Deneb, in the constellation Cygnus, is a blue supergiant. Although it is about 6,000 light-years away, it is almost as bright as Sirius, which is only about 8 light-years away.

Most stars are between red dwarfs and blue supergiants in size and brightness. These stars are called **main sequence stars**. The sun is a main sequence star and so is Sirius. The sun has a temperature of about 10,000°F (5500°C), and its light is white. The temperature of Sirius is about 18,000°F (10,000°C), and it shines with a blue-white light.

Another type of star, the **white dwarf**, is extremely hot, hotter than a star like Sirius. But white dwarf stars appear dim because they are extremely small. For example, the Pup, a companion star to Sirius, has a temperature of about 180,000°F (100,000°C), but it is 100 times smaller than the sun so it does not give off much light. At the opposite extreme, **red giants** and **red supergiants** are cool, but they shine brightly because they are enormous. The star Betelgeuse, which is in the constellation Orion, is a red supergiant. Its temperature is 5400°F (3000°C), and it gives off 1,000 times more light than the sun. Some stars do not always shine with the same brightness. They become brighter or dimmer over a period of time and are called **variable stars**.

It is unclear exactly how large a star must be to shine. In 2005, the smallest known star was found. It was just 16 percent larger than Jupiter, but its mass was 96 times as great.

Binary and Multiple Star Systems

Many stars have companion stars. In fact, astronomers think that about one-half of the stars in the sky have one or more companions. In a **binary star system**, two stars orbit each other, bound by their gravitational attraction to one another. Binary stars that are close together orbit each other very rapidly—some of them take only a few hours to complete an orbit. Binary stars that are far apart may take thousands of years to complete an orbit around one another.

Astronomers can determine the mass of the stars in a binary system by considering the strength of their gravitational forces and the speeds of their orbits. The more massive a star, the faster it orbits around its companion star and the greater its gravitational effect on the companion star. The least massive binary stars known are about $\frac{1}{12}$ the mass of the sun. The most massive ones known are about 80 times the mass of the sun.

The universe also contains **multiple star systems**. The star Castor, in the constellation Gemini, is actually made up of six stars—three binary systems orbiting one another. However, if you look at Castor without a telescope, it appears as a single star.

▶ THE FORMATION OF STARS

Stars are created in vast clouds of dust and gases. Some of the gas is made up of debris from old stars that have exploded, and some is original gas from the formation of the universe. A star begins to form when heavy elements in these gases condense to form tiny grains of interstellar dust. When enough gas and dust collects, a vast cloud can form. These

WONDER QUESTION

What are stars made of?

Stars are made of the same chemical elements that humans and other objects on Earth are made of. The elements in the stars, however, often exist in a different physical state. The atoms of the different chemical elements on Earth combine to form water, carbon dioxide, and the complex molecules that make up the human body. In most stars, molecules such as these cannot exist. It is so hot, the atoms exist as a hot gas called **plasma**. (Some cool stars have molecules in their atmospheres.)

About 90 percent of the atoms in a star are hydrogen and 9 percent are helium, the two most common elements in the universe. Only about 1 percent of the atoms in the universe are the other types of elements, such as carbon, oxygen, nitrogen, sulfur, silicon, nickel, and iron, which are found in people and other objects on Earth.

When stars grow old they explode and disperse different elements throughout space. These elements become the building blocks of new stars and planets.

clouds are called **nebulas**. (For more information, read the article NEBULAS in Volume N.)

Over very long periods of time, the gravitational pull of the particles in the nebula draws them toward one another, and parts of the nebula begin to collapse and to spin slowly. In these denser knots, the gas and particles fall inward ever faster, causing the temperature and pressure to rise and gases to glow. When the temperature and pressure become high enough, **nuclear reactions** occur that begin to generate energy. A star is born.

Several theories try to explain the formation of binary and multiple star systems. One suggests that gas clouds break into fragments, with each piece forming a star. In large gas clouds, hundreds of stars may form at once, thereby forming clusters of stars. Stars may form at different times as well. In the Orion Nebula, for example, some stars have already formed and others are still forming. The stars that have already formed illuminate and heat the surrounding gases. They glow and light up the nebula like a neon sign in the sky.

Planets form from materials that are left over from a star's formation. Although our solar system is the only collection of planets that is known with certainty to exist, astronomers think it is possible that other stars have planets, too.

How Stars Get Their Energy

Stars give off enormous amounts of energy in the form of heat, light, and other types of radiation. This energy is generated by natural reactions occurring deep within the star. These reactions are nuclear reactions, which take place between the **nuclei**, or centers, of the atoms that make up the star.

The temperature at the center of a star is extremely high. At the center of the sun, for example, the temperature is about 27,000,000°F (15,000,000°C). At such high temperatures, the atoms that make up the star move very rapidly, and their nuclei crash into one another. When the nuclei of hydrogen atoms collide, some of them fuse together to form helium nuclei. This reaction, which is called a **nuclear-fusion reaction**, produces energy. During the nuclear-fusion reactions inside a star, hydrogen is used up and helium and energy are created.

▶THE LIFE AND DEATH OF STARS

After a star has formed and nuclear fusion begins, the star begins a long life converting hydrogen into helium. But all stars do not live the same amount of time. A star's life span depends on how fast it uses up its sources of energy.

The most massive stars use up their hydrogen the fastest. Stars with 30 times more mass than our sun convert all of their hydrogen to helium in a few million years. Most main sequence stars, however, use hydrogen more slowly. Stars like our sun have enough hydrogen to last about 10 billion years. Red dwarf stars, the coolest and least massive stars, consume their hydrogen so slowly that they will shine for trillions of years. Eventually, every star uses up all of its hydrogen. At that point, a number of things can happen, depending on the size of the star.

Supernovas

Most main sequence stars become red giants when they use up their hydrogen. But what happens after that varies. When a massive, blue main sequence star uses up all of its hydrogen, its core shrinks and its temperature rises. As the core becomes hotter, helium nuclei fuse together forming carbon, and the core shrinks as a result. The area around the core, however, expands because of the heat that is generated, and the star becomes a red giant.

As the red giant continues to burn, nuclear fusion converts more helium to carbon, and in time, carbon is converted into other heavier elements. This process continues until the core has been converted to iron. Although iron nuclei can fuse with other iron nuclei, these nuclear reactions do not give off energy. With no more fuel to keep it going, the star collapses and then explodes. When it explodes, it becomes a **supernova**. Supernovas are extremely bright. In 1987, a giant star in a nearby galaxy called the Large Magellanic Cloud became a supernova. Even though this supernova was about 160,000 light-years from Earth, it could be seen without a telescope.

Supernovas are very important because they provided the elements that made life possible on Earth. When the universe first formed, it consisted almost entirely of hydrogen and helium. As stars developed and then exploded as supernovas, other elements that make life possible, such as carbon, nitrogen, oxygen, sulfur, silicon, nickel, and iron, were formed and blasted far into space. The Earth was formed out of these same elements.

White Dwarfs

When a star like the sun uses up most of its hydrogen and becomes a red giant, it expands from ten to one hundred times larger than its original size. Unlike more massive main sequence stars, however, a sun-like star never gets hot enough to convert all of its matter into the heavier elements. Instead, its energy supply becomes unsteady, causing it to pulsate from bright to dim and to change in size every few months. As the star runs out of energy, its interior shrinks and an outer envelope of gas surrounding the interior expands until it looks like a gigantic bubble surrounding the star— what astronomers call a **planetary nebula**. This planetary nebula lasts about 100,000 years and it then dissipates into space. The inner core that is left behind is called a **white dwarf** star.

In a white dwarf star, a volume of matter as great as the sun is crushed into a size no larger than the Earth. The nuclei of its atoms are thus squeezed extremely close together, and the matter is very dense. About $\frac{1}{10}$ cubic inch of this matter may weigh 1,000 tons. Because the white dwarf has no hydrogen for fusion, it no longer generates any energy, and the star begins to cool—a process that can take billions of years. No one knows what happens when a white dwarf has cooled because it gives off no light and thus cannot be seen.

Perhaps the dark, burned-out cinders of old white dwarf stars are scattered throughout the universe.

Novas. If a white dwarf star is part of a binary system, it may put up a lively fight before fading away. In a binary system, one star usually changes into a red giant and then into a white dwarf before the other star does. When the second star becomes a red giant and expands, some of its hydrogen flows to the white dwarf if the two stars are close together. When this hydrogen accumulates on the surface of a hot white dwarf, it explodes. This explosion of surface hydrogen is called a **nova**. The nova shines brightly for a few months or years and then fades away. A white dwarf may shine as a nova many times before its companion becomes a white dwarf and both stars cool and fade.

Neutron Stars, Black Holes, and Pulsars

Stars like the sun become red giants and eventually white dwarfs. Stars more massive than the sun explode as supernovas and leave an expanding cloud of elements that help create the next generation of stars. But what happens to stars more massive than the sun but not as massive as those that blow themselves apart?

When such stars use up their hydrogen, they also become red giants and create planetary nebula. But the cores of these stars are too big for them to become white dwarfs. Instead, they become neutron stars or black holes.

Neutron Stars. Although the matter in a white dwarf is extremely dense and packed together very tightly, it still contains the ordinary nuclei of atoms. However, when a star with a mass of more than $1\frac{1}{2}$ times that of the sun tries to become a white dwarf, the tremendous pressure squeezes the nuclei together, forming particles called neutrons. The resulting

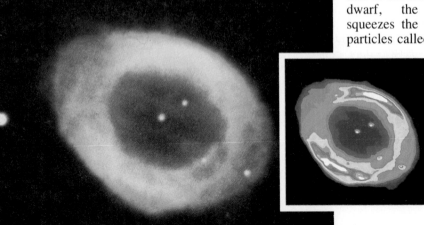

Materials released by the explosion of a star created these glowing rings of gases, called the Ring Nebula (*far left*). A computer-generated image of this planetary nebula (*inset*) helps astronomers analyze the composition of the gases released by the star.

object, called a **neutron star**, is smaller and denser than a white dwarf. A typical neutron star is only 6 miles (10 kilometers) in diameter, and ¹/₁₀ cubic inch of its matter might weigh 1 billion tons.

Astronomers have detected neutron stars in some binary star systems. When hydrogen from a companion star falls on a neutron star, the temperature becomes so great that a powerful burst of X-ray or gamma-ray radiation is emitted. Satellite observatories are able to detect these types of radiation, and astronomers hope to learn more about neutron stars by studying the radiation coming from these binary systems.

Black Holes. When a particularly massive star collapses at the end of its life, the gravitational force may become so great that the star's matter continues to collapse until it is squeezed into an infinitely small space, which scientists refer to as a **singularity**. Surrounding this point in space is a spherical gravitational boundary called an **event horizon**. Within this boundary, nothing can ever escape the tremendous gravitational forces. Space itself is bent inward and even light cannot escape. Such a phenomenon is called a **black hole**. If the Earth were compressed into a singularity, the sphere of its event horizon would be about the size of a small marble. A star-sized black hole would be only about 1 mile (1.6 kilometers) in diameter.

Since nothing, not even light, escapes a black hole, a black hole cannot be "seen." Astronomers are certain, however, that black holes exist. Astronomers can detect black holes indirectly. They can observe the effects of a black hole's gravitational forces. They can also observe what happens when matter falls into a black hole: It emits bursts of high-energy gamma rays and X rays before disappearing. Usually, it is difficult to tell whether an object that emits intense X rays and gamma rays is a neutron star or a black hole. Nonetheless, many black holes have been identified. The first object suspected of being a black hole was found within the constellation Cygnus—a source of intense X-ray radiation near a star named Cygnus X-1. Some evidence suggests that large black holes lie at the center of the Milky Way galaxy and in the midst of other galaxies as well.

Pulsars. Since 1967, astronomers have detected unusual radio waves coming from

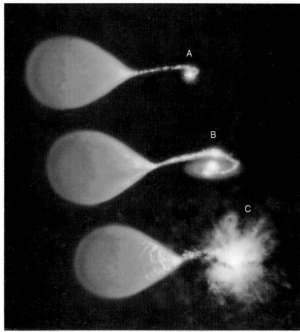

(A) When a star in a binary system expands into a red giant, some of its hydrogen flows to its smaller companion star. (B) Over time, this hydrogen accumulates on the surface of the smaller star. (C) Eventually, the accumulation of the hydrogen causes an explosion, called a nova, on the surface of the smaller star.

space in bursts, or pulses. These pulses are coming from neutron stars known as **pulsars**.

A pulsar is a neutron star that spins rapidly and has a strong magnetic field. When gas from space falls onto a pulsar, the gas becomes very hot. This hot gas and the star's strong magnetic field act like a radio transmitter sending out a narrow beam of radio waves. As the pulsar spins, the beam also spins, somewhat like the rotating beam of a lighthouse. The star always transmits its signal, but radio telescopes on Earth usually detect the signal when it sweeps past our planet as regularly spaced pulses of radio energy. This is why these stars are called pulsars.

Although astronomers have learned much about such phenomena and the birth, life, and death of stars, many secrets about them and the rest of the universe remain for the next generation of astronomers to discover.

RICHARD BERRY
Author, *Discover the Stars*

See also ASTRONOMY; ATOMS; BLACK HOLES; ELEMENTS, CHEMICAL; LIGHT; NUCLEAR ENERGY; PULSARS; QUASARS; RADIO ASTRONOMY; SUN; UNIVERSE.

STAR-SPANGLED BANNER, THE. See NATIONAL ANTHEMS AND PATRIOTIC SONGS.

STATE, UNITED STATES DEPARTMENT OF

The Department of State is the oldest of the 15 executive departments of the United States government. Its purpose is to negotiate treaties, to communicate with foreign governments, and to recommend and execute foreign policies that will promote security in the United States and around the world.

The department is headed by the secretary of state, who is appointed by the president with the consent of the Senate. The secretary, who is the highest-ranking member of the president's cabinet, also sits on the National Security Council. At the department, the secretary is assisted by a deputy secretary, a counselor, an inspector general, four under secretaries, and numerous assistant secretaries, bureau directors, and ambassadors.

Department Headquarters

State Department headquarters are located at 2201 C Street, N.W., in Washington, D.C. Employees communicate with U.S. embassies, consulates, and missions around the world and serve as the official contacts for foreign diplomats stationed in the United States.

Department headquarters are divided into two types of bureaus. **Regional bureaus** implement foreign policy in different parts of the world. They are the bureaus of African Affairs, European and Eurasian Affairs, East Asian and Pacific Affairs, Western Hemisphere Affairs, Near Eastern Affairs, and South Asian Affairs. **Functional bureaus** handle issues that are global in nature, such as human rights, the environment, international drug trafficking, and terrorism.

The Department of State also provides consular services to U.S. citizens traveling abroad. These include issuing passports and travel advisories (to warn Americans of potential dangers in unstable areas of the world); assisting U.S. businesses in their overseas operations; and providing emergency assistance to American travelers overseas.

Foreign Service

The Department of State operates more than 250 embassies, consulates, and missions in the more than 180 countries with which the United States has formal diplomatic relations.

Embassies are located in the capital cities of foreign countries. Although they are built on foreign soil, they are considered United States territory. Embassies are run by ambassadors, who are the president's personal representatives. An ambassador's top assistant is called a Deputy Chief of Mission (DCM). During an ambassador's absence from his or her embassy, the DCM takes control under the title *chargé d'affaires*.

U.S. secretary of state Condoleezza Rice (left) met with Afghan president Hamid Karzai in 2005 to pledge a long-term U.S. commitment to the newly democratic Afghanistan. Meeting with foreign leaders is one of the secretary's most important responsibilities. Rice, a former national security adviser, is the first African American woman to serve as U.S. secretary of state. She was appointed by President George W. Bush in 2005.

Secretaries of State

Name	Took Office	Under President
*Thomas Jefferson	1790	Washington
Edmund Randolph	1794	Washington
Timothy Pickering	1795	Washington, J. Adams
*John Marshall	1800	J. Adams
*James Madison	1801	Jefferson
Robert Smith	1809	Madison
*James Monroe	1811	Madison
*John Quincy Adams	1817	Monroe
*Henry Clay	1825	J. Q. Adams
*Martin Van Buren	1829	Jackson
Edward Livingston	1831	Jackson
Louis McLane	1833	Jackson
John Forsyth	1834	Jackson, Van Buren
*Daniel Webster	1841	W. H. Harrison, Tyler
Abel P. Upshur	1843	Tyler
*John C. Calhoun	1844	Tyler
*James Buchanan	1845	Polk
John M. Clayton	1849	Taylor
*Daniel Webster	1850	Fillmore
Edward Everett	1852	Fillmore
William L. Marcy	1853	Pierce
Lewis Cass	1857	Buchanan
Jeremiah S. Black	1860	Buchanan
*William H. Seward	1861	Lincoln, A. Johnson
Elihu B. Washburne	1869	Grant
Hamilton Fish	1869	Grant
William M. Evarts	1877	Hayes
*James G. Blaine	1881	Garfield, Arthur
F. T. Frelinghuysen	1881	Arthur
Thomas F. Bayard	1885	Cleveland
*James G. Blaine	1889	B. Harrison
John W. Foster	1892	B. Harrison
Walter Q. Gresham	1893	Cleveland
Richard Olney	1895	Cleveland
John Sherman	1897	McKinley
William R. Day	1898	McKinley
John M. Hay	1898	McKinley, T. Roosevelt
Elihu Root	1905	T. Roosevelt
Robert Bacon	1909	T. Roosevelt
Philander C. Knox	1909	Taft
*William J. Bryan	1913	Wilson
Robert Lansing	1915	Wilson
Bainbridge Colby	1920	Wilson
*Charles E. Hughes	1921	Harding, Coolidge
Frank B. Kellogg	1925	Coolidge
Henry L. Stimson	1929	Hoover
*Cordell Hull	1933	F. D. Roosevelt
Edward R. Stettinius, Jr.	1944	F. D. Roosevelt, Truman
James F. Byrnes	1945	Truman
*George C. Marshall	1947	Truman
Dean G. Acheson	1949	Truman
*John Foster Dulles	1953	Eisenhower
Christian A. Herter	1959	Eisenhower
Dean Rusk	1961	Kennedy, L. B. Johnson
William P. Rogers	1969	Nixon
*Henry A. Kissinger	1973	Nixon, Ford
Cyrus R. Vance	1977	Carter
*Edmund S. Muskie	1980	Carter
Alexander M. Haig, Jr.	1981	Reagan
George P. Shultz	1982	Reagan
James A. Baker III	1989	G. Bush
Lawrence S. Eagleburger	1992	G. Bush
Warren M. Christopher	1993	Clinton
*Madeleine K. Albright	1997	Clinton
*Colin L. Powell	2001	G. W. Bush
*Condoleezza Rice	2005	G. W. Bush

*Subject of a separate article or profile. Consult the Index.

Consulates general (headed by consuls general) and **consulates** (headed by consuls) are agencies smaller than embassies that are located in key foreign cities other than capitals. The agencies that represent the United States at international organizations—such as the United Nations (UN) and the Organization of American States (OAS)—are called **missions**.

Personnel

The Department of State employs about 25,000 people worldwide. Career foreign service officers (FSO's) work side by side with civil servants and political appointees, bringing together skills and experience.

In recent years, an aggressive equal employment opportunity campaign has sought to bring more women and minorities into leadership positions at the Department of State to ensure a broader representation of American society.

History

The Department of State was created by the Continental Congress in 1781. Originally called the Department of Foreign Affairs, it was renamed in 1789. Thomas Jefferson was the first secretary of state and the first of six who later were elected president.

The Department of State grew rapidly following World War I (1914–18), when the United States became a world power. During World War II (1939–45) and the Cold War that followed, the department's responsibilities continued to expand. From 1945 to 1950 the department added the Policy Planning Staff, the Bureau of International Organization Affairs, and the Bureau of Economic Affairs. It made various other organizational changes, which were based in part on the recommendations of the first Hoover Commission, led by former president Herbert Hoover.

Since 1901, when the prizes were first awarded, five U.S. secretaries of state have won the Nobel Peace Prize. They include Elihu Root (1912), Frank B. Kellogg (1929), Cordell Hull (1945), George C. Marshall (1953), and Henry Kissinger (1973).

ANTHONY ANAND DAS
Director of Public Communication
United States Department of State

See also FOREIGN SERVICE.

Each U.S. state has a legislature made up of elected officials, chosen by the voters of the state. These representatives work with the state's chief executive (the governor) and the court systems to create laws to benefit the residents of the state. Every state (except Nebraska) has two legislative chambers, which are generally known as the senate and the house of representatives, or assembly. Most state legislatures, including the New York State Assembly (*pictured right*), meet annually.

STATE GOVERNMENTS

Government in the United States is divided among fifty state governments and the tremendously complex and powerful federal (national) government that is centered in Washington, D.C. The state governments existed long before the federal government was created. Before the United States was established, each colony was governed under the laws of its own charter. When independence was declared in 1776, these charters served as models for the new states' constitutions.

In 1789, when the Founding Fathers drafted the Constitution, they gave the federal government many powers. At the same time they wanted to make sure that each state's government would retain a certain amount of authority over its own citizens, but they did not resolve this issue before the Constitution was ratified. As a result, in 1791 when the First Congress met, it drafted and adopted the Tenth Amendment to the Constitution. It specifies that any powers not specifically assigned to the federal government belong to the states or the people. This sharing of responsibilities also gives the states the freedom to address the particular needs and problems of their own communities, with which they are more familiar than the national government.

▶STATE CONSTITUTIONS

Each of the fifty states, like the federal government, has a written constitution that provides the framework for its government. Generally, the state constitutions are more specific than the federal constitution, for they provide detailed blueprints for state government operations as well as define the basic laws and duties of each state's government.

A state's constitution may not conflict with the Constitution of the United States or with federal laws. In turn, every act of a state's legislature, order of its governor, or local law must agree with the terms of the state's constitution. Finally, the municipal, or local, governments—the counties, cities, towns, and townships—must operate under the authority of the state.

If the people of a state wish to rewrite their constitution, a group of delegates is specially elected to a constitutional convention, either at the request of the citizens or on the demand of the state's legislature. It is not common to completely rewrite a constitution; usually the custom is for the state legislature to propose amendments to alter it. In every state except Delaware, the people themselves have to approve an amendment to their state constitution before it can go into effect. Such amendments are voted on at the polls on Election Day.

▶ HOW STATE GOVERNMENTS ARE ORGANIZED

When the new states were formed in the days of the Revolutionary War, there were many grievances against England. These grievances and complaints were often directed at the king and the colonial governors. As a consequence, in the new states there was strong distrust of powerful rulers. So, as the new governments were created, governors were given much less power than they had been granted in colonial times. As a result, the state governments became dominated by the legislatures.

In the 1800's the nation grew rapidly. The states flourished under the demands of the new industrial society. Mammoth projects—turnpikes, canals, modern highways, vast educational systems—increased the need for action by state governments. Local governments, faced with new scientific problems, needed more and closer supervision. All these activities of the states called for a more powerful chief or leader. Therefore, the governors gradually regained power from the legislatures, and the state governments began focusing more and more on the governor's office.

State governments are organized in much the same way as the national government, with power divided among three branches—the executive, the legislative, and the judicial. This system is called separation of powers.

The Governor

The governor, like the president of the United States, is the head of the executive branch. He or she is responsible for making sure that the laws of the state are carried out. The political qualifications of a governor are very important. Governors must be prepared for leadership and have the support of their political parties. Most will have gained experience by having served previously in some local office or in the state legislature.

Legal qualifications for the governorship vary from state to state. Most states require that their governor be at least 30 years of age, although a few states permit election at the age of 21. The governor must be a resident of the state in which he or she is elected. In most states, the governor is elected to a 4-year term; however, a few states have 2-year terms of office.

When candidates campaign for the office of governor, they must let the voters know what plans they have for the future of their state because the voters elect a candidate based on

---

POWERS BELONGING TO THE STATE GOVERNMENTS

State governments have the authority (within their own states) to:

Raise taxes
Regulate municipal governments
Supervise public education and library services
Maintain law and order
Enforce criminal laws
Maintain a state police force to ensure public safety
Protect property rights
Regulate business and labor
Provide public welfare programs
Control public health facilities
Build and maintain state roads and highways
Operate state parks, forests, and recreation areas
Conserve natural resources

GOVERNORS OF THE UNITED STATES, COMMONWEALTHS, AND TERRITORIES

State	Governor	State	Governor	State	Governor
Alabama	Bob Riley (R)	Louisiana	Kathleen Blanco (D)	Oklahoma	Brad Henry (D)
Alaska	Frank H. Murkowski (R)	Maine	John Baldacci (D)	Oregon	Ted Kulongoski (D)
American Samoa	Togiola Tulafono (D)	Maryland	Robert L. Ehrlich, Jr. (R)	Pennsylvania	Ed Rendell (D)
		Massachusetts	Mitt Romney (R)	Puerto Rico	Aníbal Acevedo-Vilá (PDP)
Arizona	Janet Napolitano (D)	Michigan	Jennifer Granholm (D)	Rhode Island	Donald Carcieri (R)
Arkansas	Mike Huckabee (R)	Minnesota	Tim Pawlenty (R)	South Carolina	Mark Sanford (R)
California	Arnold Schwarzenegger (R)	Mississippi	Haley Barbour (R)	South Dakota	Mike Rounds (R)
Colorado	Bill Owens (R)	Missouri	Matt Blunt (R)	Tennessee	Phil Bredesen (D)
Connecticut	M. Jodi Rell (R)	Montana	Brian Schweitzer (D)	Texas	Rick Perry (R)
Delaware	Ruth Ann Minner (D)	Nebraska	Mike Johanns (R)	Utah	Jon Huntsman (R)
Florida	Jeb Bush (R)	Nevada	Kenny Guinn (R)	Vermont	Jim Douglas (R)
Georgia	Sonny Perdue (R)	New Hampshire	John Lynch (D)	Virginia	Timothy M. Kaine (D)
Guam	Felix Camacho (R)	New Jersey	Jon Corzine (D)	Virgin Islands	Charles W. Turnbull (D)
Hawaii	Linda Lingle (R)	New Mexico	Bill Richardson (D)	Washington	Christine O. Gregoire (D)
Idaho	Dirk Kempthorne (R)	New York	George E. Pataki (R)	West Virginia	Joe Manchin (D)
Illinois	Rod Blagojevich (D)	North Carolina	Michael F. Easley (D)	Wisconsin	Jim Doyle (D)
Indiana	Mitch Daniels (R)	North Dakota	John Hoeven (R)	Wyoming	Dave Freudenthal (D)
Iowa	Tom Vilsack (D)	Northern Mariana Islands	Benigno Fitial (C)		
Kansas	Kathleen Sebelius (D)			(D) Democrat	
Kentucky	Ernie Fletcher (R)	Ohio	Bob Taft (R)	(R) Republican (C) Covenant (PDP) Popular Democratic Party	

this information. Once the candidate becomes governor, the people expect that the campaign promises will be carried out. This popular support gives the governor power with the legislature.

The Legislature

Legislatures make the basic decisions for the states. It is they who are responsible for the vast business of the state. They make policy decisions dealing with schools and parks, universities and courts, roads and hospitals, insurance and banking, and many other matters that the U.S. Constitution does not assign to the federal government.

Except for the state of Nebraska, state legislatures consist of two houses. (Nebraska has a one-house, or unicameral, legislature.) The legislatures go by such names as "general assembly," "legislature," "legislative assembly," and "general court." The upper house, which is generally known as the senate, has less than half as many members as the lower house, which is generally known as the house of representatives. But in practice the powers of the two houses are about the same. In most states they are organized to do business on a party basis, with the majority party or faction taking control, usually under the guidance of the governor.

The majority of the state legislatures, particularly those of the larger states, meet annually. However, many hold sessions only every two years. More recently, the number of state legislatures meeting every year has increased. This is the result of a heavier workload and the growing number of serious problems facing state governments.

The Judiciary

Most legal cases in the United States are tried in state courts. Each state has a court system that includes trial courts and courts of appeal. The trial courts are the first step in the judicial process. They handle both criminal and civil cases.

Once a verdict has been reached in a trial court, the parties involved may appeal the decision to a higher court, which is known as an appellate court.

The highest state court is the supreme court. In some states, this court may be called the court of appeals or the supreme judicial court. Several states also have a middle group of appellate courts that assist the supreme court in handling the large number of cases that come before it. Appellate courts may change (reverse) the decision of a lower court.

Lower court judges generally serve terms of eight years or less. A few serve for twelve years. State supreme courts have from three to nine judges who serve terms ranging from six to 14 years, except in Rhode Island where they are elected for life. In more than half the states, supreme court judges are elected by the people. In several states they are appointed by the governor. Appointed judges usually must be approved by the state legislature, popular vote, or an executive council.

▶PROBLEMS FACING STATE GOVERNMENTS

State governments are responsible for providing a number of basic services, including education, health care, highway maintenance and construction, police protection, and welfare. All of these services are expensive and the money for them comes mainly from taxes on personal income, goods and services, and retail sales.

Taxes must be approved by a majority vote in the state legislatures. Legislators, however, are often reluctant to impose new taxes because they do not want to displease the voters. Yet the demand for services continues to increase, and this has strained the financial resources of many states.

Cities are particularly expensive for the states to maintain. Many cities now have larger populations than they can adequately support. This has resulted in housing shortages; inadequate transportation, education, and sanitation facilities; higher crime rates; and a larger number of people dependent on public welfare. The state must provide funds to modernize and expand its services and facilities to keep up with the demands.

Although additional money is often provided by the federal government, it is unlikely there will ever be enough to meet every need. Therefore, co-operation is necessary at all levels of government—federal, state, and municipal—to use the available resources as efficiently as possible.

ROBERT RIENOW
Author, *New York State and Local Government*

See also MUNICIPAL GOVERNMENT; UNITED STATES, GOVERNMENT OF THE; and the Government sections in the articles on the individual states.

STATISTICS

Statistics is the science of collecting, organizing, displaying, and analyzing information. It helps people answer questions and make decisions about many things. For example, in education, statistics can be used to determine average grades. In the field of medicine, statistics are used to collect information about patients and diseases and to make decisions about the use of new drugs or treatments. Meteorologists use statistics to find patterns in the weather and to make predictions about what future weather will be like. Another important use of statistics is in demographics, the study of the size and vital characteristics of populations and how they might change over time. Perhaps most familiar to us are the statistics reported in the news media telling us what most people think about important issues.

▶ THE STATISTICAL PROCESS

The process of using statistics always begins with a question. We may ask "Who will probably become the next president?" or "How long will a Brand X battery last?" or "Which soft drinks are popular with teenagers in our town?" Once questions like these have been asked, the next step is to collect information about the subject. The kind of information we get from statistics is called **data** and the people who collect, organize, and analyze the data are called **researchers**.

Collecting Data

We could find answers to the questions above by conducting a survey of all the registered voters in the United States, or by testing all of the batteries made by Brand X, or by conducting a taste test with all of the teenagers in our town. This type of survey is called a **census**, and it involves an entire group, or **population**, of people or things. A census, however, can be extremely costly in time, money, and other resources.

Taking a Sample. An alternative to a census is a **sample**, a smaller group of people or things that can represent the whole group. As long as the sample is **unbiased**, or fair, we can rely on the accuracy of the information we get. The best way to get an unbiased sample is to choose it in a random fashion, so that no one person or thing has any greater chance of being selected than any other. This type of sample is called a **random sample**.

Suppose you wanted to buy a crate of oranges. To make sure that all of the oranges in the crate were sweet and juicy, you might sample a few. You could take your sample from the top of the crate, but that might not give you accurate information about all the oranges. Those in the middle or at the bottom of the crate might be bruised or spoiled. To be sure you get the best information you can about the oranges, you would want to take a random sample that would give you a few from the top, some from the middle, and a few from the bottom of the crate.

One way to choose a random sample of people from a large group is to put the names of all the people into a hat, and then draw the names out one at a time until you have a sample size you can work with. If the population is very large, however, this method is not practical. One technique sometimes used to survey very large populations is based on telephone numbers. First, researchers determine the first three digits of the telephone numbers of the people living in the area they want to survey. Then a computer chooses the last four digits for each number randomly until the sample is obtained. Since almost everyone owns a telephone today, this technique is fair because every household with a telephone in that area has an equal likelihood of being called.

Avoiding Bias. A survey in which people's opinions on a particular subject are collected is called a **poll**. Polls may be conducted face-to-face, by telephone, or through the mail. Besides making sure that a random sample is obtained, the researcher must also pay careful attention to the wording of the questions that will be asked of the people in the sample. For example, when asked the question, "You don't like that television show, do you?" some people might answer "No" because they think that is what they are expected to say, not because it is their honest opinion. A question like this is called **biased**, or unfair, because the answer may not tell you what people really think.

Another way in which a poll can be biased has to do with the time and place in which it is conducted. Asking people who are stuck in traffic on a rainy day what they think about commuting may give different results from posing the same question to those same people on a sunny day with little traffic.

There are many other ways in which polls can be biased. Researchers must be able to anticipate such problems before they collect their data.

Organizing and Displaying Data

In order to make sense of data once it has been collected, the data must be summarized, organized, and presented in appropriate ways.

Frequency Distributions. Suppose you want to know how much time students in your class spend on math homework each day. You might conduct a survey and then make a list showing how many minutes each student worked on math, as in the following: 35, 30, 45, 25, 30, 50, 25, 35, 25, 30, 40, 25, 30, 30, 60, 20, 40, 35, 30, 20. Each of the numbers in this list is called an **observation**. Just by looking at the observations you may be able to get some idea of the study habits of students in your class, but it would be more helpful to organize the observations. One way to organize them would be to put the numbers in numerical order from least to greatest or greatest to least: 20, 20, 25, 25, 25, 25, 30, 30, 30, 30, 30, 30, 35, 35, 35, 40, 40, 45, 50, 60. This is better than an unordered list because you can begin to see some patterns. But there are still a lot of numbers to look at, so you may want to make a table by arranging the numbers into groups. A commonly used table in statistics is a **frequency distribution**, a table that shows what was observed and the frequency, or number of times each observation was made. The frequency distribution table in Figure 1 has four columns. The first column on the left shows the number of minutes studied, given in five-minute intervals. In the second column a tally mark is drawn for each student next to the number of minutes studied by that student. The frequency, or total number of students for each number of minutes, is written as a number in the third column. The relative frequency, which gives the percentage of the time that each observation was noted, is shown in the last column.

In Figure 1 you can see that out of 20 students in the class, the results range from 2 students, or 10%, who study math for 20 minutes, to 6 students, or 30%, who study for 30 minutes, to 1 student, or 5%, who studies for 60 minutes.

Finding the Average. Another way to summarize data you have collected is to find an **average**. You have probably heard people discussing such averages as average temperature, baseball batting averages, the average height of people in a group, and so on. An average is a typical observation, a single number that represents a larger group of numbers. Statistics that give some indication of the overall average are called measures of central tendency. Three measures are the mean, the median, and the mode.

Perhaps the most commonly used average is the **mean**, sometimes called the arithmetic mean. To find the mean of a set of observations, add the numbers up and then divide by the total number of observations. For example, to find the mean grade for quiz grades of 82, 88, 84, and 86, first add the grades together. You get 340. Then divide 340 by 4, the total number of grades, to get a mean quiz grade of 85.

Let us go back now to the math homework example above. Try to figure out the mean study time. You must first determine the total number of minutes studied by all 20 students. Do this by multiplying the minutes studied by the frequency (number of students). Add those numbers and divide the result by 20. Your answer should be 33 minutes.

There are times when the mean is not the best way to show the average of a distribution of numbers. Suppose I am teaching a piano class and I

Figure 1. Frequency Distribution Table

Minutes Studied	Tally Marks	Frequency	Relative Frequency
20	II	2	10%
25	IIII	4	20%
30	JHt I	6	30%
35	III	3	15%
40	II	2	10%
45	I	1	5%
50	I	1	5%
55		0	0%
60	I	1	5%
Total	**20**	**20**	**100%**

HOW TO TELL IF STATISTICS ARE RELIABLE

Here are some questions you should ask yourself about statistical surveys or opinion polls.

1. Who conducted the survey and who is publicizing it? What interest does this person or group have in the results?
2. Where and when was the survey conducted?
3. How was the sample chosen? Was the sample representative of the whole population, representing different ages, genders, races, and economic groups?
4. How large was the sample? In general, the larger the sample size the better, but you can also gain important information from a small random sample.
5. How was the survey conducted? Did people call in their responses? Was there a telephone charge for responding? Were surveys conducted by mail or by interview? What are the advantages and disadvantages of the method chosen?

6. What were the exact questions asked? Do the questions appear to be biased or slanted?
7. Do the results give very specific information? Is the information so general that it is open to different interpretations?

must report the average age of my students. The ages of the 7 students in my class are 8, 8, 8, 9, 10, 11, and 65 years. I could find the mean:

8 + 8 + 8 + 9 + 10 + 11 + 65 = 119 ÷ 7 = 17

The mean age of 17 would lead someone to believe that typical students in this class are older than they actually are. The 65-year-old person pulls the mean upward and misrepresents, or distorts, the average. To overcome this effect, the **median**, or the middle value of a distribution, would be a more reasonable way to measure the average age. To find the median, the numbers are placed in order from least to greatest. The median is simply the number in the middle—in this case, 9 years of age, which would be considered more typical than 17.

8, 8, 8, (9,) 10, 11, 65

The **mode**, or most common observation, is a third way to determine the average. For this example, 8 is the age that occurs most frequently, so it is the mode. This, too, is a reasonable answer.

8, 8, 8, 9, 10, 11, 65

Although the three measures in this example are different numbers, sometimes the mean, median, and mode have the same value. When they are different, it is useful to try to determine why.

The average that should be used to describe a particular set of data depends on the situation. In most cases the mean is used because it takes all of the information into account. It is best used when there are no extremes at either end of the data. If you are looking for a typical observation when there are extremes in the data, the median should be used. Average incomes are usually given by the median because very large incomes distort the mean and make it less typical. The mode is not used as often as the others, but it is useful when one value is observed with greater frequency than any other.

Graphs. Graphs are very useful ways to display data that has been collected and organized. Graphs condense information and help the reader see patterns in the data quickly. Graphs that are not done properly, however, can actually be misleading.

Many different kinds of graphs are used to display statistics. You may be familiar with the type called a circle graph, or pie chart.

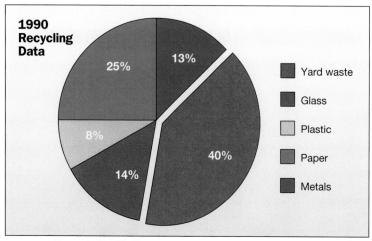

Figure 2. Pie Chart

The pie chart in Figure 2 presents information on materials collected in one community for recycling. Note that the slices of the pie show parts of the whole recycling picture. For example, it shows that 40% of the materials recycled were leaves and other yard waste turned into compost.

Other types of graphs commonly used in statistics include bar charts (see Figure 3), line graphs, histograms, and pictograms. (For more information, see the article GRAPHS in Volume G.)

Analyzing Data

In many ways the most important and most difficult stage of statistical research involves analyzing, or looking carefully at, the data that has been collected and summarized, and then asking questions about the results— What do these results mean? Are they accurate? Are there patterns in the data? What conclusions can be drawn from the results?

Making Comparisons. Look at the bar graph in Figure 3. It shows the study habits of two classes. Class A is the one we looked at earlier in this article, and Class B is from the Studihard School. Which class seems to spend more time on homework? Before using the graph to find the answer, you would have to make sure that both classes were in the same grade and were studying the same subject. Assume both are 7th grade math classes. A quick glance at the graph tells you that most of the students in Class A are clustered at the lower end of the minutes scale, and that more students in Class B are arranged at the higher end. You would conclude that, in general, the Studihard class appears to devote more time to math homework.

Misleading Statistics. Most statistical research is done correctly and produces accurate results. As consumers, however, we need to be sure that we are not deceived by faulty statistics. In the field of advertising, for instance, data may not always be presented in a way that provides the consumer with all the necessary information. You might be presented with the claim, "Almost all of the doctors we interviewed favored Gastromin to treat an upset stomach." At first glance, it may seem that Gastromin is the right product to use for an upset stomach, but the statement is missing important information: How many doctors were interviewed out of the total population of doctors? How were they chosen? What exact percentage of doctors favored Gastromin? Over what other treatments was Gastromin favored? Information that answers these questions would give you a better idea as to the truth of the claim.

The particular wording of survey questions and reported results is also important. Words like "almost all," "many," and "few" have different meanings for different people, and their use should be avoided in questionnaires or summaries.

When the data is reliable, statistics can help you make informed judgments about all kinds of things. Looking carefully at the information and asking questions about it will help you decide whether you can trust the statistics.

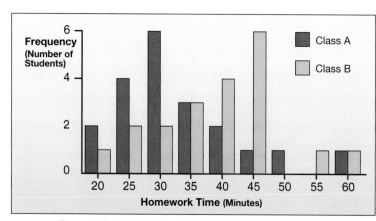

Figure 3. Bar Graph

The history of statistics goes back at least to the times of ancient Egypt, Greece, and Rome. As long ago as 3500 B.C., statistics were collected and recorded for the number of sheep or cattle owned, the amount of grain produced, or the number of people living in a particular city. In more modern times, statistical methods have been used to record and predict such things as birth and death rates, economic and social trends, and sports achievements. They have even been used to unlock secret codes.

Modern statistics is said to have begun with John Graunt (1620–74), an English tradesman. Graunt collected published records called bills of mortality that included information about the numbers and causes of deaths in the city of London. Graunt analyzed more than fifty years of data and created the first mortality table, a table that shows how long a person may be expected to live after reaching a certain age.

Others who made important contributions to statistics were Carl Friedrich Gauss (1777–1855), the brilliant German mathematician who used statistical methods in making predictions about the positions of the planets in our solar system; Adolphe Quetelet (1796–1874), the Belgian astronomer who developed the idea of the "average man" from his studies of the Belgian census; Florence Nightingale (1820–1910), the famous English nurse who pioneered the use of statistical methods to further a social cause, namely the improvement of conditions in military hospitals; Karl Pearson (1857–1936), a mathematician, also English, who made important links between probability and statistics; and the American George Gallup (1901–84), who was instrumental in making statistical polling a common tool in political campaigns.

Powerful new methods and tools continue to be developed that help make statistics more accurate and useful.

JIM O'KEEFE
Assistant Professor of Mathematics
Lesley College

See also GRAPHS; MATHEMATICS; NUMBER PATTERNS; OPINION POLLS.

STATUE OF LIBERTY. See LIBERTY, STATUE OF.

STEAM ENGINES

When water turns into steam, it expands to about 1,700 times its original volume. Steam engines use the tremendous energy of expanding steam to do their work. The steam turbine, in which steam causes big, fanlike wheels (called rotors) to spin, is one type of steam engine. But the term "steam engine" usually means a reciprocating engine—one in which the steam drives a piston back and forth in a cylinder.

▶ HOW A STEAM ENGINE WORKS

A steam engine is a heat engine. That is, it depends on heat as its ultimate source of energy. The heat energy comes from fuel that is burned beneath a boiler. The heat of the burning fuel turns the water in the boiler into steam, which is led through a pipe to the working parts of the engine. Steam engines are classified as external-combustion engines, because the fuel is burned outside the engine, under a boiler, and not inside the engine itself, as in gasoline and diesel engines.

A simple steam engine consists of a hollow cylinder, a piston that slides back and forth inside the cylinder, and valves to let the steam in and out. High-pressure steam from the boiler enters at one end of the cylinder. The steam expands, pushing the piston toward the other end of the cylinder. This is called a "stroke" or a "power stroke." At the end of the stroke, steam is let into the other end of the cylinder, and it pushes the piston back again. A rod passing through one end of the cylinder connects the piston to a crankshaft. The crankshaft changes the back-and-forth motion of the piston into rotary, or turning, motion. Since the steam engine shown in the diagram produces power on both forward and return strokes, it is called a double-acting (reciprocating) engine.

▶ HISTORY

The story of the steam engine begins with the troubles of mineowners in England in the 1600's. Many mines had become so deep that water poured into them constantly. If the water was not pumped out, the mines would become flooded and have to be abandoned. Therefore mineowners installed huge pumps, usually operated by horses. The pumps kept the mines dry, but it was very expensive to feed and care for the horses.

A number of men began experimenting with steam as a substitute source of power for the mines. In 1712 Thomas Newcomen (1663–1729), an English dealer in ironware, built the first practical steam engine. It was used to pump out a flooded coal mine.

Newcomen's engine was very different from anything in use today. It had a big vertical cylinder open at the top. The piston was connected by a chain to one end of a huge wooden rocker beam overhead. The other end of the beam was connected to the pump mechanism. When the pump was not working, the weight of the pump rod pulled the piston to the top of the cylinder. To operate the engine, steam was let into the cylinder beneath the piston. Then cold water was sprayed into the cylinder to condense the steam. This produced a partial vacuum, and the weight of the atmosphere on the open top of the piston pushed the piston down and moved the pump. Then more steam was let in, the pump rod dragged the piston up, and the cycle was repeated.

Diagram of a Newcomen steam engine, used at mines in the 1700's.

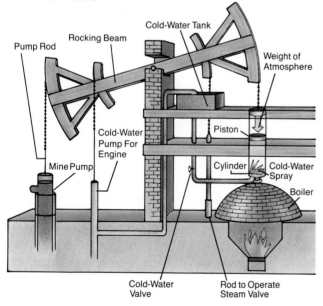

Pump Rod
Rocking Beam
Cold-Water Tank
Weight of Atmosphere
Cold-Water Pump For Engine
Piston
Mine Pump
Cylinder
Cold-Water Spray
Boiler
Cold-Water Valve
Rod to Operate Steam Valve

Newcomen's engine did far more work than horses, and far more cheaply. At one mine a Newcomen engine pumped as much water in 48 hours as 50 horses and 20 mineworkers, working in shifts around the clock, had been able to pump in an entire week.

After Newcomen's death a number of other men made improvements on his engine, gradually increasing its efficiency. But the man who is regarded as the true father of the modern steam engine was a Scotsman named James Watt (1736–1819).

In 1763 Watt, who made scientific instruments for the University of Glasgow, was asked to repair a model of the Newcomen engine. He decided that the Newcomen engine was inefficient because it wasted heat. Each time steam was admitted into the cylinder, a great deal of heat was used up in warming the cylinder to the temperature of the steam. This meant that more steam was needed for each stroke. Yet if the cylinder was not cooled by spraying cold water into it, the steam would not condense and the engine would not work. Suddenly Watt saw the solution: condense the steam outside the cylinder.

Watt built a small model to try his idea out. He led the steam from the cylinder through a pipe into a separate condensing chamber. In 1769, after several years of experimenting, Watt patented an improved version of his first engine. In the new engine both ends of the cylinder were covered over. The space above the cylinder was kept filled with low-pressure steam from the boiler. Each time the steam was condensed below the piston, the pressure of the steam above forced the piston down for the power stroke.

Watt's engine proved extremely successful and was soon in demand at mines. Iron works and factories, too, found use for this improved steam engine. The engine was used to raise water, which then turned waterwheels that drove machinery. Since Watt's customers naturally wanted to know how much work their engines could do compared to horses, Watt devised the unit called the horsepower as a measure of the engines' capacity.

But Watt's engine still produced a power stroke in one direction only. This gave it a jerky motion and it could not be used to drive machines directly. In 1782 Watt overcame the problem by making his engine double-acting. He invented a sliding valve that admitted

How A Simple Steam Engine Works

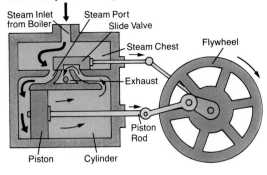

Steam entering the left-hand side of the chamber will move the piston to the right.

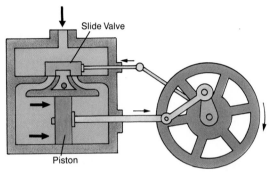

As expanding steam continues to push the piston to the right, the slide valve closes and no more steam enters the chamber.

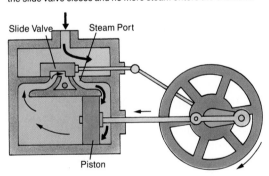

When the piston is all the way to the right again, the steam rushes into the right-hand side of the chamber and pushes the piston back to the left.

steam alternately to each side of the piston in turn, making every stroke a power stroke. To save steam, he used the "cutoff" principle— instead of letting steam into the cylinder for the whole length of the piston stroke, the steam was let in for only part of the stroke. The force of the steam's expansion drove the piston the rest of the way. The cutoff became a standard feature of steam engines. Watt also made a number of other improvements, such as an automatic governor to keep the engine running at a constant speed.

At the beginning of the 1800's, two men working separately on different sides of the Atlantic Ocean each designed and built high-pressure steam engines that did not need condensers. They were Oliver Evans (1755–1819) of Philadelphia, Pennsylvania, and Richard Trevithick (1771–1833), a mining engineer of Cornwall, England. High-pressure engines developed much more power, pound for pound, than low-pressure engines, so they could be made smaller and lighter. They also did much more work for each pound of fuel that was burned.

The use of high pressure led to efforts to get more work out of the steam. Compound engines were built, with more than one cylinder. After the steam had done its work in the small high-pressure cylinder, it passed into a big low-pressure cylinder, where it drove another piston. Toward the end of the century, compound engines with three and even four cylinders were built. Compound engines were more efficient than engines that used the steam only once. They were widely used in ships and factories, and in some locomotives.

Improvements in boilers went hand-in-hand with the development of the steam engine. The first boilers were simply huge kettles with a fire underneath. Then it was learned that the boiler's heating surface could be increased by letting the hot gases from the fire pass through tubes running through the boiler. This enabled the boiler to make steam much faster. This type of boiler is called the fire-tube boiler. Another type is the water-tube boiler, in which the tubes hold the water and the hot gases pass around the tubes.

At the beginning of the 1900's, the reciprocating steam engine was our chief source of power. Today, the steam engine has been replaced by more efficient sources of power. Electric motors drive the machines of factories. Internal-combustion engines are used in power trucks, cars, buses, airplanes, and locomotives. But the steam turbine is still important. Generators driven by steam turbines produce most of our electric power. Steam turbines drive many ships. Nuclear power systems depend on steam turbines to operate their generators.

JOSEPH P. KELLEHER
Product Engineering Magazine

See also ENGINES; LOCOMOTIVES; TURBINES.

STEEL. See IRON AND STEEL.

This portrait of Gertrude Stein was painted by Pablo Picasso, one of the many modern artists she influenced. Among the other figures who gathered at her Paris home were American writers of the post-World War I years, whom she described as the "lost generation." Stein's own writing is highly experimental.

STEIN, GERTRUDE (1874–1946)

The American writer Gertrude Stein was born in Allegheny, Pennsylvania, on February 3, 1874, and spent her childhood in Europe and California. She attended Radcliffe College and completed four years of medical school at Johns Hopkins University. In 1903 she moved to France, where she lived most of the rest of her life.

Stein was an early and influential collector of modern art; she and her companion, Alice B. Toklas, frequently entertained artists in their Paris home. Modern writers also gathered around Stein, including the Americans Ernest Hemingway, F. Scott Fitzgerald, and Sherwood Anderson.

Stein's early fiction was highly experimental. *Three Lives* (1909) offers a series of character sketches that ignore conventional rules of plot and development. *Tender Buttons* (1914) is even more difficult; her efforts to capture the innermost quality of objects led to passages that many readers have found impossible to understand. Stein insisted that she was reinventing language to express the more complex reality of the modern world. Despite the neglect of critics, she continued writing throughout her life. Her works include stories, novels, operas, travel books, and essays.

Stein's most commercially successful book was *The Autobiography of Alice B. Toklas* (1933), which was actually Stein's own autobiography. The book provides a colorful, often funny history of the Paris art world in the early 1900's. In part because of the popularity of this work, Stein received increasing recognition in her later years. Even more than her own fiction, her opinions and advice earned her a place in the front ranks of modern writers. She died in Paris on July 27, 1946.

PETER CONN
University of Pennsylvania

STEINBECK, JOHN (1902–1968)

The American writer John Ernst Steinbeck was born in Salinas, California, on February 27, 1902. His father was the treasurer of Monterey County. His mother, a teacher, encouraged John to read, and he later described her in his novel *East of Eden* (1952).

Steinbeck was a track and basketball star in high school, but he always found time to read. He attended Stanford University between 1919 and 1925, but he left without a degree. While there, he contributed poems and other writing to university publications.

After leaving Stanford, Steinbeck held a wide variety of jobs, ranging from bricklaying to newspaper reporting. In 1929, after two years as caretaker of an estate in the High Sierras, he published his first novel, *Cup of Gold*, a romantic tale of piracy.

His short-story collection, *The Pastures of Heaven* (1932), was an account of farm life in the Salinas valley. *Tortilla Flat* (1935), which humorously described the life of the Mexican-American inhabitants of a California town, was his first best-seller. He expressed his concern for uprooted migrant farm workers in 1936 in the novel *In Dubious Battle*.

Steinbeck's 1939 novel *The Grapes of Wrath* presented a grim picture of a life of poverty and despair. It tells the story of "Okies" who, evicted from their farms in Oklahoma, try to resettle in California. The book won the 1940 Pulitzer prize.

Among Steinbeck's other works are the novel *Of Mice and Men* (1937), which became a play, and the stories about the boy Jody in *The Red Pony* (1937). Steinbeck's last novel was *The Winter of Our Discontent* (1961).

In 1962, Steinbeck became the sixth American to win the Nobel prize for literature. He died in New York City on December 20, 1968.

Reviewed by JEROME H. STERN
Florida State University

STEINEM, GLORIA (1934–   )

American writer, editor, and political activist Gloria Steinem became the most prominent spokesperson of the women's rights movement when she founded *Ms.* magazine, an influential feminist publication.

Steinem was born on March 25, 1934, in Toledo, Ohio. As a child, she attended school while caring for her invalid mother. She graduated with honors from Smith College in 1956.

Steinem began her writing career at *Esquire* magazine in 1960 and later contributed to the major women's magazines. When *New York* magazine was founded in 1968, she became a contributing editor and soon had her own column, "The City Politic."

In 1968, for research purposes, Steinem attended a meeting of Redstockings, a New York City feminist organization. Inspired by their message, she wrote an award-winning story and joined the women's rights movement. Two years later she helped Betty Friedan organize the Women's Strike for Equality to bring attention to women's issues. In 1971 she helped organize both the National Wom-

en's Political Caucus and the Women's Action Alliance, to encourage women to enter politics and to fight against discrimination.

In 1972, Steinem founded *Ms.* magazine, which she also edited. Its first issue contained articles such as "Down With Sexist Upbringing." In 1989, due to financial losses, *Ms.* went out of business; but devoted readers demanded that the magazine be resurrected, and a new *Ms.*—free of advertising and supported entirely by its readers—appeared in 1990, with Steinem as consulting editor.

Steinem's other publications included *Outrageous Acts and Everyday Rebellions* (1983), *Marilyn: Norma Jeane* (1986), and *Revolution from Within: A Book of Self-Esteem* (1992).

KATHRYN CULLEN-DUPONT
Coauthor, *Women's Suffrage in America: An Eyewitness History*

STEINMETZ, CHARLES PROTEUS (1865–1923)

Charles Proteus Steinmetz was a brilliant electrical engineer whose work made possible the growth of the modern electric power industry. During his 30-year career with the General Electric Company in Schenectady, New York, his engineering genius earned him the nickname the Wizard of Schenectady.

Karl August Rudolf Steinmetz was born in Breslau, Germany, on April 9, 1865. When he became an American citizen in the 1890's, he decided to change his first names to Charles Proteus Steinmetz.

Steinmetz was hunchbacked from birth, but his great intelligence and courage helped him overcome his handicap. He entered the University of Breslau in 1883 and studied mathematics, science, and engineering.

In 1888, Steinmetz had to flee Germany to escape arrest for political activities. In 1889 he went to the United States and found work with a manufacturer of electrical machinery, who soon provided him with a laboratory for research. Within two years, Steinmetz solved

the problem of power loss caused by magnetism in alternating-current electrical equipment. Shortly after this he joined the General Electric Company.

Steinmetz' studies of alternating current led to the building of a practical system of long-distance electric power transmission. He also did research into the effect of lightning on power lines.

Steinmetz never married, but he legally adopted a son and enjoyed a happy family life. He died in Schenectady on October 26, 1923.

Reviewed by DAVID C. COOKE
Author, *Inventions That Made History*

STEPHENS, ALEXANDER HAMILTON. See CIVIL WAR, UNITED STATES (Profiles: Confederate).

STEPHENSON, GEORGE. See RAILROADS (Profiles).

STEREO. See HIGH-FIDELITY SYSTEMS.

STEUBEN, BARON VON. See REVOLUTIONARY WAR (Profiles).

STEVENS, JOHN PAUL. See SUPREME COURT OF THE UNITED STATES (Profiles).

STEVENS, THADDEUS. See UNITED STATES, CONGRESS OF THE (Profiles: House Representatives).

STEVENS, WALLACE (1879–1955)

The American poet Wallace Stevens was born in Reading, Pennsylvania, on October 2, 1879. He attended Harvard University and New York University Law School, taking his law degree in 1903. In 1916 he began a long and successful career as an executive with a Hartford, Connecticut, insurance company. Although he published a few poems while still in college, Stevens began his career as a poet rather late in life. Most of his poems were published when he was past 50.

Stevens' first volume of verse, *Harmonium*, was published in 1923. It sold fewer than one hundred copies but was enthusiastically received by critics and other poets. *Harmonium* established Stevens as a major literary figure.

Stevens' early verse was elaborate, filled with foreign phrases, and often hard to understand. He was sometimes accused of using poetry as an escape from reality, but he insisted that he was committed to exploring serious issues. Several of his poems look bravely at the terrors of death, and many confront questions raised by the violence of modern life. Other poems dealt with the question of religious faith. In "Sunday Morning," one of his most famous poems, he argued that each person must look within to find divinity.

Stevens published several new volumes in the 1930's. *Ideas of Order* (1935) and *Owl's Clover* (1936) addressed the special problems raised for Americans by the suffering of the Great Depression. In his later years, Stevens' verse continued to explore questions of reality, imagination, and belief. He received a series of major awards, including the Pulitzer prize, the National Book Award, and the Bollingen Prize. He died in Hartford on August 2, 1955.

PETER CONN
University of Pennsylvania

STEVENSON, ADLAI EWING.   See VICE PRESIDENCY OF THE UNITED STATES.

STEVENSON, ADLAI EWING II (1900–1965)

American politician and diplomat Adlai Ewing Stevenson II was born on February 5, 1900, in Los Angeles, California. His interest in public service was no doubt inspired by his grandfather, Adlai Ewing Stevenson, who had served as vice president (1893–97) under President Grover Cleveland.

Stevenson obtained a law degree from Northwestern University in 1926 and later joined the Chicago Council on Foreign Relations, where he gained knowledge of international affairs. After World War II, having served as special assistant and counsel (1941–44) to Secretary of the Navy Frank Knox, Stevenson helped plan the conference that organized the United Nations in 1945.

In 1948, Stevenson ran for governor of Illinois and won by a huge margin. As governor (1949–53) he initiated widespread reforms. He reorganized the state police force and mental hospitals, modernized the highway system, and more than doubled aid for education.

By 1952, Stevenson had become a national figure, and the Democrats chose him as their presidential candidate. Although Dwight D. Eisenhower won the election handily, Stevenson remained the popular choice among liberal

intellectuals, and his party renominated him in 1956. Again he lost to Eisenhower.

In 1961, President John F. Kennedy made Stevenson U.S. Ambassador to the United Nations. Stevenson worked diligently to improve international relations during this period of cold-war tensions until his sudden death on July 14, 1965.

JAMES T. PATTERSON
Brown University

STEVENSON, ROBERT LOUIS
(1850–1894)

Robert Louis Stevenson's Samoan name was Tusitala, "teller of tales." It was probably the name he liked best, for he was a teller of tales all his life.

He was born in Edinburgh, Scotland, on November 13, 1850. His father was a civil engineer, and Louis was expected to be one, too. But when he was very young, he vowed to learn to write. Louis' poor health kept him from attending school regularly, but tutors gave him his lessons. He entered Edinburgh University when he was 16. The same year, his first piece of writing appeared in print. A pamphlet, *The Pentland Rising,* was published at his father's expense. To please his parents, Louis took engineering courses at the university. But he seldom attended classes. He was more interested in a literary and debating club and a theatrical group. Dressed in a velvet coat, his hair long, he explored the slums of Edinburgh with his cousin Bob.

Louis wrote verses and contributed to the *Edinburgh University Magazine.* Then he decided to study law instead of engineering. He was admitted to the bar in 1875, but he never practiced law. His first book, published in 1878, was *The Inland Voyage,* an account of a canoe trip he took through Belgium and France in 1876.

In France, Stevenson met Fanny Osbourne, an American woman older than he, who was married. He followed her to America and married her in 1880 after her divorce. He was then very ill with tuberculosis. He returned to Europe with his wife and stepson, Lloyd. Much of the time they lived at health resorts.

Despite his illness, Stevenson never stopped writing. *Treasure Island* (1883), an adventure tale of pirates and buried treasure, was his first popular success. It had originally appeared in the boys' magazine *Young Folks,* which then printed *The Black Arrow* (published in book form in 1888). In 1885, Stevenson's books *A Child's Garden of Verses* and *Prince Otto* were published. However, his complete success with both critics and public came a year later with *The Strange Case of Dr. Jekyll and Mr. Hyde,* a suspense story about a respected doctor who has another, evil, personality—Mr. Hyde. Also published in 1886 was Stevenson's *Kidnapped.*

After his father died in 1887, Stevenson took his mother to America with him and his wife and stepson. He was welcomed as a celebrity in New York City. In 1888 the Stevensons traveled to San Francisco and set sail on a schooner to the South Seas. During the voyage, Stevenson completed *The Master of Ballantrae,* which was published in 1889. The family stopped in the Marquesas, Tahiti, and Hawaii. Another schooner took them to Samoa. In December, 1889, Stevenson bought an estate there, which he named Vailima ("Five Rivers"). It was Stevenson's home for the rest of his life.

Stevenson and Lloyd Osbourne wrote three works of fiction together. In 1893, Stevenson published *Catriona* (called *David Balfour* in America), a sequel to *Kidnapped.* Although his last novel, *Weir of Hermiston,* was unfinished at Stevenson's death on December 3, 1894, it is often considered his best work.

Stevenson's poem "Requiem" was inscribed on his monument in Samoa:

Under the wide and starry sky,
Dig the grave and let me lie.
Glad did I live and gladly die,
    And I laid me down with a will.

This be the verse you grave for me:
Here he lies where he longed to be;
Home is the sailor, home from the sea,
    And the hunter home from the hill.

Reviewed by ERWIN HESTER
East Carolina University

Some poems from Robert Louis Stevenson's *A Child's Garden of Verses* and an excerpt from *Kidnapped* follow.

Selections from
A CHILD'S GARDEN OF VERSES

MY SHADOW

I have a little shadow
    that goes in and out with me,
And what can be the use of him
    is more than I can see.
He is very, very like me
    from the heels up to the head;
And I see him jump before me,
    when I jump into my bed.

The funniest thing about him
    is the way he likes to grow—
Not at all like proper children,
    which is always very slow;
For he sometimes shoots up taller
    like an india-rubber ball,
And he sometimes gets so little
    that there's none of him at all.

He hasn't got a notion
    of how children ought to play,
And can only make a fool of me
    in every sort of way.
He stays so close beside me,
    he's a coward you can see;
I'd think shame to stick to nursie
    as that shadow sticks to me!

One morning, very early,
    before the sun was up,
I rose and found the shining dew
    on every buttercup;
But my lazy little shadow,
    like an arrant sleepy-head,
Had stayed at home behind me
    and was fast asleep in bed.

LOOKING-GLASS RIVER

Smooth it slides upon its travel,
    Here a wimple, there a gleam—
      O the clean grave!
      O the smooth stream!

Sailing blossoms, silver fishes,
    Paven pools as clear as air—
      How a child wishes
      To live down there!

We can see our coloured faces
    Floating on the shaken pool
      Down in cool places,
      Dim and very cool;

Till a wind or water wrinkle,
    Dipping marten, plumping trout,
      Spreads in a twinkle
      And bolts all out.

See the rings pursue each other;
    All below grows black as night,
      Just as if mother
      Had blown out the light!

Patience, children, just a minute—
    See the spreading circle die;
      The stream and all in it
      Will clear by-and-by.

THE SWING

How do you like to go up in a swing,
Up in the air so blue?
Oh, I do think it the pleasantest thing
Ever a child can do!

Up in the air and over the wall,
Till I can see so wide,
Rivers and trees and cattle and all
Over the countryside—

Till I look down on the garden green,
Down on the roof so brown—
Up in the air I go flying again,
Up in the air and down!

THE GARDENER

The gardener does not love to talk,
He makes me keep the gravel walk;
And when he puts his tools away,
He locks the door and takes the key.

Away behind the currant row
Where no one else but cook may go,
Far in the plots, I see him dig
Old and serious, brown and big.

He digs the flowers, green, red, and blue,
Nor wishes to be spoken to.
He digs the flowers and cuts the hay.
And never seems to want to play.

Silly gardener! summer goes,
And winter comes with pinching toes,
When in the garden bare and brown
You must lay your barrow down.

Well now, and while the summer stays,
To profit by these garden days
O how much wiser you would be.
To play at Indian wars with me!

BED IN SUMMER

In winter I get up at night
And dress by yellow candle-light.
In summer, quite the other way,
I have to go to bed by day.

I have to go to bed and see
The birds still hopping on the tree,
Or hear the grown-up people's feet
Still going past me in the street.

And does it not seem hard to you,
When all the sky is clear and blue,
And I should like so much to play,
To have to go to bed by day?

▶ KIDNAPPED

Stevenson considered *Kidnapped* his best story. It is set in the Highlands of Scotland during the troubled times of 1751. David Balfour, the hero, who is kidnapped, has many adventures that have a true basis in history.

David's father has died, leaving a letter for David to deliver to his uncle, Ebenezer Balfour of the house of Shaw, the family estate. David goes there, eager to be reconciled with his father's estranged family. But the estate is in poor repair and no one is there to welcome him. The eccentric Ebenezer Balfour is hated by his neighbors, and David begins to suspect that his uncle cheated his father out of his rightful inheritance. Before David can find out more, however, his uncle tricks him into boarding the *Covenant*, a slave ship bound for America.

One night the *Covenant* runs down a small boat, from which only one man is rescued— Alan Breck, a Highlander with a price on his head. The captain of the *Covenant* plots to turn Alan in to the authorities and collect the reward money, but David overhears him and warns Alan. Together, Alan and David hold the ship's crew at bay in the round-house, an enclosed room on the ship's deck.

Alan drew a dirk [dagger], which he held in his left hand in case they should run in under his sword. I, on my part, clambered up into the berth with an armful of pistols and something of a heavy heart, and set open the window where I was to watch. It was a small part of the deck that I could overlook, but enough for our purpose. The sea had gone down, and the wind was steady and kept the sails quiet; so that there was a great stillness in the ship, in which I made sure I heard the sound of muttering voices. A little after, and there came a clash of steel upon the deck, by which I knew they were dealing out the cutlasses and one had been let fall; and after that, silence again.

I do not know if I was what you call afraid; but my heart beat like a bird's, both quick and little; and there was a dimness came before my eyes which I continually rubbed away, and which continually returned. As for hope, I had none; but only a darkness of despair and a sort of anger against all the world that made me long to sell my life as dear as I was able. I tried to pray, I remember, but that same hurry of my mind, like a man running, would not suffer me to think upon the words; and my chief wish was to have the thing begin and be done with it.

It came all of a sudden when it did, with a rush of feet and a roar, and then a shout from Alan, and a sound of blows and some one crying out as if hurt. I looked back over my shoulder, and saw Mr. Shuan in the doorway, crossing blades with Alan.

"That's him that killed the boy!" I cried.

"Look to your window!" said Alan; and as I turned back to my place, I saw him pass his sword through the mate's body.

It was none too soon for me to look to my own part; for my head was scarce back at the window, before five men, carrying a spare yard for a battering-ram, ran past me and took post to drive the door in. I had never fired with a pistol in my life, and not often with a gun; far less against a fellow-creature. But it was now or never; and just as they swang the yard, I cried out: "Take that!" and shot into their midst.

I must have hit one of them, for he sang out and gave back a step, and the rest stopped as if a little disconcerted. Before they had time to recover, I sent another ball over their heads; and at my third shot (which went as wide as the second) the whole party threw down the yard and ran for it.

STEWART, JAMES. See MOTION PICTURES (Profiles: Movie Stars).

STIEGLITZ, ALFRED. See PHOTOGRAPHY (Great Photographers).

STILL, WILLIAM. See UNDERGROUND RAILROAD (Profiles).

STOCKHOLM

Stockholm is the capital and largest city of Sweden and the country's commercial, industrial, and cultural center. Its population is about 800,000. Greater Stockholm, which includes the city and its suburbs, has a population of about 1.9 million.

Located on Sweden's eastern coast, Stockholm lies between Lake Mälaren and the Baltic Sea and is built on 14 islands and parts of the mainland. Because of the presence everywhere of islands and water, it has often been called the Venice of the North.

The City. The oldest part of Stockholm is known as Gamla Stan (Old Town). Visitors are drawn to its old, narrow streets, as well as to such historic sites as the Royal Palace (completed in 1754) and Storkyrkan (the Stockholm Cathedral). On the small island of Riddarholmen is the Riddarholm Church, where many of Sweden's monarchs are buried. The Swedish parliament building, the Riksdagshuset, is located on the island of Helgeandsholmen. Norrmalm, on the mainland to the north, is the commercial heart of the city and home to the Royal Opera, the National Theater, and many major museums. Söder, to the south, developed as an industrial and commercial area; Stockholm University is located there. The city is noted for its many open spaces and parks, including the popular Skansen open-air museum.

Convenient ground transportation and an extensive subway system make getting around the city easy. Bridges link the various islands, and ferries provide service to the inner city, Lake Mälaren, and the Baltic Sea.

Economic Activity. Stockholm is an important manufacturing city, the country's second largest port, and a center of finance, international trade, and commerce. Research and development, electronics, and tourism are other areas of economic activity.

History. Stockholm was founded in the 1200's, probably as a commercial and transit point and as a fortress to defend its merchants. During the later Middle Ages, the Hanseatic League, an alliance of mainly north German trading cities, dominated trade and craft production in Stockholm; the German presence had a strong influence on life and culture in the city. When the Swedish union with Denmark ended in 1523, Stockholm became the major city and effective capital of the new Swedish kingdom. It rose to international importance during the 1600's, when Sweden became, for a time, a great European power.

Stockholm's fortunes declined along with Sweden's during the 1700's and early 1800's, but recovery followed as a result of industrial development starting in the mid-1800's. The city continued to grow in the 1900's, particularly after World War II. Its population has since become increasingly diverse due to immigration. All Nobel Prizes except the peace prize are awarded each year in Stockholm.

Reviewed by BYRON J. NORDSTROM
Gustavus Adolphus College

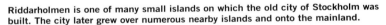
Riddarholmen is one of many small islands on which the old city of Stockholm was built. The city later grew over numerous nearby islands and onto the mainland.

Brokers buy and sell stocks for investors on the trading floor of the New York Stock Exchange. Computer monitors show the current buy and sell prices of the stocks.

STOCKS AND BONDS

Much of the world's business activity would be impossible without stocks and bonds. Stocks and bonds are certificates that are sold to raise money for starting a new company or for expanding an existing company. Stocks and bonds are also called **securities**, and people who buy them are called **investors**.

▶STOCKS

Stocks are certificates of ownership. A person who buys stock in a company becomes one of the company's owners. As an owner, the stockholder is eligible to receive a **dividend**, or share of the company's profits. The amount of this dividend may change from year to year depending on the company's performance. Well-established companies try to pay stockholders as high a dividend as possible.

There are two types of stock: **common stock** and **preferred stock**. Owners of common stock may vote for company directors and attend annual stockholders' meetings. At these meetings they have the chance to review the company's yearly performance and its future plans, and to present their own ideas. Owners of preferred stock do not usually have voting rights or the right to attend stockholders' meetings. They do, however, have priority when dividends are paid. The dividends on preferred stocks are paid according to a set rate, while the dividends on common stocks fluctuate according to the company's performance. If the company does well, however, preferred stocks do not usually gain in value as much as common stocks. If a company goes out of business, preferred stockholders are paid off first.

▶BONDS

Bonds are certificates that promise to pay a fixed rate of interest. A person who buys a bond is not buying ownership in a company but is lending the company money. The bond is the company's promise to repay that money at the end of a certain time, such as ten, fifteen, or twenty years. In return for lending the company money, the bondholder is paid interest at regular intervals. The interest rate is based on general interest rates in effect at the time the bonds are issued, as well as on the company's financial strength. Bonds generally pay more money than preferred stocks do, and they are usually considered a safer investment. If a company goes bankrupt, bondholders are paid before both preferred and common stockholders.

Local, state, and national governments also issue bonds to help pay for various projects, such as roads or schools. The interest the bondholder receives from state and local bonds—also called municipal bonds—is usually exempt from taxes.

▶HISTORY OF STOCKS AND BONDS

The trading of goods began in the earliest civilizations. Early merchants combined their money to outfit ships and caravans to take goods to faraway countries. Some of these merchants organized into trading groups. For thousands of years, trade was conducted either by these groups or by individual traders.

During the Middle Ages, merchants began to gather at annual town fairs where goods from many countries were displayed and traded. Some of these fairs became permanent, year-round events. With merchants from many countries trading at these fairs, it became necessary to establish a money exchange, or bourse, to handle financial transactions. (*Bourse* is a French word meaning "purse.")

One important annual fair took place in the city of Antwerp, in present-day Belgium. By the end of the 1400's, this city had become a center for international trade. A variety of financial activities took place there. Many merchants **speculated**—that is, they bought goods for certain prices and hoped that the prices would rise later so they could make profits when they sold the goods. Wealthy merchants or moneylenders also lent money at high rates of interest to people who needed to borrow it. They then sold bonds backed by these loans and paid interest to the people who bought them.

The Beginning of Modern Stocks

The real history of modern-day stocks began in Amsterdam in the 1600's. In 1602, the Dutch East India Company was formed there. This company, which was made up of merchants competing for trade in Asia, was given power to take full control of the spice trade. To raise money, the company sold shares of stock and paid dividends on them. In 1611 the Amsterdam Stock Exchange was set up, and trading in Dutch East India Company shares was the main activity there for many years.

Similar companies were soon established in other countries. The excitement over these new companies made many investors foolhardy. They bought shares in any company that came on the market, and few bothered to investigate the companies in which they were investing. The result was financial instability. In 1720, financial panic struck in France when, after a rush of buying and selling, stockholders became frightened and tried to sell their stocks. With everyone trying to sell and no one buying, the market crashed.

In England, a financial scandal known as the South Sea Bubble took place a few months later. The South Sea Company had been set up in 1710 to trade with Spanish South America. The proposed size of company profits was exaggerated, and the value of its stocks rose very high. These high stock prices encouraged the formation of other companies, many of which promoted farfetched schemes. In September 1720, South Sea stockholders lost faith in the company and began to sell their shares. Stockholders of other companies began to do the same, and the market crashed as it had in France. These companies became known as "bubble companies" because their stock was often as empty and worthless as a bubble and the companies collapsed like burst bubbles.

Even though the fall of bubble companies made investors wary, investing had become an established idea. The French stock market, the Paris Bourse, was set up in 1724, and the English stock market was established in 1773. In the 1800's, the rapid industrial growth that accompanied the Industrial Revolution helped stimulate stock markets everywhere. By investing in new companies or inventions, some people made and lost huge fortunes.

Rise of the Small Investor

For many years, the main buying and selling of stocks was done by a few wealthy individuals. It was not until after World War I that increasing numbers of small investors began to invest in the stock market. There was a huge rise in speculative stock trading during the 1920's, and many people made fortunes. However, the Roaring Twenties came to an abrupt end in October 1929, when stock markets crashed and fortunes were wiped out overnight. The crash was followed by the

WONDER QUESTION

What are blue chip stocks?

Blue chip stocks are common stocks issued by companies with long histories of rising profits and dividends and strong finances. The most famous and most commonly used indicator of blue chip stock performance is the **Dow Jones industrial average**. The Dow Jones average is compiled by averaging the value of 30 of the largest and most respected blue chip stocks.

Left: Anxious crowds gather on Wall Street during the collapse of the stock market in October 1929. *Right:* The New York Stock Exchange is an important marketplace for financial transactions. It is one of the three largest exchanges in the world.

Great Depression of the 1930's, a period of severe economic crisis throughout much of the world.

Since the end of World War II, small investors have begun investing again in stocks, and stock markets have been relatively stable. A sharp fall in prices in 1987 led to another stock market crash. Initially, this frightened many people away from stock investments. But within a few months the market recovered and investor confidence returned.

Stock Exchanges Today

Today, the largest and most important stock exchanges are the New York Stock Exchange, the London Stock Exchange, and the Tokyo Stock Exchange. These exchanges act as marketplaces for the buying and selling of stocks. Another important source of stock transactions is the NASDAQ system. NASDAQ, which stands for National Association of Securities Dealers Automated Quotations, allows stock transactions to be made over computer terminals simultaneously in many cities around the world. Thousands of stocks are now traded over the NASDAQ system.

▶THE NEW YORK STOCK EXCHANGE

In colonial America there were no stock exchanges. People who wanted to buy and sell securities met in auction rooms, coffeehouses,

or even on street corners. Stock trading was unorganized, and people were reluctant to invest because they could not be sure they would be able to resell their securities.

In 1792, a small group of merchants made a pact that became known as the Buttonwood Tree Agreement. These men decided to meet daily to buy and sell stocks and bonds. This was the origin of America's first organized stock market, the New York Stock Exchange (NYSE).

Today there are more than 1,000 members of the New York Stock Exchange. Each of these members "owns a seat" on the exchange. This term comes from early years, when members had to stay seated while the exchange's president called out the list of securities to be traded. Despite the change and growth of the New York Stock Exchange over the years, its basic purpose has remained much the same—to allow companies to raise money and to allow the public to invest and make their money grow.

The New York Stock Exchange operates under a constitution and a set of rules that govern the conduct of members and the handling of transactions. The members elect a board of directors that decides policies and handles any discipline problems. The exchange is controlled by its own rules and by federal regulations set up by the Securities and

Exchange Commission, which was established by the U.S. government in 1934 under the Securities and Exchange Act.

Until 1869 it was easy for a company to have its securities listed on the exchange. A broker simply had to propose that a certain security be traded and get the consent of a majority of the other members. As business expanded, however, greater regulation became necessary, and the exchange established its first requirement for listing a company—that it be notified of all stock issued and valid for trading. In the years that followed, the exchange added more requirements, including company reports on earnings and other financial information. This helps potential investors make investment decisions more wisely.

To qualify for a listing on the exchange today, a company must be in operation and have substantial assets and earning power. The exchange considers a company's permanence and position in its industry as well. All common stocks listed on the exchange must have voting power, and companies must issue important news in such a way that all investors have equal and prompt access to it.

In addition to the New York Stock Exchange, which is the largest exchange in the United States, investors can also buy and sell stocks on the American Stock Exchange and several regional exchanges. The American Stock Exchange, also located in New York, trades stocks of small and medium-sized companies that do not meet the requirements for listing on the NYSE. Regional exchanges in Boston, Philadelphia, San Francisco, and other U.S. cities handle stocks listed on the NYSE as well as local securities.

How the Stock Exchange Works

The New York Stock Exchange itself neither buys, sells, nor sets prices of any securities that are listed. It simply provides the marketplace in which stocks and bonds are bought and sold.

Placing an Order. Suppose an investor in Iowa decides to buy 2,000 shares of XYZ Corporation. The investor calls a stockbroker—a registered representative of a stock exchange member—whose job is to provide investors with information and carry out investors' orders to buy and sell. The investor asks the broker the price of XYZ stock. The broker checks the price on a computer terminal and learns that XYZ Corporation is quoted at 25 to a quarter. This means that, at the moment, the highest bid to buy XYZ is $25 a share and the lowest offer to sell is $25.25 a share. The investor tells the broker to buy "at the market," which means to buy shares at the best available price at the time the order reaches the stock exchange. If the investor sets an exact price he or she is willing to pay, the order is called a "limit order," and no sale can take place unless another stockholder wants to buy or sell at that price.

By telephone or computer, the broker in Iowa sends the investor's order through a trad-

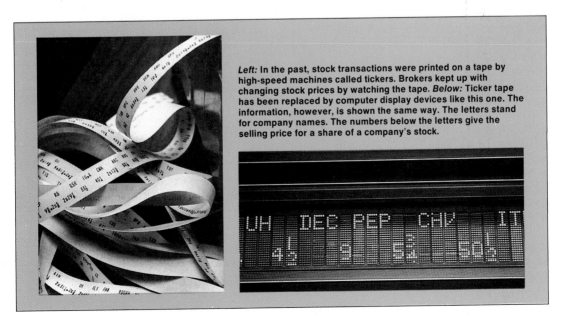

Left: In the past, stock transactions were printed on a tape by high-speed machines called tickers. Brokers kept up with changing stock prices by watching the tape. *Below:* Ticker tape has been replaced by computer display devices like this one. The information, however, is shown the same way. The letters stand for company names. The numbers below the letters give the selling price for a share of a company's stock.

ing desk at his or her firm's main office to a clerk on the floor of the stock exchange in New York. The clerk alerts the firm's floor broker by putting the broker's call number on two boards, one on each side of the trading floor. These boards are visible no matter where the floor broker is standing. The broker sees the call number and immediately goes to take the order.

Trading Stock. Small orders, such as those under 1,000 shares, often are executed automatically by computer at the best possible price at the time. Larger orders, however, are traded on the floor of the exchange, with a floor broker bargaining on the investor's behalf. This is the case with the Iowa investor's order of 2,000 shares of XYZ Corporation stock.

After receiving the order, the floor broker hurries to the place, called the **trading post**, where XYZ Corporation shares are traded. Other brokers with orders to buy or sell stocks will also be gathered there. Each trading post handles about 85 different stocks. This is where the exchange's member-brokers make transactions for investors.

At the trading post, the floor broker looks up at a video monitor above the post to see the current buy and sell prices for XYZ stock: Or he asks loudly, "How's XYZ?" and a specialist in that stock answers, "Twenty-five to a quarter." This means that the order could be filled immediately at a price of 25¼, or $25.25. It is the broker's job, however, to get the best possible price for an investor. The broker believes that a bid of 25⅛ will be accepted, so he loudly makes that bid. Another broker who has an order to sell 2,000 shares of XYZ at 25⅛ accepts the bid and says, "Sold." A trade has taken place at 25⅛.

Completing a Trade. Each broker completes the agreement by writing the price and the name of the other broker's firm on an order slip. The brokers report the transaction to their telephone clerks, so that the investors can be notified. Meanwhile, a record of the transaction is entered into the exchange's huge computer. This allows the transaction to be displayed, with all others, on thousands of computer terminals throughout the United States and around the world.

Specialists. Specialists are stock exchange members who help maintain an orderly market in the stocks for which they are registered. They do this by buying and selling for their own accounts whenever there is a temporary gap between supply and demand. In this way, they smooth the way for investors, allowing them to sell when there are few buyers or to buy when there are few sellers.

Specialists also act as brokers. A floor broker may choose to leave an order with a specialist, to be carried out when the stock reaches a certain price. Specialists are especially helpful with limit orders (orders with set prices). The price on a limit order may not come up for a week or longer, or not at all. It would be impractical for a floor broker to wait until a matching bid was made.

Odd Lots. Although a few stocks are sold in lots of 10 shares, most are sold in lots of 100. Many people, however, may want to buy only a few shares of stock rather than a complete lot. Shares sold in lots other than 10 or 100 are called odd lots. Orders in odd lots are not matched against other orders. They are carried out by specialists or by brokerage firms for their own accounts. The odd-lot system makes it possible for people with limited incomes to invest in the stock market.

Buying on Margin. Sometimes investors may wish to buy stocks but would prefer not to pay the total market price at the time of purchase. In such cases, the investors may buy on margin—that is, they pay only part of the price (usually at least half) when the stocks are purchased, and get credit for the rest from the brokerage firm. Buying on margin is very risky because the loan must be repaid to the broker, with interest, even if the price of the stock falls. To protect buyers and sellers, therefore, the federal government and the stock exchange regulate the buying of stocks on margin.

Right: In the trading room of the New York Stock Exchange, traders take orders for their firms and send them to the trading floor. *Below:* Here, a floor broker uses hand signals to buy and sell stocks for the firm.

Bulls and Bears. Bulls and bears refer to investors. A bull is someone who believes the market will rise; a bear anticipates a decline. Bulls and bears buy or sell hoping that the market will follow the pattern they predict. As optimists, bulls generally buy stocks expecting the value to rise, at which point they can sell and make a profit. As pessimists, bears sell stocks at a high price because they anticipate a market decline.

Selling Short. Investors who can satisfy certain securities regulations may sell short, or sell shares of stock they do not actually own. In selling short, an investor borrows shares from a broker who is willing to lend stock. The investor finds a buyer for the stock at the current market price, and then hopes that the price drops. When the price drops low enough, the investor buys the shares needed to complete the short sale and returns the borrowed shares to the lender. Selling short is risky. If the price drops, investors can make a profit on the difference between the high selling price and the low buying price. But if the price does not drop as expected, the investor not only does not make a profit, but can lose money buying shares at a higher price in order to return them to the lender.

▶ **MAKING INVESTMENTS**

Before investing in securities, people should understand the risks as well as the rewards. Investors should be sure that, in addi-

tion to their regular income, they have money set aside for personal emergencies. Investments often require time to increase in value. A careful study of the products, financial histories, and future plans of companies can help investors choose stocks that will allow their wealth to grow. Investors who prefer less risk might consider a money market fund where their original investment is safe and earns current rates of interest.

Many investors today invest in **mutual funds**—pools of money (from thousands of investors) that are invested in various stocks or bonds by professional managers. By having a professional buy and sell for them, investors benefit from that person's expertise. In addition, a mutual fund offers a diversified group of stocks or bonds, which means that a single investor can own pieces of many companies with a relatively small monetary investment. Such diversification also means that fund shareholders, unlike owners of individual stocks, are at less risk when a single stock drops sharply in value. Because of these features, mutual funds have become a popular alternative for many investors.

JORDAN E. GOODMAN
Senior Reporter, *Money*; Coauthor, *Barron's Dictionary of Finance and Investment Terms*

See also BANKS AND BANKING; ECONOMICS.

STOKES, CARL BURTON. See OHIO (Famous People).

STOKOWSKI, LEOPOLD. See ORCHESTRA CONDUCTING (Profiles).

STOMACH

To live and be healthy, you must eat food. But no matter how long you chew a piece of food, you can never shred, mash, or grind the food into small enough particles for your body to use. The food must travel through the digestive system before it can be used as nourishment. One part, or organ, of the digestive system that helps perform the important task of breaking down food is the stomach.

▶THE PARTS OF THE STOMACH

Because the stomach works automatically, you may not think much about the task it performs or even know where it is—at least not until you get a stomachache! Then you can readily tell that it is located at the top of the abdomen, on the left side. It is a muscular pouchlike organ that lies between the **esophagus** and the **duodenum**, the first part of the small intestine. The size and shape of the stomach vary greatly from one person to another and depend on how much food the stomach contains. An empty stomach is shaped like a letter J. But as it fills with food, the stomach bulges out to the shape of a boxing glove. An average adult's stomach can hold as much as 2½ pints (1.2 liters) of food.

The **cardiac orifice**, or opening, (which gets its name from its position close to the heart) is the entrance to the stomach from the esophagus. From there, the stomach projects upward on the left, forming an area known as the **fundus**. The middle part of the stomach is the

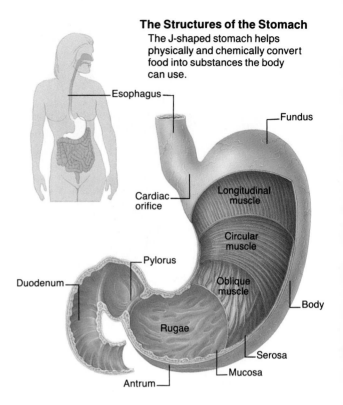

The Structures of the Stomach
The J-shaped stomach helps physically and chemically convert food into substances the body can use.

Esophagus — Fundus — Cardiac orifice — Longitudinal muscle — Circular muscle — Pylorus — Oblique muscle — Duodenum — Body — Rugae — Serosa — Mucosa — Antrum

body, and the lower region is the **antrum**. The outlet into the duodenum, called the **pylorus**, is guarded by a thick ring of muscle.

When the stomach is empty, its inner walls are drawn up into long, soft folds called **rugae**, which disappear when the stomach fills. Most of the stomach wall consists of three separate layers of muscle made up of stretchy, threadlike cells. The outside of the muscular wall is wrapped in a layer of tissue called the **serosa**, and the inside is lined with a soft, moist layer called the **mucosa**. Special cells in the mucosa are actually tiny glands that produce acid, enzymes, and other secretions that help in digestion.

▶HOW THE STOMACH WORKS

The action of the teeth, tongue, and saliva changes a mouthful of food into a moist ball, called a **bolus**. After swallowing, the bolus passes down the esophagus and into the stomach. Once the bolus reaches the stomach, circular muscles at the opening of the stomach help to keep food from backing up into the esophagus.

The folds, or rugae, of the stomach's inner lining form hills and valleys that will flatten out as the stomach fills with food.

As food continues to enter the stomach, the fundus expands to hold it. Meanwhile, contractions of the muscular wall in the middle of the stomach mix and churn the food. These mixing contractions occur in a regular rhythm. However, emotions such as excitement, anger, or fear can change the rate and strength of the stomach's contractions.

While the food is being mixed, special cells in the lining of the body of the stomach pour out their secretions. **Parietal cells** produce **hydrochloric acid**, which helps break down food proteins. **Chief cells** secrete **pepsinogen**. Pepsinogen is then changed by hydrochloric acid into **pepsin**, a protein-digesting enzyme. (In children, stomach cells produce another enzyme, called **rennin**, which helps to digest milk.) Still other cells in the mucosa produce **mucus**, a thick, gooey liquid that helps to moisten the food and protect stomach tissues. **Intrinsic factor** is another secretion. It helps the body use the vitamin B_{12} found in food to build red blood cells. Together, all these secretions are called **gastric juice**.

The flow of gastric juice is stimulated by **gastrin**, a hormone that is released when food enters the stomach. Gastric juice is strong enough to digest the tissues of the stomach itself. However, the thick mucus forms a protective layer. Even so, the lining cells soon wear out. They are quickly replaced by new ones. In fact, the entire stomach lining is replaced in about three days.

It takes about three to six hours for the food in the stomach to be churned into a soupy liquid called **chyme**. Waves of contractions, called **peristalsis**, move food down toward the antrum. As each wave reaches the pylorus, the muscle surrounding it relaxes and a bit of chyme is squirted through the opening into the duodenum.

As the stomach empties, the peristaltic contractions get stronger and begin higher up toward the fundus, until the last bit of chyme is squeezed out. The stomach muscles also contract when the stomach has been empty for a long time. These contractions produce the feeling of hunger.

▶ **DISORDERS OF THE STOMACH**

Many "stomachaches" are actually problems in the intestine or other abdominal organs. But various disorders of the stomach can produce pain or discomfort. Eating too much

or eating spoiled foods can cause indigestion, with feelings of pain, bloating, or nausea.

Heartburn, an intense pain in the middle of the chest, occurs when the cardiac orifice opens and stomach acid splashes up into the esophagus. Heartburn may be due to overeating, emotional upsets, or foods and drugs that relax the muscle surrounding the opening.

Peptic ulcers are sores that can develop in the lining of the stomach and other parts of the digestive tract that are exposed to acid-pepsin secretions. Gastric (stomach) ulcers may form when the mucosa is damaged or when the replacement of the mucosal cells cannot keep up with the daily damages.

Cancer can also occur in the stomach. It is more common in some countries than in others. Both diet and heredity are believed to play a role in its development.

A variety of treatments are used to combat stomach disorders. Drugs can be used to decrease acid production or neutralize the acid secreted. Because stress can increase the production of acid, techniques that help control emotional stress, such as meditation and biofeedback, are also used. Surgery to remove diseased or malfunctioning parts of the stomach is an additional method of treatment.

ALVIN SILVERSTEIN
VIRGINIA SILVERSTEIN
Co-authors, *The Digestive System*

See also BODY, HUMAN; BODY CHEMISTRY; DIGESTIVE SYSTEM; GLANDS.

STONE. See ROCKS.

STONE, LUCY. See WOMEN'S RIGHTS MOVEMENT (Profiles).

STONE AGE. See PREHISTORIC PEOPLE.

Stonehenge, England's most mysterious monument, has fascinated people for centuries. Today's scholars are not certain why it was built or what purposes it served. It was built in three stages over a period of 2,000 years. The drawing below shows Stonehenge as it probably appeared when completed, around 1100 B.C.

STONEHENGE

Stonehenge is one of the world's most famous and mysterious prehistoric monuments. The structure, built toward the end of the Stone Age, is located on the rolling grasslands of Salisbury Plain in southeastern England.

For centuries people have tried to determine why Stonehenge was built. It was long believed to be a temple for druids, the priests of the ancient Britons, and a place of human sacrifice. But Stonehenge was finished a thousand years before the druidic religion flourished in Britain. Nevertheless, it is still assumed to have had some ceremonial or religious significance. The location of the monument's entrance, in addition to the placement of certain boulders, has led some modern scholars to think that Stonehenge was used as a giant device to measure the heavens and forecast eclipses of the sun and moon. But to this day, Stonehenge's true purpose remains a mystery.

Stonehenge was built and rebuilt in three distinct stages over a period of about 2,000 years. Stonehenge I began about 3100 B.C. as a simple circular ditch with a high inner bank. Inside the bank were 56 pits now known as Aubrey holes, after John Aubrey (1626–97), Stonehenge's earliest scholarly investigator.

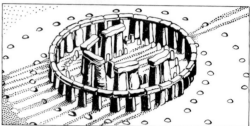

Outside the northeast entrance was placed a sarsen (a large boulder of English sandstone).

The modifications of Stonehenge II were made approximately one thousand years later, about 2150 B.C. At this time, two circles of bluestone pillars were placed in the center of the original circle but were never completed. The entrance path, called the Avenue, and the bluestones were aligned to coincide with the location of the sunrise at the summer solstice (which takes place around June 21).

Stonehenge III began shortly after, about 2000 B.C., and was built in three phases, the last ending about 1100 B.C. At this time, Stonehenge took its now familiar form (see diagram above). The huge sarsens were transported from the Marlborough Downs, 20 miles (32 kilometers) away; the bluestones, from southeastern Wales, were brought 280 miles (450 kilometers) by sea and over land. Skilled surveyors and engineers must have supervised whole communities to carve the stones (with stone and bone tools); raise the sarsens with ramps; and build scaffolding to lift the lintels that formed the archways. While it is unclear who created Stonehenge and why, it is quite evident that its builders were very determined and dedicated to their task.

VERONICA PALMER
Co-author, *Chronology of British History*

STORES. See DEPARTMENT STORES; RETAIL STORES.
STORMS. See HURRICANES; THUNDER AND LIGHTNING; TORNADOES.

WONDER QUESTION

Who built Stonehenge?

The medieval writer Geoffrey of Monmouth (?–1155) claimed that Merlin, the fabled sorcerer of King Arthur's legendary reign, raised the boulders of Stonehenge by magic.

Modern theorists suggest that the monument was built by Phoenician traders or by the Romans. But radiocarbon dating methods show that the building and remodeling of Stonehenge took place over so many generations, no single cultural group could have been responsible.

STORYTELLING

It is an ancient story
Yet it is ever new.

Heinrich Heine
Lyrisches Intermezzo

An honest tale speeds best being plainly told.

William Shakespeare
Richard III, Act IV, scene 4, line 358

The first law of story-telling . . . "Every man is bound to leave a story better than he found it."

Mrs. Humphry Ward
Robert Elsmere, Book 1, Chapter 3

An Ancient Art

Storytelling is one of the oldest of all the arts. Before writing was invented, before books were printed, there were stories. People of every race made up stories. In caves, huts, cabins, wigwams, and tents people told stories, handing them down by word of mouth from one generation to another. Perhaps the first tales told of some event of importance to a tribe or of a tribe member's brave deeds. As peoples became more civilized, they began to wonder more and more about the world around them, and stories became more than mere records of events and deeds. The tales took on deeper meaning. They expressed the hopes and fears, the beliefs and ideals of the people.

So over hundreds of years, everywhere in the world, there grew an enormous body of stories. This mass of stories is called **folk literature**, a literature made by the folk of many races. The stories are of many different kinds. There are simple nursery folktales, such as "The Old Woman and the Pig" and "The Three Pigs"; fairy tales, such as "Sleeping Beauty" and "Cinderella"; myths, such as those of the Greeks and the Norsemen; ballad stories, such as those of Robin Hood; legends of heroes, saints, and places; and epics, such as *Beowulf* and Homer's *Odyssey*.

As stories became more advanced in form the act of storytelling developed into an art. In every tribe, in every community, certain storytellers showed more ability than others. These were master storytellers, who recognized that different stories required different methods of telling. The masters studied ways of expression that would strengthen the spirit and meaning of their stories. They realized that a story, to be tellable, must be strong in plot, action, imagination, and colorful expression. In some countries—Ireland and Wales, for example—young people studied with master storytellers, who passed their skills on to them.

During the Middle Ages storytelling was the chief means of entertainment for people. Storytellers, often called minstrels or troubadours, journeyed everywhere, from castle to castle, inn to inn, marketplace to marketplace. Some of the minstrels were famous and wealthy. Others, less well off, wandered up and down the roads, telling their tales wherever they could gather a crowd. Rich or poor, they kept alive the art of storytelling and the wealth of stories that had come down through the ages. Their experience in telling gave the stories new vigor. In order to please their audiences, they added new qualities of imagination and beauty to the stories. When the time came for these tales to be collected and published, they had been enriched and polished by hundreds of tellers and hundreds of years of telling.

New Interest in Storytelling

The 1800's brought a strong awareness of the beauty and importance of every country's folk literature. The Grimm brothers were largely responsible for this. Jacob (1785–1863) and Wilhelm (1786–1859) Grimm spent a long time collecting and writing down the folktales of the German people. Following the work of the Grimms, people elsewhere began to collect tales of their countries. They got the stories from ancient manuscripts and from the folk themselves. In the British Isles, Joseph Jacobs (1854–1916) published English and Irish stories in his *English Fairy Tales* and *Celtic Fairy Tales*. Andrew Lang (1844–1912) brought together the stories of many countries in his famous "color" fairy-tale books: *Red Fairy Book*, *Yellow Fairy Book*, and others.

Doubtless the publication of such collections had something to do with the revival of the art of storytelling in the 1900's. At this same time library work with children was being developed and new methods of education were being considered. Librarians and teachers had the idea that storytelling offered children not only recreation but also a pleasant introduction to great literature. This belief received a boost from an Englishwoman, Marie Shedlock (1854–1935). A great storyteller, she visited the United States in 1915 to tell stories and to lecture on storytelling. Audiences of adults and children found her storytelling tremendously exciting.

Within a few years many public libraries organized story hours for children. Teachers and librarians told stories in schools. Youngsters in camps, playgrounds, and settlement houses heard stories. Gradually parents, teachers, librarians, and social workers came to recognize the value of storytelling.

Libraries now conduct story hours for preschool children, as well as for children of school age. Library schools, teachers colleges, and universities' schools of education offer courses in storytelling. Some radio and television stations also present programs of storytelling.

How to Tell a Story

There are three basic steps that are followed in storytelling.

The First Step. First comes the selection of the story. The chief materials for storytelling are the folktales of many different countries, modern fairy tales (like those of Hans Christian Andersen and Howard Pyle), and picture-book stories. The library is the best place to start. Children's libraries have many collections of folktales, short stories, and picture books. If the storyteller has trouble choosing a story, he or she may want to consult lists of stories that will help in making a selection. Some books on storytelling, such as Marie Shedlock's *Art of the Storyteller* (1915) and Ruth Sawyer's *Way of the Storyteller* (1942), include stories and lists of stories suitable for various age groups. Some United States libraries publish lists of stories especially selected for telling. There are, for example, the Carnegie Library of Pittsburgh's "Stories to Tell to Children," the New York Public Library's "Stories," and Baltimore's Enoch Pratt Free Library list, "Stories to Tell."

The Second Step. The second step in storytelling is learning the story. Learning a story does not mean learning it by heart. Knowing a story word by word is a mistake because the teller is likely to remember only words. The flavor, color, and spirit of the story will be lost, and the telling will be lifeless. Instead the storyteller should try to see the story as a series of pictures and make the events come vividly to life in the telling. In order to achieve this effect, it is best to read the story over and over, each time trying to see with the mind's eye the scenes, the characters, and the action that is taking place.

After several readings the storyteller should try telling the story aloud, noticing any places where the narrative is weak or unclear. In rereading the story, the teller should pay particular attention to these spots. As far as possible it is best to read the story as a whole and to think of it as a whole. A story read or learned in sections will be uneven when it is told.

The Third Step. The third step in storytelling is the actual telling of the story. Storytelling, a folk art, is simple, direct, and creative. It is creative in that a storyteller re-creates a story in the telling of it. No two tellers tell the same story the same way. Each gives his or her own feeling and own way of expressing feeling. The storyteller's chief goal is to bring the story alive. The audience should be drawn into the telling in such a way that they live within the world of the story.

The storyteller's voice should reflect the mood of the story—cheerful or sad, humorous or serious, nonsensical or realistic. The teller must speak clearly, carefully pronouncing each word. He or she will remember that children, especially younger children, may have difficulty keeping up with the action of a story told too fast. The storyteller must speak at different rates of speed. When a story is told without pause or change in pace, it becomes monotonous. Timing is important. Some stories move quickly from beginning to end. Others proceed slowly. The action in many stories quickens at times, slows down at other times. There is frequently a moment of suspended action before a crisis in a story, when the narrative seems to hold its breath. Aware of these things, the storyteller must adapt the telling to the movement of the story.

The storyteller is particularly conscious of the value of occasional pauses. The pauses should be brief—about the length of one long, indrawn breath—but they should be fairly frequent. They have the advantage of indicating a change in the story, of allowing children to relax and to get ready for what is to come. They also permit the teller to relax for a second or two.

Children, particularly small children, respond to the sounds of words, to rhythm, to rhyme. In "The Three Little Pigs" the phrase "I'll huff and I'll puff and I'll blow your house in" delights them. Their pleasure comes from the sound rather than the meaning. The storyteller should be sensitive to qualities of sound in the written story and should re-create these qualities in the story that is told. This is one more way of making the story come alive, one more way of making it a worthwhile experience for both the listener and the storyteller.

ELIZABETH NESBITT
Co-author, *A Critical History
of Children's Literature*

STOWE, HARRIET BEECHER (1811–1896)

When Harriet Beecher Stowe met President Lincoln in Washington, he said, "So you're the little woman who wrote the book that made this great war!" *Uncle Tom's Cabin*, Stowe's first novel, helped to bring about the U.S. Civil War.

Harriet Beecher was born on June 14, 1811, in Litchfield, Connecticut. Her father was Lyman Beecher, a well-known minister. Five of her six brothers, including her favorite, Henry Ward, also became ministers. Her sister Catharine became a notable educator.

Harriet began writing when she was very young. At 13 she won a prize for composition at school. After that, her two older sisters had her come to Hartford to prepare for teaching in their school.

When Lyman Beecher moved to Cincinnati in 1832 to become president of Lane Theological Seminary, Harriet went with him. Her older sister Catharine asked her to write a geography for young children. It was published in 1835. She also wrote stories for a literary club. One of them won a prize from *Western Monthly Magazine*.

In 1836 Harriet married Calvin Stowe, a professor at Lane. Lane's students became active in the antislavery movement. Their activities angered the board of trustees so much that they abolished the school's anti-slavery society. As a result, the school began losing its students. To help her husband and family during the hard times, Harriet decided to write for money. She sold a number of her stories.

The Stowes moved to Maine in 1850, when Calvin began teaching at Bowdoin. Harriet's sister-in-law in Boston wrote to her concerning slavery incidents and suggested that Harriet "write something that would make this whole nation feel what an accursed thing slavery is." She began writing *Uncle Tom's Cabin, or—Life Among the Lowly* in 1851 and published it as a book the following year.

The book's success at home and abroad was amazing. By treating blacks as human beings and showing that white southerners were also victims of slavery, Harriet convinced thousands that slavery was "accursed." She even made the villain, Simon Legree, a northerner.

Mrs. Stowe published *A Key to Uncle Tom's Cabin* in 1853 to prove her story was based on fact. She wrote a number of other novels, essays, and stories for children, but she will always be remembered as the author of *Uncle Tom's Cabin*. She died on July 1, 1896.

Reviewed by ARI HOOGENBOOM
City University of New York, Brooklyn College

STRATOSPHERE. See ATMOSPHERE.

STRAUSS, JOHANN, JR. (1825–1899)

Johann Strauss, Jr., known as the Waltz King, was born in Vienna, Austria, on October 25, 1825. His father, Johann Strauss, Sr., was a famous waltz composer and conductor. The boy developed an early love for music and wrote his first waltz at the age of 6. His father wanted him to follow a business career, but his mother encouraged him to take violin lessons and study composition.

In 1844 Strauss organized his own orchestra, which played in a fashionable restaurant. He composed waltzes that won the applause of the public—and finally, of his father.

When the elder Strauss died in 1849, his son combined their two orchestras and made a successful tour of Austria, Poland, Germany, and Russia. In 1862 Strauss married Henriette Treffz, a singer. The following year he was appointed conductor of the imperial court balls at Vienna, for which he wrote many waltzes that are still great favorites. Among these are *Tales from the Vienna Woods* (1868), *Artist's Life* (1867), and most famous of all, *The Blue Danube* (1867). While he was court conductor, Strauss visited Paris, London, and Italy. After he resigned this post in 1872, he went to the United States, where he conducted several concerts in Boston and New York.

Back in Vienna, Strauss turned his attention to composing for the musical stage. One successful operetta after another flowed from his pen. His masterpiece, *Die Fledermaus* (*The Bat*), written in 1874, is perhaps the most famous of all operettas. Also outstanding are *A Night in Venice* (1883) and *The Gypsy Baron* (1885). All the Strauss operettas are filled with tuneful dance numbers, such as polkas, galops, and especially waltzes.

After the death of his first wife, Strauss married an actress, Angelica Dietrich, from whom he was divorced several years later. His third wife, Adele, was at his side when he died in Vienna on June 3, 1899.

Reviewed by WILLIAM ASHBROOK
Philadelphia College of the Performing Arts

See also OPERETTA.

STRAUSS, RICHARD (1864–1949)

The German composer Richard Strauss was born into a musical family in Munich on June 11, 1864. His father, Franz Strauss, was the principal horn player in the Munich Court Orchestra; the younger Strauss later wrote many wonderful works for horn. Like many composers of the 1800's, Strauss also became an orchestra conductor. His earliest works were instrumental compositions, similar in style to those of German composers Johannes Brahms and Felix Mendelssohn.

After his exposure to the music of two other German composers, Richard Wagner and Franz Liszt, Strauss became interested in writing music that could express nonmusical ideas from literature, history, or even philosophy. During the 1880's, Strauss wrote a series of symphonic works that he called **tone poems** to indicate the poetic or dramatic ideas in the music. His most famous tone poems include *Don Juan* (1889), in which a brash musical theme portrays the adventures of Don Juan, and *Don Quixote* (1897), in which a cello represents the idealistic Don Quixote and a viola represents his servant Sancho Panzo. In *Thus Spake Zarathustra* (1895–96), the power of the orchestra is used to express the ideas of the German philosopher Friedrich Nietzsche.

At the beginning of the 1900's, Strauss turned his attention to opera. He shocked audiences with his highly dramatic operas *Salome* (1905) and *Electra* (1909). In both of these works, Strauss used an expressive and modernistic musical language to convey the extreme passion of the characters. In his charming *Der Rosenkavalier* (*Cavalier of the Rose*; 1911), Strauss captured the romantic and elegant spirit of Austria in the 1700's with a lighter music style, complete with Viennese waltzes. In *Ariadne auf Naxos* (1912), an opera composer and a singer participate in the production of an opera within the opera.

Strauss died on September 8, 1949, at the age of 85, after completing one of his most uplifting and poetic works, *Four Last Songs* (1949) for voice and orchestra. His operas and tone poems are performed regularly throughout the world today.

WENDY HELLER
New England Conservatory of Music

STRAVINSKY, IGOR (1882–1971)

Igor Fyodorovich Stravinsky was one of the most important composers of the 1900's. He was born in Oranienbaum (now Lomonosov), Russia, on June 17, 1882. As a child, he loved music. But his father, a singer at the Imperial Opera, wanted him to become a lawyer. Igor studied law at the University of St. Petersburg. He also studied composition with the well-known Russian composer Nikolay Rimsky-Korsakov.

A performance of Stravinsky's orchestral work *Fantastic Scherzo* in 1909 attracted the attention of Sergei Diaghilev, director of the Ballets Russes in Paris. Diaghilev commissioned the young composer to write ballets for him. Stravinsky composed *The Firebird* (1910) and *Petrouchka* (1911), based on Russian folktales. They were highly successful. But the startling rhythms and daring harmonies of his next ballet, *The Rite of Spring*, shocked the audience at its first performance in 1913. Today, the work is recognized as a masterpiece of modern music.

Stravinsky settled in Switzerland during World War I. There he wrote *The Soldier's Tale* (1918), a musical play using Russian folk material, with Spanish and ragtime influences. During the 1920's, he adopted a simpler style, later known as neoclassicism. In 1925 he made his first tour of the United States, conducting his own music. He returned to France, where he wrote one of his finest works, the *Symphony of Psalms* (1930). At the outbreak of World War II, he moved permanently to the United States.

Stravinsky's continued interest in writing for the ballet resulted in the popular *Card Party* (1937), *Orpheus* (1948), and *Agon* (1957). His opera *The Rake's Progress* was first performed in 1951. After the death that same year of the Austrian composer Arnold Schoenberg, Stravinsky adopted the older master's twelve-tone method of composition. One of his finest twelve-tone choral compositions is *Threni* (1958). Stravinsky died in New York City on April 6, 1971.

Reviewed by DIKA NEWLIN
Virginia Commonwealth University

STREEP, MERYL.   See MOTION PICTURES (Profiles: Movie Stars).
STREP THROAT.   See DISEASES (Descriptions of Some Diseases).

STRINDBERG, AUGUST (1849–1912)

The playwright and novelist August Strindberg is considered to be one of Sweden's greatest authors. He was born in Stockholm on January 22, 1849. Strindberg began to write plays while attending the University of Uppsala. His first important play, written after he had left the university, was *Master Olof* (1872), a historical drama.

Strindberg first gained wide recognition with *The Red Room* (1879), a satirical novel that ridiculed Swedish society. This work is considered to be Sweden's first naturalistic novel. In naturalistic writing, a form of realistic writing, people are viewed as having little free will or moral choice. Rather, their fates are determined by forces over which they have no control. *The Red Room* caused a scandal and quickly made Strindberg famous.

Strindberg lived outside Sweden much of the time from 1883 to 1898. His dislike of women and opposition to the feminist movement began to merge in such works as *Married* (1884), a collection of short stories.

Beginning in the late 1800's, he wrote some of his best dramas: *The Father* (1887), *Miss Julie* (1888), and *Creditors* (1889). These naturalistic works are bitter accounts of troubled marriages and love-hate relationships between men and women. Strindberg's own three marriages ended in divorce. Following the end of his second marriage he suffered a mental breakdown, which is described in his autobiographical novel *Inferno* (1897).

Later in his life, Strindberg experimented with the literary style known as expressionism, which is characterized by disturbing subject matter, emotional intensity, and the expression of inner states of mind. Strindberg's expressionist plays, such as *A Dream Play* (1902) and *The Ghost Sonata* (1908), had a major influence on the development of modern drama. Strindberg died in Stockholm on May 14, 1912.

Reviewed by MARILYN BLACKWELL
Author, *Structures of Influence: A Comparative Approach to Strindberg*

STRINGED INSTRUMENTS

All stringed instruments consist of one or more strings stretched over a sound box or soundboard, which amplifies the sound. The sound box or soundboard is necessary because a string vibrating alone cannot be heard more than a few centimeters away. Some stringed instruments, such as the electric guitar, are also amplified electronically.

Strings are made to vibrate in three ways. They may be plucked, struck, or bowed. The strings on stringed instruments are made of such materials as silk, gut, wire, nylon, or plastic. Some strings are also wound, or overstrung, with wire.

▶**PLUCKED STRINGED INSTRUMENTS**

The group of stringed instruments that are plucked is the largest. The harp, which comes in many sizes, leans against the body of the player, leaving the player free to pluck the strings with the fingers of both hands. The lute, the guitar, the ukelele, the mandolin, and the banjo are all held against the body of the player. The fingers of the player's left hand press the strings to change their pitch, while the fingers of the right hand pluck the strings.

The violin *(left)* is the smallest member of the violin family, which also includes *(left to right)* the viola, violoncello (cello), and double bass.

VIOLONCELLO (CELLO)

HARP

PIANO

CLAVICHORD

The harpsichord is a keyboard instrument on which a pick plucks each string when the key for that string is pressed. Both the zither and the American mountain, or Appalachian, dulcimer are placed on the player's lap or on a table while being played. The fingers of the player's left hand are used to change the pitch of the four or five melody strings on the zither, or the one melody string on the dulcimer, while the fingers of the right hand pluck or strum the melody and accompaniment.

▶STRINGED INSTRUMENTS THAT ARE STRUCK

The best-known stringed instrument whose strings are made to vibrate by being struck is the piano. Each key controls a hammer that strikes one, two, or three strings when that key is pressed. An older member of this group is the clavichord. Each key on this instrument also controls a hammer, or tangent, that strikes the proper string. The last member of this group is the type of dulcimer shaped like a trapezoid. Its larger, European version is called a cimbalom, while the smaller, American version is called the hammered dulcimer.

Both these instruments are played with two curved wooden sticks called hammers, which are held by the player.

▶BOWED STRINGED INSTRUMENTS

Bowed stringed instruments are played with a wooden bow that has horsehair, or sometimes a plastic substitute, stretched from end to end. The hair of the bow causes the strings of the instrument to vibrate when the bow is drawn across them. The player changes the pitch of the strings with the fingers of the left hand while bowing with the right hand. Instruments in the group of bowed stringed instruments include the older family called the viols and the modern orchestral strings, which include the violin, viola, violoncello (popularly called the cello), and the string bass or bass viol.

JEAN CRAIG SURPLUS
Author, *The Heart of the Orchestra*

See also GUITAR; KEYBOARD INSTRUMENTS; MUSICAL INSTRUMENTS; PIANO; VIOLIN.

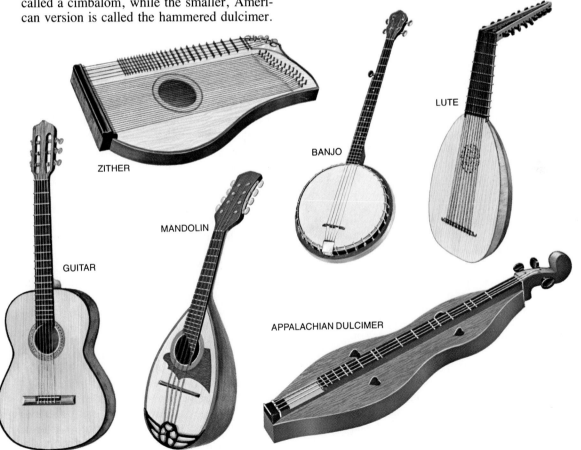

ZITHER

LUTE

BANJO

MANDOLIN

GUITAR

APPALACHIAN DULCIMER

STUART, GILBERT.
See Rhode Island (Famous People).

STUART, JEB (1833–1864)

Jeb Stuart is one of the true legendary heroes of the American Civil War. He was born James Ewell Brown (J.E.B.) Stuart on February 6, 1833, on Laurel Hill Plantation in Patrick County, Virginia. Religious, romantic, and charismatic, Jeb was full of dash and good humor. After graduating 13th in his class from West Point Military Academy in 1854, he joined the U.S. cavalry on the western frontier, but resigned to join the Confederate forces when the Civil War began in 1861.

In the spring of 1862, when Union general George McClellan tried to capture the Confederate capital of Richmond, Brigadier-General Stuart embarked on one of his most brilliant campaigns. On a three-day scouting expedition, he and 1,200 of his cavalrymen rode around McClellan's army, learning the exact strength and location of the enemy's forces. Thereafter, Confederate general Robert E. Lee called him the "eyes of the army" and placed him in command of the entire cavalry of the Army of Northern Virginia. Stuart fought at Antietam, Fredericksburg, and Chancellorsville. With his flowing beard and plumed hat, he was the very model of a Southern cavalier, a modern-day knight on horseback. Even his horses, Virginia and Highfly, became legendary.

In June 1863, at the start of the Gettysburg campaign, Stuart's forces were engaged by Union horsemen at Brandy Station, Virginia, in the largest cavalry battle in American history. Stuart did not reach Gettysburg until the second day of the battle. Some historians argue that his absence at this critical time contributed to the Confederates' defeat at Gettysburg, a turning point of the war.

Stuart went on to fight in the Wilderness Campaign but was mortally wounded at Yellow Tavern, Virginia, on May 11, 1864. He died in Richmond the following day.

GABOR S. BORITT
Director, Civil War Institute
Gettysburg College

STUDY, HOW TO

All good students have one thing in common. They know how to study. No one is born knowing how to do this. Studying is a skill, and it must be learned. In this article, you will discover many different methods to improve your own study skills. This will help you become a better student.

Choosing a Place to Study

Good organization is crucial to good studying. Start by organizing a place to work. It could be a desk or a kitchen table or anywhere you want. But there must be good light for reading and a tidy surface where you can spread out your books and papers. The place you choose should be quiet—at least while you are studying. You want to avoid all distractions when you work. You also need a collection of study tools. Here is a supply list: pencils, erasers, sharpener, pens, ruler, glue, scissors, paper clips, highlighter, stapler, staples, rubber bands, tape, hole punch.

If you have a computer, add these items to your supply list: disks, computer paper, printer ribbon.

If you do not have a desk, keep your supplies in a shoebox. Bring it with you whenever you are ready to settle down to work. Every few days, check your supplies. Replace any items that are used up, broken, or missing. If you check your supplies frequently, you will be sure to have them when you need them.

Choosing the Right Time to Study

You must also select a time for studying. Some people like to get their work done as soon as they get home from school. Some prefer to wait until after dinner. Others like to wake up early in the morning and work before school starts. Should you do all of your work at one time? Many people like to work this way. Other people prefer to work for awhile, take a break, and then get back to work. There are no set rules. The best way is the method that works best for you. But once you have selected a time and a place for studying, do

STUDY METHODS

These four study methods can help you understand your work.

1. *Scan.* When you have a reading assignment, start by scanning the material. Suppose you are reading a chapter on the American Revolution. First look at all the headings in bold type. You may come across the words "The First Battle," "The Midnight Ride," or "Jefferson's Ideas." Then study the illustrations. Perhaps there are pictures of Paul Revere, George Washington, or Thomas Jefferson. Next, read the captions. Scanning headings and captions for a few minutes gives you a preview of what the chapter contains before you read it.

2. *Think about the facts you know.* You probably already know some facts about the American Revolution. Spend one minute thinking about them. By reviewing this material, you prepare your mind to learn new information.

3. *Summarize as you read.* After you read a paragraph or two, stop and try to think of the most important information you learned in that small section. Try to guess what information you will learn next. Reading in this way ensures that you will understand your assignment.

4. *Take notes.* For some assignments, you need to take notes about the material you read. Usually a list of important people, dates, and events will do to remind you of the main points.

USE YOUR MEMORY!

Memorizing vocabulary words, multiplication tables, and historical dates can be difficult. Fortunately, there are ways to make this aspect of studying easier.

1. *Start small.* If you must memorize the meanings of twenty vocabulary words, do not try to learn all twenty at once. Study five of them for a few minutes. Then select five more words. Study these words. Combine both sets of words. Study all ten together. Add two more words, then two more. Keep adding a small number of words while you review the words you have already studied until you have mastered the whole list.

2. *Time to forget.* It is almost impossible to remember a list of words or facts with just one study session. When you turn to your vocabulary list tomorrow, do not be surprised if many of the definitions seem to have flown right out of your head. No matter how well you study on Monday, you will probably have to study this material again on Tuesday. Expect this to happen. Leave time to forget and time to restudy.

3. *Flash cards.* When you have a lot of information to memorize, make flash cards. Write a vocabulary word or name on one side of the card and its definition on the other. Then read one side of the card and try to remember the words on the opposite side. Tape the cards around your room; then you can study them as you get ready for school.

not change your routine. Follow the same schedule every day—even when you do not want to.

Preparing a Calendar

It is a good idea to organize a schedule for your assignments, too. Your teacher will probably give you three kinds of homework assignments. Homework that must be done overnight is one kind. An assignment that is due several days after you receive it is another. A third kind is a long-term project—you might be given a month to complete a book report, a social studies paper, or a science project. How can you organize your work so that you finish all of it on schedule?

One way is to make a special homework-assignment calendar. You need a calendar that shows an entire month on one page. You can buy this kind of calendar or you can make one at home. You will write your assignments on your calendar in a special way. First, in red, write the subject of the assignment on the day it is due in school. Then, in green, write the subject on the day (or days) you plan to work on the assignment. You might study for Friday's spelling test on Tuesday and Thursday. You might prepare for Monday's social studies test on Tuesday, Thursday, Saturday, and Sunday. In order to complete a book for a book report, you might read a chapter a day for two weeks. Update your calendar whenever necessary. Every day before you start to study, check your calendar and you will know your work load for the day.

Understanding Your Work

A habit is something you do again and again without thinking. If you have good study habits, your mind can concentrate on the important job, the content of your assignments.

To do your best work on almost any school assignment, you must understand the ideas and concepts that are part of every lesson. In social studies, it is not enough to know that colonial Americans were angry with the British. You must also understand why they were angry. In mathematics, it is not enough to know that fractions and decimals are part of the numerical system. You must also understand how fractions and decimals are alike and how you use them to solve math problems.

Learning How to Memorize

Understanding is only one part of a student's job. In addition, every student must memorize, or learn by heart, a considerable amount of information. In social studies you must understand the causes of the American Revolution, but you must also memorize the date the Declaration of Independence was signed. In mathematics you have to understand how fractions and decimals are alike, but you also have to memorize the way to change fractions into decimals.

It takes effort to be good at your studies. You must be organized. You must work to understand what you are studying and develop the ability to memorize information. If you keep trying, you will master these skills and become the best student you can possibly be.

PEGGY KAYE
Author, *Games for Learning*

See also LEARNING.

STUYVESANT, PETER (1592–1672)

Peter Stuyvesant (pronounced STI-ve-sent) was the last governor of *Nieuw Nederlandt* (New Netherland), a group of colonies once settled by the Dutch in the regions we now know as New York, New Jersey, Connecticut, Delaware, and Pennsylvania. Although his exact birthdate is not known, Stuyvesant was born in Scherpenzeel, Holland, in 1592.

Stuyvesant was a stocky man with a hot temper and an authoritarian nature. But he was an able administrator, and the Dutch West India Company appointed him governor of the Caribbean islands of Curaçao, Bonaire, and Aruba. In 1644, in a battle with the Portuguese, Stuyvesant's right leg was shattered by a cannonball. Thereafter, people called him "Old Silver Leg," as his wooden peg leg was ringed with silver bands.

In 1646, Stuyvesant was chosen to govern New Netherland. When he arrived the following year, he found its main settlement, New Amsterdam, in chaos. Pigs wallowed in muddy streets, the sod walls of Fort Amsterdam were used to feed cows, and one quarter of the 150 dwellings were used as taverns.

Stuyvesant was an unpopular governor, but he turned New Amsterdam into a thriving town during his 18-year administration. The streets were paved and brick houses were built. Orphanages, homes for the poor, a secondary school, and America's first fire department were established. At the same time, other Dutch settlements flourished in the surrounding areas.

On September 5, 1664, while Holland and England were at war, British soldiers invaded New Netherland, took over the colony, and renamed it New York. Stuyvesant lost his governorship, but the British agreed to let him stay on his *bouwerie* (farm) in New Amsterdam (now New York City) with his wife, Judith, and their two sons. He died there in 1672 at the age of 80. The area of New York City where he lived is still known as the Bowery. The names of other regional streets and towns, such as Peekskill and Yonkers, also recall a time when the Dutch and a man with a wooden leg ruled New Netherland.

ROBERT QUACKENBUSH
Author, *Old Silver Leg Takes Over*

SUBMARINES

Submarines are unusual ships. They can travel deep beneath the surface of the ocean or on the ocean's surface. They have many uses: Scientists and explorers can use them to study undersea plants and animals and sail under polar ice caps; historians and archaeologists can descend to the ocean bottom in them to examine ships that sank in earlier times; armed with torpedoes and missiles, they are the most powerful and feared of warships.

▶HISTORY OF SUBMARINES

People have tried to perfect an undersea vessel for almost 2,000 years. The earliest recorded attempt was during the 300's B.C., when Alexander the Great was lowered into the sea in a barrel with glass portholes. By

A.D. 1620, Cornelius van Drebbel of Holland had actually built a self-propelled submarine —a wooden boat covered with greased leather that he sailed in the Thames River in London.

Early in the history of submarines, people recognized their usefulness as warships. During the American Revolutionary War, a one-person submarine, the *Turtle*, was used to attack the British fleet. Built by David Bushnell (1742?–1824) of Connecticut, the *Turtle* was a small, oval-shaped craft powered by hand-cranked propellers. It carried a time bomb that was supposed to be attached to the hull of an enemy ship by a spike. Because the wooden hulls of British vessels were covered with copper, however, the spike for attaching the bomb could not be driven successfully through the metal, and the attack failed.

During the United States Civil War, the Confederate ship *Hunley* became the first submarine to make a successful attack on an enemy ship. The *Hunley* was powered by a hand-cranked propeller that needed eight men to turn it. It was an unlucky ship that had sunk several times during testing, each time drowning most of its crew. In 1864 it was, nonetheless, sent to attack the Union gunboat

The finlike tower on top of a nuclear submarine is known as a "sail" because it has diving planes on each side. It is used as an observation bridge by the captain and navigator when the ship is on the surface (*below*). When the submarine is underwater, information about its position can be monitored in the control room (*left*).

The *Turtle*, a one-person submarine powered by hand-cranked propellers, was used during the American Revolutionary War.

Housatonic in the harbor of Charleston, South Carolina.

The *Hunley*'s weapon was a bomb on a long pole projecting from its bow. The submarine was supposed to ram the bomb into the *Housatonic*'s hull, back off, and detonate the explosive by pulling on a rope. The bomb was rammed into the *Housatonic* as planned, but it exploded immediately, sinking both ships.

The USS *Nautilus*, the first nuclear-powered submarine, was launched in 1954.

Submarines were neither safe nor practical until the late 1800's. At that time John Holland (1840–1914), an Irish-American inventor, produced submarines with a greatly improved design. In 1900 the U.S. Navy bought its first submarine, the *Holland*, from the designer.

During the 1900's, submarines played an important role in World War I and especially in World War II. German U-boat submarines took a heavy toll on Allied shipping during World War II, and American and British submarines inflicted great damage on German and Japanese fleets. For protection, ships on both sides traveled together in convoys, accompanied by destroyers armed with depth charges—explosives set to go off well below the surface of the ocean at predetermined depths—which were often very effective weapons against submarines.

▶THE SUBMARINE'S STRUCTURE

Because of their unusual nature, submarines are designed and built differently than other types of ships. A submarine must have an especially strong hull to withstand the tremendous pressure exerted on it as it descends. It also has special ballast tanks that can be filled with water or emptied. These tanks make the ship heavier or lighter so that it can either descend toward the sea bottom or rise to the surface. To keep the submarine at a certain depth in the ocean and to guide its course, there are rudderlike fins called hydroplanes at its bow and stern.

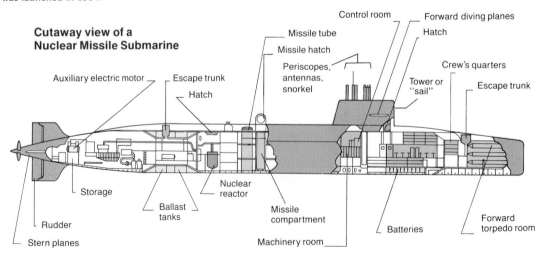

Cutaway view of a
Nuclear Missile Submarine

Control room
Forward diving planes
Missile tube
Hatch
Missile hatch
Periscopes, antennas, snorkel
Crew's quarters
Tower or "sail"
Escape trunk
Auxiliary electric motor
Escape trunk
Hatch
Storage
Nuclear reactor
Ballast tanks
Missile compartment
Batteries
Forward torpedo room
Rudder
Stern planes
Machinery room

The design of submarines has changed greatly since 1900. Today's naval submarines are larger, improved in many ways, and very expensive. Some are more than 550 feet (170 meters) long, weigh more than 17,000 metric tons, and cost more than $1 billion. In contrast, the first U.S. naval submarine was 54 feet (16.5 meters) long, weighed 68 metric tons, and cost about $150,000. Other types of submarines, used for nonmilitary purposes, come in a variety of shapes and sizes, depending on their purpose and use.

▶ TYPES OF NAVAL SUBMARINES

There are two main types of naval submarines—**conventional** and **nuclear-powered**. Conventional submarines are powered by large diesel engines. These engines need air to operate, so they can be used only when the ship is on the surface of the ocean or when it uses a snorkel, or air tube, that reaches the surface. The diesel engines turn generators that supply power to electric motors that turn the ship's propellers. The generators also supply power for charging large storage batteries. When the submarine descends beyond snorkel depth of about 30 feet (9 meters), the engines are shut off, and the batteries supply the power. The problem with conventional submarines is that they have to surface frequently to refuel and to recharge their batteries.

Nuclear-powered submarines, on the other hand, do not need air to generate power. They can go for months without having to refuel.

The living space aboard a submarine is very tight, but it is made as livable and enjoyable as possible by comfortable bunk beds, excellent food, a library, movies, and televison.

WONDER QUESTION

How is a submarine navigated underwater?

The navigator cannot actually see where a submarine is going when it is deeply submerged. Instead, electronic devices become the navigator's "eyes." Information about the course the submarine is to take is fed into an automatic navigating system, and changes in how the ship is following its course are monitored by sensitive gyroscopes. All information is relayed by computer to the navigator, who can make necessary corrections and adjustments to keep the submarine on course.

An object in the submarine's path is detected by sonar (*so*und *na*vigation *r*anging) equipment. Active sonar equipment sends out high-frequency vibrations or pulses of sound that bounce off an object and are reflected back to the submarine to determine the distance an object is from the submarine. Passive sonar equipment listens for and uses sounds to detect and identify an object and the direction in which it may be located. United States naval submarines generally use passive sonar.

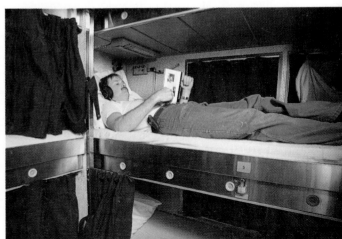

The *Alvin* is a submersible research vessel designed to conduct underwater research and exploration. In 1986 it helped divers explore the sunken luxury liner *Titanic*. Photographs of the ship's interior were taken by J. J. (*below*) a robot connected to the *Alvin* by a yellow tether. J. J. was guided through the Titanic's stairwells by remote control.

Modern nuclear submarines can cruise for 400,000 miles (about 650,000 kilometers) on one charge of fuel, and can stay submerged for months at a time. Nuclear submarines have performed feats that conventional submarines could never accomplish. In August 1958, the USS *Nautilus* cruised underwater from the Pacific to the Atlantic Ocean by passing under the north polar ice cap. In the same month the USS *Seawolf* set a record for long-submersion runs after staying underwater continuously for 60 days and traveling 14,500 miles (23,300 kilometers). That record has been bettered many times since then. Underwater cruises of two or three months are now quite common.

Naval Submarine Duty

Complex equipment and long undersea voyages make naval submarine duty quite difficult. Although modern naval submarines are large, much of the inside space is occupied by machinery, missiles, torpedoes, sonar, and other equipment. As many as 160 people must live, work, and relax in the space that remains. All submariners in the United States Navy are volunteers. Before being accepted for training, they must pass rigorous tests to make sure they can withstand the many hardships of submarine life.

Certain submarines, such as the strategic ballistic missile submarines of the United States Navy, have two crews. While one crew is at sea, the other is retraining ashore. When the submarine comes into port, the crews exchange places. The life of crew members is made as enjoyable as possible.

▶ NONMILITARY SUBMARINES

In recent years submarines have been used for many nonmilitary purposes. Special submarines have been designed for use in underwater scientific research and exploration. Oceanographers use submarines to study marine life, to determine the speed and direction of ocean currents, and to explore and map the ocean floor. Geologists use them to detect and monitor underwater mineral resources and oil deposits. Explorers and archaeologists use submarines to discover and study ancient shipwrecks or the ruins of submerged cities.

In the future, submarines may become even more important for such activities. Workers and researchers would be taken to and from work sites in submarines, and their supplies and materials would be transported by submarines as well. Submarine designers also look forward to the day when huge underwater vessels glide beneath the seas, carrying goods and people from one continent to another.

Reviewed by Lt. Robert T. Ross
Office of Information
U.S. Department of the Navy

See also Oceanography; Underwater Exploration.

SUBTRACTION. See Arithmetic.

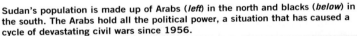

SUDAN

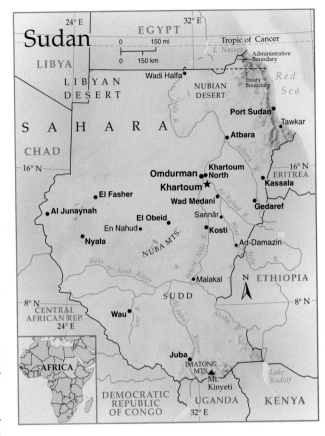

Sudan, the largest country in Africa, is approximately one-quarter the size of the United States. It is situated in northeastern Africa, on the Red Sea coast, and is bordered by nine other African nations. Sudan gained its independence in 1956 after six decades of joint colonial rule by Britain and Egypt.

Sudan is not densely populated but has great religious and ethnic diversity. Most of the wealth is in the south, but the political power is in the north. About 1780, northern Sudanese and Muslims from the west penetrated southern Sudan, raiding for slaves. Since that time, southern wealth has been forcibly taken by northern raiders. This and other factors have frustrated the efforts of post-independence governments to build lasting national unity.

Civil war raged in Sudan perhaps longer than anywhere else in history. The first civil war began at independence in 1956 and lasted until 1972. War flared again in 1983 when the Islamic government declared that all of Sudan, including the non-Islamic and partially Christian south, would be subject to Islamic laws. Southern opposition was headed by the Sudan People's Liberation Army and Movement (SPLA/M), a military and politi-

cal organization. The war, which continued until 2005, killed at least 2 million Sudanese and devastated the lives of millions more. Crops were destroyed, leading to famine and disease. Northern Sudanese militias enslaved southern peoples, forcing them into labor in the north. Many southerners fled their home-

Sudan's population is made up of Arabs (*left*) in the north and blacks (*below*) in the south. The Arabs hold all the political power, a situation that has caused a cycle of devastating civil wars since 1956.

Most Sudanese are farmers. Sorghum, millet, and other grains are among the country's chief crops.

25 percent of the country's population is concentrated in this area.

Sudan's climate varies. The north is hot and dry, with temperatures reaching 120°F (49°C) in summer. Rainfall is heaviest in the south, where 50 inches (1,270 millimeters) may fall in a year. Too little rain falls in the north to allow farming without irrigation.

lands to live in refugee camps in Kenya, Uganda, and the Central African Republic.

▶ PEOPLE

Sudan's population is made up of two distinct groups—northerners and southerners. Most of the population in the north is made up of different ethnic groups of Africans of Arabic origins. They speak Arabic, the country's official language, and practice the Sunni Muslim religion.

The southern population is made up of numerous ethnic groups, who speak different languages and practice Christianity in addition to a variety of traditional African religions. The largest and most powerful ethnic group is the southern Nilotic Dinka.

▶ LAND

Most of Sudan consists of a vast plain, bordered in the east, south, and west by hills and mountains. The highest point is Mount Kinyeti in the south, which rises 10,453 feet (3,186 meters). Elsewhere in the south, Sudan has savanna (grasslands), tropical rain forests, and the world's largest swamp. In the north are the Nubian and Libyan deserts, which make up about one-quarter of Sudan's total land area.

Sudan's most important physical feature is the Nile River, which flows the length of the country. Its two main branches are the White Nile and the Blue Nile. An island, known as the Gezira, lies between these two branches. It is Sudan's most fertile region. More than

▶ ECONOMY

Many ambitious development plans were launched after independence, but progress was limited by political instability and civil war. Oil reserves in the south, which could transform the country from an energy importer to an exporter, were seized by the northern Sudanese government, which used the profits to buy weapons. Plans to build a canal between Jonglei and Malakal in the south were also interrupted. Thus, although it

FACTS and figures

REPUBLIC OF THE SUDAN is the official name of the country.

LOCATION: Northeastern Africa.

AREA: 967,495 sq mi (2,505,813 km²).

POPULATION: 40,200,000 (estimate).

CAPITAL: Khartoum.

LARGEST CITY: Omdurman.

MAJOR LANGUAGES: Arabic (official), Nubian and various other African languages, English.

MAJOR RELIGIOUS GROUPS: Muslim, traditional African religions, Christian.

GOVERNMENT: Republic. **Head of state and government**—president. **Legislature**—National Assembly.

CHIEF PRODUCTS: Agricultural—cotton, peanuts, sorghum, millet, wheat, gum arabic, rice, sugarcane, fruits, livestock. **Manufactured**—ginned cotton, textiles, cement, edible oils, refined sugar, soaps, shoes, refined petroleum. **Mineral**—petroleum, iron ore, gold.

MONETARY UNIT: Sudanese dinar (1 dinar = 10 Sudanese pounds).

had great potential, Sudan became one of the poorest nations in the world. For many years, Sudan received international emergency food aid. But warfare and corruption blocked much of this help from reaching the neediest people in the south.

Sudan's economy is based mainly on services and agriculture. Most of the people are farmers, who raise livestock and grow such food crops as sorghum, millet, and other grains. Sudan's acacia trees produce most of the world's gum arabic, used in making ink, glue, and medicines.

Manufacturing. For centuries, artists have handcrafted rugs, tapestries, and gold jewelry. More recently, Sudan has adopted such light industries as leather tanning, cement making, sugar refining, beverage canning, and textile weaving.

Agriculture. With irrigation, the river valley soil of the Gezira is ideally suited for growing cotton, the main cash crop. Rice, wheat, peanuts, and vegetables are also grown there. But Sudan has few roads or railroads to transport agricultural goods to market. Five sugar mills currently produce 700,000 tons of sugar per year. The Kenana plant is perhaps the largest in the world.

Mining. Gold, iron ore, copper, and other minerals are mined in Sudan's mountains. With the discovery of significant deposits of petroleum in southern Sudan, 200,000 barrels a day are shipped by pipeline to Port Sudan on the Red Sea.

▶ **MAJOR CITIES**

Khartoum, the capital of Sudan, is situated at the junction of the White and Blue Nile rivers. It is the country's primary center of finance and transportation. To the north are **Khartoum North**, an industrial city, and **Omdurman**, Sudan's largest city and primary commercial center. These three cities are connected by bridges. Together they form one large urban complex with a population of about 3 million.

Other important cities include **Port Sudan**, the country's principal port, situated on the Red Sea; **El Obeid** (or **Al Ubayyid**), located in central Sudan; and **Kassala** in eastern Sudan. The chief cities of southern Sudan are **Juba**, **Wau**, and **Malakal**.

▶ **CULTURAL HERITAGE**

All the people of Sudan share a rich heritage rooted in the distant past. However, various outside influences encouraged the adoption of different sets of customs and be-

Khartoum, the capital of Sudan, spans the junction of the White and Blue Nile rivers. The Gezira, a fertile island, lies between the two branches.

liefs in different areas. In the northern and central parts of the country, cultural innovations often came from the Mediterranean world, including the religions of Christianity and Islam.

▶ **HISTORY AND GOVERNMENT**

About 7000 B.C. farmers and herders appeared along the Nile River in Nubia, in what is now northern Sudan. The Egyptians, who called the land Kush, added it to their empire. In 538 B.C., the capital of Kush was moved from Napata to Meroë, where Egyptian influences were preserved for nearly 1,000 years.

During the Middle Ages, the Nubians established several new kingdoms and adopted Christianity.

In the early 1500's, a new realm called Sinnar was founded by a Muslim African dynasty called the Funj. Its sultans ruled a large part of central Sudan until 1821, when Egypt reconquered the country. In 1885 the Sudanese drove out the Egyptians. But in 1898, British and Egyptian forces took control of Sudan and remained until the country achieved independence in 1956.

Independence. Sudan had a parliamentary form of government until the army seized power in 1958. Civilians regained control in 1965, but in 1969, Gaafar al-Nimeiry led a successful military coup and set up a revolutionary council to act as head of state. Nimeiry was later elected president.

Conflict raged between northern Islamic Sudanese, who controlled the government, and the non-Muslims in the south, who were denied democratic rights. In 1972, Nimeiry gave southerners a measure of self-rule. But in 1983, under pressure by Islamic fundamentalists, he decreed that Islamic religious laws (Sharia) applied to the whole country. Under Sharia law, non-Muslims were prohibited from holding political office.

Renewed rebellion in the south and economic difficulties led to Nimeiry's overthrow by the army in 1985. A northern civilian government took office in 1986, but it was unable to end the civil war. General Omar Hassan Ahmad al-Bashir, a Muslim fundamentalist, seized power in 1989.

In 2002, the government and the rebel forces signed a temporary cease-fire, and humanitarian aid was distributed in the south for the first time in 13 years. But by 2004, a crisis had developed in the Darfur region. Arab militants began raiding villages in a campaign against black Africans that human rights groups described as genocide. More than 2 million were displaced from their homes, and at least 50,000 were killed. Another 180,000 died from starvation and disease. The African Union (AU) sent forces in to help protect civilians as international committees met to decide what further action should be taken.

On January 9, 2005, the Sudanese government signed a peace agreement with the rebels, ending the 21-year-old civil war. The agreement gives the south the right of self-government, and in six years it may hold a referendum to decide whether to remain part of Sudan. Oil revenues were to be shared. The United Nations sent peacekeeping forces, and international donors pledged more than $4 billion in aid.

In July, a new constitution was approved to admit non-Muslims into the government. Dr. John Garang de Mabior, a Christian and the longtime leader of the Sudan People's Liberation Army and Movement, was sworn in as vice president. But within three weeks, Garang was killed in a helicopter crash. Riots broke out, as demonstrators accused the government of causing his death.

STEPHANIE BESWICK
Ball State University

SUEZ CANAL

The Suez Canal, one of the world's most important artificial waterways, is both a bridge and a boundary line between Asia and Africa. Located in northeastern Egypt, it runs from the city of Port Said (pronounced sah-EED) on the Mediterranean Sea to the city of Suez on the Gulf of Suez, an arm of the Red Sea. To the west lies the Nile River Delta and to the east is the Sinai Peninsula.

Few canals can rival the Suez in economic importance or in colorful history. Ships sailing from Europe to Asia once had to travel around the southern tip of Africa. The Suez

Canal shortened this journey by thousands of miles and, in effect, brought Europe and Asia closer together. For example, the route from London to Bombay around the coast of Africa is approximately 12,500 miles (20,000 kilometers). Using the canal, the same trip is only 7,270 miles (11,700 kilometers).

The canal has been expanded several times since it was first opened in 1869. By 2002, the depth had been increased from its original 26 feet (8 meters) to 62 feet (19 meters). Bypass channels now let ships travel in opposite directions at the same time. Dry cargo is now more important than oil, but the canal has been enlarged so that it can handle smaller supertankers.

Today annual revenues from the canal are about $2 billion. Approximately 40 ships pass through daily, although traffic has declined in recent decades.

Early History. A canal connecting the Nile River and the Red Sea was built in Egypt nearly 4,000 years ago. Small boats could travel from the Mediterranean through the Nile River into the Red Sea. In the centuries that followed, the canal was rebuilt and its course was changed several times, but sometime about the A.D. 700's, the ancient canal was filled in and abandoned.

For centuries thereafter, people continued to dream of a canal that would connect the Mediterranean and Red seas. In the early 1800's, French emperor Napoleon Bonaparte expressed interest in such a canal, but his engineers discouraged the project. They believed that the Red Sea was higher than the Mediterranean and that a sea-level canal would cause parts of Egypt to be flooded.

Building the Canal. In 1832 French diplomat Ferdinand de Lesseps started making plans to build a sea-level canal. He later formed a private corporation called the Suez Canal Company to sell shares of stock to pay for its construction. Most of the money came from private French investors and the Egyptian government.

Construction began on April 25, 1859, but de Lesseps had to solve many problems. Millions of tons of earth had to be moved with crude tools. Thousands of unskilled workers had to be supervised. Transporting water and food for the laborers across desert lands was perhaps the greatest problem. This was solved by digging a temporary freshwater canal from the Nile River into the desert and then running it parallel to the Suez route.

On November 17, 1869, the Suez Canal was opened, at a cost of nearly $100 million. It was 105 miles (169 kilometers) long and 177 feet (54 meters) wide. Its maximum depth was 26 feet (8 meters). No locks were needed, as the Mediterranean and Red seas are, indeed, at almost the same level. To commemorate the opening, the Egyptian khedive (ruler) commissioned Giuseppe Verdi to write the opera *Aïda*, which was first performed in Cairo in 1871.

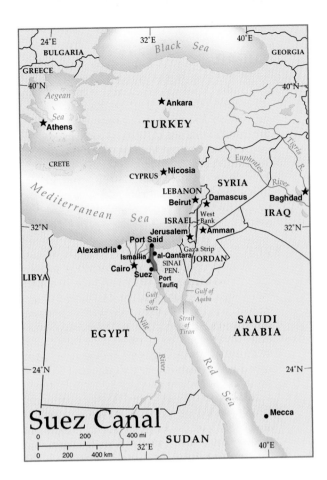

Suez Canal

From the start, the Suez Canal was a very profitable venture. And when heavy debts finally forced the Egyptian government to sell its shares of stock, Great Britain bought them out. By 1875, Britain owned almost half the shares in the Suez Canal Company.

The Canal in the Arab-Israeli Crisis. The original charter gave the Suez Canal Company a 99-year lease on the canal and on the land through which it passed. According to an international agreement (the Convention of Constantinople, October 29, 1888), all nations would have the right to use the canal. However, from 1948 (the year Israel became a nation) until 1979, Egypt violated this international law by refusing to let Israeli ships use the canal. The canal played a subsequent role in three major Arab-Israeli wars: the Suez Crisis of 1956, the Six-Day War of 1967, and the Yom Kippur War of 1973.

IRA M. SHESKIN
University of Miami (Florida)

See also CANALS; EGYPT; ISRAEL; LESSEPS, FERDINAND DE.

SUGAR

Candies, cookies, cakes, and pies—all these foods taste good because they are sweet. They are sweet because they are made with sugar. Some foods, especially fruits, contain natural sugar. Often we add sugar to foods, perhaps sprinkling it on cereal or grapefruit. And in many cases, manufacturers add sugar to the foods they process and package for sale.

Sugar comes from sugarcane or sugar beets. Different varieties of sugar, like those shown above, are generated by different amounts of processing.

▶ WHAT IS SUGAR?

When people speak of sugar, they usually mean **sucrose**, or table sugar, which comes from sugarcane or sugar beets. But there are also other kinds of sugar. All of them are **carbohydrates**—that is, they are made up of carbon, hydrogen, and oxygen arranged in different ways. A sugar's sweetness and the speed with which it dissolves in water depend upon its chemical makeup.

Next to sucrose, the most commonly known and used sugar is **dextrose**, which is also called **glucose** or grape sugar. Others are **lactose**, milk sugar; **maltose**, malt sugar; and **fructose (levulose)**, fruit sugar. Fructose is the sugar you taste when you eat honey or most kinds of fruit. It is many times as sweet as sucrose. The form of fructose that is used in the manufacture of bakery goods, confectionery items, preserves, and beverages is called high fructose corn syrup (HFCS, for short).

Most fruits and vegetables contain sugars. In addition to simple sugars, grains and dry seeds of plants contain a high percentage of starch (also a carbohydrate), which can be changed by chemical treatment or by the action of an enzyme into simple sugars.

▶ THE FORMS OF SUGAR

Sucrose is obtained from either sugarcane or sugar beets. Today about 70 percent of the world's output of sugar is from sugarcane and about 30 percent from sugar beets.

Pure sucrose refined in the crystalline form with which we are familiar is called **granulated sugar**. When sugar crystals are ground into a fine powder, the sugar is called **confectioners' sugar**. It is used to make cake frostings and some candies.

Granulated sugar that is not refined all the way to pure whiteness is called **brown sugar**.

The brown color comes from the traces of molasses that are still in the sugar. Brown sugars have a special flavor and fragrance that white sugar does not have. They are used to sweeten cookies, breads, and baked beans.

Syrup made from sugarcane is highly prized in the southern United States, where it is used for cooking or as a topping for pancakes. **Molasses** is a product that is left over from the processes of sugar manufacture. This heavy, dark syrup may be as much as 50 percent sucrose, and it also has a high content of organic and mineral substances. The highest grades of cane molasses are used to add flavor and sweetness to candies, cookies, and gingerbreads. The lower grades of molasses, including blackstrap molasses, are chiefly used for livestock feed and by the distilling industries for alcohol production.

▶ CANE SUGAR

Sugarcane is a giant member of the grass family. Sugarcane stalks are about 13 percent sucrose. Mature stocks are harvested and sugar is separated from the cane in two stages—at sugar mills and sugar refineries.

Growing Sugarcane. Sugarcane is grown in tropical and subtropical areas. In the United States, four states produce sugarcane: Florida, Hawaii, Louisiana, and Texas. In these areas, sugarcane looks much like very heavy stands of tall corn. In tropical areas, the growing season is longer and canes become very long. Instead of standing erect, the plants sprawl along the ground, with only about 5 feet (1.5 meters) at the tip end growing erect.

When a crop of cane is ready for harvest, the field may be intentionally set on fire to burn out the dried leaves. This makes it easier to do the harvesting. In hand harvesting, the stalks are cut with a heavy knife, the tops are cut off, the leaves are stripped, and the cleaned canes are piled. Harvesting machines now perform all these steps and have largely replaced hand labor.

Milling. Sugarcane stalks are brought to the mill, cleaned, cut into pieces, and then crushed by two enormous steel rollers called crushers. The crushers press the juice out of the cane. Next the juice is strained and clarified by the addition of chemicals such as lime. Then the clarified juice is concentrated into a thick syrup by removing some of the water under a vacuum.

Sugar is crystallized from the concentrated syrup by boiling the syrup in vacuum pans. The boiling is carefully controlled so that crystals build up to a suitable size. After this, the contents of the vacuum pan are dumped into a tank with stirrers. As the mass cools, further crystallization takes place.

The mass of crystallized sugar and the liquid still with it are centrifuged (spun at high speed), to separate the liquid (molasses) from the crystallized sugar. The molasses is collected and the process repeated until no more sugar can be extracted.

From the centrifuges, the moist sugar goes to cylindrical dryers. A current of hot, dry air blows through the sugar as it is tossed. After the sugar is dry, it is cooled, weighed, and readied for shipment as raw sugar.

Refining. The raw sugar shipped to a refinery is about 96 percent pure sucrose. To make it entirely pure, it is crushed, washed, centrifuged, melted into a clear, yellow liquid, and clarified. Next it is filtered until it is pure and colorless. Then it is recrystallized. The final product is dried and sifted through screens into bins for the different sizes of crystals. Then it is packaged.

▶ BEET SUGAR

Sugarcane cannot be grown in the cool climates of northern countries. In these areas and in some regions of South America, sugar is produced in commercial quantities from sugar beets.

Growing Sugar Beets. Sugar beets are large white roots—not the red beets used as a table vegetable. The seed for the beets is planted early in the growing season. The beets are harvested when the sugar content is high, usually very late in the season.

Processing. At the factory the roots of the sugar beets are carefully washed, drained, and weighed. Then they are sliced by machines into **cossettes**—slender pieces that look like french fries. The sugar is soaked out of the cossettes with hot water. The soaking is done in a diffuser, which turns the beets into pulp from which almost all sugar has been extracted.

The juice from the diffuser is clarified by adding lime and by filtering. The clear beet juice is then treated in the same way as the clear juice from sugarcane.

▶ SUGAR HISTORY

Sugarcane was probably growing wild on the island of New Guinea (just north of Australia) thousands of years ago. The stalks were highly prized as food. As people advanced in

Sugarcane grows well in tropical and subtropical regions. Today most sugarcane is harvested by machines, but at one time it was cut by hand.

Sugar beets are grown in climates that are too cool to grow sugarcane. The sugar they produce is identical to that from sugarcane.

culture, the stalks of sugarcane were traded for other goods, and their use spread. Traders carried sugar throughout the islands of the South Pacific and eventually to Indonesia and the Philippines.

Cane sugar was in general use in India in 400 B.C. and probably much earlier. The first Europeans to see the sugarcane were the invaders who went to India with Alexander the Great in 325 B.C. One of them described it as a grass that produced honey without the help of bees.

From India, sugarcane culture and sugar manufacture spread to Persia (Iran) and westward between A.D. 500 and 700. When the Muslims from Persia conquered Arabia, Syria, Palestine, Egypt, and the Mediterranean areas, they introduced the use of sugar in those countries. In the centuries that followed, these areas became the important sources of sugar for European countries.

In the 1400's, the commerce of European cities was expanding and new trade routes were needed. Christopher Columbus set out to discover a new trade route and found the New World. On his second voyage he carried, among other plants, sugarcane from the Canary Islands. But the transplanted canes failed. Explorers who came soon after him were able to introduce sugarcane successfully to the West Indies, Brazil, and Mexico. In 1751, Jesuit missionaries took sugarcane from Haiti to New Orleans, Louisiana. By 1795 the commercial production of sugar had begun in what was shortly to become part of the United States.

Northern countries, where sugarcane cannot be grown, had imported their sugar over the centuries. But in times of war, the supply of sugar was often cut off by naval blockades. In 1747, Andreas Sigismond Marggraf, director of the Prussian Academy of Science, found that the sugar in the beet and in certain other plants was the same as that in sugarcane. Fifty years later, Franz Carl Achard, his pupil and successor in the academy, was able to extract sugar from beets. Achard's early attempts to produce sugar from beets in commercial quantities failed, but others in Germany and elsewhere were successful.

This was the period of the Napoleonic Wars. In 1806 and 1807, Napoleon closed all European ports to goods carried by British ships or ships of neutral countries sympathetic to the British. The shortage of sugar became severe. But the French had heard of Achard's work. Under Napoleon's orders in 1811, thousands of acres of beets were planted, and factories were built to process the roots. By 1813 more than 150 factories were producing beet sugar. Thus the industry began.

▶ **ARTIFICIAL SWEETENERS**

Artificial sweeteners are synthetic substances used in place of sugar in foods and beverages. They are often used by people with diabetes and others who must avoid sugar for health reasons.

Aspartame is the most commonly consumed artificial sweetener. The U.S. Food and Drug Administration approved the use of aspartame in many food products in 1981. Saccharin has been used as a sweetener in foods since 1900. In the United States, foods and beverages that contain saccharin must carry a warning label because saccharin was shown to cause cancer in laboratory animals given very high amounts. Foods containing saccharin cannot be sold in Canada. Acesulfame potassium, or acesulfame-K, was approved for use in the United States in 1988. Sucralose is made from sucrose that has been chemically altered so that the body does not recognize it and does not digest it. Sucralose was approved for use in the United States in 1998.

DEWEY STEWART
United States Department of Agriculture

See also HONEY; MAPLE SYRUP AND MAPLE SUGAR.

SUICIDE

Suicide is the act of intentionally killing oneself. In the United States, it is the eighth major cause of death among adults and the major cause of death among teenagers.

People commit suicide for many reasons, but it is usually because they are severely depressed and feel hopeless about their lives. In some cases, this occurs when someone is suffering from a fatal illness and believes there is no hope of recovery. When suicide is committed with the help of a doctor, it is called physician-assisted suicide. Although this practice is against the law in most countries—as is suicide in general—some people believe it should be permitted. In recent years, the topic of physician-assisted suicide has generated much debate.

In a few cultures people commit suicide for political or religious reasons. In such instances, suicide is (or was) viewed as an honorable act. In Japan, for example, the practice of hara-kiri (death by one's own sword) was once considered obligatory for disgraced nobles and warriors.

Research has shown that certain groups are at higher risk for suicide than others. These include those who have experienced some recent loss and those who are socially isolated. Also at higher risk for suicide are people who have thought about it, have talked about it, or have already attempted it.

Since the 1960's and 1970's, many communities in the United States, Canada, and other countries have developed suicide prevention programs. These programs frequently include counseling for individuals and, sometimes, their families.

Suicide prevention programs are particularly important for teenagers. Unlike adults, they may not fully comprehend the consequences of suicide or that they will be dead forever. Instead, they get so caught up in their feelings of anger, sadness, loneliness, or shame, they do not think about the future. Prevention measures can help them realize that suicide is not a way to solve problems, even those that seem overwhelming.

MARIA TROZZI
Director, Good Grief Program
Boston Medical Center

SULFUR

Sulfur is a nonmetallic chemical element. It has the chemical symbol S, an atomic number of 16, and an atomic weight of 32.064. It is one of the few elements found in nature both as the free element and in compounds with other elements.

At room temperature, sulfur is a bright yellow solid. In this state, the sulfur atoms are arranged in puckered rings; each ring contains eight sulfur atoms. The sulfur rings stack together to form a stable solid. When sulfur is heated above its melting point of 239°F (115°C), the rings begin to slide over one another and sulfur becomes a thin liquid. As the temperature gets even hotter, the rings break apart and become tangled, causing the liquid to become more viscous (sticky). If this viscous liquid is cooled quickly—for example, by being poured into cold water—it solidifies into a dark, rubbery mass called amorphous, or plastic, sulfur. If left at room temperature, this plastic sulfur will slowly return to the yellow solid form.

The elemental form of sulfur is found in volcanic deposits throughout the world. It is also found in sedimentary deposits that are common on the northern coast of the Gulf of Mexico. Sulfur is extracted from these deposits by the Frasch process. In this process, superheated water is piped into the buried deposit to melt the sulfur, and the mixture of liquid sulfur and hot water is pumped to the surface.

FACTS ABOUT SULFUR

Chemical Symbol: S

Atomic Number: 16

Atomic Weight: 32.064

Density: 2.07 grams per cubic centimeter (about twice as dense as water).

Properties: Chemically reactive, nonmetallic yellow solid; sulfur does not conduct electricity.

Occurrence: Sulfur is found in nature both as the free element and in compounds with many other elements.

Sulfur forms compounds with nearly all other elements. Most metals combine with sulfur to form **sulfides**. Many of these sulfides are important ores of metals such as iron, nickel, copper, cobalt, zinc, and lead. For example, iron pyrite, also known as fool's gold, is a sulfide made up of sulfur and iron. **Sulfates** contain sulfur, oxygen, and other elements. The principal natural sulfates are gypsum (calcium sulfate) and kieserite (magnesium sulfate).

Sulfur combines with hydrogen to form hydrogen sulfide gas, which has the odor of rotten eggs. Sulfur burns in oxygen to form sulfur dioxide gas. Sulfur dioxide dissolves in water to form sulfurous acid, which is the acid found in acid rain. The burning of sulfur-containing fossil fuels can release sulfur dioxide gas into the air and cause acid rain.

Sulfur's most important industrial compound is sulfuric acid. Sulfuric acid is produced in larger quantities than any other chemical. Over 40 million tons are produced annually in the United States. Sulfuric acid is used in producing agricultural fertilizers, steel, plastics, and pharmaceuticals. Another industrial use of sulfur is the vulcanization of rubber. In this process, sulfur is added to rubber to strengthen it and make it more resistant to temperature change.

Sulfur is also important biologically. It is a component of several amino acids—the building blocks of proteins. In proteins, bonds between sulfur atoms help maintain the shape of the protein molecule, which is important to the protein's function. Eggs contain a high proportion of proteins that contain sulfur, and when the eggs spoil, the sulfur is released from these proteins in the form of hydrogen sulfide, which is responsible for the rotten-egg odor.

RODNEY SCHREINER
BASSAM SHAKHASHIRI
University of Wisconsin, Madison

SULLIVAN, LOUIS (1856–1924)

Louis Henri Sullivan is regarded as the first great modern architect of the United States and one of the founders of the modern architectural movement. He gave beauty of form to the skyscraper and other early modern buildings.

Sullivan was born on September 3, 1856, in Boston, Massachusetts. He decided at an early age that he wanted to be an architect. At the age of 16, he entered the Massachusetts Institute of Technology. But he left after a year to work for architects in Philadelphia and Chicago. In 1879 he began working with the Chicago architect and engineer Dankmar Adler.

Sullivan and Adler helped pioneer the design of tall office buildings and skyscrapers. Sullivan rejected the idea that these buildings should resemble buildings of the past. He said that "form follows function," meaning each building should have a shape and appearance that reflect its structure and its use. He strived to emphasize the soaring vertical lines of tall buildings and to provide horizontal contrasts.

Sullivan and Adler designed many important buildings. Among the best known are the Auditorium Building in Chicago and the Guaranty Building in Buffalo, New York.

Sullivan's career declined in the early 1900's, and he died in poverty in Chicago on April 14, 1924. But his two books on the philosophy of architecture, *Kindergarten Chats* (1901–02) and *The Autobiography of an Idea* (1924), greatly influenced younger architects.

WILLIAM DUDLEY HUNT, JR.
Author, *Encyclopedia of American Architecture*

The Auditorium Building in Chicago, designed by Louis Sullivan, is a landmark of early modern architecture.

SUMATRA. See INDONESIA.

SUMER

Sumer was an ancient region located in what is now southeastern Iraq. It was part of a larger region called Mesopotamia. Sumer was the birthplace of civilization; its people were among the first to cultivate crops, construct large buildings and cities, and create a writing system.

People. The Sumerian economy was based on agriculture. Because of the region's dry climate, irrigation systems were created to bring water from the Tigris and Euphrates rivers that bordered Sumer on the east and west. Cows, sheep, goats, and other animals were raised. Agricultural products and textiles were traded for stone and metals, which were scarce in the area.

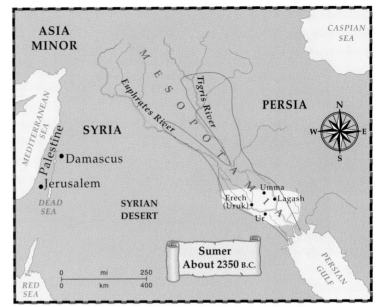

Sumer About 2350 B.C.

About 3200 B.C., the Sumerians invented cuneiform, one of the first writing systems in the world. Its wedge-shaped characters were typically pressed into clay tablets. See the article CUNEIFORM in Volume C.

The Sumerians were skilled artisans. Figurines were sculpted from stone or metal. Ziggurats, large pyramid-shaped towers built of baked clay bricks and topped with a temple, originated in Sumer and later spread throughout Mesopotamia. These monumental structures were dedicated to the Sumerians' many gods.

Sumerian mathematics was based on the number sixty. Traces of this number system survive today in timekeeping (60 minutes in an hour, 60 seconds in a minute) and in geometry (360, or 60 x 6, degrees in a circle).

History. People may have lived in the Sumer region as early as 5500 B.C. Between 3500 and 3000 B.C., the development of large cities, efficient irrigation systems, monumental (large-scale) architecture, and writing signaled the beginning of civilization. By 2600 B.C.,

This gold bull's head adorns a lyre (a type of harp) found in a royal tomb in the Sumerian city of Ur.

cities such as Uruk, Ur, Lagash, and Umma had developed into larger city-states that often fought one another for control of the region. About 2350, the region was unified for a brief time by Umma's ruler Lugalzaggesi.

Between 2340 and 2300, Sumer was conquered by the ruler Sargon, who was from Akkad, a region just north of Sumer. His Akkadian Empire lasted for about 100 years, after which an Iranian people called the Gutians controlled much of the land. About 2210 B.C., the Third Dynasty of Ur rose to power and set up a new empire in Mesopotamia.

Ur was overthrown by the Elamites, a people from the east, about 2004 B.C. This marked the end of Sumerian political power. The city-states became independent but were governed by the Amorites, who came from Syria. The Sumerian language was no longer spoken, but it continued as a language of science and religion and was taught in the area's schools until the A.D. 100's.

JOHN BRINKMAN
The Oriental Institute

See also MESOPOTAMIA.

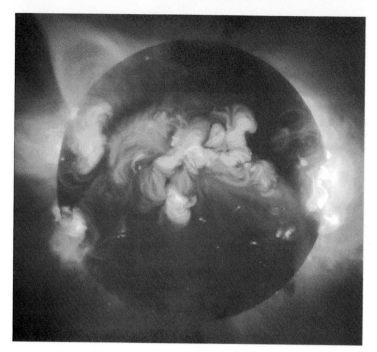

If you had X-ray eyes, you too might be able to see these spectacular, intensely hot loops of gas streaming out of the sun's corona. A special telescope orbiting in the Yohkoh space satellite can observe such X-ray emissions. The images made from the data the telescope collects provide important views of the sun's corona for astronomers to study.

SUN

The sun is a star. It is a star like all of the other stars that are visible in the night sky. Like them, the sun is a great ball of extremely hot gases that shines with its own light and gives off its own heat. Unlike other stars, however, the sun is relatively close to the Earth. The sun is about 93 million miles (150 million kilometers) away, while the next closest star to Earth, Alpha Centauri, is more than 250,000 times farther away. Light from the sun takes about eight minutes to reach the Earth, while light from Alpha Centauri takes about four years. Since the sun is so close to Earth, astronomers can study it more easily than other stars. This allows them to learn a great many details about stars that they could only imagine otherwise. Astronomers also study the sun with great interest because of its importance to our planet. The sun's light and heat are necessary to all life on Earth, and any changes in how much light and heat the sun produces could have tremendous consequences for everything on Earth.

▶OBSERVING THE SUN

While it is possible to look directly at the stars at night because they are so far away, it is very dangerous to look directly at the sun. Its intense brightness can seriously injure the eyes. Because of this danger, astronomers never observe the sun through telescopes like those used to study the planets and distant stars. These telescopes would so concentrate the sun's light that using them to observe the sun would be very dangerous. Instead, astronomers use special telescopes called solar telescopes that spread out the sun's light. They also use other types of telescopes and equipment that detect forms of radiation other than sunlight that are emitted by the sun.

Solar telescopes are very different from the telescopes used to study other objects in space. For one thing, they are very long and must be housed in special buildings. Their great length allows them to spread out light from the sun as much as possible so that it can be studied safely. One of the instruments that form part of a solar telescope is a **spectrograph**, a sensitive instrument used to analyze the different colors in sunlight. When sunlight passes through the spectrograph, it emerges as

The heliostat, or tracking mirror, (*opposite page*) atop the McMath solar telescope at Kitt Peak National Observatory (*above*) reflects an image of the sun down the telescope's tower to a mirror about 300 feet underground. This mirror then reflects that image to an observing room for study.

a narrow beam of light. The light is then reflected from a diffraction grating, which spreads the light into a band of colors called a spectrum. Also appearing on this spectrum are dark lines, called absorption lines, which are places where the light is less intense. The patterns of these absorption lines in the spectrum reveal the different chemical elements in the object from which the light is coming. Each chemical element has its own pattern of absorption lines, and the amount of absorption depends on how much of each element is present in the sun. By analyzing these lines, astronomers can determine the chemical composition of the sun. We now know that the sun is composed mostly of hydrogen and helium, but it also contains small amounts of other elements found on the Earth.

In addition to light, the sun also emits other types of radiation, including infrared radiation (heat), radio waves, ultraviolet rays, and X rays. To study radio waves, astronomers use large ground-based radio telescopes. Not all radiation reaches the Earth, however. Some infrared radiation, most ultraviolet rays, and all X rays are stopped by the Earth's atmosphere. To study these

types of radiation, scientists use a variety of different types of satellite observatories that are orbiting the Earth.

▶THE HISTORY OF THE SUN

Scientists estimate that the sun is about 4.55 billion years old, about the same age as the Earth and the other planets. While this is very old to us, it is quite young compared to the age of the universe, which is thought to be more than 15 billion years old. Scientists think they understand some of the details of how the sun and planets were formed from observing how similar stars are being formed today.

Scientists think that the sun and the planets condensed long ago out of a swirling cloud of dust and gases. Somewhere within that cloud the dust and gases were pushed more tightly together, perhaps because of a disturbance from a passing star. This dense region exerted a strong gravitational pull on nearby dust and gases in space, causing all of these materials to come together until a large mass was formed. Gravitational forces caused the center of this collapsing mass to become hotter and

An astronomer uses a spectrograph to study an image of the sun almost 33 inches across in the observing room of the McMath (*above left*). In a spectrogram (*below right*), the sun's light is spread into a band of colors called a spectrum. Each band contains patterns of dark absorption lines that represent different chemical elements in the sun.

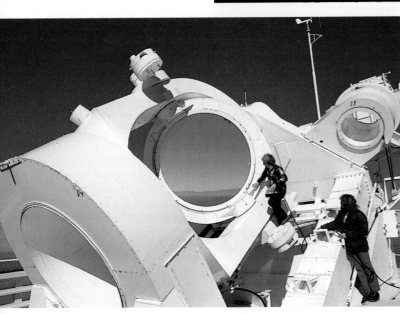

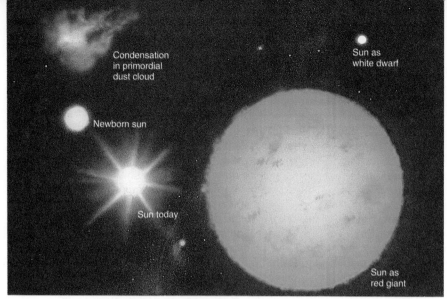

Labels in image:
Condensation in primordial dust cloud
Newborn sun
Sun today
Sun as white dwarf
Sun as red giant

Over a period of about 10 billion years, the sun will burn up its nuclear fuel, reach the end of its cycle as a medium-sized yellow star, and expand into an immense red giant. At that stage, its remaining gases will slowly drift off into space until only its hot core is left, and it becomes a white dwarf.

hotter, eventually reaching a temperature so great that the mass began to generate its own energy. In this way, the sun was born. Eventually, the surrounding dust and gases dissipated, leaving the newborn sun surrounded by smaller condensing masses that became the Earth and other planets.

Although the sun has shone steadily for more than 4.55 billion years, it will not live forever. After another 5 billion years or so, the sun will begin to expand and will become cooler and redder, so that it will change into what is known as a **red giant** star. Eventually the sun will expand further, enlarging until it becomes more than 100 times its present size. When this happens, the sun will swallow the inner planets, including Earth, and destroy any life that remains on our planet. Material in the sun's outer regions will gradually drift off into space because gravitational forces will not be strong enough to hold the material once it drifts to such a great distance. In time, much of the remaining material in the sun will also dissipate, leaving behind only a tiny hot core. The cores of other such stars, known as **white dwarf** stars, can be observed throughout the universe.

▶ THE SUN'S SIZE AND COLOR

The sun is enormous compared to the Earth and other planets. Astronomers have calculated that it is about 865,000 miles (1.4 million kilometers) in diameter—more than 100 times greater than the Earth's diameter. More than 1.3 million globes the size of the Earth could fit inside the sun. Yet despite this huge size, the sun is only a medium-sized star. Some stars have diameters more than 1,000 times larger than that of the sun; others have diameters ten times smaller.

The sun is a yellow star. While stars emit all colors of the spectrum, each star emits one color more strongly than the others. This depends on the star's temperature. Very hot stars appear bluish, while the coolest stars appear deep orange or red. Astronomers have measured the brightness of the sun's many colors and have learned that its surface temperature is about 10,000°F (5500°C). This temperature is so hot that all solids would melt and all liquids would evaporate. As a result, scientists know that the materials that make up the sun must be in a gaseous state.

▶ THE SUN'S INTERIOR

Every second, the sun produces as much energy as all the power plants on Earth would be able to produce in more than 2 million years. At one time, scientists thought that this enormous energy was the result of the ordinary combustion, or burning, of material in the sun, like the burning of material in a furnace. Scientists have calculated, however, that with ordinary combustion the sun would burn itself up in only 10,000 years, much too fast considering the sun's age. As a result, they began to search for a different source of the sun's energy, one that could last for billions of years. They found this source of energy by studying the basic structure of matter.

Particles Inside the Sun

Astronomers have learned a great deal about what takes place in the sun's interior. They know atoms in the form of gas particles are packed together tightly inside the sun. The deeper inside the sun these atoms are, the more closely packed together they are because of the pressure caused by the weight of other atoms above them. The tremendous pressures on these densely packed atoms also cause the sun's interior to be extremely hot, so that at the center of the sun we would find a very hot core with a temperature that reaches about 27,000,000°F (15,000,000°C). At such temperatures, the atoms break apart, so that their outer parts are completely stripped away from their inner parts, or **nuclei**. The temperature is also so high that the nuclei of the atoms react in ways that can produce energy. These reactions are known as **nuclear reactions**.

Nuclear Fusion Inside the Sun

Scientists now know that the sun's energy comes from a type of nuclear reaction called a **nuclear-fusion** reaction. In a nuclear-fusion reaction, the nuclei of two or more atoms fuse, or join together, forming a larger and heavier atomic nucleus. In the process some energy, known as **binding energy**, is released. Within the sun's interior, billions of atomic nuclei fuse every second, fusing nuclei of hydrogen into helium nuclei.

The fusion of hydrogen and helium can occur only at extremely high temperatures like those in the sun's interior. If the sun had less mass, there would be less pressure in the interior and the temperature would be lower. This would result in fewer nuclear reactions, and the sun would be dimmer and redder. If the sun had more mass, the pressure in the interior would be greater and the temperature would be higher. This would result in more nuclear reactions, and the sun would be brighter and bluer.

As nuclear fusion occurs within the sun's interior, it converts hydrogen to helium, which causes the sun's composition to change over time. When the sun was very young, it was composed of about 71 percent hydrogen and 27 percent helium, and this is still the composition of its outer regions today. However, as a result of nuclear-fusion reactions over billions of years, the deep interior of the sun now contains about 64 percent helium and 34 percent hydrogen. When the sun has used up the remaining hydrogen "fuel" in its deep interior, a few billion years from now, nuclear-fusion reactions will no longer occur there. Instead, such reactions will begin occurring outside the interior, and this will trigger the expansion of the sun into a red giant.

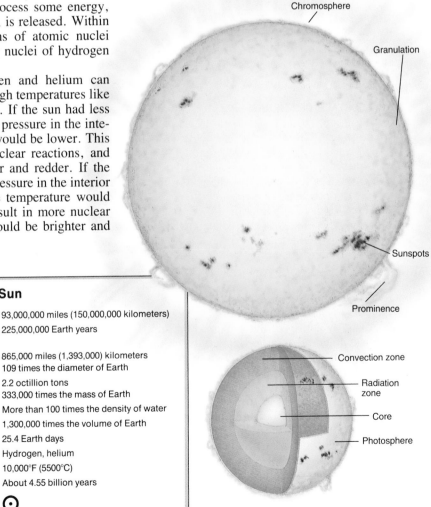

Sun	
Distance from the Earth (average)	93,000,000 miles (150,000,000 kilometers)
Revolution around the nucleus of the Milky Way Galaxy	225,000,000 Earth years
Diameter	865,000 miles (1,393,000) kilometers 109 times the diameter of Earth
Mass	2.2 octillion tons 333,000 times the mass of Earth
Density (at center)	More than 100 times the density of water
Volume	1,300,000 times the volume of Earth
Rotation on its axis (at equator)	25.4 Earth days
Atmosphere	Hydrogen, helium
Temperature (at surface)	10,000°F (5500°C)
Age	About 4.55 billion years
Symbol	

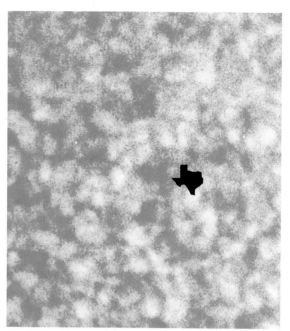

Volumes of hot gases, called granules (the bright areas), constantly erupt through the sun's photosphere and then fade back toward its interior (the dark areas), causing the mottled look known as granulation. Many granules are about the size of the state of Texas, drawn to scale on the photograph.

▶ THE SURFACE OF THE SUN

The bright surface of the sun is called the **photosphere**, from Greek words meaning "light" and "sphere." The average temperature of this region of the sun is about 10,000°F (5500°C). The light we see in the photosphere comes from the energy created by the nuclear reactions in the sun's interior. In the interior, however, this energy is not radiated as visible light but as high-energy X rays. During the passage from the interior to the photosphere, this X-ray radiation is absorbed and re-emitted by cooler and cooler matter, which causes it to be converted to other forms of radiation, including visible light.

About two thirds of the way from the sun's interior, the radiation flowing outward encounters an obstacle—the solar gases there are not hot enough to be easily penetrated by radiation. When the radiation meets these gases, it causes patches of gas to heat up and begin rising toward the surface in a process known as **convection**. These rising patches of gas bring heat upward from the sun's interior to its surface. When we look at the photosphere, we see the tops of these heated patches of gas, which are called **granules**.

Granulation

Photographs of the sun's surface reveal a pattern of bright granules separated by darker spaces called intergranular lanes. This mottled appearance is called granulation. While individual granules are tiny compared to the size of the sun, they are huge by Earth standards. A typical granule is about 900 miles (1,500 kilometers) across—about the size of the state of Texas.

Even more impressive than the large size of the granules is their violent motion. The surface of the photosphere moves constantly like a giant cauldron of seething liquid. Granules erupt and then fade in a matter of minutes. Measurements have shown that the granules erupt through the surface at speeds of about 1,000 miles (1,600 kilometers) per hour. Upon breaking the surface, larger granules often explode into smaller pieces. After eruption, the flowing gases then cool and fall back toward the sun's interior along the intergranular lanes.

All this violent activity in the photosphere makes pressure waves, which are like sound waves. We cannot hear these sound waves because sound cannot travel through the empty space between the sun and the Earth. In addition, the pitch of the solar sound waves is too low for the human ear to hear. But if we could hear the sounds from the sun, they would make a constant roar something like the sound of an erupting volcano. The sound would dwarf anything ever heard on Earth.

An ultraviolet image of the sun produced by instruments aboard the *Skylab* space station shows how fiery prominences shooting out of the sun's chromosphere cause violent disturbances in the atmosphere surrounding it.

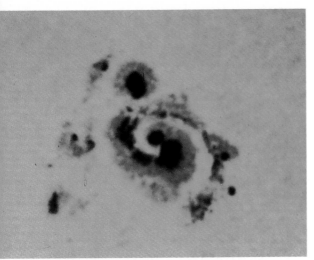

Sunspots form over magnetic fields rising to the sun's surface. An unusual spiral-shaped sunspot seen in 1982 (*above*) had a diameter of about 50,000 miles, almost six times the diameter of the Earth. Smaller features related to solar magnetic fields can be seen in the sun's upper atmosphere. This image (*right*), colored by computer, shows the north (red) and south (blue) magnetic poles in each group of spots.

esting phenomenon. In the sun's northern hemisphere, the leading sunspot of a pair—the one that moves ahead of the other—has one polarity and the other sunspot has the opposite polarity. In the southern hemisphere, the polarities of a leading spot and its companion are reversed. Astronomers believe this pattern may hold clues to the origin of the sun's magnetic field.

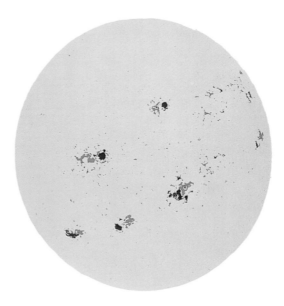

Sunspots

Dark spots often appear on the surface of the sun. These spots, called sunspots, may be up to 30,000 miles (48,000 kilometers) wide, more than three times the size of the Earth.

Sunspots are created when very strong magnetic fields—about 10,000 times stronger than the Earth's magnetic field—rise to the sun's surface from deep in the interior. These magnetic fields block the process of convection that normally brings energy to the sun's surface and makes it bright. As a result, sunspots are a bit cooler and appear dimmer than their surroundings. They look dark because of the contrast with brighter areas around them. After being formed, sunspots grow larger, reaching a maximum size within a few days. Sunspots also move across the solar surface from east to west. This movement is due to the sun's rotation on a roughly north–south axis. After a few weeks, sunspots generally fade away as their magnetic fields disperse.

Sunspots often occur in pairs. When they do, the magnetic fields of the two spots are usually of opposite polarity—that is, one spot would attract the north end of a compass needle and the other spot would attract the south end. Surrounding the sunspots are areas with slightly weaker magnetic fields called **active regions**. In studying sunspot pairs and active regions, astronomers have discovered an inter-

The Sunspot Cycle

Sunspots do not appear regularly on the solar surface. During some years many sunspots appear, but during others there may be few or none. In observing the changing frequency of sunspots over hundreds of years, astronomers have found that they vary on approximately an eleven-year cycle. During half of this cycle, sunspots increase in number until a sunspot maximum is reached. Then for the next half of the cycle, they decrease in number to a sunspot minimum. This sunspot cycle is far from regular, however. Since the 1600's, when sunspots began to be observed regularly, the full cycle has varied from about 8 to 15 years. The number of spots in a sunspot cycle varies as well. Cycles in 1980 and 1991 contained among the greatest number of sunspots on record.

Astronomers have found that the magnetic polarity pattern of sunspots changes between successive sunspot cycles. If the leading spots

in the sun's northern hemisphere have north magnetic polarity during one sunspot cycle, they will have south magnetic polarity during the next cycle. The polarity also reverses in the southern hemisphere. After two sunspot cycles, the original magnetic polarities return. When these patterns of magnetic polarity are taken into account, the basic sunspot cycle is actually about 22 years rather than 11. This is another mysterious clue to the origin of the sun's magnetic field.

▶THE SUN'S MAGNETIC FIELD

While the origin of the sun's magnetic field is not completely understood, astronomers think it is almost certainly produced by the sun's rotation. Because the sun is a ball of gases, it does not rotate rigidly or uniformly like a solid object such as the Earth does. In fact, parts of the sun rotate faster than other parts. The sun's equatorial regions, for example, rotate about 40 percent faster than its polar regions. Scientists think that this varying rotation, combined with the process of convection in the sun's outer layers, is what generates magnetic fields deep within the sun's interior. These magnetic fields then rise to the surface, where they break through as sunspots and active regions. The process is very complicated, however, and astronomers are not yet able to answer all the questions they have about solar magnetism.

▶THE SUN'S ATMOSPHERE

Above the sun's photosphere is an atmosphere—much less dense than Earth's—that is composed of different gases. This atmosphere is difficult to observe from Earth because it is hidden by the bright light of the photosphere. However, during a solar eclipse, when the moon passes between the Earth and the sun and blocks the sun's light, astronomers are able to observe the sun's atmosphere more easily.

WONDER QUESTION

Does sunspot activity affect the Earth's climate?

For a period of about 75 years, from 1640 to 1715, sunspots were very rare. This period of sunspot inactivity is known as the Maunder Minimum, named after the English astronomer Walter Maunder (1851–1928), who first noted sunspots in historical records. Records from this time also show that these same years were unusually cold on Earth, and the period became known as the Little Ice Age. The coldest decade of the period, 1690–1700, was one during which no sunspots were recorded. Because the Maunder Minimum and the Little Ice Age coincided, some scientists have questioned whether there is a connection between the Earth's climate and sunspot activity. While the answer to that question is not yet known for sure, evidence for such a connection is growing.

Measurements of the sun taken from observatories in space reveal that the sun's brightness is not constant. It decreases by a small amount during periods of the least sunspot activity and increases again during periods of the most activity. The change is very small, only a difference of about 0.1 percent, which is probably not enough to affect the Earth's climate significantly. However, many astronomers think that a major decrease in temperature could occur during a period of greatly reduced sunspot activity, such as occurred during the Maunder Minimum, and that this might have caused the Little Ice Age.

Records show that very little sunspot activity occurred from the 1640's to the 1700's compared to the level and variety of sunspot activity that occurred from the 1860's to the 1990's.

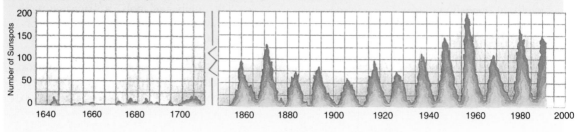

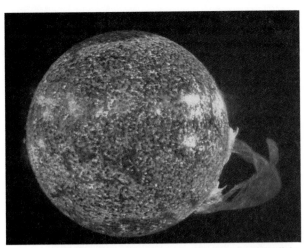

An image of a solar prominence taken in ultraviolet light reveals how solar flaring can erupt into spectacular twisting arcs of hot gases. This one extended 350,000 miles across the sun—a distance 45 times the diameter of the Earth—before it was pulled by the sun's magnetic fields back to its surface.

The Chromosphere

Starting about 100 miles (160 kilometers) above the photosphere and extending outward for about 9,000 miles (15,000 kilometers) is the chromosphere, which is a bright reddish-pink region of the atmosphere. As in the rest of the sun, the gases in the chromosphere are mainly hydrogen and helium. The base of the chromosphere is a little cooler than the surface itself. But farther above the sun's surface, the chromosphere gets hotter and hotter, reaching temperatures of 36,000°F (20,000°C) or more.

Solar Prominences

During eclipses, astronomers can see what look like giant flames extending outward from the sun. These features, which are called prominences, are actually great sheets of hot glowing gases extending outward from the top of the chromosphere. Prominences sometimes stretch out into space for distances of 250,000 miles (402,000 kilometers) or more. One prominence in 1946 extended for more than 1 million miles (1.6 million kilometers). The gases in solar prominences are always in motion, traveling along great curved paths at 10 miles (16 kilometers) a second or faster. Most prominences fall back into the sun, but some of them shoot their gases far out into space at speeds of hundreds of miles a second. Solar prominences may last for a few days or even for a few months depending on their size and shape.

The Solar Corona

One of the most beautiful sights in astronomy is a total eclipse of the sun, when the moon blocks out all the light of the sun's bright photosphere. For a few moments during a total eclipse, it is possible to glimpse the solar corona, the outer layer of the sun's atmosphere. This part of the atmosphere is called the corona, from a Latin word meaning "crown," because it looks like a shining crown, or halo, around the sun. The corona can be seen only during an eclipse, however, because it is about a million times fainter than the photosphere and is normally lost in the sun's bright glare. The inner part of the corona extends nearly 300,000 miles (483,000 kilometers) above the sun. The outer part consists of delicate streamers and loops that extend millions of miles into space.

The solar corona is visible only because it reflects sunlight; it does not emit light of its own. It does, however, emit invisible X-ray radiation, which astronomers can detect with special instruments aboard Earth-orbiting satellites. In studying this radiation, astronomers have learned that the corona contains loop-like structures of all sizes, with the two ends of a loop anchored close to the sun's surface and the middle of the loop stretching high above it. The two ends of these coronal loops always

A total eclipse of the sun makes it possible to view the faint but extremely hot outer layer of the sun's atmosphere called the corona.

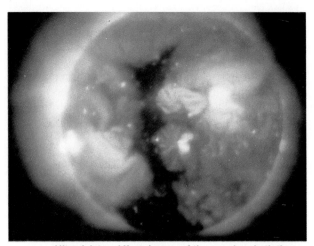

Ultraviolet and X-ray images of the sun show both the turbulence that affects the intensely hot gases in the sun's corona and the dark areas known as coronal holes, through which the hot gases and electrified particles known as the solar wind escape into space.

in the corona. The process of convection at and beneath the sun's surface twists magnetic fields there, creating electromagnetic waves and currents that move upward along the magnetic fields in the coronal loops. As these waves and currents travel upward, their energy is dissipated in the corona, and enough heat is generated in the process to heat the corona to its very high temperature.

Solar Flares

During periods of great magnetic activity on the sun's surface, X-ray emissions from the sun can become very strong. At such times, the process of convection often twists the magnetic fields in coronal loops so much that they "snap" like rubber bands that have been stretched too far. The result is a sudden release of tremendous energy called a solar flare. In a large solar flare, as much energy is released in a few minutes as would be used by the entire United States in 100,000 years.

Solar flares produce huge increases in the amount of X-ray radiation emitted from the solar corona. When this happens, it can affect the Earth, temporarily disrupting our upper atmosphere and causing interruptions in television and radio transmissions all around the planet. Solar flares also accelerate particles of matter in the solar corona to very high speeds —as much as one third the speed of light—

lie in active regions of opposite magnetic polarity, and the loops trace the patterns of magnetic fields arching upward into the corona.

It might naturally be expected that the corona would be cooler than the chromosphere, which lies much closer to the sun. However, this is not the case. Temperatures in the corona reach millions of degrees. These high temperatures are almost certainly caused by strong magnetic fields that act to heat the gases

Solar flares can accelerate streams of electrically charged particles flowing out of the sun's corona and send them far out into space. When some of these particles reach the Earth's atmosphere in the area of the Northern Hemisphere, they create an effect known as the aurora borealis, or northern lights (*left*). When they reach our atmosphere in the area of the Southern Hemisphere, they create similar effects known as aurora australis, or southern lights.

sending them far out into space. When some of these particles strike the Earth, they can cause **auroras,** or very bright lights. They can also create geomagnetic effects, such as strong electric currents in power grids. A large solar flare in 1989, for example, caused an overload in the power grid serving Quebec, Canada, and left 6 million people without power for many hours.

The Solar Wind

In some places on the sun where the magnetic field is particularly weak, the lines of the magnetic field open out into space rather than loop back to the surface. These "open" magnetic field regions provide a channel in which particles of hot matter from the solar corona can flow outward from the sun at very high speeds. This is called the solar wind.

The path of the solar wind can be traced to Earth and far beyond. Near the Earth, the solar wind is traveling at about 1 million miles (1.6 million kilometers) per hour. When it strikes the Earth's magnetic field, the solar wind produces a ring of northern and southern auroras surrounding the Earth's magnetic poles. These auroras are similar to, but not as bright as, the auroras created by solar flares.

▶ **THE SUN'S IMPORTANCE**

The sun is an important star to study not only because it reveals so much about distant stars, but also because it is so important for life on Earth. It can affect Earth in numerous ways, from creating the spectacular displays of the northern and southern auroras to disrupting worldwide communications. Its light and heat are essential for life. It may even affect the Earth's climate in ways that are not yet fully understood. The sun is the one object in the universe, other than the Earth itself, that really matters to human beings. As we become more aware of the many forces shaping our planet's environment, we realize how important it is to study the sun and its effects on the Earth.

ROBERT W. NOYES
Harvard-Smithsonian Center for Astrophysics

See also ASTRONOMY; ATOMS; COSMIC RAYS; LIGHT; NUCLEAR ENERGY; OBSERVATORIES; RADIATION BELTS; RADIO ASTRONOMY; SOLAR SYSTEM; SPACE TELESCOPES; STARS.

SUN YAT-SEN (1866–1925)

Sun Yat-sen is often called "the George Washington of China." Both Nationalist and Communist Chinese consider him to be the founder of the Chinese republic.

Sun was born near Guangzhou, China, on November 12, 1866. When he was 13, he went to school in Hawaii, where he stayed for 4 years. Soon after his return to China he entered medical school in Hong Kong. At that time the Chinese were suffering under the ineffectual, corrupt Manchu government. After graduating from medical school, Sun began to work for reform and the overthrow of the Manchu rulers.

During the 20 years from 1890 to 1910 Sun made several trips to America and Europe, seeking support among Chinese living abroad. Several unsuccessful uprisings took place under his direction in China. On October 10, 1911, when the rebellion that finally overthrew the Manchus took place in China, Sun was on a fund-raising tour in the United States. Sun returned home and was immediately chosen provisional president of the new Republic of China.

To bring unity to the country, Sun stepped down from the presidency in favor of Yuan Shikai, a military leader. But Yuan quickly proceeded to use the presidency to extend his own power. Sun led a protest against Yuan and was forced into a brief exile in Japan. In 1921 Sun established a rival republican government in Guangzhou and looked to the Soviet Union for aid to reorganize his army and political party, the Nationalist Party. Sun's Three People's Principles—nationalism, democracy, socialism—became the Nationalists' basic ideology.

In 1924 Sun went to Beijing to attend a meeting on the reunification of China. There, on March 12, 1925, he died of cancer. His body now lies in state in a magnificent mausoleum on a hillside just outside of Nanjing.

SAMUEL CHU
University of Pittsburgh

SUPERIOR, LAKE. See GREAT LAKES.

At some supermarket checkouts, a laser scanner "reads" the Universal Product Code (UPC) on the merchandise and sends price and inventory data into a computer.

SUPERMARKETS

Supermarkets are found in almost every city and town in the United States and in many countries around the world. But they are a comparatively new idea.

In the early 1800's, most people shopped for food at a general store where barrels, bins, and sacks were filled with everything from crackers to pickles. As cities grew and the number of food items increased, specialty stores developed. Shoppers bought meat at one store and vegetables at another.

In the 20th century, chain food stores (several food stores owned by the same company) began to sell all kinds of groceries in the same store. Customers liked one-store shopping, and by the 1920's about 40 percent of the nation's food was sold by chain stores.

Because they had so many customers, chain stores were able to introduce new business methods called mass merchandising. This al-

lowed the retailer to buy cheaply and sell cheaply. Increased sales made lower prices possible. And lower prices meant more sales.

In 1930, Michael Cullen opened a food store in an empty warehouse in New York City. The merchandise was piled everywhere. There were no counters or clerks, and customers helped themselves. Hard-pressed by the Depression, shoppers flocked to Cullen's store. His idea was quickly copied, and by 1936 there were 1,200 such self-service supermarkets in the United States.

World War II slowed the growth of the supermarket industry. Food was scarce. Grocers filled their empty shelves with cosmetics and medicines—the first major line of nonfood items. When the war ended, the country began to build and grow. Supermarkets opened in new shopping centers in the suburbs. Self-service was expanded, and new departments were added. Prepackaged meats, frozen foods, and bakeries appeared.

In the 1970's the supermarket encountered new problems. Inflation raised grocery prices. A decrease in population growth slowed the growth of sales.

Today supermarket operators have introduced innovations that help reduce the cost of running a store. The most important of these is a computer with a scanner that checks out what a shopper has bought by reading symbols on the merchandise. The scanner then matches the product to a price recorded in the computer, and the price flashes on a screen near the cash register. This system processes sales rapidly and accurately.

New kinds of stores have developed to meet new needs. Warehouse stores, like those of the 1930's, have done away with luxury items and passed the savings on to the customers. Some stores now offer cereals and other foods "in bulk"—that is, in barrels from which shoppers serve themselves and pay by weight. Larger stores carry more nonfood items, and many chain stores are introducing foreign and "gourmet" foods.

All this offers greater convenience for busy shoppers. In the future, markets will continue to change to meet the demands of a changing population.

ROBERT O. ADERS
Food Marketing Institute

Reviewed by BRYAN MILLER
Food Reporter, *The New York Times*

The F-14 aircraft in flight (*right*) ready for midair refueling. A computer-generated image (*below*) uses contour lines to show high (red) and low (blue) air pressure areas around the F-14 flying at supersonic speeds. Contour lines clustered close together show where pressures are changing rapidly and a shock wave may be forming.

F-14 Supersonic Mach 1.5

SUPERSONIC FLIGHT

In the early days of airplane flight, the top speed of airplanes was about 50 miles (80 kilometers) an hour. Today some airplanes exceed the speed of sound by two or three times, or even more. Flight at speeds greater than the speed of sound is called **supersonic flight**. Flight at speeds lower than the speed of sound is called **subsonic flight**. These terms come from Latin words meaning "above sound" and "under sound."

▶ THE SOUND BARRIER

By the mid-1940's, the fastest airplanes were flying close to the speed of sound. Flight at such speeds is called **transonic flight**. At sea level the speed of sound is 760 miles (1,224 kilometers) per hour. This speed decreases as altitude increases. For example, at altitudes of 36,000 to 59,000 feet (about 11,000 to 18,000 meters), the speed of sound is 660 miles (1,060 kilometers) an hour.

As airplanes approached the speed of sound, strange things began to happen. Unknown forces could cause violent shaking. An improperly designed airplane might be twisted out of shape and part of it torn away. Because of these forces, aeronautical engineers and pilots said that airplanes came up against a "sound barrier." Before airplanes could "break" this barrier, engineers had to determine the causes of the strange effects and then learn how to stop them.

Engineers now know what causes the strange effects. When an airplane flies, it pushes air out of its way. At low speeds, this displaced air flows smoothly over the airplane's surfaces. But when an airplane flies near the speed of sound, shock waves appear on the wing. If not guided properly, the air will flow past the shock waves in uneven whirls and eddies, which batter the airplane. Having found the causes of the sound barrier, aeronautical engineers knew how to modify the configuration of airplanes that fly close to the speed of sound. Most modern long-distance airliners, such as the Boeing 747 and the McDonnell Douglas DC-10, are designed for smooth flight at transonic speeds.

On October 14, 1947, Major Charles E. Yeager flew a specially designed airplane, the X-1, faster than the speed of sound. His flight proved that an airplane could safely break the sound barrier.

From left to right: The F-111 aircraft after takeoff, rising to the proper altitude for supersonic flight.
As speeds increase, the plane's variable sweep wings slant back toward its body to reduce friction drag.
At supersonic speeds, the wings are in a swept-back position, giving the aircraft a streamlined shape.

▶ MACH NUMBERS

When people talk of the speed of airplanes flying at or beyond the speed of sound, they say the airplane is flying at a certain **Mach number**. Mach numbers were named for Austrian scientist Ernst Mach (1838–1916), who performed many experiments on the speed of air flow. An airplane flying at the speed of sound has a speed of Mach 1. At twice the speed of sound, the speed is Mach 2. At half the speed of sound, it is Mach 0.5. The Mach number is the airplane's speed divided by the speed of sound at that altitude. For example, an airplane flying at 546 miles (880 kilometers) an hour at an altitude of 36,000 feet (about 11,000 meters) is flying at Mach 0.83 (546 divided by 660, the speed of sound at that altitude).

High-speed airplanes are equipped with a **machmeter**, an instrument that gives the airplane's speed in Mach numbers. An airplane may be designed for safe operation only up to a certain Mach number. A pilot must be careful not to fly faster than this Mach number or the airplane may be badly damaged.

▶ PROBLEMS OF SUPERSONIC FLIGHT

One of the major problems of supersonic flight is "drag"—the resistance of air to the forward motion of the airplane. Another serious problem is heat caused by friction as an airplane flies through the air.

WONDER QUESTION

What was the Concorde?

The Concorde was a commercial Supersonic Transport (SST) built jointly by France and Great Britain. Twenty aircraft were built between 1966 and 1979; some were used for tests only. Each Concorde could carry about 100 passengers, reach an altitude of about 11 miles (18 kilometers), and travel at about 1,350 miles (2,200 kilometers) an hour—more than twice the speed of sound. The nose of the aircraft could be bent down to allow the pilots a better view of the runway on takeoffs and landings. Concorde flights were discontinued in 2003 because they were no longer profitable.

The main cause of drag is the **shock wave** produced as an airplane flies at supersonic speeds. This shock wave also causes a loss in **lift**—the upward force that keeps an airplane from falling. A shock wave can also produce a lift. For example, the design of the recently developed hypersonic aircraft called a wave-rider generates lift by using the shock wave produced under its wing.

Shock Waves

To understand what a shock wave is, imagine a boat moving along the surface of a lake. If the boat moves slowly, it makes waves that radiate away from the boat in a circular pattern. If it moves quickly, the waves move out in straight lines in a cone-shaped pattern behind the boat. A similar thing happens to an airplane. As it flies, it creates waves of air that move outward. At subsonic speeds, the waves form a circular pattern around the airplane. But at supersonic speeds, a cone-shaped airwave pattern is created that trails behind the airplane. This airwave, which consists of compressed air, is called a shock wave. In the air next to the wings, it causes disturbances that add to the drag on the airplane.

Sonic Booms

The shock wave may produce a sonic boom—a loud, thunderlike noise—that is caused by air disturbances resulting from differences in pressure between the air in a shock wave's cone and the air near the ground. If the cone sweeps close to the ground, people as far as 30 miles (50 kilometers) away on either side of the airplane's path may hear the boom.

The strength of a sonic boom depends on an airplane's size, speed, and altitude. If supersonic speed is reached at a low altitude, the boom may be strong enough to break windows.

Heat of Friction

The outside surfaces, called "skins," of supersonic airplanes get very hot because of friction with the air. At a speed of Mach 2, the skin temperature may be 195°F (90°C), at Mach 3 it may be 570°F (300°C), and at Mach 4, almost 1200°F (650°C). Therefore, the skins of supersonic airplanes must be made of metals that tolerate very high temperatures. The aluminum used on subsonic airplanes would lose its strength and stretch, snap, or melt at speeds above Mach 2.

HIGH-ALPHA RESEARCH

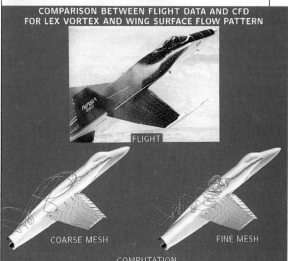

COMPARISON BETWEEN FLIGHT DATA AND CFD FOR LEX VORTEX AND WING SURFACE FLOW PATTERN

FLIGHT

COARSE MESH   FINE MESH

COMPUTATION

Aerodynamics experts use both flight data and special computer programs to improve the performance of supersonic aircraft at extreme attitudes, or angles, of flight—also known as high-alpha flight. In these sequences, an F-18 High Alpha Research Vehicle (HARV) with smoke-flow generators and video systems produces flight data and images that show air-flow patterns at various attitudes. Supercomputers using computational fluid dynamics (CFD) calculations also produce data and images that predict and evaluate flow patterns around the aircraft. Flight and CFD images are then compared. In the top photograph, computed flow lines (yellow, blue, and red) were superimposed over the flight image showing the white smoke flows around the aircraft. They all show strong vortex (swirl) patterns above the forebody and at the leading-edge extension (LEX) of the wings. In the bottom photograph, images are shown separately. The flight smoke flow is shown above the computed flows. Coarse mesh lines indicate the main feature of the surface flows and the fine mesh lines show additional features. Both the flight and computed images show similar breakups of the vortex patterns above the wings and at their LEX's. In each sequence the similarities between the flight and computed flows demonstrate the usefulness of the CFD process to designers, who use it to develop improvements in the maneuverability and safety of supersonic aircraft.

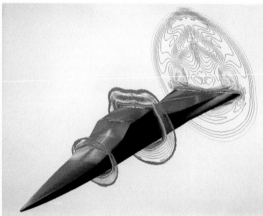

The X-30 research vehicle (*top*) being developed by the National Aero-Space Plane Program may pave the way to hypersonic flight. Supercomputers create and evaluate models of possible designs for sections of the X-30—an aircraft that may take off from a runway like an airplane, reach speeds of at least 17,500 miles per hour to achieve low-Earth orbit, then return to Earth through our atmosphere and land again on a runway. A computer-generated image (*bottom*) studies engine nozzle performance and exhaust effects on proposed "scramjet" engine tail surfaces. The image simulates wind tunnel test conditions at Mach 10, about 6,500 mph. Red to pink lines show areas of highest air density.

Solving Problems of Supersonic Flight

Engineers have designed airplanes that overcome most of the problems associated with supersonic flight. Supersonic airplanes have thin, sharp-edged wings that move through the air with less drag than thick, blunt-edged wings. The wings often slant back toward the tail of the airplane as well. Some supersonic airplanes have movable variable sweep wings that can be turned forward for easy takeoff and put into a backward-slanting position for high-speed flight. Supersonic airplanes are also designed with very smooth outside surfaces. Engineers have found that a tiny mark or dent can increase drag and affect an airplane's performance.

To withstand the heat caused by friction, many supersonic airplanes have skins made of titanium. This metal is very strong at high temperatures and does not melt as easily as aluminum. Titanium must be used for airplanes designed for speeds higher than Mach 2.

▶ENGINES FOR SUPERSONIC AIRPLANES

Early supersonic research airplanes used rocket engines for power. These airplanes were attached to the undersides of large bombers called mother ships. At an altitude of 29,000 feet (about 9,000 meters), the airplane was released from the mother ship, its rockets were fired and operated for a few minutes, and the airplane then glided down to the ground.

Most supersonic airplanes today use jet engines. In the atmosphere, a jet engine is more efficient than a rocket engine. An airplane powered by a jet engine can also stay aloft longer and take off from the ground more easily than one powered by a rocket engine.

▶HYPERSONIC FLIGHT

Flight at speeds above Mach 4 or 5 is usually called **hypersonic flight**, which means "very much above the speed of sound." In the United States, research in hypersonic flight was carried out in the 1960's with an experimental airplane called the X-15. The X-15 reached a speed of 4,520 miles (7,273 kilometers) an hour (Mach 6.7) at an altitude of 67 miles (108 kilometers). The airplane was used to test methods of flying and materials that could withstand the temperatures encountered at hypersonic speeds. Some of the knowledge gained from the X-15 program was put to use in the Apollo spacecraft that reached the moon. The regular or commercial use of hypersonic flight remains a dream that may come true sometime during the 21st century.

WILLIAM C. VERGARA
Chief Engineer, Microelectronics
The Bendix Corporation

See also AERODYNAMICS; AVIATION; JET PROPULSION; SOUND AND ULTRASONICS.

SUPERSTITION

Do you carry a rabbit's foot for luck? Have you ever knocked on wood after talking about something pleasant? Do you avoid walking under a ladder, or do you throw spilled salt over your left shoulder? These are all superstitions, many of which have been around for centuries.

Many superstitious beliefs can be traced to ancient times when people had no understanding of nature and natural phenomena. Surrounded by mysteries they could not understand, events in nature such as lightning, rain, and eclipses of the sun, and human events such as birth and death, they believed that unseen spirits, both good and bad, were at work in the world around them. To enlist the help of good spirits and keep evil spirits happy and content, they invented all kinds of magical charms and tokens.

Ancient people believed in the power of magical charms and in sympathetic magic, or "like brings like." They believed that a wish would come true if it was made while looking at or touching something that had experienced good fortune. The rabbit's foot, for example, became a good luck charm because people were impressed by the power and movement of a rabbit's hind legs. The hind legs came to be viewed as powerful charms against evil forces.

Few people today are completely free of superstitious beliefs. In spite of scientific fact and common sense, superstitions still influence the thoughts and actions of people throughout the world.

People in different countries, in fact, often have their own unique superstitious beliefs and customs. A lucky charm or superstitious belief may give someone a feeling of confidence, but such charms and superstitions really have no power beyond what human thinking and actions give them.

▶ SOME COMMON SUPERSTITIONS

Knocking on Wood. People knock on wood after speaking of good fortune or future hopes. This superstition came from early beliefs that trees, the source of wood, were the homes of kindly gods who would grant favors if asked nicely. When asking a favor, a person touched the tree bark and then knocked on it as thanks. Another belief was that jealous spirits were always nearby. The knocking noise would keep these spirits from overhearing any good news and trying to alter it.

Crossing Your Heart. Sometimes people assure others that they are telling the truth by saying "Cross my heart and hope to die" while making a cross over the heart. In ancient folklore the heart was considered the seat of wisdom and therefore a witness to the fact that the person was not lying.

Opening an Umbrella. Some people believe that opening an umbrella indoors will bring bad luck and disappointment. This superstition began long ago when umbrellas were much larger than today. When opened indoors, these large, clumsy umbrellas could hurt someone or break something in the house.

Walking Under a Ladder. Superstitions about walking under ladders have a number of sources. One early belief was that a leaning ladder made a triangle, a symbol of life, with the wall and the floor.

Anyone walking through this triangle would be punished unless countercharms, such as making a wish or crossing the fingers, were used. In some Asian countries, criminals were hanged from the seventh rung of a ladder propped against a tree. Since death was thought to be contagious, people who walked under the ladder would be in danger of catching death from the hanged person's ghost. The superstition also has a sensible basis. A ladder can collapse, or tools lying on its rungs can fall and hurt someone underneath.

Spilling Salt. Many superstitions are based on salt. Ancient people thought that salt was magical and could perform good or evil. When they discovered that salt could preserve food, they believed it could protect them also. Spilling salt was believed to be a warning from friendly spirits that evil was nearby. Since people thought that good spirits lived on the right side of the body and evil ones on the left, they threw a pinch of salt over the left shoulder to satisfy evil spirits who could harm them.

Breaking a Mirror. Some people think that breaking a mirror will mean seven years of bad luck. This superstition started long before mirrors were known, when people believed that a reflection in a pool of water was really the soul, or "other self," of a person. This other self would be injured if disturbed in any way. After the invention of mirrors, breaking one and harming the reflection in it continued to mean bad luck to the other self. The ancient Romans believed that breaking a mirror meant seven years of bad luck. That number was chosen because they thought that life renewed itself every seven years, and it would take a person that long to recover from any harm.

The Number 13. The number 13 has been considered an unlucky number among many cultures for thousands of years. Friday the 13th is considered the unluckiest day except for those people born on the 13th, for whom it is a good day. The superstition about Friday the 13th may be based on a Norse legend about the goddess Freya, who was banished for being a witch. It was believed that each Friday, a day called "witches' Sabbath," twelve witches and the devil met to make mischief and to do evil deeds.

Black Cats. The superstition about the evil that can happen when a black cat crosses someone's path goes back to the Middle Ages. At that time, it was believed that black cats were the companions of witches and warlocks and eventually were changed into witches themselves. A black cat coming toward someone could therefore be a witch intent on causing harm or mischief. The safest thing to do was to avoid the cat.

Sneezes. When a person sneezes, someone is likely to say, "God bless you" or "*Gesundheit*" (the German word for "good health"). This custom of asking God's blessing or wishing good health began in early times when people believed that a person's spirit or soul was in the form of air or breath contained in the head. A person's sneeze might accidentally expel this spirit unless God prevented it from escaping.

Breaking a Wishbone. The hen and rooster were popular in ancient folklore. Since hens cackled when laying eggs and roosters crowed at the beginning of day, it was believed that these birds had special powers and could even answer questions. After someone asked a question, the bird was sacrificed to a special god and its collarbone was saved and hung to dry. The person seeking an answer from the god made a wish on the dried bone, which became known as the "wishbone." Two people then snapped the dry wishbone, each making a wish. After the bone snapped, the person holding the longer end was supposed to get his or her wish.

CLAUDIA DE LYS
Co-author, *Superstitious? Here's Why!*

SUPPLY AND DEMAND. See ECONOMICS.

SUPREME COURT OF CANADA

The Supreme Court of Canada is the highest institution in the nation for settling legal disputes. Its essential roles are to present final court decisions in difficult cases and to bring some consistency to decisions given by the many courts below it.

The Supreme Court meets in Ottawa, Canada's capital city. It hears appeals from across the land on questions concerning the precise meaning of a law or whether government officials have acted within the range of their authority. In addition, the court plays an important role as a constitutional referee between the federal and provincial governments when disputes arise between them.

Perhaps the best-known part of the Supreme Court's work is its handling of cases under the **Canadian Charter of Rights and Freedoms**, Canada's Bill of Rights, which was adopted in 1982. Since that time, the court has played an important political role, deciding what rights are protected by the charter and what limitations government may put on those rights. It also has nullified many federal and provincial laws that violated citizens' rights under the new charter's provisions. The court declared these laws **unconstitutional** (contrary to the constitution).

Another important part of the Supreme Court's work concerns answering "reference questions," in which a government can ask a court to give its opinion on a constitutional or other legal question. The Supreme Court can decide the constitutionality of a proposed law before it is passed or of an existing law without having to wait several years for another case to raise the issue.

How the Court Is Organized

The Supreme Court has grown in size over the years. Originally there were only six

Current Justices	
Justice	**Year Appointed**
Beverley McLachlin (chief justice)	1989
John C. Major	1992
Michel Bastarache	1997
W. Ian Binnie	1998
Louis LeBel	2000
Marie Deschamps	2002
Morris J. Fish	2003
Rosalie Silberman Abella	2004
Louise Charron	2004

Top: Canada's Supreme Court building is located in Ottawa, Ontario, the nation's capital.

Right: Canada's Supreme Court justices. Front row, from left: W. Ian Binnie, John C. Major, Beverley McLachlin (chief justice), Michel Bastarache, Louis LeBel. Back row, from left: Rosalie Silberman Abella, Marie Deschamps, Morris J. Fish, Louise Charron.

members of the court, but this number grew to seven in 1927 and finally to nine in 1949.

By law, three judges must be chosen from the province of Quebec. This is because Quebec has a legal system based on the old **civil code** of France, which is quite different from the British-type **common law** system used in the other provinces, and there have to be some members on the court who are familiar with it. The other judges are chosen to make sure that all regions of the country also are represented.

Judges are appointed to the Supreme Court by the federal government. The prime minister and the justice minister consult widely before choosing a new judge, but there are no public hearings before a judge is appointed. Because the Supreme Court has become much more important, provincial governments now want to be given a formal role in suggesting candidates when a vacancy occurs in their region.

How the Court Operates

All nine judges of the Supreme Court rarely hear a case together. Usually they divide into panels of five or seven. Although anyone who has been through a provincial or federal appeals court can ask the Supreme Court to hear their case, the Supreme Court usually selects only the most important cases to hear. About 500 people ask for an appeal each year, but the court agrees to hear only about 125 of these cases.

Once all the arguments are heard for a case, the judges go into a meeting room and explain their reactions to each other. The most junior judge says how he or she would decide the case, then the others take their turns according to increasing seniority. The outcome of the case is settled by how the majority of judges vote in this meeting. Then the judges decide who will write the judgment explaining their decision. Sometimes the judges cannot agree on a case, and several opinions are written.

History

Despite its name, the Supreme Court has not always been Canada's highest court. In fact, the court was only established in 1875, eight years after Canada itself was established in 1867. For many years, Canada continued to use as its final appeal court a body called the Judicial Committee of the Privy Council, located in England, Canada's mother country. This committee acted as the appeal court for all British colonies and overseas lands.

Even after the Supreme Court of Canada was set up, any decisions it made could be appealed and overturned by the Privy Council. In fact, many cases could go directly from the provincial appeal courts to England, without ever being heard by the Supreme Court in Canada. Only in 1949 was the Supreme Court made the final court for Canada. With the ending of appeals to England, the Court gained an importance it never had before.

ANDREW HEARD
Simon Fraser University

Important Canadian Supreme Court Cases

Regarding the Meaning of "Persons" (1928) ruled that women were not "qualified persons," and therefore could not be appointed to the Senate. This decision was later overturned by the Privy Council in England.

A.G. Nova Scotia v. *A.G. Canada* (1951) ruled that the national parliament and provincial legislatures cannot transfer their powers to each other.

Big M Drug Mart Inc. v. *The Queen* (1985) struck down the Lord's Day Act, which required most businesses to close on Sunday, agreeing it limited non-Christians' freedom of religion.

Morgentaler v. *The Queen* (1987) held that the process that women must go through to terminate a pregnancy violated their rights under the Charter of Rights and Freedoms.

Ford v. *A.G. Quebec* (1988) struck down a Quebec law that required all signs in stores to be only in French, ruling that it violated freedom of speech.

McKinney v. *University of Guelph* (1990) ruled it is acceptable to require workers to retire at age 65.

Chief Justices

Name	Term of Office
Sir William B. Richards	1875–79
Sir William J. Ritchie	1879–92
Sir Samuel H. Strong	1892–1902
Sir Henri E. Taschereau	1902–06
Sir Charles Fitzpatrick	1906–18
Sir Louis H. Davies	1918–24
Francis A. Anglin	1924–33
Sir Lyman P. Duff	1933–44
Thibaudeau Rinfret	1944–54
Patrick Kerwin	1954–63
Robert Taschereau	1963–67
J.R. Cartwright	1967–70
J. Honoré G. Fauteaux	1970–73
Bora Laskin	1973–84
Brian Dickson	1984–90
Antonio Lamer	1990–2000
Beverley McLachlin	2000–

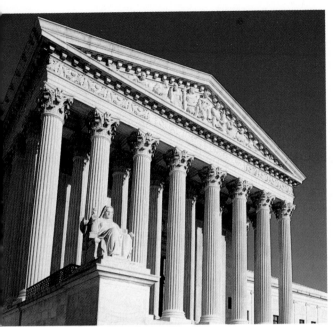

The Supreme Court Building in Washington, D.C., was designed by Cass Gilbert in the Greek Revival style. It has housed the nation's highest court since 1936.

SUPREME COURT OF THE UNITED STATES

The Supreme Court is the most powerful court of law in the United States. It heads the judicial branch of the federal government and shares power with the legislative branch (Congress) and the executive branch (headed by the president). The court was authorized by the Constitution of the United States. Article III, Section 1, decrees that "the judicial Power of the United States, shall be vested in one supreme Court, and in such inferior Courts as the Congress may from time to time ordain and establish." The Supreme Court itself was established by the Judiciary Act of 1789.

The court's most vital function is to determine whether or not local, state, and federal laws are in agreement with the Constitution. Its interpretation of the meaning of the Constitution and of laws is final and authoritative. Its decisions serve as guidelines for every other court in the nation and can be changed only by constitutional amendment or by the Supreme Court itself.

In its role as guardian of the Constitution, the Supreme Court possesses the power of **judicial review**. This gives it the authority to declare null and void any act of government (local, state, or federal) that the presiding justices determine violates the Constitution. Chief Justice John Marshall, in asserting this power for the first time in *Marbury* v. *Madison* (1803), made it clear that the Constitution is binding on all branches of government as the "superior, paramount law." The court has used the power of judicial review more than 1,000 times since the early 1800's, and in about 90 percent of these cases, it has been used to invalidate state laws.

Constitutional Status of the Supreme Court

The unique status of the Supreme Court as an independent branch of government, coexisting and sharing power with the executive and legislative branches, is an American contribution to the art of the government. Prior to this innovation, the judiciary had been regarded, in both theory and practice, as a mere extension of the executive branch of government. But the Founders believed that combining legislative, executive, and judicial powers would lead to an oppressive government. By making the judicial branch independent, they protected the court from domination by either Congress or the president. Consequently, although presidential nominees to the Supreme Court must be confirmed by a majority vote of the Senate, once they are appointed to the court, they may serve for life and can only be removed for serious wrongdoing, and only through a cumbersome impeachment process.

Jurisdiction of the Supreme Court

According to Article III, Section 2, the Supreme Court is the first court, state or federal, to hear "all Cases affecting Ambassadors, other public Ministers and Consuls, and those in which a State shall be Party. . . ." Such cases, which are relatively few in number, make up a category known as the court's **original jurisdiction**.

In all other cases the Supreme Court exercises **appellate jurisdiction**, meaning it is free to confirm or overrule a lower court's decision. The vast majority of cases heard by the Supreme Court come from the lower courts, principally the U.S. appellate courts and the state supreme courts. Most of these cases are brought before the court only after four or more Supreme Court justices vote to grant a **writ of certiorari**, which is an order to the lower courts to forward the case records for review.

Stephen Gerald Breyer (1934–), born San Francisco, Calif. A graduate (1964) of and later a professor at Harvard Law School, Breyer was appointed in 1980 to the U.S. Court of Appeals, First Circuit, and named chief judge in 1990. Considered fair-minded and moderate in his views, Breyer earned a reputation as a peacemaker. He was appointed to the Supreme Court by President William (Bill) Clinton in 1994.

Ruth Bader Ginsburg (1933–), born Brooklyn, N.Y. After receiving her law degree from Columbia University Law School (1959), she taught law at Rutgers University (1963–72) and then returned to Columbia as the school's first tenured female law professor (1972–80). She later served as a judge for the U.S. Court of Appeals for the District of Columbia (1980–93). Ginsburg was appointed to the Supreme Court by President William (Bill) Clinton in 1993.

Anthony McLeod Kennedy (1936–), born Sacramento, Calif. A graduate of Harvard Law School (1961), Kennedy served as judge for the U.S. Court of Appeals, Ninth Circuit (1976–88). He was appointed to the Supreme Court by President Ronald Reagan in 1988.

Sandra Day O'Connor (1930–), born El Paso, Tex. She received her law degree from Stanford University Law School in 1952. She served in the Arizona state senate as Republican majority leader (1972–74) and later as judge of Arizona's Maricopa County Superior Court (1974–79) and state court of appeals (1979–81). In 1981 she was appointed to the Supreme Court by President Ronald Reagan; she was the first woman ever chosen. In 2005, O'Connor announced her retirement but agreed to remain on the Court until the Senate could confirm a successor.

John Glover Roberts, Jr. (1955–), born Buffalo, N.Y. He received his law degree from Harvard Law School in 1979. He worked as a clerk (1979–81) for the judge of the U.S. Court of Appeals, Second Circuit, and Associate Supreme Court Justice William Rehnquist. He served as special assistant (1981–82) to Attorney General William French Smith and as associate counsel (1982–86) to President Ronald Reagan. He joined the Washington, D.C., law firm Hogan & Hartson, then left to serve as deputy solicitor general (1989–93) under President George Bush. In 2003 he was named to the U.S. Court of Appeals. Roberts was appointed Chief Justice of the Supreme Court by President George W. Bush in 2005.

Antonin Scalia (1936–), born Trenton, N.J. After receiving his law degree from Harvard Law School in 1960, he taught law at the University of Chicago and at Stanford University. He later served as judge for the U.S. Court of Appeals for the District of Columbia (1982–87). He was appointed to the Supreme Court by President Ronald Reagan in 1986.

David Hackett Souter (1939–), born Melrose, Mass. A Rhodes scholar, Souter obtained his law degree from Harvard Law School in 1966. He served as attorney general of New Hampshire (1976–78), as a state supreme court justice (1983–90), and as a judge for the U.S. Court of Appeals, First Circuit (1990). Souter was appointed to the Supreme Court by President George Bush in 1990.

John Paul Stevens (1920–), born Chicago, Ill. Stevens received his law degree from Northwestern University in 1947. He served as law clerk to former Supreme Court justice Wiley B. Rutledge, then practiced law in Chicago. In 1970 he was appointed to the U.S. Court of Appeals, Seventh Circuit. President Gerald Ford appointed him to the Supreme Court in 1975.

Clarence Thomas (1948–), born Savannah, Ga. He graduated from Yale University Law School in 1974 and was later appointed by President Ronald Reagan to head the Equal Employment Opportunity Commission (EEOC) (1982–89). He then served as judge for the U.S. Court of Appeals for the District of Columbia (1990–91). Thomas was appointed to the Supreme Court by President George Bush in 1991.

U.S. Supreme Court justices: Front row, from left: Antonin Scalia, John Paul Stevens, John G. Roberts, Jr. (chief justice), Sandra Day O'Connor, Anthony M. Kennedy. Back row, from left: Ruth Bader Ginsburg, David H. Souter, Clarence Thomas, Stephen Gerald Breyer.

SELECTED SIGNIFICANT U.S. SUPREME COURT DECISIONS

Judicial Review
Marbury v. *Madison* (1803) established the Supreme Court's right to declare a law passed by Congress unconstitutional.

Congressional Powers
McCulloch v. *Maryland* (1819) ruled that the Constitution gives Congress certain "implied" (unspecified) powers in order to carry out its specified powers.

Freedom of Speech
Schenck v. *United States* (1919) established that the government may curb the freedom of speech if it leads to "clear and present danger."

Racial Discrimination
Brown v. *Board of Education of Topeka* (Kans.) (1954) rejected the doctrine of "separate but equal" and declared that racial segregation in the public schools is unconstitutional.

Government Representation
Baker v. *Carr* (1962) held that the courts may provide remedies for harm due to the unequal apportionment of representatives in a legislative district. The following year, in *Wesberry* v. *Sanders* (1963), in agreement with the principle of "one person, one equal vote," the court also ruled that congressional districts must be of equal population size "as nearly as is practicable." In *Reynolds* v. *Sims* (1964), the court decreed that both houses of state legislatures "must be apportioned on a population basis."

School Prayer
Engel v. *Vitale* (1962) held that a voluntary, non-denominational prayer in the New York public schools violated the First Amendment clause that states, "Congress shall make no law respecting an establishment of religion. ..." Subsequently, the court banned recitation of the Lord's Prayer or verses from the Bible in all public schools.

Rights of the Accused
Gideon v. *Wainwright* (1963) guarantees that any person accused of criminal activities must be provided legal counsel by the state if the defendant cannot afford a lawyer. *Miranda* v. *Arizona* (1966) established rules that police must follow when questioning a suspect. They include informing individuals that they have the right to remain silent and the right to an attorney.

Women's Rights
Roe v. *Wade* (1973) ruled that a state cannot prevent a woman from having an abortion in the first three months of pregnancy.

Every year the court hears fewer than 250 cases, which is less than 5 percent of the total number it is petitioned to review. Of those cases, approximately 10 percent come to it on **appeal** in particular situations, such as when a state or lower federal court declares a federal law unconstitutional; when a state law is held to violate the Constitution; or when a state law is upheld against the challenge that it violates a federal law or the Constitution. Such cases demand resolution by the Supreme Court.

Organization and Procedures of the Supreme Court

The first Supreme Court, established by the Judiciary Act of 1789, consisted of a chief justice and five associate justices. For a period during the Civil War (1861–65), the court consisted of ten members (the most it has ever had), but in 1869 Congress fixed the size at nine, where it has since remained. The annual sessions of the court begin on the first Monday of October and run until late June.

Oral arguments before the court are normally limited to an hour—a half hour for each side—during which the justices may ask questions. In addition to oral argument, the parties submit briefs, or summaries, which forcefully present the reasonings, legal and otherwise, that justify their positions. In addition, *amicus curiae* ("friend of the court") briefs are commonly filed by organizations and individuals who are not directly involved in the lawsuit but are sympathetic to positions taken by one side or the other.

CHIEF JUSTICES OF THE SUPREME COURT

Name	Year Appointed	By President
*John Jay	1789	Washington
†John Rutledge	1795	Washington
Oliver Ellsworth	1796	Washington
*John Marshall	1801	J. Adams
Roger B. Taney	1836	Jackson
Salmon P. Chase	1864	Lincoln
Morrison R. Waite	1874	Grant
Melville W. Fuller	1888	Cleveland
Edward D. White	1910	Taft
*William Howard Taft	1921	Harding
*Charles Evans Hughes	1930	Hoover
Harlan F. Stone	1941	F. D. Roosevelt
Frederick M. Vinson	1946	Truman
Earl Warren	1953	Eisenhower
Warren E. Burger	1969	Nixon
William H. Rehnquist	1986	Reagan
John G. Roberts, Jr.	2005	G. W. Bush

† Was rejected by the U.S. Senate after serving briefly during a Senate recess.
* Subject of a separate article in *The New Book of Knowledge*.

On Wednesdays and Fridays, the justices hold conferences to discuss the cases they have just heard argued and indicate their tentative decisions. At the end of the discussion, the justices vote. The chief justice, when voting with the majority, may write the **majority opinion** or, what is more common, assign this task to another justice in the majority. If the chief justice is not a member of the majority, the senior justice voting with the majority will make the assignment. Those in the minority often write a **dissenting opinion**. Justices who agree with the conclusion of the majority opinion but not with its reasoning may write a **concurring opinion**. Most decisions of the court are usually handed down on Mondays during the last few weeks of the term.

The Supreme Court and Constitutional Development

Almost from the outset, the Supreme Court has played a major role in the development of the constitutional system. In particular it has upheld the extension of authority of the federal government over the state governments.

Since *Gitlow* v. *New York* (1925), the court has increasingly reviewed state legislation to make sure that the states do not violate the provisions of the 14th Amendment (1868), which provides that "no State shall make or enforce any law which shall abridge the privileges or immunities of citizens of the United States." (For more information, see the article BILL OF RIGHTS in Volume B.)

The Court at the Center of Controversy

In virtually every era of American history, the court has had its critics, including some highly renowned presidents. Thomas Jefferson, James Madison, Andrew Jackson, and their followers were extremely critical of the Marshall court because they feared its decisions gave too much power to the federal government; Abraham Lincoln attacked the decision rendered by Chief Justice Roger Taney in *Dred Scott* v. *Sandford* (1857), which declared that African Americans could not become citizens of the United States and that Congress did not have the constitutional authority to outlaw slavery in the federal territories. In Lincoln's view, the court's decision was not faithful to the Constitution. (For more information, see the article DRED SCOTT DECISION in Volume D.)

Perhaps the most famous confrontation between a president and the Supreme Court occurred in 1937, during the presidency of Franklin D. Roosevelt at the time of the Great Depression. Angered and frustrated because the court had declared many of his key New Deal programs unconstitutional (often by a 5–4 vote), Roosevelt sought to enlarge the court by appointing one additional justice for every sitting justice over the age of 70, up to a maximum of 15. This proposal was clearly designed to enable President Roosevelt to appoint six new justices favorable to his programs, a number more than sufficient to secure a majority. However, this "court packing" legislation, as it came to be known, was decisively defeated in the Senate.

Activists Versus Traditionalists

In recent decades, issues concerning the court have been debated between judicial activists and traditionalists in both academic and political circles. The main focus of these debates rests on the issue of how the court should interpret the Constitution.

Activists argue that the court must look to the "spirit of the constitution" in making its decisions. They contend that the Constitution is a "living" document, whose guidelines must be interpreted in light of the beliefs, needs, and circumstances of the day. For this reason, activists are inclined to expand the interpretation of certain rights to encompass ideas that are not specifically expressed in the Constitution.

Traditionalists maintain that the court should confine itself to the precise language of the Constitution, not its "spirit." Whenever possible, they contend, the court should try to determine what the Founders' intentions were and make its decisions accordingly. When this is not possible, they believe the court should defer to the judgment of the executive and legislative branches and declare null and void only those laws (state or federal) that are unmistakably contrary to the Constitution. Most of the justices now seated on the court are, to varying degrees, traditionalists who reject judicial activism.

GEORGE CAREY
Georgetown University

See also BILL OF RIGHTS; FIRST AMENDMENT FREEDOMS; UNITED STATES, CONSTITUTION OF THE.

SURFBOARDING. See SURFING.

Surfers need balance and split-second timing to ride ocean waves.

SURFING

Surfing is the sport of riding ocean waves on a long, narrow surfboard. For safety, all surfers must be good swimmers.

The sport apparently originated in the Pacific islands hundreds of years ago. When Captain James Cook reached Hawaii in 1778, surfing was a very popular sport among the Hawaiians. Contests were held, with prizes and acclaim for the winners. The islanders used very heavy boards up to 18 feet (5.5 meters) in length.

Today the sport is enjoyed at beaches all over the world, and its popularity has increased rapidly since 1957 with the widespread use of lightweight boards. These boards—which are 7 to 8 feet (2.1 to 2.4 meters) long and weigh as little as 8 pounds (3.6 kilograms)—have made it possible for more people to take up surfing. The new boards are generally made of plastic foam coated with fiberglass. A surfboard is the only special equipment the sport requires.

When riding a wave, accomplished surfers stand on the board and maneuver right and left. The surfer must first take the board out past the surf line—the point where the waves begin to break. Kneeling or lying prone on the board, the surfer waits for a set, or series of swells, to form. When the right wave appears, the surfer paddles quickly toward shore. As the wave moves under the board, it first rises and then slides down the unbroken front of the wave. Having "caught" the wave, the surfer rises to a standing position, one foot forward, and steers away from the breaking part of the wave.

Racing toward shore, the surfer has a tricky job staying balanced and controlling the board. To give the best ride, the board must be kept just ahead of the tumbling white surf, or "soup." This requires good timing and an excellent "feel" for surfing.

The board is controlled by the rider's shifting weight. The rider may turn by moving the rear foot to either side while keeping the forward, or balance, foot in place near the center of the board. If the board is moving too fast for the wave, the rider turns back and waits for the swell to build up again.

Skilled surfers travel at an angle to the shore rather than directly toward it. In this way they get a longer ride—sometimes more than ¼ mile (400 meters) at speeds up to 35 miles (55 kilometers) an hour.

Most surfing is done on waves that average over 1 meter high, although smaller waves can be ridden. The giant breakers of Hawaii, which sometimes reach about 25 feet (8 meters), provide the most challenging rides.

The United States Surfing Association, formed in 1961, has done much to organize the amateur aspect of the sport and increase interest in it. Professional competition moves around the world, following the hemispheric surf seasons to Hawaii, Australia, Japan, South Africa, Brazil, the eastern United States, and California. Other competitions are held in Peru and Europe.

STEPHEN PEZMAN
Editor and Publisher, *Surfer* magazine

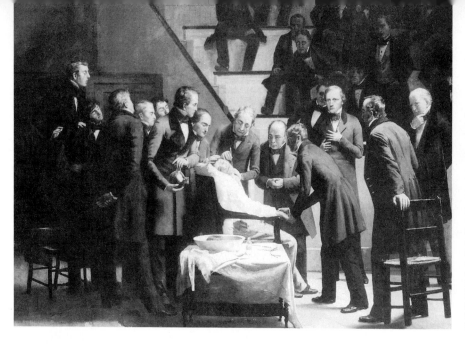

It was in 1846 that doctors gathered at Massachusetts General Hospital to witness the first public demonstration of the use of ether as an anesthetic. An American dentist named William Morton administered the drug before Dr. John Warren removed a tumor from a patient's jaw. The successful use of anesthetics was a major contribution to the development of modern surgery. Other advances included an increased knowledge of the body and the development of methods to prevent and treat wound infection.

SURGERY

Surgery is the branch of medicine in which specially trained doctors, called surgeons, treat patients using their hands. The use of their hands in treating people is the single most important thing that makes the surgeon different from every other medical specialist. Surgeons perform procedures and operations to treat peoples' injuries, diseases, and other disorders. Medicines, exercises, diet, and other forms of treatment may be used, but the most important work is done with the hands.

▶ THE EARLY PRACTICE OF SURGERY

As far back as historians can trace, people have used their hands to treat injuries and diseases. Even in the Stone Age, it was necessary to remove flint arrows and to bandage the heads of those who had been clubbed with rocks. Working with their hands, these primitive healers performed the first operations. In those times, thousands of years before scalpels (surgical knives) were invented, the first surgeons used knives made of flint stone in order to cut into injured parts. The first known surgical treatment involved cutting a hole in the skull—a procedure called trephining. Prehistoric people most likely practiced trephining to let out the evil spirits that they thought caused diseases and strange behaviors. Fossils of skulls with circular

sections removed have been found dating as far back as 10,000 years.

During the time of the pharaohs, Egyptian surgeons became very skilled at treating head injuries by trephining. Whatever the reason for the procedure, it could have helped because it allowed surgeons to drain blood that was pressing on the brain after an injury. The Egyptians also were skillful in devising ways of bandaging injuries. They used splints to help heal fractured arms and legs.

Although ancient practices, such as trephining (*left*), continued during the 1500's, significant advances also occurred. A way to close wounds by stitching cloth glued to the skin (*above*) was one of the many new techniques introduced.

As time passed, surgeons began to develop special instruments to help them do their work. Ancient Greeks and Romans used primitive forms of scalpels and forceps (grasping instruments). They also used special saws for removing a limb, during a procedure called amputation. If chemicals and tight bandaging did not stop the bleeding of a wound or an amputation, a red-hot iron called a cautery was pressed into the wound to seal it.

It was not until the 1500's that large arteries and veins were tied with thread or stitched with special needles to control bleeding. By that time, surgical clamps had been invented to hold blood vessels while they were being tied.

In those early days of medicine, surgeons and physicians were separate groups. Surgeons did not go to medical schools but learned their craft by an apprenticeship. It was not until about the 1700's that things began to change and the surgeons and physicians grew closer together. Finally, they arrived at the system that now exists: Today all students who want to be doctors complete medical school and then decide on the branch of medicine in which they will specialize.

Even though there were many instruments by the 1700's, there were two important factors that limited surgery as a treatment—pain and infection. Until 1846, the only way to decrease the pain of surgery was to give the patient drugs, such as opium, or enough alcohol to make the patient drunk. These methods were not very effective. Patients still suffered a great deal of pain and often had to be held down during surgery. Surgeons had to work very quickly. Most operations were performed in 10 or 15 minutes, and sometimes such speed could be dangerous.

Everyone recognized that some method was needed to produce deep, pain-free sleep. It was in the 1840's that a method was discovered to put patients to sleep using gases, such as nitrous oxide, ether, and chloroform. The gases, known as **anesthetics**, reduced the pain and shock of operations. Following the development of anesthetics, surgeons could work more slowly and carefully on their sleeping patients.

There was still the problem of infection. Many patients continued to die after their operations. Because of the risk of infection, it was impossible to work deep inside the body.

The only surgical procedures that could be done safely were amputations and the removal of tumors on the body's surface.

A discovery by the French chemist Louis Pasteur led to safer operations. Pasteur discovered that bacteria could cause spoilage of wine and beer. In 1867, the English surgeon Joseph Lister used Pasteur's findings to prove that

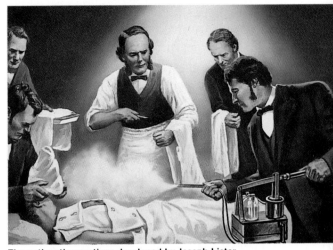

The antiseptic practices developed by Joseph Lister (shown with scalpel in hand) included spraying surgical wounds with carbolic acid to prevent infection.

bacteria could also spoil human tissue and cause infection after injury or operation. By spraying wounds with a powerful chemical called carbolic acid, he was able to kill the bacteria and stop infection.

Following the development of ways to reduce pain and help prevent infection, many new operations were attempted. Before long, surgeons were able to operate in the abdomen, skull, and chest. With the introduction of penicillin in the 1940's, surgery became even safer. Penicillin was among the first **antibiotics**—drugs that kill disease-causing organisms—to be used.

Advances in other fields, such as engineering, also have expanded the scope of surgery. Engineers have developed many instruments and machines that have helped surgeons create new life-saving techniques. The heart-lung machine is one such device. It circulates blood throughout the body when the heart and lungs are stopped. Then defects within the heart itself can be repaired.

MAJOR BRANCHES OF SURGERY

About one hundred years ago, doctors began to realize that more could be done for sick people if certain groups of surgeons concentrated their efforts on specific types of surgery. Gradually, the profession began to divide itself into a number of separate specialties. Today most surgeons specialize in a particular kind of problem. For example, a patient goes to an abdominal surgeon if an appendectomy is needed, an orthopedic surgeon if a bone is fractured, or a plastic surgeon if part of the body is being rebuilt or restored.

A TYPICAL OPERATION

Amazing progress has been made since the first operations were performed thousands of years ago. However, the process begins in the same way: The surgeon makes a diagnosis.

The Diagnosis. The steps in making a diagnosis include finding out about the patient's symptoms and complaints and conducting an examination of the patient's physical condition. The surgeon may also request that certain laboratory tests of blood or urine be performed or that X rays, CT scans, or other diagnostic images be made.

Once the diagnosis is made, the surgeon can recommend a treatment. Sometimes surgery is the only treatment. At other times, an operation may be combined with another treatment, such as the use of drugs, or chemotherapy. An appendectomy, which is the removal of the

An operation consists of three main elements: an examination to establish a diagnosis, which can include diagnostic imaging (*below*); the performance of the surgical procedure (*below right*); and the return to a normal life-style, which begins as the patient awakens in the recovery room (*right*).

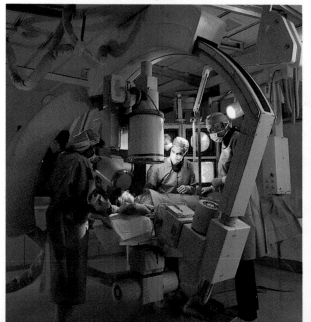

appendix, is an example of a completely surgical treatment.

The Surgery. After the diagnosis of appendicitis is made, and with the patient's written permission, a time for the surgery is scheduled. The surgeon will direct the surgical team, which consists of an anesthesiologist, nurses, and technicians. In preparation for the surgery, the operating room is cleaned and scrubbed. The equipment needed during the operation is sterilized and put into place.

The patient is brought to the operating room after being given a pre-operative medication. The medication makes the patient a little drowsy and less nervous. The surgical team is assembled and ready to begin. The anesthesiologist, who is the person responsible for providing the patient with a safe, pain-free sleep, administers the anesthetic. There are many kinds and combinations of anesthetics that can be used—some are injected, others are inhaled. The anesthesiologist chooses the ones that are best for the patient.

Once the patient is asleep, the skin of the abdomen is sterilized with an antiseptic solu-

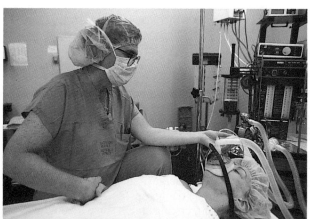

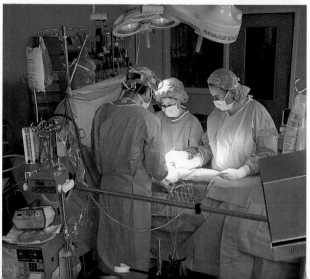

tion. Towels and drapes are put around the area to be operated on; for an appendectomy, that is the right lower quarter of the abdomen. Then an incision, or opening, is made to expose the appendix.

When the diagnosis is appendicitis, that means that the appendix is inflamed. It is swollen and red and sometimes has some decay in it. During the appendectomy, the appendix is picked up and cut away from the intestine. The surgeon stitches the intestine where it was attached. Any arteries or veins that might bleed are tied with thread or touched with a thin electric needle—the modern form of a cautery.

After the appendix is removed, the incision is stitched up and a dressing is put on the wound. Usually the whole operation takes 30 minutes to an hour. But it may take longer if the inflammation is very bad. When everything is completed, the anesthesiologist discontinues the anesthetic and the patient wakes up in a few minutes.

The Recovery. After the surgery is completed, the patient is taken to the Recovery Room. The purpose of the Recovery Room is to allow the patient to become fully awake. There are many specially trained nurses there, and their job is to be sure that each patient is comfortable and recovering well from the anesthesia. After about an hour, the patient is transferred to a hospital room. Medication is used to ease any pain that may be felt from the surgical wound. Most individuals return home within two to four days.

This is the general way in which all operations are done. Of course, some are much more complicated than an appendectomy. Complicated operations may involve a great deal of cutting, stitching, and separating of internal structures. Patients who need these more complex operations will have larger incisions. They will also have to stay longer in the hospital. But, the modern methods and skilled surgeons that now exist mean that almost everyone recovers without any problems, or complications.

▶ **FUTURE DEVELOPMENTS**

What will surgery be like in the future? In certain ways, the future is already here. Two fascinating new techniques—microsurgery and laparoscopy—have greatly increased surgical capabilities.

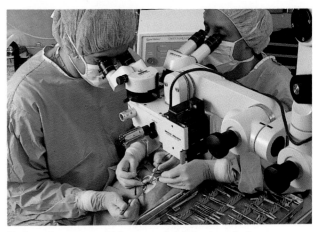

During microsurgery, doctors use miniaturized surgical tools and a special zoom-lens microscope that magnifies tiny, delicate body structures.

Microsurgeons use high-magnification lenses and small, specialized instruments to operate on tiny structures that they would otherwise not be able to cut, separate, and stitch. This has allowed them to do extraordinarily delicate procedures, such as reattaching an amputated finger.

Laparoscopy is a method in which it is possible for a surgeon to operate within a body cavity, such as the abdomen, without the surgeon's hands ever entering the cavity. Although the surgery still requires that incisions be made, they are very small. A special viewing camera, called a laparoscope, and very fine operating instruments are inserted into the cavity through the incisions. The images from the laparoscope are projected onto a video screen. By watching the screen, the surgeon and the surgical assistants are able to guide their instruments and monitor the entire procedure. Patients who undergo laparoscopic surgery have very little pain afterwards, and they are usually able to go home within 24 hours.

Together, microsurgery and laparoscopy give us a hint about what surgery of the future will be like. The constantly evolving technology will allow more complicated procedures to be performed. Surgery will also be less painful. Other benefits from new techniques include shorter hospital stays, which mean lower health costs.

SHERWIN B. NULAND, M.D.
Associate Clinical Professor of Surgery
Yale School of Medicine

See also DOCTORS; HOSPITALS; MEDICINE (Medical Milestone: The Rise of Modern Surgery).

SURINAME

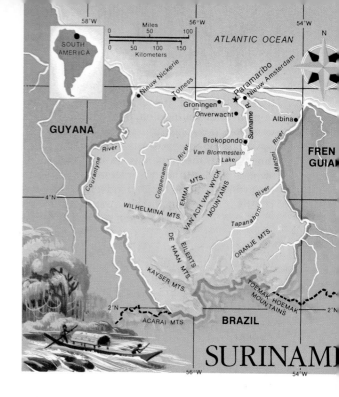

SURINAM

Suriname is a nation of many different peoples. South American Indians and the descendants of black African slaves, Europeans, and people from India, Pakistan, Indonesia, and China make up a multi-racial society. Located on the northeastern coast of South America, Suriname was long a colony of the Netherlands and once was known as Dutch Guiana. It gained its independence in 1975.

▶ THE PEOPLE

The original inhabitants of Suriname were Carib and Arawak Indians. Several thousand are still believed to live in the dense forests of the interior. Some of the Indians are nomadic, moving from place to place; others live in villages along the inland rivers. The Indians speak their own languages and have little contact with the rest of the population.

The Bush people are descendants of black African slaves who escaped from plantations before slavery was abolished in 1863. They live much as do the people in the African regions from which their ancestors came. Bush

FACTS
and figures

REPUBLIC OF SURINAME (Republiek Suriname) is the official name of the country.

LOCATION: Northeastern coast of South America.

AREA: 63,037 sq mi (163,265 km²).

POPULATION: 400,000 (estimate).

CAPITAL AND LARGEST CITY: Paramaribo.

MAJOR LANGUAGES: Dutch (official), English, Sranan Tongo.

MAJOR RELIGIONS: Hindu, Muslim, Christian.

GOVERNMENT: Republic. **Head of state and government**—president. **Legislature**—National Assembly. A Council of State exercises supervisory authority over the government.

CHIEF PRODUCTS: Agricultural—rice, sugarcane, citrus fruits, bananas. **Manufactured**—refined aluminum, processed agricultural products, lumber, processed shrimp. **Mineral**—bauxite.

MONETARY UNIT: Suriname guilder (1 guilder = 100 cents).

people are noted for the beauty of their woodcarving. Other blacks live in the coastal areas. They are descendants of slaves who, when slavery ended, left the plantations to become skilled workers in the towns.

The early Dutch settlements were in time enlarged by groups of other Europeans. Jews fleeing persecution made their way to the colony in the 1600's and established one of the first synagogues in the Americas. Some Chinese arrived in the 1800's.

After slavery was abolished, new sources of labor had to be found. Contract laborers were brought into the country, chiefly from India and the island of Java in what is now Indonesia. When the immigrant workers had fulfilled the terms of their contracts, most of them remained. Many descendants of immigrants from India and from what is now Pakistan live in the countryside, where they have become rice and dairy farmers. Others are engaged in industry, trade, and the professions. Many of the sizable Javanese population are farmers.

For many generations each of the separate groups maintained its own religious and cultural customs. But over the years the sharp lines that once clearly marked each group have become blurred, and the number of intermarriages is increasing rapidly.

The largest group of people in Suriname are called Creoles. The Creoles are not a separate

Suriname is a nation made up of the descendants of people from many lands. The diversity of the population can be seen in Paramaribo, the capital city.

ethnic group but a people of mixed ancestry. Most Creoles live in the populated areas along the coast. They make up a large proportion of the nation's lawyers, teachers, doctors, and government officials.

Suriname's official language is Dutch, but many people cling to their original tongues. English and Sranan Tongo—a mixture of English, Dutch, Portuguese, Spanish, and African languages—are also widely spoken. Hindus, Muslims, and Christians make up the major religious groups.

▶ THE LAND AND THE ECONOMY

Most of the interior of Suriname is covered with tropical rain forests and hills, which rise to a height of about 4,200 feet (1,280 meters) in the Wilhelmina Mountains. A band of savanna, or grassland, runs along the south. Most of the country's population and farms are concentrated on a low, narrow coastal plain in the north. Suriname has a tropical climate, with heavy rainfall and generally high temperatures and humidity.

The capital and largest city is Paramaribo, which lies near the coast on the Suriname River. About half of Suriname's people live in and around Paramaribo.

Suriname is a leading producer of bauxite, the chief ore of aluminum. Exports of bauxite and aluminum are a mainstay of the economy, providing most of the country's income. The great majority of the people, however, are farmers. Rice is the main food crop and also is exported. Sugarcane, citrus fruits, and bananas are important commercial crops. Some timber is harvested, and shrimp is processed for export.

▶ HISTORY AND GOVERNMENT

Spanish explorers first sighted the Suriname coast in the late 1400's, but no permanent settlements were established until the British arrived in the 1600's. Britain ceded the territory to the Dutch in 1667, in exchange for the colony of New Netherland (now New York). Except for a brief return to British rule, the Netherlands governed Suriname until its independence in 1975.

Suriname was governed as a parliamentary democracy until 1980, when the government was overthrown in a military coup and the constitution suspended. A Supreme Council of military officers then governed the country through appointed civilian prime ministers.

A new constitution adopted in 1987 legalized the political power of the army, but it was amended in 1992 to end the influence of the army on the government. Since 1991, power has passed peacefully from one elected civilian government to another. The members of the legislature are elected by the people for 5-year terms. They select the president and vice president, who also serve for five years.

HELEN WATSON-MALM
Suriname Consulate-General, New York

SURREALISM

Surrealism is a style of modern art in which images are based on fantasy and the world of dreams. It flourished in Europe from the mid-1920's to well after the end of World War II (1939–45).

The stage was set for surrealism by an earlier movement known as **dada**. Dadaists were disillusioned with modern society after the outbreak of World War I in 1914. They wrote nonsense poetry and created nonsense art to express their belief that traditional values had become meaningless. Like dada, surrealism was also in conflict with social values, although the two movements differed greatly.

Surrealism first appeared about 1924 as a literary movement led by the French poet André Breton. Breton's writings caught the attention of many artists, including the German painter Max Ernst and the Spanish painter Salvador Dali. These artists created strange pictures consisting of totally unrelated objects, sometimes chosen by pure chance, placed against mysterious backgrounds. These were exciting works, at times giving the impression that the artists who created them were in touch with another world. What was the inspiration for such unusual paintings?

From its beginnings, surrealism was influenced by the theories of Sigmund Freud, the father of psychoanalysis. Freud believed that many important thoughts and feelings are buried deep in the unconscious mind. Surrealist artists tried to liberate these buried thoughts and feelings and use them as subjects for their art. They claimed that the images produced by this process were actually more real than images seen by the eye in everyday life. The surrealists wanted to fuse unconscious forces with everyday reality in order to produce a super-reality, or "surreality."

In order to reach this unconscious world, the surrealists analyzed their dreams and underwent hypnosis. They also used such techniques as doodling and automatic drawing, putting down on paper whatever images came into their minds. Another method developed by the surrealists is **frottage**, in which rubbings of wood or other rough surfaces produce unexpected shapes and textures.

Two different kinds of surrealist art emerged. Artists such as Dali, Belgium's René Magritte, and France's Yves Tanguy painted

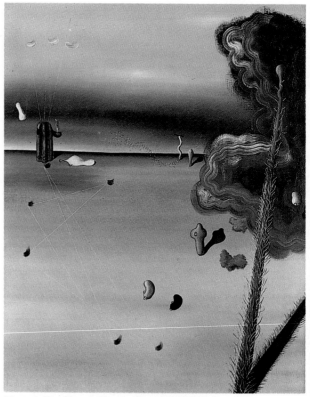

The painting *Mama, Papa Is Wounded!* (1927), by French artist Yves Tanguy, has a mysterious and dreamlike quality that is characteristic of surrealistic art.

dreamlike images using a highly realistic technique. So meticulously painted are these works that they are sometimes called "hand-painted dream photographs." Other artists, such as Spanish painter Joan Miró, Swiss-born painter Paul Klee, and the French sculptor Jean Arp, did not use a realistic style. Their works often consist of abstract shapes that have no intended resemblance to familiar objects. In their freshness and vitality, these works resemble children's art.

Surrealism influenced much later art, especially the movement known as abstract expressionism. The American painter Jackson Pollock, for example, allowed chance to dictate where his dripping paints would fall on his canvas. Surrealism also found expression in the writings of Breton and others, in the architecture of Spain's Antonio Gaudí, and in the films of Spain's Luis Buñuel.

HOWARD E. WOODEN
Director Emeritus
Wichita Museum of Art

SURVEYING

Surveying is the measuring of the size, shape, or location of any part of the earth's surface—land or sea. Surveyors look over an area of land or a body of water very carefully to measure mountains, lowlands, rivers, lakes, oceans, and islands. Different heights of land and different depths of water are also recorded. Anything from a homeowner's small lot to the entire surface of the earth may be measured. Scientists are even trying to survey the surface of other planets.

What are these surveys used for? They are needed for many purposes, and each purpose requires a different type of survey.

Land or property surveying, the measuring of small tracts of land, is needed to determine the ownership of real estate and to draw up legal property boundaries.

Engineering surveys are used for laying out highways, railroads, electric power lines, and similar engineering work. Tunnels, bridges, and missile sites are laid out true and square by engineering surveys. Even the structure of large airplanes is aligned by the use of surveying instruments.

To measure large portions of the earth, such as whole continents, **geodetic surveying** is needed. Through it, national or state boundaries can be established, as well as lines and measurements that can be used for surveys of smaller areas. The word "geodetic" comes from two Greek words meaning "earth" and "to divide."

Another important type of surveying is **cartographic surveying**, used in making maps, atlases, and geographic charts. Maps and charts are used for various purposes, so different features may be surveyed for each. **Topographic maps** emphasize the earth's natural terrain—hills, forests, valleys, rivers—as well as structures made by people, such as highways, railroads, dams, and canals. For **hydrographic charts**, needed for navigating ships, waterways with shallows, deeps, reefs, and sandbanks are surveyed. The contours (outlines) of the earth beneath those waterways must also be recorded. The information obtained in topographic and hydrographic surveys is also used in preparing **aeronautical charts**. In addition, these charts have to show special features, such as radio beacons, that will guide pilots. For **geological maps** and **soil survey maps**, the structure of the earth under its visible surface is determined. Such maps are useful to mining experts.

How Surveying Is Done

All surveying is done with the help of tools and instruments that measure distances, angles, and elevations (heights). The simplest surveying tool is a tape measure made of a long, flexible band of steel. This **surveyor's tape** is stretched over the ground, and distances are read off quickly and easily. Differences in height are measured with a telescope called a **surveyor's level** and with rods that have height markings painted on them. The telescope gets its name from the built-in level—a device that

Instruments used to measure elevations include the surveyor's level, tape, and rod (left) and a transit to measure angles (below left). The electronic total station and field book (below right) combine the functions of many surveying tools for greater accuracy in collecting, calculating, and storing measurements.

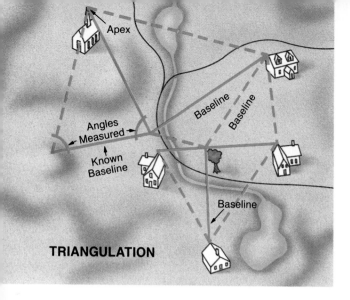

TRIANGULATION

shows when the whole instrument is perfectly horizontal. The first step is to sight a point of known elevation through the telescope's lens. The telescope's height can then easily be calculated. Once this is known, the surveyor takes a sight on a rod that is held upright on the point whose elevation is to be measured. Where the horizontal line of the surveyor's vision meets the rod, the marking on the rod indicates the difference in height of the two points. Long distances cannot be measured directly, especially if the ground has obstacles like rivers or hills. A method called **triangulation** is therefore employed for surveying large areas.

Triangulation consists of measuring angles and triangles. First, a certain stretch of land is measured very accurately. This becomes the **baseline** of a triangle. Then a prominent point in the distance, such as a church steeple or mountain peak, is singled out. This point will be the **apex** (tip) of the triangle. The distances between the apex and the ends of the baseline form the sides of the triangle. The lengths of these sides are as yet unknown. From both ends of the baseline the surveyors then sight the apex through telescopes called **transits**. A transit is much like a surveyor's level, but it has an added advantage: It can measure angles. When the apex is sighted through its lens, the transit automatically measures the angle between baseline and side. Knowing the baseline and the two angles, the surveyors can work out the lengths of the sides and other distances within the triangle. These known distances become the new baselines for other triangles, until a whole series is created.

Surveying small areas is also called **plane surveying**, because the ground is treated as a flat plane. In geodetic surveys, which may cover hundreds of square miles, the curvature of the earth's surface has to be taken into consideration. Such work requires a more complicated transit, called a **theodolite**. Today, theodolites are often part of instruments known as **electronic total stations**, which combine several devices and make it possible for a surveyor to take much more precise measurements. They are also used with **electronic field books** that can transmit the measurements to computers in the surveyor's office. In geodetic surveys, specially built steel towers are often used as sighting points. Helicopters, which may be used in difficult terrain, can hover over one particular spot, and this spot can be used as a point in triangulation.

Modern cartographic surveying depends on photographs and other information gathered by airplanes and satellites. Hydrographic surveys are made by ships that are really floating laboratories. Underwater depths are measured almost entirely by electronic equipment.

A sensing device called the **magnetometer** is used for geological surveys. It may be fixed inside an airplane, or it may be hung from the plane on a cable so that it trails above the ground. It records magnetic readings from which scientists can determine the structure of the earth under the surface.

History of Surveying

Surveying is one of the world's oldest professions. About 5,000 years ago, surveys were conducted in the river valleys of Egypt, India, and China, to re-establish boundaries washed away by the annual floodwaters. Over the centuries the art of surveying progressed steadily. The invention of the telescope in the 1600's made it possible to develop modern surveying methods.

Today surveying is becoming more and more adventurous. The earth, moon, and other planets are mapped from satellites put in space for just that purpose. Under the polar ice caps, surveys are conducted by sonar from nuclear submarines.

WALTER S. DIX
American Congress on Surveying and Mapping

See also MAPS AND GLOBES; OPTICAL INSTRUMENTS.

SWAMPS. See WETLANDS.

SWANS. See DUCKS, GEESE, AND SWANS.

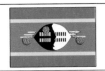

SWAZILAND

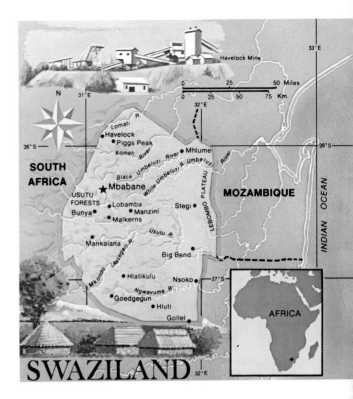

SWAZILAND

Swaziland is a small kingdom located in southeastern Africa. It is bounded by the Republic of South Africa on the north, west, and south and by Mozambique on the east. Swaziland takes its name from the Swazi, the people who make up most of the country's population. A former British protectorate, Swaziland gained full independence in 1968.

▶ THE PEOPLE

Aside from the Swazi, the population includes other black African peoples, several thousand whites (mainly from South Africa), and people of mixed race. Most Swazi follow a traditional way of life. The great majority are farmers, who grow food for their own use on land that is held in common. They also raise livestock, particularly cattle. Some Swazi work on the large farms and in the mines of neighboring South Africa.

The official languages of the country are Siswati (the Swazi language) and English. The majority of the people are Christians; others practice traditional African religions.

FACTS AND FIGURES

KINGDOM OF SWAZILAND is the official name of the country.

THE PEOPLE are known as Swazi.

LOCATION: Southeastern Africa.

AREA: 6,704 sq mi (17,363 km²).

POPULATION: 700,000 (estimate).

CAPITAL: Mbabane (administrative); Lobamba (traditional).

LARGEST CITY: Mbabane.

MAJOR LANGUAGES: Siswati, English (both official).

MAJOR RELIGIONS: Christian, traditional religions.

GOVERNMENT: Monarchy. **Head of state**—king. **Head of government**—prime minister (appointed by the king). **Legislature**—House of Assembly and the Senate.

CHIEF PRODUCTS: Agricultural—sugarcane, rice, corn, cotton, citrus fruits, tobacco, pineapples, livestock. **Manufactured**—refined sugar, wood pulp. **Mineral**—asbestos, coal, gold, tin, diamonds.

MONETARY UNIT: Lilangeni (1 lilangeni = 100 cents).

NATIONAL ANTHEM: Begins: "O God, bestower of the blessings of the Swazi."

▶ THE LAND

Swaziland has four distinct regions. The easternmost region is the Lebombo Plateau, which averages about 2,000 feet (610 meters) in height. Next are three regions of increasing elevation, called the low veld, the middle veld, and the high veld. The high veld rises sharply to about 6,000 feet (1,800 meters) in the west. Most of Swaziland's people live in the middle and high veld regions. The country's main rivers provide water to irrigate croplands.

The climate varies with elevation. The high veld has fairly moderate temperatures and the heaviest rainfall. The low veld is the hottest and driest region.

Cities. Mbabane is the administrative capital and largest city, with a population of about 39,000. Manzini is second in size. Lobamba is the traditional Swazi capital.

▶ THE ECONOMY

The economy is based mainly on agriculture, with mining and the production of timber also of importance. Sugar is the country's chief export. The sugarcane, along with rice and citrus fruits, is grown on irrigated lands.

Tobacco, cotton, and pineapples are major cash crops in the middle and high velds. Corn is the most important food crop. Cattle are a sign of wealth among the Swazis. Tanned hides and processed meat are exported.

Near Piggs Peak and around the Usutu River, huge forests of pine and eucalyptus trees have been planted. Wood pulp has become an important export. Iron ore was once the chief export, but the high-grade ore has been used up. Asbestos, gold, tin, and diamonds are mined. Coal provides power for a growing number of small industries. Mountain scenery, game preserves, and gambling casinos attract tourists in increasing numbers.

▶ HISTORY AND GOVERNMENT

Hunters using iron tools settled in the area about 40,000 years ago. The Swazis were driven southward into what is now Swaziland by the Zulus, a related tribe, in the early 1800's. A series of great kings united the Swazi peoples during this time.

White settlers began to move into the area in the 1840's. King Mbandzeni gave them agricultural and mining rights over much of the country to preserve Swazi independence. As a result, the white minority still controls most of Swaziland's exports. In 1903, after the Boer War, the area became a British protectorate. Local government stayed in the hands of Swazi chiefs, and the British resisted demands that Swaziland be incorporated into South Africa. Swaziland gained internal self-government in 1967 and independence in 1968.

Swaziland is a monarchy. Under a new constitution adopted in 1978, the king is both head of state and has ultimate power over the government. The legislature is composed of the House of Assembly and the Senate. The House of Assembly has 50 members; 40 are chosen by an electoral college and 10 are appointed by the king. The Senate has 20 members, of which 10 are chosen by the electoral college and 10 appointed by the king. The king also appoints the prime minister, who acts as the head of government. All legislation must be approved by the king before it can become law.

For many years Swaziland was ruled by King Sobhuza II, who became leader of the Swazi people in 1921. After Sobhuza's death in 1982, the country was ruled first by one and then another of his queens. A son of Sobhuza came to the throne as King Mswati III in 1986.

HUGH C. BROOKS
Director, Center for African Studies
St. John's University (New York)

A wide variety of crops is grown in Swaziland's middle veld. The use of irrigation on farms like this one has increased agricultural production.

SWEDEN

Sweden is the largest of the Scandinavian countries and the fifth largest European nation. In area, it is exceeded only by Russia, Ukraine, France, and Spain. Sweden occupies the larger part of the Scandinavian Peninsula of northern Europe, which it shares with Norway. Denmark, another Scandinavian country, lies to Sweden's southwest and is part of the European mainland. Finland, sometimes considered a Scandinavian country, lies to the east.

▶ PEOPLE

The Swedes are closely related to the Danes, Icelanders, Faeroe Islanders, Norwegians, and Swedish-speaking Finns. Their origins lie in several migrations of people, some of whom likely came from or through Russia, between 9000 and 2500 B.C. Sweden's population has become ethnically diverse in recent decades. The Finns are the country's largest ethnic minority, but there are many people from South America, Africa, the Middle East, and Asia. About 17,000 Sami (formerly called Lapps) live in the far northern region of Sweden known as Lapland.

Although large in area, Sweden has a relatively small population. Most of Sweden's people live in the southern part of the country, its most fertile region and the site of its major cities.

Language. Swedish is the national language and is related to Danish, Faeroese, Icelandic, and Norwegian. The Swedish alphabet is the same as that used in English, except that there are three extra vowels: *å*, *ä*, and *ö*. Many Swedes also speak English and German. The native languages of ethnic minorities are preserved through special education programs. The Sami speak one of three dialects of a language also called Sami.

Religion. Most Swedes belong to the Evangelical Lutheran Church of Sweden, which was the state church until 2000. Few, however, are active members. Considerable numbers of Roman Catholics,

Right: A young Swedish girl in traditional dress. **Below:** Colorful houses line a harbor in the Swedish port town of Smögen.

Swedes enjoy a variety of outdoor activities and organized sports. *Left:* A couple hike through mountainous terrain in northern Sweden. *Above:* Young soccer fans celebrate a Swedish victory in a World Cup tournament game.

Orthodox Christians, and Muslims live in Sweden.

Education and Libraries. Education is highly valued in Sweden, and almost all of it is free. After pre-school, Swedish children begin their nine-year compulsory schooling at age 7. Then most students continue at an upper secondary school of their choice. Each of these offers a basic core of studies and either an academic or practical specialty. About one-third of all students then go on to a professional school or university. Sweden has over a dozen universities, including Uppsala University, the country's oldest university, founded in 1477, and Lund University, which dates from 1668. There are also many vocational schools that prepare students for particular skilled jobs. The country has an extensive library system. The Royal Library is located in Stockholm, the capital.

Home Life. The great majority of Swedes live in cities and towns, mostly in apartments. Sweden has one of the highest rates of computer and cell phone ownership in the world, and most families have several televisions and at least one automobile.

Sports and Recreation. Swedes love the outdoors and enjoy hiking, camping, skiing, and water sports. Organized sports are also popular, with soccer, ice hockey, and bandy (which resembles field hockey on ice) leading the list.

Food and Drink. Swedes enjoy both traditional fare and a growing number of international dishes. The country's surrounding waters provide abundant fish; favorite seafood includes cod, salmon, and shrimp. In addition to beef, pork, and chicken, reindeer and moose are popular. A common way to serve food is the *smörgåsbord* (which literally means "sandwich table"). This is a buffet offering a wide variety of foods, including breads, fish, meats, cheeses, salads, and desserts. Favorite beverages include wine, beer, and *aquavit* (meaning "water of life"), a vodka flavored with berries or spices.

▶ **LAND**

Sweden stretches some 1,000 miles (1,600 kilometers) from south to north and about 300 miles (480 kilometers) from east to west. Much of Sweden's land is covered with forests. Numerous rivers and approximately 90,000 lakes make up nearly one-tenth of its total area.

Land Regions. Geographically, Sweden can be divided into five regions: the South, the Southern Highland, the Central Lowland, the North (Norrland), and the islands.

The South is a lowland region of fertile plains, with the warmest climate in Sweden. Many of Sweden's best farms are in this area.

To the north rise the hills of the Southern Highland, which reach their highest point near Lake Vättern. The soils of the region are thin and stony, making farming difficult. It has dense forests and countless small lakes and swamps.

The Central Lowland stretches across the middle of Sweden. It has broad, rolling plains broken by rocky, forested ridges and large blue lakes. Sweden's largest lake, Lake Vänern, is located in this region. The Central Lowland is the historic heart of the country. After the southern provinces, it is Sweden's most important farming region.

The North is a vast region that makes up almost two-thirds of the country. Its hilly terrain becomes mountainous along the Norwegian border. The highest point in Sweden, Kebnekaise, rises 6,965 feet (2,123 meters) and is located in the Kölen Mountains. Spilling down from the mountains out of deep glacial lakes are dozens of rushing rivers, which form countless rapids and waterfalls on their way to the sea.

The islands of Öland and Gotland lie off the eastern coast of Sweden in the Baltic Sea. They form a region in themselves because their land, composed of limestone and sandstone, is so different from the mainland. The islands have no true rivers and their soils are too dry for crops to be grown. Sweden also has two large archipelagoes (island groups). One is along the west coast and the other reaches east into the Baltic from Stockholm.

FACTS and figures

KINGDOM OF SWEDEN (Konungariket Sverige) is the official name of the country.

LOCATION: Northern Europe.

AREA: 158,662 sq mi (410,934 km²).

POPULATION: 8,900,000 (estimate).

CAPITAL AND LARGEST CITY: Stockholm.

MAJOR LANGUAGE: Swedish (official).

MAJOR RELIGIOUS GROUP: Evangelical Lutheran, Roman Catholic, Orthodox Christian, Muslim.

GOVERNMENT: Constitutional monarchy. **Head of state**—monarch (king). **Head of government**—prime minister. **Legislature**—Parliament (Riksdag).

CHIEF PRODUCTS: Agricultural—barley, wheat, sugar beets, meat, milk. **Manufactured**—iron and steel, precision equipment (bearings, radio and telephone parts, armaments), wood pulp and paper products, processed foods, motor vehicles. **Mineral**—zinc, iron ore, lead, copper, silver, uranium.

MONETARY UNIT: Krona (1 krona = 100 öre).

Climate. Sweden lies as far north as Alaska but generally has a milder climate. This is because the warm waters of the North Atlantic Drift flow nearby and because the prevailing winds are from the southwest during all seasons. Winter temperatures in the central and southern part of the country average slightly below freezing. In the far north the average winter temperature is 7°F (–14°C). Summer temperatures are cool but comfortable. Rainfall averages about 24 inches (610 millimeters) a year. There is considerable snowfall in winter.

Natural Resources. Only about 7 percent of Sweden's land is suitable for farming. The country's most valuable natural resources are its mineral deposits, forests, and rivers. Sweden's most important mineral is iron ore, which is exported and is vital to its iron, steel, engineering, and shipbuilding industries. Other mineral deposits include zinc, lead, copper, silver, and uranium. The forests, mainly spruce and pine, provide the raw ma-

Sweden's most valuable natural resources include its thick forests, which cover much of the country, and its swift-flowing rivers, which provide hydroelectric power to generate much of the country's electricity.

terial for lumber, wood pulp, and paper industries. Sweden has no petroleum and virtually no coal, but its swift-flowing rivers provide hydroelectric power. On the west coast, wind power is becoming increasingly important in generating electricity.

▶ ECONOMY

As late as 1900, Sweden's economy was still mainly agricultural. Rapid industrialization began after about 1870 and was very important for most of the 1900's. It helped give Sweden one of the highest standards of living in the world.

Services. Today Sweden has what some call a post-industrial economy. Government social programs, commercial and retail customer services, education, and tourism account for nearly 70 percent of the economy.

Manufacturing. About one-fifth of the workforce is employed in manufacturing. The leading manufactures include metals and metal products; industrial machinery; and high-technology products. Products that originated in Sweden and are known worldwide include Volvo and Saab automobiles, Saab aircraft, and Ericsson mobile phones.

Agriculture, Forestry, and Fishing. Although less than 5 percent of the labor force is engaged in agriculture, Swedish farms are highly mechanized and supply most of the country's demand for barley, wheat, sugar beets, meat, and milk. Sweden also exports some food products, including cheeses, lingonberries (a kind of small, sweet cranberry), coffee, chocolate, and vodka.

Wood, wood pulp, paper, and paper products were vital to the Swedish economy for many decades. Today precision equipment and high-technology goods have replaced those products in importance as exports.

Sweden's long coastline has made fishing a traditional economic activity, although it is not as important as in the past. Much of the catch is consumed at home, but some canned fish is exported.

Timber from Sweden's forests flows through a processing plant. Wood pulp, paper products, and lumber have traditionally been important export products.

Mining. Sweden has been an important producer of high-grade iron ore since the Middle Ages. Today the center of the mining industry is based at the enormous open-pit mine at Kiruna in the far north. In addition to supplying its own industries, Sweden exports iron ore in large quantities, chiefly to the industrialized nations of western Europe.

Energy. Because of its lack of petroleum and coal, Sweden's early industrial development was dependent on imported fuels and water power to generate electricity. Hydroelectric power now provides just over half of Sweden's total energy. To reduce its import dependency, Sweden began a nuclear power program in the 1970's. By the mid-1980's, hydroelectric and nuclear power were supplying almost all of Sweden's energy requirements. In 1980, safety concerns led to a national referendum and a plan to phase out Sweden's nuclear generating plants, but only one has since been decommissioned. Until alternative sources of energy are developed, Sweden's nuclear plants will remain essential.

Transportation. The transportation system in Sweden is well developed. A rail network connects most of the country. Sweden's highway systems and foreign and domestic air services are also well developed; the main international airports include Arlanda, in Stockholm, and Göteborg-Landvetter, near Göteborg. In July 2000, the Öresund Bridge opened, connecting Sweden and Denmark and completing a ground-based travel network that runs from far northern Scandinavia to southern Italy.

Communication. Sweden is a leader in information technology, based on studies of personal computer, Internet, and wireless phone use, as well as telecommunications systems, freedom of the press, and education levels. There are about 170 television stations and about 270 radio stations. In Stockholm, the most widely read daily newspapers include *Dagens Nyheter* and *Expressen*.

▶ MAJOR CITIES

Stockholm is Sweden's capital and largest city, as well as its commercial, industrial, and cultural center. Situated on the country's eastern coast, it is built on islands as well as part of the mainland. The city's population is about 800,000. Because of its many waterways, it is often called the Venice of the

Riddarholmen is one of the many islands on which the old city of Stockholm was built. It is the site of Riddarholm Church, where Sweden's kings are buried.

North. Stockholm was founded in the mid-1200's and became the capital in 1523. See the article on Stockholm in this volume.

Göteborg is a seaport on the Kattegat, an arm of the North Sea, at the mouth of the Göta River. It is the country's second largest city with a population of about 500,000. Göteborg was founded in the early 1600's. It is a center for shipbuilding, engineering, automobile manufacturing, and education.

Malmö is part of a growing economic, cultural, and educational region that includes the Danish capital of Copenhagen. It is Sweden's third largest city, with a population of approximately 300,000.

▶ CULTURAL HERITAGE

Literature. Sweden has contributed important figures to the world of literature. August Strindberg revolutionized the drama with such plays as *The Father* (1887), *Miss Julie* (1888), and *The Ghost Sonata* (1907). Pär Lagerkvist was a poet and novelist as well as a dramatist. Selma Lagerlöf, best known for her novel *Gösta Berling* (1891), was the first Swede (and the first woman) to win the Nobel Prize for literature, in 1909. The creator of the Nobel Prizes, Alfred Nobel, was a Swedish industrialist. Author Astrid Lindgren is well-known for her children's book, *Pippi Longstocking* (1945). (See the article SCANDINAVIAN LITERATURE and the biographies of Nobel and Strindberg in the appropriate volumes.)

Music. In music, two of Sweden's leading composers were Franz Berwald and Hugo Alfvén. Several Swedish singers have gained international fame in opera roles, including Jenny Lind (called the Swedish Nightingale) in the 1800's and Birgit Nilsson, Jussi Björling, and Nicolai Gedda in the 1900's. The famous Swedish rock music group ABBA first became popular in the 1970's.

Art. Talented painters emerged in Sweden in the 1600's, including David Klocker Ehrenstrahl. Major artists of the 1700's include C. G. Pilo, Alexander Roslin, and J. T. Sergel. Leading figures of the 1800's and 1900's include painters Anders Zorn and Carl Larsson and the sculptor Carl Milles. Swedes also helped develop the Scandinavian Modern design style, characterized by its clean lines and functionality.

Film. Among Sweden's best-known film directors are Ingmar Bergman, Victor Sjöström, and Mauritz Stiller. Famous actors Greta Garbo, Ingrid Bergman, and Max von Sydow began their careers in Sweden.

▶ **GOVERNMENT**

Sweden has been a constitutional monarchy since 1809. The monarch is the official head of state but, under a constitution that went into effect in 1975, performs only ceremonial duties. The present monarch, King Charles XVI Gustav, came to the throne in 1973. Executive authority rests with the prime minister, who is the head of government and leads the cabinet of ministers. The prime minister and cabinet are responsible to the legislative body, the Riksdag, which consists of 349 members elected for 4-year terms. The Speaker of the Riksdag nominates the prime minister, who must then be approved by the full membership of the legislature.

Seven political parties are represented in the Swedish parliament; additional parties participate in elections. The largest party, the Social Democrats, has held power since the early 1930's, except for the periods between 1976–82 and 1991–94, when the country was governed by non-Socialist coalitions.

The Swedes have a long tradition of local self-government. The country is divided into 2 regions, 18 counties, and 290 municipalities, all of which have authority over local matters.

▶ **HISTORY**

Little is known of Swedish history before the Viking period (about A.D. 800–1000). Sweden was not yet united as a country, and people were organized along family, tribal, and regional lines. Two important groups were the Svear and the Götar, and warfare was common between them. In the 800's, the Svear seem to have won control over most of the center of modern-day Sweden. The Swedish name for Sweden—Sverige—comes from *Svea rike,* meaning "realm of the Svear."

Swedish Vikings traveled eastward across the Baltic Sea and into the rivers of Russia. In the 800's and 900's their trade contacts reached Constantinople (modern Istanbul), the Caspian Sea, and Asia. Some believe a Swedish Viking chieftain, Rurik, was the founder of the first Russian royal dynasty. Finland came under Swedish rule in the 1100's.

In 1397, the Union of Kalmar joined the kingdoms of Sweden, Denmark, and Norway under the Danish monarchy. The Swedes resisted Danish domination, which was ended in 1523, when Gustav Vasa came to the Swedish throne as King Gustav I.

Rise and Decline of Swedish Power. Under Gustav I and his successors, Sweden became a military and economic power. Gustav II Adolf, known as Gustavus Adolphus, won brilliant victories in the Thirty Years' War (1618–48) before his death in battle in 1632. At this time, his daughter and only

An angel sculpture by Carl Milles, Sweden's best-known modern sculptor. Many of Milles's works are exhibited at Millesgården, a park on an island near Stockholm.

heir, Christina, became queen of Sweden at age 6. (See the article CHRISTINA.) As a result of the war, Sweden gained territory in northern Germany and became a leading force in the Baltic region. In 1638, Sweden founded a short-lived colony in America called New Sweden, in what are now parts of Delaware, Pennsylvania, and New Jersey.

Constantly challenged by its neighbors, Sweden fought a series of wars, mainly with Denmark, Russia, and Poland, to maintain its Baltic empire. The last of these, the Great Northern War (1700–

Victories by Gustavus Adolphus in the Thirty Years' War helped make Sweden a leading Baltic power in the 1600's.

21), was disastrous for Sweden. The Swedish king Charles XII at first won spectacular successes. But his defeat by the Russians under Czar Peter the Great at the Battle of Poltava in 1709 marked the beginning of Sweden's decline as a great power. By the time the war ended in 1721, Sweden had lost most of its Baltic empire.

Constitutional Monarchy. The loss of Finland to Russia in 1809 during the Napoleonic Wars (begun by the French emperor and general Napoleon, in an attempt to conquer Europe) contributed to the overthrow of King Gustav IV. A new constitution was adopted and the Riksdag chose a foreigner—Jean Baptiste Bernadotte, a talented marshal of Napoleon's army—as crown prince. In 1814, after Napoleon's defeat, Norway was acquired from Denmark to offset the loss of Finland. The union of Sweden and Norway lasted until 1905, when Norway gained its independence. Bernadotte, the founder of the present Swedish royal house, came to the throne in 1818 as King Charles XIV John.

Emigration. Rapid population growth, lack of religious freedom, and other conditions led large numbers of Swedes to emigrate. Between about 1850 and 1930 some 1.3 million Swedes left, mainly for the United States. Although some emigration from Sweden continues today, the country has attracted many immigrants since the 1960's.

Foreign Affairs. Since 1815, Sweden has chosen to remain nonaligned during times of peace and neutral during wars. It has built up its armed forces to protect its neutral status. Swedes have been involved in humanitarian activities and international organizations such as the United Nations. Raoul Wallenberg worked to rescue Hungarian Jews from the Holocaust in 1944 and probably died in a Soviet prison. (See the article WALLENBERG, RAOUL.) Count Folke Bernadotte was assassinated while trying to mediate an end to the Arab-Israeli war in 1948. Dag Hammarskjöld, the second Secretary-General of the United Nations, was killed in a plane crash while on a peace mission in Africa in 1961. Swedish troops often serve in the United Nations peacekeeping efforts.

Modern Times. The growth of Swedish industry, beginning in the early 1900's, brought great change. From the 1930's on, Sweden, led for almost half a century by the Social Democrats, developed a social welfare system that guaranteed the necessities of life to all Swedes. In the late 1900's, Swedes often enjoyed the highest standard of living in the world.

Sweden Today. Sweden faces many problems similar to other developed nations, including economic slowdown and rising welfare-system costs. In a country where violence is rare, Swedes were shocked by the assassinations of Prime Minister Olof Palme in 1986 and Foreign Minister Anna Lindh in 2003.

But the country remains affluent. In 1995, Sweden joined the European Union (EU) but voted against adopting the common currency (the euro) in 2003. Sweden's membership in the EU, along with the country's government reform programs and its ability to adapt well to economic change, are important factors in keeping its prosperity. So, too, are Swedish efforts to build greater cooperation in Scandinavia and the Baltic.

Reviewed by BYRON J. NORDSTROM
Gustavus Adolphus College

See also LAPLAND; SCANDINAVIA.

Jonathan Swift is best known as the author of *Gulliver's Travels* (1726). Enjoyed by children for its fantasy, the book can also be read as a powerful satire.

SWIFT, JONATHAN (1667–1745)

Jonathan Swift, best known as the author of *Gulliver's Travels,* was born in Dublin, Ireland, on November 30, 1667. His father, an Englishman who had come to Ireland to seek his fortune, had died a few months before. For most of his life, Swift traveled back and forth between England and Ireland. He was educated at Kilkenny School and at Trinity College, in Dublin.

Swift stayed at Trinity to earn his master's degree until the Irish rebellion of 1689 forced him, as an English subject, to leave Ireland. He then became companion and secretary to Sir William Temple, a distant relative and retired diplomat. At Moor Park, Temple's home in Surrey, England, Swift met and tutored Esther Johnson, whom he called Stella. His letters to her were published after his death as the *Journal to Stella.* Swift never married.

Swift was ordained a priest in the Anglican Church and in 1701 received his doctor of divinity degree. In 1713 he was appointed dean of St. Patrick's Cathedral in Dublin.

After the publication of *A Tale of a Tub* (1704), which makes fun of some of the practices and teachings of the church, Swift began building a reputation as a wit. When Queen Anne's Tory ministers needed someone to write political pamphlets, they asked Swift. He wrote attacks against the Whigs, but when Queen Anne died in 1714, Swift's friends fell from power.

Swift returned to Dublin, feeling as though he had been exiled from England. About 1720 he began writing *Gulliver's Travels,* an imaginative work that was an immediate success when it was published in 1726. It has been considered a classic ever since, read by children as a fantasy and by adults as a satire, and it ensured Swift's place as the grand master of 18th-century prose style.

Swift's other satires include *The Drapier's Letters* (1724–25) and *A Modest Proposal* (1729), a humorous but bitter condemnation of the ways in which England, in Swift's view, made poor slaves of the Irish.

Swift died on October 19, 1745, and was buried in St. Patrick's Cathedral, under an epitaph he had composed himself.

Reviewed by DORIS L. EDER
Yale University

▶GULLIVER'S TRAVELS

Jonathan Swift's *Gulliver's Travels,* published in England in 1726, tells the story of Lemuel Gulliver and his travels through imaginary lands. The following excerpt is taken from Gulliver's first adventure, which was in Lilliput, a country whose inhabitants are only 6 inches tall.

It would not be proper, for some reasons, to trouble the reader with the particulars of our adventures in those seas: let it suffice to inform him, that in our passage from thence to the East Indies, we were driven by a violent storm to the northwest of Van Diemen's Land. By an observation, we found ourselves in the latitude of 30 degrees 2 minutes south. Twelve of our crew were dead by immoderate labor and ill food, the rest were in a very weak condition. On the fifth of November, which was the beginning of summer in those parts, the weather being very hazy, the seamen spied a rock, within half a cable's length of the ship; but the wind was so strong, that we were driven directly upon it, and immediately split. Six of the crew, of whom I was one, having let down the boat into the sea, made a shift to get clear of the ship, and the rock. We rowed by my computation about three leagues, till we

Gulliver's Travels describes the adventures of Lemuel Gulliver, an Englishman, on four voyages to imaginary lands. In this scene Gulliver has been shipwrecked on the island of Lilliput and captured by its inhabitants, tiny humanlike creatures only six inches tall.

were able to work no longer, being already spent with labor while we were in the ship. We therefore trusted ourselves to the mercy of the waves, and in about half an hour the boat was overset by a sudden flurry from the north. What became of my companions in the boat, as well as of those who escaped on the rock, or were left in the vessel, I cannot tell; but conclude they were all lost. For my own part, I swam as fortune directed me, and was pushed forward by wind and tide. I often let my legs drop, and could feel no bottom: but when I was almost gone, and able to struggle no longer, I found myself within my depth; and by this time the storm was much abated. The declivity was so small, that I walked near a mile before I got to the shore, which I conjectured was about eight o'clock in the evening. I then advanced forward near half a mile, but could not discover any sign of houses or inhabitants; at least I was in so weak a con-

dition, that I did not observe them. I was extremely tired, and with that, and the heat of the weather, and about half a pint of brandy that I drank as I left the ship, I found myself much inclined to sleep. I lay down on the grass, which was very short and soft, where I slept sounder than ever I remember to have done in my life, and, as I reckoned, above nine hours; for when I awakened, it was just daylight. I attempted to rise, but was not able to stir: for, as I happened to lie on my back, I found my arms and legs were strongly fastened on each side to the ground; and my hair, which was long and thick, tied down in the same manner. I likewise felt several slender ligatures across my body, from my armpits to my thighs. I could only look upwards; the sun began to grow hot, and the light offended my eyes. I heard a confused noise about me, but in the posture I lay, could see nothing except the sky. In a little time I felt something alive moving on my left leg, which advancing gently forward over my breast, came almost up to my chin; when bending my eyes downwards as much as I could, I perceived it to be a human creature not six inches high, with a bow and arrow in his hands, and a quiver at his back. In the meantime, I felt at least forty more of the same kind (as I conjectured) following the first. I was in the utmost astonishment, and roared so loud, that they all ran back in a fright; and some of them, as I was afterwards told, were hurt with the falls they got by leaping from my sides upon the ground. However, they soon returned, and one of them, who ventured so far as to get a full sight of my face, lifting up his hands and eyes by way of admiration, cried out in a shrill but distinct voice, *Hekinah degul:* the others repeated the same words several times, but I then knew not what they meant. I lay all this while, as the reader may believe, in great uneasiness: at length, struggling to get loose, I had the fortune to break the strings, and wrench out the pegs that fastened my left arm to the ground; for, by lifting it up to my face, I discovered the methods they had taken to bind me, and at the same time, with a violent pull, which gave me excessive pain, I a little loosened the strings that tied down my hair on the left side, so that I was just able to turn my head about two inches. But the creatures ran off a second time, before I could seize them; whereupon there was a great shout in a very shrill accent, and after it ceased, I heard one of them cry aloud, *Tolgo phonac;* when in an instant I felt above a hundred arrows discharged on my left hand, which pricked me like so many needles; and besides they shot another flight into the air, as we do bombs in Europe, whereof many, I suppose, fell on my body (though I felt them not) and some on my face, which I immediately covered with my left hand. When this shower of arrows was over, I fell a groaning with grief and pain, and then striving to get loose, they discharged another volley larger than the first, and some of them attempted with spears to stick me in the sides; but, by good luck, I had on me a buff jerkin, which they could not pierce. I thought it the most prudent method to lie still, and my design was to continue so till night, when, my left hand being already loose, I could easily free myself: and as for the inhabitants, I had reason to believe I might be a match for the greatest armies they could bring against me, if they were all of the same size with him that I saw. But fortune disposed otherwise of me.

SWIMMING

Swimming is one of the most healthful of sports. Nearly every muscle of the body is used and regular practice helps a person develop coordination and strength. Millions of people swim regularly in rivers, lakes, and oceans all over the world. Indoor pools have made swimming a year-round sport.

▶ LEARNING TO SWIM

The best place to learn to swim is in a pool, where supervision and coaching are easiest. The first thing a beginner should learn is how to float and tread water. Floating allows a swimmer to stay on top of the water with little or no effort, and it is necessary when swimming long distances. Treading water is something like walking in deep water.

The Strokes

After the beginner has learned to float, the exciting part of swimming—learning the strokes—begins.

It is important to learn how to swim from a good instructor and in a safe place, such as a pool, where advice and rescue are close by.

In competitive swimming, getting a good start and maintaining strong, accurate strokes throughout a race are essential. Constant practice helps a swimmer achieve good form and endurance.

Breaststroke. This is the easiest stroke to use for long distances. It allows you to take a breath during each stroke as you lift your head above water. In the breaststroke, your arms and legs bend deeply and then straighten out quickly to propel you forward.

Backstroke. Learning how to float on your back helps you learn the backstroke, which is restful and useful in distance swimming. Its movements are similar to those of the crawl except that you are lying faceup in the water, so breathing is not difficult. Because you are on your back, your arms move in a backward circular motion to help propel you forward. Both strokes use the flutter kick, in which your feet alternate moving up and down in the water with your knees slightly bent.

Sidestroke. In this stroke, your body is turned sideways, to whichever side is more comfortable, and your lower arm sweeps through the water in a forward circular motion. Using the scissors kick, your legs separate, knees bent, and then come together and straighten out quickly to propel you forward.

Crawl, or Freestyle. You use the flutter kick as your arms alternate moving in and out of the water in a forward circular motion. You breathe as you lift your head above the water and exhale when your head is under the water.

Butterfly Stroke. Although classified as a breaststroke, the butterfly has arm movements similar to those used in the crawl, except that both arms make the stroke at the same time. You breathe as you lift your head out of the water and exhale as you move it under the water. You use what is called a dolphin kick —your feet move up and down in the water at the same time—during each stroke. The butterfly is used mostly in competition.

▶**CONDITIONING FOR COMPETITIVE SWIMMING**

A championship swimmer must have physical endurance and strength, as well as flexibility of the joints of the shoulders, ankles, thighs, and backs of the legs. There are many exercises that will help develop the flexibility necessary to be a good swimmer.

Strength can be developed by a good general physical conditioning program. Exercises that develop specific muscles can also be helpful to the aspiring champion.

Endurance can be built up by constant practice and correct execution of the various swimming strokes. Learn to swim about a mile—first in broken stages—using all the different strokes. After a while you will be able to swim a mile with little or no rest between changes in the strokes.

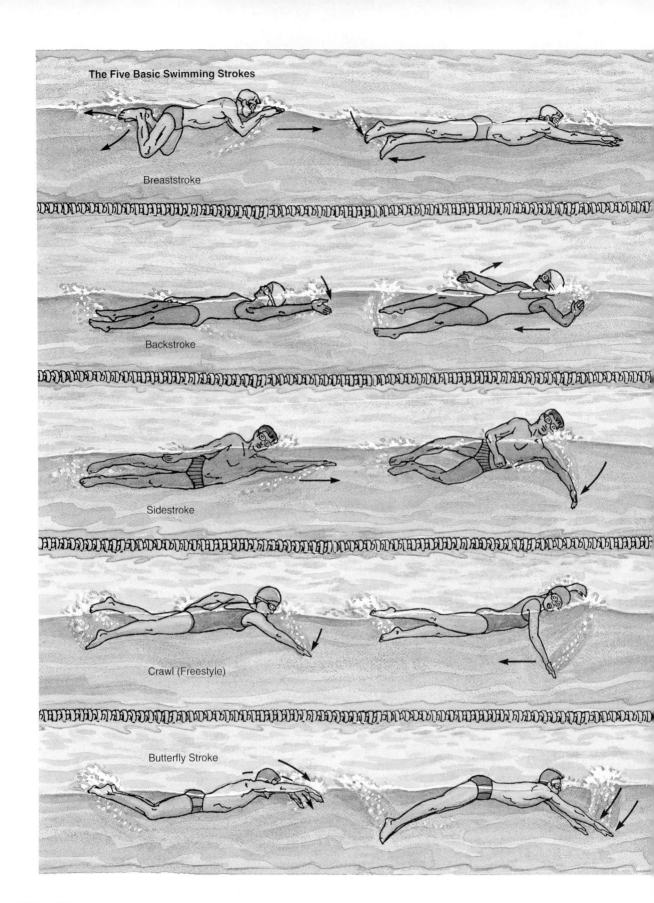

The Five Basic Swimming Strokes

Breaststroke

Backstroke

Sidestroke

Crawl (Freestyle)

Butterfly Stroke

Human beings are not natural swimmers. Originally they must have learned to swim by watching animals that swim by instinct. Swimming was undoubtedly important to the survival of early humans, but its rise as a sport has been comparatively recent.

Swimming as a sport goes back only to the early 1800's. By 1837 there were six swimming pools in London. The popularity of the sport continued to grow, and in 1869 the formation of the Amateur Swimming Association of Great Britain was the first step toward organized swimming competition.

In the United States, competitive swimming became organized with the founding of the Amateur Athletic Union in 1888. The sport grew rapidly, and by the 1920's the United States dominated most international swimming events. Outstanding in the development of swimming were Sydney Cavill (?–1945), coach of the Olympic Swimming Club in San Francisco; Robert J. H. Kiphuth (1890–1967), swimming coach at Yale University and frequent Olympic coach; and the Women's Swimming Association in New York City, whose coach, Lewis de B. Handley (?–1956), produced many stars, including Gertrude Ederle (1906–2003), the first woman to swim the English Channel. Today, many nations besides the United States have strong competitive swimmers, especially Australia, Canada, Germany, and some of the countries of the former Soviet Union, which swam as a single team, the Unified Team, in the 1992 Summer Olympics.

The international popularity of competitive swimming has gone hand in hand with the revival of the Olympic Games. Swimming was included in the first modern games in Athens in 1896, and swimming is now second in popularity only to track-and-field events.

Gertrude Ederle set many world swimming records and won several U.S. freestyle swimming championships. At the 1924 Olympic Games she won one gold medal and two bronze medals. In 1926, she became the first woman to swim the English Channel.

At first, only the breaststroke was used in racing. In time, other strokes were used as well, and racers developed new ways to swim faster. The first important new stroke was the sidearm stroke, or sidestroke. This was an alternating arm stroke in which the swimmer lay on his or her side in the water. The kick was changed from a frog action to a more propulsive scissors action. Then some swimmers found that by lifting the top arm out of the water during the recovery and reaching straight out overhead, they could make a full 180-degree arm stroke. This became known as the overarm sidestroke.

Sometime in the late 1800's an Englishman named John Trudgen visited South America. There he saw people swimming with a two armed alternating stroke. Trudgen mastered this method and taught it to swimmers in England, most notably to J. H. Derbyshire, who in 1897 swam 100 yards in 60 seconds. Derbyshire's feat brought great fame and the stroke became known as the trudgen. The scissors kick was still used.

In 1902 Richard Cavill (?–1938), an Australian, set a new world's record by swimming 100 yards in 58.6 seconds. Cavill used an arm stroke similar to Trudgen's, but he changed the kick from the scissors to an up-and-down flutter kick. His style became known as the Australian crawl. Cavill had learned this kick from his father, Frederick Cavill (1839–1927), an Englishman who had emigrated to Australia in 1878. The elder Cavill noticed that people on islands in the Pacific Ocean used a flutter kick, and he taught it to his sons.

Richard Cavill's brother Sydney moved to San Francisco, California, in 1903 to coach the Olympic Club there. Among his first students was J. Scott Leary, who in 1905 became the first American to swim 100 yards in 60 seconds. Leary's success attracted the attention of Charles M. Daniels, an athlete at the New York Athletic Club, who developed a flutter kick with six beats to each full arm cycle. Using this method, Daniels lowered the 100-yard record to 54.8 seconds in 1910. It became known as the American crawl.

Duke Kahanamoku (1890–1968) of Hawaii went to San Francisco in 1913, and using a crawl stroke with a six-beat flutter kick, lowered the 100-yard record to 54.6 seconds. A self-taught swimmer, Kahanamoku said he learned the stroke from Hawaiian islanders.

GREAT SWIMMERS IN THE HISTORY OF THE SPORT

The International Swimming Hall of Fame, established in 1965, is located in Fort Lauderdale, Florida. Many of the best swimmers are honored in the Hall of Fame, and some of them are profiled here. Some of the American swimmers also have received the James E. Sullivan Memorial Trophy. Inaugurated in 1930, the Sullivan Trophy is given annually by the AAU to the amateur athlete in any sport who "has done the most during the year to advance the cause of sportsmanship."

MATT BIONDI (1965–) won 7 medals, including 5 golds, at the 1988 Olympic Games. He was the first U.S. swimmer to win gold medals in 3 Olympiads and the first to win gold medals in the same Olympic event (the 400-meter freestyle relay). During his career, he broke 7 world and 16 American records, earned 15 international titles, 17 U.S. national crowns, and 8 NCAA national championships. Biondi was elected to the International Swimming Hall of Fame in 1997.

TRACY CAULKINS (1963–) was the first swimmer—male or female—to hold American records in every stroke. During her career, she set 63 American records, including 4 (200-meter and 400-meter individual medley, 100-meter breaststroke, and 200-meter butterfly) in her final year of competition. The winner of 3 gold medals at the 1984 Olympics, she received the Sullivan Trophy in 1978 and was elected to the International Swimming Hall of Fame in 1990.

MATT BIONDI

TRACY CAULKINS

FLORENCE CHADWICK (1918– 95) was an American swimmer known for her outdoor distance swimming. She was the second woman to swim across the English Channel, making the crossing in 1950 from France to England in a then-record time of 13 hours and 23 minutes, and the first to cross it both ways, making the England to France

FLORENCE CHADWICK

DONNA DE VARONA

JANET EVANS

DAWN FRASER

crossing 3 times, in 1951, 1953, and 1955. At one time she held the men's and the women's world records for swimming across the Catalina Channel, off the California coast, making the first successful attempt by a woman in 1952. Her many achievements included successfully swimming the Strait of Gibraltar, the Dardanelles, and the Bosporus. Chadwick was elected to the International Swimming Hall of Fame in 1970.

DONNA DE VARONA (1947–), considered one of the best American female swimmers of the early 1960's, went on to become the first female sportscaster on network TV. During her swimming career, she held 8 world and 10 American records. In 1964, she won 2 Olympic gold medals (400-meter individual medley and 400-meter freestyle relay) and was voted America's Outstanding Woman Athlete. She was elected to the International Swimming Hall of Fame in 1969.

JANET EVANS (1971–) won 3 gold medals (400-meter individual medley, 400-meter freestyle, and 800-meter freestyle) at the 1988 Olympics and another gold (800-meter freestyle) at the 1992 Olympics. In 1989, Evans received the Sullivan Trophy and also was named Sportswoman of the Year by the U.S. Olympic Committee. During her career, she won 5 national and 17 international titles. She was elected to the International Swimming Hall of Fame in 2001.

DAWN FRASER (1937–), one of Australia's greatest swimmers, won 8 Olympic medals—4 gold and 4 silver—at the 1956, 1960, and 1964 Olympic Games. She won the same event (the 100-meter freestyle) in all three of those Olympics. In 1962, she became the first woman to break the 1-minute barrier in 100 meters, swimming the distance in 59.9 seconds. In 1965, she became one of the charter members of the International Swimming Hall of Fame.

MICHAEL GROSS (1964–), nicknamed the Albatross for his long armspan, won multiple world and European titles and set 4 world records during his career. At the 1984 Olympics, he won the 200-meter freestyle by more than two body lengths and set a world record in the process. In doing so, he became the first German to win an Olympic swimming title. He also won a silver medal in the 200-meter butterfly. In 1988, Gross won that butterfly event and set an Olympic record. He was elected to the International Swimming Hall of Fame in 1995.

MARY T. MEAGHER (1964–) was known as Madame Butterfly for her excellence in that stroke. In 1981, she set a world record in the 200-meter butterfly that stood for 19 years. Her world record in the 100-meter butterfly, also set in 1981, lasted 18 years. At the 1984 Olympic Games, she won the gold medal in both the 100-meter and 200-meter butterfly. She won another gold medal as a member of the United States' 400-meter medley relay team. Meagher was also a two-time world champion (1982, 100-meter butterfly; 1986, 200-meter butterfly). She was elected to the International Swimming Hall of Fame in 1993.

PABLO MORALES (1964–) was a top American swimmer for over a decade. His rivalry with Michael Gross in the 1980's was one of the most exciting in the sport. At the 1984 Olympics, Morales beat his own world record in the 100-meter butterfly only to be outdone by Gross. At the 1992 Olympics, he won gold medals in the 100-meter butterfly and the 400-meter medley relay. He was elected to the International Swimming Hall of Fame in 1998.

JOHN NABER (1956–) won 4 gold medals at the 1976 Olympics, 2 of which (the 100- and 200-meter backstroke) set world

MICHAEL GROSS

MARY T. MEAGHER

PABLO MORALES

JOHN NABER

MARK SPITZ

AMY VAN DYKEN

JOHNNY WEISSMULLER

records. He also won a silver in the 200-meter freestyle. For his efforts, he was named 1976 Male Swimmer of the Year. In 1977, he won 3 gold medals at the Pan Am Games and received the Sullivan Trophy. He was elected to the International Swimming Hall of Fame in 1982.

MARK SPITZ (1950–) will always be remembered as the first person to win 7 gold medals at a single Olympics, setting world records in each of the events at the 1972 Games. During his career, he won 11 Olympic medals, set 26 world and 25 American records, and won 8 national titles, including 4 for the 100-meter butterfly. Spitz was awarded the Sullivan Trophy in 1971 and was elected to the International Swimming Hall of Fame in 1977.

AMY VAN DYKEN (1973–) was the first American woman to win four gold medals at one Olympics (1996). In addition to her individual triumphs in the 50-meter freestyle and 100-meter butterfly, she was a member of the teams that won the 400-meter freestyle relay and the 400-meter medley relay. At the 2000 Olympic Games, she won a fifth gold medal in the 400-meter freestyle relay as her team set a new world record. Prior to the Olympics, Van Dyken was named 1994 Swimmer of the Year by the National Collegiate Athletic Association (NCAA). She then won three gold medals at both the 1995 Pan Am Games and the 1998 world championships.

JOHNNY WEISSMULLER (1904–84) was the first swimmer to win 5 gold medals in Olympic competition. In 1924, he won the 100-meter freestyle, the 400-meter freestyle, and the 800-meter freestyle relay. Four years later, at the 1928 Games, he again won the 100-meter freestyle and the 800-meter freestyle relay. During his career, he set 51 world records. His 100-meter freestyle record of 51 seconds stood for 17 years. In 1965, he became one of the charter members of the International Swimming Hall of Fame.

AAU   Amateur Athletic Union
NCAA   National Collegiate Athletic Association

SWIMMING WORLD RECORDS—MEN*

Event	Record	Holder	Country
FREESTYLE			
50 meters	21.64 sec.	Alexander Popov	Russia
100 meters	47.84 sec.	Pieter van den Hoogenband	Netherlands
200 meters	1 min. 44.06 sec.	Ian Thorpe	Australia
400 meters	3 min. 40.08 sec.	Ian Thorpe	Australia
800 meters	7 min. 38.65 sec.	Grant Hackett	Australia
1,500 meters	14 min. 34.56 sec.	Grant Hackett	Australia
BACKSTROKE			
100 meters	53.17 sec.	Aaron Peirsol	United States
200 meters	1 min. 54.66 sec.	Aaron Peirsol	United States
BREASTSTROKE			
100 meters	59.30 sec.	Brendan Hansen	United States
200 meters	2 min. 09.04 sec.	Brendan Hansen	United States
BUTTERFLY			
100 meters	50.40 sec.	Ian Crocker	United States
200 meters	1 min. 53.93 sec.	Michael Phelps	United States
INDIVIDUAL MEDLEY			
200 meters	1 min. 55.94 sec.	Michael Phelps	United States
400 meters	4 min. 08.26 sec.	Michael Phelps	United States
FREESTYLE RELAY			
400 meters	3 min. 13.17 sec.	Roland Schoeman, Lyndon Ferns, Darian Townsend, Ryk Neethling	South Africa
800 meters	7 min. 04.66 sec.	Ian Thorpe, William Kirby, Grant Hackett, Michael Klim	Australia
MEDLEY RELAY			
400 meters	3 min. 30.68 sec.	Aaron Peirsol, Ian Crocker, Brendan Hansen, Jason Lezak	United States

SWIMMING WORLD RECORDS—WOMEN*

Event	Record	Holder	Country
FREESTYLE			
50 meters	24.13 sec.	Inge de Bruijn	Netherlands
100 meters	53.52 sec.	Jodie Henry	Australia
200 meters	1 min. 56.64 sec.	Franziska Van Almsick	Germany
400 meters	4 min. 03.85 sec.	Janet Evans	United States
800 meters	8 min. 16.22 sec.	Janet Evans	United States
1,500 meters	15 min. 52.10 sec.	Janet Evans	United States
BACKSTROKE			
100 meters	59.58 sec.	Natalie Couglin	United States
200 meters	2 min. 06.62 sec.	Kristina Egerszegi	Hungary
BREASTSTROKE			
100 meters	1 min. 06.20 sec.	Jessica Hardy	United States
200 meters	2 min. 21.72 sec.	Leisel Jones	Australia
BUTTERFLY			
100 meters	56.61 sec.	Inge de Bruijn	Netherlands
200 meters	2 min. 05.61 sec.	Otylia Jedrzejczak	Poland
INDIVIDUAL MEDLEY			
200 meters	2 min. 09.72 sec.	Wu Yanyan	China
400 meters	4 min. 33.59 sec.	Yana Klochkova	Ukraine
FREESTYLE RELAY			
400 meters	3 min. 35.94 sec.	Alice Mills, Lisbeth Lenton, Petria Thomas, Jodie Henry	Australia
800 meters	7 min. 53.42 sec.	Natalie Coughlin, Carly Piper, Dana Vollmer, Kaitlin Sandeno	United States
MEDLEY RELAY			
400 meters	3 min. 57.32 sec.	Giaan Rooney, Leisel Jones, Petria Thomas, Jodie Henry	Australia

*Records as of September 2005, recognized by the Fédération Internationale de Natation (FINA). All records for long-course (50-meter) pool.

Along with development in the crawl, or freestyle, came growth and change in other swimming strokes: the breaststroke, the backstroke, and in 1935 the butterfly. No sport proves the old saying that "records are made to be broken" better than swimming.

Today there are many different national and international events in competitive swimming. At the Olympic Games there are four basic racing categories—freestyle, backstroke, breaststroke, and butterfly—as well as relay and medley races made up of combinations of these four. Each category is run at more than one distance.

Perhaps the most significant event in the history of competitive swimming occurred in 1908 with the formation of the Fédération Internationale de Natation (FINA), or the International Federation of Swimming. The creation of FINA came about largely in response to disorganized and questionable swimming events at the 1900 and 1904 Olympic Games. Since its formation, FINA has been the world governing body for swimming, with authority over all international swimming competitions. FINA's responsibilities now also include competitive diving, water polo, and synchronized swimming.

ROBERT J. H. KIPHUTH
Author, *Swimming*
Former Head Swimming Coach
Yale University

SWITZERLAND

Switzerland is a small nation located in west central Europe. It is bordered by the nations of France, Germany, Austria, Liechtenstein, and Italy. A mountainous country, Switzerland is known for the scenic grandeur of its snowcapped Alps, which are among the highest mountain peaks in western Europe.

Switzerland is in many ways a land of contradictions. It has few mineral resources and little good soil for farming. Yet it is a prosperous country, with one of the world's highest standards of living. It is one of Europe's oldest republics, whose people are all called Swiss. But it has no single Swiss language. Instead, its people speak four different national languages. The Swiss are proud of their individuality, yet they have learned to co-operate with each other to make their democratic society work effectively. The Swiss were once famed throughout Europe as soldiers, and Swiss men must still undergo military training. Yet Switzerland has long followed a policy of neutrality and has not been involved in a foreign war in nearly two centuries.

▶ THE PEOPLE

Most Swiss come from three distinct cultural backgrounds: German, French, and Italian. Each group has preserved its own language, traditions, and customs.

Language. The official languages of Switzerland are German, French, Italian, and Romansch. German is spoken by about 65 percent of the population, mainly in the central and northern cantons (states). Approximately 19 percent of the Swiss, mostly in the western cantons, speak French. Italian is spoken by about 10 percent of the people, most of whom live in the southern canton of Ticino. Romansch, a very old language derived from Latin, is spoken by less than one percent of the people, mostly in the canton of Grabünden (Grisons) in eastern Switzerland. Schools use the language spoken by the people of the region, but a second language is always taught.

Religion. The Swiss are about equally divided between Roman Catholics and Protestant sects. Religious freedom is guaranteed to all the people.

Cattle graze on lush pastures in Switzerland's picturesque mountain villages during the summer months. Dairy products are the most important part of the country's agricultural economy.

Education. Swiss children must attend school full-time until they are 16. After completing primary school, some students enter a three- or four-year apprenticeship program to learn a trade. Those who do must continue their general education at night on a part-time basis until the age of 19. Other students continue studying full-time, either at vocational (trade) schools or at schools that train them for admission to a university. Swiss universities have a worldwide reputation for excellence, and they attract many students from foreign countries.

In addition to the public school system, Switzerland is known for its private schools, many of them very expensive, which draw students from all over the world.

Way of Life. More than 60 percent of Switzerland's people live in cities. As in cities elsewhere, most Swiss work in commerce and industry. The work day and the school day both traditionally begin early—7:00 A.M. in summer and 8:00 A.M. in winter. Offices and schools usually have a two-hour lunch break at noon, when the entire family comes home for the main meal of the day. The business day usually ends at 6:00 P.M.

Most Swiss farmers live in villages situated on the country's central plateau or in the valleys and lower slopes of the Alps. The raising of dairy cattle is their most important activity. In winter, however, when many mountain villages are snowbound, outdoor work stops. Indoors, the men work at wood carving and other handicrafts, while the women spin and weave woolen cloth and make lace and embroidery. When spring comes, farming resumes. Cowherds begin the yearly drive of cattle up the mountain slopes, following the melting snow, in search of pasture.

Cultural Activities. Almost every city and large town in Switzerland has its own library, theater, and orchestra. The Zurich Playhouse and the Orchestre de la Suisse Romande in Geneva are probably the country's best-known theater and symphony orchestra. Opera, ballet, symphony, and dramatic companies come from all over Europe to Zurich's June festival. Lugano, Lausanne, Lucerne, and other cities and towns have music, ballet, or film festivals.

Each year the town of Interlaken presents special open-air performances of *William Tell*, the play about Switzerland's 14th-century legendary hero. According to legend, Tell was

SWITZERLAND

FACTS and figures

SWISS CONFEDERATION is the official name of the country.

LOCATION: West central Europe.

AREA: 15,943 sq mi (41,293 km²).

POPULATION: 7,000,000 (estimate).

CAPITAL: Bern.

LARGEST CITY: Zurich.

MAJOR LANGUAGES: German, French, Italian, Romansch (all official).

MAJOR RELIGIOUS GROUPS: Roman Catholic, Protestant.

GOVERNMENT: Republic. **Head of state and government**—president (elected annually from membership of the Federal Council). **Legislature**—Federal Assembly (consisting of the National Council and the Council of States).

CHIEF PRODUCTS: Agricultural—dairy products, potatoes, wheat, barley, and other grains, sugar beets, wine grapes, apples, and other fruits. **Manufactured**—textiles, watches, precision optical instruments, cheese, chocolate, machinery, electrical and engineering equipment, chemicals. **Mineral**—salt, limestone.

MONETARY UNIT: Swiss franc (1 franc = 100 centimes, or rappen).

forced to shoot an apple off his son's head with a crossbow, as punishment for resisting the orders of a foreign governor of the canton of Uri. No one knows if the story is true, or even if William Tell ever lived. But he remains a symbol of Swiss independence and determination to resist foreign rule.

Swiss folk culture has been strongly influenced by the traditions developed in the small mountain villages. These traditional activities include flag tossing, folk dancing, yodeling, and music played on Alpine horns, some of which may be 15 feet (4.5 meters) in length.

Sports. From December to April, winter sports enthusiasts are drawn to Switzerland, especially for skiing. In summer, mountain climbers come from all over the world to test their skill against the peaks of the Swiss Alps.

Many people sail and wind surf on the country's many beautiful lakes. Soccer is a favorite sport, as is target shooting with rifles and pistols.

▶ THE LAND

Switzerland has three major geographic regions. The Jura Mountains, which range from about 3,000 to 4,000 feet (900 to 1,200 meters) in height, run along the Swiss-French border. The Swiss Plateau, bounded by Lake Constance in the north and Lake Geneva in the south, is a hilly but not mountainous region that covers about 30 percent of the country. It is the most densely populated region and the site of most of Switzerland's major cities. The mountain ranges known as the Swiss Alps cover more than half the country. Many Al-

Below: Winter resorts, often nestled in small valleys among the Swiss Alps and Jura Mountains, bring thousands of skiers and other winter sports enthusiasts to Switzerland every year. *Right:* National and regional folk festivals and contests, such as Alpine-horn blowing and flag throwing (*above right*) and yodeling (*below right*), help preserve ancient customs, folklore, and costumes. These events are also popular tourist attractions.

pine peaks exceed 12,000 feet (3,600 meters) in height. The highest, Dufourspitze, on the Italian-Swiss border, reaches 15,203 feet (4,634 meters). Slightly lower in elevation but better known are the Matterhorn and the Jungfrau.

The Alps are a continental watershed. Rain, snow, and melted water from the permanent Alpine glaciers (ice fields) feed Switzerland's rivers and lakes. Two of western Europe's most important rivers, the Rhine and the Rhône, rise in the Swiss Alps. Switzerland's many lakes include Geneva, Constance, Neuchâtel, Lucerne, Zurich, and Maggiore.

Land Use. Switzerland has little fertile land. Less than 10 percent is cultivated for crops. About 40 percent is meadow and pasture, used for grazing cows, sheep, and goats.

More than 26 percent of the land is forested. Swiss law requires that all land presently forested must remain so permanently as a conservation measure.

Climate. Switzerland's climate varies considerably, depending on elevation and the amount of protection provided to the valleys by the surrounding mountain ranges. In general, winters are cold and summers mild, but not hot. The mildest winters and warmest summers are found in the area bordering Italy. The higher Alpine peaks are covered with snow year-round.

Switzerland receives a great amount of rain and snow each year. Lower elevations often can be quite damp and foggy. However, there are lengthy periods of sunshine in both winter and summer, especially at higher elevations.

Above: The Rhône River flows through the city of Geneva in southwestern Switzerland near the French border. Geneva is a financial center and the headquarters of many world organizations. It has frequently been the site of important diplomatic conferences. *Left:* The towering peak of the Matterhorn has long challenged mountain climbers.

Most of the people of Zurich, Switzerland's largest city, are German speaking. The city is the country's principal center for commerce and industry and also offers an impressive variety of educational and cultural institutions.

Major Cities. Bern is Switzerland's federal capital. Founded in the 12th century, the city is noted for its buildings dating from the Middle Ages as well as for being the seat of government. Zurich is Switzerland's largest city. A modern city, located in the German-speaking northern part of the country, it is a center of Switzerland's banking, commerce, and manufacturing. See the article on Zurich in Volume W-X-Y-Z.

Basel is a port city on the Rhine River, situated at a point where Switzerland, Germany, and France all meet. It is also a center of Switzerland's chemical industry.

Geneva is perhaps Switzerland's most famous city. Located on Lake Geneva in the French-speaking western part of the country, it was long an independent republic and did not join the Swiss Confederation until 1815. Between World Wars I and II, Geneva was the site of the League of Nations, the forerunner of the United Nations. The city is still frequently chosen as the setting for international diplomatic conferences. It is the headquarters of the International Red Cross, the World Council of Churches, and other organizations. Lausanne, another largely French-speaking city on Lake Geneva, is noted for its beauty, its music festivals and art exhibits, and its many fine private schools.

▶**THE ECONOMY**

Although it is small in size and poor in natural resources, Switzerland is one of the world's most prosperous and highly industrialized nations. Its economy is based chiefly on manufacturing and trade, tourism, and banking.

Manufacturing. Manufacturing is the mainstay of the Swiss economy, providing about 90 percent of the country's exports. Because Switzerland has so few natural resources of its own, it must import industrial raw materials from other countries, which it then fashions into high quality finished products for sale abroad. Switzerland has long been noted for its fine watches, textiles, and precision optical instruments (such as microscopes). Machinery, electrical and engineering equipment, chemicals (especially dyes and drugs), and fabricated metal products are among its chief manufactured goods as well.

Agriculture. Agriculture employs only about 7 percent of the Swiss workforce. Dairy products—milk, butter, and cheese—are by far the most important part of the agricultural economy. Switzerland is known particularly for its cheeses. The chief crops are potatoes, wheat, barley, and other grains, sugar beets, wine grapes, apples, and other fruits. Swiss agriculture can supply only 60 percent of the country's food needs; the rest of Switzerland's food must be imported.

Tourism. Tourism is one of Switzerland's most important industries. Millions of tourists visit Switzerland each year, attracted by the beauty of its Alpine peaks, lakes, and picturesque mountain villages. Resort towns such as St. Moritz, Locarno, Lugano, Interlaken, and Zermatt are world famous.

The Swiss are noted for the high quality and fine crafts-manship of their manufactured goods. Swiss watches (*left*), considered among the finest in the world, are one of the country's chief exports. The Swiss are also famous for making delicious cheeses (*above*), particularly Emmentaler (Swiss cheese) and Gruyère.

Banking. Switzerland is a center of international banking and finance. Swiss banks are closely regulated by the government to ensure privacy. Noted for their stability, they draw wealthy depositors from all over the world.

Energy. Switzerland has no oil and practically no coal with which to fuel its manufacturing industries. However, its many swift mountain streams are an abundant source of hydroelectric power, which provides much of the country's energy needs. Most of the rest is supplied by nuclear power plants.

Transportation. In spite of its mountainous terrain, Switzerland has an excellent transportation network. Tunnels cut through the Alps have enabled the Swiss to build an extensive network of railroads and highways. The St. Gotthard Tunnel, which is more than 10 miles (16 kilometers) in length, is the world's longest highway tunnel. Switzerland's international airline, Swissair, flies to many countries.

▶**GOVERNMENT**

Switzerland is a confederation of 20 cantons and six half cantons, which are somewhat similar to the states of the United States. The newest canton, Jura, was created in 1978. Each canton has its own government. In several of the smaller cantons, citizens gather in open-air meetings to decide local issues by direct vote. The cantons originally were independent states and still retain a good deal of power.

The Federal Government. The Federal Assembly, or federal legislature, is made up of two houses, the National Council and the Council of States. The 200 members of the National Council are elected on the basis of the number of votes cast for each political party in national elections. Each canton elects two representatives to the Council of States. Half cantons elect one representative.

Every four years the Federal Assembly elects a seven-member Federal Council, which acts as the executive branch of the government. Each year the Federal Assembly elects one member of the Federal Council to serve as president and one to serve as vice president.

The Referendum. A unique aspect of Swiss government is the system of the national referendum. By submitting a petition with 30,000 signatures, citizens can vote on any law passed by the Federal Assembly.

Status of Women. Until 1971, Switzerland was the only nation in Europe in which women could not vote in national elections. After years of debate, a referendum was approved in that year extending the vote to women in all national elections and referenda. However, two half cantons continue to resist women's participation in local government.

Defense. The Swiss often refer to their position in international affairs as one of "armed neutrality." Geared entirely to fighting a defensive war if attacked, the Swiss have developed plans for destroying every tunnel, bridge, and mountain pass leading into Switzerland. Unless exempted, all Swiss men between the ages of 20 and 50 are required to participate in active military service, followed by membership in the military reserves.

Early History. The land that is now Switzerland was ruled by various peoples before it emerged as an independent state. The Romans conquered the region, which they called Helvetia, in the 1st century B.C. Germanic tribes invaded the area in the 5th and 6th centuries A.D. Until the end of the 13th century, present-day Switzerland remained under the control of foreign rulers.

Alliance of Three Cantons. In 1291 three cantons—Uri, Schwyz, and Unterwalden—formed an alliance in which they swore to assist each other against foreign domination. The alliance marks the beginning of the Swiss confederation. Switzerland takes its name from one of these cantons, Schwyz.

The confederation fought many battles against the Habsburg rulers of Austria, who claimed Swiss territory. Because of its mountains, however, Switzerland was a natural fortress—easier to defend than to conquer. Though they were usually outnumbered, the Swiss generally were victorious. Other cantons joined the confederation, and Switzerland expanded in size. By 1499 the Swiss had achieved their independence, although it was not officially recognized by other European states until the Peace of Westphalia was signed in 1648.

Religious Wars. During the years between 1500 and 1648, Switzerland was divided by the religious conflicts between the established Roman Catholic Church and the newer Protestant sects. Two leaders of the Protestant Reformation, Huldreich Zwingli and John Calvin, lived in what is now Switzerland during this period. Civil wars continued to threaten Switzerland's stability in the centuries that followed. But the Swiss gift for compromise kept the confederation intact.

Toward a Policy of Neutrality. Because of their skill on the battlefield, Swiss troops were sought after by many European countries. For a time, soldiers became one of Switzerland's main exports. However, in 1515, at the Battle of Marignano (now Melegnano) in Italy, Swiss troops serving as allies of the Italians suffered severe losses fighting against the French. This defeat taught the Swiss that their only chance to survive as a free nation was to stay out of wars between other European countries. Thus, the idea of permanent Swiss neutrality was born.

French Invasion and the Congress of Vienna. In 1798, French troops occupied Switzerland. France established what was called the Helvetic Republic, placing the Swiss cantons under a strong central government. The discontent of many Swiss at the loss of their individual liberties, however, led the French Emperor Napoleon I to restore the confederation in 1803. In 1815, at the Congress of Vienna, a meeting of the European powers, Switzerland's permanent neutrality and present borders were recognized.

The Constitution of 1848. During the 1830's and 1840's, a movement for political change swept over much of Switzerland. Many of the cantons sought liberal reforms within a stronger federal government. Some of the cantons resisted, and a brief civil war broke out in 1847. The victory of the reform group led to the adoption of a constitution in 1848 that provided for a careful balance between the federal government and the governments of the cantons. As revised in 1874, this constitution still governs Switzerland today.

Switzerland Today. Switzerland's history since then has been marked by peace and growing prosperity. Although its neighbors were caught up in two world wars—from 1914 to 1918 and 1939 to 1945—Switzerland was able to keep its neutrality. As a neutral country, it has been a haven for refugees from war and has served as a channel of communications between hostile nations. The city of Geneva has also been the site of arms-control talks.

In order to maintain its position of strict neutrality, Switzerland did not join the United Nations when it was formed in 1945. However, the country became active in many U.N. agencies, and the organization's European headquarters were founded in Geneva.

In a 1986 national referendum, Swiss voters again declined to join the association. But in 2002 they reversed their decision, and after 57 years Switzerland finally joined the United Nations. However, they overwhelmingly rejected a proposal to join the European Union (EU).

JEAN RAMSEYER
Contributor, Neue Zürcher Zeitung
Revised and updated by PAUL C. HELMREICH
Wheaton College (Massachusetts)

See also ALPS.

SYDNEY

Sydney, the capital of the state of New South Wales, is Australia's largest city and chief seaport. This bustling, vigorous metropolis, with a population of about 3.5 million, is spread over an area of 1,573 square miles (4,074 square kilometers). Sydney is Australia's oldest city. It was founded as a penal colony in 1788.

Sydney is located on the southeastern coast of Australia on an inlet of the South Pacific Ocean. The city's natural deepwater harbor is one of the world's finest. A huge single-arch bridge spans the harbor. From the time it was built in 1932, this famous bridge has been a Sydney landmark. At one point Sydney Harbour Bridge soars to a height of 440 feet (134 meters) above the blue inlet.

Many people of the city and its outlying suburbs are employed in the bustling harbor. This area is alive with the sounds of cranes and ship whistles and with the movement of trucks and of snub-nosed tugs guiding ocean-going ships into their berths. There are extensive wharves to accommodate the large passenger ships and freighters. Most of these vessels come long distances—from Europe, Asia, and North and South America—and make Sydney a regular port of call.

▶ INDUSTRY AND COMMERCE

Sydney is the leading industrial and commercial city of Australia. Its factories turn out about 30 percent of the country's entire production. The city has many textile and knitting mills, brass foundries, and automobile plants. Among the other leading industries are sawmilling, engineering, chemical manufacture, telephone and electrical cable production, and oil refining.

Sydney is a city of skyscrapers, large department stores, and a huge variety of business enterprises. One of its proudest boasts is that practically anything on sale anywhere else in the world can also be bought in Sydney. During the day the downtown area of Sydney—an area of several square miles—swarms with activity. One of the busiest sections is around Martin Place, the financial heart of the city. Here the greatest banking, insurance, and commercial institutions of Australia make their headquarters. Just a short distance from Martin Place, on Bond Street, is the Sydney Stock Exchange. Many people come to visit the public gallery of the exchange.

A network of railroad lines and highways links Sydney with other communities in New South Wales and the rest of Australia. The city is also a major port. Kingsford Smith Airport, just outside of Sydney, is the largest and busiest air terminal in Australia.

▶ CULTURE, EDUCATION, AND RECREATION

The Art Gallery of New South Wales is one of the many museums and art galleries in Sydney. It has a widely representative collec-

The graceful arches of the Sydney Opera House, overlooking the harbor, contrast with the skyscrapers. Sydney Tower at Centrepoint, left, is the nation's tallest structure.

tion of Australian painting and sculpture. The largest library in the city is the State Library of New South Wales. Its Mitchell Library division has one of the world's most comprehensive collections of books, documents, and pictures relating to Australasia and the South Pacific. Among the educational institutions in Sydney are the University of Sydney, the University of New South Wales, and Macquarie University.

There are many theaters, concert halls, and motion picture houses. The Sydney Opera House at Bennelong Point in Sydney Harbour was completed in 1973. It includes an opera house, a complex of theaters and concert halls, and an exhibition area. It is the home of the famed Sydney Symphony Orchestra. Many concerts are given in the auditorium of the State Conservatorium of Music on Macquarie Street.

Many people go to see the birds, fish, and animals in the Taronga Zoological Park. The city also has beautiful beaches and botanical gardens. The mild climate and many waterways around the city make water sports, such as surfing and sailing, a popular activity. The restored shopping area known as The Rocks, the site of many historic buildings, attracts numerous visitors. Another notable landmark is Sydney Tower at Centrepoint, the tallest structure in Australia. Many new sports facilities were built in the Homebush section of the city for the 2000 Summer Olympic Games, which were held in Sydney.

▶ HISTORY

The first European settlers in Australia were the British convicts, soldiers, and free settlers who arrived on the shore of what is now Sydney Harbour in 1788. The harbor and the city were named after Lord Sydney, who was at that time British home secretary. In 1842, Sydney was incorporated as a municipality. Today this city, which began as a tiny community in a vast land, has grown into Australia's leading metropolis.

Reviewed by Sharyn Kalnins
Australian Capital Territory Schools Authority

SYMPHONY. See Music (Musical Forms).

SYNONYMS AND ANTONYMS

Words that are similar in meaning are called synonyms. Words that are opposite in meaning are called antonyms. Using synonyms and antonyms allows speakers and writers to express themselves in a more exact and interesting way than they would if they repeated the same word over and over.

Suppose a speaker wants a different way of saying that something is "nice." In a book of synonyms and antonyms, the speaker will find synonyms such as *pleasant, agreeable, likable, satisfactory, delightful,* and *charming,* and antonyms such as *unpleasant, disagreeable, nasty, hateful, horrid,* and *unbearable.* Using synonyms, the speaker can say that he or she spent an agreeable afternoon in a pleasant place with people who were quite charming. This is better than saying that it was a nice time in a nice place with nice people. Or, if it were not a nice time, the speaker could use antonyms and say that it was an unbearable afternoon in an unpleasant place with nasty people.

Lists of synonyms and antonyms are given in a thesaurus. *Roget's Thesaurus* is one of the best known. A thesaurus does not define words or discuss shades of meaning. Dictionaries do that. There are also special dictionaries just for synonyms and antonyms.

Here are some synonyms and antonyms of words used quite often.

Synonyms

sad—unhappy—gloomy	strong—mighty—powerful
fat—stout—plump	
big—great—large	happy—joyous—jubilant
fast—swift—rapid	
thin—slim—lean	little—small—tiny

Antonyms

many—few	wise—foolish
strong—weak	long—short
sweet—sour	certain—doubtful
generous—stingy	plain—fancy

Reviewed by Mary Morris
Coauthor, *Harper Dictionary of Contemporary Usage*

SYPHILIS. See Diseases (Descriptions of Some Diseases).

SYRIA

Syria is a nation of southwest Asia. About the size of the U.S. state of North Dakota, it is located in the heart of the region known as the Middle East, along some of the oldest and most important routes linking Asia, Europe, and Africa. An ancient land, Syria has been influenced by many of the world's great civilizations. Syria's modern history as a nation dates from 1946, when, after centuries of foreign domination, it became an independent nation. The Golan Heights, a small region along the country's southwestern border, has been occupied by Israel since 1967.

▶ **PEOPLE**

The great majority of the people of Syria are Arabs. The two main minority groups are the Kurds and Armenians.

Language. Arabic is the official language of the country. Kurds and Armenians speak Arabic as well as their own languages. Most educated Syrians also speak French or English, or both.

Religion. Most Syrians are Muslims. The majority belong to the Sunni (orthodox) branch and a minority to the Shia (Shi'i) branch of Islam. Among the Shia are the Alawis (Alawites) and Ismailis, who hold religious views considered extremist by other Muslims. About 10 percent of the people are Christians, belonging to many sects. Syria also has a small Jewish community.

Education. Syria's education is free and compulsory for children ages 6 to 12. Major universities and libraries are located in the cities of Damascus, Aleppo, Homs, and Latakia. The Damascus University Library has more than 150,000 volumes.

A craftsman sells his textiles in a marketplace, or *souk*, on a narrow city street. Syria is famed for its varied handicrafts.

Way of Life. More than half of Syria's people live in cities and small towns. The rest of the people are mainly farmers. Although some large state-run farms are mechanized, most plots are small and many farmers use traditional wooden plows drawn by teams of oxen or horses.

Most Syrians in the cities work in trade or commerce or in the growing manufacturing and service industries. A distinctive feature of city life is the marketplace, or *souk*, where each narrow street is devoted to a particular trade or craft.

Syria's farmlands are among its greatest natural resources. Many farmers still use traditional tools to tend and harvest their crops.

The borders of Syria's desert regions are the home of the Bedouin. A nomadic or semi-nomadic people, the Bedouin have traditionally traveled with their livestock in search of pasture. Most Bedouin today live in permanent communities for parts of the year, selling wool and dairy products to nearby towns.

▶ **LAND**

Syria consists of a semi-arid desert plateau, narrow coastal plains, and a mountain range in the west. The country has several distinct land regions: mountains, fertile valleys and lowlands, and deserts and plains.

Land Regions. The Anti-Lebanon mountains form Syria's western border with Lebanon. This range contains Mount Hermon, the country's highest peak, which rises 9,232 feet (2,814 meters) above sea level.

Fertile valleys follow the Orontes River, which runs parallel to the Mediterranean coast, and the Euphrates River, which runs through the northeastern region of the country. The coastal lowlands are also well-watered and are ideal for agriculture.

More than half of Syria's land is desert. The great Syrian Desert spreads from the southeastern interior, across the border, and into Iraq and Jordan. Southwest of the desert is the plain of Hawrān, which extends to the Golan Heights.

Rivers and Lakes. The Euphrates River and its tributaries form the longest river system in Syria. Syria's other major rivers are the Khābūr and the Orontes. Syria's largest lake is Lake Al-Asad, which was created after the completion of the Euphrates (Tabka) Dam in 1973.

Climate. Western Syria has a mild climate, with cool wet winters and warm summers. Rainfall varies from 12 inches (300 millimeters) in the far southeast to 40 inches (1,000 millimeters) on the Mediterranean coast. The mountain regions and highlands are much cooler than the plains, and they receive frequent snowfall.

The interior plains have hotter summers and colder winters, with moderate rainfall. Eastern Syria has a hot, dry desert climate.

Natural Resources. Among Syria's most important natural resources are its farmlands. These are located along the Mediterranean coast near Latakia, on the Hawrān plain and in the Orontes River valley, in the valley of the Euphrates River, and around the cities of Damascus and Aleppo.

Petroleum is the country's most important mineral resource, although production is small compared with some other Middle Eastern countries. Phosphates are mined for commercial uses and export, and there are deposits of iron ore, chromite, and marble.

▶ ECONOMY

Until recently, lack of economic reforms by the government held back Syria's economic growth. Areas with poor soil could not be made suitable for agriculture due to problems in distributing water, much of which was polluted. In addition, the production of oil—the country's greatest export—had declined, while other exports did not make up for the difference in revenue. About 24 percent of the population is unemployed.

Services. Among the employed, about 40 percent work in the service industries. These industries include restaurants, hotels, and tourism.

Manufacturing. Manufactured products account for about 20 percent of Syria's exports. Textiles are the chief manufactured product. Other products include processed foods, furniture, chemicals, tobacco products, soap, glass, and handicrafts.

Agriculture. Agriculture employs about 40 percent of the country's workforce. Wheat and barley are the main commercial crops. Other important crops are cotton, lentils, chickpeas, olives, and sugar beets.

Mining. Petroleum and petroleum products account for more than 60 percent of the country's exports. Phosphate rock, marble, and salt are also mined, but in smaller amounts.

▶ MAJOR CITIES

Damascus is Syria's capital and second largest city, with a population of nearly 1.4 million. It lies at the foot of the Anti-Lebanon mountains in a fertile area watered by the Barada River. Damascus is the oldest continuously inhabited city in the world. After the Arab conquest in the A.D. 600's, the city was the capital of the entire Muslim world for nearly 100 years.

Aleppo (Halab) is Syria's largest city, with a population of nearly 1.6 million. It is an important center of commerce and is home to a number of sites with great religious and historical importance. One of these sites—the

Damascus, Syria's capital, is located at the foot of the Anti-Lebanon mountains. It is the oldest continuously inhabited city in the world.

Mosque of Zacharias—is believed to house the tomb of Saint John the Baptist's father.

▶ CULTURAL HERITAGE

Syria is well known for its handicrafts. Their varied styles reflect the many migrations, invasions, and battles the region has seen over time. Textiles, as well as wood and metal (particularly gold) products are skillfully made and very popular. The decorative technique called damask (used on textiles and metal and characterized by flowing lines) takes its name from the city that popularized it, Damascus.

▶ GOVERNMENT

Syria is a republic that has been under military control since 1963. The president, who is the head of state, is elected to 7-year terms. A prime minister, appointed by the president, is the head of government. Members of the legislature, the People's Council, are elected to 4-year terms. A Council of Ministers is appointed by the president.

▶ HISTORY

Syria has been fought over, conquered, and settled by many different peoples. Following the Arab conquest in the 600's, Syria became part of a vast Islamic empire. Islam gradually replaced Christianity, and Arabic gradually replaced Aramaic as the national and official language of Syria. During the Middle Ages, Syria was invaded by Crusaders from Europe and by Mongols from Central Asia. In the 1500's, Syria fell to the Ottoman Turks, who ruled it for 400 years.

French Rule and Independence. During World War I (1914–18), the Arabs revolted against Turkish rule. With the breakup of the Ottoman Empire after the war, the region then known as Greater Syria was divided into four separate states: Syria and Lebanon under the administration of France, and Palestine and Transjordan under Britain. Syria gained complete independence from France in 1946. In the years following independence, successive Syrian governments were overthrown by the military. Officers and their allies founded the Ba'th Party to establish a Socialist state in Syria. Following a military takeover in 1963, the Ba'th Party dominated the government.

The Assad Government. In 1970, General Hafez al-Assad, a Ba'thist, seized power. First elected president in 1971, he won all subsequent elections through 1999. Under the Socialist system he imposed, the old ruling classes lost their power, and Syria received economic and military aid from the Soviet Union. During the Persian Gulf War (1991), Syria joined the anti-Iraq coalition.

Relations with Israel and Lebanon. Syria opposed the creation of the nation of Israel and took part in three wars against Israel, in 1948, 1967, and 1973. As a result of the 1967 war, Israel first occupied, then annexed, Syria's Golan Heights. Syria opposed the peace accords of the 1990's between Israel and the Palestine Liberation Organization (PLO) and continued to demand the return of the Golan Heights. (See PALESTINE in Volume P.)

In 1976, at the request of the Lebanese government, Syria sent peacekeeping forces to Lebanon, where civil war raged. Syrian troops stayed in the country after the war ended in 1991. (See the article on Lebanon in Volume L.) That same year, Assad died and his son, Bashar al-Assad, succeeded him as president. Bashar initiated some economic, agricultural, and educational reforms.

Syria condemned the September 11, 2001, terrorist attacks on the United States but strongly opposed the 2003 U.S. military intervention in neighboring Iraq. In 2004 the United States imposed trade sanctions on Syria in response to its support for anti-Israeli terrorist groups. In 2005, mass protests by the Lebanese, along with international pressure, forced Syria to agree to remove its remaining troops from Lebanon. Meanwhile, the United Nations investigated Syria's possible involvement in the assassination of a former Lebanese prime minister.

ALEXANDER MELAMID
New York University

Reviewed by ALAM PAYIND
JENNIFER NICHOLS
Middle East Studies Center
The Ohio State University

FACTS and figures

SYRIAN ARAB REPUBLIC (Al Jumhuriyah al Arabiyah as Suriyah) is the official name of the country.

LOCATION: Southwest Asia.

AREA: 71,498 sq mi (185,180 km²).

POPULATION: 18,500,000 (estimate).

CAPITAL: Damascus.

LARGEST CITY: Aleppo.

MAJOR LANGUAGES: Arabic (official), Kurdish, Armenian, French, English.

MAJOR RELIGIOUS GROUPS: Muslim, Christian, Jewish.

GOVERNMENT: Republic under a military regime. **Head of state**—president. **Head of government**—prime minister. **Legislature**—People's Council.

CHIEF PRODUCTS: Agricultural—wheat, barley, cotton, lentils, chickpeas, olives, sugar beets, livestock. **Manufactured**—textiles, processed foods. **Mineral**—petroleum, phosphates.

MONETARY UNIT: Syrian pound (1 pound = 100 piastres).

Index

Safety (cont.)
elevator safety system **E:**185–86
exercise, protective equipment for **P:**227
experiments and other science activities **E:**384
eye protection **E:**432
fire, what to do in case of **F:**149–51
fire prevention **F:**152–54
fireworks should be set off only by trained people **F:**155
food additives **F:**342–43
food inspection **F:**335
food safety at picnics **O:**262
gene splicing, concerns about **G:**83, 84
genetically engineered foods, questions about **F:**338
government regulation of businesses **B:**473
guns **G:**426
gymnastics **G:**430
Halloween safety **H:**14
health precautions **H:**76
hiking and backpacking **H:**136
How dangerous are bears? **B:**106
How safe is your food? **F:**343
hunting **H:**301
iceboating rules **I:**20
ice-skating **I:**39
jogging and running **J:**111
kite flying **K:**270
Little League Baseball **L:**265
maritime safety is responsibility of Coast Guard **U:**124–25
microwaves **M:**288
mining **M:**322
motorcycles **M:**499
nuclear reactors **N:**371–72
occupational health and safety **O:**13
ocean liners **O:**32, 33
playgrounds **P:**80
poison prevention **P:**356
quicksand **Q:**20–21
railroads **R:**84, 89
road and highway devices **R:**250
robots **R:**253–54
safety tips **S:**5
sailing **S:**11
school bus safety laws **B:**461
signal devices of railroads **R:**85–86
skateboarding **S:**182
skiing **S:**184c, 184f
skin diving **S:**188
skydiving **S:**190
snakes, venomous **S:**215
spelunking **S:**401
sun, looking at the **S:**488
thunderstorm safety precautions **T:**187
tires **T:**212
tornado safety rules **T:**242
toys **T:**247–48
transformers reduce electrical voltage **T:**271
Transportation, United States Department of **T:**293
transportation regulations **T:**290
tsunami preparedness **T:**328
waterskiing **W:**72
woodworking **W:**231
X-rays, protection against accumulated doses of **X:**351
Safety (scoring play in football) **F:**358
Safety bicycles B:177
Safety glass A:544; **G:**230
Safety lamp (used by miners) **D:**44
Safety Last (silent movie)
picture(s) **M:**489
"Safety net" programs (to reduce poverty) **P:**419–20
Safety valves V:270
Saffir-Simpson hurricane scale H:305
Saffron (plant) **D:**376, 377, 378; **H:**121
picture(s) **D:**377
Sagamore Hill National Historic Site (New York) **N:**214

Sagan, Carl Edward (American astronomer, educator, and author) **N:**233 *profile*
Sagas (in northern European literature) **S:**58h
Eric the Red **E:**312
Icelandic literature **I:**33, 36
Ireland, literature of **I:**325
Norse version of Nibelungenlied **N:**281
source of our knowledge of Leif Ericson **E:**311
Vikings **V:**340
Sage (herb) **H:**121
picture(s) **H:**121
Sagebrush (plant) **N:**127
picture(s) **N:**123; **P:**319
Sagebrush State (nickname for Nevada) **N:**122, 123
Sage grouse (bird)
picture(s) **B:**227
Saginaw (Michigan) **M:**268
Sagittarius (constellation) **C:**529; **Z:**387
Saguaro (cactus plant) **A:**396, 400; **C:**5; **D:**129
picture(s) **A:**393, 396; **C:**4
Saguaro National Park (Arizona) **A:**400
Sahaptian (Native American language) **I:**188
Sahara (desert in Northern Africa) **A:**47; **D:**126, 127, 128; **S:**6–7
Algeria **A:**185–86, 187
nomadic herders **A:**63
oases **O:**2–3
petroleum deposits **A:**49
picture(s) **A:**46; **D:**125; **S:**6, 7
Berber encampment **M:**458
prehistoric art **P:**437
Sahel (region of Africa) **A:**52; **S:**6
Burkina Faso **B:**453
drought **D:**328–29
livestock raising **A:**63
Mauritania **M:**179–80
Saho (a people of Eritrea) **E:**316
Sahrawis (people of Western Sahara) **W:**124
Sa'id, Seyyid (sultan of Zanzibar) *see* Seyyid Said
Saigon (Vietnam) *see* Ho Chi Minh City
Sailboarding (sport) *see* Boardsailing
Sailboats P:329; **S:**8, 11
diagram(s) **S:**9, 10
picture(s) **G:**216; **S:**8, 11
Sailfish F:186
Sailing S:8–12; **T:**283–84 *see also* Boardsailing
glossary of terms **S:**12
iceboating **I:**19–20
pirates **P:**262–64
trade winds help sailors **T:**268
Sailing ships S:153, 157–58
early ocean liners **O:**32
Viking ships **V:**339
picture(s)
Viking ships **V:**340
Sailor King *see* William IV (king of England)
Sailplanes *see* Gliders
Sails (for boats) **S:**8, 156–57, 158
Saimaa Canal (Finland) **F:**135–36
Saint *see* Saints; the names of saints, as Paul, Saint, and Xavier, Francis, Saint. Place names beginning with Saint are under Saint, as Saint Louis, Missouri
Saint Andrew's (church, Kiev, Ukraine)
picture(s) **K:**245
Saint Andrews (New Brunswick) **N:**138f
Saint Andrews (Scotland) **G:**255, 257
Saint Anthony at Nuremberg (engraving by Albrecht Dürer)
picture(s) **G:**167
Saint Anthony Falls (on the Mississippi River) **M:**325, 364
Saint Augustine (Florida) **F:**260, 270, 272; **T:**166; **U:**173
St. Bartholomew's Day Massacre (1572) **H:**279
Saint Basil's Cathedral (Moscow, Russia) **M:**466
picture(s) **C:**133; **R:**357
Saint Bernard Pass, Great *see* Great Saint Bernard Pass

Saint Bernards (dogs)   D:245, 247
  picture(s)   D:244
Saint Christopher and Nevis   *see* Saint Kitts and Nevis
Saint Clair, Arthur (American soldier)   I:204
Saint Clair, Lake (Michigan–Ontario)   L:33; M:260
Saint Clair River (Michigan–Ontario)   L:33
Saint Croix (Virgin Islands, United States)   C:114, 115; U:84
Saint Croix River (Maine–New Brunswick)   M:38
Saint Croix River (Minnesota–Wisconsin)   W:194
Saint Denis, Abbey of (Paris)   A:371; F:422; G:267
Saint Denis (St. Denis), Ruth (American dancer)   D:31, 32
      profile
Sainte-Chapelle (church, Paris)   F:423; P:73
Sainte-Foy (Quebec)   Q:19
Sainte Genevieve (Missouri)   M:379
Saint Elias, Mount (Alaska)   N:49
Saint Elias Mountains (Yukon Territory)   Y:370
  picture(s)   Y:371
Saint Elmo's fire (kind of lightning)   T:187
Sainte-Madeleine, Church of (Vézelay, France)
  picture(s)   S:97
Saint Eustatius (island in the Caribbean)   C:114
Saint-Exupéry, Antoine de (French aviator and writer)   F:443
Saint Francois Mountains (Missouri)   M:368
Saint-Gaudens, Augustus (American sculptor)   N:158, 163
      profile; U:131
Saint George, Church of (Sofia, Bulgaria)   B:444
Saint George's (Saint George) (capital of Grenada)   G:378
  picture(s)   C:113
Saint-Germain, Treaty of (1919)   W:291
Saint Gotthard Pass (Swiss Alps)   A:194d
Saint Gotthard Tunnel (Switzerland)   A:194d; S:545
Saint Helena (island in the South Atlantic)   I:367; N:14
Saint Helens (Oregon)   O:211
Saint Helens, Mount (Washington)   E:15; M:502; V:379;
      W:16, 22
  picture(s)   N:31
      plant regrowth after eruption   F:375
Saint Isaac, Cathedral of (Saint Petersburg, Russia)   S:18a
Saint James's Park (London, England)   L:296
Saint Jerome in his Study (engraving by Albrecht Dürer)   D:354
Saint Joan (play by George Bernard Shaw)   S:146
Saint John (New Brunswick)   N:138c, 138e, 138f, 138g
  picture(s)   N:138c, 138f
Saint John (Virgin Islands, United States)   C:114, 115; U:84
Saint John River (Maine–New Brunswick)   C:54, 56; M:38;
      N:138a, 138f; R:245
Saint Johns (capital of Antigua and Barbuda)   A:314
Saint John's (capital of Newfoundland and Labrador)   N:141,
      145–46
  picture(s)   N:146
St. Johnsbury Athanaeum and Library (Vermont)
  picture(s)   V:311
Saint John's College (Annapolis, Maryland)   M:124
Saint John's Eve (holiday in Latvia)   L:80
Saint Johns River (Florida)   F:262
Saint-John's-wort (Klamath weed) (plant)   W:106
Saint John the Baptist in the Wilderness (painting by Geertgen
      tot Sint Jans)
  picture(s)   D:362
Saint John the Divine (cathedral, New York City)   C:135
Saint Joseph River (Michigan)   M:260
Saint Kitts and Nevis (Caribbean nation)   C:114, 115; S:13
  map(s)   S:13
  picture(s)
      flag   F:238
Saint Laurent, Louis Stephen (Canadian prime minister)   C:77
      profile; Q:15
  picture(s)   C:77
Saint Lawrence, Gulf of   C:57
Saint Lawrence, Lake   S:15
Saint Lawrence Lowlands (region of Canada)   Q:10, 10a
Saint Lawrence River   S:14–15
      Atlantic Basin of Canada   C:56

Cartier, Jacques, discovered   C:126
Montreal   M:444–45
New France (early Canada)   C:79–80
New York   N:213
Quebec   Q:10, 10b
Quebec railway bridge   B:401
  map(s)   S:14
  picture(s)   S:15
Saint Lawrence Seaway   S:15; U:95
      Army Corps of Engineers   U:106
      Canada   C:56, 85
      canals, history of   C:90
      Chicago open to ocean going ships   C:219
      Great Lakes   C:66; G:326–28
      Michigan   M:258
      Ontario   O:130
      Quebec   Q:10b
  map(s)   S:14
Saint Lawrence Seaway Development Corporation   T:294
Saint Leger, Barry (British soldier)   R:203
Saint-Lô (France)   W:311
Saint Louis (Missouri)   M:366, 368, 371, 373, 375, 380;
      S:16
      Chouteau family   F:522
      first public-school kindergarten (1873)   E:84
      floodplain of Missouri and Mississippi rivers   R:241
      Jefferson National Expansion Memorial   M:370
      Louisiana Purchase Exposition (1904)   F:16
      Wainwright Building   A:373
  picture(s)   U:98
      Gateway Arch   M:367; S:16
      Missouri Botanical Garden   M:370
      Wainwright Building   U:131
Saint-Louis (Senegal)   S:118
Saint Louis Missouri Fur Company   F:521
Saint Louis *Post-Dispatch* (newspaper)   M:375; P:533
Saint Louis River (Minnesota)   M:328
Saint Louis University (Missouri)   M:371, 373
Saint Lucia (Caribbean nation)   C:114, 115; S:17–18
  picture(s)   S:18
      flag   F:238
Saint Mark's Basilica (Venice, Italy)   B:492; V:300–301
  picture(s)   I:379
Saint Martin (one of the Leeward Islands)   C:114
Saint Martin, Alexis (French-Canadian Indian)   B:109
Saint Martin's Day (religious holiday)   *see* Martinmas
Saint Mary's Cathedral (San Francisco, California)
  picture(s)   C:135
Saint Marys City (Maryland)   M:128, 133
Saint Mary's Lake (Montana)
  picture(s)   G:220
Saint Marys River (Florida–Georgia)   F:262
Saint Marys River (Michigan–Ontario)   M:267
  picture(s)   M:267
Saint Matthew Passion (by Bach)   C:283
Saint Michael's (Maryland)
  picture(s)   M:128
Saint Michael's Russian Orthodox Cathedral (Sitka, Alaska)
      A:148
Saint Moritz (Switzerland)   B:270
Saint Nicholas (magazine)   M:17
St. Pancras train station (London, England)   A:373
Saint Patrick's Day   H:165
Saint Paul (capital of Minnesota)   M:325, 326, 329, 331,
      335
  picture(s)   M:330, 336
Saint Paul's Cathedral (London)   B:68; E:259; L:292
  picture(s)   B:68; W:323
Saint Paul's School (Concord, New Hampshire)   N:155
Saint Peter's (basilica, Rome, Italy)   V:280
      baroque style   A:372; B:65
      Bernini, Giovanni Lorenzo   B:152
      Italian baroque art and architecture   I:400
      Michelangelo   I:397; M:257

Saint Peter's (cont.)
  not officially a cathedral   **C:**135
  original church architecture   **A:**369
  Renaissance architecture   **A:**371–72; **R:**167
  picture(s)   **E:**356; **R:**305; **V:**280
    baroque style   **A:**372
    Bernini's Throne of Saint Peter   **I:**400
    high altar designed by Bernini   **V:**281
Saint Petersburg (Florida)   **F:**271
Saint Petersburg (Russia)   **R:**359, 364, 365, 369; **S:**18a–18b;
    U:34, 35
  Hermitage Museum   **H:**122
  revolutions (1917)   **R:**371; **U:**40–41
  Russia, art and architecture of   **R:**376–77
  World War II siege of Leningrad   **R:**372; **W:**300, 309
  picture(s)
      canal   **S:**18a
      Nevsky Prospekt   **R:**365; **S:**18b
      parade of labor workers (1917)   **U:**40
      statue of Peter the Great   **S:**18a
      Winter Palace   **H:**122
Saint Pierre and Miquelon   **I:**367; **N:**145, 147
Saint Roch (schooner)   **N:**339
Saint Rombold, Cathedral of (Mechelen, Belgium)   **B:**142
Saints (in Christianity)   **S:**18c–18d *see also* names of saints
  Roman Catholic beliefs   **R:**284, 291
Saints (in Islam)   **I:**347
Saints (of the Plymouth Colony)   **P:**345
Saint Sabina Church (Rome, Italy)   **I:**392
Saint-Saëns, Camille (French composer)   **F:**446; **O:**163
Saint Sebastian (painting by Terbrugghen)
  picture(s)   **D:**367
St. Serapion (painting by Zurbarán)
  picture(s)   **B:**65
Saint-Simon, Claude Henri de Rouvroy, Comte de (French social
    scientist)   **S:**224
Saint-Simon, Louis de Rouvroy, Duc de (French social critic)
    F:439
Saint Sophia (Byzantine church) *see* Hagia Sophia
Saint Sophia Cathedral (Kiev, Ukraine)   **R:**374
  picture(s)   **U:**11
Saints Peter and Paul, Cathedral of (Saint Petersburg, Russia)
    R:376
Saint Stephen's Cathedral (Vienna, Austria)   **V:**333
Saint Swithin's Day   **H:**162–63
Saint Thais (engraving by Parmigianino)
  picture(s)   **E:**294
Saint Thomas (Virgin Islands, United States)   **C:**114, 115;
    U:84
Saint Valentine's Day Massacre (Chicago, 1929)   **I:**76
Saint Vincent and the Grenadines   **C:**114, 115; **S:**19–20
  map(s)   **S:**19
  picture(s)
      flag   **F:**238
Saint Vith (Belgium)   **W:**314
Saipan (island in Pacific)   **U:**85; **W:**308, 313, 317
  picture(s)
      World War II, campaigns of   **P:**7
Saïs (ancient Egyptian capital)   **E:**117
Sajudis (Lithuanian reform movement)   **L:**263
Sakakawea, Lake (North Dakota)   **N:**325
Sakartvelo *see* Georgia, Republic of
Sakhalin (island off Siberian coast)   **I:**367–68
Sakharov, Andrei Dimitriyevich (Soviet nuclear physicist and
    dissident)   **U:**37 *profile*
Salaberry, Charles de (British colonel)   **Q:**13
Salad dressings   **O:**81
Saladin, Yūsuf ibn-Ayyūb (sultan of Egypt and Syria)   **C:**600;
    E:104; **I:**352; **J:**84; **M:**295 *profile*
  picture(s)   **M:**295
Salamanca (Spain)   **S:**371
Salamanders (land-water animals)   **A:**222–24
  acid rain's effects   **A:**10
  blind cave dwellers   **C:**158

reproduction   **R:**177
  tiger salamander   **L:**201
  picture(s)   **A:**222, 224, **C:**157
Salamis (island, in Aegean Sea)   **G:**343
Salamis, Battle of (480 B.C.)   **B:**103e
Salaries (pay for work done) *see* Wages and salaries
Salary arbitration (in major league sports)   **A:**349
Salat (Islamic duty to pray)   **I:**348
Salazar, António de Oliveira (Portuguese dictator)   **P:**395
Salé, Jamie (Canadian athlete)   **O:**117
  picture(s)   **O:**117
Saleh, Tayeb (Sudanese writer)   **A:**342
Salem (capital of Oregon)   **O:**208, 211
  picture(s)   **O:**207, 212
Salem (Massachusetts)   **M:**144; **T:**173
  colonial sites you can visit today   **C:**422
  witch-hunting in the 1600's   **C:**418; **P:**551; **W:**209
Salerno (Italy)   **M:**208; **W:**308
Sales (of products and services)   **S:**20–21 *see also* Food
    shopping
  advertising   **A:**29–35
  automobile dealers   **A:**556
  book sales conferences   **B:**333
  commercial art   **C:**456–58
  department stores   **D:**118
  Internet   **C:**488
  mail order   **M:**34–35
  retail stores   **R:**188–89
  picture(s)
      Cameroon town market   **C:**40
      Panamanian vendors   **P:**44
      Turkish market stall   **T:**347
      Vietnamese floating markets   **V:**334b
Sales tax   **S:**146; **T:**25
Salgado, Sebastião (Brazilian photographer)   **P:**217 *profile*
Salicin (natural pain reliever)   **P:**297
Salicylic acid (aspirin ingredient)   **M:**208g
Salinas, Pedro (Spanish poet)   **S:**392
Salinas de Gortari, Carlos (Mexican political leader)   **M:**252
Saline conversion *see* Water desalting
Salinger, J. D. (American author)   **A:**218; **N:**363
Salinity (of ocean water)   **O:**17, 35, 38
Salisbury (Zimbabwe) *see* Harare
Salish (Native American language)   **I:**188
Saliva   **B:**279; **D:**163; **P:**103
Salivary glands   **B:**291; **D:**197; **G:**226–27
  of insects   **I:**237–38
Salk, Jonas Edward (American medical researcher)   **C:**33
    profile; **D:**201; **S:**75
  picture(s)   **M:**279
Salk Institute (La Jolla, California)   **A:**375
Salmon (fish)   **F:**183, 195, 199
  British Columbia   **B:**405; **C:**64
  egg laying   **A:**285
  fishing industry   **F:**217, 218, 219, 220
  Indians, American   **I:**188–89
  migration   **H:**199–200
  Native American mythology   **M:**577
  Norway's salmon industry   **F:**208
  Oregon   **O:**206
  Washington fisheries   **W:**18, 28
  picture(s)   **A:**148; **F:**183, 194; **N:**295
  table(s)
      United States aquaculture production   **F:**208
Salmonella (bacteria)   **T:**357
  picture(s)   **B:**12; **F:**340
Salmon Falls (New Hampshire)   **N:**152
Salome (in the New Testament)   **B:**161; **J:**125
Salome (opera by Richard Strauss)   **O:**163
Salonika (Greece) *see* Thessaloníki
Salons (meetings of notable people at the home of a prominent
    person)   **F:**437
Salsa (condiment)   **F:**333
Salsa (Latin-American dance)   **F:**323
SALT *see* Strategic Arms Limitation Treaty

Salt (Sodium chloride)   S:22–23
    aluminum damaged by   A:195
    Atlantic Ocean content   A:478
    body chemistry   B:295
    breads and bakery products   B:387
    crystals   C:603, 605
    curing of meat   M:198
    fish, preservation of   F:220–21
    food preservation   F:344
    How do we get salt?   S:22
    hypertension   D:195
    iodine added   I:287
    ionic solids   I:288
    Kansas is a major supplier   K:180
    leather curing   L:109–10
    melting point of ice, effect on   I:4
    money, early form of   M:413
    porcupines look for salt   P:389
    salt lakes   L:24, 28, 29–30, 31
    seasoning in cooking   C:544
    superstition about   S:504
    table salt is a product of ionization   C:203
    taste, one of the senses of   B:290
    West Virginia deposits   W:130, 138, 139
    picture(s)
        crystals   C:604
Saltatorial locomotion (of snakes)   S:210–11
Saltbox houses   C:416
    picture(s)   C:415; H:194
Salt domes (geologic formations)   L:316; M:356; P:168;
        S:22; T:124
Salter, Susanna Madora (first woman mayor in the United
        States)   K:189 profile
    picture(s)   K:188
Salt Lake City (capital of Utah)   S:24; U:242, 247, 249, 251,
        255
    Mormons   M:457; P:493
    Temple Square   U:250
    Winter Olympic Games (2002)   O:117–18
    Young, Brigham   Y:363
    picture(s)   S:24; U:251
        capitol building   U:252
        Mormon Temple   M:457
        Temple Square   U:250
Salt lakes   L:24, 28, 29–30, 31; O:17
    California   C:21
    Poopó, Lake (Bolivia)   B:307
Salt licks (salt deposits used by animals)   S:23
Salt marshes   W:148
Salto (Uruguay)   U:240
Salton Sea (southern California)   C:21; L:26, 33
Saltpeter (Potassium nitrate)   E:420; I:287
Salt River (Arizona)   A:395
Salt River Project (conservation plan)   A:400, 404, 405
Salts (chemical compounds)   C:204; O:17
Salt water see Seawater
Saltwater swamps   W:146
Salukis (dogs)
    picture(s)   D:248
Salvador (Bahia) (Brazil)   B:379, 381
Salvage logging (of lumber)   L:340
Salvarsan (chemical compound)   E:118
Salvation (in theology)   C:292; P:490, 491
Salvation Army   S:25
    picture(s)   S:25
Salween River (Asia)   M:559; R:245
Salyut (Soviet space station)   S:54, 350, 352, 355, 366
Salzburg (Austria)   A:521
Salzburg Festival (Austria)   A:522; M:555
SAM (surface-to-air missiles)   M:345, 349; U:102
Samaritans (a people of the Middle East)   B:157
Samarium (element)   E:176; R:75
Samarkand (Uzbekistan)   U:257
Samba (Brazilian dance music)   L:72
Sambo (form of wrestling)   W:324

Same-sex unions   H:204; P:494
Samgam literature (of India)   I:141
Sami (a people of far northern Europe)   L:44–45 see also
        Lapland
    Arctic   A:380
    Finland   F:134, 138–39
    nomads   N:272
    Norway   N:344, 346
    Sweden   S:523
    picture(s)   L:44
Samnites (a people of Europe)   R:313
Samo (Frankish king)   Y:367
Samoa see American Samoa; Western Samoa
Samoset (Abnaki chief)   I:177 profile; M:148; P:346; S:25
Samothrace, Victory of see Winged Victory of Samothrace
Samoyeds (dogs)   D:245, 247
Samp (corn dish of colonial America)   C:411
Sampaio, Jorge (president of Portugal)   P:395
Sampans (Chinese boat-homes)   H:189
Sample fairs (in medieval Europe)   F:15
Samplers (form of needlecraft)   A:317; N:97
    picture(s)   N:98
Sampling (in statistics)   M:158; O:169–70; S:439
Sampras, Pete (American tennis player)
    picture(s)   T:88
Sampson, William T. (American admiral)   S:392c, 392d
Samsara (cycle of death and rebirth in Buddhism)   B:424
Samskaras (Hindu life-cycle rituals)   H:141
Samson (Biblical character)   B:161
Samson et Dalila (opera by Camille Saint-Saëns)   O:163
Samuel I and II (books of the Old Testament)   B:160
Samuel Book, The (Yiddish poem)   Y:360
Samuel ibn Nagrela (Hebrew poet) see Ha-nagid, Shmuel
Samuelson, Paul (American economist)   E:62–63 profile
    picture(s)   E:63
Samuelson, Ralph (American founder of waterskiing)   W:71
Samurai   J:41–42, 43, 44
Samut Prakan (Thailand)   T:151
San (a people of Africa)   A:55; B:344
    cave and rock paintings   A:70, 73, 75
    folk dance   F:300
    language   A:56
    music   A:77
    Namibia   N:8, 9
    South Africa   S:269
    picture(s)   A:70
San, Aung (Burmese political leader) see Aung San
Sana (capital of Yemen)   Y:358
    picture(s)   Y:357
San Agustín (archaeological site, Colombia)
    picture(s)   S:293
San Andreas fault (California)   E:40; G:114; L:303
    picture(s)   E:14, 34; G:115
San Antonio (Texas)   S:26; T:132, 134, 138
    picture(s)   S:26; T:129, 132
San Carlos de Borromeo Mission (Carmel-by-the-Sea, California)
    picture(s)   C:28
Sánchez de Lozada, Gonzalo (president of Bolivia)   B:310
San Christobel (one of the Solomon Islands)   S:252
Sanctions (penalties against a country that violates
        international law)   I:268
    against Iraq   H:307; I:316a
    against Rhodesia   Z:384
    against South Africa   C:327
    against Syria   S:552
Sanctoral cycle (in Christian calendar)   S:18c
Sand   S:235
    ceramics   C:176
    glassmaking   F:143
    optical glass   O:185
    quartz sand   Q:7
    quicksand   Q:20–21
Sand, George (French novelist)   D:149; F:440–41
Sandalwood   H:61
Sandblasting (to decorate glass)   G:231

Santa Cruz Islands (southwestern Pacific) S:252
Santa Fe (capital of New Mexico) N:180, 185, 187, 192
  picture(s) H:145; N:181, 189
Santa Fe Opera (New Mexico) N:185
  picture(s) N:185
Santa Fe Railroad see Atchison, Topeka, and Santa Fe Railway
Santa Fe Trail O:272, 274–75
  beginning in Missouri M:380
  Kansas K:183, 184
  New Mexico N:187, 193
  map(s) O:273
  picture(s) K:184
Santa Isabela (one of the Solomon Islands) S:252
Santa Lucia Day (Swedish holiday) C:300; H:162
Santa Maria (ship of Christopher Columbus) C:446, 448;
  E:404
Santamaría, Juan (national hero of Costa Rica) C:567
Santa Maria della Salute (church in Venice, Italy)
  picture(s) V:300
Santana, Carlos (American musician) H:147
Santana, Rafael (American baseball player)
  picture(s) H:147
Santander, Francisco de Paula (president of New Granada)
  C:408
Santa River (Peru) P:162
Santa Sophia (Byzantine church, now a museum) see Hagia
  Sophia
Santa Tecla (El Salvador) see Nueva San Salvador
Santayana, George (American poet and philosopher) H:152
Santee River (South Carolina) S:298, 299, 300
Santería (Cuban religious practices) C:606; H:145; L:50
Santiago (capital of Chile) C:250, 253, 254; S:37, 289
  picture(s) C:253
Santiago de Compostela (Spain) S:382
Santiago de Cuba (Cuba) C:608; S:392d
Santillana, Marquis of (Spanish poet) S:387
Santo Domingo (capital of Dominican Republic) D:282
  picture(s) D:282
Santo Domingo (Indians of North America) I:183
Santo Domingo, University of see Autonomous University of
  Santo Domingo
Santorini Island A:236
Santos-Dumont, Alberto (Brazilian aviator) A:562
Santo Stefano Rotondo (church, Rome) I:392
Santo Tomás, University of (Manila, Philippines) M:79; P:184
  picture(s) P:187
San Vitale church (Ravenna, Italy) I:392
  picture(s) B:488
San Xavier del Bac (mission, Arizona) A:400
  picture(s) A:400
São Francisco River (Brazil) B:378; R:245–46; S:280
São Paulo (Brazil) B:375, 379, 381; S:38–39, 289
  picture(s) B:380; S:38, 288, 289
São Tiago (island, Cape Verde) C:102
São Tomé (capital of São Tomé and Príncipe) S:40
São Tomé and Príncipe S:40–41
  picture(s)
    flag F:238
Sap (of plants) M:91; T:306–7
Sapodilla (tropical fruit) T:317
  picture(s) T:317
Sapphires (gems) G:69, 70, 71, 73, 74
  amulets and talismans G:72
  picture(s) G:70, 72, 74
Sappho (Greek lyric poet) G:353, 355
  picture(s) G:354
Sapporo (Japan) J:36
Saprobes (in biology) F:498
Sapsucker (bird)
  picture(s) B:221
Sapwood (of trees) T:306; W:222–23
Saqqara (Sakkara) (Egypt) A:365; E:108, 110, 112; P:556
  picture(s) P:557
Sara (a people of Chad) C:180
Saracens (Muslim Arabs) I:388

Saragossa, Treaty of (1529) E:405
Sarah (wife of Abraham) A:8, 9; B:161
Sarah Constant (ship) see Susan Constant
Sarajevo (capital of Bosnia and Herzegovina) B:338; W:276
Sarakolé (a people of Africa) M:179
Saraswati River (Pakistan) A:240
Saratoga, Battle of (1777) N:222; R:204; W:40
Saratoga National Historical Park (New York) N:214
Sarawak (state of Malaysia) B:336, 337; M:56, 57, 58, 59
Sarazen, Gene (American golf champion) G:259 profile
  picture(s) G:259
Sarcodines (protozoans) P:496
Sarcomas (cancers) C:92
Sarcophagi (burial chests) S:96
Sard (chalcedony quartz) Q:8
Sardines (fish) F:200, 202, 218
  picture(s) P:393
Sardinia (island, west of Italy) I:368
Sardonyx (chalcedony quartz) Q:8
Sargasso Sea (Atlantic Ocean) A:479; E:94; F:201; O:47
Sargassum fish
  picture(s) F:200
Sargent, John Singer (American painter) P:30; S:41; U:130;
  W:57
  picture(s)
    Portrait of Madame X (painting) S:41
Sargonid dynasty (of Assyria) A:462
Sargon of Akkad (ancient Mesopotamian ruler) A:231;
  M:231; S:487
  picture(s) A:231
Saris (garments worn by women in Bangladesh) B:49
  picture(s) B:49
Sarkisian, Vazgen (Armenian prime minister) A:422
Sarmatians (a people of Europe) R:366
Sarmiento, Domingo F. (writer and president of Argentina)
  A:386c; L:68
Sarney, José (president of Brazil) B:384
Sarnia (Ontario) O:128
Sarnoff, David (American radio and television executive) R:59
Saro (South American giant otter) O:252
Saroyan, William (American author and playwright) A:421
Sarrette, Bernard (French bandmaster) B:43
SARS (Severe acute respiratory syndrome) A:457; C:273;
  D:202–3
Sarsen (sandstone boulder) S:462
Sartre, Jean-Paul (French writer and philosopher) D:305;
  F:443
Saskatchewan (Canada) C:64; S:42–51
  map(s) S:46
  picture(s)
    farmer C:51
    farmland S:45
    grain elevators S:48
    Regina S:50
    Royal Canadian Mounted Police S:45
    Ukrainian Orthodox church S:44
    wheat field C:56
Saskatchewan River (Canada) C:57; R:246; S:43
Saskatoon (Saskatchewan) S:47, 49
Sasquatch see Bigfoot
Sassafras Mountain (South Carolina) S:297, 298
Sassafras trees
  picture(s) T:303
Sassandra River (Ivory Coast) I:419
Sassanians (rulers of Persia) A:234; I:308; P:156–57
Sassoon, Siegfried (English poet)
  "Everyone Sang" (poem) F:124
Sassou-Nguesso, Denis (president of the People's Republic of
  the Congo) C:506
Sastre, Alfonso (Spanish dramatist) S:392
Satan A:258
Satellites (moons) P:275; S:52, 247
  astronomy, history of A:471
  Jupiter's satellites J:161–62; P:279–80; S:360

Satellites (cont.)
Mars' satellites   **M:**109; **P:**278–79
moon   **M:**446–55; **P:**278
Neptune's satellites   **N:**113–14; **P:**282
Pluto's satellite   **P:**282, 342–43
Saturn's rings may have come from   **S:**57
Saturn's satellites   **P:**280; **S:**58, 360
Uranus' satellites   **P:**281; **U:**233
Which planet has the strangest moon in the solar system?
U:233
Satellites, artificial   **S:**53–54, 351, 353
archaeological use   **A:**352
balloon satellites   **B:**37
carried in space shuttle's cargo bay   **S:**365
communications satellites   **C:**469–70; **T:**55, 66
"Earth Science Enterprise"   **S:**363
geography   **G:**106
Global Positioning System (GPS)   **R:**51
navigation   **N:**77
oceanographic research   **O:**37, 38, 40
orbiting observatories   **O:**10–12
petroleum deposits, search for   **P:**169
photographic spies   **S:**407
photography, special uses of   **P:**209
powered by solar batteries   **B:**103c
radiation-belt probes   **R:**48
railroad signals   **R:**86
satellite radio service   **R:**61
space research and technology   **S:**361–62
space stations   **S:**366
telecommunications   **T:**48
volcanoes monitored with   **V:**386
weather satellites   **H:**305; **W:**90–91, 94
wind measurement   **W:**189
picture(s)
communication   **C:**470
leaving a space shuttle   **E:**160
mobile phone networks   **T:**56
oceanographic research   **O:**36
photograph of hurricane   **P:**209
Satellites, political   **I:**102; **U:**39
Satellite telephones   **T:**47, 56
Satie, Erik (French composer)   **F:**448
Satin stitch (in embroidery)   **N:**98
picture(s)   **N:**99
Satire (a form of humor)   **H:**291–92
Aristophanes' comedies   **D:**299
English literature   **E:**276, 277, 278, 289
fiction, origins of   **F:**114
Gulliver's Travels   **E:**278
Hogarth, William   **H:**159a
Latin America, literature of   **L:**67
Swift, Jonathan   **S:**530
Satraps (governors of ancient Persia)   **P:**154
Satsuma (mandarin orange grown in Japan)   **O:**189
Saturated fats   **N:**425; **O:**80
Saturation (of pigment colors)   **C:**425–26
Saturation current (maximum current generated by a photovoltaic cell)   **P:**197
Saturation temperature *see* Dew point
Saturday (day of the week)   **D:**46; **R:**153
Saturday Evening Post (magazine)   **R:**272
Saturday Night Fever (motion picture, 1977)   **D:**29
Saturn (planet)   **P:**280; **S:**55–58
auroras   **R:**49
experiments and other science activities   **E:**390
Galileo discovered rings   **A:**470
Huygens, Christiaan   **H:**310
observing Saturn   **P:**281
radiation belts   **R:**49
radio astronomy   **R:**69
space probes   **O:**10; **S:**360
Where did Saturn's rings come from?   **S:**57
diagram(s)   **S:**56

picture(s)   **S:**55
false-color images of rings   **P:**280; **S:**57
moon Dione   **O:**11
radio image   **R:**69
Saturn (Roman god) *see* Cronus
Saturn EV1 (automobile)
picture(s)   **A:**545
Saturn rockets   **R:**257; **S:**340a, 340f, 362; **V:**391
diagram(s)   **R:**259
picture(s)   **S:**340c, 340f–340g, 340h, 361
Satyrs (in Greek mythology)   **G:**363
Saud (king of Saudi Arabia)   **S:**58e
Saud, House of (ruling family of Saudi Arabia)   **S:**58e
Saudi Arabia   **M:**199, 303; **O:**222; **S:**58a–58e
map(s)   **S:**58c
picture(s)
computer operator   **M:**298
desert   **S:**58a
flag   **F:**239
man with cellular telephone   **A:**444
Mecca   **S:**58d
oil refineries   **A:**452; **D:**131; **M:**303; **S:**58d
people   **S:**58a, 58b
water pipeline   **M:**301
Saugus (Massachusetts)   **I:**337; **M:**144
Sauk (Indians of North America)   **I:**74–75, 179, 204, 302, 303
Saul (first Hebrew king)   **B:**161; **D:**42; **J:**102
Saul of Tarsus *see* Paul, Saint
Sault Sainte Marie (Michigan)   **M:**269
Sault Sainte Marie (Ontario)   **O:**133
Sault Sainte Marie (Soo) Canals (Michigan–Ontario)   **G:**327; **M:**267; **O:**130
picture(s)   **G:**326; **M:**267
Saund, Dalip Singh (American political figure)   **A:**459
Saunders, Keith (American ballet dancer)
picture(s)   **B:**33
Saurischia (group of dinosaurs)   **D:**170–73
Sauropoda (group of dinosaurs)   **D:**172–73
Savai'i (island of Samoa)   **W:**124
Savang Vatthana (king of Laos)   **L:**43
Savannah (early American steamship)   **O:**32; **S:**158–59
Savannah (Georgia)   **C:**343; **G:**141; **T:**178
picture(s)   **G:**141
Savannah, NS (nuclear-powered ship)   **S:**159
Savannah buffalo   **B:**430
Savannah elephants   **E:**180
Savannah River (United States)   **S:**298, 299
Savannas (grasslands)   **A:**52; **B:**207; **C:**362; **S:**277, 283
picture(s)   **A:**52; **B:**198
Sava River (Europe)   **C:**588
Savater, Fernando (Spanish philosopher)   **S:**392
Savery, Thomas (English inventor)   **I:**221
Savimbi, Jonas (Angolan political figure)   **A:**260
Savings accounts   **B:**56; **I:**255
Savings and loan associations   **B:**54, 55
Savings Association Insurance Fund (SAIF)   **B:**58–59
Savings banks   **B:**55
Savi's pygmy shrew (animal)   **S:**166
Savonarola, Girolamo (Italian reformer)   **O:**191
Savoy, House of (Italian ruling family)   **V:**332
Savoye House (Villa Savoye) (Poissy-sur-Seine, France)   **A:**374
picture(s)   **L:**124
Savoy operas (of Gilbert and Sullivan)   **G:**209
Sawda, Jabal (mountain in Saudi Arabia)   **S:**58c
Sawfish   **S:**145
Sawm (Islamic duty to fast)   **I:**349
Sawmilling   **L:**341–42
Saws (tools)   **T:**228, 233, 234
lumber and lumbering   **L:**342
mechanical saws   **T:**231
power saws   **T:**230
woodworking   **W:**231
picture(s)   **T:**228

circular saw **T:**231
lumber and lumbering **L:**340
table saw **T:**232
Sawtooth National Recreation Area (Idaho) **I:**54
picture(s) **I:**47
Sawyer, Ruth (American author) **S:**464
Sawyer, Tom (fictional character) **T:**361–62
Sax, Adolphe (Belgian inventor) **B:**133
Saxe, John Godfrey (American poet)
"The Blind Men and the Elephant" **F:**7
Saxe-Coburg-Gotha, House of (English royal family) **E:**248, 250
Saxo Grammaticus (Danish historian) **D:**112; **N:**277; **S:**58h
Saxons (Germanic people) **C:**188; **E:**236; **G:**159
Saxophone (musical instrument) **M:**550; **O:**193–94; **W:**184
picture(s) **I:**279; **M:**530, 549; **W:**185
Sayers, Dorothy L. (English writer) **M:**565 *profile*
Sayers, Gale (American football player) **F:**363 *profile*
picture(s) **F:**363
Sayre, Woodrow Wilson (American author and mountain climber) **E:**371
SBR (synthetic rubber) **R:**346
Scafell Pike (highest point in England) **E:**233
Scala, La (opera house, Milan) *see* La Scala
Scalawags (Southern whites who supported Republicans during Reconstruction Period) **R:**119
Scalding *see* Burns and scalds
Scale (in interior design) **I:**258
Scale (of maps) **M:**95
Scale insects *see* Scales (sucking insects)
Scale models
automobile models **A:**534
interior decorator's scale drawing **I:**259, 260
standard dollhouse scale **D:**264
picture(s)
Hubble Space Telescope **P:**272
solar system **P:**272
Scales (constellation) *see* Libra
Scales (for measuring weight) **G:**324
picture(s) **W:**114
Scales (in music) **M:**531–32, 537
ancient music **A:**237
how to play on the harmonica **H:**34
modal jazz **J:**63
Scales (of animals)
butterflies and moths **B:**475, 476
fish **F:**188–89
sharks and rays **S:**142
picture(s)
how to determine the age of a fish **F:**189
Scales (sucking insects) **A:**324; **F:**482
Scalia, Antonin (American jurist) **S:**508 *profile*
picture(s) **U:**171
Scallions (onions) **O:**123
Scallops (mollusks) **M:**405; **O:**290–91; **S:**150
picture(s) **S:**150
Scalpel (surgical instrument) **S:**513
Scandals, political *see* Corruption, political
Scandentia (order of mammals)
picture(s)
pen-tailed shrew as example **M:**74
Scandinavia (region in northern Europe) **S:**58f–58g *see also* Denmark; Norway; Sweden; Vikings
Christmas customs **C:**300
education **E:**74
emigration to Minnesota **M:**330
English language, history of **E:**265–66
furniture **F:**517
homes and housing **H:**187
northwestern uplands of Europe **E:**344
tapestry, art of **T:**22
witches, laws against **W:**208
Scandinavian literature **S:**58h–58i
drama **D:**303, 304

fairies **F:**10–11, 12
giants in myths and legends **G:**201, 202
Norse mythology **N:**277–81
Scandium (element) **E:**176
Scanner (electronic instrument) **B:**331; **C:**481; **D:**263; **P:**216
Scanning (in reading) **S:**471
Scanning electron microscopes **E:**164; **M:**155, 285
Scanning transmission electron microscopes **M:**285
Scanning tunneling microscopes **A:**484; **E:**164; **M:**155, 285
picture(s)
images of atoms **A:**489
Scaphopods (mollusks) **M:**407; **S:**151
picture(s) **S:**151
Scapula (shoulder blade) **S:**183
Scarabs (dung beetles) **B:**125
picture(s) **B:**123, 126
Scarborough (Tobago) **T:**315
Scarlatti, Alessandro (Italian composer) **B:**70, 71; **I:**412; **O:**141
Scarlatti, Domenico (Italian composer and musician) **B:**72
Scarlet fever (disease) **D:**203, 204
Scarlet king snakes **S:**213
picture(s) **S:**216
Scarlet Letter, The (novel by Hawthorne) **A:**210; **H:**65
Scarpa, Carlo (Italian architect) **G:**234
Scarps (cliffs on Mercury) **M:**228; **P:**276
Scarry, Richard (American author and illustrator) **C:**235 *profile*
Scarves (clothing accessories) **P:**337
Scat singing (in jazz) **J:**60; **L:**326
Scattering of light **L:**215–16, 222
Scatter plots (style of graph) **G:**311–12
Scavenger beetle
picture(s) **I:**234
Scavengers (animals) **A:**279; **F:**199; **L:**206; **V:**394
Scenery (of plays) *see* Stage scenery and lighting
Scenes (in motion pictures) **M:**481
Scenic designers (of plays) *see* Set designers
Scents (of animals)
ants communicate with scent **A:**318
butterflies and moths **B:**476, 478
how animals communicate **A:**284
insect trap baiting **I:**250
skunks **O:**253
Schaan (Liechtenstein) **L:**192
Schaeffer, Pierre (French composer) **E:**156
Schaeffer, Vincent J. (American scientist) **W:**95
Schechter, Solomon (American Jewish leader) **J:**146
Schedules **T:**205–6
study, how to **S:**471–72
Scheele, Carl Wilhelm (Swedish chemist) **N:**262; **O:**288; **T:**332
Schefferville (Quebec) **Q:**10b
Scheherazade (heroine of *Arabian Nights*) **A:**339
Schelde River (Europe) **N:**120a; **R:**236, 246
Schenck* v. *United States (1919) **F:**163; **S:**509
Schenectady (New York) **F:**463
Schiller, Friedrich von (German dramatist, poet, and philosopher) **D:**302; **G:**178; **S:**58j
Schimmel, Wilhelm (woodcarver)
picture(s)
eagle **F:**296
Schindler, Oskar (German industrialist) **S:**58j
Schindler's List (motion picture, 1993) **S:**58j
picture(s) **M:**497
Schipperkes (dogs) **D:**247, 255
Schirrmann, Richard (German founder of hosteling) **H:**254–55
Schisms (within the church)
Great Schism or Eastern Schism **E:**45
Great Western Schism, two popes during **R:**290
Schist (metamorphic rock) **R:**270–71
Schizoid personality disorder **M:**224
Schizophrenia (form of mental illness) **M:**223, 224
Schlafly, Phyllis (American anti-feminist) **W:**213

Schleiden, Matthias (German scientist)   B:202
   picture(s)   B:202
Schleswig-Holstein (area of Europe)   D:113
Schley, Winfield S. (American commodore)   S:392d
Schlieffen, Alfred von (German general)   W:280
Schliemann, Heinrich (German archaeologist)   A:236–37;
   S:59; T:316
Schmeling, Max (German boxer)   B:351
Schmidt, Helmut (West German political leader)   G:165; S:59
Schmidt-Cassegrain telescope   T:59
   diagram(s)   T:59
Schmitt, Harrison H. (American astronaut)   S:342
Schnitger, Arp (German organ builder)   O:219
Schnitke, Alfred (Russian composer)   R:386
Schnitzler, Arthur (Austrian writer)   D:303; G:180
   picture(s)   A:522
Schoellkopf, Jacob (German-born American businessman)
   N:243
Schoenberg, Arnold (Austrian-born American composer)
   G:189; S:60
   Berg, Alban   B:145
   chamber music   C:184
   choral music   C:285
   modern music   M:397–98, 544
   opera   O:148
Schoenbrunn Village State Memorial (Ohio)   O:70
Scholarships   U:224
Scholastic aptitude tests   T:118, 120–23
Schomburgk, Sir Robert (British explorer)   E:409
Schönbein, Christian Friedrich (German chemist)   O:292
Schönberg, Arnold (Austrian-born American composer) see
   Schoenberg, Arnold
Schönbrunn Palace (Vienna, Austria)   V:332j
   picture(s)   V:332j
Schongauer, Martin (German artist)   G:170
"School-at-home" programs   H:196
School boards   E:76, 130
School books see Textbooks
School buses   B:461
   picture(s)   B:461; E:75
Schoolcraft, Henry Rowe (American explorer and specialist in
   Indian cultures)   M:334
School districts   E:76, 87; M:517
School for Scandal, The (play by Sheridan)   E:277
Schooling (form of behavior in fish)   F:201
School libraries   L:177–78
School nurses   N:418–19
School of Athens, The (painting by Raphael)
   picture(s)   I:398; R:168
Schools   S:60–61 see also Education; Universities and
   colleges; the education section of country, province,
   state, and city articles
   cheerleading   C:193–94
   child development   C:226
   colonial America   C:412, 418
   education, history of   E:74–88
   elementary schools   E:74
   ethics   E:328
   high schools   E:76
   juvenile crime, causes and prevention of   J:168, 170
   kindergarten and nursery schools   K:246–50
   kinds of schools, list of   S:61
   land grants for schools   P:517
   libraries   L:177–78
   National Honor Society   N:42
   parent-teacher associations   P:66–67
   parochial schools   E:76
   physical education programs   P:222–23
   preparatory schools   P:443–44
   private schools   E:77
   programmed instruction   P:483
   public schools   E:76
   public schools (independent schools) in the United
      Kingdom   U:48

   secondary schools   E:74
   Supreme Court rulings on segregation   C:328; N:26;
      S:509
   teachers and teaching   T:37–38
   time management at school   T:206
   universities and colleges   U:219–26
   violence in schools   E:88
   vocational schools   E:72; S:58b
   volunteerism   V:390
   picture(s)
      frontier school   P:257
      juvenile crime   J:167
      one-room schoolhouse   E:83
      village school in India   I:119
Schools (of fish)   F:201, 217
Schooners (early American ships)   S:157–58
Schooners (sailboats)   S:8
Schröder, Gerhard (German chancellor)   G:166; S:62
Schrödinger, Erwin (Austrian physicist)   P:231, 238 profile
   influence on Watson and Crick   G:86
   picture(s)   P:238
Schubert, Franz (Austrian composer)   S:62
   chamber music   C:184
   choral music   C:284
   classical age, compositions of   C:349, 351, 352
   romanticism   G:186–87; R:304
   picture(s)   A:522; M:542
Schuckburgh, Richard (British army doctor)   N:22
Schultz, Augustus (American inventor)   L:111
Schultz, Dutch (American mobster)   O:224 profile
Schultz, Peter (American scientist)   F:107
Schulz, Charles M. (American cartoonist)   C:128; M:339
   profile
   picture(s)   M:339
Schulze, Johann (German doctor)   P:211
Schumann, Clara (German pianist)   P:242
   picture(s)   G:187
Schumann, Robert (German composer)   B:361; G:187; R:304;
   S:63
Schurz, Carl (American statesman and journalist)   W:207
   profile
Schurz, Margarethe Meyer (American educator)   W:197, 207
Schuster, Rudolf (president of Slovakia)   S:202
Schütz, Heinrich (German composer)   B:70; C:283; G:184
Schwa (vowel sound)   P:486
Schwabe, Heinrich S. (German astronomer)   A:471
Schwalbe, Louis (English chemist)   N:439
Schwann, Theodor (German physiologist)   B:202
   picture(s)   B:202
Schwartz, I. I. (Yiddish poet)   Y:361
Schwarzenegger, Arnold (Austrian bodybuilder and actor)
   B:294; M:497
Schwarzkopf, H. Norman (American general)   P:158
Schweitzer, Albert (French medical missionary, philosopher,
   and musician)   G:3; S:63
Schwerner, Michael (American civil rights volunteer)   M:363
Schwitters, Kurt (German artist)   M:393
   picture(s)
      Merzbild mit Regenbogen (collage)   M:396a
Sciascia, Leonardo (Italian author)   I:409
Science   S:64–75
   children's books, list of   C:247
   computer graphics, uses of   C:484
   Enlightenment, Age of   E:295
   experiments and other science activities   E:380–97
   forensic science   F:372–73
   Internet, uses of   C:488–89
   mathematics in careers   M:161
   museums   M:523–24
   myth and science   M:573–75
   National Geographic Society   N:41
   Nobel prizes   N:263–65, 268–70
   science fairs   S:76–78
   technology and science   T:39–41
   What is pseudoscience?   S:67

Science (journal)   **S:**68
Science, history of   **S:**68–75 *see also* individual headings
    beginning with the word Scientific; the names of
    scientists
    astronomy, history of   **A:**468–75
    biology   **B:**195–204
    chemistry, history of   **C:**206–11
    evolution   **E:**372–79
    Galileo   **G:**5–6
    Galton, Sir Francis   **G:**7
    geology   **G:**107–19
    Italy's contributions to science   **I:**387
    language growth with scientific terms   **W:**241
    mathematics, history of   **M:**162–70
    Muslim role in medieval education   **E:**80
    nuclear energy, research in   **N:**366–73
    physics, history of   **P:**233–39
    Priestley, Joseph   **P:**454
    relativity   **R:**139–44
    Renaissance   **E:**81; **R:**162
Science, Office of (United States)   **E:**218
Science and society
    computers and society   **C:**494
    fundamentalism   **F:**492
    robots' impact on society   **R:**255–56
Science and Technology Policy, Office of (United States)
        P:451
Science fairs   **E:**386–87; **S:**76–78
Science fiction   **F:**114; **S:**79–83
    Le Guin, Ursula K.   **O:**214–15
    motion pictures   **M:**492–93
    robots   **R:**256
    Verne, Jules   **V:**320
    Vonnegut, Kurt, Jr.   **V:**391
    Wells, H. G.   **W:**123
    writing science fiction   **C:**478
Scientific classification (of living things)   **A:**264–65
Scientific instruments
    electron microscope   **E:**163–64
    Geiger counters   **G:**67–68
    microscopes   **M:**281–86
    weather instruments   **W:**87–90
Scientific method   **S:**64–65
    basic research   **R:**181
    contributions of Bacon   **B:**9
    experiments and other science activities   **E:**380–97
    four-step process   **R:**139–40
    science-fair experiments   **S:**76
Scientific research *see* Research, scientific
Scientific revolution   **S:**64, 70–71; **W:**266–67
Scilly Islands (southwest of England)   **I:**368
Scintillation counters (instruments to detect radiation)   **U:**229
Scion (tree bud)   **O:**188
Scipio Africanus (the Elder) (Roman general)   **H:**26; **S:**408
        profile
        picture(s)   **S:**408
Scissors   **S:**129
Scissor-tailed flycatcher (bird)
        picture(s)   **O:**83
Scituate Reservoir (Rhode Island)   **R:**214
SCLC *see* Southern Christian Leadership Conference
Sclera (of the eye)   **E:**429
Sclerosis *see* Multiple sclerosis
Scobee, Francis Richard (American astronaut)   **S:**352
Scoliosis (spinal condition)   **D:**204
        picture(s)   **D:**204
Scolosaurus (dinosaur)   **D:**175–76
Scoop (type of dredge)   **D:**321
Scooter (cloud on Neptune)   **N:**112–13
Scooters (type of iceboat)   **I:**19, 20
Scopas (Greek sculptor)   **G:**350
Scopes, John T. (American teacher of biology) *see* Scopes trial
Scopes trial (Tennessee, 1925)   **E:**379; **S:**84; **T:**87
    American Civil Liberties Union   **A:**199

    Bryan, William Jennings   **B:**416
    Darrow, Clarence   **D:**36
Score (in music)   **M:**537; **O:**199–200
Score following (in electronic music)   **E:**157
Scores (of tests)   **T:**118–19
Scoria (lava rock)   **N:**326; **R:**266; **V:**383
Scorpion (constellation) *see* Scorpius
Scorpions (arachnids)   **A:**348; **S:**84
        picture(s)   **A:**348; **I:**231; **S:**84
Scorpius (Scorpio) (constellation)   **C:**529; **Z:**387
Scorsese, Martin (American film director)   **M:**496 *profile,*
        497
Scotch drum   **D:**339
Scotch pine trees
        picture(s)   **L:**113
Scotland   **S:**85–88 *see also* United Kingdom
    ballads   **F:**309
    curling (game), origin of   **C:**615
    dances   **F:**302
    education   **E:**74, 81
    fairs, history of   **F:**18
    golf developed in   **G:**253, 256–57
    Hebrides   **I:**365
    historical, cultural, and scenic places   **U:**54
    holidays   **H:**160, 162
    home rule   **E:**255; **U:**61
    James (kings)   **J:**19
    Knox, John   **K:**289
    land features   **U:**51–52, 53
    Loch Ness monster   **L:**281
    lochs   **L:**31, 32
    Mary, Queen of Scots   **M:**118
    New Year   **N:**209
    Orkney Islands   **I:**366–67
    Reformation   **R:**131, 132
    Robert I (the Bruce)   **R:**251
    Rob Roy   **O:**264
    Royal Highland Games   **U:**50
    Shetland Islands   **I:**368
    map(s)   **S:**86
    picture(s)
        bagpipes   **S:**85
        Edinburgh   **S:**88; **U:**58
        Eilean Donan   **S:**85
        Glasgow   **S:**87
        highland dancers   **F:**302
        kilts   **C:**373; **U:**46
        Loch Leven   **U:**53
        Loch Lomond   **L:**25
        Royal Highland Games   **U:**51
        sheep   **S:**86
        Urquart Castle   **C:**131
Scotland, Church of   **S:**85; **U:**48
Scotland Act (1998)   **S:**88
Scotland Yard (London)   **P:**368
Scott, David R. (American astronaut)   **S:**347 *profile*
Scott, Dred (American slave)   **C:**335; **D:**323
Scott, Duncan Campbell (Canadian poet and public servant)
        C:86
Scott, Mount (Oklahoma)
        picture(s)   **O:**84
Scott, Robert Falcon (British explorer)   **A:**226, 295; **E:**415
Scott, Thomas (Canadian executed by Louis Riel)   **C:**84;
        R:232
Scott, Sir Walter (Scottish author)   **S:**89
    historical fiction   **F:**114
    quotation from *The Lay of the Last Minstrel*   **Q:**22
    romanticism in English literature   **E:**283
    style and themes of his novels   **N:**359
Scott, Winfield (American army chaplain and homesteader)
        A:401
Scott, Winfield (American army officer)   **C:**338; **M:**239b; **S:**89
        picture(s)   **S:**89
Scott Brown, Denise (African-born American architect)   **A:**376
Scotti (Celtic tribe)   **S:**85

Scottish deerhounds (dogs)   D:241–42
Scottish literature   E:278, 283, 286; S:89 *see also* the names
    of Scottish poets and novelists
Scotts Bluff National Monument (Nebraska)   N:90
Scottsdale (Arizona)   A:401
    picture(s)   W:326
Scott Tournament of Hearts (in curling)   C:615
Scout dogs (Patrol dogs) (used by the armed forces)   U:114
Scout promise and law   B:358
Scouts *see* Boy Scouts; Girl Scouts
Scouts Canada   B:360
Scowcroft, Brent (American public official)   B:465
Scrabble (word game)   G:16–17; W:237
Scrambled eggs   C:543
Scramjet (Supersonic combustion ramjet)   J:92
Scranton (Pennsylvania)   P:135
Scrapers (early tools)   T:233
Scrapers (earth-moving machinery)   E:32
Scrapie (disease of sheep)   D:208
Scrap metal   W:301
Scream, The (lithograph by Munch)   G:307
    picture(s)   E:424
Screech owls (birds)   O:285
Screen painting (in Japanese art)   J:49
    picture(s)
        The Old Plum   J:51
Screenplays (for motion pictures)   M:479, 480
Screen printing *see* Silk-screen printing
Screwball comedy (type of motion picture)   M:492
Screwdrivers (tools)   T:229; W:231
Screws (hardware)   N:2–3; W:250
    picture(s)   N:3
Scriabin, Alexander (Russian composer)   R:386
Scribes (professional writers of letters and accounts)   E:77,
    106, 107; P:478
Scrimmage (in football)   F:354
Scrimshaw (ivory or bone with carved designs)   F:295; I:416
    picture(s)   F:295
Script (style of typeface)   T:369, 370
Scriptoria (rooms for writing)   B:321; I:77; L:173
Scripts (short for "manuscripts")
    animation   A:288, 289
    planetarium shows   P:273
Script supervisors (for motion pictures)   M:483
Scriptures *see* Sacred books
Scrolls (oldest form of books)   B:319; D:47; I:79; J:49; L:171
Scroobious Pip (book by Edward Lear)
    picture(s)
        Burkert illustration   C:237
Scrotum (male anatomy)   B:287; R:178
Scrubbers (to remove sulfur dioxide from coal smoke)   C:391
Scrummage (in rugby)   R:351
Scuba diving   S:186–88 *see also* Skin diving
    ancient scuba devices   U:26
    Cousteau, Jacques-Yves   C:577
    underwater archaeology   U:18
    underwater exploration   E:416; U:22–23
    picture(s)   U:18, 21
Scud missiles   M:348–49
Sculling (rowing)   R:340
Sculpture   S:90–105 *see also* the names of individual artists
    and of art of specific countries, such as Italy, art and
    architecture of
    Africa, art of   A:71–73; P:411
    art as a record   A:429, 431
    art of the artist   A:431–32, 433
    baroque period   B:65
    Byzantine carving   B:490–91, 493–94
    Canada, art of   C:72–73
    Chinese sculpture   C:277
    Chinese tomb figures   P:409–10
    design techniques   D:136–37
    Egypt, ancient   E:108, 112, 113, 115–16
    English art   E:257

folk art   F:294–96
fountains   F:393–94
Futurism   M:391
Gothic   G:269–70
Great Sphinx at Giza is one of the largest sculptures ever
    made   E:108
Greece, ancient   G:345, 346–47, 349–50, 351–52
Inuit carvings   I:275
Italian art and architecture   I:392, 393, 395, 400, 403
ivory carving   I:416
Japanese tomb figures   P:410
joined wood block technique   J:48
Latin America   L:62
Michelangelo   M:255–57
modern art   M:387–96b
Nok culture of Nigeria   A:70–71
Olmec head sculptures   I:167
pre-Columbian pottery   P:412
Renaissance art   R:163–71
Rodin, Auguste   R:281
Romanesque art   R:295
Rome, art of   R:319
Spanish sculpture   S:380, 383, 384
surrealism   M:394
United States   U:128
wood carving   W:228
    picture(s)
        acid rain's effects   A:10
        Chinese tomb figures   P:409
        early South American Indians   S:293
        Hawaiian gods   H:52
        Ifé, kingdom of   N:257
        Inuit carvings   I:275
        Mesopotamian bronze   M:231
        from Mohenjo-Daro   A:453
        Olmec pottery   P:412
        terra-cotta sculpture of Nok culture   P:411
Scup (fish) *see* Porgy
Scurvy (nutritional disease)   L:138; V:370a, 370d
Scutage (feudal tax)   F:103
Scutari, Lake (Europe)   S:124
Scylla (sea monster in Greek mythology)   O:53
Scyphozoans (coelenterates)   J:76–77
Scytale (instrument used in code writing)   C:393
Scythians (a people of Europe)   R:366
SDI *see* Star Wars (Strategic Defense Initiative)
Sea anemones (coelenterates)   J:73, 76, 77; K:255
    aging process   A:83
    picture(s)   J:73; K:255; O:25
Sea birds *see* Water birds
Seabiscuit (racehorse)   H:235 *profile*
    picture(s)   H:235
Sea blubbers (jellyfish)   J:76
Seaborgium (element)   E:177
Sea breezes   W:82, 86, 187
Seabrook nuclear power plant (New Hampshire)   N:163
Sea caves   C:156–57
Sea cows *see* Sirenia
Sea cradles *see* Chitons
Sea dogs (pirates)   P:263–64
Seadragon (nuclear submarine)   N:339
Sea elephants *see* Elephant seals
Sea Explorer Ship groups (division of Scouting)   B:359
Sea fans (coelenterates)   J:77
Seafarer, The (Old English poem)   E:268
Sea farming *see* Aquaculture
Seaga, Edward P. G. (prime minister of Jamaica)   J:19
Seagram Building (New York City)   J:123; U:136
    picture(s)   U:136
Sea Gull, The (play by Anton Chekhov)   C:196
Sea gulls (birds)   U:246
    picture(s)   B:198; U:243
Sea hares (mollusks)   M:406
Sea horses (fish)   E:96; F:186, 194
Sea ice (around Antarctica)   A:292

Sea Islands (United States) G:135; S:296
Sea kayaks (boats) *see* Touring kayaks
Sealants, dental T:44
Sea-launched cruise missiles (SLCM) *see* SLCM
Seale, Bobby G. (Black Panther leader) A:79o
Sea level G:240; H:91; T:193
Sea lilies (marine invertebrates) *see* Crinoids
Sea Lion Cave (Oregon) C:156
Sea lions M:68, 72; S:106
Seal of the United States *see* Great Seal of the United States
Seals (animals) S:107–8
　adaptations for water living M:72
　Antarctic A:293
　Arctic region's natural resources A:380
　furs F:502
　Inuit hunting I:273
　migration H:199
　picture(s) I:6; M:71; O:25
Seals (designs)
　Comics Code seal C:454
　Great Seal of the United States G:329
　Harappan civilization A:240
　Japanese signatures J:30
　state *see* individual state articles
　picture(s)
　　Harappan clay seals A:231, 240
SEALS (United States Navy special military force) U:113
Sealskin (fur)
　picture(s) F:501, 502
Seamen (of the Merchant Marine) U:126
Sea mounts (underwater volcanic peaks) O:21, 23, 38
Seam rippers (to remove stitches in sewing) S:129
Seams (layers of coal) C:389
Séance (gathering to communicate with spirits) G:200
Sea otters A:144, 156; E:306; F:502; O:252
　picture(s) O:252
Sea pens (coelenterates) J:77
　picture(s) J:73
Seaplanes A:114; S:30
　picture(s) A:151, 569
Search and rescue teams
　disaster relief D:184–85
　police P:365
Search and seizure (in the Fourth Amendment to the United
　States Constitution) B:182; J:170
Search engines (on the Internet) C:489
Searchers, The (motion picture, 1956) M:492
Search for Extraterrestrial Intelligence *see* SETI
Search radar R:39–40
Search warrants (orders authorizing search of specific
　premises) F:89
Sea robin (fish) F:194
Sears, Minnie Earl (American librarian) L:180
Sears, Roebuck and Company M:35
Sears Tower (building, Chicago, Illinois) B:437; C:218;
　U:136
　picture(s) B:432; C:218; W:220
Seas O:43–47 *see also* the names of seas and oceans
　inland seas *see* individual names in the article Lakes
　maria (singular *mare*) on moon M:450
　What seas are actually lakes? L:26
Seas (of grass) G:314; N:325
Sea scorpions (early invertebrates) *see* Eurypterids
Seashells *see* Shells (of mollusks)
Seashores E:54; L:26; N:55 *see also* Beaches
　picture(s) B:240; N:165
Sea snakes O:25; S:211, 212, 216, 217
　picture(s) S:217
Seasonal unemployment U:28
Seasoning (of wood) W:226
Seasonings (for food) C:544; H:119–21
Seasons S:109–11 *see also* Climate; individual month
　articles
　biological clocks L:204

constellations C:530–32
Earth's motions in space E:9
farmers must conform to the cycle of F:48
flowers for spring, summer, and fall G:42, 46, 49
growing seasons *see* individual country, province, and state
　articles
hemispheres compared *see* individual month articles
hibernating animals H:128
holidays mark the passing seasons H:161–62
jet streams change with the seasons J:93
length of a shadow changes with the seasons E:383
on Mars M:105, 108
migration of animals B:237–38; H:198, 200
religious holidays by season R:153–55
time T:200
trade wind belts shift with changing seasons T:268
Why is it hotter in summer than it is in winter? S:110
picture(s)
　plant's life cycle P:311
Sea Sparrow (radar-guided missile) U:115
Sea squirts (sea animals) P:285
Sea stars (echinoderms) *see* Starfish
Seat belts A:552; B:366; H:76; M:474
SEATO *see* Southeast Asia Treaty Organization
Seattle (Native American chief) W:27 *profile*
Seattle (Washington) S:112–13; W:17, 18, 21, 27
　museums W:19, 20
　rainfall pattern D:328
　Space Needle F:17; W:22
　picture(s) S:112; W:23
　　Pike Place Market W:19
　　Space Needle F:16; L:230; W:22
　　totem in Occidental Park W:19
　　Washington, University of U:75
Sea turtles H:199, 202; O:25
　picture(s) P:9
　　migration route H:201
Sea urchins (echinoderms) A:281
Seaver, Tom (American baseball player)
　picture(s) B:93
Sea wasps (coelenterates) J:73, 77
　picture(s) J:77
Seawater (salt water) O:16–17; W:51–52
　common salt S:22
　freezing point I:4; U:21
　magnesium in M:27
　not potable (drinkable) W:73
　oceanographic studies O:35
　solution contains salt crystals C:605
　water desalting M:302; W:75
　table(s)
　　composition of O:17
Seaweeds A:180; O:28
Seawolf, USS (nuclear submarine) S:476
SeaWorld (marine park, Orlando, Florida) F:270
　picture(s) F:267
Sea World (marine park, San Diego, California) C:28; S:30
Sebaceous glands G:226
Sebhorrea *see* Dandruff
Sebring (Florida) sports-car race A:537
Sebum (oily substance produced by glands in the skin) D:123
SEC *see* Securities and Exchange Commission
Secant (ratio in trigonometry) T:312, 313
Secession (group of Austrian artists) K:271
Secession (in United States history) U:185
　Civil War issue C:336, 347
　Confederate States C:495
　Davis, Jefferson D:43
　Johnson, Andrew, opposes J:116
　Kentucky and Virginia Resolutions K:227
　Lincoln, Abraham L:244–45
　states' rights in 10th amendment to Constitution B:179
　Tyler was president of Peace Conference (1861) T:368
Second (measure of time) T:201; W:115–16

Selective Service Act (United States, 1917)   D:293
Selective Service System (in the United States)   D:293
Selectmen, board of (governing body of towns)   M:515
Selenga (river in Mongolia)   M:417
Selenium (element)   E:177; P:478
Seles, Monica (American tennis player)
    picture(s)   T:95
Seleucids (Hellenistic dynasty of Syria)   G:344; I:308; P:40c,
    155
Self-assembly (of viruses)   V:363
Self-contained cartridges (for guns)   G:419
    picture(s)   G:420
Self-contained underwater breathing apparatus see Scuba diving
Self-coordination (of automated equipment)   A:530
Self-defense
    judo   J:149–50
    karate   K:194–95
    violence and society   V:344
Self-determination
    United Nations policies   U:70–71
Self-employment   L:3
Self-government (of the body)   B:287
Self-hypnosis   H:328
Self-incrimination (in the Fifth Amendment to the United States
    Constitution)   B:182
Self-instruction see Programmed instruction
Self-pollination (of plants)   F:284; P:308
Self Portrait (drawing by Leonardo da Vinci)
    picture(s)   L:153
Self Portrait (painting by Dürer)
    picture(s)   R:170
Self Portrait (painting by Goya)
    picture(s)   P:27
Self-Portrait (painting by Rembrandt)
    picture(s)   R:156
Self-Portrait with Model (painting by Ernst Ludwig Kirchner)
    picture(s)   G:172
Self-recognition (of animals looking in mirrors)   D:278
Self-sequencing (of automated equipment)   A:530
Self-service stores   S:21, 498
Self-tapping screws   N:3
Self-teaching (educational principle)   K:249
Self-winding watches   W:45
Selim I (Ottoman sultan)   O:259
Seljuks (Turkish tribes)   T:348
Selkirk (Manitoba)   M:82
Selkirk, 5th Earl of (Thomas Douglas) (Scottish colonizer in
    Canada)   M:85; N:334
Selkirk, Alexander (Scottish seaman)   S:281
Selkirk Mountains (British Columbia–Washington)   W:16–17
Selknam (Indians of South America)   I:199
Selling see Sales
Selling short (on the stock exchange)   S:459
Selma (Alabama)
    civil rights march (1965)   A:79o; C:330
Selva (rain forest of Brazil)   B:378
Selznick, David O. (American film producer)   L:308 profile
SEM see Scanning electron microscopes
Semantics (science of meanings)   S:116
Semaphore (device for sending messages)   T:51, 270
Semele (in Greek mythology)   G:363
Semester (division of an academic year)   U:221
Semiarid areas   D:128, 130, 131
Semiautomatic guns   G:423, 424
    picture(s)   G:423
Semicircular canals (of the inner ear)   E:4, 5, 6
Semicolons (punctuation marks)   P:542
Semiconductor lasers   L:46b
Semiconductors (of electricity)   E:139; M:153–54
    automation used in processing   A:530
    electronics   E:159
    lasers   L:46b
    photoelectricity   P:196, 197
    robots used in their processing   R:254

thermistors   T:164
thermoelectric refrigeration   R:135
transistors, diodes, and integrated circuits   I:285;
    T:274–78
Semilunar valves (of the heart)   H:80, 82
Semimetals see Metalloids
Seminole (Indians of North America)   F:265, 272, 274;
    I:178, 179
    doll making   D:272
    Indian wars   I:205
    Jackson, Andrew   J:5
    Osceola   O:237
Seminole War (1835–1842)   F:274; O:237; T:31
Semipermeable membranes   O:240
Semi-postal stamps (to raise money for special causes)   P:399
Semiprecious gems   J:95
Semisynthetic antibiotics   A:307
Semitic languages   L:39
    Arabic   A:344
    Hebrew   H:98–99
    Mesopotamia   M:231, 232
    spoken in Asia   A:445
    syllabic writing systems   A:194a
Semitrailers   T:318–19, 322
Semmelweis, Ignaz (Hungarian doctor)   M:208b, 208c
Semolina (wheat product)   G:281; W:156
Semper Fidelis (Marine Corps motto and march)   U:122
Semper Paratus ("Always Prepared") (Coast Guard motto)
    U:124
Semple, Letitia (acting first lady for Tyler)   F:169
    picture(s)   F:169
Senanayake, D. S. (Ceylonese prime minister)   S:416
Senat (ancient game)   G:10, 11
Senate (of ancient Rome)   R:310
Senate, Canadian   C:75
Senate, United States see United States Senate
Senate War Investigating Committee   T:324
Sendak, Maurice (American artist and children's book writer)
    I:83; S:116
    picture(s)
        illustrations from Where the Wild Things Are   C:243;
            S:116
Sender, Ramón (Spanish novelist)   S:392
Seneca (Indians of North America)   I:175
Seneca, Lucius Annaeus (Roman philosopher and writer)
    D:299; L:76; M:286
Seneca Falls Convention (for women's rights, 1848)   W:212
Seneca Rocks (West Virginia)   W:134
    picture(s)   W:129
Senefelder, Aloys (German inventor)   G:308; P:474
Senegal   A:76d; G:8, 9; S:117–18
    picture(s)
        Dakar   S:117
        flag   F:239
        schoolgirls   A:54
Senegal River (western Africa)   G:406a; M:180
Senegambia (confederation of Senegal and The Gambia)   G:9;
    S:118
Senescence (aging of leaves)   L:114–15
Senghor, Léopold Sédar (poet and president of Senegal)
    A:76d; S:118
Senior Branches (Canadian Girl Guides)   G:217–18
Senior Girl Scouts   G:215–16
    picture(s)   G:216
Seniority (principle of job security for labor)   L:8
Sennett, Mack (American film producer and director)   C:185
Sénoufo (a people of Africa)   M:61
Sensation   B:289–91
    sensory areas of the brain   B:366
Sensation novel (in literature)   M:563
Senses
    amphibians   A:222
    birds   B:224
    body, human   B:289–91

Senses (cont.)
brain function   **B:**365, 366
butterflies and moths   **B:**476, 478
cats   **C:**142–43
communication   **C:**462
dogs   **D:**242–43
dolphins   **D:**276–77
ear   **E:**4–6
experiments and other science activities   **E:**394
eye   **E:**429–32
fish   **F:**193–94
horses   **H:**237
insects   **I:**234–35
lateral system of fish   **F:**192
mammals   **M:**67
Montessori's training method for children   **K:**249
nervous system receives information through sense organs
    N:115
organisms' response to their environment   **B:**197
snakes   **S:**213–14
turtles   **T:**358
Sensitive plant
picture(s)   **P:**315
Sensorineural hearing loss   **D:**49
Sensors (computer peripherals)   **M:**346; **O:**37; **R:**253; **S:**340L
Sensory neurons (Sensory nerves)   **B:**362; **N:**116, 118
Sensory register (of the brain)   **L:**101
Sentence (in law)   **C:**576, 586
Sentences (in grammar)   **G:**288
aptitude test questions   **T:**121
parts of speech   **P:**92–94
punctuation   **P:**541–44
sentence outlines   **O:**266, 267
Sentence starters (in grammar)   **G:**289
Sentinel Range (mountains, Antarctica)   **M:**506
Sentry dogs (used by the armed forces)   **U:**114
Seoul (capital of South Korea)   **K:**298, 300, 302, 303; **S:**119
Korean War   **K:**304, 305, 306
picture(s)   **K:**299; **S:**119
Sepals (of flowers)   **F:**282; **P:**306
Separate system (of punishment) *see* Pennsylvania system
Separation of powers (in government)   **U:**145
American system   **G:**275, 276; **S:**437; **U:**162–63
Separatists (Church of England) *see* Pilgrims
Sephardim (Jews of Asian or African origin)   **I:**369; **J:**145;
    S:370
Sepia (secretion of cuttlefish)   **I:**229
Sepia print (photographic reproduction method)   **B:**263
Sepoy Mutiny (1857)   **E:**47; **I:**132
September (ninth month of year)   **S:**120–21
September 11, 2001, terrorist attacks *see* Terrorist attacks on
    the United States
Septic tanks (for waste disposal)   **P:**339; **S:**33
Septuagint (early Greek translation of Bible)   **B:**157; **J:**103
Septum (wall dividing chambers of the heart)   **H:**80
Sequence (in music)   **M:**537
Sequences (in mathematics) *see* Number sequences
Sequential movement puzzles   **P:**554
Sequim (Washington)   **W:**18
Sequoia (giant evergreen)   **C:**21; **N:**291–92; **P:**294
ancient forests   **T:**311
bark   **P:**316
How big can a plant grow?   **P:**302
Yosemite National Park   **Y:**363
picture(s)   **K:**256; **L:**197; **T:**302
Sequoia National Park (California)   **C:**28; **N:**44
Sequoya (George Gist; George Guess) (Cherokee Indian leader)
    I:178 *profile;* **S:**122
picture(s)   **I:**178; **S:**122
Serapis (British warship)   **J:**128
picture(s)   **U:**116
Serbia and Montenegro   **S:**123–27
Balkans   **B:**22, 23
Belgrade   **B:**136

World War I   **W:**278, 285
Yugoslavia   **Y:**364, 365–66, 367, 369
map(s)   **S:**124
picture(s)
    Belgrade   **B:**136; **S:**125
    flag   **F:**239
    Golubac Castle   **S:**123
    people   **S:**123
Serbo-Croatian (language)   **S:**123
Serbs (a people of Europe)   **B:**338; **S:**123, 127
racism   **G:**96; **R:**34c
Yugoslavia   **Y:**364, 365, 369
Serenade (musical form)   **M:**541
Serengeti National Park (Tanzania)   **A:**53
picture(s)   **N:**57; **W:**217
Serengeti Plain (Kenya and Tanzania)   **T:**17
picture(s)   **T:**17
Serer (a people of Africa)   **S:**117
Serfs (workers bound in servitude to feudal lords)   **F:**102;
    M:292
Catherine II of Russia   **C:**136
Peasants' Revolt in England   **E:**241
Russia   **R:**357, 369, 370; **U:**39
Russian emancipation by Alexander II   **A:**176
serfdom was a kind of slavery of the Middle Ages   **S:**193
Sergeant at arms (officer of organizations)   **P:**81, 82
Sergeant major (fish)   **F:**196
Sergius I, Saint (pope)   **R:**292
Sergius II (pope)   **R:**292
Sergius III (pope)   **R:**292
Sergius IV (pope)   **R:**292
Serialism (in modern music)   **F:**448; **M:**398–99
Serials (periodicals) *see* Magazines
Seriation classification (of archaeological artifacts)   **A:**355
Sericulture (care of silkworms)   **S:**174–75
Series connection (of batteries)   **B:**103a
Serifs (on type)   **T:**369
Serigraphy *see* Silk-screen printing
Serkin, Rudolf (American pianist)   **M:**556
Sermisy, Claude de (French composer)   **F:**445
Sermons (religious lectures)   **A:**202; **P:**550, 551
Serosa (tissue of the stomach wall)   **S:**460
Serotonin (neurotransmitter)   **B:**363
Serpens (constellation)
picture(s)   **U:**215
Serpentine (mineral)   **A:**438c
Serpentine, The (artificial lake, London, England)   **L:**296
Serpent Mound State Memorial (Ohio) *see* Great Serpent Mound
Serra, Junípero (Spanish missionary in America)   **C:**29, 33
profile; **S:**30
Serum (watery portion of a fluid left after coagulation)
antiserums   **A:**313
blood serum in transfusions   **T:**273
snakebite serums developed in Brazil   **S:**39
Servals (wild cats)   **C:**145
picture(s)   **C:**142, 144
Servants, indentured *see* Indentured servants
Serve (Service) (tennis stroke)   **T:**88, 90–91
picture(s)   **T:**90
Servers (powerful computers)   **C:**480, 491
Service, Robert W. (Canadian poet)   **P:**353
Service industries and occupations   **I:**225 *see also* the
    economy section of province and state articles
hotels and motels   **H:**256–59
Servicemen's Readjustment Act (U.S., 1944) *see* GI Bill
Service module (SM) (section of Apollo spacecraft)   **S:**340g,
    340h–340i
Service stations (for automobiles)   **A:**555, 556
Service wells (in the oil industry)   **P:**171
Servomotors (small electric or compressed air motors)   **A:**105
Sesame Street (television program)   **F:**391; **T:**71
picture(s)   **T:**71
Sesostris III (king of ancient Egypt)
picture(s)
    sculpted portrait   **E:**113

Sesotho (language) **L:**156
Sesquicentennial Exposition (Philadelphia, 1926) **F:**16–17
Sessile benthos (organisms permanently attached to the ocean bottom) **O:**26
Sestet (last six lines of a sonnet) **P:**352
Set (in tennis) **T:**88
Set designers (Scenic designers) **M:**481; **P:**336; **T:**158
SETI (Search for Extraterrestrial Intelligence) **A:**476b; **R:**70; **S:**340c
SETI@home (radio astronomy project) **R:**70
Seton, Ernest Thompson (Canadian writer) **C:**86
Seton, Saint Elizabeth Ann Bayley (first native-born American to be canonized) **S:**18d profile
Sets (in mathematics) **M:**158, 169–70; **S:**128–28a
Sets (scenery for plays) see Stage scenery and lighting
Setswana (Bantu language) **B:**344
Setters (dogs) **D:**252
Setting (of hair) **H:**8
Setting (of novels) **N:**358
Settlement, Act of see Act of Settlement
Settlement houses (centers for social welfare) **A:**21
Setúbal (Portugal) **P:**393
Seurat, Georges (French painter) **F:**431; **I:**106; **M:**387
Seuss, Dr. (Theodor Seuss Geisel) (American author and illustrator) **I:**83; **S:**128b
    picture(s) **S:**128b
       illustration from The Cat in the Hat **C:**244
Sevareid, Eric (American broadcaster and author) **N:**334 profile
    picture(s) **N:**335
Sevastopol (Russia) **C:**587; **W:**308
Seven, Group of (Canadian painters) see Group of Seven
Seven bridges of Königsberg (topological problem) **T:**237
    picture(s) **T:**237
Seven Cities of Cíbola **C:**559
Seven Days' battles (1862, Civil War) **C:**339
Seven Hills of Rome **R:**305
Seven Pines, Battle of (1862) see Fair Oaks, Battle of
Seven Sisters (star cluster) see Pleiades
Seventeenth Amendment (to the United States Constitution) **B:**183; **U:**139, 158
Seventh-Day Adventists **P:**494; **V:**293
Seventy, The see Septuagint
78-rpm phonograph records **R:**123
Seven Weeks' War (1866) **B:**252
Seven wonders of the ancient world **W:**216–20 see also individual wonders by name
Seven Years' War (1756–1763) **G:**160; **I:**203 see also French and Indian War (1754–1763)
    Canada, history of **C:**81
    Frederick II of Prussia **F:**459–60
    French and Indian War in North America **F:**464, 465
    Pitt, William, Earl of Chatham **P:**265
Severe acute respiratory syndrome see SARS
Severe combined immunodeficiency (SCID) **B:**190; **G:**88
Severin, Tim (British adventurer) **E:**401
Severini, Gino (Italian artist) **I:**403
Severinus (pope) **R:**292
Severn River (United Kingdom) **E:**233; **T:**197; **U:**52
Severus, Septimius (Roman emperor) **R:**317
Sevier, John (American statesman) **T:**84, 86, 87 profile
Sévigné, Marquise de (French literary figure) **F:**439
Seville (Spain) **S:**372, 375, 376
    architecture **S:**381
    dance **D:**26
    Expo '92 **F:**17
    Jews, history of **J:**104
Sèvres, Treaty of (1920) **W:**291
Sèvres porcelain **P:**413
    picture(s) **P:**413
Sewage disposal **S:**33 see also Solid-waste disposal
    ancient Rome's water and sewer systems **M:**208
    community helps in prevention of disease **D:**211–12
    detergent pollution **D:**141

environment, problems of **E:**301–2
fermentation **F:**92
ocean pollution **O:**29
organic fertilizer **F:**97
plumbing **P:**339–40
water pollution **W:**66–67
wetlands purify water **W:**148
"Sewage farming" (using treated sewage water for irrigation) **W:**53
Sewall, Samuel (American colonial judge) **A:**203; **W:**209
Seward, William Henry (American statesman) **A:**157 profile; **E:**201; **J:**118; **L:**244; **M:**427
Seward's Folly (purchase of Alaska) **A:**157; **T:**109
Sewers (in plumbing) **P:**339, 340
Sewing **N:**97–101; **S:**129–30
    bookbinding methods **B:**332–33
    connecting parts of a knitted article **K:**281
    fur garments **F:**503–4
    needles **N:**102
Sewing machines **C:**378, 380; **S:**129, 130
    automation, history of **A:**533
    Howe, Elias, was one of the inventors **H:**272–73
    shoemaking **S:**160
Sex
    adolescence **A:**24, 25–26
    baby's sex determined by chromosomes **B:**3
    birth control **B:**250a–251
    bivalves change their sex **O:**290
    endocrine glands and hormones **G:**228
    homosexuality **H:**204
    hormones influence development **D:**194; **H:**227, 228
    how AIDS spreads **A:**100b
    human reproduction **B:**287
    reproduction **R:**175–79
    sexual abuse of children **C:**222
Sex-linked diseases **D:**193; **G:**81
    hemophilia **D:**193–94
Sextants (navigation instruments) **N:**75; **O:**183
    picture(s) **N:**76
Sexual harassment (unwelcome sexual conduct)
    Jones, Paula **C:**367, 368
Sexually transmitted diseases
    condoms reduce risk of **B:**250b; **D:**210
    gonorrhea **D:**193
    herpes simplex II **D:**194
    syphilis **D:**205–6
Sexual reproduction **A:**285; **B:**197; **L:**198; **R:**176–79
    birth control **B:**250a–251
    genetics and heredity **G:**77–91
    human **B:**286–87
    mammals **M:**68
    plants **P:**308, 310
    protozoans **P:**496, 497
    picture(s)
       plants **P:**309
Seychelles **S:**131
    map(s) **S:**131
    picture(s)
       flag **F:**239
Seyfert galaxies **A:**474
Seymour, Jane (third queen of Henry VIII of England) **E:**242; **H:**114
Seyyid Said (sultan of Zanzibar) **T:**19
Sezer, Ahmet Necdet (president of Turkey) **T:**349
Sfax (Tunisia) **T:**335, 336
Sforzando (musical term) **M:**537, 538
Sfumato (painting technique) **L:**154; **P:**21
Shaba (province, Democratic Republic of Congo) see Katanga
Shabuoth (Jewish holiday) **J:**146a, 146b; **R:**153
Shackleton, Sir Ernest (English explorer) **E:**415
Shades (of colors) **C:**426
Shading (in art) **D:**311, 317; **E:**294
Shadow clocks see Sundials
Shadow mask (of a television receiver) **T:**63
Shadow of a Gunman (play by O'Casey) **I:**327

Shadow puppets M:58; P:545
  picture(s) P:548
Shadows L:212, 216, 217
  eclipses E:50–52
  how the length changes with the seasons E:383
  photography, light sources for P:212
Shadows, The (house, New Iberia, Louisiana) L:322
Shadow skating (in pair figure skating) I:41
Shaffer, Peter (English dramatist) D:305; E:290
Shafter, William R. (American general) S:392d
Shaftesbury, Lord (English statesman) E:246
Shaft mining C:389; I:330
Shafts (in mines) M:321
Shagbark hickory trees
  picture(s) T:304
Shahadah (Islam's creed) I:348; R:148
Shah Jahan (Mogul emperor) I:132; T:12
  picture(s) I:116, 132
Shahn, Ben (American painter)
  picture(s)
    mural depicting refugees I:92
    Triple Dip (print) G:306
Shah-nameh (Persian epic)
  picture(s) I:78
Shah of Iran *see* Mohammed Reza Pahlavi; Reza Shah Pahlavi
Shakers A:315; F:297
  picture(s)
    furniture F:296
Shaker Village (Canterbury, New Hampshire) N:158
Shakespeare, William (English poet and dramatist) S:132–39
  Elizabethan drama dominated by D:301
  England, his description of E:232
  English literature, place in E:272–73
  Hamlet (tragedy), excerpt from E:266
  Midsummer Night's Dream, A (comedy) F:9, 12
  nonsense verse and prose N:276
  plot outlines of his plays S:135–39
  quotations from plays Q:22
  Renaissance literature R:160
  Romeo and Juliet, metaphor used in P:351
  signature prized A:527
  Sonnet 18 P:352
  theater in England T:160; U:49
  What is the most frequently performed drama in history? D:298
  picture(s) E:363; P:351
    Olivier, Laurence, as Hamlet D:297
    Romeo and Juliet, scene from W:265
    signature prized A:527
    statue U:48
Shakespearean sonnet P:352
Shakespeare memorial theaters A:135; C:69; T:160
  picture(s) O:131
Shale (rock) G:117; R:268–69, 270
Shallots (plants of onion family) O:123; V:290
Shallow-water swamps W:146
Shalmaneser III (king of Assyria) A:462
Shalmei (medieval musical instrument) *see* Shawm
Shalyapin, Feodor *see* Chaliapin, Feodor
Shamanism (primitive religion) A:449; I:275; K:295, 299; P:437
Shamir, Yitzhak (Israeli political leader) I:376
Shamisen (stringed instrument) D:24
Shamma (Ethiopian garment) E:331
Shampoos (for hair) A:330; H:7, 8
Shamrock (cloverleaf symbol of Ireland) H:165; P:100
Shan (a people of Myanmar) M:557, 561
Shang (Yin) dynasty (in Chinese history) A:240–41; C:268, 276; D:74
  picture(s)
    bronze vessel A:231
Shanghai (China) C:265, 270; S:140–41
  picture(s) C:265; S:140, 141
Shannon (British warship) W:10
Shannon, Claude (American mathematician) T:49

Shannon River (Ireland) I:318–19; R:246
Shantytowns (poor settlements) H:190; L:53
Shapers (tools) F:515; T:232
Shapley, Harlow (American astronomer) A:476a *profile*
  picture(s) A:476a
Shapur I (Persian king) P:156
Shapur II (Persian king) P:157
Sharchops (a people of Bhutan) B:155
Sharecroppers A:79i
Share Our Wealth plan (of Huey Long) L:300
Shares (in television ratings) T:69
Shariah (Muslim laws) I:348; S:480
Sharif, Nawaz (Pakistani prime minister) P:40a
Shari River (central Africa) C:170, 180, 181; L:29
Sharkey, Jack (American boxer) B:351
Sharks F:219; S:142–45; U:22
  freshwater sharks in Lake Nicaragua L:32; N:245
  picture(s) E:378; F:188; N:168; U:22
Shark suckers *see* Remoras
Sharon, Ariel (prime minister of Israel) I:376
Sharon, Plain of (Israel) I:371
Sharp, Becky (character in Thackeray's *Vanity Fair*) T:146–47
Sharp, Granville (British abolitionist) S:172
Shar-peis (dogs) *see* Chinese shar-peis
Sharpeville Massacre (South Africa, 1960) M:78; S:273
Sharps breech-loading carbine
  picture(s) G:420
Sharpsburg, Battle of *see* Antietam, Battle of
Sharp-shinned hawks (birds) H:64
Sharp sign (in musical notation) M:534, 537
Shasta (Indians of North America) I:186
Shasta, Mount (California) C:18
Shasta daisies (flowers) B:452
  picture(s) G:50
Shasta Lake (California) C:21
Shastri, Lal Bahadur (prime minister of India) I:133
Shatt al Arab (river between Iraq and Iran) I:312, 316
Shavante (Native American language) I:197
Shaver, Phillip (American psychologist) P:510
Shavu'ot (Jewish holiday) *see* Shabuoth
Shaw, Bernard (American news broadcaster)
  picture(s) T:71
Shaw, George Bernard (Irish playwright) I:322; S:146
  leading English-language playwright E:289
  realism in drama D:303; R:114
  Shaw Festival (Ontario, Canada) C:69
  spelling "fish" as "ghoti" S:398
Shaw, T. E. *see* Lawrence of Arabia
Shaw, USS (battleship)
  picture(s) W:293
Shawm (Shalmei) (medieval musical instrument) M:297
  picture(s) M:297
Shawn, Ted (American dancer) D:31, 32 *profile*
Shawnee Prophet *see* Tenskwatawa
Shawnees (Indians of North America) I:178, 179
  Indian wars I:204
  Kentucky K:225
  Shawnee Sun was first newspaper in Kansas K:185
  Tippecanoe, Battle of H:42
Shawnee Trail (cattle trail) C:578
Shays' Rebellion U:145–46
Shchedrin, Rodion (Russian composer) R:386
Shea, George Beverly (American gospel singer) H:326
Shea, Jim (American athlete) O:117
Shearing (Clipping) (of sheep) W:234
  picture(s) W:234
Shearlings (skins of sheared sheep) L:110
Shear walls (in construction) B:437
Shear waves (of earthquakes) *see* S-waves
Sheaves (pulleys) E:185
Sheba, Queen of (Ethiopian princess) A:76c; C:465; E:333; S:251
Shedlock, Marie (English lecturer and writer) S:464
Sheen, Fulton (American bishop) O:191

Shevardnadze, Eduard (political leader of republic of Georgia) G:148
Shi (in classical Chinese literature) C:278
Shichi-Go-San (Japanese holiday) J:32
Shields (in tunnel building) T:338
Shields (kind of armor) A:423, 424
  picture(s) A:425; H:117; P:2
Shield volcanoes M:107; V:380
Shifting cultivation see Migratory agriculture
Shifts (changes in viruses) I:228
Shift workers B:194
Shigatse (Tibet) T:190
Shih tzus (dogs) D:246
Shi Huangdi (Shih Huang Ti) (Chinese emperor) A:242; C:268–69
  burial sculptures near his tomb A:356; C:259, 277; F:495; P:409–10
  Great Wall of China A:241
  picture(s) A:233; C:268
    burial sculptures A:242, 356; C:277; P:409; W:219
Shi'ites (major sect of Islam) I:346, 350, 351
  Arabs A:343–44
  Iran I:305, 307, 308, 309
  Iraq I:311, 316, 316a
  Khomeini, Ruhollah K:240
  Middle East M:299
Shikoku (island of Japan) J:35
Shiloh, Battle of (1862, Civil War) C:338; G:295
Shiloh National Military Park T:82
  picture(s) T:82
Shimin, Symeon (American illustrator) C:240
Shimmers (beats in tempered tuning) S:262
Shinbone see Tibia
Shingles (disease) D:200; V:367
Shingles (on a house) B:433; F:105; H:188
  picture(s) B:435; F:105
Shining Path (Peruvian guerrilla movement) P:165
Shinkansen (Japanese turbo train system) O:235
  picture(s) T:285
Shinto (Shintoism) (religion of Japan) R:146, 151–52
  Asian religions A:448
  Japan J:27, 32, 40
  Japanese architecture A:366
  marriage rites W:103
  picture(s) J:31; R:152; W:101
Ship canals C:88–90
Shipibo (Native American language) I:197
Ship Island (Mississippi)
  picture(s) M:352
Shipley, Jenny (prime minister of New Zealand) N:242
Shipp, Ellis Reynolds (American physician) U:255 profile
Ships and shipping S:153–59
  Bermuda Triangle disappearances B:152
  Canada C:66
  canals C:88–90
  containerized cargo R:85
  diesel engines D:162
  fishing ships for processing the catch F:220
  freight transportation T:289
  gyroscopes G:437, 438
  icebergs a danger I:17–18
  insurance from Lloyd's of London I:252
  International Code of Signals, use of F:247
  Japan is world leader in shipbuilding A:451
  lanterns I:233
  lighthouses and lightships L:227–29
  Maine shipbuilding M:43, 50
  navigation N:72–77
  ocean liners O:30–33
  oceanographic research O:34, 37, 39, 41
  radio, importance of I:284
  Saint Lawrence Seaway S:15
  speed measured in knots K:286
  steam turbines T:342

submarines S:473–76
United States Merchant Marine U:126
United States Navy: types of ships U:114–15
Viking ships V:339
whaling ships W:154–55
What are flotsam, jetsam, and lagan? S:158
Why are ships christened with champagne? S:156
Why are the left and right sides of a ship called port and starboard? S:154
why boats float F:253
picture(s)
  Bath Iron Works (Maine) M:42
  being loaded with grain O:209
  going through locks on a canal M:267
  Jamestown colonists' ships J:22
  Viking ships V:339, 340
  welder in Finnish shipyard F:137
Shipworms (Teredo worms) (clams) M:407; O:291
Shipwrecks U:18–20, 24
Shiraz (Iran) I:309
Shire Highlands (Malawi) M:52, 53
Shire horses H:241
Shire River (Malawi–Mozambique) L:32; M:52
Shirley Temple dolls D:270
Shish kebab (popular food) T:345
Shiva (Hindu god) A:240; H:139, 140, 142
  picture(s)
    bronze statue I:135
Shivah (Jewish period of mourning) F:494; J:147
Shivering (snakes' incubation process) S:214
Shivering thermogenesis (production of body heat by shivering the muscles) H:126
Shkhara, Mount (highest peak in the Republic of Georgia) G:147
Shkumbi River (Albania) A:159
Shmuel Ha-nagid (Hebrew poet) see Ha-nagid, Shmuel
Shneur, Z. (Yiddish author) Y:361
Shock (drop in body's blood pressure) F:159
  picture(s)
    first aid for F:159
Shock absorbers (of an automobile) A:551
Shockley, William (American inventor) I:285
Shock waves (in physics)
  aerodynamics of compressed air A:40
  measuring the depth of ice I:7
  nuclear blast N:376
  oil deposits located with seismographs P:169
  seismic waves of earthquakes E:14
  supersonic flight S:499, 501
Shoemaker-Levy, Comet J:162; S:368
Shoes S:160
  bowling B:349
  exercise, shoes for P:227
  folk dance F:302
  hiking and backpacking H:134–35
  ice-skating boots I:38, 39, 40
  industry's needs I:224
  leather L:109, 110, 111
  Massachusetts industry M:140, 142, 150
  New Hampshire industry N:156, 162
  running shoes J:111
  ski boots S:184c
  synthetic materials L:111
  track shoes T:253
  picture(s)
    Chinese factory I:224
    Dutch clogs N:119
    leather, uses of L:109
Shoes (of drum brakes) A:550
Shofar (ram's horn) J:148
  picture(s) J:143; M:299
Shoguns (early Japanese military governors) J:42, 43–45
Sholem Aleykhem (Jewish writer and humorist) see Aleykhem (Aleichem), Sholem

Sholes, Christopher Latham (American printer, journalist, and
    inventor)   **T:**374
Sholokhov, Mikhail (Russian author)   **N:**363; **R:**384
Shona (language)   **Z:**381
Shooting (sport)   **H:**300–301
    Oakley, Annie   **O:**2
"Shooting of Dan McGrew, The" (poem by Service)   **P:**353
Shootings (crimes)   **J:**168
    picture(s)   **J:**167
Shooting stars (meteors) *see* Meteors
Shopping *see also* Food shopping
    airport shops   **A:**127
    department stores   **D:**118
    mail order   **M:**34–35
    retail stores   **R:**188–89
    Soviet system   **U:**36
Shopping centers (malls)   **R:**188
    Mall of America (Bloomington, Minnesota)   **M:**335
    Southdale, first fully enclosed, environmentally controlled
        shopping center   **A:**376
    world's largest (Edmonton, Canada)   **E:**73
    picture(s)   **R:**188
        Galleria (Houston, Texas)   **T:**133
        São Paulo (Brazil)   **S:**288
Shore Establishment (of the United States Navy)   **U:**112
Short circuits (in electricity)   **E:**148
Short-day plants   **F:**287
Shortening (cooking ingredient)   **B:**387; **O:**79, 81
Shorter, Wayne (American jazz saxophonist)   **J:**63
Shorthaired cats   **C:**138, 139
Shortleaf pine trees
    picture(s)   **A:**407
Short Parliament (English, 1640)   **E:**245
Short sale (of stock not actually owned)   **S:**459
Short-statured persons *see* Dwarfism
Short Stirling (British bomber plane)   **A:**565
Shortstop (in baseball)   **B:**80
Short stories   **S:**161–65
    Arabic literature   **A:**342
    Australian literature   **A:**500–501
    book reports on   **B:**316
    fiction, development of   **F:**115, 116
    Hawthorne, Nathaniel   **H:**65
    Henry, O.   **H:**112
    Poe, Edgar Allan   **P:**348
    types of literature   **L:**259
Short-term memory   **B:**367
Short ton (measure of weight)   **W:**114, 115
Shortwave radio   **R:**51–52
Shoshone Falls (Snake River, Idaho)   **I:**54; **W:**59
    picture(s)   **I:**49
Shoshone National Forest (Wyoming)
    picture(s)   **N:**30
Shoshoni (Indians of North America)   **I:**46, 180, 186
    Nevada   **N:**128, 134
    Wyoming   **W:**338
    picture(s)   **F:**141; **I:**50, 175; **W:**339
Shostakovich, Dmitri (Soviet composer)   **O:**148; **R:**386
Shotcreting (in tunnel building)   **T:**337
Shotguns (pellet-firing guns)   **G:**419; **H:**300
    picture(s)   **G:**419
Shot lists (in motion pictures)   **M:**481
Shot put (field event)   **O:**120; **T:**252, 257, 258, 261
    picture(s)   **O:**120
Shots (photographic components of motion pictures)   **M:**481
Shoulder arms (guns that are held to the shoulder when fired)
    G:415, 423
Show Boat (musical by Kern and Hammerstein)   **M:**554
Showboats (steamboats with theater and a company of actors)
    T:159
Showers (baths) *see* Baths and bathing
Show Me State (nickname for Missouri)   **M:**366, 367
Showy lady's slipper (flower)
    picture(s)   **M:**327
Shredders (office machines)   **O:**60

Shreve, Henry Miller (American steamboat pioneer)   **L:**323
Shreveport (Louisiana)   **L:**319, 323, 328
    picture(s)   **L:**323
Shrews (animals of insectivore group)   **A:**271; **H:**128; **S:**166
    picture(s)   **M:**74; **S:**166
Shrewsbury, Battle of (1403)   **H:**109
Shrike missiles   **M:**349
Shrimps (crustaceans)   **C:**601, 602; **S:**167–68
    benthic ocean life   **O:**26
    fishing industry   **F:**217
    glands control molting   **G:**226
    picture(s)   **L:**320
    table(s)
        United States aquaculture production   **F:**208
Shrine of the Book (Jerusalem)   **D:**47; **J:**81
Shrines
    Guadalupe, Basilica of the Virgin of   **M:**241; **R:**155
    Kyoto (Japan), City of a Thousand Shrines   **K:**312
    Our Lady of the Angels   **C:**564–65
    saints   **S:**18c
    Shinto shrines rebuilt every twenty years   **A:**366
Shriver, Eunice Kennedy (founder of Special Olympics)   **S:**394
Shrouds (coverings to protect satellites)   **S:**54
Shrouds (on sailboats)   **S:**11
Shrove Tuesday (religious holiday) *see* Mardi Gras
Shrubs (low, usually several-stemmed woody plants)   **G:**29
Shrunken heads (Jivaro Indian custom)   **I:**198
Shuar (Indians of South America)   **I:**197
Shubra Khit, Battle of (1798)   **N:**10
Shuffleboard (game)   **S:**169
Shula, Don (American football coach)   **F:**359
Shulevitz, Uri (American author and illustrator)
    picture(s)
        One Monday Morning (book)   **I:**84
Shulhan Arukh (Orthodox Jewish law)   **J:**148
Shunga dynasty (India)   **I:**136
Shunning (practice of the Amish)   **A:**220
Shushan (Iran) *see* Susa
Shushkevich, Stanislav (president of Belarus)
    picture(s)   **C:**459
Shuswap (Indians of North America)   **I:**188
Shutters (in cameras)   **L:**148; **P:**200–201, 213
Shuttle (device of a loom to pass threads)   **I:**216–17; **R:**353;
    W:98b
Shuttle, space *see* Space shuttles
Shuttlecock (used in playing badminton)   **B:**13
Shuwaykh (Kuwait)   **K:**310
Shwe Dagon Pagoda (in Yangon, Myanmar)   **M:**560
    picture(s)   **M:**557
SI *see* Metric system
Siad Barré, Mohammed (president of Somalia)   **S:**255
Siam *see* Thailand
Siamang gibbons   **A:**325
Siamese cats   **C:**138
    picture(s)   **C:**138; **P:**177
Siamese fighting fish   **F:**204
Siamese twins (twins whose bodies are joined together)
    C:485; **T:**364
Sibelius, Jean (Finnish composer)   **A:**249; **S:**169
Siberia (Asian region of Russia)   **A:**441; **R:**362, 363; **S:**170
    Arctic region   **A:**379, 380
    Inuit   **I:**272–76
    prairies   **P:**427–28
    winter temperatures   **A:**443
    picture(s)   **A:**444; **R:**243, 361
Siberian huskies (working dogs)   **D:**245, 247
Siberian tigers   **C:**144, 145; **R:**363; **T:**198
Sibling relationships (in the family)   **B:**4
Sichuan Basin (China)   **C:**262
Sicily (island off southwestern tip of Italy)   **I:**368
    Frederick II (king)   **F:**459
    Middle Ages   **M:**291
    Two Sicilies, Kingdom of the   **R:**157
    World War II   **W:**308
    picture(s)   **I:**383

flags of the world **F:**225–48
heraldry **H:**116–18
hieroglyphic writing systems **H:**129–31
map legends or keys **M:**96
mathematical notations **M:**168
musical notation **M:**533–39
numerals and numeration systems **N:**403–9
Olympic symbol **O:**108
Paralympic symbol **O:**115
sets in mathematics **S:**128
trademarks **T:**266–67
traffic signs and signals **D:**326; **T:**270
weather map symbols **W:**92–93
Who invented mathematical signs? **M:**165
word writing systems **A:**194
zodiac signs for each month *see* individual month articles
picture(s)
    corporate design **C:**458
    map legends or keys **M:**92, 93, 95
    political parties, cartoon about **P:**371
    snake is a symbol of the medical profession **M:**205
    tavern sign **C:**412
table(s)
    chemical elements **C:**200
Sigurd (Siegfried) (Norse hero) **N:**281
Sigurdsson, Jón (Icelandic scholar and politician) **I:**37
Sihamoni, Norodom (king of Cambodia) **C:**38
Sihanouk, Norodom (king of Cambodia) **C:**38
picture(s) **C:**38
Sikharulidze, Anton (Russian athlete) **O:**117
picture(s) **O:**117
Sikhs (religious group of India) **I:**123, 134; **R:**146, 150–51
    United Kingdom **U:**48
picture(s) **I:**117, 118
Si Kiang (river, China) *see* Xi Jiang
Sikkim (state, India) **I:**134
Sikorsky, Igor Ivanovich (Russian-American aeronautical engineer) **H:**104
Sikorsky Aircraft Company **A:**565
Silage (Ensilage) (livestock feed) **D:**5; **F:**52
Silas Marner (novel by George Eliot) **E:**190
Silberman, Gottfried (German piano builder) **O:**219; **P:**241
Silent Cal (nickname for Calvin Coolidge) **C:**545
"Silent Night, Holy Night" (carol) **A:**522; **C:**118
Silent pictures (early movies) **C:**185–86; **M:**487–90
Silent Spring (book by Rachel Carson) **C:**121, 526; **S:**75
Silent system (of punishment) *see* Auburn system
Silent World, The (book by Cousteau and Dumas) **C:**577
Siles Zuazo, Hernán (president of Bolivia) **B:**310
Silhouette (in fashion design) **F:**65
Silhouette (island, Seychelles) **S:**131
Silica (Silicon dioxide) **G:**229, 318; **O:**17; **P:**302; **R:**347
Silicate slag **I:**332
Silicon (element) **E:**177
    conductor of electricity **C:**211; **S:**250
    integrated circuits **T:**278
    photovoltaic cells **P:**196
    semiconductors **M:**154; **T:**274–75
    solar cells **B:**103c
    solid-state devices **E:**159
    picture(s)
        arrangement of atoms **A:**489
        crystal **M:**154
        electron shells **C:**203
Silicon bronze (alloy) **B:**409–10
Silicon carbide *see* Carborundum
Silicon chips *see* Computer chips
Silicon dioxide *see* Silica
Silicones (chemical compounds) **L:**335; **R:**346; **S:**173
Silicon Valley (area around San Jose, California) **G:**104; **S:**34
Silicosis (lung disease) **D:**197; **M:**322
Silisili, Mount (Samoa) **W:**124
Silk **S:**174–75
    decorative arts **D:**75, 78

natural fibers **F:**109
needlecraft **N:**97
Oriental watercolor painting **W:**55
silk-screen printing **S:**176
spider genes used to grow silk-producing cells **B:**214
spiders' silk **S:**403, 404
textiles, history of **T:**143, 144, 146
thread **S:**129
picture(s)
    drying of dyed threads **D:**378
    industry **S:**175
Silk cotton tree *see* Ceiba
Silko, Leslie Marmon (American writer) **A:**219
Silk Road (trade route) **A:**242; **P:**410; **U:**257
Silk-screen printing **G:**308; **P:**478; **S:**176; **T:**143; **W:**7
Silkworms **F:**109; **K:**198; **P:**98; **S:**174–75
picture(s) **B:**482; **F:**109; **I:**249
Silky anteaters (mammals) **A:**296
Silla kingdom (Korea) **K:**297, 302–3
Silliman, Benjamin, Jr. (American chemist) **P:**168
Sills, Beverly (American opera singer) **O:**141 *profile*
Silmarillion (book by Tolkien) **T:**220
Silos (underground structures for storing missiles) **M:**348
Silt (soil) **C:**89; **D:**321–22; **S:**235
Silurian period (in geology) **E:**25, 27
table(s) **F:**384
Silver **S:**177–78
    antique **A:**316a
    batteries **B:**103b
    coins and coin collecting **C:**399, 400
    dolls made of **D:**268
    electroplating **E:**165
    elements **E:**177
    free coinage was Bryan's political issue **B:**416
    Hayes administration restored limited coinage **H:**71
    Idaho production **I:**46
    jewelry **J:**96
    Mexico is world's leading exporter **M:**243
    money **M:**413
    Nevada mines **N:**122, 131, 135, 136
    North American mineral resources **N:**293
    photographs, developing of **P:**199, 211
    Revere, Paul, as silversmith **R:**192, 193
    Sherman Silver Purchase Act (1890) **C:**360
    Why is high-quality silver called "sterling"? **S:**178
    picture(s)
        baby's rattle made of **C:**410
        teapot made by Paul Revere **C:**414
    table(s) **M:**235
"Silver" (poem by Walter de la Mare) **F:**123
Silver bromide (chemical compound) **P:**204
Silver dollar (coin) **D:**263
Silverfish (insects) **H:**262
picture(s) **I:**231
Silver iodide (chemical used in cloud seeding) **W:**95
Silverius, Saint (pope) **R:**292
Silver-plating (electroplating process) **E:**165
Silver Star (American award)
picture(s) **D:**70
Silver State (nickname for Nevada) **N:**122, 123
Silverstein, Shel (American writer, illustrator, cartoonist, and composer) **C:**235 *profile*
picture(s)
    illustration from *Where the Sidewalk Ends* **C:**248
Silver Strand Fall (California) **W:**59
Silversword (plant) **H:**52
Silverware **I:**314–15; **K:**283–85; **S:**178
Silviculture (control of tree growth in forests) **F:**377
Sima Qian (Chinese author) **C:**278
Simchat Torah (last day of Sukkoth festival) **J:**146a
Simcoe, John Graves (British colonial governor) **O:**137; **T:**243
Simenon, Georges (Belgian writer) **B:**134; **M:**565 *profile*
Simeon I (czar of Bulgaria) **B:**445
Simeon II (czar of Bulgaria, in exile) **B:**446
Simeon of Polozk (Russian writer) **R:**380–81

Simeon Stylites, Saint   B:491
Similarity (in geometry)   G:125
Similar triangles (in trigonometry)   T:312
Simile (figure of speech)   F:122; P:351
Simitis, Costas (Greek political leader)   G:338
Simla (India)   I:123
Simmental (breed of beef cattle)   C:151
Simmering (method of cooking)   C:542
Simms, William Gilmore (American novelist)   A:208
Simon, Claude (French novelist)   F:443
Simon, Herbert (American social scientist)   P:507
Simón, Moisés (Cuban musician)   C:609
Simon, Paul (American singer and songwriter)   R:263 profile
Simon, Theodore (French psychologist)   I:253, 254; P:508
Simon Bar Kokhba (Jewish military leader) see Bar Kokhba
Simone di Martino (Italian painter) see Martini, Simone
Simonides (Greek poet)   G:356
Simonov, Konstantin (Russian author)   R:384
Simon Peter see Peter, Saint
Simon Says (game)   G:19
Simon the Cananaean, Saint (one of the Apostles)   A:329
Simon Wiesenthal Center (Los Angeles, California)   H:174
Simony (sale of sacred things)   L:151; R:289
Simple leaves   L:112; P:306
   picture(s)   L:113
Simple machines   W:247–51
Simplicius, Saint (pope)   R:292
Simplification (in algebra)   A:182–83
Simplon Pass (through the Alps)   A:194d
Simplon Tunnel (through the Alps)   A:194d
Simpson, George (American paleontologist)   E:375
Simpson, James Young (English doctor)   A:255; M:208a
Simpson, Wallis Warfield (Duchess of Windsor)   E:92
Simpson Desert (Australia)   D:126
Simulations (video games)   V:332c
Simulators (machines to imitate certain conditions)
   astronaut training   A:466–67; C:486; S:340a
   computers, uses of   C:485, 486
   driver education   D:326
   simulation programs   C:491
   space museums' programs   P:274
   picture(s)
      astronaut training   S:340a
Simulcasting (broadcasting of a program through more than
      one medium at the same time)   R:61
Sin   C:287; J:144; R:283
Sinai Peninsula (Egypt)   E:102; P:42
   wars in   E:105; I:375, 376
Sinatra, Frank (American singer)   N:179 profile
Sinclair (Wyoming)   W:340
Sinclair, Upton Beall (American author)   A:214; C:534
Sindebele (language)   Z:381
Sindhis (a people of Pakistan)   K:193; P:35
   picture(s)   P:35
Sine (ratio in trigonometry)   T:312, 313
Singapore (capital of Singapore)   S:179, 181
   picture(s)   S:179, 180
Singapore (island nation, Southeast Asia)   S:179–81
   economy   S:332
   ethnic Chinese population   S:328
   Indian Ocean trade   I:161
   World War II   W:304
   map(s)   S:179
   picture(s)   S:334
      flag   F:239
      Singapore (capital city)   S:179, 180
Singapore Strait   S:180
Singer, I. J. (Yiddish novelist)   Y:361
Singer, Isaac Bashevis (American writer)   Y:361
Singer, Isaac Merrit (American inventor)   C:380; S:129
Singh, Gulab (Dogra prince of Kashmir)   K:198
Singh, Maharajah Sir Hari (Hindu ruler)   K:198
Singh, Manmohan (prime minister of India)   I:134

Singing   V:377–78 see also Choral music
   Africa, music of   A:77, 79
      folk music   F:320–28
      jazz singers   J:60
Singing telegrams   T:52
Singin' in the Rain (motion picture, 1952)   M:492
Single-acting cylinders (in hydraulic systems)   H:313
Single Action Army Colt (revolver)   G:422
Single crochet stitch (in crocheting)   C:590
Single-leaf piñon (tree)
   picture(s)   N:123
Single-lens reflex (SLR) cameras   P:202, 207, 213
   diagram(s)   P:200
Single-member districts (in United States electoral system)
      E:130
Single-mode fibers (fiber optics)   F:107
Single-parent families   F:38; P:419
Single photon emission computed tomography   I:86
Singspiel (German half-spoken opera)   O:143
Singularity (in physics)   S:433
Sinhalese (a people of Sri Lanka)   S:413, 416
Siniora, Fouad (prime minister of Lebanon)   L:123
Sinkers (weights used in fishing)   F:211
Sinkholes (in Earth)   F:262; K:214; L:27; W:73
Sinkiang (China) see Xinjiang
Sinks see Sinkholes
Sinnar (former African kingdom)   S:480
Sinn Féin party (of Ireland)   I:324; N:337
Sinoatrial node (SA node; Pacemaker) (heart structure that
      regulates heartbeat)   C:306; H:81
Sino-Japanese War (1894–1895)   J:45; T:9
Sino-Japanese War (1937–1945)   C:217; M:90
Sino-Tibetan languages   A:445; L:40; T:189
Sinte Gleska University (South Dakota)   S:318
Sintering (of ores)   M:233
Sinterklaas see Nicholas, Saint
Sinuses (open spaces in the bodies of invertebrates)   C:306
Sinusoids (in the liver)   L:268
Sioux (Indians of North America)   I:178, 179–80, 182
   Bozeman Trail   O:282
   Indian wars   I:205
   Minnesota   M:330, 331, 338
   North Dakota   N:334
   South Dakota   S:312, 324, 325
   Wyoming uprisings   W:344
   picture(s)
      children in computer class   I:200
      Indian wars   I:203
      Lakota Sioux in 1890 photograph   S:325
Sioux City (Iowa)   I:299
Sioux Falls (South Dakota)   S:312, 318, 319, 321, 322, 324
   picture(s)   S:321
Sioux State (nickname for North Dakota)   N:322, 323
Sipadan (island in Celebes Sea)   M:59
Sipán (Peruvian archaeological site)   A:245, 354
Siphons (necks of clams)   M:406; O:290
Sir (British title)   K:277
Sira (Mohammed's biography)   I:347
Sirach (book of Wisdom literature) see Ecclesiasticus
Sirenia (Sea cows) (order of mammals)   H:216; M:72, 77
   picture(s)
      manatee as example   M:71
Sirens (in Greek mythology)   M:77; O:53
Sirens (signals)   C:466
Sirhan, Sirhan B. (Jordanian assassin of Robert Kennedy)
      K:211
Siricius, Saint (pope)   R:292
Sirionú (Indians of South America)   I:197
Sirius (Dog Star)   C:531; D:256; S:428, 429
Sirius (early steamship)   T:284
Sirius Satellite Radio   R:61
Sirk, Douglas (American film director)   M:492
Sirocco (dry wind from the Sahara)   A:186; E:318; M:212
Sisal (tropical plant)   F:109; R:334; T:18
Sisinnius (pope)   R:292

Siskiyou Mountains (California–Oregon) *see* Klamath Mountains
Sisley, Alfred (French painter)   I:103
picture(s)
   The Bridge at Sevres (painting)   I:104
Sissinghurst Gardens (Kent, England)
picture(s)   P:77
Sister Carrie (novel by Theodore Dreiser)   A:214; D:324
Sistine Chapel (Vatican, Rome, Italy)   V:280–81
   art museums   M:525
   Botticelli's wall paintings   B:345
   Michelangelo's work   I:397; M:257; R:169
   Raphael's tapestries   I:397; R:106
picture(s)
   Michelangelo's work   M:255–56; V:281
Siswati (language)   S:521
Sisyphus (in Greek mythology)   G:367
Sita (wife of Rama in Hindu literature)   I:140
Sitar (musical instrument)   I:143; M:544
Sitcoms (Situation comedies) (television programs)   G:357;
   T:69–70
Sit-down strikes (labor tactic)   O:77
Sitecast construction (of buildings)   B:438
Site fidelity (return of animals to a location where they have
   lived before)   H:197
Sites (areas chosen by archaeologists for digging)   A:351–57
Sit-ins (to protest discrimination in public places)   A:79n;
   C:330; N:321
Sitka (Alaska)   A:148, 151, 156
Sitka National Historical Park (Alaska)   A:148
Sitka spruce trees
picture(s)   A:145
Sittang River (in Myanmar)   M:559
Sitters (spies)   S:407
Sitting Bull (Sioux chief)   I:181 *profile*; S:326, 327 *profile*
   Buffalo Bill's Wild West shows   B:431
   Indians defended North Dakota hunting grounds   N:334
   Indian wars   I:182
picture(s)   I:180; S:327
Sitting war (Phony war) (1939–1940)   W:296
Situation comedies *see* Sitcoms
Sit-ups (exercise)   P:225
Sitwell, Dame Edith (English poet and critic)   E:287
Six, The (French composers)   F:448
Six-Day War (1967)   I:376; S:481
Six Dynasties period (in Chinese history)   C:274
Six Flags over America (amusement parks)   N:172; P:79
Six Nations of the Iroquois *see* Five Nations
Sixteenth Amendment (to the U.S. Constitution)   I:111; U:158
Sixth Amendment (to the U.S. Constitution)   B:182, 183
Sixtine edition (of the Bible)   B:157
Sixtus I, Saint (pope)   R:292
Sixtus II, Saint (pope)   R:292
Sixtus III, Saint (pope)   R:292
Sixtus IV (pope)   R:293
Sixtus V (pope)   R:293
Size (bigness)
   American lobster was heaviest crustacean ever caught
      L:280
   animals, large and small   A:271
   dog breeds vary greatly   D:255
   How big can a plant grow?   P:302
   How big do fish grow?   F:186
   How big do flowers grow?   F:283
   How big do mammals grow?   M:66
   human beings' physical traits   H:281
   mollusks   M:408
   plants   P:294
Size (coating for paper)   W:54
Skadi (giant in Norse mythology)   N:279
Skaggs, Ricky (American singer)   C:573
picture(s)   C:573
Skagit (Indians of North America)   I:188
Skagway (Alaska)
picture(s)   A:157
Skaldic poetry (early Scandinavian poetry)   N:277; S:58h

Skalds (medieval Scandinavian singers)   M:297
Skanderbeg (Albanian hero) *see* Kastrioti, George
Skansen (Sweden)   M:524
Skate (American nuclear submarine)   E:414
Skateboarding   S:182
Skates (fish)   S:145
Skating *see* Ice-skating; Roller-skating
Skating, figure *see* Figure skating
Skavronskaya, Marfa (Russian empress) *see* Catherine I
Skeena River (Canada)   B:402
Skeeter class (of iceboats)   I:19
Skeletal muscles   B:279, 280; M:518–19
   fish   F:190
Skeletal system (of the body)   S:183–84b
   bat's skeleton is the framework for its wings   B:100
   birds   B:222
   body, human   B:278
   coral polyps   C:555, 556
   dinosaurs   D:168–69, 172–73
   fish   F:189–90
   insects   I:231–32
   racial differences   R:30, 33
   sharks, rays, and chimaeras   S:142
   sponge skeleton   S:412
picture(s)
   bat's skeleton   B:101
Skeleton (sledding)   O:117
picture(s)   O:117
Skeleton construction (of buildings)   B:437
Skeleton keys   L:284
Skeps (medieval beehives)   H:212
Skepticism   H:288
Skerrit, Roosevelt (prime minister of Dominica)   D:279
Sketching *see* Drawing
Skidding (in logging)   L:339, 341
Skidmore, Owings, and Merrill (American architects)   A:375;
   U:136
Skiffs (boats)   F:218
Skiing   S:184c–185
   artificial snow   W:95
   Austria   A:519
   avalanche prevention and control   A:558
   first ski club formed at Berlin (New Hampshire)   N:159
   National Ski Hall of Fame and Ski Museum   M:262
   Olympic Games   O:117–18
   Switzerland   S:542
   Vermont tourism   V:319
   waterskiing   W:71–72
picture(s)   F:108
   California   C:28
   Colorado   C:435
   disabilities, people with   D:178
   Europe   E:357
   high jump   O:106
   Utah   U:248
   Vermont   V:312
   West Virginia   W:130
Ski lifts   S:185
Skills (abilities gained by practice and knowledge) *see also*
   Child development
   social studies   S:227
   time management   T:205–6
Skim milk   D:8; M:307
Skin
   allergic reactions   A:190, 191
   blushing   B:300
   body, human   B:276–77
   body chemistry   B:295
   cancer of   A:482; C:95; D:123–24, 199
   defense against disease   D:210
   dermatology   D:123–24
   exocrine glands   G:226
   fish   F:186–87
   goose bumps   B:301

Skin (cont.)
  senses **B:**290
  skin foods (cosmetics) **C:**560
  What is the largest organ of your body? **B:**276
Skin diseases
  dermatology **D:**123–24
  poisonous plants **P:**317
Skin diving (underwater swimming) **S:**186–88, 401 *see also*
    Scuba diving
Skinheads (white supremacists) **R:**34c
Skinks (lizards) **L:**275
  picture(s) **L:**277
Skinner, B. F. (American psychologist) **L:**99; **P:**507
  picture(s) **P:**507
Skinner, Eugene F. (American founder of Eugene, Oregon)
    O:211
Skin-on-skin process (in making fur garments) **F:**504
Skin tests (medical tests) **D:**204
  allergies **A:**191
  tuberculosis **T:**329
Skipjack (fish) **F:**217
Ski-planes (aircraft) **A:**115
  picture(s) **A:**114
Ski touring **S:**184d
Skopje (capital of Macedonia) **M:**4
Skua (bird) **B:**244
Skull (bones of the head) **S:**183
  picture(s)
    anthropologist studies ancient skull **A:**301
Skullcaps (hats) **H:**46; **J:**148
Skunks **A:**283; **H:**128; **M:**74; **O:**252–53; **S:**189
  picture(s) **M:**73; **O:**253
Sky
  blue is a structural color **C:**426–27
  clouds, types of **C:**385
  constellations **C:**528–32
  planetarium projectors **P:**270–72
  seen from moon **M:**454
  Why is the sky blue? **A:**482
  picture(s)
    clouds, types of **C:**384
    COBE satellite photo **U:**211
    map showing positions of stars and galaxies **U:**212
Skydiving (parachuting for fun) **S:**190
Skykje waterfalls (Norway) **W:**59
Skylab (orbiting observatory) **S:**54, 350, 355, 366
  prototype at U.S. Space and Rocket Center **S:**340a
  replica at National Air and Space Museum **P:**274
  picture(s) **S:**351
Skyline Drive (Shenandoah National Park) **V:**354
Skyline logging **L:**341
Sky lobbies (for elevators) **E:**187
Skyscrapers (tall buildings) **C:**321; **U:**131, 133, 136
  Canada, architecture of **C:**73
  elevators **E:**185, 186–87
  fire, how to escape **F:**150
  first construction methods **B:**440
  high-rise apartment buildings **H:**195
  Home Insurance Building (Chicago) **I:**76
  Mies van der Rohe, Ludwig **M:**306
  modern architecture **A:**373, 375
  New York City **N:**230
  Sullivan, Louis **S:**486
  Why don't tall buildings blow down in a strong wind?
    B:437
**"Skyscraper to the Moon and How the Green Rat with the
    Rheumatism Ran a Thousand Miles Twice, The"** (story
    by Carl Sandburg) **S:**28
Slab avalanches **A:**557
Slabs (ingots of steel) **I:**334
Slag (waste from refining of metals) **I:**331, 332, 333; **M:**234
Slalom (in kayaking) **K:**199
Slalom (in skateboarding) **S:**182
Slalom (in skiing) **S:**184e
  picture(s) **S:**184c

Slang **F:**307; **L:**40; **S:**191 *see also* Figures of speech
Slap shot (in ice hockey) **I:**26
Slapstick (form of humor) **H:**290; **M:**489
Slash-and-burn agriculture *see* Migratory agriculture
Slate (metamorphic rock) **G:**118; **R:**270; **V:**312
  picture(s) **R:**269
Slater, Samuel (English-born American manufacturer) **I:**221
  profile, 222; **R:**226; **T:**145
Slater Mill Historic Site (Pawtucket, Rhode Island) **R:**220
Slaughterhouse-Five (novel by Vonnegut) **V:**391
Slave cylinder (in a hydraulic system) **H:**312
Slave narratives (American literature) **A:**208
Slave River (Canada) **A:**171
Slavery **S:**192–97 *see also* Abolition movement; Slave trade;
    Underground Railroad
  abolition movement **A:**6–6b
  African American history **A:**79a–79b, 79e–79g
  African American spirituals **H:**325
  Alabama **A:**140
  American colonies **C:**414, 415; **T:**166, 178
  ancient civilizations **A:**229
  Arthur, Chester Alan, opposed **A:**434–35
  Brazil **B:**383, 384
  civil rights violations **C:**327
  Civil War issue **C:**332–36, 347
  Compromise of 1850 **C:**479
  Confederate States of America **C:**496
  Cuba **C:**609
  Declaration of Independence **D:**62
  Delaware, history of **D:**102
  Dred Scott decision **D:**323
  drums not allowed **A:**79
  Emancipation Proclamation **E:**200–201
  Greece, ancient **G:**341
  Haiti **H:**9, 11; **T:**246
  human rights violations **H:**285
  Indians, American **I:**178, 193, 194
  Kansas-Nebraska Act (1854) **K:**191
  Libreville (Gabon) **G:**3
  Lincoln-Douglas debates **L:**243–44
  Lincoln opposes Kansas-Nebraska Act **L:**243
  Mason-Dixon line **M:**135
  Mississippi, history of **M:**350, 362
  Mississippi River **M:**365
  Missouri, history of **M:**366, 371, 379–80
  Missouri Compromise **M:**381
  Ottoman Empire **O:**259
  Pierce supported Kansas-Nebraska Act **P:**247
  political parties **P:**371
  Protestant churches divided by **P:**493
  racism **R:**34b–34c
  rights, slaves' lack of **D:**59
  Rome, ancient **R:**311
  segregation of slaves **S:**113–14
  serfdom of feudalism **F:**102
  South Carolina **S:**309–10
  sugarcane's introduction to New World **F:**337
  Taylor, Zachary, opposed compromise **T:**32–33
  Thirteenth Amendment **U:**157
  Tubman, Harriet **T:**329
  Uncle Tom's Cabin (novel) **A:**211; **S:**465
  Underground Railroad **U:**15–17
  United States, history of the **U:**173, 180–81, 183,
    184–86
  Viking society **V:**341
  Virginia, history of **V:**358, 360
  Washington, D.C., history of **W:**36
  What were the fugitive slave laws? **U:**17
  picture(s)
    engraving of slaves picking cotton **A:**140
Slavery (in ants) **A:**321, 322–23
Slave trade **A:**66, 79d–79e
  abolished in District of Columbia **C:**479
  abolition movement **A:**6

Smell, sense of (cont.)
  dolphins have no sense of smell   D:276
  fish, smell and taste in   F:194
  insects   I:235
  migrating animals navigate by   H:202
  primates   P:456
  sense of taste affected by   E:394
  sharks, rays, and chimaeras   S:143
Smelting (of ores)   I:218; M:233–34; O:217
Smet, Pierre-Jean de (Belgian-born missionary) see De Smet, Pierre-Jean
Smetana, Bedrich (Czech composer, conductor, and pianist)   C:621
  The Bartered Bride (opera)   O:150–51
  picture(s)   C:621
Smiley, George (fictional character)   M:565
Smilodon (saber-toothed cat) see Saber-toothed cats
Smith, Adam (Scottish political economist)   E:60, 62 profile; T:26
  capitalism   C:103
  Enlightenment, Age of   E:298
  Hume, David   H:288
  picture(s)   E:62
Smith, Alfred Emanuel (American statesman)   H:224; N:225
Smith, Anna Deavere (American playwright)   D:307
Smith, Bessie (American blues singer)   J:58; T:87 profile
  picture(s)   J:58; T:86
Smith, David (American sculptor)   M:396b; S:105; U:135
  picture(s)
    Cubi IX (steel sculpture)   S:103
    sculpture exhibit at the National Gallery of Art   N:38
Smith, Doris Buchanan (American author)   C:238
Smith, George (American scientist)   P:218
Smith, Harry B. (American librettist)   M:553
Smith, Horace (American gunsmith)   G:419
Smith, Howard Worth (American politician)   U:143 profile
Smith, Ian Douglas (prime minister of Rhodesia)   Z:384
Smith, James (American political figure)   D:68 profile
Smith, Jedediah Strong (American explorer and trapper)   F:522 profile, 523; N:135; O:272, 274, 279
Smith, John (English soldier and explorer)   S:205
  explored Eastern Shore of Maryland   M:132
  Jamestown settlement   J:22; T:169, 170; V:356
  Massachusetts, history of   M:146; T:171
  New England named by   N:139
  published account of Jamestown settlement   A:201
  picture(s)   A:202
Smith, Joseph (American founder of Mormons)   M:457; P:493; S:205; Y:363
Smith, Kate (American singer)   N:23
Smith, Margaret Chase (American political figure)   M:49 profile; U:139 profile
  picture(s)   M:49; U:139
Smith, Mary Ellen Spear (Canadian reformer)   B:406d
Smith, Michael J. (American astronaut)   S:352
Smith, Samuel Francis (American clergyman)   N:22
Smith, Stan (American tennis player)   T:97 profile
  picture(s)   T:97
Smith, Tommie (American athlete)   O:111
  picture(s)   O:111
Smith, Tony (American sculptor)   S:105
Smith, Walker, Jr. (American boxer) see Robinson, Sugar Ray
Smith, William (English geologist)   G:110
Smith, William Alexander see De Cosmos, Amor
Smith, William Jay (American poet)   F:123
Smith, Willoughby (English scientist)   P:196
Smithfield (Virginia)   V:352
Smithson, James (English scientist)   S:206
Smithsonian (magazine)   S:206
Smithsonian Astrophysical Observatory (Cambridge, Massachusetts)   S:206
Smithsonian Environmental Research Center   S:206
Smithsonian Festival of American Folklife   F:312

Smithsonian Institution (Washington, D.C.)   S:206; W:33
  Adams, John Quincy, helped establish   A:19
  Division of Numismatics   C:399
  Goddard's rocket experiments   G:245
  National Air and Space Museum   P:273–74
  vice president of United States is member of board   V:330
Smithsonian Tropical Research Institute (Panama)   S:206
Smog (form of air pollution)   A:123; E:303–4; F:290, 291
  bronchitis   D:189–90
  fire and the environment   F:144
  Los Angeles   L:303
  Santiago (Chile)   S:37
  picture(s)   A:124
Smoke
  acid rain   A:9, 10
  air pollution   A:122–23
  dust   D:355
  fires, dangers of   F:148
  meat-curing process   F:344; M:198
  smoke candles for search parties   F:155
Smoke detectors (to warn people of fire)   F:149, 152
  picture(s)   E:159
Smoked sheets (of rubber)   R:345
Smokeless powder (used in guns)   G:419
Smoke signals   C:466
Smokey the Bear (symbol of forest fire prevention)   N:188
Smoking (of meat)   F:344; M:198
  fish, preservation of   F:220
  picture(s)
    fish   F:221
Smoking (of tobacco)   S:207; T:215
  avoiding health hazards   H:75
  bronchitis and emphysema   D:190, 192
  cancer   C:93, 95
  drug abuse, form of   D:329, 330
  fires, smoking-related   F:146
  heart diseases   H:84
  hypnosis used to help people stop smoking   H:329
  introduced to the Old World   T:170
  lung diseases   L:345
  public health issue   D:213
Smoky Night (book by Bunting)
  picture(s)
    illustration by David Diaz   C:11
Smoky quartz (Cairngorm) (gemstone)   Q:8
Smollett, Tobias (English novelist)   E:280; N:359
Smoot-Hawley Tariff see Hawley-Smoot Tariff
Smoothbore guns   G:418
Smooth muscles   B:279; M:519–20
Smörgåsbord (Swedish meal)   S:524
Smørrebrød (Danish sandwich)   D:109
Smudge pots   F:482
  picture(s)   F:483
Smuggler's Notch (Vermont)   V:314
Smuggling   U:124
Smurfs (cartoon characters)   B:134
Smuts (fungi)   C:558; F:499; O:4
  picture(s)   P:289
Smyrna (Tennessee)   T:80
Smyrna (Turkey) see Izmir
Smyrna figs   F:121
Smyth sewing (in bookbinding)   B:332–33
Snag boats (to clear obstructions from riverbeds)   L:323
Snails (mollusks)   M:405, 406, 407; S:150, **208**
  Tyrian purple dye   D:377
  picture(s)   S:149, 208
Snake River (North America)   I:48; O:205; W:17, 336
  picture(s)   I:49; W:336
Snake River Birds of Prey Natural Area   I:54
Snakes   R:180; S:**209–18**
  Asia's wildlife   A:442
  desert animals   D:129
  leather made from skins   L:109

Soft coal *see* Bituminous coal
Soft drinks
    stains, removal of **L:**82
    picture(s)
        large servings **F:**338
Soft ice cream (frozen dessert) **I:**22
Soft landing (of spacecraft) **S:**340d
"Soft law" **O:**220
Soft light **L:**236
Soft-paste porcelain **P:**412, 413
Soft-shelled turtles **T:**356, 357
    picture(s) **T:**355
Soft-tip pens **P:**143
Software (instructions telling computers what to do) **C:**480, 483, 489, 491 *see also* Hardware
    digital darkroom **P:**216–17
    Gates, Bill **W:**27
    genealogical programs **G:**76, 76b
    Internet **C:**488
Softwood trees **W:**225
Soglo, Nicephore (Benin president) **B:**144
Soho (district in London, England) **L:**294
Soil Conservation Service **C:**526; **D:**356
Soils **S:**234–38 *see also* the natural resources section of continent, country, province, and state articles
    acid rain's effects **A:**9, 10
    alluvial soil deposited by rivers **R:**238
    antibiotics obtained from **A:**306
    Can changes in temperature break up rocks? **S:**234
    conservation of **C:**524
    desert environments **D:**128
    different plants for different soils **L:**203
    Do growing plants break up rocks? **S:**235
    dust **D:**355
    Dust Bowl **D:**355–56
    earthworms **E:**42; **W:**320
    erosion **E:**319
    fertilizers and soil tests **F:**96
    floods **F:**254, 255
    forensic science **F:**372
    gardens and gardening **G:**30, 39
    grasses beneficial to **G:**319
    houseplant potting soil **H:**265–66, 269
    land management **A:**95–96; **F:**62
    landslides **A:**557, 558
    Martian soil experiments **S:**362
    moon samples **M:**453; **S:**340h
    mosses help to form and enrich soil **M:**473
    plants help to renew and conserve soil **P:**295
    prairie soil **I:**297; **P:**426
    preparing soil for planting **F:**48–49
    rain forests **R:**99
    river deltas **R:**236
    space probes gather samples from Mars **S:**358
    Why should topsoil be conserved? **S:**237
Soissons, Battle of (486) **P:**74
Sojourner (Martian surface rover) **C:**485; **M:**106; **R:**254; **S:**358, 359
    picture(s) **R:**254
Sokodé (Togo) **T:**217
Solanin (bitter substance in green potatoes) **P:**404
Solar, Xul (Argentine painter) **L:**63, 64
    picture(s)
        Mundo (painting) **L:**64
Solar batteries (devices made up of solar cells) **B:**103c; **S:**240
Solar cells (devices using sunlight to generate electricity) **B:**103c; **E:**222; **S:**240, 340d; **T:**276
Solar Challenger (solar-powered airplane) **A:**117
Solar eclipses **E:**50–51, 52; **M:**448, 449; **S:**494–95
    diagram(s) **E:**51
    picture(s) **E:**51, 52
Solar energy **E:**213, 216–17, 222; **S:**239–40
    air pollution's effects **A:**124

Earth receives light and heat from the sun **E:**9
    electric generators **E:**142
    experimental aircraft powered by **A:**117, 572
    heating systems **H:**96–97
    homebuilding **H:**195
    influence on Earth studied during solar eclipse **E:**52
    nuclear fusion within the sun **S:**490–91
    photoelectricity **P:**197
    renewable resource **N:**64
    spacecraft powered by **S:**362
    space shuttles have solar panels **S:**365
    sun's energy is our most basic natural resource **N:**63
    picture(s)
        apartment buildings with solar panels **H:**195
        electric generators **E:**143
        floating lighthouse **P:**197
        house with solar panels **C:**526
        photovoltaic cells **P:**196
Solar energy collectors **S:**239
Solar flares **R:**48, 49; **S:**345, 496–97
Solar furnace
    picture(s) **E:**222
Solar heat *see* Solar energy
Solar heating systems **E:**222; **H:**96–97
Solar Maximum (space satellite) **S:**355
Solar observatories **O:**9
Solar plexus (of the nervous system) **N:**117
Solar power *see* Solar energy
Solar salt **S:**23
Solar storms **C:**562
Solar system **S:**241–49 *see also* Sun; the names of planets
    astronomy, history of **A:**470–72
    comets, meteorites, and asteroids **C:**449–52
    Copernicus **C:**552–53
    Earth's place in the system **E:**8
    geology in the solar system **G:**118–19
    gravity and gravitation **G:**320–25
    moon **M:**446–55
    Newton's findings **A:**470
    place in our galaxy **U:**211
    planets **P:**275–82
    satellites **S:**52
    space probes **S:**357–60
    sun **S:**488–97
    theories of formation **E:**22–23; **M:**454; **S:**248–49
    volcanoes **V:**386
    What is the outermost planet in the solar system? **N:**113
    picture(s)
        Milky Way, position in **S:**245
        museum display **P:**272
Solar telescope **S:**488
    picture(s) **O:**9
Solar tides (caused by the sun's gravitational pull) **O:**19
Solar wind (flow of electrified particles) **S:**497
    comets **A:**471; **C:**452; **S:**248
    eclipse studies **E:**52
    interaction with planets' magnetic fields **R:**69
    moon, detection devices placed on **S:**340h
    radiation belts **R:**48, 49
Solar year **T:**202
Soldering **T:**209, 278; **W:**118
Soldiers
    Geneva Conventions **G:**93
    United States Army **U:**102–6
    picture(s)
        Confederate (U.S. Civil War) **C:**332, 339
        infantry **U:**102
        radio use by **C:**469
        Union (U.S. Civil War) **C:**333
Soldiers Home National Cemetery (Washington, D.C.) **N:**27
Sole (fish) **F:**193, 217
Sole (of the foot) **F:**81, 82
Solemn Land, The (painting by J. E. H. MacDonald)
    picture(s) **C:**73
Solheim Cup (golf) **G:**260

Solidarity (Polish labor union)　**P:**362; **W:**4
　picture(s)　**L:**18
Solid geometry　**G:**123–24; **M:**157
Solid-propellant rockets　**M:**344; **R:**259–60, 262
　diagram(s)　**R:**261
Solids (in design)　**D:**137
Solids (pieces of matter that have a definite shape)　**S:**250
　chemical term　**C:**204
　crystals　**C:**603–5
　how heat changes matter　**H:**89–92
　and liquids　**L:**254
　materials science　**M:**151
　matter, states of　**M:**172, 175
　states of matter compared　**M:**174–75
Solid solution (in chemistry)　**A:**193
Solid-state devices　**E:**159 *see also* Integrated circuits;
　Transistors
Solid-state physics　**S:**74, 250; **W:**118
Solid-state watches *see* Electronic watches
Solid-waste disposal　**S:**33 *see also* Sewage disposal
　community helps in prevention of disease　**D:**212
　environment, problems of　**E:**305–6
　fuel generation　**F:**489
　genetically engineered bacteria　**G:**86
　water pollution　**W:**66
　picture(s)
　　seagulls at garbage dump　**B:**198
Solís, Juan Díaz de (Spanish explorer)　**A:**386b; **E:**409; **H:**208;
　U:241
Solitaire card games (for one person)　**C:**108–9
Solo (in music)　**M:**537
Solomon (king of Israel)　**B:**161; **J:**102; **S:**251
　carrier pigeons used by　**C:**465
　Ethiopian epic story　**A:**76c
　Jerusalem　**J:**84
　Sheba, Queen of　**E:**333
　Song of Solomon (book of the Bible)　**B:**163
Solomon ibn Gabirol *see* Ibn Gabirol, Solomon
Solomon Islands (Pacific Ocean)　**S:**252–53
　Bougainville　**P:**8
　Buka　**P:**8
　Guadalcanal　**P:**9
　map(s)　**S:**253
　picture(s)
　　carved shield　**P:**2
　　flag　**F:**239
Solomos, Dionysios (Greek poet)　**G:**359
Solon (Athenian lawgiver)　**S:**253
Solstice ("stand-still" position of the sun)　**S:**110
Solti, Sir Georg (Hungarian orchestra conductor)　**O:**201
　profile
　picture(s)　**I:**70; **O:**201
Solute (in chemistry)　**C:**204
Solution (chemical term)　**C:**204, 605; **L:**254, 255
Solution caves (caverns)　**C:**156
Solvent extraction (of fats and oils)　**O:**80
Solvents (in chemistry)　**C:**204; **D:**341; **W:**50
Solway Firth (England–Scotland)　**U:**52
Sólyom, László (president of Hungary)　**H:**299
Solzhenitsyn, Aleksandr (Soviet novelist)　**N:**363; **R:**384; **U:**37
　profile
　picture(s)　**N:**362; **U:**37
Somalia　**E:**334; **S:**254–55; **W:**299
　map(s)　**S:**254
　picture(s)
　　flag　**F:**239
　　food distribution to famine victims　**P:**419
　　people　**A:**345; **S:**254
　　United States Marines　**B:**462
Somali jet stream　**J:**93
Somalis (a people of Africa)　**E:**330; **S:**254
Somas (of neurons) *see* Cell bodies
Somatic cells (of the body)　**G:**78
Sombrero (Mexican hat)　**H:**46
　picture(s)　**H:**47

Sombrero Galaxy
　picture(s)　**U:**213
Somers, Sir George (English sea captain)　**B:**152
Somers Islands *see* Bermuda
Somme, Battles of the (1916, 1918)　**T:**15; **W:**287, 289
　picture(s)　**W:**276, 281
Sommeiller, Germaine (Italian engineer)　**T:**339
Somoza Debayle, Anastasio (president of Nicaragua)　**N:**247
Somoza Debayle, Luis (Nicaraguan political leader)　**N:**247
Somoza Garcia, Anastasio (president of Nicaragua)　**N:**247
Sonar (SOund NAvigation Ranging)　**R:**40–41
　dolphins' echolocation　**D:**277
　echo　**E:**49
　ocean bottom, mapping of　**O:**37–38
　submarine navigation　**S:**475
　underwater archaeology　**U:**18–19
　uses of ultrasound　**S:**265
　picture(s)　**O:**34, 37
Sonata (in music)　**B:**71–72; **C:**350; **M:**540–41
Sondheim, Stephen (American composer and lyricist)
　M:554–55
Son et lumière *see* Sound and light shows
Song cycles (groups of songs)　**G:**187; **M:**542
Song dynasty (Chinese dynasty)　**C:**269, 274–75, 277; **P:**410
Songe (a people of Africa)
　picture(s)
　　mask　**A:**73
Songhaï (a people of Africa)　**A:**66, 79d; **M:**61
Songhua (Sungari) River (Asia)　**R:**246
Songkhla (Thailand)　**T:**151
Song of Germany *see* Deutschlandlied
Song of Hiawatha (poem by Henry Wadsworth Longfellow)
　A:209; **L:**301
"Song of Myself" (poem by Walt Whitman)
　excerpt from　**A:**211
Song of Solomon (book of the Old Testament)　**B:**163
Song of the South (motion picture, 1946)　**D:**216
Songs　**M:**542–43
　Africa, music of　**A:**78
　African American spirituals　**A:**79f
　art songs　**V:**378
　Aztecs　**A:**578
　ballad (form of folk song)　**B:**24
　Berlin, Irving　**B:**150
　carols　**C:**118
　Chinese poems　**C:**279
　communication, history of　**C:**463
　folklore in song　**F:**308–9
　folk music　**F:**320–28
　Foster, Stephen　**F:**389
　France, music of　**F:**447
　German and Austrian music　**G:**186–87
　history of Western musical forms　**M:**538
　hymns　**H:**320–26
　lied (art song)　**C:**351
　lullabies　**L:**336–37
　national anthems　**N:**18–23
　patriotic songs　**N:**18–23
　rock music　**R:**262a–264
　Schubert, Franz　**S:**62
　spirituals and other folk hymns　**H:**324–26
　state songs *see* individual state articles
Songs of Chu, The (poems by Qu Yuan)　**C:**279
Songs of Experience (poems by William Blake)
　picture(s)
　　engraving from　**E:**278
Songtsan Gampo (Tibetan king)　**T:**191
Sonic boom (during supersonic flight)　**A:**40; **S:**501
Soninké (a people of Africa)　**M:**61
Sonnets　**P:**352
　English verse forms　**E:**271–72
　"How do I love thee?" by Elizabeth Barrett Browning
　　B:412
　Italian poetry　**I:**405

Southern Cross (constellation)   C:530; N:75
Southern Hemisphere   E:308
   air motion   W:81
   constellations   C:529, 530
   hurricanes   H:302, 303
   latitude and longitude   L:77
   month by month *see* individual month articles
   ocean currents   E:19
   seasons   E:9; S:109, 111
   trade winds   T:268
   winds   W:187, 188, 189
   picture(s)
      constellations   C:529
Southern hognose snakes   S:218
Southern lights *see* Aurora australis
Southern magnolia (tree)
   picture(s)   M:351
Southern pine trees
   picture(s)   A:131
Southern Poverty Law Center   C:326
Southern Rhodesia *see* Zimbabwe
Southern Tenant Farmer's Union   A:418
Southern University (Baton Rouge, Louisiana)   L:319
South Korea *see* Korea, South
South Pacific (musical by Rodgers and Hammerstein)   M:554
South Pass (Wyoming)   O:272, 276, 278; W:342, 343
South-pointing chariot (ancient type of compass)   G:66
   picture(s)   G:66
South Pole
   Amundsen, Roald   A:226
   Antarctic exploration   A:295
   Earth's axis   E:9
   exploration and discovery   B:485; E:414–15
   Hillary, Sir Edmund   H:136
   seasonal positions   S:109
South Sandwich Trench (in the Atlantic Ocean)   A:478
South Saskatchewan River (Canada)   S:43
South Sea *see* Pacific Ocean
South Sea Bubble (English financial scandal)   S:455
South Sea Islands *see* Pacific islands and island groups
South Vietnam *see* Vietnam, Republic of
Southwest, the (region of the United States)
   homes and housing   H:194
South-West Africa *see* Namibia
South-West Africa People's Organization (SWAPO)   N:9
Southwest Asia *see* Middle East
Southwestern Power Administration   E:218
Sou'wester (waterproof hat)   H:46
Sovereign equality (principle of the United Nations)   U:64
Sovereignty, popular *see* Popular sovereignty
Soviet literature   N:363; R:383–84
Soviets (councils of workers organized during the Russian
   Revolution)   C:473; L:140
Soviet Union *see* Union of Soviet Socialist Republics
Sovkhoz (Soviet state farm)   U:38
Sows (female pigs)   H:219; P:248
Soybeans   S:337; V:290
   Asian diet   F:332
   breakfast cereals with soy protein   H:79
   food from plants   P:296
   genetically altered foods   A:100
   Illinois is leading producer   I:62, 71
   important agricultural products   A:90, 94
   soybean oil   O:79
   picture(s)   S:337
Soyinka, Wole (Nigerian poet, novelist, and playwright)
   A:76d; N:257
Soy milk   S:337
Soyuz (series of piloted Soviet space flights)   S:352, 355
Space
   flower arranging principles   F:278
   living organisms need space   E:301
   matter takes up space   M:172
   modern architecture   A:374

   relativity   P:231; R:143–44
   space as a design element in sculpture   D:137; M:391
Space, outer   S:340c *see also* Space exploration and travel
   aerial photography   P:216
   cosmic rays, studies of   C:562
   how rockets work in space   R:258
   nuclear weapons   N:377
   Piccard's balloon ascents   B:36
   radiation belts   R:48–49
   radio astronomy   R:66–73
   research using balloons   B:37
   United States Navy   U:193
   vacuum   V:262
Space agencies and centers   S:338–40a
Space and Rocket Center, United States (Huntsville, Alabama)
   A:138; S:340a
Space Camp, United States   S:340a
Space centers *see* Space agencies and centers
Spacecraft *see also* Satellites, artificial
   accidents and disasters   S:352
   famous meetings in space   S:355
   gyroscopes   G:437
   radio, uses of   R:51
   space exploration and travel   S:340b–356
   space probes   S:357–60
   space shuttles   S:364–65
   temperature control   S:356
   picture(s)
      hypersonic plane   A:121
Space debris (material in orbit around Earth)   L:46d
Space Defense Initiative *see* Star Wars (Strategic Defense
   Initiative)
Space exploration and travel   S:340b–356 *see also* Astronauts
   accidents and disasters   S:352
   algae may be food on spaceships   P:221
   astronauts   A:466–67
   automation   A:532
   China's first manned space capsule   C:273
   exploration and discovery   E:417
   famous meetings in space   S:355
   gases in industry   G:60
   inventions   I:286
   lasers, uses of   L:46d
   liquid gases, use of   L:253
   moon landing   E:417
   National Air and Space Museum   P:273–74
   navigation in space   N:77
   observatories in space   O:10–12
   radiation belts   R:48
   radio, uses of   R:51
   robots   C:485; R:254–55
   rockets   R:257–62
   satellites, artificial   S:53–54
   space agencies and centers   S:338–40a
   space probes   S:357–60
   space research and technology   S:361–63
   space shuttles   S:364–65
   space stations   S:366
   terms, list of   S:340d
   Venus probes   V:303a
   veterinarians, contributions of   V:323
   Von Braun, Wernher   V:391
   weightlessness due to lack of gravity   G:324
   What kinds of animals have traveled in space?   S:350
Space Infrared Telescope Facility *see* Spitzer Space Telescope
Space museums   P:273–74; S:340–40a
Space Needle (symbol of the Seattle World's Fair)   F:17;
   S:112; W:22
   picture(s)   F:16; L:230; S:112; W:22
Space probes   S:351, 353, **357–60**
   astronomers' tools   A:476a
   comets, studies of   C:452
   gyroscopes   G:437
   important space probes, list of   S:359

Spain, music of   S:392a–392b see also the names of Spanish
    composers
  ballads   B:24; F:309
  opera   0:147
Spalding, A. G. (American athlete and businessman)   G:242
Spalding, Henry and Eliza (American missionaries in Idaho)
    0:276–77
Spallanzani, Lazzaro (Italian zoologist)   B:103
Spam (unwanted e-mail)   A:32
Spandex (synthetic fiber)   N:437
Spaniels (dogs)   D:246, 253
Spanish-American literature see Latin America, literature of
Spanish-American War (1898)   S:392c–392d; U:189–90
  American overseas possessions   T:110–11
  Armed Forces history, important dates in   U:116
  Cuba, history of   C:609
  Dewey, George   D:144
  kites used to take pictures from the air   K:270
  McKinley's administration   M:192–93
  Philippines   P:188
  "Rough Riders" in Cuba   R:329
  veterans' organizations   U:121
  picture(s)
    "Rough Riders" in Cuba   R:330
Spanish architecture see Spain, art and architecture of
Spanish Armada (1588)   B:103f; E:244; S:377, 393
  Drake defeats King Philip's fleet   D:296
  first naval battle fought entirely under sail   S:157
  picture(s)   B:103e
Spanish art see Spain, art and architecture of
Spanish Civil War (1936–1939)   S:379, 393; U:14; W:295
  aviation   A:565
  Barcelona   B:60a
Spanish dollar (monetary unit)   D:261
Spanish Flu (worldwide epidemic, 1918–19)   I:228
Spanish Guinea see Equatorial Guinea
Spanish Hour, The (opera by Ravel) see Heure espagnole, L'
Spanish language and literature see Spain, language and
    literature of
Spanish Main (mainland of South America)   P:264
Spanish Merino sheep see Merino
Spanish moss (air plant)   L:317; M:473
  picture(s)   G:34, 135; L:315
Spanish music see Spain, music of
Spanish Sahara see Western Sahara
Spanish Steps (Rome, Italy)   R:306
  picture(s)   I:385; R:306
Spanish Succession, War of the (1701–1713)   A:524;
    E:247–48; L:313; M:104; S:377–78
Spanish Town (Jamaica)   J:18
Spares (in bowling)   B:349–50, 350a
Spark, Muriel (English writer)   E:290
Spark chamber (used to observe cosmic rays)   C:563
Spark-ignition engines see Gasoline engines
Sparklers (fireworks)   F:155
Sparkling wines   W:190, 190a
Spark plugs (spark-producing devices)   A:548; E:231; I:264
Sparks (Canadian Girl Guides)   G:217
Sparrow hawk
  picture(s)   B:215
Sparrows (birds)
  picture(s)   B:246
Spars (of airplane wings)   A:111
Spars (of sailboats and sailing ships)   S:8, 156
Spars (transportable steel towers)   L:341
Sparta (city of ancient Greece)   A:238; G:343, 344
  Athens, rivalry with   A:476d
  Olympic Games   0:102
  Peloponnesian War   P:120a
  physical education programs   P:223
Spartacus (Roman slave and gladiator)   S:196 profile
Spartanburg (South Carolina)   S:306
Spas (mineral water health resorts)   C:620; G:192
Spasm (of muscles)   M:521
Spawn (egg laying of fish)   E:94; F:194–95; R:177

Spawn (of mushrooms)   M:529
Spaying (of dogs)   D:260
Speakeasies (illegal bars and nightclubs during Prohibition)
    C:547; 0:224; P:485
Speaker of the House of Representatives   U:137, 144, 168
Speakerphones (kind of telephone)   0:58
Speakers (audio equipment) see Loudspeakers
Speaker's Corner (Hyde Park, London, England)   L:296
  picture(s)   L:298
Speaking (one of the language arts)   L:36 see also Debates;
    Public speaking; Speech
Spearbearer (statue by Polyclitus)   G:349
Speare, Elizabeth George (American author)   C:235 profile
Spearfish (South Dakota)   S:319
Spear guns (for underwater use)   S:187
Spearman, Charles (English psychologist)   P:508
Spear-nosed bats   B:101
Spears, stone
  picture(s)   I:278
Special agents (of Federal Bureau of Investigation)   F:76–77
Special courts (of the United States government)   U:171
Special districts (units of municipal government)   M:517
Special Education and Rehabilitative Services, Office of (United
    States)   E:89
Special effects (in motion pictures)   M:484, 487
Special effects (in planetarium shows)   P:273
Special elections   E:129
Special Forces (in the United States Armed Forces)   U:102,
    113
Special-interest groups (of political parties)   P:373
Special-interest magazines   A:30; M:16, 19, 20
Special libraries   L:179
Special Libraries Association   L:181
Special Olympics (athletic program for people with mental
    retardation)   S:394
Special theory of relativity   P:231, 236; R:139, 141–43
Specialty networks (cable television)   T:71
Specialty stores   R:188
Special weapons units (in police departments)   P:365
Speciation (process by which one species branches into two or
    more new species)   E:378
Specie Circular (United States, 1836)   J:7
Specie payment   B:53
Species (divisions of biological classification)   A:265; B:202;
    L:207
  endangered species   E:208–11
  evolution   E:374, 375, 376, 378
  genetics   G:77, 81, 86
  How many kinds of living things are there?   K:259
  taxonomy   T:27, 28, 29
Specific heat (amount required to raise the temperature of a
    fixed weight of a substance by a given amount)   H:88
Specific impulse (of a rocket)   R:259, 260
Specified commands (of the United States military)   D:83;
    U:101
Spectacle (circus parade)   C:307
Spectacled bears   B:104, 106
  picture(s)   B:107
Spectacles see Eyeglasses
Spectaculars (advertisements)   A:30
Spectator, The (English journal)   E:278–79, 321; M:19
Spectrograph (optical instrument)   A:355; 0:12, 184; S:488
  Hubble Space Telescope   S:367–68
Spectrography (use of a camera with a spectroscope to analyze
    light)   P:209
Spectrometer (optical instrument)   A:302, 476; C:563; S:428
    see also Mass spectrometer
  picture(s)   I:289
Spectrophotometer (optical instrument)   0:184
  picture(s)   0:185
Spectroscopes (optical instruments)   E:394; L:225; 0:184;
    P:209; U:215

Spectrum (plural: spectra) (band of colors formed by light going through a prism)   L:213
   atomic spectrum   P:231, 238
   classification of stars   A:472–73
   Doppler effect studied with   L:225–26
   electromagnetic spectrum   L:220; R:44–46
   How do astronomers measure distances in space?   A:476
   Kirchhoff discovered   C:210
   line spectrum   L:223–24
   Newton's experiments   C:424; N:207; P:235
   observing the sun   S:489
   red shift   U:215–16
   X-rays   X:349
Specular reflection (of light)   L:213
Speculation (buying and selling involving risk)   S:455
Speech   S:395–96 see also Languages
   Bell, Alexander Graham   B:140
   communication   C:462, 463
   deaf people   D:50
   human beings   H:281
   learning disorders   L:107
   linguistic anthropology   A:302–3
   lungs help in forming sounds   L:345
   phonics   P:194
   speech disorders   S:397–98
   ventriloquism   V:302
   voice   V:377–78
Speech, freedom of see Freedom of speech
Speech disorders   S:397–98; T:225
Speeches
   Bryan's "Cross of Gold" speech   B:416; O:191
   Henry's "Give me liberty, or give me death"   H:113
   how to prepare and give a speech   P:519–20
   oratory   O:190–91
   public speaking   P:518–20
Speech pathologists (therapists)   H:249; S:398
Speechreading (Lipreading) (by the deaf)   D:50
Speed (in physics)
   airspeed and ground speed of airplanes   A:118
   animals   A:278–79
   antelopes   A:297
   automobile racing   A:536, 538, 542
   aviation records   A:567
   cheetah is the fastest land animal   C:149
   conversion of mass and energy   M:173
   falling bodies, laws of   F:34
   How fast can the fastest elevators climb?   E:187
   iceboating   I:19
   of light   L:219
   mammal locomotion   M:71
   measurement   W:116
   relativity   R:141–42
   satellite orbits and orbital velocities   S:53
   sound   S:256, 259
   speed of fish related to size   F:199
   stalling speed of airplanes   A:39
   supersonic flight   S:499–502
   picture(s)
       peregrine falcon is fastest animal   A:279
Speed-detector units (used by police)   P:364
Speed dialers (of telephones)   O:58
Speed increasers (gears)   G:66
Speed reducers (gears)   G:66
Speed skating   I:38, 39, 42–43; O:118; W:198
Speedway racing   A:537
   picture(s)   A:536
Speedwell (Pilgrims' ship)   P:345; T:170
Speed (of photographic film) see Film speed
Speer, Albert (German architect and Nazi)   N:81 profile
Speke, John Hanning (English explorer)   B:457; E:412
Spektor, Mordecai (Yiddish novelist)   Y:361
Speleology   C:158 see also Caves and caverns; Spelunking
Spellbound (motion picture, 1945)   D:13

Spelling   S:398–400
   homonyms   H:203
   name variations   N:5
   Webster, Noah, and spelling reform   W:99
Spelunking (sport of cave exploring)   C:158; S:400–401
Spencer, Diana (princess of Wales) see Diana, Princess of Wales
Spencer, Herbert (English philosopher)   S:231
Spender, Stephen (English poet)   E:288
Spenser, Edmund (English poet)   E:271–72; S:401
   Faerie Queene   F:12
Spenser, Willard (American composer)   O:167
Spenserian stanza (in poetry)   E:271
Spermaceti (substance from sperm whales)   C:96; W:78, 154, 155
Spermaceti organs (of sperm whales)   W:150
Spermatophore (of amphibians)   A:224
Sperm cell (male reproductive cell)   R:176–79
   birth control   B:250a, 250b
   genetics and heredity   G:78, 81
   human reproduction   B:2, 3, 286, 287
   plants   F:282
Spermicide (for birth control)   B:250b
Sperm whales   W:149, 150, 154
   picture(s)   W:150
Sperry, Elmer Ambrose (American inventor)   G:438
Speusippus (ancient Greek encyclopedist)   E:207
Sphagnum moss   M:472, 473; W:147
Sphalerite (zinc ore)   Z:385
Sphere (geometric figure)   G:123–24; L:255
Spherical aberration (of lenses)   L:148; M:286
Spherical mirrors   T:59
Spherical trigonometry   T:313
Sphincter (muscle)   M:520
Sphinx (mythological monster, half lion, half human)
   Great Sphinx of Giza   C:8; E:108, 112; S:93
   riddle of solved by Oedipus   G:364; J:126
   picture(s)
       Great Sphinx of Giza   E:111; W:258
Sphinx moths
   picture(s)   B:483; I:244, 245
Sphygmomanometer (to measure blood pressure)   H:85; M:204
Sphynx (cat)   C:138
   picture(s)   C:138
Spice Islands see Moluccas
Spices (dried plant parts used for flavoring)   H:119–21
   Asian food   F:331–32
   baked goods, ingredient in   B:388
   food preservation by pickling   F:344
   microscope, some things to see with   M:283
   seasonings in cooking   C:544
Spider conchs (mollusks)
   picture(s)   S:149
Spider crabs (crustaceans)   C:581, 601
Spider King see Louis XI (king of France)
Spiderlings (young spiders)   S:406
Spider monkeys
   picture(s)   A:277; M:421
Spider plant (houseplant)
   picture(s)   H:268
Spiders (arachnids)   A:348; S:402–6
   genes used to grow silk-producing cells   B:214
   household pests   H:263
   insects eaten by   A:280
   reproduction   R:177
   species harmful to people   S:406
   What is the largest spider?   S:405
   picture(s)
       compared to insects   I:231
       silk production   A:348
Spiders (Internet search engines)   C:489
Spider webs   S:403–4, 405
   Charlotte's Web, excerpt from   W:163
   picture(s)
       rhythmic design, example of   D:132

Spiegelman, Art (American comics artist) C:454
  picture(s)
    Maus: A Survivor's Tale C:454
Spielberg, Steven (American film director) M:496 profile, 497
Spies S:407–9 see also Bugging
  aerial photography P:216
  Federal Bureau of Investigation F:77
  Hale, Nathan H:12
  kites, people-carrying K:270
  military spying by satellite S:53
  shortwave radio has been used by R:51
  tongue twisters used to catch spies T:225–26
  Trojan horse T:316
  Tubman, Harriet T:329
  What are some types of espionage agents? S:407
Spies, Adolph (German gymnast) P:223
Spikes (large nails) N:2
Spikes (of viruses) V:363
Spilling salt (superstition) S:504
Spillway (surplus water escape passage) D:18; F:257
Spilsbury, John (English mapmaker) P:553
Spin (magnetism created by orbiting electrons) M:31
Spina bifida (birth defect) V:370c
Spinach (vegetable) V:286, 289, 290
Spinal anesthesia A:256
Spinal cord (links brain and body) B:367; N:116, 118
  injuries to the head and neck F:160
Spinal curvature D:204
Spinal nerves N:116
Spin-casting (fishing) F:209, 210, 212
Spindle (part of cell division) C:161, 162
Spindletop oil field (Texas) T:124, 140
Spine (Backbone) (of animals) A:265
  birds B:222
  human beings H:281
  mammals M:66
  spinal curvature D:204
  vertebrae provide flexibility S:183
Spinel (gem mineral) G:71, 74
Spines (sharp projections)
  animal defense A:283
  cactus C:4
  hedgehogs H:101, 102
  leaves, special functions of L:117
  plants P:305, 316
  porcupines R:278
Spinets (keyboard instruments) K:237
Spingarn, Joel (American educator) S:409
Spingarn Medal S:409–10
  list of winners S:410
Spinks, Leon (American boxer) A:189; B:351
Spinks, Michael (American boxer) B:351, 352
Spinnakers (sails) S:8
  picture(s) S:8
Spinneret (kind of nozzle) N:438, 439
  manufactured fibers F:111
  organs of spiders that produce silk S:403
  picture(s)
    synthetic fibers, extrusion of F:111
Spinners (lures for fishing) F:211
Spinning (fishing) F:209–10, 212
Spinning (of yarns) F:112 see also Weaving
  cotton industry C:569
  Hargreaves' spinning jenny I:217
  Industrial Revolution I:216, 217
  manufactured fibers F:111
  textile industry T:141
  wool W:235
  picture(s)
    ancient Iranian sculpture T:143
    Arkwright's spinning frame I:217; W:268
    wool being spun on frame W:235
Spinning jenny (machine) I:217
Spinning mule (machine) I:217, 220–21

Spínola, António de (Portuguese leader) P:395
Spinoza, Baruch (Dutch philosopher) P:190; S:410
Spiny anteaters (Echidnas) A:506; E:96; H:127; M:68, 69; P:331–32
  picture(s) P:332
Spiny dogfish (sharks) see Dogfish
Spiny lobsters (crustaceans) H:199; L:279, 280
  picture(s) H:199
Spiracles (breathing holes of animals)
  ants A:320
  beetles B:124
  insects I:239, 240
Spiral arrangement (of leaves) see Alternate arrangement
Spiral galaxies M:308; U:213–14
  picture(s) P:239
Spiral screwdriver (tool) T:229
Spirillum (corkscrew-shaped bacterium) B:12; D:188; M:275
Spirit (space probe) M:107; O:10; P:279; S:358, 359
Spirited Away (motion picture, 2001)
  picture(s) A:291
Spirit level (instrument for determining if a surface is level) S:519–20; T:230, 234
  picture(s) T:230
Spirit of Saint Louis (airplane) A:563; L:249
Spirit of '76, The (painting by Archibald M. Willard)
  picture(s) R:194
Spiritualism (ghost belief movement) G:200
Spirituals (African American folk hymns) H:324–25
  African American music A:79f
  American folklore and folk songs F:324
  religious folk songs F:324
  rock music, development of R:262a
Spirit worship R:147
  Africa, art of A:70, 73
  African tribal religions A:60
  dance, purpose of D:22
  ghosts G:199
  Inuit religion I:275
  Laos L:42
  Southeast Asia S:329
Spirogyra (protist) K:258
Spitfire (British fighter plane) A:115, 565
Spitsbergen see Svalbard Islands
Spittle bugs
  picture(s) I:233
Spitz, Mark (American swimmer) O:113; S:538 profile
  picture(s) S:538
Spitzer, Lyman Jr. (American astrophysicist) S:368
Spitzer Space Telescope (formerly Space Infrared Telescope Facility) O:12; S:367, 368
  picture(s)
    supernova remnant O:11
Spitzes (dogs) D:247
Spleen (organ of the lymphatic system) L:350
"Splendid little war" (Spanish-American War, 1898) S:392c
Splicing (joining pieces of film) M:485
Splicing (of magnetic tape) E:156
Splints (for broken bones) F:160
Split (Croatia) C:589
  picture(s) C:588
Split letter system (of arranging encyclopedias) E:206
Splitrock caves see Boulder caves
Split Rock Lighthouse (on Lake Superior)
  picture(s) M:334
Splits (in bowling) B:350
Split stitch (in embroidery) N:98
  picture(s) N:99
Splitting (of hides in leather preparation) L:110–11
Spock, Benjamin (American pediatrician) C:521 profile
Spode, Josiah, II (English porcelain maker) A:316a; P:413
Spohr, Louis (German composer and conductor) O:197
Spoil (mud and silt excavated by dredges) D:321, 322
Spoilage of food see Food spoilage and contamination
Spoils system (political patronage) A:434, 435–36; C:331; H:69, 71; J:6

Spokane (Washington)   F:17; W:23
    picture(s)   W:23
Spokane (Spokan) Indians (of North America)   I:188
Spokes (of wheels)   W:160
Spoleto Festival, U.S.A.   M:556; S:301
Spoleto (Italy) Festival of Two Worlds   M:555
Sponge, vaginal see Vaginal sponge
SpongeBob Squarepants (animated television program)
    picture(s)   A:291
Sponge method (of making yeast bread)   B:388
Sponges   A:267; F:268; O:26; S:411–12
    diagram(s)   S:412
    picture(s)   A:285; S:411
Spongiform encephalopathies (diseases)   D:208–9
Spongin (protein of sponge skeleton)   A:267
Spontaneous abortion see Miscarriage
Spontaneous combustion   F:141
Spontaneous emission (of radiation)   L:46a
Spontaneous generation (biological theory)   L:209–10; P:98
    Leeuwenhoek helps discredit the theory   L:128
Spontini, Gasparo (Italian composer)   I:412
Spoonerisms (transposing of initial sounds of words)   H:290
Spoons (eating utensils)   E:165, 338; K:283–85
Spoons (lures for fishing)   F:211
Spore prints   F:498
Spores (reproductive cells)   R:176
    algae   A:181
    ferns   F:95
    fungi   F:497; M:276
    mosses   M:473
    mushrooms   M:529
    photosynthesis, role in   P:220
    travel long distances   L:196
    picture(s)
        ferns   F:95
Sporophyte generation   F:94–95; M:473
Sporozoans (protozoans)   P:497
Sporting dogs   D:246
Sports see also Games; Gymnastics; the names of sports; the
        people section of country articles
    archery   A:360–62
    automobile racing   A:536–38
    badminton   B:13–14
    ballooning   B:38
    balls for different sports   B:23
    baseball   B:76–94
    basketball   B:95–99
    bicycling   B:175–78
    billiards   B:179–80
    boardsailing   B:264–65
    boats and boating   B:266–69
    bobsledding   B:270–71
    bodybuilding   B:293–94
    bowling   B:348–50a
    boxing   B:350b–354
    canoeing   C:99–101
    cheerleading   C:193–94
    child development   C:225
    children see Children's sports
    cricket   C:583
    croquet   C:595–96
    curling   C:615
    diving   D:220–29
    fencing   F:85–87
    field hockey   F:119–20
    fishing   F:209–15
    football   F:352–64
    gloves worn for protection   G:242
    golf   G:253–61
    gymnastics   G:428b–433
    handball   H:17–20
    hiking and backpacking   H:134–36
    Hispanic Americans   H:147–48
    horseback riding   H:229–32

horse racing   H:233–36
horseshoe pitching   H:246
hunting   H:300–301
ice boating   I:19–20
ice hockey   I:23–32
ice-skating   I:38–45
injuries   S:5
jai alai   J:12–13
jogging and running   J:111
judo   J:149–50
karate   K:194–95
karting   K:196
kayaking   K:199
kite flying   K:266b–270
lacrosse   L:20–21
Little League Baseball   L:264–67
martial arts   M:116
mathematics in everyday life   M:160
mountain climbing   M:499–500
Olympic Games   O:102–20
paddleball   R:35
paddle tennis   P:11
parachuting   P:60
percents, use of   P:145–46
physical education   P:222–23
platform tennis   R:37
play   P:334
playground activities   P:80
polo   P:379
racing   R:34a
racket sports   R:34d–37
racquetball   R:36
rodeos   R:279–80
roller-skating   R:282
rowing   R:340–41
rugby   R:350–52
sailing   S:8–12
scuba diving   S:186–88
skateboarding   S:182
skiing   S:184c–185
skin diving   S:186–88
skydiving   S:190
snowboarding   S:218
Soap Box Derby   S:218a
soccer   S:218b–223
softball   S:233
Special Olympics   S:394
spelunking   S:400–401
sportsmanship   H:301
squash   R:34d–35
sumo wrestling   J:33
surfing   S:511
swimming   S:532–39
table tennis   T:2
Tee Ball, Little League   L:266
tennis   T:88–99
track and field   T:252–63
violence and society   V:344
volleyball   V:387
water polo   W:68
waterskiing   W:71–72
weight lifting   W:107
wrestling   W:324–25
youth soccer   S:222–23
Sports-car racing   A:537
Sportsmanship (in hunting)   H:301
Sportsman's Paradise (nickname for Louisiana)   L:314, 315
Sports medicine
    picture(s)   F:160
Sports video games   V:332c
Sport utility vehicles   W:75
Spot-bellied bobwhites (birds)   Q:4a
Spotswood, Alexander (English colonial governor)   W:136
Spotted hyenas see Laughing hyenas
Spotted owls   O:285

Spotted skunks   O:253
   picture(s)   O:253
Spotted Tail (Sioux Indian chief)   I:181 *profile*
Spotted turtles   T:355
Sprains (injuries to ligaments)   F:160
Spraying
   apple trees   A:332–33
   controlling farm pests   F:56–57
   controlling pests on fruit   F:482
   paint spraying   P:34
   weeds   W:106
   picture(s)
      insecticides   E:301; I:250
Spray skirts (kayaking equipment)   K:199
Spring (painting by Botticelli) *see* Primavera
Spring (season)   S:109, 110, 111 *see also* the names of
      months
   constellations   C:531
   Easter customs derived from early spring festivals   E:44
   flowers for spring   G:42
   holidays celebrating spring   H:161, 169
   picture(s)
      constellations   C:530
Spring balance (instrument)   F:251, 365, 366, 366a
   picture(s)   F:366
Springbok (antelope)   A:298
Spring clips (of railroad tracks)   R:78
Springfield (capital of Illinois)   I:71, 74
   picture(s)   I:71
      Lincoln's home   L:244
Springfield (Massachusetts)   M:143, 145
   picture(s)   M:145
Springfield (Missouri)   M:375–76
Springfield dolls (made of wood)   D:266
Springfield rifle   G:421
Spring Hill (Tennessee)   T:80
Spring peeper (frog)   F:476
Springs (mechanical devices)
   clocks   C:370
   furniture, use in   U:228
   suspension systems   A:551
   watches   W:45
Springs (of water) *see also* Hot springs
   Florida's first-magnitude springs   F:262
   Missouri has eleven of nation's largest springs   M:369
   picture(s)
      Florida   F:262
Springsteen, Bruce (American singer)   R:263 *profile*, 264
   picture(s)   M:531; R:264
Spring tides   O:19; T:195
Spring training (in baseball)   B:83
Spring Water (ballet)
   picture(s)   B:30
Spring wheat   W:157
Sprinkler method (of irrigation)   I:340
Sprinting *see* Running (sport)
Sprint racing (of cars) *see* Drag racing
Spritsail (small sail on a ship)   S:157
Sprockets (wheel projections)   E:187–88
Spruance, Raymond (American admiral)   W:314
Spruce Goose (airplane)   N:134
Spruce Knob–Seneca Rocks National Recreation Area   W:134
Spruce trees   C:434; W:227
   picture(s)   A:145; C:431; S:313; T:302; U:243
      uses of the wood and its grain   W:224
Spuds (beams for holding dredges in place)   D:322
Spur gears   G:66
   picture(s)   G:65, 66
Spurgeon, Charles (English orator)   O:191
Spurges (plants)   P:317
Spurr, Mount (volcano in Alaska)
   picture(s)   C:485
Sputnik (space satellite)   S:340, 340e, 350, 357, 359
   Khrushchev era in Soviet history   U:43

satellites, artificial   S:54
space research and technology   S:361–62
Spying *see* Spies
Spy stories   M:564–65
SQ4R method (of learning)   L:105
Squabs (young pigeons)   B:250a
Squad (army troop unit)   U:104
Squadron (Air Force unit)   U:109
Squadron (army troop unit)   U:104
Squamish (Indians of North America)   I:188
Squam Lake (New Hampshire)
   picture(s)   N:151
Squamous cell carcinoma (type of skin cancer)   D:124
Squanto (Native American)   I:177; M:148; P:346; S:25
Square (geometric figure)   G:121
Square (tool for measuring)   T:230, 234; W:231
Square dances (Barn dances)   D:27; F:299, 300, 303
   picture(s)   K:217
Square Deal (program of Theodore Roosevelt)   R:330
Square (Reef) knots   M:7b
   picture(s)   K:286; M:7a
Square measure (of area)   W:112–13
Square numbers   A:183; G:121; N:386–87
Square-rigging (on a ship)   S:158
Square root (of a number)   N:402
Squash (Squash racquets) (sport)   R:34d–35
Squash (vegetable)   I:165; V:290, 291
Squatters (settlers on land not legally their own)   L:53; P:260
Squatter sovereignty *see* Popular (Squatter) sovereignty
Squeeze play (in baseball)   B:83
Squids (mollusks)   M:405, 406, 407, 408; O:50, 51
   deep-sea life   O:27
   locomotion   A:278
   reproduction   R:177
Squire (Shield bearer) (knight's apprentice)   A:424; K:276–77
Squirrel monkeys   P:456
   picture(s)   M:421
Squirrels   R:275
   hibernation of ground squirrels   H:126, 127, 128
   squirrels' fleas can carry plague   D:212
   picture(s)   A:269
      flying squirrel   A:269
      red squirrel   B:209
SRAM (missile)   M:349
Sranan Tongo (language)   S:517
Sri Lanka   S:413–16
   Buddhism   B:424
   gems found in   G:71
   pearls   P:115
   tsunami (2004)   D:183
   picture(s)
      flag   F:240
      girl gathering tea leaves   A:444
      nurse caring for disaster victim   D:185
Srinagar (capital of Kashmir)   K:198
Sriwidjaya (former Indonesian kingdom)   I:211
SS (Hitler's official police)   N:80, 81
SS-18 (Russian missile)   M:348
SSI *see* Supplemental Security Income
SSM (surface-to-surface missiles)   M:345, 348–49; U:102,
      110
SST's (supersonic transport planes) *see* Supersonic flight;
      Supersonic Transports
St. (Ste.) (abbreviation for Saint and Sainte) *see* individual
      names as Paul, Saint, and Xavier, Francis, Saint. Place
      names beginning with St. are under Saint, as Saint
      Louis, Missouri
Stabiae (Italy)   P:381
Stabilator (of an airplane)   A:114
Stabiles (stationary sculpture of Calder)   M:396b; S:104–5
Stabilizers (of airplanes and ships)   A:113; G:437
Staccato notes (in musical notation)   M:537, 538
Stacking fault (defect in a crystal)   M:153
Stack pipes (in plumbing)   P:340
Stadacona (early Indian village, now Quebec City)   C:126

Stadholders (Dutch governors) **N**:121
Staël, Madame de (French writer) **F**:440
Staff (in musical notation) **M**:534, 537
Staff officers, United States Navy **U**:113
"Staff of life" (bread) **B**:385
Staffordshire pottery **A**:316a
Staff writers (of businesses) **W**:331
Stage *see* Plays; Theater
Stagecoaches **T**:282
Stage crews (of plays) **P**:338
Stagehands (of a theater) **T**:158
Stage managers (of plays) **P**:336; **T**:158
Stage scenery and lighting **P**:335, 337; **T**:158
 picture(s) **M**:480
Staghorn ferns **F**:94
Staging (medical evaluation of cancer patients) **C**:93
Staging (of rockets) **R**:261
Stag of Ceryneia (in Greek mythology) **G**:366
Stahl, Georg E. (German chemist) **C**:208
Stained-glass windows **S**:417–18
 Chagall, Marc **C**:182
 communication, history of **C**:463
 decorative arts of the Middle Ages **D**:77
 French Gothic architecture **F**:423
 Gothic tracery **G**:267–69
 medieval glassmaking **G**:233
 Spanish Gothic architecture **S**:382
 picture(s) **D**:77
  Canterbury Cathedral **G**:269
  Chartres Cathedral **G**:269
Stainless steels (alloys) **A**:192; **I**:329, 333
 Faraday produced first stainless steel **F**:47
 knives, forks, and spoons **K**:285
 nickel **N**:250
Stain removal **L**:82
 dry cleaning **D**:341
 dyeing and staining **D**:376
Stains (for microscope specimens) **M**:282
Staking (in leather preparation) **L**:111
Stalactites (cave formations) **C**:156
Stalagmites (cave formations) **C**:156
Stalemate (chess term) **C**:215
Stalin, Joseph (Soviet dictator) **R**:372; **S**:419; **U**:42, 43
 Cold War **C**:400, 401
 communism in the Soviet Union **C**:473–74
 de-Stalinization **K**:241
 Tito, dispute with **Y**:365, 368
 Ukraine, history of **U**:12
 picture(s)
  Tehran conference (1943) **W**:293
  toppled statue **U**:33
  Yalta Conference (1945) **R**:326
Stalingrad, Battle of (1942) **B**:103f; **W**:308
 picture(s) **W**:293
Stalking (hunting technique of cats) **C**:148
Stalling speed (in an airplane) **A**:39
Stallions (male horses) **H**:237
Stallone, Sylvester (American actor) **M**:497
Stalwarts (political group) **A**:436; **G**:54
Stamens (of flowers) **F**:282, 286; **P**:307
Stamford (Connecticut) **C**:517
 picture(s) **C**:518
Stamford Bridge, Battle of (1066) **V**:343
Stamitz, Johann (Bohemian composer) **O**:196
Stamp Act (Britain, 1765) **U**:176
 Adams, John, protests **A**:12–13
 Adams, Samuel, protests **A**:20
 American colonies protest **D**:58
 Franklin testifies against **F**:456
 Otis' role in repealing **O**:246
 Revolution, background of **R**:195–96
 Virginia's resistance **V**:359
Stamp Act Congress (1765) **R**:196
Stampede (of cattle) **C**:578
Stamping (in metalworking) **J**:97

Stamps and stamp collecting **S**:420–23
 Andorra **A**:252
 Bhutan **B**:155a
 Liechtenstein **L**:192
 Olympic Museum exhibits **O**:116
 postal service **P**:399
 San Marino **S**:35
 picture(s)
  commercial art **C**:458
Stanchions (type of barn housing for cattle) *see* Tie-stalls
Stand (area on which only one type of tree grows) **L**:338
Standard A mail **P**:399
Standard B mail **P**:399
Standardbred racing *see* Harness racing
Standard Fruit and Steamship Company **H**:207
Standardization
 automobile manufacturing **A**:542–43
 clothing sizes **C**:380
 Industrial Tool Period **T**:235
 interchangeability of parts in manufacturing **M**:88
 weights and measures **W**:108–17
Standardized tests **E**:86–87; **T**:119
 picture(s) **E**:87
Standard missiles **U**:115
Standard model (in quantum physics) **P**:232, 239
Standard of living **E**:61
 budgets, family **B**:427–28
 changes over time **P**:419
 Consumer Price Index **C**:533
 developing countries **D**:143
 effects of overpopulation **P**:387
 United States **U**:99
Standard of value (in economics) **M**:412
Standard Oil Company **R**:256; **T**:23
Standard Periodical Directory, The **M**:19
Standards (carried as flags) **F**:225; **H**:118
Standards and Technology, National Institute of **W**:110
Standard time **T**:202–3
Standard unit cubes (geometric measurements) **G**:125
Standard unit squares (geometric measurements) **G**:124–25
Standing committees (of organizations) **P**:82; **U**:165
Standish, Miles (English soldier and Pilgrim) **P**:345; **T**:171
Stanford, Leland (American railroad pioneer) **C**:33 *profile*
 picture(s) **C**:33
Stanford-Binet intelligence test **I**:253
Stanishev, Sergei (Bulgarian prime minister) **B**:446
Stanislaus River (California) **O**:280
Stanislavski, Konstantin (Russian actor) **T**:161 *profile*, 161–62
Stanley, Henry Morton (English-American explorer) **A**:66; **E**:412–13; **S**:424
 Congo River exploration **C**:502, 507
 Uganda, history of **U**:7
 picture(s) **S**:424
Stanley, Wendell (American biochemist) **V**:363
Stanley, William (American engineer and inventor) **T**:272
Stanley Cup (ice-hockey championship) **I**:28
 picture(s) **I**:28
Stanley Falls (Democratic Republic of Congo) **W**:59
Stanley of Preston, Frederick Arthur, Lord *see* Arthur, Frederick, Lord Stanley of Preston
Stanley Steamer (automobile) **A**:542
 picture(s) **A**:541
Stannous fluoride (toothpaste additive) **T**:209
Stannum *see* Tin
Stanton, Edwin McMasters (American politician) **B**:335; **C**:344 *profile*; **J**:118; **R**:118
 picture(s) **C**:344
Stanton, Elizabeth Cady (American suffragist) **A**:299; **S**:424; **W**:212, 212a, 214
 picture(s) **W**:214
Stanza (group of lines of poetry) **P**:350
Staphylococcus (bacteria) **A**:310; **D**:188
 picture(s)
  antibiotic's effects on **A**:308

Stapledon, Olaf (English writer)   **S:**82
Staple (Short) fibers   **C:**568; **F:**112; **N:**438
Staples (fasteners)   **N:**2
Starboard (right side of a boat or ship)   **S:**11, 154
Starch   **S:**425
  body chemistry of   **B:**296
  digestion of   **B:**280, 281
  fermentation   **F:**90
  grain and grain products   **G:**281, 282, 284, 285
  made up of glucose units   **L:**199
  nutrition   **N:**424, 428
  potatoes   **P:**403
  shopping for starchy foods   **F:**348–49
Star charts (of constellations)   **C:**528, 529, 530, 531
Stardust (space probe)   **C:**452; **S:**360
Star Festival (Japan)   **J:**32
Starfish (echinoderms)   **M:**237; **S:**426–27
  picture(s)   **S:**426, 427
Starflight clubs (of Camp Fire Boys and Girls)   **C:**43
  picture(s)   **C:**42
Stargazer (fish)   **F:**192
  picture(s)   **F:**192
Stargazer's Stone (marker where Pennsylvania, Maryland, and
    Delaware meet)   **M:**135
Stark, John (American Revolutionary War hero)   **R:**199, 204
Starley, John (English inventor)   **I:**281
Star maps *see* Star charts
Starnose mole (animal)   **M:**404
Star of Africa (gem)
  picture(s)   **E:**235
Star of David (symbol of Judaism)   **H:**173; **J:**148
  picture(s)   **J:**149
Star projectors (in planetariums)   **P:**270–72
Starr, Belle (American outlaw)   **O:**264 *profile*
  picture(s)   **O:**264
Starr, Kenneth (American lawyer)   **C:**368
Starr, Ringo (English musician and singer)   **B:**108
  picture(s)   **B:**108
Star Route frauds (post office scandal)   **A:**436; **G:**55
Star routes (in the United States Postal Service)   **P:**398
"Starry Night, A" (poem by Paul Dunbar)   **D:**353
Starry Night, The (painting by Vincent Van Gogh)
  picture(s)   **V:**278
Stars   **S:**428–33
  black holes   **B:**252–53
  constellations   **C:**528–32
  cosmic rays   **C:**563
  discoveries and classification in astronomy   **A:**472–74
  experiments and other science activities   **E:**389, 390–91
  gravity and star formation   **S:**249
  How do astronomers measure distance in space?   **A:**476
  Milky Way   **M:**308–9; **U:**211–13
  navigation by   **N:**75
  nebulas   **N:**96
  night-migrating birds navigate by the stars   **H:**202
  orbiting space colonies   **S:**356
  planetariums   **P:**269–73
  pulsars (neutron stars)   **P:**539
  quasars   **Q:**8–9
  radio astronomy   **R:**69–71
  solar system of our sun   **S:**241–49
  sun   **S:**488–97
  twinkling, cause of   **S:**367
  universe and our galaxy   **U:**211–18
  What are stars made of?   **S:**430
  Why do stars twinkle?   **S:**432
  picture(s)
    artist's impression of X-ray binary system   **B:**252
Stars (leading actors and actresses)   **M:**489, 497
Stars and Bars (Confederate flag)
  picture(s)   **C:**495; **F:**243
Stars and Stripes (flags) *see also* Pledge of Allegiance
  picture(s)   **F:**243

"Star-Spangled Banner, The" (national anthem of the United
    States)   **F:**248; **N:**18, 19; **W:**11
  picture(s)
    flag for which it was written   **F:**243
START *see* Strategic Arms Reduction Treaty
Starters, electric (of automobiles)   **A:**543
Star Trek (television program)   **S:**81, 83
  picture(s)   **T:**70
Starvation *see* Famine
Starving time (in Jamestown)   **J:**23; **T:**169
Star Wars (motion picture series)   **A:**289; **M:**497; **S:**83
  picture(s)   **D:**271; **R:**255; **S:**83
Star Wars (Strategic Defense Initiative) (space-based defense
    system)   **N:**379
State, United States Department of   **F:**371; **P:**447; **S:**434–35;
    T:290
State aid (for schools)   **E:**76
State banks   **B:**53
State farms (in the former Soviet Union)   **U:**38
State governments (United States)   **S:**436–38 *see also* States'
    rights; the government section of state articles
  civil service   **C:**331
  courts   **C:**574
  education   **E:**76
  elections   **E:**128, 130
  income tax   **I:**111
  Indian reservations exempt from some rules   **I:**201
  initiative, referendum, and recall   **O:**212, 214
  law and law enforcement   **L:**85–86
  legal holidays   **H:**164
  libraries   **L:**178
  marijuana, medical use of   **D:**330
  municipal and state government relations   **M:**515, 517
  National Guard   **N:**41–42
  Nebraska's unicameral legislature   **N:**91
  power of impeachment   **I:**99
  powers, list of   **S:**437
  public-assistance programs   **W:**119–20
  state police   **P:**366
  taxation powers limited   **T:**25
  Tenth Amendment defines powers left to the states
    B:182
  wills   **W:**177
State House (Annapolis, Maryland)
  picture(s)   **M:**130
Statelessness   **C:**324; **R:**136–37
Statement of financial position *see* Balance sheet
Staten Island (New York City)   **N:**226, 228
State of siege *see* Martial law
State of the Union message (of the United States president)
    P:450
State police (in the United States)   **P:**366
State prisons   **P:**480
States' rights (in United States history)
  Bill of Rights: Tenth Amendment   **B:**182
  Calhoun, John C.   **C:**17
  Civil War issue   **C:**335, 347
  Davis, Jefferson, changes his viewpoint   **D:**43
  The Federalist interprets the constitution   **F:**78
  Johnson, Andrew, supports   **J:**117
  Kentucky and Virginia Resolutions   **K:**227
  laws, each state has its own   **C:**584
  Missouri Compromise   **M:**381
  nullification issue   **J:**6–7
  political parties   **P:**371
  Reconstruction Period (1866–1877)   **R:**117–18
  Supreme Court and constitutional development   **S:**510
  weaknesses of the Articles of Confederation   **U:**145–46
States' Rights (Dixiecrat) Party (in United States history)
    P:372; **T:**326
Static (electrical interference in radio or television reception)
    R:57, 72; **T:**56
Static electricity   **E:**136–37; **P:**478; **T:**184
Static stretching (of the muscles and ligaments)   **P:**226
Stationary front (in meteorology)   **W:**85, 93

Stationers (medieval book dealers)   B:321
Stations (ranches in Australia)
   picture(s)   A:498
Statistical Abstract of the United States, The   C:167
Statistics   M:158; S:439–43
   census information   C:167
   graphs   G:309–13
   Mendel's experiment combining biology with   M:218
   opinion polls' sampling techniques   O:169–70
   percents, use of   P:146
   population statistics   P:385–88
   statistical weather forecasting   W:94
Statistics Canada (agency that takes the census)   C:167
Stators (of machines)   E:154
Statue of Liberty see Liberty, Statue of
Statues see Monuments; Sculpture
Status Indians (of Canada) see First Nations peoples
Status offenses (juvenile crimes)   J:167
Statute miles (measure of distance)   L:78; W:115
Statutes (written laws)   L:85, 86
Statutory days (in Canada)   H:164
Staubbach waterfall (Switzerland)   W:59
Stays (of sailboats)   S:11
Stealing bases (in baseball)   B:82
Stealth advertising   A:32
Steam (hot water vapor)   H:91
   croup treatment   D:191
   geysers and hot springs   G:192, 193
   volcanoes   V:379, 384
   picture(s)
      boiling point   H:90
Steam automobiles   A:539–40, 541–42
Steamboats   T:284
   Fulton, Robert   F:491; I:220
   Mississippi River   M:360, 365
   Ohio River   O:78
   South Dakota   S:321
   picture(s)   M:351
Steamboat Willie (animated cartoon)   A:290; D:215
Steam distillation   D:219
Steam engines   S:443–45
   airplanes, experimental   A:561
   automobiles, history of   A:539–40, 541–42; T:286
   Boulton, Matthew   I:220
   compared to steam turbines   T:342
   Corliss, George Henry   R:225
   engines, types of   E:229; I:262
   Evans, Oliver   D:100
   Industrial Revolution   I:218, 219–20
   inventions   I:280–81
   kinetic energy, source of   E:216
   locomotives   L:285–86
   military uses   B:103f
   ocean liners   O:32
   Stanley Steamer (automobile)   A:542
   steam-powered dredges   D:322
   Watt, James   W:77
   diagram(s)
      Newcomen's   S:444
   picture(s)   I:218
      textile factory   I:281
Steam fog   F:290
   picture(s)   F:291
Steaming (method of cooking)   C:542
Steam locomotives   L:285–86, 288; R:80–81, 87
   picture(s)   L:286; R:80
Steam power plants see Thermal power plants
Steamships   S:158–59; T:284 see also Steamboats
   battles   B:103f
   early ocean liners   O:32
   Industrial Revolution   I:220
Steam turbines   E:229; P:422; S:443, 445; T:342, 343
Steam vents (in the Earth) see Fumaroles
Stearic acid   C:96
Stearin (paraffin product used in candles)   L:232

Steel   I:329–38 see also Iron
   Alabama   A:136
   alloy steels   A:192; I:329
   armor   A:423–24
   Belgian industry   B:132
   Bessemer, Sir Henry   B:154
   building material   B:433, 437, 440
   cheap production, importance of   M:88
   Chicago area's manufacturing capacity is world's largest
      C:219
   coal used in refining iron   C:391
   Damascus steel   I:337; T:332
   decorative arts   D:79
   galvanized steel   Z:385
   Indiana's industry   I:150
   Industrial Revolution   I:218–19, 223
   jewelry making   J:96
   metallurgy   M:236
   Pennsylvania's industry   P:139
   Pittsburgh   P:267
   railroad tracks   R:77, 78, 89
   reinforcing rods in concrete   C:166
   Sheffield (England)   U:60
   shipbuilding   S:159
   stainless see Stainless steels
   tools   T:235
   United States production   U:93
   water used to produce steel   W:53
   picture(s)
      buildings of steel construction   B:438
      China's industry   C:264
      Colombia's industry   S:291
      fire, uses of   F:142
      grinding   G:391
      helical gears of hot mill rollers   G:65
      Indiana's industry   I:151
      India's industry   I:128
      industry in 1800's   U:188
      Japan's industry   J:39
      Ohio's industry   O:69
      Ontario's industry   O:129
      Pennsylvania's industry   P:133
Steele, Cecily (American farmer)   D:102
Steele, Sir Richard (English essayist and dramatist)   E:278,
   321; M:19
Steel King (nickname for Andrew Carnegie)   C:115
Steel plates   I:336–37
Steel wool (an abrasive)   G:392
Steen, Jan (Dutch painter)   D:365
Steeplechase (horse race)   H:235
Steeplechases (track events)   T:255, 261
Steer, Wilson (English painter)   I:105
Steerage (section of ships)   O:32
Steerage, The (photograph by Alfred Stieglitz)
   picture(s)   P:203
Steering systems (of automobiles)   A:546, 550
Steering systems (of missiles)   M:346–47
Steering vanes (in rockets)   R:260
Steers (cattle)   C:151; I:129; M:196
   picture(s)   I:121
Steer wrestling (at rodeos)   R:280
Ŝtefánik, Milan (Slovak political leader)   S:201
Stegosaurus (dinosaur)   D:175
   picture(s)   D:175; P:433
Steig, William (American artist and cartoonist)
   picture(s)
      illustration from *Doctor De Soto*   C:242
Stein, Clarence (American architect)   U:236
Stein, Gertrude (American writer)   A:214a; S:446
Stein, Johann Andreas (Viennese piano builder)   P:241
Steinbeck, John (American author)   A:216; N:362; S:446
   The Grapes of Wrath (book)   O:96
   quoted on dogs   D:259
   picture(s)   C:32
      The Grapes of Wrath (book)   N:361

Steinem, Gloria (American writer and political activist) **S:447**
  picture(s) **S:**447; **W:**213
Steinmetz, Charles Proteus (American engineer) **S:447**
Steinway and Sons (piano builders) **P:**242
Stela (stone pillar or slab) **M:**184
Stella, Frank (American artist) **M:**396b; **P:**32
  picture(s)
    Ctesiphon II (painting) **M:**396a
Stellar transit (of extrasolar planets) **P:**282
Steller sea lions **S:**106
Steller's jay (bird)
  picture(s) **B:**402
Steller's sea cows (extinct mammals) **M:**77
Stem and leaf graphs **G:**312
Stem cell research **B:**214; **G:**91; **M:**208h–209; **O:**227
Stem cells (immature blood cells) **B:**261; **C:**94; **S:**184a
Stems (of plants) **F:**329; **P:**297, 304–5
Stem stitch (in embroidery) **N:**100
  picture(s) **N:**99
Stencil printing, silk-screen (graphic art) **P:**478; **S:**176
Stendhal (French writer) **F:**441; **N:**360
Steno, Nicolaus (Danish scientist) **G:**109
Step dancing (Irish folk dance) **F:**300; **I:**322
  picture(s) **F:**301
Step-down transformers (of electric currents) **T:**271, 272
Stephanopoulos, Costas (president of Greece) **G:**338
Stephen (king of England) **H:**108
Stephen, Saint (first king of Hungary) **H:**298
Stephen I, Saint (pope) **R:**292
Stephen (II) (pope) **R:**292
Stephen II (III) (pope) **R:**292
Stephen III (IV) (pope) **R:**288, 292
Stephen IV (V) (pope) **R:**292
Stephen V (VI) (pope) **R:**292
Stephen VI (VII) (pope) **R:**292
Stephen VII (VIII) (pope) **R:**292
Stephen VIII (IX) (pope) **R:**292
Stephen IX (X) (pope) **R:**292
Stephen Dushan (Dušan) (Serbian king) **S:**126; **Y:**367
Stephen Nemanja (overlord of Serbia) **S:**125; **Y:**367
Stephens, Alexander Hamilton (American political figure)
    C:336, 345 profile, 495
  picture(s) **C:**345
Stephens, Helen (American runner) **M:**379 profile
Stephens, Uriah S. (founded Knights of Labor) **L:**13
Stephenson, George (English inventor) **R:**78, 87, 88 profile
  picture(s) **R:**88
Step leader (first stroke of lightning in a storm) **T:**187
Stepparents **F:**37–38
Steppenwolf (book by Hermann Hesse) **H:**125
Steppes (plains regions)
  Africa **A:**52
  Asia **A:**438f
  climate **C:**362
  Moldova **M:**402
  prairies **P:**426–29
  Russia **R:**361, 362
  semiarid lands **D:**126
  Ukraine **U:**9
  picture(s)
    Central Asia **A:**438g
Step Pyramid (Saqqara, Egypt) **A:**365; **E:**108, 110–11;
    P:556
  picture(s) **A:**365; **P:**557
Step-roofed houses **H:**194
Steps (in dancing) **D:**22–23
Steptoe, John (American writer) **C:**238
Step-up transformers (of electric currents) **T:**271, 272
Stereo (kind of sound reproduction) **H:**131
  phonographs **P:**195
  radio broadcasting **R:**61
  recording industry **R:**123
  sound recording **S:**267
  videocassette recorders **H:**133

Stereolithography (plastics manufacturing technology)
    P:328–29
Stereomicroscopes (optical instruments) **O:**180
Stereophonic reproduction of sound see Stereo
Stereoscopic microscopes **M:**282
Stereoscopic motion pictures see Three-dimensional motion
    pictures
Stereoscopic (Binocular) vision **E:**429
Sterility (inability to have children) see Infertility
Sterilization (to make things germfree) **D:**214
  canning of food **F:**342
  milk **D:**8
  modern surgery, rise of **M:**208b
  ultraviolet radiation **L:**221
Sterilization (to prevent pregnancy) **B:**250b
  neutering or spaying of pets **C:**140; **D:**260
Sterling silver (high-quality alloy of silver and copper) **J:**96;
    K:285; **S:**177, 178
Stern (rear of a boat) **C:**99
Sternberg, Robert (American psychologist) **I:**253; **P:**509
Sterne, Laurence (English theologian and novelist) **E:**280;
    N:359
Stern-steerers (iceboats) **I:**19–20
Sternum (breastbone) **B:**222
Steroids (lipids in body cells) **B:**296; **H:**228; **O:**116 see also
    Corticosteroids
Stesichorus (Greek poet) **G:**356
Stethoscope (instrument used by doctors) **D:**203; **H:**85;
    M:204
Stetson, John B. (American hatmaker) **H:**47
Stetson hats **C:**577
Stettheimer dollhouse **D:**265
Stettin (Poland) see Szczecin
Stettinius, Edward (United States secretary of state)
  picture(s) **U:**64
Steuben, Friedrich, Baron von (German general, volunteer aid to
    Americans) **R:**203, 209 profile
Steunenberg, Frank (governor of Idaho) **I:**59
Stevens, Isaac (American soldier and first governor of
    Washington territory) **W:**26–27
Stevens, John (American inventor) **R:**87
Stevens, John Paul (American jurist) **S:**508 profile
  picture(s) **U:**171
Stevens, Siaka (first president of Sierra Leone) **S:**172
Stevens, Thaddeus (American political leader) **R:**116; **U:**143
    profile
  picture(s) **R:**117; **U:**142
Stevens, Wallace (American poet) **A:**215; **S:**448
Stevens-Murphy party (of pioneers) **O:**280
Stevenson, Adlai Ewing (vice president of the United States)
    V:328 profile
Stevenson, Adlai Ewing II (American political leader) **S:**448
Stevenson, Robert Louis (Scottish author) **S:**449–52
  adventure fiction **F:**114
  "Bed in Summer" (poem) **S:**451
  children's literature **C:**237
  A Child's Garden of Verses, poems from **S:**450–51
  essays **E:**321
  "The Gardener" (poem) **S:**451
  Kidnapped, excerpt from **S:**452
  "Looking-Glass River" (poem) **S:**450
  "My Shadow" (poem) **S:**450
  place in English literature **E:**286
  "Requiem" (poem) **S:**449
  "The Swing" (poem) **S:**451
  Treasure Island as an adventure story **M:**563
Stewardesses, airline see Airline flight attendants
Stewards (on cruise ships) **O:**32
Stewart, James (American actor) **M:**491 profile
Stewart, William Morris (American lawyer) **N:**135 profile
Stewart Island (New Zealand) **N:**237
Sticklebacks (fish) **F:**197
  picture(s) **F:**195
Stickley, Gustav (American furniture designer) **F:**514
Stick puppets see Rod puppets

Stiegel, Henry William (American glassmaker)   G:233
Stieglitz, Alfred (American photographer)   O:81; P:203 *profile*
  picture(s)
    The Steerage (photograph)   P:203
Stigma (part of a flower)   F:282, 285; P:307
Stikine River (Canada)   B:402
Still, Clyfford (American painter)   N:335 *profile*
Still, James (American practitioner of herbal medicine)
    N:179 *profile*
Still, William (American civil rights leader)   U:16 *profile*
Stillbirth (natural early ending of pregnancy)   A:8
Still life (in art)   D:365
  picture(s)
    development of a still life drawing   D:309
Stills (distilling equipment)   D:218; W:161
Stilt houses   H:188
  picture(s)   H:188; M:558
Stimson, Henry Lewis (American statesman)   W:317
Stimson Doctrine (in international relations)   H:225; T:297
Stimulants (drugs)
    abuse of   D:330–31; O:114
    ADHD, treatment of   A:23
    caffeine in coffee   C:397
    how drugs work   D:334
Stimulated emission of radiation (of lasers)   L:46a
Stine, R. L. (American author)   C:239
Stingrays (fish)   A:276; F:201; S:145
  picture(s)   A:276; S:145
Stings   S:3
    bees   B:116
    first aid   F:161
    insects   I:243
    jellyfish   A:280
Stink badgers *see* Teledus
Stippling (drawing technique)   D:311
Stipules (of leaves)   L:112; P:306
  picture(s)   L:113
Stirling, Battle of (1297)   S:88
Stirling, Robert (Scottish clergyman and inventor)   E:229
Stirling engine   E:229
Stirrup (bone in the ear)   E:4, 6
  picture(s)   E:5
Stitches (in sewing)
    crocheting stitches   C:590–91
    embroidery stitches   N:98
    needlepoint stitches   N:100
  picture(s)   S:130
    embroidery stitches   N:99
Stoas (in Greek architecture)   A:368; G:349
Stoats (type of weasels)   O:254
Stock (of a rifle)   G:415
Stockade (frontier fort)   F:379
Stock agencies (providers of photographs to magazines and
    advertisers)   P:210
Stock-car racing   A:537–38
Stock cars (of railroads)   R:84
Stock companies (theater)   T:159–60
Stocker cattle   C:153
Stock exchanges (places where stocks and bonds are bought
    and sold)   S:456
    Toronto's is world's largest market for mining shares
      O:133
    Wall Street (New York City)   N:232
  picture(s)
    New York Stock Exchange   N:218; U:91
Stockholders   B:313, 471; E:128
Stockholm (capital of Sweden)   S:453, 524, 527
  picture(s)   S:453
    Riddarholm Church   S:527
Stockholm Bloodbath (in Swedish history)   C:286
Stockinette stitch (in knitting)   K:281
Stocking dolls   D:268
Stock market *see* Stock exchanges

Stocks (certificates representing shares in a company)
    S:454–59
    corporations   B:471
    Depression, Great   D:119
    investment banks   B:55
    prices fall in recessions   D:122
    What are blue chip stocks?   S:455
    What is cornering the market?   S:458
Stocks (used for punishment)   P:347
Stock ticker (device giving information on stock exchange)
    E:71
Stockton, John (American basketball player)
  picture(s)   B:95c
Stockton, Richard (American lawyer)   D:66
Stockton and Darlington Railway   R:78, 88; T:285
Stoker, Bram (Anglo-Irish writer)   F:114; L:130
Stokes, Carl Burton (American public official)   A:79c; C:356;
    O:77 *profile*
  picture(s)   O:76
Stokes, Louise (American athlete)   O:112
Stoking (fueling an engine)   L:285–86
Stokowski, Leopold (British orchestra conductor)   O:201
    profile
  picture(s)   O:201
Stolons (creeping stems of plants)   P:305
  picture(s)   G:316
Stomach   S:460–61
    birds   B:222–23
    burps and growls   B:301
    digestive system   B:280–81; D:163–64
    peptic ulcer   D:198–99
    research by Beaumont   B:109
    ruminants (cud-chewing animals)   H:218
    What makes a stomach growl?   S:461
  diagram(s)
    ruminants   H:219
  picture(s)
    peptic ulcer damage   D:198
Stomachache (discomfort in the abdomen)   D:165
Stomata (of plants)   L:113, 116; P:306
Stone
    Africa, architecture of   A:76
    Africa, art of   D:73
    ancient Egyptian art   D:73; E:108
    ancient stonework   B:439
    architecture, history of   A:365, 367, 368
    building material   B:432
    gems   G:69–75
    houses of   H:187
    natural resources   N:62
    Pennsylvania is a leading producer   P:133
    quarrying   Q:6
    stone masonry   B:393–94
Stone (measure of weight)   W:114, 115
Stone, Edmund (English clergyman)   M:208g
Stone, Edward Durell (American architect)   A:419 *profile;*
    U:136
Stone, Lucy (American suffragist and reformer)   W:212, 212a,
    215 *profile*
Stone, Thomas (American political figure)   D:66 *profile*
Stone Age   P:438–42
    Chinese ornamental pottery   C:274; P:409
    fire, use of   F:141
    invention through the ages   I:278–79
    prehistoric art   C:463; D:72; P:435–37
    surgery, early practice of   S:512
    tools   T:232–33
    toys, history of   T:250
  picture(s)
    Chinese earthenware pot   P:409
    lighting   L:231
    tools   T:233
Stonefish   F:201
Stone fruits   P:107–9

Stonehenge (England)   **E:**235; **S:462; U:**54
   astronomy, history of   **A:**468
   Who built Stonehenge?   **S:**462
   picture(s)   **A:**468; **E:**236; **W:**216
Stone implements   **P:**440; **T:**232–33
   picture(s)   **P:**441
Stonemasons   **B:**393; **G:**271
Stone Mountain Park (Georgia)   **G:**140
   picture(s)
      Confederate Memorial   **G:**140
Stoner, Eugene Morrison (American inventor)   **G:**424
Stones River (Tennessee)   **C:**340
Stone's sheep   **S:**147
Stonewall Riot (beginning of modern lesbian and gay
      movement)   **H:**204
Stoneware (pottery)   **A:**316a; **C:**177; **P:**408
   picture(s)   **A:**316
Stool *see* Feces
Stop, drop, and roll (what to do if your clothing catches fire)
      F:150
Stop ERA (organization)   **W:**213
Stopes (underground excavations for mining)   **M:**321–22
Stop in the Country, A (painting by Prilidiano Pueyrredón)
   picture(s)   **L:**63
Stop-motion photography   **A:**289; **M:**484, 487
   picture(s)   **P:**199
Stoppard, Tom (British playwright)   **D:**305; **E:**290
   picture(s)   **D:**305
Stoppers (knots)   **K:**287
"Stopping by Woods on a Snowy Evening" (poem by Robert
      Frost)   **F:**480
Stopping potential (in photoelectricity)   **L:**223
Stops (of pipe organs)   **K:**236, 238; **M:**551
Stopwatches   **W:**45–46
Storage (of food)   **F:**52
   grain   **G:**285–86
   Tupperware, invention of   **I:**283
   vegetables   **V:**289–90
Storage batteries *see* Secondary batteries
Storage dams   **D:**16, 21
Store of value (in economics)   **M:**412
Stores *see* Department stores; Retail stores; Shopping;
      Supermarkets
Stories (told in full) *see also* Children's literature; Fables; Fairy
      tales; Fiction; Folklore; Greek mythology; Legends;
      Mystery and detective stories; Storytelling; excerpts
      from longer works by name, as *Oliver Twist*
   "The Ant and the Grasshopper" (by Aesop)   **F:**5
   "The Blind Men and the Elephant" (in verse)   **F:**7
   "Boy Jesus"   **B:**168–69
   "Daniel in the Lions' Den"   **B:**172–73
   "David and Goliath"   **B:**169–70
   "The Elephant's Child" (by Kipling)   **K:**261–64
   "The Emperor's New Clothes"   **A:**247–49
   "The Enchanted Princess"   **F:**23–25
   "The Four Oxen and the Lion" (by Aesop)   **F:**5
   "Hansel and Gretel"   **G:**384–90
   "Jonah"   **B:**171–72
   "The Lion and the Mouse" (by Aesop)   **F:**4
   "Little Red Riding-Hood"   **F:**29–32
   "The Moth and the Star" (by Thurber)   **F:**6
   "Noah's Ark"   **B:**168–69
   "The Princess on the Pea" (by Andersen)   **F:**26
   "Rapunzel"   **G:**382–84
   "Roland and Oliver" (legend)   **L:**131–34
   "The Skyscraper to the Moon and How the Green Rat With
      the Rheumatism Ran a Thousand Miles Twice" (by
      Sandburg)   **S:**28
   "Sleeping Beauty"   **F:**27–29
   "The Tyrant Who Became a Just Ruler" (by Bidpai)   **F:**8
Storks (birds)   **E:**350; **H:**124
   picture(s)   **E:**351
Storm, Gale (American singer)   **R:**262c
Storm Prediction Center (Norman, Oklahoma)   **T:**242; **W:**93

Storms   **W:**81–82, 85–86
   climate   **C:**361
   cumulonimbus clouds   **C:**385
   Dust Bowl   **D:**355–56
   dust storms on Mars   **M:**107, 108
   hurricanes   **H:**302–6
   thunder and lightning   **T:**184–87
   tornadoes   **T:**241–42
   United States has most severe storms   **W:**85
   weather forecasting   **W:**93
   weather-instrument monitoring   **W:**90
   weather satellites track tropical storms   **W:**91
   picture(s)
      cumulonimbus clouds   **C:**384
      warning lights and flags for boats   **B:**268
Storm surges   **H:**305
Storm troopers (name for Nazi private army)   **N:**79, 80
Storting (Norway's national parliament)   **N:**348
Storyboards (series of pictures with captions)   **A:**33, 288;
      I:84; **M:**481
Story of the King: Louis XIV Entering Dunkirk (Gobelins tapestry)
   picture(s)   **T:**21
Story strips (form of comic strips)   **C:**128
Storytelling   **S:**463–65   *see also* excerpts from longer works by
      name, as *Little Women*
   The Arabian Nights, excerpt from   **A:**339–40
   Arthur, King, legends of, excerpt from   **A:**438a–438b
   Bible stories   **B:**168–74
   Charlotte's Web, excerpt from   **W:**163
   children's literature, history of   **C:**228
   early form of communication   **C:**463
   fables   **F:**2–8
   fairy tales   **F:**19
   folklore   **F:**307
   Grimm brothers' storyteller (Gammer Grethel)   **F:**21
   Indian dance-drama   **T:**162
   Just So Stories (by Kipling), excerpt from   **K:**261–64
   kindergarten activities   **K:**247
   legends   **L:**129–36
   library story hour   **L:**177
   mythology   **M:**568
   oral tradition in African literature   **A:**76a–76c
   origin of the *Iliad* and *Odyssey*   **H:**184
   Sanskrit literature   **I:**141
   picture(s)   **F:**304
      Africa   **A:**76a, 76c; **C:**463
      early childhood education   **K:**249
      Kyrgyzstan   **K:**313
      library story hour   **L:**176
Story theater (in which a narrator tells the story)   **P:**335
Stourbridge Fair (England)   **F:**18
Stourbridge Lion (locomotive)   **L:**287; **R:**87–88
   picture(s)   **L:**287
Stout (type of beer)   **B:**115
Stowe, Harriet Beecher (American writer)   **A:**211; **C:**334, 514;
      S:465
   picture(s)   **A:**6a
Strabismus (eye disorder)   **E:**431
Strabo (Greek geographer)   **G:**105
Strachan, John (Canadian educator and bishop)   **O:**137
Strachey, Lytton (English biographer)   **E:**288
Stradivari, Antonio (Italian violin-maker)   **B:**71; **V:**345
   picture(s)   **I:**411; **M:**540
Straight billiards (game)   **B:**180
Straightening (of the hair)   **H:**8
Straight pool (pocket billiards game)   **B:**180
Straight stitch (in embroidery)   **N:**98
   picture(s)   **N:**99
Straight truck (with cab and cargo space on one chassis)
      T:318
Strains (injuries to muscles or tendons)   **F:**160; **M:**521
Strait (geographic term) *see* the names of straits, as Magellan,
      Strait of
Strand casting (in steelmaking)   **I:**334–35
Strandings (of whales on beaches)   **W:**151

Strange attractor (mathematical pattern)
picture(s) **M:**170
Strange Interlude (play by Eugene O'Neill) **O:**122
Strange quark (subatomic particle) **A:**488
Strangers (of the Plymouth Colony) **P:**345
Strangling fig (rain-forest plant) **R:**99
Straparola, Giovanni (Italian writer) **F:**20
Strap-on boosters (small rockets on launch vehicles) **R:**261
Strasbourg (France) **F:**410
picture(s) **C:**284
Strasser, Gregor (German Nazi leader) **N:**80
Strassmann, Fritz (German chemist) **F:**222
Strata (layers of rock) **G:**109, 110; **R:**267–69
Strategic Arms Limitation Treaty (SALT) **D:**182; **N:**378–79
Strategic Arms Reduction Treaty (START) (1991) **D:**182; **N:**379
Strategic Arms Reduction Treaty II (START II) (1993) **B:**465; **N:**379
Strategic Defense Initiative *see* Star Wars (Strategic Defense Initiative)
Strategic nuclear weapons **N:**375
Strategy games **G:**12–13
Stratford-on-Avon (England) **E:**272; **S:**132, 134; **T:**160
Stratford Shakespearean Festival (Stratford, Ontario) **C:**69
picture(s) **C:**131
Stratigraphy (study of archaeological site's layers) **A:**354
Stratigraphy (study of the arrangement of rock strata) **P:**168
Stratocumulus clouds **C:**385; **W:**87
picture(s) **C:**384
Stratopause (atmospheric boundary) **A:**482
Stratosphere (second layer of Earth's atmosphere) **A:**482; **E:**21; **J:**93
ozone layer **O:**292
Stratospheric Observatory for Infrared Astronomy (SOFIA) **O:**10
Stratovolcanoes **V:**380
Stratum corneum (outermost layer of skin) **B:**277
Stratus clouds **C:**385; **W:**87
picture(s) **C:**384
Strauss, Johann, Jr. (Austrian composer) **S:**466
The Bat (operetta) **O:**166, 167–68
The Gypsy Baron (operetta) **O:**168
musical theater **M:**553
operetta **O:**166
Strauss, Richard (German composer) **S:**466
opera **O:**148
romanticism in music **R:**304
Rosenkavalier, Der (opera) **O:**163
Salome (opera) **O:**163
symphonic poems **G:**187
Stravinsky, Igor (Russian-born American composer) **S:**467
ballet music **B:**30
choral music **C:**285
French music, influence on **F:**448
modern music **M:**398
opera **O:**148
Russia, music of **R:**386
Straw (for drinking through) **V:**263
Straw (used in brickmaking) **B:**391
Strawberries **G:**51, 298; **P:**305
picture(s) **F:**52; **G:**299
flowers **F:**287
stolons **P:**310
Strawberry cacti *see* Hedgehog cacti
Strawbery Banke (Portsmouth, New Hampshire) **N:**158
Streaking (to identify minerals) **M:**316
Streak lightning **T:**187
Stream erosion **E:**318
Streamers (fly-fishing lures) **F:**215
picture(s) **F:**214
Streaming (of sound through the Internet) **R:**61, 124
Streamlining
airplane design to reduce drag **A:**39–40
fish, shape of **F:**186
industrial design **I:**215
locomotion in animals **A:**276, 278

Stream of consciousness (in literature) **E:**289; **F:**116; **N:**361
Joyce's technique of the novel **I:**327; **J:**142
Streep, Meryl (American actress) **M:**492 *profile*
Street, George Edmund (English architect) **E:**263
Streetcar Named Desire, A (play by Tennessee Williams) **W:**176
picture(s) **A:**218; **D:**306
Streetcars and trolleycars **T:**288
electric motors **E:**145; **L:**287
San Diego **S:**30
San Francisco's cable cars **S:**31
Seashore Trolley Museum (Kennebunkport, Maine) **M:**44
streetcar companies built the first American amusement parks **P:**78
wide-gauge railways **R:**78
picture(s)
San Francisco's cable cars **S:**32
Zagreb (Croatia) **E:**362
Streeter, Ruth Cheney (American military official) **N:**163
Street of Silver (Delhi, India) *see* Chandni Chowk
Streets *see* Roads and highways
Strength (the amount of force muscles can exert) **P:**224–25
Strep throats **D:**188
Streptococci (bacteria) **B:**12; **D:**204
nephritis **D:**198
rheumatic fever can follow strep infections **D:**202
scarlet fever **D:**203
picture(s) **B:**12
Streptomycin (drug) **M:**206
Stresemann, Gustav (German statesman) **G:**162
Stress (in psychology and biology) **D:**202, 209
electrocardiograph test **H:**85
spaceflight, dangers of **S:**344
stomach disorders **S:**461
zoo animals **Z:**393
Stretching (of the muscles and ligaments) **P:**226, 227
Striations (in muscle fiber)
picture(s) **M:**518
Strike (in baseball) **B:**81–82
Strike (in bowling) **B:**349, 350
Strikebreakers **L:**8
Strikes (workers' refusal to work) **L:**8, 10
California grape workers **H:**148
Flint "sit-down" strike **M:**273
Great Strike of 1877 (Baltimore) **M:**134
major league baseball **B:**94
Ohio, history of **O:**76, 77
Pennsylvania, history of **P:**141
professional basketball **B:**99
Pullman strike **D:**53; **R:**88
railroad workers (1922) **R:**90
West Virginia coal miners **W:**139
Winnipeg General Strike (1919) **M:**86
picture(s)
New York Daily News **L:**10
Strindberg, August (Swedish dramatist) **D:**304; **S:**58i, **467,** 527
String beans **V:**292
Stringed instruments **M:**546, 547–49; **S:**468–69
Africa, music of **A:**78
baroque period **B:**71
chamber music **C:**183–84
dance accompaniment **D:**24
guitar **G:**411–12
harp **H:**35–36
luthiers build stringed instruments **W:**232
orchestra **C:**350; **O:**193
orchestra seating plan **O:**196
piano **P:**240–42
violin **V:**345
picture(s)
students learning to become luthiers **G:**405
Stringfellow, John (English engineer) **A:**561
String orchestra **O:**192, 193

Subsidies (grants made by governments)   **T:**159
Subsistence farming   **A:**62, 63
Subsistence hunting   **H:**300
Subsoil   **S:**237
Subsonic flight (under the speed of sound)   **S:**499, 501
Substance (in chemistry)   **C:**198; **M:**151–55
Substance Abuse and Mental Health Services Administration
   (United States)   **H:**78; **P:**514
Substance abuse *see* Alcoholism; Drug abuse
Substitution ciphers (in secret writing)   **C:**393–94
Subsurface methods (of irrigation)   **I:**340–41
Subtraction (in mathematics)   **A:**389
   abacus   **A:**2
   algebra   **A:**182, 183
   decimals   **F:**401
   fractions   **F:**398–99
   number systems   **N:**398
   picture(s)
      abacus   **A:**3
Subtractive primaries (pigment colors)   **C:**425
Subtrahend (in subtraction)   **A:**389
Subtropical deserts   **C:**362; **D:**127
Subtropical fruits   **F:**481
Subtropical jet stream   **J:**93
Suburbs (of cities)
   expansion of cities and suburbs forms megalopolis   **C:**321
   GI Bill and growth of   **U:**125
   homes and housing   **H:**188–89, 195
   Maryland counties near Washington, D.C.   **M:**120, 124,
      129
   modern architecture   **A:**375–76
   traffic problems   **T:**269
Subways   **R:**81; **T:**288, 289
   Cairo's first in Africa   **C:**8
   London   **L:**297, 298; **P:**396
   Moscow's Metro   **M:**467
   New York City   **N:**233
   Paris Métro   **P:**73
   Rome's are limited by catacombs   **R:**308
   Russia   **R:**364
   Washington, D.C.   **W:**34
Succession (in botany)   **F:**376
   picture(s)   **F:**375; **P:**300–301
Succession, line of (for the United States presidency)   **P:**448
Succession myth (in Greek mythology)   **G:**361–62
Succulents (plants)   **B:**207; **C:**5; **H:**269; **L:**117
Suckers (of plants)   **P:**249; **T:**305
Sucket forks   **K:**285
Sucking pests   **P:**288, 291
Sucralose (artificial sweetener)   **S:**484
Sucrase (digestive enzyme)   **D:**164
Sucre (legal capital of Bolivia)   **B:**309
Sucre, Antonio José de (South American liberator)   **B:**310;
   P:165; **V:**298
Sucrose (table sugar)   **B:**296; **H:**211; **L:**199; **P:**315; **S:**482,
   483
   diagram(s)   **B:**296
Suction (Hydraulic) dredge   **D:**322
Suction pumps   **P:**540
Sudan   **S:**477–80
   folktales   **A:**76b
   human rights violations   **H:**286
   irrigation by Nile River   **N:**261
   pyramids   **P:**557
   wedding dances   **F:**303
   World War II   **W:**299
   map(s)   **S:**477
   picture(s)
      farmland   **S:**478
      flag   **F:**240
      Khartoum   **S:**479
      people   **S:**477
      warrior   **A:**55
Sudan region (African culture)   **A:**71–72
Sudbury (Ontario)   **O:**133, 138

Sudbury district (mining region, Ontario)   **O:**128
Sudbury Neutrino Observatory (Ontario)
   picture(s)   **S:**64
Sudd (swamp region of the Sudan)   **N:**260, 261
Sudetenland (region of former Czechoslovakia)   **C:**623; **W:**295
Suetonius (Roman historian)   **L:**76
Suez Canal (Egypt)   **C:**90; **S:**480–81
   Arab-Israeli wars   **E:**105; **I:**375
   dividing line between Asia and Africa   **A:**438d
   Egypt   **E:**102, 103, 104–5
   Indian Ocean trade   **I:**161
   Lesseps, Ferdinand de   **L:**157
   Mediterranean Sea, history of   **M:**212
   Nasser, Gamal Abdel   **N:**17
   map(s)   **S:**481
Suez Crisis (1956)   **S:**481
Suffixes (additions to the end of words)   **W:**239
Suffocation   **S:**4
Suffolk Resolves (in American history)   **A:**20
Suffrage (right to vote in political elections)   **G:**276
   Fifteenth Amendment   **U:**157
   26th Amendment granted vote to 18-year-olds   **U:**160
   woman suffrage *see* Woman suffrage
Suffragists (Suffragettes) (advocates of votes for women) *see*
   Woman suffrage
Sufism (Islamic mysticism)   **I:**346
Sugar   **S:**482–84 *see also* Honey
   baked goods, ingredient in   **B:**387
   body chemistry of   **B:**296
   candy and candy making   **C:**97–99
   carbohydrates formed from   **L:**199
   cereal foods, nutritional value of   **G:**284
   Cuba, production in   **C:**608
   fermentation   **F:**90
   food preservation   **F:**344
   important agricultural products   **A:**90
   keeping the body well   **H:**75
   lactose (milk sugar)   **M:**307
   leaves make   **L:**116
   Louisiana refineries   **L:**321
   maple sugar   **M:**91
   nutrition   **N:**424
   starch digested as sugar   **S:**425
   starch sugars in the food industry   **G:**285
   Sudanese industry   **S:**479
Sugar Act (Britain, 1764)   **R:**195
Sugar beets   **S:**482, 483, 484
   picture(s)   **S:**484
Sugar Bowl (football game, New Orleans, Louisiana)   **F:**361
Sugarcane   **S:**482–83, 483–84
   Australia   **A:**509, 512
   Crusaders introduced to Europe   **C:**599
   important crop to Hawaii   **H:**48, 56
   Puerto Rican economy   **P:**529
   slavery in the New World   **F:**337
   sweet grasses   **G:**319
   wax   **W:**78
   picture(s)   **A:**90; **G:**318; **L:**316; **P:**38; **S:**483
      Cuban harvest   **C:**114, 608
      Jamaica   **J:**16
Sugaring Off (painting by Grandma Moses)
   picture(s)   **M:**470
Sugarloaf Mountain (Rio de Janeiro, Brazil)   **R:**233
   picture(s)   **B:**381
Sugar maple trees   **M:**91; **P:**304
   picture(s)   **N:**211; **T:**303; **V:**307; **W:**127, 193
Sugar pine trees
   picture(s)   **T:**301
Sugar State (nickname for Louisiana)   **L:**315
Sugata (name for Buddha)   **B:**422b
Suger, Abbot (French monk)   **A:**371; **F:**422; **G:**267
Suggestion, mental *see* Mental suggestion
Suharto (Indonesian political leader)   **I:**212; **S:**336
   picture(s)   **I:**212

Suicide (intentionally killing oneself)   S:231, **485**
   Islamic prohibition against   I:353
   kamikaze pilots   W:315
   mood disorders can result in   M:221
   poisons   P:355
Suicide bombings (terrorist acts)   T:114–15
Sui Dynasty (in Chinese history)   P:410
Suite (in music)   M:540
Suits (in card games)   C:107
   What is the origin of the suits in a deck of playing cards?
      C:107
Suits, law   C:574–76
Sukarno (Indonesian political leader)   I:212; J:14
Sukarnoputri, Megawati (Indonesian political leader) *see*
      Megawati Sukarnoputri
Sukhe Bator (Mongolian leader)   M:418
Sukiyaki (Japanese food)   J:29
Sukkoth (Feast of the Tabernacles) (Jewish holiday)   J:146a;
      R:154
Sukuma (a people of Africa)   T:16
Sulawesi *see* Celebes
Sulci (grooves on the cerebral cortex)   B:364
Suleiman I (Suleiman the Magnificent) (sultan of Turkey)   J:83;
      O:259, 260
   picture(s)   A:455; O:260
Sulfa drugs   M:209
Sulfate pulping process (of papermaking)   P:55
Sulfates (sulfur-oxygen compounds)   S:486
Sulfides (sulfur-metal compounds)   C:198, 199; S:486
Sulfite pulping process (of papermaking)   P:55
Sulfur (element)   E:177; S:485–86
   acid rain   A:10
   air pollution   A:123; E:304
   coal, high-sulfur   C:391
   Louisiana mines by Frasch process   L:318, 321
   onions' flavor and odor caused by   O:123
   petroleum-product content   P:176
   rubber ingredient   R:347
   vulcanization process, Goodyear's discovery of   R:348
   picture(s)   M:316
Sulfur dioxide (polluting agent)   E:304; S:486; V:385
Sulfuric acid   A:9; O:289; S:486
   automobile batteries   B:103b
   gold treated in refining process   G:249
   Venus' atmosphere   V:303, 303b
Sulfurous acid   S:486
Sulfur oxides (air pollutants)   A:9, 123
Sulkies (carts for harness racing)   H:234
   picture(s)   H:234
Sulla, Lucius Cornelius (Roman general)   C:6; R:315
Sullivan, Anne (teacher of Helen Keller)   K:203
Sullivan, Sir Arthur (English composer)   G:208–9
Sullivan, John L. (American boxer)   B:351, 352
Sullivan, Kathryn D. (American astronaut)
   picture(s)   S:341
Sullivan, Louis (American architect)   A:373; I:214; S:486;
      U:131, 133; W:326
   picture(s)
      Wainwright Building   U:131
Sullivan, Thomas (American tea merchant)   T:36
Sullivan Brothers (five brothers killed in World War II)   W:306
Sullivans Island (South Carolina)   S:296, 309
Sullivan Trophy (amateur athletic award)   S:537
Sulphides *see* Sulfides
Sulphur *see* Sulfur
Sultana grapes   G:297
Sultan Ahmed (Blue) Mosque (Istanbul)   I:378
   picture(s)   I:356; T:348
Sultan of Swat (nickname for Babe Ruth)   R:387
Sulu Archipelago (in the Philippines)   P:184, 185
Sum (in addition)   A:388
Sumac (tree used as a source of yellow dye)   D:377; L:111
Sumac, poison *see* Poison sumac
Sumatra (island of Indonesia)   I:208, 209, 210, 211, 212

Sumatran orangutans
   picture(s)   E:211
Sumatran rhinoceroses (mammals)   H:217; R:211
Sumatran tigers
   picture(s)   T:198
Sumatras (thunderstorms)   M:57
Sumer (the birthplace of civilization)   A:230–31; M:231,
      304; S:487
   archaeological discoveries   A:353
   architecture, history of   A:364–65
   clothing, history of   C:374
   cuneiform   C:613; I:280
   grain surplus led to record keeping   F:336
   influenced the Babylonians   B:5
   mathematics, history of   M:162
   writing, history of   A:194; B:318; W:258
   picture(s)
      artifact   W:258
      gold bull's head   S:487
      mosaic of musician   A:237
      shell plaque   A:230
      stone statue   A:231
Summer (season)   S:109, 110, 111 *see also* the names of
      months
   constellations   C:531
   estivation   H:128
   flowers for summer bloom   G:46
   What are the dog days?   D:256
   picture(s)
      constellations   C:531
      tree in summer   T:300
Summer camps *see* Camping, organized
Summer fallow (Saskatchewan crop practice)   S:44
Summer melons (muskmelons)   M:214
Summer Palace (Beijing, China)   B:127d
Summerside (Prince Edward Island)   P:466
Summer theaters   T:159–60
Summer Triangle (pattern of stars)   C:531
Summit Series (in ice hockey)   I:30
Sumner, Charles (United States senator)   K:191
Sumner, William G. (American sociologist)   S:231
Sumo (Japanese wrestling)   J:33; M:116; W:324
Sumter, Thomas (American soldier)   S:304
Sumter National Forest (South Carolina)   S:299
Sun   S:488–97
   absorption spectrum   L:225
   astronomy, discoveries in   A:471–72
   classified as a star   A:472
   climatic changes, sources of   C:364
   comets   C:452
   cosmic rays   C:562
   distance from Earth   E:8
   Does sunspot activity affect the Earth's climate?   S:494
   dust-cloud hypothesis   E:22–23
   Earth receives light and heat from the sun   E:9
   Earth's geology affected by   G:115
   eclipses of *see* Solar eclipses
   heat   H:94
   How hot is the sun?   H:87
   ice age theories   I:16
   ions and ionization   I:289
   light   L:212, 215
   looking at   S:488
   main sequence star   S:429
   navigation   N:75
   obelisk was sacred Egyptian symbol of   E:112
   ozone layer of atmosphere absorbs radiation   A:482
   radiant energy source of other forms of energy   E:216–17
   radio astronomy studies   R:69
   seasons   S:109–11
   solar energy   S:239–40
   solar observatories   O:9
   solar system   S:241–49
   solar tides   O:19

nebulas **N:**96
pulsars **P:**539
radio astronomy **R:**70–71
picture(s) **O:**11; **R:**70
Superphosphates (fertilizers) **F:**97
Superpressure balloon (used in scientific research) **B:**37
Superrealism (in art) *see* Photorealism
Supersonic combustion ramjet *see* Scramjet
Supersonic flight **A:**567, 568; **S:**499–502; **T:**287; **U:**57
What was the Concorde? **S:**500
Supersonic speed (faster than sound) **A:**40–41, 538
Supersonic Transports (airplanes) **S:**500
Superstition **S:**503–4 *see also* Magic; Voodoo
colonial New England **C:**417–18
ghosts **G:**199–200
good luck customs for weddings **W:**100
Groundhog Day **F:**74
knots thought to have magical powers **K:**286
zodiac, signs of *see* individual month articles
Supertankers (cargo ships) **P:**173; **S:**155
picture(s) **S:**153
Suppawn (Hasty pudding) (colonial American dish) **C:**411
Suppé, Franz von (Austrian composer) **O:**166
Suppiluliumas (Hittite king) **A:**236
Supplemental Security Income (SSI) **I:**93; **W:**120
Supply, law of (in economics) **E:**56
Support services (for older people) **O:**100
Suppressor T cells (in the immune system) **I:**97
Supremacy, Act of (England, 1534) **H:**114
Suprematism (in art) *see* Constructivism
Supreme Allied Commander, Europe **N:**305
Supreme Court of Canada **C:**78; **P:**84; **S:**505–6
Supreme Court of the United States **C:**576; **S:**507–10; **U:**170, 171
abortion **A:**8
African American civil rights **A:**79h, 79i, 79L, 79m
Bill of Rights, rulings on **B:**184
Black, Hugo La Fayette **A:**142
Blackmun, Harry Andrew **I:**74
building **V:**312–13; **W:**32
Burger, Warren Earl **M:**338
Bush, George W., nominations by **B:**469
capital punishment **C:**104
Chase, Salmon Portland **O:**76
civil rights movement **C:**328
Douglas, William O. **D:**288
Dred Scott decision **D:**323
First Amendment freedoms **F:**163
Holmes, Oliver Wendell, Jr. **H:**172
Hughes, Charles Evans **H:**275
Jay, John, was first chief justice **J:**55
Jefferson's struggle with Federalist justices **J:**70
Marshall, John **M:**111
Roosevelt, Franklin D. **N:**138h; **R:**325; **U:**195
school integration decision (1954) **S:**114
Taft, William Howard, as chief justice **T:**6
voucher program decision **E:**87
Warren, Earl **L:**308
Watergate **W:**60–61
women's rights, rulings on **W:**213
picture(s) **C:**574
Supremes (musical group) **R:**262c
Supreme Soviet (national legislature, USSR) **U:**36–37
Surabaya (Indonesia) **I:**211
Surahs (chapters of the Koran) **K:**293
Surati (cheese made from buffalo's milk) **C:**195
Surdas (Indian poet-saint) **I:**141
Surface mining **M:**322–23
Surface Mining, Reclamation, and Enforcement, Office of (United States) **I:**256
Surface runoff (of irrigation water) **I:**339
Surface tension (of liquids) **E:**394–95; **L:**255; **W:**49–50
Surface-to-air missiles *see* SAM
Surface-to-surface missiles *see* SSM
Surface water (in streams or lakes) **W:**73, 121, 122

Surface waves (of earthquakes) **E:**34–35
Surfactants (cleansing agents of detergents) **D:**139, 140–41
air sacs of lungs coated with **L:**343
Surfboarding *see* Surfing
Surfboards **S:**511
Surfboating (sport)
picture(s) **A:**500
Surfing (sport) **S:**511 *see also* Boardsailing
picture(s) **H:**49; **O:**28
Surgeon General (of the United States) **D:**213, 236; **P:**514
smoking, report on **S:**207
Surgery **S:**512–15 *see also* Organ transplants
anesthesia **A:**254–57; **M:**208b–208c
appendicitis corrected by **D:**189
cancer treatment **C:**93
circulatory system disorders, treatment of **C:**306
computers, uses of **C:**485
deafness, treatment of **D:**49, 50
dental specialties **D:**115
disabilities, rehabilitation of people with **D:**179
diseases, treatment of **D:**207–9; **M:**204
hospitals **H:**247–48, 253
hypnotism as an anesthetic **H:**328, 329
laser beams **L:**46c
liquid gases, uses of **L:**253
Lister's antiseptics **L:**257
modern surgery, rise of **M:**208b
nurses in operating rooms **N:**417, 418
organ transplants **I:**97; **M:**208d; **O:**226–27
prehistoric medicine **M:**206
Renaissance medicine **M:**208
robots, medical **M:**208f; **R:**255
stomach disorders **S:**461
surgeons' needles **N:**102
surgical insurance **I:**252
Taussig, Helen Brooke **T:**24
tonsillectomy **D:**207
Williams, Daniel Hale **I:**75
picture(s) **M:**203; **T:**131
hospitals **H:**249
nurse assisting surgeons **N:**418
operating room **D:**208
television, uses of **T:**61
Suricates (animals) *see* Meerkats
Suriname (formerly **Dutch Guiana**) **L:**49, 50, 57; **N:**121; **S:**516–17
picture(s)
flag **F:**240
Paramaribo **S:**517
Surnames (family names) **N:**4
Surratt, Mary (American conspirator in Lincoln's assassination) **B:**335
Surrealism (in art) **M:**394–95; **S:**518
Dali, Salvador **D:**13
Italy, art of **I:**403
Klee, Paul **K:**271
Latin America **L:**64
Miró, Joan **M:**343
sculpture **S:**104
Spain, art of **S:**385
Surrealism (in literature) **F:**442
Surround-sound processors (in home theater) **H:**133
Surtr (Norse fire giant) **N:**281
Surtsey (volcanic island off Iceland) **I:**34
picture(s) **I:**361; **O:**20
Surveying **S:**519–20 *see also* Maps and globes
aerial photography **P:**206
early methods of public land survey **P:**516
geography **G:**98
lasers, uses of **L:**46c
Mason-Dixon line **M:**135
optical instruments **O:**182–83
pioneer life **P:**260
roads **R:**249

Surveying (cont.)
tunnel building   T:337
Washington's early career   W:37
picture(s)   G:98
Washington, George   W:38
Surveyor (moon probe)   S:359
Survival (in space)   S:340L–345
Survival of the fittest (theory of evolution)   E:376
Susa (city of ancient Persia)   P:155
picture(s)
relief sculpture   T:143
Susan Constant (ship)   J:22; T:168
Susanna (apocryphal book of the Bible)   B:164
Su Shi (Chinese poet)   C:275
Suspension (in music)   M:537
Suspension bridges   B:397–98
Humber Bridge (England)   U:57
Verrazano-Narrows Bridge   N:233
picture(s)
Golden Gate Bridge   B:398; S:32
table(s)
notable bridges of the world   B:400
Suspension system (of an automobile)   A:546, 551
Susquehanna River (United States)   M:122; P:128
Susquehannock (Indians of North America)   I:175
Sussex (New Brunswick)   N:138b, 138c
Sussex County (Delaware)   D:88, 90, 91, 95
Sustainable agriculture   F:351
Sustainable development   D:143
Sustainer (rocket engine)   S:340d
Susu (a people of western Africa) *see* Sosso
Sutherland, Joan (Australian soprano)   O:141 *profile*
picture(s)   A:501; O:157
Sutherland Falls (New Zealand)   N:237; W:58, 59
Sutras (Buddhist scriptures)   B:425; P:430
Sutter, John Augustus (early California settler)   C:30
Sutter's Fort (near Sacramento, California)   G:250
Sutzkever, Abraham (Yiddish poet)   Y:361
Suu Kyi, Aung San (political leader in Myanmar) *see* Aung San Suu Kyi
Suva (capital of Fiji)   F:125
Suwannee (river in Florida)   F:262–63
Suzor-Coté, Marc-Aurèle (Canadian sculptor)   C:72
Suzuki Harunobu *see* Harunobu, Suzuki
Svalbard Islands (Norway)   I:368; N:346
Svevo, Italo (Italian author)   I:408
Swahili (Bantu language)   A:56; K:229; T:16; U:4
Swallows (birds)
picture(s)   B:218, 229
Swallowtail butterflies
picture(s)   B:480, 481
caterpillar   I:243
chrysalis   I:233
Swamp Fox (name for Francis Marion)   M:103; R:207
Swamps   L:27; W:145, 146
Great Dismal Swamp (Virginia)   V:346
picture(s)
cranberry bogs   G:300
Swan (constellation) *see* Cygnus
Swan, Sir Joseph Wilson (British physicist and chemist)   F:110; L:234; N:439
"Swanee River" (song by Foster) *see* "Old Folks at Home"
Swan Lake (ballet)   B:28–29; D:348
picture(s)   D:30
Swan River (first free colony in Australia)   A:516
Swans (birds)   D:345, 348 *see also* Trumpeter swans
picture(s)   B:215, 226
Swansea (Wales)   W:3
Swanson, Gloria (American film actress)   C:221 *profile*
SWAPO *see* South-West Africa People's Organization
Swarming (of bees)   B:120–21
Swarte Piet (Saint Nicholas' helper)   C:301
Swastika (emblem of Nazism)   N:79, 81
picture(s)   N:78
Swather (farm machine)   F:58

S-waves (of earthquakes)   E:14, 36, 37
Swazi (a people of Africa)   S:521, 522
Swaziland   S:521–22
picture(s)
flag   F:240
Sweat glands   B:291; D:191; G:226
Sweatshops (in the clothing industry)   C:380
picture(s)   L:12
Sweden   S:58f–58g, **523–29**
Charles VIII-XVI   C:190
Christian II (king of Denmark and Norway)   C:286
Christina   C:295
Christmas customs   C:300
Finland, history of   F:139
holidays   H:162
income tax   I:111
Lapland   L:44–45
postal service   P:397
Scandinavian literature   S:58h, 58i
Stockholm   S:453
Thirty Years' War   T:179
map(s)   S:525
picture(s)
farm woman   E:352
flag   F:240
forest and river   S:526
girl in traditional costume   S:523
lumber industry   S:526
maypole dance   F:300–301
palace guard   E:352
people   S:523, 524
Smögen   S:523
Stockholm   S:453, 527
Swedes in America   D:93, 96, 100; P:138; S:529; T:175
picture(s)   D:101
Swedish language   F:134; S:523
Sweelinck, Jan Pieters (Dutch composer and organist)   D:373
Sweeney Todd (musical by Sondheim)   M:554–55
Sweep rowing   R:340
Sweet (a sense of taste)   B:290
Sweet alyssum (flowers)
picture(s)   G:27, 28
Sweetbreads (variety meat)   M:196
Sweet corn   C:558
Sweeteners, artificial   S:484
Sweet grasses   G:319
Sweet pea (plant)
picture(s)   G:47
Sweet potatoes   C:130; V:287
Sweyn Forkbeard (king of the Danes)   V:343
Swift, Jonathan (English author)   S:530–32
children's literature   C:232
essays   E:321
Gulliver's Travels   G:203
place in Irish literature   I:326
satire and political writings   E:278; H:292
Swift Current (Saskatchewan)   S:49
"Swifter, Higher, Stronger" (Olympic motto)   O:108
Swift Gamma-Ray Burst Mission   S:368
Swifts (birds)   H:128
Swigert, John L., Jr. (American astronaut)   S:352
Swim bladder (of a fish)   F:192; U:25
Swim fins (Flippers) (for skin diving) *see* Flippers
Swimmerets (small appendages of animals)   L:280; S:167
Swimming   S:532–39 *see also* Diving
from boats   B:268
fish   A:278; F:198–99
Olympic events   O:107, 119
safety measures   S:5
skin diving   S:186–88
water polo   W:68
world records   S:539
picture(s)
how fish swim   F:198
Icelandic pastime   I:33

Swinburne, Algernon Charles (English poet) E:285

Swine see Pigs

"Swing, The" (poem by Robert Louis Stevenson) S:451

Swing era (in popular music) D:29; J:61

Swiss chard (vegetable) V:290

Swiss cheese D:10

Swiss Guard (of Vatican City) V:281

Switch, electric E:148; P:197

Switchboards, telephone T:55

Switch-hitter (in baseball) B:83

Switching systems (in electronic communications) T:49, 53–54

picture(s)

telephone operator T:47

Switching yards (of railroads) see Classification yards

Swithin, Saint, Feast of H:162–63

Switzerland S:540–46

chocolate consumption highest in the world C:281

Geneva G:92

lakes L:30, 31, 32

La Tène culture C:164

Liechtenstein, relation to L:192

railroads L:288; R:80, 81

Reformation C:292

refugee resettlement R:137

romanticism in art R:303

Swiss and German literature G:180, 181

Zurich Z:395

picture(s)

cattle grazing S:540

elections D:106

flag F:240

flag throwing S:542

Geneva G:92; S:543

Geneva, Lake L:30

Grand Dixence Dam D:17

hostelers H:253

Matterhorn S:543

skiing S:542

yodeling S:542

Zurich S:544; Z:395

Sword dance F:300, 302

picture(s) F:302

Swordfish F:219, 220; L:32

Swords

King Arthur legends A:438a, 438b

knights' swords K:273

Sycamore Shoals, Treaty of (1775) K:225

Sycamore trees W:224

picture(s) T:303

Sydney (capital of New South Wales, Australia) A:511, 515; S:547–48

aquarium A:337

Opera House A:503

world's fair (1879) F:16

picture(s) A:513, 515, 517; B:397

first British settlement in Australia I:94

maglev train M:33

Olympic Games O:102

Opera House A:496; S:547

Sydney (Nova Scotia) N:353

Syllabaries (syllabic writing systems) A:194a; C:613; S:122

Syllables (speech sounds pronounced as a unit) A:194–94a; P:194, 486

Syllabus of Errors (document issued by Pope Pius IX) R:294

Syllogisms (in logic) L:289–90

Sylphide, La (ballet by Taglioni) B:27

Sylphides, Les (ballet by Fokine) B:29

Sylvester IV (antipope) R:292

Sylvester I, Saint (pope) R:292

Sylvester II (pope) H:177; R:292

Sylvester III (pope) R:292

Symbiosis (co-operative living arrangement between unlike plants or animals) L:206

ants and the bull-horn acacia P:317

cleaner shrimps and fish S:167

clownfish and sea anemones J:76

corals and zooxanthellae C:556

lichens F:498

mollusks M:406

plants and fungi P:313; R:99

picture(s)

sharks and remoras F:188

Symbolic logic see Mathematical logic

Symbolism (in Flemish art) D:359

Symbolism (in literature) D:304; F:441, 442; R:383

Symbols see Signs and symbols

Symbols, chemical see Chemical symbols

Symmachus, Saint (pope) R:292

Symmes, Susannah Livingston (American patriot) L:274

Symmetry (in geometry) G:125

Sympathetic nerves N:117

Sympathetic vibrations (of sound) S:261

Sympathy notes L:160a–160b

Symphonic poem (Tone poem) (in music) M:543

developed by Franz Liszt L:257

German music G:187

romanticism in music R:304

Strauss, Richard S:466

Symphony (in music) G:185; M:541, 543; R:304 see also the names of composers

Symphony orchestra O:192–95

picture(s) O:192–93

Symptoms (of a disease) D:186, 200

Synagogues (congregations of Jews) J:103, 145, 146

choral music C:282

Curaçao has oldest in New World L:50

Touro Synagogue (Newport, Rhode Island) R:220

picture(s)

Touro Synagogue J:145; R:220

Synapses (points where axons pass impulses to other cells) B:362; N:117–18

Synaptic terminals (of nervous system cells) B:362

Synchronized diving (sport) D:229; O:119–20

Syncopation (in music) J:57; M:537

Syncytium (network of cells) M:519

Syndication (of newspaper features) C:128; N:200

Syndics of the Cloth Merchants' Guild, The (painting by Rembrandt) B:68

picture(s) B:68; D:367

Synge, John Millington (Irish playwright) D:305; I:322, 327

Synonyms (words) S:548

Synoptic maps (in meteorology) W:92–94

Synovial fluid (in the joints of the skeleton) S:184b

Syntax (grammatical word order) G:288–90

Biblical Hebrew language parallelisms H:98

English language word order E:267

Synthesis (in chemistry) C:204

Synthesizers see Electronic synthesizers; Voice synthesizers

Synthetic cubism (art style) C:612

Synthetic elements see Artificial elements

Synthetic fibers F:108, 109–12; N:436–40

clothes today C:380–81

cotton and synthetic fibers C:569

dyeing D:378–79, 380

fashion F:65–66

How are synthetic fibers named? N:437

imitation furs F:505

manufacturing of M:89

rugs and carpets R:356

textiles T:141, 146

Synthetic materials M:89

adhesives G:243

antibiotics A:307

chemical industry C:197

detergents D:139–41

PHOTO CREDITS

The following list credits the sources of photos used in THE NEW BOOK OF KNOWLEDGE. Credits are listed, by page, photo by photo—left to right, top to bottom. Wherever appropriate, the name of the photographer has been listed with the source, the two being separated by a dash. When two or more photos by different photographers appear on one page, their credits are separated by semicolons.

340j North American Space and Information Systems, North American Aviation, Inc.; North American Space and Information Systems, North American Aviation, Inc.; NASA.
340k NASA—Johnson Space Center
340l NASA—Johnson Space Center
341 NASA—Johnson Space Center
342 NASA—Johnson Space Center (all photos on page).
343 NASA—Johnson Space Center
344 NASA—Johnson Space Center.
345 NASA—Johnson Space Center
346 NASA; Bettmann/Corbis; Bettmann/Corbis; Bettmann/Corbis; Bettmann/Corbis.
347 NASA (all photos on page).
348 NASA; NASA; Digital Image © 1996 Corbis, original image courtesy NASA.
349 NASA/AP/Wide World Photos; NASA.
350 NASA; Bettmann/Corbis.
351 NASA (all photos on page).
352 © Dr. Scott Lieberman—AP/Wide World Photos
353 © Michael Carroll
354 NASA
355 NASA
356 © Martin Marietta
357 NASA
359 NASA; © Julian Baum—Photo Researchers.
361 © Bruce Mathews—Midwestock; NASA—Goddard Space Flight Center; NASA—Johnson Space Center.
362 © Frank Rossotto—Stocktrek
363 NASA—Johnson Space Center (all photos on page).
365 © Frank Rossotto; © Frank Rossotto—Stocktrek.
366 NASA
367 NASA (all photos on page).
369 © Pedro Coll—The Stock Market; © Nik Wheeler—Black Star; © Joe Viesti—The Viesti Collection, Inc.; © David Ball—The Stock Market.
370 © Bruno Barbey—Magnum Photos
371 © Brooks Kraft—Corbis-Sygma
372 © Jean-Pierre Laffont—Corbis-Sygma; © John F. Mason—The Stock Market.
373 The Granger Collection (all photos on page).
374 The Granger Collection
378 © Erich Lessing—Art Resource; Bettmann/Corbis.
379 © David Burnett—Contact Press Images/PNI
380 Art Resource; © Odyssey Productions/Chicago.
381 © Robert Frerck—Odyssey Productions/Chicago; © Robert Frerck—Stone.
382 © Robert Frerck—Odyssey Productions/Chicago; © Glenn Knudsen—Stone.
383 Scala/Art Resource; Giraudon/Art Resource.
384 Scala/Art Resource; The Metropolitan Museum of Art—The Jules Bach Collection, 1949.
385 MAS, Barcelona
386 The Granger Collection
387 Partimonio Nacional, Madrid from MAS, Barcelona
388 The Granger Collection
389 MAS, Barcelona
390 MAS, Barcelona
391 Ambassade d' Espagne a' Paris
392 Reuters/Bettmann
392a © Jose L. Pelaez—The Stock Market; © Jacques Lowe—Woodfin Camp & Associates.
392b MAS, Barcelona; The Granger Collection.
392c The Granger Collection
392d © Rick Stewart—Allsport
397 © Billy Brown—Comstock
400 © Peter & Ann Bosted—Photo 20-20
402 © Kim Taylor—Bruce Coleman Inc.; © H. L. Fox—Animals Animals; © E. S. Ross.
403 © Grant Heilman Photography
404 © Stephen Dalton—Animals Animals; © Stephen P. Parker—Photo Researchers; © E. S. Ross.
405 © E. R. Degginger—Bruce Coleman Inc.; © E. S. Ross.
406 © Hans Pfletschinger—Peter Arnold, Inc.; ©

408 Larry West—Bruce Coleman Inc.
408 The Bettmann Archive; The Bettmann Archive; The Granger Collection.
409 UPI/Bettmann Newsphotos
411 © Doug Perrine; © Andrew J. Martinez; © Fred Bavendam.
414 © Loc Bouchage—Rapho Guillumette; © Ed Drews—Photo Researchers; © Frederick Ayers III—Photo Researchers.
417 © Sonia Halliday & Laura Lushington—Sonia Halliday Photographs (all photos on page).
418 Art Resource; © Robert Llewellyn.
419 Courtesy of the Harry S. Truman Library
420 © Mickey Pfleger—Photo 20-20; © Susan Grayson—Keim Publishing; © Susan Grayson—Keim Publishing; © Susan Grayson—Keim Publishing.
421 © Paul H. Segnitz—Photo Researchers; © Finbar Kenny—J & H Stowlow; © Paul H. Segnitz—Photo Researchers; © Paul H. Segnitz—Photo Researchers.
422 © Susan Grayson—Keim Publishing (all photos on page).
423 © Susan Grayson—Keim Publishing (all photos on page).
424 Hulton/Bettmann; Brown Brothers.
426 © Joyce Burek—Animals Animals; © Carl Roessler—Animals Animals; © Fred McConnaughey—Photo Researchers; © Brock May—Photo Researchers; © Neil G. McDaniel—Photo Researchers.
427 © Fred Bavendam—Peter Arnold, Inc. (all photos on page).
428 National Optical Astronomy Observatories; Space Telescope Science Institute—NASA—Photo Researchers; C. R. O'Dell (Rice University)—NASA.
429 NASA; © National Solar Observatories—SEL/Ressmeyer/Corbis.
432 National Optical Astronomy Observatories; © Rudolph Schild—Smithsonian Astrophysical Observatory—Photo Researchers.
434 Tomas Munita—AP/Wide World Photos
436 © Paul Costin—New York State
446 The Metropolitan Museum of Art, Bequest of Gertrude Stein, 1946
447 © Rich Bard
448 UPI/Bettmann Newsphotos
449 The Granger Collection
450– Illustrations by Brian Wildsmith from A Child's
451 Garden Of Verses by Robert Louis Stevenson. 1966 Oxford University Press. Permission of Oxford University Press.
452 The Granger Collection
453 © David Buffington—Photodisc Green/Getty Images
454 © Jon Riley—Stone
456 UPI/Bettmann Newsphotos; © Doug Armand—Stone.
457 © Joan Sydlow—FPG International; © Everett C. Johnson—Leo de Wys.
459 © Cathy Ursillo—Leo de Wys; © Jon Riley—Stone.
460 Boehringer Ingelheim International GmbH
462 © Dave Jacobs—Robert Harding Picture Library
463 © Anne Zane Shanks
470 The Granger Collection
473 © Steve Kaufman (all photos on page).
474 © Photri
475 © Steve Kaufman; © Yogi Kaufman; © Steve Kaufman.
476 Rodney Catanach—Woods Hole Oceanographic Institution; Woods Hole Oceanographic Institution.
477 © Betty Press—Woodfin Camp & Associates; © Michael Yamashita—Woodfin Camp & Associates.
478 © Martin Rogers—Stone/Getty
479 © Robert Caputo—Aurora/PictureQuest
482 © C Squared Studios/PhotoDisc/Getty Images
483 © SuperStock
484 © Inga Spence—Visuals Unlimited, Inc.
486 © 2002 Churchill & Klehr/Danita Delimont, Agent

487 © Scala/Art Resource, NY
488 Palo Alto Research Laboratories; © Dennis di Cicco.
489 © Dan McCoy—Rainbow; © Dan McCoy—Rainbow; National Optical Astronomy Observatories—National Solar Observatory.
492 Courtesy of the Mt. Palomar Observatories—California Institute of Technology; © NASA—Mark Marten—Photo Researchers.
493 National Optical Astronomy Observatories; NASA.
495 Naval Research Laboratory—NASA—Starlight; © Dennis di Cicco.
496 NASA; © Perka Parvia—Science Photo Library—Photo Researchers.
498 © John Zoiner—International Stock
499 © Photri; Grumman Corporation—Corporate Research Center; © Photri.
500 © Photri; © Photri; © Photri; © Brian Parker—Tom Stack & Associates.
501 Courtesy of NASA Ames Research Center; Courtesy of NASA Ames Research Center.
502 Courtesy of NASA; Courtesy of NASA Langley Research Center.
505 © Reuters/Landov
507 © Jon Feingersh—The Stock Market
508 © J. Scott Applewhite—AP/Wide World Photos
511 © Leo Aarons
512 Brown Brothers; Brown Brothers; Culver Pictures.
513 The Bettmann Archive
514 © Tom Tracy—Photo Network; © David Wells—The Image Works; © Al Cook—Photo Network.
515 © Vito Palmisano—Photri
517 © J. Alex Langley—DPI
518 Collection, The Museum of Modern Art, New York, Purchase. Photograph © 1992 The Museum of Modern Art, New York
519 © David Sailors—The Stock Market; © Thomas Stewart—The Stock Market; © Eric R. Berndt—Unicorn Stock Photo.
522 © Julian Bryan—Photo Researchers
523 © Sips Image—eStock Photos; © F. Damm—The Zefa Collection/Masterfile.
524 © Malcolm Hanes—Bruce Coleman Inc.; © Bertil Ericson—AP/Wide World Photos.
526 © Roine Magnusson—Stone/Getty Images; © Richard Bullard—Stone/Getty Images.
527 © Yoshio Tomii—SuperStock
528 © Nicolas Sapieha—The Art Archive
529 Mary Evans Picture Library
530 The Granger Collection
531 The Granger Collection
532 © Peggy Daly—ProFiles West/Index Stock
533 © Ron Sherman—Uniphoto Picture Agency; © Ed Slater—Southern Stock/Index Stock Photos.
536 UPI/Bettmann Newsphotos
537 © Focus on Sports; © Tony Duffy—Allsport; Corbis-Bettmann; Corbis-Bettmann; Reuters/Will Burgess/Archive Photos; UPI/Corbis-Bettmann.
538 © Simon Bruty—Allsport; © UPI/Corbis-Bettmann.
540 © Dennis Hallinan—FPG International
542 © Kurt Scholz—SuperStock; Courtesy of Swiss National Tourist Office; Courtesy of Swiss National Tourist Office.
543 © Cotton Coulson—Woodfin Camp & Associates; Courtesy of Swiss National Tourist Office.
544 © Fred Mayer—Woodfin Camp & Associates
545 Courtesy of Swiss Watch Industry Association, Bramaz; Courtesy of The Swiss Cheese Industry.
547 Cameramann International Ltd.
549 © Siegfried Tauqueur—eStock Photo
550 © Daniel O'Leary—Panos Pictures
551 © Siegfried Tauqueur—eStock Photo